The Cambridge Handbook of Corrective Feedback in Second Language Learning and Teaching

Corrective feedback is a vital pedagogical tool in language learning. This is the first volume to provide an in-depth analysis and discussion of the role of corrective feedback in second and foreign language learning and teaching. Written by leading scholars, it assembles cutting-edge research and state-of-the-art articles that address recent developments in core areas of corrective feedback including oral, written, computer-mediated, nonverbal, and peer feedback. The chapters are a combination of both theme-based and original empirical studies carried out in diverse second and foreign language contexts. Each chapter provides a concise review of its own topic, discusses theoretical and empirical issues not adequately addressed before, and identifies their implications for classroom instruction and future research. It will be an essential resource for all those interested in the role of corrective feedback in second and foreign language learning and how it can be used to enhance classroom teaching.

Hossein Nassaji is Professor of Applied Linguistics in the Department of Linguistics at the University of Victoria, Canada. He maintains an active research agenda across various areas of second language teaching and learning and has authored numerous publications on these topics.

Eva Kartchava is Associate Professor in the School of Linguistics and Language Studies at Carleton University, Canada. She has published research on the relationship between corrective feedback and second language learning, noticeability of feedback, and the role of individual differences in the language learning process.

CAMBRIDGE HANDBOOKS IN LANGUAGE AND LINGUISTICS

Genuinely broad in scope, each handbook in this series provides a complete state-of-the-field overview of a major sub-discipline within language study and research. Grouped into broad thematic areas, the chapters in each volume encompass the most important issues and topics within each subject, offering a coherent picture of the latest theories and findings. Together, the volumes will build into an integrated overview of the discipline in its entirety.

Published titles

The Cambridge Handbook of Phonology, edited by Paul de Lacy
The Cambridge Handbook of Linguistic Code-switching, edited by Barbara E. Bullock and Almeida Jacqueline Toribio
The Cambridge Handbook of Child Language, Second Edition, edited by Edith L. Bavin and Letitia Naigles
The Cambridge Handbook of Endangered Languages, edited by Peter K. Austin and Julia Sallabank
The Cambridge Handbook of Sociolinguistics, edited by Rajend Mesthrie
The Cambridge Handbook of Pragmatics, edited by Keith Allan and Kasia M. Jaszczolt
The Cambridge Handbook of Language Policy, edited by Bernard Spolsky
The Cambridge Handbook of Second Language Acquisition, edited by Julia Herschensohn and Martha Young-Scholten
The Cambridge Handbook of Biolinguistics, edited by Cedric Boeckx and Kleanthes K. Grohmann
The Cambridge Handbook of Generative Syntax, edited by Marcel den Dikken
The Cambridge Handbook of Communication Disorders, edited by Louise Cummings
The Cambridge Handbook of Stylistics, edited by Peter Stockwell and Sara Whiteley
The Cambridge Handbook of Linguistic Anthropology, edited by N.J. Enfield, Paul Kockelman and Jack Sidnell
The Cambridge Handbook of English Corpus Linguistics, edited by Douglas Biber and Randi Reppen
The Cambridge Handbook of Bilingual Processing, edited by John W. Schwieter
The Cambridge Handbook of Learner Corpus Research, edited by Sylviane Granger, Gaëtanelle Gilquin and Fanny Meunier
The Cambridge Handbook of Linguistic Multicompetence, edited by Li Wei and Vivian Cook
The Cambridge Handbook of English Historical Linguistics, edited by Merja Kytö and Päivi Pahta
The Cambridge Handbook of Formal Semantics, edited by Maria Aloni and Paul Dekker
The Cambridge Handbook of Morphology, edited by Andrew Hippisley and Greg Stump
The Cambridge Handbook of Historical Syntax, edited by Adam Ledgeway and Ian Roberts
The Cambridge Handbook of Linguistic Typology, edited by Alexandra Y. Aikhenvald and R. M. W. Dixon
The Cambridge Handbook of Areal Linguistics, edited by Raymond Hickey

The Cambridge Handbook of Cognitive Linguistics, edited by Barbara Dancygier
The Cambridge Handbook of Japanese Linguistics, edited by Yoko Hasegawa
The Cambridge Handbook of Spanish Linguistics, edited by Kimberly L. Geeslin
The Cambridge Handbook of Bilingualism, edited by Annick De Houwer and Lourdes Ortega
The Cambridge Handbook of Systemic Functional Linguistics, edited by Geoff Thompson, Wendy L. Bowcher, Lise Fontaine and David Schönthal
The Cambridge Handbook of African Linguistics, edited by H. Ekkehard Wolff
The Cambridge Handbook of Language Learning, edited by John W. Schwieter and Alessandro Benati
The Cambridge Handbook of World Englishes, edited by Daniel Schreier, Marianne Hundt and Edgar W. Schneider
The Cambridge Handbook of Intercultural Communication, edited by Guido Rings and Sebastian Rasinger
The Cambridge Handbook of Germanic Linguistics, edited by Michael T. Putnam and B. Richard Page
The Cambridge Handbook of Discourse Studies, edited by Anna De Fina and Alexandra Georgakopoulou
The Cambridge Handbook of Language Standardization, edited by Wendy Ayres-Bennett and John Bellamy
The Cambridge Handbook of Korean Linguistics, edited by Sungdai Cho and John Whitman
The Cambridge Handbook of Phonetics, edited by Rachael-Anne Knight and Jane Setter
The Cambridge Handbook of Corrective Feedback in Second Language Learning and Teaching, edited by Hossein Nassaji and Eva Kartchava

The Cambridge Handbook of Corrective Feedback in Second Language Learning and Teaching

Edited by
Hossein Nassaji
University of Victoria, Canada
Eva Kartchava
Carleton University, Canada

Shaftesbury Road, Cambridge CB2 8EA, United Kingdom

One Liberty Plaza, 20th Floor, New York, NY 10006, USA

477 Williamstown Road, Port Melbourne, VIC 3207, Australia

314–321, 3rd Floor, Plot 3, Splendor Forum, Jasola District Centre, New Delhi – 110025, India

103 Penang Road, #05–06/07, Visioncrest Commercial, Singapore 238467

Cambridge University Press is part of Cambridge University Press & Assessment, a department of the University of Cambridge.

We share the University's mission to contribute to society through the pursuit of education, learning and research at the highest international levels of excellence.

www.cambridge.org
Information on this title: www.cambridge.org/9781108450577

DOI: 10.1017/9781108589789

© Cambridge University Press & Assessment 2021

This publication is in copyright. Subject to statutory exception and to the provisions of relevant collective licensing agreements, no reproduction of any part may take place without the written permission of Cambridge University Press & Assessment.

First published 2021
First paperback edition 2024

A catalogue record for this publication is available from the British Library

Library of Congress Cataloging-in-Publication data
Names: Nassaji, Hossein, editor. | Kartchava, Eva, editor.
Title: The Cambridge handbook of corrective feedback in second language learning and teaching / edited by Hossein Nassaji, University of Victoria, British Columbia ; Eva Kartchava, Carleton University, Ottawa.
Description: Cambridge, UK ; New York : Cambridge University Press, 2020. | Series: Cambridge handbooks in language and linguistics | Includes bibliographical references and index.
Identifiers: LCCN 2020039500 (print) | LCCN 2020039501 (ebook) | ISBN 9781108499101 (hardback) | ISBN 9781108589789 (ebook)
Subjects: LCSH: Second language acquisition – Study and teaching – Research. | Language and languages – Study and teaching – Foreign speakers – Evaluation. | Communication in foreign language education. | Feedback (Psychology) | Language teachers – Training of.
Classification: LCC P118.2 .C3553 2020 (print) | LCC P118.2 (ebook) |DDC 418.0071–dc23
LC record available at https://lccn.loc.gov/2020039500
LC ebook record available at https://lccn.loc.gov/2020039501

ISBN   978-1-108-49910-1   Hardback
ISBN   978-1-108-45057-7   Paperback

Cambridge University Press & Assessment has no responsibility for the persistence or accuracy of URLs for external or third-party internet websites referred to in this publication and does not guarantee that any content on such websites is, or will remain, accurate or appropriate.

Contents

List of Figures	page x
List of Tables	xi
List of Contributors	xiii
Acknowledgments	xxi

Introduction: Corrective Feedback in Second Language Teaching
and Learning   Hossein Nassaji and Eva Kartchava   1

Part I   Theoretical Perspectives on Corrective Feedback   21
1 Corrective Feedback from Behaviorist and Innatist
   Perspectives   ZhaoHong Han   23
2 Interactionist Approach to Corrective Feedback in Second
   Language Acquisition   Rebekha Abbuhl   44
3 Cognitive Theoretical Perspectives of Corrective
   Feedback   Ronald P. Leow and Meagan Driver   65
4 Corrective Feedback from a Sociocultural Perspective
   Hossein Nassaji   85

**Part II   Methodological Approaches in the Study
   of Corrective Feedback**   109
5 Tools to Measure the Effectiveness of Feedback   Alison
   Mackey, Lara Bryfonski, Özgür Parlak, Ashleigh Pipes,
   Ayşenur Sağdıç, and Bo-Ram Suh   111
6 Laboratory-Based Oral Corrective Feedback   Shawn Loewen
   and Susan M. Gass   130
7 Classroom-Based Research in Corrective Feedback
   Antonella Valeo   147
8 Meta-Analysis and Research Synthesis   Dan Brown   164

Part III Different Delivery Modes of Corrective Feedback   185
9 Oral Corrective Feedback   Rhonda Oliver and Rebecca Adams   187
10 Written Corrective Feedback   John Bitchener   207
11 Technology-Mediated Corrective Feedback   Trude Heift, Phuong Nguyen, and Volker Hegelheimer   226
12 Gestures, Corrective Feedback, and Second Language Development   Kimi Nakatsukasa[†]   251

Part IV Feedback Provider, Feedback Intensity, and Feedback Timing   273
13 Peer Feedback in Second Language Oral Interaction Noriko Iwashita and Phung Dao   275
14 Focused versus Unfocused Corrective Feedback   Catherine van Beuningen   300
15 Corrective Feedback Timing and Second Language Grammatical Development: Research, Theory, and Practice Paul Gregory Quinn   322
16 Explicit and Implicit Oral Corrective Feedback   Rod Ellis   341

Part V Corrective Feedback and Language Skills   365
17 Corrective Feedback and the Development of Second Language Grammar   Helen Basturkmen and Mengxia Fu   367
18 Corrective Feedback and the Development of Second Language Vocabulary   Nobuhiro Kamiya and Tatsuya Nakata   387
19 Effects of Corrective Feedback on Second Language Pronunciation Development   Kazuya Saito   407
20 Corrective Feedback in Instructional Pragmatics Kathleen Bardovi-Harlig and Yucel Yilmaz   429
21 Alphabetic Print Literacy Level and Noticing Oral Corrective Feedback in SLA   Elaine Tarone   450

Part VI Contexts of Corrective Feedback and Their Effects   471
22 Corrective Feedback in Second versus Foreign Language Contexts   Maria del Pilar García Mayo and Ruth Milla   473
23 Corrective Feedback in Computer-Mediated versus Face-to-Face Environments   Luis Cerezo   494
24 Corrective Feedback in Mobile Technology-Mediated Contexts   Eva Kartchava and Hossein Nassaji   520
25 Oral Corrective Feedback in Content-Based Contexts Susan Ballinger   539

Part VII Learners' and Teachers' Feedback Perspectives, Perceptions, and Preferences   559
26 Teachers' and Students' Beliefs and Perspectives about Corrective Feedback   YouJin Kim and Tamanna Mostafa   561

27	Written Corrective Feedback and Learners' Objects, Beliefs, and Emotions Neomy Storch	581
28	The Role of Training in Feedback Provision and Effectiveness Eva Kartchava	598
29	Perceptions and Noticing of Corrective Feedback Reiko Yoshida	620

Part VIII   Individual Differences, Tasks, and Other Language- and Learner-Related Factors — 643

30	Age and Corrective Feedback Alyssa Vuono and Shaofeng Li	645
31	Gender Effects Rebecca Adams and Lauren Ross-Feldman	668
32	Feedback, Aptitude, and Multilingualism Beatriz Lado and Cristina Sanz	689
33	Corrective Feedback and Affect Jaemyung Goo and Takaaki Takeuchi	713
34	Corrective Feedback, Developmental Readiness, and Language Proficiency Miroslaw Pawlak	733
35	Corrective Feedback and Grammatical Complexity: A Research Synthesis Gisela Granena and Yucel Yilmaz	754
36	The Role of Task in the Efficacy of Corrective Feedback Pauline Foster and Martyn McGettigan	777

Index — 796

Figures

3.1	Feedback processing framework based on Leow's (2015) Model of the L2 Learning Process in ISLA	page 80
6.1	Defining lab studies	134
6.2	Differentiating between lab, interventionist, and noninterventionist classroom studies	135
10.1	Cognitive processing stages for a single written CF episode	216
10.2	Factors that may moderate the cognitive processing of written CF across the stages of a single written CF episode	217
11.1	Grammarly interface	233
11.2	The Writing Mentor interface	236
11.3	The Writing Mentor post-use checklist	236
11.4	Audacity's waveform of the word "paragraph" produced by a female native speaker of English	238
11.5	PRATT's spectrogram of "paragraph" produced by a female native speaker of English	239
11.6	Pitch contour generated by PRATT	239
16.1	The explicit/implicit continuum (from Lyster & Saito, 2010, p. 278)	345
25.1	Continuum of content and language integration (Lyster, 2017; Met, 1998)	540
27.1	Second generation (G_2) model of AT (adapted from Engeström 2001)	584

Tables

0.1	A taxonomy of oral feedback (from Nassaji, 2015)	page 4
3.1	A synopsis of the cognitive processes and variables postulated to play important roles in processing CF	67
4.1	Regulatory Scale from implicit feedback to more explicit feedback (Aljaafreh & Lantolf, 1994, p. 471)	95
6.1	Manipulation in lab and classroom research	136
8.1	Domain definitions and outcomes across meta-analyses of corrective feedback	172
8.2	Methodological recommendations in meta-analyses involving oral CF research	177
10.1	Studies comparing direct written CF and indirect written CF	211
10.2	Studies comparing direct written CF and direct plus metalinguistic feedback	212
14.1	Characteristics of CF options	301
16.1	Explicit and implicit corrective strategies	342
16.2	Implicit and explicit recasts (based on Loewen & Philp, 2006)	346
16.3	Implicit and explicit recasts and prompts (based on Nassaji, 2009)	355
17.1	Taxonomy of CF strategies based on Lyster and Ranta (1997)	369
17.2	Classification of CF strategies	369
17.3	Grammar targets and CF studies	382
18.1	Categorization of oral corrective feedback	389
18.2	Categorization of written corrective feedback	393
21.1	Participant profiles (table modified from Bigelow et al., 2006)	455
21.2	Mean correct or modified recalls by literacy level (table modified from Bigelow et al., 2006, p. 680)	456
21.3	Participant literacy levels (table modified from Martin-Mejia, 2011, p. 34)	460

21.4	Recall of recasts of questions in spot-the-difference task (table modified from Martin-Mejía, 2011, p. 41)	461
21.5	Participant literacy levels (table modified from Mueller, 2013, p. 41)	462
30.1	Types of corrective feedback with examples of correction to a student's erroneous utterance *"Yesterday, I play in the park"	649
30.2	Feedback provided by age in the classroom	650
30.3	Feedback forms with the most reported uptake in classroom observational studies	656
30.4	Findings of experimental effectiveness studies	658
35.1	Study features	768
35.2	Feedback effects by time and target complexity	771

Contributors

Rebekha Abbuhl is Associate Professor of Linguistics at California State University, Long Beach where she teaches courses in language acquisition, research methods, and pedagogy. She has taught English as a Foreign Language and worked as a teacher trainer in Hungary, Japan, Ukraine, and Vietnam.

Rebecca Adams is Associate Professor of Applied Linguistics at the University of Memphis. Her research focuses on peer interaction, feedback, and focus on form in instructed second language contexts in classrooms and online. She has published two co-authored books on second language peer interaction, both with Routledge.

Susan Ballinger is Assistant Professor of Second Language Education in McGill University's Department of Integrated Studies in Education. Her research is situated in bilingual education contexts, and her interests include language transfer and crosslinguistic pedagogy, classroom interaction, and teacher training for content and language integrated instruction.

Kathleen Bardovi-Harlig is Provost Professor of Second Language Studies at Indiana University where she teaches and conducts research on pragmatics (including speech acts, conventional expressions, and pragmatic routines), second language acquisition, and tense-aspect systems. Her recent work on instructional pragmatics has explored the use of corpora to teach pragmatic routines.

Helen Basturkmen lectures at the University of Auckland, New Zealand. Her research interests include spoken discourse, classroom interaction, and English for Specific Purposes. She is currently researching language-related interaction in content classes in English-medium instruction. She also convenes courses on discourse analysis and English for Specific Purposes at the University of Auckland.

John Bitchener is Emeritus Professor of Applied Linguistics at Auckland University of Technology, New Zealand. He has published over 100 articles and book chapters in leading publications, and delivered over 150 plenary and invited papers, seminars, and workshops on feedback at renowned universities and colleges in the USA, the UK, and parts of Europe, Southeast Asia, Australia, and New Zealand. His books include *Written Corrective Feedback for L2 Development* (with Storch, 2016) and *Written Corrective Feedback in Second Language Acquisition and Writing* (with Ferris, 2012). He runs an academic writing consultancy in New Zealand.

Dan Brown is Assistant Professor at Grand Valley State University, Michigan. His research interests focus on interactionist and corrective feedback, second language writing for academic purposes, meta-analysis in applied linguistics research, and second language teaching methodology. He has taught ESL/EFL and trained English teachers in the United States, Thailand, Chile, and Japan.

Lara Bryfonski is Assistant Professor of Linguistics at Georgetown University, Washington, DC, where she conducts research on a variety of topics in second language acquisition, including interaction and corrective feedback, task-based language teaching, language teacher training, individual differences, and language learning in study abroad contexts.

Luis Cerezo is Associate Professor of Applied Linguistics and director of the Spanish Language Program at American University, Washington, DC. His research investigates how to maximize additional language learning through videogames, computer-mediated communication, and hybrid and online curricula premised on instructional approaches such as guided induction, metacognitive instruction, and vicarious learning.

Phung Dao is a lecturer in TESOL and Applied Linguistics in the Department of Languages, Information and Communications, Manchester Metropolitan University. His research interests include second language acquisition and pedagoy, task-based language teaching, and computer-mediated communication.

Meagan Driver is Assistant Professor in the Spanish and Second Language Studies programs at Michigan State University. Her research focuses on heritage language education, multilingualism, and emotion and motivation within foreign language and study abroad contexts.

Rod Ellis is Research Professor at Curtin University, Western Australia, visiting professor at Shanghai International Studies University, and Emeritus Distinguished Professor at the University of Auckland, New Zealand. He is also a fellow of the Royal Society of New Zealand. He has written extensively on second language acquisition and task-based language teaching. His most recent (co-authored) book is *Task-based Language Teaching: Theory and Practice* (Cambridge University Press, 2020).

Pauline Foster is Professor of Applied Linguistics at St. Mary's University, London. Her research focuses on second language acquisition, especially task-based learning, classroom interaction, and formulaic language.

Mengxia Fu is an honorary post-doctoral research fellow of the School of Cultures, Languages and Linguistics at the University of Auckland, New Zealand. Her research interests include task-based language teaching, corrective feedback, and the role of individual differences in foreign and second language learning.

Maria del Pilar García Mayo is Professor of English Language and Linguistics at the University of the Basque Country, Spain. She has published widely on the acquisition of English L2/L3 morphosyntax and interaction in EFL settings. She is the co-editor of the journal *Language Teaching Research* and director of the research group *Language and Speech*.

Susan M. Gass is University Distinguished Professor in the Second Language Studies program at Michigan State University. She has published widely in the field of second language acquisition and is currently editor of the journal *Studies in Second Language Acquisition*.

Jaemyung Goo is Associate Professor of English Education at Gwangju National University of Education, Gwangju, South Korea. He received his Ph.D. in Linguistics from Georgetown University in May 2011. His research interests include corrective feedback, cognitive individual differences, implicit and explicit instruction, and task-based language teaching.

Gisela Granena is Associate Professor of English as a Second Language and director of the technology-mediated language teaching and learning program at the Universitat Oberta de Catalunya. Her research interests include the role of cognitive aptitudes in naturalistic and instructed contexts; aptitude-treatment interactions; task-based language teaching; measures of implicit and explicit language knowledge; and the effects of early and late bilingualism on long-term L2 achievement.

ZhaoHong Han is Professor of Applied Linguistics at Teachers College, Columbia University. Her research interests lie broadly in second language learnability and teachability across life span. Among her recent works are *Profiling Learner Language as a Dynamic System* (2019) and a special issue on instructed SLA in the journal *Language Teaching Research*.

Volker Hegelheimer is Professor of Applied Linguistics in the Department of English at Iowa State University. He teaches courses on technology in language teaching and research, language assessment, and research methodology. His research interests include applications of technologies in language learning and language testing.

Trude Heift is Professor of Linguistics in the Department of Linguistics at Simon Fraser University, Canada. Her research focuses on the design as well as the evaluation of CALL systems with a particular interest in learner-computer interactions and learner language. She is co-editor of the journal *Language Learning & Technology*.

Noriko Iwashita is an associate professor in the School of Languages and Cultures, at the University of Queensland, Brisbane, Australia. Her research interests include the role of interaction in second language learning, task-based language teaching, learning and assessment, the construct of oral proficiency in second language acquisition and assessment, and testing research and peer interaction assessment.

Nobuhiro Kamiya is Professor of English Education in the Department of International Communication at Gunma Prefectural Women's University, Japan. His interests are in instructed second language acquisition and English education in Japan. His recent papers focus on oral corrective feedback and nonverbal behaviors, recasts, and teacher gesture *inter alia*.

Eva Kartchava is Associate Professor in the School of Linguistics and Language Studies at Carleton University, Canada. She is interested in, and has published research on, the relationship between corrective feedback and second language learning, noticeability of feedback, and the role of individual differences in the language learning process.

YouJin Kim is a professor in the Department of Applied Linguistics and ESL at Georgia State University. She specializes in instructed second language acquisition, task-based language teaching, and classroom-based research. She is a co-author (with Casey Keck) of *Pedagogical Grammar* (2014) and a co-editor (with Naoko Taguchi) of *Task-based Approaches to Teaching and Assessing Pragmatics* (2018).

Beatriz Lado is Associate Professor and director of the Linguistics program at Lehman College, City University of New York (CUNY). She is also affiliated with LAILaC at The Graduate Center (CUNY). Her interests include: Bi/multilingual language acquisition; individual differences and pedagogical interventions; critical approaches to language learning; and language placement. She has published in journals such as *Applied Psycholinguistics*, *Bilingualism: Language & Cognition*, *Language Learning*, and *International Journal of Multilingualism*.

Ronald Leow is Professor of Applied Linguistics and director of Spanish Language Instruction at Georgetown University, Washington, DC. His areas of expertise include language curriculum development, teacher education, instructed language learning, psycholinguistics, cognitive processes in language learning, research methodology, and CALL.

Shaofeng Li is Associate Professor of Foreign and Second Language Education at Florida State University and an honorary professor at Zhengzhou University. He received his Ph.D. from Michigan State University. Prior to his appointment at Florida State University, he worked as senior lecturer in Applied Language Studies at the University of Auckland, New Zealand. His main research interests include corrective feedback, language aptitude, working memory, task-based instruction, and meta-analysis.

Shawn Loewen is Professor at Michigan State University in the MATESOL and Second Language Studies programs. His research interests include instructed second language acquisition, classroom interaction, and quantitative research methodology. He is currently the associate editor of *The Modern Language Journal*.

Alison Mackey is Professor of Linguistics at Georgetown University in Washington, DC and Professor of Applied Linguistics at Lancaster University in the UK. She is also editor-in-chief of the *Annual Review of Applied Linguistics* (Cambridge University Press). Her interests include second language acquisition and research methodology in applied linguistics.

Martyn McGettigan recently completed an MA in Applied Linguistics at St. Mary's University, London. He currently teaches EFL at a Japanese elementary school and is interested in the implementation of task-based language teaching in Japanese elementary school classrooms.

Ruth Milla teaches undergraduate courses on EFL didactics in the Faculty of Education at the University of the Basque Country, Spain. Her research and publications deal with EFL teaching and learning in multilingual contexts, developed within the research group *Language and Speech*.

Tamanna Mostafa is a Ph.D. candidate in the Department of Applied Linguistics and ESL at Georgia State University. Her research interests include second language (L2) speaking, L2 writing, individual cognitive differences in L2 acquisition, and application of natural language processing tools for analyzing learner language.

Tatsuya Nakata is an associate professor at the College of Intercultural Communication, Rikkyo University, Japan. His research interests include second language vocabulary acquisition and computer-assisted language learning. His research has appeared in publications such as *Studies in Second Language Acquisition*, *The Modern Language Journal*, and *Language Teaching Research*.

Kimi Nakatsukasa[†] was Assistant Professor in the Department of Classical and Modern Languages and Literatures at Texas Tech University. Her research interests included the analysis of gestures and second language development, classroom interaction, and interaction between linguistic and nonlinguistic abilities. She tragically passed away before the publication of this volume.

Hossein Nassaji is Professor of Applied Linguistics in the Department of Linguistics at the University of Victoria, Canada. He maintains an active research agenda across various areas of second language teaching and learning (e.g., corrective feedback, form-focused instruction, task-based teaching, classroom discourse, L2 reading processes) and has authored numerous publications on these topics.

Phuong Nguyen is a Ph.D. candidate in applied linguistics and technology at Iowa State University. She also works as a language assessment specialist at the University of Chicago. Her research interests include language assessment, CALL, and corpus linguistics.

Professor Rhonda Oliver is Head of the School of Education, Curtin University, Western Australia. She has researched extensively about second language acquisition, especially in relation to child language learners, but has also conducted research on language learners in high schools and universities. Recently she has undertaken work in the area of Aboriginal education.

Özgür Parlak is Assistant Professor of Linguistics at the American University of Sharjah. His research focuses on the relationship between interaction and the development of second language phonology, second language speech production and perception, second language pronunciation and intelligibility, and task-based language teaching.

Mirosław Pawlak is Professor of English at the State University of Applied Sciences, Konin, Poland, and Adam Mickiewicz University, Kalisz, Poland. His research interests include classroom interaction, form-focused instruction, corrective feedback, learner autonomy, language learning strategies, motivation, willingness to communicate, boredom, pronunciation teaching, and study abroad.

Ashleigh Pipes is Adjunct Professor at the University of Tennessee at Chattanooga. She is interested in individual differences in second language acquisition, with a particular focus on creativity.

Paul Gregory Quinn is an English for Academic Purposes professor in the English Language Learning Program at Centennial College and a TESL instructor for the Toronto District School Board. He researches how language is learned through production and corrective feedback. He is particularly interested in the timing of corrective feedback.

Lauren Ross-Feldman's work at Princeton University explores how cognitive, social, and individual factors mediate the experience and effects of communicative interaction on language learning. Her research has appeared in the journal *Language Learning* and in books published by John Benjamins and Oxford University Press.

Ayşenur Sağdıç is a doctoral candidate in applied linguistics at Georgetown University, Washington, DC. Her research focuses on L2 pragmatics in instructional and study abroad contexts and task-based language teaching, particularly the role of technology-mediated tasks and feedback on L2 pragmatic development. She has taught ESL, EFL, and linguistics courses.

Kazuya Saito is Associate Professor in Applied Linguistics at University College London. His research interests include how second language learners develop various dimensions of their speech in naturalistic settings; and how instruction can help optimize such learning processes in classroom contexts.

List of Contributors   xix

Cristina Sanz is Professor of Spanish & Linguistics, director of the Intensive & School of Foreign Service (SFS) Spanish Programs, the Barcelona Summer Program, and coordinator of the Catalan Lectureship at Georgetown University. Her area of expertise is multilingualism across the life span, with a focus on the interactions between individual differences and contexts of acquisition. She has published almost 100 articles in such journals as *Journal of Cognitive Neuroscience*, *Bilingualism Language and Cognition*, *Language Learning*, and *Applied Psycholinguistics*. Her most recent volume *The Routledge Handbook of Study Abroad Research and Practice* appeared in 2018.

Neomy Storch is Associate Professor in ESL and Applied Linguistics in the School of Languages & Linguistics, University of Melbourne. Her research focuses on topics related to L2 writing, including collaborative writing, corrective feedback, writing development, and authorial voice. She has published and presented extensively on her research.

Bo-Ram Suh is Associate Teaching Professor in the Faculty of Liberal Education at Seoul National University in South Korea. Her interests include second language acquisition, corrective feedback, cognitive processes in language learning, research methodology in applied linguistics, computer-assisted language learning, and task-based language teaching.

Takaaki Takeuchi is Professor of Foreign Language at Aichi University of Education, Japan. He is interested in second language learning and second language teaching, particularly the role of working memory and the role of individual differences.

Elaine E. Tarone is Distinguished Teaching Professor Emerita, University of Minnesota-Twin Cities. She is widely published in the area of second language acquisition research, on such topics as the variationist theory of SLA, the impact of literacy level on oral L2 processing, learner language analysis, and L2 language play, particularly in constructed dialogue. Dr. Tarone served as director of the Center for Advanced Research on Language Acquisition (CARLA) at the University of Minnesota from 1993 to 2016, offering an annual summer institute at CARLA on learner language analysis for teachers.

Antonella Valeo is an associate professor at York University where she teaches graduate courses in applied linguistics, TESOL, and ESL to undergraduate students. Her research explores language teaching and learning with a focus on classroom-based interaction, corrective feedback, and teacher education and development.

Catherine van Beuningen is senior researcher within the Research Centre for Learning and Innovation at the University of Applied Sciences Utrecht and Associate Professor within the Faculty of Education at the Amsterdam University of Applied Sciences. Her research interests include instructed second language learning, second language writing, and teaching in multilingual classrooms.

Alyssa Vuono is a doctoral student at Florida State University, majoring in Curriculum and Development in Foreign and Second Language Education. Her research interests include oral and written forms of corrective feedback as well as peer feedback on student writing.

Yucel Yilmaz is Associate Professor of Second Language Studies at Indiana University. His research focuses on second language interaction and corrective feedback; computer-mediated communication; task-based language teaching; individual differences in second language acquisition; and explicit and implicit learning processes.

Reiko Yoshida is a lecturer of Japanese in the School of Education at the University of South Australia. Her interests include perceptions of corrective feedback, corrective feedback between peers, and private speech in language classrooms, which are discussed in her book *Learners in Japanese Language Classrooms: Overt and Covert Participation* (2009).

Acknowledgments

This handbook would not have been possible without the help of many people. First, we would like to extend our sincere gratitude to the leading scholars in various areas of corrective feedback research, who eagerly answered our invitation to contribute to the project and produced chapters of the highest caliber. The editorial team at Cambridge University Press, ably headed by Rebecca Taylor, proved extremely supportive across all the stages of the process: from recognizing the need for this collection to providing insightful guidance during its preparation and production. We are grateful for their dedication and professionalism. The three anonymous reviewers of the book proposal for the volume are also to be acknowledged for their cogent assessment and expert advice on ways to improve the final product – we sincerely hope that this handbook lives up to their expectations. Finally, we would like to dedicate this volume to the memory of one of its contributors, Kimi Nakatsukasa, who, unfortunately, did not live long enough to see its publication. An exceptional scholar and colleague, Dr. Nakatsukasa leaves behind a rich and inspiring body of research on gesture and corrective feedback that should be learned from, built on, and added to.

Introduction

Corrective Feedback in Second Language Teaching and Learning

Hossein Nassaji and Eva Kartchava

Background

Current theory and research in second language acquisition (SLA) have widely advocated activities that involve a focus on meaning and at the same time provide opportunities for noticing and attention to language forms. Practitioners have also become increasingly aware of the importance of drawing learners' attention to form in classroom instruction. There are different ways of doing so, one of which is through corrective feedback.

Corrective feedback refers to any signal that a learner's utterance may be erroneous in some way. In the SLA literature, it is also known as negative evidence, defined as the information about what is not possible in a given language (e.g., Gass, 2003). This is opposed to positive evidence, which provides information about what is possible in a given language. The difference between corrective feedback and negative evidence is that corrective feedback is mainly provided in response to errors. Therefore, it is reactive. Negative evidence, however, can be both reactive and preemptive. That is, it can be obtained through corrective feedback on errors and also through explanation and presentation of grammatical rules that intend to inform the learner of nontarget-like uses of the language (see Nassaji, 2015, 2016). When negative evidence occurs reactively (i.e., corrective feedback), it can be either in the form of overt responses with a primary intention to correct that form or in the form of implicit feedback in which the correction occurs when the primary focus is on meaning.

Theoretical Issues

Theoretically, corrective feedback has long been a controversial topic in the field of both first and second language (L2) acquisition (see Part I of this volume). While some have argued that corrective feedback is necessary and assists language acquisition, others have contended that there is no need for corrective feedback and that it has little impact on L2 development. In the field of first language acquisition, for example, one theoretical position known as the nativist theory claims that there is limited explicit corrective feedback in oral language input and that it does not help child language acquisition (Brown & Hanlon, 1970; Demetras, Post & Snow, 1986). In this view, children are born with a genetically determined capacity that predisposes them to acquire the language through exposure to input. This innate capacity is referred to as Language Acquisition Device (LAD) or, more formally, Universal Grammar (UG). While the theory of UG has been used mainly to explain first language acquisition, a number of SLA researchers have extended it to SLA (e.g., Flynn, 1988, 1996; Schwartz, 1993; White, 1991), arguing that similar innate principles are also available to L2 learners either fully or partially and that since L2 learners have access to these principles corrective feedback hardly plays any role.

Other perspectives in L2, on the other hand, such as the cognitive views or cognitive interactionist views, hold that corrective feedback is both needed and facilitative of language acquisition. From a cognitive perspective, corrective feedback promotes noticing of language forms and also helps learners to test their hypotheses about the language they are learning. Making a distinction between declarative and procedural knowledge, skill acquisition theories, for example, argue that language knowledge is first declarative and then becomes procedural through practice (e.g., Anderson, 1985). Declarative knowledge is knowledge about language, and procedural knowledge is knowledge of how to use the language. From this perspective, corrective feedback is essential as it helps the formation of our initial declarative knowledge. Information-processing theories and skill acquisition theories consider corrective feedback crucial as it facilitates forming a mental representation of the target language.

Corrective feedback is also important from an interactionist perspective. This perspective emphasizes the centrality of interaction, particularly negotiation of meaning, which refers to conversational strategies (such as confirmation checks, reformulation, and clarification requests) used to signal or repair problems in communication (e.g., Pica, 1994). From this perspective, interaction with nonnative speakers contains many instances of such interactional modifications, and these modifications provide learners with important sources of comprehensible input and negative evidence (e.g., Gass, 2003; Gass & Varonis, 1994; Long, 1991, 1996; Pica, 1994, 1998). The notion of interactional feedback in SLA is based on an interactionist perspective and the assumption that through interactional feedback learners not only communicate their meaning but also receive negative evidence through the use of the above-mentioned negotiation strategies. Corrective feedback also provides opportunities for output (e.g., Swain, 1995, 2005). When learners receive feedback, they may be pushed to produce new language and also have opportunities to revise their original utterance to be more accurate and comprehensible. In the SLA literature, this is called modified output and considered as facilitative of language acquisition.

Types and Modes of Corrective Feedback

Corrective feedback can be written and oral and can be provided both verbally and nonverbally (through, for example, body language such as gestures) by the teacher, the computer, or the learner (peer feedback) (see Part III and Part IV of this volume). Oral feedback is verbal and can be provided both during and after oral production. When corrective feedback occurs immediately after an error during conversation, it requires more dependence on online processing and, as such, is usually more cognitively demanding than when feedback is provided after the error. Written feedback, compared to oral feedback, is often delayed, and for that reason, it may be less cognitively demanding as learners have more time to process the feedback. Oral feedback often has the purpose of increasing the accuracy of learners' utterances, whereas written feedback focuses on not only the accuracy of language forms but also the overall quality of writing, including content, ideas, and organization.

There are different ways of providing corrective feedback. In general, feedback types can be classified into reformulation and elicitation. Reformulation strategies are those that rephrase the learner's erroneous utterance into a correct form. They have also been called input-providing because they provide the learner with target-like input (Ellis, 2009). Elicitation strategies do not provide the correct form but rather attempt to prompt the learners to correct their original erroneous output. Therefore, they are called output-prompting (Ellis, 2009). Since elicitations do not supply the correct form, they allow the learner to discover it for themselves. In other words, they provide opportunities for self-repair. Table 0.1 provides a taxonomy of oral corrective feedback.

Written feedback has been typically classified as direct, indirect, and metalinguistic comment or explanation. Direct feedback provides the correct form, whereas indirect feedback indicates the presence of an error without any correction. Both direct and indirect feedback can take different forms and can be used either alone or in combination with other feedback types. Direct feedback, for example, can occur in the form of crossing out the wrong or unnecessary words or phrases, supplying the missing form, highlighting the wrong form and indicating the accurate form by writing the correct form above, beside, or across from the error (Ferris, 2006). Indirect feedback can occur in the form of underlining the error, using codes to indicate the type of error, commenting on the error in the margin, or color-coding the error. Lira Gonzales and Nassaji (2018), for example, found a very frequent use of

Table 0.1 *A taxonomy of oral feedback (from Nassaji, 2015)*

Reformulation (Input providing)	Elicitation (output-prompting)
Recasts: Rephrase all or part of an erroneous utterance into a correct form.	Clarification requests: Occur when an utterance is not fully understood and the learner is asked for clarification.
Direct correction: Rephrases an erroneous utterance into a correct form and also clearly indicates the erroneous part.	Repetition: Repeats the erroneous utterance with a rising intonation.
	Direct elicitation: Elicits the correct form, for example, by repeating the erroneous utterance up to the error and waiting for the correction.
	Metalinguistic cue: Provides metalinguistic information.

direct feedback compared to indirect feedback on students' writings by teachers in such different instructional contexts as elementary, secondary, and college-level settings. Written feedback can also be provided electronically via the computer or any other technological devices to correct an error or provide an indication that an error has occurred.

Nonverbal feedback occurs through body movements such as gestures, facial expressions, head, hand, and finger movements. For example, frowning or shaking the head could be used to show that an error has taken place. Body movements could be used to indicate where the error has occurred or the nature of the error.

As noted earlier, feedback can also be provided by the student, both orally and in written form (called peer feedback or peer review). Research indicates that peer feedback is being increasingly used in recent years in language classrooms and that it has positive effects on students' learning, particularly if students are trained to provide it. What's more, both teachers and students consider it a valuable resource.

Corrective feedback can vary in terms of its focus. In this respect, a distinction has been made between extensive and intensive feedback in the oral feedback literature (e.g., Nassaji, 2017) and between focused and unfocused (comprehensive) feedback in the written feedback literature (e.g., Sheen, Wright & Moldawa, 2009). Extensive or comprehensive feedback is provided on a wide range of linguistic forms, whereas intensive or focused feedback is provided on a single or a small number of linguistic targets. Theoretically, intensive/focused feedback has been viewed to be more effective than extensive feedback because learners may be more likely to notice the feedback when it targets a single error repeatedly. However, it is possible that extensive feedback might also be effective, for when the feedback is provided extensively, learners may be exposed to additional instances of the feedback and therefore may become better aware of the presence of the feedback, particularly if it is implicit in nature (e.g., Nassaji, 2017).

Researching Corrective Feedback

Owing to both the theoretical and the pedagogical importance of corrective feedback and also the debate around its usefulness, many studies have examined its role in various contexts. This research has been both descriptive (observational) and experimental, conducted inside and outside the classroom, targeting different language forms including grammar, vocabulary, and pragmatics. Observational or descriptive research has attempted to determine the degree to which feedback occurs in the different L2 learning contexts, its distributional patterns, and the types of response, if any, learners provide to such feedback. In much of the descriptive research on oral feedback, the usefulness of feedback has been measured by learner responses, which has been called uptake or repair. In written feedback, this has been measured by the degree to which learners revise their text or transfer their knowledge into new texts (e.g., Karim & Nassaji, 2020; Suzuki, Nassaji & Sato, 2019). The aim of experimental research, in turn, has been to determine more directly the effects of feedback on learning and the factors that might mediate feedback effectiveness. It has also investigated the effect of different types of feedback on different target structures and/or on different types of knowledge (i.e., both explicit and implicit knowledge, see, for example, Nassaji, 2015, 2020).

Depending on its purpose, the findings of corrective feedback research have been summarized in a number of recent reviews and meta-analyses (e.g., written feedback: Kang & Han, 2015; oral feedback: Li, 2010; Lyster & Saito, 2010; Lyster, Saito & Sato, 2012; Mackey & Goo, 2007; Nassaji, 2015, 2016; Russell & Spada, 2006; computer-mediated feedback: Yousefi & Nassaji, 2019; Ziegler, 2016, see also the various chapters of this volume). The overall conclusions are that corrective feedback is helpful in general. Descriptive studies, for example, have shown that corrective feedback occurs frequently in L2 classrooms and that learners revise their erroneous output in response to feedback. Experimental studies have also confirmed the beneficial effects of feedback, but at the same time, they have shown that these effects are not the same across feedback types and contexts and, as such, may vary depending on a number of other factors, including the type of target structure (see below).

Additionally, studies have explored learners' perspectives and/or perceptions of both oral and written feedback and their relationship to feedback types and feedback targets (Amrhein & Nassaji, 2010; Egi, 2010; Fu, 2012, see also Part VII of this volume). Using various forms of retrospective and introspective data collection tools – such as think-aloud, stimulated, or immediate recall as well as various kinds of self-report data (e.g., questionnaires, diaries, journals) – perception studies have helped us understand the relationship between teachers' intention for feedback and learners' interpretation of that feedback. Some of the chapters of this handbook have examined these issues in detail.

As noted earlier, corrective feedback can also occur via the computer and other technological devices. In recent years, a number of studies as well as meta-analyses and reviews have examined the use and effectiveness of feedback through technology (e.g., Felix, 2005a, 2005b; Liu et al., 2002; Nassaji & Kartchava, 2019; Yousefi & Nassaji, 2019; Ziegler, 2016, see also Part VI of this volume). These studies have shown that technology-mediated feedback can promote L2 learning and that its effectiveness may be different from that of face-to-face feedback (see Yousefi & Nassaji, 2019).

Factors Affecting the Role of Feedback

The findings of all feedback studies, including those of the meta-analyses, confirm that corrective feedback is beneficial for L2 learning in general and that such feedback promotes L2 learning. However, they have also found notable variability in results, which suggests that the role of corrective feedback is not universal and can differ depending on a number of factors, including the type of feedback, the nature of the target form, learners' level of language proficiency, and their developmental readiness. Mackey and Philp (1998), for example, found that learners who were developmentally more advanced benefited more from recasts than those who were developmentally less advanced. Ammar and Spada (2006) found that high-proficiency learners benefited more from recasts than lower-proficiency learners. The effectiveness of feedback has also been shown to vary depending on the way learners' attention is directed to the feedback (Nabei & Swain, 2002), the type of tasks used (Gass, Mackey & Ross-Feldman, 2005), and even learners' gender (Ross-Feldman, 2007). Individual differences – such as learners' working memory, age, anxiety, aptitude, analytic ability, and learner literacy (Bigelow et al., 2006) – may also impact the degree to which learners benefit from feedback (see Part VIII on the role of individual differences). In their meta-analysis of oral feedback studies in the classroom, Lyster and Saito (2010) found an important effect for age, with younger learners benefiting more from feedback than older learners.

Both the instructional and the interactional contexts may also mediate feedback effectiveness. Mackey and Goo's (2007) meta-analysis found that interactional feedback had a significantly greater effect in foreign language contexts than in second language contexts; this was also true for the laboratory versus classroom settings. The effect of both oral and written feedback may not be the same for different target structures either (Long, Inagaki & Ortega, 1998) and may also vary depending on whether the learners are required to revise their previous errors or use their knowledge in new contexts. For example, examining the effect of both direct and indirect written corrective feedback on the English indefinite article and the past perfect tense, Suzuki et al. (2019) found that while both feedback types improved the accuracy of the two target structures in revision, the transfer effect of feedback to new pieces of writing was found only for the past perfect.

Another important mediating factor is the feedback focusedness, that is, whether the feedback is provided extensively on a wide range of errors or intensively on certain preselected errors (see Part IV of this volume). Some researchers have suggested that intensive recasts may be more effective than extensive feedback, as it draws learners' attention to form more efficiently (e.g., Ellis & Sheen, 2006; Lyster et al., 2012). However, studies that have compared focused versus unfocused (or comprehensive) feedback or extensive versus intensive feedback have shown variable results. For example, comparing the effectiveness of focused and unfocused written feedback, Ellis et al. (2008) found similar gains for both feedback types. Sheen et al. (2009), however, found more effects for focused than unfocused written feedback. Kamiya (2015) found no clear-cut difference between extensive and intensive oral recasts. Yet, Nassaji (2017) found extensive recasts to be generally more effective than intensive recasts. Part of the reason for these differences could be the way feedback focusedness has been operationalized. For instance, Ellis et al. used a range of different feedback types in their study. Therefore, it is unclear whether the results were because of the focus of the feedback or the differences in the types of feedback used. Sheen et al. used the feedback very explicitly, providing the correct form and drawing the learners' attention to the error through metalinguistic explanation. Nassaji, however, used implicit recasts.

Last but not least, the effectiveness of feedback may also vary depending on how it is measured (see Nassaji, 2020 for a discussion). Some studies, for example, have found that recasts may have more positive effects on oral measures than written ones (e.g., Révész, 2012) or on tests that measure implicit rather than explicit knowledge (e.g., Lyster & Saito, 2010; Mackey & Goo, 2007). Of course, the effects of outcome measures might also interact with those of other variables, such as the context of feedback and/or the type of target structure (e.g., Norris & Ortega, 2001).

All these and many other issues on corrective feedback are addressed in detail in the various chapters of this handbook. In what follows, we describe the aims and content of the volume as well as what each chapter covers.

The Aims of the Volume

The role and importance of various forms of corrective feedback have been examined in numerous studies in different instructional contexts and with different L2 learners and languages. The results of most of these studies have been published in many individual journal articles and book chapters. Yet, until now, there has been only one collection (Nassaji & Kartchava, 2017) that has drawn the findings of some of these investigations together and discussed their applications in real-world learning situations. This collection, however, was subject to space limitation and as a result could not provide a thorough treatment of the topic. Recognizing the burgeoning need to communicate the findings of current research on corrective feedback to various audiences, including researchers and teachers, we decided to put together this handbook, which is intended to provide the first comprehensive source of information on corrective feedback in a single volume. The specific aims are to (a) provide an in-depth analysis and discussion of research and theory in this area, (b) bring together state-of-the-art chapters that address recent developments in a range of core areas of corrective feedback, including oral, written, computer-mediated and nonverbal feedback as well as studies of various factors that may influence feedback effectiveness, including learner and teacher perception and the role of various individual learner differences, (c) examine the current methodological tools and perspectives that have been used to study the contributions of corrective feedback to L2 learning and pedagogy, and (d) connect theory and research with classroom practice – a link that is timely, yet currently noticeably absent from most of the writings in the field.

The Intended Audience

This handbook provides a key single-volume resource for all those interested in gaining insight into the role of corrective feedback in L2 learning and how it can be used to enhance L2 teaching. Given its scope, it will appeal to a broad set of readers, including researchers and graduate students in applied linguistics and TESL as well as teachers, teacher educators, and materials developers, who are interested in learning about the role of feedback in second language teaching and learning. Since the chapters are theme-based, each one can be read as a stand-alone piece or as part of an integrated whole that seeks to enable the reader to develop a coherent understanding of the themes covered. It can also be used as a textbook in courses on second language acquisition and/ or those concerned specifically with corrective feedback. Hence, the collection could prove useful for both introductory and more specialized courses. Finally, since the volume includes a comprehensive reference on theory and research in a range of core areas of corrective feedback, it can be used as a guide among nonacademic audiences, such as school boards and individual practitioners, as well as appeal to numerous other stakeholders internationally.

The Organization of the Book

The handbook contains thirty-six chapters that examine various theoretical, empirical, and methodological issues currently addressed in the field of L2 corrective feedback. For ease of access, we have organized these chapters into the following eight parts.

    Part I: Theoretical perspectives on corrective feedback
    Part II: Methodological approaches in the study of corrective feedback
    Part III: Different delivery modes of corrective feedback
    Part IV: Feedback provider, feedback intensity, and feedback timing
    Part V: Corrective feedback and language skills
    Part VI: Contexts of corrective feedback and their effects
    Part VII: Learners' and teachers' feedback perspectives, perceptions, and preferences
    Part VIII: Individual differences, tasks, and other language and learner-related factors

Part I
Part I contains four chapters that discuss the different theoretical perspectives on corrective feedback including the behaviorist, the innatist, the interactionist, the cognitive, and the sociocultural perspective. In Chapter 1, Han examines the behaviorist and innatist perspectives. Arguably, these are the most established yet polarizing perspectives, which have profoundly impacted all aspects of second language inquiry, including the role of error correction. The chapter begins by describing each of the paradigms individually, highlighting their underlying tenets, orientations toward second/additional language development, and their views on errors and their treatment. It also compares and discusses the similarities and differences in these approaches while at the same time underscoring their contributions to past and present error correction research and pedagogy. In Chapter 2, Abbuhl examines the interactionist approach to corrective feedback. The chapter first discusses the basis of the theory with respect to error correction and then evaluates these against other extant research paradigms. After reviewing the early and current research evidence within the paradigm, the chapter suggests directions for future interactionist investigations on both known and developing issues and the contributions these may make to classroom teaching. In Chapter 3, Leow and Driver consider cognitive theoretical perspectives on corrective feedback. Here, they use a coarse-grained theoretical feedback processing framework to illuminate how cognitive processes involved in error correction are viewed within major cognitive viewpoints on L2 development. For each viewpoint, the authors first present its theoretical underpinnings and

then examine the importance that the theory assigns to corrective feedback as well as the type of processing it requires for feedback delivery. Nassaji, in Chapter 4, considers the role of corrective feedback from a sociocultural perspective. Following an examination of the theoretical underpinnings, the chapter reviews empirical evidence on corrective feedback offered by the research conducted from this perspective and suggests pedagogical implications for the delivery of effective feedback.

Part II

Part II focuses on the methodological approaches in the study of corrective feedback. It consists of four chapters (Chapters 5 to 8). In Chapter 5, Mackey, Bryfonski, Parlak, Pipes, Sağdıç, and Suh discuss tools that have been used to elicit and examine the effectiveness of feedback for language learning. The authors consider established and novel instruments to collect learner-external and learner-internal data across feedback modes, in both classroom and laboratory settings. Each instrument is considered in terms of its purpose, utility, and effective administrative procedures; illustrative studies that employed the tool in their design are also cited and/or explained. Implications and special considerations for the implementation of these instruments in research and teaching are provided at the end. Chapter 6 and Chapter 7 address research methodologies used to explore corrective feedback in the laboratory and classroom settings, respectfully. Loewen and Gass (Chapter 6) begin by suggesting an expanded guideline on how to distinguish between the classroom and laboratory contexts, arguing that the traditional differentiation is limiting and often difficult to apply. They propose that laboratory-based research, regardless of focus, should be distinguished from classroom research in terms of the physical location, the one who provides instruction (i.e., instructor/researcher/different interlocutor), and the nature of instructional tasks employed. Drawing on the existing corrective feedback research, the authors first illustrate the application of these principles and then show how their manipulation, even unintentional, could yield conflicting results. Hence, they urge caution and call on future studies to adopt improved and more overt contextual operationalizations. In Chapter 7, Valeo explores the impact of classroom-based research on our understanding of the role and contributions of oral and written corrective feedback. Examining key studies in this area, the chapter considers how specific research methodologies (including descriptive and experimental types) applied within particular instructional settings can be affected by the various contextual features present (even if unaccounted for) and in turn, affect the findings. Reiterating the importance of context in feedback provision, the author urges both researchers and teachers to reflect and expand on their practices, suggesting possible directions to consider.

Brown, in Chapter 8, discusses the use of research synthesis, and more specifically meta-analysis and methodological synthesis, to evaluate the effectiveness of corrective feedback. Following an explanation of the differences between these methodological tools, the reader is provided with a guideline on how to conduct the syntheses and is informed of potential benefits and limitations that each approach may offer. The chapter concludes with suggestions of ways in which these tools could benefit future corrective feedback studies.

Part III

Part III focuses on the various modes through which corrective feedback could be delivered including oral, written, technology-mediated, and nonverbal modes. This part consists of four chapters, Chapters 9 to 13. Chapter 9, by Oliver and Adams, concerns oral feedback. This chapter discusses the importance of this delivery mode as well as the various issues that surround it. Following a presentation of the possible oral corrective feedback strategies, the chapter also examines current evidence for their effectiveness and evaluates ways in which additional social and individual factors can impact the utility of the feedback. Pedagogical implications of this body of research are provided. In Chapter 10, Bitchener examines written corrective feedback. The chapter begins with an examination of the various types of feedback used to address learners' errors in second language writing and then examines their effectiveness in terms of both product and cognitive processing involved in accurate output. Pedagogical insights drawn from this discussion are provided. Heift, Nguyen, and Hegelheimer (Chapter 11) consider technology-mediated corrective feedback. They describe the different technologies that have been developed to provide learners with feedback in the areas of spelling, grammar and writing, and pronunciation during computer-based interactions. The chapter examines effectiveness of the technological tools discussed and offers recommendations for language instruction. The final chapter in this section, Chapter 12, examines the role of nonverbal feedback in language learning and teaching. Nakatsukasa posits that corrective feedback investigations would be complemented by analysis of nonverbal features, such as gestures, that may occur alongside oral corrective episodes. It is argued that the information they convey may be as important as the information provided through their verbal counterparts. To illustrate this, the chapter first discusses the facilitative role of gestures in learning in general and language learning more specifically and then examines current evidence on the impact of gesture in the development of different language skills including vocabulary, pronunciation, grammar, and comprehension. Directions for future research on gesture (and other nonverbal features) and feedback as well as guidelines for gesture use in the classroom are also provided.

Part IV

Part IV includes four chapters (Chapters 13 to16) that examine issues related to feedback provider, feedback intensity, and feedback timing. Chapter 13, by Iwashita and Dao, considers the role of oral peer feedback in language learning. A description of the types and benefits of this feedback type opens the chapter, and then empirical findings on its effectiveness are reviewed. Directions for future research and the practical applications of peer feedback in the classroom conclude the chapter. In Chapter 14, Van Beuningen addresses the focusedness of corrective feedback. While, in general terms, focused corrective feedback entails attention to one or a limited number of preselected linguistic features, unfocused feedback is unrestricted in scope and error count. Yet, because the application of this distinction in practice is not clear-cut, the chapter first examines the various terms as well as their particular nuances and characteristics advanced in the SLA literature and then posits that focusedness should be considered as a matter of degree and as two sides of a continuum, not as a dichotomy. Theoretical, pedagogical, and methodological arguments that support the use and/or investigation of focused and unfocused corrective feedback are presented followed by a discussion on their impact in verbal and written communication. The chapter concludes by outlining pedagogical implications and possible directions for future research. Chapter 15, by Quinn, discusses the issue of feedback timing – i.e., whether to address errors immediately after an error is made or at a later time. Here, theoretical proposals and empirical evidence on the timing of both oral and written feedback are discussed and implications for research and pedagogy are considered. In Chapter 16, Ellis discusses the issue of feedback explicitness. The chapter begins by examining the theoretical and empirical issues as well as the confounding matters that can plague explicit/implicit distinction and then discusses the variables that need to be considered when doing research in this area.

Part V

Part V (Chapters 17 to 21) examines how corrective feedback impacts the development of various L2 skills. In Chapter 17, Basturkmen and Fu consider the development of grammar, which they define as the learning of morphological and syntactic forms and form–meaning mappings. The chapter reviews research that has considered grammar development in relation to feedback and the implication of this research for classroom pedagogy. Chapter 18, by Kamiya and Nakata, examines the role of feedback with respect to the development of L2 vocabulary. The chapter first reviews available research on how oral and written feedback affect vocabulary learning. It then, centering on each feedback type (oral vs. written) individually, examines evidence for vocabulary-focused feedback effectiveness, outlines observed corrective feedback practices, and suggests ways to improve such practices. Directions for future investigations are also identified. Chapter 19, by Saito, explores the role of corrective feedback on L2 pronunciation. It examines both experimental and descriptive research on the topic and also the impact of such factors as learner readiness, feedback strategies, instructional targets, and attitudes on research findings. Topics for future investigations conclude the chapter. In Chapter 20, Bardovi-Harlig and Yilmaz discuss the potential role of corrective feedback in L2 pragmatics. They begin by arguing that current research is too limited to provide any recommendations for or against the implementation of corrective feedback in L2 instruction. In search of additional evidence, the authors draw on research on corrective feedback in general and on L2 pragmatics in particular to offer guidelines for research on the relationship between corrective feedback and learning L2 pragmatics. Finally, in Chapter 21, Tarone examines the issue of corrective feedback in relation to language literacy (including alphabetic print literacy), an area of L2 development that has received less attention in current research. Drawing on research from cognitive psychology and the studies in SLA, the chapter discusses issues related to low-literate adults' phonemic and phonological awareness as well as their ability to notice and benefit from corrective feedback. The chapter concludes with a discussion on the impact of feedback on these learners' language development and calls for sustained interest in investigating the utility of corrective feedback for assisting language development among low-literate/illiterate populations.

Part VI

Part VI consists of four chapters, Chapters 22 to 25, and explores the relationship between context and corrective feedback. Chapter 22, by Garcia Mayo and Milla, examines the impact of instructional context on the delivery and perception of corrective feedback. With a focus on second and foreign language settings, the chapter reviews studies on oral feedback in each of these contexts and also those that compare the two settings. The chapter concludes with pedagogical implications drawn from this body of research as well as directions for additional research. Cerezo, in Chapter 23, examines the effectiveness of corrective feedback in computer-mediated settings and also compares it with feedback effectiveness in face-to-face interactions. A critical synthesis of forty-one studies that compared the impact of written corrective feedback in the two environments is provided. The findings point to diverging results, which the author explains in terms of methodological issues and lack of focus. Suggestions on possible ways to overcome these drawbacks as well as ideas for future research are outlined. Chapter 24, by Kartchava and Nassaji, explores the role of corrective feedback in mobile technology-mediated contexts. The chapter examines the ways in which mobile technology can assist language learning in general and when used to deliver feedback in particular. Although findings from the currently limited body of research on mobile-assisted corrective feedback are encouraging, the authors call for more investigations to assess the use of this technology in delivering feedback as well as the factors and processes that mediate its effectiveness. The final chapter in this section, Chapter 25 by Ballinger, considers corrective feedback in content-based contexts. The author reviews current research in this area and also calls for more studies not only on feedback effectiveness in content-based settings but also on educating teachers of the value of corrective feedback and the ways in which it can be provided in such contexts.

Part VII

Part VII addresses learners' and teachers' feedback perspectives, perceptions, and preferences. Chapter 26, by Kim and Mostafa, reviews teachers' and learners' beliefs about oral and written corrective feedback and how they affect the provision or reception of the feedback. The findings are synthesized and directions for additional investigations in each area are offered. Chapter 27, by Storch, focuses on the language learner and his or her response (or lack thereof) to written corrective feedback provided by the teacher. Using the Activity Theory lens, Storch examines how learners' individual factors and learning goals in conjunction with various elements of their immediate and broader learning contexts may explain the outcomes of the feedback they receive on their writing. Suggestions for the classroom and empirical explorations in this area conclude the chapter. Continuing the theme of factors that may underlie behavior in relation to corrective feedback, Kartchava, in Chapter 28, investigates how targeted training in corrective feedback may assist both teachers and learners in improving their understanding of and relationship with feedback. For teachers, this entails adopting effective practices for feedback provision, and for learners – becoming informed consumers and users of the information the corrective feedback contains. The chapter concludes with calls for additional studies that probe the effectiveness and implications for teacher and student training in corrective feedback, and to this end, it outlines possible directions that these might take. In Chapter 29, Yoshida explores perceptions and noticeability of oral (and some chat-based) feedback in various contexts (teacher–learner, learner–learner, and learner–computer) and considers factors that may impact it. The synthesis highlights what is already known about the complex notion of noticing and corrective feedback and also points to potentially fruitful and timely explorations on the topic in need of implementation.

Part VIII

Part VIII includes seven chapters (Chapters 30 to 36) and examines the role of individual differences, task, and language-related factors in the efficacy of corrective feedback. Age is the topic of Chapter 30, where Vuono and Li explore its importance and impact in relation to feedback effectiveness from a variety of perspectives. They provide an extensive review that outlines and critically evaluates the findings, approaches, and contexts targeted in researching the role of corrective feedback in both child and adult L2 learners. The chapter concludes with a discussion of implications for both researchers and teachers. Chapter 31, by Adams and Ross-Feldman, considers the role of gender. Presenting arguments for the need to consider gender in feedback research, the authors posit that it may be a determinant in how feedback is supplied and responded to in learner interactions with native speakers, teachers, and peers. They argue that the limited body of available research on corrective feedback and gender, however, is currently unable to provide concrete conclusions on how gender may affect opportunities to learn a second language through feedback on error, and thus the authors suggest several directions that researchers interested in the subject area could pursue. The role of two cognitive factors of aptitude and prior language experience (here, dubbed "multilingualism") in the efficacy of corrective feedback is examined by Lado and Sanz in Chapter 32. The chapter considers each variable separately by situating its role and function in general L2 learning and in relation to feedback, synthesizing available research across learning conditions and outlining research gaps as well as implications that extant findings may carry for language pedagogy. Chapter 33, by Goo and Takeuchi, explores how affective variables such as language anxiety, emotions, as well as other related factors, such as motivation, learner beliefs, and self-efficacy, shape and are shaped by L2 learning and teaching. The comprehensive review of the literature points to the potentially important role these affective variables may play in mediating the effectiveness of corrective feedback. The authors end with a discussion of pedagogical implications and ways to positively influence corrective feedback provision in light of the discussed factors. Pawlak, in Chapter 34, examines the role of developmental readiness and language proficiency in the efficacy of corrective feedback. Following a description of the two constructs and their relationship to L2 knowledge, a critical review of the research conducted on the factors in relation to feedback is presented and suggestions about how the findings could inform classroom practice are offered. A call for additional well-designed studies that examine these variables across instructional contexts and conditions is also made. Chapter 35, by Granena and Yilmaz, presents a synthesis of primary studies to examine the effectiveness of corrective feedback in relation to the grammatical complexity of particular morphosyntactic features in English. Although, on the whole, the results point to feedback being more effective with simple grammatical structures, the authors warn against rush conclusions, calling for dedicated studies that specifically set out to investigate the relationship between complexity of target structure and corrective feedback effectiveness. They also submit a method to categorize the complexity of formal and semantic features. The final chapter in the collection, Chapter 36, considers the role of task in the efficacy of corrective feedback. After defining the notion of "task" and specifying the theoretical underpinnings, Foster and McGettigan show how task design has generally not been examined in studies on corrective feedback and, instead, been relegated to a means of generating output. Positing fruitful intersections between task design and opportunities for task-based attention to form, they put forth proposals that may promote a role for feedback across the various stages of task performance. Given that research on the topic is currently scant, the authors also call on researchers to invest in investigations that explore the proposed intersections.

References

Ammar, A. & Spada, N. (2006). One size fits all? Recasts, prompts, and L2 learning. *Studies in Second Language Acquisition*, 28(4), 543–574.

Amrhein, H. & Nassaji, H. (2010). Written corrective feedback: What do students and teachers prefer and why? *Canadian Journal of Applied Linguistics*, 13(2), 95–127.

Anderson, J. (1985). Cognitive psychology and its implications. New York: Freeman.

Bigelow, M., Delmas, R., Hansen, K. & Tarone, E. (2006). Literacy and the processing of oral recasts in SLA. *TESOL Quarterly*, 40(4), 665–689.

Brown, R. & Hanlon, C. (1970). Derivational complexity and order of acquisition in child speech. In J. Hayes (ed.), *Cognition and the development of language* (pp. 11–53). New York: Wiley.

Demetras, M., Post, K. & Snow, C. (1986). Feedback to first language learners: The role of repetitions and clarification questions. *Journal of Child Language*, 13(2), 275–292.

Egi, T. (2010). Uptake, modified output, and learner perceptions of recasts: Learner responses as language awareness. *Modern Language Journal*, 94(1), 1–21. doi:10.1111/j.1540-4781.2009.00980.x.

Ellis, R. (2009). Corrective feedback and teacher development. *L2 Journal*, 1(1), 3–18.

Ellis, R. & Sheen, Y. (2006). Reexamining the role of recasts in second language acquisition. *Studies in Second Language Acquisition*, 28(4), 575–600.

Ellis, R., Sheen, Y., Murakami, M. & Takashima, H. (2008). The effects of focused and unfocused written corrective feedback in an English as a foreign language context. *System*, 36(3), 353–371.

Felix, U. (2005a). Analyzing recent CALL effectiveness research: Towards a common agenda. *Computer Assisted Language Learning*, 18(1–2), 1–32.
Felix, U. (2005b). What do meta-analyses tell us about CALL effectiveness? *ReCALL*, 17(12), 269–288.
Ferris, D. R. (2006). Does error feedback help student writers? New evidence on the short- and long-term effects of written error correction. In K. Hyland & F. Hyland (eds.), *Feedback in second language writing* (pp. 81–104). Cambridge: Cambridge University Press.
Flynn, S. (1988). Nature of development in L2 acquisition and implications for theories of language acquisition in general. In S. Flynn & W. O'Neill (eds.), *Linguistic theory in second language acquisition* (pp. 277–294). Dordrecht: Kluwer.
Flynn, S. (1996). A parameter-setting approach to second language acquisition. In W. Ritchie & T. Bhatia (eds.), *Handbook of second language acquisition* (pp. 121–158). San Diego: Academic Press.
Fu, T. (2012). Corrective feedback and learner uptake in a Chinese as a foreign language class: Do perceptions and the reality match? Unpublished MA thesis, University of Victoria, Victoria, BC.
Gass, S. (2003). Input and interaction. In C. Doughty & M. Long (eds.), *The handbook of second language acquisition* (pp. 224–255). Oxford: Blackwell.
Gass, S., Mackey, A. & Ross-Feldman, L. (2005). Task-based interactions in classroom and laboratory settings. *Language Learning*, 55(4), 575–611.
Gass, S. & Varonis, E. (1994). Input, interaction, and second language production. *Studies in Second Language Acquisition*, 16(3), 283–302.
Kamiya, N. (2015). The effectiveness of intensive and extensive recasts on L2 acquisition for implicit and explicit knowledge. *Linguistics and Education*, 29, 59–72.
Kang, E., & Han, Z. (2015). The efficacy of written corrective feedback in improving L2 written accuracy: A meta-analysis. *Modern Language Journal*, 99(1), 1–18.
Karim, K. & Nassaji, H. (2020). The revision and transfer effects of direct and indirect comprehensive corrective feedback on ESL students' writing. *Language Teaching Research*, 24(4), 519–539.
Li, S. (2010). The effectiveness of corrective feedback in SLA: A meta-analysis. *Language Learning*, 60(2), 309–365.
Lira Gonzales, M., & Nassaji, H. (2018). Teachers' written corrective feedback and students' revision in the ESL classroom. Paper presented at the American Association for Applied Linguistics 4–27 March, Chicago, USA.
Liu, M., Moore, Z., Graham, L. & Lee, S. (2002). A look at the research in computer-based technology use in second language learning: A review of literature from 1990–2000. *Journal of Research on Technology in Education*, 34(3), 250–273.

Long, M. (1991). Focus on form: A design feature in language teaching methodology. In K. DeBot, R. Ginsberge & C. Kramsch (eds.), *Foreign language research in cross-cultural perspective* (pp. 39–52). Amsterdam: John Benjamins.

(1996). The role of the linguistic environment in second language acquisition. In W. Ritchie & T. Bhatia (eds.), *Handbook of second language acquisition* (pp. 413–468). San Diego: Academic Press.

Long, M., Inagaki, S. & Ortega, L. (1998). The role of implicit negative feedback in SLA: Models and recasts in Japanese and Spanish. *Modern Language Journal*, 82(3), 357–371.

Lyster, R. & Saito, K. (2010). Oral feedback in classroom SLA: A meta-analysis. *Studies in Second Language Acquisition*, 32(2), 265–302.

Lyster, R., Saito, K. & Sato, M. (2012). Oral corrective feedback in second language classrooms. *Language Teaching*, 46(1), 1–40. doi:10.1017/S0261444812000365.

Mackey, A. & Goo, J. (2007). Interaction research in SLA: A meta-analysis and research synthesis. In A. Mackey (ed.), *Conversational interaction in second language acquisition: A collection of empirical studies* (pp. 407–452). Oxford: Oxford University Press.

Mackey, A. & Philp, J. (1998). Conversational interaction and second language development: Recasts, responses, and red herrings? *Modern Language Journal*, 82(3), 338–356.

Nabei, T. & Swain, M. (2002). Learner awareness of recasts in classroom interaction: A case study of an adult EFL student's second language learning. *Language Awareness*, 11(1), 43–63.

Nassaji, H. (2015). *Interactional feedback dimension in instructed second language learning*. London: Bloomsbury Publishing.

(2016). Anniversary article: Interactional feedback in second language teaching and learning: A synthesis and analysis of current research. *Language Teaching Research*, 20(4), 535–562.

(2017). The effectiveness of extensive versus intensive recasts for learning L2 grammar. *Modern Language Journal*, 101(2), 353–368.

(2020). Assessing the effectiveness of interactional feedback for L2 acquisition: Issues and challenges. *Language Teaching Research*, 53(1), 3–28.

Nassaji, H. & Kartchava, E. (eds.). (2017). *Corrective Feedback in Second Language Teaching and Learning: Research, Theory, Applications, Implications*. New York; London: Routledge.

(2019). Technology-mediated feedback and instruction. *International Journal of Applied Linguistics*, 170(2), 151–153.

Norris, J. & Ortega, L. (2001). Does type of instruction make a difference? Substantive findings from a meta-analytic review. *Language Learning*, 51(1), 157–213.

Pica, T. (1994). Research on negotiation: What does it reveal about second-language learning conditions, processes, and outcomes? *Language Learning, 44*(3), 493–527.

(1998). Second language learning through interaction: Multiple perspectives. In V. Regan (ed.), *Contemporary approaches to second language acquisition in social context* (pp. 9–31). Dublin: University College Dublin Press.

Révész, A. (2012). Working memory and the observed effectiveness of recasts on different L2 outcome measures. *Language Learning, 62*(1), 93–132. doi:10.1111/j.1467-9922.2011.00690.x.

Ross-Feldman, L. (2007). Interaction in the L2 classroom: Does gender influence learning opportunities? In A. Mackey (ed.), *Conversational interaction in second language acquisition: A collection of empirical studies* (pp. 53–77). Oxford: Oxford University Press.

Russell, J. & Spada, N. (2006). The effectiveness of corrective feedback for second language acquisition: A meta-analysis of the research. In J. Norris & L. Ortega (eds.), *Synthesizing research on language learning and teaching* (pp. 131–164). Amsterdam: John Benjamins.

Schwartz, B. (1993). On explicit and negative data effecting and affecting competence and linguistic behavior. *Studies in Second Language Acquisition, 15*(2), 147–163.

Sheen, Y., Wright, D. & Moldawa, A. (2009). Differential effects of focused and unfocused written correction on the accurate use of grammatical forms by adult ESL learners. *System, 37*(4), 556–569. doi:10.1016/j.system.2009.09.002.

Suzuki, W., Nassaji, H. & Sato, K. (2019). The effects of feedback explicitness and type of target structure on accuracy in revision and new pieces of writing. *System, 81,* 135–145.

Swain, M. (1995). Three functions of output in second language learning. In H. G. Widdowson, G. Cook & B. Seidlhofer (eds.), *Principle and practice in applied linguistics: Studies in honour of H. G. Widdowson* (pp. 125–144). Oxford: Oxford University Press.

(2005). The output hypothesis: Theory and research. In E. Hinkel (ed.), *Handbook on research in second language teaching and learning* (pp. 471–483). Mahwah, NJ: Lawrence Erlbaum.

White, L. (1991). Adverb placement in second language acquisition: Some effects of positive and negative evidence in the classroom. *Second Language Research, 7*(2), 133–161.

Yousefi, M. & Nassaji, H. (2019). A meta-analysis of the effects of instruction and corrective feedback on L2 pragmatics and the role of moderator variables: Face-to-face vs. computer-mediated instruction. *International Journal of Applied Linguistics, 170*(2), 277–308.

Ziegler, N. (2016). Synchronous computer-mediated communication and interaction: A meta-analysis. *Studies in Second Language Acquisition, 38*(3), 553–586.

Part I

Theoretical Perspectives on Corrective Feedback

1

Corrective Feedback from Behaviorist and Innatist Perspectives

ZhaoHong Han[*]

Corrective feedback has consistently ranked among the most resilient topics in second language acquisition (SLA) research over its five decades of existence, garnering attention transcending theoretical boundaries (and research and practice divide, for that matter). Yet theoretical perspectives on corrective feedback did not always coexist; rather, they superseded their predecessors, mirroring paradigmatic shifts writ large. Therefore, a look at corrective feedback through a theoretical lens may yield insights into the epistemological differences underlying the seemingly common denominating construct or phenomenon and provide a useful pathway to understanding the waxing and waning of the general perception of corrective feedback that the field has witnessed to date. The focus of this chapter is on two polarized theoretical perspectives on corrective feedback, the behaviorist and the innatist.

The Behaviorist Perspective on Corrective Feedback

Chronologically, behaviorism predated innatism and was, in fact, the earliest theoretical paradigm dominating the field of second language (L2) studies in the 1950s through much of the 1960s, if not beyond (cf. VanPatten & Williams, 2015). Behaviorism, coupling the psychology theory of behaviorism (Skinner, 1957) with the then prevalent linguistic theory of structuralism (see, e.g., Fries, 1952; Lado, 1957), views L2 learning as quintessentially a process of responding to environmental stimulation (hence, the moniker of "stimulus and response theory") and of habit formation through reinforcement. Learning, if it happens, manifests itself as formation of new behaviors or habits. Environment is germane to

[*] This chapter has benefited from the thoughtful suggestions and comments of the editors and anonymous reviewers. Any errors are exclusively my own.

inducing behavioral change and shaping new linguistic habits. In fact, "the environment was seen as the controlling factor in any kind of learning" (VanPatten & Williams, 2015). The content of language instruction centers around explicit training on grammatical patterns and structures (Lee, 1957).

Corrective feedback – a type of information given to the L2 learner on what is not sanctioned in the target language (TL) – is part of the environmental stimulation, a form of negative reinforcement, and it allegedly helps the learner realign his or her behavior with the grammatical norms of the TL. According to the Thorndike Law of Effect (Hernstein, 1970), responses that produce a negative reaction from the environment are less likely to continue than otherwise, i.e., responses receiving positive reaction. Such reinforcing effect (or lack thereof) is context-specific. Thus, a learner behavior, if it receives positive reinforcement, will be repeated; conversely, it will be abandoned if it receives negative reinforcement through corrective feedback (VanPatten & Williams, 2015). In addition, since learning is construed as a process of habit formation, corrective feedback needs to be omnipresent and repetitive in order for correct habits to be established.

Thus, just as learning demands the participation of both learner-external linguistic influence and learner-internal formation of habit, corrective feedback requires both external (e.g., the teacher's) and internal (e.g., the learner's) efforts. However, for behaviorists, the balance between the two is decidedly tipped toward the external. Hence, in the feedback process it is the feedback giver (e.g., the teacher) that should have towering influence on the learner, the feedback receiver. It is assumed that once feedback is delivered, learning will ensue *ipso facto*.

Such conception entails much attention to what the teacher does with corrective feedback, while giving short shrift to what the learner does with it. Indeed, this was the ethos of the corrective feedback literature in the 1950s through the 1960s, a literature characterized by zero tolerance of learner errors, insistence on learner conformity to the structural norms of the TL, and a singular fixation on first language (L1) influence as a source of learner errors.

An overarching puritanical attitude to learner errors seemed to grip the minds of scholars and practitioners alike in the behaviorist era. Brooks (1960), for instance, likened error to "sin," admonishing that "error is to be avoided and its influence overcome" (p. 58). Errors should be nipped in the bud. *The Teachers Manual for German, Level One*, prepared by the Modern Language Development Center (1961), mandated that teachers should correct all errors immediately and that learners should neither be required nor permitted to discover and correct their own errors. And so on.

The behaviorist approach to corrective feedback has been rightfully called a "mechanistic approach" (Hendrickson, 1978). It treats learners as passive recipients of information. The Audio-Lingual Method (ALM) of language pedagogy prevalent in the 1950s and 1960s embodied this approach to its fullest. ALM promotes learners' rote memorization of teacher-fed chunks and patterns of language, stressing accurate and fluent production thereof. Accuracy is, in turn, cultivated through immediate and thorough teacher correction of learner errors, and fluency by promoting habit formation – or "operant conditioning" – through engaging learners in repetition of the same utterances in the same exact context. Teaching and learning, consequently, largely revolve around correction and repetition. The typical terms used to describe this type of teaching are *drill*, *reinforcement*, *mechanical*, and *audiolingual* (Fanselow, 1977).

Further, a behaviorist approach to correction is essentially a crusade on L1 interference. Learners' L1 represents an existing set of language habits, which comes to interfere with the formation of a new set of habits as the learner begins to learn an L2. Lee (1957) noted:

> No language is ever studied in a linguistic vacuum. The environment of learning includes at least that same language or another, and may include several languages, audible and perhaps visible on every side. When a second language is attempted, it is usually in an environment of the learner's first language, acquired as a child, so that all around him are linguistic patterns whose tyranny he is struggling to escape. And even in a community using the second language he needs, a learner has his home-language habits to combat. (p. 77)

By extension, L1 constitutes a primary, if not an exclusive, source of L2 errors. Differences and similarities between the L1 and the L2 matter in that differences (including absences of crosslinguistic counterparts) will lead to difficulty of learning, while similarities will ease the process of learning, according to the Contrastive Analysis Hypothesis (Lado, 1957).

Early empirical research did produce descriptive evidence of L1 as a substantial source of learner errors. In the field's first experimental study on language transfer, Selinker (1969) examined the statistical trends of syntactic patterns in Hebrew-English as compared to trends in L1 Hebrew, reporting that "of eight syntactic combinations tested, seven specific interlanguage arrangements produced by Israeli students were transferred from their native language, Hebrew" (p. 88). Syntactic transfer here was defined as "a process which occurred whenever a statistically significant arrangement in the Israeli's Hebrew sentence reappeared in his interlanguage behavior, i.e., in his attempted production of English sentences" (p. 86). The study yielded the first scientific definition of language transfer that is frequency based, which is still relevant today.

> Whenever there are such binary choices [e.g., syntactic arrangements of a-b or b-a, as in *I live in Tel Aviv now* or *I live now in Tel Aviv*], LANGUAGE TRANSFER may be operationally defined as a process occurring from the native to the foreign language if frequency analysis shows that a statistically significant trend in the speaker's native language appears

toward one of these two alternatives, which is then paralleled by a significant trend toward the same alternative in the speaker's interlanguage behavior, i.e., in his attempted production of the foreign language sentences, phonetic features, phonetic sequences, etc. (p. 86)

Not all learner errors, however, are L1-inspired, as shown in other contemporary studies. For instance, in her study of Czech-English interlanguage Duskova (1969) concluded:

Categories that exist in both languages but display differences in their functions and distribution, although giving rise to many errors, do not seem to be the most potent source of errors, i.e., they do not represent the greatest difficulties in the foreign language being learnt. What proves to be still more difficult is a category nonexistent in the mother tongue. Here *the learner has no frame of reference to which he can relate his expression in the foreign language.* (p. 29, emphasis added)

Those errors due to "a category nonexistent in the mother tongue," such as the subsystem of articles, according to Duskova, "remain the last sphere" eluding learners even with a near-native command of English (cf. Lee, 1957).

Duskova sampled written production data from fifty postgraduate students – who were proficient in English – performing three communicative tasks: producing a written request for correction of an English letter, briefly retelling their last journey abroad, and concluding a scientific article on a given topic. Analyses of grammatical and lexical errors in the writings revealed that L1-interference errors were indeed many, some directly due to L1–TL crosslinguistic difference (e.g., word order and prepositions) and some indirectly to absence of counterparts in the L1 (e.g., articles). Moreover, the study showed that some of these errors, notably the ones resulting from absence of L1 counterparts, were particularly persistent.

But the Duskova study was illuminating also in another regard. She identified a large number of errors that did not seem to be L1-related. Errors such as omission of the plural ending in the noun, lack of agreement between the subject noun and its verb, confusion of the infinitive and the past participle, and so on appeared to arise from the complexity of the TL. As she put it, "they are interferences between the other terms of the English subsystem in question" (p. 21). The study, therefore, expanded on the sources of "interference" to include not only the L1 but also the learner's developing knowledge of the TL, TL-internal complexity, and even TL-internal (lexical) similarity (e.g., case – cause, clearly – cleanly).

But above all, the study signaled a broadening of the scope of learner errors, and by the same token, of corrective feedback. Errors are no longer seen as resulting only from transfer of old habits from the L1, but rather, as products of a complex learning process involving multiple sources of influence on the learner.

The evolving view on learner error, in time, upended the conception of error as a negative phenomenon. Researchers, instead, embraced errors as a window onto the learning process. Corder (1967) was credited for being the first to elaborate on the psycholinguistic significance of learner errors. Some of the distinctions he made, then, such as input versus intake, error versus mistake, external versus internal syllabus, have been among the long-lasting legacies from the SLA research in the 1960s and have since served as the bedrock for much of the theoretical enterprise in SLA (see VanPatten & Williams, 2015).

It was widely believed, at the time that an adequate analysis of learner errors would be critical to effective instruction. Lee (1957) conveyed the sentiment the best when noting:

> A broadly based and representative collection of spoken and written errors, sufficiently classified, may help to determine several things – the scope and nature of pronunciation teaching, the time given to practice with certain structures, the time given to practice with certain expressions and words, and even the order in which these structures, expressions, and words are introduced. (p. 78)
>
> Through an examination of learners' mistakes, a teacher may enter more fully into the environment of teaching and put on, as it were, his pupils' linguistic spectacles. (p. 83)

Of note, early research also called out meaning as a potential source of error, which, in today's terms, would be errors in meaning and form mapping. For instance, a Czech speaker may say *I don't know already* when he or she means "I no longer know." A French speaker may say *They have arrived there are three days* when he or she means "They arrived three days ago." Corder (1967) discussed yet another type of form–meaning mapping error that he dubbed "covert errors." These errors are grammatically accurate but mis-encode meanings. A typical example of a covert error would be an utterance of *You must not take off your hat* for *You don't have to take off your hat*. The early attention to learner meaning, unfortunately, did not catch on in time with later researchers. Corrective feedback, up to now, has mostly focused on correcting surface grammatical errors, with learner meaning largely sidelined (Han & Ekiert, 2017).

An equally valuable insight from early research, which has, sadly, fallen by the wayside, is the need to achieve a system view on learner errors. Lee (1957) maintained that knowledge of the learner's L1 may aid the teacher's understanding of the systematic nature of learner error: "Teaching English tense usage to learners whose language has only one past tense form is apt to perplex a teacher unaware of the fact, but errors in several tenses are seen to be linked by one who is so aware" (p. 84). The behaviorist influence on corrective feedback, especially the conception of corrective feedback as resting mostly in the hands of the teacher or in the environment, remained pronounced well into the 1970s, as captured in Hendrickson (1978), the first synthesis of corrective feedback research, addressing five questions:

1. Should learner errors be corrected?
2. If so, when should learner errors be corrected?
3. Which learner errors should be corrected?
4. How should learner errors be corrected?
5. Who should correct learner errors?

These questions reflect the general research interest, in that era, in what teachers do, not what learners do. And they still appear to drive much of current research on corrective feedback (see, e.g., Nassaji & Kartchava, 2017).

While recognizing the lack of a sufficient number of studies to shed adequate light on each of these questions, Hendrickson (1978) made do with what was available then and painted an emerging picture. With respect to the first question, it seemed that researchers were shifting away from "zero tolerance" of learner errors to *selective correction*. The prevailing belief was that error correction would improve L2 proficiency more so than noncorrection.

But the timing of correction was a point of contention among researchers. While rejecting "the obsessive concern with error avoidance," many began to embrace the notion that errors were a natural, and even necessary, phenomenon in language learning (Corder, 1967), some going so far as to suggest that teachers should "accept a wide margin of deviance from so-called 'standard' forms and structures of the target language" (Hendrickson, 1978, p. 390). This change of the conception of error struck a chord in others harboring considerations toward the affective dimension of learning. Fear of dampening learners' confidence or curbing their willingness to take risks led them to suggest the need to consider the "economics of intervention" or reserving error correction for manipulative grammar practice and tolerating errors during communicative practice (Birckbichler, 1977; George, 1972; Walker, 1973). Despite the abundance of opinions, little experimental research existed in the meantime on the question of when to correct.

With respect to which errors to correct, there were likewise a multitude of suggestions. A noteworthy suggestion was made by Burt (1975), who contended that corrective feedback should target global or lexical errors (i.e., errors that hamper communication) before tackling local or grammatical errors, arguing that "only when their product in the foreign language [is] to become relatively free of communicative errors, should learners begin to concentrate on remediating local errors, if the learners are to approach near-native fluency" (p. 58). Alternative suggestions were many, ranging from correcting errors that would stigmatize foreign language learners to correcting high-frequency errors or "fossilized" errors (Birkbichler, 1977; Corder, 1975; Hanzeli, 1975; Johansson, 1973; Richards, 1973; Sternglass, 1974). The question of what to correct was far from settled, and similarly, there had been little empirical research to support any of the suggestions.

As for how learner errors should be corrected, the literature by then had garnered a number of descriptive studies on teachers' correction behaviors (Allwright, 1975; Chaudron, 1977; Fanselow, 1977). It was generally found that teachers' behaviors were inconsistent, imprecise, and ineffective. There was a notable lack of agreement over whether correction should be systematic. Some argued that systematic correction should fare better than random correction (e.g., Cohen & Robbins, 1976), but others saw value not so much in systematic correction as in selective correction tailored to individual learners' developmental needs (e.g., Dulay & Burt, 1977). An array of strategies was proffered on how to correct, from specific procedures to more general pointers. Wingfield (1975), for instance, provided five options specific to correcting errors in learner writing: (1) the teacher gives sufficient clues to enable self-correction to be made; (2) the teacher corrects the script; (3) the teacher deals with errors through marginal comments and footnotes; (4) the teacher explains orally to individual students; and (5) the teacher uses the error as an illustration for a class explanation. Allwright (1975) offered a set of nine steps: (1) indicating that an error has occurred; (2) identifying the error type; (3) showing the location of the error; (4) indicating who made the error; (5) selecting a remedy; (6) providing a correct model; (7) giving an opportunity for a new attempt; (8) indicating improvement; and (9) offering praise. Neither Wingfield's nor Allwright's proposals derived from experimental research, however. It, therefore, came as no surprise that Hendrickson (1978) questioned the credibility of these recommendations and saw the need for more questions to be asked. For instance, "What effects do corrections in natural versus artificial settings have upon learners' language proficiency?" "Do native-speaking and nonnative-speaking teachers evaluate deviant speech and writing differently?" These kinds of questions are still relevant today.

Lastly, who should correct the errors? The literature yielded the understanding that the primary agent of error correction should be the teacher. Corder (1973) conceived of the role of the teacher as "[providing] data and examples, and where necessary [offering] explanations and descriptions, and, more importantly, verification of the learner's hypothesis" (p. 336). Aside from the teacher, peer correction was also considered possible, though its effects might be selective. Corder (1975) observed that the modality of communication seemed to matter: with spoken errors, students were able to help each other out with lexical errors but not grammatical ones, the reverse with written errors. Other researchers noticed that errors were more salient to peers in a heterogeneous class than in a homogeneous class (Burt & Kiparsky, 1972; Corder, 1975; Valdman,

1975). According to Witbeck's (1976) experimental study, peer feedback resulted in greater sensitivity to accuracy in individual learners as well as greater predisposition toward teacher correction. Aside from the teacher and the peer as agents of corrective feedback, learners might correct their own errors. Wingfield (1975) noted that self-correction was more effective when the errors were grammatical rather than lexical.

Hendrickson (1978) concluded his review of literature by underscoring the lack of empirical research. Much of what he gleaned from the literature was, at best, in the form of insights from descriptive studies but, mostly, from speculations based on intuition. A logical next step would be for experimental research to substantiate the existing ideas "before corrections can be recommended or rejected as being effective for dealing with students' written or oral errors" (p. 396). Hendrickson was surely prescient when he wrote:

> It may well be that the specific effects on a learner's language proficiency in terms of *who* corrects his errors will depend upon *when* they are corrected, *which* ones are corrected, and especially *how* they are brought to the learner's attention. (p. 396)

This insight could well have served as the roadmap for a systems approach to investigating corrective feedback, but it never did. The preponderance of corrective feedback research, as repeatedly attested in meta-analyses (Kang & Han, 2015; Li, 2010; Lyster & Saito, 2010; Mackey & Goo, 2007; Russell & Spada, 2006), has pursued the question of whether or not corrective feedback is helpful to learning, and if so, which type of correction is more helpful and, to a much lesser extent, for which type of linguistic item (e.g., Ferris, 1999; Shintani, Ellis & Suzuki, 2014). Moreover, the research has mostly focused on what the feedback giver does, not what the learner (as receiver) does, and much less how the two processes interact (Han, 2001). The skewed attention to the feedback giver is, at its core, a function of the lingering influence of behaviorism.

The Innatist Perspective on Corrective Feedback

Behaviorists' exclusive focus on observable behavior such as learner errors and on the role of environment in changing the behavior was challenged by innatists who view language learning as arising more from internal, mental operations than from an external, environmental influence.

In a poignant and elaborate critique of Skinner's (1957) behaviorism, Chomsky (1959) argued that human learning is a complex phenomenon, non-analogous to animal learning or learning by low organisms. Extrapolations across the two learning contexts are, therefore, not legitimate due to their marked differences. One obvious difference is that human learning requires much mental operation. Another striking difference is that stimulus and response do not form a linear causal relationship in human learning. Chomsky wrote:

> Stimuli are no longer part of the outside physical world; they are driven back into the organism. We identify the stimulus when we hear the response ... the talk of "stimulus control" simply disguises a complete retreat to mentalistic psychology. *We cannot predict verbal behavior in terms of the stimuli in the speaker's environment, since we do not know what the current stimuli are until he responds.* Furthermore, since we cannot control the property of a physical object to which an individual will respond, except in highly artificial cases, Skinner's claim that his system ... permits the practical control of verbal behavior is quite false. (p. 32, emphasis added)

Taking exception to the behaviorist view that environmental reinforcement induces learning, Chomsky invoked two commonly observed facts about humans learning a second language. First is that children are able to acquire a new language rapidly and effortlessly in spite of the fact that they have not heard or experienced everything in the language. Second, adults, in spite of their relative lack of such ease in acquiring a new language, are nevertheless able to decipher new sentences and utterances. For Chomsky, "These abilities indicate that there must be fundamental processes at work quite independently of 'feedback' from the environment" (p. 42), and the behaviorist embrace of environment as the sole driver of learning is nothing but flimsy.

The theoretical pivot from the environment to the organism or the (language) learner is veritably the *sine qua non* of innatism. Unlike behaviorists, innatists are fixated on mental properties, some of which do not externalize, properties that they argue are genetically endowed. Under the premise that humans have an innate disposition to learn language, innatists are singularly interested in exploring Universal Grammar (UG), a mental faculty or module that is language-specific rather than domain-general. This view has come to be known as a modular view on the human mind, according to which the human mind contains multiple modules such as one for vision, one for language, etc.

UG as the language module is an abstract entity, complex and sophisticated, that underlies the speaker's ability to, *inter alia*, distinguish sentences from nonsentences, detect ambiguities, etc., and this ability is acquired "in an astonishingly short time, to a large extent independently of intelligence, and in a comparable way by all children" (p. 57). Chomsky stated:

> The fact that all normal children acquire essentially comparable grammars of great complexity with remarkable rapidity suggests that human beings are somehow *specially designed to do this*, with data handling or 'hypothesis-formulating' ability of unknown character and complexity. (p. 57, emphasis added)

That UG is responsible for the remarkable feat of first language acquisition is widely accepted as a theory of first language acquisition (L1A). But whether UG also guides and enables second language acquisition (L2A), especially L2A by adult learners, has been a contentious question. The theoretical debate began in the late 1980s and lasted more than a decade (see, e.g., Bley-Vroman, Felix & Ioup, 1988; Clahsen & Muysken, 1989; DuPlessis et al., 1987; Eubank, 1991; Schwartz, 1986), resulting in a reasonable consensus that UG is still relevant to the development of L2 grammar (Thomas, 2003; White, 2015), though the extent of relevance remains far from clear. It looks as if any claim on substantive engagement of UG in L2A is destined to be undercut by two widely observed phenomena: the general lack of full attainment of the L2 and the variable attainment among and within L2 learners (Bley-Vroman, 1989; Han, 2004, 2014; Schachter, 1991; VanPatten & Williams, 2015).

Still, innatists maintain that UG illuminates the nature of interlanguage *competence* – how it develops and how it differs from *performance*. Competence here refers to a system of knowledge that underlies linguistic behavior or performance. It underlies performance, but performance may not always implicate competence. Mechanical imitation of utterances heard in the environment, for instance, may not involve competence. In Chomsky's terms, competence is I-language – internal to the speaker, and performance is E-language – what the speaker externalizes in specific contexts.

Given its exclusive concern about a linguistic knowledge system or competence, UG–L2 researchers generally recognize input as critical – more in a qualitative than quantitative sense – but downplay the role of corrective feedback or negative data (ND), deeming the latter as capable of affecting performance rather than competence. In a seminal discussion on the relationship between input and UG vis-à-vis L2 competence, Schwartz (1993) argued that UG can only interact with primary linguistic data (PLD) – exemplars of natural, contextual, and communicative use of language.

> For the knowledge system of a particular language to grow, the acquirer must have exposure to instances or exemplars of that particular language. Without such exposure language development will not take place... PLD are *necessary* for growth of the system of linguistic knowledge.
>
> (p. 148, emphasis added)

On this view, PLD, not ND, are what enables the development of L2 competence. This competence or system of linguistic knowledge is what allows the speaker of the language to tell not only what kinds of sentences are possible *but also what are not*. Such competence underlies native speakers' use of language but is typically lacking in L2 learners. In order to know what is not permissible in the TL, learners generally rely on corrective feedback or ND (Bley-Vroman, 1989).

Schwartz maintained, however, that when learners are fed with ND, it results in learned linguistic knowledge (LLK), a different entity from competence. Much of this has to do with the propositional content of ND versus PLD: ND is about language, and PLD is the language itself. ND (and explicit metalinguistic data, for that matter) leads to LLK and learned linguistic behavior (LLB), thereby ultimately affecting performance, but hardly competence (cf. Krashen, 1982; Truscott, 1998). Schwartz wrote:

> [G]iven the distinction between LLK and competence, the fact that explicit data and ND can cause changes in L2 behavior implies that there are (at least) two possible knowledge sources that could underlie the change: interlanguage competence or (merely) LLK. In short, the fact that explicit data and ND (can) give rise to observable changes in L2 behavior does not necessarily entail that one and the same knowledge source as underlies L1 (i.e., UG) underlies the L2 behavior ... The fact that ND are made (even abundantly) available to L2ers does not entail that the developing interlanguage systems are able to incorporate ND to initiate changes.
> (pp. 152–153)

The whole line of argument boils down to the hypothesis that "ND cannot initiate reorganization of the (L2) grammar (viz., competence – not LLK)" (pp. 152–153).

Further explicating the lack of interface between ND and competence, Schwartz (1993), invoking Fodor's (1982) modular view of language, argued that UG, like every other mental module, features "information encapsulation," in that it can only work with PLD or natural, contextualized, communicative input. ND, by virtue of it being a different type of information, does not and cannot engage with UG, and, hence, does not promote L2 competence. Schwartz cited empirical evidence to show that ND is not helpful (see, e.g., Cohen & Robbins, 1976; White, 1991).

This line of reasoning has, ostensibly, left unanswered the question of why ND is not needed in L1A. This question has, in fact, been framed as the logical problem of language acquisition (Hornstein & Lightfoot, 1981). It is claimed that native speakers' linguistic knowledge or competence far exceeds the amount of PLD they have been exposed to, and the gap between the input and the resultant linguistic system is filled by UG. Simply put, UG guides the learner to retrieve from errors through interaction with PLD and detecting what is or is not permissible (Baker, 1979; see, however, Braine, 1971). It sends the learner *en route* to developing an organic linguistic system of knowledge, so to speak.

There are two important fallouts from Schwartz's perspective on ND. One is that certain elements of the TL may never be acquirable for L2 learners, given there is no interface between UG and ND – ND affects LLK and LLB only. As is clear from the discussion above, LLK (and LLB, for that matter) is not on a par with competence and performance. A way to differentiate them is to think of the former, LLK and LLB, as contrived and the latter, competence and performance, as natural and organic. Second, not all aspects of the TL are equally susceptible to the influence of ND. Schwartz hypothesized that things that are outside the reign of UG, such as vocabulary, should be more susceptible to the influence of ND than those that are within, such as syntax and morphology (cf. Schachter, 1991). This claim has been, to some extent, borne out in empirical research on corrective feedback. For example, study after study on recasts – a type of corrective feedback involving a reformulation of the learner's erroneous utterance – has shown that recasts are more effective on lexical errors than on morphological errors, in spite of morphological recasts greatly outnumbering lexical recasts (for discussion, see Han, 2008). Moreover, L2 research on fossilization or persistent errors has consistently isolated grammatical morphemes as the last holdouts (DeKeyser, 2005; Franceschina, 2005; Han, 2011, 2013, 2014).

The view that L1 and L2 linguistic knowledge are epistemologically different resonates within the wider field of SLA (see, e.g., Krashen, 1982; Truscott, 1998, 2001, 2007; VanPatten, 2014, 2017). Krashen (1982) famously differentiated between *learning* and *acquisition*. Learning involves exposure to ND and explicit grammar explanation, while acquisition involves exposure to PLD only. There are two distinct pathways to two very different types of knowledge, known as explicit knowledge and implicit knowledge. Learning, by virtue of being a conscious process, results in explicit knowledge, learned knowledge or LLK, as Schwartz called it; acquisition, an unconscious process, results in implicit knowledge or competence in Schwartz's terms. For Krashen, development of implicit knowledge should be the goal of learners since it is what underwrites fluent communicative use of language. Accordingly, acquisition should take precedence over learning, and the role of ND and the resultant learned knowledge should be marginal and circumstantial. Learned knowledge may function as a monitor, Krashen claimed, only to be turned on when (a) the learner knows the form, (b) desires accuracy, and (c) has the time to achieve it. Error correction (and grammar instruction, for that matter), if anything, works only – or not even – for forms involving simple grammatical rules.

Furthermore, like Schwartz, Krashen claimed that not everything is learnable, and that explicit and implicit knowledge are mutually exclusive and neither can substitute for the other (see Han & Finneran, 2014, for discussion on three positions on the interface between explicit and implicit knowledge). Citing the case study by Krashen and Pon (1975), Krashen (1982) noted:

> P was an excellent Monitor user ... an adult with a BA in Linguistics with honors, whose written English appeared nearly native-like. In casual conversation, however, P made occasional "careless" errors on "easy" rules

that she had known consciously for twenty years. Thus, even well-learned, well-practiced rules may not turn into acquisition. (p. 86)

Several hallmarks of innatism are emerging from the discussion so far. First, innatists differentiate between LLK and competence. Second, innatists value PLD and discredit ND or corrective feedback. Third, innatists believe that language development is fundamentally an unconscious process. Fourth, conscious learning does not aid the development of competence. Fifth, language is too complex to be learned explicitly.

These characteristics of innatism are in full display in Truscott's writings (e.g., 1996, 1998, 1999, 2001, 2005, 2007, 2014). In his seminal critique of the Noticing Hypothesis (Schmidt, 1990, 1993, 1995),[1] Truscott (1998), after delving into its conceptual and empirical bases in cognitive psychology and second language acquisition, arrived at the following conclusions:

1. The Noticing Hypothesis is weak in theoretical basis and empirical support.
2. The construct of noticing is so vague that it has little testability.
3. The hypothesis is too strong to be of value to understanding the relevance of noticing (and consciousness for that matter) to language development.
4. L2 research on form-focused instruction and corrective feedback (considering its conceptual and methodological flaws) provides little evidence in support of the hypothesis but considerable counter evidence (e.g., Cohen & Robbins, 1976; DeKeyser, 1993; Ellis, 1984; Harley, 1989; Liou, 1989; Kadia, 1988; Kepner, 1991; Lightbown et al., 1980; Lightbown, 1983; Plann, 1977; Rob et al., 1986; Sciaorone & Meijer, 1995; Schumann, 1978; Semke, 1984; Sheppard, 1992; Spada, 1986; Terrell et al., 1987; VanPatten, 1988; White, 1991).
5. The hypothesis is valid only in that it affects development of metalinguistic knowledge, but not linguistic knowledge or competence.

Summing up, Truscott wrote:

> Throughout the discussion, I dealt with the stronger version of the [noticing] hypothesis, according to which conscious awareness of form is a necessary condition for its acquisition. If one adopts the weaker version – that noticing is helpful but not necessary – only minor adjustments are needed in the arguments. The application of cognitive research remains problematic, and vagueness continues to be a problem. Research on form-focused instruction and feedback suggests that awareness of form is not only unnecessary but also unhelpful. (p. 126)

---

[1] Schmidt advanced that everything we come to know about language was first noticed consciously, and that noticing is both a necessary and a sufficient condition for L2 learning.

This viewpoint about the role of consciousness, form-focused instruction, and corrective feedback reverberates elsewhere in Truscott's writings, a review of which is beyond the scope of this chapter.

Conclusion and Implications

Behaviorism and innatism both have had a profound impact on L2 research. While neither presently serves as the seeming mainstream theoretical framework, because neither is sustainable without the other, their influences have lingered on.

Both borrowed from external disciplines, behaviorism from psychology and innatism from linguistics, behaviorism directs the attention of L2 research to environment, and innatism to a mind-based language-specific faculty – UG. The two theories view ND or corrective feedback through starkly different lenses. For behaviorists, ND is an indispensable part of the environment and it goes to change and reinforce behavior, and behavior is construed as the sole indicator of learning – including language learning. Conversely, innatists believe that language is subserved by a specific mental faculty and development comes out of its interaction with PLD – more commonly known as natural samples of language. On this account, ND, if of any use, is on the fringe of language development for two important reasons – these often get lost in the shuffle as the literature touts the value of corrective feedback. First, the mental faculty, or UG, is information encapsulated such that it can only interact with PLD, but not with ND. Second, UG interacting with – or instantiated by – PLD leads to development of competence, while ND results in metalinguistic knowledge, or LLK and LLB, as Schwartz called it. Competence drives language behavior, whereas ND leads to language-like behavior (cf. Long, 2015). Fluent, accurate, and appropriate use of language, as seen in native speakers, is enabled by competence, not by metalinguistic knowledge, the latter having merely a supplemental role. Simply put, UG interacting with PLD is considered an organic pathway to language development; in contrast, ND plus explicit grammar-based instruction is an artificial form of intervention by a third party to steer development. The former underlies L1A, while the latter drives much of L2A (see, e.g., Bley-Vroman, 1989).

Selinker (1972) noted:

> The second language learner who actually achieves native-like competence cannot possibly have been taught this competence, since linguists are daily ... discovering new and fundamental facts about particular languages. Successful learners, in order to achieve this native-speaker competence, must have acquired these facts (and most probably important principles of language organization) *without* having explicitly been taught them.
>
> (pp. 212–213, emphasis added)

More than forty years later, echoing Selinker (1972) yet taking an even stronger stance on the lack of relevance of explicit instruction (and ND for that matter) to development of L2 competence, VanPatten (2014) wrote:

> Selinker [1972] was correct in that underlying competence is not derived from explicit instruction/learning. As argued here, all underlying knowledge is the result of complex interplays between input, language specific mechanisms, and input processing mechanisms. My argument is that Selinker's claim holds true for all learners and all stages of development, not just those who have reached native-like or super-advanced levels of knowledge and proficiency ... In short, the effects of instruction, particularly form-focused instruction, are marginally related (at best) to how an internal grammar grows over time. (p. 123)

The question at stake for L2A, however, is whether the UG plus PLD pathway is viable. Both the variable outcome of L2A and the pervasive presence of ND in the L2 environment (along with the heavy dependence on grammar instruction) serve to demonstrate that it is not (cf. Schachter, 1991). The questions that then ensue are these: How useful is ND? How usable is it? And to whom, and at which stage of development?

While these questions are amply addressed in the remainder of this volume and elsewhere (e.g., Kang & Han, 2015; Kang, Sok & Han, 2019; Li, 2010; Lyster & Sato, 2010; Mackey & Goo, 2007; Nassaji & Kartchava, 2017; Russell & Spada, 2006), future research on corrective feedback should benefit greatly from heeding the eclectic insights from behaviorism and innatism, which I highlight below:

1. L2 development results from interaction between the environment and the learner.
2. The quality of environment matters.
3. PLD should constitute the primary input to the L2 learner.
4. L2 development has two dimensions: competence and performance.
5. Competence is not the same as learned linguistic knowledge via grammar explanation and corrective feedback.
6. Competence drives communicative use of language and should therefore remain the goal of L2 development.
7. Empirical research on corrective feedback and its effects should target systems or clusters of linguistic elements rather than isolated linguistic elements.
8. Empirical research on corrective feedback should, *inter alia*, measure learners' natural, spontaneous, and communicative use of language whereby learners use the L2 to communicate their *own* meaning instead of regurgitating what is fed to them.
9. Empirical research on corrective feedback and its effects should be longitudinal to shed light on the nature of the effects – has corrective feedback affected learned linguistic knowledge or competence (i.e., underlying system of linguistic knowledge)?

10. Corrective feedback is more effective on lexical errors than on morphosyntactic errors, especially where there is an absence of a counterpart morphosyntactic subsystem in the learner's L1.

In closing, five decades of research on corrective feedback have generated a sizable yet heterogeneous empirical database, with mixed findings. Research-based pedagogical recommendations are abundant but have mostly been vague and unhelpful, if not sometimes irresponsible. More studies will not necessarily change the scenario unless they are undergirded by solid theoretical work. Revisiting the theories in this chapter reminds us that theories are a treasure trove of insights, especially if we are not embracing one to the exclusion of others (as is a common practice in SLA), but rather engaging, dialogically, with diverse theories.

References

Allwright, R. (1975). Problems in the study of the language teacher's treatment of learner error. In M. Burt & H. Dulay (eds.), *On TESOL' 75: New directions in second language learning, teaching and bilingual education* (pp. 96–109). Washington, DC: TESOL.

Baker, C. L. (1979). Syntactic theory and the projection problem. *Linguistic Inquiry*, 10(4), 533–581.

Birckbichler, D. (1977). Communication and beyond. In J. Phillips (ed.), *The language connection: From the classroom to the world*. Skokie, IL: National Textbook Company.

Bley-Vroman, R. (1989). The logical problem of foreign language learning. In S. Gass & J. Schachter (eds.), *Linguistic perspectives on second language acquisition* (pp. 41–68). Cambridge: Cambridge University Press.

Bley-Vroman, R., Felix, S. & Ioup, G. (1988). The accessibility of Universal Grammar in adult learning. *Second Language Research*, 4(1), 1–32.

Braine, M. D. S. (1971). On two types of models of the internalization of grammars. In D. Slobin (ed.), *The ontogenesis of grammar* (pp. 153–186). New York: Academic Press.

Brooks, N. (1960). *Language and language learning*. New York: Harcourt, Brace and World.

Burt, M. (1975). Error analysis in the adult EFL classroom *TESOL Quarterly*, 9(1), 53–63.

Burt, M. & Kiparsky, C. (1972). *The gooficon: A repair manual for English*. Rowley, MA: Newbury House.

Chaudron, C. (1977). A descriptive model of discourse in the corrective treatment of learners' errors. *Language Learning*, 27(1), 29–46.

Chomsky, N. (1959). Review of Skinner (1957). *Language*, 35(1), 26–58.

Clahsen, H. & Muysken, P. (1989). The UG paradox in L2 acquisition. *Interlanguage Studies Bulletin*, 5(1), 1–29.

Cohen, A. & Robbins, M. (1976). Toward assessing interlanguage performance: The relationship between selected errors, learners' characteristics, and learners' explanations. *Language Learning*, 26, 45–66.

Corder, S. P. (1967). The significance of learners' errors. *International Review of Applied Linguistics*, 5(4), 161–170.

— (1973). *Introducing applied linguistics*. Harmondsworth: Penguin.

— (1975). The language of second-language learners: The broader issues. *Modern Language Journal*, 59(8), 409–413.

DeKeyser, R. (1993). The effects of error correction on L2 grammar knowledge and oral proficiency. *Modern Language Journal*, 77(4), 501–513.

— (2005). What makes learning second language grammar difficult? A review of issues. *Language Learning*, 55(S1), 1–25.

Dulay, H. & Burt, M. (1975). Creative construction in second language learning. In M. Burt & H. Dulay (eds.), *On TESOL '75: New directions in second language learning, teaching and bilingual education* (pp. 21–32). Washington, DC: TESOL.

— (1977). Remarks on creativity in language acquisition. In H. Dulay & M. Burt (eds.), *Viewpoints on English as a second language* (pp. 95–126). New York Regents Publishing Company.

DuPlessis, J., Solin, D., Travis, L. & White, L. (1987). UG or not UG, that is the question: A reply to Chlahsen & Muysken. *Second Language Research*, 56 (3), 56–75.

Duskova, L. (1969). On sources of errors in foreign language learning. *International Review of Applied Linguistics*, 7(1), 11–36.

Ellis, R. (1984). Can syntax be taught? A study of the effects of formal instruction on the acquisition of WH questions by children. *Applied Linguistics*, 5(2), 138–155.

Eubank, L. (1991). *Point counterpoint: Universal grammar in the second language*. Amsterdam: John Benjamins.

Fanselow, J. (1977). The treatment of error in oral work. *Foreign Language Annals*, 10(4), 583–593.

Ferris, D. (1999). The case for grammar correction in L2 writing classes: A response to Truscott (1996). *Journal of Second Language Writing*, 8(1), 1–10.

Franceschina, F. (2005). *Fossilized second language grammars: The acquisition of grammatical gender*. Language Acquisition & Language Disorders 38. Amsterdam: John Benjamins.

Fries, C. (1952). *The structure of English: An introduction to the construction of English sentences*. New York: Harcourt, Brace & Company.

George, H. V. (1972). *Common errors in language learning*. Rowley, MA: Newbury House.

Han, Z.-H. (2001). Fine-tuning corrective feedback. *Foreign Language Annals*, 34(6), 582–599.

— (2004). *Fossilization in adult second language acquisition*. Clevedon: Multilingual Matters.

(2008). On the role of meaning in focus on form. In Z.-H. Han (ed.), *Understanding second language process* (pp. 45–79). Clevedon: Multilingual Matters.

(2011). Fossilization – A classic concern of SLA research. In S. Gass & A. Mackey (eds.), *The Routledge handbook of second language acquisition* (pp. 476–490). New York: Routledge.

(2013). [State-of-the-art article] Forty years later: Updating the Fossilization Hypothesis. *Language Teaching*, 46(2), 133–171.

(2014). From Julie to Wes to Alberto: Revisiting the construct of fossilization. In Z.-H. Han & E. Tarone (eds.), *Interlanguage: Forty years later* (pp. 47–74). Amsterdam: John Benjamins.

Han, Z.-H. & Ekiert, M. (2017). Beyond focus on form: Giving learner meaning its proper place. *Second Language Learning Research*, 3(1), 1–12.

Han, Z.-H. & Finneran, R. (2014). Re-engaging the interface debate: Strong, weak, none, or all? *International Journal of Applied Linguistics*, 24(3), 370–389.

Hanzeli, V. (1975). Learner's language: Implications of recent research for foreign language instruction. *Modern Language Journal*, 59(8), 426–432.

Harley, B. (1989). Functional grammar in French immersion: A classroom experiment. *Applied Linguistics*, 10(3), 331–360.

Hendrickson, J. (1978). Error correction in foreign language teaching: Recent theory, research and practice. *Modern Language Journal*, 62(8), 387–398.

(1981). *Error analysis and error correction in language teaching*. Singapore: SEAMO Regional Language Center.

Hernstein, R. (1970). On the law of effect. *Journal of Experimental Analysis of Behavior*, 13(2), 243–266.

Hornstein, N., & Lightfoot, D. (1981). Introduction. In N. Hornstein & D. Lightfoot (eds.), *Explanation in linguistics* (pp. 9–31). New York: Longman.

Johansson, S. (1973). The identification and evaluation of errors in foreign languages: A functional approach. In J. Svartvik (ed.), *Errata: Papers in error analysis* (pp. 102–114). Lund: CWK Gleerup.

Kadia, K. (1988). The effect of formal instruction on monitored and spontaneous naturalistic interlanguage performance. *TESOL Quarterly*, 22, 509–515.

Kang, E. Y. & Han, Z.-H. (2015). The efficacy of written corrective feedback in improving L2 written accuracy: A meta-analysis. *Modern Language Journal*, 99(1), 1–18.

Kang, E.Y., Sok, S., & Han, Z-H. (2019). Thirty-five years of ISLA on form-focused instruction: A meta-analysis. *Language Teaching Research*, 23(4), 403–427.

Kepner, C. (1991). An experiment in the relationship of types of written feedback to the development of second language writing skills. *Modern Language Journal, 75*(3), 305–313.

Krashen, S. (1982). *Principles and practice in second language acquisition.* Oxford: Pergamon.

Krashen, S. & Pon, P. (1975). An error analysis of an advanced learner of ESL: The importance of the monitor. *Working Papers in Bilingualism, 7,* 125–129.

Lado, R. (1957). *Linguistics across cultures: Applied linguistics for language teachers.* Ann Arbor: University of Michigan Press.

Lee, W. (1957). The linguistic context of language teaching. *English Language Teaching Journal, 11,* 77–85.

Li, S. (2010). The effectiveness of corrective feedback in SLA: A meta-analysis. *Language Learning, 60*(2), 309–365.

Lightbown, P. M. (1983). Exploring relationships between developmental and instructional sequences in L2 acquisition. In H. Seliger & M. H. Long (eds.), *Classroom oriented research in second language acquisition* (pp. 217–243). Rowley, MA: Newbury House.

Lightbown, P., Spada, N. & Wallace, R. (1980). Some effects of instruction on child and adolescent ESL learners. In S. D. Krashen & R. Scarcella (eds.), *Research in second language acquisition: Selected papers of the Los Angeles Second Language Research Forum* (pp. 162–172). Rowley, MA: Newbury House.

Loiou, H.-C. (1989). The impact of formal instruction on second language grammatical accuracy. Unpublished doctoral dissertation, University of Illinois, Urbana-Champaign.

Long, M. (2015). *Second language acquisition and task-based language teaching.* New York: John Wiley & Sons.

Lyster, R. & Saito, K. (2010). Oral feedback in classroom SLA. *Studies in Second Language Acquisition, 32*(special issue 2), 265–302.

Mackey, A. & Goo, J. (2007). Interaction research in SLA: A meta-analysis and research synthesis. In A. Mackey (ed.), *Conversational interaction in second language acquisition: A series of empirical studies* (pp. 407–453). Oxford: Oxford University Press.

Nassaji, H. & Kartchava, E. (2017). *Corrective feedback in second language teaching and learning.* New York: Routledge.

Plann, S. (1977). Acquiring a second language in an immersion classroom. In H. D. Brown, C. Yorio & R. Crymes (eds.), *On TESOL' 77: Teaching and learning English as a second language: Trends in research and practice* (pp. 213–225). Washington, DC: TESOL.

Richards, J. (1973). Error analysis and second language strategies. In J. Oller & J. Richards (eds.), *Focus on the learner: Pragmatic perspectives for the language teacher* (pp. 114–135). New York: Newbury House.

Robb, T., Ross, S. & Shortreed, I. (1986). Salience of feedback on error and its effect on EFL writing quality. *TESOL Quarterly, 20,* 83–93.

Russell, J., & Spada, N. (2006). The effectiveness of corrective feedback for the acquisition of L2 grammar: A meta-analysis of the research. In J. M. Norris & L. Ortega (eds.), *Synthesizing research on language learning and teaching* (pp. 133–164). Amsterdam; Philadelphia: John Benjamins.

Schachter, J. (1991). Corrective feedback in historical perspective. *Second Language Research*, 7(2), 89–102.

Schmidt, R. (1990). The role of consciousness in second language learning. *Applied Linguistics*, 11(2), 129–158.

(1993). Consciousness, learning and interlanguage pragmatics. In G. Kasper & S. Blum-Kulka (eds.), *Interlanguage pragmatics* (pp. 21–42). New York: Oxford University Press.

(1995). Consciousness and foreign language learning. In R. Schmidt (ed.), *Attention and awareness in foreign language learning* (pp. 1–64). Honolulu: University of Hawai'i at Manoa, Second Language Teaching and Curriculum Center.

Schumann, J. (1978). *The pidginization process: A model for second language acquisition*. Rowley, MA: Newbury House.

Schwartz, B. (1986). The modular basis of second language acquisition. Unpublished doctoral dissertation, University of Southern California.

(1993). On explicit and negative data effecting and affecting competence and linguistic behavior. *Studies in Second Language Acquisition*, 15(2), 147–163.

Sciarone, A. & Meijer, P. (1995). Does practice make perfect? On the effect of exercises on second/foreign language acquisition. *ITL Review of Applied Linguistics*, 107–108, 35–57.

Selinker, L. (1969). Language transfer. *General Linguistics*, 9, 67–92.

(1972). Interlanguage. *IRAL*, 10(2), 209–231.

Semke, H. (1984). The effects of the red pen. *Foreign Language Annals*, 17(3), 195–202.

Sheppard, K. (1992). Two feedback types: Do they make a difference? *RELC Journal*, 23, 103–110.

Shintani, N., Ellis, R. & Suzuki, W. (2014). Effects of written feedback and revision on learners' accuracy in using two English grammatical structures. *Language Learning*, 64(1), 103–131.

Skinner, B. F. (1957). *Verbal behavior*. New York: Appleton-Century-Crofts.

Spada, N. (1986). The interaction between types of content and type of instruction: Some effects on the L2 proficiency of adult learners. *Studies in Second Language Acquisition*, 8(2), 181–199.

Sternglass, M. (1974). Close similarities in dialect features of black and white college students in remedial composition classes. *TESOL Quarterly*, 8, 271–283.

Terrell, T. (1991). The role of grammar instruction in a communicative approach. *Modern Language Journal*, 75(1), 52–63.

Terrell, T., Baycroft, B. & Perrone, C. (1987). The subjunctive in Spanish interlanguage: accuracy and comprehensibility. In B. VanPatten,

T. Dvorak & J. Lee (eds.), *Foreign language learning: A research perspective* (pp. 23–48). New York: Newbury House.

Thomas, M. (2003). Two textbook representations of second language acquisition and Universal Grammar: "access" and "constraint." *Second Language Research, 19*(4), 359–376.

Truscott, J. (1996). The case against grammar correction in L2 writing classes. *Language Learning, 46*(2), 327–369.

(1998). Noticing in second language acquisition: A critical review. *Second Language Research, 14*(2), 103–135.

(1999). Unconscious second language acquisition: Alive and well. *Studies in English Literature and Linguistics, 25*(1), 114–131.

(2001). Selecting errors for selective error correction. *Concentric: Studies in English Literature and Linguistics, 27*(2), 93–108.

(2005). The continuing problems of oral grammar correction. *International Journal of Foreign Language Teaching, 1*(2), 17–22.

(2007). The effect of error correction on learners' ability to write accurately. *Journal of Second Language Writing, 16*(4), 255–272.

(2014). *Consciousness and second language learning*. Clevedon: Multilingual Matters.

Valdman, A. (1975). Learner systems and error analysis. In G. Jarvis (ed.), *Perspective: A new freedom* (pp. 219–258). Skokie, IL: National Textbook Company.

VanPatten, B. (1988). How juries get hung: Problems with the evidence for a focus on form. *Language Learning, 38*(2), 243–260.

(2014). The limits of instruction: 40 years after "Interlanguage". In Z.-H. Han & E. Tarone (eds.), *Interlanguage: Forty years later* (pp. 105–126). Amsterdam: John Benjamins.

(2017). Situating instructed language acquisition: Facts about second language acquisition. *Instructed Second Language Acquisition, 1*(1), 45–60.

VanPatten, B. & Williams, J. (eds.). (2015). *Theories in second language acquisition* (2nd ed.). New York: Routledge.

Walker, J. (1973). Opinions of university students about language teaching. *Foreign Language Annals, 7*(1), 102–105.

White, L. (1991). Adverb placement in second language acquisition: some effects of positive and negative evidence in the classroom. *Second Language Research, 7*(2), 133–161.

(2015). Linguistic theory, universal grammar, and second language acquisition. In B. VanPatten & J. Williams (eds.), *Theories in second language acquisition* (pp. 34–53). New York: Routledge.

Wingfield, R. (1975). Five ways of dealing with errors in written compositions. *English Language Teaching Journals, 29*(4), 311–313.

Witbeck, M. (1976). Peer correction procedures for intermediate and advanced ESL composition lessons. *TESOL Quarterly, 10*(3), 321–326.

2

Interactionist Approach to Corrective Feedback in Second Language Acquisition

Rebekha Abbuhl

Introduction

The interactionist approach to corrective feedback (CF) stems from the Interaction Hypothesis (Long, 1996), which argues that communicative breakdowns during meaning-focused conversational interaction can become sites for L2 learning. In particular, when nonnative speakers fail to understand an interlocutor's message or have difficulties making themselves understood, there may be opportunities for "negotiation for meaning," when the two parties take a time out from the conversation to focus on form (the structure of the language). Here, the nonnative speaker may ask for clarification and in turn receive modified input (language that has been simplified to be more readily understood); alternatively, the interlocutor may request that the learner restate her or his original utterance, which may prompt the learner to pay particular attention to form as she or he attempts to produce a more target-like reformulation. The learner may also receive CF on the original utterance, which can provide crucial negative evidence or information on what is not possible in the L2 (Gass, 1997, 2003; Long, 1996; Pica, 1996).

For interactionist researchers, the importance of negative evidence in second language acquisition (SLA) is in large part due to the insufficiency of positive evidence – i.e., the input, or the language to which a learner is exposed (Long, 1996, 2015; White, 1987, 1991). On the surface, this view of input resembles claims made by generativists regarding first language (L1), and to a lesser extent, second language (L2) acquisition – namely, that the input is impoverished and thus something else is needed to account for language development. However, the generativist use of the term "impoverished" to describe the input is quite different from the interactionist claim that the input is insufficient. For generativists, the input is labeled impoverished as it is deemed incomplete (in the sense that it does not typically contain the full array of grammatical structures that L1, and to a lesser extent, L2 learners end up knowing), but also because it is riddled with errors, fragments, slips of the tongue, and the like. Generativists argue that the only way to explain language learners' apparent ability to go beyond the input is to posit that innate linguistic knowledge (i.e., Universal Grammar or UG) is involved. Negative evidence plays little, if any, role in this account since UG is believed to be activated and maintained by positive evidence and positive evidence alone (e.g., Guasti, 2009; Pinker, 1989).

Early days of SLA interactionist research witnessed a similar claim being made for L2 learners. Krashen (1985) argued that L1 and L2 learners are fundamentally similar, and since the former do not require or benefit from negative evidence, neither should the latter. Krashen insisted that simple exposure to input was sufficient for language acquisition, particularly if this input was comprehensible (understandable to the learner). This became the basis of his Comprehensible Input Hypothesis, which, as we will see below, is problematic but has nonetheless influenced the current interactionist approach.

In contrast to both generativist and Krashenesque approaches to L2 acquisition, current interactionist researchers maintain that L2 learners are unable to exploit positive evidence to the same extent as child L1 learners. This may be due to a host of reasons, including a lack of (full) access to UG, ineffective pattern detection abilities, cognitive declines associated with aging, interfering L1 structures, and/or negative affective states (such as anxiety and demotivation), among many other factors. Although agnostic on the exact reasons for L1/L2 differences (Gass, 2003), interactionist researchers assert that these differences make negative evidence useful, or perhaps even necessary in SLA – and particularly for aspects of the L2 that are irregular, infrequent, semantically opaque, dissimilar to the L1, and/or lacking in transparency with respect to form–meaning mapping (e.g., White, 1987, 1991). Thus, for interactionist researchers, the input is not impoverished in the sense of being incomplete or flawed, but rather, just *inadequate* in light of L2 learners' compromised abilities to extract regularities from positive evidence and to retreat from overgeneralizations.

In discussing the insufficiency of positive evidence in L2 acquisition (and the importance of negative evidence), interactionist researchers invoke the concept of attention. It has been commonly noted that children acquire their native language implicitly, or without conscious attention. Children are not aware of what they are learning, cannot verbalize what they have learned, and do not employ conscious processes, such as hypothesis testing, to construct the rules of the language. Although debate continues as to whether (and to what extent) implicit learning is possible in SLA, interactionist researchers argue that it plays a minimal role. In one early view, Schmidt's (1990) highly influential Noticing Hypothesis, attention was "the necessary and sufficient condition for the conversion of input to intake" (p. 129). Implicit learning for L2 learners was deemed impossible. Later versions of this hypothesis (e.g., Schmidt, 1994) and treatments of attention (e.g., Robinson, 1995) deemed attention facilitative rather than necessary, arguing that attention helps encode input into working memory, which in turn is a prerequisite for long-term storage. It was noted that unattended linguistic stimuli quickly exit short-term memory, making it unlikely that the learner will be able to retrieve the stimuli at a later time for further analysis or use.

Although lively debate continues on the exact operationalization of attention, and how it differs from similar constructs, such as awareness and noticing (as well as on its exact role in SLA – see, for example, Leow & Donatelli, 2017 for a review), interactionist researchers argue that CF during interaction can be an efficient mechanism for consciously orienting learners to features of the L2, and in particular, to problems with their own output (production) – problems that may go otherwise unnoticed and unaddressed. For instance, in the conversation below (Example 1), the learner produces an error with the past tense of the verb *to lose*. As the interlocutor gives no indication that a grammatical error was present, a question can be raised as to how the learner would be able to recognize her or his deviation from the target-like norm. The error has not disrupted communication, and, given that the interlocutor has provided no signals of nonunderstanding, the nonnative speaker might be led to believe that her or his utterance was grammatically correct.

Example 1
LEARNER: I losed my button.
INTERLOCUTOR: Oh, that's too bad.

Researchers have suggested that learners could theoretically notice the absence of a particular structure in the input (in this case, "losed"); however, this may result in a learning process that is slow and inefficient (e.g., White, 1991). The provision of some kind of CF, such as a recast, metalinguistic explanation, or prompt, could more efficiently draw learners' attention to the error, helping them "notice the gap," or the mismatch between the interlanguage and target-like forms. For instance, in Example 2 below, the NS interlocutor provides an enhanced recast to the learner, stressing the past tense of the verb *to lose* in order to signal that there was an error with the learner's verb form. This appears to help the learner recognize her or his error with the verb, as suggested by the production of modified output (i.e., a reformulation of the original utterance) in line 3.

Example 2
LEARNER: I losed my button.
INTERLOCUTOR: You **lost** your button?
LEARNER: Yeah lost my button.

It has been long noted that modified output in and of itself cannot be taken as irrefutable evidence of noticing, as learners may simply be parroting back the correction they heard, without understanding (Gass, 2003). Studies examining the relationship between noticing and the production of modified output have also yielded mixed results (see Gurzynski-Weiss & Baralt, 2015 for a recent review). However, recent work has helped the field advance its understanding of the relationship between the two by creating finer-grained operationalizations of modified output. For example, McDonough and Mackey (2006) operationalized modified output not as the full, immediate repetition of the feedback given, but rather as primed production. This refers to the learner using the syntactic structure targeted in the CF to form a new utterance, either immediately after the CF or several turns later. For instance, in Example 3 below, the learner, after receiving a recast targeting the omission of the auxiliary verb "did" in the original question, forms a new question that contains this auxiliary verb.

Example 3 (from McDonough & Mackey, 2006, p. 705)
LEARNER: Why he hit the deer?
INTERLOCUTOR: Why did he hit the deer? He was driving home and the deer ran out in front of his car.
LEARNER: What did he do after that?

In McDonough and Mackey's (2006) study, primed production was found to be a significant predictor of the learners' development of the target structure. Another refining of the concept of modified output can be seen in Gurzynski-Weiss and Baralt's (2015) bipartite distinction between full modified output (repeating the feedback in its entirety) and partial modified output (when learners repeat only the structures that had been targeted in the feedback). Finding that the latter was the strongest predictor of accurate noticing of feedback, the researchers argued that partial modified output may indicate that the learners have focused their attention specifically on the error (as opposed to the entire correction).

Although the relationship between noticing and modified output remains contentious, it has been claimed that modified output may have several benefits beyond suggesting that the learner has noticed the CF. For example, in striving to produce an utterance that is more comprehensible or target-like after receiving CF, learners may be forced to consider syntactic form, a deeper level of processing than just processing for meaning (i.e., semantic processing) (Swain, 1995). Modified output also allows the learner to test interlanguage hypotheses: in particular, production after CF allows the learner to experiment with various reformulations of the original utterance, which in turn can yield additional CF. Practicing with a correct form after CF can also pave the way to automatization (Swain, 1995).

These claims regarding the utility of modified output are the foundation of Swain's (1995, 2005) Output Hypothesis. This hypothesis was developed after a series of studies on French immersion classrooms in Canada that focused primarily on providing input (e.g., Swain, 1985, 1993). In these studies, Swain found that the students' productive abilities lagged considerably behind their receptive abilities, leading her to conclude that (1) input is not sufficient for L2 learning (contra Krashen's 1985 Comprehensible Input Hypothesis); and (2) output is a necessary (but not sufficient) component of L2 learning. In addition to its potential for stretching learners' linguistic repertoires, its hypothesis-testing function, and its role in promoting automaticity, Swain noted that output can also serve a consciousness-raising function. In particular, in struggling to produce target-like utterances, learners may notice "gaps" (areas of deficiency, such as unknown or partially known grammatical structures). Alerted to areas needing improvement, learners may be encouraged to seek help or to pay increased attention to the input (Swain, 1995, 2005).

In light of the role that output and modified output are believed to play in SLA, some interactionist researchers have hypothesized that output-prompting feedback (such as elicitations, clarification requests, repetitions of the error, and paralinguistic signals) may be particularly beneficial in terms of facilitating noticing and L2 development (e.g., Lyster, 2004). Arguments for output-prompting CF often draw upon skill acquisition theory (see Chapter 3, this volume), which hypothesizes that CF which withholds the correct form and instead encourages learners to self-correct leads to "a gradual shift of knowledge from declarative to procedural (i.e., proceduralization) during which repeated practice plays an essential role" (Sato & Lyster, 2012, pp. 593–594).

Arguments have also been advanced concerning the value of input, including input-providing CF such as recasts (Leeman, 2003). Although current researchers do not subscribe to Krashen's (1985) Comprehensible Input Hypothesis, they recognize the importance of helping learners understand their interlocutors' message, as input from which learners can extract no meaning is unlikely to be retained by the learner (e.g., Gass & Mackey, 2015). Learners can play an active role in obtaining comprehensible input by providing signals of non-understanding and by making clarification requests (e.g., *Can you say that again?*), as these can prompt the interlocutor to use modified input (i.e., input with simpler sentences, more frequent vocabulary items, and a slower rate). With respect to input-providing feedback, and in particular, recasts, researchers have noted that the immediate juxtaposition of the target-like and nontarget-like forms (as in Examples 2 and 3 above) extends an opportunity for the learner to conduct a close comparison of the two.

The recast also provides a model, and since the CF is a reformulation of what the learner just said, her or his comprehension of the CF is likely to be facilitated, allowing scarce attentional resources to be temporarily diverted from meaning to form (e.g., Leeman, 2003; Long, 2007; see Goo & Mackey, 2013 for a review).

Over the past twenty years, considerable journal space has been devoted to comparing output-prompting and input-providing CF (see Pawlak & Tomczyk, 2013 for a review), as well as feedback differing along other dimensions, such as explicit/implicit (see Chapter 16, this volume). This body of work has yielded valuable insights into the complex nature of the relationship between CF and noticing/learning outcomes, with researchers providing evidence that "one size does not fit all" with respect to CF (Ammar & Spada, 2006, p. 566). As detailed in Parts VI and VIII of this volume, the characteristics of the learners, the context, the target, and the feedback itself all need to be considered when evaluating the effectiveness of any given type of CF.

Together, these components – attention, output, and input – are believed to be helpfully combined in conversational interaction involving CF, and in particular, negotiation for meaning. As noted by Long (1996), negotiation for meaning "facilitates acquisition because it connects input, internal learner capacities, particularly selective attention, and output in productive ways" (pp. 451–452). Researchers taking an interactionist approach use this hypothesis to help explain why CF, when given during meaning-focused activities, has the potential to promote L2 learning outcomes: it draws learners' attention to form while still prioritizing meaning; it provides information on what is not possible in the L2, and in the process, draws learners' attention to gaps in their L2 knowledge (and possible differences between the L1 and L2); it may provide a model of the correct form or encourage learners to arrive at that form themselves; finally, it may prompt learners to produce modified output.

Comparison to Other Approaches

The interactionist approach to feedback differs considerably from the behaviorist approaches to CF described in Chapter 1. For behaviorists, errors were seen as a sign of faulty learning needing immediate redress lest fossilization occur. A strong emphasis was placed on correcting all errors as well as on having students complete drills and other decontextualized activities that allowed them to focus on one particular form at a time. This synthetic approach to L2 instruction, labeled as "Focus on Form" by Long (1991), has been criticized on the grounds that it not only fails to lead to fluency but is also based on an untenable view of L2 learning – namely, that linguistic forms are acquired in an additive fashion, with the error-free mastery of one being the prerequisite for the learning of another (see Nassaji, 2015 for a discussion).

However, interactionist researchers also do not adhere to a pedagogical position at the other end of the continuum: a pure focus on meaning. Here, communicative activities and exposure to comprehensible input are prioritized over any focus on form, including grammar-focused lessons and CF (e.g., Lightbown, 2000). In such classrooms, the primary emphasis is on building fluency and the students' self-confidence. At best, CF is seen here as a contributor to students' knowledge *about* the language (i.e., explicit knowledge), but not to the largely unconscious, automatic knowledge believed to underlie fluent language use and processing (i.e., implicit knowledge) (e.g., Krashen, 1981). At worst, CF is viewed as anxiety-inducing, inconsistent, and ambiguous (e.g., Truscott, 1999).

While valuing meaning-focused activities and the importance of fluency, interactionist researchers would argue that pedagogical approaches that focus solely on meaning do not adequately address grammatical accuracy, and as such, ill-prepare learners for real-world language tasks (Ellis, 2015). Interactionist researchers thus support a "focus on form" approach, originally defined by Long (1991) as one that gives importance to addressing form incidentally and implicitly during meaning-focused communication (for example, by recasting grammatical errors as they arise). Over the years, the focus on form approach has been expanded to include not only incidental focus on form, but also planned focus on form (where instructors have lessons primarily focused on meaning but may designate part of the lesson to focus on a particular area of difficulty for the students), as well as a wider range of CF moves, such as prompts and metalinguistic explanations (e.g., Doughty & Varela, 1998; Doughty & Williams, 1998). Researchers and practitioners who advocate this approach argue that learners have a default tendency to focus solely on meaning when engaged in communicative activities (e.g., VanPatten, 2002), and thus some mechanism is needed to periodically shift their attention to form. Because a focus on form approach allows this shift to occur *within* a meaning-focused activity, learners are more likely to be able to map form to meaning here than they would be, for example, in a decontextualized grammar activity where little importance is placed on communication (Doughty, 2001; Nassaji, 2013).

In reaching a better understanding of interactionist approaches to CF, it is also useful to contrast this approach to its close cousin, the sociocultural approach to CF. The interactionist approach has been labeled "cognitivist," as it tends to highlight the learner-internal cognitive processes (such as noticing) engendered by interaction. Sociocultural researchers, on the other hand, place more emphasis on the interaction itself, arguing that learning is not the *result of* interaction, but rather a socially mediated activity that occurs *within* it (Ellis, 2009; Vygotsky, 1978). On this view, linguistic development occurs through scaffolding, or support, from a more proficient partner to a learner. This scaffolding can take many forms, including models, simplifications, encouragement, and feedback. Collectively, they help the learner accomplish a (linguistic) task that she or he would find difficult to complete alone and thus provide a foundation for future learner autonomy and self-regulation (e.g., Donato, 1994; Ohta, 2013). Over the years, there has been considerable debate over the relative explanatory power of cognitivist and sociocultural approaches. However, it is commonly recognized today that the two are complementary rather than in competition, with both being necessary to address the diverse questions raised by researchers interested in CF (see, for example, Batstone, 2010; Hulstijn et al., 2014; King & Mackey, 2016; Ortega, 2011).

Early and Current Research

The interactionist approach to corrective feedback draws upon a long line of research, including early descriptive studies on the types and frequency of negotiation of meaning moves in NS–NNS and NNS–NNS dyads (e.g., Pica, Young & Doughty, 1987; Varonis & Gass, 1985), as well as studies specifically focusing on the incidence of corrective feedback within these dyads (e.g., Gass & Varonis, 1989) and in classrooms (e.g., Lyster & Ranta, 1997) (for detailed historical overviews, see Mackey, 2012; Nassaji, 2015). These studies became the foundation for later experimental research seeking to establish the effect of that feedback on L2 production and comprehension (e.g., Carroll & Swain, 1993; Doughty & Varela, 1998; Leeman, 2003; Long, Inagaki & Ortega 1998; for recent meta-analyses, see Li, 2010 and Lyster & Saito, 2010). Collectively, these studies have provided evidence not only that corrective feedback occurs in a range of contexts, but also that it has the potential to effect positive changes in L2 learning outcomes.

Current interactionist research is investigating CF from a wide variety of angles, including the effect of CF on different linguistic targets. Studies on CF and morphosyntax are particularly well represented in the literature (see Chapter 17). Examinations of other linguistic targets – including vocabulary (see Chapter 18), phonology (Chapter 19), and pragmatics (Chapter 20) – are less common but have seen increased attention in recent years. A particularly productive strand of recent research (especially with morphosyntax) has been to investigate variables that may mediate the effectiveness of CF, such as learners' experience or familiarity with the linguistic target (e.g., Ellis, 2007; Li, 2014; van de Guchte et al., 2015; Yang & Lyster, 2010) as well as learner-difference characteristics such as working memory capacity, attentional control, language analytic ability, phonemic coding ability, explicit language aptitude, and anxiety (see Part VIII of this volume for more discussion of individual differences).

For example, in one recent study, Li (2014) compared recasts and metalinguistic explanations (the latter operationalized as a recast and then an explanation in the learners' L1 about the linguistic rule) with respect to the ability of Chinese as a second language learners at two levels of proficiency to learn two linguistic targets, the relatively simple classifiers and the more complex perfective marker *-le*. For the low-proficiency learners, the results depended on the linguistic target: recasts did not impact the perfective *-le* in this group, but metalinguistic explanations led to durable effects. For the high-proficiency learners, both recasts and metalinguistic explanations were equally beneficial for both targets. Commenting on the interaction between proficiency level and linguistic target, Li (2014) noted that relatively implicit recasts can work for lower-proficiency learners, provided that the linguistic target is transparent and salient. For more difficult targets, feedback that additionally contains information about the rule involved may help lower-proficiency learners (whose cognitive and linguistic resources are likely to be already stretched) to notice the feedback and process that information. Similarly, van de Guchte et al. (2015) compared the effects of recasts and prompts on German as a foreign language learners' ability to acquire two new constructions: a relatively simple construction (the comparative, formed in German very similarly to the way it is formed in the students' L1 of Dutch) and a more difficult construction (the dative case after a preposition of place, something that had no L1 analog). In this study, a prompt was defined as metalinguistic feedback plus an elicitation (a request for a reformulation). The researchers found that although the recasts helped the students learn about both structures, the effect of that form of feedback was more pronounced on the simpler comparative structure than on the more complex dative structure. For the more complex structure, the students appeared to need a form of feedback that gave them explicit information (i.e., the prompt).

The effect of context has been investigated as well, with studies comparing face-to-face and computer-mediated contexts, as well as various types of classrooms (see Ellis, 2010; Nassaji, 2015 for reviews; see also Part VI of this volume). One observation commonly made in this body of work is that while CF does have the potential to promote L2 development in a wide variety of contexts, especially with morphosyntax, its overall effect may be more pronounced in laboratory and text-based computer-mediated settings (where learners may be attuned to form and where the CF is likely to be given in a consistent and intensive manner) than in classroom settings (where the CF may take a number of different forms and may overlap with non-corrective discourse moves). CF studies have also considered the pedagogic orientation of the classroom and whether the language is being taught in a second or foreign language context (e.g., Azkarai & Imaz Agirre, 2016; Sheen, 2004). As noted by Philp and Tognini (2009), there are substantial differences across classrooms around the world with respect to their pedagogic orientation, as well as the amount of L2 input and practice opportunities available outside the classroom. In one study to compare four different contexts (French immersion, Canadian ESL, New Zealand ESL, and Korean EFL contexts), Sheen (2004) found that there were notable differences with respect to the amount of feedback given as well as the students' uptake and repair after that feedback. Mackey and Goo's (2007) meta-analysis revealed that there were greater effects for interaction and CF in foreign language settings than in second language settings on immediate post-tests, but not on delayed post-tests, perhaps due to the second language learners' greater exposure to the target linguistic items after the treatment.

Future Research

The findings discussed above, especially in light of the growing body of literature documenting differences in foreign language learning outcomes across contexts (e.g., study abroad vs. stay-at-home) (see, for example, Håkansson & Norrby, 2010), point to the need for additional research that addresses the intersections between the context of CF, learner-internal differences, and learning outcomes.

Additional suggestions may be put forth to expand these lines of inquiry. For example, although mediating variables have been addressed in numerous CF studies on morphosyntactic targets, these variables have scarcely been addressed in CF studies of phonology or pragmatics. With respect to phonology, studies to date have tended to concentrate on the overall effect of CF rather than considering the differential impact of CF on various phonological targets. For example, Gooch, Saito, and Lyster (2016) compared recasts and prompts (the latter operationalized as a request to say the nontarget-like word again) with respect to Korean EFL learners' ability to pronounce /ɹ/. The researchers found that recasts led to gains in controlled production, but that prompts helped learners improve their pronunciation in both controlled and spontaneous tasks. Given the well-documented differences across L2 phonological targets in terms of their perceptual saliency, articulatory complexity, L1–L2 similarity, and frequency (among other dimensions) (see Major, 2001 for a review), along with the mounting evidence that L2 learners can be distinguished in terms of their phonemic coding ability, articulatory knowledge, sensitivity to sound contrasts, and sound sequence recognition (e.g., Hu et al., 2013), future CF research that investigates the intersection between the characteristics of the phonological target and learner-internal variables – as well as considerations of the context – will help assess the generalizability of previous studies on morphosyntax (Gooch et al., 2016; Lee & Lyster, 2016).

A similar argument can be made with pragmatics. Of the limited number of studies that have examined CF and pragmatic targets, not only have few isolated the effect of the CF, but none to date have investigated the mediating role of individual difference variables (including identity, motivation, and personality; see Kuriscak, 2010 for a review of variables that are believed to influence L2 pragmatic development) and only one has considered the relative difficulty of the target (Nguyen, Pham & Pham, 2017). In this latter study, the researchers examined the effects of input enhancement (defined in the study as exposure to language for expressing constructive criticism) and recasts on EFL learners' use of constructive criticism in peer review activities. Using a pre-test, post-test, delayed post-test design, Nguyen et al. (2017) found that the combination of enhanced pragmatic input and recasts on pragmatic errors helped their students, pre-service EFL teachers in Vietnam, improve their use of both the relatively easier-to-notice external modifiers (such as compliments) and the more difficult internal modifiers (e.g., past tense, modal verbs, and expressions of uncertainty) in their use of constructive criticisms. However, by the delayed post-test, the effect of the treatment was only observed for the external modifiers, a finding which supports the claim that the relative difficulty of the speech act or its components may moderate the effect of the CF.

Another suggestion concerns the types of feedback moves that have been investigated. As noted above, there has been ample research and spirited debates on the relative effectiveness of one type of feedback over another. There have been suggestions in the literature, however, to expand this focus so as to include mixed feedback practices, as employing a range of CF techniques in a single lesson is not only common practice in L2 classrooms (Lyster, Saito & Sato, 2013) but a potentially effective method of addressing the needs and learning profiles of diverse students (Ellis, 2010), particularly when decisions regarding CF type are based on considerations of the learners' prior knowledge of the target and the communicative goals of the lesson (Nassaji, 2016). There may also be a synergistic effect between different types of feedback, such that the presence of one type enhances the noticeability or effectiveness of another (Goo & Mackey, 2013; Kartchava & Ammar, 2014). The few existing studies to date on mixed CF have provided evidence of the heightened noticeability of mixed CF (Kartchava & Ammar, 2014) and its potential for promoting gains in L2 performance, at least in the short term (Yilmaz, 2013) and on some measures (Sarandi, 2017), but more research is needed that addresses the effect of learners' prior knowledge of the target, different combinations of feedback types, and the durability of the effects.

Strides have also been made in recent years to address previous criticisms regarding the treatment of social and interpersonal factors in the interactionist approach. In the mid-1990s, cognitivist perspectives on CF were taken to task for not having a framework that was adequately socially informed (see Block, 2003 for a review). These criticisms were not without controversy (Long himself had previously argued that "[c]hange the social setting altogether, e.g., from street to classroom, or from a foreign to a second language environment, and, as far as we know, the way the learner acquires does not change much either," 1998, p. 93), but for many, these criticisms justified what has been labeled a "social turn" – namely, a greater attention to the socially mediated and situated nature of CF in interaction (e.g., Mackey, 2006). To this end, sociocognitive CF researchers have expanded their research focus to include interpersonal dynamics (e.g., the learner's perceived competence of the interlocutor and the degree of cooperation between the two) (e.g., Philp & Mackey, 2010; Philp, Adams & Iwashita, 2017; Sato, 2017; Sato & Ballinger, 2016; Solon, 2017; see Chapter 13, this volume), student engagement within the interaction (e.g., Storch, 2008), and learners' perceptions of interaction (e.g., Mackey, 2012; see Chapter 26, this volume). Studies such as these have provided evidence that the amount and type of CF, as well as rates of uptake, are impacted by interpersonal variables.

Another issue worthy of further discussion in interactionist studies is the problem of narrow sampling. It has been noted that in most social science research, the majority of participants are university students, and concerns have been raised regarding the generalizability of studies based on this population (e.g., Hanel & Vione, 2016; Peterson & Merunka, 2014). CF studies also tend to rely on university students: For example, of the forty-five unique studies targeted in two recent meta-analyses that focused exclusively on oral CF (Li, 2010; Lyster & Saito, 2010), thirty-four were conducted with university students (individuals who may be highly invested in learning the formal features of the target language as well as being attuned to various forms of CF through their years of schooling). Although some progress has been made in recent years to include other populations of learners, including elderly learners (e.g., Mackey & Sachs, 2012), children (e.g., Mackey & Silver, 2005), and learners in developing countries (Sherris & Burns, 2015), flags have been raised concerning the field's continued reliance on highly educated participants in university contexts (e.g., Tarone, 2010). For example, in one of the only CF studies to date to include literacy as a variable, Bigelow et al. (2006) found that the more literate group of Somali immigrants in their study recalled the recasts they received significantly more accurately than the less literate group. The researchers speculated that literacy influences metalinguistic awareness, which in turn impacts participants' ability to consciously notice and recall CF targeting the formal features of the L2.

Concerns regarding narrow sampling also tie into increased calls in the field of psychology for research on individuals in non-WEIRD (Western, educated, industrialized, rich, democratic) contexts, as there is accumulating evidence undermining the long-held assumption that cognitive processes, such as attention, function independently of external influences (e.g., Masuda, 2017; Nielsen et al., 2017; Nisbett & Miyamoto, 2005). This work in psychology hopefully will serve as an impetus for the field to investigate whether – and to what extent – social, cultural, and interpersonal factors impact the cognitive processes believed to be engendered by interaction-driven CF.

Investigating diverse populations can also help researchers address "'macro' or global forces – including, for instance, ... dynamics of race, gender, class, sexuality, and political inequality – [and how they] impact what have been described as 'micro'-level language learning processes" (King & Mackey, 2016, p. 213). The intersection between these two forces has been frequently addressed in studies of *written* CF (see Chapter 10 this volume); in this body of work, researchers commonly highlight learners' life histories, identities, and experiences in the larger social and national context to illuminate the ways in which they actively initiate, co-construct, and respond to (and sometimes resist) CF. Although the intersection between these two forces has yet to be systematically investigated by interactionist researchers, the beginnings of this line of inquiry can be seen in the studies of contextual and interpersonal factors, as well as in examinations of CF practices outside of instructed settings (see, for example, Kasper & Burch, 2016; Kunitz, 2018; Theodórsdórttir, 2018).

These varied concerns necessitate both epistemological and methodological diversity (e.g., King & Mackey, 2016; Larson-Freeman, 2018; Ortega, 2011, 2012). Detailed, longitudinal case studies on CF can help address the dynamic intersection of macro- and micro-level factors in L2 learning over time (Larson-Freeman, 2018). Longitudinal studies are also needed to assess the durability of CF effects. For example, in Li's (2010) meta-analysis of thirty-three studies, the researcher noted that explicit feedback was more effective than implicit feedback on immediate post-tests (seven days or less after the treatment) and short-delayed post-tests (eight to twenty-nine days after treatment); however, on the long-delayed post-tests (thirty days or more), he found a statistically nonsignificant, but slightly greater effect size for implicit feedback than for explicit. Li (2010) urged caution in interpreting the results, however, as there were only four studies on explicit feedback with long-delayed post-tests.

Small-scale studies can play a role in what Sakaluk (2016) refers to as "explor[ing] small and confirm[ing] big" (p. 47). Here, small-scale studies can help CF researchers take a deep dive into the cognitive, affective, interpersonal, sociopolitical, and contextual factors that may mediate the effectiveness of CF. Larger-scale studies (including replications and multi-site replications) can be used to test hypotheses and assess the generalizability of previous results. Replications are also needed given the preponderance of CF studies that focus on highly literate adults in school settings (Tarone, 2010) learning grammar with English as a target language (Kim, 2017).

Conclusions and Pedagogical Implications

The interactionist approach – with its emphasis on drawing learners' attention to form by providing feedback during meaning-focused activities – has been the subject of much research over the past thirty years. There have also been numerous pedagogical suggestions based on this research. For example, Lyster (2004) has recommended that explicit forms of feedback be used with younger learners, as they may have difficulties recognizing the corrective intent of implicit forms of feedback. More difficult linguistic targets – such as those that are irregular or semantically opaque – may also call for CF types that provide explicit information on the nature of the error. This may help learners not only recognize that they have produced a nontarget-like utterance but also understand how the nontarget-like and target-like forms differ. Explicit, output-prompting feedback may also allow learners to practice partially acquired forms during accuracy-based activities (Pawlak, 2014).

Recommendations have also been made for the classroom use of more implicit, input-providing forms of CF, such as recasts. Long (2007), for example, has advocated for the use of recasts in lessons focused on fluency, as they provide a model of the target-like form while not disrupting the primary focus on meaning in the lesson. The juxtaposition of the target-like and nontarget-like forms may also help learners notice the difference between the two. To facilitate this noticing, focal intonation can be used to highlight the error; for less proficient learners or learners with lower working memory capacities, recasts can be made shorter with one error targeted as opposed to several (e.g., Loewen & Philp, 2006). Teachers can also employ mixed CF practices within a single lesson, such as beginning with a prompt to encourage learners to self-correct and then using a recast if that self-correction does not take place.

As researchers have oft remarked, there is no one-size-fits-all form of CF (e.g., Ammar & Spada, 2006; Ellis, 2009). Teachers' decisions on how and when to respond to learner errors will depend on the goals of the lesson, the characteristics of the learners, and the difficulty of the target – as well as their own professional experiences and teaching beliefs. The research to date can serve as a useful starting point for these pedagogical decisions.

References

Ammar, A. & Spada, N. (2006). One size fits all? Recasts, prompts, and L2 learning. *Studies in Second Language Acquisition*, 28(4), 543–574.

Azkarai, A. & Imaz Agirre, A. (2016). Negotiation of meaning strategies in child EFL mainstream and CLIL settings. *TESOL Quarterly*, 50(4), 844–870.

Batstone, R. (2010). *Sociocognitive perspectives on language use and language learning*. Oxford: Oxford University Press.

Bigelow, M., delMas, B., Hansen, K. & Tarone, E. (2006). Literacy and the processing of oral recasts in SLA. *TESOL Quarterly, 40*, 1–25.

Block, D. (2003). *The social turn in second language acquisition*. Edinburgh: Edinburgh University Press.

Carroll, S. & Swain, M. (1993). Explicit and implicit negative feedback: An empirical study of the learning of linguistic generalizations. *Studies in Second Language Acquisition, 15*(3), 357–386.

Donato, R. (1994). Collective scaffolding in second language learning. In J. Lantolf & G. Appel (eds.), *Vygotskian approaches to second language research* (pp. 33–56). Norwood, NJ: Ablex.

Doughty, C. (2001). Cognitive underpinning of focus on form. In P. Robinson (ed.), *Cognition and second language instruction* (pp. 206–257). Cambridge: Cambridge University Press.

Doughty, C. & Varela, E. (1998). Communicative focus on form. In C. Doughty & J. Williams (eds.), *Focus on form in classroom second language acquisition* (pp. 114–138). Cambridge: Cambridge University Press.

Doughty, C. & Williams, J. (1998). *Focus on form in classroom second language acquisition*. Cambridge: Cambridge University Press.

Ellis, R. (2007). The differential effects of corrective feedback on two grammatical structures. In A. Mackey (ed.), *Conversational interaction in second language acquisition* (pp. 339–360). Oxford: Oxford University Press.

(2009). Corrective feedback and teacher development. *L2 Journal, 1*, 3–18.

(2010). Cognitive, social, and psychological dimensions of corrective feedback. In R. Batstone (ed.), *Sociocognitive perspectives on language use and language learning* (pp. 151–165). Oxford: Oxford University Press.

(2015). The importance of focus on form in communicative language teaching. *Eurasian Journal of Applied Linguistics, 1*(2), 1–12.

Gass, S. (1997). *Input, interaction, and the second language learner*. Mahwah, NJ: Laurence Erlbaum.

(2003). Input and interaction. In C. Doughty & M. Long (eds.), *The handbook of second language acquisition* (pp. 224–255). Oxford: Blackwell.

Gass, S. & Mackey, A. (2015). Input, interaction, and output in second language acquisition. In B. VanPatten & J. Williams (eds.), *Theories in second language acquisition: An introduction* (pp. 180–206). New York: Routledge.

Gass, S. & Varonis, E. (1989). Incorporated repairs in NNS discourse. In M. Eisenstein (ed.), *The dynamic interlanguage: Empirical studies in second language variation* (pp. 71–86). New York: Plenum.

Goo, J. & Mackey, A. (2013). The case against the case against recasts. *Studies in Second Language Acquisition, 35*(1), 127–165.

Gooch, R., Saito, K. & Lyster, R. (2016). Effects of recasts and prompts on L2 pronunciation development: Teaching English /ɹ/ to Korean adult EFL learners. *System, 60*, 117–127.

Guasti, M. (2009). Universal grammar approaches to language acquisition. In S. Foster-Cohen (ed.), *Language acquisition* (pp. 87–108). London: Palgrave Macmillan.

Gurzynski-Weiss, L. & Baralt, M. (2015). Does type of modified output correspond to learner noticing of feedback? A closer look in face-to-face and computer-mediated task-based interaction. *Applied Psycholinguistics*, 36(6), 1393–1420.

Håkansson, G. & Norrby, C. (2010). Environmental influence on language acquisition: Comparing second and foreign language acquisition of Swedish. *Language Learning*, 60(3), 628–650.

Hanel, P. & Vione, K. (2016). Do student samples provide an accurate estimate of the general public? *PLoD One*, 11. DOI:10.1371/journal.pone.0168354.

Hu, X., Ackerman, H., Martin, J., Erb, M., Winkler, S. & Reiterer, S. (2013). Language aptitude for pronunciation in advanced second language (L2) learners: Behavioural predictors and neural substrates. *Brain & Language*, 127(3), 366–376.

Hulstijn, J., Young, R., Ortega, L., Bigelow, M., DeKeyser, R., Ellis, N., Lantolf, J., Mackey, A. & Talmy, S. (2014). Bridging the gap: Cognitive and social approaches to research in second language learning and teaching. *Studies in Second Language Acquisition*, 36(3), 361–421.

Kartchava, E. & Ammar, A. (2014). The noticeability and effectiveness of corrective feedback in relation to target type. *Language Teaching Research*, 18(4), 428–452.

Kasper, G. & Burch, A. (2016). Focus on form in the wild. In R. van Compernolle & J. McGregor (eds.), *Authenticity, language, and interaction in second language contexts* (pp. 198–232). Bristol: Multilingual Matters.

Kim, Y. (2017). Cognitive-interactionist approaches to L2 instruction. In S. Loewen & M. Sato (eds.), *The Routledge handbook of instructed second language acquisition* (pp. 126–145). New York: Routledge.

King, K. & Mackey, A. (2016). Research methodology in second language studies: Trends, concerns, and new directions. *Modern Language Journal*, 100(S1), 209–227.

Krashen, S. (1981). *Second language acquisition and second language learning*. Oxford: Oxford University Press.

(1985). *The input hypothesis: Issues and implications*. New York: Longman.

Kunitz, S. (2018). Collaborative attention work on gender agreement in Italian as a foreign language. *Modern Language Journal*, 102(S1), 64–81.

Kuriscak, L. (2010). The effect of individual-level variables on speech act performance. In A. Martínez-Flor & E. Usó-Juan (eds.), *Speech act performance: Theoretical, empirical and methodological issues* (pp. 23–39). Amsterdam: John Benjamins.

Larson-Freeman, D. (2018). Looking ahead: Future directions in, and future research into, second language acquisition. *Foreign Language Annals*. DOI:10.1111/flan.12314.

Lee, A. & Lyster, R. (2016). Effects of different types of corrective feedback on receptive skills in a second language: A speech perception training study. *Language Learning*, 66(4), 809–833.

Leeman, J. (2003). Recasts and second language development: Beyond negative evidence. *Studies in Second Language Acquisition*, 25(1), 37–63.

Leow, R. & Donatelli, L. (2017). The role of (un)awareness in SLA. *Language Teaching*, 50(2), 189–211.

Li, S. (2010). The effectiveness of corrective feedback in SLA: A meta-analysis. *Language Learning*, 60(2), 309–365.

  (2014). The interface between feedback type, L2 proficiency, and the nature of the linguistic target. *Language Teaching Research*, 18(3), 373–396.

Lightbown, P. (2000). Anniversary article: Classroom SLA research and language teaching. *Applied Linguistics*, 21(4), 431–462.

Loewen, S. & Philp, J. (2006). Recasts in the adult English L2 classroom: Characteristics, explicitness, and effectiveness. *Modern Language Journal*, 90(4), 536–556.

Long, M. (1991). Focus on form: A design feature in language teaching methodology. In K. De Bot, R. Ginsberg & C. Kramsch (eds.), *Foreign language research in cross-cultural perspective* (pp. 39–52). Amsterdam: John Benjamins.

  (1996). The role of the linguistic environment in second language acquisition. In W. Ritchie & T. Bhatia (eds.), *Handbook of second language acquisition* (pp. 413–468). New York: Academic Press.

  (1998). SLA: Breaking the siege. *University of Hawai'i Working Papers in ESL*, 17, 79–129.

  (2007). *Problems in SLA*. Mahwah, NJ: Lawrence Erlbaum.

  (2015). *Second language acquisition and task-based language teaching*. Oxford, England: Wiley-Blackwell.

Long, M., Inagaki, S. & Ortega, L. (1998). The role of implicit negative feedback in SLA: Models and recasts in Japanese and Spanish. *Modern Language Journal*, 82, 357–371.

Lyster, R. (2004). Differential effects of prompts and recasts in form-focused instruction. *Studies in Second Language Acquisition*, 26(3), 399–426.

Lyster, R. & Ranta, L. (1997). Corrective feedback and learner uptake: Negotiation of form in communicative classrooms. *Studies in Second Language Acquisition*, 19(1), 37–66.

Lyster, R. & Saito, K. (2010). Oral feedback in classroom SLA: A meta-analysis. *Studies in Second Language Acquisition*, 32(2), 265–302.

Lyster, R., Saito, K. & Sato, M. (2013). Oral corrective feedback in second language classrooms. *Language Teaching*, 46(1), 1–40.

Mackey, A. (2006). Epilogue: From introspections, brain scans, and memory tests to the role of social context: Advancing research on interaction and learning. *Studies in Second Language Acquisition*, 28(2), 369–379.

(2012). *Input, interaction and corrective feedback in L2 classrooms*. Oxford: Oxford University Press.

Mackey, A. & Goo, J. (2007). Interaction research in SLA: A meta-analysis and research synthesis. In A. Mackey (ed.), *Conversational interaction in second language acquisition: A series of empirical studies* (pp. 407–453). Oxford: Oxford University Press.

Mackey, A. & Sachs, R. (2012). Older learners in SLA research: A first look at working memory, feedback, and L2 development. *Language Learning*, 62(3), 704–740.

Mackey, A. & Silver, R. (2005). Interactional tasks and English L2 learning by immigrant children in Singapore. *System*, 33, 239–260.

Major, R. (2001). *Foreign accent: The ontogeny and phylogeny of second language phonology*. Mahwah, NJ: Lawrence Erlbaum.

Masuda, T. (2017). Culture and attention: Recent empirical findings and new directions in cultural psychology. *Social and Personality Psychology Compass*, 11(12). DOI:10.1111/spc3.12363.

McDonough, K. & Mackey, A. (2006). Responses to recasts: Repetitions, primed production, and linguistic development. *Language Learning*, 56(4), 693–720.

Nassaji, H. (2013). Participation structure and incidental focus on form in adult ESL classrooms. *Language Learning*, 63(4), 835–869.

(2015). *The interactional feedback dimension in instructed second language learning: Linking theory, research, and practice*. London: Bloomsbury.

(2016). Interactional feedback in second language teaching and learning: A synthesis and analysis of current research. *Language Teaching Research*, 20(4), 535–562.

Nguyen, M., Pham, H. & Pham, T. (2017). The effects of input enhancement and recasts on the development of second language pragmatic competence. *Innovation in Language Learning and Teaching*, 11(1), 45–67.

Nielsen, M., Huan, D., Kärtner, J. & Legare, C. (2017). The persistent sampling bias in developmental psychology: A call to action. *Journal of Experimental Child Psychology*, 162, 31–38.

Nisbett, R. & Miyamoto, Y. (2005). The influence of culture: Holistic versus analytic perception. *Trends in Cognitive Sciences*, 9(10), 467–473.

Ohta, A. (2013). Sociocultural theory and the zone of proximal development. In J. Herschensohn & M. Young-Scholten (eds.), *The Cambridge handbook of second language acquisition* (pp. 648–669). Cambridge: Cambridge University Press.

Ortega, L. (2011). SLA after the social turn: Where cognitivism and its alternatives stand. In D. Atkinson (ed.), *Alternative approaches to second language acquisition* (pp. 167–180). London: Routledge.

(2012). Epistemological diversity and moral ends of research in instructed SLA. *Language Teaching Research*, 16(2), 206–226.

Pawlak, M. (2014). *Error correction in the foreign language classroom: Reconsidering the issues*. Berlin: Springer.

Pawlak, M. & Tomczyk, E. (2013). Differential effects of input-providing and output-inducing corrective feedback on the acquisition of English passive voice. In E. Piechurska-Kucial & E. Szymanska-Czaplak (eds.), *Language in cognition and affect* (pp. 133–149). Berlin: Springer.

Peterson, R. & Merunka, S. (2014). Convenience samples of college students and research reproducibility. *Journal of Business Research, 67*(5), 1035–1041.

Philp, J. (2003). Constraints on "noticing the gap": Nonnative speakers' noticing or recasts in NS-NNS interaction. *Studies in Second Language Acquisition, 25*(1), 99–126.

Philp, J. & Mackey, A. (2010). Interaction research: What can socially informed approaches offer to cognitivists (and vice versa)? In R. Batstone (ed.), *Sociocognitive perspectives on language use and language learning* (pp. 210–228). Oxford: Oxford University Press.

Philp, J. & Tognini, R. (2009). Language acquisition in foreign language contexts and the differential benefits of interaction. *International Review of Applied Linguistics in Language Testing, 47*(3–4) 245–266.

Philp, J., Adams, R. & Iwashita, N. (2017). *Peer interaction and second language learning.* London: Routledge.

Pica, T. (1996). Do second language learners need negotiation? *International Review of Applied Linguistics in Language Teaching, 34*(1), 1–21.

Pica, T., Young, R. & Doughty, C. (1987). The impact of interaction on comprehension. *TESOL Quarterly, 21*(4), 737–758.

Pinker, S. (1989). *Learnability and cognition: The acquisition of argument structure.* Cambridge, MA: MIT Press.

Robinson, P. (1995). Attention, memory, and the noticing hypothesis. *Language Learning, 45*(2), 283–331.

Sakaluk, J. (2016). Exploring small, confirming big: An alternative system to the new statistics for advancing cumulative and replicable psychological research. *Journal of Experimental Social Psychology, 66,* 47–54.

Sarandi, H. (2017). Mixed corrective feedback and the acquisition of third person "-s." *The Language Learning Journal.* DOI:10.1080/09571736.2017.1400579.

Sato, M. (2017). Oral peer corrective feedback: Multiple theoretical perspectives. In H. Nassaji & E. Kartchava (eds.), *Corrective feedback in second language teaching and learning: Research, theory, applications, implications* (pp. 19–34). New York: Routledge.

Sato, M. & Ballinger, S. (2016). *Peer interaction and second language learning: Pedagogical potential and research agenda.* Amsterdam: John Benjamins.

Sato, M. & Lyster, R. (2012). Peer interaction and corrective feedback for accuracy and fluency development: Monitoring, practice, and proceduralization. *Studies in Second Language Acquisition, 34*(4), 591–626.

Schmidt, R. (1990). The role of consciousness in second language learning. *Applied Linguistics, 11*(2), 129–158.

(1994). Implicit learning and the cognitive unconscious: Of artificial grammars and SLA. In N. Ellis (ed.), *Implicit and explicit learning of languages* (pp. 165–209). London: Academic Press.

Sheen, Y. (2004). Corrective feedback and learners' uptake in communicative classrooms across instructional settings. *Language Teaching Research*, 8(3), 263–300.

Sherris, A. & Burns, M. S. (2015). New border crossings for the interaction hypothesis: The effects of feedback on Gonja speakers learning English in a rural school in Ghana. *Pedagogies: An International Journal*, 10(3), 238–255.

Solon, M. (2017). Interaction and phonetic form in task completion: An examination of interlocutor effects in learner-learner and learner-heritage speaker interaction. In L. Gurzynski-Weiss (ed.), *Expanding individual difference research in the interaction approach: Investigating learners, instructors, and other interlocutors* (pp. 121–147). Amsterdam: John Benjamins.

Storch, N. (2008). Metatalk in pair work activity: Level of engagement and implications for language development. *Language Awareness*, 17(2), 95–114.

Swain, M. (1985). Communicative competence: Some roles of comprehensible input and comprehensible output in its development. In S. Gass & C. Madden (eds.), *Input in second language acquisition* (pp. 235–253). Rowley, MA: Newbury House.

(1993). The output hypothesis: Just speaking and writing aren't enough. *Canadian Modern Language Review*, 50(1), 158–164.

(1995). Three functions of output in second language learning. In G. Cook & B. Seidlhofer (eds.), *Principles and practice in applied linguistics* (pp.125–144). Oxford: Oxford University Press.

(2005). The output hypothesis: Theory and research. In E. Hinkel (ed.), *Handbook on research in second language teaching and learning* (pp. 471–483). Mahwah, NJ: Lawrence Erlbaum.

Tarone, E. (2010). Second language acquisition by low-literate learners: An under-studied population. *Language Teaching*, 43(1), 75–83.

Theodórsdóttir, G. (2018). L2 teaching in the wild: A closer look at correction and explanation practices in everyday L2 interaction. *Modern Language Journal*, 201(S1), 30–45.

Truscott, J. (1999). What's wrong with oral grammar correction. *Canadian Modern Language Review*, 55(4), 437–456.

van de Guchte, M., Braaksma, M., Rijlaarsdam, G. & Bimmel, P. (2015). Learning new grammatical structures in task-based language learning: The effects of recasts and prompts. *Modern Language Journal*, 99(2), 246–262.

VanPatten, B. (2002). Processing instruction: An update. *Language Learning*, 52(4), 755–803.

Varonis, E. & Gass, S. (1985). Non-native/non-native conversations: A model for negotiation of meaning. *Applied Linguistics*, 6(1), 71–90.

Vygotsky, L. (1978). *Mind in society: The development of higher psychological processes*. Cambridge, MA: Harvard University Press.

White, L. (1987). Against comprehensible input: The input hypothesis and the development of second-language competence. *Applied Linguistics*, 8(2), 95–110.

(1991). Adverb placement in second language acquisition: Some effects of positive and negative evidence in the classroom. *Second Language Research*, 7(2), 133–161.

Yang, Y. & Lyster, R. (2010). Effects of form-focused practice and feedback on Chinese EFL learners' acquisition of regular and irregular past tense forms. *Studies in Second Language Acquisition*, 32(2), 235–263.

Yilmaz, Y. (2013). The relative effectiveness of mixed, explicit and implicit feedback in the acquisition of English articles. *System*, 41, 691–705.

3

Cognitive Theoretical Perspectives of Corrective Feedback

Ronald P. Leow and Meagan Driver

Introduction

Corrective feedback (CF) is a response that is provided by a teacher, a researcher, or a peer in reaction to an error committed by the second/foreign language (L2) learner.[1] The response may be delivered in the first language (L1) or L2 and in the oral, written, and/or computerized or digital mode. There are various types of CF that have been empirically addressed for either or both modes in the CF literature (implicit or explicit, direct or indirect feedback, positive or negative, input-providing or output-prompting feedback, direct or indirect, focused or unfocused, intensive or extensive, metalinguistic, and so on). What is noteworthy is that CF appears to be firmly situated within the instructed setting given that the bulk of studies conducted within this CF strand of research draw their sample populations from the formal L2 context. Indeed, the role of CF in the L2 learning process has for decades remained a dominant issue in the second language acquisition (SLA) (naturalistic) and instructed SLA (ISLA) strands of research, albeit with some overlapping between these two contexts. This chapter (1) traces the early roots of CF; (2) presents a coarse-grained theoretical feedback processing framework to discuss the cognitive theoretical underpinnings postulated to account for the role of CF in L2 development; (3) provides a list of cognitive processes assumed to play a role during CF provision; and (4) reports on each theoretical underpinning followed by a commentary on each theoretical underpinning's ability to account for the role of CF in L2 development.

---

[1] Corrective feedback has also been provided via problem-solving tasks (e.g., Leow, 2001), the computer (e.g., Nagata, 1993), synchronous computer-mediated communication (SCMC) (Gurzynski-Weiss, Al Khalil, Baralt & Leow, 2016), and so on. Computerized corrective feedback will not be discussed in this chapter.

Early Roots of CF

An early focus on the role of errors in L2 learning began in the mid-1950s around the advent of Lado's (1957) contrastive analysis that systematically compared the L1 and L2 languages to identify potential difficulties in learning the L2, which may lead to learner error. This contrastive analysis approach was heavily influenced by two theoretical underpinnings: Structural linguistics (Bloomfield, 1933) that viewed language as a rule-governed system divided into hierarchically and individually arranged subsystems and behaviorism (Skinner, 1957) that viewed L2 learning as habit formation, which could be potentially affected by L1-based learner error. Pedagogically, contrastive analysis allowed teachers to anticipate and prevent potential learner error, which, it was assumed, needed to be corrected immediately while carefully guiding L2 learning via rote learning (e.g., the audiolingual approach). However, the assumed association between learning difficulty and error prediction and the assumption that errors were L1-based were not empirically supported. At the same time, behaviorism began to lose its appeal due to a shift to a rationalist/mentalist/nativist (e.g., Chomsky, 1957) perspective of learning that viewed the student as a more active participant in the learning process. Consequently, the field began to focus more on internal processes to explain the occurrence of errors.

Two major publications (Corder, 1967 and Selinker, 1972) that provided the foundation for current research in (I)SLA were both learner-centered and repudiations of a behaviorist approach to language learning. Corder underscored the need to investigate the role of errors from the perspective of language processing and learning. Selinker suggested that the learner internal system that L2 learners possess as their ability to learn the L2 develops, which he called "interlanguage," needed to be acknowledged. As the term connotes, interlanguage is a system that is somewhere between the L1 and the L2. Given the status of interlanguage being a system with its own rules, it raises the question of whether errors produced by learners are "really systematically 'correct' according to their own interlanguage system, but are being graded from a native or near-native speaker's perspective" (Leow, 2015, p. 3).

Error analysis became popular in this period, as errors were viewed as an inevitable and necessary feature of the learning process without which L2 development would not take place. However, like contrastive analysis, error identification became problematic in accurately identifying, for example, type of error (e.g., errors vs. mistakes, variability in errors), error classification (e.g., overlapping of linguistic domains), the origin of psycholinguistic causes (e.g., language transfer, L1-based), error evaluation, and so on.

Theoretical Underpinnings

Errors are a natural feature of both the L1 and L2 learning process and several meta-analyses have reported beneficial effects of CF (e.g., Brown, 2016; Li, 2010; Lyster & Saito, 2010; Russell & Spada, 2006) in (I)SLA. Currently, there are several cognitive theoretical underpinnings cited by empirical CF studies (e.g., Egi, 2007; Loewen, 2005; Lyster, 1998; Mackey, 2006; Manchón & Vasylets, 2019) to account for the role or lack thereof of CF in the L2 learning process, for example, the Monitor Model (Krashen, 1982), the Interaction Hypothesis (Long, 1996), the Noticing Hypothesis (Schmidt, 1990), the Output Hypothesis (Swain, 2005), Skill Acquisition Theory (DeKeyser, 2015), and the Model of the L2 Learning Process in ISLA (Leow, 2015), be it oral, written, or computerized or digital. These theoretical underpinnings can be viewed from, minimally, three perspectives: (1) whether the underpinning is grounded in SLA (naturalistic) or ISLA (instructed setting); (2) the importance or lack thereof of CF in the process of learning an L2; and (3) the type of learning (implicit or explicit) assumed to be associated with the processing of CF. It is also useful to keep in mind a coarse-grained feedback processing framework (Leow, 2020) that underlies most underpinnings, as seen below:

Feedback > Feedback processing > Internal system (prior knowledge) > Output

Whether CF is indeed processed by L2 learners may depend on several cognitive processes. Table 3.1 (adapted from Leow, 2015, pp. 98–99)

Table 3.1 *A synopsis of the cognitive processes and variables postulated to play important roles in processing CF*

FEEDBACK			---processing---			→OUTPUT
	WM	attention	awareness	levels of awareness	levels of processing	prior knowledge
Monitor Model	no	(yes)[a]	no (acquisition) yes (learning)	no	no	no
	no	yes		no	(yes)	yes
Output Hypothesis	no	yes	yes	no	yes	yes
Noticing Hypothesis	no	yes	yes	yes	(yes)	(no)
Interaction Hypothesis	no	yes	(no)	no	no	yes
Skill Acquisition	no	yes	(yes)	no	(yes)	yes
Model of L2 Learning	yes	yes	yes	yes	yes	yes

WM = Working memory
( )[a] = not clearly stated but gleaned from postulation

presents the cognitive processes postulated to account for the role of CF and in relation to their roles in the theoretical underpinnings mentioned above.

The Monitor Model

Krashen's (1982) Monitor Model is derived from child L1 acquisition and postulates five hypotheses, of which the Acquisition-Learning Hypothesis is pertinent to the potential role of CF. The Acquisition-Learning Hypothesis postulates that adult learners have two distinct and different ways to develop their knowledge of the L2 with no interface between the two. The first is language *acquisition*, which simulates the way children acquire their first language. This type of learning is subconscious, that is, learners are unaware of the rules of the L2, and acquisition is also associated with "implicit learning, informal learning, and natural learning. In non-technical language, acquisition is 'picking-up' a language" (Krashen, 1982: 10). *Acquisition* feeds into acquired knowledge.

The second way to learn the L2 is by language *learning*, which is associated with conscious processing, knowing the rules, being aware of such rules, and being able to discuss them. *Learning*, then, is associated with explicit metalinguistic learning that may be associated with awareness at the level of understanding (Schmidt, 1990) and feeds into learned knowledge.

Key Features
1. The Monitor Model appears to be situated in both SLA (acquisition) and ISLA (learning).
2. There are two ways to develop L2 knowledge: subconsciously via *acquisition* and consciously via *learning*. There is no interface between the two.
3. CF may only impact *learning* but not *acquisition* given that CF is situated at the output stage, while *acquisition* is input-based or at the input processing stage.
4. The *acquisition* process is implicit, while the *learning* process is explicit.

Comments on the Monitor Model

Krashen's Monitor Model makes an arguably important distinction between two learning processes, if viewed from *how* L2 data are processed and the context in which they occur: *Acquisition* that simulates the type of processing that is typically found in the naturalistic setting and *learning*, the type of processing that is typically evidenced in the instructed setting (Leow, 2015; Leow & Cerezo, 2016). Krashen does afford the role of CF within the explicit learning process given that it affects the learners' learned knowledge by informing them that their prior L2 knowledge is incorrect. Consequently, if the focus of the instruction is on *learning*, and more specifically metalinguistic learning, then Krashen views CF as positive though it should not occur for every error committed or for all the grammar rules.

By describing *learning* as being rule-based or reflecting awareness at the level of understanding (Schmidt, 1990) or metalinguistic awareness, which may also indicate a high depth of processing of the linguistic information, the Monitor Model is unable to account for any potential noticing or lower level of awareness of the feedback that may lead to a potential restructuring of the learner's interlanguage. Krashen's Monitor Model has not been a popular source for a theoretical underpinning in the CF strand of research perhaps due to the (I)SLA field's conflation of the two types of processing (acquisition and learning) in the current literature, which implicitly assumes that the type of processing involved in *acquisition* and *learning* is essentially the same.

The Output Hypothesis

Swain's (2005) Output Hypothesis is a direct rebuttal to Krashen's (1982) Input Hypothesis which postulates that learning takes place during exposure to comprehensible input, that is, during the early stages of the L2 process (the input-processing stage). This hypothesis was postulated after Swain observed that the L2 productive ability of students in content-based L2 French classrooms in immersion schools in Canada was quite low even after a lot of exposure to comprehensible input and when compared to their comprehension ability. Swain felt that allowing students to have more opportunities to produce the L2 would improve their productive ability by allowing them to move away from semantic processing or processing for meaning and become more consciously and cognitively engaged in grammatical (e.g., syntactic and morphological) processing.

Swain makes three major claims in her Output Hypothesis regarding the functions of learner production during the learning process at this production stage. While the first two claims are psycholinguistic in nature, the third is sociocultural. The first claim addresses the actual process of producing the L2 and potential cognitive processes involved during this production while the second is associated with cognitive processes associated with the potential role of feedback.

Claim #1: A Noticing/Triggering Function, or What Might Be Referred to as a Consciousness-Raising Role

Given the opportunity to produce the L2, this noticing/triggering function may push learners to raise their awareness of or recognize potential gaps between their current interlanguage (or knowledge) and the L2. This, in turn, may encourage them to process relevant L2 data associated with these linguistic problems. Swain also claims that this awareness triggers cognitive processes associated with learning, namely, "ones in which learners generate linguistic knowledge that is new to them, or that consolidate their current existing knowledge" (Swain, 2005: 474). At the same time, learner awareness may also depend upon several other variables that may prevent such awareness-raising.

Noticing in this claim may refer to attention plus a low level of awareness (Schmidt, 1990), attention due to saliency or frequency of the feature (Gass, 1997), in addition to noticing the gap (Schmidt & Frota, 1986), that is, noticing that one's L2 usage is different from the target language, or noticing the hole (Swain, 1985). In other words learners may notice that they are unable to say what they want to convey in the L2. Included in this claim is the notion of depth of processing (Craik & Lockhart, 1972), which is associated with the amount of analysis and elaboration L2 learners perform on the L2 data with the belief that deeper processing leads to better retention of L2 knowledge.

Claim #2: A Hypothesis-Testing Function

This function is related to the opportunity to experiment with new forms and structures and see whether they are correct or need correction. This function appears to be more relevant to learners willing to consciously produce the language for feedback. According to Swain, if learners are not testing hypotheses, then changes in their output would not be expected following feedback. However, changes could also originate from conversational moves or CF, such as clarification requests, confirmation checks, etc. Swain's assumption here is that the provision of opportunities to produce the L2 will reduce learners' focus on the task of communication. This production will increase the time they have to explicitly analyze the mismatches they identify during output. This increase in consciously processing the feedback can potentially lead to modifying or "reprocessing" their output.

Claim #3: A Metalinguistic Function, or What Might Be Referred to as Its "Reflective" Role

Swain (2005) frames this third function within Vygotsky's sociocultural theory of mind (Vygotsky, 1978), which posits that using language to reflect on language produced by the self or others mediates the process of L2 learning. Given that sociocultural theory is premised on people operating with mediating tools, of which speaking is one, Swain also views output as speaking, writing, collaborative dialogue, and/or verbalizing. Collaborative dialogue involves speakers engaged in problem solving and knowledge building and, in the case of L2 learners, solving linguistic problems and building knowledge about language.

Key Features
1. This hypothesis is situated within ISLA.
2. It views output as a part of the L2 learning process. Output provides the opportunity to elicit feedback, which, in turn, if processed, loops back as input to be further processed.
3. Feedback, consciously sought, allows L2 learners to restructure their prior knowledge.
4. It postulates the notion of effort or depth of processing during output processing.
5. The learning process is explicit.

Comments on the Output Hypothesis
Although the Output Hypothesis (Swain, 2005) addresses the output stage of the L2 learning process, the hypothesis claims that "the act of producing language (speaking or writing) constitutes, under certain circumstances, part of the process of second language learning" (Swain, 2005: 471). In other words, while it is usually assumed that output or production is a product and, for many, outside of the L2 learning process, Swain includes this process of producing as part of the learning process, which appears to involve quite a high depth of processing in all three claims. In addition, Swain claims that the processes involved in producing language are quite different from those employed during the early stages of the L2 learning process (e.g., comprehension).

The Output Hypothesis lends itself quite easily to the role of CF given that it is situated primarily at the output stage of the L2 learning process, where the provision of CF occurs, and it is classroom-based in which the type of processing is typically explicit. According to the hypothesis, it is the hypothesis-testing function that affords the benefits of CF although the recipients may be restricted to only those L2 learners who are willing to invest more effort into explicitly processing the L2 data via production. However, how the feedback is further processed and whether L2 learning rests solely on production (the notion of "reprocessing" the feedback at the input-to-intake stage arguably weakens the primary tenet of the Output Hypothesis) are questions that remain unanswered in this hypothesis.

The Noticing Hypothesis
Arguably one of the most influential theoretical underpinnings employed by many corrective feedback studies is Schmidt's (1990, 1993, 1994, 1995, 2001) Noticing Hypothesis, which is typically framed within the need to minimally "notice" feedback before any potential restructuring may take

place. The Noticing Hypothesis is premised upon a commonly held view in the SLA field that the absence of awareness precludes the possibility of any processing of input beyond short-term memory.

It should be noted that Schmidt's (1990 and elsewhere) Noticing Hypothesis was originally situated at the early stage of the L2 learning process (the input-to-intake stage) and addresses new linguistic information in the L2 input. According to the Noticing Hypothesis, attention controls access to awareness and is responsible for the subjective experience of noticing, which, in an earlier statement, was "the necessary and sufficient condition for the conversion of input to intake" (Schmidt, 1993, p. 209). His position is that focal attention is isomorphic with awareness and that learning without awareness must be ruled out. While Schmidt does admit the existence of processes that stand outside of awareness (e.g., implicit learning), he rejects the possibility of abstraction without awareness and contends that abstraction is always associated with conscious cognitive functions (Schmidt, 1995).

Schmidt (1994) concedes that the crucial role of noticing in input processing is controversial, since there is a widespread belief that learners can somehow pick up elements of the language without being aware of it (Tomlin & Villa, 1994). In addition, given the methodological problem of establishing zero awareness at the point of noticing or processing, Schmidt has withdrawn from his original postulation of noticing as the necessary and sufficient condition for the conversion of input into intake to one of more noticing leads to more learning (Schmidt, 1994), underscoring the facilitative nature of noticing in the early stages of the learning process.

Besides noticing, Schmidt (1990) distinguishes a higher level of awareness, which he calls understanding and which is related to the ability to analyze, compare, and test hypotheses about the linguistic input leading to rule formulation. In the researcher's view, whereas noticing is necessary for intake and potential learning to take place, understanding may act as a facilitator for learning, but its presence is not necessary. The crucial difference between noticing and understanding, according to Schmidt (1993), is that the former results in intake and in item learning, while the latter leads to restructuring and system learning. In other words, understanding seems to be a more sophisticated process than noticing although they both allow for storage of linguistic material in long-term memory.

Key Features
1. The Noticing Hypothesis is situated within both SLA and ISLA.
2. Focal attention accompanied by a low level of awareness is called *noticing*, and this is crucial for intake and, as an extension, learning.

3. While not necessary for subsequent processing of the input, there is also a higher level of awareness involved during the learning process, namely, awareness at the level of understanding.
4. CF provides an opportunity for L2 learners to notice the gap or mismatch between their output and their current prior knowledge.
5. The learning process is mainly explicit.

Comments on the Noticing Hypothesis

The notion of noticing à la Schmidt permeates most of the oral, written, or computerized/digital CF literature in addition to the role of attention in this strand of research. At the same time, any reference to noticing to explicate findings in this strand of research acknowledges the need to process CF with a minimal low level of awareness given that noticing subsumes both attention and awareness. Schmidt's Noticing Hypothesis was proposed to address new linguistic information at the input processing stage of the L2 learning process with the potential of noticed information leading to intake. When the Noticing Hypothesis is employed at the output stage, the premise is that, like new linguistic information, the feedback provided at this stage also needs to be minimally noticed. However, at this output stage noticing has to be necessarily linked to the learner's prior knowledge. In other words, learners notice the mismatch between what they just produced (from prior knowledge already lodged in their internal system) and the different linguistic information contained in the corrective feedback. At the same time, the Noticing Hypothesis fails to account for; (1) the potential for processing the CF without awareness; (2) any subsequent processing of the feedback; or (3) what role prior knowledge plays in any interaction with the CF noticed.

The Interaction Hypothesis

Long's (1996) Interaction Hypothesis is an updated version of Long's (1981, 1983, 1989) previous hypothesis that was originally grounded in the following process: Comprehensible input (Krashen, 1982) > comprehension > acquisition. To promote the acquisition process, modifications made during a problem-solving segment of a natural conversation can assist in making the L2 more comprehensible. The Interaction Hypothesis, then, centers itself on the facilitative adjustments that a native or expert speaker of a language may offer a novice language learner during social, communicative interactions. As part of his hypothesis, Long (1996) posits that *negotiation for meaning* leads the competent speaker to provide interactional feedback to the language learner, aiding acquisition efforts by productively drawing a connection between input and attention, among other internal abilities, and output. Interaction provides the opportunity for L2 learners to recreate or modify their knowledge and extend it to further contexts according to their understanding (Bitchener & Storch, 2016). The hypothesis holds the negotiation for meaning and feedback that arises during *semantically contingent speech* as the primary trigger and driver of SLA (Long, 1996).

Long (1996) identifies the high frequency of semantically related speech during instances of feedback, or negotiation for meaning, as an important factor in language acquisition. Given that negotiation aims to solve a problem through repetitions, extensions, reformulations, and recasts of the same or similar linguistic items, the saliency of these target forms is assumed to increase, which in turn is assumed to increase the learners' attention to the key form. Negotiation can also lend information on the arrangement and segmentation of utterances and give hints as to the meaning of new words, making acquisition attainable for the learners.

Long (1996) bases his hypothesis on Tomlin and Villa's (1994) neuroscience-based discussion of attention to support the benefits of communicative interactions on SLA. Briefly, Tomlin and Villa propose a functionally based, fine-grained analysis of attention for input processing in SLA "that integrates these related conceptions of attention into a system that allows investigation of SLA data at the moment of acquisition" (p. 190). In their model of input processing in SLA, attention has three components (all of which have neurological correlates): (1) alertness (an overall readiness to deal with incoming stimuli whose function is related to the speed of information selection; (2) orientation (the direction of attentional resources to a certain type of stimuli; and (3) detection (the cognitive registration of stimuli or the process that selects, or engages, a particular and specific bit of information). According to Tomlin and Villa, it is detection alone that is necessary for further processing of input and subsequent learning to take place. The other two components can enhance the chances that detection will occur, but neither is necessary.

Grounded in this model, Long claims that, because learners are more likely to be alert during conversation, potentially interested in seeing the effect their utterance has had on their interlocutor, and know what they have intended to communicate, they are free to orient their attention and processing resources to the form of the native or advanced speaker's response. Any reformulation offered by the interlocutor will most likely require little semantic change, which allows the learners to focus attentional resources on forms of even greater complexity. While Long admits that it cannot be assured that the novice learners will apply any spare resources to processing form, it is more probable that the learners will detect and understand any modifications offered by their interlocutor and incorporate them into their own speech with higher frequency when they are not required to simultaneously process both form and meaning that are ambiguous or unfamiliar.

The effort to link the linguistic environment and input features with learners' internal factors (cognitive processes) is indeed laudable and is succinctly observed in this statement:

> It is proposed that environmental contributions to acquisition are mediated by selective attention and the learner's developing L2 processing capacity, and that these resources are brought together most usefully, although not exclusively during *negotiation of meaning*. Negative feedback obtained during negotiation work or elsewhere may be facilitative of L2 development, at least for vocabulary, morphology and language-specific syntax, and essential for learning certain specifiable L1–L2 contrasts.
> (Long, 1996, p. 414)

Long (1996) thus hypothesizes that language development and acquisition are contingent on establishing the best input features and linguistic environment for interaction with learners' cognitive processes.

Key Features
1. This hypothesis appears to be situated within both SLA and ISLA.
2. Language acquisition and cognitive development are dependent on the feedback gained by novice learners during their interactions with expert speakers.
3. There is an effort to incorporate learner cognitive processes.
4. The learning process appears to be both implicit and explicit.

Comments on the Interaction Hypothesis

The Interaction Hypothesis provides the theoretical underpinning for many oral CF studies although at this point it is not clear where the hypothesis is situated theoretically in terms of type of processing. Long argues that recasts, arguably the most well-known and researched interactional type of CF, are ideal for promoting acquisition or implicit learning. As can be seen, this argument appears to fall quite easily within Tomlin and Villa's (1994) notion of detection of linguistic information by learners that allows intake to occur without any level of awareness involved. However, Tomlin and Villa's notion of detection is associated with new information becoming intake and also not linked to the learners' prior knowledge (see discussion of noticing above). In addition, it is assumed that the level of processing of the difference between learner production and potential subsequent restructuring is quite low. However, there appears to be a mismatch between the type of processing assumed in Tomlin and Villa's (1994) notion of detection (attention and cognitive registration without awareness) and Long's description of novice learners being primed (aware) of any potential feedback provided. Indeed, Long's description would fall within Schmidt's notion of noticing (focal attention plus a low level of awareness) (see Gass & Mackey, 2015 for a similar interpretation) and Swain's (2005) Output Hypothesis in which she presents the notion of motivated learners primed to test their hypotheses on their output via feedback, which is clearly grounded in explicit processing. It is, then, not surprising to note that in several oral CF studies there is some uncertainty as to whether the researchers are assuming that learners are detecting (à la Tomlin and Villa) or noticing (à la Schmidt) the CF provided; in other words, whether the depth of processing is very low (as in *acquisition*) or relatively high (as in *learning*). This may also raise the issues of quantity and quality of feedback provided by the interlocutor (e.g., Ellis, 1991) and whether the SLA or ISLA context is being considered given that the affordances in each context are not equal (Leow, 2019).

The Interaction Hypothesis clearly posits a role for cognitive processes (e.g., selective attention and the learners' developing L2 processing capacity) during the interactional exchange but does not provide much description of how such processes or capacity interact with CF and whether their roles are indeed important or even crucial for successful processing of CF. There is an obvious assumption within the Interaction Hypothesis that feedback provides L2 learners with the important opportunity to cognitively process the feedback provided within a conversational exchange, but the question is whether such feedback is indeed processed by the learners and, if so, how and whether it is processed similarly or differentially.

Skill Acquisition Theory

Skill Acquisition Theory concerns itself with the path learners take in order to gain a new skill and explains how explicit/declarative L2 knowledge becomes proceduralized over time until it is converted into implicit/procedural knowledge (DeKeyser, 2015). Emphasizing the importance of explicit/declarative knowledge during earlier stages of learning, this psychology-based theory applies principally to adept adult learners who find themselves at the early stage of learning relatively simple structures in, specifically, an instructed setting. Under Skill Acquisition Theory, researchers characterize knowledge by type and use this to propose three principal stages of development, commonly referred to within SLA as the acquisition of declarative knowledge, proceduralization, and automatization stages (see Anderson, 1982, 1993, 2007).

The learning process begins with learners acquiring declarative knowledge *about* a skill (language), most often through observation and analysis of expert behavior as well as a verbal and explicit explanation (DeKeyser, 2015), without attempting to engage in any kind of language perception or production. Once the learners have acquired enough knowledge about a skill, typically associated with much cognitive effort, they may begin the process of forming a behavior where declarative knowledge is transformed into procedural knowledge during *proceduralization*. DeKeyser (2015) explains that even after little time and few trials learners may begin to develop from slow understanding of a task to quick and fluid task completion. Once the learners have proceduralized their declarative knowledge, they can retrieve specific information with less dependence on declarative knowledge and, consequently, less cognitive effort.

In order to develop spontaneous and fluid speech and proceduralize knowledge, a great deal of meaningful, contextualized practice is required (DeKeyser, 2015). As a result of this intensive practice or "overlearning," reaction times, the time required to carry out a task, and attention requirements as well as error rates are all reduced if the learners are led into the stage of automatization. To describe the process of acquisition, DeKeyser posits a qualitative change in knowledge retrieval that resembles a power curve, representing a shift from declarative to procedural knowledge through automatization and shows the change over time as explicit knowledge becomes acquired. Automaticity may depend, however, on the task, making automatization useful in select cases. As a result, there is a requirement to promote both specific procedural knowledge and more abstract declarative knowledge that may be applied in a broader sense.

Skill Acquisition Theory does not necessarily claim an evolution from explicit to implicit knowledge but focuses on how explicitly learned declarative knowledge carries learners through the proceduralization stage by way of carefully formatted tasks, to more implicit or procedural knowledge and into the initial stages of automatization. Through this theory, one may see how learners may simultaneously acquire declarative knowledge of one element while moving differently through or never reaching some stages for others. However, under this theory, learners cannot reach a practical proficiency level without moving through each stage (DeKeyser, 2015).

Key Features
1. This theory is situated within ISLA.
2. Skill Acquisition Theory is concerned with learners' behavior at the output stage (practice).
3. Explicitly acquired, declarative knowledge about a skill is required for learners to arrive at specific, procedural knowledge, and, ultimately, automatization of this knowledge.
4. Feedback may allow L2 learners the opportunity to practice correctly the L2 during the stages of the acquisition of declarative knowledge, proceduralization, and automatization.
5. The learning process is explicit.

Comments on the Skill Acquisition Theory

Skill Acquisition Theory lies at the output stage of the L2 learning process and falls within the belief that CF provides learners with the opportunity to practice the L2 more accurately until they convert declarative knowledge into procedural knowledge (e.g., Bitchener, 2016). There appears to be quite a high level of processing and potential awareness during the early stages of practice that is reduced as the grammatical knowledge becomes automatized. Leeman (2007) suggests that feedback may play a role at the three stages postulated within the theory, namely, the acquisition of declarative knowledge, proceduralization, and automatization. At the initial stage, feedback can promote the development of declarative knowledge while during the stages of proceduralization and automatization, feedback can "indicate the need for greater attention and reliance on declarative knowledge as well as the need to change the scope of a given rule or procedure. Furthermore, feedback may be useful in avoiding the automatization of non-target L2 knowledge" (Leeman, 2007, p. 117). While it may be proposed that feedback associated with subsequent corrected and consistent practice promotes a type of L2 knowledge during the three stages, it is noteworthy that Skill Acquisition Theory is premised on constant practice of declarative knowledge (assumed to be accurate) until it is proceduralized or automatized. Whether CF plays an important role in this theory is not well explicated.

Model of the L2 Learning Process in ISLA

Leow's (2015) model views the notion of learning as consisting of both processes and products and elaborates on three processing stages (input processing stage, intake processing stage, knowledge processing stage) in light of the cognitive processes postulated to play important roles during these stages. This model is crucially situated within the instructed setting and is premised on the role of attention in the process of learning an L2. However, while attention is central to the model, depth of processing, defined as "the relative amount of cognitive effort, level of analysis, elaboration of intake together with the usage of prior knowledge, hypothesis testing and rule formation employed in decoding and encoding some grammatical or lexical item in the input" (p. 204), plays an important role at several stages of the L2 learning process. The three processing stages are succinctly described below.

Input Processing Stage

The first stage (*input processing*) is between the input and the intake of specific linguistic information, and what is taken in (intake) is initially stored in working memory. This stage is largely dependent upon the level of attention (peripheral, selective, or focal) paid to such information by the learner and may be accompanied by depth of processing, cognitive registration, and level of awareness. Based on these variables, intake lodged into working memory may be of three types: attended intake, detected intake, and noticed intake. Crucially, unless further processed in the intake processing stage, any type of intake will be discarded from working memory.

Intake Processing Stage

This second stage of further processing occurs between preliminary intake (attended, detected, and noticed) and the internal system. New preliminary intake, be it attended, detected, or noticed, may be processed in one of two ways depending upon depth or level of processing and/or cognitive effort: (1) Minimal data-driven processing associated with a very low depth of processing that allows the data to be entered into learners' L2 developing system encoded as a non-systemized chunk of language or (2) conceptually driven processing, or consciously encoding and decoding the linguistic information, associated with higher levels of processing and potential higher levels of awareness. Activation of old or recent (new exemplars) prior knowledge also plays a role in the intake processing stage. Dependent upon the depth of processing or amount of cognitive effort and/or levels of awareness, new linguistic information may lead to either implicit or explicit systemized learning of the L2 information, which is stored in the grammatical system within the system learning component. For example, a low level of processing may potentially lead to implicit systemized learning. However, this kind of processing "depends heavily on many factors that include the provision of large amounts of exemplars in meaningful contexts and quite a long period of time to process, internalize the exemplars, and have the knowledge available for subsequent usage" (Leow, 2015, p. 244).

Knowledge Processing Stage

The third and final processing stage occurs between the L2 developing system and what is produced by the learner (*knowledge processing*, e.g., assigning phonological features to the L2 in oral production, monitoring production in relation to learned grammar, etc.). Depth of processing and potential level of awareness may also play a role at this stage together with the ability to activate (appropriate) prior knowledge. Like Swain (2005), Leow also views this knowledge processing stage as part of the L2 learning process given that learners' output may also serve as additional input. Learners may monitor what they produce or use potential feedback based on what they have just produced as confirmation or disconfirmation of their L2 output or prior knowledge. Consequently, feedback may serve as additional L2 input to the L2 learner. Dependent upon depth of processing or level of awareness, they may reinforce their current knowledge or restructure their current interlanguage.

Based on his model, Leow (2020) provides a feedback processing framework that offers a cognitive explanation for the role of feedback, whether oral or written, in subsequent L2 development in direct relation to how L2 learners or writers process such feedback, as seen in Figure 3.1.

In this framework, as reported in Leow (2020), Feedback is the L2 information that learners need to process and *Feedback Processing*

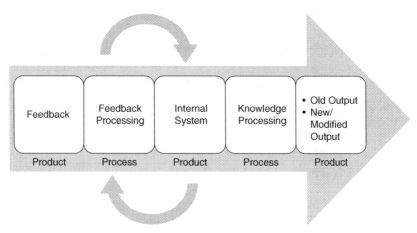

Figure 3.1 Feedback processing framework based on Leow's (2015) Model of the L2 Learning Process in ISLA

> encompasses *how* the learner cognitively processes the feedback (if at all) in relation to the current learner knowledge or interlanguage. If further processed at this stage, whether with a low or high depth of processing or level of awareness, the information in the feedback allows for reinforcement of accurate prior knowledge or, based on corrective feedback, for the potential of restructuring of previously learned inaccurate knowledge stored in the learner's *Internal System*. The new restructured information (accurate or still inaccurate) then replaces or joins the original knowledge in the *Internal System*, which is then available for the *Knowledge Processing* stage. There is, then, the possibility that the learner still retains the previous inaccurate L2 data and now holds both (accurate and inaccurate) options in the system. (p. 104)

Old output represents a potential absence or low depth of prior processing of the corrective feedback provided or not much confidence in the newly restructured knowledge. New or Modified output represents the learners' production of the restructured L2, which is assumed to represent the L2 knowledge (as a chunk of language/item learning or systemized) present at that point in time in their internal system. Whether a complete accurate restructuring took place (as in system learning) or whether such restructuring was temporary, immediate or reflective of item learning may be observed in delayed performance. In other words, accurate performance was evidenced immediately after the corrective feedback was provided, but the learners later reverted back to their previous inaccurate interlanguage. Whether feedback is indeed processed by L2 learners may depend on several cognitive processes and variables, for example, depth of processing, levels of awareness, activation of appropriate prior knowledge, hypothesis testing, rule formulation, and/or metacognition.

Key Features
1. The model is situated within ISLA.
2. All types of intake may disappear from working memory unless further processed.
3. There is activation of two types of prior knowledge (old and new).
4. The learning process is mainly explicit in the instructed setting.
5. It views output as a part of the L2 learning process. Output provides the opportunity to elicit feedback, which, in turn, if processed, loops back as input to be further processed.
6. It postulates the notion of effort or depth of processing during output processing.
7. The feedback processing framework provides a cognitive explanation for the role of feedback (oral or written) in subsequent L2 development in direct relation to how L2 learners or writers process such feedback.
8. Both implicit and explicit learning are possible, with the former dependent upon specific conditions.

Comments on the Model of the L2 Learning Process in ISLA

Like Swain's (2005) Output Hypothesis, Leow's model views the learning process to include the knowledge processing stage that allows potential feedback to loop back to the early input processing stage. It is situated also within the instructed setting. According to the model (and its feedback processing framework), whether the feedback has been attended to, detected, or noticed once again depends upon the attentional resources allocated to the feedback by the learner in addition to the depth of processing and level of awareness involved to make the connection between the learner's prior inaccurate knowledge or output and the information in the feedback received. In other words, whether the feedback processed allows for potential restructuring of the inaccurate knowledge may depend upon how deeply the feedback is processed or the level of awareness in relation to the mismatch between the learner's prior knowledge and the feedback. Feedback can be processed implicitly, that is, without much cognitive effort expended in doing so, but may depend upon many instances of the same feedback for implicit learning or restructuring to take place. However, in the instructed setting it will most likely be processed explicitly, especially in the written mode.

Conclusion

This chapter began with a brief report of the early roots of corrective feedback, presented a coarse-grained feedback framework that underlies most theoretical underpinnings, and provided a list of cognitive processes assumed to play a role during CF provision and in relation to their roles in these underpinnings. A description of each theoretical underpinning and its key features was provided followed by a commentary on each, which was viewed from minimally three perspectives: (1) whether the theoretical underpinning is grounded in SLA (naturalistic setting) or ISLA (instructed setting); (2) the importance or lack thereof of CF in the process of learning an L2; and (3) the type of learning (implicit or explicit) assumed to be associated with the provision of CF. While almost all the theoretical underpinnings agree that CF does play a role in L2 development and the type of processing of feedback is explicit, they are almost split between being SLA- or ISLA-based.

References

Anderson, J. R. (1982). Acquisition of cognitive skill. *Psychological Review*, 89(4), 369–406.
  (1993). *Rules of the mind*. Hillsdale, NJ: Lawrence Erlbaum.
  (2007). *How can a human mind occur in the physical universe?* New York: Oxford University Press.
Bitchener, J. (2016). To what extent has the published written CF research aided our understanding of its potential for L2 development? *ITL – International Journal of Applied Linguistics*, 167(2), 111–131.
Bitchener, J. & Storch, N. (2016). *Written corrective feedback for L2 development*. Bristol: Multilingual Matters.
Bloomfield, L. (1933). *Language*. Chicago: University of Chicago Press.
Brown, D. (2016). The type and linguistic foci of oral corrective feedback in the L2 classroom: A meta-analysis. *Language Teaching Research*, 20(4), 436–458.
Chomsky, N. (1957). *Syntactic structures*. The Hague: Mouton and Company.
Corder, S. (1967). The significance of learners' errors. *International Review of Applied Linguistics*, 5(4), 161–170.
Craik, F. I. M. & Lockhart, R. S. (1972). Levels of processing: A framework for memory research. *Journal of Verbal Learning and Verbal Behavior*, 11(6), 671–684.
DeKeyser, R. M. (2015). Skill acquisition theory. In B. VanPatten & J. Williams (eds.), *Theories in second language acquisition* (pp. 94–112). London: Routledge.
Egi, T. (2007). Interpreting recasts as linguistic evidence. *Studies in Second Language Acquisition*, 29(4), 511–537.
Ellis, R. (1991). The interaction hypothesis: A critical evaluation. Paper presented at the Regional Language Center Seminar, Singapore, April 22–28, 1991. (ERIC document no. ED338037).
Gass, S. M. (1997). *Input, interaction, and the second language learner*. Mahwah, NJ: Lawrence Erlbaum.
Gass, S. M. & Mackey, A. (2015). Input, interaction, and output in second language acquisition. In B. VanPatten & J. Williams (eds.), *Theories in second language acquisition* (pp. 175–200). London: Routledge.

Gurzynski-Weiss, L., Al Khalil, M., Baralt, M. & Leow, R. P (2016). Levels of awareness in relation to type of recast and type of linguistic item in computer-mediated communication: A concurrent investigation. In R. P. Leow, L. Cerezo & M. Baralt (eds.), *A psycholinguistic approach to technology and language learning* (pp. 151–170). Berlin: De Gruyter Mouton.

Krashen, S. D. (1982). *Principles and practice in second language acquisition.* Oxford: Pergamon Press.

Lado, R. (1957). *Linguistics across cultures: Applied linguistics for language teachers.* Michigan: University of Michigan Press.

Leeman, J. (2007). Feedback in L2 learning: Responding to errors during practice. In R. DeKeyser (ed.), *Practicing in a second language: Perspectives from applied linguistics and cognitive psychology* (pp. 111–137). New York: Cambridge University Press.

Leow, R. P. (2001). Attention, awareness and foreign language behavior. *Language Learning, 51*(Suppl. 1), 113–155.

(2015). *Explicit learning in the L2 classroom: A student-centered approach.* New York: Routledge.

(2019). ISLA: How implicit or how explicit should it be? Theoretical, empirical, and pedagogical/curricular issues. *Language Teaching Research, 23*(4), 476–493.

(2020). L2 writing-to-learn: Theory, research, and a curricular approach. In Rosa M. Manchón (ed.), *Writing and language learning: Advancing research agendas* (pp. 95–117). Amsterdam: John Benjamins.

Leow, R. P. & Cerezo, L. (2016). Deconstructing the "I" and "SLA" in ISLA: One curricular approach. *Studies in Second Language Learning and Teaching, 6*(1), 43–63.

Li, S. (2010). The effectiveness of corrective feedback in SLA: A meta-analysis. *Language Learning, 60*(2), 309–365.

Loewen, S. (2005). Incidental focus on form and second language learning. *Studies in Second Language Acquisition 27*(3), 361–386.

Long, M. H. (1981). Input, interaction, and second language acquisition. *Annals of the New York Academy of Sciences, 379,* 259–278.

(1983). Native speaker/non-native speaker conversation and negotiation of comprehensible input. *Applied Linguistics, 4*(2), 126–141.

(1989). Task, group, and task-group interactions. *University of Hawaii Working Papers in ESL, 8* 2), 1–26.

(1996). The role of the linguistic environment in second language acquisition. In W. C. Ritchie & T. K. Bhatia (eds.), *Handbook of second language acquisition* (pp. 413–467). San Diego, CA: Academic Press.

Lyster, R. (1998). Recasts, repetition and ambiguity in L2 classroom discourse. *Studies in Second Language Acquisition, 20*(1), 51–81.

Lyster, R. & Saito, K. (2010). Oral feedback in classroom SLA: A meta-analysis. *Studies in Second Language Acquisition, 32*(2), 265–302.

Mackey, A. (2006). Feedback, noticing and instructed second language learning. *Applied Linguistics*, 27(3), 405–430.

Manchón, R. M. & Vasylets, O. (2019). Language learning through writing: Theoretical perspectives and empirical evidence. In J. W. Schwieter & A. Benati (eds.), *The Cambridge handbook of language learning* (pp. 341–362). Cambridge: Cambridge University Press.

Nagata, N. (1993). Intelligent computer feedback for second language instruction. *The Modern Language Journal*, 77(3), 330–339.

Russell, J. & Spada, N. (2006). The effectiveness of corrective feedback for the acquisition of L2 grammar. In J. M. Norris (ed.), *Synthesizing research on language learning and teaching* (pp. 133–162). Philadelphia, PA: John Benjamins.

Schmidt, R. W. (1990). The role of consciousness in second language learning. *Applied Linguistics*, 11(2), 129–158.

(1993). Awareness and second language acquisition. *Annual Review of Applied Linguistics*, 13, 206–226.

(1994). Implicit learning and the cognitive unconscious: Of artificial grammars and SLA. In N. Ellis (ed.), *Implicit and explicit learning of languages* (pp. 165–209). London: Academic Press.

(1995). Consciousness and foreign language learning: a tutorial on the role of attention and awareness in learning. In R. Schmidt (ed.), *Attention and awareness in foreign language learning and teaching*, Second Language Teaching and Curriculum Center Technical Report No. 9 (pp. 1–64). Honolulu: University of Hawai'i Press.

(2001). Attention. In P. Robinson (ed.), *Cognition and second language instruction* (pp. 3–32). New York: Cambridge University Press.

Schmidt, R. & Frota, S. (1986). Developing basic conversational ability in second language. In R. Day (ed.), *Talking to learn* (pp. 237–326). Rowley, MA: Newbury House.

Selinker, L. (1972). Interlanguage. *International Review of Applied Linguistics*, 10(3), 219–231.

Skinner, B. F. (1957). *Verbal behavior*. New York: Appleton-Century-Crofts.

Swain, M. (1985). Communicative competence: Some roles of comprehensible input and comprehensible output in its development. In S. Gass & C. Madden (eds.), *Input in second language acquisition* (pp. 235–253). Rowley, MA: Newbury House.

(2005). The output hypothesis: Theory and research. In E. Hinkel (ed.), *Handbook of research in second language teaching and learning* (pp.471–483). Mahwah, NJ: Lawrence Erlbaum.

Tomlin, R. S. & Villa, V. (1994). Attention in cognitive science and second language acquisition. *Studies in Second Language Acquisition*, 16(2), 183–203.

Vygotsky, L. S. (1978). *Mind in society: The development of higher psychological processes*. Cambridge, MA: Harvard University Press.

4

Corrective Feedback from a Sociocultural Perspective

Hossein Nassaji

Introduction

Traditionally, the role of corrective feedback has been viewed primarily from a cognitive or cognitive-interactionist perspective (see Chapters 2 and 3, this volume). From a cognitive perspective, second language (L2) acquisition is essentially a mental process. Learning is more about how individuals develop language "in response to an environment defined fairly narrowly as a source of linguistic information" (Mitchell & Myles, 1998, p. 163). The idea is that language knowledge "results from the cognitive processing of linguistic input which is then used for producing output" (Ellis, 2003, p. 175). Two important sources of input are positive and negative evidence. Positive evidence refers to information that tells the learner what is possible in a given language, and negative evidence provides information about what is not possible. Consequently, the beneficial effects of feedback are considered to be more due to how feedback offers learners positive and negative evidence or how feedback facilitates other cognitive mechanisms, such as noticing, awareness, input, output, uptake, intake, or retrieval and rehearsal of language forms.

From a cognitive-interactionist perspective, the beneficial role of feedback is attributed to a process called negotiation. Negotiation refers to various interactional modifications that occur during interaction to repair possible communication breakdowns, such as repetitions, clarification requests, confirmation checks, and reformulations, which take place in meaning-focused interaction. There are two types of negotiation: meaning negotiation and form negotiation. Meaning negotiation refers to the side sequences to the conversational interaction to deal with communication problems and to make input more comprehensible (Nassaji, 2015, 2016; Pica, 1994; Van den Branden, 1997). Form negotiation, on the other hand, is triggered by an attention to form and occurs when "one interlocutor tries to 'push' the other towards producing a formally more correct and/or appropriate utterance" (Van den Branden, 1997, p. 592).

Within the field of second language acquisition (SLA), a main source of argument for the importance of negotiation has come from Long's (1996) Interaction Hypothesis, which emphasizes negotiated interaction as an essential factor in L2 learning. Within this perspective, negotiation facilitates L2 acquisition in a number of ways including making input more comprehensible, highlighting linguistic forms, and pushing learners to modify their erroneous output. During negotiation learners not only have opportunities for interaction but can also receive feedback on their errors through various forms of interactional feedback (see for example Nassaji, 2016, 2015 for a discussion). In this context, the role of negotiation links closely with the argument that the effectiveness of corrective feedback depends largely on the degree to which it is integrated with meaning-focused communication (Doughty & Williams, 1998; Long, 1996). The value of negotiation is also associated with several attentional factors that may affect learning, including learners' selective attention, negative evidence, and L2 processing capacity. Thus, what the cognitive and cognitive-interactionist perspectives have in common is that both emphasize the facilitative role of attentional resources or how feedback draws learners' attention to language forms. They both focus on the cognitive mechanisms that may facilitate or constrain people's learning of specific language forms (Nassaji & Cumming, 2000). The difference is that the cognitive-interactionist perspective emphasizes the role of interactional negotiation in facilitating cognitive processes.

Although much of the theoretical argument for feedback and negotiation has been within a cognitive or cognitive-interactionist perspective, another theoretical framework for understanding the role of feedback comes from the sociocultural theory (Vygotsky 1978, 1986). The following sections discuss this perspective.

A Sociocultural Perspective on Corrective Feedback

The sociocultural theory is a theoretical perspective on learning that originates mainly from the work of Vygotsky (Vygotsky, 1978, 1981, 1986). This theory emphasizes that human cognition is socially mediated and constructed. As noted above, from a cognitive-interactionist perspective, L2 learning develops as a result of interactional processes. The sociocultural theory also stresses the importance of interaction. However, it differs from other theories such as the cognitive-interactionist perspective in a number of ways. First, it provides a different argument for how interaction assists learning by placing a particular emphasis on the social and dialogic nature of interaction (Nassaji & Swain, 2000). The sociocultural approach considers language development as essentially a socially situated process and therefore the focus is more on the social dimension of learning. It considers that "while human neurobiology is a necessary condition for higher order thinking, the most important forms of human cognitive activity develop through interaction within social and material environments" (Lantolf & Thorne, 2007, p. 201). In this view, interaction does not simply facilitate mental processing but is an integral and inherent part of it. In other words, language development "occurs in rather than as a result of interaction" (Ellis, 2009, p. 12). For the same reason, corrective feedback is not viewed as a unilateral strategy to correct learners' errors but a dialogic endeavor carried out between the learner and a more capable person with the aim of assisting the learner to achieve what he or she is not able to accomplish without assistance.

Second, the sociocultural perspective differs from other interactionist theories in how the role of language itself is conceptualized. In this perspective, language is not merely a means of communication. It is a powerful semiotic tool that mediates higher-order thinking and mental functioning (Lantolf & Thorne, 2006). As Wells (2007, p. 244) puts it, "Language is the principal mode of meaning making; it mediates both the communication through which thinking with others is made possible and also the inner speech through which individual thinking is brought under conscious control." Thus, language is both what should be learned and a tool for use in learning the 'second' or 'additional' language (see below for more detail).

Third, from a sociocultural perspective, the focus is more on the process rather than the product of learning. Process in this approach is viewed as "a dynamic interaction of person-environment" (Ohta, 2001, p. 3). Consequently, feedback is viewed as a process embedded in and affected by the social context of learning. Thus, to understand how feedback helps learners, we need to consider both the learners and also the complexity of the circumstances in which they operate, including, for example, the classroom, the teacher, other learners, and their shared knowledge, experiences, and background. Since the focus is on the process of learning, the effectiveness of feedback is not viewed merely in terms of its effect on the accurate production of language forms but in terms of how it assists language development over time.

A number of key concepts are closely connected with the sociocultural perspective, which are central to understanding how language development is conceptualized and how the role of feedback should be interpreted in this process. These include the notions of Zone of Proximal Development (ZPD), mediation, scaffolding, and regulation. They are briefly discussed below.

The Notion of ZPD

One of the notions that are key to the sociocultural perspective is that of the Zone of Proximal Development (ZPD). The ZPD refers to "the distance between the actual developmental level as determined by independent problem solving and the level of potential development as determined through problem solving under adult guidance or in collaboration with more capable peers" (Vygotsky, 1978, p. 86). The concept of ZPD emphasizes learners' both current and potential level of development. The current level of development refers to what the learner can achieve without assistance, and the potential level of development is what he or she can achieve with assistance. Vygotsky has called the potential functions "buds" or "flowers" of development (as they are still in the process of maturation and can lead to growth with guidance) and the actual development as "fruits" of development.

To appreciate the importance of ZPD more fully, as Lantolf explained, it is also crucial to understand the distinction that Vygotsky (1978) made between *learning* and *development*. Learning, according to Vygotsky, is when the learner is not able to perform without the assistance of another person or an artifact. It can be in the form of direct or indirect instruction provided by an expert or assistance provided by a tool such as a computer. "Development, on the other hand, results from the appropriation and internalization of that assistance, which in turn, enables individuals to function independently of specific concrete circumstances and to therefore extend their abilities to a broader range of circumstances" (Vygotsky, 1978, p. 698). The concept of ZPD captures this critical role that assistance plays and its relationship with independent performance. Even when learners have similar actual levels of development, they may need different amounts of assistance to achieve their potential levels of development. Therefore, they may have different developmental gaps and, hence, different ZPDs.

Another important feature of ZPD is the emphasis on collaborative interaction. ZPD provides a dialogic activity sphere for the potential mental processes to develop through a collaborative process rather than an individualistic one. In other words, "the ZPD is the developmental space where learning is dialogical" (Marchenkova, 2005, p. 179). However, although the ZPD stresses dialogic collaboration, from a Vygotskian perspective, the focus of the collaboration is not on the product of learning, but on the process of how higher-level mental functioning arises through collaborative interaction (Appel & Lantolf, 1994). Thus, not all collaborative interactions are helpful for development. Only when interaction occurs in the learner's ZPD does it become effective because it would trigger the functions that are in the process of maturation (see above). When learners interact within their ZPD, they can use their existing linguistic ability to develop what they have not yet mastered independently (Appel & Lantolf, 1994; Donato, 1994).

When it comes to feedback, it is through such ZPD-based interaction that the teacher or a more capable other can discover a learner's developmental level and provide appropriate assistance. Here is when new knowledge is constructed as the more knowledgeable interlocutor can provide the kind of assistance that helps a less knowledgeable one reach a higher level of competence (Donato, 1994). At every stage of the learning process, those who receive feedback within their ZPD are likely to achieve more sophisticated developmental levels beyond their actual linguistic ability but again within their potential developmental level (Nassaji & Cumming 2000).

Scaffolding

Another related concept is that of scaffolding. The term scaffolding was originally used by Bruner (1986) whose work was influenced by Vygotsky's notion of the assistance given to a novice by an expert. Bruner initially used the term to demonstrate how language development occurs as a result of help parents provide to children. He subsequently used it to define the kind of support students receive from their teachers in the initial stages of their learning. However, although Vygotsky did not introduce the term "scaffolding," there is agreement that it was Vygotsky that used scaffolding to refer to the kind of assistance provided by a more capable peer, and thus Vygotsky offered the "theoretical anchoring" for the concept (Bliss, Askew & Macrae 1996, p. 38, as cited in Engin, 2012, p. 12).

Effective scaffolding is not random assistance, but it is assistance that is negotiated within the learner's ZPD. Thus, it is contingent on the learner, because to be effective "it should be appropriate to the learner at a particular time in the interaction" (Engin, 2012, p. 13). For the same reason, it is not unidirectional; instead, it is a reciprocal process jointly constructed on the basis of the learner's developmental needs and capacity (Nassaji & Swain, 2000). It is through such collaborative interaction that learners become able to master what they are not able to learn independently, particularly when they interact with a more capable person.

Thus, from the above perspective, the value of feedback lies in the opportunities it provides for scaffolding. It is through such collaborative support that feedback can further learners' interlanguage growth and ability (Aljaafreh & Lantolf, 1994). The following from Donato (1994, p. 44) provides an example of scaffolding when three learners of French are working together on a collaborative task. As can be seen, on their own, learners were unable to produce "You remembered" ("Tu as souvenu") in French accurately, but through the scaffolded feedback, they became able to do so. In this case, the feedback has enabled the learner to achieve a level of competence that he or she has not been able to achieve alone.

SPEAKER 1: ... and then I'll say... tu as souvenu notre anniversaire de mariage ... or should I say mon anniversaire?
SPEAKER 2: Tu as ...
SPEAKER 3: Tu as ...
SPEAKER 1: Tu as souvenu ... you remembered?
SPEAKER 3: Yea, but isn't that a reflexive? Tu t'as ...
SPEAKER 1: Ah, tu t'as souvenu.
SPEAKER 3: Oh, it's tu es ...
SPEAKER 1: Tu es ...
SPEAKER 3: Tu es, tu es, tu ...
SPEAKER 1: T'es, tu t'es ...
SPEAKER 3: Tu t'es ...
SPEAKER 1: Tu t'es souvenu.

Although there is a relationship between scaffolding and ZPD, there are different views on what scaffolding is. Lantolf and Thorne (2006, p. 203) pointed out that scaffolding "refers to any type of adult–child (expert–novice) assisted performance." As such, in scaffolding "the goal is to complete the task rather than to help the child develop, and therefore the task is usually carried out through other-regulation, whereby the adult controls the child's performance instead of searching for opportunities to relinquish control to the child" (Lantolf & Thorne, 2007, p. 203). According to Donato, however, scaffolding is based on the idea that "a knowledgeable participant can create, by means of speech, supportive conditions in which the novice can participate in, and extend current skills and knowledge to higher levels of competence" (Donato, 1994, p. 40). Verity (2005) argued that scaffolding should not be taken to refer to any help, but it "should be limited to describing the cognitive support given to a novice learner to reduce the cognitive load of the task" (p. 4). According to this author, "[t]o scaffold a task is to take over the part of a task that is cognitively beyond the learner, so that he is free to focus on what he can do independently" (p. 4). Despite these different interpretations, from a Vygotskian perspective, effective scaffolding is the kind of assistance that is negotiated within the learner's ZPD.

Mediation

Another critical component of the Vygotskian sociocultural theory is the notion of mediation. According to this view, higher-order mental activities are all socially mediated. Mediation refers to the various forms of physical and symbolic tools and artifacts that allow us to establish a link between ourselves and the world around us (Wells, 2007). Among mediating artifacts, Vygotsky has stressed the role of language, seeing it as essential for the emergence of higher mental functioning (Wertsch, 1985). According to

Vygotsky, language serves both as a means through which social interaction takes place and also as a tool to mediate mental activities. What happens during language-mediated activities is the development of mutual understanding between participants, or what Rogoff (1990) called "intersubjectivity." Language is also a mediation tool that can be used to reflect on language use. Therefore, language learning entails developing the means for mediating learning (e.g., the tool for learning) and learning the language itself (i.e., the object of learning) (Ellis, 2003).

Three types of mediation have been distinguished in the sociocultural theory: mediation taking place by others, mediation by the self, and mediation by artifacts (Lantolf, 2000). Mediation by others happens in social interaction when language learning is facilitated by interaction with peers or experts, such as the teacher or a native speaker. One way through which language use mediates our mental functioning is through private speech (Lantolf & Thorne, 2006). Private speech is speech directed at self rather than others, and it is an important mediational tool through which self-regulation and internalization take place. According to Lantolf, "Self-talk functions not only as a means to mediate and regulate mental functioning in complex cognitive tasks, but it also serves to facilitate the internalization of mental functions" (Lantolf, 2006, p. 28). Other mediation through artifacts refers to mediation taking place via external tools. As Lantolf and Thorne (2007) pointed out, in performing physical activities, such as digging a hole, the tool could be the shovel, which is used to assist us to perform the task. In performing higher-level mental activities, such as learning, it could be, for example, language or other tools such as tasks or even technology. For example, teachers may design a task or use a particular kind of technology with which learners may interact to mediate their L2 development.

Within this perspective, feedback can be conceptualized as another kind of mediation provided by the teacher. L2 teachers may provide feedback during task-based interaction as a tool in order to mediate learning and to support learners' internalization of language forms (see below for a discussion of the notion of internalization).

Regulation

The fourth concept developed from a Vygotskian framework is the notion of regulation. Regulation is a form of mediation, which conceptualizes learning as a process of moving from object-regulation to other-regulation to self-regulation. Object-regulation is a stage where learners' behavior is controlled by objects in their environment. In other words, the behavior is mediated by an object. At this stage, learners are often controlled by the objects in their environment to perform a task. Lantolf and Thorne (2007) gave an example of a child who is requested by his or her parents to perform a task such as going and getting a toy. If the child is at the stage of object-regulation, he or she may be easily distracted by other objects in the environment, such as another more colorful toy, and therefore, may thus fail to perform the request. For mental activities such as learning an L2 at the early stages, learners may be able to respond to only the stimuli that are available in here-and-now contexts. As they progress, they can perform tasks that involve more abstract entities.

Other-regulation refers to situations when the learner has gained some control over the object, but still needs the help, guidance, or instruction from others. This assistance or instruction can come from the teacher, other learners, or other activities that guide the learner to achieve their goals. For example, when given a classroom task, learners may not be able to complete it successfully unless they have clear instructions or other forms of assistance from the teacher. The teacher may need to provide the learners with the kind of vocabulary that they will require to complete the task or provide feedback on aspects of the task so that the learners will be able to perform it.

Self-regulation occurs when the learner becomes skilled and able to act autonomously. One way self-regulation can be achieved is through internalization – "a process of making what was once external assistance a resource that is internally available to the individual (though still very much social in origin, quality, and function)" (Lantolf & Thorne, 2006, p. 200). To explain these processes, Vygotsky (1981) put forward what has been called "general genetic law of cultural development":

> Any function in the child's cultural development appears twice, or on two planes. First, it appears on the social plane, and then on the psychological plane. First, it appears between people as an interpsychological category, and then within the child as an intrapsychological category. This is equally true with regard to voluntary attention, logical memory, the formation of concepts, and the development of volition. (p. 163)

This law explains the transition from the inter-mental ability that originates in interaction to intra-mental ability (such as intentional thinking) that occurs inside the learner. Vygotsky emphasizes that internalization is achieved when people are able to "create" in their internal planes what has been performed in external social planes. Thus, internalization not only transforms social functions to internal psychological functions but also changes the structure and functions of the process (Vygotsky, 1981). This intra-mental ability is evident when someone begins to act independently (Appel & Lantolf, 1994; Donato, 1994). In this process, the role of imitation has also been emphasized as an important contributing factor to internalization, particularly in instructional contexts. According to Vygotsky, "a central feature for the psychological study of instruction is the analysis of the child's potential to raise himself to a higher intellectual level of development through collaboration to move from what he has to what he does not have through imitation" (Vygotsky 1988, p. 210). Vygotsky, however, defines imitation, not as a mechanical activity involving copying or mimicking, but as an intellectually active and creative process through which the learner becomes able to do what he or she is not able to do alone.

The notion of regulation and the concepts associated with it highlight a number of important themes in the sociocultural theory that can have significant implications for how feedback can be conceptualized. First, it confirms that new knowledge not only originates in interaction but also becomes internalized through interaction. Second, the concept of regulation reveals the inherent association between interpsychological and intrapsychological functioning (Wertsch, 1985). intrapsychological functioning has to do with the interaction that occurs between and among people whereas intrapsychological functioning refers to processes that are internal and occur within the learner (Wertsch, 1985). As noted earlier, according to Vygotsky, cognitive development cannot be achieved through isolated learning. Rather, people's intellectual development begins from social interaction and then moves towards becoming internalized and consolidated within the learner. Such engagement in sociocultural activities results in the "transformation of participation" (Rogoff, 1990); that is "individuals develop as they participate with others in shared endeavors" (p. 687). This intersubjectivity contributes to the emergence of originally social functions on the individual level.

Third, the concepts of other- and self-regulation, in particular, explain how someone who first needs assistance begins to act autonomously, showing control over his or her own behavior (Appel & Lantolf, 1994; Donato, 1994). The process begins with when the expert has full control over the novice's performance, and then the novice will gradually appropriate the control to the point where they do not need to rely on the expert and move toward relying on the self (Aljaafreh & Lantolf, 1994).

Within the above conceptualization, feedback can be considered as an important instructional strategy to provide opportunities for the learner to move from reliance on the expert (other-regulation) to no reliance (self-regulation). How this can be achieved can be seen in the following five transitional levels of guidance proposed by Aljaafreh and Lantolf (1994) in a study examining the role of corrective feedback within a sociocultural perspective.

Level 1: The learner is not aware that he or she has made an error and does not know how to correct it even with assistance. At this stage, the expert should assume full responsibility for making the learner aware of the error and correcting the error.

Level 2: The learner is able to notice the error but is unable to correct it. Thus, the learner may have some knowledge of the error but still needs assistance to correct it. The kind of the feedback needed here would be toward the explicit end of the implicit–explicit continuum.

Level 3: The learner is able to notice and also to correct the error but only with help. When help is provided, the learner is able to understand and react to it. The help needed here would be less explicit, as the learner has started to gain some control.

Level 4: The learner is able to notice the error and correct it, but he or she is not yet self-regulated and needs some assistance. At this stage, the learner often produces the form incorrectly and may need the expert to confirm the correct form.

Level 5: The learner has reached a level where he or she is able to notice and correct the error without any assistance. For example, the learner is able to self-correct and therefore does not need the expert's intervention. At this stage, the learner can be said to have become self-regulated.

Studies of Feedback within a Sociocultural Perspective

As noted above, the sociocultural perspective conceptualizes corrective feedback as a collaborative and dialogic process rather than an individualistic one, in which the nature of interaction determines the quality and quantity of the feedback. This process involves identifying the learner's ZPD and tailoring assistance to the level of learners' linguistic needs and ability based on the learner's responsiveness to feedback. Thus, the amount of assistance the learner needs can be at times highly variable, and the effect of feedback on self-regulation may differ from learner to learner. In what follows, I will review a sample of studies that have examined the role of corrective feedback within the sociocultural perspective along with their conclusions and implications.

Two foundational and widely cited studies that examined corrective feedback within this theoretical approach are those by Aljaafreh and Lantolf (1994) and Nassaji and Swain (2000). Aljaafreh and Lantolf (1994) examined the effectiveness of corrective feedback on L2 learning in oral interactions that occurred between three ESL writers and one tutor. The data came from five one-on-one tutorial sessions to review the learners' written texts. The aim was to show how negotiation and corrective feedback within the learner's ZPD promote L2 development. Corrective feedback was defined as a form of other-regulation negotiated between the learner and the tutor. It was operationalized in terms of a "regulatory scale" consisting of thirteen feedback moves (0–12), beginning with broad implicit feedback and gradually moving toward more specific direct/explicit help in a scaffolding manner (Table 4.1).

The effectiveness of the feedback was analyzed for the following four grammatical errors: articles, tense marking, modal verbs, and prepositions. The results showed that when feedback was negotiated within the

Table 4.1 *Regulatory Scale from implicit feedback to more explicit feedback (Aljaafreh & Lantolf, 1994, p. 471)*

0. Tutor asks the learner to read, find the errors, and correct them independently, prior to the tutorial.
1. Construction of a "collaborative frame."
2. Prompted or focused reading of the sentence that contains the error by the learner or the tutor.
3. Tutor indicates that something may be wrong in a segment (e.g., sentence, clause, line) – "Is there anything wrong in this sentence?"
4. Tutor rejects unsuccessful attempts at recognizing the error.
5. Tutor narrows down the location of the error (e.g., tutor repeats or points to the specific segment which contains the error).
6. Tutor indicates the nature of the error but does not identify the error (e.g., "There is something wrong with the tense marking here").
7. Tutor identifies the error (e.g., "You can't use an auxiliary here").
8. Tutor rejects learner's unsuccessful attempts at correcting the error.
9. Tutor provides clues to help the learner arrive at the correct form (e.g., "It is not really past but something that is still going on").
10. Tutor provides the correct form.
11. Tutor provides some explanation for use of the correct form.
12. Tutor provides examples of the correct pattern when other forms of help fail to produce an appropriate responsive action.

learners' ZPD, it facilitated their learning and, over time, also increased their control over already known forms. The researchers then concluded that learners are able to advance their knowledge of the targeted form through a process of collaboration during which feedback is negotiated between the novice and the expert.

Aljaafreh and Lantolf's study was descriptive with a focus on documenting how feedback occurred within the ZPD. Building and expanding on this study, Nassaji and Swain (2000) used a comparative design to compare the effectiveness of feedback negotiated within the learners' ZPD with feedback that occurred regardless of the ZPD. The data came from tutorial sessions between a tutor and two intermediate ESL learners who received feedback on their article errors in their compositions. One of the learners received feedback in a random manner and the other one within the ZPD. The ZPD feedback was defined as feedback provided according to the learners' level of development and moved, using prompts from Aljaafreh and Lantolf's (1994) regulatory scale, from indirect and less implicit help toward more direct and explicit help as needed. The non-ZPD student received nonnegotiated help in the form of single prompts which were provided regardless of the learner's ZPD. The prompt was randomly selected from the list of levels of help from Aljaafreh and Lantolf's Regulatory Scale.

To examine feedback effectiveness, the data were analyzed using both microgenetic and macrogenetic analyses. Microgenetic analysis examined developmental changes that occurred within a session. For that purpose, learner's performance was compared on the target structure on two episodes within the same session. Macrogenetic growth was operationalized as growth that occurred over time, and for that purpose learners' performance was compared across sessions. Consistent with the notion of regulation, reduction in the amount of assistance needed within and across sessions was taken as evidence for learners' improvement. When learners are able to correct an error with less assistance than before, they can be considered to have developed (Lantolf & Thorne, 2006). In addition to these qualitative analyses, quantitative process-product analyses of the data were also conducted in which the performance of the learner during the interaction was compared to his or her performance in final individualized post-tests. The results of the qualitative and quantitative analyses showed that negotiated feedback was more effective than random feedback in improving learners' accuracy. It also showed that help within the ZPD increased the learner's control over the target form both within and across sessions. Examples of such microgenetic and macrogenetic growths are illustrated in the following excerpts.

Examples 1 and 2 show the amount of assistance the ZPD learner needed to overcome the same error on two occasions within the same session. As can be seen, in Episode A, the learner needed several levels of help to be able to correct the error. However, in the second encounter with the same error (Episode B) in the same session, the amount of help was reduced considerably.

Example 1: Episode A, Session 1

1	T:	"Most of Korean have same name." So do you see anything wrong with this sentence?
2	S:	uhm ... I imagine that... uhm ... but ... in this position... I imagine that ... I think it's ok [laughing].
3	T:	It's ok?
4	S:	Yes.
5	T:	Ah... what about this part, "most of Korean." Do you see ... Do you see anything wrong with this phrase?
6	S:	Most of a Korean ... Korean [whispering] ... mmm ...
7	T:	Anything wrong within this part [referring to the place of the error]?
8	S:	Korean?
9	T:	No.
10	S:	No? Uhm ...
11	T:	Yes there is something wrong with this [referring to the word "Korean"].
12	S:	Yes. I think ... ah ... Korea means Korean people, yes?
13	T:	Ok.
14	S:	Yes?
15	T:	But grammatically, is there anything wrong?

16	S:	Of the? No?
17	T:	Yes, what?
18	S:	Of the?
19	T:	The, yeah.
20	S:	Yes.

Example 2: Episode B, Session 1

1	T:	"Most of the Koreans have same name." Do you see anything wrong with this?
2	S:	Have the ... same name?
3	T:	Ok, yes.
4	S:	I'm ... my article is bad [laughing].

(Nassaji & Swain, 2000, pp. 40–41)

Examples 3 and 4 provide a comparison between the amount of assistance needed to overcome the same error on two occasions across sessions. As can be seen, in Episode C, the learner needed several levels of help. However, in the second encounter of the same error (Episode D) in the subsequent session, the amount of help has been reduced considerably. This suggests that the help in the first session made the learner able to identify the same error with less help in the subsequent session. Such improvements were not observed in the non-ZPD learner.

Example 3: Episode C, Session 2

1	T:	"I think I am such stupid girl." There is something wrong with this sentence. Can you see?
2	S:	Such stupid the girl?
3	T:	No.
4	S:	No?
5	T:	There is something wrong with "stupid".
6	S:	Uh ... stupidary?
7	T:	I mean there is something wrong with "stupid girl".
8	S:	Article? Need article?
9	T:	Yes.
10	S:	But ... but ...
11	T:	Which ... what article?
12	S:	Ah ... a?

Example 4: Episode D, Session 4

1	T:	"It is such stupid idea." There is something still wrong.
2	S:	Yes.
3	T:	"It is such stupid idea" is wrong. Can you make it correct?
4	S:	Such a? ... such a stupid idea?

(Nassaji & Swain, 2000, pp. 41–42)

In both Aljaafreh and Lantolf's study and Nassaji and Swain's study, the data were collected outside the classroom. In a subsequent study, Nassaji (2007) investigated the role of feedback when negotiated within the ZPD in an L2 classroom setting. The data were collected when students were writing weekly journals on topics of their interest. Initial observations of the classroom and the student–teacher interaction revealed that the teacher made a combination of both negotiated and less negotiated feedback in response to students' written errors. The study then video-recorded these sessions and analyzed the student–teacher interaction for the nature and the degree of negotiated feedback and their effect on learners' written accuracy. Three types of feedback were distinguished and compared: nonnegotiated feedback, feedback with limited negotiation, and feedback with extended negotiation. Nonnegotiated feedback resolved the error unidirectionally with no negotiation (Example 5). Limited feedback negotiation involved some negotiation (Example 6), and feedback with extended negotiation involved guiding the learner to discover the correct form step by step by first providing indirect help and then moving progressively toward more direct help as needed (Example 7). The following provides examples of each type of feedback.

Example 5: Nonnegotiated feedback
TRIGGER: "Victoria, one of the most beautiful city in Canada."
TEACHER: Ah, city becomes cities, one of the most beautiful cities in Canada. OK?

Example 6: Feedback with limited negotiation
TRIGGER: It's cheaper than Canadian's one.
TEACHER: It's cheaper than Canadian's one?
KEIL: Canadians.
TEACHER: The Canadian. The S is in the wrong place. A pack of cigarettes is cheaper than Canadian ones.

Example 7: Feedback with extended negotiation
TRIGGER: "Teachers in class like our friend ..."
TEACHER: So who can make a correction? Who's got an idea to correct this? Mitny what would you do to correct this? Any idea?
MITNY: I don't know. I don't know.
TEACHER: Just try. Just try. Just try your best.
MITNY: Okay, okay. Their.
TEACHER: OK so there is "their"?
MITNY: Their teachers?
TEACHER: How about I'll help here. How about 'our teachers'?
MITNY: Our teachers?
TEACHER: Can you start with that?

MITNY:	Our teachers?
TEACHER:	Yeah.
MITNY:	Hm. Hm. They are?
TEACHER:	OK. So we have 'teachers', so we don't need 'their'. We just need 'teachers are.'

(Nassaji, 2007, pp. 125–126)

In Example 5, the feedback was triggered in response to the problematic use of the word "city." The teacher corrects the error immediately with no negotiation. In Example 6, the feedback was triggered in response to the incorrect use of the word "Canadian." The teacher corrects the error with some negotiation but after a few turns, the teacher provides the correct form. In Example 7, the teacher guides the learner gradually and progressively toward the correct form by first providing indirect cues and then moving toward more direct help as needed. The data were analyzed for the learners' correction of the same error during interaction and also in tailor-made student-specific tests that were administered after the interaction. The results revealed a significant effect for negotiated feedback by showing that feedback with extended negotiation resulted in more successful or partially successful correction of the error than feedback with limited or no negotiation during interaction. Also, feedback with extended negotiation resulted in more successful corrections of the same errors in subsequent tests than feedback with no or limited negotiation.

While Nassaji's (2007) study was an observational classroom study in which the feedback occurred incidentally, Nassaji's (2011) investigation examined the role of negotiated feedback in an experimental classroom-based study. Data were collected from two ESL classes over a four-week period. The study examined whether the effectiveness of feedback differed according to the degree of negotiation and also whether the type of the target structure would make a difference. Two frequently used linguistic targets were used: English articles and prepositions. Three types of feedback were compared: direct reformulation with no negotiation (scaffolding), prompt plus reformulation, and feedback with negotiation. To test the effects of feedback, the study used tailor-made learner-specific error identification/correction tasks that asked learners to identify and correct their own erroneous sentences in subsequent sessions. The results showed a clear advantage for feedback that involved scaffolded negotiation. It also showed an effect for the type of the target structure, with the effect of scaffolded negotiation being stronger for article errors than preposition errors.

As noted earlier, an important concept in the sociocultural theory is that of private speech as a tool that facilitates self-regulation. Using such a perspective, Ohta (2000) investigated the role of private speech among adult foreign language learners of Japanese when learners responded to recasts. Private speech was defined as "oral language addressed by the student to himself or herself" (Ohta, 2000, p. 52). The data consisted of audio and video recording of thirty-four hours of classroom interaction collected from seven learners. The analysis found that all the learners produced private speech in response to recasts with four of them producing it at a fairly frequent rate. The characteristics of such responses included reduced volume and individual learner responses within a choral context. The following provides an example of such responses (Example 8). In this example, the student (K) has made an error (line 2) *hima* in response to the teacher's query (line 1). The teacher has provided a recast (line 3) and the student who has been addressed has provided uptake by repeating the recast (line 4). A second student (C), however, has also repeated the recast silently through private speech (line 5).

Example 8

1	T:	Kon shuumatsu hima desu ka? Kim san
		This weekend are you free? Kim
2	K:	Um (..) iie (.) um (.) uh:: (.) hima- (.) hima: (.) <u>hima nai</u>
		Um (...) no (.) um (.) uh:: (.) not (.) not (.) not free
		((ERROR–"hima nai"))
3	T:	<u>Hima ja ^ arimasen</u>
4	K:	"You're not free" ((corrects form to "Hima ja arimasen"))
		Oh ja arim (asen
		Oh cop neg
5	C:	["hima ja^ arimasen"
		"not free" ((correct form))

(Ohta, 2000, p. 60)

Ohta's findings provide important insights into how learners use private speech in response to feedback to learn language forms. It indicates that learners are able to privately engage in classroom interaction and benefit from corrective feedback even when the feedback is not directed at them or when they are not directly participating in the interaction. Her findings also suggest that the traditional definition of corrective feedback and uptake is inadequate to capture the complexity of interactional feedback exchanges. Feedback in the classroom is not simply an utterance to address a specific learner's erroneous utterance, but also a social move that can have an effect on all the learners in a classroom setting. In such contexts, both the learners who are the direct target of the feedback and those who are not may become cognitively engaged and respond to it.

The above studies have so far examined various aspects of the sociocultural theory as related to corrective feedback in different language learning settings. There are also a few studies that have compared feedback as operationalized within a cognitive-interactionist perspective with feedback operationalized within a sociocultural perspective. As noted earlier, a cognitive-interactionist perspective conceptualizes feedback in terms of discrete feedback strategies, such as elicitations, recasts, explicit correction, and attempts to find out which one is more effective. A sociocultural perspective, on the other hand, defines feedback in terms of the degree of support learners need to become self-regulated. Feedback in this perspective often takes the form of graduated scaffolding that begins with implicit help and moves toward explicit help as needed. One of the studies that compared these two perspectives is Erlam, Ellis, and Batstone (2013), who examined the effectiveness of graduated feedback versus explicit correction. The data were collected in L2 conferencing sessions between a teacher and two groups of adult pre-intermediate L2 learners – a graduated feedback group and an explicit correction group. The analysis of the data revealed an advantage for graduated feedback in promoting self-correction. However, no evidence was found for a systematic reduction of the level of assistance needed over time, and the amount of feedback required was highly variable. Not surprisingly, explicit correction was found to be more efficient in correcting the errors although it did not lead to consistent uptake. Another study of this kind is Rassaei (2014), which compared the effectiveness of scaffolded (graduated) feedback with recasts. The data came from seventy-eight Persian EFL learners divided into three groups: a control group that received no feedback and two experimental groups, with one receiving recasts and the other receiving scaffolded feedback. The target structure was English *wh*-question forms. The study used two measures to evaluate the effectiveness of feedback: an untimed grammaticality judgment task and an oral production task. The findings showed an advantage for scaffolded feedback over recasts on both measures.

Researchers working within the sociocultural perspective have also examined the role of feedback under the rubric of what has been called dynamic assessment (DA). DA integrates feedback and assessment as a unified activity with the aim of understanding learners' developmental potentials and providing feedback in ways that assist learners' development (see Poehner, 2008 for a discussion and also Davin & Donato, 2013, Lantolf & Poehner, 2007; Poehner, 2009). Rahimi, Kushki, and Nassaji (2015), for example, conducted a qualitative case study exploring the role of DA in the development of conceptual L2 writing skills. The data came from three advanced EFL students, who each produced ten writing tasks and then received scaffolded feedback in tutorial sessions with their teacher. Two research questions were addressed. One concerned how scaffolded feedback assisted learners in diagnosing their writing problems and the other focused on how effective the feedback was in helping learners improve their writing ability. The findings showed notable diagnostic as well as developmental effects for scaffolded feedback. That is, it helped learners both to identify the sources of their problems and also to become less reliant on the teacher's feedback over time.

In sum, the findings from studies within the sociocultural perspective indicate that the effectiveness of corrective feedback depends to a great extent on the opportunities it provides for effective scaffolding within the learner's ZPD. More specifically, they suggest that the amount of learning brought about depends largely on how the learner and the novice participate in the interaction as well as the degree to which the feedback they receive is tuned to their emerging needs and abilities. Research within the sociocultural perspective also highlights the importance of the various social and cultural factors that can affect feedback effectiveness. It suggests that learners' development is closely related to not only the people they interact with but also the way they interact. The effectiveness of the feedback is also highly affected by the dynamic context of learning. Context here involves all aspects of the social setting including the school, the learner, the teacher, classroom tasks and activities, and the various individual differences that exist among the teacher and the learners. Different learners would also vary in the way they respond to different types of corrective feedback because of the individual differences that exist among them (see Part VIII of this volume).

Conclusion and Implications

The sociocultural perspective and the findings of research in this area have significant implications for how corrective feedback should be viewed and used in language teaching. I will conclude by summarizing a number of characteristics gleaned from this research for the delivery of effective feedback.

As discussed earlier, central to the sociocultural theory is the notion of ZPD, which highlights the importance of developmentally appropriate interaction in the process of language learning. It is believed that interaction within the ZPD enables learners to use their existing linguistic knowledge to develop what they have not yet mastered independently. It is through such interaction that the teacher or a more capable other is able to discover the learner's actual developmental level and then provide feedback in ways that enable the learner to reach his or her potential level of development. Another assumption is that learning is fundamentally a mediated process, in which the interaction between the teacher and students plays a very important part (among other forms of mediation including instructional tools and tasks). Dialogic interaction is crucial to accurately identifying learners' developmental needs and helping them move from other-regulation to self-regulation, that is, a process that begins with the help or guidance of others and ends in a situation when the learner becomes able to act autonomously with no more help from others.

When students obtain feedback through interaction within their ZPD, they take a more active part in the feedback process and, hence, become more capable of attending to and processing the feedback provided in response to their errors. Pedagogically, this suggests the importance of the creation of such opportunities in the classroom. One way of achieving this would be through designing and using various collaborative tasks and activities that promote student–teacher and student–student interaction.

In the sociocultural perspective, feedback effectiveness does not depend much on the type of feedback but on how feedback is constructed. The focus is also not on the product but on the process of learning and on how feedback is negotiated between the novice and the expert. Effective feedback is also scaffolded. That is, it is in the form of guided assistance. When the feedback is scaffolded, it becomes relevant and appropriate (Aljaafreh & Lantolf, 1994). It also enables the teacher to determine how much control the learner has over his or her performance and what degree of scaffolding is needed to help the learner arrive at self-regulation. Thus, the role of the teacher is not simply correcting errors but creating supportive conditions in which the novice can participate and extend his or her current skills and knowledge to higher levels of competence.

Research within a cognitive paradigm suggests that feedback becomes effective if it targets language forms for which learners are developmentally ready (e.g., Pienemann, 1998; Pienemann, 2005). Pedagogically, this indicates that teachers should take into account learners' developmental readiness and provide feedback that matches learners' linguistic ability. However, it is not always easy to determine the developmental readiness of individual learners. To address this issue, a cognitive perspective suggests that teachers should be flexible and use a combination of different feedback types so that learners can be exposed to a variety of feedback forms (see Nassaji, 2015). Another option, however, would be to provide scaffolded feedback based on the learner's ongoing needs. This need is determined by how the learner responds to the feedback (Aljaafreh & Lantolf, 1994). When feedback is scaffolded, the teacher would be able to discover the cause of the error more effectively and at the same time, fine-tune the feedback to the learner's level of interlanguage competence (Nassaji, 2011).

An important characteristic of scaffolded feedback is that it is gradual rather than sudden (Aljaafreh & Lantolf, 1994). That is, it is progressive, starting with the least direct or explicit assistance and then gradually moving toward more direct and explicit feedback as needed. The aim is to help learners step by step as they appropriate the feedback and gain control over their performance over time. One limitation of such feedback is that it may be time-consuming. However, if scaffolding assists acquisition, the time spent on such a procedure is justified (Nassaji, 2017).

Effective feedback is also contingent (Aljaafreh & Lantolf, 1994). There are at least two implications that can be drawn from this contingency idea.

First, the assistance provided should attempt to provide the learners with opportunities to self-correct if possible. Second, no more help should be given than is necessary, thus allowing the learner to exercise his or her agency (Aljaafreh & Lantolf, 1994). As learners become more developmentally advanced, they need increasingly less assistance to use a particular language form correctly.

Finally, from a sociocultural perspective, no feedback type is intrinsically better than the other, and every feedback type can be beneficial as long as it can assist the learner to move toward self-regulation. As noted earlier, the sociocultural perspective stresses the connection between inter-mental and intra-mental functioning (Wertsch, 1985). Effective feedback is thus a process that helps this transition. In other words, it is a process of other-regulation to self-regulation. When receiving feedback, learners may first rely more on the assistance and the intervention of the other (i.e., the teacher or the expert). However, as they become more proficient, they become more independent and able to perform the task with little or no assistance.

In such cases, the learner can be said to have become more self-regulated.

References

Aljaafreh, A. & Lantolf, J. (1994). Negative feedback as regulation and second language learning in the zone of proximal development. *Modern Language Journal*, 78(4), 465–483.

Appel, G. & Lantolf, J. (1994). *Vygotskian approaches to second language research*. Norwood, NJ: Ablex.

Bliss, J., Askew, M. & Macrae, S. (1996). Effective teaching and learning: Scaffolding revisited. *Oxford Review of Education*, 22(1) 37–61.

Bruner, J. S. (1986). *Actual minds, possible worlds*. London: Harvard University Press.

Davin, K. & Donato, R. (2013). Student collaboration and teacher-directed classroom dynamic assessment: A complementary pairing. *Foreign Language Annals*, 46(1), 5–22.

Donato, R. (1994). Collective scaffolding in second language learning. In J. Lantolf & G. Appel (eds.), *Vygotskian approaches to second language research* (pp. 33–59). Norwood, NJ: Ablex.

Doughty, C. & Williams, J. (1998). Pedagogical choices in focus on form. In C. Doughty & J. Williams (eds.), *Focus on form in classroom second language acquisition* (pp. 197–261). Cambridge: Cambridge University Press.

Ellis, R. (2003). *Task-based language learning and teaching*. Oxford: Oxford University Press.

(2009). Corrective feedback and teacher development. *L2 Journal*, 1, 2–18.

Engin, M. (2012). Trainer talk: Levels of intervention. *ELT journal*, 67(1), 11–19.

Erlam, R., Ellis, R. & Batstone, R. (2013). Oral corrective feedback on L2 writing: Two approaches compared. *System*, 41(2), 257–268.

Lantolf, J. (2000). *Sociocultural theory and second language learning*. Oxford: Oxford University Press.

(2006). Sociocultural theory and L2: State of the art. *Studies in Second Language Acquisition*, 28(1), 67–109.

Lantolf, J. & Poehner, M. (2007). Dynamic assessment of L2 development: Bringing the past into the future. *Journal of Applied Linguistics and Professional Practice*, 1(1), 49–72.

Lantolf, J., & Thorne, S. L. (2006). *Sociocultural theory and the genesis of second language development*. Oxford: Oxford University Press.

(2007). Sociocultural theory and second language learning. In. B. van Patten & J. Williams (eds.), *Theories in second language acquisition* (pp. 201–224). Mahwah, NJ: Lawrence Erlbaum.

Long, M. (1996). The role of the linguistic environment in second language acquisition. In W. Ritchie & T. Bhatia (eds.), *Handbook of second language acquisition* (pp. 413–468). San Diego: Academic Press.

Marchenkova, L. (2005). Language, culture, and self: The Bakhtin – Vygotsky encounter. In J. K. Hall, G. Vitanova & L. Marchenkova (eds.), *Dialogue with Bakhtin on second and foreign language learning* (pp. 171–188). Mahwah, NJ: Lawrence: Lawrence Erlbaum.

Mitchell, R. & Myles, F. (1998). *Second language learning theories* (2nd ed.). London: Arnold.

Nassaji, H. (2007). Reactive focus on form through negotiation on learners' written errors. In S. Fotos & H. Nassaji (eds.), *Form focused instruction and teacher education: Studies in honour of Rod Ellis* (pp. 117–129). Oxford: Oxford University Press.

(2011). Correcting students' written grammatical errors: The effects of negotiated versus nonnegotiated feedback. *Studies in Second Language Learning and Teaching*, 1(3), 315–334.

(2013). Interactional feedback: Insights from theory and research. In A. Benati, C. Laval & M. Arche (eds.), *The grammar dimension in instructed second language learning: Theory, research and practice* (pp. 103–123). London: Bloomsbury.

(2015). *Interactional feedback dimension in instructed second language learning*. London: Bloomsbury.

(2016). Anniversary article: Interactional feedback in second language teaching and learning: A synthesis and analysis of current research. *Language Teaching Research*, 20(4), 535–562.

(2017). Negotiated oral feedback in response to written errors. In H. Nassaji & E. Kartchava (eds.), *Corrective feedback in second language* teaching and learning: Research, theory, applications, implications (pp. 114–128). New York: Routledge.

Nassaji, H. & Cumming, A. (2000). What's in a ZPD? A case study of a young ESL student and teacher interacting through dialogue journals. *Language Teaching Research*, 4(2), 95–121.

Nassaji, H. & Swain, M. (2000). Vygotskian perspective on corrective feedback in L2: The effect of random versus negotiated help on the learning of English articles. *Language Awareness*, 9(1), 34–51.

Ohta, A. (2000). Rethinking interaction in SLA: Developmentally appropriate assistance in the zone of proximal development and the acquisition and L2 grammar. In J. Lantolf (ed.), *Sociocultural theory and second language learning* (pp. 51–78). Oxford: Oxford University Press.

(2001). *Second language acquisition processes in the classroom: Learning Japanese*. Mahwah, NJ: Lawrence Erlbaum.

Pica, T. (1994). Research on negotiation: What does it reveal about second-language learning conditions, processes, and outcomes? *Language learning*, 44(3), 493–527.

Pienemann, M. (1998). *Language processing and second language development: Processability theory*. Amsterdam: John Benjamins.

(2005). Discussing processability theory. In M. Pienemann (ed.), *Crosslinguistic aspects of processability theory* (pp. 61–83). Amsterdam: John Benjamins.

Poehner, M. (2008). *Dynamic assessment: A Vygotskian approach to understanding and promoting L2 development*. Berlin: Springer.

(2009). Group dynamic assessment: Mediation for the L2 classroom. *TESOL Quarterly*, 43(3), 471–491.

Rahimi, M., Kushki, A. & Nassaji, H. (2015). Diagnostic and developmental potentials of dynamic assessment for L2 writing. *Language and Sociocultural Theory*, 2(2), 185–208.

Rassaei, E. (2014). Scaffolded feedback, recasts, and L2 development: A sociocultural perspective. *Modern Language Journal*, 98(1), 417–431.

Rogoff, B. (1990). *Apprenticeship in thinking: Cognitive development in social context*. New York: Oxford University Press.

Van den Branden, K. (1997). Effects of negotiation on language learners' output. *Language Learning*, 47(4), 589–636.

Verity, D. P. (2005). Vygotskian concepts for teacher education. In *Lifelong learning: Proceedings of the 4th annual JALT Pan-SIG conference*. May 14–15, 2005. Tokyo: Tokyo Keizai University.

Vygotsky, L. S. (1978). *Mind in society: The development of higher psychological processes*. Cambridge, MA: Harvard University Press.

(1981). The genesis of higher mental functions. In J. V. Wertsch (ed.), *The concept of activity in soviet psychology* (pp. 144–188). Armonk, NY: M. E. Sharpe.

(1986). *Thought and language*. Cambridge, MA: MIT Press.

(1988). *The collected works of L. S. Vygotsky.* Vol. I: *Problems of general psychology.* New York: Plenum Press.

Wells, G. (2007). Semiotic mediation, dialogue and the construction of knowledge. *Human Development, 50*(5), 244–274.

Wertsch, J. V. (1985). *Vygotsky and the social formation of mind.* Cambridge, MA: Harvard University Press.

Part II

Methodological Approaches in the Study of Corrective Feedback

5

Tools to Measure the Effectiveness of Feedback

Alison Mackey, Lara Bryfonski, Özgür Parlak,
Ashleigh Pipes, Ayşenur Sağdıç, and Bo-Ram Suh

Introduction

In this chapter, we describe some of the tools that are typically used to measure the effectiveness of corrective feedback, ranging from tools such as tasks which have been used since the early days of corrective feedback research, to tools that have been more recently adopted from related fields like psychology and educational measurement. As part of describing these tools, we also consider the importance of factors like the instructions given, the participants, and their roles in assessing the effectiveness of feedback. We cover tools used in classrooms and laboratory settings, discussing introspective tools as well as external measurements.

We will first define corrective feedback as it is understood in Long's (1996) Interaction Hypothesis and discuss each data collection tool as it relates to the measurement of corrective feedback. This hypothesis notes that interaction "connects input, internal language capacities, particularly selective attention, and output in productive ways" (1996, pp. 451–452). Interaction, as Long and many others have noted, involves input, corrective feedback, and output, and has been theoretically claimed and empirically shown to lead to learning in a very wide variety of studies. Exactly how interaction and corrective feedback lead to learning is an active research topic. In this chapter, corrective feedback is understood as being any sort of indication showing that there is an error in a learner's oral or written production. Corrective feedback may provide positive or negative evidence (or both) to the learner; for example, the feedback may point out the error and provide a grammatical explanation. Alternatively, feedback could also simply be the provision of the corrected form.

Using Tasks to Examine the Effectiveness of Corrective Feedback

Second language acquisition (SLA) researchers are often interested in the external features of the second language (L2) learning process; namely, the input and corrective feedback that learners receive, the output they produce, and any learning that results. So a typical design for measuring the effectiveness of corrective feedback involves a pre-test (which can take the form of a communicative task), several days of treatment, where a series of tasks have been engineered and conditions constructed for learners to receive feedback on targeted language forms, and an immediate and delayed post-test, also typically tasks, of the same type but different examples, as for the pre-test. Measurement of the targeted forms from pre- to post-tests would indicate the degree of effectiveness (or not) of corrective feedback, given that a control group would have carried out similar tasks to the treatment group, but without corrective feedback on targeted forms.

A wide array of elicitation tools, especially interaction-based tools, have been used to investigate the role of corrective feedback on L2 learning and teaching. Tasks are among the most common and have been used to both assess the effectiveness of corrective feedback and provide opportunities for interaction and corrective feedback to occur (e.g., Cobb, 2010; Mackey & Goo, 2007). Because there are so many options, deciding on a task to elicit appropriate data to assess the effectiveness of corrective feedback is no easy feat. Some of the most frequently used instruments in the literature include picture description tasks, story completion tasks, consensus tasks, jigsaw tasks, consciousness-raising tasks, and any of these can be used as more direct or more indirect formats. Some of these tasks are one-way, meaning that the information is conveyed by one person to the other, and some are two-way, indicating that both partners have some information, and they are asked to communicate with each other about their piece of knowledge. Commonalities among these tasks are that they are interaction-based, and they facilitate meaningful language production and opportunities for corrective feedback. How that feedback occurs, more implicitly or explicitly, can also often be controlled in the design of the tasks, the instructions, and how the tasks are administered. The following subsections provide overviews of common tasks used to elicit and assess the effectiveness of corrective feedback for SLA.

Picture Description Tasks

This sort of task typically involves asking Learner A to describe a picture to Learner B, who may or may not be able to see the picture. Learner B can then be asked to draw the picture being described by Learner A if they cannot see it (e.g., Mackey, 1999). This is considered a one-way task because only one of the learners (i.e., Learner A) can see the picture and has the information. Picture descriptions can also be utilized to elicit the target structure during treatments and investigate the effects of different types of written feedback. An example of a study is Stefanou and Révész (2015) which used picture description tasks in a pre-test, treatment, post-test, delayed post-test design to investigate the effects of direct written corrective feedback for acquiring articles for generic and specific plural references. Eighty-nine Greek English as a Foreign Language (EFL) students received either direct feedback, direct feedback with metalinguistic commentary, or no feedback on their descriptions of pictures that were designed to elicit the target structures. The learners were able to review the comments after carrying out the task. They were later tested on their knowledge of generic and plural references through truth value judgment tasks and assessments.

Picture sequencing is another type of picture description task that prompts learners to work on a set of pictures and to sequence them in a way to create a meaningful story. This task has been used in several studies to investigate the role of corrective feedback on L2 development (e.g., Nassaji, 2009, 2011). An example of a two-way picture description task is a spot-the-difference task. In this task, each learner is given a picture that slightly differs from the picture provided to the other learner, and they are asked to describe their pictures to each other in order to spot all the differences between the two pictures. In another type of picture description task known as a story completion, information also flows two ways. Each partner is given a different portion of a story, and they are asked to work together to complete the story by asking and answering each other's questions about their parts of the story (e.g., Bigelow et al., 2006; Mackey & Oliver, 2002; Mackey et al., 2002).

Consensus Tasks

This two-way task prompts L2 learners to work on a problem and agree on a solution to solve the problem. An example for a consensus task could be a dictogloss task (e.g., Swain & Lapkin, 2001). In this task, learners are asked to work together to reconstruct a story that they have just heard. This type of task can be used for participants of many ages, as in Li, Zhu, and Ellis's (2016) study of the effects of immediate and delayed corrective feedback with middle school students of English in China. Participants listened to a teacher tell a story three times following presentation of vocabulary and brainstorming about the topic. The first telling was strictly oral, the second telling included slides with the text and vocabulary enhancement, and the third telling was again oral. Students retold the story in pairs with the additional task of jointly creating an ending for the story. Then they performed the story in front of the class and shared the endings they had agreed upon in their pairs. Students who received immediate corrective feedback showed an advantage over students who received delayed feedback, and both showed an advantage over a control group on explicit knowledge of a new grammatical structure as measured by a grammaticality judgment post-test. Other types of consensus tasks involve asking learners to debate and arrive at a common outcome based on a statement. Often, to increase learners' motivation and task engagement, the statement may be somewhat controversial, for example "Climate change is fake news." Learners are given the conversational job of arguing one way or the other. Alternatively, learners could be given a hypothetical scenario that requires them to discuss a number of options and choose one in order to complete the task. An example of this type of consensus task can be found in Loewen and Wolff's (2016) study. The task required learner dyads to review the profiles of three hypothetical scholarship candidates who wanted to study in the United States, and then to discuss which one should be given the scholarship.

Jigsaw Tasks
In this type of two-way task, each learner is provided with different pieces of information, and have to work together to combine their respective pieces of knowledge to solve a problem. A map task is an example of a jigsaw task (e.g., Gass, Mackey & Ross-Feldman, 2005). Learners are given a map of a place (e.g., a city) with different information (e.g., road closings, accidents), and they are asked to work together to choose the best route to go from point A to point B. Jigsaw tasks are similar to picture description tasks, in that critical information for task completion is not uniformly distributed among participants. However, typically in jigsaw tasks, all participants have some information they must share, while in picture description tasks, there is usually a single participant with all the information who must explain it to their partner or partners. An example of a study that utilized jigsaw tasks to examine the role of corrective feedback in task-based interaction is the one carried out by Iwashita (2003). This study used both two-way spot-the-difference tasks and one-way picture description tasks (see above). In a spot-the-difference task, learner–native speaker (NS) dyads have pictures that differ in predetermined ways. The pair must work together to determine what differences exist without looking at their partner's picture. In Iwashita's study, the pictures were used to elicit particular Japanese grammatical structures (objects and their locations) while the NS provided implicit corrective feedback and positive evidence. Results indicated that NSs provided positive evidence more often than implicit negative evidence. However, positive evidence only benefited learners with above-average scores on pre-

tests. Implicit negative evidence (specifically recasts) benefited all learners, regardless of pre-treatment proficiency.

Direct and Indirect Tests

Direct and indirect tests are commonly used to investigate implicit and explicit learning which may result from corrective feedback (e.g., Ellis, 2005; Rebuschat & Williams, 2012). While it is argued that direct tests require learners to make use of their conscious linguistic knowledge to perform a task, indirect tests prompt learners to perform a task without making it explicit to them that their performance is being measured. This is to ensure that the elicited production draws on their unconscious knowledge. For example, learners can be presented with artificial or unknown language excerpts and can be asked to perform an elicited imitation task as an indirect test (see Rebuschat, 2013 for an overview). An elicited imitation task usually requires participants to repeat information after hearing it. Participants can then gain knowledge about the linguistic rules governing the language excerpts provided to them, even without being told about them, and can be asked to perform an untimed grammaticality judgment task as a direct test (see Ellis, Loewen & Erlam, 2006 for examples of using oral imitation and grammaticality judgment tests). Grammaticality (or acceptability) judgment tasks involve learners rating language as grammatical/acceptable or not, and sometimes confidence intervals are also used (how sure are you that your answer is right?), and reaction times (how long did it take you to make the judgment?) provide more information.

Instructions and the Role of Participants in Tasks

As important as the tasks (materials) themselves are at providing opportunities for corrective feedback to occur, it is also important to understand that the instructions for carrying out tasks can play an important role in providing opportunities to assess the effectiveness of corrective feedback. Task instructions can be manipulated to uncover information about the provision and use of corrective feedback in tasks, and the outcomes, or effectiveness of such feedback.

The Confederate Scripting Technique in Tasks

Originating in the field of social psychology, confederate scripting techniques have been used in SLA studies for a variety of purposes. In this technique, one of the task participants is "directing the linguistic traffic," without the other participant(s) realizing. They typically involve the researcher training a conversational partner to act as a confederate to interact with unknowing learners (who do not know the confederates are working with the experimenters) during a communicative task (e.g., McDonough & Mackey, 2008) . The confederates elicit data from learners and provide them with input and output opportunities. The advantage of this technique is the ability to control one side of the conversation (e.g., utterances, questions), which then makes it possible to elicit specific linguistic data and to make comparisons across all study participants. Confederate scripting has previously been utilized in priming studies where learners need to repeat previously heard utterances during interactions (McDonough, 2006; McDonough & Mackey, 2008). Confederates in priming studies are scripted to produce developmentally advanced forms such as question forms or other syntactic constructions. McDonough (2006), for example, found that learners who demonstrated high levels of priming by a confederate were more likely to advance to higher stages in the developmental stages for ESL question formation. Although confederate scripting has mainly been utilized in priming studies, it can easily be adopted in corrective feedback studies. The confederate can carry out both the function of controlling the direction of the interaction through scripted questions or statements in order to elicit the target language feature from learners, and the function of providing corrective feedback on nontarget-like production that may emerge during elicitation.

So far, the tools we have been describing, and the techniques for manipulating them, have been mainly used for oral corrective feedback. However, when tasks are mediated by technology, for example, computers, apps, websites, and so on, written corrective feedback is often studied in terms of its effectiveness, so we will turn to a discussion of this next.

Computer-Mediated Environments

Many language learning tasks that are carried out in a face-to-face environment can actually be carried out in a computer-mediated environment. Similar to face-to-face language learning, computer-mediated language learning (Chappelle, 1998; Ziegler, 2016) also promotes negotiation for meaning and, hence, provides opportunities for corrective feedback and language learning. A number of meta-analyses have shown that L2 learning that takes place in computer-mediated environments has the potential to be as effective as L2 learning that occurs in face-to-face environments (Grgurović, Chapelle & Shelley, 2013; Lai & Li, 2011; Plonsky & Ziegler, 2016). Some examples of tasks that have been commonly used for face-to-face language learning and can be directly incorporated into computer-mediated language learning environments include decision-making, jigsaw, information-gap tasks (e.g., Blake, 2000; Smith, 2003), picture description tasks (e.g., Loewen & Erlam, 2006), dictogloss (e.g., Yilmaz, 2011), and collaborative writing tasks (e.g., Sauro, 2009).

When performed in a computer-mediated environment, tasks can be carried out during a synchronous text-chat interaction (Blake, 2000; Yilmaz, 2011; Yilmaz & Sağdıç, 2019), meaning learners are working together, in real time, chatting, but in text. This falls somewhere between speaking and writing. There are also audiovisual interactions using video-conferencing software such as Skype (e.g., Parlak & Ziegler, 2017; Yanguas, 2010) as vehicles through which to measure corrective feedback and its impact on learning. From a research perspective, one advantage of computer-mediated environments over face-to-face environments is that it is much easier to analyze learners' productions during the task. For example, various text-chat software programs developed for research purposes allow all textual input entered into the computer to be recorded, including the text that has been deleted by learners. This particular software feature provides a window into learners' cognitive processes allowing researchers to gain access not only to learners' production data but also to process-related internal mechanisms such as online planning (e.g., Sauro & Smith, 2010). In addition to synchronous communication, computer-mediated environments also allow tasks to be carried out asynchronously (e.g., Abrams, 2003; Kitade, 2006). Not carried out in real time, asynchronous tasks provide learners with more time for planning and revising what they are going to say based on feedback.

Introspective Measurements of the Effectiveness of Corrective Feedback

An often-asked question in the corrective feedback line of research after the linguistic outcomes have been measured, frequently using communicative tasks, is *why* does corrective feedback lead to learning (given that it often does). One way to address this question is to use introspective methods and tools.

To that end, when measuring the effectiveness of corrective feedback, it is useful to also gather data on the internal cognitive processes learners engage in as they interact and hear corrective feedback. Introspective methods seek to obtain information on what participants are thinking at the time of interaction. These methods might be concurrent – from an online, real-time perspective – or retrospective, occurring after the interaction or task. We now turn to a description of some of the most commonly used methods for gathering introspective data in the field of SLA – think-alouds (e.g., Leow, 1997), immediate recall (e.g., Philp, 2003), stimulated recall (e.g., Gass & Mackey, 2017) as well as some exciting and relatively new tools such as eye-tracking (e.g., Smith, 2010), reaction times (e.g., Lyster & Izquierdo, 2009), and other new technologies.

Think-Alouds

Think-aloud protocols (see Leow et al., 2014 for an overview) are an example of concurrent (real-time) introspective data collection. Researchers who employ think-alouds are interested in why learners process L2 input in the way they do, including what they notice or how they focus their attentional resources during interaction. In think-alouds, learners are trained to verbalize their thoughts as they complete a task or activity. In studies of corrective feedback, learners might reveal why they modified their output in a particular manner, or what aspects of the corrective feedback they received were most salient. For example, in the domain of written corrective feedback, Sachs and Polio (2007) had learners think aloud as they reviewed feedback they received on a draft of their writing. Learners who verbalized their understanding of why an item was reformulated (during the think-aloud) were more likely to revise that item on subsequent drafts than learners who did not notice the reformulations. However, one disadvantage of think-alouds is that they are incompatible with oral interaction tasks as participants cannot simultaneously think aloud and complete an oral task.

Immediate Recall

Immediate recall methods tap into what learners notice and store in their short-term memory as they receive input. The method is grounded in the fact that the information that has been recently attended to (i.e. noticed) is available for conscious recall, whereas input that has not been noticed is not stored in short-term memory and is not further processed by the learner (see Egi, 2004 for an overview). This method can be used to examine whether or not learners notice the corrective feedback they receive and if that noticing is constrained by how long and complex the correction is or by such individual differences as the learners' L2 proficiency. A study by Philp (2003) utilized immediate recall as a way of testing whether L2 English learners noticed recasts provided in oral interaction. Noticing was operationalized as accurate immediate recall of the recasts by the learners. In this study, participants were prompted to recall the NS's previous utterance after hearing the sound of two knocks. In this way, interaction was interrupted following recasts with the knocking sound and learners repeated the last thing they heard. Findings demonstrated that learners interacting in NS–NNS dyads noticed 60–70 percent of the recasts provided in the input, but that accurate recall was moderated by the learner's proficiency level and the length and number of changes made within the recast.

Stimulated Recall

Where think-alouds and immediate recall methods happen concurrently with a task or interaction, stimulated recall interviews are retroactive and ask participants to recall what they were thinking during a prior task or activity. These thoughts are elicited, in as short a time period as possible after the original interaction, by presenting participants with a stimulus, such as a video or audio recording, of the task the participant previously performed (Gass & Mackey, 2017 provide an overview). During the stimulated recall, learners are asked to orient their verbalizations to what they were thinking at the time the interaction occurred, rather than at the time of the interview. The researcher can choose selected stimuli, such as episodes of corrective feedback and modified output, or let the participant pause the video or audio recording whenever they wish to share what they were thinking at a given point in time. Because it does not interrupt the initial interaction, stimulated recall has the potential to tap into learners' thought processes, learning strategies, or other cognitive processes that are not evident through simple observation. Stimulated recall interviews are also useful when processing cannot be practically measured or observed during task completion, such as when a participant is teaching or completing an interactive task.

Stimulated recall protocols have been profitably applied to the domain of corrective feedback (e.g., Egi, 2010; Mackey, 2006; Mackey et al., 2007; Yoshida, 2008). For example, a study by Mackey (2006) investigated how and when learners noticed interactional corrective feedback on selected target forms during in-class activities. Learners participated in stimulated recall interviews, during which video clips from the classroom activities that included feedback episodes and distractors were presented. Results indicated a connection between noticing and L2 development, in that features that were noticed by participants in stimulated recall interview data resulted in greater development on post-tests.

Retrospective measures pose some limitations, however, as participants must be trained to orient their verbalizations to what they were thinking at the time the event in question occurred. Care should be taken to avoid the pitfalls of reactivity, or the act of recall potentially triggering changes in participants' cognition, by ensuring that participants take post-tests before participating in stimulated recall interviews. This way, researchers can ensure that the act of performing stimulated recall does not influence the interviewees' noticing of forms on a post-test and vice versa. Another option is to have focal students participate in stimulated recall interviews and not take post-tests. This would eliminate the potential of one form of data, either stimulated recall or post-test results, influencing the other. However, having several participants only complete stimulated recall interviews could be limiting to the sample size of the post-tests.

Interviews

Other forms of introspection that may shed light on the effectiveness of corrective feedback include interviews, which may be structured, unstructured, or semi-structured. A structured interview will be the same for every participant, like a questionnaire delivered orally instead of on paper or electronically. An unstructured interview, on the other hand, is more like a regular conversation in which the interviewer can freely pursue discussion about the research topic, as it is personally relevant to the participant. In a semi-structured interview, the interviewer starts with a list of preliminary questions to guide the conversation. However, in this format the interviewer has flexibility to delve deeper into fruitful topics by adding new questions as the interview progresses if the participant has thoughts or ideas the researcher had not anticipated. If the participant is unresponsive to a particular topic, the interviewer can skip some questions. Semi-structured interviews were used by Bryfonski and Sanz (2018) while investigating corrective feedback in conversation groups during a study abroad program in Spain. These interviews corroborated quantitative data concerning the decreased amount of feedback over time and also provided deeper insights into the dynamics of student attitudes toward corrections from native versus nonnative Spanish-speaking peers and the use of English in conversation groups.

In terms of how interviews are carried out, it is important to be careful in the scheduling and execution of them. If participants are more comfortable speaking in their L1, it is useful to have an interviewer available who can communicate comfortably in that language. No matter what language they use, researchers should try to find a place that is comfortable and quiet enough for recording devices to pick up sound, especially in multi-participant interviews or focus groups (Creswell, 2013). The time when the interview is conducted can impact its effectiveness as well. Getting participants' thoughts immediately after a class, as in a structured exit-questionnaire interview, can gauge participants' perceptions of corrective feedback episodes before their memories of an occasion start to fade, as pointed out by Hall and Rist (1999). Sometimes several days or weeks are necessary for participants to process interactions, as the effects of corrective feedback are sometimes delayed rather than immediate.

This is especially true if the research involves delayed post-tests or other measures of development, as in Bryfonski and Sanz's (2018) study above.

Journals and Blogs

Other helpful introspective data collection tools that offer a means of collecting both L2 data and learners' thoughts on the language learning process are journals and blogs. Capitalizing on the familiarity of blogs to many of today's language learners, Delgado and McDougald (2013) used a combination of blogs and journals to examine the effects of peer corrective feedback on narratives. A group of five Colombian pre-service English teachers created personal narrative blogs and simultaneously provided corrective feedback on one another's blogs. The same pre-service teachers kept learning journals to document the effects of the peer corrective feedback on the coherence of their subsequent blog entries. Integrated analysis of the blogs and journals showed positive results in terms of coherence of blog content as well as community building among the participants. In other words, the provision of peer feedback was found to enhance or maintain coherence features in blog posts by developing the participants' awareness of coherence in texts as well as increasing their motivation and engagement with peers through collaborative writing. Blogs combine the advantages of being modern and publicly accessible, which can be motivating for participants who want to showcase their best work in an L2. Journals provide a more personal account that gives participants a chance to reflect on their personal reactions to successes, challenges, and feedback, knowing that only the researcher will see what they write. Whatever choice or combination a researcher uses, though, providing an appropriate level of guidance and detailed instructions to the participants will help generate usable and consistent data.

Uptake Sheets

Another very interesting way of collecting data on efficacy of feedback is known in the SLA literature as uptake sheets. Allwright (1984) defined uptake as learners' reports about their learning and devised uptake sheets as a method to gauge it (1984, 1987; see also Slimani, 1989, 1992). SLA researchers have employed uptake sheets as a methodological technique to elicit learners' viewpoints about what they are learning in the classroom (e.g., Jones, 1992; Palmeira, 1995). Recently, Nabei (2013) asked Japanese EFL learners to fill out an uptake sheet (Slimani, 1992) in order to investigate their own L2 learning experiences in a reading classroom. The uptake sheet was distributed approximately 10 minutes before each of the two class meetings ended. The learners in the study were asked to write down anything they remembered learning during that day's class about grammar, vocabulary, spelling, pronunciation, English expressions, and others specifically on a chart in the sheet. The findings of this study showed that the learners tended to focus primarily on vocabulary and that they could learn and report teacher-initiated target linguistic items. Uptake sheets have considerable potential for further use in research on interaction and corrective feedback, as demonstrated by Mackey et al.'s (2001) comparison of several possible formats. They considered three charts – one that focused on language, one on language and context, and one on structure. The results for each format varied in terms of quantity and quality of detail provided by students, and the timing of when the sheets are completed by students also arose as a point to consider. However, this tool would be easily adaptable to corrective feedback research by adding columns for learners to report the feedback they heard and its effectiveness.

Having discussed both tasks and introspective tools, we will move to one more common technique for assessing feedback. This is observations, and they are one of the oldest tools for classroom investigations. We will briefly describe common features of observations here.

Observations in Determining the Effectiveness of Corrective Feedback

Observations of student–teacher and peer-to-peer interactions are also helpful in collecting authentic data concerning corrective feedback. Observation tools range from detailed protocol schemes to more free-form field notes. Some schemes may include rows and columns arranged as a grid for the observer to tally each instance of the variables under study, such as "Elicitation of self/peer correction session," "Scaffolding," or even "Class applause" (Guilloteaux & Dörnyei, 2008) divided by time segments or individual student actions. Other schemes may be loosely structured worksheets for the observer to make field notes, with categories such as "Metalinguistic information given for linguistic awareness building" (Bailey & Marsden, 2017) and space to elaborate on thoughts or questions that occur during an observation. Video recording is often necessary in order to thoroughly document a phenomenon under study, especially for studies that investigate visual data such as the effectiveness of gestures in supporting recasts (e.g., Nakatsukasa, 2016). Video is used as a backup to ensure observers do not miss anything while looking down to take notes. Most of these techniques can be used or modified to collect information on corrective feedback and its outcomes.

New Directions in Measuring the Effectiveness of Corrective Feedback

Studies of corrective feedback are increasingly employing methodological tools such as response or reaction times (e.g., Li, 2013; Loewen & Erlam,

2006; Lyster & Izquierdo, 2009) and eye-tracking (e.g., Smith, 2010) to investigate the noticing, processing, and effectiveness of corrective feedback. Other technologies such as electro-encephalography (EEG) and functional magnetic resonance imaging (fMRI) have been highlighted as potential avenues for interdisciplinary collaboration and utilized to investigate topics in corrective feedback processing (see Mackey, Abbuhl & Gass, 2013 for an overview).

Eye-tracking, for example, is an increasingly popular method of gathering data for second language researchers (Winke, Godfroid & Gass, 2013). It records where a participant's gaze focuses for a period of time. Eye-tracking data can be represented by heatmaps showing where on the screen learners tended to focus their gaze the most, as well as videos that track where and how learners' gaze moves throughout a task. When coupled with audio recordings, screen capture, and keystroke capture (e.g., Smith, 2008), the research can, rather comprehensively, capture the multimodal aspects of an online interaction involving written corrective feedback. Eye-tracking has been productively applied to corrective feedback research. For example, a study by Smith (2010) utilized eye-tracking to measure the noticing of recasts provided during synchronous computer-mediated-communication (SCMC). Findings demonstrated that 60 percent of all recasts were noticed in the SCMC environment as measured by fixation times and that lexical recasts were noticed more often than grammatical recasts. In this study, eye-tracking was deemed to provide a robust measure of noticing of corrective feedback.

EEG and fMRI are also being used to study language learning and use. Although high costs and training requirements have been impediments to widespread EEG and fMRI use in corrective feedback research, there is tremendous potential. For example, EEG could be used to capture differences in responses to implicit and explicit feedback. Likewise, fMRI could help reveal activation patterns, as learners either receive or observe feedback. Results from these studies will need to be interpreted cautiously as the methodology develops within the study of corrective feedback, but careful and thorough research could yield informative and interesting results.

Pedagogical Implications

Having described all these different tools for capturing data that can shed light on the effectiveness of corrective feedback, an obvious point that should also be addressed by researchers using these tools is to determine what effectiveness might look like. In other words, how do we know, from the data we collect, that learning has taken place? In its most obvious form, a measure of effectiveness would provide evidence that a learner's language developed as a result of corrective feedback (in comparison with another learner's language, when that other learner did not receive feedback, but was also exposed to similar language and had similar time on task and input and output opportunities did not develop). What counts as development (or acquisition, or learning) is obviously a complex construct and a full discussion is beyond the scope of the current chapter. However, it is important to point out that studies should carefully operationalize linguistic development in order to investigate the effectiveness of feedback.

Also, while the emphasis here has been on tools and their effectiveness for measuring feedback, it is worth noting that linguistic development can be a fortunate by-product of the use of the tools for research study participants. In the comparison of several formats of uptake sheets, for example, Mackey et al.'s (2001) participants commented that filling out the sheets was beneficial in helping them pay attention to the teacher, and helpful for learning grammar and vocabulary. Introspective activities also appeared to help participants in the study carried out by Mackey (2006), which showed learners demonstrating higher gains on post-tests for features they had noticed in stimulated recall sessions. Delgado and McDougald (2013), as mentioned above, also found that pre-service English teachers who participated in peer-to-peer corrective feedback created more cohesive blog entries over the course of a six-week study.

In this chapter, we have outlined some of the measures that are commonly used in feedback research, including tasks which have been used since the early days of corrective feedback research, and are used as pedagogical tools by many teachers as well as by researchers to collect data. Factors important to research, such as the nature and type of the instructions, and how to pair up learners or put them into small groups, are also issues that teachers need to grapple with. We believe research on corrective feedback benefits from these close instructional–experimental connections.

References

Abrams, Z. I. (2003). The effect of synchronous and asynchronous CMC on oral performance in German. *The Modern Language Journal*, 87(2), 157–167.

Allwright, D. (1984). Why don't learners learn what teachers teach? The interaction hypothesis. In D. Singleton & D. Little (eds.), *Language learning in formal and informal contexts* (pp. 3–18). Dublin: IRAAL.

(1987). Classroom observation: Problems and possibilities. In B. K. Das (ed.), *Patterns of classroom interaction in Southeast Asia* (pp. 88–102). Singapore: SEAMEO Regional Language Center.

Bailey, E. G. & Marsden, E. (2017). Teachers' views on recognizing and using home languages in predominantly monolingual primary schools. *Language and Education*, 31(4), 283–306.

Bigelow, M., Delmas, R., Hansen, K. & Tarone, E. (2006). Literacy and the processing of oral recasts in SLA. *TESOL Quarterly*, 40(4), 665–689.

Blake, R. (2000). Computer mediated communication: A window on L2 Spanish interlanguage. *Language Learning & Technology*, 4(1), 120–136.

Bryfonski, L. & Sanz, C. (2018). Opportunities for corrective feedback during study abroad: A mixed methods approach. *Annual Review of Applied Linguistics*, 38, 1–32.

Chapelle, C. A. (1998). Multimedia CALL: Lessons to be learned from research on instructed SLA. *Language Learning & Technology*, 2(1), 22–34.

Cobb, M. (2010). Meta-analysis of the effectiveness of task-based interaction in form-focused instruction of adult learners in foreign and second language teaching. Unpublished doctoral dissertation, University of San Francisco.

Creswell, J. W. (2013). *Qualitative inquiry and research design: Choosing among five approaches* (3rd edn.). Thousand Oaks, CA: Sage Publications.

Delgado, O. & McDougald, J. S. (2013). Developing writing through blogs and peer feedback. *Íkala*, 18(3), 45–61.

Egi, T. (2004). Verbal reports, noticing, and SLA research. *Language Awareness*, 13(4), 243–264.

— (2007). Recasts, learners' interpretations, and L2 development. In A. Mackey (ed.), *Conversational interaction in second language acquisition: A series of empirical studies* (pp. 249–267). Oxford: Oxford University Press.

— (2010). Uptake, modified output, and learner perceptions of recasts: learner responses as language awareness. *Modern Language Journal*, 94 (1), 1–22.

Ellis, R. (2003). *Task-based language learning and teaching*. Oxford: Oxford University Press.

— (2004). The definition and measurement of L2 explicit knowledge. *Language Learning*, 54(2), 227–275.

— (2005). Measuring implicit and explicit knowledge of a second language: A psychometric study. *Studies in Second Language Acquisition*, 27(2), 141–172.

Ellis, R. & Barkhuizen, G. P. (2005). *Analyzing learner language*. Oxford: Oxford University Press.

Ellis, R. & He, X. (1999). The roles of modified input and output in the incidental acquisition of word meanings. *Studies in Second Language Acquisition*, 21(2), 285–301.

Ellis, R., Loewen, S. & Erlam, R. (2006). Implicit and explicit corrective feedback and the acquisition of L2 grammar. *Studies in Second Language Acquisition*, 28(2), 339–368.

Gass, S. M. (1979). Language transfer and universal grammatical relations. *Language Learning, 29,* 327–344.

   (1982). From theory to practice. In M. Hines & W. Rutherford (eds.), *On TESOL '81* (pp. 129–139). Washington, DC: TESOL.

Gass, S. M. & Mackey, A. (2017). *Stimulated recall methodology in applied linguistics and L2 research.* New York: Routledge.

Gass, S., Mackey, A. & Ross-Feldman, L. (2005). Task-based interactions in classroom and laboratory settings. *Language Learning, 55*(4), 575–611.

Grgurović, M., Chapelle, C. A. & Shelley, M. C. (2013). A meta-analysis of effectiveness studies on computer technology-supported language learning. *ReCALL, 25*(2), 165–198.

Guilloteaux, M. & Dörnyei, Z. (2008). Motivating language learners: A classroom-oriented investigation of the effects of motivational strategies on student motivation. *TESOL Quarterly, 42*(1), 55–77.

Hall, A. & Rist, R. (1999). Integrating multiple qualitative research methods (or avoiding the precariousness of a one-legged stool). *Psychology and Marketing, 16*(4), 291–304.

Iwashita, N. (2003). Negative feedback and positive evidence in task-based interaction: Differential effects on L2 development. *Studies in Second Language Acquisition, 25*(1), 1–36.

Jones, F. (1992). A language-teaching machine: Input, uptake, and output in the communicative classroom. *System, 20*(2), 133–150.

Kitade, K. (2006). The negotiation model in asynchronous computer-mediated communication (CMC): Negotiation in task-based email exchanges. *CALICO Journal, 23*(2), 319.

Lai, C. & Li, G. (2011). Technology and task-based language teaching: A critical review. *CALICO Journal, 28*(2), 498–521.

Leow, R. P. (1997). Attention, awareness, and foreign language behavior. *Language Learning, 47*(3), 467–505.

Leow, R. P., Grey, S., Marijuan, S. & Moorman, C. (2014). Concurrent data elicitation procedures, processes, and the early stages of L2 learning: A critical overview. *Second Language Research, 30*(2), 111–127.

Li, S. (2013). The interactions between the effects of implicit and explicit feedback and individual differences in language analytic ability and working memory. *Modern Language Journal, 97*(3), 634–654.

Li, S., Zhu, Y. & Ellis, R. (2016). The effects of the timing of corrective feedback on the acquisition of a new linguistic structure. *Modern Language Journal, 100*(1), 276–295.

Loewen, S. & Erlam, R. (2006). Corrective feedback in the chatroom: An experimental study. *Computer Assisted Language Learning, 19*(1), 1–14.

Loewen, S. & Wolff, D. (2016). Peer interaction in F2F and CMC contexts. In M. Sato & S. Ballinger (eds.), *Peer interaction and second language learning: Pedagogical potential and research agenda* (pp. 163–184). Philadelphia: John Benjamins.

Long, M. H. (1996). The role of the linguistic environment in second language acquisition. In W. C. Ritchie & T. K. Bhatia (eds.), *Handbook of second language acquisition* (pp. 413–468). San Diego, CA: Academic Press.

Lyster, R. & Izquierdo, J. (2009). Prompts versus recasts in dyadic interaction. *Language Learning*, 59(2), 453–498.

Mackey, A. (1999). Input, interaction, and second language development: An empirical study of question formation in ESL. *Studies in Second Language Acquisition*, 21(4), 557–587.

  (2006). Feedback, noticing and instructed second language learning. *Applied Linguistics*, 27(3), 405–430.

Mackey, A., Abbuhl, R. & Gass, S. M. (2013). Interactionist Approach. In S. M. Gass & A. Mackey (eds.), *The Routledge handbook of second language acquisition* (pp. 7–23). New York: Routledge.

Mackey, A., Al-Khalil, M., Atanassova, G., Hama, M., Logan-Terry, A. & Nakatsukasa, K. (2007). Teachers' intentions and learners' perceptions about corrective feedback in the L2 classroom. *Innovations in Language Learning and Teaching*, 1(1), 129–152.

Mackey, A. & Gass, S. M. (2015). *Second language research: Methodology and design* (2nd edn.). London: Routledge.

Mackey, A. & Goo, J. (2007). Interaction research in SLA: A meta-analysis and research synthesis. In A. Mackey (ed.), *Conversational interaction in second language acquisition: A collection of empirical studies* (pp. 407–452). Oxford: Oxford University Press.

Mackey, A., McDonough, K., Fujii, A. & Tatsumi T. (2001). Investigating learners' reports about the L2 classroom. *International Review of Applied Linguistics in Language Teaching*, 39(4), 285–308.

Mackey, A. & Oliver, R. (2002). Interactional feedback and children's L2 development. *System*, 30(4), 459–477.

Mackey, A., Philp, J., Egi, T., Fujii, A. & Tatsumi, T. (2002). Individual differences in working memory, noticing of interactional feedback and L2 development. In P. Robinson (ed.), *Individual differences and instructional language learning* (pp. 181–209). Philadelphia: John Benjamins.

Mackey, A. & Sachs, R. (2012). Older learners in SLA research: A first look at working memory, feedback, and L2 development. *Language Learning*, 62(3), 704–740.

McDonough, K. (2006). Interaction and syntactic priming: English L2 speakers' production of dative constructions. *Studies in Second Language Acquisition*, 28(2), 179–207.

McDonough, K. & Mackey, A. (2008). Syntactic priming and ESL question development. *Studies in Second Language Acquisition*, 30(1), 31–47.

Nabei, T. (2013). Learner uptake reports on an EFL reading class in Japan. *Gaikokugo Kyouiku Fouramu (Foreign Language Education Forum)*, 12, 47–62.

Nakatsukasa, K. (2016). Efficacy of recasts and gestures on the acquisition of locative prepositions. *Studies in Second Language Acquisition*, 38(4), 771–799.

Nassaji, H. (2009). Effects of recasts and elicitations in dyadic interaction and the role of feedback explicitness. *Language Learning*, 59(2), 411–452.

(2011). Immediate learner repair and its relationship with learning targeted forms in dyadic interaction. *System*, 39(1), 17–29.

Palmeira, W. K. (1995). A study of uptake by learners of Hawaiian. In R. Schmidt (ed.), *Attention and awareness in foreign language learning* (pp. 127–161). Honolulu: University of Hawaii.

Parlak, Ö. & Ziegler, N. (2017). The impact of recasts on the development of primary stress in a synchronous computer-mediated environment. *Studies in Second Language Acquisition*, 39(2), 257–285.

Payant, C. & Kim, Y. (2015). Language mediation in an L3 classroom: The role of task modalities and task types. *Foreign Language Annals*, 48(4), 706–729.

Philp, J. (2003). Constraints on "noticing the gap": Nonnative speakers' noticing of recasts in NS–NNS interaction. *Studies in Second Language Acquisition*, 25(1), 99–126.

Plonsky, L. & Ziegler, N. (2016). The CALL–SLA interface: Insights from a second-order synthesis. *Language Learning & Technology*, 20(2), 17–37.

Rebuschat, P. (2013). Measuring implicit and explicit knowledge in second language research. *Language Learning*, 63(3), 595–626.

Rebuschat, P. & Williams, J. N. (2012). Implicit and explicit knowledge in second language acquisition. *Applied Psycholinguistics*, 33(4), 829–856.

Sachs, R. & Polio, C. (2007). Learners' uses of two types of written feedback on a L2 writing revision task. *Studies in Second Language Acquisition*, 29(1), 67–100.

Sato, M., & Loewen, S. (2018). Metacognitive instruction enhances the effectiveness of corrective feedback: Variable effects of feedback types and linguistic targets. *Language Learning*, 68(2), 507–545.

Sauro, S. (2009). Computer-mediated corrective feedback and the development of L2 grammar. *Language Learning & Technology*, 13(1), 96–120.

Sauro, S. & Smith, B. (2010). Investigating L2 performance in text chat. *Applied Linguistics*, 31(4), 554–577.

Slimani, A. (1989). The role of topicalization in classroom language learning. *System*, 17, 223–234.

(1992). Evaluation of classroom interaction. In J. C. Alderson & A. Beretta (eds.), *Evaluating Second Language Education* (pp. 197–221). Cambridge: Cambridge University Press.

Smith, B. (2003). Computer-mediated negotiated interaction: An expanded model. *The Modern Language Journal*, 87(1), 38–57.

(2008). Methodological hurdles in capturing CMC data: The case of the missing self-repair. *Language Learning & Technology*, 12(1), 85–103.

(2010) Employing eye-tracking technology in researching the effectiveness of recasts in CMC. In F. M. Hult (ed.), *Directions and prospects for educational linguistics* (pp. 79–97). Dordrecht: Springer.

Stefanou, C. & Révész, A. (2015). Direct written corrective feedback, learner differences, and the acquisition of second language article use for generic and specific plural reference. *Modern Language Journal, 99*(2), 263–282.

Swain, M. & Lapkin, S. (2001). Focus on form through collaborative dialogue: Exploring task effects. In M. Bygate, P. Skehan & M. Swain (eds.), *Researching pedagogic tasks: Second language learning, teaching and testing* (pp. 99–118). Harlow: Pearson Education.

Winke, P. M., Godfroid, A. & Gass, S. M. (2013). Introduction to the special issue. *Studies in Second Language Acquisition, 35*(2), 205–212.

Yanguas, Í. (2010). Oral computer-mediated interaction between L2 learners: It's about time! *Language Learning & Technology, 14*(3), 72–93.

Yilmaz, Y. (2011). Task effects on focus on form in synchronous computer-mediated communication. *The Modern Language Journal, 95*(1), 115–132.

Yilmaz, Y., & Sağdıç, A. (2019). The interaction between inhibitory control and corrective feedback timing. *ITL-International Journal of Applied Linguistics, 170*(2), 205–228.

Yoshida, R. (2008). Learners' perception of corrective feedback in pair work. *Foreign Language Annals, 41*(3), 525–541.

Ziegler, N. (2016). Taking technology to task: Technology-mediated TBLT, performance, and production. *Annual Review of Applied Linguistics, 36*, 136–163.

6

Laboratory-Based Oral Corrective Feedback

Shawn Loewen and Susan M. Gass

Introduction

Research methodology plays a critical role in how researchers investigate and understand the construct(s) that they are investigating. For corrective feedback research in particular, and interaction research more generally, there has been a long-standing debate about the strengths and weaknesses of research conducted in the classroom compared to research in a laboratory setting[1] (e.g., Eckerth, 2009; Foster, 1998; Gass, Mackey & Ross-Feldman, 2005, 2011; Loewen & Sato, 2018). On the one hand, lab-based research allows researchers to control numerous aspects of the interaction and treatment. However, critics have countered that such control is at the expense of ecological validity, and at the extreme, critics suggest that the results of lab-based research differ from those of classroom-based research and therefore reveal little about the effectiveness of corrective feedback as a pedagogical technique (Foster, 1998). This chapter explores various aspects of lab-based research and considers its merits and limitations. It should be noted that although this chapter focuses on corrective feedback research, we begin with a discussion of definitions of lab-based and classroom-based research.[2] In particular, we ask the question: what are the factors that distinguish classroom from lab-based research?

---

[1] The precise definition of laboratory-based studies is often lacking with studies being classified as either lab-based or classroom-based. Typically, however, lab-based studies are those that take place outside of the classroom context and involve manipulation of variables.

[2] It is important to recognize that the distinctions we make between the two types of research can be made for most instructed second language acquisition research and are not limited to corrective feedback.

Defining Lab-Based Research

The term *laboratory-based research* is frequently used but not often defined or clearly operationalized in corrective feedback research studies. However, one exception is Lyster, Saito, and Sato (2013), who in their synthesis of classroom-based oral corrective feedback defined classroom research as "involving interaction between a teacher and an intact class of students" (p. 2) and laboratory studies as "involving interaction between two individuals, usually a researcher and a learner" (p. 2). Lyster et al. stated that the reason they chose to examine only classroom contexts in their meta-analysis was because of "the contextual and pragmatic differences between laboratory and classroom settings" (p. 2). For example, in laboratory studies, feedback is likely to be more directed at a participant, whereas in a classroom setting, there are numerous distractions and feedback may be directed toward one student only with others being just observers (e.g., Mackey, 1999). The definition provided by Lyster et al. is limiting in that lab-based research may involve multiple participants, not just two, as they suggested. In another description of classroom research, Williams (2012) helpfully points out that classroom research involves these characteristics: (a) the purpose is educational, (b) an instructor is present, and (c) more than one learner is present. More recently, Plonsky (personal communication, July 26, 2018) reports operationalizing classroom-based research or lab-based research for purposes of meta-analysis studies as depending on whether the studies were conducted with or without intact classes, regardless of physical location. This operationalization allows for the inclusion of computer-mediated instruction (CMC) studies in the category of classroom-based even though the research is not carried out in a physical classroom.

In contrast to *classroom-based research*, the term *laboratory-based research* may conjure up images of researchers in white lab coats administering treatments to unwitting research subjects. The reality of lab-based research in instructed second language acquisition (ISLA) is much more mundane, and several aspects may not differ all that much from classroom research, as we discuss below. There are some characteristics that clearly differentiate classroom-based research and lab-based research, but there are others where it is best to think of lab-based and classroom-based research existing on a continuum, with one critical feature being the amount of control the researcher has over the research context (e.g., Lyster & Saito, 2010; Mackey, 2012). In classroom-based research, researchers often do little, if anything, to manipulate the classroom context, often investigating the interaction and corrective feedback that occurs naturally between teachers and students (e.g., Brown, 2016). Alternatively, researchers might minimally ask teachers to provide corrective feedback either as teachers deem fit, or on specific linguistic items or in a specific way (e.g.,

Sato & Loewen, 2018). In this way, classroom-based studies need not be exclusively observational or descriptive. However, the more control researchers exert over the instructional context, the less the research context can be considered a naturally occurring classroom.

In contrast, in lab-based research, researchers attempt to control multiple aspects of the research context, including the type(s) of corrective feedback that are provided to learners (e.g., recasts, metalinguistic comments, comprehension checks), the activities that are used (e.g., tasks that are one-way versus two-way, closed versus open), the timing of the corrective feedback (immediately following an incorrect utterance versus delayed feedback), the target of the corrective feedback (e.g., phonology, morphosyntax, vocabulary), and the interactional patterns between or among classroom participants.

Another important feature to consider in lab-based research is the difference between the research context and the learners' regular instructional context. The significance of this difference comes from the likely possibility that novel activities or instructional contexts may cause learners to behave and react differently than they would in their day-to-day classes (e.g., Gass & Mackey, 2007). For example, assume a research project in which an instructor wants to understand the nature of corrective feedback in peer interaction. One way of collecting appropriate data would be through the use of a dictogloss (e.g., Swain & Lapkin, 2000). However, if students had never participated in a dictogloss before, their behavior might be different from what it would be if this pedagogical practice had been a regular part of their classroom activities (cf. Gass & Plough, 1993). Thus, any oral corrective feedback that is administered might be perceived differently by learners, and thus might have a different effect on their second language (L2) development. Similarly, if learners are not used to engaging in communicative tasks during their regular classroom activities but, instead, are typically exposed to decontextualized grammar activities and explicit metalinguistic instruction, it will be difficult for researchers to determine if any treatment effects are due to the novelty of the research conditions or the corrective feedback itself.

This effect of research context is especially important for corrective feedback research because of the importance of noticing, attention, and awareness in the effectiveness of different types of feedback (Gass & Mackey 2020; Schmidt, 1995, 2001). Being in a novel context outside of their regular classroom might cause learners to pay more attention to linguistic features that they might not have noticed if the same interaction had occurred during normal classroom activities. In those different settings, there is a heightened awareness that something "different" is taking place which in turn may lead to the so-called Halo effect whereby a participant is trying to give the researcher what the participant thinks he or she wants. In order to please the researcher, the participant needs to figure out what it is that is being looked at. Trying to figure out the focus of the research necessitates a heightened awareness of what the study is about.

The act of interacting with a researcher or research assistant one-on-one outside of the classroom may be very daunting for learners. First, there is the fact that the researcher or assistant is typically not known to the learner. This unfamiliarity might result in two, not mutually exclusive, possibilities. First, learners might be very nervous speaking in the target language with a stranger, especially if they come from classes in which communicative tasks are not a regular part of the curriculum. Therefore, learners might be more hesitant to speak; their fluency, in such instances, is affected. As noted above, research participants often act differently in order to please the researcher (see discussion of the Halo and Hawthorne effects in Gass & Mackey, 2016). Even though learners might not know the purpose of the research, they might engage in behaviors that they imagine the researcher is looking for. Thus, they might pay closer attention to the accuracy of their language production or use less common vocabulary items than they ordinarily would in their regular classroom. One reason for this is because they may be eager to impress the researcher by showing their high level of proficiency. In general, they feel positive about being a participant in a research project (Hawthorne effect).

Thus far, we have identified characteristics of lab-based studies. We now turn to distinguishing them from classroom-based studies. We recognize that the issues discussed are not unique to corrective feedback research; rather, they are relevant to any discussion of research conducted in labs and classrooms.

Distinguishing Lab-Based from Classroom-Based Studies

As mentioned earlier, there are clearly studies that are lab-based and others that are classroom-based. In general, it is useful to think of distinguishing these two by a set of initial questions. These represent ways in which classroom versus lab studies have been distinguished, some of which are implied in the definition by Lyster et al. (2013). This is illustrated in Figure 6.1.

Throughout this section we focus on three characteristics: physical location, interlocutor/instructor, instructional tasks. Considering Figure 6.1, the questions are ordered in such a way that the physical location is dominant, although we also believe that this may not be the most interesting division for understanding the classroom. It is for this reason that further questions must be asked. A second question to be asked is who is providing the instruction. Is it the regular teacher or has a researcher been inserted into the classroom? If the latter, is this a truly accurate description of what happens normally in that particular classroom? A third question that needs to be asked is the question of task. Does the task itself interrupt the

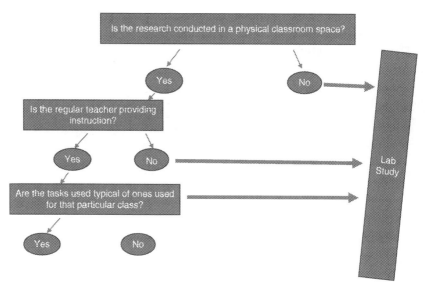

Figure 6.1 Defining lab studies

normal procedures and expectations of the classroom? Implied in questions two and three is the further question of the behavior of the teacher. Is it altered as a result of the experiment? For example, is he or she intentionally providing a particular type of feedback? This set of questions is useful in distinguishing many instances of classroom- versus laboratory-based research. However, it portrays this genre of research as dichotomous, and even the two names suggest a dichotomy. Unfortunately, it belies the true nature of this research which often includes elements of both.

Another way of thinking of the classroom versus lab distinction is to view certain aspects as a continuum. This view provides a clearer understanding of the appropriate ways to describe behaviors that take place in classrooms. For example, a classroom where the regular instructor changes his or her behavior minimally (e.g., focusing on extensive recast usage on a particular grammatical structure when recasts are a part of the instructor's normal repertoire) is quite different from a classroom where a "stranger" (researcher) provides the instruction and does an activity (e.g., a spot-the-difference task) that has never been done before.

Loewen and Philp (2012) provide a useful way of distinguishing among different types of classroom-based research: (a) observational, (b) noninterventionist quasi-experimental, (c) interventionist quasi-experimental, and (d) action research. We focus on (b) and (c) because they differ in the important dimensions of control and manipulation that take place in setting up the research. In a noninterventionist approach, the researcher does not make any "attempt to manipulate the variables that are of interest to the researcher" (p. 58). In other words, the attempt is to collect naturalistic classroom data. On the other side are interventionist studies. In these studies, the researcher makes a priori decisions about the classroom to be investigated. For example, she or he decides what will be tested and measured and how such measurement will take place; she or he decides what types of structures (phonological, lexical morphosyntactic) will be targeted; and she or he decides what the intervention will be and what the timing of the intervention will be. These studies may or may not be reflective of typical classroom activities.

In sum, there are features of research methodology that can be viewed on a continuum, with research in intact, regularly occurring classrooms with no researcher manipulation on one end of the continuum. On the other end, there is lab-based research with researchers tightly controlling the research context, which was explicitly created for the research study. Within the continuum, studies might have more or less of the extreme components of either type of research. Figure 6.2 is a revised version of what was presented in Figure 6.1 (which provided a typical view of the classroom versus lab dichotomy).

Figure 6.2 represents an attempt to consider a more elaborated view of what has typically been a dichotomous perspective of lab versus classroom research. We propose three types of study environments (lab, interventionist classroom, noninterventionist classroom). The first question that is still asked is about the context, but here we bring in the notion of an intact class and we ask if one is being used. If the

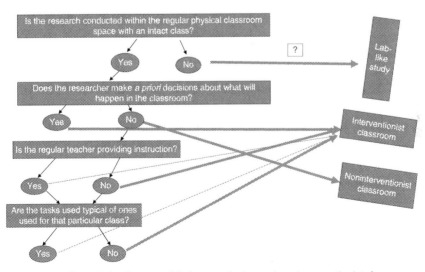

Figure 6.2 Differentiating between lab, interventionist, and noninterventionist classroom studies

answer is "yes," it is in the classroom category and additional questions are posed; if no, it is a lab-like study. The question mark ("?") indicates a "fuzzy" situation in which participants may be recruited for a specific purpose, although an existing class is not being used. This is considered a classroom quasi-experimental study and could fall into either a lab-like or, depending on the circumstances, a classroom study. The next question addresses the level of control that a researcher exerts over the study. Here, the answer determines whether it is an interventionist or a noninterventionist study. If the answer is "yes," it is classified as an interventionist study; if the answer is "no," additional questions are asked. The next question addresses the instructor and is asked only if the prior question was in the negative because a "yes" response to the question about control has already indicated that the study is an interventionist study. Both "yes" and "no" responses are suggestive of interventionist studies although the thickness of the lines also suggests that those that have a different instructor reflect studies where the researcher has greater control than those where the regular instructor is in place. Regardless of the response, further elaboration is needed to fully understand the type of research and to determine the degree of manipulation by the researcher. Again, the line width suggests that if the answer is "yes," there is less control than when the answer is "no." In other words, the thick lines indicate greater intervention. By bringing in the distinction between interventionist and noninterventionist classroom studies, we are better able to conceptualize the continuous nature of corrective feedback studies from lab- to classroom-based. This is illustrated in Table 6.1, where manipulation of the environment becomes primary in understanding the types of research that are relevant to the classroom.

As discussed above, there are three characteristics that we have identified as being the most salient with regard to distinguishing lab-based and

Table 6.1 *Manipulation in lab and classroom research*

		Manipulation	
		Yes	No
Lab study		✓	✓
Classroom intervention study			
	space	✓	
	Instructor	✓	
	Task	✓	
Classroom nonintervention			
	Space		✓
	Instructor		✓
	Task		✓

both types of classroom-based studies (interventionist and noninterventionist) from one another:

The Physical Location of the Research

The actual physical space in which the research is conducted is important when comparing classroom and laboratory studies. The more removed the research context is from participants' regularly occurring classrooms, the more lab-like the study will be. If participants are taken from their own regular classroom to a nearby room, the space may still be familiar to them. However, learners might also be requested to come to a location they have never been to before, such as the researcher's office or a room, perhaps in another building, that is specifically designated for research. This unfamiliarity might heighten learners' feelings of nervousness and anxiety, which may affect their interactional patterns and their attention to corrective feedback. Toward the middle of the classroom/laboratory continuum is research that is conducted in participants' regular classroom space, but the researcher exerts control over different aspects of the instruction. This, in our view, is an interventionist classroom study and has characteristics of both pure lab studies and pure classroom studies. Finally, it is also important to point out that not all naturally occurring L2 classes occur within the four walls of a physical classroom. Virtual classrooms are becoming more common, including classrooms that rely on written and audiovisual CMC, and three-dimensional virtual learning environments (e.g., Hartwick, 2018). The difference between lab-based and classroom-based studies extends to this context. Research done in preexisting, intact online classes constitutes classroom-based research, while online contexts that are arranged specifically for research are lab-based. Even though online classes do not have four walls, we place them in the same category as those that do given their other characteristics (e.g., a regular teacher with a steady group of students who are meeting virtually rather than face-to-face).

The Interlocutor

Lab-based research often involves researchers or their proxy taking over the role of teacher in order to provide the treatment consistently and in accordance with the goals of the research. This is so because the regular teacher often will not have the research goal as primary during the lesson given his or her general daily classroom responsibilities. Researchers can be more focused in carrying out the research as planned. Additionally, researchers might bring in other interlocutors, such as native speakers of the target language, who otherwise would not be in the classroom. Again, the lack of familiarity with the interlocutor can influence the dynamics of the interaction. Regular classroom teachers might also be involved in research that could be considered lab-based, if they engage in interactional patterns that are not normally part of their regular classroom. For example, researchers might train teachers to provide specific types of corrective feedback.

In addition to the researcher or teacher, participants often interact with other students. In some research studies, participants might interact with their regular classmates. However, in some lab-based research, students may be brought in from multiple classes, or even noninstructional contexts. For example, researchers might want to find out the effects of interacting with first language (L1) speakers. Typically, there is only one L1 speaker, if any, in the classroom, namely the teacher. Therefore, if researchers want to investigate interaction with L1 speakers, they must constitute some type of artificial context for the interaction. Similarly, learners are typically grouped in classes according to proficiency levels. Thus, if researchers want to investigate the effects of interaction and the provision of feedback to and by learners of differing proficiency levels, then they need to do so in a lab-based context. Similarly, learners are also typically grouped by age, especially during their primary, secondary, and to a lesser extent, tertiary education. If researchers want to examine the effects of age on interaction and the provision of feedback, then they need to bring learners of different ages together in a nonclassroom environment.

The Instructional Tasks

In many cases, researchers use specific instructional tasks and activities to induce certain types of interaction and/or to elicit specific linguistic structures that are the target of the research study. In some cases, the types of activities might be familiar to participants, but at other times, the activities, especially if they are communicative tasks, might be noticeably different from instruction that focuses more on the development of explicit knowledge about the target language. The novelty of the tasks might make participants behave differently during the interaction. Participants may be uncomfortable with communicative tasks if they are not used to conversing in the L2. Again, participants might also pay more attention to the language that is being used during these unfamiliar tasks.

When considering corrective feedback, or other targeted pedagogical interventions, the distinction between lab-based and classroom-based studies is not easy. We have argued that there are many different types of studies that have corrective feedback as their focus. What is more important in understanding the differences is how much deviation there is from what happens on a day-to-day basis in the classroom. We turn now to examples of corrective feedback lab-based studies.

Examples of Lab-Based Studies

This section examines exemplar corrective feedback studies that manipulated the features of lab-based research to varying degrees. Perhaps the clearest example of lab-based research is that of researchers bringing together learners from different classes. The regular teacher is not the interlocutor, and the participants are engaged in a task that is not familiar to them. In this regard, Lee and Lyster's (2017) study might be a quintessential example of a lab-based corrective feedback study. Participants for the study came from "private or university language institutions" (p. 375), meaning that they were not all from the same intact classroom. Subsequently, participants were randomly assigned to one of five groups, each with a different type of corrective feedback. Each participant engaged in a computer-assisted perception training session that targeted two pairs of English vowels. Learners' errors in perception were provided with a specific type of feedback by the computer program. Thus, almost every aspect of the research study was controlled and manipulated by the researchers. Although Lee and Lyster did not describe their research as lab-based, they did mention that it would be interesting to replicate the study "with different learning contexts, such as laboratory versus classroom settings" (p. 389). However, they did not provide suggestions for research designs in these different contexts. In fact, it seems that the parameters of the study would need to be altered significantly for the study to be conducted in a classroom context due to the provision of computer-based feedback.

A slightly less controlled option for lab-based studies is to have either pairs or small groups of learners come out of class to engage in treatment activities. In this case, learners typically have one or more individuals with whom they are familiar to help ameliorate some of the anxiety they might feel if they were to interact with the researcher one-on-one. Additionally, although they might not be in their own classroom, learners might be in a location that is familiar to them. However, the rest of the research study might still be strictly controlled by the researcher. One study that was conducted in this fashion is Loewen and Nabei (2007), who had groups of four learners leave the classroom to engage in interactive tasks with a researcher. The groups were randomly assigned one of four conditions: (a) recasts, (b) elicitations, (c) metalinguistic information, (d) task only. In addition, one group of students was left to do their regular classroom activities and thus served as a control group. Even though the participants were interacting in groups with other students from their class, they were outside of their regular classroom, and they were engaging in tasks that had been designed to target specific linguistic features, namely English question formation. Thus, the context was still fairly removed from their regular classroom.

A slightly different approach to a lab study was conducted by Gass, Mackey, and Ross-Feldman (2005, 2011). Their manipulation involved only the physical location given earlier arguments questioning the relevance of lab studies to the classroom context. Their participants came from four intact classes of third-semester Spanish, divided into two groups: classroom and lab. The classroom group, in our scheme, was an intervention study. As in Loewen and Nabei's (2007) study, the difference was the physical location where the interaction took place and who was describing to the students what had to be done: in the classroom group, it was the teacher and in the lab group, it was the research assistant.

The examples so far have been of research that takes students out of their physical classroom and locates them physically in a different space. Indeed, the terms classroom-based and lab-based research typically raise notions of different physical locations in which the research is conducted. However, if a characteristic of lab-based research is how much control the researcher exerts on the context, then it is also possible to consider instances in which the researcher takes over a preexisting, intact class for research purposes. In this case, it is not the physical location that is changed, nor are participants interacting with learners who are unfamiliar to them. However, obviously, teachers have a profound impact on their learners, and replacing the regular teacher with a researcher may again cause learners to behave in ways that are different from their regular classroom routine. Thus, such types of studies fall somewhere in the middle of the lab-based/classroom-based continuum. One such study is Ellis, Loewen and Erlam (2006), which provided different types of feedback, namely recasts and metalinguistic feedback, to students in intact classes. Although the types of tasks were considered to be familiar to the students, a researcher led the tasks and provided the corrective feedback according to the assigned type. Thus, it was not the students' regular teacher who was interacting with them or providing the feedback. On the one hand, this arrangement ensured that the desired type of feedback was given to the participants; additionally, it removed the teacher as a source of variability in the study. If different classroom teachers gave different types of feedback, it would not be clear if it was the teacher or the feedback that was most important. On the other hand, the participants' lack of familiarity with the researcher might have affected their interactional patterns during the tasks.

Another study that could be considered interventionist but took place in intact classrooms is Sato and Loewen (2018). In this study, the researchers asked teachers in English L2 classes in a Chilean university to provide a specific type of oral corrective feedback (either input-providing or output-prompting) in addition to metacognitive instruction. The researchers first observed several classes to select teachers who naturally provided corrective feedback to their learners. Then, the researchers asked the teachers to provide their preferred type of feedback to learner errors on English third person -s and possessive determiner pronouns (*his* and *her*). Compared to other studies, the intervention was minimal; however, the researchers were still attempting to control specific aspects of the classroom interaction for research purposes.

Comparing Lab-Based and Classroom-Based Studies

It is clear that different research studies can be classified as more classroom-like or more lab-like, but it is important to consider whether these distinctions influence the findings of research studies on corrective feedback. There have been few individual studies that have directly compared the two contexts; however, one exception is Gass, Mackey, and Ross-Feldman (2005) who investigated the differences between tasks conducted in a "typical foreign language classroom and a typical interaction laboratory experiment, with a comparable population" (p. 597). Participants in the classroom condition worked in dyads to complete "the tasks during regular class time in their classroom with their regular instructor" (p. 583). The teacher presented the tasks as part of regular classroom instruction, and then walked around the classroom monitoring the groups. Participants in the laboratory condition "completed the tasks in a laboratory setting with a research assistant" (p. 584). The research assistant, who was a native speaker, read the instructions to each dyad as they came for the task. The research assistant left the room after the task directions had been clarified. Gass et al. (2005) found that "there were very few differences in the classroom and laboratory contexts in terms of interactional features" (p. 597).

However, in spite of the fact that few studies have directly compared the two contexts, several corrective feedback meta-analyses have included research context as one of the factors that they investigated. For example, Russell and Spada (2006) conducted a meta-analysis with fifteen corrective feedback studies. Six were considered lab-based, and nine were classroom-based, although Russell and Spada did not detail how they operationalized classroom versus laboratory. The meta-analysis showed that both laboratory and classroom studies had large effects for L2 development, but the two contexts were not significantly different from each other.

In another meta-analysis of interaction research, Mackey and Goo (2007) also examined the difference between classroom and laboratory studies. Again, no explicit operationalization of the two contexts was included in the study. Mackey and Goo found that out of twenty-eight studies, only 36 percent were conducted in classrooms, leaving 64 percent that were laboratory-based. Results of the comparison showed that interaction in lab-based research studies had significantly larger effect sizes on immediate, short delayed, and long delayed post-tests; however, Mackey and Goo suggest caution when considering the differences in the short and long delayed post-tests due to the low number of studies with such tests. In terms of explaining these results, Mackey and Goo (2007) state that "experimental research often involves dyadic interactions which are arguably free from many of the distractions and the wide variety of linguistic issues which occur in classrooms" (p. 415).

Li's (2010) meta-analysis also investigated the differences between lab-based and classroom-based studies of corrective feedback. Of the thirty-three studies included in his meta-analysis, 55 percent were lab-based, 33 percent were classroom-based, and 12 percent were conducted in small groups. Although Li did not specify his inclusion criteria for what constituted lab or classroom studies, he did provide a post hoc list of characteristics that differed between the two contexts. For example, lab-based studies typically involved "dyadic interaction between a native speaker and a nonnative speaker" (p. 332); consequently, corrective feedback was directed at individual learners. In addition, Li found that lab-based treatments tended to last less than 50 minutes. In contrast, classroom-based research studies were generally conducted with small groups of participants and feedback was intended for the whole class or group. Furthermore, treatments tended to be longer than 50 minutes. The results of Li's meta-analysis showed that lab-based studies had a significantly higher effect size than classroom or group studies; however, no significant difference was found between classroom and group studies. Li attributed the larger effects for lab-based studies on the fact that there is less distraction in the lab compared to the classroom; furthermore, corrective feedback provided in the lab is directed at individual learners, whereas in the classroom, corrective feedback is often provided to the entire class, which may make it less salient to individual learners. Li suggests that the quality of treatment might also be better in the lab because "in the laboratory, distraction is minimized and instructional interventions can be better implemented than in the classroom" (p. 316).

In summary, it appears that lab-based corrective feedback studies might be more likely to provide evidence for the effectiveness of corrective feedback (e.g., Li, 2010; Mackey & Goo, 2007), but that is not to say that classroom studies have not also found feedback to be effective. At least a few studies (e.g., Gass et al., 2005; Russell & Spada, 2006) suggest that the effects of interaction and corrective feedback may not be different in the lab and classroom. In coming to this conclusion, it is important to note the difficulties that Plonsky and Brown (2015) point to when drawing conclusions from meta-analytic studies regarding feedback. In particular, they note that the search techniques are not uniform across studies and there are different definitions of the domain known as corrective feedback. Finally, meta-analytic effects vary across subdomains (e.g., pronunciation instruction, grammar instruction) (see Chapter 8, this volume).

Calls for Future Research

In light of these conflicting findings, it is important to consider how future research might clarify the effects of lab-based and classroom-based research. One reason for the ambiguity of research findings is that the differences between the two contexts is often not clearly operationalized. Individual studies sometimes do not self-identify as either lab-based or classroom-based, making it unclear as to how different meta-analyses decide on inclusion criteria. However, it is also the case that the difference between lab-based and classroom-based research is not a dichotomy, but a continuum, with some studies being more or less lab-like. Instead, future research would do well to consider the degree to which the amount of control and manipulation exerted by the researcher on the context of the research study might affect the results. In many cases, researchers do describe the contexts of their studies: the physical location of the research, the interlocutors, and the types of tasks. Still, there should be an acknowledgment that some purported lab-based studies might not be all that different from classroom-based studies. Additionally, researchers in some supposed classroom-based studies might come very close to the control that is present in a lab-based study. In fact, Loewen and Philp (2012) use the terms interventionist and noninterventionist research, instead of lab-based or classroom-based research to better capture the amount of control that researchers exert on the details of the study.

Additionally, there are few studies that have directly compared the two contexts; rather, it has been left to meta-analyses to explore any differences. Designing corrective feedback research that clearly identifies the characteristics of classroom- and lab-based research and that can be conducted and compared in both settings is important for understanding the effects of each research context. For example, researchers could vary different aspects of lab-based and classroom-based research to address questions like the following:

- Does it make a difference if the regular teacher or a researcher provides the corrective feedback to an intact class?
- Does the physical location of the research, either in students' regular classroom or a specially designated research space, affect students' interactional behavior and the effects of feedback?
- What is the effect of students engaging in activities that are similar to or different from their regularly occurring classroom activities?
- What is the difference between interaction and corrective feedback in regularly occurring virtual classrooms compared to groups of learners placed together in a virtual space for research purposes?

Even though lab-based research might not be entirely similar to classroom-based research, it does not mean that research from the lab is uninformative about the effects of corrective feedback. Rather it is the case that the lab-based context may not provide as accurate a picture of how corrective feedback works when certain factors are not manipulated, which is typically the case when teachers and learners go about their everyday business in the classroom. Mackey (2017) states, "While [laboratory] studies offer important scientific advantages, much real-world language learning does not occur in laboratories, but in authentic contexts... In order to better understand the relationship between instructional methods, materials, treatments, and second language learning outcomes, research needs to be carried out with the instructional settings where learning occurs" (p. 541).

Corrective feedback researchers will continue to investigate the factors that make feedback more or less effective. Lab-based studies can provide a degree of control that might help isolate the effects of specific feedback features. However, it would be useful to follow up lab-based studies with classroom studies to determine if the effects found in more controlled environments are also found in contexts in which individuals actually engage in L2 learning. By gradually reducing the amount of control exerted in corrective feedback studies, researchers can better tease apart the important and impactful characteristics of each research context.

References

Brown, D. (2016). The type and linguistic foci of oral corrective feedback in the L2 classroom. *Language Teaching Research, 20*(4), 436–458.

Eckerth, J. (2009). Negotiated interaction in the L2 classroom. *Language Teaching, 42*(1), 109–130.

Ellis, R., Loewen, S. & Erlam, R. (2006). Implicit and explicit corrective feedback and the acquisition of L2 grammar. *Studies in Second Language Acquisition, 28*(2), 339–368.

Foster, P. (1998). A classroom perspective on the negotiation of meaning. *Applied Linguistics, 19*(1), 1–23.

Gass, S., & Mackey, A. (2020). In VanPatten, W., Keating, G., & Wulff, S. Theories of second language acquisition: An introduction (3rd ed.) (pp. 192–222). New York: Routledge.

Gass, S. M. & Mackey, A. (2007). *Data elicitation for second and foreign language research.* Mahwah, NJ: Lawrence Erlbaum.

(2016). *Second language research: Methodology and design.* New York: Routledge.

(2020). Input, interaction, and output in second language acquisition. In B. VanPatten, G. Keating & S. Wulff (eds.), *Theories in second language acquisition: An Introduction* (3rd ed., pp. 192–222). New York: Routledge.

Gass, S., Mackey, A. & Ross-Feldman, L. (2005). Task-based interactions in classroom and laboratory settings. *Language Learning*, 55(4), 575–611.
   (2011). Task-based interactions in classroom and laboratory settings. *Language Learning*, 61(S1), 189–220.
Gass, S. & Plough, I. (1993). Interlocutor and task familiarity: Effects on interactional structure. In S. Gass & G. Crookes (eds.), *Tasks and language learning: Integrating theory and practice* (pp. 35–56). Clevedon: Multilingual Matters.
Hartwick, P. (2018). Investigating research approaches: Classroom-based interaction studies in physical and virtual contexts. *ReCALL*, 30(2), 161–176.
Lee, A. H. & Lyster, R. (2017). Can corrective feedback on second language speech perception errors affect production accuracy? *Applied Psycholinguistics*, 38(2), 371–393.
Li, S. (2010). The effectiveness of corrective feedback in SLA: A meta-analysis. *Language Learning*, 60(2), 309–365.
Loewen, S. & Nabei, T. (2007). The effect of oral corrective feedback on implicit and explicit L2 knowledge. In A. Mackey (ed.), *Conversational interaction and second language acquisition: A series of empirical studies* (pp. 361–378). Oxford: Oxford University Press.
Loewen, S. & Philp, J. (2012). Instructed second language acquisition. In A. Mackey & S. M. Gass (eds.), *Research methods in second language acquisition: A practical guide* (pp. 53–73). Malden, MA: Wiley-Blackwell.
Loewen, S. & Sato, M. (2018). State-of-the-art article: Interaction and instructed second language acquisition. *Language Teaching*, 51(3), 285–329.
Lyster, R. & Saito, K. (2010). Oral feedback in classroom SLA: A meta-analysis. *Studies in Second Language Acquisition*, 32(2), 265–302.
Lyster, R., Saito, K. & Sato, M. (2013). Oral corrective feedback in second language classrooms. *Language Teaching*, 46(1), 1–40.
Mackey, A. (1999). Input, interaction, and second language development: An empirical study of question formation in ESL. *Studies in Second Language Acquisition*, 21(4), 557–587.
   (2012). Input, interaction, and corrective feedback in L2 learning. Oxford: Oxford University Press.
   (2017). Classroom-based research. In S. Loewen & M. Sato (eds.), *The Routledge handbook of instructed second language acquisition* (pp. 541–561). New York: Routledge.
Mackey, A., Fujii, A., Biesenbach-Lucas, S., Weger, H., Jacobsen, N., Fogle, L., Lake, J., Sondermann, K., Tagarelli, K., Tsujita, M., Watanabe, A., Abbuhl, R. & Kim, K. (2013). Tasks and traditional practice activities in a foreign language context. In K. McDonough & A. Mackey (eds.), *Second language interaction in diverse educational contexts* (pp. 71–87). Philadelphia: John Benjamins.

Mackey, A. & Goo, J. (2007). Interaction research in SLA: A meta-analysis and research synthesis. In A. Mackey (ed.), *Conversational interaction in second language acquisition: A collection of empirical studies* (pp. 407–449). Oxford: Oxford University Press.

Plonsky, L. & Brown, D. (2015). Domain definition and search techniques in meta-analyses of L2 research (Or why 18 meta-analyses of feedback have different results). *Second Language Research*, 31(2), 267–278.

Russell, J. & Spada, N. (2006). The effectiveness of corrective feedback for the acquisition of L2 grammar: A meta-analysis of the research. In J. Norris & L. Ortega (eds.), *Synthesizing research on language learning and teaching* (pp. 133–164). Philadelphia: John Benjamins.

Sato, M. & Loewen, S. (2018). Metacognitive instruction enhances the effectiveness of corrective feedback: Variable effects of feedback types and linguistic targets. *Language Learning*, 68(2), 507–545. DOI: 10.1111/lang.12283.

Schmidt, R. (1995). *Attention and awareness in foreign language learning*. Honolulu: University of Hawai'i Press.

(2001). Attention. In P. Robinson (ed.), *Cognition and second language instruction* (pp. 3–32). Cambridge: Cambridge University Press.

Swain, M. & Lapkin, S. (2000). Task-based second language learning: The uses of the first language. *Language Teaching Research*, 4(3), 251–274.

Williams, J. (2012). Classroom research. In S. M. Gass & A. Mackey (eds.), *The Routledge handbook of second language acquisition* (pp. 541–554). New York: Routledge.

7

Classroom-Based Research in Corrective Feedback

Antonella Valeo

Introduction

For many teachers and learners, corrective feedback is a defining feature of the language classroom. The practice of corrective feedback has been an area of intense interest for researchers as well. For both teachers and researchers, the classroom is the focal point for learning and teaching and presents an opportunity to investigate pedagogical questions in the context of teaching and learning. Classroom-based research is carried out in intact classrooms constructed by and existing within a community that includes learners, teachers, program developers, administrators, and numerous other stakeholders invested in the activity. Within the classroom, corrective feedback is one of many instructional strategies provided alongside a range of other strategies embedded within variable unpredictable classroom environments. The context of this classroom environment is an important dimension of corrective feedback practice and is increasingly being recognized as an important consideration for researchers. Contextual factors influence the results but are not always accounted for in the design of the study, the analysis, or the discussion, making it difficult to compare findings across studies.

Researchers and scholars in second language acquisition have, over the years, called for attention to context in research in general and corrective feedback research in particular (e.g., Allwright, 1975; Bastone, 2002; Ferris, 2009, 2012; Storch, 2010). The term "context," however, is used broadly to include many different aspects of the classroom that shape conditions for teaching and learning. Context can be considered on a macro or micro level. The macro context is shaped by the community outside the classroom, such as the linguistic setting (e.g., ESL vs. EFL), institutional policies and practices, and the sociopolitical landscape in education and language. All these factors exert an influence on what goes on inside the classroom for teachers and learners. Micro-level contextual factors are embedded within curriculum at the lesson and program level, and reflected in classroom interaction between and among teachers and learners.

Classroom-based research is best positioned to examine the micro and macro contextual factors that moderate and shape the experience of teaching and learning. Researchers choose a classroom setting, or they may choose to carry out research outside the classroom in conditions that are considered to be laboratory settings. The most common distinction is that laboratory-based studies usually take place outside of the classroom in a setting created by the researcher; learners and teachers are invited to step into a setting created by the researcher in order to investigate research questions, whereas in classroom-based research, the researcher reaches out to teachers and is invited to step into the classroom community. There has been much debate and discussion about the relative benefits and challenges of research conducted in laboratory settings versus classroom settings. Some researchers have raised questions about the degree to which findings from research carried out in laboratory settings can be applied to classroom practice (e.g., Foster, 1998). Others have highlighted the benefit of being able to control conditions of the learning and teaching context in laboratory settings, helping to ensure "rigour" in experimental research (e.g., Hulstijn, 1997) and avoid the "distraction" of the classroom. A more in-depth discussion of laboratory research is included in Chapter 6 of this volume. The focus of this chapter is on classroom-based research, carried out in *intact* classrooms created for teaching and learning outside of a research agenda.

In this chapter, I will draw on selected studies to describe how research carried out in classrooms has contributed to our understanding of corrective feedback. Specifically, the goal is to highlight how classroom context has and continues to play a role in the questions we ask as researchers, the studies we design, and what the findings may mean to us as teachers and researchers. The scope of this chapter does not allow for a comprehensive review of the literature, nor for a discussion of a full range of contextual features. I will draw on studies that illustrate how contextual features have emerged and played a role in how we understand corrective feedback through classroom-based research. I will also explore what characterizes the classroom context and how the notion of the classroom as language learning and teaching *in situ* has become increasingly complex.

Classroom-Based Research: What Do We Know?

Contextual factors in classroom-based research have generally been either ignored, treated as a complication, or investigated as a feature of interest. The same is true of research in corrective feedback where a range of contextual features have emerged in both descriptive and experimental studies carried out in intact classrooms, on both a macro and a micro level. While individual learner differences are embedded within the micro context and play a role, there is a large body of research that addresses the role of individual differences in second language learning. Within the scope of this chapter, I will highlight some of these differences.

Observing the Classroom "in Action": Descriptive Studies

Descriptive studies are ideally situated to classroom-based research approaches. In such studies, researchers observe and document classroom interaction, allowing them to see the "real" classroom "in action." Well-designed descriptive studies can help us to understand the classroom in ways that are genuine to the teacher and learner experience and to lay the groundwork to ask about the relationship between learning and teaching. Data from classroom observations can be analyzed qualitatively, describing classroom interaction, events, and behaviors, or quantitatively, in which the same behaviors are coded and "measured" to determine how frequently one strategy or behavior occurs in relation to other events in the classroom.

Early classroom-based studies, though not concerned exclusively with corrective feedback, drew attention to classroom interaction as a feature of the micro context by highlighting the complexity of teacher and learner behavior in the classroom (e.g., Allwright, 1975; Chaudron, 1977). In corrective feedback specifically, a highly influential study of this kind was carried out by Lyster and Ranta (1997) who drew on classroom observations in an attempt to understand how teachers provided corrective feedback and how learners responded. They identified a number of corrective feedback strategies used by the teacher and created a typology of feedback types. They observed that while teachers provided corrective feedback using a range of different strategies, there was a strong preference for the use of a specific type: *recasts*, a strategy in which the teacher provides feedback by reformulating the learner's error correctly, with no explicit reference or indication of the error. They also observed that learners responded to recasts less often than to other types of corrective feedback. This early work by Lyster and Ranta provided a foundation from which to ask questions about what type of corrective feedback to use, when, how, and under what conditions; it also encouraged other researchers to examine how teachers and learners use corrective feedback in other contexts, in both classroom-based and laboratory settings.

Out of Lyster and Ranta's typology of strategies, recasts attracted intense interest on the part of researchers and became a focal point for further investigation. As a corrective feedback strategy deeply embedded in classroom interaction it also highlighted the role of context. Lyster and Ranta (1997) conducted their research in a French immersion program in

Canada, a content-based program in which curriculum and teaching focused heavily, if not exclusively, on content meaning rather than language form. The distinct nature of this setting cannot be overstated. Early research by Swain (1985) drew attention to the nature of classroom discourse in such programs, specifically French immersion programs for children in Canada. Her work showed that a concern for content over language form often dominated instruction and therefore classroom interaction. Today, it is widely recognized that a content-based program that includes both a focus on subject matter and language as in an immersion program will often encourage a very different focus for both teachers and learners from one in which content is secondary to language (see Nicholas, Lightbown & Spada, 2001).

Lyster and Ranta's study encouraged researchers to explore how contextual features such as curriculum and program might play a role in how teachers and learners use corrective feedback, specifically recasts. Pica (2002), for example, observed similar patterns in theme-based programs for adults in a university setting. In both settings the relationship between content and language had a significant impact on teacher–student interactions. Researchers carried out observational studies in a range of other contexts to see if the same patterns emerged. Some studies carried out in diverse contexts have echoed the findings of the original study, including a study carried out in an adult ESL program in Canada (Panova & Lyster, 2002), a study with secondary school students studying English in Hong Kong (Tsang, 2004), and another in an academic ESL program in an American university (Lee, 2013). Like the study by Lyster and Ranta (1997), these investigations found that teachers used recasts more often than any other feedback strategy. However, how often learners responded to recasts by correcting themselves differed. Learners in the American ESL program (Lee, 2013) responded to recasts with self-correction and the learners in Hong Kong (Tsang, 2004) responded to neither recasts nor explicit correction.

A more nuanced understanding of context, however, emerged in other studies. For example, Lochtman (2002) examined how teachers teaching German as a Foreign Language in a school in Belgium used feedback in their classrooms. She compared this context to French immersion classrooms, and described the German foreign language context as "analytic" in that the focus was entirely on language and not on content. The findings showed that metalinguistic feedback, rather than recasts, was the type of feedback used most often by teachers. Interestingly, the teaching task was a consideration for teachers: they used recasts more often when engaged in comprehension, meaning-based activities, and metalinguistic feedback when they were engaged in structure-based activities.

Sheen (2004) took a closer look at the classroom context to examine how teachers' use of corrective feedback varied across four classroom contexts: Canadian French immersion with children; adults in English as a Second

Language (ESL) in Canada; ESL with young adults in New Zealand; and English as a Foreign Language (EFL) with adults in Korea. Sheen's findings confirmed that teachers across all four contexts tended to use recasts more often than other corrective feedback types. However, there were differences in how often students responded to teacher feedback provided in a recast. Students responded more often to recasts in the Korean and New Zealand context than in the Canadian contexts, and adults in the Canadian ESL context responded the least often. One suggestion was that the experiences and backgrounds of the learners may have been an important factor: learners in the Canadian ESL classroom had less experience with formal education than those in the New Zealand or Korean programs and as such were not as attuned to the teacher's behaviors when providing corrective feedback.

While such comparisons are valuable, other research has shown that they are not dichotomous in that immersion contexts are not monolithic and classroom discourse can vary considerably across programs that identify as immersion. Lyster and Mori (2006) compared the findings of the Canadian French immersion context with a Japanese immersion program in the United States. Both programs were content based and highly meaning focused, and in both contexts teachers used recasts more often than other types of corrective feedback. However, learner response to recasts differed: learners in the Japanese language classrooms responded to recasts more often than those in the French language classrooms. It was suggested that learners in the Japanese language classroom, despite the immersion context, were more oriented toward accuracy. A number of factors may have played a role. In this study, classroom observations documented that unlike the French language teachers, those in the Japanese context used repetition tasks in the classroom to address accuracy, which may have oriented the learners to attend to form despite the overall orientation of the program to meaning. Another suggestion considered the broader macro context in which these classrooms operated – the French language program operated in a French-speaking community, in the French-speaking province of Quebec, while the Japanese language program was situated in an English language majority context in the United States. Learners in French immersion had access to the language outside the classroom while the Japanese learners did not and as such needed to focus on accuracy during classroom time.

More recently, Llinares & Lyster (2014) examined corrective feedback across three programs that were all described as content oriented but in different instructional settings: French immersion in Canada, Japanese immersion in the United States, and content and language integrated learning (CLIL) English classes in Spain. They examined classroom discourse to understand how learners responded to corrective feedback by self-correcting or not. They found that learners differed in the degree to which they responded to different corrective feedback, including recasts, prompts (a corrective feedback strategy that provides a clue to encourage the learner to self-correct without providing a reformulation), and more explicit types of corrective feedback. Japanese immersion learners responded to all corrective feedback equally, CLIL learners responded best to recasts, and French immersion learners tended to ignore the recasts over prompts. The authors suggest the nature of recasts was mediated by the context, in that recasts can serve a conversational or didactic purpose in different classroom contexts. What precisely determines this is unclear. They point to the mediating role of teacher beliefs and experiences as they make pedagogical decisions that may prioritize content or language in their teaching and signal these as primary foci for the learners.

The "messaging" provided to learners by teachers can be influential even when it is not planned or explicitly acknowledged as part of a program. Interactional context within lessons has also emerged as a factor influencing how learners respond to corrective feedback, specifically the nature and focus of learner–teacher exchanges. In a study situated in ESL classes in an Australian secondary school, Oliver and Mackey (2003) observed that corrective feedback depended on the purpose of the exchange between learners and teachers. These exchanges included: classroom management, a focus on language, information about content, and general communication. Not surprisingly, teachers provided the least corrective feedback when engaged in classroom management and the most when focusing on language. However, recasts were used less in language-focused interaction than in any of the other three. The authors suggest a variety of reasons for this finding. Most importantly, however, this analysis of interaction within a lesson highlighted the importance of considering interactional context when analyzing and interpreting research findings.

Sometimes, however, descriptive research can be challenged by contextual factors that are unexpected, specifically from participants. For example, while classroom observation is often premised on the assumption that the researcher is an outsider who is unobtrusive and will not have an impact on the "natural" state of the classroom, there is evidence that teacher or learner behavior changes when they are aware of the research goals or activities; they may behave as they believe the researcher expects and provide the "right" outcomes. In a meta-analysis of twenty-eight studies on corrective feedback, Brown (2016) notes that when teachers were informed that the study investigated feedback, they provided 40 percent fewer recasts than when they were told the focus was interaction. Research in corrective feedback, in particular, may be susceptible to this effect: for students, corrective feedback tends to be a point of stress, as it indicates error and language struggle, and for teachers, it is often central to teaching activity.

"Testing" Learning and Teaching in the Classroom: Experimental Studies

Researchers may adopt an experimental design for a study when they want to test a theory or examine the impact of specific pedagogical strategies and approaches. Experimental designs are directed by a specific aim, and researchers may select an intact class in which to create specific teaching and learning conditions that will allow them to do this. Experimental studies often create teaching described as an "intervention" in which the researcher instructs the teacher or teachers as to what strategies to use with different classes or groups of learners. The researcher establishes a baseline of knowledge in a pre-test that carefully targets the goals of the instruction and determines learning outcomes with a post-test after the instruction has ended, sometimes followed by another (delayed) post-test to determine the extent to which learning gains have been retained. In corrective feedback, experimental studies explore both theoretical and pedagogical questions. The focus here will be on pedagogical questions.

A number of core pedagogical questions continue to be the focus of much experimental research, generally aimed at determining what type of feedback might be more effective than another and under what conditions. Increasingly, there has been greater interest in the "conditions" of this investigation. Overall, findings from experimental studies in the classroom have shown that a variety of corrective feedback strategies are effective *depending on* how a myriad of contextual factors interact with each other to have an impact on teaching and learning. This includes instructional setting, curriculum, program goals, and institutional constraints, all of which play a role in what happens in the classroom and, as such, the findings of corrective feedback research carried out in the classroom.

Meta-analyses help us understand findings across experimental studies and many also highlight the role of context in making these comparisons. One feature of the context that is often considered by researchers is the distinction between second and foreign language settings. How this aspect of setting plays a role, however, is still inconclusive and debated among researchers. For example, Li (2010) carried out a meta-analysis that included eleven classroom-based studies and found that the studies carried out in foreign language settings reported stronger language gains than those in second language contexts. The suggestion was that learners and teachers in foreign language settings were more oriented toward a focus on linguistic form. In contrast, Lyster and Saito (2010) examined fifteen classroom-based experimental studies and distinguished between those carried out in second and foreign language contexts. They found no significant differences: all three types of corrective feedback – recasts, prompts, and explicit feedback – had significant effects. They suggested, however, that the distinctions between the two settings may have been "too fluid" to yield clear findings (p. 292). A closer look shows that one of the studies (Dekeyser, 1993) classified as second language was with Dutch speakers learning French in the Dutch-speaking part of Belgium and another (Ammar & Spada, 2006) with French speakers learning English in Montreal, Canada.

It may be, then, that while this distinction between second and foreign language contexts is valuable, it is not as distinct as it may appear. Foreign and second language designations are determined by the sociopolitical framing of the teaching and learning context and the role of the particular language, as much as by the extent to which the target language is in the community. Socioeconomic, political, and historical contexts vary, as in the case of studying English in a country with a strongly homogenous language such as Japan, versus studying English in a former British colony such as Hong Kong. The English language, in particular, occupies very different sociopolitical spaces in different international contexts. French language education in Canada illustrates how this distinction can be complex. In Canadian French immersion classes, French might be considered a second language because it is one of the two official languages of Canada. Yet when French immersion is taught in Ontario, where English is a dominant language, there is little opportunity for learners to use it on a daily basis, much like a foreign language setting. Context then, whether it is described as foreign language, second language, immersion, or core, demands more nuanced interpretation.

In a number of studies, the tension between experimental research that assumes controlled conditions and the context of the classroom that is characterized by changing conditions has been well illustrated. Challenges can include somewhat "technical" challenges, such as when learners leave the course during the term and life of the research project, leaving the researcher with a reduced number of participants. They can also include the impact of "rogue" teachers who do not carry out the instruction as intended by the researcher. For example, in a study by Spada and Lightbown (1993), three experimental groups were taught by three different teachers. Two were assigned specific instructions to include form-focused instruction and corrective feedback, while the third was intended as a comparison group and not given any instructions. Based on extensive classroom observation in the program, the researchers had concluded that error correction and explicit instruction were rare. However, when the data were analyzed, they revealed that the teacher in the comparison group had in fact given learners in that class explicit instruction and error correction. The researchers responded by considering the group nonetheless a comparison group in that it was the only one that had received this instruction throughout the duration of the study; the other two teachers had been asked to provide corrective feedback only during the stage between pre-test and post-test.

In addition, experimental studies are designed with the assumption that learners will behave in a particular way if they are exposed to particular instruction. Yet learners may not only reinterpret and modify activities but also redirect the focus of their own learning. The degree to which the research "interferes" with "usual" classroom conditions can have an impact on learner engagement and motivation. Some studies, such as Ellis, Loewen, and Erlam (2006), have designed communicative tasks for the teacher to provide corrective feedback, drawing on the knowledge that the program emphasized communication. Ammar and Spada (2006) adapted a grammaticality judgment task, usually designed for research, to embed it within a meaningful context; the story about a 12-year-old boy was better suited for learners in an elementary school.

Another feature of experimental research that is confronted by contextual challenges is that related to decisions about how long the experimental phase should be. The duration of the intervening instruction can vary considerably, from a few hours to as much as a year (see Dekeyser, 1993). Often, however, because of the difficulty of sustaining the "intrusion" into the classroom, they are often carried out as "short bursts" of intervention. This doesn't allow the researcher to examine, understand, or consider the community. Spada (2005) highlights this critical dimension by describing how she and her colleagues "spent the first few years of our research watching, listening, and documenting the instructional behaviour of many different intensive ESL teachers in interaction with learners in their classrooms" (p. 331). This type of investment, however, is often not possible for many researchers.

Corrective Feedback on Writing

Though much of the discussion in this chapter has centred on research concerned with oral corrective feedback, context plays a role in classroom-based research concerned with corrective feedback in writing as well, though it may be framed differently. Written corrective feedback studies are not commonly identified as laboratory or classroom-based. Studies carried out in laboratory conditions may consist of learners recruited for the study, as in oral corrective feedback, and corrective feedback may be provided in tutorial sessions with researchers (e.g., Aljaafreh & Lantolf, 1994; Nassaji & Swain, 2000). In some cases, researchers carrying out research in intact classrooms adopt laboratory-like conditions by selecting tasks that are not ordinarily used for corrective feedback in the classroom, such as in Fazio (2001), who collected data from journal assignments in his study. Contextual factors are commonly related to their impact on learner goals and motivation regarding writing and the focus on accuracy. The literature on written corrective feedback is vast and beyond the scope of this chapter (but see Chapter 10, this volume). The focus here will be on contextual features that are, in some ways, unique to written corrective feedback. The studies are chosen as examples to illustrate this point.

In the Classroom

A complexity surrounding the classroom context in written corrective feedback research is the question of whether the research was carried out in a class dedicated to writing or in a language classroom that included writing as part of the program, along with other skills. This context can have an enormous impact on research design and interpretation. For researchers, it determines the amount of writing accessible, learners' goals and motivations, teachers' focus and experience, curriculum mandates such as assessment, and the relationship between oral and written corrective feedback. In other cases, researchers struggle to reconcile the context. For example, in a study investigating the effect of focused written corrective feedback with ESL learners in a college program in the United States, Sheen (2007) noted that it was not necessary to create ecologically valid writing tasks because it was not a writing class. She opted to use tasks that would collect the information needed for the study instead. She later cited the context – in a language class and not a writing class – as a limitation because it was not ecologically valid. Yet in contexts outside of higher education, writing is integrated with other skills. Teachers in those contexts also provide corrective feedback and may benefit from research that speaks to their teaching context.

The distinction between second and foreign language classrooms has attracted some attention in research concerned with written corrective feedback. Hedgcock and Lefkowitz (1994) examined learner responses to content and linguistic feedback across a range of EFL and ESL classes. They found that the EFL learners in the study focused more strongly on linguistic accuracy than the ESL students, who seemed to value feedback on content and composition more. The authors suggested that the two groups had different goals for their writing but also that EFL teachers were more focused on linguistic accuracy in their pedagogy, both of which likely had an impact on how the learners responded to feedback.

Ferris (2009), however, drew attention to the diversity of the student population in higher education in the ESL context, in particular the distinction between international students and residents, including long-term and more recent newcomers. She suggested international students and residents may have different goals and perceptions and that learners who live in an ESL context may have acculturated to the local context in ways that may have an impact on how they respond to feedback. Bitchener and Knoch (2008) carried out one of the few studies that has attempted to examine the effect of corrective feedback in writing with these different groups of learners in a classroom setting.

Two intact classes of learners enrolled in a private language school in New Zealand participated in an experimental classroom-based study investigating the effectiveness of different corrective feedback strategies in writing. One class consisted of international students who were in New Zealand for the purpose of study, and the other consisted of adults who had migrated to the country for settlement. The authors hypothesized that the international students were more focused on accuracy and would respond more readily to corrective feedback on form, while the residents would focus on the communicative value of language, in response to their community context. However, the study did not support this hypothesis: both groups benefited equally from all the corrective feedback strategies. The authors suggested that this finding may have been a result of mixed groups in that there may have been some international students in the resident class and vice versa. Bitchener and Knoch did report a difference in learning outcomes at the post-test stage, at which point the international students outperformed the residents. When speculating on this finding, the authors suggested that students' previous learning experiences may have had an impact: the international students were from Asian countries that may have emphasized a focus on accuracy and were accustomed to receiving corrective feedback on form, while the other group of learners were not. In addition, they noted that the residents were generally older than the international students and suggested that age may have prevented older learners from remembering what they had learned in the classroom. While this may be true, it is also important to look at their lives outside the classroom and examine the context in which they live. International students often study abroad without the responsibilities of family and are able to focus on their studies in a way that residents who may have families to care for are not able to do.

In noting that there may have been some overlap between the two groups with international and migrant students attending both programs, the authors highlight one of the challenges that face classroom-based researchers. In another example, Park, Song, and Shin (2016) faced the same issue when trying to compare heritage (learners who grew up hearing Korean spoken at home) and non-heritage learners of Korean. Park et al. found that heritage learners responded better to corrective feedback in all areas of language except for orthography. When comparing groups, however, it turned out that one of them was mixed and heritage learners were also enrolled in the non-heritage class. While it is not clear why this was the case, it is not entirely surprising and may reflect an aspect of institutional context: course enrollment is mediated through institutional financial needs as well as learner needs. If there aren't enough learners to create a class, the enrollment criteria may be adjusted. It is important that researchers acknowledge the complexity of programming and do not adopt a monolithic approach to characterizing both how classes are formed and the diversity within groups classified by unitary concepts such as residents, international, or heritage and non-heritage.

One example of research that has examined the sociopolitical contexts of written corrective feedback is a study by Lee (2008). Lee examined how teacher beliefs and practices were embedded within the context of English language teaching in Hong Kong. The author described how teachers' decision-making in the classroom, concerned with how and when to deliver corrective feedback, was mediated through sometimes conflicting pedagogical knowledge and institutional policy. Findings showed that the exam-driven culture of the context leads teachers to give detailed feedback on accuracy over content or organization.

Connecting Research and Practice: The Role of Context

The primary agenda of this chapter has been to examine classroom-based research concerned with corrective feedback by highlighting the important role of context. Corrective feedback will likely continue to be of intense interest to teachers and researchers. It is intimately connected with the act of teaching, a core activity that defines classroom instruction for many practitioners, and it provides fertile ground from which to explore theoretical and pedagogical questions that drive research. As such it is well positioned to connect research and practice in meaningful ways, with implications for both researchers and teachers.

Considerations for Researchers

Explore New Territory
Researchers are becoming increasingly aware of the role of context to make research findings meaningful and many have called for greater attention to the ways in which studies are contextualized. Yet, in the initial design of classroom-based research, there has been little variation in terms of context and setting (e.g., see Ferris, 2012). While studies are increasingly being carried out in both second and foreign language settings, the vast majority of studies have taken place in university or college programs. For example, community-based programs that provide government-funded language instruction to newcomers for settlement are generally ignored as potential settings for research. Yet these contexts may allow us to examine the impact of the broader sociopolitical landscape that dictates policy and how the lived experiences of learners play a role in learning and teaching.

Leverage the Strengths of the Classroom
Research in corrective feedback on writing has struggled with criticism that studies are not designed with rigor and therefore do not provide evidence of the value of written corrective feedback (see Ferris, 1999; Truscott, 1996). Although the same arguments have been made on oral

corrective feedback, it resonates more loudly on written corrective feedback where corrective feedback takes up teacher time and energy. The response has been to "tighten" conditions in the classroom, which has had an impact on the role of context in these studies. A fine balance, however, is necessary to avoid compromising the conditions that characterize studies as classroom-based and relevant to teachers. The dynamic classroom environment enriches research and encourages deeper inquiry.

Anticipate Diversity

Much research in the classroom aims to classify and categorize. Yet this act threatens to ignore and create research that is blind to the realities of learners, teachers, and their experiences. For example, it is important that researchers do not ignore the complexity of programming and adopt a monolithic approach to characterizing classrooms and learners through unitary concepts such as residents, international, and heritage.

Look Beyond the Classroom

Researchers may not capture what is not overtly observed in the classroom, and there may be forces outside the classroom influencing how teachers and learners behave. For example, institutional practices and policies direct teaching, and while it may be possible to gather information about stated policies outside the classroom, in the classroom context, teachers enact policy rather than follow it (see Ball et al., 2011). Why teachers make the choices they make in relation to their context must be considered by researchers in any analysis of classroom observation data.

What Does This Mean for Teachers?

While this chapter did not provide a comprehensive overview of the classroom-based research, this snapshot suggests that, (a) corrective feedback is useful, and (b) there is likely no one strategy that is always more effective than another. Rather, different strategies and options are suited to different learners and, importantly, in *different contexts*.

While researchers explore both theoretical and pedagogical questions and theories, the ultimate goal of research in applied linguistics in general and in corrective feedback specifically is to be useful to teachers. If there is no "uptake" on the part of teachers, classroom-based research becomes a cycle of inquiry that becomes irrelevant to application. Teachers are the final arbiters who decide what is useful or not, and as experts in their own contexts, individual teachers must critically examine research to see if contextual factors are accounted for and if the findings are transferable to their own. In addition, like researchers, teachers should access and engage with research situated in a variety of contexts, outside of their own. No study will mirror any one pedagogical reality, but teachers can make decisions about the applicability of research to their own context by asking: *Where was the study situated? How similar is it to my own context? How does it differ? Is this pedagogy feasible in my classroom, program, institution, location, and community?*

Lightbown (2000) summed up a review of classroom-based research reminding us that pedagogical innovations arising from research "must be implemented and adapted to local conditions" (p. 454), conditions that include the resources available for teaching and learning. All this merits a call encouraging teachers to become engaged in research through an approach sometimes referred to as *action research*. This approach to research is teacher initiated, rooted in questions in the teacher's own practice, and aimed at responding to questions with action. It draws on the teacher's expertise and knowledge about the classroom context. This approach brings its own set of challenges (see Mackey & Gass, 2005) but holds promise for its own set of rewards as well.

The Changing Classroom: What Will Classroom-Based Research Look Like in the Future?

Moving forward, any close examination of classroom context raises questions about our understanding of the classroom. Is a classroom defined by its organization, its composition, or its physicality? More recent research has explored how corrective feedback plays a role in the virtual classroom (e.g., Monteiro, 2014; Rassaei, 2017; Sauro, 2009; Zhang, 2017). While much of it draws on the same core theories that underpin research in corrective feedback in general, this line of research challenges our notion of the classroom and presents the potential for us to reconceptualize feedback and the role of teacher and learner. As researchers we will need to look at classroom-based research through a new lens and ask, *What characterizes the classroom? What questions will emerge in these new contexts? How will research in the virtual classroom be meaningful and relevant to diverse contexts?* An important direction will be the development of a framework to help us understand the many dimensions of the classroom context and how to critically engage with contextual features that are important to teaching and learning. Given the complexity and dynamic nature of the classroom interaction, challenges related to context are unlikely to be addressed in their entirety. However, an awareness that they exist may encourage both researchers and teachers to interpret research with more nuanced and critical perspectives.

References

Aljaafreh, A. & Lantolf, J. P. (1994). Negative feedback as regulation and second language learning in the zone of proximal development. *The Modern Language Journal, 78*(4), 465–483.

Allwright, R. L. (1975). Problems in the study of the language teacher's treatment of learner error. In Burt and Dulay (eds.), *New directions in second language learning, teaching and bilingual education* (pp. 96–109). Washington, DC: TESOL.

Ammar, A. & Spada, N. (2006). One size fits all? Recasts, prompts and L2 learning. *Studies in Second Language Acquisition*, 28(4), 543–574.

Ball, S. J., Maguire, M., Braun, A. & Hoskins, K. (2011). Policy actors: Doing policy work in schools. *Discourse: Studies in the Cultural Politics of Education*, 32(4), 625–639.

Bastone, R. (2002). Contexts of engagement: A discourse perspective on "intake" and "pushed output." *System*, 30, 1–14.

Bitchener, J. & Knoch, U. (2008). The value of written corrective feedback for migrant and international students. *Language Teaching Research* 12 (3), 409–431.

Brown, D. (2016). The type and linguistic foci of oral corrective feedback in the L2 classroom: A meta-analysis. *Language Teaching Research*, 20(4), 436–458.

Chaudron, C. (1977). A descriptive model of discourse in the corrective treatment of learners' errors. *Language Learning*, 27(1), 29–46.

DeKeyser, R. (1993). The effect of error correction on L2 grammar knowledge and oral proficiency. *Modern Language Journal*, 77(4), 501–514.

Ellis, R., Loewen, S. & Erlam, R. (2006). Implicit and explicit corrective feedback and the acquisition of L2 grammar. *Studies in Second Language Acquisition*, 28(2), 339–368.

Fazio, L. L. (2001). The effect of corrections and commentaries on the journal writing accuracy of minority- and majority language students. *Journal of Second Language Writing*, 10(4), 235–249.

Ferris, D. R. (1999). The case for grammar correction in L2 writing classes: A response to Truscott (1996). *Journal of Second Language Writing*, 8(1), 1–11.

(2009) *Teaching college writing to diverse student populations*. Ann Arbor: University of Michigan Press.

(2012). Written corrective feedback in second language acquisition and writing studies. *Language Teaching*, 45(4), 446–459.

Foster, P. (1998). A classroom perspective on the negotiation of meaning. *Applied Linguistics*, 19(1), 1–23.

Hedgcock, J. & Lefkowitz, N. (1994). Feedback on feedback: Assessing learner receptivity to teacher response to L2 composing. *Journal of Second Language Writing*, 3(2), 141–163.

Hulstijn, J. (1997). Second language acquisition research in the laboratory. *Studies in Second Language Acquisition*, 19(2), 131–143.

Lee, E. J. (2013). Corrective feedback preferences and learner repair among advanced ESL students. *System*, 41, 217–230.

Lee, I. (2008). Understanding teachers' written feedback practices in Hong Kong secondary classrooms. *Journal of Second Language Writing*, 17(2), 69–85.

Li, S. (2010). The effectiveness of corrective feedback in SLA: A meta-analysis. *Language Learning, 60*(2), 309–365.

Lightbown, P. (2000). Anniversary article. Classroom SLA research and second language teaching. *Applied Linguistics, 21*(4), 431–462.

Llinares, A. & Lyster, R. (2014). The influence of context on patterns of corrective feedback and learner uptake: A comparison of CLIL and immersion classrooms. *The Language Learning Journal, 42*(2), 181–194.

Lochtman, K. (2002). Oral corrective feedback in the foreign language classroom: How it affects interaction in analytic foreign language teaching. *International Journal of Educational Research, 37*(3–4), 271–283.

Lyster, R. & Mori, H. (2006). Interactional feedback and instructional counterbalance. *Studies in Second Language Acquisition, 28*(2), 269–300.

Lyster, R. & Ranta, L. (1997). Corrective feedback and learner uptake. *Studies in Second Language Acquisition, 19*(1), 37–66.

Lyster, R. & Saito, K. (2010). Oral feedback in classroom SLA: A meta-analysis. *Studies in Second Language Acquisition, 32*(2), 265–302.

Mackey, A. & Gass. S. M. (2005). *Second language research: Methodology and design*. Mahwah, NJ: Lawrence Erlbaum.

Monteiro, K. (2014). An experimental study of corrective feedback during video-conferencing. *Language Learning & Technology, 18*(3), 56–79.

Nassaji, H. & Swain, M. (2000). A Vygotskian perspective on corrective feedback in L2: The effect of random versus negotiated help on the learning of English articles. *Language Awareness, 9*(1), 34–51.

Nicholas, N., Lightbown, P. & Spada, N. (2001). Recasts as feedback to language learners. *Language Learning, 51*(4), 719–758.

Oliver, R. & Mackey, A. (2003). Interactional context and feedback in child ESL contexts. *Modern Language Journal, 87*(4), 519–532.

Panova, I. & Lyster, R. (2002). Patterns of corrective feedback and uptake in an adult ESL classroom. *TESOL Quarterly, 36*(4), 573–595.

Park, E. S., Song, S. & Shin, Y. K. (2016). To what extent do learners benefit from indirect written corrective feedback? A study targeting learners of different proficiency and heritage language status. *Language Teaching Research, 20*(6), 678–699.

Pica, T. (2002). Subject-matter content: How does it assist the interactional and linguistic needs of classroom language learners? *Modern Language Journal, 86*(i), 1–19.

Rassaei, E. (2017). Video chat vs. face-to-face recasts, learners' interpretations and L2 development: A case of Persian EFL learners. *Computer Assisted Language Learning. 30*(1–2), 133–148.

Sauro, S. (2009). Computer-mediated corrective feedback and the development of L2 grammar. *Language Learning and Technology, 13*(1), 96–120.

Sheen, Y. (2004). Corrective feedback and learner uptake in communicative classrooms across instructional settings. *Language Teaching Research, 8*(3), 263–300.

(2007). The effect of focused written corrective feedback and language aptitude on ESL learners' acquisition of articles. *TESOL Quarterly, 41*(2), 255–283.

Spada, N. (2005). Conditions and challenges in developing school-based SLA research programs. *Modern Language Journal, 89*(3), 328–338.

Spada, N. & Lightbown, P. M. (1993). Instruction and the development of questions in L2 classrooms. *Studies in Second Language Acquisition, 15*(2), 205–224.

Storch, N. (2010). Critical feedback on written corrective feedback. *International Journal of English Studies, 10*(2), 29–46.

Swain, M. (1985). Communicative competence: Some roles of comprehensible input and comprehensible output in its development. In S. Gass & C. Madden (eds.), *Input in second language acquisition* (pp. 235–253). Rowley, MA: Newbury House.

Truscott, J. (1996). The case against grammar correction in L2 writing classes. *Language Learning, 46*(2), 327–369.

Tsang, W. K. (2004). Feedback and uptake in teacher-student interaction: An analysis of 18 English lessons in Hong Kong secondary classrooms. *RELC Journal, 35*(2), 187–209.

Zhang, Z. (2017). Student engagement with computer-generated feedback: A case study. *ELT Journal, 71*(3), 317–328.

8

Meta-Analysis and Research Synthesis

Dan Brown

An Introduction to Research Synthesis

The general aim of this book is to synthesize recent developments and current research on corrective feedback (CF). But the term *synthesis* carries a more specific meaning from a methodological perspective. *Research synthesis*, as a methodological practice, is the systematic (i.e., replicable, exhaustive) integration of existing research on a given topic that aims to provide a comprehensive view of patterns in findings across studies and/or methods used (Cooper, 2010; Norris & Ortega, 2006). The traditional approach to reviewing research, a narrative literature review, relies on authors' judgments in identifying the most relevant existing research to include, address, and build from. Although experts tend to be aware of most relevant literature in their domain and provide wisdom, experience, and keen judgment to identify important themes, the approach to carrying out a narrative review is inherently subjective. As a result, a narrative literature review is limited by representations and analyses of previous research that are selective and incomplete, that favor certain theoretical positions, and/or that lack the precision available in quantitative estimates of the effects or relationships of interest. Research synthesis, on the other hand, has formalized approaches to combining data from existing studies by following a thorough and transparent quantitative approach in gathering relevant literature to establish a complete summary of existing findings on a particular research question or variable. While research synthesis has gained prominence across most established scientific areas of study, it has only recently been substantially integrated into applied linguistics research (Norris & Ortega, 2006). A research synthesis approaches the existing literature on a topic as a researcher would approach an empirical study with access to an entire population of subjects (Lipsey & Wilson, 2001). No data point (or in the case of research synthesis, no existing study) is left unturned, aiming for a comprehensive view across a selected domain. Following this analogy, in a research synthesis each existing study within a domain is like a participant in a primary study, and data for each study are collected and analyzed to determine patterns and inconsistencies concerning variables of interest.

As a broad methodological approach of systematic review, research synthesis includes under its umbrella the more focused methodologies of *meta-analysis* (now used extensively in CF research, see Plonsky & Brown, 2015) and *methodological synthesis* (Liu & Brown, 2015; Plonsky, 2013). A methodological synthesis aims to take inventory of methodological practices that have been used in a research domain with intent to provide guidance and direction for the substance and methods in future studies (e.g., Derrick, 2016; Liu & Brown, 2015; Plonsky & Kim, 2016). Following a brief introduction to these two forms of research synthesis (meta-analysis and methodological synthesis) and an overview of their potential value, this chapter will describe the process involved in conducting them and highlight their contributions and limitations in our current understanding of CF research. The chapter will conclude by offering suggestions for how these methods can continue to help guide development of theoretical and practical knowledge in the role of CF in second language learning and teaching.

The value of research synthesis rests on the accumulation of primary studies that investigate a similar topic. And in light of exponential growth in research on second language learning and teaching (relatively young fields of study), a range of subtopics within these fields have only recently become ripe for the application of synthetic research techniques (Norris & Ortega, 2006). In turn, the need for research synthesis has taken root in applied linguistics, albeit well behind other domains in the social sciences (Plonsky & Oswald, 2014), and since the first meta-analyses in applied linguistics drew substantial attention (e.g., Norris & Ortega, 2000, 2006), interest in this methodological approach has developed quickly. In the last decade, fueled in part by Luke Plonsky's efforts (e.g., Plonsky, 2013), research synthesis has taken spotlight as a preferred method of review as the field rapidly matures, with over 100 meta-analyses conducted in applied linguistics to date.

Meta-analysis

Meta-analysis, the most common form of research synthesis used in CF research (at least twenty-one meta-analyses have been conducted on CF), is essentially used to find the average overall effects of a given phenomenon across all existing studies (Lipsey & Wilson, 2001). To perform a meta-analysis, data from all the primary studies on a topic (e.g., development in grammatical accuracy resulting from written corrective feedback) are aggregated using effect sizes to quantify and estimate the patterns in findings across studies. With enough studies accumulated on a topic, a meta-analysis can allow researchers to overcome the limitations of small sample sizes (often ubiquitous in classroom-based research).

Perhaps an even more valuable feature of a meta-analysis is the ability to conduct moderator analyses, which are the examination of variability in overall effects as a function of study and/or methodological features. In other words, we can isolate the potential impact that peripheral study variables (i.e., those that were not necessarily the focus of individual studies) have on the overall effects of CF. For example, meta-analyses have shown that, overall, grammar and pronunciation, as targets of oral CF, have been more susceptible to development than other linguistic features, e.g., lexis (Li, 2010), and the data that show such patterns come from studies that may intentionally compare linguistic target types, but also from studies that only focus on a single target type. Such findings can be revealed through a bird's-eye perspective across many studies as too few individual studies may focus on such a question (i.e., the role of target feature) in their research design, or sample sizes for individual studies often limit statistical confidence in their findings. Moderator analyses also allow systematic analysis of methodological practices that have been used in a domain. For example, we can compare the differential effects of CF depending on the use of a delayed post-test (Plonsky & Gass, 2011), which can offer insight into the durability of effects for different types of CF. As a by-product of moderator analyses, we can also uncover patterns of interaction between variables that were never the focus of investigation in any single study (Cooper, 2010). For example, Brown (2016), a meta-analysis on L2 teachers' oral feedback practices, revealed that when teachers who participated in such studies were informed of the focus of the research (e.g., feedback type), they provided significantly fewer recasts in favor of prompts, suggesting that researchers should avoid informing teachers of the research focus when conducting these types of studies. Although teachers' awareness of research focus was not the explicit focus of any of the primary studies on that topic, a view of the totality of studies with different methodological design features among them can reveal patterns untenable for exploration in the individual studies themselves. So, not only does meta-analysis involve averaging the main effects across studies, with enough aggregated data it can reveal novel insights into the nuances of effectiveness by exposing relationships between outcomes and variables previously unstudied, or variables that have been examined but on limited samples.

Methodological Synthesis

Methodological synthesis, another form of research synthesis that has more recently surfaced in applied linguistics (e.g., Plonsky, 2013; Plonsky

& Gonulal, 2015; Plonsky & Kim, 2016), and in CF research specifically (Liu & Brown, 2015), shares many characteristics of a meta-analysis. While meta-analyses often include a systematic methodological analysis and critique (e.g., Norris & Ortega, 2000; Plonsky & Gass, 2011), methodological syntheses focus attention exclusively on a quantitative description of research and reporting practices within a domain or subdomain of study. A methodological synthesis illuminates trends in general study designs, sampling practices, variables of interest, methods of analysis, reporting practices, or even theoretical positions that have been applied to previous research in an area for the purpose of guiding future research efforts (Norris & Ortega, 2006; Plonsky, 2013). While many of these outcomes are also presented in meta-analyses, a methodological synthesis does not aim to aggregate findings and can therefore cast a wider net on the types of studies to include (i.e., not being limited to those lacking certain features required for quantitative analysis).

In recent years, methodological syntheses have been conducted examining general practices in applied linguistics research (e.g., Plonsky, 2013), practices within a specific journal (e.g., Riazi, Shi & Haggerty, 2018), and specific research practices such as instrument reporting (Derrick, 2016) or use of a particular statistical analysis (Plonsky & Gonulal, 2015). Methodological syntheses have also focused on substantive subdomains in the field, such as interaction in second language acquisition (Plonsky & Gass, 2011), form-focused instruction (Sok, Kang & Han, 2018), task-based learner production (Plonsky & Kim, 2016), self-paced reading (Marsden, Thompson & Plonsky, 2018), and written corrective feedback (Liu & Brown, 2015; Yousefi & Nassaji, 2018).

In the domain of written CF specifically, several narrative reviews have highlighted methodological shortcomings and inconsistencies that have slowed progress in our understanding of the effectiveness of written CF over decades, such as the lack of control groups, exclusive focus on edited texts rather than new writings, and incomparability due to inconsistent treatments and accuracy measures (e.g., Bruton, 2010; Ferris, 2004, 2010; Storch, 2010). With systematic methodological review, these concerns can be accurately quantified and described. Through methodological synthesis, researchers can clearly track decisions and patterns in the rationales, variables of interest, study contexts, decision-making in sampling, instrument design, data collection, analysis, and reporting practices, and track how these practices may change over time (e.g., Liu & Brown, 2015; Plonsky, 2013; Sok et al., 2018). Such systematic reporting allows us to evaluate current practices and trends in methodology across studies with precision, as well as clarify construct definitions and methods of operationalization. This insight can add clarity in guiding future methodological decision-making to help standardize methodological practices, increase transparency, and ultimately, add validity to our research (Plonsky, 2013).

The Process of Research Synthesis

A brief introduction to how research syntheses are conducted can help in understanding and interpreting the results of the growing number of such studies on CF research (and their often disparate findings). Different approaches to research synthesis (e.g., meta-analysis, methodological synthesis) follow similar fundamental processes, but the approach to conducting a meta-analysis will be introduced here first because of its prominence in applied linguistics (and in CF research, especially). For a practical and more comprehensive introduction to conducting meta-analyses, there are several useful general guides available (e.g., Borenstein et al., 2009; Cooper, 2010; Cooper, Hedges & Valentine, 2009; Lipsey & Wilson, 2001) and recommended resources specific to second language research (e.g., Plonsky & Oswald, 2012). In short, the process begins with a principled search and selection of primary studies within a defined research domain. Protocol for sampling here is just as important as in any other empirical research – random for experimental designs, purposeful for qualitative, and a complete sample for research syntheses (Ortega, 2015). Perhaps the most important feature of synthetic research is that a rigorous research synthesis aims to gather all the studies (including unpublished literature to the extent possible) that have investigated the same set of variables and/or relationships. The literature search, then, must be transparent and comprehensive to identify the complete set of studies that are relevant. This first step involves defining domain parameters through principled and specific inclusion and exclusion criteria. For example, in Russell and Spada's (2006, pp. 140–141) meta-analysis on CF for the acquisition of L2 grammar, studies needed to: "(a) include empirical data; (b) be published in English; (c) include a measure of form-focused CF of grammar as an independent variable; (d) include a measure of learning as a dependent variable; (e) clearly isolate the corrective feedback from other forms of instruction that may have been included; and (f) clearly isolate CF in response to errors in grammatical form from CF in response to other types of errors (e.g., sociolinguistic, discourse, phonological)." Studies are typically excluded from meta-analyses if not enough data are reported to calculate effect sizes, or in some cases if certain methodological features are not adopted, such as those lacking a control group in (quasi-) experimental studies. Domain definitions for meta-analyses on CF also differ in terms of mode of delivery (e.g., spoken, written, computer mediated), research method (e.g., limited to classroom or experimental studies or outcome measurement), or provider of CF (e.g., teacher or peer), among other choices. All potentially relevant studies should be examined to decide on inclusion/exclusion based on the defined criteria and rationale (Cooper, 2010; Ortega, 2015; Oswald & Plonsky, 2010). As Plonsky and Brown (2015) highlight, the subtle differences in choices at the domain definition stage in setting parameters (e.g., written CF vs. oral, the inclusion of computer-mediated CF) have led to wide variability in findings (these will be discussed in more detail in the following section). Once the domain is explicitly defined, an exhaustive search must be carried out which is fully explained and replicable (Norris & Ortega, 2006). The search should include electronic searches through databases, manual searches of relevant journals, reference chasing, forward searches, and email requests to authors as needed.

Once a comprehensive sample of studies is collected (i.e., as close as possible to a full data set), the meta-analyst then systematically codes the studies using a coding scheme that has been developed specifically for that domain. The coding scheme includes the main variables across studies, such as publication details (e.g., year, authors, journal/book/dissertation, published or unpublished), features of the research contexts (e.g., classroom or lab, elementary/K-12/university, SL or FL), methodological procedures adopted (e.g., sample size, reliability, statistical procedures, outcome measures), and main variables investigated (e.g., type of feedback, duration of feedback, durability of effects on delayed tests). After systematic coding of each study with use of interrater reliability, the evidence reported comprehensively across the full sample allows consumers of research a more objective view, rather than relying on author's interpretations of accumulated knowledge as in narrative literature reviews (Norris & Ortega, 2006).

To aggregate existing findings across studies in a meta-analysis, effect sizes and confidence intervals are used to show the magnitude and variability of quantitative findings, as averages alone do not allow for stable or maximally informative interpretations of aggregate effects. An effect size answers the question "to what extent" rather than seeking a yes/no answer, as is the case in null-hypothesis significance testing (Oswald & Plonsky, 2010). The most commonly used measure of effect size in applied linguistics research, Cohen's d, represents the difference between the mean of two groups measured in standard deviations. For example, if the effect of CF on an experimental group results in a mean score that is two standard deviations greater than the mean of the control group, then d would equal 2.0. A crucial characteristic of effect sizes is that they are standardized (through standard deviation units) and can therefore be compared or averaged with d values from a group of studies that have investigated the same variable under the same resolution of domain specification. Another key measure used to interpret overall average effect sizes is a confidence interval, which is the range around the observed average effect size, typically reported with a 95 percent likelihood of containing the true average effect size. With an average effect size across studies, we can then interpret that value relative to typical findings in the subdomain (when enough studies exist) or relative to the general area of behavioral sciences. As Plonsky and

Oswald (2014) argue, effect sizes are most useful when interpreted within the context of a particular domain or discipline, so rather than following the traditional guidelines set by Cohen for interpreting d values (0.2 as small, 0.5 medium, and 0.8 large), they suggest field-specific guidelines for interpreting effect size values in L2 research: 0.4 as small, 0.7 medium, and 1.0 large. Their proposed scale corresponds more closely to the 25th, 50th, and 75th percentiles in L2 research, respectively, and helps in more meaningful interpretations of effect sizes.

As will be described in more detail in the following section, meta-analysis has generally provided robust evidence in support of the overall effectiveness of CF in second language learning and teaching, as well as indications of patterns that can help practitioners better understand the factors that influence effectiveness. For example, moderator analysis in Lyster and Saito (2010) revealed that the overall impact of CF in classroom settings might be greater for younger learners than for older learners.

The process of conducting a methodological synthesis follows the same systematic procedures as a meta-analysis in terms of setting search criteria and conducting a comprehensive and transparent search of the literature, but without the goal of aggregating effect sizes across studies. This type of summative description typically relies on frequencies and percentages to track study features as a central method of analysis. Without aggregating effects, which requires reporting of certain study features, such as effect sizes or the data required to extract an effect size (i.e., means and standard deviations), a methodological synthesis can describe a wider scope of studies and their design features with the goals of accurate description of methods used, evaluation of patterns in study quality, and a historical account of change in methods used over time (Plonsky & Gonulal, 2015). For example, Liu and Brown (2015) surveyed the methods used in forty-four studies on written CF to provide a detailed account of how research had been conducted in that domain, with a focus on trends that were both concerning and encouraging to guide future design.

While traditional reviews of CF research have certainly helped identify trends and patterns in CF research (e.g., Ferris, 2004; Nassaji, 2015, 2016; Nicholas, Lightbown & Spada, 2001), they have also proven limited in shedding an accurate light on the full range of research findings. For example, the debate over the efficacy of written CF (see Ferris, 1999; Truscott, 1996) continued for years despite improvements in the rigor of research methodology (Storch, 2010), leading Bruton (2010) to describe the ongoing debate as "sterile," "tedious," and without practical relevance to L2 writing teachers. In the last decade, however, meta-analytic findings have clarified our understanding of the effectiveness of CF, which will be explored in the next section.

The Contribution of Meta-analyses to CF Research

The fascination with the topic of CF leading to a breadth of research, coupled with the growing popularity of meta-analysis in applied linguistics has led to twenty-one unique meta-analyses at the time of this publication (see Table 8.1). Although the majority of these studies present their findings tentatively as the respective domains are still growing, this body of research has generally verified the overall effectiveness of both oral and written CF. Meanwhile, the variability in findings among these CF meta-analyses have likely led to some confusion.

As Plonsky and Brown (2015) highlight, the subjectivity involved in the meta-analytic process (inherent in any methodological approach), specifically at the level of defining a domain of inquiry, has resulted in wide variability in findings across these meta-analyses of CF. Table 8.1 summarizes the domain parameters and their respective outcomes (aggregate effects) of the twenty-one meta-analyses of CF to date (which is updated from Plonsky & Brown, 2015, that presented eighteen studies). The twenty-one meta-analytic studies presented are divided into (a) meta-analyses of broader domains of research that include CF (e.g., CF as a type of grammar instruction in Norris & Ortega, 2000), and (b) meta-analyses with a dominant focus on CF specifically. Table 8.1 compares the unique domain definitions operationalized, such as oral feedback (Lyster & Saito, 2010), written feedback (Truscott, 2007; Kang & Han, 2015), both oral and written feedback (Russell & Spada, 2006), and a combination of these subdomains along with computer delivered feedback (Li, 2010; Ziegler, 2016), or peer delivered written feedback (Chen & Lin, 2012). Aside from mode of feedback, another distinguishing feature between the foci of these studies has been the target skill or feature; for example, a focus on grammatical accuracy in Kang and Han (2015) and Russell and Spada (2006), or on pronunciation in Lee, Jang, and Plonsky (2015), and so on. The wide range of summary effects found across these meta-analyses of CF (d values ranging from weak negative effects, −0.16, to large positive ones, 1.16) reflect the diversity and scope of the subdomains of inquiry. Note that interpretation of effect sizes follow Plonsky and Oswald's (2014) guidelines for L2 research (presented earlier for comparing groups).

As a result, the findings presented by meta-analyses must be interpreted with the same caution as in primary studies, particularly in domains that are newly ripe for synthesis. For instance, Truscott (2007) meta-analyzed written CF (WCF) research to find an aggregate small *negative* effect for WCF on the development of accuracy in writing with 95 percent confidence that "if it has any actual benefits, they are very small" (p. 255). Only eight years later, Kang and Han's (2015) meta-analysis on studies within a similar domain parameter included twenty-two studies and found a moderate to large effect of WCF. An explanation for the disparate

Table 8.1 *Domain definitions and outcomes across meta-analyses of corrective feedback*

Author (k^a)	Domains	Effects (*d*) [95% CIs]
Meta-analyses of broader domains that include CF		
Mackey & Goo, 2007 (45)	CF as a type of interaction; classroom and laboratory-based studies; face-to-face and computer-delivered CF; grammar and vocab	0.71 [0.63–0.80]
Lee et al., 2015 (44)	Oral and computer-delivered CF; pronunciation only	0.76 [0.52–0.99]
Norris & Ortega, 2000 (13)	CF as a type of instruction; grammar only	0.89 [N/A]
Keck et al., 2006	CF as a type of interaction but not examined separately; grammar and vocab	N/A[b]
Cobb, 2010	Oral CF as a type of interaction; task-based; grammar only	N/A[b]
Plonsky & Gass, 2011	Oral feedback as a type of interaction	N/A[b]
Ziegler, 2013	Oral and written CF among studies of computer-mediated and face-to-face interaction; grammar, vocab, and pragmatics	N/A[b]
Meta-analyses of CF		
Truscott, 2007 (9)	Written CF; classroom contexts only; not grammar learning	−0.16 [N/A]
Poltavtchenko & Johnson, 2009 (9)	Written CF; classroom contexts only; included peer revision	0.33 [0.14–0.50]
Kao & Wible, 2011 (12)	Written CF; focused vs. unfocused CF*	0.37 [0.09–0.64]
Miller & Pan, 2012 (13)	Written and oral CF; grammar and pragmatics only; recasts only; class- and lab-based	0.38 [N/A]
Chen & Lin, 2012 (11)	Peer feedback; L2 writing only; ESL/EFL learners only	0.48 [0.32–0.64]
Li, 2010 (33)	Oral and computer-delivered CF; classroom and lab; grammar and vocab	0.64 [0.47–0.81]
Kang & Han, 2015 (22)	Written CF provided by teachers in classroom based-studies; grammar only	0.68 [0.42–0.93]*
Lyster & Saito, 2010 (15)	Oral CF; classroom-based studies only	0.74 [0.58–0.90]
Thirakunkovit & Chamcharatsri, 2019 (27)	Written CF; teacher and peer CF	0.79 [0.64–0.95]*
Biber et al., 2011 (23)	Written CF; L1 and L2 users; multiple outcome types (e.g., revisions, attitude measures, syntactic and lexical complexity)	0.88 [0.08–1.34]
Miller, 2003 (8)	Oral CF; effects of learners' noticing of errors	1.08 [1.01–1.15]
Russell & Spada, 2006 (15)	Oral and written CF; grammar only	1.16 [0.70–1.38]
Brown, 2016	Proportion of different feedback types and target features; Classroom-based studies only; oral only	N/A[c]

Note. Cohen's *d* effect size was reported in this set of studies with two exceptions: * Kang and Han (2015) and Thirakunkovit and Chamcharatsri (2019) reported effect size as Hedges *g*. [a] Number of studies of CF that contributed to the meta-analytic results presented here; [b] These studies meta-analyzed primary studies of CF, but they did not present meta-analytic results for the effect of feedback separately. [c] The focus of this study is not on the effects of CF, but rather the types of linguistic foci of classroom-based studies of feedback. Adapted from Plonsky and Brown (2015).

findings between these two studies is not limited by the additional dozen studies conducted in the eight years between them. Truscott's (2007) findings supported one side of an ongoing debate over the value of WCF, but they were, in part, the result of the literature search procedures and inclusion/exclusion criteria (domain parameters) set to arrive at the seven studies that comprised his data set. This study lacked a comprehensive (and transparent) literature search – a hallmark of meta-analyses – and described the procedures used for retrieval of inclusion studies as "a general look at published sources, relying primarily on reviews by Ferris … and Truscott" (p. 257). As described above, standard procedures in searching for relevant studies in meta-analyses are far more systematic, typically including description of databases searched, specific search terms used in those databases, other methods of identifying unpublished studies and conference presentations, and a timeframe when the search was conducted. Truscott (2007), like Kang and Han (2015), included classroom studies, authentic writing samples (rather than grammar exercises), and comparison in new writings over time. Both excluded studies that focused only on revision as an outcome, but Truscott (2007) also excluded one-shot treatments with reasoning that these studies "have generally gotten little respect in this literature" (p. 257), but as Kang and Han (2015) argue, effects of treatment duration can only be determined with consideration of other design features (i.e., moderator variables). These slight differences in inclusion/exclusion criteria resulted in disparate data sets; unlike Kang and Han (2015), Truscott (2007) included Sheppard (1992), which utlized student–teacher conferences, arguing that these conferences should be considered a natural part of the feedback process and therefore not excluded on this ground. Truscott (2007) also did not include Chandler (2003) or Bitchener et al. (2005), although it is unclear if Bitchener et al. (2005) was available for inclusion, as Trucott's meta-analysis did not describe when the search was conducted. Furthermore, by excluding unpublished work, including dissertations, Duppenthale (2002) and Hendrickson (1977) did not contribute to Truscott's findings even though they should have met inclusion requirements. Although Truscott made clear that the estimates found in his meta-analysis should not be interpreted as certain, audiences should be aware of the role of domain definition when interpreting meta-analytic results (see Plonsky & Brown, 2015, for a more detailed discussion).

In the case of the effects of written CF on grammatical accuracy, with reliable evidence from enough accumulated studies, we can now end the debate over "the big question" (Ferris, 2004) and shift attention to how and when WCF can be most efficiently applied. Although the array of meta-analyses on CF define their domains differently, together they substantiate the overall effectiveness of CF in L2 learning and teaching and position researchers to focus on investigating the variables and contexts that play the most important roles in moderating effectiveness of CF.

Apart from overall effect sizes, perhaps the most intriguing value of meta-analysis comes from moderator analysis (Cooper, 2010; Norris & Ortega, 2006). By aggregating data on a range of study features and comparing them against outcome effects, researchers can detect the influence of variables in research context or design features that may influence or be associated with the relationship(s) of interest. This type of analysis can help provide more reliable answers to research questions involving the relationships between common study variables. Despite the variability in overall effects of the meta-analyses of CF, there are patterns that represent consistencies across subdomains as well as differences according to mode and context of delivery of CF, target features, CF type, and learner characteristics. Updated from Plonsky and Brown (2015), we found the following trends among the CF meta-analyses:

- Studies focusing on WCF in classroom settings resulted in relatively smaller effects (−0.16, 0.33, 0.37, 0.48, 0.68) than studies in controlled conditions. As Lyster and Saito (2010) suggest, more control over study environment tends to result in stronger magnitude of outcomes.
- Oral and computer-mediated CF studies resulted in relatively larger effects ($d = 0.64, 0.71, 0.74$) compared to written CF, although these are considered medium-sized effects when considering differences between groups in L2 research (Plonsky & Oswald, 2014). A possible explanation for this advantage could be a greater treatment length or intensity, or perhaps a tendency to include a more limited scope of features as targets of oral or computer-mediated CF, thus amplifying the focused effects.
- Grammar learning as an outcome of CF, compared to vocabulary or pronunciation learning, yielded the largest effects in the sample ($d = 1.16$ and 0.89). As Plonsky and Gass (2011) suggest, grammatical features' frequency (and systematicity) of occurrence likely explains their greater susceptibility to development in response to CF than lexis, while pronunciation has been connected more closely to a critical period of development.
- Pronunciation instruction involving CF also resulted in relatively large effects ($d = 0.91$) compared to vocabulary. This difference might be explained in terms of outcome measures (i.e., uptake of CF on pronunciation could occur relatively frequently in repeating recasted pronunciation, without necessarily leading to acquisition).
- Oral CF as recasts resulted in a relatively smaller effect ($d = 0.38$) relative to other forms of oral CF, such as prompts. A probable explanation here is that recasts often go unnoticed, while prompts have been argued to result in deeper cognitive processing that may be optimal for long-term gains (Lyster & Saito, 2010).
- Oral CF in classrooms may have greater benefits for younger learners ($r = -0.51$ in between-group contrasts and $r = -0.40$ in within-groups

contrasts). As Lyster and Saito (2010) argue, it could be that younger learners are more sensitive to the effects of CF "because it engages implicit learning mechanisms that are more characteristic of younger than older learners" (p. 293). It could also be that younger learners generally receive relatively longer instructional treatments, or they are generally less anxious about being corrected in public than adults.

In addition to these trends, it appears that the general effect sizes show an advantage for oral CF (medium to large effect sizes) over written CF (generally small to medium). This pattern may be partially explained due to the challenges in measuring development in L2 writing. As Plonsky and Brown (2015) highlight, studies of oral feedback, comparatively, tend to employ relatively constrained outcome measures (see Chapter 5 of this volume for details of outcome measures) which seem more likely to result in larger effects (also see Norris & Ortega, 2000).

Moderator analysis also speaks to the common concerns of meta-analysis regarding "garbage in, garbage out" or questioning the value of boiling down so many different studies into a single effect size value (Cooper, 2010). Through moderator analysis, we can study features of methodological design to determine their potential effect on overall outcomes. For instance, Li's (2010) meta-analysis of classroom-based oral CF found greater mean effects for between-group contrasts in lab-based than in classroom-based studies (d = 1.08 and 0.5, respectively), suggesting that (perhaps implicit) feedback may be more noticeable in a more controlled, focused environment. Furthermore, meta-analyses should not exclude studies with apparent methodological weakness (e.g., small sample size, lack of reliability measures, absence of delayed post-tests), and instead should investigate how these features impact overall outcomes as potential moderator variables. Plonsky and Gass (2011) found that when experimental studies included delayed post-tests they resulted in substantially larger effects on immediate post-tests than when they did not include delayed post-tests in both classrooms and lab-based studies. They also found greater effects for studies that randomly assigned individual participation conditions. These relationships between methodological features and study outcomes can help distinguish the impact of and inform future methodological decisions.

The Contribution of Methodological Synthesis to CF Research

Most of the synthetic evidence concerning methodological practices in CF research to date has been obtained as part of meta-analyses (e.g., Lyster & Saito, 2010), with the exceptions of Liu and Brown (2015) and Chen (2016), which focused exclusively on methods and reporting practices in CF research. In Liu and Brown, which focused on WCF and development in accuracy over time, we chose to quantitatively account for methodological features in that domain in an effort to help standardize methodological choices so that more research can be systematically aggregated on the topic. In other words, despite hundreds of studies on WCF, very few were carried out with consistent design features to be adequately compared. For instance, among the set of forty-four primary studies that investigated gains in written accuracy in new writings over time, we found over ten combinations of CF types examined and over half of the studies contained at least one group that received a mix of feedback types (e.g., direct feedback with metalinguistic comments, coded with symbols and metalinguistic comments, direct feedback with oral metalinguistic comments) making it challenging to tease apart the effects of individual feedback types. We also found six types of outcome measures employed across the studies: percentage of correct uses in obligatory contexts, normed errors per number of words, sum of errors or mean scores for accuracy, error-free T-units over total T-units, length of error-free T-units over length of total T-units, or holistic ratings (14 percent of the studies did not report the outcome measure used). Additionally, we found that a "one-shot" treatment design was most common with a quarter of the studies using a single writing to provide feedback before measuring development between pre- and post-tests. In examining reporting practices, we found inconsistent reporting on moderating variables such as length of writings, length of intervals between writing tasks, presence of explicit grammar instruction, and training in the use of codes. In other trends, we found that studies in the last decade have increasingly compared multiple types of CF against a control group and more studies have included a wider range of (unfocused) errors, perhaps representing concern over ecological classroom validity. But despite the breadth of studies in this area, replication efforts have provided limited value as comparison across studies remains problematic. Precise description of these study features can help guide this domain as well as other areas of CF research.

Meta-analyses of oral CF research also often include dedicated sections that report on methodological patterns and developments and routinely offer recommendations to help advance this line of research. The recommendations, summarized in Table 8.2, have largely echoed concerns raised in WCF research regarding sampling practices, design features, substantive features, and reporting practices. Although the differences in domain definition limit comparison, it should be noted that several recommendations persist even a decade later (e.g., inconsistencies in how study variables have been operationalized). It should also be noted that several meta-analyses in this sample reported improved research design over time, such as improved reporting of effect sizes and greater use of delayed post-tests in (quasi-)experimental design (e.g., Plonsky & Gass, 2011), which support general trends in WCF research (Liu & Brown, 2015). Continued use of methodological synthesis should continue to guide methodological

Table 8.2 *Methodological recommendations in meta-analyses involving oral CF research*

Sampling practices	More studies needed that involve child learners, learners of L2s other than English, and high-proficiency learners	Keck et al., 2006; Li, 2010; Mackey & Goo, 2007; Russell & Spada, 2006; Miller & Pan, 2012
Design features	Inconsistency in how study variables have been defined and operationalized	Keck et al., 2006; Li 2010; Miller & Pan, 2012; Norris & Ortega, 2000
	Lack of measurement of learners' knowledge about target structures prior to treatments	Li, 2010
	Lack of a control group	Keck et al., 2006; Miller & Pan, 2012; Norris & Ortega, 2000
Substantive features	More studies needed that include feedback types other than recasts (for more balanced data)	Li, 2010
	Need for larger subgroups based on study context, feedback type, and mode of feedback.	Russell & Spada, 2006
	More studies needed involving peer-generated feedback	Keck et al., 2006; Mackey & Goo, 2007
	More studies needed on computer-mediated CF	Li, 2010, Mackey & Goo, 2007
	Greater nuance needed in classification of feedback types to tease apart effects of prompts / explicit correction.	Lyster & Saito, 2010; Miller, 2003
Reporting practices	More consistent reporting of learner characteristics (e.g., proficiency, literacy levels, degree of anxiety, L1 background).	Lyster & Saito, 2010; Miller, 2003
	More consistent reporting of reliability, validity, and interrater reliability	Norris & Ortega, 2000; Russell & Spada, 2006
	More consistent reporting of data that can allow for calculation of effect sizes (i.e., means and standard deviations) and confidence intervals	Keck et al., 2006; Norris & Ortega, 2000; Miller, 2003; Russell & Spada, 2006
	Reporting of task type used to measure L2 learning	Keck et al., 2006; Russell & Spada, 2006

progress, particularly in terms of transparency in methodological choices, and ultimately, help to make research on CF more trustworthy and useful.

Conclusion and Recommendations

Research synthesis and meta-analysis hold great promise to help make sense of research on CF as it rapidly expands in size and scope. Despite the bulge of meta-analyses on CF relative to other subdomains in L2 research,

research syntheses in this domain is unlikely to subside. In fact, in some areas we have only scratched the surface. Synthetic researchers have so far ignored nonverbal feedback modes (the focus of Chapter 12), and more synthetic qualitative research on CF could help reveal variables that require more attention in exploring the relative effectiveness of CF. In terms of methodological synthesis, there is great room for study across subdomains of CF research following Liu and Brown (2015) and Chen (2016). As witnessed from the comparison of Truscott (2007) and Kang and Han (2015), both investigating effectiveness of WCF over time, research synthesis makes contributions in waves. As more studies build in the same domain, and as methods evolve and research questions become increasingly refined, updated syntheses are needed for a more generalizable representation of the full population of learners and study contexts (Cooper, 2010; Norris & Ortega, 2006; Plonsky, 2012). As the population of studies on CF grows, so do the subdomains, the size, and added power of the subgroups aggregated for meta-analyses, which will also allow deeper investigation into more nuanced relationships between study variables and outcomes that could not be explored within individual studies. In this spirit, it is important to emphasize the value of replication in CF research, as we need findings from more studies that incorporate similar methods across a wider context of environments and learner populations in order to be able to generalize findings and uncover more nuanced moderator analyses (e.g., Marsden et al., 2018; Porte, 2012).

Of course, there are dangers to avoid amidst the explosion of research synthesis on CF. If a subdomain is not yet fully ripe for synthesis, with too few studies on a topic, we risk premature closure to a topic when more research may be urgently needed (e.g., Truscott, 2007 vs. Kang & Han, 2015), especially when audiences focus on main effects and ignore moderating variables (Plonsky, 2012). For this reason, it is the meta-analyst's responsibility to avoid overstating results, while at the same time, emphasizing substantive and methodological gaps that remain. In conducting research syntheses, we also need to be aware of the inflation of effects due to publication bias, as studies without significant results unfortunately still have lower chances of being published, although there are techniques that can measure and mitigate these effects such as funnel plots (see Cooper, 2010 and Plonsky & Oswald, 2012).

Findings from meta-analyses in CF should provide practitioners with a clearer sense of our general confidence in the overall effectiveness of CF in instructional contexts (ranging from moderate to large) based on cumulative data from hundreds of studies in this area. These findings should lend assurance to language teachers who spend a great deal of time providing feedback to their students. Meta-analyses can also help reveal patterns in the data on CF to date that highlight factors influencing the effectiveness of CF (e.g., a seemingly stronger effect for oral CF relative to written, particularly on grammar and pronunciation; greater benefit for younger learners in classroom contexts). These patterns, studied through moderator analysis, could be used to inform policy and practice with the awareness that much more research is needed to build confidence in our understanding of the factors that affect the utility of CF. As researchers and practitioners become more familiar with synthetic research techniques, the results should guide researchers' future methodological efforts to result in more systematicity, replicability, and reduced bias (Norris & Ortega, 2006, 2007). These attributes of research synthesis will lead to more orderly knowledge building and more efficient extraction of pedagogical implications from research findings.

References

Biber, D., Nekrasova, T. & Horn, B. (2011). The effectiveness of feedback for L1-English and L2-writing development: A meta-analysis. *TOEFL iBT Research Report No. TOEFLiBT-14*. Princeton, NJ: Educational Testing Service.

Bitchener, J., Young, S. & Cameron, D. (2005). The effect of different types of corrective feedback on ESL student writing. *Journal of Second Language Writing*, 14(3), 191–205.

Borenstein, M., Hedges, L. V., Higgins, J. P. T. & Rothstein, H. R. (2009). *Introduction to Meta-analysis*. Chichester: Wiley.

Brown, D. (2016). The type and linguistic foci of oral corrective feedback in the L2 classroom: A meta-analysis. *Language Teaching Research*, 20(4), 436–458.

Bruton, A. (2010). Another reply to Truscott on error correction: Improved situated designs over statistics. *System*, 38, 491–498. DOI:10.1016/j.system.2010.07.001.

Chandler, J. (2003). The efficacy of various kinds of error feedback for improvement in the accuracy and fluency of L2 student writing. *Journal of Second Language Writing*, 12(3), 267–296.

Chen, T. (2016). Technology-supported peer feedback in ESL/EFL writing classes: A research synthesis. *Computer Assisted Language Learning*, 29(2), 365–397.

Chen, T. & Lin, H. (2012, March). Effects of peer feedback on EFL/ESL writing improvement: A meta-analysis. Paper presented at the Georgetown University Roundtable on Linguistics and Languages (GURT), Georgetown University, Washington, DC.

Cobb, M. (2010). Meta-analysis of the effectiveness of task-based interaction in form-focused instruction of adult learners in foreign and second language teaching. Unpublished doctoral dissertation, University of San Francisco.

Cooper, H. (2010). *Research Synthesis and Meta-analysis: A Step-by-Step Approach* (4th edn.). Los Angeles: Sage.

Cooper, H., Hedges, L. V. & Valentine, J. C. (eds.). (2009). *The handbook of research synthesis and meta-analysis* (2nd ed.), New York: Russell Sage Foundations.

Derrick, D. J. (2016). Instrument reporting practices in second language research. *TESOL Quarterly, 50*, 132–153. DOI:10.1002/tesq.217.

Duppenthale, P. (2002). Feedback and Japanese high school English language journal writing. Unpublished doctoral dissertation, Temple University.

Ferris, D. R. (1999). The case for grammar correction in L2 writing classes: A response to Truscott (1996). *Journal of Second Language Writing, 8* (1), 1–11.

(2004). The "Grammar correction" debate in L2 writing: Where are we, and where do we go from here? (and what do we do in the meantime...?). *Journal of Second Language Writing, 13*(1), 49–62.

(2010). Second language writing research and written corrective feedback in SLA. *Studies in Second Language Acquisition, 32*(2), 181–201.

Hendrickson, J. M. (1977). The effects of error correction treatments upon adequate and accurate communication in the written compositions of adult learners of English as a second language. Unpublished doctoral dissertation, Ohio State University.

Kang, E. & Han, Z. (2015). The efficacy of written corrective feedback in improving L2 written accuracy: A meta-analysis. *Modern Language Journal, 99*(1), 1–18.

Kao, C. W. & Wible, D. (2011). The distinction between focused and unfocused grammar feedback matters: A meta-analysis. Paper presented at the Second Language Research Forum, Ames, IA, October.

Keck, C. M., Iberri-Shea, G., Tracy-Ventura, N. & Wa-Mbaleka, S. (2006). Investigating the empirical link between task-based interaction and acquisition: A meta-analysis. In J. M. Norris and L. Ortega (eds.), *Synthesizing research on language learning and teaching* (pp. 91–131). Philadelphia: John Benjamins.

Lee, J., Jang, J. & Plonsky, L. (2015). The effectiveness of second language pronunciation instruction: A meta-analysis. *Applied Linguistics, 36*(3), 345–366.

Li, S. (2010). The effectiveness of corrective feedback in SLA: A meta-analysis. *Language Learning, 60*(2), 309–365. DOI:10.1111/j.1467-9922.2010.00561.x.

Lipsey, M. W. & Wilson, D. B. (2001). *Practical meta-analysis*. Thousand Oaks, CA: Sage.

Liu, Q. & Brown, D. (2015). A methodological synthesis of research on the effectiveness of corrective feedback in L2 writing. *Journal of Second Language Writing, 30*, 66–81.

Lyster, R. & Saito, K. (2010). Oral feedback in classroom SLA: A meta-analysis. *Studies in Second Language Acquisition*, 32(2), 265–302. DOI:10.1017/S0272263109990520.

Mackey, A. & Goo, J. (2007). Interaction research in SLA: A meta-analysis and research synthesis. In A. Mackey (ed.), *Conversational interaction in second language acquisition: A collection of empirical studies* (pp. 407–451). New York: Oxford University Press,

Marsden, E., Morgan-Short, K., Thompson, S. & Abugaber, D. (2018). Replication in second language research: Narrative and systematic reviews, and recommendations for the field. *Language Learning*. Advance online publication. DOI:10.1111/lang.12286.

Marsden, E., Thompson, S. & Plonsky, L. (2018). A methodological synthesis of self-paced reading in second language research. *Applied Psycholinguistics*. Advance online publication. https://doi.org/10.1017/S0142716418000036.

Miller, P. C. (2003). The effectiveness of corrective feedback: A meta-analysis. Unpublished doctoral dissertation, Purdue University, West Lafayette, IN.

Miller, P. C. and Pan, W. (2012). Recasts in the L2 classroom: A meta-analytic review. *International Journal of Educational Research*, 56, 48–59. doi: 10.1016/j.ijer.2012.07.002.

Nassaji, H. (2015). *Interactional feedback dimension in instructed second language learning*. London: Bloomsbury Publishing.

  (2016). Anniversary article: Interactional feedback in second language teaching and learning: A synthesis and analysis of current research. *Language Teaching Research*, 20(4), 535–562.

Nicholas, H., Lightbown, P. M. & Spada, N. (2001). Recasts as feedback to language learners. *Language Learning*, 51(4), 719–758.

Norris, J. M. & Ortega, L. (2000). Effectiveness of L2 instruction: A research synthesis and quantitative meta-analysis. *Language Learning*, 50(3), 417–528.

  (eds.). (2006). *Synthesizing research on language learning and teaching*. Philadelphia: John Benjamins.

  (2007). The future of research synthesis in applied linguistics: Beyond art or science. *TESOL Quarterly*, 41(4), 805–815.

Ortega, L. (2015). Research synthesis. In B. Paltridge & A. Phakiti (eds.), *Research methods in applied linguistics: A practical resource* (pp. 225–244). London: Bloomsbury.

Oswald, F. L. & Plonsky, L. (2010). Meta-analysis in second language research: Choices and challenges. *Annual Review of Applied Linguistics*, 30, 85–110.

Papaioannou, D., Sutton, A., Carroll, C., Booth, A. & Wong, R. (2009). Literature searching for social science systematic reviews: Consideration of a range of search techniques. *Health Information and Libraries Journal*, 27, 114–122. DOI: 10.1111/j.1471-1842.2009.00863.x.

Plonsky, L. (2012). Replication, meta-analysis, and generalizability. In G. Porte (ed.), *Replication Research in Applied Linguistics* (pp. 116–132). Cambridge: Cambridge University Press.

(2013). Study quality in SLA: An assessment of designs, analyses, and reporting practices in quantitative L2 research. *Studies in Second Language Acquisition*, 35(4), 655–687.

(2014). Study quality in quantitative L2 research (1990–2010): A methodological synthesis and call for reform. *Modern Language Journal*, 98(1), 450–470.

Plonsky, L. & Brown, D. (2015). Domain definition and search techniques in meta-analyses of L2 research (Or why 18 meta-analyses of feedback have different results). *Second Language Research*, 31(2), 267–278.

Plonsky, L. & Gass, S. (2011). Quantitative research methods, study quality, and outcomes: The case of interaction research. *Language Learning*, 61 (2), 325–366.

Plonsky, L. & Gonulal, T. (2015). Methodological synthesis in quantitative L2 research: A review of reviews and a case study of exploratory factor analysis. *Language Learning*, 65(Suppl. 1), 9–36.

Plonsky, L. & Kim, Y. (2016). Task-based learner production: A substantive and methodological review. *Annual Review of Applied Linguistics*, 36, 73–97.

Plonsky, L. & Oswald, F. L. (2012). How to do a meta-analysis. In A. Mackey, S. M. Gass, L. Plonsky & F. L. Oswald (eds.), *Research methods in second language acquisition: A practical guide* (pp. 275–295). Blackwell Publishing.

(2014). How big is "big"? Interpreting effect sizes in L2 research. *Language Learning*, 64(4), 878–912.

Poltavtchenko, E. & Johnson, M. D. (2009). *Feedback and second language writing: A meta-analysis*. Poster session presented at the annual meeting of TESOL, Denver, CO, March.

Porte, G. (ed.). (2012). *Replication research in applied linguistics*. Cambridge: Cambridge University Press.

Riazi, M., Shi, L. & Haggerty, J. (2018). Analysis of the empirical research in the journal of second language writing at its 25th year (1992–2016). *Journal of Second Language Writing*, 41, 41–54.

Rothstein H. R., Sutton A. J. & Borenstein M. (eds.). (2005). *Publication bias in meta-analysis: Prevention, assessment and adjustments*. Hoboken, NJ: Wiley.

Russell, J. & Spada, N. (2006). The effectiveness of corrective feedback for the acquisition of L2 grammar: A meta-analysis of the research. In J. M. Norris and L. Ortega (eds.), *Synthesizing research on language learning and teaching* (pp. 133–164). Philadelphia: John Benjamins.

Sheppard, K. (1992). Two feedback types: Do they make a difference? *RELC Journal*, 23, 103–110.

Sok, S., Kang, E. Y. & Han, Z. (2018). Thirty-five years of ISLA on form-focused instruction: A methodological synthesis. *Language Teaching Research.* Advance online publication. DOI:10.1177/1362168818776673.

Storch, N. (2010). Critical feedback on written corrective feedback research. *International Journal of English Studies*, 10(2), 29–46. DOI:10.6018/ijes/2010/2/119181.

Thirakunkovit, S. P. & Chamcharatsri, P. B. (2019). A meta-analysis of effectiveness of teacher and peer feedback: Implications for writing instructions and research. *Asian EFL Journal*, 21(1), 140–170.

Truscott, J. (1996). The case against grammar correction in L2 writing classes. *Language Learning*, 46(2), 327–369.

⎯ (2007). The effect of error correction on learners' ability to write accurately. *Journal of Second Language Writing*, 16(4), 255–272. DOI:10.1016/j.jslw.2007.06.003.

Yousefi, M. & Nassaji, H. (2018). The effect of computer-mediated vs. face-to-face instruction on L2 pragmatics: A meta-analysis. *International Journal of Cognitive and Language Sciences*, 12(7), 620–624.

Ziegler, N. (2013). Synchronous computer-mediated communication and interaction: A research synthesis and meta-analysis. Unpublished doctoral dissertation, Georgetown University.

⎯ (2016). Synchronous computer-mediated communication and interaction: A meta-analysis. *Studies in Second Language Acquisition*, 38(3), 553–586.

Part III

Different Delivery Modes of Corrective Feedback

9

Oral Corrective Feedback

Rhonda Oliver and Rebecca Adams

Introduction

A number of features in our language environment, especially those that occur when we engage in conversation with others, can play an important role in facilitating second language learning. Such features include opportunities to receive comprehensible input, chances to focus on language form in the context of meaning, and conversational space to apply emergent language abilities to produce comprehensible linguistic output. When learners produce language output during communication within and beyond the language classroom, it opens up the possibility for them to receive corrective feedback (CF) from a communication partner about the language they have produced. This feedback, oral CF, is the focus of the current chapter. A further chapter (Chapter 10) in this volume will provide an overview of feedback provided for written output.

Researchers working from multiple theoretical perspectives have come to regard feedback as an essential component in the second language acquisition equation as it optimises learner language development. For instance, those subscribing to a cognitive-interactionist perspective (e.g., Gass, 2013; Long, 1996; Mackey, 2013; Ranta & Lyster, 2007) deem input to be necessary, but on its own insufficient for the acquisition of second language competence beyond basic proficiency. Rather, by giving learners the chance to produce output and then to receive feedback on their growing language knowledge, their attention is drawn to the language forms they are using. This process is purported to make important contributions to language learning. Those subscribing to a sociocultural position also support the view that feedback, as part of interaction, creates a context for acquisition because through feedback teachers can provide scaffolding to the learners, helping them to produce language that they could not do successfully on their own (e.g., Ellis, 2009; Lantolf & Thorne, 2006; Swain 2010).

From a pedagogical perspective, teachers and scholars continue to consider what is most useful for language learners in terms of feedback. This includes questions about what form the feedback should take, how frequently it should be provided, and when it should be provided (e.g., whether the timing of feedback should be immediate or delayed). These issues are discussed below, beginning with a description of what oral feedback is. We then discuss evidence of the importance of oral CF to language learning, the range of forms that feedback can take, and current understandings of factors that make feedback effective for learning. We conclude by describing some of the pedagogical implications of oral CF research.

What Is Oral Corrective Feedback?

Oral CF is the response provided by teachers or other conversational partners to language learners when their output is erroneous, nontarget-like, and/or not appropriate or ambiguous. It indicates to them in an oral mode, either implicitly or explicitly, that something is not right with what they have said. This information has been described as negative evidence, as it provides data for learners about what is not acceptable in the target language (Gass, 2013; Long, 1996). Negative evidence stands in contrast to positive evidence, which is information about what is possible and acceptable in the language. (It should be noted that some forms of CF, such as recasts, provide both positive and negative evidence, as discussed below.) It is hypothesized that feedback is also necessary for second language acquisition as there are aspects of learning a second language that are unlikely to be learned from exposure to input alone, that is, positive evidence on its own is insufficient. This was illustrated by Gass and Madden (1985) using crosslinguistic examples of adverb placement.

Example 1
(i) *Lentamente Giovanni beve il caffè.*
   Slowly, John drinks the coffee.
(ii) *Giovanni lentamente beve il caffè.*
   John slowly drinks the coffee.
(iii) *Giovanni beve il caffè lentamente.*
   John drinks the coffee slowly.
(iv) *Giovanni beve lentamente il caffè.*
   *John drinks slowly the coffee.   (p. 122)

Each of the italicized Italian examples demonstrates an allowable position for the adverb in that language. The first three are likewise acceptable in English, but the fourth is not. Gass and Madden point out that English speakers learning Italian could learn the fourth pattern simply by hearing it in the input (positive evidence). However, Italian speakers learning English would need to notice that the fourth example was missing from the input, which is unlikely to occur. What is more likely is for them to amend their interlanguage knowledge of adverb placement restrictions when presented with some corrective feedback (negative evidence) because this alerts them to the fact that adverbs cannot be located between verbs and their objects in English.

A key part of second language CF is that it is generally reactive, provided in response to learner output. In a conversational exchange, a learner may say something that does not conform to native-speaker expectations. Researchers have described such output as "triggering" feedback from a teacher or other interlocutor (Pica, 1994). Because feedback is always a response to learner efforts, it is considered by educational scholars as a learner-centered form of instruction (Hattie, 2009). In terms of linguistic research about feedback, there is some debate about what conversational partners are responding to. For example, some such as Ellis, Loewen, and Erlam (2006), describe CF as being provided in *response to error* (italics added). This may involve feedback about errors related to pronunciation, as in Example 2 below:

Example 2
LEARNER 1: No tiene flores ... uh un bosco.
 It doesn't have flowers ... uh, a forest [mispronunciation]
LEARNER 2: Bosque.
 Forest. [correct pronunciation]
LEARNER 1: Bosque.
 Forest. [correct pronunciation]
 (Gass, Mackey & Ross-Feldman, 2011, p. 199)

Learner 1 was describing a picture as part of a conversational task, mispronounced a Spanish word, and received a recast correcting his pronunciation from his conversational partner. He repeated the correct pronunciation. Feedback can also respond to lexical errors, as in Example 3:

Example 3
NNS: He broke his surfing board.
NS: He broke his surfboard.
 (Carpenter et al., 2006, p. 227)

The learner (nonnative speaker, NNS) in this excerpt is working with the native speaker (NS) on a picture-based task about waves. He misnames a surfboard and receives a short recast with the correct lexical form. CF can also be targeted to grammatical errors, as in the morphological feedback given in Example 4 below:

Example 4
L: Yesterday Joe and Bill ah went to ah Bill's grandmother and visit their grandmother and
T: 'Visit you need past tense.'

L: Visited, yes.

(Ellis, Loewen & Erlam, 2006, p. 353)

The feedback in this instance provides the learner with an explicit correction and explanation of a regular past tense morphology error, which the learner is able to correct once he is attending to it.

In contrast, Oliver and Mackey (2003) describe oral CF as being provided when the learner's initial production is nontarget-like. This can include feedback in response to production that is unacceptable or inappropriate, either grammatically or pragmatically, as in Example 5.

Example 5
S: "x" said he ride the bike with "x" and – and he fall in – and then he fall in the bum.
T: Oh he fell down, oh dear.
S: And I fall on the botty.

(Oliver & Mackey, 2003, p. 524)

In this example, a class of child ESL learners are sharing "morning news" with their classmates. One student shares a story of a bicycle accident. The teacher provides her with past tense feedback (fall → fell) but also rephrases her contribution to be more nativelike ("fall in the bum" → "fell down").

Whether directed at errors or nonnative constructions, oral CF provides information to learners about the target language they are learning.

Why Is CF Important?

Many empirical studies as well as meta-analyses have indicated that oral CF actually promotes language acquisition (e.g., Goo & Mackey, 2013; Leeman, 2003; Li, 2010; Lyster & Saito, 2010; Mackey & Goo, 2007; Oliver, 1995; Russell & Spada, 2006; Sheen, 2004). In this section, we discuss how this is achieved. It should be remembered, however, that the effects of CF can be constrained by the context in which it is provided and also by individual differences of the learners (Li, 2014), factors which also will be discussed. Even with these caveats, instruction has been found to be more effective when it involves oral CF than when it does not (Doughty & Varela, 1998; Loewen & Nabei, 2007; Lyster & Saito, 2010; McDonough, 2007).

A variety of reasons for the effectiveness of CF have been proffered. As we have indicated above, the key component of oral CF is that it provides learners with negative evidence and does so by alerting them to what is not possible in the target language – indicating what is unacceptable or erroneous. This pushes learners to notice the gap between the target language and their own developing interlanguage knowledge (Gass, 2013; Long, 1996). According to the Noticing Hypothesis (e.g., Schmidt, 1990), drawing attention to what is problematic in this way can promote cognitive processing necessary for learning. Some forms of oral CF also provide additional positive evidence, demonstrating models of what is acceptable and/or correct in the target language.

The effectiveness of oral CF lies in its reactiveness, given as a response to what learners need for their language development right at the time when they need it (Lightbown, 1998). In many ways, this is the very essence of learner-centered teaching (as described in the general education literature), as the feedback is based on what the learner actually needs rather than what we might imagine they need (Hattie, 2009). This helps learners to reconsider and restructure their interlanguage knowledge, leading it closer to the target language system.

Lyster, Saito, and Sato (2013) suggest that, through the re-presentation of the target language, oral CF helps learners to develop a "network of associations" (p. 13). They also suggest that it helps learners develop "self-regulation" in their use of the target language, especially when the feedback involves negotiation – either of meaning or form. Aljaafreh and Lantolf (1994) found that when feedback was negotiated in interaction to match a student's Zone of Proximal Development (ZPD), what has been described in other studies as learner developmental readiness (Mackey & Oliver, 2002; Mackey & Philp, 1998), students were increasingly able to control their production of target forms. Nassaji and Swain (2000) tested this by providing feedback matched to the student's emergent knowledge of form with feedback that was provided randomly, finding that students who received negotiated feedback were increasingly able to control the use of the targeted form. Sato and Ballinger (2012) similarly found that training learners to negotiate feedback with one another enhanced their language awareness.

Despite its apparent effectiveness, there remains some contention about the contribution of oral CF to second language learning. There is debate, for example, about how it contributes to language development, whether it simply consolidates partially acquired knowledge or whether it contributes to new learning (Goo & Mackey, 2013). However, considerably more argument has centered around the effectiveness of the various types of oral CF; as a result there has been a large amount of research attention focused on determining how effective these different types of CF are in terms of language learning.

Types of Oral Corrective Feedback

Oral CF is described as ranging from those types that are implicit (Long, 1996) or indirect (Lantolf, 2000) to those that are explicit or direct. (It should be noted these categorizations are not uniform; for example, Long, 1996, describes recasts as implicit, Li, 2014, suggests they are direct, and Lyster & Mori, 2006 believe them to be more explicit than implicit.)

Lyster and Ranta (1997) identified six types of CF including recasts, explicit correction, elicitation, clarification requests, metalinguistic clues, and repetition. Ranta and Lyster (2007) later sorted these into two categories: reformulations (recasts and explicit correction) – which supply learners with both positive and negative evidence – and prompts (elicitations, clarification requests, metalinguistic clues, and repetitions), which provide only negative evidence, pushing the learner to fill in the correct form themselves. In this section, we define and exemplify different types of oral CF, beginning with feedback that reformulates learner utterances.

Recasts

These are described as a reformulation of the learner's erroneous production that is done in such a way as to maintain the meaning of the learner (Long, 1996). One example, taken from one of the earliest second language studies of this type of CF (Oliver, 1995, p. 475), is shown below. In this example, a child NNS is describing a simple line drawing picture for an age-matched NS interlocutor.

Example 6
NNS: The boy is holding the girl hand and the boy ...
NS: The boy is holding the girl's hand?
NNS: Yer.

The child's omission of possessive marking is recast by the interlocutor, in this case, with rising question intonation. This provides the child both with negative evidence (that his original production was not target-like) and positive evidence (of how to correctly use the possessive in that sentence). The child confirms that the recast reflects his intended meaning, and the interaction moves on. This example demonstrates how recasts not only indicate to learners that there is a problem with what they have said but also provide a model of how it should be said. Leeman (2003) has suggested that this juxtaposition raises the salience of the form during the interaction.

Explicit Correction

As the name suggests, in explicit corrections, a teacher or another interlocutor explicitly indicates to learners that there is something wrong with what they have said. Ranta and Lyster (2007) categorize explicit corrections along with recasts as feedback that reformulates learner utterances to make them more target-like; other researchers have considered any feedback with an explicit statement that the learner utterance was not acceptable as explicit feedback, even if no reformulation is offered, as in the following example of teacher–student discourse collected from a full class discussion of pictures of aquatic animals.

Example 7
S: Octopus?
T: No, because an octopus has teeth.
S: Jelly fish?

(Oliver & Mackey, 2003, p. 523)

The student incorrectly guessed the name of the animal in the picture. The teacher explicitly stated that her suggestion was incorrect, including a reason the word given did not meet the semantic requirements. Although mostly associated with feedback provided by teachers, peers are also capable of providing explicit correction, as in Example 8, taken from a dyadic classroom task requiring learners to write out a story that occurred in the past tense.

Example 8
LEARNER 1: She's sad.
LEARNER 2: No, she was sad.
LEARNER 1: She was sad, because she thinking?

(Adams, Nuevo & Egi, 2011, p. 51)

While some studies have found that learners rarely provide explicit corrections (likely because of the social equality among learners in a classroom), others have found that adolescent and adult learners do provide substantial amounts of explicit correction. Adams et al. (2011) found that 45 percent of the feedback provided by learners to their peers was in the form of explicit corrections. The grammatical focus of the language learning program as well as the use of tasks that required collaborative writing may have influenced this result (see Adams & Ross-Feldman, 2008). On the other hand, even for teacher–student interactions, explicit corrections have been found to be relatively rare. Lyster et al. (2013) suggest that it is generally the least common form of CF.

Prompts

Ranta and Lyster (2007) consider all feedback moves that push learners to reformulate their own erroneous utterances as prompts. This includes elicitations, clarification requests, repetitions, and metalinguistic cues. Elicitations are most often provided by teachers and encourage learners to self-repair, rather than relying on "other repair" as is the case of explicit correction or recasts (McDonough, 2005). They may provide either explicit or implicit negative evidence that an error has occurred and encourage the learner to reformulate their own nontarget-like output, however, they do not provide a model (positive evidence) of how to do this. An elicitation, for example, does this directly by asking questions or pausing to allow the student to complete their interlocutor's utterance, as in Example 9.

Example 9
Student: Ben y a un jet de parfum qui sent pas très bon ... [lexical error]
"Well there's a stream of perfume that doesn't smell very nice."
Teacher: Alors un jet de parfum, on va appeler ça un ...?
"So a stream of perfume, we'll call that a ...?"

(Lyster & Mori, 2006, p. 272)

The teacher forms a question about the correct lexical items and waits for the learner to try to self-correct. This is a relatively explicit prompt. Similarly, in metalinguistic cues, the interlocutor provides linguistic information about the target-likeness of the learner's production. They can do this by, for example, reminding the learner about grammar forms, as in Example 10.

Example 10
LEARNER 1: the man prepare for the trip
LEARNER 2: E-D
LEARNER 1: E-D he prepared

(Adams, 2007, p. 40)

Like elicitations, metalinguistic cues are an explicit form of correction; they both explicitly indicate that there is something unacceptable about the learner's utterance and provide a metalinguistic description of why their output is erroneous or inappropriate. Other prompts are more implicit. For example, clarification requests (like Example 11, below) act as implicit feedback. They provide negative evidence that there is an issue with the learner's production but do so indirectly by suggesting that the message was not understood. Through questioning about intended meaning, the conversation partner conveys to the learner that there is something problematic with their output.

Example 11
LEARNER: What happen for the boat?
NS: What?
LEARNER: What's wrong with the boat?

(McDonough, 2005, p. 86)

The native speaker's question ("what?") serves as a prompt to the learner to reconsider his or her prior utterance and attempt to phrase the message in a more understandable way, although the learner is never explicitly told that something is wrong. A similar implicit prompt is repetition, in which the interlocutor repeats part or all of the problematic utterance, often with rising intonation, as in Example 12.

Example 12
STUDENT: La chocolat ...
"(F) Chocolate."
TEACHER: La chocolat?
"(F) Chocolate?"
STUDENT: Le chocolat.
"(M) Chocolate."

(Lyster, 2004, p. 405)

The teacher repeats the student's erroneous use of a feminine article with a masculine noun, using a rising intonation to suggest that an error has been made (providing implicit negative evidence). The student recognizes the repetition as correction and corrects the error in the following turn.

As we have seen, both types of feedback (feedback that reformulates and feedback that prompts) can exist in relatively implicit and relatively explicit formats, and all types of feedback provide negative evidence. There has been, however, a long-running debate within applied linguistics research on the effectiveness of different types of feedback, which we summarize next.

Effective Feedback

As indicated previously, there has been considerable research effort expended to determine which CF moves are most effective. The question of whether or not feedback is effective hinges on whether it enhances learning outcomes. For oral CF in second language studies, this question has frequently been framed in terms of whether or not feedback leads to modified output or repair (in the case of feedback that reformulates, this has been framed in terms of whether the learner repeats the linguistic model; this conversational move has been labelled "uptake") (Lyster & Ranta, 1997). In both cases, learner moves that repair their initial utterances following feedback are taken as evidence that they have noticed the feedback, a process that is facilitative of acquisition (cf. Schmidt, 2001). Research has connected uptake and modified output with increased learning gains (e.g., Loewen, 2005; McDonough, 2005), suggesting that uptake can be at least a contributing factor for learning. However, the lack of immediate uptake does not necessarily mean that learning has not occurred – in their seminal work, Mackey and Philp (1998) demonstrated how learning can occur as a delayed response, yet one still emanating from corrective feedback.

Perhaps more than any other type of CF, recasts have been the subject of considerable attention (summarized in Goo & Mackey, 2013, and in Han &

Kim, 2008). As a consequence of this body of research, support for the effectiveness of recasts has been found in both laboratory and classroom settings, particularly in the former, where they have been found to support second language development (Iwashita, 2003; Leeman, 2003; Long, Inagaki & Ortega, 1998; Mackey, 1999; Mackey & Oliver, 2002; Mackey & Philp, 1998). Theoretical explanation for the utility of recasts comes mainly from a cognitive perspective. Specifically, by maintaining the learner's meaning, they lighten the processing load, allowing cognitive space for a focus on form to occur and, in particular, for the learner to notice the "gap" between the language they produce and that of the target language form. Loewen and Philp (2006) also point out that recasts increase the saliency of the feedback and are pedagogically expeditious, as they can be provided without interrupting the flow of conversation and in this way meaningful interaction can be maintained, as the learner's production is scaffolded to allow them to produce language that they could not produce independently.

Others taking a more sociocultural perspective claim, however, that because prompts push the work of reformulating utterances onto the learners (Lyster et al., 2013), they are a useful way of scaffolding learner production (this only works, of course, if the modifications needed are within the learners' ZPD; self-correction after prompts is only possible if it is within the learner's ability to do so). In this way, the contribution of prompts is explained from a sociocultural perspective of language learning, as they are seen as a way learners can be encouraged to self-regulate.

Lyster and Mori (2006), in their review, indicate that prompts in most, but not all, classroom contexts are more effective than recasts, promoting uptake and modified output. Similarly, Ammar (2008) suggests that learners are more likely to notice prompts than recasts. It should be noted, however, that other studies have called the connection between uptake/repair and noticing into question, suggesting that immediate uptake can actually be a "red herring" – pointing to short-term awareness that does not necessarily lead to long-term learning (Mackey & Oliver, 2002; Mackey & Philp, 1998). The debate about the utility of recasts continues (cf. Goo & Mackey, 2013, and Lyster & Ranta, 2013, for different perspectives). Those suggesting a positive contribution for recasts (e.g., Leeman, 2003) suggest their utility may lie in salience; that is, because the meanings expressed in the recast reflect the meaning the learner intended, it makes it easier for them to focus on language form.

This debate is complicated by the different forms that both recasts and prompts can take. Recasts have often been further subdivided into more specific categories based on several different aspects of the context and manner in which they are provided (see Han & Kim, 2008, for an overview). These factors generally moderate the implicitness or explicitness of the recasts and include the presence or absence of question intonation, whether the feedback provider pauses for the learner to modify their production (i.e., provides opportunity as described by Oliver, 1995) or simply continues the discourse, and whether the recast was provided with a corrective or communicative intent (what Sheen & Ellis, 2011, refer to as didactic and conversational recasts).

Sheen (2004) examined the provision of recasts across four teaching settings to determine which types of recasts were more likely to be noticed and used in the output by adult language learners. She found several characteristics of recasts more likely to lead to repair of nontarget-like utterances. These included *length*, with a shorter recast (of a specific word or phrase) more likely to lead to repair than a longer recast; *language target* (with more repairs following recasts of phonological rather than grammatical or lexical errors), and *intonation* (with interrogative recasts leading more often to acknowledgment than uptake). A replication by Oliver and Grote (2010) with child learners corroborated Sheen's assertion that the way that recasts are provided significantly influences whether they lead to repair. Mackey et al. (2007) collected student and teacher perceptions of previously recorded feedback episodes. They found that learners were more likely to correctly perceive the corrective intent of interrogative recasts. Other studies have explored learner perceptions about CF, with some such as Lyster and Ranta (1997) arguing against the effectiveness of recasts based on learners' inability to perceive them as feedback and also because of their pragmatic ambivalence. Others dispute the centrality of noticing to learning from recasts. Mackey's (2006) study, for example, found no connection between noticing recasts and learning from them. A later study, Mackey et al. (2007), found that only 36 percent of CF perceived the way the teacher intended, but again this did not negate the potential for learners to develop their L2.

Even so, debate continues about why some CF moves have greater utility than others. Some suggest that the effectiveness of the feedback relates not to whether the feedback reformulates or prompts, but how explicitly it does so. Ellis (1994) hypothesizes that this is because it triggers learners to engage in cognitive comparison; this perhaps explains why some have found that learners are more likely to notice explicit than implicit CF (Mackey et al., 2007; Nassaji, 2009). Despite this, others (e.g., Li, 2010; Long, 1996; Mackey & Goo, 2007) claim that the impact of implicit feedback is longer lasting. This is further illustrated by Li's (2010) meta-analysis of feedback studies which found that explicit feedback led to greater gains on immediate post-tests, while implicit feedback like recasts led to greater effects on delayed post-tests, suggesting that implicit feedback in the form of either prompts or recasts may have longer-term effects in promoting language learning.

The diversity of findings on the effectiveness of different types of feedback has led some researchers to call for a more pragmatic position of using a variety of feedback moves in teaching (e.g., Saito, 2013), rather than advocating specific types of feedback over others, or considering the ways that feedback affects noticing and learning differently in different classroom settings (Lyster & Mori, 2006). A wide range of individual and contextual factors influence the effectiveness of these different CF moves (e.g., age, target language) – a point we turn to in the next section.

Individual and Social Factors Impacting Upon the Effectiveness of CF

A number of factors including age and learning context have been found to impact the effectiveness of CF. Oliver (2000) explored these factors, finding that both teachers and NS partners provided abundant levels of CF, but regardless of age, learners were more likely to modify their output following CF in teacher-fronted contexts than in pairwork settings, although the opportunity to do so was greater in the latter context. There were, however, differences in the type of CF provided: Teachers were more likely to negotiate with adult learners (through the use of clarification requests, confirmation checks, and repetition) than with child learners. In the pairwork context, adults provided more recasts to their partners than did children. These results were then corroborated by Panova and Lyster (2002).

The effectiveness of feedback is also influenced by who provides the feedback – teachers, other learners, or native speakers. Mackey, Oliver, and Leeman (2003), for example, found that native speakers provided more feedback than fellow learners, but when learners provided each other with feedback, they were more likely to do so in a way that allowed for uptake or repair. The effectiveness of feedback also varies according to the language and learning context in which it is provided. For example, in an adult EFL setting in Korea, Sheen (2004) found that feedback provided was nearly always recasts (83% recasts, 6% prompts, and 11% explicit correction); in a secondary French setting, Simard and Jean (2011) found a different proportion of feedback types (25% recasts, 29% prompts, and 46% explicit correction). In their review of a series of studies examining these features, Lyster, et al. (2013) found a wide divergence in both the amount of feedback provided in different settings (ranging from six to forty-one corrective feedback moves per hour) and in the distribution of feedback types (prompts, for example, could account for anywhere between 6 percent and 77 percent of the feedback provided). Feedback provision seems to be closely tied to specific learning settings, with wide variance between settings. Lyster and Mori (2006) found that whether or not feedback led to uptake or repair differed not just according to the type of feedback, but also according to how that feedback fit with the overall teaching context, with implicit feedback taken up in classrooms with a more explicit focus, and explicit feedback leading to repair in more communicative settings.

More recently there has been a series of investigations examining the timing of feedback. Lyster and Saito (2010) claim that when oral CF is provided at the point of need (defined as when the learner has produced something problematic) there is a greater likelihood that the information provided will be transferred to similar contexts as they appear in the future. This is in contrast to delayed CF, where such decontextualized language use is less likely to contribute to the incorporation of that information in learner future language use.

Other studies have examined whether oral CF provided in isolation is more or less effective than when it provided with other feedback or instruction (Nassaji, 2009). Research has also examined whether CF is better when it is provided intensively, focusing on just a few features, as suggested by Doughty (2001) and as investigated by Kamiya (2015). Mackey and Goo (2007) provided support for this, showing that intensive CF has a greater effect, particularly in the delayed post-tests. However, Russell and Spada (2006) found no evidence of any difference between intensive and extensive treatments, whereas Ellis and Sheen (2006) noted that "extensive recasts directed at whatever errors learners happen to make might be of greater practical value" (p. 255), serving to remind us that the goal of research on CF is to provide teachers with information on how to use feedback effectively. We examine this in the final section.

Pedagogical Implications

Based on the body of research as described above, it is clear that CF has an important role to play in second language acquisition, indicating to teachers the benefit of providing feedback at the point of need. However, as discussed above, the effectiveness of CF for learning is related both to the context in which it is provided and to the type of feedback, making it impossible to issue blanket statements on how feedback should be provided across learning settings and likely leaving educators confused about how to provide CF in their particular classrooms.

The findings of tightly controlled laboratory studies cannot be simply transferred to classroom situations (e.g., Lyster et al., 2013), but the results of such studies coupled with those that are classroom based do provide teachers at the very least with insights that can guide them to reflect on CF in their setting, directing them to important considerations that can guide their practice. Because of the myriad of CF options available to them, teachers will first need to consider some basic questions about the role of CF in their classrooms. For example, will they provide CF to all errors or target only a few – that is, will they provide extensive or intensive CF? How frequently will they provide CF? Li (2014) points to the fine balance between providing sufficient CF, but not to the extent of risking it reducing learner motivation and learner autonomy. Teachers will also need to consider at what point to provide the feedback, whether to do so immediately, potentially interrupting the flow of conversation, or do so later (what Li, 2014, describes as "online" or "offline") when the effectiveness of use is diminished. And depending on whether they provide CF straight away or delay will then require them to consider the type which is best to use for their learners in their teaching context (e.g., recasts and prompts may be most effective immediately during communicative exchanges, whereas explicit CF may be best utilised at a later point).

In order to make choices about what is most appropriate for their particular learners, especially in terms of the how and when to provide CF, teachers need to consider who the learners are. This includes considering their age and motivations for learning the target language, whether this language is a second language or a foreign language, and the classroom context in which they are learning. Some researchers also suggest catering for the CF preferences of learners, taking into consideration learners' expectations with regards to receiving CF. This does not necessarily mean providing only the type of CF learners prefer, but targeting CF so that it is useful and uptake is possible. It is important to keep in mind, however, that learners cannot always accurately articulate their feedback preferences, and their stated preferences may not actually be most helpful in promoting their learning. For example, learners may express a desire to be explicitly and consistently corrected (Plonsky & Mills, 2006) but in actuality find frequent explicit corrections embarrassing and intimidating, leaving them less likely to take up feedback and apply it. The use of constant CF may also inhibit the natural flow of the conversation and diminish communicative opportunities within the classroom (Lasagabaster & Sierra, 2009). Another issue to consider is the compatibility of learner perceptions about CF compared to the teacher's intentions. Mismatches between how the teacher intended the feedback and how students perceive it can have a negative effect on learning (Nunan, 1989).

How and when CF should be provided depends to a large extent on the teacher's objectives. If they are targeting instruction at learning specific language forms that have been identified as learner needs, they may use more frequent feedback focused on the specific form. If they are trying to push their students to develop confidence in their communication abilities or to practice a range of communication strategies to allow them to use the second language, they may use less intrusive, more implicit feedback, such as clarification requests that provide feedback while moving the conversation forward. Spada and Lightbown (1993), Lightbown (1998), and Long (1996) have all claimed that CF is most effective when it is embedded in meaningful language use. Teachers should take care to provide CF in ways that allow learners to focus on language in the context of meaningful communication, rather than allowing frequent, explicit feedback to draw learner attention away from using language to make and understand meanings. It is important that educators weigh these possibilities to ensure the CF they provide is most appropriate for the needs of their learners as well as targeted in ways that allow learners to attend to it during classroom communication (Li, 2010).

In addition, choosing which feedback is appropriate for their learners will require teachers to consider learner developmental needs. CF targeted below the zone of the learners' development is unnecessary, CF targeted too far above this range is inaccessible. Hedge (2000), for example, suggests responding only to those errors that occur because they are currently not part of learners' interlanguage repertoire, rather than providing CF to "mistakes" (e.g., slips of the tongue) and simple errors that the learners can correct themselves. As we indicated previously, the effectiveness of CF is related to the readiness of learners, with immediate uptake not necessarily indicative of usefulness (Mackey & Oliver, 2002; Mackey & Philp, 1998).

CF should require some degree of effort on the part of the learners. This helps learners to develop their skills of self-monitoring and self-correction, creating opportunities for learners to develop a degree of autonomy so that they do not become accustomed to relying only on teachers to oversee the correctness of their production. Lyster (2004) claims that promoting self-correction is often more motivating for learners and leads to classes that are more interactive, although he does acknowledge that this also depends on how the classes are set up. For instance, even reformulation feedback makes demands of learners, asking them to compare their own output with the reformulation and, in so doing, to notice differences. Furthermore, cognitive effort in processing feedback increases the likelihood that it will be retained (Aljaafreh & Lantolf, 1994; Nassaji & Swain, 2009).

Although teachers may feel they shoulder the burden for CF within the classroom, it also can be provided by others, especially by peers. Dyadic and group work situations have been shown to provide a rich source of CF (Mackey & Goo, 2007). (See Adams and Oliver, 2019, for an overview of how teachers can create pair and group work opportunities that promote classroom interactions, facilitating the provision of peer CF.) Peer CF offers different opportunities than CF provided by teachers or native speakers; for example, it is provided in ways that give learners more opportunities to modify their own language use (e.g., Oliver, 2000) and in ways that more effectively push students to do so (McDonough, 2007). Of course, this may require teachers to stage the introduction of such an approach – if not used previously – and to provide feedback training for learners (Sato & Lyster, 2012) as well as guidance during interactions to support learners as they provide CF to their peers (Oliver, Philp & Mackey, 2008).

This chapter has touched on a number of issues that can help guide teacher decision-making in providing CF in language learning classrooms, and understandably many will have ongoing concerns about whether CF is effective in their classrooms and how it can best be provided. Professional development for teachers that introduces them to CF practices, along with the benefits and drawbacks of different types and uses of CF, allows them to develop their own awareness and be supported as they reflect on developing the role of CF in their classroom practices.

Conclusion

Our review has described how oral CF contributes to language learning, showing that, as a communicative feature, it is potentially a significant part of the acquisition equation. Although the effectiveness of feedback is dependent on a wide range of factors associated with the feedback itself, the contexts in which it is provided, and the learners it is provided to, CF has the potential to expedite language learning in classroom settings. While a considerable body of research has focused on the usefulness of different types of CF and how they can contribute to second language acquisition, more is needed to provide teachers with guidance on how different types of feedback in different settings help learners learn different aspects of language.

References

Adams, R. (2007). Do second language learners benefit from interacting with each other? In A. Mackey (ed.), *Conversational interaction in second language acquisition* (pp. 29–51). Oxford: Oxford University Press.

Adams, R., Nuevo, A. M. & Egi, T. (2011). Explicit and implicit feedback, modified output, and SLA: Does explicit and implicit feedback promote learning and learner–learner interactions? *Modern Language Journal*, 11(Suppl. issue), 42–63.

Adams, R. & Oliver, R. (2019). *Teaching through peer interaction*. New York: Routledge.

Adams, R. & Ross-Feldman, L. (2008). Does writing influence learner attention to form? In D. Belcher & A. Hirvela (eds.), *The oral–literate connection: Perspectives on L2 speaking, writing, and other media interactions* (pp. 243–265). Ann Arbor: University of Michigan Press.

Aljaafeh, A. & Lantolf, J. (1994). Negative feedback as regulation and second language learning in the zone of proximal development. *Modern Language Journal*, 78(4), 465–483.

Ammar, A. (2008). Prompts and recasts: Differential effects on second language morphosyntax. *Language Teaching Research*, 12(2), 183–210.

Carpenter, H., Jeon, S., MacGregor, D. & Mackey, A. (2006). Learner's interpretations of recasts. *Studies in Second Language Acquisition*, 28(2), 209–236.

Doughty, C. (2001). Cognitive underpinnings of focus on form. In P. Robinson (ed.), *Cognition and second language instruction* (pp. 206–257). Cambridge: Cambridge University Press.

Doughty, C. & Varela, E. (1998). Communicative focus on form. In C. Doughty & J. Williams (eds.), *Focus on form in classroom second language acquisition* (pp. 114–138). Cambridge: Cambridge University Press.

Ellis, R. (1994). A theory of instructed second language acquisition. In N. C. Ellis (ed.), *Implicit and explicit language learning* (pp. 79–114). San Diego, CA: Academic Press.

(2009). Corrective feedback and teacher development. *L2 Journal*, 1 (1), 3–18.

Ellis, R., Loewen, S. & Erlam, R. (2006). Implicit and explicit corrective feedback and the acquisition of L2 grammar. *Studies in Second Language Acquisition*, 28(2), 339–368.

Ellis, R. and Sheen, Y. (2006). Reexamining the role of recasts in second language acquisition. *Studies in Second Language Acquisition*, 28(5), 575–600.

Gass, S. (2013). *Input, interaction, and the second language learner*. New York: Routledge.

Gass, S., Mackey, A. & Ross–Feldman, L. (2011). Task-based interactions in classroom and laboratory settings. *Language Learning*, 61(S1), 189–220.

Gass, S. & Madden, C. (eds.). (1985). *Input in second language acquisition*. Rowley, MA: Newbury House.

Goo, J. & Mackey, A. (2013). The case against the case against recasts. *Studies in Second Language Acquisition*, 35(1), 127–165.

Han, Z. & Kim, J. (2008). Corrective recasts: What teachers might want to know. *Language Learning Journal*, 36(1), 35–44.

Hattie, J. (2009). *Visible learning: A synthesis of over 800 meta-analyses relating to achievement*. London: Routledge.

Hedge, T. (2000). *Teaching and learning in the language classroom*. Oxford: Oxford University Press.

Iwashita, N. (2003). Negative feedback and positive evidence in task-based interaction: Differential effects on L2 development. *Studies in Second Language Acquisition*, 25(1), 1–36.

Kamiya, N. (2015). The effectiveness of intensive and extensive recasts on L2 acquisition for implicit and explicit knowledge. *Linguistics and Education*, 29, 59–72.

Lantolf, J. P. (ed.). (2000). *Sociocultural theory and second language learning*. Oxford: Oxford University Press.

Lantolf, J. P. & Thorne, S. L. (2006). *Sociocultural theory and the genesis of second language development*. Oxford: Oxford University Press.

Lasagabaster, D. & Sierra, J. M. (2009). Error correction: Students' versus teachers' perceptions. *Language Awareness*, 14(2–3), 112–127.

Leeman, J. (2003). Recasts and L2 development: Beyond negative evidence. *Studies in Second Language Acquisition*, 25(1), 37–63.

Li, S. (2010). The effectiveness of corrective feedback in SLA: A meta-analysis. *Language Learning*, *60*(2), 309–365.

(2014). Oral corrective feedback. *ELT Journal*, *68*(2), 196–198.

Lightbown, P. (1998). The importance of timing in focus on form. In C. Doughty & J. Williams (eds.), *Focus on form in classroom second language acquisition* (pp. 177–196). Cambridge: Cambridge University Press.

Loewen, S. (2005). Incidental focus on form and second language learning. *Studies in Second Language Acquisition*, *27*(3), 361–386.

Loewen, S. & Nabei, T. (2007). Measuring the effects of oral corrective feedback on L2 knowledge. In A. Mackey (ed.), *Conversational interaction in second language acquisition: A collection of empirical studies* (pp. 361–377). Oxford: Oxford University Press.

Loewen, S. & Philp, J. (2006). Recasts in the adult English L2 classroom: Characteristics, explicitness, and effectiveness. *Modern Language Journal*, *90*(4), 536–556.

Long, M. H. (1996). The role of linguistic environment in second language acquisition. In W. Ritchie and T. K. Bhatia (eds.), *Handbook of second language acquisition* (pp. 413–468). San Diego, CA: Academic Press.

Long, M., Inagaki, S. & Ortega, L. (1998). The role of implicit negative feedback in SLA: Models and recasts in Japanese and Spanish. *Modern Language Journal*, *82*(3), 357–371.

Lyster, R. (2004). Differential effects of prompts and recasts in form-focused instruction. *Studies in Second Language Acquisition*, *26*(3), 399–432.

Lyster, R. & Mori, H. (2006). Interactional feedback and instructional counterbalance. *Studies in Second Language Acquisition*, *28*(2), 269–300.

Lyster, R. & Ranta, L. (1997). Corrective feedback and learner uptake. *Studies in Second Language Acquisition*, *19*(1), 37–66.

(2013). Counterpoint piece: The case for variety in corrective feedback research. *Studies in Second Language Acquisition*, *35*(1), 167–184.

Lyster, R. & Saito, K. (2010). Oral feedback in classroom SLA: A meta-analysis. *Studies in Second Language Acquisition*, *32*(2), 265–302.

Lyster, R., Saito, K. & Sato, M. (2013). Oral corrective feedback in L2 classrooms. *Language Teaching*, *46*(4), 1–40.

Mackey, A. (1999). Input, interaction and second language development: An empirical study of question formation in ESL. *Studies in Second Language Acquisition*, *21*(4), 557–587.

(2006). Feedback, noticing and instructed second language learning. *Applied Linguistics*, *27*(3), 405–430.

(2013). *Input, interaction and corrective feedback in L2 learning*. Oxford: Oxford University Press.

Mackey, A., Al-Khalil, M., Atanassova, G., Hama, M., Logan-Terry, A. & Nakatsukasa, K. (2007). Teachers' intentions and learners' perceptions about corrective feedback in the L2 classroom. *Innovations in Language Learning and Teaching*, *1*(1), 129–152.

Mackey, A. & Goo, J. (2007). Interaction research in SLA: A meta-analysis and research synthesis. In A. Mackey (ed.), *Conversational interaction in second language acquisition: A collection of empirical studies* (pp. 407–452). Oxford: Oxford University Press.

Mackey, A. & Oliver, R. (2002). Interactional feedback and children's L2 development. *System, 30*(4), 459–477.

Mackey, A., Oliver, R. & Leeman, J. (2003). Interactional input and incorporation of feedback: An exploration of NS–NNS and NNS–NNS adult and child dyads. *Language Learning, 53*(1), 35–66.

Mackey, A. & Philp, J. (1998). Conversational interaction and second language development: Recasts, responses, and red herrings? *Modern Language Journal, 82*(3), 338–356.

McDonough, K. (2005). Identifying the impact of negative feedback and learners' responses on ESL question development. *Studies in Second Language Acquisition, 27*(1), 79–103.

(2007). Interactional feedback and the emergence of simple past activity verbs in L2 English. In A. Mackey (ed.), *Conversational interaction in second language acquisition: A collection of empirical studies* (pp. 323–338). Oxford: Oxford University Press.

Nassaji, H. (2009). Effects of recasts and elicitations in dyadic interaction and the role of feedback explicitness. *Language Learning, 59*(2), 411–452.

Nassaji, H., & Swain, M. (2000). A Vygotskian perspective on corrective feedback in L2: The effect of random versus negotiated help on the learning of English articles. Language awareness, 9(1), 34–51.

(2009). A Vygotskyan perspective on corrective feedback in L2: The effect of random versus negotiated help in the learning of English articles. *Language Awareness, 9*(1), 34–51.

Nunan, D. (1989). *Designing tasks for the communicative classroom.* Cambridge: Cambridge University Press.

Oliver, R. (1995). Negative feedback in child NS–NNS conversation. *Studies in Second Language Acquisition, 17*(4), 459–481.

(2000). Age differences in negotiation and feedback in classroom and pair work. *Language Learning, 50*(1), 119–150.

Oliver, R. & Grote, E. (2010). The provision and uptake of different types of recasts in child and adult ESL learners. *Australian Review of Applied Linguistics, 33*(3), 21.1–26.22.

Oliver, R. & Mackey, A. (2003). Interactional context and feedback in child ESL classrooms. *Modern Language Journal, 87*(4), 519–533.

Oliver, R., Philp. J. & Mackey, A. (2008). Age, teacher guidance and the linguistic outcomes of task-based interaction. In J. Philp, R. Oliver & A. Mackey (eds.), *Child's play? Second language acquisition and the younger learner* (pp. 131–147). Amsterdam: John Benjamins.

Panova, I. & Lyster, R. (2002). Patterns of corrective feedback and uptake in an adult ESL classroom. *TESOL Quarterly, 36*(4), 573–595.

Pica, T. (1994). Research on negotiation: What does it reveal about second-language learning conditions, processes, and outcomes? *Language Learning*, 44(4), 493–527.

Plonsky, L. & Mills, S. V. (2006). An exploratory study of differing perceptions of error correction between a teacher and students: Bridging the gap. *Applied Language Learning*, 16(1), 55–74.

Ranta, L. & Lyster, R. (2007). A cognitive approach to improving immersion students' oral language abilities: The Awareness–Practice–Feedback sequence. In R. DeKeyser (ed.), *Practice in a second language: Perspectives from applied linguistics and cognitive psychology* (pp. 141–160). Cambridge: Cambridge University Press.

Russell, J. & Spada, N. (2006). The effectiveness of corrective feedback for the acquisition of L2 grammar. In J. Norris. & L. Ortega (eds.), *Synthesizing research on language learning and teaching* (pp. 133–142). Amsterdam: John Benjamins.

Saito, K. (2013). Re-examining effects of form-focused instruction on L2 pronunciation development: The role of explicit phonetic information. *Studies in Second Language Acquisition*, 35(1), 1–29.

Sato, M. & Ballinger, S. (2012). Raising language awareness in peer interaction: A cross-context, cross-method examination. *Language Awareness*, 21(1–2), 157–179.

Sato, M. & Lyster, R. (2012). Peer interaction and corrective feedback for accuracy and fluency development, monitoring, practice and proceduralization. *Studies in Second Language Acquisition*, 34(4), 591–626.

Schmidt, R. (1990). The role of consciousness in second language learning. *Applied Linguistics*, 11(2), 129–158.

(2001). Attention. In P. Robinson (ed.), *Cognition and second language instruction* (pp. 3–32). Cambridge: Cambridge University Press.

Sheen, Y. (2004). Corrective feedback and learner uptake in communicative classrooms across instructional settings. *Language Teaching Research*, 8(3), 263–300.

Sheen, Y. & Ellis, R. (2011). Corrective feedback in language teaching. In E. Hinkel (ed.), *Handbook of research in second language teaching and learning* (Vol. II, pp. 593–610). London: Routledge.

Simard, D. & Jean, G. (2011). An exploration of L2 teachers' use of pedagogical interventions devised to draw L2 learners' attention to form. *Language Learning*, 61(3), 759–785.

Spada, N. & Lightbown, P. (1993). Instruction and the development of questions in L2 classrooms. *Studies in Second Language Acquisition*, 15(2), 205–244.

Swain, M. (2010). Talking it through: Languaging as a source of learning. In R. Batstone (ed.), *Sociocognitive perspectives on language use and language learning* (pp. 112–130). Oxford: Oxford University Press.

10

Written Corrective Feedback

John Bitchener

Feedback delivery in the form of written corrective feedback (CF) on linguistic errors in second language (L2) learners' written texts has been central to much of the L2 writing and second language acquisition (SLA) literature since the 1970s. A range of feedback options are available to teachers and others providing feedback, including focused (targeted) written CF or unfocused (comprehensive) written CF and direct written CF, indirect written CF, and metalinguistic feedback. Decisions about which of the options to provide tend to be influenced by (1) whether or not feedback is being given to a class or group of learners or to individual learners and (2) whether or not the purpose of the feedback is for L2 learning/acquisition/development or composition writing.

The first main section of this chapter provides a description of the various feedback options and an explanation of their typical pedagogical purposes. The next section devotes most of its ongoing discussion to what we know from the available research and recent theoretical proposals about the ways in which the various feedback options may facilitate or impede the L2 learning process. Readers who are interested in the use of the different feedback options for composition writing should refer to earlier discussions in books by Bitchener and Ferris (2012) and Ferris (2003). The final section presents a range of pedagogical options for teachers based on what has been discussed in the chapter.

Description and Purposes of Different Types of Written CF

The range of pedagogical options available to those providing written CF has been described in detail over the years (e.g., Bitchener & Storch, 2016; Ellis, 2009), so only an overview of the options available to teachers and others will be provided here. When deciding what type of written CF to provide L2 learners with, teachers typically find themselves making two types of decision. The first is whether or not to provide feedback on only one or a few targeted/focused categories of error (e.g., verb tense; article use) or comprehensive/unfocused feedback on a wider range of error categories (e.g., lexis, syntax, morphology). The second decision to be made concerns the choice of feedback: direct written CF (error correction), indirect written CF (e.g., those that circle or underline where an error has occurred), or metalinguistic feedback (i.e., feedback on what may have caused an error and on how the error may be corrected). Metalinguistic information may be provided in the form of an abbreviation such as PT for past tense error or in the form of a more elaborate description, including explanations and examples of correct usage.

A number of factors may be considered when teachers decide on which of the feedback types to use when responding to the errors in their learners' written texts. The first factor is the focus of the class or instruction being offered. In classes such as composition classes or written literacy classes where one of the criteria of target-like writing is linguistic accuracy of expression, teachers over the years have tended to favor comprehensive written CF so that as many errors as possible can be corrected (Bitchener & Ferris, 2012). In classes such as these, teachers then need to decide how explicit their feedback is to be. For instance, if they think that learners may be able to self-correct their errors, teachers may be more likely to provide one of the indirect feedback options, but if they think their learners are unlikely to be able to self-correct, they will usually provide direct error correction and/or metalinguistic explanation. Concerning the second option, it would be fair to say that writing teachers are more likely to provide direct error correction as it is a quick and efficient form of feedback. However, if they think their learners are unlikely to understand the cause of their errors, they may decide to provide some form of metalinguistic explanation even though this option is more time-consuming. Writing teachers may also decide to provide both metalinguistic explanation with direct error correction.

On the other hand, in language learning classes, the decisions that teachers make may be different to some extent. In order to avoid information overload, language teachers are more likely to provide focused feedback on one or a few error categories so that their learners are able to focus their attention on a range of instances within a single text where a particular language error has been made. Often the choice of error coincides with the grammar focus of lessons leading up to the writing of texts in which learners have a range of opportunities to demonstrate the extent to which they can use a particular form or structure with target-like accuracy. A range of factors may then determine how explicit the feedback needs to be. Indirect feedback may be considered more appropriate if the targeted form or structure has recently been taught. More explicit types of feedback might be given if it is clear that learners need more detailed feedback. Language teachers are more likely to employ metalinguistic options than writing or composition teachers given that their primary focus is on helping learners understand and learn what is acceptable and not acceptable in the target language. Thus, the decisions that teachers make center around (1) how much feedback to give (focused or unfocused), (2) how explicit the feedback needs to be (direct or indirect options), and (3) what level of information is considered necessary (metalinguistic feedback or direct/indirect feedback). In some language learning contexts, teachers may not always be permitted to operate according to their individual understanding of what is most effective for their learners. Some contexts (e.g., Hong Kong secondary schools) may be more prescriptive than others about the focus of feedback to be given (Lee, 2008, 2017).

Because there are options available to them, it is to be expected that teachers and researchers will want to find out whether one type of delivery is more effective or beneficial than another type for L2 development. Research on the relative effectiveness of different types of feedback has evolved over the years from the early pedagogical focus on what type of feedback to deliver, when to provide it, and who should provide it (see Hendrickson, 1980, for an overview of this work) to the more important investigations in to how and why one type might be more effective than another for L2 development. If the question about *why* cannot be answered, there is less likelihood that discussions about the pedagogical *how* factors can be theorized and then empirically investigated for their effectiveness for L2 development. This evolution has very much been aligned to the development of theories of SLA. The nature and findings of the empirical research, as it has emerged over time, and the evolving theoretical focus on how and why written CF and its delivery may contribute to L2 development are therefore discussed in the following sections.

Written CF and Its Forms of Delivery for L2 Development

This section of the discussion is divided into two main subsections. The first considers the research literature on the role of the different feedback delivery options for facilitating modified and new, accurate output. The focus here is on the product rather than the process involved in arriving at the output or product. The second main subsection considers theoretical explanations about how and why the cognitive processing of written CF and its delivery options may contribute to modified and new, accurate output.

Research on the Extent to Which Different Feedback Delivery Options May Facilitate Modified and New, Accurate Output

Within this first subsection, consideration is given to (1) the feedback delivery literature in the early years of published research on written CF,

(2) the research on direct, indirect and metalinguistic written CF for developing accuracy output, and (3) the research on focused and unfocused written CF for developing accuracy output.

The Early Research Focus on Written CF and Its Delivery Options on Modified and New, Accurate Output

The early literature during the 1970s was focused on the role that different types of written CF could play in helping learner-writers improve the accuracy of their written texts. Writing or composition teachers sought to find out which types of written CF might be more effective for their learners so that they could develop the knowledge and skills to edit their texts according to target language accuracy norms (Hendrickson, 1980).

During the early 1980s, with the emergence of SLA theories like Krashen's Input Hypothesis (1985), the research focus moved to language teachers and their interest in understanding whether or not certain types of written CF might better facilitate L2 development than other types. In order to measure the relative effectiveness of different types of written CF, most empirical investigations employed a pre-test/treatment (different types of written CF and no written CF)/post-test design to determine whether the linguistic accuracy demonstrated in an initial piece of text (the pre-test) improved as a result of the treatment (the written CF type) in a revision of the text and/or in the writing of a new text (the post-tests) immediately after written CF had been provided and over time. These studies were therefore interested in comparing the accuracy of the *output* rather than the extent to which the different types of written CF might moderate a learner's cognitive *processing* of the written CF input. The primary reason for focusing on the output rather than on the processing was the desire to empirically test the claim made by Truscott (1996) that written CF cannot be expected to contribute to L2 learning and to determine whether or not written CF has the potential to bring about change or development in the learner's knowledge and use of the target language. Thus, the focus of teacher-researchers was on whether written CF "works" and on whether certain types of written CF may be more facilitative of L2 development than other types.

Research on Direct, Indirect, and Metalinguistic Written CF for Developing Accuracy Output

Several of the early studies (Lalande, 1982; Semke, 1984; Sheppard, 1992) compared the effectiveness of providing learners with direct written CF and indirect written CF on a limited range of linguistic error categories (e.g., the English article system, the simple past tense) and reported no difference between the two types of feedback in terms of their effect on accuracy improvement. However, a number of methodological shortcomings in the design of these studies (including, for example, the absence of a true control group that did not receive written CF feedback) means that the findings cannot be accepted as clear evidence of the relative effectiveness for L2 development (Guenette, 2007). However, more recent studies (Bitchener & Knoch, 2010b; Van Beuningen, De Jong & Kuiken, 2008, 2012) have reported that direct written CF may have a more significant long-term effect on accuracy development than indirect written CF. Table 10.1 provides a summary of these studies.

In the same way that it is not possible to draw any firm conclusions about the relative effectiveness of direct and indirect written CF, studies of the relative effectiveness of direct written CF and metalinguistic feedback have also not produced consistent findings. Bitchener (2008) and Bitchener and Knoch (2008) found no difference in effect for direct written CF and metalinguistic feedback. Shintani and Ellis (2013) reported that metalinguistic feedback was more effective in their study than direct written CF in the short term but not over time, but Shintani, Ellis, and Suzuki (2014) found that direct written CF was more effective than metalinguistic

Table 10.1 *Studies comparing direct written CF and indirect written CF*

Studies	Linguistic focus	Proficiency level	Feedback types	Effectiveness
Lalande (1982)	Unfocused	Intermediate	1. Direct 2. Indirect (coding)	Indirect more effective than direct but not significant
Semke (1984)	Unfocused	Intermediate	1. Direct 2. Content comments 3. Direct & content comments 4. Indirect (coding)	No difference
Sheppard (1992)	Unfocused	Upper intermediate	1. Direct + conference 2. Content comments + conference	No difference
Bitchener & Knoch (2010b)	Definite & indefinite articles	Advanced	1. Written metalinguistic 2. Indirect (underlining or circling) 3. Written & oral metalinguistic 4. Control	No difference in immediate post-test BUT both metalinguistic groups more effective than indirect (10 weeks)
Van Beuningen et al. (2008)	Unfocused	High school	1. Direct 2. Indirect 3. Writing practice 4. Self-correction	Direct more effective long-term; Direct and indirect effective short-term
Van Beuningen et al. (2012)	Unfocused	High school	1. Direct 2. Indirect 3. Writing practice 4. Self-correction	Direct more effective for grammar; indirect more effective for non-grammar items

feedback over time. Further complicating these observations, Bitchener et al. (2005), Sheen (2007), and Stefanou and Revesz (2015) reported that a combination of direct written CF and metalinguistic feedback was more effective than the provision of only one of these two types of feedback. These studies are summarised in Table 10.2 below.

For teachers seeking some form of clear and consistent guidance about whether certain types of written CF may be more effective for L2

Table 10.2 *Studies comparing direct written CF and direct plus metalinguistic feedback*

Studies	Linguistic focus	Proficiency level	Feedback types	Effectiveness
Bitchener et al. (2005)	Definite & indefinite articles; simple past tense; prepositions	Advanced	1. direct 2. direct + written metalinguistic 3. direct and oral metalinguistic	Direct + oral and written metalinguistic more effective than direct only for articles and simple past tense
Bitchener (2008)	Definite & indefinite articles	Intermediate	1. direct 2. direct + written metalinguistic 3. direct and oral metalinguistic	Direct + written and oral metalinguistic as well as direct alone more effective than direct + written metalinguistic
Bitchener & Knoch (2008)	Definite & indefinite articles	Intermediate	1. direct 2. direct + written metalinguistic 3. direct and oral metalinguistic	No difference
Sheen (2007)	Definite & indefinite articles	Intermediate	1. direct 2. direct + written metalinguistic	Direct + written metalinguistic more effective than direct alone
Shintani & Ellis (2013)	Indefinite article	Low intermediate	1. direct 2. metalinguistic 3. control	Metalinguistic more effective than direct alone in immediate post-test but not in 2 week delayed post-test
Shintani et al. (2014)	Indefinite article; hypothetical conditional	Low intermediate	1. direct 2. direct + revision 3. metalinguistic 4. metalinguistic + revision 5. control	Direct more effective than metalinguistic in 2 week post-test
Stefanou & Revesz (2015)	Articles with generic & specific plural referents	Upper intermediate	1. direct 2. direct + metalinguistic	Direct + metalinguistic more effective than direct

development than others, these findings may not be particularly helpful unless teachers realize that each of these studies included other variables (e.g., proficiency level and targeted linguistic focus as well as other individual difference factors discussed in the next section) that may have had a moderating effect on the output they reported. Thus, the difference in findings across the studies does not mean that any of them are necessarily flawed.

Research on Focused and Unfocused Written CF for Developing Accuracy Output

The other written CF distinction to have been considered in the output-oriented written CF research is between focused/targeted written CF and unfocused/comprehensive written CF. All of the focused written CF studies (Bitchener, 2008; Bitchener & Knoch, 2008, 2010a, 2010b; Ellis et al., 2008; Rummel, 2014; Sheen, 2007; Sheen, Wright & Moldawa, 2009; Shintani & Ellis, 2013; Shintani et al., 2014; Stefanou & Revesz, 2015) found it to be effective in facilitating improved accuracy in the use of rule-based features like the English article system and the past simple tense. On the other hand, unfocused written CF studies have produced mixed findings: Semke (1984), Robb, Ross & Shortreed (1986), Kepner (1991), Sheppard (1992), and Truscott and Hsu (2008) reported that unfocused feedback did not result in accuracy improvement but Frear and Chiu (2015) and Van Beunigen et al. (2008, 2012) found it to be effective. Only three studies have actually compared the effectiveness of focused and unfocused written CF: whereas Ellis et al. (2008) reported that both types of feedback were effective and Sheen et al. (2009) reported that focused feedback was more effective than unfocused feedback, Frear and Chiu (2015) reported benefits for both. Little can be concluded from only two studies with conflicting results and from studies that did not distinguish their two constructs sufficiently for a valid comparison to be made.

Considering these focused and unfocused studies as a whole, there is insufficient evidence to claim that one type is more effective for accuracy improvement than the other type even though intuitively one might expect targeted feedback on one or a few linguistic error categories to be more effective for L2 development when learners are able to focus their attention on a more limited range of input than is the case with comprehensive feedback. This view would seem to be supported theoretically by an understanding that a learner's cognitive processing will be eased if the load is reduced (Skehan, 1998) when feedback processing is lower for focused than unfocused CF, especially in the offline condition.

In order to produce more consistent findings on the relative merits of both categories of written CF, one would need to investigate more carefully designed research questions and take into account the potential effect of different variables interacting with the two categories of written CF. For example, one research question might be: To what extent do prior learning experiences have an interactional effect on the effectiveness of different types of written CF? Research such as this would be expected to yield more consistent results, but ultimately the question needs to be asked about how important it is to investigate the interactional effect of different types of written CF and other variables on output. Given that most of the published research has been conducted with groups of learners, the question needs to be asked about why some learners within the groups are unable to produce accurate output. Thus, as research has shown and as classroom teachers are aware, it would seem to be as important to understand why some learners benefit from written CF but others do not. In order to understand why learners are successful or unsuccessful in using the written CF input they receive, it is necessary to understand the cognitive processes that learners go through as they seek to modify their erroneous output and/or produce new, accurate output in a new piece of writing. Once the cognitive processing stages are understood on a theoretical level, it will then be possible to consider whether and how various variables like different written CF types and other contextual and individual difference factors may impact upon a learner's processing across stages. Once theoretical proposals have been established, empirical evidence of their validity and completeness can then be tested. Thus, the next section of this chapter considers from a theoretical perspective how and why written CF and potentially moderating variables like written CF type may impact upon a learner's processing trajectory.

Theoretical Explanations about How and Why the Cognitive Processing of Written CF and its Delivery Options May Contribute to Modified and New, Accurate Output

Within this section, first the influence of cognitive processing in the oral context on cognitive processing within the written CF context is discussed and then, in the following subsection, the potentially moderating effect of different types of written CF and other variables on the cognitive processing of written CF across the various stages is discussed.

The Influence of the Cognitive Processing of Written CF in the Oral and Written Contexts

Earlier SLA literature (e.g., the Gass 1997 framework) has been informative about the various stages of cognitive processing that learners need to traverse if they are to turn oral input into modified or new, accurate output. Although there are some differences and unique characteristics associated with the processing of *written* CF input, the same key stages of processing are required in both contexts even though there are some unique differences within each stage. Thus, it is relevant to consider what the oral SLA literature tells us about the various processing stages within a single written CF episode. Tomlin and Villa (1994) explain that learners need to be motivated and oriented toward a focus on form (accuracy) when receiving CF input if they are to attend to it and notice the difference between their own output and that which the CF has provided (Schmidt, 2001). Because written CF is explicit, it is likely that learners will notice it more than they might notice oral CF input given that the latter, as recasts, for example, may be seen as an alternative but equally acceptable version of their output (Lyster, 1998).

In the next stage, learners need to comprehend or understand what the CF input is telling them. With regard to oral CF input, Gass (1997) explained that two levels of analysis are required for understanding at this stage: analysis to understand the meaning and analysis to understand the form. Because written CF is off-line (compared with online oral CF) and more time is available for the learner to engage in a deeper type of processing than is possible during the online condition, it is likely that the learner will proceed to the next stage, that is, intake, and consider the hypothesis he/she wishes to test for accuracy. Again, because the learner is processing written CF rather than oral CF, he/she has the luxury of time and the permanence of record to permit a considered analysis before producing output for testing. During this cognitive process, learners have the opportunity to consider any relevant knowledge that is stored in their long-term memory. The fourth stage, involving the integration of new knowledge, is first demonstrated in either the modified output that results from hypothesis-testing or in the accurate use of the new knowledge in new pieces of writing.

Figure 10.1 provides a visual summary of the stages involved in the cognitive processing of written CF within a single episode. For readers who are interested in the consolidation phase of learning beyond the initial processing episode described above, Bitchener (2019) provides a model of some of the key stages involved in the accessing and use of a learner's new knowledge resulting from written CF processing.

The cognitive processing described here, of course, does not take into account the fact that learners are not robots. A range of factors may influence how successful a learner is in traversing all of the stages and producing modified accurate output in a text revision and/or new accurate output in a new text. The next subsection considers the potential of these factors.

The Potentially Moderating Effect of Different Types of Written CF and Other Variables on the Cognitive Processing of Written CF

A range of variables or factors may moderate the processing of written CF and its delivery options. It may do so at any of the key stages identified in Figure 10.1. A detailed discussion of various individual difference factors and wider contextual factors that may have an influence on a learner's

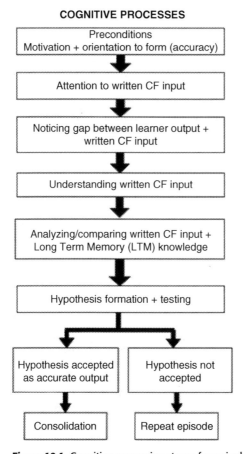

Figure 10.1 Cognitive processing stages for a single written CF episode

processing trajectory can be found in Bitchener (2019). The focus of this subsection is an overview of (1) the extent to which different types of written CF may have such an influence and (2) the interacting role that variables or factors may have on the extent to which different types of written CF may facilitate or impede a learner's cognitive processing.

Figure 10.2 identifies some of the variables that may moderate the cognitive processing of a learner, including those that specifically identify at what processing stages written CF types may have an influence.

In column 2, the cognitive processing stages (referred to earlier in Figure 10.1) are presented again and, in column 1, some of the variables that may have an influence on different stages of processing are presented. It can be seen that learners may or may not attend to the feedback they are given if they have a negative response to the particular type of written CF they have been given. Some learners, for example, may decide to ignore the feedback if they are given indirect written CF rather than direct feedback or metalinguistic feedback. It may be that learners of a lower L2

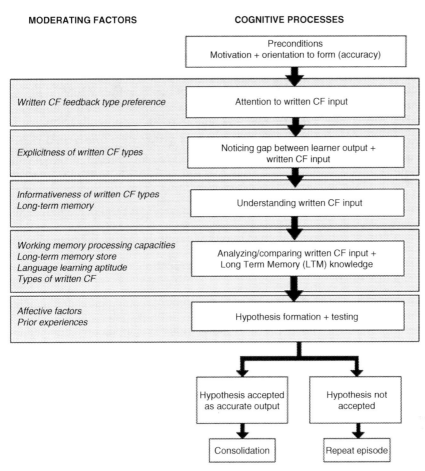

Figure 10.2 Factors that may moderate the cognitive processing of written CF across the stages of a single written CF episode

proficiency level (such as a beginner or elementary level) will not be interested in feedback that only identifies where an error has occurred. On the other hand, more proficient L2 learners may not want to be given direct written CF if they think they know what the correction should be. Such learners may only want indirect feedback.

In both of these scenarios, it is likely that other variables may be further influencing their preference. For instance, learners' prior learning experiences may mean that, based on earlier occasions in which they found the feedback was not particularly helpful for them or in which they found they were unsuccessful in producing accurate output, they had a negative attitude toward that type of feedback or a low self-efficacy belief in their ability to use the feedback effectively and so were unwilling to attend to that same type of feedback on subsequent occasions. Rummel and Bitchener (2015) have reported that learners who had developed stronger beliefs about the effectiveness of certain types of written CF tend to produce more accurate output, especially when given the type of feedback they prefer. If learners decide to not attend to the feedback, it is clear that they will not proceed to the next stage of cognitive processing.

On the other hand, learners who do attend to the feedback they have been given can move to the next stage and compare their erroneous output with the target-like version or information they have been given in the written CF input. The degree of explicitness of the type of written CF learners are given may have an effect on whether they notice that there is a difference between their own output and the feedback they have been given. Because explicitness refers to the salience and linguistic marking of the written CF type, it may be that one type of feedback for some learners is more facilitative of noticing that there was an error with the accuracy of their output. For example, direct written CF that provides a correct version of a learner's error may be necessary, particularly if, for the same learners, indirect underlining or circling does not indicate to them that an error is being identified.

Different types of written CF may also convey different levels of information. For some learners, metalinguistic feedback (that explains the cause of an error and/or indicates how an error can be corrected and/or provides illustrations of accurate usage) may be necessary if they are to progress to the next stage where understanding and comprehension are required. Such learners may find indirect written CF is not informative enough for them to be able to modify their own output.

Another variable that may be expected to play a role in this context and impact upon a learner's noticing of the difference is the linguistic form or structure that is being targeted. More complex structures (e.g., the hypothetical conditional and the passive voice) that comprise two or more linguistic elements or components (as opposed to simple rule-based forms) may be more effectively targeted if metalinguistic feedback is provided (together with or without direct error correction) and some form of explanation is offered (Bitchener & Storch, 2016; Li, 2017).

Another variable, long-term memory, may further interact with the type of written CF that a learner is given. More advanced L2 learners are likely to have a more developed long-term memory store. If they do and if information about a particular form or structure is contained in their long-term memory as information about the particular linguistic feature that has been targeted with written CF, indirect written CF may be all that they need to understand the feedback they have been given. It is more likely that lower proficiency learners will have less information stored in their long-term memory and may not have any information in it about the targeted linguistic form or structure. In this situation, these learners may be more reliant upon a combination of the most explicit type of written CF (direct written CF) and the most informative type of feedback (metalinguistic explanation) for their understanding of the difference between their erroneous output and the target-like information conveyed in the feedback.

When it comes to the hypothesis-formation stage of processing, the role of a particular written CF type is likely to be similarly important in the analysis that a learner engages in before forming a hypothesis about what the modified version or a new accurate version should be. As Figure 10.2 shows, there are other variables that may also interact with the type of feedback that is given and these may strengthen or weaken the influence that a particular type of written CF has on the formation of a particular hypothesis. The working memory capacity of learners will likely influence the extent to which they are able to juggle a number of variables (e.g., language learning aptitude and analytic ability) during their analyses. Sheen (2007, 2011) as well as Stefanou and Revesz (2015) have observed that learners with high language learning aptitude, especially those with strong analytical capacity, may be able to make more effective use of metalinguistic information, and this may mean that learners with less language learning aptitude benefit more from direct written CF or a combination of direct and metalinguistic feedback.

The theoretical model described in Figure 10.2 has identified a number of factors or variables that may interact with different types of written CF at particular cognitive processing stages. Apart from studies by Shintani et al. (2014) and Stefanou and Revesz (2015), the various proposals in the model have yet to be empirically tested. It is important that we understand what happens in *each* of the processing stages (e.g., what kind of analysis of the written CF input and knowledge in the learner's long-term memory is undertaken and how do learners decide what hypothesis to test in their modified or new output). It is also important to understand the extent to which different factors may interact with different types of written CF and lead to accurate output.

In order to elicit data that are relevant to these types of questions, some form of intrusion during the processing will need to occur. For instance, it will be necessary to employ think-aloud and stimulated recall approaches as well as self-report interviews and questionnaires at particular processing stages. Because some learners may be uncomfortable with some of these approaches, it will be necessary to secure ethical consent before these types of data are collected.

Although the validity of the proposals has yet to be tested, this does not mean that language learning teachers cannot think about how the various factors might interact as their learners process the types of feedback they are given. Teachers are sometimes critical of the written CF research because it seems to provide so few "one-size-fits-all" answers to their questions. This chapter has endeavoured to explain that a wide range of factors may moderate the extent to which learners find the written CF they receive to be effective. The research presented in the earlier sections of this chapter has also shown that at least one "one-size-fits-all" guideline can be given, namely, that focused feedback does enable learners to process the feedback and produce accurate modifications and/or accurate uses of the targeted form or structure in new texts over time. Additionally, the research so far has not provided any evidence that any type of written CF is harmful (a claim made by Truscott, 1996). Based on what the chapter has presented, the aim of the final section is to identify some specific pedagogical approaches that teachers may find helpful when they think about the type of written CF to give their classes, groups, and individual learners.

Some Pedagogical Suggestions for Teachers

The early written CF research was motivated by pedagogical issues about whether certain types of written CF might be more effective than other types. In seeking a type of "one-size-fits-all" answer to these questions, it was perhaps, in hindsight, a rather naïve and simplistic type of question to have asked. Subsequent research findings about the relative efficacy of different types of written CF for L2 development have now revealed that other variables need to be considered in conjunction with the different types of written CF.

That said, however, there have been a couple of findings that would seem to be consistent for language learners. First, the discussion of focused and unfocused approaches to giving written CF has shown that while there is currently insufficient research about the relative merits of these two approaches, there are consistent and compelling findings among the many studies that took a focused approach to conclude that focused feedback is effective for targeting at least simple rule-based forms and some evidence that this approach is also beneficial for learners seeking to overcome more complex structural errors. Second, the earlier composition-oriented studies were quite consistent in finding that an unfocused approach was beneficial to certain learners (especially those of a more advanced level of proficiency), but the limited number of unfocused studies with mixed findings in more recent research (that has generally been regarded as more carefully designed than the earlier studies) means that the unfocused approach for language learners (especially those at lower levels of proficiency) may not be the most effective for developing accuracy.

A considerable amount of research has investigated the relative merits of providing learners with either direct written CF, indirect written CF, metalinguistic feedback, or combinations of these types (e.g., direct written CF and metalinguistic feedback). Considering the studies of the two main comparisons (between direct written CF and indirect written CF and between direct written CF and metalinguistic feedback), the findings have been completely inconsistent. However, this does not mean that they should be ignored. Even though the direct–indirect comparison studies in the early years were significantly flawed from a design and analytical perspective, recent studies, even though they are still limited in number, suggest that direct written CF may be more effective than indirect written CF over time. Certainly, more research is needed on this comparison but, in the meantime, teachers may find the use of direct written CF to be more effective for their lower proficiency learners, especially if the targeted form or structure has been recently taught. More advanced learners, who might be expected to have received instruction of the targeted form or structure on earlier occasions, may find in the first instance that indirect underlining or circling of their errors is sufficient for them to self-correct. If it proves to be ineffective, teachers can then follow up with more explicit feedback.

The comparison between direct written CF and metalinguistic feedback has reported inconsistent findings. This is more than likely the result of the moderating influence of other variables on the effectiveness of the two approaches. Studies comparing these two approaches have been popular in recent years, so if this level of research interest continues, further guidance may be possible over time. In the meantime, however, teachers can reflect upon the different variables in the reported findings and decide whether or not they think their learners possess some of the characteristics and, if so, think about whether they might have a moderating influence on the effectiveness of certain types of written CF. Intuitively, teachers may decide that learners, who are unlikely to have been taught the targeted form or structure or who have only recently been taught it, should be given metalinguistic feedback together with direct written CF. This is because studies examining the effectiveness of this combination have consistently reported that learners benefit from this practice rather than from just one of these feedback types.

If metalinguistic feedback is considered by teachers, they may decide to provide it initially in its coded form (e.g., PT for past tense error or PV for passive voice error). If something more detailed and explanatory is considered necessary, an outline of the causes of the error and further information about how to correct it, including examples of correct usage, may be necessary in an end-of-text statement as long as an in-text method of referring learners to where the error occurs has been made.

In conjunction with these pedagogical suggestions, teachers would also do well to think about other points raised in the theoretical proposals of this chapter. First, it has been suggested that preconditions, such as motivation and an orientation to form-focused learning, may determine whether or not learners respond to the feedback they are given and start to cognitively process the written CF input. Teachers could advise learners before their texts are returned to them that the feedback they have provided is on linguistic accuracy. Second, the theoretical models presented in this chapter have shown that individual difference factors across learners may further impact on the way in which they cognitively process the different types of written CF they are given. Considering these factors before making a decision about the type of written CF to provide may not always be possible if there are a large number of learners in a class, but they should certainly be considered when any intensive one-on-one feedback is given to learners who may not be responding positively to the feedback that others in a class are managing to benefit from. There may be individual difference factors (e.g., lower proficiency level and less developed long-term memory stores) that may indicate to the teacher that certain individual learners need more detailed feedback than others (e.g., more metalinguistic feedback, including that which is discussed in one-on-one conference sessions).

The final piece of advice for teachers is the need to try different approaches with individual students and see whether they are effective or not. Learners are individuals and may respond to and process different types of written CF in ways that are different to other individuals. Additionally, individual learners may respond to and process different types of written CF in different ways on different occasions. Thus, teachers need to understand that a degree of experimentation will sometimes be required. Follow-up questions (orally and/or in writing), after the feedback has been provided and modifications have been attempted (but unsuccessfully), could help teachers gain insights into the needs and preferences of individual learners and the most effective ways of giving feedback from the learners' perspectives.

References

Bitchener, J. (2008). Evidence in support of written corrective feedback. *Journal of second language writing*, 17(2), 102–118.

(2019). The intersection between SLA and feedback research. In K. Hyland & F. Hyland (eds.), *Feedback in second language writing: Contexts and issues* (2nd ed., pp. 85–105). Cambridge: Cambridge University Press.

Bitchener, J. & Ferris, D. (2012). *Written corrective feedback in second language acquisition and writing*. London: Routledge.

Bitchener, J. & Knoch, U. (2008). The value of written corrective feedback for migrant and international students. *Language Teaching Research*, 12(3), 409–431.

(2010a). The contribution of written corrective feedback to language development: A ten month investigation. *Applied Linguistics*, 31(2), 193–214.

(2010b). Raising the linguistic accuracy level of advanced L2 writers with written corrective feedback. *Journal of Second Language Writing*, 19(4), 207–217.

Bitchener, J. & Storch, N. (2016). *Written corrective feedback for L2 development.* Bristol: Multilingual Matters.

Bitchener, J., Young, S. & Cameron, D. (2005). The effect of different types of corrective feedback on ESL student writing. *Journal of Second Language Writing, 14*(3), 191–205.

Ellis, R. (2008). *The study of second language acquisition* (2nd ed.). New York: Oxford University Press.

(2009). A typology of written corrective feedback types. *ELT Journal, 63*(2), 97–107.

Ellis, R., Sheen, Y., Murakami, M. & Takashima, H. (2008). The effects of focused and unfocused written corrective feedback in an English as a foreign language context. *System, 36*(3), 353–371.

Ferris, D. (2003). *Response to student writing: Implications for second language students.* Mahwah, NJ: Lawrence Erlbaum.

Frear, D. & Chiu, Y. (2015). The effect of focused and unfocused indirect written corrective feedback on EFL learners' accuracy in new pieces of writing. *System, 53*, 24–34.

Gass, S. (1997). *Input, interaction, and the second language learner.* Mahwah, NJ: Lawrence Erlbaum.

Guenette, D. (2007). Is feedback pedagogically correct? Research design issues in studies of feedback in writing. *Journal of Second Language Writing, 16*(1), 40–53.

Hendrickson, J. (1980). The treatment of error in written work. *Modern Language Journal, 64*(2), 216–221.

Kepner, C. G. (1991). An experiment in the relationship of types of written feedback to the development of second-language writing skills. *Modern Language Journal, 75*(3), 305–313.

Krashen, S. D. (1985). *The input hypothesis: Issues and implications.* London: Longman.

Lalande, J. F. (1982). Reducing composition errors: An experiment. *Modern Language Journal, 66*(2), 140–149.

Lee, I. (2008). Understanding teachers' written feedback practices in Hong Kong secondary classrooms. *Journal of Second Language Writing, 17*(2), 69–85.

(2017). Working hard or working smart: Comprehensive or focused written corrective feedback in L2 academic contexts. In J. Bitchener, N. Storch & R. Wette (eds.), *Teaching writing for academic purposes to multilingual students* (pp. 168–180). New York: Routledge.

Li, S. (2017). The efficacy of written corrective feedback on second language development: The impact of feedback type, revision type, learning motivation and strtaegies. Unpublished Ph.D. thesis, Auckland University of Technology, Auckland, New Zealand.

Lyster, R. (1998). Negotiation of form, recasts, and explicit correction in relation to error types and learner repair in immersion classrooms. *Language Learning, 48*(2), 183–218.

Qi, G. (2015). The impact of explicitness of written CF, targeted linguistic form and proficiency level on the effectiveness of written CF: A mixed-methods study. Unpublished doctoral thesis, AUT University, Auckland, New Zealand.

Robb, T., Ross, S. & Shortreed, I. (1986). Salience of feedback on error and its effect on EFL writing quality. *Tesol Quarterly, 20*(1), 83–95.

Rummel, S. (2014). Student and teacher beliefs about written CF and the effect these beliefs have on uptake: A multiple case study of Laos and Kuwait. Unpublished doctoral thesis, AUT University, Auckland, New Zealand.

Rummel, S. & Bitchener, J. (2015). The effectiveness of written corrective feedback and the impact Lao learners' beliefs have on uptake. *Australian Review of Applied Linguistics, 38*(1), 64–82.

Schmidt, R. (2001). Attention. In P. Robinson (ed.), *Cognition and second language instruction* (pp. 3–32). Cambridge: Cambridge University Press.

Semke, H. D. (1984). Effects of the red pen. *Foreign Language Annals, 17*(3), 195–202.

Sheen, Y. (2007). The effect of focused written corrective feedback and language aptitude on ESL learners' acquisition of articles. *Tesol Quarterly, 41*(2), 255–283.

(2011). *Corrective feedback, individual differences and second language learning*. London: Springer.

Sheen, Y., Wright, D. & Moldawa, A. (2009). Differential effects of focused and unfocused written correction on the accurate use of grammatical forms by adult ESL learners. *System, 37*(4), 556–569.

Sheppard, K. (1992). Two feedback types: Do they make a difference? *RELC Journal, 23*(1), 103–110.

Shintani, N. & Ellis, R. (2013). The comparative effect of direct written corrective feedback and metalinguistic explanation on learners' explicit and implicit knowledge of the English indefinite article. *Journal of Second Language Writing, 22*(3), 286–306. DOI:http://dx.doi.org/10.1016/j.jslw.2013.03.011.

Shintani, N., Ellis, R. & Suzuki, W. (2014). Effects of written feedback and revision on learners' accuracy in using two English grammatical structures. *Language Learning, 64*(1), 103–131. DOI:10.1111/lang.12029.

Skehan, P. (1998). *A cognitive approach to language learning*. Oxford: Oxford University Press.

Stefanou, C. & Revesz, A. (2015). Direct written corrective feedback, learners differences and the acquisition of second language article use for generic and specific plural reference. *Modern Language Journal, 99*(2), 263–282.

Tomlin, R. S. & Villa, V. (1994). Attention in cognitive science and second language acquisition. *Studies in Second Language Acquisition, 16*(2), 183–203.

Truscott, J. (1996). The case against grammar correction in L2 writing classes. *Language Learning, 46*(2), 327–369.

Truscott, J. & Hsu, A. Y. (2008). Error correction, revision, and learning. *Journal of Second Language Writing, 17*(4), 292–305.

Van Beuningen, C. G., De Jong, N. H. & Kuiken, F. (2008). The effect of direct and indirect corrective feedback on L2 learners' written accuracy. *ITL-Review of Applied Linguistics, 156*, 279–296.

(2012). Evidence on the effectiveness of comprehensive error correction in second language writing. *Language Learning, 62*(1), 1–41.

11
Technology-Mediated Corrective Feedback

Trude Heift, Phuong Nguyen, and Volker Hegelheimer

Introduction

Corrective feedback, "an indication to the learner that his or her use of the target language is incorrect" (Lightbown & Spada, 1999, p. 172), has been considered an important aspect of second language (L2) pedagogy and has drawn extensive scholarly attention in L2 acquisition over the past decades (Bitchener, 2012; Bitchener & Ferris, 2012). Language instructors and second language acquisition (SLA) researchers have expressed a keen interest in assessing the feasibility and efficacy of providing corrective feedback to learner errors (Ferris, 1999, 2010; Lyster, Lightbown & Spada, 1999; Truscott, 1999). While the role of corrective feedback in L2 acquisition and instruction has been a controversial topic, many researchers have argued that under certain conditions, corrective feedback can play a beneficial role in facilitating the acquisition of the L2, which may be difficult to learn through input alone (see Bitchener, 2008; Nassaji & Kartchava, 2017).

With the integration of technology in language instruction, the provision of corrective feedback also remains a central topic among researchers who work in the field of computer-assisted language learning (CALL). Not only is technology-mediated corrective feedback an efficient way for language instructors and peers to comment on the learner's L2 output (Lavolette, Polio & Kahng, 2015), it also holds great promise for the learning of especially complex or low-salient forms, for instance (Sauro, 2009). Ideally, technology-mediated corrective feedback is individualized, as it can help learners notice their errors in their L2 production and consequently facilitate L2 development, something that cannot be as easily achieved in the traditional language classroom.

Since the late 1960s, corrective feedback in CALL has mainly focused on learner–computer interactions in contrast to computer-mediated learner–learner interactions, in which L2 learners, instructors, and speakers interact with each other via the computer. Learner-computer feedback, or computer-generated corrective feedback through Tutorial CALL systems, has exploited the advantages of different technology-mediated pedagogical approaches to L2 learning and teaching in providing explicit and implicit feedback to learners by focusing language practice on graded and discrete grammatical points (Heift & Hegelheimer, 2017). However, technological advancements over the past decades have facilitated the changes and diversity in CALL applications employed to identify, process, and communicate L2 errors to learners.

More specifically, improvements in the computer hardware's storage capacity and processing speed, along with the proliferation of multimedia-capable computers and the emergence of the World Wide Web, have allowed for more detailed, individualized corrective feedback that is no longer restricted to simplistic computer responses to mechanical practice of selected grammatical phenomena and lexical items. Instead, these newer technologies have made it possible to provide L2 learners with visual and more contextual, error-specific feedback in other language areas and skills such as pronunciation (or oral communication), writing, and testing. However, these technological innovations face the challenge of being robust and comprehensive.

This chapter reviews research on technology-mediated corrective feedback through learner–computer interactions by mainly focusing on spelling, grammar and writing, and pronunciation (or oral communication). For each area, we describe the different types of technologies that have been developed for L2 learners to provide them with technology-mediated corrective feedback. We also examine existing research and discuss implications for L2 instruction.

Spelling

Knowing how to spell is important not only for native speakers but also for language learners. Studies have indicated that difficulties with spelling may impact or even restrict progress in other writing skills. Scott (2000), for instance, states that "cognitive resources directed to spelling compete with those needed for generating content, with attendant rate and quality implications" (p. 67). Moats (2005) further notes that poor spellers might prefer to choose words simply because they know how to spell them thereby limiting their lexical range. This, in turn, may lead not only to a loss of verbal power but also to incoherent expressions.

Yet, and despite its importance, spelling is a skill that is generally not taught in the L2 classroom. For this reason, students often rely on technology-mediated corrective feedback for their spelling by autonomously employing generic spell checkers (e.g., Microsoft Word). Generic spell checkers, however, are not specifically designed for L2 learners and thus have their limitations with regards to identifying L2 misspellings and providing effective corrective feedback.

Word processors generally have a built-in spell and grammar checker. The spell checker scans a text for *all* unknown words, that is, all words that are not contained in the spell checker's dictionary. Once these words have been identified and resolved (e.g., the user modifies the original input or tells the system that the word is spelled correctly such as a proper noun), the grammar checker examines the text for grammatical errors such as subject-verb agreement or passive constructions, for instance.

A number of studies have focused on the performance of generic spell checkers (see, for instance, Lawley, 2016; Rimrott & Heift, 2008). Generic spell checkers (e.g., the one built into Microsoft Word) target L1 writers and assume that misspellings mainly involve accidental mistypings, which are fairly predictable minimal deviations from the correct spellings (Dagneaux, Denness & Granger, 1998; Helfrich & Music, 2000; Pollock & Zamora, 1984). Specifically, the algorithms of generic spell checkers are largely based on the empirical finding that the vast majority of L1 misspellings involve an edit distance of *one*[1]. Edit distance is defined as the number of additions, omissions, substitutions, or transpositions needed to convert a misspelling into its target word. Accordingly, most L1 misspellings contain only a *single* error of omission (e.g., *<spel>/<spell>), addition (*<sspell>), substitution (*<soell>), or transposition (*<sepll>) (Damerau, 1964; Pollock & Zamora, 1984). Apart from problems with proper nouns, rare words, and real-word errors (e.g., *<their>/<there>), generic spell checkers successfully handle the majority of misspellings made by typical native speakers. Kukich (1992) notes that when the first three guesses in a spell checker's list of suggested corrections are considered, accuracy levels above 90 percent are reported (see also Hodge & Austin, 2003).

In L2 writing, however, in addition to these accidental mistypings, learners produce words unknown to the word processor due to misconceptions of the L2. For example, a learner might make a morphologically triggered error by inflecting a verb incorrectly, which results in a nonexistent word (e.g., *<goed>/<went>). However, the fact that a spell checker identifies these morphological errors does not imply that the suggestions for error repair should focus on spelling. On the contrary, learner feedback for a morphology-triggered misspelling ideally explains the morphological nature of the error without making reference to spelling. From a computational point of view, this, however, requires that the error can be identified as such by the computer program, which is generally not the case with a generic spell checker designed for native speakers.

Rimrott and Heift (2008) conducted a study with a corpus of 1,027 unique misspellings from forty-eight anglophone learners of German and classified these into three error taxonomies: linguistic competence

---

[1] For more sophisticated methods use spelling error correction models, see, for instance, Brill & Moore (2000).

(competence versus performance misspellings), linguistic subsystem (lexical, morphological or phonological misspellings), and target modification (single-edit versus multiple-edit misspellings). The study then evaluated the performance of the Microsoft Word spell check on these misspellings. Results indicate that only 62 percent of the L2 misspellings are corrected and that the spell checker, independent of other factors, generally cannot correct multiple-edit misspellings although it is quite successful in correcting single-edit errors. In contrast to most misspellings by native writers, many L2 misspellings are multiple-edit errors and are thus not corrected by a spell checker designed for native writers (see also Burston, 1998; Hovermale, 2008).

Similarly, Stirling (2011) found with her corpus of adult EFL writing that 16 percent of the spelling errors were homophones or other real words which were overlooked by the generic spell checker. Furthermore, for 15 percent of the misspellings the spell checker suggested inappropriate replacement words (see also Mitton & Okada, 2007). A generic spell checker may also undertake the correction itself assuming that this is the word the writer intended. However, as found by Dikli (2010) and Bestgen and Granger (2011), the lack of feedback might not only be confusing but, from a pedagogical perspective, it is also not very helpful because the error is corrected so quickly that the learner may not even notice that an automatic correction occurred (see also Lawley, 2016).

In contrast to the studies that show that generic spell checkers are not very effective with L2 learners, Flor and Futagi (2012) report that their generic spell checker, ConSpel, has almost the same success rate for native and L2 writers. However, ConSpel is specifically designed to correct misspellings with an edit distance of greater than *one* and thus one may argue that the spelling errors the system targets are more in line with those made by L2 writers.

Given the limited performance of generic spell checkers with L2 learners, several spell checkers especially aimed at second language learners have been developed. Most of these programs specifically target certain error classes, such as phonology-triggered or morphology-triggered misspellings. An example of such a spell checker is FipsOrtho (L'haire, 2007) for learners of French that developed out of FipsCor (Ndiaye & Vandeventer Faltin, 2003). Regarding morphological misspellings, the program, for instance, can correct the incorrect plural regularization in *<animals>/<animaux>. Nadasdi and Sinclair's Spellcheckplus (http://spellcheckplus.com/) and BonPatron (http://bonpatron.com/) are online L2 English and L2 French spell and grammar checkers, respectively. In addition to correcting typographical and some phonological misspellings, the two programs are able to correct morphologically triggered errors (e.g., in English, *<goed>/<went>). SCALE, Spelling Correction Adapted for Learners of English, is an L2 spell checker that addresses phonological confusion and morphological overregularization (e.g., *<feeled>/<felt>) by Japanese learners of English (Hovermale, 2008).

L2 spell checkers may also anticipate errors by incorporating complete lists of commonly misspelled words in the target language (e.g., Antidote, a spell checker for learners of French) or may even be based on a corpus of learner misspellings (see Bestgen & Granger, 2011; Flor & Futagi, 2013). We also find computational algorithms which adaptively create spelling error correction models from raw learner corpora to address errors in which the intended word results in a nonexistent word. Here the assumption is that the misspelled word has the same meaning as its correct form, and thus they appear in similar semantic environments (see Brill & Moore, 2000).

Mitton and Okada (2007), for instance, based their spell checker for Japanese learners of English on an analysis of a corpus of L2 spelling errors. Sakaguchi et al. (2012) used the spelling corpus of the Cambridge Learner Corpus (CLC) to train their spelling algorithm along with part-of-speech tagging. Lawley (2016) also describes the creation of the Prototype Pedagogical Spell Checker (PPSC) for Spanish learners of English for which a corpus of common misspellings was first collected, and then for each of the errors pedagogical feedback was encoded. When PPSC was tested, the researcher found that the handcrafted feedback for the L2 errors provided an initial coverage of 62 percent of all learner errors. For the remaining 32 percent, the system nonetheless informed the learner that the word was misspelled.

Finally, there are also L2 spell checkers that, instead of targeting certain error classes, provide learners with additional tools to overcome the limitations of generic spell checkers. For instance, the Penguin (Fallman, 2002) is a descriptive grammar and spell checker that uses the Internet as a reference database. If a learner is unsure of the spelling of a particular word, the number of hits for alternative spellings, as retrieved by a search engine, can be compared to determine the correct spelling (i.e., the alternative with the most hits is likely to be correct).

From the studies on generic spell checkers, it is evident that they do not provide appropriate corrective feedback for L2 learners. However, even if a spell checker identifies the majority of errors correctly, it is equally important to study the learner's interaction and usage of spell checkers. Furthermore, research that investigates learning gains, especially in the long-term, as well as studies that focus on learner autonomy are needed in order for students to get the most benefit from this writing tool.

In addition to developing targeted spell checkers and studies that assess learner behavior, there are pedagogical measures that L2 instructors can take in the L2 classroom. For instance, the number of misspellings students produce in the first place can be reduced. For example, learners can be taught about L2-specific phoneme–grapheme correspondences (e.g., <ie> versus <ei> in German) and, more generally, orthography. The CALL program eSpindle (www.espindle.org, reviewed by Olmanson,

2007), for instance, helps learners of English practice spelling (see also Nicholas, Debski & Lagerberg, 2004). In addition, typical L2 competence misspellings can be discussed in the classroom. These strategies may also lead to more successful students' long-term self-monitoring, which is not limited to spelling but also extends to grammar and writing (see Burston, 2001).

Grammar and Writing

Almost all research and development in CALL in the 1960s to 1990s can be labeled Tutorial CALL. In Tutorial CALL, the computer is commonly used for sentence-based practice activities in the form of multiple choice or multiple select, fill-in-the-blank, match or rank answers, and reassembling or translating small chunks of text.

In early learning approaches of Tutorial CALL, learners were provided with mainly mechanical practice of selected grammatical phenomena and lexical items (DeKeyser, 2007). The programs were limited to simplistic knowledge-of-result feedback generated by monolithic string-matching algorithms and binary holistic answer processing (Right vs. Wrong, Try again) in addition to more sophisticated matching to regular expressions ("Regular expression" 2013). More detailed corrective feedback on error location was achieved by leaving the anticipated character substring of the student answer intact and highlighting or deleting the substring that deviated from the model answer.

Changes that did occur within the research and development efforts of Tutorial CALL focused on the individualization of the learning experience. Tutorial CALL packages paid particular attention to branching, the individualization of practice sequences. Based on calibrated item difficulty – a tenet of classical testing theory, which depends on scores for a completed activity – students would be presented with more difficult practice material after achieving a high score and less difficult and remedial practice material after obtaining a low score. The main challenge for Tutorial CALL activities that rely on more or less sophisticated string-matching algorithms to provide students with contextual corrective feedback and/or additional instructional guidance is that they have to be based on the anticipation of each and every possible correct and erroneous answer in order for them to be robust and comprehensive. Of course, the number of well-formed utterances in a language is infinite and the number of erroneous utterances is then infinitely infinite. In the absence of comparing the student's input string to the strings of anticipated answers, the computer needs to be capable of a linguistic analysis of student input to detect errors and to provide corrective feedback and contextual instructional guidance. Broadly speaking, this research approach is taken in intelligent computer-assisted language learning (ICALL).

ICALL is the label of predominantly Tutorial CALL applications at the nexus of Artificial Intelligence (AI) and CALL. ICALL relies on natural language processing (NLP), student modeling, and expert systems. NLP produces a formal linguistic representation of learners' linguistic input with the goal to provide corrective feedback and instructional guidance. The record of this information over time, which is maintained in student profiles, provides the basis for inferring interrelated facets of the student's cognitive belief system about the learned language, that is, the construction of a student model. Information from the student model, in turn, provides some basis for the tailoring of learning sequences and contingent guidance. Expert systems model the learning domain, such as aspects of the grammar of a language, and are a rich source of structured (linguistic) knowledge that can guide and scaffold the students' learning processes. They enable learners to query this knowledge base during task completion, thus serving as a comprehensive reference tool in learner–computer interactions.

Most research in ICALL is aimed at grammar checking for language learners by focusing on error detection and correction of learner input with the goal to provide more informative, metalinguistic learner feedback. A number of ICALL systems are used in regular L2 curricula: E-Tutor (Heift, 2010) for L2 German, Robo-Sensei (Nagata, 2009) for L2 Japanese, and Tagarela (Amaral & Meurers, 2011) for L2 Portuguese, and these applications provide metalinguistic and/or individualized feedback on spelling, morphological, syntactic, and semantic errors for L2 grammar practice. Owing to their more sophisticated NLP analysis, their learning environments and activity types are also less restricted than those found in online L2 workbooks and especially those found in more traditional Tutorial CALL activities. Nevertheless, the CALL activities contained in these systems are generally limited to the sentence level. However, due to technological advances as well as shifts in language teaching pedagogy, automatic writing evaluation (AWE) systems that target and provide technology-mediated corrective feedback for L2 writing are increasingly used in the L2 classroom (Leacock et al., 2010).

Indeed, the last thirty years have seen a dramatic change in the approach to writing as well as in the approach to the teaching of writing. The introduction of word processing applications in the 1980s impacted how teachers and learners thought about writing. The focus shifted from viewing writing as a product – a finished text – to seeing writing as a process – developing a text via writing, revising, editing, etc. Chapelle (2018) argues that "when writing is viewed as a process, feedback is an important tool for learning; feedback is intended to be formative and to help students to reconsider what they have written and to advance as writers" (p. 2).

Feedback has also dramatically shifted from critiquing the product and assigning a grade to a finished paper to informing and evaluating the process of writing. Technology-mediated feedback on writing has played a major role in this endeavor and ranges from teacher-provided process feedback to automatically provided feedback as learners write in real time or as they complete their writing (episodic mode). Likewise, the last thirty years have seen tremendous growth in the development of systems that provide automated feedback on writing. These automated writing evaluation (AWE) tools utilize error detection algorithms and can "analyze a wide range of lexical, syntactic, semantic and discourse structures and provide feedback on the linguistic features of student writing" (Heift & Hegelheimer, 2017).

A number of these AWE tools have been employed in language learning classrooms to provide technology-mediated corrective feedback to developing writers. At the more ubiquitous end of the continuum is word processing software that often comes with basic grammar and spell checkers that can provide some feedback, albeit often the kind that only identifies an error or is not specifically aimed at L2 learners (see previous section on spelling). Using web-based writing, applications such as Google Docs expands the opportunities for feedback. On the one hand, this tool allows the easy creation of a collaborative writing experience as multiple authors can plan, write, revise, and edit concurrently the same document or leave feedback in the form of comments and suggestions. Yet another added benefit is the ability to look at how a writer (or a group of writers) arrived at the final product. Taking a closer look at the version history, it is possible to see how a writer went about the construction of the text.

By becoming increasingly more widespread, AWE tools such as Grammarly (Figure 11.1) are being used to assist developing writers with their writing, nonnative and native speakers alike. Grammarly works as an add-on for most popular web browsers or within Microsoft Word to help writers "automatically detect grammar, spelling, punctuation, word

Figure 11.1 Grammarly interface

choice, and style mistakes in [their] writing" (Grammarly, 2018). Its user-friendly interface coupled with feedback that detects errors and suggests solutions as well as its price tag (a free basic version) make it an attractive tool. The approach to offer Grammarly as its own text editor, browser extension for most popular browsers, and as an add-on to Microsoft Word has increased its popularity among teachers and learners. The software developers describe Grammarly's approach as follows: "Grammarly's algorithms flag potential issues in the text and suggest context-specific corrections for grammar, spelling, wordiness, style, punctuation, and even plagiarism. Grammarly explains the reasoning behind each correction, so you can make an informed decision about whether, and how, to correct an issue" (Grammarly.com).

When using Grammarly, it first identifies errors by underlining them in red (Figure 11.1) and by providing one or multiple suggestions for corrections in the right margin of the text. As with any tool, the error identification rate is not 100 percent accurate. For instance, removing the word "about" in the text in Figure 11.1 does not result in a correct sentence. Any time such tools are included in classroom practice, however, it is essential to investigate their impact on instruction and learning. A number of researchers have studied the use of AWE tools to provide written corrective feedback, more generally (Dikli & Bleyle, 2014; Lavolette et al., 2015; Ranalli, Link & Chukharev-Hudilainen, 2017; Stevenson & Phakiti, 2014), while others have investigated the potential of timely written corrective feedback to support language learning (Hartshorn et al., 2010; Shintani & Aubrey, 2016).

Ranalli, Yamashita, and Bappe (2017), for instance, report on a study comparing the quantity and quality of automated corrective feedback provided by Grammarly versus Microsoft Word. In particular, they examined episodic feedback and compared it to real-time feedback. In the episodic mode, they considered twenty-four texts written by intermediate ESL writers. In real-time mode, Ranalli et al. (2017) used twenty intermediate ESL writers. The researchers utilized a complex data-capturing approach that consisted of capturing the computer screen, the learner in front of the computer, and the audio. The compiled media file was then used as the basis for a retrospective think-aloud session with the learner. In both cases, they compared the accuracy of the error identification and classification as well as the accuracy of the suggestion(s). Their study found that on their learner samples of written data, Grammarly performed in line with AWE developers' benchmarks and was marginally less accurate than Microsoft Word (in the episodic mode only). Yet, Grammarly identified more grammar errors than Microsoft Word across a wider range of issues. The results support differential uses of the AWE tool Grammarly by recommending the episodic mode for discursive writing (i.e., learning-to-write) tasks and the real-time mode for L2 practice (i.e., writing-to-learn) tasks (Ranalli et al., 2017). Ranalli et al. (2017) conjecture "that this will not only help support our students' self-regulation of writing but also allow them to spend more time interacting with the feedback and thus create better opportunities for learning from it" (p. 11). Their additional observation that writers made "the same mistake repeatedly despite accepting Grammarly's real-time suggestions" further supports this approach.

For many writers, especially younger writers, the drafting of a text occurs less frequently on a stand-alone word processing application than in the context of a ubiquitous web application. In the North American context, that application is often Google Docs. While Google Docs does provide grammar and spell checking on its own, the add-on tool Grammarly unfortunately does not work on that platform even though it works for other web writing tasks, including blog posts. The Educational Testing Service (ETS) released a free add-on AWE tool for Google Docs, the *Writing Mentor*, in late 2017. The Writing Mentor takes a slightly different approach to providing technology-mediated corrective feedback to developing writers. Rather than focusing on grammar and spelling mistakes, this free add-on claims to help writers examine if their writing is convincing, well-developed, coherent, and well-edited, with editing being the last stage of the writing process. A welcome addition is a checklist that learners can submit along with their paper that provides aspects of what the writers have double-checked with the Writing Mentor. This type of integration is crucial to help learners and teachers recognize the value of AWE writing tools.

In the classroom, any tool requires appropriate support to be successful. This is even more important when a piece of technology such as an automated writing evaluation tool is allocated authority that previously resided with the teacher. Ranalli and Davis (personal communication, February 27, 2018) provide usage guidelines for instructors teaching writing to nonnative speakers of English in an English for Academic Purposes (EAP) setting. These suggestions are based on Hubbard's (2013) work on learner training and on Ranalli and Davis's experience with integrating Grammarly into multiple sections of ESL writing courses. In particular, they suggest tasks to help illustrate the affordances and the shortcomings of the tool. Specifically, with Grammarly, they recommend that students work in pairs to examine a carefully constructed sample essay that contains fifteen errors, of which ten errors are typically identified by Grammarly and five are typically overlooked. In the first phase, the learners are asked to identify the errors. The learners then run the text through Grammarly and discuss the feedback it provides on the errors it detected. Lastly, the learners discuss the type of feedback a teacher or writing tutor might provide on the same text. Here, it is particularly important for learners to understand that any tool has limitations and that it continues to be important to critically question any suggestions a tool provides. Yet another way to integrate a tool that provides technology-mediated writing feedback is by integrating its output into the assignment. For example, learners could be asked to submit the feedback they received from Grammarly along with their writing sample so that teachers have

Figure 11.2 The Writing Mentor interface

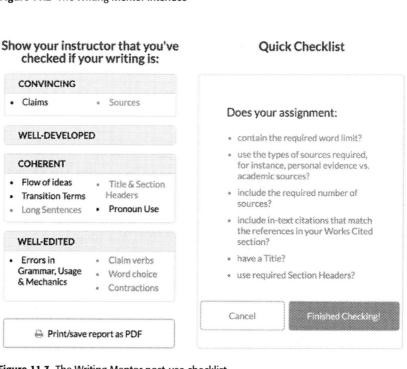

Figure 11.3 The Writing Mentor post-use checklist

a better sense and understanding of how the AWE feedback shaped the writing and revising process.

It is interesting, however, that several tools that provide automated feedback on writing are filtering down to the instructor and the learners from high and medium-stake language testing operations. For example, the ETS has years of experience with rating written texts automatically using a scoring algorithm trained on essays written by test takers. This scoring engine – e-rater – was then also employed in the classroom application Criterion which is being marketed for use in K-12 settings as well as in post-secondary settings. Unlike this fee-based service, the Writing Mentor is made available for free and has clearly benefited from prior work in AWE tools.

Technology-mediated feedback on writing has seen decades of development, and the tools which analyze writing and provide corrective feedback have clearly become more sophisticated. Much of the research aimed at learning when and how to provide meaningful writing feedback is heading in a useful direction in that the results can inform pedagogical decisions in the classroom. The questions surrounding when and how to use such automated tools remain fruitful paths of inquiry. The competition among products like Grammarly, Criterion, and others that aim to enter the lucrative market of classroom instruction will no doubt lead to more accurate and responsive writing feedback. In addition to exploring and determining the use and usefulness of these tools to help with the completion of a writing assignment, an even more important research avenue is the transfer of such feedback provision to students' writing ability over time. In other words, the next series of investigations should include longitudinal studies closely looking at how students interact with these tools and at students' writing development from assignment to assignment and semester to semester. The end goal has to remain to improve students' ability to write. Work in other areas, such as pronunciation, is similarly ramping up to becoming more effective.

Pronunciation

The feedback provided to learners in pronunciation is different in nature from that in spelling, grammar, or writing. While corrective feedback in those areas generally provides responses to learners' errors, technology-mediated feedback provided by computer-assisted pronunciation training (CAPT) systems is not always corrective. Quite often, these systems provide feedback to inform learners about their pronunciation accuracy even though no error has occurred. Current CAPT systems exploit various techniques for technology-mediated feedback presentation, focus on different aspects of pronunciation, and differ in the extent to which feedback is explicit and informative. Although feedback provision on pronunciation can be achieved in various ways, approaches to feedback in CAPT systems primarily include the use of speech visualization and automatic speech recognition (ASR).

Visual Feedback

The use of visual technology-mediated feedback in the form of oscillo-grams (i.e., waveforms), spectrograms, and pitch contours (i.e., pitch tracings) has been supported for decades (Anderson-Hsieh, 1994; Neri et al., 2002) although the instruments for creating these visuals were originally developed as a clinical instrumentation tool used by speech-language pathologists. In fact, these types of visual display are still popular in more recent CAPT systems.

In an oscillogram, the speech waveform is displayed as the amplitude or loudness on the vertical axis and by time on the horizontal axis (Figure 11.4).

A spectrogram shows degrees of amplitude (represented light-to-dark, as in white = no energy, black = lots of energy) at various frequencies on the vertical axis by time on the horizontal axis (Figure 11.5). Waveforms and spectrograms of learners' acoustic speech signal can be generated and edited by various programs such as Audacity (Audacity, n.d), Better Accent Tutor (Kommissarchik & Komissarchik, 2000), Kay Sona-Match (Carey, 2004), PRAAT (Brett, 2004; Offerman & Olson, 2016; Olson, 2014), Syntrillium's Cool Edit 2000 (now called Cool Edit Pro) (Coniam, 2002), and WinPitch (WinPitch, n.d). Meanwhile, spectrograms can be displayed in PRATT (Brett, 2004; Offerman & Olson, 2016; Olson, 2014), Cool Edit Pro (Coniam, 2002), and WinPitch (WinPitch, n.d).

While waveforms and spectrograms are mostly used for the teaching of segmental features, in combination with oscillograms or spectrograms, they are commonly employed for the instruction of suprasegmentals (Chun, 1998). Pitch contours display rising, falling, and level lines that correspond to rises, falls, and levels in a speaker's voice pitch (Figure 11.6). They can be generated from software and CAPT packages such as Better Accent Tutor (Kommissarchik & Komissarchik, 2000), PRATT, Kay Elemetrics' CSL-Pitch Program (Hirata, 2004), and WinPitch (WinPitch, n.d).

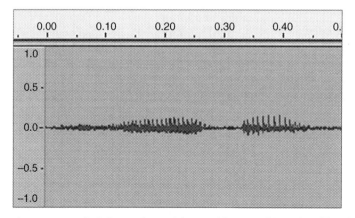

Figure 11.4 Audacity's waveform of the word "paragraph" produced by a female native speaker of English

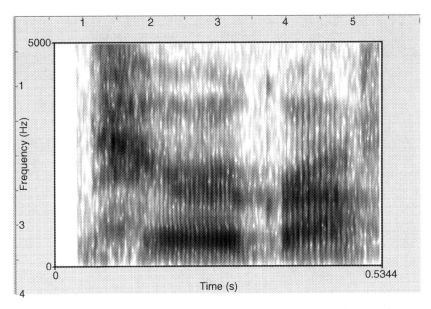

Figure 11.5 PRATT's spectrogram of "paragraph" produced by produced by a female native speaker of English

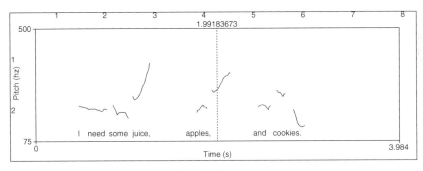

Figure 11.6 Pitch contour generated by PRATT

Pitch contours have proven to be effective for the teaching of prosodic features, including intonation, stress, and rhythm (Anderson-Hsieh, 1994; Eskenazi, 1999; Neri, et al., 2002) and are generally considered especially valuable for the teaching of intonational paragraph markers, that is, paratones (Levis & Pickering, 2004).

Systems that employ speech visualization for pronunciation training commonly first present learners with the model speech before learners record their production of the target feature. The CAPT system then analyzes the speech recording and presents the visual display of their acoustic speech signal together with those produced by the model speaker. Sometimes, learners are also presented with a diagram depicting a sagittal section and an animation of the movement of the tongue within the oral cavity (Carey, 2004; Engwall, 2012) or with audio feedback giving explicit instruction on how to improve articulation (Engwall, 2012). Learners then practice their pronunciation by repeatedly recording their speech to achieve a more native-like pronunciation.

The provision of visual feedback during pronunciation training is based on two assumptions: First, learners are able to interpret the visuals from which they can identify the similarities and differences between their speech and that of a native speaker. Second, once they have successfully identified the differences, they are able to work on the errors and improve their pronunciation. However, interpreting the visual feedback is not always straightforward, especially for L2 learners. Although waveforms and spectrograms are often included in CAPT packages and have been employed in the training of segmental features, they have been widely criticized for not providing enough useful information for L2 learners to improve their pronunciation (Ehsani & Knodt, 1998; Godwin-Jones, 2009; Neri et al., 2002). Without some basic training in phonetics, a language learner is generally not capable of interpreting waveforms and spectrograms and inasmuch as pitch contours are easier for learners to read, training is nonetheless necessary (Chun, 2007; Hardison, 2004). Moreover, even if the learner is capable of interpreting the graphic displays, there is still the step of knowing where exactly to alter their articulation of the sound to approximate the model speaker.

Automatic Speech Recognition

Although the use of spectrograms for technology-mediated corrective feedback for pronunciation is still prevalent in many CAPT packages, researchers (Eskenazi, 1999; Hincks, 2003; Kim, 2006; Neri et al., 2002) have been advocating and focusing on the use of ASR techniques for pronunciation training. In fact, the last two decades have witnessed an increasing popularity of CAPT systems employing ASR because of their ability to provide individualized feedback in a more autonomous environment.

ASR, a computer-based technology that processes and converts speech into text in real time, can be classified into several categories.

First, and based on the type of training model needed, they can be *speaker-dependent, speaker-independent,* or *speaker-adaptive*. Speaker-dependent ASR systems have to learn the unique characteristics of the user's voice first before they are able to analyze their speech. While speaker-dependent ASR technology yields higher recognition accuracy than its speaker-independent counterpart, it requires training for every new user which can be exhaustive and time-consuming. In contrast, speaker-independent ASR systems are trained with a corpus of model speakers' spoken language to recognize any user's speech (Wachowicz & Scott, 1999). In the third type of ASR system, speaker-adaptive, input from one speaker is first analyzed using the parameters given from the training corpus before the system parameters are adapted to the new speaker's voice (O'Shaughnessy, 2008).

Second, ASR applications can also be classified as *discrete* or *continuous* (Wachowicz & Scott, 1999). Discrete ASR systems, which aim at recognition of individual sounds or words and require input to be separated by pauses, are more appropriate for individual sound-based or word-based language tasks. Continuous ASR systems are intended to process longer phrases and utterances, and thus are more suitable for activities that extend beyond the word level.

A common type of technology-mediated corrective feedback provided by ASR systems is the orthographic representation of learners' speech. An example of this type of software is Dragon Systems' Naturally Speaking (Coniam, 1999), a speaker-dependent ASR package for continuous speech. After a learner records their sample, the software then transcribes the oral input and presents the transcription to the learner. Another example of such a type of ASR software is Nuance's Dragon Dictation, which is a speaker-independent dictation system designed for continuous speech recognition and has been used in a study by Liakin, Cardoso, and Liakina (2015). In their system, learners practiced the French sound /y/ in words, phrases, and sentences and received an immediate transcription of their pronunciation of their input. The feedback given by both CAPT systems is, however, implicit as learners need to infer that any mismatch between the transcription and the intended output is due to a pronunciation error.

Feedback to learners' pronunciation can also be given as a score informing learners about their pronunciation quality and accuracy. An example of this type of corrective feedback is provided in Pronto, speaker-dependent, discrete ASR software which was developed by the Indiana Speech Training Aid (ISTRA) research program for speech-language pathologists and educators and aimed at people with impaired hearing (Dalby & Kewley-Port, 1999). The system combines ASR technology with speech drills which are organized in game-like formats (i.e., baseball, moonride, and bowling). In the bowling game, for instance, learners' pronunciation is presented with a score and its level of quality is illustrated by the number of pins knocked down.

In addition to providing technology-mediated corrective feedback orthographically, or in the form of a score, ASR-based CAPT systems also display a combination of different types of feedback to learners. For example, Dutch-CAPT, which provides feedback on Dutch phonemes that are problematic for adult learners of Dutch (Neri, Cucchiarini & Strik, 2008), not only presents an orthographical transcription of the learner's utterance but also includes an emoji (e.g., smiley face) along with a written comment highlighting problematic sounds. Another example of an ASR system that provides multiple forms of feedback is FluSpeak, a speaker-independent, continuous ASR system that employs IBM's ViaVoice recognizer (Kim, 2006). This software is designed for the practice of sounds, words, and intonation. During intonation practice, when learner speech is recognized by the software, a spectrogram or pitch contour of their utterance is displayed visually for learners to compare their pronunciation to that of a native speaker. In addition, a score for each individual word of the utterance as well as the average score are also presented.

Finally, Wang and Young (2015) employed an ASR-based CAPT system which provides a variety of corrective feedback types: an audio recast of the learner's utterance displayed with a waveform and a score, words pronounced correctly or incorrectly, a model pronunciation of the full sentence at normal speed and slow speed, and a model pronunciation of single words. Learners can also listen to their speech production and compare it with the model speaker's speech.

Although ASR systems are of great pedagogical value for pronunciation instruction, such as providing learners with immediate feedback and limitless opportunities for self-paced, autonomous practice (Eskenazi, 1999; Godwin-Jones, 2009; Neri et al., 2002), they are not free from limitations. First, there is evidence that ASR systems are not foolproof and thus provide erroneous feedback (Kim, 2006), especially when used to analyze nonnative speech (Coniam, 1999; Ehsani & Knodt, 1998; Levis, 2007). From a pedagogical perspective, this may result in incorrect uptake of the knowledge and skills as well as frustration on the part of the learner. Second, the feedback provided by these systems is not always useful to learners. For instance, while providing a single score to learners to evaluate their pronunciation has its benefits, it makes no suggestion as to how to repair the error. Similarly, speech visualization is not completely transparent to learners in communicating the source of the error and how to fix it (Levis, 2007; Neri et al., 2002). Therefore, for learners to gain the maximum benefits from pronunciation technology, it is essential that ASR systems accurately pinpoint specific errors and provide detailed, meaningful feedback on how to address the learners' pronunciation errors.

In addition to further research to explore ways to improve the accuracy and comprehensibility of computer-delivered pronunciation feedback, more studies should be done to investigate the long-term effect of this type of feedback on learners' pronunciation. Most studies to date have focused on learners' attitudes toward ASR-based pronunciation feedback (see, for example, Neri et al., 2008; Walker et al., 2011; Wang & Young, 2014) or its short-term effect on learners' pronunciation (Cucchiarini, Neri & Strik, 2009; Hincks, 2003; Neri et al., 2008; Walker et al., 2011). Longitudinal studies with larger sample sizes, together with research on the effects of ASR applications on learner motivation and autonomy, will provide evidence about the benefits of language learners' usage of ASR systems in the long term. Such studies have significant pedagogical value because long-term learning effects are the goal of language education by encouraging language teachers to make use of ASR-based systems in their pronunciation teaching.

Pedagogical Implications and Future Directions

In this chapter, we discussed technologies that have been developed to provide technology-mediated corrective feedback to L2 learners by focusing on spelling, grammar and writing, and pronunciation. Our overview of the technologies along with the research that has been conducted shows that significant progress has been made over the past decades in assisting students with their L2 language studies. Nevertheless, there is room for further research, some of which we identified in each respective section above. Most importantly, however, studies need to investigate the long-term efficacy of technology-mediated feedback when students use these tools in the language learning classroom or outside independently.

In addition, technology-mediated corrective feedback is by no means 100 percent accurate, and learners need guidance from language instructors, especially with regards to learning not to overly rely on the technology. Learners must be made aware of its caveats and learn to appropriately interpret the feedback they receive from the technology. In the case of corrective feedback for pronunciation, for instance, students might even benefit from some linguistic training to make best use of the technology-mediated corrective feedback provided by speech technologies. In addition to concrete examples, training on how to interpret visual feedback is critical since waveforms, spectrograms, and pitch contours are not always straightforward to students. Therefore, teachers should first train students on how to interpret the visual feedback (e.g., darker areas on a spectrogram imply stressed syllables). More importantly, they need to equip students with knowledge about the expected pronunciation of a word, phrases, and sentences; for example, where a stress should be placed on a multisyllabic word. With this kinds of training, students will be more able to comprehend the feedback and make their own inference about the appropriateness of their pronunciation from the feedback provided.

Similarly, in the areas of grammar and writing, the grammatical terminology used in the feedback also needs to be exemplified to the learner, especially if the tools themselves do not provide additional examples and/or explanations. Undoubtedly, students will use these tools outside the classroom and unless they have an understanding of the kind of feedback that the system provides, the tool will be less effective. Link et al. (2014) outline several ways of integrating automated writing and grammar feedback tools, including helping students improve the quality of initial drafts prior to submission and alerting students to specific errors they are working on, so to speak as a diagnostic tool. For these ways to be effective, they need to be illustrated by the instructor. Clearly, and as is the case with any supplementary course material, the language instructor plays a central role in that students need guidance on how and when to use the technologies most effectively. Ideally, this is done at the beginning of the semester where the instructor provides an introduction to the tools that are useful to the course. For instance, samples of technology-mediated feedback as provided by each tool could be chosen and then explained to students. As for grammar and writing, a sample text could be selected which the class corrects first manually and then compares it to the computer-corrected version. Most likely, this will include examples where the computer-generated feedback deviates from the manual correction, and these examples could then be highlighted and discussed. Any concrete examples that the instructor can provide will most likely lead to a better understanding of the caveats of the tools and their effective use. Carefully designed learning training (Hubbard, 2004) is therefore the most critical aspect of success, as it can help to counteract a possible mismatch between "natural" use of technology versus the "ideal" use of technology for learning (Reinders & Hubbard, 2013).

References

Amaral, L. and Meurers, D. (2011). On using intelligent computer-assisted language learning in real-life foreign language teaching and learning. *ReCALL*, 23(1), 4–24.

Anderson-Hsieh, J. (1994). Interpreting visual feedback on suprasegmentals in computer assisted pronunciation instruction. *CALICO Journal*, 11(4), 5–21.

Audacity (n.d.). www.audacityteam.org/ (accessed on March 6, 2018).

Bestgen, Y. & Granger, S. (2011). Categorising spelling errors to assess L2 writing. *International Journal of Continuing Engineering Education and Life Long Learning*, 21(2–3), 235–252.

Bitchener, J. (2008). Evidence in support of written corrective feedback. *Journal of Second Language Writing*, 17(2), 102–118. DOI:10.1016/jslw.2007.11.004.

(2012). Written corrective feedback for L2 development: Current knowledge and future research. *TESOL Quarterly*, 46(4), 855–860. DOI:10.1002/tesq.62.

Bitchener, J. & Ferris, D. R. (2012). *Written corrective feedback in second language acquisition and writing*. New York: Routledge.

Bon Patron (n.d.). http://bonpatron.com/ (accessed March 15, 2018).

Brett, D. (2004). Computer generated feedback on vowel production by learners of English as a second language. *ReCALL*, 16(1), 103–113. DOI:10.1017/s0958344004000813.

Brill, E. & Moore, R.C. (2000). An improved error model for noisy channel spelling correction. In *Proceedings of 38th Annual Meeting of the Association for Computational Linguistics, Hong Kong, China, October 2000* (pp. 286–293). Stroudsburg, PA: Association for Computational Linguistics.

Burston, J. (1998). Antidote 98 [review]. *CALICO Journal*, 16(2), 197–212.

(2001). Exploiting the potential of a computer-based grammar checker in conjunction with self-monitoring strategies with advanced level students of French. *CALICO Journal*, 18(3), 499–515.

Carey, M. (2004). CALL Visual feedback for pronunciation of vowels: Kay Sona-Match. *CALICO Journal*, 21(3), 1–32.

Chapelle, C. A. (2018, March 26). Week 5: Technology & Writing (Part 1). [Video file]. https://youtu.be/vJ5KSMT5m8A.

Chun, D. M. (1998). Signal analysis software of teaching discourse intonation. *Language Learning & Technology*, 2(1), 74–93. http://llt.msu.edu/vol2num1/article4/.

(2007). Come ride the wave: But where is it taking us? *CALICO Journal*, 24(2), 239–252.

Coniam, D. (1999). Voice recognition software accuracy with second language speakers of English. *System*, 27(1), 49–64.

(2002). Technology as an awareness-raising tool for sensitising teachers to features of stress and rhythm in English, *Language Awareness*, 11(1), 30–42. DOI:10.1080/09658410208667044.

Cucchiarini, C., Neri, A. & Strik, H. (2009). Oral proficiency training in Dutch L2: The contribution of ASR-based corrective feedback. *Speech Communication*, 51(10), 853–863.

Dagneaux, E., Denness, S. & Granger, S. (1998). Computer-aided error analysis. *System*, 26(2), 163–174.

Dalby, J. & Kewley-Port, D. (1999). Explicit pronunciation training using automatic speech recognition technology. *CALICO*, 16(3), 425–445.

Damerau, F. J. (1964). A technique for computer detection and correction of spelling errors. *Communications of the ACM*, 7(3), 171–176.

DeKeyser, R. (ed.). (2007). *Practice in a second language: Perspectives from applied linguistics and cognitive psychology*. Cambridge: Cambridge University Press.

Dikli, S. (2010). The nature of automated essay scoring feedback. *CALICO Journal*, 28(1), 99–134.

Dikli, S. & Bleyle, S. (2014). Automated essay scoring feedback for second language writers: How does it compare to instructor feedback? *Assessing Writing*, 22, 1–17. http://dx.doi.org/10.1016/j.asw.2014.03.006.

Ehsani, F. & Knodt, E. (1998). Speech technology in computer-aided language learning: Strengths and limitations of a new CALL paradigm. *Language Learning & Technology*, 2(1), 54–73.

Engwall, O. (2012). Analysis of and feedback on phonetic features in pronunciation training with a virtual teacher. *Computer Assisted Language Learning*, 25(1), 37–64. DOI:10.1080/09588221.2011.582845.

Eskenazi, M. (1999). Using Automatic Speech Processing for foreign language pronunciation tutoring: Some issues and a prototype. *Language Learning & Technology*, 2(2), 62–76.

eSpindle (n.d.). www.espindle.org/ (accessed March 15, 2018).

Fallman, D. (2002). The Penguin: Using the web as a database for descriptive and dynamic grammar and spell checking. Paper presented at the CHI 2002, Conference on Human Factors in Computing Systems, Minneapolis, MN, April 20–25, 2002.

Ferris, D. (1999). The case for grammar correction in L2 writing classes: A response to Truscott (1996). *Journal of Second Language Writing*, 8 (1), 1–11.

(2010). Second language writing research and written corrective feedback in SLA. *Studies in Second Language Acquisition*, 32(2), 181–201. DOI:10.1017/s0272263109990490.

Flor, M. & Futagi, Y. (2012). On using context for automatic correction of non-word misspellings in student essays. In *Proceedings of the 7th Workshop on Innovative Use of NLP for Building Educational Applications* (BEA), 105–115, Montréal, Canada, June 3-8, 2012.

(2013). Producing an annotated corpus with automatic spelling correction. In S. Granger, G. Gilquin & F. Meunier (eds.), *Twenty years of learner corpus research: Looking back, moving ahead. corpora and language in use* (pp. 139–154). Louvain-la-Neuve: Presses universitaires de Louvain.

Godwin-Jones, R. (2009). Emerging technology: Speech tools and technologies. *Language Learning & Technology*, 13(3), 4–11. http://llt.msu.edu/vol13num3/emerging.pdf.

Hardison, D. (2004). Contextualized computer-based L2 prosody training: Evaluating the effects of discourse context and video input. *CALICO Journal*, 22(2), 175–190.

Hartshorn, K. J., Evans, N. W., Merrill, P. F., Sudweeks, R. R., Strong-Krause, D. & Anderson, N. J. (2010). Effects of dynamic corrective feedback on ESL writing accuracy. *TESOL Quarterly*, 44(1), 84–109. DOI:10.5054/tq.2010.213781.

Heift, T. (2010). Developing an intelligent tutor. *CALICO Journal*, 27(3), 443–459.

Heift, T. & Hegelheimer, V. (2017). Computer-assisted corrected feedback and language learning. In H. Nassaji & E. Kartchava (eds.), *Corrective feedback in second language teaching and learning* (pp. 51–65). New York: Routledge.

Heift, T. & Schulze, M. (2015). Tutorial computer-assisted language learning. *Language Teaching*, 48(4), 471–490. DOI:10.1017/S0261444815000245.

Helfrich, A. & Music, B. (2000). Design and evaluation of grammar checkers in multiple languages. In *Proceedings of the 18th International Conference on Computational Linguistics (COLING 2000), Vol. II* (pp. 1036–1040). Stroudsburg, PA: Association for Computational Linguistics. www.aclweb.org/anthology/C00-2153/.

Hincks, R. (2003). Speech technologies for pronunciation feedback and evaluation. *ReCALL, 15*(1), 3–20. DOI:10.1017/s0958344003000211.

Hirata, Y. (2004). Computer assisted pronunciation training for native English speakers learning Japanese pitch and durational contrasts. *Computer Assisted Language Learning, 17*(3–4), 357–376. https://doi.org/10.1080/0958822042000319629.

Hodge V. J. and Austin J. (2003): A comparison of standard spell checking algorithms and a novel binary neural approach. *IEEE Transactions on Knowledge and Data Engineering, 15*(5), 1073–1081.

Hovermale, D. J. (2008). SCALE: Spelling correction adapted for learners of English. Poster presentation at ICALL Special Interest Group pre-conference workshop, CALICO conference, March 18–22, San Francisco, USA.

Hubbard, P. (2004). Learner training for effective use of CALL. In S. Fotos & C. Browne (eds.), *New perspectives on CALL for second language classrooms* (pp. 45–67). Mahwah, NJ: Lawrence Erlbaum.

(2013). Making a case for learner training in technology enhanced language learning environments. *CALICO Journal, 30*(2), 163–178.

Kim, I. S. (2006). Automatic speech recognition: Reliability and pedagogical implications for teaching pronunciation. *Educational Technology and Society, 9*(1), 322–344.

Kommissarchik, J. & Komissarchik, E. (2000). Better accent tutor: Analysis and visualization of speech prosody. *Proceedings of InSTILL 2000* (pp. 86–89). Dundee, Scotland.

Kukich, K. (1992). Techniques for automatically correcting words in text. *ACM Computing Surveys, 24*(4), 377–439.

Lavolette, E., Polio, C. & Kahng, J. (2015). The accuracy of computer-assisted feedback and students' responses to it. *Language Learning & Technology, 19*(2), 50–68.

Lawley, J. (2016). Spelling: Computerised feedback for self-correction. *Computer Assisted Language Learning, 29*(5), 868–880. DOI:10.1080/09588221.2015.1069746.

Leacock, C., Chodorow, M., Gamon, M. & Tetreault, J. (2010). *Automated grammatical error detection for language learners*. San Rafael, CA: Morgan & Claypool Publishers.

Levis, J. (2007). Computer technology in teaching and researching pronunciation. *Annual Review of Applied Linguistics, 27*, 184–202. DOI:10.1017/S0267190508070098.

Levis, J. & Pickering, L. (2004). Teaching intonation in discourse using speech visualization technology. *System, 32*(4), 505–524.

L'haire, S. (2007). Fipsortho: A spell checker for learners of French. *ReCALL, 19*(3), 137–161.

Liakin, D., Cardoso, W. & Liakina, N. (2015). Learning L2 pronunciation with a mobile speech recognizer: French /y/. *CALICO Journal, 32*(1), 1–25.

Lightbown, P. M. & Spada, N. (1999). *How languages are learned*. Oxford: Oxford University Press.

Link, S., Dursun, A., Karakaya, K. & Hegelheimer, V. (2014). Towards best ESL practices for implementing automated writing evaluation. *CALICO Journal*, 31(3), 323–344.

Lyster, R., Lightbown, P. M. & Spada, N. (1999). A response to Truscott's "What's wrong with oral grammar correction." *Canadian Modern Language Review*, 55(4), 457.

Mitton R. & Okada T. (2007). *The adaptation of an English spellchecker for Japanese writers. Paper presented at the Symposium on Second Language Writing*. Nagoya, Japan, September 15–17, 2007.

Moats, L. (2005).How spelling supports reading and why it is more regular and predictable than you may think. *American Educator*, 29(4), 12–22.

Murphy-Judy, K. (2003). Sans-faute writing environment [review]. *CALICO Journal*, 21(1), 209–220.

Nagata, N. (2009). Robo-Sensei's NLP-based error detection and feedback generation. *CALICO Journal*, 26(3), 562–579.

Nassaji, H. & Kartchava, E. (2017). *Corrective feedback in second language teaching and learning: Research, theory, applications, implications*. Milton Park: Routledge.

Ndiaye, M. & Vandeventer Faltin, A. (2003). A spell checker tailored to language learners. *Computer Assisted Language Learning*, 16(2–3), 213–232.

Neri, A., Cucchiarini, C. & Strik, H. (2008). The effectiveness of computer-based speech corrective feedback for improving segmental quality in L2 Dutch. *ReCALL*, 20(2). DOI:10.1017/s0958344008000724.

Neri, A., Cucchiarini, C., Strik, H. & Boves, L. (2002). The pedagogy–technology interface in computer assisted pronunciation training. *Computer Assisted Language Learning*, 15(5), 441–467.

Nicholas, N., Debski, R. & Lagerberg, R. (2004). Skryba: An online orthography teaching tool for learners from bilingual backgrounds. *Computer Assisted Language Learning*, 17(3–4), 441–458.

Offerman, H. M. & Olson, D. J. (2016). Visual feedback and second language segmental production: The generalizability of pronunciation gains. *System*, 59, 45–60. https://doi.org/10.1016/j.system.2016.03.003.

Olmanson, J. (2007). Review of eSpindle vocabulary & spelling program online. *Language Learning & Technology*, 11(3), 18–28.

Olson, D. J. (2014). Benefits of visual feedback on segmental production in the L2 classroom. *Language Learning & Technology*, 18(3), 173–192. http://llt.msu.edu/issues/october2014/olson.pdf

O'Shaughnessy, D. (2008). Invited paper: Automatic speech recognition: History, methods and challenges. *Pattern Recognition*, 41(10), 2965–2979. https://doi.org/10.1016/j.patcog.2008.05.008.

Pollock, J. J. & Zamora, A. (1984). Automatic spelling correction in scientific and scholarly text. *Communications of the ACM*, 27(4), 358–368.

Ranalli, J., Link, S. & Chukharev-Hudilainen, E. (2017). Automated writing evaluation for formative assessment of second language writing: Investigating the accuracy and usefulness of feedback as part of argument-based validation. *Educational Psychology, 37*(1), 8–25. DOI:10.1080/01443410.2015.1136407.

Ranalli, J., Yamashita, T. & Bappe C. (2017). Comparing the quantity and quality of automated corrective feedback provided by Grammarly versus MS Word. Paper presented at *CALICO 2017*, Flagstaff, USA.

Regular expression. (2018). In *Wikipedia*. http://en.wikipedia.org/wiki/Regular_expression.

Reinders, H. & Hubbard, P. (2013). CALL and learner autonomy: Affordance and constraints. In M. Thomas, H. Reinders & M. Warschauer (eds.), *Contemporary computer-assisted language learning* (pp. 359–376). London: Bloomsbury Academic.

Rimrott, A. & Heift, T. (2008). Evaluating Automatic Detection of Misspellings in German. *Language Learning & Technology, 12*(3), 73–92.

Sakaguchi, K., Mizumoto, T., Komachi, M. & Matsumoto, Y. (2012). Joint English spelling error correction and POS tagging for language learners writing. In *Proceedings of the 24th International Conference on Computational Linguistics (COLING 2012), Mumbai, India* (pp. 2357–2374).

Sauro, S. (2009). Computer-mediated corrective feedback and the development of L2 grammar. *Languge Learning & Technology, 13*(1), 96–120.

Scott, C. (2000). Principles and methods of spelling instruction: Application for poor spellers. *Topics in Language Disorders, 20*(3), 66–82.

Shintani, N. & Aubrey, S. C. (2016). The effectiveness of synchronous and asynchronous written corrective feedback on grammatical accuracy in a computer-mediated environment. *Modern Language Journal, 100*(1), 296–319.

Spellcheckplus (n.d.). http://spellcheckplus.com/ (accessed March 15, 2018).

Stevenson, M. & Phakiti, A. (2014). The effects of computer-generated feedback on the quality of writing. *Assessing Writing, 19*, 51–65. http://dx.doi.org/10.1016/j.asw.2013.11.007.

Stirling, J. (2011). *Teaching spelling to English language learners*. Raleigh, NC: Lulu.

Truscott, J. (1999). What's wrong with oral grammar correction. *Canadian Modern Language Review, 55*(4), 437.

Wachowicz, K., & Scott, B. (1999). Software that listens: It's not a question of whether, it's a question of how. *CALICO Journal, 16*(3), 253–276. www.jstor.org/stable/24147843.

Walker, N. R., Trofimovich, P., Cedergren, H. & Gatbonton, E. (2011). Using ASR technology in language training for specific purposes: A perspective from Quebec, Canada. *CALICO Journal, 28*(3), 721–743.

Wang, Y.-H. & Young, S. S.-C. (2014). A study of the design and implementation of the ASR-based iCASL system with corrective feedback to facilitate English learning. *Educational Technology & Society, 17*(2), 219–233.

(2015). Effectiveness of feedback for enhancing English pronunciation in an ASR-based CALL system. *Journal of Computer Assisted Learning, 31*(6), 493–504. DOI:10.1111/jcal.12079.

WinPitch (n.d). Pitch Instruments Inc. www.winpitch.com (accessed on March 6, 2018).

12

Gestures, Corrective Feedback, and Second Language Development

Kimi Nakatsukasa[†2019]

Introduction

This chapter introduces the significance of nonverbal features, such as gestures, in second and foreign language teaching and learning, particularly in relation to corrective feedback. It is human nature to use various nonverbal features during communication, and it is not surprising that nonverbal features are as important as what is conveyed verbally in teaching. To date, a growing number of corrective feedback studies have been published; however, the number of corrective feedback studies that also systematically incorporated nonverbal features is extremely limited. This chapter is written to complement existing studies on corrective feedback by presenting the findings from descriptive and experimental studies on nonverbal features, particularly gestures, and to suggest research directions by relating the findings from gestural studies to feedback studies.

In this chapter, first a brief overview of studies on oral corrective feedback is provided followed by a summary of the evidence from educational psychology that showed the facilitative roles of gestures in learning in math education. Next, how gestures are used in a language classroom is introduced. In the subsequent four sections, the evidence from empirical studies that demonstrate whether gestures help the development of a second language (L2) in three linguistic domains (vocabulary, pronunciation, and grammar) and then L2 comprehension is explained. Each section concludes with suggestions for research direction by bridging the

I am extremely grateful to the anonymous reviewers who shared valuable comments on the earlier version of the manuscript. Thank you Dr. Hossein Nassaji and Dr. Eva Kartchava for organizing a colloquium at Second Language Research Forum 2018 in which a part of this manuscript was presented. The feedback given during the colloquium was immensely insightful. I would also like to extend my gratitude to the graduate students who attended the course Nonverbal Features and L2 Learning in spring 2018 for their enthusiastic discussion of many studies reviewed in this chapter. Lastly, I would like to thank Women Faculty Writing Program at Texas Tech University for providing me with a place and time to write this manuscript and encouraging me during the process of writing.

gestures and corrective feedback studies. In the final section, the relationship between learners' individual differences, gestures, and corrective feedback is introduced.

Corrective Feedback

Studies on corrective feedback have flourished in the past thirty years. Several recent meta-analyses have confirmed that receiving corrective feedback is helpful for L2 development overall because such feedback helps learners notice linguistic structures, and it leads to L2 development (Li, 2010; Lyster & Saito, 2010; Lyster, Saito & Sato, 2013; Russell & Spada, 2006).

The studies on corrective feedback began by identifying how an instructor provides corrective feedback in a language classroom and provided a framework for classifying feedback types. For example, Lyster and Ranta (1997), in a seminal study about corrective feedback, observed a French as a Foreign Language classroom for 18.3 hours to find out what type of corrective feedback is used in a language classroom and how students respond to teachers' feedback. The authors identified six types of corrective feedback (explicit correction, recasts, clarification requests, metalinguistic feedback, elicitation, and repetition) and found that recast is the most commonly used type. However, they found that other feedback types allowed students to repair their own utterances, which is arguably helpful for L2 learning.

To find out the optimal type of corrective feedback, researchers examined various features of corrective feedback: input-providing or output-prompting qualities (Goo & Mackey, 2013; Lyster & Ranta, 2013), the degree of implicitness (Ellis, Loewen & Erlam, 2006), and the linguistic targets (Brown, 2014). Additionally, some studies reported that the discoursal features of corrective feedback influence student–teacher interaction. Loewen and Philp (2006), for example, investigated the prosody used by teachers during the provision of recasts. The authors found that students produced uptake more frequently following recasts with *declarative* intonation. Interestingly, however, learners were able to provide correct answers on a subsequent post-test when the learners received recasts with *interrogative* intonation, as in the following example:

> **Example 1: Recast with interrogative intonation (Loewen & Philp, 2006, p. 556)**
> STUDENT: Somebody steal my paper (.) stolen
> TEACHER: Someone stole your paper?

A recent meta-analysis by Li (2010) showed that an explicit type of feedback, such as metalinguistic feedback, is more effective than an implicit type of feedback, such as recasts. However, implicit feedback tends to have stronger long-lasting effects than explicit feedback. The major difference between implicit and explicit feedback concerns the saliency of the feedback, that is, how noticeable the linguistic target in jeopardy is to the learners. Explicit feedback, such as metalinguistic feedback, is more salient than implicit feedback, and the explicitness or implicitness of feedback depends not only on a general feedback type but also on how feedback is provided in terms of prosody and intonation, as Loewen and Philp (2006) reported. The gestural studies have reported that some types of gestures, such as beat and deictic gestures, co-occur with speech and that timing of occurrence of these gestures coincides with when the speaker emphasizes a part of his or her speech using stress (Leonard & Cummins, 2011). If such gestures are also used during corrective feedback to cue the linguistic targets, it is possible that gestures affect the saliency of corrective feedback.

Gesture and Learning

Researchers have developed different types of classifications of gestures depending on the research purposes. Among them, McNeill's (1992) classification is one of the most commonly used in various disciplines. Emblems are gestures that have specific meanings that are culturally determined and do not need to be accompanied by speech to convey their meaning. A typical example is the gesture of the thumb and index finger making a circle with the other fingers extended upward that means "okay" in the United States but signifies "money" in Japan. Iconic gestures are those that present images of concrete entities and/or actions. Metaphoric gestures also present an image but of abstract concepts. Deictic gestures are pointing with the finger or other body parts and are used to index concrete and abstract entities. Beat gestures refer to vertical or horizontal hand movements that are made with the rhythm of speech (McNeill, 1992). McNeill (2005) further elaborated the gesture's characteristics by adding the concept of dimensions, such as *deixis* (deictic) and *metaphoricity* (metaphoric), and emphasized that gestures can have more than one category.

Because gestures play an integral role in communication, researchers in various disciplines have investigated the functions of gestures. Researchers in the field of education and educational psychology, for example, reported that teachers often incorporate gestures during teaching (Alibali, Flevares & Goldin-Meadow, 1997; Crowder, 1996; Perry, Birch & Singleton, 1995; Roth, 2001; Roth & Lawless, 2002a, 2002b) and use gestures to manage the classroom and to tell students when and what to pay attention to in class (Flevares & Perry, 2001).

Researchers in the field of developmental psychology took a further step to investigate the impact of gestures on learning in nonlinguistic domains

(Cook, Yip, & Goldin-Meadow, 2010; Goldin-Meadow, Cook, & Mitchell, 2009; Goldin-Meadow & Sandhofer, 1999; Goldin-Meadow & Singer, 2003). Susan Goldin-Meadow and her colleagues have been examining how gestures impact learning of mathematical concepts. In a 2009 study, Goldin-Meadow et al. investigated how seeing and producing gestures facilitate children's understanding of mathematical concepts. The children were directed to point out the relevant numbers of a math equation in one condition. For example, they were asked to point out numbers 4 and 5 of an equation such as 4 + 5 + 7 = __ + 7. The second group was told only to point out another set of numbers (4 and 7 or 5 and 7). The third group did not use any gestures. After the treatment, the children completed a math test that tested their understanding of the mathematical concept introduced. The findings suggested that producing appropriate gestures are beneficial for learning the equation. Following such findings, I speculate that gestures as a part of instructions, if used appropriately, play a significant role in language teaching.

Gestures in Language Classrooms

Extending this line of research, the studies in the field of second language acquisition also investigated the relevance of gestures in relation to L2 learning. Since the late 1990s, researchers have investigated how language instructors use gestures in second and foreign language classrooms (Allen, 1995, 2000; Hudson, 2011; Inceoglu, 2015; Lazaraton, 2004; Smotrova, 2014; Smotrova & Lantolf, 2013; Tellier, 2006; Wang, 2009; Zhao, 2007). In one of the early works, for example, Lazaraton (2004) used a conversation analysis approach and provided rich information about how gestures were used during a five-hour observation of an English as Second Language (ESL) classroom taught by a Japanese graduate student. In a detailed analysis, she reported that gestures functioned as comprehensive input during vocabulary instruction. The instructor used gestures to show the meaning of the verbs without verbal explanations. For example, when introducing the word *weave*, the instructor moved her hands close to each other to show a knitting motion while simultaneously asking "What does weave mean?" Similarly, in an analysis of six 55-minute recordings of a Spanish as a Foreign Language classroom, Allen (2000) reported that gestures were used to help learners understand the meaning of teachers' utterances (e.g., "Close the textbook"). She also reported that the instructor used gestures to indicate the accent pattern, to maintain turn-taking, and to identify the referent point, such as people or objects.

Following these precursor studies, a growing number of descriptive classroom studies have been published in the past ten years. The first group of studies used focus on form as a theoretical framework and reported the ratio of gesture use (Inceoglu, 2015; Kamiya, 2012). Kamiya

(2012) investigated the quality and frequency of teachers' gestures during focus-on-form instruction, an instruction style that enables learners to map form and function by shifting learners' attention from meaning to form during a meaning-focused instructional setting, which is considered to play a significant role in L2 development. In an observation of an ESL classroom, he found that 36 percent of focus on form concerned proactive focus on form, and 14 percent of reactive focus on form incorporated gestures. This study is important as it not only measured gestural use during instruction, which is directly tied to language learning, but also provided the different proportions of gesture use.

A similar study was conducted by Inceoglu (2015), but she focused on the focus-on-form episodes (FFEs) targeting vocabulary words. In a ten-hour observation, she identified a total of 110 FFEs targeting lexical items. Almost half of the FFEs were accompanied by gestures. Interestingly, she found that the word class affected the incorporation of gestures. Specifically, her data showed that FFEs were mediated by gestures frequently for verbs and nouns. When teaching collocations, the instructor almost always used gestures. The author further identified that how FFEs were initiated influenced the types of gestures being used. Iconic gestures were frequently used regardless of whether the FFEs were being initiated by students or teachers. However, deictic gestures were more frequently used when FFEs were initiated by the students than by the instructor. Such studies are important because they collectively identified several variables which affected the teachers' use of gestures. In a similar line of study, Davies (2006) also observed how frequently nonverbal cues were used during FFEs. Although the specifics of nonverbal cues were not revealed in the study, it was reported that 47 percent of FFEs were accompanied by nonverbal cues.

Wang and Loewen (2016) specifically reported how teachers used nonverbal behaviors, including gestures, during the provision of corrective feedback in the ESL classrooms. They observed about 65 hours of nine ESL classrooms taught by eight instructors. They identified that more than 60 percent of corrective feedback was accompanied by various nonverbal behaviors, including head movements, such as nodding and head shaking, and deictic gestures, such as pointing at an artifact or at a person. Specifically, as for the explicitness of feedback, they found that the more explicit form of feedback was accompanied by nonverbal behaviors, as shown in the following example:

Example 2: Deictic gesture used with explicit feedback (Wang & Loewen, 2015, pp. 14–15)
CADI: While he was studying at the ELC, he was playing basketball.

TEACHER: <While he **was** studying>, but [he] (right hand points at the students' partner) still **is**. That's when we can't use the past because [he is still studying and he still is playing basketball]. (Right hand repeatedly moves up and down.) That's present.
CADI: (Nods).

The second group of researchers used sociocultural theory as the theoretical framework and investigated how students and teachers use gestures in a classroom, a shared community, and how such use plays a role in classroom interaction (McCafferty & Rosborough, 2014; Smotrova, 2014; Smotrova & Lantolf, 2013; van Compernolle & Smotrova, 2014). Smotrova and Lantolf (2013) examined interactions between instructors and students in English as a Foreign Language (EFL) classrooms in Ukraine and found that the students in the classroom began to reciprocate a gestural feature. Such recurrent gestural features continued to be used while the new gestural features were constructed and shared. The authors also found that gestures were used as a mediating tool to facilitate students' understanding of lexical items by disambiguating their meaning, and such gestures were mirrored by students. The authors argued that such imitations of gestures are helpful for L2 development because they allow learners to confirm their understanding but also function as enactment. A similar finding, that students incorporated teachers' gestures, was reported by Matsumoto and Dobbs (2017). They found that the instructor used gestures for teaching English tense and aspect in a 56-hour observation of an ESL classroom in the United States. The data showed that the students continued to use the gestures introduced by the instructor, which helped the students learn tense and aspect.

These observational studies showed how gestures are used by instructors and students in a language classroom. The studies showed how different variables affect the quantity and quality of teachers' gestures. Furthermore, the studies provided indications that teachers' gestures, especially when they are shared by students, are potentially helpful for L2 development. The future descriptive study could also investigate how students use gestures as a part of their uptake. Wang (2009), for instance, reported that students use head movement, such as nodding, when responding to feedback. It is possible that the response could be given also gesturally. For example, students may use thumbs up to show their acknowledgment and repeat teachers' pedagogical gesture, such as a point-back gesture, to show their understanding of missing past tense. To better understand whether this exposure to and production of gestures truly help L2 learning, the findings need to be complemented with intervention studies. In the next section, the findings from experimental studies that investigated whether gestures help different linguistic areas are introduced.

Gesture and Vocabulary Learning

Researchers in the field of psycholinguistics investigated the facilitative role of gestures, and studies have collectively shown that seeing and repeating the instructor's gestures are helpful for L2 vocabulary acquisition as well. The two common theoretical frameworks used in these studies are Clark and Paivio's (1991) *dual coding theory*, which suggests that learning is reinforced when verbal and nonverbal modalities co-occur, and *enactment theory*, which argues that recalling enacted action and phrases has been found to be superior to recall of action phrases without enactment (Cohen & Otterbein, 1992; Engelkamp & Cohen, 1991). These theories suggest that receiving input in multiple modalities and/or enacting the gestures which represent the meaning of the target vocabulary promote learning because the multimodal input and enactment aid better memory retention. Following these theoretical notions, the researchers specifically examined the effects of "seeing then repeating" instructors' gestures during vocabulary instruction.

An early study conducted by Tellier (2008) investigated whether seeing and repeating the instructor's gestures impacts learning English vocabulary by L1 French adolescents. In Week 1, after the target words (*house, swim, cry, snake, book, rabbit,* and *scissors*) were introduced once with pictures and gestures to assure that children understood the meaning, the researcher introduced the words with either gestures or pictures. All the children were instructed to repeat the target words orally, but the children in the gesture condition were told to repeat the gestures as well. The vocabulary lesson was repeated twice over two weeks. The researcher measured children's passive knowledge (Weeks 1 and 3) and active knowledge (Weeks 2 and 3). The results showed that there was no difference between the children in the two conditions on a passive knowledge test in Week 1, but the children in the gesture condition outperformed the children in the picture condition for all the remaining tests. This finding indicates that "seeing and repeating" gestures were more effective than seeing no gestures at all. In other words, the effects of enactment, as reported in enactment theory, were stronger than multimodal input, as argued in dual coding theory.

Researchers have also investigated what kinds of gestures help vocabulary learning. Manuela Macedonia and her colleagues examined the effectiveness of enactment by teaching a list of Vimmi vocabulary, an artificial corpus that conforms to Italian phonotactics (Macedonia & Klimesch, 2014; Macedonia, Müller & Friederici, 2011). In Macedonia et al. (2011), a total of thirty-three L1 German participants learned twenty-nine Vimmi concrete nouns. The target vocabulary was presented in a video recording with iconic gestures, which described the meaning of the words, or with meaningless gestures which were just physical activity without including any iconic or symbolic image that potentially illustrated the meaning of target words. The participants orally and gesturally repeated the target words. After viewing the video, the participants were asked to translate the target words. The results showed that the participants significantly remembered the target items better when presented with iconic gestures than with meaningless gestures, and the learning was maintained long-term, sixty days after the intervention. Kelly, McDevitt, and Esch (2009) also found similar results. They tested the learnability of vocabulary words in Vimmi with a total of twenty-eight university students. They were randomly assigned to one of the following conditions: (1) listen to the word, (2) repeat the word, (3) repeat the word and perform a congruent gesture, or (4) repeat the word and perform an incongruent gesture. According to the memory test, the authors found that the learners who repeated the word and performed congruent gestures learned the best. These studies highlight that not all gestures are helpful for vocabulary teaching and suggest incorporating iconic gestures that illustrate target words during vocabulary instruction.

Recent studies on gestures also explored whether the benefits of enactment can be found for abstract words. In Macedonia and Knösche (2011), a total of twenty participants were taught thirty-two sentences that consisted of four words each. All sentences included a concrete subject, an adverb, a verb, and a noun as in this example: *Pilot genießt wirklich Aussit* ([The] pilot really enjoys [the] view). Sixteen sentences were presented with iconic gestures which described the semantic content of the concrete words and with arbitrary gestures for the abstract words. For example, for a concrete noun *nunun* (seal), the researcher imitated balancing a ball on her nose. For an abstract word such as preposition *gito* (at), the researcher pointed at the floor in the direction of her right foot. The remaining sixteen sentences were presented without gestures. Using the data obtained from the recall tests in which the participants were asked to write as many items as possible in Vimmi and German (L1), the researchers found that learners benefited from gestures when learning concrete and abstract words. Repetto, Pedroli, and Macedonia (2017) also examined the possibility of teaching abstract words through gestures. They taught a total of thirty abstract words to a total of twenty learners divided into one of three conditions: (1) reading only, (2) reading and matching the word and picture, and (3) reading and enacting the corresponding gestures. The memory tests revealed that learners who read and enacted the corresponding gestures performed the best. In sum, these studies showed that gestures can be used as a memory-enhancing tool for concrete and abstract words.

The studies previously mentioned showed that gestures help vocabulary learning, but to what extent such gestures are helpful during corrective feedback in a daily language classroom is not yet known. One way to examine the efficacy of gestures during corrective feedback on vocabulary development is to carry out a quasi-experimental study which targets individual learners' linguistic development after receiving corrective feedback. Loewen (2005) conducted this type of study by examining ESL learners' L2 development following FFEs. Each learner received individual test items asking them to recall the linguistic target mentioned during the FFEs. He found that learners retained the information about the linguistic target even two weeks after receiving the FFEs. A future study could replicate this research solely focusing on corrective feedback targeting the vocabulary. A video recording of the class may be used to identify whether the corrective feedback included iconic and congruent gestures. Then, the accuracy rate of the recalled information could be compared between the two corrective feedback conditions (gesture vs. no-gesture). Adding a delayed post-test would also be informative, as studies on vocabulary development specifically identified the long-term effect of gestures.

Gesture and Pronunciation Learning

The findings regarding the effectiveness of using gestures to teach pronunciation are mixed, although language teachers often incorporate gestures when teaching pronunciation (Hudson, 2011). Hudson (2011) observed an ESL classroom at a university to identify how teachers used gestures in general. One finding was that the instructor used various types of gestures when teaching. Iconic gestures were used to present a mouth shape when teaching short and long vowels (*ship* vs. *sheep*), beat gestures when teaching syllable stress, and deictic (pointing) gestures to teach intonation, to name a few. Visual input is considered essential in pronunciation learning as it has been shown in a classic McGurk effect, which explains how humans perceive sound visually and auditory. When a listener is presented with a sound with a mismatched visual, seeing a lip movement of /ba/ while the sound is /va/, for example, the listener often interprets the sound as /va/.

To examine whether using gestures is helpful for pronunciation learning, researchers have examined the effects of gestures in intervention studies. Significant work regarding Japanese phonological features has been conducted by Spencer Kelly and his colleagues (Hirata & Kelly, 2010; Hirata et al., 2014; Kelly & Lee, 2012). Other researchers have examined gestural effects on teaching Chinese tones (Morett & Chang, 2015) and Spanish intonation (Yuan et al., 2019). The theoretical constructs of these studies involve dual coding theory (described in the vocabulary learning section) and embodied cognition, which argues that our cognition, understanding of phonological features, for example, is influenced by our experiences with the physical world, such as producing corresponding gestures.

Following dual coding theory, some studies have examined whether seeing the instructor's gestures that metaphorically illustrate the sound patterns affects the development of pronunciation learning. Studies regarding the acquisition of English prosody or speech patterns collectively illustrate the favorable impact by incorporating gestures (Gluhareva & Prieto, 2017; Yuan et al., 2019), but that is not always the case for learning Japanese short and long vowels (Hirata & Kelly, 2010; Kelly & Lee, 2012). Gluhareva and Prieto (2017), for example, investigated the effectiveness of seeing beat gestures in the acquisition of English speech patterns. L1 Spanish students were given a video training in which an instructor spoke with or without beat gestures. The participants were asked to talk spontaneously before and after the video training, and their speech was rated by native speakers. The rating suggested that in the accentedness ratings the learners who saw an instructor's beat gestures outperformed those who saw an instructor with no gestures. Such favorable findings were not found in the series of studies targeting phonemic contrasts. For example, Hirata and Kelly (2010) investigated whether seeing gestures in pronunciation instructions could help learners distinguish short and long vowels in Japanese. A total of sixty learners viewed one of four videos: (1) audio only (control), (2) audio and mouth movement, (3) audio and gesture which indicated the sound pattern, and (4) audio, mouth movement, and gestures. The results indicated that the learners who saw mouth movements only showed significant improvement between the pre- and post-test. Collectively, the results indicate the limited effects of *seeing* gestures, and the effectiveness seems to vary depending on phonological targets.

Researchers have further examined the effectiveness of *repeating* instructors' gestures, following embodiment theory (Hirata et al., 2014; Morett & Chang, 2015). Morett and Chang (2015), for example, taught a total of twenty Mandarin words to fifty-seven L1 English speakers in three video conditions: (1) using pitch gestures, illustrating pitch used in the target words; (2) using semantic gestures, illustrating the meaning of target words; and (3) no gestures. As the participants viewed the videos, the participants in Conditions 1 and 2 were asked to repeat the gestures. The participants also completed a tone-identification test and a word–meaning association test. The results showed that learners benefited from pitch gestures and semantic gestures for tone identification. Interestingly, the researchers found that pitch gestures were more helpful for connecting meaning and target words. In contrast, Hirata et al. (2014) found that observing gestures was as effective as mimicking gestures. They asked a total of eighty-eight L1 English speakers to learn short and long vowels in Japanese in one of four conditions: (1) watch an instructor's syllabic gestures, (2) watch an instructor's moraic gestures, (3) watch and repeat an instructor's syllabic gestures, or (4) watch and repeat an instructor's moraic gestures. Moraic gestures represent the number of moras, a basic rhythmic unit of Japanese, and a long vowel is counted as two moras, whereas a short vowel is counted as one mora (see Hirata et al., 2014, p. 2092). According to the discrimination test the participants completed after the intervention, all learners improved equally regardless of gesture type and of whether they watched or repeated the gestures.

Owing to the mixed findings, it may be premature to conclude that gestures are helpful for teaching all the aspects of pronunciation. In addition, the results may be interpreted with caution because the participants were not necessarily actual L2 learners in some studies, and the studies took place in a lab setting, not language classrooms. In other words, participants may not have been ready to learn the phonological contrasts because it was the first time they had been exposed to the target language's phonology, and the effects of gestures on pronunciation learning in a classroom setting remain unclear. Consequently, further studies with real L2 learners and in a real classroom are needed to better examine the effects of gesture on pronunciation learning.

As mentioned, the effectiveness of gestures in pronunciation teaching is still inconclusive. The trend, however, is that gestures are particularly helpful for teaching tones and prosody. To examine whether gestures' facilitative functions hold during corrective feedback, a semi-replication study of Saito and Lyster (2012) may be helpful. They conducted an intervention study to examine the effectiveness of oral recasts on the development of English /r/ by L1 Japanese speakers. Specifically, the authors compared the effectiveness of recasts provided during a meaningful discourse following form-focused instruction. The results from the pre-tests and post-tests showed that the learners who received recasts improved significantly compared to those who did not receive recasts. A future study could replicate this investigation by targeting tone or prosody and by adding one more variable, such as oral recasts, with gestures which indicate the difference in the tongue placement in mouth and oral recasts alone in a language classroom. Then, one could compare the learners' development via pre-tests and post-tests that assess the correct choice of tone or prosody in controlled and spontaneous speech and/or perception by a native speaker. Such study would better inform us whether teachers' gestures are helpful in the development of L2 pronunciation.

Gesture and Comprehension

It may be intuitive that seeing a speaker's gestures is helpful for understanding the contents of speech in general and even more so in the case of L2 speech. Studies have shown that L2 learners report that seeing an instructor's gestures help learners understand better in class (Sime, 2006, 2008). To find out how L2 learners perceive teachers' gestures, Sime (2006) interviewed a total of twenty-two EFL learners using stimulated recall, which is a retrospective measure to elicit participants' concurrent thoughts. Typically, the participants viewed a recorded classroom interaction immediately after class, and the researcher asked them to verbalize their thoughts at the time of the interaction. The participants watched a five-minute video segment that included student–teacher interaction in an ESL classroom. The students reported that seeing gestures was helpful because they helped the students learn and understand the instructors' emotions and attitudes, and intention for classroom management.

Some researchers have further investigated to what extent seeing gestures helps learners' comprehension (Dahl & Ludwigsen, 2014; Sueyoshi & Hardison, 2005). Dahl and Ludwigsen (2014), for example, investigated the different effects of seeing gestures between seventh- and eighth-grade native speakers of English from the United States and EFL speakers in Norway. The participants watched a series of short videos that described cartoon images either with or without speakers' gestures. Then the participants were asked to draw corresponding images. The authors found that although the visibility of gestures did not affect the native speakers' drawings, seeing gestures helped the L2 speakers understand the speech contents as well as the native speakers. Sueyoshi and Hardison (2005) also compared the roles of gestures in comprehension, particularly in relation to learners' proficiency levels. In their study, a total of forty-two EFL learners at beginning and advanced levels viewed a video of a lecture in three conditions: audiovisual including gestures and faces, audiovisual with faces only, and audio only. The participants answered a set of comprehension questions after listening to the lecture. The researchers found that learners with low proficiency benefited the most from the gesture-face audiovisual presentation of data and the no-gesture audiovisual condition helped the advanced learners most. Although the number of studies is still limited, these studies confirm that seeing speakers' gestures is helpful for understanding the contents of L2 speech, particularly for beginning learners.

If seeing gestures helps comprehension, it is possible that seeing gestures also allows learners to perceive teachers' intentions for corrective feedback more accurately if the gestures used in corrective feedback illustrate the contents of feedback, such as linguistic targets. Partially replicating a study such as Mackey, Gass, and McDonough (2000) can clarify whether gestures play a role in learners' perception of feedback. Mackey et al. asked a total of ten English as a Second Language learners and seven Italian as a Foreign Language learners to provide their concurrent thoughts when receiving corrective feedback using a stimulated recall. The authors found that the learners' accuracy in perception depended on linguistic targets (e.g., feedback targeting lexis, semantic, and phonology was perceived more accurately than morphosyntax). A future replication study could incorporate teachers' gestures as a possible variable and compare

Gesture and Grammar Learning

Classroom studies have collectively reported how teachers use gestures when teaching grammatical aspects, such as present and past tense (Hudson, 2011). For example, a teacher incorporates deictic gestures "to point to the past as if it were located behind her, often pointing with her thumb" (p. 124) or to point "to the ground to indicate the present time" (p. 130).

Unlike studies on pronunciation, vocabulary, and comprehension, not many studies have examined whether using gestures helps development of L2 grammar except Nakatsukasa (2019). Using dual coding theory as the theoretical framework, she investigated whether the instructor's use of gestures during the provision of recasts helps learners' acquisition of locative pronouns. A total of fifty-nine ESL learners were assigned to one of the following conditions: (1) recast only, (2) recast with gestures, and (3) no feedback. The learners received recasts when they made a mistake in locative prepositions during hour-long communicative tasks. Learners in the recast with gestures condition received oral recasts which were followed by a gesture that iconically illustrated the incorrect use of prepositions. The results showed that the learners who received recasts with and without gestures performed similarly at the time of immediate post-test, but learners in the recast with gestures condition were able to maintain learning significantly better than those who received the recast only condition. The results indicate that seeing gestures facilitates retaining learned information. Similarly, Nakatsukasa (2019) investigated whether gestures incorporated in recasts help learners use the regular past tense in English. Unlike for locative prepositions, she did not find significant differences between the two experimental conditions. She concluded that this may be because that learners did not need to reconceptualize their understanding of the past tense during the task, unlike locative prepositions, because the learners did not need to use contrastive tenses during the task. These studies seem to be the only ones that investigated the effectiveness of recasts on L2 grammar development during the provision of corrective feedback, and the effectiveness of gestures remains inconclusive.

To argue whether gestures are effective for teaching grammar during corrective feedback, more intervention studies are needed. Although Nakatsukasa (2016) found that using gestures during corrective feedback is helpful for teaching locative prepositions, it is not clear whether similar findings can be obtained for metaphoric use of prepositions (e.g., temporal) because form–meaning mapping is potentially more complex. Additional replication studies that target grammatical features with different types of gestures would provide a more accurate picture of the function of gestures during corrective feedback. For instance, one could construct a communicative task (e.g., scheduling activity) with intermediate-level ESL learners which requires use of the subjunctive (*I would join the party, if I could finish my homework*) and indicative structures (*I will join the party after I finish my homework*). After providing an explicit explanation for these structures and corrective feedback either with or without gestures, learning could be measured by implementing pre- and post-tests, targeting the explicit and implicit knowledge of these two structures, and comparing the learning in two conditions to identify the efficacy of gestures on grammatical development. One could further investigate learners' uptake following the feedback to find out if a learner incorporates teacher's gestures and if learners who incorporated gestures exhibit better learning than those who did not.

Individual Differences, Gestures, and Corrective Feedback

In the previous sections, the works on gestures that examined the effectiveness of gestures on various linguistic targets were introduced and what other studies could be conducted in the future were summarized. Aside from these studies, researchers have begun to investigate how learners' individual differences play a role in the perception of and the effectiveness of gestures in an L2 setting, such as the contrast between a native speaker and a nonnative speaker (Dahl & Ludvigsen, 2014), proficiency levels of nonnative speakers (Sueyoshi & Hardison, 2005), age (e.g., Kamiya, 2018), and gender (Nakatsukasa, 2017).

The first two studies examined whether seeing a speaker's gestures help comprehension. Dahl and Ludvigsen (2014) asked a native speaker of English and L1 Norwegian L2 English children to watch a speaker describing a cartoon image. Then the children were asked to draw a picture that illustrated the scene they just heard. The researchers found that overall seeing gestures had a facilitative role in comprehension for L1 Norwegian L2 English children but not for L1 Norwegian children. Similarly, as described in the earlier section, Sueyoshi and Hardison (2005) (as summarized in the section "Gesture and Comprehension") found that proficiency plays a role in comprehension when it comes to the effectiveness of seeing gestures. The authors found that beginning learners benefit from seeing gestures more than advanced learners.

The second variable reported in a recent study by Kamiya (2018) is that participants' age played a role in understanding teachers' speech. Kamiya asked thirty-six elementary school students and thirty university students in Japan to judge whether the teacher was asking a question or making a statement using a silent video clip. He found that university students were able to use nonverbal cues, including gestures, more frequently to judge more correctly than the elementary school students. Similarly, Mohan and Helmer (1988) reported that the 5-year-old ESL learners were better able to interpret the meaning of English speakers' common emblematic gestures than 4-year-old learners. However, the effect of age on interpretation of gestures is not as straightforward as it seems. In the aforementioned study by Dahl and Ludvigsen (2014), the participants were recruited from the seventh- and eighth-grade population. The researchers found no significant differences in their comprehensions due to the presence of gestures.

Gender has also been reported to affect the effectiveness of gestures during corrective feedback. Nakatsukasa (2017) reanalyzed the data obtained from her 2016 study and found that female students were able to better retain learning than male students when the recasts were given with gestures. She argued that this may be a result of better long-term memory, which women are reported to have compared to men. Although this is the only study that has examined the different effects of seeing gestures on L2 learning, a number of studies have reported differences in cognitive constructs between men and women. Therefore, further investigations of whether feedback with gestures work equally for men and women would be worthwhile.

These studies illustrate how some individual difference factors affect the efficacy of gestures. However, additional studies are needed to understand the effects of other individual difference variables and to figure out how to maximize the effectiveness of corrective feedback for learners with different characteristics. For instance, the relationship between the gesture-enhanced corrective feedback and learners' visual short-term memory could be explored. Recent studies on working memory have shown that learners' working memory capacity plays a significant role in the efficacy of recasts but not in metalinguistic feedback (Goo, 2012). Goo argued that learners with a high working memory capacity were better able to contrast their interlanguage and the target form because they have better control of attentional resources. As gesture is visual, it makes sense to investigate whether learners' visual short-term memory plays a significant role in the perception and efficacy of gesture-incorporated corrective feedback. It is possible that learners with higher visual short-term memory capacity may benefit more from seeing gestures during corrective feedback.

Conclusions and Implications

This chapter introduced gestural studies conducted in the second and foreign language contexts. A number of descriptive studies have confirmed that teachers incorporate gestures in teaching, and experimental studies have shown that gestures overall play a facilitative role in L2 learning in various linguistic domains. Although the number of studies is still too limited to generalize the findings, gestures, when used along with verbal corrective feedback, potentially facilitate learning.

Future research studies are encouraged to consider gestures and other nonverbal features as one of the variables. In an observational study, a researcher could examine how students respond to corrective feedback when pedagogical gestures are used. Specifically, one could observe the characteristics of learners' uptake following corrective feedback, as done in Lyster and Ranta (1997). Additionally, one could use a similar research design as Loewen (2005) and incorporate individual tests that measure learning of linguistic targets of corrective feedback. For the experimental studies, it is worthwhile investigating if seeing teachers' gestures affects learners' noticing of linguistic targets and of the corrective nature of feedback. One could incorporate a stimulated recall for a study that includes verbal and gestural corrective feedback, or an eye-tracking and/or think-aloud protocols if the feedback is given visually on screen. In both settings, observing learners' gestural responses may reveal what they have understood about the feedback. For example, a learner's noticing may be expressed by repeating the instructor's pedagogical gestures.

Pedagogically, a language teacher may benefit from being aware of how gestures are used in their own teaching. Furthermore, the existing studies recommend using gestures when teaching some linguistic areas, including prosodic features and vocabulary items. When teaching prosodic features, an instructor may metaphorically illustrate the sound patterns using gestures. An instructor of a tone-based language may find illustrating pitch (e.g., high and low) using gestures helpful. Positioning and movements of hand can also teach stress patterns or intonations. When teaching vocabulary items, an instructor may gesture to describe the meaning of target vocabulary and then have the students repeat them during the lesson. As for teaching grammar, there is no clear consensus regarding the effectiveness of seeing teacher's pedagogical gestures which depict the grammatical features; however, one could observe what pedagogical gestures students tend to continue using in class to identify types of gestures which seem to help learning.

References

Alibali, M., Flevares, L. & Goldin-Meadow, S. (1997). Assessing knowledge conveyed in gesture: Do teachers have the upper hand? *Journal of Educational Psychology*, 23(1), 183–194.
Allen, L. Q. (1995). The effects of emblematic features on the development and access of mental representations of French expressions. *Modern Language Journal*, 79(4), 521–529.

(2000). Form–meaning connections and the French causative. *Studies in Second Language Acquisition*, 22(1), 69–84.

Brown, D. (2014). The type of linguistic foci of oral corrective feedback in the L2 classroom: A meta-analysis. *Language Teaching Research*, 20(4), 436–458.

Clark, J. M. & Paivio, A. (1991). Dual coding theory and education. *Educational Psychology Review*, 3(3), 149–210.

Cohen, R. L. & Otterbein, N. (1992). The mnemonic effect of speech gestures: Pantomimic and non-pantomimic gestures compared. *European Journal of Cognitive Psychology*, 4(2), 113–139.

Cook, S. W., Yip, T. K. & Goldin-Meadow, S. (2010). Gesturing makes memories that last. *Journal of Memory and Language*, 63(4), 465–475.

Crowder, E. M. (1996). Gestures at work in sense-making science talk. *Journal of the Learning Sciences*, 5(3), 173–208.

Dahl, T. I. & Ludvigsen, S. (2014). How I see what you're saying: The role of gestures in native and foreign language listening comprehension. *Modern Language Journal*, 98(3), 813–833.

Davies, M. (2006). Paralinguistic focus on form. *TESOL Quarterly*, 40(4), 841–855.

Ellis, R., Loewen, S. & Erlam, R. (2006). Implicit and explicit corrective feedback and the acquisition of L2 grammar. *Studies in Second Language Acquisition*, 28(3), 339–368.

Engelkamp, J. & Cohen, R. L. (1991). Current issues in memory of action events. *Psychological Research*, 53(3), 175–182.

Flevares, L. M. & Perry, M. (2001). How many do you see? The use of nonspoken representations in first-grade mathematics lessons. *Journal of Educational Psychology*, 93(2), 330–345.

Gluhareva, D. & Prieto, P. (2017). Training with rhythmic beat gestures benefits L2 pronunciation in discourse-demanding situations. *Language Teaching Research*, 21(5), 609–631.

Goldin-Meadow, S., Cook, S. W. & Mitchell, Z. A. (2009). Gesturing gives children new ideas about math. *Psychological Science*, 20(3), 267–272.

Goldin-Meadow, S. & Sandhofer, C. M. (1999). Gesture conveys substantive information to ordinary listeners. *Developmental Science*, 2(1), 67–74.

Goldin-Meadow, S. & Singer, M. A. (2003). From children's hands to adults' ears: Gesture's role in the learning process. *Developmental Psychology*, 39(3), 509–520.

Goo, J. (2012). Corrective feedback and working memory capacity in interaction-driven L2 learning. *Studies in Second Language Acquisition*, 34(3), 445–474.

Goo, J. & Mackey, A. (2013). The case against the case against recasts. *Studies in Second Language Acquisition*, 35(1), 1–39.

Hirata, Y. & Kelly, S. D. (2010). Effects of lips and hands on auditory learning of second-language speech sounds. *Journal of Speech, Language, and Hearing Research*, 53(2), 298–310.

Hirata, Y., Kelly, S. D., Huang, J. & Manansala, M. (2014). Effects of hand gestures on auditory learning of second-language vowel length contrasts. *Journal of Speech, Language, and Hearing Research*, 57(6), 2090–2101.

Hudson, N. (2011). Teacher gesture in a post-secondary English as a second language classroom: A sociocultural approach. Unpublished doctoral dissertation, University of Nevada, Las Vegas.

Inceoglu, S. (2015). Teacher gesture and lexical focus on form in a foreign language classroom. *Canadian Modern Language Review*, 71(2), 130–154.

Kamiya, N. (2012). Proactive and reactive focus on form and gestures in EFL classrooms in Japan. *System*, 40(3), 386–397.

 (2018). The effect of learner age on the interpretation of the nonverbal behaviors of teachers and other students in identifying questions in the L2 classroom. *Language Teaching Research*, 22(1), 47–64.

Kelly, S. D. & Lee, A. (2012). When actions speak too much louder than words: Gesture disrupts word learning when phonetic demands are high. *Language and Cognitive Processes*, 27(6), 793–807.

Kelly, S. D., McDevitt, T. & Esch, M. (2009). Brief training with co-speech gesture lends a hand to word learning in a foreign language. *Language and Cognitive Processes*, 24(2), 313–334.

Lazaraton, A. (2004). Gesture and speech in the vocabulary explanations of one ESL teacher: A microanalytic inquiry. *Language Learning*, 54(1), 79–117.

Leonard, T. & Cummins, F. (2011). The temporal relation between beat gestures and speech. *Language and Cognitive Processes*, 26(10), 1457–1471.

Li, S. (2010). The effectiveness of corrective feedback in SLA: A meta-analysis. *Language Learning*, 60(2), 309–365.

 (2013). The interactions between the effects of implicit and explicit feedback and individual differences in language analytic ability and working memory. *Modern Language Journal*, 97(3), 634–654.

Loewen, S. (2005). Incidental focus on form and second language learning. *Studies in Second Language Acquisition*, 27(3), 361–386.

Loewen, S. & Philp, J. (2006). Recasts in the adult English L2 classroom: Characteristics, explicitness, and effectiveness. *Modern Language Journal*, 90(4), 536–556.

Lyster, R. & Ranta, L. (1997). Corrective feedback and learner uptake: Negotiation of form in communicative classrooms. *Studies in Second Language Acquisition*, 19(1), 37–66.

 (2013). Counterpoint piece: The case for variety in corrective feedback research. *Studies in Second Language Acquisition*, 35(1), 1–18.

Lyster, R. & Saito, K. (2010). Oral feedback in classroom SLA: A meta-analysis. *Studies in Second Language Acquisition*, 32(2), 265–302.

Lyster, R., Saito, K. & Sato, M. (2013). Oral corrective feedback in second language classrooms. *Language Teaching*, 46(1), 1–40.

Macedonia, M. & Klimesch, W. (2014). Long-term effects of gestures on memory for foreign language words trained in the classroom. *Mind, Brain, and Education*, 8(2), 74–88.

Macedonia, M. & Knösche, T. R. (2011). Body in mind: How gestures empower foreign language learning. *Mind, Brain, and Education*, 5(4), 196–211.

Macedonia, M., Müller, K. & Friederici, A. D. (2011). The impact of iconic gestures on foreign language word learning and its neural substrate. *Human Brain Mapping*, 32(6), 982–998.

Mackey, A., Gass, S. & McDonough, K. (2000). How do learners perceive interactional feedback? *Studies in Second Language Acquisition*, 22(4), 471–497.

Matsumoto, Y. & Dobs, A. M. (2017). Pedagogical gestures as interactional resources for teaching and learning tense and aspect in the ESL grammar classroom. *Language Learning*, 67(1), 7–42.

McCafferty, S. G. & Rosborough, A. (2014). Gesture as a private form of communication during lessons in an ESL-designated elementary classroom: A sociocultural perspective. *TESOL Journal*, 5(2), 225–246.

McNeill, D. (1992). *Hand and mind: What gestures reveal about thought*. Chicago: University of Chicago Press.

(2005). *Gesture and thought*. Chicago: University of Chicago Press.

Mohan, B. & Helmer, S. (1988). Context and second language development: Preschoolers' comprehension of gestures. *Applied Linguistics*, 9(3), 275–292.

Morett, L. M. & Chang, L. Y. (2015). Emphasising sound and meaning: Pitch gestures enhance Mandarin lexical tone acquisition. *Language, Cognition and Neuroscience*, 30(3), 347–353.

Nakatsukasa, K. (2016). Efficacy of recasts and gesture on the acquisition of locative prepositions. *Studies in Second Language Acquisition*, 38(4), 771–799.

(2017). Interlocutors' gender impact on L2 acquisition: Analysis of L2 grammar acquisition via communicative tasks. In L. Gurzynski-Weiss (ed.), *Expanding individual difference research in the interaction approach: Investigating learner, instructor and researcher IDs* (pp. 100–119). New York: Routledge.

(2019). Gesture-enhanced recasts have limited effects: A case of the regular past tense. *Language Teaching Research*, 1–26. https://doi.org/10.1177/1362168819870283.

Perry, M., Birch, D. & Singleton, J. (1995). Constructing shared understanding: The role of nonverbal input in learning contexts. *Contemporary Legal Issues*, 6, 213–235.

Repetto, C., Pedroli, E. & Macedonia, M. (2017). Enrichment effects of gestures and pictures on abstract words in a second language. *Frontiers in Psychology*, 8, 2136.

Roth, W. (2001). Gestures: Their role in teaching and learning. *Review of Educational Research*, 71(3), 365–392.

Roth, W. & Lawless, D. V. (2002a). Signs, deixis, and the emergence of scientific explanations. *Semiotica*, 138(1–4), 95–130.

(2002b). When up is down and down is up: Body orientation, proximity, and gestures as resources. *Language in Society*, 31(1), 1–28.

Russell, J. & Spada, N. (2006). The effectiveness of corrective feedback for the acquisition of L2 grammar: A meta-analysis of the research. In J. Norris & L. Ortega (eds.), *Synthesizing research on language learning and teaching* (pp. 133–164). Philadelphia: John Benjamins.

Saito, K. & Lyster, R. (2012). Effects of form-focused instruction and corrective feedback on L2 pronunciation development of /ɹ/ by Japanese learners of English. *Language Learning*, 62(2), 595–633.

Sime, D. (2006). What do learners make of teachers' gestures in the language classroom? *International Review of Applied Linguistics*, 44(2), 211–230.

(2008). "Because of her gesture, it's very easy to understand": Learner's perceptions of teachers' gestures in the foreign language class. In S. G. McCafferty & G. Stam (eds.), *Gesture in second language acquisition and classroom research* (pp. 259–279). London: Routledge.

Smotrova, T. (2014). Instructional functions of speech and gesture in the L2 classroom. Unpublished doctoral dissertation, Pennsylvania State University, Pennsylvania.

Smotrova, T. & Lantolf, J. P. (2013). The function of gesture in lexically focused L2 instructional conversations. *Modern Language Journal*, 97(2), 397–416.

Sueyoshi, A. & Hardison, D. M. (2005). The role of gestures and facial cues in second language listening comprehension. *Language Learning*, 55(4), 661–699.

Tellier, M. (2006). L'impact du geste pédagogique sur l'enseignement/apprentissage des langues étrangères: Etude sur des enfants de 5 ans [The impact of pedagogic gesture on teaching/learning foreign languages]. Unpublished doctoral dissertation, Université Paris-Diderot Paris VII, Paris, France.

(2008). The effect of gestures on second language memorisation by young children. *Gesture*, 8(2), 219–235.

van Compernolle, R. A. & Smotrova, T. (2014). Corrective feedback, gesture, and mediation in classroom language learning. *Language and Sociocultural Theory*, 1(1), 25–47.

Wang, W. (2009). The noticing and effect of teacher feedback in ESL classrooms. Unpublished doctoral dissertation, Michigan State University, East Lansing, MI.

Wang, W. & Loewen, S. (2016). Nonverbal behavior and corrective feedback in nine ESL university-level classrooms. *Language Teaching Research*, 20(4), 459–478.

Yuan, C., González-Fuente, S., Baills, F. & Prieto, P. (2019). Observing pitch gestures favors the learning of Spanish intonation by Mandarin speakers. *Studies in Second Language Acquisition, 41*(1), 5–32.

Zhao, J. (2007). Metaphors and gestures for abstract concepts in academic English writing. Unpublished doctoral dissertation, University of Arizona, AZ.

Part IV

Feedback Provider, Feedback Intensity, and Feedback Timing

13

Peer Feedback in Second Language Oral Interaction

Noriko Iwashita and Phung Dao

Introduction

Peer feedback has recently gained significant attention in second language (L2) acquisition research. Studies have found that despite being lower in quality and frequency than teacher or native-speaker (NS) feedback, peer feedback given in oral interaction promotes L2 production accuracy and development by triggering learners' attention to language form, increasing language modifications, and proceduralizing learners' declarative linguistic knowledge through meaningful practice (see Philp, Adams & Iwashita, 2014; Sato & Balinger, 2016 for reviews). The impact of these cognitive processes on language learning is, however, mediated by different social and contextual factors, such as the role of conversational partners (e.g., presumably equal in terms of language expertise; provider and receiver of peer feedback), learner perceptions of the interlocutors' relationship during interaction, approach to task, and previous experiences of working with partners (Coughlan & Duff, 1994; Philp & Mackey, 2010; Watanabe & Swain, 2008). Peer feedback is also perceived as dialogic scaffolding or language mediation, which creates learning opportunities whereby learners assist each other in performing intended communication and/or co-constructing language knowledge (van Compernolle, 2015).

This chapter presents an overview of the research on peer feedback in L2 oral interaction. The first section of the chapter describes the types and characteristics of peer feedback, followed by a discussion of the theoretical underpinnings of peer feedback to explain the benefits of peer interaction in L2 development. The third section presents a review of the studies on peer feedback that have focused on the effect of peer feedback on L2 development and factors affecting this type of feedback. The chapter concludes with some pedagogical implications and suggestions for future research on peer feedback in L2 oral interaction.

Peer Oral Feedback Types and Characteristics

Feedback involves a learner receiving corrective information on his or her speech from a teacher, native speaker, or peer(s) during an interaction. Like teacher or native-speaker feedback, peer feedback refers to all response information that informs the learner about their actual stage of language use and/or communication issues. However, peer feedback is unique because it is given by peers who hold an equal status of being a learner, and learners are both active feedback providers and receivers (see van Popta et al., 2017). This (more) equal relationship both positively and negatively affects the frequency and quality of the feedback observed in peer interaction and L2 development when compared to learner–teacher or learner–NS interaction (Philp et al., 2014).

Feedback Types

Following recent categorizations of teacher corrective feedback (Lyster, Saito & Sato, 2013; Sato & Loewen, 2018; Sheen & Ellis, 2011; also see Lyster & Ranta, 1997), peer feedback can be classified into two broad types – input-providing and output-prompting – in terms of evidence it provides (i.e., negative and positive). Input-providing peer feedback supplies learners with positive evidence that contains linguistic information about what is acceptable in the target language. Two representative types of input-providing peer feedback are the recast, which is a reformulation (either partial or full) of learners' errors, and the explicit correction, which provides the correct form and explicit indication of an error (Lyster & Ranta, 1997; Lyster, Saito & Sato, 2013; Sheen & Ellis, 2011). In contrast to input-providing peer feedback, output-prompting peer feedback does not supply learners with a target-like form or positive evidence. Instead, it creates opportunities for learners to self-correct or modify their output by indicating that there are comprehension and/or language issues. Different forms of output-prompting peer feedback have been documented in empirical studies, including repetition, clarification request, elicitation, and metalinguistic comment (Lyster, Saito & Sato, 2013).

Apart from the input-providing and output-prompting dimensions, the degree of feedback explicitness is another aspect of feedback categorization (Lyster & Satio, 2010; Nassaji, 2009; Sheen & Ellis, 2011; Sato & Loewen, 2018). The degree of feedback explicitness refers to the extent to which the feedback is salient to learners in discourse. The salience of feedback has been shown to depend on various factors, such as the nature of peer feedback, metalinguistic information (linguistic salience), intonation (auditory salience), and gesture and body language (visual salience) (see Loewen & Philp, 2006; Yilmaz, 2011). Although it may be possible to manipulate the explicitness externally to a certain extent, whether it is salient enough for learners depends on individual perceptions.

Examples of the different feedback types introduced here will be given in the next section which describes the characteristics of peer feedback. While the feedback types observed in peer interaction are similar to teacher and NS feedback, peer feedback has several characteristics that set it apart from the teacher's and native speakers' feedback.

Feedback Orientation

The first distinctive characteristic of peer feedback is its orientation. Often, teacher feedback informs learners of their erroneous utterances, expecting that learners will notice and correct the errors, which may possibly result in language modification and accurate output. However, peer feedback with the same explicit corrective intention as teacher feedback is rare in peer interaction (Philp et al., 2014; Sato, 2013). During the course of communication, the learners' main focus is often on meaning (e.g., Philip et al., 2014) and task completion (Philp et al., 2010). Information given by learners in peer feedback usually serves as a tool for others to understand them and to achieve intended communication.

However, it is notable that there are cases in which learners explicitly provide feedback to correct their partner's erroneous utterances. Examples 1 and 2 demonstrate two instances of talk segments where learners explicitly correct each other during an interaction.

Example 1: Explicit peer feedback in the form of reformulation and metalinguistic information

s1: 아버지가 선생님이다?
(Abu-ji-ga sun-saeng-nim-i-da?)
[Father is a teacher?]

s2: 아버지는 선생님이었다 현재 아니고과거
(a-bu-ji-nun sun-saeng-nim-i-et-da. hyun-jae a-ni-go, gwa-guh)
[Father was a teacher, not present, past] ◄──── explicit correction
(Kim & McDonough, 2008, pp. 217–218, commentary added)

In Example 1, S2 learner explicitly corrected their partner's utterance (e.g., "father is a teacher") by reformulation (e.g., "father was a teacher") and provided metalinguistic information (e.g., "not present, past"). Similarly, Example 2 shows that learner C explicitly questioned his partner's language use (e.g., "why is 'ly'?"), which led learner M to reconsider his choice of language (line 4).

Example 2: Explicit peer feedback in the form of a question

1   M: the immigrants particular
2   C: south

```
3   M:  is particularly
4   C:  why is "ly"? ←——— clarification request
5   M:  or in particular... because is, is adjective and this context this
        not adjective here
6   C:  mm (some agreement)
7   M:  yeah... particularly... in south... maybe in... in
8   C:  the immigrants particularly
```
(Storch, 2008, p. 101, commentary added)

However, the corrective intention is not always clear, as demonstrated in Example 3.

Example 3: Peer feedback in the form of recast
```
S1:  Non, boutelle [mispronunciation of the word] euh (.) deux bouteilles,
     s'il vous plait
     "No, bootle ah (.) two bottles, please."
S2:  Deux bouteilles ←——— recast
     "Two bottles."
```
(Philp, Walter & Basturkmen, 2010, p. 267)

While S2 reformulated S1's phonological error, it is not certain whether the reformulation was recognized. Thus, the pedagogical intention of feedback is not as clear as the corrective feedback from a teacher, which suggests a need for possible intervention to improve the effectiveness of peer feedback (Sato & Lyster, 2012).

When the goal of interactions is to complete a task or perform certain types of communication, learners tend to provide feedback on the linguistic areas that cause difficulties in completing a task or address communication breakdowns caused by language problems. Consequently, learners provide one another with feedback that targets multiple aspects of language rather than consistent and intensive feedback on one aspect of language, as shown below.

Example 4, which is taken from an interaction in which learners collaborated to sequence and describe pictures, shows peer feedback that targets multiple features of language during task completion.

Example 4: Feedback targeting multiple aspects of language
```
1   P1:  This is a phone... then she call to the hospital because her cat
         is uh...
2   P2:  is broke broken is broke head
3   P1:  cái gì [what?]... broken leg ←——— recast (multiple errors:
         grammar and lexis)
4   P2:  Uh broke leg... and then they are...
5   P1:  in the hopital [wrong pronunciation]
6   P2:  in the hospital [right pronunciation] ←——— recast (phonological
         error) and the doctor khám bệnh là gì? [what is "examine"]
```
(Dao, Nguyen & Chi, 2020, unpublished data)

In this example, when learner P2 said "broke head'" (line 2) to describe a cat with a broken leg, learner P1 did not understand the intended meaning and expressed his confusion with "what?" (line 3). Later, learner P1 reformulated his partner's errors with "broken leg" (line 3). This recast targeted multiple errors (lexical and grammatical) in the partner's erroneous utterance. However, learner P2 only noticed one aspect of the correction (lexical), as reflected in his uptake "broke leg" (line 4). In a subsequent turn, learner P1 made a phonological error (line 5), which was immediately corrected by learner P2. Overall, Example 4 demonstrates two important characteristics of peer feedback. First, peer feedback is spontaneous and targets various emerging language issues in interaction, with its main function being to allow each person to be understood so that they can complete the task (i.e., describe and sequence pictures to create a story). It is unclear whether having the focus of feedback on multiple aspects or a single aspect of language is more beneficial to L2 learning; however, research suggests that peer feedback tends to show "inconsistency in attention to target form" (Toth, 2008, p. 296). Second, peer feedback is easily accepted by peer partners when learners are collaborative and share the same goal of completing a task, as reflected by both learners in Example 4 providing and receiving feedback on each other's language issues.

Feedback Quality

It is well acknowledged that peer feedback is perceived as less reliable than the feedback learners receive from teachers or native-speaker interlocutors (Pica et al., 1996). Peer feedback may contain incorrect information, as seen in Example 5.

Example 5: Peer feedback (explicit feedback) with inaccurate input

s2: Muchos ... emigré? Pretérito?
[Many ... emigrated (first-person sing.) preterit?]

s1: Creo que emigré a Estados Unidos y España. Feedback ◄──── with inaccurate input.
[I think that emigrated (first-person sing.) to the United States and Spain.]

s2: Sí. emigré.
[Yes, emigrated (first-person sing.)]

s1: Emigré gente. Emigré.
[emigrated (first-person sing.) people. Emigrated.]

(Leeser, 2004, p. 66)

In Example 5, when asked for feedback, S1 provides S2 with inaccurate information about the correct form of the verb *emigrar*; that is, using the first-person singular form. However, the correct form of *emigrar* is the third-person plural preterit to agree with *muchos* and the third-person singular preterite form to agree with *gente*. Incorrect information in peer feedback is one reason why the benefits of peer feedback for L2 learning tend to be discounted.

Although learners may provide peer feedback that contains incorrect information, it can create opportunities for learners to attend to language features. Example 6 demonstrates how peer feedback with incorrect information increases learners' attention to form.

Example 6: Peer feedback (recast) with inaccurate input
P1: not some many many projector break down–
P2: ya out of date ◄——— recast with incorrect information
P1: out of work recast with incorrect information
P2: ya ok [laugh] out of work
P1: ... a lộn xin lỗi [*mistake sorry*] out of order sorry [laugh] ◄——— recast with correct information
P2: [laugh] ...

(Dao, 2017)

In Example 6, learner P1 made a grammatical error (e.g., plural form of "projector"). Learner P2 provided recast with incorrect information on word choice (e.g., "out of date") instead of addressing the grammatical issue. Although it contained incorrect information, this peer feedback led learner P1 to reformulate learner P2's nontarget-like utterance (e.g., "out of work"), which was also nontarget-like. Learner P1 recognized the inaccurate information (e.g., "mistake sorry") and reformulated it again (e.g., "out of order"). Example 6 shows that although the learners provided inaccurate information, the peer feedback increased the attention of the feedback provider, possibly resulting in learning. The learners were then able to correct inaccurate information, which is considered to result in the restructuring of their L2 knowledge (see also Philp et al., 2014; Sato & Loewen, 2018; Sato & Lyster, 2012).

However, compared to teacher or native-speaker feedback – which manifests in different forms such as recast, prompt, clarification request, and explicit elicitation (e.g., Lyster & Ranta, 1997) – feedback provided by a fellow learner may include segmentation, repetition of previous utterances, and/or non-specification of errors (McDonough, 2004; Pica et al., 1996). Peer feedback in the form of segmentation and repetition of the interlocutor's previous utterance is often less noticed by learners if it is implicit. This, therefore, may not promote language modification (Pica et al., 1996). The non-specification of errors in peer feedback also signifies fewer modifications. Example 7 provides an example of peer feedback that does not specify what information needs to be elicited.

Example 7: A non-specified clarification request
L9: if the city build more bicycle lane
L11: again please ◄——— clarification request

(McDonough, 2004, p. 217)

In Example 7, L11 requested clarification; however, it is not clear whether the requester is asking for clarification of the information provided in the previous statement or signaling that there is a grammatical error (i.e., subject/verb agreement). This excerpt shows that peer feedback is not effective if learners do not recognize the corrective intention.

As explained above, in terms of orientation and correctness, the quality of peer feedback is not the same as that of teacher or native-speaker feedback, and the frequency of peer feedback is often not as high either. However, the overall quality of feedback is important in studies drawing on the cognitive perspective of SLA because feedback provided by learners is seen as positive/negative evidence; that is, it is information that helps them to revise their interlanguage system. Furthermore, for studies based on skill acquisition theory, repeated practice in meaning-focused contexts would help learners restructure their current knowledge and further proceduralize it. Thus, through meaningful practice, learners may be better able to recognize the incorrectness of linguistic information in peer feedback and more likely to correct and improve its quality as they progress to higher levels of proficiency. Theoretical accounts that explain the benefits of oral peer feedback and a review of empirical studies are presented in the following sections.

Benefits of Oral Peer Feedback for L2 Development – Theoretical Accounts

Theoretical accounts of oral peer feedback that explain its benefits for L2 development can be viewed from multiple perspectives: educational (e.g., van Popta et al., 2017), cognitive (including both cognitive-interactionist, e.g., Gass & Mackey, 2007; Long, 1981, 1983, 1996, 2007, and skill acquisition theory, e.g., Anderson, 2005; DeKeyser, 1998), and sociocognitive (e.g., Philp & Mackey, 2010).

Educational Perspective

Providing peer feedback to each other can help learners to improve their overall output, which may then lead to transformation in their L2 knowledge. For instance, in education literature, peer feedback has been shown to promote a higher level of learning skills and critical insight in learners, as well as engender active reflection on the learners' own performance and that of their peers (Ertmer et al., 2007; Liu et al., 2001;

van Popta et al., 2017). The process of providing peer feedback entails meaning making and knowledge building (Nicol, 2009) and triggers different metacognitive processes such as evaluating, suggesting modifications, reflecting, planning, and regulating learners' own thinking. These metacognitive processes enable learners to build their reflective knowledge, which in turn results in the restructuring of their own knowledge (Liu et al., 2001; Nicol, 2009, 2014). Although learners may find it difficult to provide peer feedback (Dochy, Segers & Sluijsmans,1999; Topping et al., 2000), with careful use and training, it can generate positive impact on a learner's performance (van Popta et al., 2017; also, see Chapter 28, this volume).

In L2 acquisition studies, peer corrective feedback is believed to heighten learners' awareness of language form, especially when learners are trained and encouraged to attend to their peers' speech, to detect errors, and provide feedback (Fuji et al., 2016; Sato & Lyster, 2012). Thus, the hope is that peer feedback will encourage learners to actively engage in learning, which may then enhance their language skills and develop higher cognitive skills (Liu & Carless, 2006). Moreover, when learners are engaged in providing and receiving feedback, they are likely to have more speaking practice opportunities than in teacher–learner interactions. Detecting errors during the course of communication as a result of feedback is believed to positively affect interlanguage restructuring (DeKeyser, 2007). As a result of receiving feedback, learners have opportunities to self-correct or modify their output. The process of detecting errors and providing feedback enhances learners' monitoring of their own production, and in some cases peer feedback is believed to promote greater attention to language forms, which is positively correlated with language development (Sato & Lyster, 2012), than teacher feedback does (Sipple & Jackson, 2015). Therefore, increased attention to language form created by peer feedback is seen as showing the benefit of peer feedback and thus is expected to result in greater L2 development (Sipple & Jackson, 2015).

Cognitive Perspective

Oral interaction provides an opportunity to receive and process information. The two types of peer feedback explained above (i.e., input-providing and output-prompting feedback) draw from two theoretical orientations (i.e., cognitive-interactionist and Skill Acquisition Theory) to explain the cognitive processes that can result in learning.

Cognitive-Interactionist

The theoretical basis to guide researchers in examining a connection between input-providing/output-prompting feedback and L2 development largely draws upon Long's Interaction Hypothesis (1981, 1983, 1996, 2007) and Swain's Output Hypothesis (1995, 1998). Long proposed that conversational modifications offered in response to communication difficulties promote L2 learning. In his updated theory, Long (1996) stressed the facilitative role of input-providing feedback, such as recasts, as these interactional moves draw greater attention to the formal aspects of language while maintaining focus on meaning during interaction. Through peer interaction, learners provide feedback to one another and receive opportunities for modified output (Pica, 1994). In language production, learners are required to attend to the language, which Swain (1995) described as stretching interlanguage to meet communicative goals in her Output Hypothesis. In other words, learners engage in active deployment of their cognitive resources during production (Izumi, 2003).

As noted at the beginning of this section, the model of how interaction facilitates L2 learning was initially proposed based on interaction between native speakers and learners and was primarily examined under experimental conditions, not in classrooms. Thus, questions arise regarding the extent to which this model can be applied to explaining peer interaction in classrooms. Some may argue that the quality of peer feedback, in comparison to teacher and native-speaker feedback, decreases the effectiveness of corrective feedback in facilitating error noticeability and output modification. Additionally, peer feedback in some learning contexts may not promote as much attention to form as teacher feedback because of its unclear corrective intention and timeliness (e.g., Toth, 2008). Learners have been found more likely to provide implicit than explicit feedback (Morris, 2005). However, recent research has shown that peer feedback could promote L2 learning despite it being of lower quality and frequency than that provided by teachers and native-speaker interlocutors (Adams, 2007; Chu, 2013; McDonough, 2004; Sato & Lyster, 2012; Sipple & Jackson, 2015). In some contexts, learners reported that they appreciated peer feedback (Sato, 2013) and enjoyed interactions with peers more than with teachers (Sipple & Jackson, 2015). The findings lend support to the updated version of the Interaction Hypothesis in peer interaction contexts.

Skill Acquisition Theory

The usefulness of peer feedback (e.g., output-prompting feedback) for L2 development can be explained through Skill Acquisition Theory (SAT). Skill Acquisition Theory postulates that guided practice in conjunction with feedback transforms learners' declarative knowledge (e.g., explicit mental representation of language items such as language meanings and rules) into procedural knowledge (e.g., knowledge of how to carry out cognitive operations such as automatic language production) (Anderson, 2005). When applied to L2 learning, Skill Acquisition Theory posits that L2 learning refers to a gradual transition from the effortful to automatic use of a second language (VanPatten & Benati, 2010). This transition is brought about by feedback in meaningful communications (DeKeyser, 1998, 2007;

also see Sato & McDonough, 2019). In other words, feedback given in contextualized practice facilitates learners' proceduralization and automatization of language forms, which enables them to achieve faster and more accurate processing of L2 in both comprehension and production.

Furthermore, with the opportunity for extended and repeated production practice that peer interaction provides (Tognini, 2008), peer feedback allows learners to move from the effortful, slow production to effortless, smooth production (e.g., Ellis, 2005; Segalowitz, 2003), which can result in L2 automatic use or language growth (Ranta & Lyster, 2007). Thus, Skill Acquisition Theory emphasizes the pivotal role of peer feedback through contextualized practice in driving the restructuring and proceduralization of learners' developing knowledge of the target language. From both a cognitive-interactionist perspective and a Skill Acquisition Theory perspective, learning is largely considered individual and cognitive, and this approach has been criticized for not taking social factors into account.

Sociocognitive Perspectives

The sociocognitive approach to L2 learning considers the effect of both cognitive and social factors in understanding L2 acquisition. One line of cognitive-interactionist research further informed by the social approach suggests that the quality and quantity of information in corrective feedback given during interaction depends on the context (e.g., classroom, laboratory) and other factors, such as learner perceptions of the interlocutors' relationship in interactions and tasks (Ellis, 2010; Philp & Mackey, 2010). This body of research aims to extend understanding of the role of social and contextual factors in mediating the impact of cognitive factors on L2 acquisition during interaction. That is, the effectiveness of peer feedback depends largely on cognitive processes (e.g., attention and information processing), which are mediated by social and contextual factors of interaction in which peer feedback is given and received.

Also associated with the sociocognitive perspective, sociocultural theory could provide an alternative explanation of the contribution of peer feedback to L2 development to those offered by cognitive-interactionist and skill acquisition theories. According to the sociocultural theory, language learning is a socially situated and collaboratively co-constructed activity (Lantolf & Thorne, 2006). Within interaction, learners co-construct their L2 knowledge by providing each other with various forms of assistance or scaffolding (Donato, 2004; Ohta, 2001; Poehner, 2008; Sato & Ballinger, 2012). Scaffoldings in the form of peer feedback are believed to help learners acquire appropriate language forms, which enable them to perform intended activities such as producing language or achieving communication (e.g., Aljaafreh & Lantolf, 1994; Lantolf & Thorn, 2006; Nassaji & Swain, 2000; Ohta, 2000; Sato & Ballinger, 2012; Wertsch, 1998).

Studies of Peer Feedback

Effect of Peer Feedback on L2 Development

A considerable number of studies have investigated the effects of peer feedback on L2 development, focusing mainly on input-providing feedback. Broadly speaking, research has shown that peer feedback contributes to improving production accuracy and L2 development. For instance, using tailor-made production tests, Adams (2007) found that learners scored higher on the linguistic items they had received feedback on compared to those that were left untreated. Peer feedback, including recasts, has been shown to positively affect production accuracy of verb forms (Sato & Viveros, 2016).

Some studies have reported that peer feedback is superior to teacher feedback. For example, when comparing peer feedback with teacher feedback, Lynch (2007) found that peer feedback was more effective in developing learners' oral performance. Lynch attributed the effectiveness of peer feedback to its promotion of talk and triggering of deeper cognitive processes, which deems peer feedback superior to other types of corrective feedback. When comparing the effects of oral teacher feedback and oral peer feedback on learning German present perfect tense and past participle formation, Sipple and Jackson (2015) found that although both teacher feedback and peer feedback contributed to the improvement in accuracy of the target structures, learners who received peer feedback outperformed those receiving teacher feedback based on the pre-test/post-test scores. They attributed the superior impact of peer feedback to its characteristics of heightening learners' awareness of language form and promoting learner engagement in providing and receiving feedback from peers. Although this body of research has reported the positive impact of peer feedback on L2 production accuracy and learning, the effectiveness of peer feedback is understood to be vulnerable to social factors such as perceptions of equality of peers, comfort level, and previous partnership experience (see the next section).

To enhance the occurrence and effectiveness of peer feedback, recent research has included pedagogical interventions in peer interaction. Providing learners with a brief pedagogical training on how to give peer feedback has shown positive impact on language development, especially in terms of accuracy and fluency. For instance, in Chu's (2013) study, learners were taught a variety of peer feedback techniques and encouraged to use them in their interactions. The results showed that learners demonstrated improvement from pre-test to post-test on oral tasks (e.g., information-gap and picture-based tasks). Also teaching learners how to provide peer feedback, Sato and Lyster (2012) found a positive correlation between the frequency of peer feedback provision and L2 developmental scores (e.g., accuracy scores), suggesting that peer feedback positively impacts L2 learning. Similarly, in another study by Fujii, Ziegler, and Mackey (2016), learners received metacognitive instruction on the provision and use of interaction opportunities (e.g., providing peer feedback), which were shown to facilitate L2 development. The results revealed that compared to those who were not involved in the training session, learners who participated in the training prior to interaction provided more peer feedback and made use of the feedback that was provided, thereby benefiting more from these interactional opportunities.

Unlike input-providing feedback, very few studies have investigated the role of output-prompting feedback. In a study that compared the degree to which learners participated in peer feedback and modified output instances, McDonough (2004) reported that learners who provided more peer feedback and produced more modified output improved significantly on immediate and delayed production tests of structural targets (real and unreal conditions) than those who produced fewer instances of peer feedback and modified output. Although some positive impact of peer feedback is reported, it is not clear how the characteristics of peer feedback mentioned earlier (i.e., less clear and infrequent in comparison with teacher feedback) affects its effectiveness. Furthermore, its effectiveness largely depends on social and contextual factors, which are discussed in the next section.

Factors Affecting Peer Feedback

Social and Contextual Factors

Earlier studies comparing the occurrence of peer feedback and expert feedback (e.g., from native speakers and teachers) showed that learners provided one another with more feedback than when they interacted with other interlocutors (e.g., native speakers). Furthermore, learners were shown to address more communication breakdowns when interacting with peers than native speakers; this resulted in more peer feedback (e.g., elicitation). Pica et al. (1996) reasoned that learners may have experienced higher levels of comfort when interacting with peers than with teachers and, as such, were more likely to experiment further with language production.

As noted earlier, despite its occurrence and potential to promote L2 development, the frequency of peer feedback in peer interaction appears to be low. The low incidence of peer feedback is largely attributed to the social factors inherent in peer interaction (e.g., perceptions of equality of peers, comfort level, and previous partnership experience) that makes it distinct from teacher and native-speaker feedback. As the act of providing and receiving peer feedback entails reciprocity between peer interlocutors, the nature of peer interaction and effectiveness of peer feedback depend on how learners establish social relationships during interaction (Philp &

Mackey, 2010; Storch, 2002; Watanabe & Swain, 2007, 2008) and their mindset at the time of interaction (Sato, 2017). Regardless of the level of language repertoire, learners may perceive themselves and their peers as sharing the same and equal role of interlocutors in interaction (Philp & Mackey, 2010). Thus, when receiving peer feedback, they may feel embarrassed (Chu, 2013), or even frustrated if they are not satisfied with the quality of their interlocutors' correction (Kowal & Swain, 1994, 1997). In other words, the provision of peer feedback may be problematic for learners who have a strong sense of equality between peers (Philp & Mackey, 2010).

The low occurrence of peer feedback is also due to learners' hesitation in correcting each other's errors. Research on teachers' and learners' beliefs about corrective feedback provided by teachers and peers has suggested that learners might feel uncomfortable when providing feedback and/or being corrected by peers (Yoshida, 2010). As a result, they are hesitant about correcting partners' language errors (Philp, Walter & Basturkmen, 2010; Sato, 2013). Furthermore, learners' hesitation to provide peer feedback may be due to their inability to identify and provide comments on language errors; peer feedback may also interrupt interaction (Philp et al., 2010).

Perceptions of Peer Feedback

The relatively low incidence of peer feedback may also be attributed to learners' different attitudes toward it as opposed to native-speaker and teacher feedback. For example, in Chu's (2013) study that compared the effects of teacher and peer feedback, learners reported that they considered corrective feedback necessary and helpful; however, they expressed preference for teacher feedback over peer feedback. They believed teacher feedback to be more beneficial for L2 learning. Some learners even stated that correcting errors or providing feedback is the teachers', not the learners', role. However, learners also stated that they were willing to provide feedback to peers, but only when they themselves had confidence in their language ability. Similarly, learners in other learning contexts said that corrective feedback was imperative to L2 development (Schulz, 1996), but the majority preferred their errors to be corrected by teachers rather than peers (Brown, 2009; Cathcart & Olsen, 1976; Schulz, 1996; Yoshida, 2008), which echoes the findings of written corrective feedback studies (Miao, Badger & Zhen, 2006; Zhao, 2010).

Learners have expressed different reasons for preferring not to receive feedback from peers. First, they believe peer feedback may not be accurate, and peers who provide feedback may not understand the errors they correct (Yoshida, 2008). They are skeptical of their partner's language input, given his or her role as a learner; thus, they tend to seek teachers' help for language issues (Davis, 1997; Mackey et al., 2001; Williams, 2001). Second, because learners mistrust their peers' language ability, they do not consider them a reliable learning source (Katayama, 2007; Philp, Walter & Batsturkmen,

2010; Yoshida, 2008). Learners only believe or trust their peers when the peers show confidence when providing feedback (Katayama, 2007). This indicates that learners tend to be uncertain of the effectiveness of peer feedback.

However, it is notable that learners' views on peer feedback vary according to context. For instance, in a context in which learners have good linguistic knowledge due to their intensive experience with instruction that explicitly focuses on language forms, learners express appreciation for peer feedback. This is documented in Sato and Lyster's (2012) study on the effect of peer feedback training on improvement in L2 accuracy and fluency. They found that the learners had positive attitudes toward peer feedback. In another study, Sato (2013) asked learners, before and after receiving peer feedback training, about their perceptions of the effectiveness of peer feedback. Learners reported having positive attitudes toward peer feedback, and the peer feedback training appeared to enhance learners' trust in the feedback provided by peers. However, learners shared concerns that peer feedback impeded the conversation flow and, at times, caused peers to feel hurt or embarrassment. Overall, these studies indicate that learners' general and strong preference for teacher feedback could be rectified by training in how to provide feedback to peers, but learners' perceptions or preferences toward peer feedback may still affect its effectiveness, as reported in teacher feedback studies (Brandl, 1995; Brown, 2009; Yoshida, 2008).

Although learners generally preferred to receive feedback from teachers than peers, they reported that interactions with peers were more enjoyable. Furthermore, if past experiences of learning with a partner revealed that the partner was of high proficiency, these learners tended to appreciate and accept more feedback from the partner (Philp & Mackey, 2010). This suggests that peer feedback can be psychologically and socially acceptable to learners (Sato, 2013; Sipple & Jackson, 2015). With evidence from recent research about the positive impact of peer feedback (Chu, 2013; Sato & Lyster, 2012; Sipple, 2017; Sipple & Jackson, 2015), learners' negative beliefs could be alleviated by raising their awareness and training them to provide feedback to maximize the effectiveness of peer feedback on L2 development (Sato, 2013; Sato & Lyster, 2012).

Approach to Task Type, Task Role, and Proficiency

Apart from the influence of learners' perceptions of peer feedback, the learners' approach to tasks and task roles have also been documented as affecting the frequency and perceptions of the use of peer feedback. Based on interviews with individual learners, Philp and Mackey (2010) found that while most learners perceived a role-play task as an opportunity to practice forms learned in the textbook in a simulated, real-life context, other learners considered it as an act-out play to depict different personae.

Different approaches to the task were suggested to determine whether learners felt it was necessary to provide feedback, and how they perceived the use of peer feedback. Furthermore, the assignment of a task role to learners in pairwork has been shown to affect the amount of learner engagement with language forms, including the provision and use of peer feedback (Dao & McDonough, 2017). That is, giving the information-holder role to a lower-proficiency learner in a mixed dyad would likely result in greater engagement with language forms, (e.g., more provision of peer feedback). In sum, these studies have shown that the amount and effectiveness of peer feedback are subject to the social and contextual factors at play during interaction.

Proficiency and learners' perceptions of their partner's proficiency have also been observed to affect the frequency and impact of peer feedback on L2 development. When comparing low-proficiency and high-proficiency groups, Sato and Viveros (2016) found more instances of peer feedback and modified output following peer feedback in the low- rather than high-proficiency groups. Learners in the low-proficiency groups also demonstrated higher post-task scores, based on tense usage and vocabulary size tests. These results provide evidence that peer feedback positively affected L2 learning gains, although its impact may be mediated by the learners' mindsets (Sato, 2017). Previous research also showed that the perceived proficiency level, rather than peer's actual proficiency level, affected the amount of time learners engaged in discussing language form (e.g., including providing feedback) (Watanabe & Swain, 2007, 2008; also see Choi & Iwashita, 2016; Dao & McDonough, 2018; Young & Tedick, 2016). Overall, given that peer interaction is "a dynamic interaction phenomenon" coupled with "inherently affective and social nature" (Sato, 2017, p.19; Philp et al., 2014; Philp & Duchesne, 2016; Tognini, 2008), various social and contextual factors need to be considered when examining the effectiveness of peer feedback.

Summary

Peer feedback, especially input-providing feedback, has been found to enhance production accuracy and development by triggering learners' attention to language form compared to when no feedback is supplied. Some studies have also reported a positive relationship between frequency and accuracy rates. While the frequency of peer feedback is relatively low, some studies found more feedback provided by peers than teachers. Feedback training could compensate for the drawbacks of peer feedback in terms of the frequency and quality (Sato & Lyster, 2012; see also Chapter 28, this volume). The effectiveness of feedback depends on contextual factors and is also mitigated by social factors. Notably, in the studies discussed in this section, the language studied was predominantly

English being learned mainly by adults. Considering the impact of social and contextual factors on effectiveness of feedback, studies of different languages and diverse learners would provide further insight into the effectiveness of peer feedback for L2 development.

Pedagogical Implications

Peer feedback can serve as a pedagogical tool that has potential benefits for learners in the course of learning an L2 (Sato, 2017; Sato & Lyster, 2012). As peer feedback has been shown to be helpful, even for less proficient learners (Sato & Viveros, 2016) and for different structures (Sipple & Jackson, 2015), it is suggested that teachers should encourage learners to provide peer feedback during interactions for the sake of language development. However, the use of peer feedback should be handled with care. Peers may not perceive it positively and can discard it on the grounds that it may be of lower quality than that provided by a teacher; providing feedback to peers also entails "face-threatening" elements (Naughton, 2006).

To enhance the effectiveness of peer feedback, manipulation of peer interaction (Dao & McDonough, 2017; Kim & McDonough, 2011) or training learners to provide peer corrective feedback by shifting their attention to form may be necessary. Research has documented evidence of the positive impact that these pedagogical interventions have had on the occurrence of peer corrections (Chu, 2013; Sato, 2013; Sato & Ballinger, 2012; Sipple, 2017) and L2 development (Chu, 2013; Fujii et al., 2016; Sato & Lyster, 2012; Sipple & Jackson, 2015). Furthermore, even brief training has been shown to promote learners' positive perceptions and appreciation of peer feedback (Sato, 2013). As the occurrence of peer feedback may be low due to learners' greater focus on meaning in conversation, instructional interventions, such as modelling collaborative interaction and guided practice for producing peer feedback, might induce more peer feedback and maximize its effectiveness. This may, in turn, promote greater language development and construct a positive social relationship among learners during interaction (Gass & Varonis, 1989; Sato & Lyster, 2007).

To magnify peer feedback's effectiveness, its weaknesses need to be addressed. For example, as mentioned above, when providing peer feedback, learners may not always have explicitly corrective intentions or maintain consistent focus on the aspects of language to improve (Toth, 2008). Explicit instruction on how to carefully provide feedback so it can make the corrective intention more salient and socially acceptable to peers is important (Loewen & Philp, 2006). Additionally, as the effectiveness of peer feedback has been shown to depend on multiple social, contextual, and individual factors, such as interaction dynamics, age, proficiency, types of target forms, and perceptions (Philp & Mackey, 2010), teachers need to create a socially supportive and comfortable environment for learners to encourage the provision and appreciation of peer feedback (Philp, 2016). Overall, it is important that teachers are aware of both the weaknesses and the potential strengths of peer feedback and address them for the benefit of their learners.

Conclusion

This chapter primarily describes the types and characteristics of peer feedback in oral interaction and discusses its role in L2 acquisition. Peer feedback has some distinctive features that make it more facilitative of L2 learning as compared to teachers' or native speakers' corrective feedback. Peer feedback has also been shown to benefit learners in terms of increasing their attention to language features, which may possibly result in greater production accuracy and learning of language features. However, peer feedback also has some weaknesses that decrease its effectiveness. To address its weaknesses and harness its facilitative role in L2 learning, research suggests different pedagogical interventions that not only promote the provision of peer feedback but also show its positive impact on L2 learning. Peer feedback is shown to be subject to different social and contextual factors, which need to be considered when investing the role of peer feedback in L2 learning and using it as a pedagogical tool in the classroom.

Given the increasing attention to peer feedback, there are numerous avenues for future research in this area. For instance, although research has begun to investigate peer feedback, many studies have remained descriptive (except Adams, 2007; Chu, 2013; Sato & Lyster, 2012; Sipple & Jackson, 2015). This suggests the need for more empirical studies that examine the causal relationship between peer feedback and language production and development. Furthermore, the majority of studies have investigated the effect of input-providing feedback, and it is not known whether output-prompting feedback is as effective as input-providing feedback. It is also not known exactly what (frequency or quality of feedback) would enhance production accuracy. Whether peer feedback is more effective for certain types of linguistic forms and/or tasks than other forms/tasks targeting diverse learners and the L2 in varied contexts, is also worthy of further investigation.

Additionally, unlike teacher feedback, peer feedback has multiple drawbacks that need to be addressed. Although training has been found to promote the frequency of peer feedback, it is not clear how training enhances the quality of feedback and the extent to which the known drawbacks could be rectified. Finally, instructional interventions have been shown to improve the quality and quantity of feedback in peer interactions; however, whether the positive effects vary according to the learners and instructional contexts remains unclear. Thus, increasing understanding of peer feedback in L2 pedagogy warrants further research.

References

Adams, R. (2007). Do second language learners benefit from interacting with each other. In Mackey, A. (ed.), *Conversational interaction in second language acquisition* (pp. 29–51). Oxford: Oxford University Press.

Aljaafreh, A. & Lantolf, J. P. (1994). Negative feedback as regulation: Second language learning in the zone of proximal development. *Modern Language Journal*, 78(4), 465–483.

Anderson, J. (2005). *Cognitive psychology and its implications* (6th ed.). New York: Worth Publishers.

Brandl, K. (1995). Strong and weak students' preferences for error feedback options and responses. *Modern Language Journal*, 79(2), 194–211.

Brooks, L. & Swain, M. (2009). Languaging in collaborative writing: Creation of and response to expertise. In A. Mackey & C. Polio (eds.), *Multiple perspectives on interaction in SLA* (pp. 58–89). Mahwah, NJ: Lawrence Erlbaum.

Brown, A. (2009). Students' and teachers' perceptions of effective foreign language teaching: A comparison of ideals. *Modern Language Journal*, 93(1), 46–60.

Cathcart, R. & Olsen, J. (1976). Teachers' and students' preferences for correction of classroom conversation errors. In J. Fanselow & R. Crymes (eds.), *On TESOL '76* (pp. 41–53). Washington, DC: TESOL.

Choi, H. & Iwashita, N. (2016). Interactional behaviours of low-proficiency learners in small group work. In Sato, M. & Ballinger, S. (eds.), *Peer interaction and second language learning: Pedagogical potential and research agenda* (pp. 113–134). Amsterdam: John Benjamins.

Chu, R. (2013). Effects of peer feedback on Taiwanese adolescents' English speaking practices and development. Unpublished doctoral dissertation, The University of Edinburgh. www.era.lib.ed.ac.uk/handle/1842/8045.

Coughlan, P. & Duff, P. A. (1994). Same task, different activities: Analysis of an SLA task from an activity theory perspective. In J. Lantolf & G. Appel (eds.), *Vygotskian approaches to second language research* (pp. 173–193). Westport, CT: Ablex.

Dao, P. (2017). Learner engagement in peer task-based interaction: Identifying the effect of interlocutor proficiency and task outcome. Unpublished doctoral dissertation, Concordia University. https://spectrum.library.concordia.ca/982862/.

(2019). Effects of task goal orientation on learner engagement in task performance. *International Review of Applied Linguistics in Language Teaching*, 1–20. www.degruyter.com/view/j/iral?rskey=JOFBFp.

Dao, P. & McDonough, K. (2017). The effect of task role on Vietnamese EFL learners' collaboration in mixed proficiency dyads. *System*, 65(1), 15–24.

(2018). Effect of proficiency on Vietnamese EFL learners' engagement in peer interaction. *International Journal of Educational Research*, 88(1), 60–72.

Dao, P., Nguyen, M. X. N. & Chi, D. N. (2020). Reflective learning practice for promoting adolescent EFL learners' attention to form. *Innovation in Language Learning and Teaching*, 1–16. https://doi.org/10.1080/17501229.2020.1766467.

Davis, R. (1997). Modeling the strategies we advocate. *TESOL Journal*, 6(4), 5–6.

DeKeyser, R. (1998). Exploring automatization processes. *TESOL Quarterly*, 30(2), 349–357.

(2007). Skill acquisition theory. In B. VanPatten & J. Williams (eds.), *Theories in second language acquisition: An introduction* (pp. 97–113). Mahwah, NJ: Lawrence Erlbaum.

Dochy, F., Segers, M. & Sluijsmans, D. (1999). The use of self-, peer and co-assessment in higher education: A review. *Studies in Higher Education*, 24(3), 331–350.

Donato, R. (2004). Aspects of collaboration in pedagogical discourse. *Annual Review of Applied Linguistics*, 24, 284–302.

Ellis, N. C. (2005). At the interface: Dynamic interactions of explicit and implicit language knowledge. *Studies in Second Language Acquisition*, 27(1), 305–352.

Ellis, R. (2010). Cognitive, social and psychological dimensions of corrective feedback. In R. Batstone (ed.), *Sociocognitive perspectives on language use and language learning* (pp. 151–165). New York: Oxford University Press.

Ertmer, P., Richardson, J., Belland, B., Camin, D., Connolly, P., Coulthard, G., Lei, K. & Mong, C. (2007). Using peer feedback to enhance the quality of student online postings: An exploratory study. *Journal of Computer Mediated Communication*, 12(2), 412–433.

Fujii, A., Ziegler, N. & Mackey, A. (2016). Peer interaction and metacognitive instruction in the EFL classroom. In M. Sato & S. Ballinger (eds.), *Peer interaction and second language learning: Pedagogical potential and research agenda* (pp. 63–89). Amsterdam: John Benjamins.

Gass, S. (2003). Input and interaction. In C. Doughty & M. Long (eds.), *The handbook of second language acquisition* (pp. 224–255). Oxford: Blackwell.

Gass, S. & Mackey, A. (2007). Input, interaction, and output in second language acquisition. In B. VanPatten & J. Williams (eds.), *Theories *in second language acquisition: An introduction* (pp. 180–206). New York: Routledge.

Gass, S. & Varonis, E. (1989). Incorporated repairs in nonnative discourse. In M. R. Eisenstein (ed.), *The dynamic interlanguage: Empirical studies in second language variation* (pp. 71–86). New York: Plenum Press.

(1994). Input, interaction and second language production. *Studies in Second Language Acquisition, 16*(3), 283–302.

Iwashita, N. (1999). Tasks and learners' output in nonnative–nonnative interaction. In Kazue Kanno (ed.), *The acquisition of Japanese as a second language* (pp. 31–52). Amsterdam: John Benjamins.

Izumi, S. (2003). Comprehension and production processes in second language learning: In search of the psycholinguistic rationale of the output hypothesis. *Applied Linguistics 24*(2), 168–196. https://doi.org/10.1093/applin/24.2.145.

Katayama, A. (2007). Japanese EFL students' preferences toward correction of classroom oral errors. *Asian EFL Journal, 9*(4), 289–305.

Kim, Y. & McDonough, K. (2008). The effect of interlocutor proficiency on the collaborative dialogue between Korean as second language learners. *Language Teaching Research, 12*(2), 211–234.

(2011). Using pre-task modeling to encourage collaborative learning opportunities. *Language Teaching Research, 15*(2), 183–199.

Kowal, M. & Swain, M. (1994). Using collaborative language production tasks to promote students' language awareness. *Language Awareness, 3* (2), 73–93.

(1997). From semantic to syntactic processing: How can we promote metalinguistic awareness in the French immersion classroom? In R. Johnson & M. Swain (eds.), *Immersion education: International perspective* (pp. 284–309). Cambridge: Cambridge University Press.

Krashen, S. (1982). *Principles and practice in second language learning and acquisition.* Oxford: Pergamon.

Lantolf, J. & Thorne, S. (2006). *Sociocultural theory and the genesis of second language development.* Oxford: Oxford University Press.

Leeser, M. J. (2004). Learner proficiency and focus on form during collaborative dialogue. *Language Teaching Research, 8*(1), 55–81.

Liu, E., Lin, S., Chiu, C. & Yuan, S. (2001). Web-based peer review: The learner as both adapter and reviewer. *IEEE Transactions on Education, 44*(3), 246–251.

Liu, N. F. & Carless, D. (2006). Peer feedback: The learning element of peer assessment. *Teaching in Higher Education, 11*(3), 279–290.

Loewen, S. & Philp, J. (2006). Recasts in the adult English L2 classroom: Characteristics, explicitness, and effectiveness. *Modern Language Journal, 90*(4), 536–556.

Long, M. (1981). Input, interaction, and second-language acquisition. *Annals of the New York Academy of Sciences, 379*(1), 259–278.

(1983). Linguistic and conversational adjustments to non-native speakers. *Studies in Second Language Acquisition*, 5(2), 177–193.

(1996). The role of the linguistic environment in second language acquisition. In W. C. Ritchie & T. K. Bhatia (eds.), *Handbook of second language acquisition* (pp. 413–468). New York: Academic Press.

(2007). *Problems in SLA*. Mahwah, NJ: Lawrence Erlbaum.

Lynch, T. (2007). Learning from the transcripts of an oral communication task. *ELT Journal*, 61(4), 311–320.

Lyster, R. & Ranta, L. (1997). Corrective feedback and learner uptake: Negotiation of form in communicative classrooms. *Studies in Second Language Acquisition*, 19(4), 37–66.

Lyster, R. & Saito, K. (2010). Oral feedback in classroom SLA: A meta-analysis. *Studies in Second Language Acquisition*, 32(2), 265–302.

Lyster, R., Saito, K. & Sato, M. (2013). Oral corrective feedback in second language classrooms. *Language Teaching*, 46(1), 1–40.

Mackey, A., Abbuhl, R. & Gass, S. M. (2012). Interactionist approaches. In S. Gass & A. Mackey (eds.), *The Routledge handbook of second language acquisition* (pp. 7–23). New York: Routledge.

Mackey, A. & Gass, S. (2015). Interaction approaches. In B. VanPatten & J. Williams (eds.), *Theories in second language acquisition*. New York: Routledge.

Mackey, A., McDonough, K., Fujii, A. & Tatsumi, T. (2001). Investigating learners' reports about the L2 classroom. *International Review of Applied Linguistics*, 39(4), 285–308.

Mackey, A., Oliver, R. L. & Leeman, J. (2003). Interaction input and the incorporation of feedback: an exploration of NS–NNS and NNS–NNS adult and child dyads. *Language Learning*, 53(1), 35–66.

McDonough, K. (2004). Learner–learner interaction during pair and small group activities in a Thai EFL context. *System*, 32(2), 207–224.

Miao, Y., Badger, R. & Zhen, Y. (2006). A comparative study of peer and teacher feedback in a Chinese EFL writing class. *Journal of Second Language Writing*, 15(3), 179–200.

Morris, F. (2005). Child-to-child interaction and corrective feedback in a computer mediated L2 class. *Language Learning & Technology*, 9(1), 29–45.

Nassaji, H. (2009). The effects of recasts and elicitations in dyadic interaction and the role of feedback explicitness. *Language Learning*, 59(2), 411–452.

(2015). *Interactional feedback dimension in instructed second language learning*. London: Bloomsbury Publishing.

Nassaji, H. & Swain, M. (2000). A Vygotskian perspective on corrective feedback in L2: The effect of random versus negotiated help on the learning of English articles. *Language Awareness*, 9(1), 34–51.

Naughton, D. (2006). Cooperative strategy training and oral interaction: Enhancing small group communication in the language classroom. *Modern Language Journal*, *90*(2), 169–184.

Nicol, D. (2009). Assessment for learner self-regulation: Enhancing achievement in the first year using learning technologies. *Assessment and Evaluation in Higher Education*, *34*(3), 335–352.

(2014). Guiding principles of peer review: Unlocking learners' evaluative skills. In C. Kreber, C. Anderson, N. Entwistle & J. McArthur (eds.), *Advances and innovations in university assessment and feedback* (pp. 195–258). Edinburgh: Edinburgh University Press.

Ohta, A. (2000). Rethinking interaction in SLA: Developmentally appropriate assistance in the zone of proximal development and the acquisition of L2 grammar. In J. P. Lantolf (ed.), *Sociocultural theory and second language learning* (pp. 51–78). Oxford: Oxford University Press.

(2001). *Second language acquisition processes in the classroom: Learning Japanese*. Mahwah, NJ: Lawrence Erlbaum.

Philp, J. (2016). New pathways in researching interaction. In M. Sato & S. Ballinger (eds.), *Peer interaction and second language learning: Pedagogical potential and research agenda* (pp. 377–395). Amsterdam: John Benjamins.

Philp, J., Adams, R. & Iwashita, N. (2014). *Peer interaction and second language learning*. New York: Taylor & Francis.

Philp, J. & Duchesne, S. (2016). Exploring engagement in tasks in the language classroom. *Annual Review of Applied Linguistics*, *36*(1), 50–72.

Philp, J. & Mackey, A. (2010). Interaction research: What can socially informed approaches offer to cognitivists (and vice versa)? In R. Batstone (ed.), *Sociocognitive perspectives on language use and language learning* (pp. 210–228). New York: Oxford University Press.

Philp, J., Walter, S. & Basturkmen, H. (2010). Peer interaction in the foreign language classroom: What factors foster a focus on form? *Language Awareness*, *19*(4), 261–279.

Pica, T. (1994). Research on negotiation: What does it reveal about second language learning conditions, processes, and outcomes? *Language Learning*, *44*(3), 493–527.

Pica, T., Lincoln-Porter, F., Paninos, D. & Linnell, J. (1996). Language learners' interaction: How does it address the input, output, and feedback needs of L2 learners? *TESOL Quarterly*, *30*(1), 59–84.

Poehner, M. E. (2008). Both sides of the conversation: The interplay between mediation and learner reciprocity in dynamic assessment. In J. P. Lantolf & M. E. Poehner (eds.), *Sociocultural theory and the teaching of second languages* (pp. 33–56). London: Equinox.

Ranta, L. & Lyster, R. (2007). A cognitive approach to improving immersion students' oral language abilities: The Awareness–Practice–Feedback sequence. In R. DeKeyser (ed.), *Practice in a second language: Perspectives from applied linguistics and cognitive psychology* (pp. 141–160). Cambridge: Cambridge University Press.

Sato, M. (2013). Beliefs about peer interaction and peer corrective feedback: Efficacy of classroom intervention. *Modern Language Journal, 97* (3), 611–633.

(2017). Oral corrective feedback: Multiple theoretical perspectives. In H. Nassaji & E. Kartchava (eds.), *Corrective feedback in second language teaching and learning: Research, theory, applications, implications* (pp. 19–35). New York: Routledge.

Sato, M. & Ballinger, S. (2012). Raising language awareness in peer interaction: A cross-context, cross-method examination. *Language Awareness, 21*(1), 157–179.

(2016). Understanding peer interaction: Research synthesis and directions. In M. Sato & S. Ballinger (eds.), *Peer interaction and second language learning: Pedagogical potential and research agenda* (pp. 1–30). Amsterdam: John Benjamins.

Sato, M. & Loewen, S. (2018). Metacognitive instruction enhances the effectiveness of corrective feedback: Variable effects of feedback types and linguistic targets. *Language Learning, 68*(2), 507–545.

Sato, M. & Lyster, R. (2007). Modified output of Japanese EFL learners: Variable effects of interlocutor vs. feedback types. In A. Mackey (ed.), *Conversational interaction in second language acquisition: A collection of empirical studies* (pp. 123–142). Oxford: Oxford University Press.

(2012). Peer interaction and corrective feedback for accuracy and fluency development: Monitoring, practice, and proceduralization. *Studies in Second Language Acquisition, 34*(4), 591–626.

Sato, M. & McDonough, K. (2019). Practice is important but how about its quality? Contextualized practice in the classroom, *Studies in Second Language Acquisition, 41*(1), 999–1026.

Sato, M. & Viveros, P. (2016). Interaction or collaboration? Group dynamics in the foreign language classroom. In M. Sato & S. Ballinger (eds.), *Peer interaction and second language learning: Pedagogical potential and research agenda* (pp. 91–112). Amsterdam: John Benjamins.

Schulz, R. A. (1996). Focus on form in the foreign language classroom: Students' and teachers' views on error correction and the role of grammar. *Foreign Language Annals, 29*(3), 343–364.

Segalowitz, N. (2003). Automaticity and second languages. In C. Doughty & M. H. Long (eds.), *The handbook of second language acquisition* (pp. 382–408). Malden, MA: Blackwell.

Sheen, Y. & Ellis, R. (2011). Corrective feedback in language teaching. In E. Hinkel (ed.), *Handbook of research in second language teaching and learning* (pp. 593–610). New York: Routledge.

Sipple, L. (2017). The effects of peer interaction, form-focused instruction, and peer corrective feedback on the acquisition of grammar and vocabulary in L2 German. Unpublished doctoral dissertation,

Pennsylvania State University. https://etda.libraries.psu.edu/files/final_submissions/14444.

Sipple, L. & Jackson, C. N. (2015). Teacher vs. peer oral corrective feedback in the German language classroom. *Foreign Language Annals*, 48(4), 688–705.

Skehan, P. (1998). *A cognitive approach to language learning*. Oxford: Oxford University Press.

Storch, N. (2002). Patterns of interaction in ESL pair work. *Language Learning*, 52(1), 119–158.

  (2008). Metatalk in a pair work activity: Level of engagement and implications for language development. *Language Awareness*, 17(2), 95–114.

  (2017). Sociocultural theory in the L2 classroom. In S. Loewen & M. Sato (eds.), *The Routledge handbook of instructed second language acquisition* (pp. 69–84). New York: Routledge.

Swain, M. (1995). Three functions of output in second language learning. In G. Cook and B. Seidlhofer (eds.), *Principles and practice in applied linguistics* (pp. 125–144). Oxford: Oxford University Press.

  (1998). Focus on form through conscious reflection. In C. Doughty and J. Williams (eds.), *Focus on form in classroom second language acquisition* (pp. 61–81). Cambridge: Cambridge University Press.

  (2000). The output hypothesis and beyond: Mediating acquisition through collaborative dialogue. In J. P. Lantolf (ed.), *Sociocultural theory and second language learning* (pp. 97–114). Oxford: Oxford University Press.

Tognini, R. (2008). Interaction in languages other than English classes in Western Australian primary and secondary schools: Theory, practice and perceptions. Unpublished doctoral dissertation, Edith Cowan University, Perth, Australia.

Topping, K. J., Smith, E. F., Swanson, I. & Elliot, A. (2000). Formative peer assessment of academic writing between postgraduate students. *Assessment and Evaluation in Higher Education*, 25(2), 149–169.

Toth, P. (2008). Teacher- and learner-led discourse in task-based grammar instruction: Providing procedural assistance for L2 morphosyntactic development. *Language Learning*, 58(2), 237–283.

van Compernolle R. A. (2015). *Interaction and second language development: A Vygotskian perspective*. Amsterdam; Philadelphia: John Benjamins.

VanPatten, B. & Benati, A. (2010). *Key terms in second language acquisition*. New York: Continuum International Publishing Group.

van Popta, E., Kral, M., Camp, G., Martens, R. & Simons, R. (2017). Exploring the value of peer feedback in online learning for the provider. *Educational Research Review*, 20(1), 24–34.

Varonis, E. & Gass, S. (1985). Non-native/non-native conversations: A model for the negotiation of meaning. *Applied Linguistics*, 6(1), 71–90.

Watanabe, Y. & Swain, M. (2007). Effects of proficiency differences and patterns of pair interaction on second language learning: Collaborative dialogue between adult ESL learners. *Language Teaching Research, 11*(2), 121–142.

(2008). Perception of learner proficiency: Its impact on the interaction between an ESL learner and her higher and lower proficiency partners. *Language Awareness, 17*(2), 115–130.

Wertsch, J. V. (1998). *Mind as action.* Cambridge, MA: Harvard University Press.

Williams, J. (2001). Learner-generated attention to form. *Language Learning, 51*(1), 303–346.

Yilmaz, Y. (2011). Task effects on focus on form in synchronous computer-mediated communication. *Modern Language Journal, 95*(1), 115–132.

Yoshida, R. (2008). Learners' perception of corrective feedback in pair work. *Foreign Language Annals, 41*(3), 525–541.

(2008). Teachers' choice and learners' preference of corrective-feedback types. *Language Awareness, 17*(1), 78–93.

(2010). How do teachers and learners perceive corrective feedback in the Japanese language classroom? *Modern Language Journal, 94*(2), 293–314.

Young, A. & Tedick, D. (2016). Collaborative dialogue in a two-way Spanish/English immersion classroom. In M. Sato & S. Ballinger (eds.), *Peer interaction and second language learning: Pedagogical potential and research agenda* (pp. 135–160). Amsterdam: John Benjamins.

Zhao, H. (2010). Investigating learners' use and understanding of peer and teacher feedback on writing: a comparative study in a Chinese English writing classroom. *Assessing Writing, 15*(1), 3–17.

14

Focused versus Unfocused Corrective Feedback

Catherine van Beuningen

Introduction

As attested to by the publication of this book, corrective feedback (CF) is an issue of considerable interest for language teachers and SLA researchers alike. Apart from the overarching question as to whether CF is a worthwhile practice in second language (L2) classrooms, the attention of both researchers and teachers has also gone out to the question of what feedback type is most beneficial to learners' L2 development. Different (contrasts of) CF options have been distinguished in the literature, including implicit and explicit (oral) CF, direct and indirect (written) CF, and metalinguistic CF. Central in the current chapter is the contrast between providing either *focused* or *unfocused* CF.

When providing focused CF, a teacher targets one or a few specific (preselected) linguistic feature(s), leaving errors outside the focus category or categories uncorrected. Unfocused CF, on the other hand, refers to the feedback option in which such a specific focus is absent, and, as a result, feedback is provided on a wide(r) range of errors. The focused–unfocused distinction is not a black and white one, but rather a continuum ranging from providing feedback on just one error category to providing feedback on all errors in learners' output.

In the CF literature, other terminology has also been used to refer to focused and unfocused CF options, such as selective versus comprehensive and intensive versus extensive CF. Although there is definitely meaning overlap, and the different terms are usually used interchangeably, there are nuanced differences between the following pairs: focused and unfocused CF (e.g., Ellis, 2008), the selective–comprehensive distinction (e.g., Bitchener & Ferris, 2012), and the intensive–extensive contrast (e.g., Ellis, 2008). Table 14.1 summarizes these nuances or characteristics. Just as the focused–unfocused contrast is not a clear-cut

Table 14.1 *Characteristics of CF options*

Feedback contrasts	Feedback types	Feedback characteristics
Focused vs. unfocused CF Distinctive feature: purposeful selection of CF target error categories	Focused CF	+ focused + selective + intensive [unless the task learners are presented with does not elicit (extended) use of the target structure(s)/form(s)] +/− planned +/− systematic
	Unfocused CF	− focused +/− selective − intensive +/− planned +/− systematic
Intensive vs. extensive CF Distinctive feature: amount of CF on a particular target form/structure	Intensive CF	+/− focused + selective + intensive +/− planned +/− systematic
	Extensive CF	− focused +/− selective − intensive +/− planned +/− systematic
Selective vs. comprehensive CF Distinctive feature: number of CF target forms/structures	Selective CF	+/− focused + selective +/− intensive +/− planned +/− systematic
	Comprehensive CF	− focused − selective − intensive +/− planned +/− systematic

dichotomy, the related terminology pairs should also be seen as the extremes of a continuum.

The distinctive characteristic in the focused–unfocused pair is the (lack of) purposeful *selection* of linguistic target features. Whereas in a focused approach, a teacher consciously determines which error categories to provide feedback on (e.g., article usage, past tense conjugation), such purposive selection of specific target forms/structures is lacking in an unfocused approach to CF. The distinction between selective and comprehensive CF, on the other hand, is not as much related to the way in which target structures are selected, but to the *number* of linguistic features to which the feedback pertains. When a teacher provides (fully) comprehensive CF, he or she marks *all* error types in learners' output, whereas in a selective CF approach, only a selection of errors is marked (Bitchener & Ferris, 2012). This means that, while focused CF is by default selective (i.e., not all types of errors, but only errors within the focus domain(s) will be marked), selective feedback does not need to be focused on predefined error categories; a teacher could also, for example, decide to provide feedback on the most serious and/or most stigmatizing errors in a student's output (which do not have to belong to a specific, preselected linguistic category). Moreover, unfocused CF can be either selective (i.e., marking of a selection of errors, not based on their linguistic category; for example, the ones interfering most with communicative success) or comprehensive (i.e., marking of all error types). The final opposition, that between intensive and extensive CF, concerns the *amount* of feedback a learner receives on a particular linguistic feature. Focused CF is usually (but not necessarily) relatively intensive because this type of feedback is generally provided in an instructional context focusing on and/or a task eliciting the targeted feature(s). Unfocused and comprehensive CF types, on the other hand, are more extensive in nature because they are not aiming to target a specific error category (or a limited set of categories) but instead have a wider focus.

Two issues that are relevant in all three CF contrasts discussed are the (un)planned nature of CF and the level of feedback systematicity. The terms "planned" and "unplanned" have been used to characterize focused and unfocused CF types respectively: "planned feedback, that is, feedback provided intensively and repeatedly on certain predetermined target structures" and "unplanned feedback that is provided on any form" (Nassaji, 2016, p. 545). However, planning can take place at any level, and therefore any type of feedback (cf. Table 14.1) could be either planned or unplanned in nature. A teacher, for example, could plan only to provide feedback on tense errors (i.e., focused CF), but he or she could just as well plan to correct all errors in learners' output (i.e., unfocused CF) or not to provide any form-focused feedback at all.

The second issue pertains to the systematicity of feedback delivery. CF is systematic when a teacher provides feedback on every instance of a certain error type. Conversely, feedback is unsystematic when a teacher corrects some instances of a particular error type while leaving other instances of the same error uncorrected. Every feedback type in Table 14.1 could be delivered in either a systematic or an unsystematic way. For example, a teacher could correct all instances of errors within selected domain(s) when providing focused CF (i.e., systematic), but he or she could also leave some errors within these domains unidentified (i.e., unsystematic). In the same way, even though (fully) comprehensive CF targets all error types, that does not necessarily mean that every instance of each error type is corrected. As with focused feedback, comprehensive CF could be provided systematically or unsystematically.

The distinctions elucidated above will not all be equally relevant in different contexts. Their relevance will differ, for example, depending on the feedback mode and type of CF research. With regards to CF mode, both oral and written feedback types can be categorized along the focused–unfocused and intensive–extensive continua. However, the selective–comprehensive distinction is more relevant in characterizing written CF options than oral ones; while providing (fully) comprehensive CF is a realistic option in response to learners' written output, it is rather unlikely that a teacher will be able (and/or aiming) to target errors comprehensively in oral contexts. Oral CF will be selective (i.e., targeting only a selection of potential targets) almost by default, due to its online character and for the sake of preserving communicative flow. Likewise, providing systematic feedback (i.e., on all instances of an error type) is quite feasible when providing written CF but rather difficult in oral CF contexts.

Considering the role of the contrasts in Table 14.1 within different research contexts, we see that the focus of SLA-oriented experimental CF studies – that explore the potential of CF in aiding L2 development – has almost exclusively been on the effectiveness of CF that is focused, selective, and intensive. Only a limited number of oral CF studies (e.g., DeKeyser, 1993; Hawkes & Nassaji, 2016; Nassaji, 2017b) and a handful of written CF studies (e.g., Karim & Nassaji, 2020; Truscott & Hsu, 2008; Van Beuningen, De Jong & Kuiken, 2012) investigated the language learning potential of CF options at the other end of the spectrum. Both oral and written CF studies with a more descriptive and/or pedagogical orientation, on the other hand, also explored the use and effectiveness of less focused CF types.

By virtue of clarity, I will use the distinction *focused* versus *unfocused* CF throughout this chapter, to refer respectively to CF types that are on the highly focused, intensive, and selective or on the more unfocused, extensive, and comprehensive side of the continuum. From the array of terminology, these two terms are chosen (and not, for example, the two CF types that are maximally distinct: focused vs. comprehensive CF, see Table 14.1) because they are suitable to describe both oral and written CF practices. When significant, nuances alongside the characterizations in Table 14.1 will be added in the remainder of this chapter, which consists of a discussion of (1) different arguments favoring either focused or unfocused CF approaches; (2) insights from available relevant oral and written CF research; and (3) implications for both future research and the L2 classroom.

Arguments in Favor of Focused and Unfocused CF Options

Different types of arguments (i.e., theoretical, pedagogical, and methodological arguments) have been put forward in the literature to support either the use and/or investigation of focused or unfocused CF types.

Theoretical Arguments

Predictions have been articulated regarding the (relative) effectiveness of focused and unfocused CF approaches, both from a cognitive and a sociocultural perspective on L2 development. From a cognitive perspective on language learning, in which attention and understanding are deemed a prerequisite for acquisition (e.g., Schmidt, 1994; Ellis, 2005), many CF researchers have hypothesized the focused approach to be more beneficial to L2 development than unfocused CF (e.g., Bitchener, 2008; Ellis et al., 2008; Sheen, 2007, 2010). They have argued that, since L2 learners have limited processing capacities, students are more likely to notice and understand corrections when they target a specific (limited set of) error type(s); focused CF could therefore be expected to have greater potential in fostering the language learning process than unfocused CF because targeting a broad range of linguistic features at the same time might produce a cognitive overload, and, as such, prohibit successful feedback processing. Countering this hypothesized preferability of focused CF, one could also contend that unfocused CF is more effective in guiding learners' orientation to language form because corrections are more frequent and thereby more salient when feedback is delivered comprehensively (e.g., Nassaji, 2017b). Moreover, it has been argued that (highly) focused CF is rather a form of explicit grammar instruction than a focus-on-form intervention (e.g., Bruton, 2009; Xu, 2009), which might make it more difficult for learners to transfer what is learned from the CF received on a particular task to new speaking or writing situations (e.g., Segalowitz, 1997, 2000).

The tenability of the predictions above may vary depending on the context in which the CF is provided (e.g., CF mode, CF recipients). For example, the attentional capacity issue, as outlined in the previous paragraph, might be more prominent in the processing of oral feedback than in the handling of written CF. Whereas processing oral CF typically involves online cognitive comparison and is therefore heavily demanding on learners' short-term memory (Sheen, 2010), written corrections are nonvolatile and can be processed offline. This means that, in written CF, learners have richer opportunities to attend to, reflect on, understand, and test L2 hypotheses based on the feedback they receive (Bitchener, 2017; Williams, 2012). As such, unfocused CF may be a more promising feedback option in written than in oral contexts.

Apart from varying between CF modes (i.e., oral vs. written), cognitively oriented hypotheses about the effectiveness of (un)focused CF also differ, depending on the proficiency level of feedback recipients. While lower-proficiency learners can easily be cognitively overloaded when provided with CF on a wide range of structures, higher-proficiency learners are thought to have more attentional capacity available and are therefore expected to be more able to process CF types that are less focused (e.g.,

Bitchener & Storch, 2016). Moreover, unfocused CF will be more fit for advanced learners because they have ample linguistic knowledge stored in their long-term memory that they can draw upon for understanding the feedback they receive (Bitchener, 2017), whereas "learners with only partially developed knowledge ... may need more targeted feedback, and a more sustained approach to attend to and consciously process feedback" (Bitchener & Storch, 2016, p. 59). Bitchener and Ferris (2012) furthermore argue that for advanced learners, who have already developed a relatively high level of accuracy, non-focused CF options can be more efficient and effective because they allow for the treatment of a greater range of errors in a short period of time.

From a sociocultural perspective, CF is not seen as a facilitator of cognitive learning processes (e.g., noticing, hypothesis testing), but rather "the value of feedback lies in the opportunities it provides for scaffolding" (Nassaji, 2016, p. 358); CF can assist learners in using linguistic forms and structures they are not yet able to handle independently (Sheen, 2010). Not all types of assistance or scaffolding (e.g., CF types) are expected to be equally conducive to L2 development, however. For scaffolding – in this case CF – to be effective, it should aim to help learners perform beyond their current level of achievement, or in other words, it should fall within a learner's Zone of Proximal Development (ZPD). This influential notion of ZPD was developed by Vygotsky (1978) who defined it as

> [t]he distance between the actual developmental level as determined by independent problem solving and the level of potential development as determined through problem solving under adult guidance or in collaboration with more capable peers. (p. 86)

According to Aljaafreh and Lantolf (1994), ZPD-appropriate CF should also be graduated, contingent, and dialogic. CF is graduated if it offers learners the minimal level of guidance needed. As Bitchener and Storch (2016) argue, too much feedback (i.e., non-graduated CF) may fail to aid learners' development because they may not feel encouraged to become self-regulated and to take eventual responsibility for the accuracy of their own language production, which is the ultimate aim of scaffolding. This claim would support the use of more focused CF options, in which the teacher only provides feedback on those features learners could not be expected to self-correct.

For CF to be contingent, it has to be adaptive to learners' needs. As the level of assistance learners require will change, teachers' feedback practices should co-evolve; CF "should be offered only when it is needed, and withdrawn as soon as the novice shows signs of self-control and ability to function independently" (Aljaafreh & Lantolf, 1994, p. 468). As such, a teacher's choice of feedback type should change along with learners' development. More novice and/or lower proficiency learners might, for example, need CF that is intensive in nature to be able to progress towards more target-like use of a particular form or structure, whereas for learners with a higher level of expertise and/or proficiency just a "reminder" of a nontarget-like element in their output (i.e., extensive CF) could be enough.

Finally, CF can only be graduated and contingent if learners are actively involved in the feedback process; learners need to provide teachers with cues about their abilities to profit from the assistance they receive and about their changing scaffolding needs. Not only are these needs determined by a learner's level of expertise but they could also be dependent, for example, on his or her orientation toward CF and/or the goals he or she has set for him- or herself. To be able to cater for these needs, CF should take the shape of a dialogic activity between a more skilled individual (e.g., the teacher) and a novice (e.g., a student).

As elucidated in the above discussion, the key assumption from a sociocultural perspective on CF is that what works for one learner in one context might not benefit another learner in a different context, as feedback needs differ between individuals, contexts, developmental stages, etcetera. The ultimate goal of all scaffolding, however, is to hand over responsibility to the learner and for the learner to become self-regulated. As such, the amount of feedback should decline, and CF should be less explicit in nature with the growing expertise of a learner (Bitchener & Storch, 2016). In general, this would mean that CF could become less focused over time, as more self-regulated learners will be better able to deal with less intensive feedback on a wider range of structures. On the other hand, a teacher could also choose to take an increasingly focused CF approach as learners' capability develops, following the line of reasoning that more capable learners can self-correct most errors themselves.

Pedagogical Arguments
Different arguments have also been put forward with respect to the pedagogical value of adopting either a focused or an unfocused approach to CF. These arguments relate to, for example, the different goals teachers may pursue when giving feedback. In a context where learners produce output as a means to push their L2 development and the goal of providing CF is therefore clearly didactic in nature, focusing the CF on a (few) specific linguistic feature(s) might be most effective (e.g., Bitchener, 2008; Ellis et al., 2008; Sheen, 2007, 2010). Nevertheless, as Xu (2009) duly remarked, focused CF might not be the most authentic CF option, since it "is quite a luxury for teachers and students" (p. 275) to be able to (repeatedly) focus on one or a few specific target form(s) or structure(s). Bitchener and Ferris (2012), however, counter Xu's argument by pointing out that, since there is ample empirical evidence showing that accuracy improvement is already

visible after one treatment, teachers can introduce a wide range of new target features over the course of a semester.

If the goal of CF is communicative rather than purely L2 didactic, merely targeting a (few) preselected error type(s) "may miss the big picture of how student errors may impact their progress as successful . . . communicators" (e.g., Bitchener & Ferris, 2012, p. 115). On a related note, students in the real world need to learn to monitor their output for all types of errors (e.g., Evans et al., 2010; Hartshorn et al., 2010), so adopting a (highly) focused approach to CF might mislead learners about the amount of effort and attention it takes to monitor and self-edit their language production, and may fail to provide them with the strategies they need to be able to do so (Bitchener & Ferris, 2012). Moreover, as noted by Ellis and Sheen (2006), unfocused CF "directed at whatever errors learners happen to make might be of greater practical value" (p. 597). In this line of reasoning, unfocused CF is arguably preferable to focused feedback. A case could be made, however, for the use of CF that is *selective* in nature (but not focused on predefined error categories), only marking errors that interfere with communicative success and/or errors that are stigmatizing. Such a feedback approach would align with warnings against overcorrection, which could negatively influence communicative flow and/or fluency (e.g., Brown, 2009; Edge, 1989; Ellis, 2017; Ur, 1996).

Whereas SLA researchers have mainly shown interest in the cognitive effects (i.e., learning potential) of CF, teachers are also concerned with its affective impact (Ellis, 2017). From an affective perspective, one argument in favor of providing unfocused CF is that research into students' preferences has shown that they typically prefer to receive feedback on all their errors (e.g., Ferris & Roberts, 2001; Jean & Simard, 2011; Leki, 1991). An often repeated argument in favor of a more focused approach to CF, on the other hand, is that providing students with too much feedback may lead to learner anxiety, students' loss of confidence, and diminishing motivation (e.g., Brown, 2009; Jean & Simard, 2011; Lightbown, 2008; Truscott, 1996).

Methodological Arguments

In addition to theoretical and pedagogical arguments, methodological (i.e., research oriented) rationales have also been put forward in favor of investigating either focused or unfocused CF types. Some have argued that in order to be able to test theoretical claims about CF effectiveness, CF should be focused on a (limited set of) specific linguistic feature(s) so that acquisition can be measured precisely in terms of this/these feature(s) (e.g., Bitchener & Ferris, 2012; Sheen, 2010). However, Xu (2009) warns that when adopting such a methodology, care should be taken to check for possible trade-off effects; apart from measuring accuracy in terms of the target-like use of the focus feature(s), the overall accuracy of learners' output should also be taken into account to examine if gain on one (or a few) linguistic feature(s), as promoted by CF, did not work to the detriment of performance in other linguistic domains. Moreover, the aim of gauging CF effects precisely could also be met when the type of feedback under study is unfocused, for example by using "individualized pre- and/or post-tests" (e.g., Nassaji, 2016) or detailed sequential analyses of learner output (Bruton, 2009). Both methods provide researchers with tools to measure learners' accuracy development within (a) specific linguistic domain(s), even when the feedback participants receive is unfocused.

A methodological argument in favor of unfocused CF is that the CF provided in L2 classrooms is usually directed at a variety of errors, which makes the ecological validity of focused CF studies somewhat questionable (Ferris, 2010; Hartshorn et al., 2010; Nassaji, 2016; Van Beuningen et al., 2012). As such, one could cast doubt on the extent to which findings of studies into the effectiveness of CF that is highly focused (i.e., provided intensively and repeatedly on predetermined linguistic features) are generalizable to actual classroom contexts.

When aiming to shed light on the tenability of the hypotheses and arguments discussed in this section, the investigation of both focused and unfocused CF approaches, as well as their relative efficacy, could be considered a worthwhile undertaking. The following section will briefly outline what available research tells us about the (relative) effectiveness of both feedback types.

Research on Focused and Unfocused CF

This section will be divided into two main parts. The first part discusses *oral* CF research that provides insight into the value of focused and unfocused CF. The second part summarizes what we know about the effectiveness of focused and unfocused *written* CF. Whereas oral CF studies have always been grounded in SLA theory, written CF studies – especially the earlier ones – have also drawn on (L2) composition theories. Nevertheless, similar questions have driven both fields, such as "Does CF have the potential to stimulate L2 development?" or "What individual and contextual factors mediate CF effectiveness?"

Synthesizing what we know from empirical work about the (relative) efficacy of focused and unfocused CF, this section focuses on a third pertinent question, namely: "What CF approaches are (most) effective?" This review mainly features studies that view CF from a cognitive perspective because studies from the sociocultural strand (e.g., Aljaafreh & Lantolf, 1994; Nassaji, 2012; Nassaji & Swain, 2000; Rassaei, 2014) do not focus on the efficacy of different feedback types (e.g., focused vs. unfocused CF). Rather, these studies have been concerned with the questions as to what scaffolded CF should look like and if such negotiated feedback is more effective than non-negotiated CF.

What We Know About (Un)focused CF from Oral Feedback Studies

Within oral CF research, different strands can be discerned. On the one hand, there are observational or descriptive CF studies, exploring the use of conversational, meaning-focused feedback. Studies within this strand aim to identify the various types of feedback offered to learners in language classrooms (e.g., Lyster & Ranta, 1997; Sheen, 2006) and the amount of uptake associated with these different CF types (e.g., Lyster, 1998; Sheen, 2004). (Quasi) experimental oral CF studies (both laboratory and classroom-based), on the other hand, examine more pedagogically oriented, form-focused feedback and its effects on language learning (e.g., Ellis, Loewen & Erlam, 2006; Mackey & Philp, 1998).

Across the board, the conclusion from available individual studies from both strands as well as from a growing number of meta-analyses and narrative reviews is that oral CF has the potential to aid the acquisition of a wide range of grammatical structures (e.g., past tense, articles, question formation, passive forms, gender agreement), either in terms of uptake[1] or increased accuracy in new spoken output (e.g., Ellis & Sheen, 2006; Goo & Mackey, 2013; Li, 2010; Lyster & Ranta, 2013; Lyster & Saito, 2010; Lyster, Saito & Sato, 2013; Mackey & Goo, 2007; Nassaji, 2016; Russell & Spada, 2006).

Whereas many available oral CF studies have examined the (relative) effectiveness of different feedback types, such as implicit versus explicit or input-providing versus output-prompting feedback options, the question of whether to provide focused or unfocused oral CF has received little explicit research attention. From observational studies, it has become clear that in the teaching practice CF is generally unfocused, as "teachers are likely to address a high percentage of the errors that learners make" (Ellis, 2017, p. 8) in an unplanned and extensive manner. Most experimental oral CF work, on the other hand, has investigated the language learning potential of feedback when provided repeatedly and intensively on a specific target structure (i.e., focused CF).

These experimental oral CF studies have provided robust evidence on the efficacy of focused feedback (see aforementioned meta-analyses, e.g., Li, 2010; Lyster & Saito, 2010; Mackey & Goo, 2007). Some, however, have questioned the ecological validity of such experimental studies (e.g., Ellis & Sheen, 2006) because of the apparent mismatch between the type of feedback most commonly used in actual language classrooms (i.e., unfocused CF) and the type of feedback foregrounded in CF research (i.e., focused CF). Therefore,

---

[1] Whether successful uptake constitutes evidence of learning is an issue of debate. See, for example, discussions by Truscott (1996, 2007; Truscott and Hsu, 2008).

several studies set out to gauge the effectiveness of unfocused oral feedback, for example by using individualized pre- and/or post-tests (e.g., Hawkes & Nassaji, 2016; Nabei & Swain, 2002; Nassaji, 2011, 2013; Williams, 2001). These studies have shown that oral CF can also be effective in promoting language development when it is unfocused (i.e., extensive, but selective) in nature.

To the best of my knowledge, the only available empirical investigation that directly contrasted focused and unfocused oral feedback options is Nassaji's (2017b) study into the relative effectiveness of extensive and intensive recasts. Its findings point to the advantage of extensive oral CF over intensive recasts, thereby challenging the assumption that focused CF is more effective because of its smaller burden on learners' processing capacity (see the section on Theoretical Arguments). As Nassaji (2017b) hypothesizes, the higher frequency of CF episodes in the extensive condition might have contributed to the salience of the recasts, and, as such, to a higher level of CF uptake.

Contrary to the findings by Nassaji (2017b), Mackey and Goo (2007) found in their meta-analysis that intensive CF approaches yield larger effects than extensive feedback types (in delayed post-tests; no differences were found in immediate post-tests). When interpreting these seemingly conflicting findings, it is important, however, to take into account the type of research we are considering. As shown in a meta-analysis by Li (2010), CF-associated effect sizes tend to be larger in lab-based studies than in classroom-based studies. It has been claimed that this observation may be explained by the different ways in which feedback is delivered in laboratory and classroom settings. In lab-based studies CF tends to be highly focused (i.e., intensively targeting a single structure), whereas in classroom-based studies feedback is usually unfocused. As such, Li's (2010) findings could be interpreted as an indication of the relative preferability of focused CF; larger effects are found in lab-based studies because in such contexts CF is usually focused, and therefore more likely to be noticed and understood by learners (e.g., Lyster & Saito, 2010; Nassaji, 2016; see also Theological Arguments section). Li (2010) himself, however, provides another perspective on these findings, in contending that it might be less the (un)focused nature of the feedback that explains these outcomes, but rather contextual differences between classroom-based and laboratory studies; in laboratory studies feedback is typically provided in dyadic interaction, in a relatively distraction-free setting, "in the classroom context, there is more distraction and feedback is often not directed towards individual learners. Therefore, feedback ... might not be easily recognizable" (p. 345). Nassaji's (2017b) findings could be taken to substantiate this interpretation; when directly contrasting focused and unfocused feedback within a lab-based setting, with its favorable contextual conditions – and thereby neutralizing the confound between feedback type and research context – unfocused oral CF has the potential to be more effective than focused feedback.

Whereas laboratory and quasi-experimental classroom-based studies were able to evidence the value of both focused and unfocused oral CF options, it is still too early to draw any firm conclusions on the relative effectiveness of these feedback types; direct empirical evidence is scarce, and apparent differences between available studies in design variables such as participant type, linguistic focus, contextual factors, etc., make comparison across studies problematic. The following section will provide an overview of what written CF research tells us about the (relative) efficacy of (un)focused feedback.

What We Know About (Un)focused CF from Written Feedback Studies

Earlier written CF studies, which were grounded in L2 writing research, set out to inform composition teachers on how to support their learners in developing (self-)editing skills. As such, they investigated the role of CF in aiding learners to improve the accuracy of their texts during text revision (e.g., Ashwell, 2000; Fathman & Whalley, 1990; Ferris & Roberts, 2001). In these so-called revision studies, the feedback learners received was mostly comprehensive (and therefore unfocused), and these studies consistently showed that this type of feedback enables learners to significantly reduce the number of errors in the text they received CF on (e.g., Bitchener & Ferris, 2012).

The larger body of written CF research, however, has tried to answer the question not only of whether providing learners with feedback on one text will result in accuracy improvement of that same text (i.e., revision effect), but of whether CF leads to more accurate newly written output (i.e., learning effect). Two strands of studies dealing with this question can be distinguished: compositional studies investigating how CF benefits L2 writing development (learning-to-write perspective; e.g., Manchón, 2009), and SLA-oriented studies focusing on the question of whether CF has the potential to hone learners' L2 learning (writing-to-learn perspective).

In the composition-oriented studies investigating the effects of CF over time (e.g., Chandler, 2003; Kepner, 1991; Polio, Fleck & Leder, 1998), learners received feedback on a wide range of errors (i.e., unfocused CF). Most of these studies concluded that unfocused CF did not succeed in promoting students' written accuracy development. However, as discussed by Ferris (2004), among others, these studies were all hampered by serious methodological shortcomings (e.g., lack of a control group, time-on-task differences), which make the tenability of their conclusions questionable.

Within the strand of writing-to-learn research, great care was taken to overcome the design issues of the earlier work just mentioned. Following the oral CF tradition, the vast majority of such studies explored the effects of focused CF (e.g., Bitchener & Knoch, 2010; Ellis et al., 2008; Sheen, 2007; Shintani, Ellis & Suzuki, 2014). These tightly controlled studies all found robust and durable positive effects of focused written feedback (see, e.g., Kang & Han's 2015 meta-analysis). As noted by others (e.g., Ferris, 2010) and notwithstanding the contribution this work on focused CF has made to the field, its implications as of yet are fairly limited. First, and in contrast to the availability of evidence showing focused oral CF to be effective in targeting a wide range of grammatical structures, linguistic features targeted in written CF studies so far have typically been low in complexity, discrete, and rule-based (i.e., English articles and past tense). Second, and in line with what has been said about focused oral CF research, some have argued that such studies lack authenticity since the processing of focused written CF has more resemblance to performing a grammar exercise than to a writing task (e.g., Bruton, 2009), and because a teacher's purpose in providing feedback on learners' written work is to improve accuracy in general, not just the use of one grammatical feature (e.g., Storch, 2010; see also Pedagogical Arguments section for more (counter)arguments).

SLA-oriented studies that have investigated the long-term effectiveness of the feedback type more commonly found in actual classrooms – that is unfocused written CF – have been scarce. Of the few available studies, three found comprehensive written CF to be conducive to L2 development (Frear & Chiu, 2015; Van Beuningen, De Jong & Kuiken, 2008; Van Beuningen et al., 2012). Findings from a recent study by Karim and Nassaji (2020) were less clear-cut; learning effects were found for some tasks under some of the feedback conditions in the study (e.g., accuracy gains based on direct unfocused CF between task 1 and task 2) but not for others. A fifth study (Truscott & Hsu, 2008) reported that unfocused CF did not lead to improved accuracy in new pieces of writing. This latter finding, however, might well be attributable to a ceiling effect; since learners in Truscott and Hsu's study made very few errors to begin with, there was little room for CF-induced accuracy development (Bruton, 2009). As three out of the five studies produced clear evidence on the effectiveness of unfocused written CF, and a fourth yielded inconclusive but encouraging results, we might tentatively conclude that unfocused written CF is an effective means of promoting L2 learning. Moreover, and in contrast to Truscott's (1996, 2007) claims, there is no empirical indication that comprehensive feedback might be harmful, for example in the sense that it would incite learners to avoid corrected structures and thereby would lead to simplified future writing (e.g., Van Beuningen et al., 2012).

As is the case for oral CF, little is known about the relative effectiveness of focused and unfocused written CF. The three studies that directly addressed this issue produced mixed findings. Ellis and colleagues (2008) as well as Frear and Chiu (2015) found that both their focused and unfocused CF groups outperformed their control groups (i.e., groups not receiving any CF). They did not find any differences in accuracy gains, however, between groups receiving either focused or unfocused feedback. The third study examining the relative value of (un)focused CF approaches reported focused CF to be more beneficial to written accuracy development than the provision of unfocused feedback (Sheen, Wright & Moldawa, 2009). In the light of the inconclusiveness of these results, design differences between the studies (e.g., *indirect* (un)focused CF in Frear and Chiu's study vs. *direct* (un)focused CF in the other two studies), as well as the methodological limitations of Ellis et al.'s (2008) and Sheen et al.'s (2009) studies discussed earlier by, for example, Xu (2009) and Van Beuningen (2010), it would be ill-advised to make any statement in favor of either focused or unfocused written CF at this point.

Based on the above characterization of focused and unfocused CF, a discussion of different arguments in favor of either feedback type and a synthesis of what available research tells us about the value of these feedback options, the final section of this chapter will present suggestions for future research as well as implications for teaching practice, with a particular focus on the latter.

Suggestions for Further Research and Implications for the L2 Classroom

The first and foremost conclusion to be drawn from the synthesis presented above is that summons for the abandonment of CF from language classrooms that have been made in the literature (e.g., Truscott, 1996, 2007) seem to be unjustified; most research discussed attests to the effectiveness of CF in fostering language development, irrespective of the (un)focused nature of CF or the feedback mode (i.e., oral or written). More research is needed, however, before any conclusions can be drawn about the relative efficacy of focused and unfocused CF approaches.

That being said, the question as to which feedback type is most effective might not be the most relevant one, since "we must be careful not to oversimplify the issue, and note that there is no single answer to how or what teachers should do in L2 classrooms" (Nassaji, 2016, p. 553). As a growing body of research reveals, individual (e.g., motivation, aptitude) and contextual factors (e.g., instructional setting) mediate CF effectiveness (e.g., Brown, 2016; Bitchener, 2017): what works for one learner or in a particular setting might not be (as) beneficial to another student or in a different context. Teachers would therefore be advised to combine various CF approaches in such a way that they, for example, complement each other, by using different CF types for different goals (e.g., selective written CF on most notable error patterns to help learners to self-edit their work, or comprehensive written CF when aiming for a high-quality final product). Teachers could also differentiate their CF approaches to accommodate the needs and preferences of different learners and/or of the same learner at different points in his/her developmental process to maximize learning opportunities (e.g., Aljaafreh & Lantolf, 1994; Bitchener & Ferris, 2012; Lyster et al., 2013). It has been hypothesized, for instance, that unfocused CF might be a more appropriate feedback option for learners with higher L2 proficiency and/or more working memory capacity (see Theoretical Arguments section). Future cognitively oriented studies could systematically test such hypotheses (e.g., Ellis, 2010). Sociocultural research could explore the potential interplay between the CF characteristics elucidated in Table 14.1 and the scaffolding properties of CF (e.g., do we see a diminishing need for feedback intensity when learners become more self-regulated?). Moreover, to be able to attune CF to the specific needs of individual learners, CF could best take the form of a dialogic, collaborative activity (e.g., Nassaji & Swain, 2000). Some pedagogical tools that can be used to enhance learners' active involvement in the feedback process are one-on-one feedback conferences (Nassaji, 2017a), allowing for multiple drafts of written texts, and dialogic learning journals (Bitchener & Storch, 2016).

Relatedly, it is also interesting and necessary to gather more insight into the ways learners engage with and process (un)focused CF (e.g., Bitchener & Storch, 2016; Ellis, 2010). Observing students while using the feedback they receive (e.g., by using think-aloud protocols, stimulated recall, eye-tracking, self-reports, interviews) could further our understanding of why some learners succeed and others fail to profit from (a specific type of) CF. It could also be helpful for teachers to elicit their students' thought processes during CF processing (e.g., by asking a student to think out loud while revising a text based on the feedback he or she received) because this allows teachers to directly perceive the potential hurdles and needs of his or her student (e.g., Van Beuningen, 2016), thereby giving teachers the opportunity to adjust their feedback approaches in the appropriate direction (e.g., making feedback more salient by focusing on fewer structures, or providing additional CF on issues that were not targeted, but that the learner him- or herself considers important). In the same vein, teachers could organize class discussions and one-on-one interactions with students to unveil their CF needs and preferences. These constitute an important source of information when making pedagogical choices, since learners' beliefs about and attitudes toward feedback have been found to mediate CF efficacy (e.g., Li, 2010). A complementary direction for future research would be, for instance, to empirically test if unfocused feedback is indeed associated with hypothesized affective drawbacks, such as learner anxiety, loss of confidence, or diminishing motivation (see Pedagogical Arguments section).

An important issue for teachers to consider when providing focused CF is which error category/categories to target. Ellis (2017) notes that teachers should make this choice in a principled manner. One way of making such a principled decision would be to target those structures that are most salient (Brown, 2016), for example those structures that are also the object of instruction. Another way would be to single out errors that are interfering most with communicative success or which are the most frequent and/or most stigmatizing (note that such a feedback approach would be selective, but not focused in nature; see Introduction). A third option teachers have when they want to make an informed decision on which errors to correct is basing their choices on research insights pertaining to the CF amenability of different error categories. As discussed in the subsection on oral feedback studies, focused oral CF has been found to be effective in promoting the development of a wide range of morphosyntactic structures; errors within this linguistic domain would therefore make good candidates to be targeted in oral teacher feedback. Lyster et al.'s (2013) review of oral feedback research suggests, however, that CF might even be more effective in addressing lexical and pronunciation errors, and that this might be because such errors interfere with understanding more significantly. Given that few studies have investigated the value of CF beyond the realm of morphosyntax, exploring CF effectiveness within the lexical and pronunciation domains would make a worthwhile pursuit for future research. With respect to written focused feedback, there is an even bigger need to gather empirical evidence on the CF responsiveness of various target forms and structures since, so far, focused CF studies have exclusively targeted discrete, rule-based morphosyntactical categories (i.e., mainly use of English articles; see section on written feedback studies). Van Beuningen et al.'s (2012) study on the effectiveness of unfocused written CF does provide some evidence of the CF amenability of error types beyond the ones that have been investigated in written focused CF studies; their study showed comprehensive CF to be effective in promoting both grammatical (i.e., morphosyntactic) and nongrammatical (e.g., lexical) accuracy development. As Bitchener and Ferris (2012) rightly argue though, it is important that future studies investigating the efficacy of unfocused CF not only examine such broad categories of learner errors but also compare accuracy gains across more specific error types, because otherwise "we will never know which specific forms or structures within these categories are the reasons for observed improvement or lack of improvement" (p. 102). One way of accomplishing this would be by using individualized pre- and post-tests as has already been done in some classroom-based oral CF studies (e.g., Hawkes & Nassaji, 2016). A final approach in deciding which error categories to target would be to establish the CF focus in interaction with the learner him- or herself, considering learners are intentional agents who have their own language learning goals (e.g., Lantolf & Pavlenko, 2001).

    Two final recommendations to L2 teachers would be to inform students about their feedback choices and to use CF approaches that encourage learners to engage with the feedback they receive. The first point is particularly important when providing focused CF; without students being aware of and understanding teachers' CF priorities and practices (Bitchener, 2017), observing that some of their errors (i.e., errors belonging to particular categories) are corrected while others are not might be rather confusing for students (Van Beuningen, 2010). The second point is vital for any type of CF to be effective: to increase the likelihood of aiding acquisition, CF should be actively processed by learners. Nassaji (2016) therefore advises teachers to always use CF in ways that encourage learners to modify their output (e.g., by asking students to revise texts based on the feedback they have received in the case of written CF). An additional way to promote active engagement with CF (and thereby learning) is by having students reflect on error patterns in their output and/or on what they have learned from the CF they received on those errors (Bitchener & Ferris, 2012), for example in a learning journal.

I will end this chapter by identifying some methodological issues future investigations into the effectiveness of (un)focused CF could consider. First, there is a clear need for more longitudinal studies into the effects of (un)focused oral and written CF on L2 development, since the lion's share of studies so far have only looked into short-term learning effects (e.g., Ellis, 2017). Second, research on focused CF types should employ a design that controls or checks for possible trade-off effects; only if accuracy development within the target domain does not come at the expense of performance in other linguistic domains can focused CF be claimed to be beneficial for L2 learning (Xu, 2009). Moreover, future studies should consider assessing CF effectiveness not only in terms of accuracy improvement, but also in terms of increasing self-regulatory abilities; from a sociocultural perspective, if a learner's need for CF diminishes over time (e.g., if he or she needs less intensive feedback to identify and self-correct errors), this could also be interpreted as a sign of development (Nassaji & Swain, 2000). Finally, it is important to increase teacher involvement in the design and execution of SLA oriented (un)focused CF studies, to increase the authenticity and ecological validity of such CF research (e.g., Bitchener & Ferris, 2012).

References

Aljaafreh, A. & Lantolf, J. P. (1994). Negative feedback as regulation and second language learning in the zone of proximal development. *Modern Language Journal* 78(4), 465–483.

Ashwell, T. (2000). Patterns of teacher response to student writing in a multiple-draft composition classroom: Is content feedback followed by form feedback the best method? *Journal of Second Language Writing*, 9 (3), 227–258.

Bitchener, J. (2008). Evidence in support of written corrective feedback. *Journal of Second Language Writing, 17*(2), 102–118.

(2017). Why some L2 learners fail to benefit from written corrective feedback. In H. Nassaji & E. Kartchava (eds.), *Corrective feedback in second language teaching and learning: Research, theory, applications, implications* (pp. 129–140). New York: Routledge.

Bitchener, J. & Ferris, D. (2012). *Written corrective feedback in second language acquisition and writing.* London: Routledge.

Bitchener, J. & Knoch, U. (2010). The contribution of written corrective feedback to language development: A ten-month investigation. *Applied Linguistics, 31*(2), 193–214.

Bitchener, J. & Storch, N. (2016). *Written corrective feedback for L2 development.* Bristol: Multilingual Matters.

Brown, A. (2009). Students' and teachers' perceptions of effective foreign language teaching: A comparison of ideals. *Modern Language Journal 93* (1), 46–60.

Brown, D. (2016). The type and linguistic foci of oral corrective feedback in the L2 classroom: A meta-analysis. *Language Teaching Research, 20*(4), 436–458.

Bruton, A. (2009). Designing research into the effect of error correction in L2 writing: Not so straightforward. *Journal of Second Language Writing, 18* (2), 136–140.

Chandler, J. (2003). The efficacy of various kinds of error feedback for improvement in the accuracy and fluency of L2 student writing. *Journal of Second Language Writing, 12*(3), 267–296.

DeKeyser, R. (1993). The effect of error correction on L2 grammar knowledge and oral proficiency. *Modern Language Journal, 77*(4), 501–514.

Edge, J. (1989). *Mistakes and correction.* London: Longman.

Ellis, R. (2005). Principles of instructed language learning. *System 33*(2), 209–224.

(2008). A typology of written corrective feedback types. *ELT Journal, 63*(2), 97–107.

(2010). Epilogue: A framework for investigating oral and written corrective feedback. *Studies in Second Language Acquisition, 32*(2), 335–349.

(2017). Oral corrective feedback in L2 classrooms. In H. Nassaji & E. Kartchava (eds.), *Corrective feedback in second language teaching and learning: Research, theory, applications, implications* (pp. 3–18). New York: Routledge.

Ellis, R., Loewen, S. & Erlam, R. (2006). Implicit and explicit corrective feedback and the acquisition of L2 grammar. *Studies in Second Language Acquisition, 28*(2), 339–368.

Ellis, R. & Sheen, Y. (2006). Reexamining the role of recasts in second language acquisition. *Studies in Second Language Acquisition, 28*(4), 575–600.

Ellis, R., Sheen, Y., Murakami, M. & Takashima, H. (2008). The effects of focused and unfocused written corrective feedback in an English as a foreign language context. *System, 36*(3), 353–371.

Evans, N., Hartshorn, K., McCollum, R. & Wolfersberger, M. (2010). Contextualizing corrective feedback in second language writing pedagogy. *Language Teaching Research*, 14(4), 445–463.

Fathman, A. & Whalley, E. (1990). Teacher response to student writing: Focus on form versus content. In B. Kroll (ed.), *Second language writing: Research insights for the classroom* (pp. 178–190). Cambridge: Cambridge University Press.

Ferris, D. (2004). The "grammar correction" debate in L2 writing: Where are we, and where do we go from here...? (and what do we do in the meantime?). *Journal of Second Language Writing* 13(1), 49–62.

— (2010). Second language writing research and written corrective feedback in SLA. *Studies in Second Language Acquisition*, 32(2), 181–201.

Ferris, D. & Roberts, B. (2001). Error feedback in L2 writing classes. How explicit does it need to be? *Journal of Second Language Writing*, 10(3), 161–184.

Frear, D. & Chiu, Y. (2015). The effect of focused and unfocused indirect written corrective feedback on EFL learners' accuracy in new pieces of writing. *System*, 53, 24–34.

Goo, J. & Mackey, A. (2013). The case against the case against recasts. *Studies in Second Language Acquisition*, 35(1), 127–165.

Hartshorn, K., Evans, N., Merrill, P., Sudweeks, R., Strong-Krause, D. & Anderson, N. (2010). Effects of dynamic corrective feedback on ESL writing accuracy. *TESOL Quarterly*, 44(1), 84–109.

Hawkes, L. & Nassaji, H. (2016). The role of extensive recasts in error detection and correction by adult ESL students. *Studies in Second Language Learning and Teaching*, 6(1), 19–41.

Jean, G. & D. Simard (2011). Grammar learning in English and French L2: Students' and teachers' beliefs and perceptions. *Foreign Language Annals*, 44(4), 465–492.

Kang, E. & Han, Z. (2015). The efficacy of written corrective feedback in improving L2 written accuracy: A meta-analysis. *Modern Language Journal*, 99(1), 1–18.

Karim, K. & Nassaji, H. (2020). The revision and transfer effects of direct and indirect comprehensive corrective feedback on ESL students' writing. *Language Teaching Research*, 24(4), 519–539.

Kepner, C. (1991). An experiment in the relationship of types of written feedback to the development of second language writing skills. *Modern Language Journal*, 75(3), 305–313.

Lantolf, J. & Pavlenko, A. (2001). (S)econd (L)anguage (A)ctivity theory: Understanding second language learners as people. In M. Breen (ed.), *Learner contributions to language learning* (pp. 141–158). London: Longman.

Leki, I. (1991). The preferences of ESL students for error correction in college-level writing classes. *Foreign Language Annals*, 24(3), 203–218.

Li, S. (2010). The effectiveness of corrective feedback in SLA: A meta-analysis. *Language Learning*, 60(2), 309–365.

Lightbown, P. (2008). Transfer appropriate processing as a model for class second language acquisition. In Z. Han (ed.), *Understanding second language process* (pp. 27–44). Clevedon: Multilingual Matters.

Lyster, R. (1998). Negotiation of form, recasts, and explicit correction in relation to error types and learner repair in immersion classrooms. *Language Learning*, 48(2), 183–218.

Lyster, R. & Ranta, L. (1997). Corrective feedback and learner uptake. *Studies in Second Language Acquisition*, 19(1), 37–66.

(2013). Counterpoint piece: The case for variety in corrective feedback research. *Studies in Second Language Acquisition*, 35(1), 167–184.

Lyster, R. & Saito, K. (2010). Oral feedback in classroom SLA: A meta-analysis. *Studies in Second Language Acquisition*, 32(2), 265–302.

Lyster, R., Saito, K. & Sato, M. (2013). Oral corrective feedback in second language classrooms. *Language Teaching*, 46(1), 1–40.

Mackey, A. & Goo, J. (2007). Interaction research in SLA: A meta-analysis and research synthesis. In A. Mackey (ed.), *Conversational interaction in second language acquisition: A collection of empirical studies* (pp. 407–452). Oxford: Oxford University Press.

Mackey, A. & Philp, J. (1998). Conversational interaction and second language development: Recasts, responses, and red herrings? *Modern Language Journal*, 82(3), 338–356.

Manchón, R. (2009). Broadening the perspective of L2 writing scholarship: The contribution of research on foreign language writing. In R. M. Manchón (ed.), *Writing in foreign language contexts: Learning, teaching, and research* (pp. 1–19). Clevedon: Multilingual Matters.

Nabei, T. & Swain, M. (2002). Learner awareness of recasts in classroom interaction: A case study of an adult EFL student's second language learning. *Language Awareness*, 11(1), 43–63.

Nassaji, H. (2011). Correcting students' written grammatical errors: The effects of negotiated versus nonnegotiated feedback. *Studies in Second Language Learning and Teaching*, 1(3), 315–334.

(2012). Effects of recasts and elicitations in dyadic interaction and the role of feedback explicitness. *Language Learning*, 59(2), 411–452.

(2013). Participation structure and incidental focus on form in adult ESL classrooms. *Language Learning*, 63(4), 835–869.

(2016). Anniversary article Interactional feedback in second language teaching and learning: A synthesis and analysis of current research. *Language Teaching Research*, 20(4), 535–562.

(2017a). Oral negotiation in response to written errors. In H. Nassaji & E. Kartchava (Eds.), *Corrective Feedback in Second Language Teaching and Learning: Research, Theory, Applications, Implications* (pp. 114–128). New York: Routledge.

(2017b). The effectiveness of extensive versus intensive recasts for learning L2 grammar. *Modern Language Journal, 101*(2), 353–368.

Nassaji, H. & Swain, M. (2000). A Vygotskian perspective on corrective feedback in L2: The effect of random versus negotiated help on the learning of English articles. *Language Awareness, 9*(1), 34–51.

Polio, C., Fleck, C. & Leder, N. (1998). "If only I had more time": ESL learners' changes in linguistic accuracy on essay revisions. *Journal of Second Language Writing, 7*(1), 43–68.

Rassaei, E. (2014). Scaffolded feedback, recasts, and L2 development: A sociocultural perspective. *Modern Language Journal 98*(1), 417–431.

Russell, J. & Spada, N. (2006). The effectiveness of corrective feedback for second language acquisition: A meta-analysis of the research. In J. Norris, & L. Ortega (eds.), *Synthesizing research on language learning and teaching* (pp. 131–164). Amsterdam: John Benjamins.

Schmidt, R. (1994). Deconstructing consciousness in search of useful definitions for applied linguistics. *AILA Review 11*, 11–26.

Segalowitz, N. (1997). Individual differences in second language acquisition. In A. M. B. De Groot & J. F. Kroll (eds.), *Tutorials in bilingualism: Psycholinguistic perspectives* (pp. 85–112). Mahwah, NJ: Lawrence Erlbaum.

(2000). Automaticity and attentional skill in fluent performance. In H. Riggenbach (ed.), *Perspectives on fluency* (pp. 200–219). Ann Arbor: University of Michigan Press.

Sheen, Y. (2004). Corrective feedback and learner uptake in communicative classrooms across instructional settings. *Language Teaching Research, 8*(3), 263–300.

(2006). Exploring the relationship between characteristics of recasts and learner uptake. *Language Teaching Research, 11*(4), 361–392.

(2007). The effect of focused written corrective feedback and language aptitude on ESL learners' acquisition of articles. *TESOL Quarterly, 41*(2), 255–283.

(2010). Introduction: The role of oral and written corrective feedback in SLA. *Studies in Second Language Acquisition, 32*(2), 169–179.

Sheen, Y., Wright, D. & Moldawa, A. (2009). Differential effects of focused and unfocused written correction on the accurate use of grammatical forms by adult ESL learners. *System 37*(4), 556–569.

Shintani, N., Ellis, R. & Suzuki, W. (2014). Effects of written feedback and revision on learners' accuracy in using two English grammatical structures. *Language Learning, 64*(1), 103–131.

Storch, N. (2010). Critical feedback on written corrective feedback research. *International Journal of English Studies, 10*(2), 29–46.

Truscott, J. (1996). The case against grammar correction in L2 writing classes. *Language Learning, 46*(2), 327–369.

(2007). The effect of error correction on learners' ability to write accurately. *Journal of Second Language Writing, 16*(4), 255–272.

Truscott, J. & Hsu, A. Y. (2008). Error correction, revision, and learning. *Journal of Second Language Writing, 17*(4), 292–305.

Ur, P. (1996). *A course in language teaching: Practice and theory*. Cambridge: Cambridge University Press.

Van Beuningen, C. (2010). Corrective feedback in L2 writing: Theoretical perspectives, empirical insights, and future directions. *International Journal of English Studies, 10*(2), 1–27.

(2016). Waarom werkt de rode pen (niet altijd)? Een onderzoek naar denkprocessen en strategiegebruik van leerlingen tijdens de verwerking van correctieve feedback. [Why does(n't) the red pen (always) work? A study into thought processes and strategy use of students during the processing of corrective feedback.] *Tijdschrift Les, 34*(199), 14–16.

Van Beuningen, C., De Jong, N. H. & Kuiken, F. (2008). The effect of direct and indirect corrective feedback on L2 learners' written accuracy. *ITL-Review of Applied Linguistics, 156*, 279–296.

(2012). Evidence on the effectiveness of comprehensive error correction in second language writing. *Language Learning, 62*(1), 1–41.

Vygotsky, L. S. (1978). *Mind in society: The development of higher psychological processes*. Cambridge, MA: Harvard University Press.

Williams, J. (2001). The effectiveness of spontaneous attention to form. *System, 29*(3), 325–340.

(2012). The potential role (s) of writing in second language development. *Journal of Second Language Writing, 21*(4), 321–331.

Xu, C. (2009). Overgeneralization from a narrow focus: A response to Ellis et al. (2008) and Bitchener (2008). *Journal of Second Language Writing, 18*(4), 270–275.

15

Corrective Feedback Timing and Second Language Grammatical Development: Research, Theory, and Practice

Paul Gregory Quinn

Corrective feedback (CF) timing refers to when errors in second language (L2) are treated. CF provided directly after an error is made is immediate CF, while CF provided at a later time is delayed CF. This chapter summarizes research on the timing of written and oral CF on L2 grammatical errors. It explains theoretical proposals about how immediate and delayed CF facilitate L2 development (i.e., statistically significant increases in either explicit or implicit L2 grammatical knowledge). In addition, it discusses the potential implications that research and theory might have for L2 pedagogy, as well as what future research might best be conducted in the area of CF timing.

Researching CF Timing as an Independent Variable

CF timing has only recently begun to be investigated as an independent variable. Previously, written CF research investigated CF provided on completed texts (which just happened to be delayed CF), and oral CF research investigated CF provided immediately following spoken errors (which just happened to be immediate CF). There is currently an upsurge in studies investigating both immediate and delayed CF on written and spoken errors.

Written CF Timing Research
The position that (delayed) written CF could facilitate L2 development was criticized by Truscott (1996), who argued that methodological limitations

in early written CF research weakened the case. Subsequently, more rigidly designed studies provided better evidence that written CF could facilitate L2 development (e.g., Sheen, 2007, 2010; Van Beuningen, De Jong & Kuiken, 2012). In a meta-analysis of twenty-one written CF studies, Kang and Han (2015) investigated whether written CF facilitated L2 development and how it was affected by variables including learner proficiency, CF type, and CF focus. While learner proficiency refers to whether learners are beginners, intermediate, or advanced, CF type refers to how CF is provided. For example, indirect CF is provided by underlining or circling error location. More direct CF indicates error location and provides metalinguistic information about the error, such as whether the error is a verb tense or pronoun agreement issue. (For example, teachers often provide codes like "VT" for verb tense errors.) The most direct form of written CF involves crossing out errors and writing in accurate forms. Finally, CF focus refers to whether CF is provided on a limited number of features or all errors (see Chapter 14, this volume).

Kang and Han's (2015) meta-analysis found an overall moderate effect size for the effectiveness of written CF, supporting the position that delayed written CF facilitates L2 development. They found that written CF resulted in greater effect sizes for advanced than for intermediate and beginner learners. Additionally, they found no statistically significant differences between direct and indirect CF, and none between the effects of focused and unfocused CF.

The advent of computer-assisted language learning (CALL) facilitated ways that written CF could be provided immediately or after some delay (for an overview of CF research in CALL, see Chapter 11, this volume). This technological advance sparked interest in the investigation of timing as a variable of written CF research. Henshaw (2011) used CALL software to investigate the effects of timing on written CF. Participants completed a multiple-choice pre-test on recognizing and correctly interpreting the use of the Spanish subjunctive. Then, during a computer-based treatment task, participants selected a response from written responses to multiple-choice questions. When computerized direct written CF was provided, it stated whether the answer was correct or not and provided metalinguistic information. There were three CF conditions: (1) immediate CF after each question, (2) delayed CF at the end of the task, and (3) 24-hour delayed CF. A control group received no CF. On a post-test, Henshaw found the three CF conditions statistically outperformed the control group but not each other. She concluded that written CF was effective over time, regardless of its timing.

Lavolette, Polio, and Kahng (2015) also employed CALL software to investigate written CF timing. The software analyzed participants' completed essay drafts and then provided written feedback by highlighting and providing metalinguistic information about errors. An immediate CF condition received feedback on a completed essay in a timely manner, within 40 minutes of essay submission, while a delayed CF condition received it in a less timely manner, within one to three weeks. They compared the number of error-free T-units (a T-unit was defined as a main clause plus its dependent clauses) in texts written before and after treatment. They found no significant differences between the immediate and delayed CF conditions.

Henshaw (2011) and Lavolette et al. (2015) are less convincing comparisons of immediate and delayed written CF than the studies that followed them for two reasons. First, Henshaw (2011) is atypical because the written CF was provided on responses to multiple choices of written responses, rather than on participants' own writing. Second, Lavolette et al. (2015) investigated CF timing, but their construct of immediate CF was operationalized as the timely response to a completed text, rather than the immediate correction of individual errors as they were committed. As such, their study might more suitably be categorized as an investigation of the "timeliness" (Lavolette et al., 2015, p. 53) of CF, a term they used to describe two studies (Evans, Hartshorn & Strong-Krause, 2011; Hartshorn et al., 2010) that compared briefly delayed to more lengthily delayed CF on completed texts. Lavolette et al. found no statistical differences between their two timing conditions, while the other two studies found that sooner was significantly better than later in terms of L2 grammatical development.

Arguably, Shintani and Aubrey (2016) conducted the first study comparing the effectiveness of immediate and delayed CF on participants' written production. They used Google Docs to compare immediate (synchronous) to delayed (asynchronous) written CF. Participants wrote paragraphs that required the English hypothetical conditional. Direct focused CF was provided to the immediate CF group just after conditional errors were made, to the delayed CF group after the writing task, and CF was not provided to the comparison condition. Text reconstruction tasks were used for pre-, immediate-post-, and delayed-post-tests. Both CF conditions statistically outperformed the non-CF comparison group, but only the immediate CF condition maintained that outperformance on the delayed-post-test.

Text-based computer-mediated communication (CMC) has also been used to compare immediate and delayed written CF. In its common asynchronous form of email, CMC is similar to traditional written correspondence, but in its common synchronous form of instant text messaging, CMC is similar to oral communication. However, because the CF that is conducted in both forms of CMC is text based, in this chapter, it is classified as written CF. Arroyo and Yilmaz (2018) compared the effectiveness of synchronous CF to asynchronous CF. The treatment consisted of an online text chat where participants used gendered nouns in Spanish to provide researchers with missing information about a picture.

Participants were assigned to three conditions: immediate CF, delayed CF, and a no-CF control condition. Immediate written CF was provided within 40 seconds by an instant text message that reformulated participants' errors into accurate models. Delayed CF was provided in a Microsoft Word document containing a written list of participants' errors, each accompanied by correct reformulations. An untimed grammaticality judgment test (GJT) and a spot-the-differences oral production test (OPT) were given as pre-, immediate post-, and delayed post-tests. On the OPT, the immediate CF group statistically outperformed both the delayed CF group and the control group on both post-tests. On both GJT post-tests, the immediate and delayed CF groups outperformed the control group but not each other.

Therefore, research has demonstrated that both immediate and delayed written CF can facilitate L2 development. It also indicates that immediate written CF is sometimes more effective than delayed written CF. This sooner is better pattern is also found in the majority of the studies that are, as argued above, better referred to as "timeliness of CF" studies.

Oral CF Timing Research

There are parallels between the written and oral CF timing research. First, the timing of oral CF was also not an independent variable until much research had been conducted on oral CF that just happened to be immediate CF. Like written CF timing research, that oral CF research investigated how, not when, to provide CF.

As with written CF research, the ways to provide oral CF can be simply categorized. Oral CF can (1) provide input in the form of an accurate model, (2) push output by prompting learners to self-correct, or (3) push output and provide input in a hybrid form of CF that elicits self-correction attempts and provides accurate models. Input providing CF is called reformulation. "Recasts" are more implicit reformulations because they merely paraphrase learners' errors with a corrected model of speech. For example, if the learner explains his father's eye colour by saying *Her eyes are blue*, a teacher can provide a recast by saying *His eyes are blue*. Explicit reformulations are called "explicit correction" because learners are explicitly told that they have erred, and then they are given the accurate model of speech (with or without a metalinguistic explanation). In treating the preceding error with explicit correction, the teacher would say "Her" is incorrect. You must say *His eyes are blue*. Pushed output correction, or "prompting," is provided by teachers via elicitation (which may include metalinguistic information but will not provide an accurate model). A prompt for the eye colour error might be to repeat "Her?" with rising intonation to indicate that the learner is being asked if he has used the correct grammar.

Most oral CF research has investigated these CF types as they were provided immediately following errors. Several meta-analyses of this research found that providing (immediate) CF for errors in learners' spoken L2 facilitated L2 development (e.g., Li, 2010; Lyster & Saito, 2010; Mackey & Goo, 2007). Research also found that the efficacy of CF was affected by learners' awareness of the corrective intent of CF, or put differently, by whether learners noticed that teachers were attempting to correct their errors. Evidence of the importance of the awareness of corrective intent is that more explicit CF has proven more effective in facilitating L2 development. In comparison studies, participants who received recasts were statistically outperformed by participants who received more explicit CF in the form of prompts (Lyster, 2004; Yang & Lyster, 2010) and explicit correction (Carroll & Swain, 1993; Sheen 2007).

As in written CF research, interest in investigating the timing of oral CF as an independent variable is recent, and the oral CF timing literature also consists of studies that are more or less convincing comparisons of immediate and delayed CF. There are several reasons that the first set of oral CF timing studies reviewed below ((Azad, Farrokhi & Zohrabi, 2018; Farmani, Akbari & Ghanizadeh, 2017; Rahimi & Vahid Dastjerdi, 2012; Siyarri, 2005; Varnosfadrani, 2006) are arguably less convincing comparisons of immediate CF and delayed CF than the second set (Li, Ellis & Zhu, 2016; Quinn, 2014). First, some of these studies lack clear construct definitions for immediate and delayed CF. Second, they often plainly confound CF timing and type, such that the CF used for immediate CF differs in type from the CF used for delayed CF, which makes it difficult to claim that differences in outcomes are the result of CF timing differences. Third, many lack no-CF control groups. Without control groups, improvement over time cannot be convincingly attributed to the CF treatments.

Siyyari (2005) compared immediate and delayed oral CF on spoken errors on four English grammatical constructions: "I wish," three forms of the causative clause, second conditional sentences, and "should have + past participle." Over twelve classes, four teachers provided CF to sixty Iranian adult English learners in a series of dictogloss (Wajnryb, 1990) text reconstruction tasks that elicited the constructions. However, there was a CF type and timing confound because thirty learners received recasts for immediate CF, and thirty received explicit CF for delayed CF after the task. Moreover, there was also no control group. Pre- and post-tests featuring sentence completion questions compelled use of the constructions. For each construction, Siyyari found that immediate and delayed CF resulted in significant improvement from the pre- to post-tests, but he found no significant differences between immediate and delayed CF treatments. However, when he aggregated the scores from all constructions, Siyyari found the immediate CF group significantly outperformed the delayed CF group.

Varnosfadrani (2006) also compared immediate and delayed CF. Twenty-eight Iranian adult English learners participated in two dictogloss tasks. In the first task, learners received immediate explicit CF. In the second, the same learners received delayed CF, after the task, in the form of a reminder of the error followed by explicit CF. Varnosfadrani created tailor-made tests for each learner, composed of items with grammar errors that had been corrected. He found no significant differences between the immediate and delayed CF treatments. However, because all learners received both immediate and delayed CF, it is possible that some errors that learners were tested on might have received both immediate and delayed CF. For example, if a simple past tense error was corrected in the first task with immediate CF and then another simple past tense error received delayed CF in the second task, then simple past tense test items may have been answered correctly due to the effects of both immediate and delayed CF.

Rahimi and Vahid Dastjerdi (2012) investigated how immediate and delayed CF affected the complexity, accuracy, and fluency of twenty Iranian English learners. Over a semester, these learners discussed topics in two groups. In the first group, ten learners were provided CF immediately. In the second group, learners were provided CF "with some delay i.e. after finishing their speech" (Rahimi & Vahid Dastjerdi, 2012, p. 50). At the end of the term, each learner was recorded discussing a topic. That recording was scored on a series of criteria for complexity, fluency, and general accuracy. Then they compared the scores for immediate and delayed CF participants. They found that delayed CF participants significantly outperformed the immediate CF participants in terms of complexity and accuracy but not fluency. The lack of a pre-test to compare the two conditions is problematic because it is impossible to know if the delayed CF participants were more capable prior to the CF treatment. Furthermore, it is impossible to determine if there was a type and timing confound because the CF type or types are undefined. Another construct definition issue was that the researchers vaguely describe when the immediate and delayed CF were provided. If "immediate CF" in this study refers to an interruption of an utterance, and "delayed CF," described as "after finishing their speech" (Rahimi & Vahid Dastjerdi, 2012, p. 50), means having been supplied merely at the end of an utterance (following Long, 1977), then the "delayed CF" would seem more like a slightly different form of "immediate CF," and that makes the value of the comparison dubious.[1]

Farmani, Akbari, and Ghanizadeh (2017) compared immediate to delayed oral CF over twenty sessions for ninety Iranian English learners. There were three thirty-participant conditions: immediate CF, delayed CF, and a control condition. The activities during the sessions are not explained, but the CF is described. The immediate CF participants received explicit correction directly after making an error. The delayed CF participants also received explicit correction, but when they received it is unclear. Farmani et al. cite Long's (1977) definition of delayed CF following

---

[1] Quinn (2014) and Quinn and Nakata (2017) argue that CF becomes delayed CF when it is provided outside of Doughty's (2001) "window of cognitive opportunity" (p. 257), a construct explained in this chapter's theoretical section. Both Quinn (2014) and Arroyo and Yilmaz (2018) define delayed CF in line with what Quinn and Nakata (2017) call the "psycholinguistic demarcation" (p. 43) between immediate and delayed CF.

the end of a learner's utterance but not sooner than 10 seconds after an error. As in Rahimi and Vahid Dastjerdi (2012), the lack of clear construct definition makes it difficult to know whether the comparison was between immediate and delayed CF or between immediate CF that interrupted an utterance and immediate CF that followed a completed utterance. Another issue is that the control group was not a no-CF group, but rather a group that sometimes received delayed CF and sometimes received immediate CF. The study used the Cambridge English Proficiency test for pre- and post-tests. They found that only the immediate CF condition significantly outperformed the control group.

Azad, Farrokhi, and Zohrabi (2018) compared immediate and delayed oral CF by assigning approximately sixteen Iranian English learners in intact classes to four conditions: immediate intensive recasts (on simple past errors), immediate extensive recasts (on all errors), delayed explicit correction with metalinguistic explanation (on simple past errors), and a no-CF control group. Participants engaged in six story-retelling tasks over a semester, and CF was provided in line with the four conditions. General measures of accuracy (error-free clauses) and fluency (speech rates) in the first and sixth sessions were compared. No statistically significant differences were found. The study's clear CF type and timing confound renders it a less convincing comparison of immediate and delayed oral CF.

Quinn (2014) and Li et al. (2016) more convincingly compared immediate and delayed oral CF[2]. In Quinn's (2014) study, ninety ESL learners were randomly assigned to three conditions: immediate CF, delayed CF, and a no-CF control group. In the first week, learners completed an oral production test, a timed aural GJT, and a written error correction test on the English passive construction. In the second week, learners received a mini-lesson on the passive voice. Then, according to learners' conditions, Quinn provided or did not provide CF while each learner individually engaged with him in three 10-minute communicative tasks (an information-gap task, a picture-cued story-retelling task, and a role-play). The amount and type of CF provision were uniform for the participants in the immediate and delayed CF conditions. All participants in the CF conditions received twelve provisions of teacher-initiated student correction (Rolin-Ianziti, 2010), which is a hybrid form of CF, wherein Quinn used prompts to provoke the participant to attempt to say something she had previously said inaccurately, and then, regardless of whether she self-corrected accurately, Quinn provided the accurate language model and had her repeat it. Thus, the only differences between the three conditions were that the no-CF condition received no CF, immediate CF learners received CF immediately after an error, and the delayed CF learners received CF after each task. Following the treatment, and one week later, participants completed the

---

[2] However, see Li et al.'s (2016) criticism of Quinn's (2014) delayed CF construct and Quinn and Nakata's (2017) criticism of Li et al.'s (2016) potential CF type and timing confound.

three tests again. On all tests, Quinn found a significant improvement from pre- to post-tests. However, he found no significant differences between any conditions.

Li et al. (2016) also convincingly compared immediate and delayed oral CF. They investigated the English passive as a previously unknown structure for 120 English learners in four intact classrooms in China. These classes made up four conditions: immediate CF, delayed CF, task-only, and test-only. Learners took pre-tests one week before engaging in treatment tasks, which were followed by immediate and delayed post-tests. Knowledge of the passive was assessed with an untimed GJT to assess explicit knowledge, and an elicited imitation test was used to assess implicit knowledge. The treatment tasks engaged learners in practicing and then performing two dictogloss tasks that elicited the passive. Immediate CF learners were corrected as soon as errors were made with corrective recasts (Doughty & Varela, 1998). Thus, once an error was made, the teacher repeated the utterance using emphasis to highlight the inaccurate part. If the student self-corrected accurately, the task continued. If not, the teacher provided the accurate model. Delayed CF learners' errors were noted, and CF was delayed until after both dictogloss tasks were completed. Then, CF was provided by reminding the learner about a wrong utterance and asking him to correct it. From that juncture, CF followed the same process as the immediate CF. For the task-only learners, errors were not corrected. Finally, test-only learners took the pre- and post-tests but did not do dictogloss tasks or receive CF. Li et al. (2016) found that all their conditions improved significantly from pre- to post-tests for the elicited imitation measure of implicit knowledge. Because there were no significant differences between conditions, they concluded that the improvement came only as a result of a test practice effect.

For the GJT measure of explicit knowledge, Li et al. (2016) again found significant improvement over time. Moreover, on the delayed post-test, they found that immediate CF learners significantly outperformed the test-only but not the task-only learners. That is, they found that doing dictogloss tasks with or without CF helped learners, but they could not attribute the development solely to CF. However, they found that only immediate CF learners scored significantly better than task-only learners on test items that contained regular verbs. Moreover, only the immediate CF learners significantly outperformed the task-only learners on the delayed post-test for test items that used verbs in the dictogloss tasks. They concluded that immediate CF demonstrated advantages over delayed CF in explicit L2 knowledge development.

In summary, the oral and written CF timing research share much in common. First, in both cases, the research has indicated that immediate and delayed CF can facilitate L2 development. Second, the studies in both can be divided into studies that more convincingly compare immediate to delayed CF and those that do so less convincingly. A third parallel is that of mixed findings. Both the written and oral CF research results indicate that immediate CF is not consistently superior to delayed CF (or vice versa). However, when a difference in effectiveness has been found in written CF timing studies, and in all but one oral CF study (Rahimi & Vahid Dastjerdi, 2012), the difference has been that immediate CF has outperformed delayed CF.

Theoretical Explanations for the Effectiveness of Immediate and Delayed CF

According to the National Research Council (2000), learning is a process wherein new knowledge is constructed upon learners' existing knowledge. Therefore, teachers must focus on problems in that preexisting knowledge to assist learners construct new and improved knowledge. CF is a tool that L2 teachers employ to engage learners' preexisting inaccurate knowledge so that over time it can be transformed into, and replaced by, new accurate knowledge. The following section discusses theoretical explanations for how immediate and delayed written and oral CF are thought to facilitate that process. As is argued below, the effectiveness of immediate CF is more easily explained than the effectiveness of delayed CF by all of the cited theoretical frameworks, with the exception of Transfer Appropriate Processing (TAP) (Morris, Bransford & Franks, 1977), which predicts that immediate and delayed CF are likely to result in greater development of implicit and explicit knowledge, respectively.

Sociocultural theory (SCT) (e.g., Aljaafreh & Lantolf, 1994; Lantolf, 2000; Nassaji, Chapter 4, this volume) focuses on social interchange as the locus for language learning. According to the SCT explanation of CF effectiveness, teachers should address a learner's error with a series of CF moves that act as a mediating process through which the teacher's CF initially externally regulates the learner's knowledge gradually until the learner internalizes the regulation of the knowledge. This mediation of knowledge is hypothesized to occur in the learner's zone of proximal development, or in an area of linguistic knowledge in which the teacher's CF can be a scaffolding that bridges the gap between the knowledge of the teacher and the learner.

At the heart of SCT is the continuous social interchange which allows the teacher to carefully gauge and appropriately respond to the learner's needs. Arguably, this mediation can more easily be achieved when providing immediate CF that can be reacted to and built upon as the discourse is in process. This seems particularly to be the case for oral CF because when delayed CF is provided, the discourse is finished, so there is little opportunity for continuous tailored interchange. It also may be the case for written CF, for as Shintani and Aubrey (2016) concluded, their immediate CF learners received CF in a condition that allowed for better scaffolding than was the case for their delayed CF recipients. That is, immediate written CF allowed them to assist in the gradual development of writers because the CF was being provided while learners were composing, and not after the composition was finished, as was the case with delayed CF.

However, sometimes CF on written work is conducted through writing conferences (i.e., teacher–student meetings) about completed writing (e.g., Aljaafreh & Lantolf, 1994) which might make SCT a more suitable theoretical explanation for the effectiveness of this kind of delayed written CF. Writing conferences are somewhat different from the written CF discussed in this chapter given that they can be conducted orally, and that typically more attention is paid to individual errors (see Nassaji, 2017 for an overview). Such properties of post-task writing conferences resemble remedial instruction in ways that the rest of the CF reviewed in this chapter does not.

Whereas SCT focuses on the tailored social exchange between teachers and learners as it mediates internalization, more cognitively oriented theory focuses closely on internal mental processing. TAP (Morris, Bransford & Franks, 1977) predicts that immediate and delayed CF may result in the development of different types of L2 knowledge. TAP posits that memories are best recalled in conditions similar to those in which they were encoded. Drawing upon TAP, Spada and Lightbown (2008) hypothesized that learners who are instructed on grammar structures during communication might score better on tests of those structures that take the form of communicative tasks than on discrete point grammar tests. Concomitantly, different learners who learned the same grammar feature by learning the rules outside of communication might score higher on discrete grammar point tests than on tests in the form of communicative tasks. Another way of viewing this interpretation of TAP is that providing immediate CF that is integrated into synchronous oral or written communication may lead to an increase in procedural (or implicit) grammar knowledge while providing delayed CF following communicative discourse may lead to an increase in explicit (or declarative) knowledge.

Skill acquisition theory (SAT) (Anderson, 1982), another cognitively oriented explanation for CF effectiveness, describes how explicit knowledge becomes implicit knowledge through practice. SAT posits that humans learn by first learning factual information about a skill and then practicing until the skill is proceduralized into a behavior that eventually becomes automatic. DeKeyser (2007) argues that the theory can be applied to L2 acquisition. Drawing upon DeKeyser's argument, Ranta and Lyster (2007) proposed that oral CF in the form of prompts may facilitate proceduralization in communicative practice because prompts encourage learners to retrieve a learned grammar rule and reattempt to produce the language more accurately with that rule in mind. Continually doing so proceduralizes accurate usage. Bitchener and Storch (2016) argue that SAT might also explain the effectiveness of written CF.

However, is SAT useful in explaining the effectiveness of both immediate and delayed CF? As Bitchener and Storch note, Dekeyser (1998) argues that SAT is more likely to be effective when communicative behavior is being proceduralized, rather than when learners are solely engaged in the decontextualized mechanical practice of forming grammatically accurate structures with no other communicative intent. As such, it seems that SAT is a good explanation for the effectiveness of both written and oral immediate CF. They are both provided to learners in the midst of their attempts to meaningfully communicate a message. Then they have the chance to continue, in Dekeyser's (1998) words, "engaging in the target behaviour or procedure – while temporarily leaning on declarative crutches" (p. 49). According to SAT, repeated behavior practice of this kind would be effective. In the case of delayed CF, for SAT to serve as a suitable explanation, there needs to be some further attempt to communicate meaningfully while drawing upon the explicit knowledge. Perhaps for delayed written CF, this would involve subsequent writing of revised texts. For delayed oral CF, the CF would have to compel meaningful use of the language, as was attempted in Quinn's (2014) use of Rolin-Ianziti's (2010) teacher-initiated student-correction, where learners were asked to re-attempt something meaningfully from the communicative tasks that they had initially not been able to do accurately.

Another theoretical explanation for how CF facilitates L2 grammatical development can be broadly labelled "cognitive comparison." In SAT, the learning is hypothesized to proceed when CF provokes guided productive practice of accurate behavior. Cognitive comparison functions differently. First, when a learner makes a grammar mistake, a teacher provides them with the accurate model of that grammar structure. Then the learner's mental representation of that input (from the teacher) affects their own original inaccurate mental representation of how to form that structure when those two mental representations are adjacent to each other in their working memory (WM). According to Cowan (1995), WM is the activated component of long-term memory that facilitates the processing and storage of new sensory input. Doughty (2001) argues that recasts facilitate development by allowing for an immediate cognitive comparison which contributes to the gradual restructuring of the learner's knowledge. Doughty contends that to be effective, the comparison should occur within the "cognitive window of opportunity" (p. 257). This window refers to the less than 60 seconds that humans can maintain active mental representations in WM.

However, can cognitive comparison explain why oral CF delayed for a minute or more could cause L2 grammatical development through comparison-induced restructuring? Quinn and Nakata (2017) argue that the effectiveness of delayed (and immediate) CF might be explicable via cognitive comparison through a cognitive process called reactivation and reconsolidation (RAR) (Nader & Einarsson, 2010). In RAR, the act of reminding a participant of a previously learned pattern (which arguably could be facilitated by immediate or delayed CF, in the form of a prompt) causes a reactivation of a long-term mental representation of it. This reactivation of the mental representation makes it labile, or susceptible to influence. If that labile representation is present when a new stimulus (such as the forming of a new mental representation caused by the introduction of a similar pattern, which could be a teacher-provided accurate model of speech) occurs, the mind mixes the two mental representations together as it attempts to store, or reconsolidate, the original memory. Thus, the reactivated long-term mental representation is interfered with by the new mental stimulus, and it is altered to include some component of that new stimulus. Research has shown that this alteration effect occurs in declarative (Walker et al., 2003) and procedural memory (Hupbach et al., 2007).

To explain how written CF leads to L2 development through comparison-induced processing, Bitchener and Storch (2016) adopt Gass's (1997) five-stage model of oral CF processing. In the first stage, CF causes learners to notice that there is a difference between what they have said and what the CF provider has offered in response. The second stage is comprehending what the difference is between the two. The third stage involves the learner comparing his or her long-term mental representations about the grammatical structure with the provided CF in WM and mentally modifying his or her original output to test hypotheses about what is allowable and what is not in the L2. The fourth stage is when the outcome of hypothesis testing is resolved. A modified hypothesis is compared with the CF, and it is accepted if it matches the CF, or it is rejected if it does not. Rejection can result in more hypothesis testing and comparison, or it can result in eliminating the hypothesis. Acceptance leads to strengthening of the learner's hypothesis of how the L2 functions. Acceptance can also lead to storage. Stored material can be further tested in future output. The fifth stage involves confirming a hypothesis by orally producing it in the presence of other speakers whose responses signal that the new hypothesis is accurate or still inaccurate. If the hypothesis is inaccurate, the five-stage cycle starts again. If the hypothesis is confirmed, then the knowledge will be consolidated by the proceduralizing process described in the outline of SAT above.

Bitchener and Storch argue that this five-stage explanation of oral CF processing is not only applicable to written CF but may be even more effective in the case of written CF. They note that the cognitive comparisons in the process must occur while CF is held in WM, and as Williams (2012) has posited, the cognitive window is probably wider in the case of written CF than oral CF because written CF is provided in the form of a permanent record, unlike the more ephemeral form of oral CF. Immediate and delayed written CF both provide a permanent record.

However, because immediately provided CF occurs in the midst of a writing task, there is a greater chance that learners will have an opportunity to engage in Gass's fifth stage of confirming their new hypothesis via the written output required to complete the written task. Learners who are provided delayed CF but do not engage in any further writing would not have that chance.

Pedagogical Implications and Future Research Directions

The empirical and theoretical literature provides insights about CF timing that can inform the pedagogy of L2 teachers. However, it does not prescribe a simple model of perfect CF timing pedagogy. Instead, teachers should draw upon the literature to make informed decisions. This section organizes the empirical and theoretical literature in response to two questions that teachers are likely to ask of it: (1) Does providing immediate and delayed written and oral CF help my L2 students? and (2) Which is better, immediate or delayed CF? The section addresses those two questions before concluding with a consideration of some potential future directions for CF timing research.

The answer to the first question is "yes." Providing CF immediately and/or delaying CF provision in both written and oral modes can help your students. Both the empirical and the theoretical literature provide support for the position that written and oral immediate and delayed CF can facilitate L2 grammatical development.

The second question about whether it is better to provide immediate or delayed CF is more complex. In the case of oral CF, arguably both the empirical and theoretical literature more strongly support the use of immediate than delayed CF. In all but one comparison of immediate and delayed oral CF (Rahimi & Vahid Dastjerdi, 2012), where a difference was found between the two, immediate outperformed delayed CF. Moreover, the empirical evidence for delayed oral CF facilitating L2 development is not strong. It is based on results that demonstrated statistically significant improvement over time in studies without a clear construct definition of delayed CF (Rahimi & Vahid Dastjerdi, 2012), without a control group (Siyyari, 2005), or in which the delayed CF condition improved over time but not more so than a control group (Li et al., 2016; Quinn, 2014).

The theoretical literature also appears to support the use of immediate over delayed oral CF. That is, the theoretical conditions required for L2 development to occur via SCT, SAT, and immediate cognitive comparison are all present when CF is provided immediately (and continuously) in the midst of communicative activity. In order to meet those conditions when providing delayed CF, CF must be provided in a manner that reengages learners in communicative activity after the original discourse has ended. Doing so is challenging to operationalize, and it is likely to result in learners being more focused on language form than on meaningful communication. As a result, and as TAP predicts, delayed oral CF is more likely to result in the development of only explicit L2 knowledge.

However, potentially, delayed oral CF could facilitate implicit knowledge development via reactivation and reconsolidation, a process which has proven to affect long-term procedural memories in cognitive psychology research (Hupbach et al., 2007). To do so, a teacher would have to reengage a learner in meaningful communication so that the learner's inaccurate procedural long-term mental representation (of how to form a grammatical structure) could be reactivated by the delayed CF. If the teacher offered an accurate model, and that model was present as a new mental representation in the learner's WM, then the originally inaccurate procedural representation would be susceptible to the restructuring that would ensue in the reconsolidation process.

Is delayed oral CF ever advantageous? Here are three situations where delayed CF might be beneficial: (1) in communicative tasks in which interruption is counter-productive, (2) when learners (especially beginners) are having difficulty with a grammar structure due to a deficiency in explicit knowledge, and (3) when grammatical structures are complex due to the number of transformations they require to be formed.[3] First, the aim of teaching in some communicative tasks is to prepare learners to complete the entire task without stopping for assistance. For example, learners preparing to give an oral presentation must, at some point, practice giving the presentation completely on their own. Teachers might best record grammar errors, especially those that interfere with listeners' comprehension, and provide delayed CF after the presentation. Second, when learners (especially beginners) demonstrate deficiency in the explicit knowledge of how to form a grammar feature, then delayed CF may be useful. For example, if a learner persistently errs in using a structure and fails to accurately form it after several teacher prompts to self-correct, then probably the learner does not possess the required explicit L2 knowledge. In such a case, delaying oral CF until after a communicative task might allow the learner an opportunity to better process the explicit knowledge of the rules of how to form the feature. Unlike having to do so in the middle of attempting to communicate meaning, delayed CF might provide a time of undistracted processing. Third, for similar reasons, delayed CF might lighten the cognitive processing load and prove helpful for students making persistent errors on structures which are complex because they require multiple transformations. The English passive, for example, requires attention to inversion, verb tense, subject and verb agreement, and (sometimes) irregular verb forms. (For

---

[3] Hulstijn and de Graaff (1994) define complexity in terms of the number of criteria required to form a grammar structure accurately.

the second and third situations, combining explicit correction with metalinguistic information might be the most beneficial form of delayed CF.[4])

As to written CF timing, in comparison studies, where differences were found, immediate CF outperformed delayed CF. Nonetheless, theoretically, it is more challenging to explain why there might be a difference in the effectiveness of immediate and delayed CF in the written mode than it is in the oral mode. For example, where cognitive comparison is concerned, both immediate and delayed written CF may have a broader cognitive window, or indeed may always allow learners to reopen the cognitive window because the CF is permanently available for comparison. This permanent record is also equally beneficial for both immediate and delayed CF where the proceduralization in SAT is concerned. Notwithstanding that, proceduralization requires written output subsequent to CF provision. Learners that receive immediate CF in the midst of a writing task will practice proceduralizing accurate behavior as they complete that task. The same thing cannot be guaranteed for recipients of delayed CF. Furthermore, as Shintani and Aubrey (2016) concluded about their study, immediate CF provision may have allowed for the tailored social interchange required for SCT mediation in a manner that delayed CF provision did not. However, conducting CF through writing conferences might arguably facilitate the mediation of SCT and/or the proceduralization of SAT.

Before concluding, it is important to consider what written CF is being provided upon. On the one hand, as Arroyo and Yilmaz (2018) argue, synchronous CMC is similar to oral communication in several ways, and as such, may make immediate CF preferable. On the other hand, as Lavolette et al. (2015) argued, delaying written CF on written compositions (such as essays) until they are completed may be a more practical means of delivering CF than interrupting. This would seem to be particularly true when the writing is done with pen and paper, and/or with a large number of students. Thus, there are solid reasons for withholding a verdict on the question of which mode of written CF timing is superior.

In summary, the research and theoretical literature on CF timing can be drawn upon to inform L2 pedagogical practice. Teachers should feel some confidence that they can facilitate L2 grammatical development in their students when they provide immediate and delayed oral and written CF. Immediate oral CF appears to be more helpful than delayed CF, but there are times when delaying oral CF is potentially beneficial. It is more challenging to conclude that immediate written CF is superior to delayed written CF. Finally, the CF timing literature may prove useful for teachers

---

[4] Even though the second and third reasons are intuitively attractive, it must be noted that in Li et al. (2016) beginners with no previous knowledge of the English passive were provided with immediate and delayed CF in the form of corrective recasts. Only the immediate CF condition outperformed a control group on a measure of explicit knowledge. Perhaps adding metalinguistic information to the delayed CF in that study might have improved the performance of the delayed CF condition.

as a resource that can be drawn upon when justifying CF timing choices to themselves, their students, or to those evaluating their pedagogy. The literature can also be drawn upon by teacher trainers when educating teacher candidates about the role of CF timing in facilitating L2 grammatical development.

Turning to future CF timing research, it should investigate what causes the differences in findings in CF timing studies. Are these mixed findings due to different grammatical features, learning contexts, learner proficiency levels, and/or CF types interacting differently with CF timing? That research should employ rigorous methodology that avoids confounding CF type and timing and includes no-CF control groups. Furthermore, the CF timing constructs in those studies must be well-defined. In fact, one research question that needs investigation is whether delayed CF is a monolithic construct. That is, are there empirical differences in the effects of end-of-task, end-of-class, and subsequent-day delayed CF? Moreover, more long-term CF timing studies should also be conducted to determine whether the effects found in one-off studies are maintained over longer time periods. In addition, it would be interesting to conduct descriptive research to investigate when teachers provide feedback in authentic L2 classrooms. Finally, future CF timing researchers should follow Arroyo and Yilmaz (2018) in making their materials available, so that their studies can be easily replicated.

References

Aljaafreh, A. L. I. & Lantolf, J. P. (1994). Negative feedback as regulation and second language learning in the Zone of Proximal Development. *Modern Language Journal*, 78(4), 465–483.

Anderson, J. (1982). Acquisition of cognitive skill. *Psychological Review*, 89(4), 369–406.

Arroyo, D. C. & Yilmaz, Y. (2018). An open for replication study: The role of feedback timing in synchronous computer-mediated communication. *Language Learning*, https://doi.org/10.1111/lang.12300.

Azad, M. H. C, Farrokhi, F. & Zohrabi M. (2018). Corrective feedback, spoken accuracy and fluency, and the Trade-off Hypothesis. *International Journal of Instruction*, 11(2), 465–482.

Bitchener, J. & Storch, N. (2016). The cognitive perspective on written CF for L2 development. In J. Bitchener & N. Storch (eds.), *Written corrective feedback for L2 development* (pp. 10–33). Bristol: Multilingual Matters.

Bransford, J. D., Brown, A. L. & Cocking, R. R. (eds.). (2000). *How people learn: Brain, mind, experience, and school (expanded edn.)*. Washington, DC: The National Academies Press. https://doi.org/10.17226/9853.

Carroll, S. & Swain, M. (1993). Explicit and implicit negative feedback: An empirical study of the learning of linguistic generalizations. *Studies in Second Language Acquisition*, 15(3), 357–386.

Cowan, N. (1995). *Attention and memory: An integrated framework.* New York: Oxford University Press.

DeKeyser, R. (1998). Beyond focus on form: Cognitive perspectives on learning and practising second language grammar. In C. Doughty & J. Williams (eds.), *Focus on form in classroom second language acquisition* (pp. 42–63). New York: Cambridge University Press.

(2007). *Practice in a second language: Perspectives from applied linguistics and cognitive psychology.* New York: Cambridge University Press.

Doughty, C. (2001). Cognitive underpinnings of focus on form. In P. Robinson (ed.), *Cognition and second language instruction* (pp. 206–257). New York: Cambridge University Press.

Doughty, C. & Varela, E. (1998). Communicative focus on form. In C. Doughty & J. Williams (eds.), *Focus on form in classroom second language acquisition* (pp. 114–138). Cambridge: Cambridge University Press.

Evans, N. W., Hartshorn, K. J. & Strong-Krause, D. (2011). The efficacy of dynamic written corrective feedback for university-matriculated ESL learners. *System*, 39(2), 229–239.

Farmani, R., Akbari, O. & Ghanizadeh, A. (2017). The impact of immediate and delayed error correction on Iranian EFL learner's motivation. *European Journal of Foreign Language Teaching* 2(3), 76–86.

Gass, S. (1997). *Input, interaction, and the second language learner.* New York: Routledge.

Hartshorn, K. J., Evans, N. W., Merrill, P. F., Sudweeks, R. R., Strong-Krause, D. & Anderson, N. J. (2010). Effects of dynamic corrective feedback on ESL writing accuracy. *TESOL Quarterly*, 44(1), 84–109.

Henshaw, F. (2011). Effects of feedback timing in SLA: A computer assisted study on the Spanish subjunctive. In C. Sanz & R. Leow (eds.), *Implicit and explicit language learning: Conditions, processes, and knowledge in SLA and bilingualism* (pp. 85–99). Washington, DC: Georgetown University Press.

Hulstijn, J. H. & de Graaff, R. (1994). Under what conditions does explicit knowledge of a second language facilitate the acquisition of implicit knowledge? A research proposal. *AILA Review*, 11, 97–112.

Hupbach, A., Gomez, R., Hardt, O. & Nadel, L. (2007). Reconsolidation of episodic memories: A subtle reminder triggers integration of new information. *Learning & Memory*, 14(1–2), 47–53.

Kang, E. Y. & Han, Z. (2015). The efficacy of written corrective feedback in improving L2 written accuracy: A meta-analysis. *Modern Language Journal*, 99, 1–18.

Lantolf, J. P. (2000). Second language learning as a mediated process. *Language Teaching*, 33(2), 79–96.

Lavolette, E., Polio, C. & Kahng, J. (2015). The accuracy of computer-assisted feedback and students' responses to it. *Language, Learning & Technology*, *19*(2), 50–68.

Li, S. (2010). The effectiveness of corrective feedback in SLA: A meta-analysis. *Language Learning*, *60*(2), 309–365.

Li, S., Ellis, R. & Zhu, Y. (2016). The effects of the timing of corrective feedback on the acquisition of a new linguistic structure. *Modern Language Journal*, *100*(1), 276–295.

Long, M. H. (1977). Teacher feedback on learner error: Mapping cognitions In H. D. Brown, C. A. Yorio & R. H. Crymes (eds.), *On TESOL '77* (pp. 278–293). Washington, DC: TESOL.

Lyster, R. (2004). Differential effects of prompts and recasts in form-focused instruction. *Studies in Second Language Acquisition*, *26*(3), 399–432.

Lyster, R. & Saito, K. (2010). Oral feedback in classroom SLA: A meta-analysis. *Studies in Second Language Acquisition*, *32*(2), 265–302.

Mackey, A. & Goo, J. (2007). Interaction research in SLA: A meta-analysis and research synthesis. In A. Mackey (ed.), *Conversational interaction in second language acquisition: A collection of empirical studies* (pp. 407–452). Oxford: Oxford University Press.

Morris, D. D., Bransford, J. D. & Franks, J. J. (1977). Levels of processing versus transfer appropriate processing. *Journal of Verbal Learning and Verbal Behavior*, *16*(5), 519–533.

Nader, K. & Einarsson, E. O. (2010). Memory reconsolidation: An update. *Annals of the New York Academy of Sciences*, *1191*, 27–41.

Nassaji, H. (2017). Oral negotiation in response to written errors. In H. Nassaji & E. Kartchava (eds.), *Corrective feedback in second language teaching and learning: Research, theory, applications, implications* (pp. 114–128). New York: Routledge.

National Research Council (2000). *How people learn: Brain, mind, experience, and school* (expanded ed.). Washington, DC: The National Academies Press. https://doi.org/10.17226/9853.

Quinn, P. (2014). Delayed versus immediate corrective feedback on orally produced passive errors in English. Unpublished doctoral dissertation, University of Toronto, Canada.

Quinn, P. & Nakata, T. (2017). The timing of oral corrective feedback. In H. Nassaji & E. Kartchava (eds.), *Corrective feedback in second language teaching and learning: Research, theory, applications, implications* (pp. 35–47). New York: Routledge.

Rahimi, A. & Vahid Dastjerdi, H. (2012). Impact of immediate and delayed error correction on EFL learners' oral production: CAF. *Mediterranean Journal of Social Sciences*, *3*(1), 45–54.

Ranta, L. & Lyster, R. (2007). A cognitive approach to improving immersion students' oral language abilities: The awareness-practice-feedback sequence. In R. M. DeKeyser (ed.), *Practice in a second language:*

Perspectives from applied linguistics and cognitive psychology (pp. 141–160). Cambridge: Cambridge University Press.

Rolin-Ianziti, J. (2010). The organization of delayed second language correction. *Language Teaching Research, 14*(2), 183–206.

Sheen, Y. (2007). The effects of corrective feedback, language aptitude, and learner attitudes on the acquisition of English articles. In A. Mackey (ed.), *Conversational interaction in second language acquisition* (pp. 301–322). Oxford: Oxford University Press.

(2010). Differential effects of oral and written corrective feedback in the ESL classroom. *Studies in Second Language Acquisition, 32*(2), 203–234.

Shintani, N. & Aubrey, S. (2016). The effectiveness of synchronous and asynchronous written corrective feedback on grammatical accuracy in a computer-mediated environment. *Modern Language Journal, 100*(1), 296–319.

Siyyari, M. (2005). A comparative study of the effect of implicit and delayed, explicit focus on form on Iranian EFL learners' accuracy of oral production. Unpublished MA thesis, Iran University of Science and Technology, Tehran, Iran.

Spada, N. & Lightbown, P. M. (2008). Form-focused instruction: Isolated or integrated? *TESOL Quarterly, 42*(2), 181–207.

Truscott, J. (1996). The case against grammar correction in L2 writing classes. *Language Learning, 46*(2), 327–369.

Van Beuningen, C. G., De Jong, N. H. & Kuiken, F. (2012). Evidence on the effectiveness of comprehensive error correction in second language writing. *Language Learning, 62*(1), 1–41.

Varnosfadrani, A. D. (2006). A comparison of the effects of implicit / explicit and immediate /delayed corrective feedback on learners' performance in tailor-made tests. Unpublished Ph.D. thesis, University of Auckland, New Zealand.

Wajnryb, R. (1990). *Grammar dictation*. Oxford: Oxford University Press.

Walker, M. P., Brakefield, T., Hobson, J. A. & Stickgold, R. (2003). Dissociable stages of human memory consolidation and reconsolidation. *Nature, 425*(6598), 616–620.

Williams, J. (2012). The potential role (s) of writing in second language development. *Journal of Second Language Writing, 21*(4), 321–331.

Yang, Y. & Lyster, R. (2010). Effects of oral production practice and feedback on EFL learners' acquisition of regular and irregular past-tense forms. *Studies in Second Language Acquisition, 32*(2), 235–263.

16

Explicit and Implicit Oral Corrective Feedback

Rod Ellis

Explicit and Implicit Corrective Strategies

Researchers have investigated two dimensions of corrective feedback (CF): (1) input-providing versus output-prompting and (2) explicit versus implicit. The focus of this chapter is on the latter distinction, which is defined as follows:

> An explicit feedback move is one that makes it clear to the learner that a correction has been made or is needed while an implicit move is one where the corrective force is masked because it is potentially performing some other function (e.g. topic continuation or the negotiation of meaning).

Table 16.1 shows the strategies generally considered to be explicit or implicit. However, while to some extent it is possible to classify the main feedback strategies in terms of whether the corrective force is overt or covert (most clearly in the case of explicit correction and metalinguistic cue), for many of the strategies (recasts in particular) this is not possible because variants of these strategies can be more or less explicit. This important point is taken up in a later section of this chapter.

I will begin by examining the theoretical significance of explicit/implicit CF. I will then discuss a number of key issues that comparisons of these two kinds of CF need to take account of. This will lead into a review of the research that has investigated explicit/implicit CF.

Theoretical Significance of Explicit/Implicit Corrective Feedback

The rationale for corrective feedback draws on a number of cognitive-interactionist theories and hypotheses – the Interaction Hypothesis (Long,

Table 16.1 *Explicit and implicit corrective strategies*

Dimension	Corrective strategies
Explicit	Direct correction – e.g., *No, not "goed."*
	Explicit correction – e.g., *"Went" not "goed."*
	Elicitation – e.g., *The man ___?*
	Metalinguistic clue – e.g., *You need the correct past tense form.*
	Metalinguistic explanation – e.g., *"Go" is an irregular verb so you can't say "goed"; you need the irregular verb form "went."*
Implicit	Recast – e.g., S1: *The man goed home.*
	S2: *The man went home.*
	Clarification request – e.g., S1: *The man goed home.*
	S2: *Sorry?*
	Repetition – e.g., S1: *The man goed home.*
	S2: *The man goed home.*

1996), the Output Hypothesis (Swain, 1995), Schmidt's Noticing Hypothesis (Schmidt, 2001), Skill-learning Theory (DeKeyser, 1998) and Carroll's (2001) Autonomous Induction Theory. In addition, more recently the role of working memory (Ellis, 2001) and other learner factors, such as anxiety, have been invoked to explain differences in learners' ability to benefit from CF.

These theories have contributed to the debate regarding the effectiveness of different feedback strategies. According to Long (1996, 2007), recasts are effective precisely because they are implicit and cater to implicit learning.[1] He considers them the ideal way of conducting the focus on form that he sees as essential for connecting linguistic form to meaning in ways that promote acquisition. Recasts provide the learner with both negative evidence (i.e., they indicate there is a linguistic problem) and positive evidence (i.e., they provide the correct linguistic form) and encourage cognitive comparison (Doughty, 2001) by juxtaposing the learners' incorrect form with the correct form. Finally, according to Long, learners are likely to be strongly motivated to attend to recasts because they help learners to say what they want to say. Long is doubtful about the value of prompts such as metalinguistic clue and elicitation because they do not provide positive evidence, and so, while they may help learners to increase control over partially acquired forms, they do not help them to acquire new linguistic features. Prompts do push learners to repair their errors, but Long considers repair unimportant for acquisition. Lyster (1998) puts forward an alternative point of view. He argues that recasts often fail to provide negative evidence because learners do not recognize their corrective force (i.e., they are too implicit). Prompts, on the other hand, are more clearly corrective, and the repair work they lead to is important for acquisition. Lyster draws on skill learning theory to suggest that prompts afford learners the practice they need to convert declarative into procedural

---

[1] More recently, however, Long (2015) has recognized that explicit types of feedback can also play an important part as long as they occur in response to a problem that arises during a communicative exchange.

knowledge. This debate on the relative efficacy of recasts and prompts was revisited in Mackey and Goo (2007) and Lyster and Ranta (2013). It has motivated several experimental studies comparing recasts and prompts (see Chapter 9, this volume).

A careful inspection of these arguments in support of recasts and prompts indicates that in fact they do not rest entirely on whether the feedback is input-providing or output-prompting but also on whether it is explicit or implicit. Recasts are in general seen as implicit (but see the following section) whereas many prompts (e.g. explicit correction; elicitations; metalinguistic cues; metalinguistic explanation) are explicit. Thus the debate might be reframed in terms of the explicit/implicit distinction. Crucial to this reframing is Schmidt's Noticing Hypothesis (2001). This claims that intake and learning generally occur only when learners pay conscious attention to linguistic form. It provides an argument in favour of explicit types of feedback as learners are more likely to notice a correction if the corrective force is made salient. Recasts may go unnoticed. Schmidt (2001) is ambivalent as to whether a higher level of awareness involving understanding of a grammatical rule or regularity involved in the correction is necessary for acquisition but acknowledges that it may help. One way in which it may do so is through the explicit knowledge that results from understanding the reason for a correction. There are strong theoretical arguments to support the role that explicit knowledge plays in the acquisition of implicit knowledge (see Ellis, 1994; Ellis, 2005). This being so, it would seem that explicit feedback, especially perhaps if it involves metalinguistic information, might be more beneficial than implicit feedback. Cognitive theories, therefore, lend support to implicit CF but on balance they point to the superiority of explicit CF, which makes noticing and awareness at the level of understanding more likely to occur.

Carroll's (2001) Autonomous Induction Theory also points to an advantage for explicit feedback. Carroll argues that feedback can only work for acquisition if learners recognize that they are being corrected. She also notes that learners must be able to locate the error they have committed and that most indirect forms of feedback do not help them to do this. In order for learners to correct their errors following feedback they need to be able to detect the errors and then compare their erroneous forms with the target phonological forms. From this perspective, an explicit correction where the corrective force is directly signalled and the target phonological form provided is ideal.

Individual learner factors mediate the effect of CF. Models of working memory (WM) (e.g., Baddeley, 2000) have been used to investigate the role that both phonological short-term memory (PSTM) responsible for the temporary storage of information and executive memory (EM) involved in the analysis of this information play in the various cognitive tasks involving language. However, applying these models to CF is not straightforward (see Li, 2013; Yilmaz, 2013b). One possibility is that learners with higher PSTM capacity will find it easier to process recasts than those with lower PSTM. Another possibility is that EM will help learners to process metalinguistic feedback. However, there is an alternative possibility, namely that the provision of explicit information about a linguistic feature – as in metalinguistic cues and metalinguistic explanation – will level out differences in EM and language analytical ability in learners allowing all students to benefit equally. Language anxiety (Horwitz, 2001) may also affect learners' ability to process CF. Corrective feedback is often seen as anxiety-provoking and teachers are often exhorted to conduct it with care (Ur, 1996). All CF is potentially face-threatening and thus may arouse anxiety but implicit CF, where the corrective force is disguised, may cause less anxiety than explicit CF, where the corrective force is overt. CF may also generate anxiety when it pushes learners to self-correct, as anxiety often arises from fear of production in the L2 (Woodrow, 2006). It could be considered, therefore, more likely to occur with output-prompting CF.

Sociocultural theory affords a totally different perspective on CF. Where cognitive-interactionist theories have been utilized to develop cases for specific feedback strategies, sociocultural theory emphasizes the importance of engaging learners in a collaborative manner and of ensuring that feedback is tailored to the individual learner's developmental level (Aljaafreh & Lantolf, 1994; Poehner, 2008). The aim of CF from a sociocultural perspective, therefore, is to assist in the construction of Zones of Proximal Development; that is, to enable learners to achieve self-regulation by helping them to correct their own errors. Thus there is no "best" type of CF; the provision of CF depends on the individual learner and the specific linguistic feature involved and should provide the least assistance needed for the learner to self-correct. One way of defining the level of help needed is in terms of how explicit or implicit the CF is.

Some Key Definitional Issues

I have already pointed out that the explicit/implicit dimension of CF is confounded with the input-providing/output-prompting dimension. Direct correction, elicitation, and metalinguistic clues (all explicit strategies) are output-prompting, but recasts (the most common and frequently researched implicit strategy) are input-providing. Thus comparative studies investigating these strategies (e.g., Ammar & Spada, 2006; Lyster, 2004; Nassaji, 2009) cannot say for certain whether any differential effect on acquisition is due to the explicit/implicit or the input-providing/output-prompting dimension of CF. Ideally, then, to investigate the effect that the explicitness has on acquisition it is necessary to compare an input-providing explicit strategy (e.g., explicit correction) with an input-providing implicit strategy (e.g., recasts) or, alternatively, an explicit output-prompting strategy (e.g., elicitation) with an implicit output-prompting strategy (e.g., clarification request). However, this is not the way that most researchers have proceeded. Perhaps, from the perspective of the classroom, mixing strategies is desirable. However, it is problematic when it comes to testing theories of L2 acquisition. Whereas some theories emphasize the importance of explicitnesss, other theories emphasize the importance of input or pushed output. Only studies that avoid confounding the two dimensions of CF can address theory-based hypotheses.

The second issue concerns the definitions of explicit and implicit feedback. Li (2013) rightly argued that it is essential to decide whether the distinction is made from the perspective of the instructor/researcher or the learner. This is because what is implicit or explicit from the perspective of the former may be perceived differently by the learner. From the perspective of instruction, the difference depends on whether the feedback is intended to *direct* or just *attract* attention to the linguistic form. From the perspective of the learner, it depends on whether the learner just pays brief attention to the target of the feedback or also develops conscious understanding of the nature of the error that has been committed. Li argued that explicit/implicit feedback needs to be defined from the perspective of instruction. This is, in fact, what all the studies that have investigated this distinction have done and is the position that informs this chapter. Nevertheless, it is also clearly important to also investigate the learner's perspective. A number of studies (e.g., Egi, 2007; Mackey, 2006) have done this, using retrospective interviews to examine to what extent learners became aware of the feedback they received and the nature of this awareness.

There is wide agreement among researchers that the difference between explicit and implicit feedback is continuous rather than dichotomous. This is the third issue. On what basis can the different feedback types be placed on the continuum? Figure 16.1 from Lyster and Saito (2010) constitutes one proposal. This classification of the various feedback strategies is helpful because it takes into account the input-providing and output-prompting dimension. Lyster and Saito acknowledge, however, that the classification of prompts "is rather crude and open to further refinement" (p. 279). Classifying strategies in terms of their level of explicitness is also problematic because each strategy can vary in terms of whether it directs

Figure 16.1 The explicit/implicit continuum (from Lyster & Saito, 2010, p. 278)

or attracts attention to the target form. This is the fourth issue and the most problematic.

Recasts are generally held to be implicit, but as Ellis and Sheen (2006) noted, they can vary enormously and in many cases become quite explicit. Table 16.2 lists those characteristics that make a recast explicit or implicit. Loewen and Philp (2006) reported that the recasts in the learners they investigated were typically of the explicit kind – that is, they were short, involved just one change, were declarative in form, and included prosodic stress on the erroneous form. This points to the danger of simply treating recasts as invariably implicit and the need for researchers to specify the nature of the recasts that occurred in their study. In fact, this is rarely done (but see Nassaji, 2009). One advantage of a laboratory-based over a classroom-based study is that it is easier to narrowly prescribe the kind of recast investigated – as in Leeman's (2003) study.

It is not just recasts that manifest variety – other types of feedback do so too. Repetitions, typically viewed as implicit, can be in fact become quite explicit if the incorrect forms are stressed. Doughty and Varela (1998) used what they called "corrective recasts" in their study. These consisted of a repetition with prosodic emphasis on the errors followed by full recasts if the learner failed to correct after the repetition. The repetition by itself is arguably explicit and the following recast very clearly so, as can be seen in this example:

L: I think that the worm will go under the soil.
T: I *think* that the worm *will* go under the soil?
L: (no response)
T: I *thought* that the worm *would* go under the soil.
L: I *thought* that the worm *would* go under the soil.

Elicitations can also vary in explicitness. Lyster and Ranta (1997) distinguished three elicitation techniques: (1) elicitation completion (see example in Table 16.1), (2) a question (e.g., *How do we say X in French?*), and (3) asking students to reformulate their utterances (e.g., *Can you say that again?*). (1) and (2) very clearly direct the learner's attention to the

Table 16.2 *Implicit and explicit recasts (based on Loewen & Philp, 2006)*

Implicit recasts	Explicit recasts
Simple feedback exchange involving a single feedback move	Complex feedback exchange involving several feedback moves
No prosodic stress on erroneous form(s)	Prosodic stress on erroneous forms
Interrogative recast	Declarative recast
Full recast	Partial recast
Just one change	Two or more changes

erroneous form, but (3) is more ambiguous as it does not make it clear whether the problem is a linguistic one or the interlocutor's failure to comprehend.

These various issues make investigating the effectiveness of explicit and implicit CF problematic, as is evident in the meta-analyses of corrective feedback studies which I will now turn to.

Meta-analyses of Corrective Feedback Studies

Given the definitional issues discussed in the previous section, great care must be taken when considering what meta-analyses of corrective feedback can tell us about the relative effectiveness of explicit and implicit CF. Plonsky and Brown (2015) note that much depends on how the domain of the meta-analysis is defined. In fact, the domain relevant to the explicit–implicit distinction has been defined quite differently in different meta-analyses.[2]

Of the seventeen meta-analyses of corrective feedback identified by Plonsky and Brown, only three included an analysis of explicit/implicit feedback studies. This was not because this subdomain was not of interest, but either because of insufficient relevant studies or because of the difficulty of determining whether the CF strategies investigated in the primary studies were explicit or implicit. Brown (2016) excluded this subdomain from his meta-analysis on the grounds that "this categorization requires a more detailed analysis of CF types, particularly for recasts" (p. 441) – precisely the point made in the previous section.

Mackey and Goo (2007) included an analysis of the explicit/implicit distinction in their wider analysis of the effects of interaction in general. They calculated effect sizes for three feedback types – recasts, negotiation, and metalinguistic. Recasts were treated as a monolithic construct – "for practical reasons" (p. 413). Negotiation moves included clarification requests, comprehension checks, and confirmation checks. Both categories were viewed as close to the implicit end of the continuum, with metalinguistic feedback (not defined by Mackey and Goo) at the explicit end. There was a large effect size for recasts on immediate tests ($d = 0.96$; SD = 1.04), short-term delayed tests ($d = 1.69$; SD 1.13), and long-term delayed tests ($d = 1.22$; SD 0.85). These effect sizes were considerably larger than for prompts or metalinguistic feedback, but, as Mackey and Goo pointed out, a true comparison was not possible given that there were only four treatment conditions involving the explicit types. Noteworthy in the results for recasts were the very large standard deviations, suggesting

---

[2] The meta-analyses of CF studies considered by Plonsky and Brown (2015) included studies of oral, written, and computer-delivered CF. It should be noted that written and computer-delivered CF occurs off-line and thus is inherently explicit in nature.

considerable variation in their level of effectiveness in different studies, casting doubt on the legitimacy of coding recasts as a single CF type.

Li (2010) acknowledged the difficulty of coding some feedback types as explicit or implicit. However, while acknowledging that recasts vary in explicitness, he elected to include them as an implicit category along with clarification requests, elicitation, and repetition. However, as pointed out above, elicitation is arguably more explicit than implicit, while repetitions can be made explicit if the erroneous linguistic form is stressed. Explicit feedback included metalinguistic feedback, explicit correction, and "any feedback that overtly indicated that the learner's output was not acceptable" (p. 323). Li reported results for immediate post-tests, short-delayed post-tests, and long-delayed post-tests. The results for implicit feedback were 0.542, 0.444, 0.544 and for explicit feedback 0.693, 0.608, 0.444. These results point to a superiority of explicit feedback in immediate and short-term delayed tests but of implicit feedback in long-term delayed tests. However, Li noted that in three out of four studies involving explicit feedback the feedback was provided in mechanical drills where learners were likely to be strongly oriented to form. Given the problems of categorizing feedback as explicit and implicit – which Li acknowledged – it is difficult to see what conclusions can be drawn from this meta-analysis.

Whereas both Mackey and Goo's and Li's meta-analyses included both laboratory-based and classroom-based studies, Lyster and Saito's (2010) meta-analysis was restricted to classroom-based studies. While acknowledging that the explicit/implicit distinction is a continuum (see Figure 16.1 above), they elected to classify feedback strategies into explicit and implicit types while also including a separate category for prompts. Between-group comparisons resulted in $d = 0.53$ for recasts, 0.83 for prompts, and 0.84 for explicit correction. Within group comparisons (i.e. pre- to post-test) were recasts ($d = 0.70$), prompts ($d = 1.14$), and explicit correction ($d = 0.60$).

Perhaps the one clear conclusion possible from these meta-analyses is that both explicit and implicit feedback have a positive effect on acquisition in both the short term and the longer term. However, the relative effectiveness of explicit and implicit feedback remains unclear, as the results of the meta-analyses differ considerably. This is not surprising given that the domain was defined quite differently. The authors of these meta-analyses demonstrate an understanding of the difficulties of classifying CF types into explicit and implicit, but they did not overcome them. Arguably, the time is not yet ripe for meta-analysing studies of explicit/implicit feedback. In the following sections, therefore, I will resort to a more traditional narrative review of the research beginning with descriptive studies and then moving on to experimental studies.

Descriptive Studies of CF in Classrooms

CF is not restricted to classroom settings, but it is ubiquitous in them. Not surprisingly, then, a number of studies have investigated what happens when teachers correct their students. Much of the earliest research was descriptive in nature, the aim being to develop typologies of CF strategies (Allwright, 1975; Chaudron, 1977; Long 1977). The most cited descriptive study is Lyster and Ranta (1997), which investigated CF in French immersion classrooms in Canada. This identified a set of main CF strategies (those shown in Table 16.1) and reported the frequency of each along with the frequency of uptake-with-repair (i.e., learner production of the correct linguistic form in response to CF). Recasts were the most frequent type but also the least likely to be accompanied with uptake-with-repair. Prompts such as elicitations and metalinguistic cues were much less frequent but resulted in a higher level of uptake-with-repair. It was this finding that led Lyster (1998) to argue that prompts were preferable to recasts. Sheen (2004) compared the frequency of different CF strategies in four instructional contexts (Canada immersion; Canada ESL; New Zealand ESL; Korea EFL). Recasts were dominant in all four contexts accounting for more than 50 percent of all CF moves. The two next most frequent strategies were clarification requests and elicitations. The general picture, then, is that the students in these classrooms were most likely to experience relatively implicit feedback and that when explicit feedback occurred, it did not include metalinguistic information. Learners were, however, more likely to repair their errors when the feedback was explicit although in the Korea EFL context there was little difference between repair following recasts and explicit correction. Yoshida (2010) investigated the CF that occurred in Japanese as a Foreign Language (JFL) classes at a university in Australia. She also found that recasts were the most common, more than twice as likely to occur as explicit types of correction, and that repair following the recasts was at a similar level to that reported in Lyster and Ranta (1997).

However, differences can arise according to instructional context. Simard and Jean (2011), for example, in a study that compared the CF occurring in ESL and French as a Second Language (FSL) classrooms in Canada found that whereas recasts were the most common in the ESL classes, explicit correction was most common in the FSL classes. Lyster, Saito, and Sato (2013) warned against overgeneralizing the preference for recasts. They noted that recasts were only the most frequent type of CF in six out of the twelve contexts they investigated and suggested that their frequency depends on the social context and the communicative orientation of students. Teachers are also likely to vary in their preferred type of CF.

The problem with these descriptive studies is that they assume the legitimacy of coding CF in terms of the general corrective strategies listed in Table 16.1. But as I have shown, this is problematic. Recasts, in particular, are so varied in form as to defy coding as a single category. A more valid analysis, then, is one that attempts to identify different types of recasts and how the characteristics of the recasts affect the level of repair that occurs. Sheen (2006) undertook such an analysis. She reanalyzed all the recasts from her earlier study. She reported that the majority of recasts involved a single move as opposed to multi-moves and were declarative, isolated (as opposed to incorporated into an utterance that contained additional semantic information), focused on a single word (rather than a phrase or clause), and encoded a single change in the learner's utterance. In other words, the recasts belonged to the explicit end of the explicit/implicit continuum for recasts. She also found that when the recasts were of the more explicit kind, uptake-with-repair was more likely to occur. Loewen and Philp (2006) conducted a similar study, focusing on the recasts that occurred in New Zealand communicative ESL classes, and reported similar results to Sheen's regarding their frequency and repair.

These descriptive studies are insightful. They show that more explicit types of feedback, including explicit recasts, are more likely to lead to learners repairing their utterances. Repair can be taken as evidence of noticing. Thus, these studies support the theoretical claim that noticing is more likely to occur following explicit feedback and, given that noticing can promote acquisition, is more likely to result in learners incorporating the correct forms into their interlanguage systems. However, as Long (2007) noted, learner repair cannot be taken as indicative of acquisition. Also, noticing can occur when there is no repair. Thus, descriptive studies are limited because they cannot shed light on whether CF results in acquisition. For this reason researchers have turned to designs which potentially can show which type of CF is the more effective. Some of these studies simply administered post-tests following classroom exposure to CF to examine the relative effectiveness of the different feedback strategies that occurred. Others were experimental in nature (i.e., they involved pre- and post-tests along with manipulations of the feedback strategies learners experienced). I will begin by considering the former.

Classroom-Based Exposure to CF and Acquisition

One of the very first classroom-based studies to go beyond simply describing corrective feedback was DeKeyser (1993). He investigated two groups of twenty-five Dutch-speaking high school students learning L2 French. One group received extensive explicit corrective feedback during normal class activities, while the other received only limited explicit feedback. The learning of a set of grammatical structures was measured twice by means of three oral communication tasks and a fill-in-the-blank test. DeKeyser reported no differences between the two groups although various individual difference factors (e.g., language aptitude and language anxiety) influenced whether individual learners benefited from the CF.

Havranek and Cesnik (2003) coded 1,700 corrective feedback episodes that occurred in the normal lessons of university students studying English and administered tests of the various linguistic forms that had received feedback. The effectiveness of the CF was in the order of: (1) elicited self-correction, (2) explicit rejection + recast (i.e., explicit correction in Table 16.1), and (3) recasts alone. In other words, the study points to an advantage of explicit types of feedback over implicit.

Loewen (2005) investigated the effect of incidental focus on form (which included various types of CF) on learning. He audio-recorded communicative lessons and identified all episodes where a focus on form occurred. He then designed tailor-made tests, which were administered one day after class and again two weeks later, to assess whether the learners were able to perform the linguistic features that had been targeted in the focus-on-form episodes correctly. The main finding of interest here is that uptake-with-repair consistently predicted test scores. A limitation of this study from the perspective of this chapter, however, is that it did not distinguish focus-on-form episodes that involved CF from other ways in which the classroom participants attended to form (i.e., preemptive focus on form). However, Loewen and Philp (2006) reanalyzed the data focusing just on recasts. They reported that recasts predicted test scores if they had an interrogative intonation, involved a single change, and focused on morphological errors. However, successful uptake of recasts did not predict test scores, bearing out Long's (2007) claim that acquisition does not depend on repair.

The methodological differences in these studies make it difficult to reach any conclusion. DeKeyser's study points to the importance of considering individual difference factors in determining whether explicit CF is effective. Havranek and Cesnik's and Loewen's studies suggest that feedback that is explicit – either in terms of type or in terms of the characteristics of a single type – predicts learning.

Comparative Experimental Studies of Explicit and Implicit Feedback

Early Studies

Ellis, Loewen, and Erlam (2006) reviewed a number of early comparative studies of explicit and implicit feedback.[3] They found that implicit

---

[3] I referred to Ellis et al. (2006) for corrective feedback studies published prior to 2006. For articles published between 2006 and 2017, I consulted major journals, namely *Language Learning, Language Teaching Research, Modern Language Journal, Studies in Second Language Acquisition*, and *System*.

feedback typically consisted of recasts in these studies (Carroll, 2001; Carroll & Swain, 1993; Kim & Mathes, 2001; Leeman, 2003; Lyster, 2004). Muranoi (2000) combined recasts with requests for repetition and in Sanz (2003) the CF consisted of just requests for repetition (i.e. "Sorry, try again"), which arguably lies somewhat closer to the explicit end of the continuum. Explicit feedback was operationalized in even more different ways. In some studies (e.g. Carroll and Swain, 1993; Leeman, 2003) it consisted only of a direct signal that an error had been committed. Other studies included more extensive explicit correction involving metalinguistic information. The explicit feedback in Muranoi's (2000) study was delayed until the learners had completed performing the task.[4] Given these differences, Ellis et al. (2006) were circumspect in reaching any conclusions regarding the relative effectiveness of implicit and explicit CF. However, they did suggest that, overall, the studies pointed to an advantage for explicit feedback, especially explicit feedback including metalinguistic information, while noting that there was also clear evidence of the effectiveness of implicit feedback. Explicit feedback consisting of just indicating a problem was less effective than recasts (Leeman, 2003), while Kim and Mathes (2001), in a replication of Carroll and Swain (1993), reported no difference in the effect of the two kinds of feedback.

Ellis et al. (2006) went on to point out a major limitation of these studies, namely that they utilized tests to measure learning that were biased in favor of explicit CF. Their own study attempted to remedy this design flaw by including tests of both implicit knowledge (e.g., an oral elicited imitation test) and explicit knowledge (i.e., an untimed grammaticality judgment test and a metalinguistic knowledge test). They operationalized implicit feedback as recasts and explicit feedback as repetition of the error plus metalinguistic clues. Despite the fact that learners in the implicit feedback group received more corrections of target structure errors (past tense forms) than those in the explicit group, the explicit feedback was found to be superior to the implicit in both the oral elicited imitation test and the untimed grammaticality judgment test. The recasts in this study were of the partial kind, generally considered to be more explicit than full recasts. The fact that they were still found to be less effective than the explicit feedback suggests that it may not have been the difference in explicitness between the two CF treatments but the fact that the explicit treatment included metalinguistic information. A limitation of their study – and of many subsequent studies – was that the length of the feedback treatment was very short. Ellis et al. speculated that the benefits of recasts may become more apparent over time.

---

[4] When feedback is delayed until the instructional activity has been completed, it is inevitably explicit. See Quinn and Nakata (2017).

Later Studies

One of the points I emphasized earlier was that specific feedback strategies can vary considerably in their level of explicitness depending on how they are performed. Implicit feedback in the later studies always took the form of recasts, but the nature of the recasts differed. In Goo (2012) a complete sentence was recast with declarative intonation; in Ellis (2007) and Yilmaz (2013a), only the erroneous segment was recast; in Yilmaz (2013a) the recasts were segmental but sometimes declarative and sometimes interrogative; in Sheen (2007) the recasts were a mixture of full and partial; in Ammar and Spada (2006) the recasts were sometimes partial and sometimes full, sometimes isolated and sometimes integrated into a longer utterance. The studies also differed in terms of whether learner repair following a correction was allowed. Variation also occurred in how explicit feedback was operationalized. It is clear that although these studies purported to be comparing explicit and implicit CF, in fact they were comparing very different manifestations of these two kinds of feedback.

Six of the studies (Ammar and Spada, 2006; Ellis, 2007; Sheen, 2007; Varnosfradrani and Basturkmen, 2009; Yilmaz, 2013a and 2013b) point to an advantage for explicit types of feedback. Four of these studies were carried out in a laboratory-type setting and two in classrooms. Overall, however, these studies bear out the finding of the earlier studies – explicit feedback results in greater gains in linguistic accuracy than implicit feedback – a finding that holds true for both the laboratory-type and classroom-based studies. The superiority of explicit CF was evident in immediate and delayed tests and also in tests that required both controlled and more automatic processing. One study (Goo, 2012), however, reported no differences in the effect of explicit and implicit feedback. In this study, the learners receiving metalinguistic feedback were prevented from modifying their output even though it would be natural to do so following such a prompt. This may explain why he found no difference between the effects of metalinguistic feedback and recasts. It does point, however, to one reason why explicit feedback is more effective – it typically results in more modified output than recasts (Sheen, 2004). Li (2010) found that learning resulting from implicit feedback was better sustained over time (i.e. in the delayed post-tests), but the other studies found that the effects of explicit feedback were stronger than those of implicit feedback irrespective of the timing of the post-tests.

Explicit feedback might be more effective than implicit, but this is not to say that implicit feedback is not effective. Indeed, a number of studies reported significant differences between recast groups and control groups. Han (2002) reported an interesting quasi-experimental study of recasts in which CF was provided over a period of eight weeks, much longer than in other studies. Han reported that consistent recasting of past tense errors led to improved accuracy. But she also concluded that the recasts were only effective because they met four crucial conditions: (1) individualized attention, (2) a consistent focus on a single grammatical feature, (3) the developmental readiness of the learners, and (4) intensity. Unfortunately, there have been no similar comparative studies of recasts and explicit feedback, and without such studies it is not possible to claim explicit feedback is superior with any certainty.

The later studies also indicate that the relative effectiveness of explicit and implicit feedback depends on extraneous factors. For example, one study (Ammar and Spada, 2006) found that prompts, which were explicit in this study, were more beneficial for low-proficiency learners although this may have been because the learners had received a priori explicit instruction directed at the target structures. Li (2013) reported that low-proficiency learners of Chinese benefited more from implicit CF when the target structure was complex. Ellis (2007) reported a difference in the effect that metalinguistic feedback had on the two structures he investigated; its effects on comparative adjectives and past tense were evident in the immediate post-test but for comparatives only on the delayed post-test. However, the small number of comparative studies and the large of number of potential moderating factors (only two of which – proficiency and structural complexity – figured in these studies) preclude firm conclusions about the moderating role of such factors in determining the relative effectiveness of explicit and implicit feedback.

An alternative to comparative studies is to examine whether differences in how specific corrective strategies are utilized can shed light on the effect that explicitness has on acquisition. Nakatsukasa (2016), for example, compared a group that received recasts with a group that received recasts accompanied by gestures.[5] Nakatsukasa was interested in whether gestures enhanced the effect of recasts, but her study can also be seen as investigating the relative effects of implicit-type recasts – they were of the full type in her study – and recasts made more explicit through gestures. Gestures are likely to attract learners' attention and thus enhance the noticeability of recasts. She reported that only the group that was exposed to recasts with gestures outperformed the control group on the delayed post-test.

Another study that investigated differences in the level of explicitness of the same feedback strategies was Nassaji (2009). Learners in this study first wrote a description of pictures. They then interacted with a teacher when performing the same picture task orally. The teachers were instructed to provide feedback on the errors that occurred in accordance with their normal practice. Following this, the learners were given the written text they had completed at the start and asked to correct any errors in it. This was repeated two weeks later. To investigate the effects of the feedback,

---

[5] Wang and Loewen (2016) report a study that shows that various nonverbal behaviors accompany teachers' use of corrective feedback in classrooms.

Table 16.3 *Implicit and explicit recasts and prompts (based on Nassaji, 2009)*

	Implicit	Explicit
Recasts	Full; no intonational information; confirmatory tone	Partial; stress or rising intonation; additional verbal prompt
Prompts	Error not highlighted; clarification request or repetition; no intonation signal; no metalinguistic clue	Error highlighted by stressing or repeating it; metalinguistic information.

Nassaji first identified all the corrective episodes in the interactions between the learners and the teacher, classified them into recasts and prompts, and then distinguished implicit and explicit variants of each. Table 16.3 summarizes the implicit and explicit versions of the two basic feedback types. The key finding of this study was that more explicit forms of recasts and prompts led to higher rates of written correction than the more implicit forms of both strategy types. Also, interestingly, explicit recasts had a greater effect than explicit elicitations. This study reinforces the general view that explicit feedback is more effective than implicit but, importantly, it avoids making simplistic comparisons of strategy types that are claimed to be explicit or implicit.

All the studies considered so far involved teachers (or researchers) providing the feedback. But learners also provide feedback on each other's errors. Adams, Nuevo, and Egi (2011) asked pairs of learners to perform communicative tasks that made the use of two target structures (English past tense and locatives) essential. They analysed the oral interactions that occurred to identify instances of feedback, distinguishing implicit and explicit types. They reported very few significant correlations between instances of feedback and gains in accuracy in the target structures, as measured by tests, and concluded "feedback may not play as important a role in learner–learner interactions as it plays in NS–learner interactions" (p. 56). Clearly, though, more research is needed before any conclusion can be reached about learner-generated explicit and implicit CF.

Another interesting issue is whether feedback is only (or mainly) effective for just those learners who receive it, or whether it is also effective for learners who overhear it. In a laboratory context learners are receivers. But in a classroom context, they are both receivers and overhearers Yilmaz (2016) compared the effects of very explicit feedback (i.e., "You should say X") on learners who served as receivers (i.e., the feedback was directed at them) and non-receivers (i.e., they just listened to the feedback). Both the receivers and non-receivers benefited from the feedback, with the receivers outperforming the non-receivers on the easy structure (Turkish plurals) but with no difference on the difficult structure (Turkish locatives). It would be interesting to carry out a similar study to investigate the effects of more implicit feedback on receivers and non-receivers.

In all these later studies, the feedback of the intensive kind was directed at pre-selected target structures and for that reason alone was perhaps likely to be attended to even if it is of the implicit kind. In many communicative classrooms, however, feedback is more likely to be extensive, directed at whatever errors happen to arise, so its diffuseness may dilute its effectiveness. Nassaji (2017) compared intensive and extensive recasts. Both groups received a similar number of recasts directed at the target structure (English articles), but only the extensive group received recasts directed at other errors. Nassaji found that the extensive recast group outperformed the intensive recast group in both immediate and delayed post-tests of the target structure and suggested that this might have been because the density of the recasts in the extensive group oriented them to form.

Corrective feedback is highly complex. As these studies illustrate, there are multiple factors that influence its impact. Who provides the correction (learners or teachers), whether the learner is the receiver of the corrections or just an overhearer, and whether the feedback is intensive or extensive along with many other factors potentially impact on the level of explicitness of the feedback and the extent to which it is noticed by learners.

Scaffolded Feedback

The research discussed in the previous sections all belongs to the cognitive-interactionist paradigm. However, as I noted earlier, there is an alternative perspective on the explicit/implicit feedback distinction, which treats it as a continuum rather than a dichotomy and posits that feedback is effective when it is tailored to the individual learner.

Aljaafreh and Lantolf (1994) drew on sociocultural theory to propose a "regulatory scale" consisting of feedback moves from the very implicit to the very explicit. For example, asking learners to find and correct their own errors constitutes an implicit strategy, whereas providing examples of the correct pattern is a highly explicit strategy, and an intermediate level occurs when the tutor indicates the nature of an error without identifying it for the learner. Aljaafreh and Lantolf demonstrated learning by showing that learners needed less explicit feedback to correct particular errors in a later oral conferencing session than they had in an earlier one. In other words, the extent to which learners depended on explicit or implicit forms of feedback when correcting their errors changed, reflecting development in self-regulation.

Building on this idea of graduated feedback, Poehner and Lantolf (2005) developed the idea of "dynamic assessment." They asked learners to construct a past-tense oral narrative in French after watching a short video clip with no feedback or mediation in this first task. But when the task was repeated the mediator "offered suggestions, posed questions, made corrections, and helped them think through decisions concerning selection of lexical items, verb tense, and other language difficulties" (p. 246). This interactive assistance was "highly flexible, emerging from the interaction between the student and the mediator." Poehner and Lantolf showed how the native-speaker interlocutor (the "tester") varied the specific mediating strategies he used at different times with the same learner and also with different learners. For example, with one learner he initially used quite direct clues ("in the past") and subsequently, when addressing the same linguistic problem, more indirect means ("there's something there with the verb").

There is convincing evidence that dynamic assessment is effective (see Poehner, 2008). Nevertheless, it is necessary to ask whether scaffolded feedback is more effective than traditional feedback consisting of a single type – implicit or explicit. Rassaei (2014) compared the effect of scaffolded feedback and recasts on adult Iranian learners' acquisition of *wh*-questions. Scaffolded feedback resulted in higher scores on both an untimed grammaticality judgment test and an oral production test. In another study, Erlam, Ellis, and Batstone (2015) compared the effects of scaffolded feedback and very explicit correction on two grammatical structures – English past tense and articles. A post-test showed that scaffolded feedback resulted in greater gains in accuracy than explicit correction for articles but not for past tense. It is possible, therefore, that when the form–meaning mapping is transparent (as is the case for English past tense), scaffolded feedback is not necessary and a quick explicit correction works just as well.

A strength of the sociocultural research on corrective feedback is that it recognizes that feedback is contingent on the learner's response to it. In research based on cognitive-interactionist SLA, corrective feedback is typically of the one-shot kind. That is, every time an error occurs it is corrected briefly by a predetermined corrective strategy (e.g., recasts or explicit correction). Corrective feedback in this paradigm is something done to a learner. In contrast, in sociocultural theory, corrective feedback is seen as co-constructed between an expert and novice and as continuing over several turns in the search for a Zone of Proximal Development. But there may be times when a simple direct explicit correction may work just as well.

Conclusion

In this review of the research I have endeavored to identify the various issues and factors that researchers interested in investigating explicit/implicit feedback need to consider. Here is a summary:

1. The explicit/implicit distinction is confounded with the input-providing/output-prompting distinction such that it has not really proved possible to determine whether explicit feedback is more effective than implicit because it is explicit or because it is typically output prompting.
2. Each feedback strategy can be realized in different ways. This is most apparent with recasts, which can be more or less implicit, but is also true of explicit strategies. Thus, to investigate the explicit/implicit distinction, it is necessary to go beyond investigating general strategies and examine the level of explicitness of specific strategies.
3. Regarding the latter, the distinction between explicit feedback with and without metalinguistic information may be crucial for understanding what it is about explicit feedback that is important for learning, but this has not been investigated.
4. Both implicit and explicit feedback can only assist acquisition if learners notice the form that is corrected. We need to know what types of feedback and under what conditions feedback induces both noticing (shallow level of awareness) and understanding (deeper level of awareness).
5. The effect of explicit/implicit instruction varies according to the grammatical structure that is the target of feedback. Thus, while implicit feedback may be effective for some structures, explicit instruction may work better for others. For this reason the interaction between feedback type and structural target needs to be properly theorized and investigated.
6. The effectiveness of both implicit and explicit feedback is dependent on conditions relating to how the feedback is carried out – with and without gestures, intensively or extensively, in a single move or multiple moves – and whether it is available to just the receiver or also to overhearers.
7. The effectiveness of implicit and explicit feedback will also be mediated by various learner-internal factors, such as proficiency level, working memory capacity, and language anxiety.
8. While cognitive-interactionist research has been preoccupied with investigating the effects of different feedback strategies, sociocultural researchers have proposed graduated feedback involving the use of a range of strategies that become progressively more explicit in order to facilitate self-regulation in the learner. But questions arise as to whether graduated feedback, which is obviously time-consuming, is always needed.

As I have mentioned several times, corrective feedback is complex both inherently and in terms of the extraneous factors that impact on it. Thus, it is necessary to be cautious in reaching any conclusions about the relative effectiveness of implicit and explicit corrective feedback. That said, the research to date does point to the superiority of explicit feedback over recasts, the implicit strategy that has been most investigated. However, this conclusion is based on short-term experimental studies. What is needed is greater insight into the specific features of explicit feedback that are effective, the conditions under which they are effective, and how learner factors mediate their effectiveness. Given the diversity of factors involved and the complex interactions among them, a better way forward than short-term experimental studies might be longitudinal studies that examine how feedback types, context, and learner profiles interact to facilitate noticing and learning.

References

Adams, R., Nuevo, A. & Egi, T. (2011). Explicit and implicit feedback, modified output and SLA: Does implicit and explicit feedback promote learning and learner–learner interactions? *Modern Language Journal*, 95 (Suppl.), 42–63.

Aljaafreh, A. & Lantolf, J. (1994). Negative feedback as regulation and second language learning in the Zone of Proximal Development. *Modern Language Journal*, 78(4), 465–483.

Allwright, R. L. (1975). Problems in the study of the language teacher's treatment of error. In M. K. Burt & H. D. Dulay (eds.), *On TESOL '75: New directions in second language learning, teaching, and bilingual education* (pp. 96–109). Washington, DC: TESOL.

Ammar, A. & Spada, N. (2006). One size fits all? Recasts, prompts and L2 learning. *Studies in Second language Acquisition*, 28(4), 543–574.

Baddeley, A. D. (2000). The episodic buffer: A new component of working memory? *Trends in Cognitive Sciences*, 4(11), 417–423.

Brown, D. (2016). The type and linguistic foci of oral corrective feedback in the L2 classroom: A meta-analysis. *Language Teaching Research*, 20(4), 436–458.

Carroll, S. (2001). *Input and evidence: The raw material of second language acquisition*. Amsterdam: John Benjamins.

Carroll, S. & Swain, M. (1993). Explicit and implicit negative feedback: An empirical study of the learning of linguistic generalizations. *Studies in Second Language Acquisition*, 15(3), 357–386.

Chaudron, C. (1977). A descriptive model of discourse in the corrective treatment of learners' errors. *Language Learning*, 27(1), 29–46.

DeKeyser, R. (1993). The effect of error correction on L2 grammar knowledge and oral proficiency. *Modern Language Journal*, 77(4), 501–514.

 (1998). Beyond focus on form: Cognitive perspectives on learning and practicing second language grammar. In C. Doughty and J. Williams (eds.), *Focus on Form in Second Language Acquisition* (pp. 42–63). Cambridge: Cambridge University Press.

Doughty, C. (2001). Cognitive underpinnings of focus on form. In P. Robinson (ed.), *Cognition and second language instruction* (pp. 206–257). Cambridge: Cambridge University Press.

Doughty, C. J. & Varela, E. 1998. Communicative focus on form. In C. Doughty & J. Williams (eds.), *Focus on form in classroom second language acquisition* (pp. 114–138). Cambridge: Cambridge University Press.

Egi, T. (2007). Interpreting recasts as linguistic evidence. *Studies in Second Language Acquisition*, 29(4), 511–537.

Ellis, N. C. (2001). Memory for language. In P. Robinson (ed.), *Cognition and second language instruction* (pp. 33–68). Cambridge: Cambridge University Press.

(2005). At the interface: How explicit knowledge affects implicit language learning. *Studies in Second Language Acquisition*, 27(2), 305–352.

Ellis, R. (1994). A theory of instructed second language acquisition. In N. Ellis (ed.), *Implicit and explicit learning of languages* (pp. 79–114). San Diego: Academic Press.

(2007). The differential effects of corrective feedback on two grammatical structures. In A. Mackey (ed.), *Conversational interaction in second language acquisition* (pp. 339–360). Oxford: Oxford University Press.

Ellis, R., Loewen, S. & Erlam, R. (2006). Implicit and explicit corrective feedback and the acquisition of L2 grammar. *Studies in Second Language Acquisition*, 28(2), 339–368.

Ellis, R. & Sheen, Y. (2006). Re-examining the role of recasts in SLA. *Studies in Second Language Acquisition*, 28(4), 575–600.

Erlam, R., Ellis, R. & Batstone, R. (2013). Oral corrective feedback on L2 writing: Two approaches compared. *System*, 41(2), 257–268.

Goo, J. (2012). Corrective feedback and working memory capacity in interaction-driven L2 learning. *Studies in Second Language Acquisition*, 34(3), 445–474.

Han, Z. 2002. A study of the impact of recasts on tense consistency in L2 output. *TESOL Quarterly*, 36(4), 543–572.

Havranek, G. & Cesnik, H. (2003). Factors affecting the success of corrective feedback. In S. Foster- Cohen & A. Nizegorodzew (eds.), *EUROSLA yearbook (Vol. I*, pp. 99–122). Amsterdam: John Benjamins.

Horwitz, E. K. (2001). Language anxiety and achievement. *Annual Review of Applied Linguistics*, 21(1), 112–127.

Kartchava, E. & Ammar, A. (2014). The noticeability and effectiveness of corrective feedback in relation to target type. *Language Teaching Research*, 18(4), 428–452.

Kim, H. & Mathes, G. (2001). Explicit vs. implicit corrective feedback. *The Korea TESOL Journal*, 4(1), 1–15.

Leeman, J. (2003). Recasts and L2 development: Beyond negative evidence. *Studies in Second Language Acquisition*, 25(1), 37–63.

Li, S. (2010). The effectiveness of corrective feedback in SLA: a meta-analysis. *Language Learning*, 60(2), 309–365.

(2013). The interactions between the effects of implicit and explicit feedback and individual differences in language analytical ability and working memory. *Modern Language Journal, 97*(3), 634–654.

Loewen, S. (2005). Incidental focus on form and second language learning. *Studies in Second Language Acquisition, 27*(3), 361–386.

Loewen, S. & Philp, J. (2006). Recasts in the adult English L2 classroom: Characteristics, explicitness, and effectiveness. *Modern Language Journal, 90*(4), 536–556.

Long, M. B. (1977). Teacher feedback on learner error: mapping cognitions. In B. D. Brown, C. A. Yorio & R. H. Crymes (eds.), *Qn TESOL '77 Teaching and learning English as a second language: Trends in research and practice* (pp. 278–293). Washington, DC: TESOL.

Long, M. (1996). The role of the linguistic environment in second language acquisition. In W. Ritchie & T. Bhatia (eds.), *Handbook of second language acquisition* (pp. 469–506). San Diego: Academic Press.

(2007). *Problems in SLA*. Mahwah, NJ: Lawrence Erlbaum.

(2015). *Second language acquisition and task-based teaching*. Malden, MA: Wiley-Blackwell.

Lyster, R. (1998). Recasts, repetition and ambiguity in L2 classroom discourse. *Studies in Second Language Acquisition, 20*(1), 51–81.

(2004). Differential effects of prompts and recasts in form-focused instruction. *Studies in Second Language Acquisition, 26*(3), 399–432.

Lyster, R. & Ranta, L. (1997). Corrective feedback and learner uptake. *Studies in Second Language Acquisition, 19*(1), 37–66.

(2013). Counterpoint piece: The case for variety in corrective feedback research. *Studies in Second Language Acquisition, 35*(1), 167–184.

Lyster, R. & Saito, K. (2010). Oral feedback in classroom SLA. *Studies in Second Language Acquisition, 32* (Special issue 2), 265–302.

Lyster, R., Saito, K. & Sato, M. (2013). Oral corrective feedback in second language classrooms. *Language Teaching, 46*(1), 1–40.

Mackey, A. (2006). Feedback, noticing and instructed second language learning. *Applied Linguistics, 27*, 405–430.

Mackey, A. & Goo, J. M. (2007). Interaction research in SLA: A meta-analysis and research synthesis. In A. Mackey (ed.), *Input, interaction and corrective feedback in L2 learning* (pp. 379–452). Oxford: Oxford University Press.

Muranoi, H. (2000). Focus on form through interaction enhancement: integrating formal instruction into a communicative task in EFL classrooms. *Language Learning, 50*(4), 617–673.

Nakatsukasa, K. (2016). Efficacy of requests and gestures on the acquisition of locative prepositions. *Studies in Second Language Acquisition, 38*(4), 771–799.

Nassaji, H. (2009). Effects of recasts and elicitations in dyadic interaction and the role of feedback explicitness. *Language Learning, 59*(2), 411–452.

(2017). The effectiveness of extensive versus intensive recasts for L2 learning of grammar. *Modern Language Review*, *101*(2), 353–368.

Plonsky, L. & Brown, D. (2015). Domain definition and search techniques in meta-analyses of L2 research (Or why 18 meta-analyses of feedback have different results). *Second Language Research*, *31*(2), 267–278.

Poehner, M. (2008). *Dynamic assessment: A Vygotskian approach to understanding and promoting L2 development*. Berlin: Springer.

Poehner, M. & Lantolf, J. (2005). Dynamic assessment in the language classroom. *Language Teaching Research*, *9*(3), 233–265.

Quinn, P. & Nakata, T. (2017). The timing of oral corrective feedback. In H. Nassaji & E. Kartchava (eds.), *Corrective feedback in second language teaching and learning: Research, theory, applications, implications* (pp. 35–47). Abingdon: Routledge.

Rassaei, E. (2014). Scaffolded feedback, recasts, and L2 development: A sociocultural perspective. *Modern Language Journal*, *98*(1), 417–431.

Sanz, C. (2003). Computer delivered implicit vs. explicit feedback in processing instruction. In B. VanPatten (ed.), *Processing instruction: Theory, research, and commentary* (pp. 241–256). Mahwah, NJ: Lawrence Erlbaum.

Schmidt, R. (2001). Attention. In P. Robinson (ed.), *Cognition and second language instruction* (pp. 3–32). Cambridge: Cambridge University Press.

Sheen, Y. (2004). Corrective feedback and learner uptake in communicative classrooms across instructional settings. *Language Teaching Research*, *8*(3), 263–300.

(2006). Exploring the relationship between characteristics of recasts and learner uptake. *Language Teaching Research*, *10*(4), 361–392.

(2007). The effects of corrective feedback, language aptitude, and learner attitudes on the acquisition of English articles. In A. Mackey (ed.), *Conversational interaction in second language acquisition* (pp. 301–322). Oxford: Oxford University Press.

Sheen, Y. and Ellis, R. (2011). Corrective feedback in language teaching. In E. Hinkel (ed.), *Handbook of research in second language teaching and learning*(2nd ed., pp. 593–610). New York: Routledge.

Simard, D. & Jean, G. (2011). An exploration of L2 teacher's use of pedagogical interventions devised to draw learners' attention to form. *Language Learning*, *61*(3), 759–785.

Swain, M. (1995). Three functions of output in second language learning. In G. Cook and B. Seidlhofer (eds.), *Principle and practice in applied linguistics: Studies in honour of H. G. Widdowson* (pp. 125–144). Oxford: Oxford University Press.

Ur, P. (1996). *A course in language teaching: Practice and theory*. Cambridge: Cambridge University Press.

Varnosfadrani, A. & Basturkmen, H. (2009). The effectiveness of implicit and explicit error correction on learners' performance. *System*, *37*(1), 82–98.

Wang, W. & Loewen, S. (2016). Non-verbal behaviour and corrective feedback in nine ESL university-level classrooms. *Language Teaching Research, 20*(4), 459–478.

Woodrow, L. (2006). Anxiety and speaking English as a second language. *RELC Journal, 37*(3), 308–328.

Yilmaz, Y. (2013a). The relative effectiveness of mixed, explicit and implicit feedback in the acquisition of English articles. *System, 41*(3), 691–705.

(2013b). Relative effects of explicit and implicit feedback: The role of working memory capacity and language analytic ability. *Applied Linguistics, 34*(3), 344–368.

(2016). The role of exposure condition in the effectiveness of explicit correction. *Studies in Second Language Acquisition, 38*(1), 65–96.

Yoshida, R. (2010). How do teachers and learners perceive corrective feedback in the Japanese language classroom? *Modern Language Journal, 94* (2), 293–314.

Part V

Corrective Feedback and Language Skills

17

Corrective Feedback and the Development of Second Language Grammar

Helen Basturkmen and Mengxia Fu

Background

The development of grammar is recognized to be central in learning a second language (L2). Grammar is arguably the linguistic system that has received the most attention by researchers in second language acquisition (SLA). Loewen (2012) notes that much corrective feedback (CF) inquiry has focused on grammatical structures with English question formation and past tense being particularly popular topics. Grammar is also often prioritized in the L2 classroom. Many teachers and learners see grammar as being "at the heart of language use" and the view that language learning is essentially a process of accumulating discrete grammatical items often prevails (Thornbury, 2018, p. 183). There is thus a substantial "coincidence of interest" in grammar between researchers and practicing teachers (Bygate, 1994, p. 257). Corrective feedback in particular is an aspect of grammar teaching where the interests of teachers and researchers coincide (Ellis & Shintani, 2014).

CF can contribute to learning by being a source of positive and negative evidence. Reformulations, such as recasts and explicit correction, provide information regarding the ungrammaticality of learners' utterances (negative evidence that the utterances do not conform to target language norms) and positive evidence which provides the correct forms. Prompts, such as clarification requests and elicitations provide negative evidence only. They signal to learners that something they said does not conform to target language norms and needs modification. CF thus contrasts with other types of instructional input which generally provides positive evidence alone (Ellis & Shintani, 2014).

In this chapter, the term CF is used to refer to responses to learners' utterances that contain actual or perceived errors and the term errors to refer to nontarget-like utterances (Mackey, Park & Tagarelli, 2016). The chapter examines literature that has investigated the effectiveness of the kinds of oral CF typically provided by teachers as measured in oral and/or written tests. The following fundamental questions for the CF research agenda are listed in Mackey et al. (2016, p. 499):

1. Should learner errors be corrected?
2. If so, when should learners' errors be corrected?
3. Which learner errors should be corrected?
4. How should learner errors be corrected?
5. Who should correct learner errors?

The chapter reviews recent research that provides insights linking in particular to questions 1, 2, 3, and 4 in relation to the development of grammar, that is, the learning of morphological and syntactic forms (structures) and form–meaning mappings (Thornbury, 2018). Where possible, we suggest implications for teachers based on cumulative evidence from this body of literature. Although the topic of individual differences is not central to the present review (see reviews of this topic in Part VIII of the present volume), some discussion of proficiency factors is included in our examination of research into the effectiveness of oral CF strategies on the development of grammar.

Descriptive studies have provided taxonomies of the oral error correction strategies teachers use (Chaudron, 1977; Lyster & Ranta, 1997, Ranta & Lyster, 2007). For example, Lyster and Ranta (1997) proposed a six-part taxonomy of CF strategies (see Table 17.1) based on observations of over 18 hours of classroom transcripts.

In a later work, Ranta and Lyster (2007) grouped the strategies, combining recasts and explicit correction in one group named reformulation and the rest (repetition, elicitation, clarification requests, and metalinguistic feedback) in a second group of strategies called prompts. Prompts are also known as output-prompting strategies because the teacher/researcher withholds target forms and encourages learners to correct themselves. Reformulations are defined as input-providing strategies because the teacher/researcher replaces learners' errors with correct forms.

In addition to the distinction between input-providing and output-prompting functions, Ellis (2012) pointed out that CF strategies can be classified according to how obvious they appear as a form of correction. An explicit strategy is the one where the teacher/researcher overtly indicates that the learner has made an error (e.g., *You should say "I played basketball yesterday."*) and an implicit strategy is the one where the teacher/researcher treats an error but in less obvious manner. (e.g., *Pardon?*).

Table 17.1 *Taxonomy of CF strategies based on Lyster and Ranta (1997)*

Strategy	Definition	Example
Explicit	The teacher points out an error directly and provides the correct form.	S: I play basketball yesterday. T: You should say "I played basketball yesterday."
Recast	The teacher reformulates part or all of the initial incorrect utterance.	S: I play basketball yesterday. T: I played.
Clarification request	The teacher indicates that there has been a mistake or misunderstanding.	S: I play basketball yesterday. T: Pardon?
Elicitation	The teacher endeavors to elicit correct forms by pausing before the initial erroneous word or asking students to reformulate their utterances.	S: I play basketball yesterday. T: I … (pause) basketball yesterday.
Repetition	The teacher repeats the erroneous part.	S: I play basketball yesterday. T: Play?
Metalinguistic feedback move	The teacher indicates there is an error in learner's utterance using comments, questions, or metalinguistic knowledge of the error but does not provide the correct form.	S: I play basketball yesterday. T: Present tense or past tense? (Or) It should be past tense.

Table 17.2 *Classification of CF strategies*

	Explicit	Implicit
Output-prompting	Metalinguistic clue Elicitation	Repetition Clarification requests
Input-providing	Explicit correction only	Recasts

Note. This table is adapted from Ellis (2012).

According to Ellis (2012), explicit correction, metalinguistic clues, and elicitation are explicit and recasts, repetition, and clarification requests are implicit. For a review of explicit and implicit feedback, see also Chapter 16. Given input-providing and output-prompting CF types show various explicitness, the two dimensions of CF (see Table 17.2) intertwine with each other.

CF Strategies and Measures of L2 Grammatical Development: Should Errors Be Corrected and, If So, How?

A major area of experimental research concerns the relationship between the different types of CF strategies and grammar learning outcomes. Within this area, many studies have compared the differential effects of output-prompting CF strategies especially prompts (a combination of repetition, clarification requests, metalinguistic clues and elicitation) with input-providing CF strategies, particularly recasts (Ammar, 2008; Ammar & Spada, 2006; Guchte et al., 2015; Loewen & Nabei, 2007; Lyster, 2004; Lyster & Izquierdo, 2009; Nassaji, 2009; Sato & Lyster, 2012; Yang & Lyster, 2010). A few studies (Ellis, 2007; Ellis, Loewen & Erlam, 2006; Goo, 2012; Li, 2014; Loewen & Nabei, 2007; Nassaji, 2009; Sheen, 2007; Yilmaz, 2012) have compared the differential effects of explicit CF (e.g., metalinguistic correction) with implicit CF (e.g., recasts). Some studies (Hawkes & Nassaji, 2016; Li, Zhu & Ellis, 2016; Nassaji, 2017; Quinn, 2014; Yilmaz & Yuksel, 2011; Zhao, 2015) have focused on the effects of recasts which are the most frequent feedback type in classrooms (Lyster & Ranta, 1997). These recasts studies have compared (1) the effects of recasts with no feedback (Hawkes & Nassaji, 2016), (2) the effects of recasts delivered through different communication modes, face-to-face or computer-mediated (Yilmaz & Yuksel, 2011), (3) the effects of recasts on correcting different types of errors such as intensive recasts focusing on errors of a specific target structure and extensive recasts focusing on any errors that emerged incidentally during CF treatment (Nassaji, 2017), (4) the effects of different types of recasts such as explicit recasts (i.e., corrective recasts) involving two feedback moves (first drawing learners' attention to errors through repeating their erroneous utterances with emphasis and then using a recast) and implicit recasts which only include one recast move (Zhao, 2015), and (5) the effects of recasts provided under different timing conditions (Fu, 2019; Li et al., 2016; Quinn, 2014).

Although the studies above investigated different CF strategies, they are all concerned with assessing the effectiveness of the CF strategies in developing learners' grammatical accuracy. For example, Lyster (2004) examined the differential effects of prompts and recasts on the acquisition of French grammatical gender when form-focused instruction was provided. The form-focused instruction (FFI) drew learners' attention to the target structure and asked them to complete some practice activities. The participants were divided into four groups, a recasts+FFI group who received FFI and recasts on their gender errors, a prompts+FFI group who received FFI and prompts on their gender errors, a FFI only group who received FFI but were not provided with any CF, and a control group who did not receive FFI or CF. The four groups' accuracy of using French grammatical gender was measured before (pre-test) and after (post-test) CF treatment. Each pre-or post-test was composed of four tests, two written tests and two oral tests. After comparing the three experimental groups' (recasts+FFI, prompts+FFI, and FFI only) accuracy scores with the control group's scores on the post-tests, it was found that (1) the three experimental groups all outperformed the control group, (2) the prompts+FFI group outperformed the recasts+FFI and FFI only group, and (3) the difference between the recasts+FFI group and the FFI only group was marginal.

Following Lyster (2004), many other studies (Ammar & Spada, 2006; Ellis, 2007; Ellis et al., 2006; Fu, 2019; Goo, 2012; Guchte et al., 2015; Hawkes & Nassaji, 2016; Li, 2014; Li et al., 2016; Loewen & Nabei, 2007; Lyster & Izquierdo, 2009; Nassaji, 2009, 2017; Quinn, 2014; Sato & Lyster, 2012; Sheen, 2007; Yang & Lyster, 2010; Yilmaz, 2012; Yilmaz & Yuksel, 2011; Zhao, 2015) examined the effectiveness of different CF types by measuring learners' grammatical accuracy on written and/or oral tests. Although some studies only used one type of test to measure the efficacy of CF, either written (Goo, 2012; Nassaji, 2009) or oral tests (Sato & Lyster, 2012; Yilmaz & Yuksel, 2011), most studies have used both types of tests (Ammar & Spada, 2006; Ellis, 2007; Ellis et al., 2006; Fu, 2019; Guchte et al., 2015; Hawkes & Nassaji, 2016; Li, 2014; Li et al., 2016; Loewen & Nabei, 2007; Lyster, 2004; Lyster & Izquierdo, 2009; Nassaji, 2017; Quinn, 2014; Sheen, 2007; Yang & Lyster, 2010; Yilmaz, 2012; Zhao, 2015). It is important to note that written and oral tests tend to tap into different types of knowledge. In written tests, learners have opportunities to monitor their production and thus such tests are commonly used to measure explicit knowledge, the type of knowledge that the learner is aware of having and can explain (Basturkmen, 2017; Ellis, 2005). In contrast, in oral tests learners are usually required to use the language spontaneously, and thus such tests are most often used to measure implicit knowledge, tacit knowledge, or the type of knowledge that learners use without awareness and may not be able to explain (Ellis, 2005).

Various types of written tests have been used in the CF literature. Grammaticality judgment tests are the most frequently used type of written tests. These tests require learners to judge the correctness of a set of sentences with/without error correction (Ellis, 2007; Ellis et al., 2006; Fu, 2019; Goo, 2012; Li, 2014; Li et al., 2016; Loewen & Nabei, 2007; Nassaji, 2017; Zhao, 2015). Moreover, error correction tests require learners to identify and correct errors (Amma & Spada, 2006), such as errors in their writings/utterances (Hawkes & Nassaji, 2016; Nassaji, 2009), or to correct errors directly without judging their correctness (Sheen, 2007). There are also production tests which require learners to write sentences (Goo, 2012) or stories (Nassaji, 2017; Sheen, 2007; Yang & Lyster, 2010; Zhao, 2015), multiple-choice tests (Lyster, 2004; Lyster & Izquierdo, 2009; Yilmaz, 2012), fill-in-the-blank tests (Guchte et al., 2015; Lyster, 2004), and tests of metalinguistic knowledge that ask learners to correct underlined errors and provide reasons for their corrections (Ellis, 2007; Quinn, 2014).

A limited range of oral tests have been used. Some studies have used oral production tests which require learners to describe/compare a set of pictures (Ammar & Spada, 2006; Guchte et al., 2015; Loewen & Nabei, 2007; Lyster, 2004; Lyster & Izquierdo, 2009; Nassaji, 2017; Quinn, 2014; Yilmaz, 2012; Yilmaz & Yuksel, 2011) or to describe items using target structures (Lyster, 2004; Lyster & Izquierdo, 2009). Some studies (Ellis, 2007; Ellis et al., 2006; Fu, 2019; Li, 2014; Li et al., 2016; Zhao, 2015) have used elicited imitation tests in which sentences, either grammatical or ungrammatical, are presented one after another. After listening to each sentence, learners first judge if the sentence applies to them based on their situations (e.g., *I ate an apple yesterday*) and then repeat the sentence in correct English. Some studies (Yang & Lyster, 2010; Zhao, 2015) have used story-retelling tests to measure learners' oral performance. One study (Hawkes & Nassaji, 2016) used computerized error correction tests which asked learners to listen to their own utterances, judge the grammaticality of them, and correct the erroneous utterances orally. Note that although oral tests are often used to measure the development of learners' implicit knowledge, Ellis (2005) found that written tests can also be used to measure this type of knowledge. When written tests imposed time pressure on learners, such as timed grammaticality judgment tests (Loewen & Nabei, 2007; Quinn, 2014) and speeded dictation (Sheen, 2007), the time constraints compelled learners to draw on their tactic implicit knowledge instead of conscious explicit knowledge to complete the tests.

In order to understand the overall relationship between CF and the development of L2 grammatical accuracy, Russell and Spada (2006) and Lyster and Saito (2010) synthesized the results reported from empirical studies that investigated the effects of different CF types on promoting L2 grammatical accuracy. Russell and Spada (2006) found that oral and written CF were both beneficial for the development of L2 grammatical accuracy although written CF showed more facilitative effects than oral CF. Russel and Spada (2006) had not compared different oral feedback strategies, which led Lyster and Saito (2010) to address this gap in the research. They compared the effects of prompts, recasts, and explicit feedback in oral feedback through a synthesis of results from fifteen empirical studies. They found that (1) overall CF had moderate positive effects on L2 grammar development, (2) prompts were more beneficial than recasts, and (3) the effects of explicit correction were not significantly different from the other two CF types. These synthesized results suggest that teachers should be encouraged to use oral CF, particularly prompts, to facilitate the development of L2 grammatical accuracy.

Apart from investigating the effects of CF on accuracy development, some studies (Ammar, 2008; Guchte et al., 2015; Hawkes & Nassaji, 2016; Lyster & Izquierdo, 2009; Sato & Lyster, 2012) examined the effects of CF on fluency development as gauged by improvements in learners' speed of processing and production of grammatical structures on oral or written tests. It is important to measure fluency in the development of grammar. According to Skill Acquisition Theory (DeKeyser, 2015), the development of L2 interlanguage involves a transition from controlled knowledge processing (low fluency) to automatic processing (high fluency). Overall, the above studies showed beneficial effects of CF on promoting fluency, but mixed findings were reported regarding which type of CF strategy was more beneficial.

Three studies (Ammar, 2008; Hawkes & Nassaji, 2016; Lyster & Izquierdo, 2009) assessed fluency by recording learners' reaction time which was the average/overall time used by learners to complete each/all testing item(s) in computerized error correction tests (Hawkes & Nassaji, 2016) or computerized multiple-choice tests (Ammar, 2008; Lyster & Izquierdo, 2009). In an error detection test which required learners to judge whether there were any errors in a set of given episodes, Hawkes and Nassaji (2016) found that learners were slightly faster in detecting the errors that had received recasts than the errors that had not received recasts. Ammar (2008) found that the prompts group, the recasts group, and the control group all improved their speed (reduced reaction time) in completing a computerized multiple-choice post-test, and the prompts group achieved significantly higher fluency gains than the recasts group. This result was partially confirmed in Lyster and Izquierdo (2009) who found that both the prompts group and the recasts group completed a computerized multiple-choice test more quickly after receiving CF treatment but there was no significant difference between the recasts and the prompts group.

Two recent studies (Guchte et al., 2015; Sato & Lyster, 2012) provided further evidence regarding the positive effects of CF on fluency development in spontaneous oral production. Sato and Lyster (2012) compared the effects of prompts and recasts on developing learners' overall speech rate (the number of words per minute) in picture description tests. It was found that both the prompts group and the recasts group improved their oral fluency after CF treatment, but there was no significant difference between the two CF groups. Unlike Sato and Lyster (2012), Guchte et al. (2015) adopted a relatively subjective method to assess fluency. They asked a native speaker to rate learners' speech fluency in two picture description tests, which involved the use of a simple morphological structure and a complex syntactic structure respectively, before and after the CF treatment. The results showed that both CF groups improved their speech fluency after receiving the CF treatment; however, the recasts group spoke more fluently than the prompts group in the test focusing on the complex syntactic structure but not in the oral test focusing on the simple morphological structure.

Results from the above empirical studies which have examined fluency development suggest that teachers can be encouraged to use CF to promote learners' speed of processing and producing grammar structures. Teachers may consider selecting CF strategies in relation to types of grammar structures. For example, both recasts and prompts may enhance the speed of producing simple morphology structures while recasts could be more facilitative than prompts in promoting the speed of producing complex syntactic structures.

As has been shown, a good deal of research has assessed whether learners make gains in their accuracy in using grammatical structures. The findings from the meta-analyses described above indicate that CF does have positive effects on grammar in terms of developing accuracy. Oral CF appears to benefit learners' development of grammar compared to control groups who did not receive feedback. Research syntheses (e.g., Li, 2010; Mackey & Goo, 2007) indicate larger long-term effects of CF measured on delayed post-tests compared to the short-term effects of CF measured on immediate post-tests, which may suggest the "long-term pedagogical value of corrective feedback" (Mackey et al., 2016, p. 502). These findings should encourage teachers of the value of CF in accuracy-focused grammar instruction.

Few teachers would question the potential value of CF when the focus of instruction is on developing grammar accuracy. A review of advice for teachers in methodology books (Ellis & Shintani, 2014) suggests such works generally advocate a more positive role for the provision of CF in accuracy compared to fluency activities, such as communicative tasks. For example, Harmer (1983) advises that CF interventions, such as "telling students that they are making mistakes, insisting on accuracy and asking for repetition" (p. 44), should be avoided in fluency activities. Scrivener (2011) recommends that correction is helpful when accuracy is the aim of the activity, but when fluency is the aim, interruptions and corrections can "get in the way of the work" (p. 286) since they impede the flow of communication, which is the aim of the activity. Harmer (2007) writes, "The received view has been that when students are involved in accuracy work, it is part of the teacher's function to point out and correct the mistakes students are making" (p. 143), whereas during communicative activities where the focus is on exchanging messages "it is generally felt that teachers should not interrupt students mid-flow to point out grammatical, lexical or pronunciation error, since to do so drags an activity back to the study of language form or precise meaning" (p. 143). In this perspective, teachers' interruptions during fluency activities to provide better forms of expression can result in students no longer needing to negotiate meaning, a key process in language acquisition. Harmer (2007) recommends that during fluency activities teachers provide feedback on content (rather than language) and refrain from attempts to "untangle language problems" (p. 146) until after the activity. On those occasions during fluency work when teachers do feel a need to provide CF, they should do so using "gentle" forms of correction, such as quick reformulations or prompts and not move into the stage of the students having to get it right.

In light of findings from recent research (Guchte et al. 2015; Sato & Lyster, 2012) indicating the positive effects of CF on fluency development, the provision of CF during fluency activities may be reconsidered. The Counterbalance Hypothesis (Lyster & Mori, 2006) proposes that instructional activities and interactional feedback are likely to be particularly effective when they are in juxtaposition to rather than congruent with a classroom's mainly meaning-focused (or form-focused) orientation because they require a shift in learners' attention and thus additional attentional efforts, which can stimulate interlanguage restructuring and language development. It should be noted that this hypothesis was based on findings from research that adopted learner uptake (the extent to which learners responded to CF) as a measure of interlanguage development, unlike other studies reviewed in this chapter which used results from oral and/or written achievement tests.

The studies reported above involved a range of types of tests whereby gains or development were measured. These test types may be of interest to teachers to assess their students' learning. For example, teachers might consider new ways to assess their learners' grammar learning such as through the use of grammaticality judgment tests or tests of metalinguistic knowledge. If the instruction of a specific structure has included an element of metalinguistic information, the teacher may wish to assess learners' understanding of this information as well as their ability to produce the target structure accurately.

Although research studies have tended to indicate prompts have a greater effect on learning compared to recasts, this does not mean to say that recasts are not effective in the classroom. Findings need to be treated with caution as the research has compared "apples and oranges" or dissimilar strategies (Mackey et al., 2016, p. 504). Prompts tend to elicit modified output, whereas recasts by their nature do not. Modified output is understood to aid learning (Swain, 2005). The best advice to teachers may be to continue to implement a variety of feedback strategies (Mackey et al., 2016).

Grammar Targets: Which Errors Should be Corrected and When?

There is a considerable body of research evidence concerning the role of corrective feedback in learning specific grammatical structures. The vast majority of research studies have concerned learning English as a second or foreign language. Researchers have, for example, examined the effectiveness of CF in learning English articles (Nassaji, 2017; Sheen, 2007), third-person singular possessive determiners (Ammar, 2008; Ammar & Spada, 2006), question formations (Loewen & Nabei, 2007), *that*-trace filter (Goo, 2012), past tense (Ellis, 2007; Ellis et al., 2006; Fu, 2019; Yang & Lyster, 2010), comparative *-er* (Ellis, 2007), passive constructions (Li et al., 2016; Quinn, 2014), embedded questions, and third person *-s* (Zhao, 2015). Relatively fewer studies have examined the effects of CF on learning other second languages. These include the investigation into the effects of CF on learning grammatical gender in French (Lyster, 2004; Lyster & Izquierdo, 2009), dative and comparative structures in German (Guchte et al., 2015), classifiers and aspect marker -*le* in Chinese (Li, 2014), and plural and locative case morphemes in Turkish (Yilmaz, 2012; Yilmaz & Yuksel, 2011).

Saliency

Language teachers may wonder if it is as useful to provide CF on structures that are easy for learners to notice compared to structures that are hard to perceive. Previous CF studies (e.g., Li, 2014; Yang & Lyster, 2010) have been conducted to answer this question, and their results showed the effects of CF strategies changed when the saliency of the target structure varied. Based on the features of grammatical structures and the criteria of structural saliency introduced by previous researchers (Goldschneider & DeKeyser, 2001; Li, 2014), the term *salient structure* is used in this chapter to refer to a structure that can easily be heard or perceived in L2 input, conveys a clear one-to-one form–meaning mapping, or involves easy rule explanations; the term *non-salient structure* is used to refer to a structure that can only be heard or noticed in L2 input with difficulty, conveys an opaque form–meaning mapping, or involves complex rule explanations. Although it is acknowledged that other factors (e.g., position of a structure in treatment tasks) may also influence structural saliency, these will not be considered in the following review. We note that the distinction between salient and non-salient is relative rather than absolute. For example, English possessive determiners are relatively salient because they can be heard in L2 input clearly, their form–meaning mapping is transparent (attribute possession to someone or something), and their rule explanation is easy (agree with the gender of the possessor and come before nouns). In contrast, English articles are relatively non-salient because they are "difficult to notice in many contexts" (Nassaji, 2017, p. 357), and their form–meaning mapping is not straightforward. The indefinite article, for example, can be used in a specific or a non-specific sense (Quirk et al., 1985). Rule explanation is complicated because English articles have a range of uses.

For this review, we divided previous CF studies into three groups based on the saliency of their target structures (see Table 17.3). One group of studies investigated relatively salient structures, including English possessive determiners (Ammar, 2008; Ammar & Spada, 2006), English question formation (Loewen & Nabei, 2007), and English passive construction (Li et al., 2016; Quinn, 2014). Another group of studies examined relatively non-salient structures, including French gender (Lyster, 2004; Lyster & Izquierdo, 2009), English regular past tense -*ed* (Ellis et al., 2006), English *that*-trace filter (Goo, 2012), and English articles (Nassaji, 2017; Sheen, 2007). The third group of studies compared salient and non-salient structures, including English regular past tense -*ed* and comparative -*er* (Ellis, 2007), English irregular and regular past tense (Yang & Lyster, 2010),

Turkish plural and locative case morphemes (Yilmaz, 2012; Yilmaz & Yuksel, 2011), Chinese classifiers and aspect marker -*le* (Li, 2014), German comparative and dative morphemes (Guchte et al., 2015), and English embedded question and third person -*s* (Zhao, 2015). For example, Yang and Lyster (2010) investigated the effects of prompts and recasts on learning a salient (English irregular past tense) and a non-salient structure (English regular past tense). They assigned learners into three groups – a prompts group, a recasts group, and a control group – who received prompts, recasts, and no CF on errors of the salient and the non-salient structure respectively. Learners' knowledge of both types of structures was measured through written narrative tests and story-retelling tests before, immediately after, and two weeks following the CF treatment. The results showed prompts were more facilitative than recasts on the development of the non-salient structure, while prompts and recasts had identical effects on the development of the salient structure.

Most of the studies investigating the effects of CF on the development of salient structures reported beneficial effects of CF (Ammar, 2008; Ammar & Spada, 2006; Li et al., 2016; Loewen & Nabei, 2007). These studies can be further divided into three subgroups, studies investigating the effects of output-prompting (e.g., prompts) and input-providing (e.g., recasts) CF (Ammar, 2008; Ammar & Spada, 2006; Loewen & Nabei, 2007), studies comparing the effects of explicit and implicit CF (Loewen & Nabei, 2007), and studies exploring the timing effects of CF (Li et al., 2016; Quinn, 2014). Studies comparing the effects of output-prompting and input-providing CF on learning a salient structure found that (1) output-prompting CF was more beneficial than input-providing CF (Ammar, 2008; Ammar & Spada, 2006) and (2) output-prompting and input-providing CF were equally effective when the length of CF treatment (half an hour) was relatively short (Loewen & Nabei, 2007). In the same study, Loewen and Nabei (2007) also found that explicit and implicit CF showed identical effects on learning a salient structure. Studies (Li et al., 2016; Quinn, 2014) comparing immediate CF (provided during interaction) and delayed CF (provided after interaction), however, reported contradictory results regarding their effects on learning the same salient structure (passive construction). Quinn (2014) found the timing of CF did not have a significant impact on L2 development although Li et al. (2016) reported that immediate CF was more beneficial than delayed CF.

Overall, positive effects of CF were also reported in the studies targeting non-salient structures, although results about the effects of different CF strategies have not been consistent (Ellis et al., 2006; Goo, 2012; Lyster, 2004; Lyster & Izquierdo, 2009; Nassaji, 2017; Sheen, 2007). These studies can be further divided into three subgroups, studies investigating the effects of output-prompting and input-providing CF (Lyster, 2004; Lyster & Izquierdo, 2009), studies investigating the effects of explicit and implicit CF (Ellis et al., 2006; Goo, 2012; Sheen, 2007), and a study examining the effects of intensive and extensive recasts (Nassaji, 2017). Experimental research comparing the effects of output-prompting and input-providing CF on learning a non-salient structure found that input-providing and output-prompting CF were equally effective (Lyster & Izquierdo, 2009). However, classroom-based research found that output-prompting CF was more effective than input-providing CF (Lyster, 2004). The studies examining the effects of explicit (e.g., metalinguistic feedback) and implicit (e.g., recasts) CF on learning a non-salient structure (Ellis et al., 2006 and Sheen, 2007) found that explicit CF was more effective than implicit CF, while Goo (2012) found explicit CF was as effective as implicit CF. The beneficial effect of CF on the development of non-salient structures was also reported in Nassaji (2017) who examined the effects of intensive and extensive recasts on the acquisition of English articles. Learners were divided into three groups, an intensive recasts group who only received recasts on errors of English articles, an extensive recasts group who received recasts on errors of a wide range of structures including English articles, and a control group who did not receive CF. After comparing the three groups' scores on post-tests, Nassaji (2017) found that the extensive recasts group benefited more than the intensive recasts group as the extensive recasts group outperformed the control group while the intensive recasts group did not.

The studies exploring the effectiveness of different CF strategies on learning both salient and non-salient structures (Ellis, 2007; Guchte et al., 2015; Li, 2014; Yang & Lyster, 2010; Yilmaz, 2012; Yilmaz & Yuksel, 2011; Zhao, 2015) also reported overall beneficial effects of CF, while mixed results were found regarding which type of CF favored which kind of structure. These studies can be further divided into three subgroups, studies comparing the effects of output-prompting and input-providing CF (Guchte et al., 2015; Yang & Lyster, 2010), studies comparing the effects of explicit and implicit CF (Ellis, 2007; Li, 2014; Yilmaz, 2012; Zhao, 2015), and studies examining the effects of communication mode (Yilmaz, 2012; Yilmaz & Yuksel, 2011) on learning a salient and a non-salient structure. The studies comparing the effects of input-providing and output-prompting CF on learning both types of structures found that (1) output-prompting CF was more effective than input-providing CF in promoting the development of non-salient structures (Yang & Lyster, 2010), (2) input-providing CF was as effective as output-prompting CF in facilitating the development of salient structures (Yang & Lyster, 2010), (3) output-prompting CF was more effective than input-providing CF in learning both salient and non-salient structures (Guchte et al., 2015), and (4) input-providing CF had a greater effect on the development of the salient structure compared to the non-salient structure (Guchte et al., 2015).

Studies (Ellis, 2007; Li, 2014; Yilmaz, 2012; Zhao, 2015) comparing the effects of explicit and implicit CF on learning a salient and a non-salient structure also reported mixed results. Ellis (2007) found the non-salient structure benefited more from explicit CF than the salient structure although neither the salient nor the non-salient structure developed when implicit CF was provided. Yilmaz (2012) reported that the salient structure developed more rapidly than the non-salient structure regardless of CF type, but Zhao (2015) found structural saliency did not play a role in the effects of CF when both types of structures benefited equally from explicit and implicit CF. Moreover, Li (2014) found learners' overall language proficiency moderated the effects of different CF on learning both types of structures. That is, for high-proficiency learners, explicit and implicit CF were both effective when learning both types of structures; but for low-proficiency learners, explicit CF was more beneficial than implicit CF when learning both types of structures. In addition to the studies examining the effects of different CF strategies on learning a salient and a non-salient structure, Yilmaz and Yuksel (2011) and Yilmaz (2012) explored the development of both types of structures under two CF communication modes, a face-to-face mode where a researcher provided face-to-face CF and a computer-mediated mode where the researcher provided text-based CF through a chat tool on computers. Yilmaz and Yuksel (2011) found that the salient and the non-salient structure benefited equally from recasts under either mode when the non-salient structure appeared in a salient position (first word in each sentence) in the treatment task. However, when both types of structures appeared in the same word position, Yilmaz (2012) found the salient structure benefited more from CF than the non-salient structure regardless of communication mode.

From this body of research, classroom teachers may note that CF has been found to be effective for both salient and non-salient grammatical structures. It would seem appropriate therefore, on a practical level, that teachers provide CF on both kinds of structures. Research findings across different studies indicate that all types of CF strategy (output-prompting, input-providing, implicit and explicit) are effective for salient and non-salient structures, although findings as to whether one or another strategy is more effective appear mixed. It may thus be recommended that teachers do not adhere to only one type of feedback strategy in provision of feedback on salient and non-salient structures but rather implement various feedback strategies "even if they *think* one kind is the most effective" (Mackey et al., 2016, p. 504). However, results from Li (2014) showed strong evidence that learners' proficiency may influence the effectiveness of CF strategy types. As this indicated that low-proficiency-level learners benefit in particular from explicit feedback, teachers of low-proficiency-level learners could possibly use more explicit strategies more often. Teachers often provide CF on any number of different incorrect grammatical structures. Teachers may thus find encouraging the results from Nassaji (2017) that indicated that the group receiving extensive feedback benefited more than the group receiving feedback on only one structure.

Learners' Prior Knowledge of Grammar Targets

Language teachers may want to know if they should adopt different strategies to correct grammatical errors when learners have limited or good prior knowledge of the grammatical structures. Learners' prior knowledge might influence the efficacy of CF given that Pienemann's *Teachability Hypothesis* (1988) predicts that L2 instruction (e.g., CF) will be facilitative when learners' current developmental level (prior knowledge) is close to the developmental stage of the target structure. A series of studies (Ammar, 2008; Ammar & Spada, 2006; Mackey & Philp, 1998) have investigated the influence of learners' prior knowledge or developmental readiness on L2 learning under different CF conditions. For example, Ammar and Spada (2006) assigned their learners into two groups based on their pre-test scores of English possessive determiners, a high prior knowledge group whose accuracy was higher than 50 percent on pre-tests and a low prior knowledge group whose accuracy was lower than or equivalent to 50 percent on pre-tests. Within each experimental group, there were three subgroups, recasts low/high prior knowledge group, prompts low/high prior knowledge group, and control low/high prior knowledge group. The results showed that the high prior knowledge learners benefited equally from recasts and prompts, while the low prior knowledge learners benefited more from prompts than recasts.

For this review, we grouped previous CF studies based on their participants' pre-test scores (see Table 17.3). Please note that although these studies did not all directly address the question of learners' prior knowledge, they included information on this. As learners achieved an extensive range of pre-test scores (accuracy scores between 0% and 90%), we divided these studies into three groups: studies that recruited learners with limited prior knowledge of a target structure (mean accuracy lower than 10% on pre-tests); with moderate prior knowledge (mean accuracy between 10% and 70% on pre-tests); and with good prior knowledge (mean accuracy higher than 70% on pre-tests). The review found that CF showed overall positive effects on L2 development in studies that recruited learners with limited or moderate prior knowledge of target structures. Although studies recruiting learners with limited prior knowledge of target structures (Guchte et al., 2015; Li et al., 2016; Yilmaz, 2012; Yilmaz & Yuksel, 2011) found CF promoted L2 development, Li et al. (2016) points out that the efficacy of CF might be constrained by learners' developmental readiness. We found that the studies recruiting participants with moderate prior knowledge of target structures also indicated positive effects of CF on L2 grammar development (Ammar, 2008; Ammar & Spada, 2006; Goo, 2012; Guchte et al., 2015; Lyster, 2004; Nassaji, 2017; Sheen, 2007; Yang & Lyster, 2010). However, CF was less effective in studies recruiting participants with good prior knowledge (Ellis, 2007; Ellis et al., 2006;

Loewen & Nabei, 2007; Lyster & Izquierdo, 2009; Zhao, 2015). Loewen and Nabei (2007), for example, investigated the effects of CF on the development of English question formation when learners showed good prior knowledge of the structure on a written pre-test. The results of an untimed, written post-test indicated that CF did not facilitate the development of English question formation.

Suggestions that teachers forgo providing feedback on grammatical structures that they perceive to be well known by their learners may be premature. Further research is needed, especially research that collects evidence from oral tests as well as written tests. However, on the basis of this review, teachers might reflect on their teaching experiences to consider whether they need to provide CF on well-developed structures at all times. Possibly their CF efforts might be more usefully spent in addressing errors in those structures that are new or partially acquired by their learners. This is not to say teachers would no longer help learners with well-developed structures. They could, for example, on occasion require students to record their oral production or gather samples of their written work and ask the students to identify and correct any grammatical errors. Learners often are able to identify and remedy errors in structures they know well. For a review of research into CF in relation to language proficiency and developmental readiness, see Chapter 34.

Conclusion

In regard to the question of whether learner errors should be corrected, our review of the research suggests that CF is effective in aiding the development of L2 grammar. Overall CF appears to promote the development of L2 grammar in terms of accuracy, and some research has indicated it can contribute to fluency. Thus, teachers can use CF in both accuracy and fluency classroom tasks. In fluency tasks, teachers will of course consider factors other than grammar acquisition, such as affective factors. If teachers do opt to provide CF on grammar in fluency tasks, we suggest they draw on the kinds of CF strategies that do not overtly interrupt the communicative flow. Quick reformulations (recasts) and prompts, that is implicit CF strategies, can provide the kind of "gentle" correction alluded to in work on teaching methodology (Harmer, 2007). In regard to the question of how grammar errors should be corrected, the research indicates that all CF strategies are effective, including recasts (input providing) and prompts (which lead learners to modify their output), as well as explicit and implicit CF. At a practical level, teachers' decisions about how to provide CF is often based on multiple factors, including teaching objectives. When the lesson has accuracy objectives, explicit CF may be seen by teachers as particularly appropriate. When fluency is the objective, implicit CF may seem more

Table 17.3 *Grammar targets and CF studies*

CF types	Studies with salient grammar targets	Studies with non-salient grammar targets	Studies in which learners have limited prior knowledge of grammar targets	Studies in which learners have moderate prior knowledge of grammar targets	Studies in which learners have developed prior knowledge of grammar targets
Output-prompting CF vs. Input-providing CF	Ammar (2008)* Ammar & Spada (2006)* Guchte et al. (2015)* Loewen & Nabei (2007)* Yang & Lyster (2010)**	Guchte et al. (2015) Lyster (2004)* Lyster & Izquierdo (2009)** Yang & Lyster (2010)	Guchte et al. (2015)	Ammar (2008) Ammar & Spada (2006) Guchte et al. (2015) Lyster (2004) Yang & Lyster (2010)	Loewen & Nabei (2007) Lyster & Izquierdo (2009)
Explicit CF vs. Implicit CF	Ellis (2007)* Li (2014)* Loewen & Nabei (2007) Yilmaz (2012)**	Ellis (2007) Ellis et al. (2006)* Goo (2012)* Li (2014) Sheen (2007)* Yilmaz (2012) Nassaji (2017)*	Yilmaz (2012)	Goo (2012) Sheen (2007)	Ellis et al. (2006) Ellis (2007) Loewen & Nabei (2007)
Intensive recasts vs. Extensive recasts				Nassaji (2017)	
Explicit recasts vs. Implicit recasts	Zhao (2015)***	Zhao (2015)			Zhao (2015)
Immediate recasts vs. Delayed recasts	Li et al. (2016)* Quinn (2014) †		Li et al. (2016)	Quinn (2014)	
Computer-mediated recasts vs. Face-to-face recasts	Yilmaz & Yuksel (2011)**	Yilmaz & Yuksel (2011)	Yilmaz & Yuksel (2011)		

Note. * These studies established the effectiveness of CF based on the results of between-group comparisons on post-test scores, either between different CF groups or between CF groups and no CF groups. ** These studies established the effectiveness of CF based on the results of within-group comparisons, between pre- and post-tests scores of each group. *** These studies established the effectiveness of CF based on the results of both between-group and within-group comparisons.
† This study did not identify significant effects of CF based on the results of between-group comparisons.

appropriate. However, we suggest that teachers also consider learner proficiency level in light of findings from Li (2014) that indicate the greater effectiveness of explicit CF compared to implicit CF with low-proficiency-level learners.

To address the question of which grammar errors should be corrected and when, we reviewed findings from the studies listed in Table 17.3. Overall, the studies listed in columns 2 and 3 indicate that CF is effective with both salient and non-salient grammar structures. Among these studies, Nassaji (2017) found extensive CF (recasts on a range of structures) is more effective than intensive CF (recasts on a single structure). In our experience of teaching, extensive CF is a fairly common teaching practice. The review of studies listed in columns 4, 5, and 6 suggests that CF is particularly effective for structures that are new to or only partially known by the learners. In view of this finding, we suggested earlier that teachers might opt for self-correction activities to enable their students to correct errors on well-known structures. On a practical classroom level, structures may be better known by some compared to other students. This could complicate any decision-making about correcting grammar errors on the basis of learners' prior knowledge.

References

Ammar, A. (2008). Prompts and recasts: Differential effects on second language morphosyntax. *Language Teaching Research,12*(2), 183–210. https://doi.org/10.1177/1362168807086287.

Ammar, A. & Spada, N. (2006). One size fits all?: Recasts, prompts, and L2 learning. *Studies in Second Language Acquisition, 28*(4), 543–574. https://doi.org/10.1017/S0272263106060268.

Basturkmen, H. (2017). Explicit versus implicit grammar knowledge. In J. Liontas (ed.), *TESOL Encyclopedia of English Language Teaching* (Vol. V, pp. 2738–2743). Hoboken, NJ: John Wiley.

Bygate, M. (1994). Adjusting the focus: Teacher roles in task-based learning of grammar. In M. Bygate, A. Tonkyn & E. Williams (eds.), *Grammar and the Language Teacher* (pp. 237–259). London: Prentice Hall.

Chaudron, C. (1977). A descriptive model of discourse in the corrective treatment of learners' errors. *Language Learning, 27*(1), 29–46. https://doi.org/10.1111/j.1467-1770.1977.tb00290.x.

DeKeyser, R. (2015). Skill acquisition theory. In B. VanPatten & J. Williams (eds.), *Theories in second language acquisition: An introduction* (2nd ed., pp. 94–112). New York: Routledge.

Ellis, R. (2005). Measuring implicit and explicit knowledge of a second language: A psychometric study. *Studies in Second Language Acquisition, 27*(2), 141–172. https://doi.org/10.1017/S0272263105050096.

(2007). The differential effects of corrective feedback on two grammatical structures. In A. Mackey (ed.), *Conversational interaction in second language acquisition: A collection of empirical studies* (pp. 339–360). Oxford: Oxford University Press.

(2012). *Language teaching research and language pedagogy*. Malden, MA: Wiley-Blackwell.

Ellis, R., Loewen, S. & Erlam, R. (2006). Implicit and explicit corrective feedback and the acquisition of L2 grammar. *Studies in Second Language Acquisition, 28*(2), 339–368. https://doi.org/10.1017/S0272263106060141

Ellis, R. & Shintani, N. (2014). *Exploring language pedagogy through second language acquisition research*. Abingdon: Routledge.

Fu, M. (2019). The timing effects of corrective feedback and their associations with working memory, declarative memory and procedural memory. PhD dissertation in progress. University of Auckland, New Zealand.

Goldschneider, J. & DeKeyser, R. (2001). Explaining the "natural order of L2 morpheme acquisition" in English: A Meta-analysis of multiple determinants. *Language learning, 51*(1), 1–50. https://doi.org/10.1111/1467-9922.00147.

Goo, J. (2012). Corrective feedback and working memory capacity in interaction-driven L2 learning. *Studies in Second Language Acquisition, 34*(3), 445–474. https://doi.org/10.1017/S0272263112000149.

Guchte, M., Braaksma, M., Rijlaarsdam, G. & Bimmel, P. (2015). Learning new grammatical structures in task-based language learning: The effects of recasts and prompts. *Modern Language Journal, 99*(2), 246–262. https://doi.org/10.1111/modl.12211.

Harmer, J. (1983). *The practice of English language teaching*. London: Longman.

(2007). *The practice of English language teaching* (4th ed.). Harlow: Pearson Educational Limited.

Hawkes, L. & Nassaji, H. (2016). The role of extensive recasts in error detection and correction by adult ESL students. *Studies in Second Language Learning and Teaching, 6*(1), 19–41. http://dx.doi.org/10.14746/ssllt.2016.6.1.2.

Li, S. (2010). The effectiveness of corrective feedback in SLA: A meta-analysis. *Language Learning, 60*(2), 309–365. https://doi.org/10.1111/j.1467-9922.2010.00561.x.

(2014). The interface between feedback type, L2 proficiency, and the nature of the linguistic target. *Language Teaching Research, 18*(3), 373–396. https://doi.org/10.1177/1362168813510384.

Li, S., Zhu, Y. & Ellis, R. (2016). The effects of the timing of corrective feedback on the acquisition of a new linguistic structure. *Modern Language Journal, 100*(1), 276–295. https://doi.org/10.1111/modl.12315.

Loewen, S. (2012). The role of feedback. In S. Gass & A. Mackey (eds.), *The Routledge handbook of second language acquisition* (pp. 24–40). Abingdon: Routledge.

Loewen, S. & Nabei, T. (2007). Measuring the effects of oral corrective feedback on L2 knowledge. In A. Mackey (ed.), *Conversational interaction in second language acquisition: A collection of empirical studies* (pp. 361–376). Oxford: Oxford University Press.

Lyster, R. (2004). Differential effects of prompts and recasts in form-focused instruction. *Studies in Second Language Acquisition, 26*(3), 399–432. https://doi.org/10.1017/S0272263104263021.

Lyster, R. & Izquierdo, J. (2009). Prompts versus recasts in dyadic interaction. *Language Learning, 59*(2), 453–498. https://doi.org/10.1111/j.1467-9922.2009.00512.x.

Lyster, R. & Mori, H. (2006). Interactional feedback and instructional counterbalance. *Studies in Second Language Acquisition, 28*(2), 269–300. https://doi.org/10.1017/S0272263106060128.

Lyster, R. & Ranta, L. (1997). Corrective feedback and learner uptake. *Studies in Second Language Acquisition, 19*(1), 37–66.

Lyster, R. & Saito, K. (2010). Oral feedback in classroom SLA: A meta-analysis. *Studies in Second Language Acquisition, 32*(2), 265–302. https://doi.org/10.1017/S0272263109990520.

Mackey, A. & Goo, J. (2007). Interaction research in SLA: A meta-analysis and research synthesis. In A. Mackey (ed.), *Conversational interaction in second language acquisition: a series of empirical studies* (pp. 407–452). Oxford: Oxford University Press.

Mackey, A., Park, H. & Tagarelli, K. (2016). Errors, corrective feedback and repair. In H. Hall (ed.), *The Routledge handbook of English language teaching* (pp. 499–512). Abingdon: Routledge.

Mackey, A. & Philp, J. (1998). Conversational interaction and second language development: Recasts, responses, and red herrings? *Modern Language Journal, 82*(3), 338–356. https://doi.org/10.1111/j.1540-4781.1998.tb01211.x.

Nassaji, H. (2009). Effects of recasts and elicitations in dyadic interaction and the role of feedback explicitness. *Language Learning, 59*(2), 411–452. https://doi.org/10.1111/j.1467-9922.2009.00511.x.

(2017). The effectiveness of extensive versus intensive recasts for learning L2 grammar. *Modern Language Journal, 101*(2), 353–368. https://doi.org/10.1111/modl.12387.

Pienemann, M. (1988). Is language teachable? Psycholinguistic experiments and hypotheses. *Applied Linguistics, 10*(1), 52–79.

Quinn, P. (2014). Delayed versus immediate corrective feedback on orally produced passive errors in English. Unpublished Ph.D. dissertation, University of Toronto, Canada.

Quirk, R., Greenbaum, S., Leech, G. & Startvik, J. (1985). *A Comprehensive grammar of the English language*. London; New York: Longman.

Ranta, L. & Lyster, R. (2007). A cognitive approach to improving immersion students' oral language abilities: The awareness-practice-feedback sequence. In R. DeKeyser (ed.), *Practice in a second language: perspectives from applied linguistics and cognitive psychology* (pp. 141–160). Cambridge: Cambridge University Press.

Russell, J. & Spada, N. (2006). The effectiveness of corrective feedback for the acquisition of L2 grammar: A meta-analysis of the research. In J. Norris & L. Ortega (eds.), *Synthesizing research on language learning and teaching* (pp. 133–164). Amsterdam: John Benjamins.

Sato, M. & Lyster, R. (2012). Peer interaction and corrective feedback for accuracy and fluency development. *Studies in Second Language Acquisition*, 34(4), 591–626. https://doi.org/10.1017/S0272263112000356.

Scrivener, J. (2011). *Learning teaching: The essential guide to English language teaching* (3rd ed.). Oxford: Macmillan Educational.

Sheen, Y. (2007). The effects of corrective feedback, language aptitude, and learner attitudes on the acquisition of English articles. In A. Mackey (ed.), *Conversational interaction in second language acquisition: A collection of empirical studies* (pp. 301–322). Oxford: Oxford University Press.

Swain, M. (2005). The output hypothesis: Theory and research. In E. Hinkel (ed.), *Handbook of research in second language teaching and learning* (pp. 471–483). Mahwah, NJ: Lawrence Erlbaum.

Thornbury, S. (2018). Learning grammar. In J. Richards & A. Burns (eds.), *The Cambridge guide to learning a second language* (pp. 183–192). Cambridge: Cambridge University Press.

Yang, Y. & Lyster, R. (2010). Effects of form-focused practice and feedback on Chinese EFL learners' acquisition of regular and irregular past tense forms. *Studies in Second Language Acquisition*, 32(2), 235–263. https://doi.org/10.1017/S0272263109990519.

Yilmaz, Y. (2012). Relative effects of explicit and implicit feedback: The role of working memory capacity and language analytic ability. *Applied Linguistics*, 34(3), 344–368. https://doi.org/10.1093/applin/ams044.

Yilmaz, Y. & Yuksel, D. (2011). Effects of communication mode and salience on recasts: A first exposure study. *Language Teaching Research*, 15(4), 457–477. https://doi.org/10.1177/1362168811412873.

Zhao, Y. (2015). The effects of explicit and implicit recasts on the acquisition of two grammatical structures and the mediating role of working memory. Unpublished Ph.D. dissertation, University of Auckland, New Zealand.

18

Corrective Feedback and the Development of Second Language Vocabulary

Nobuhiro Kamiya and Tatsuya Nakata

Meara (1980) once observed that vocabulary was a "neglected aspect" in the field of second language (L2) acquisition; accordingly, a majority of second language acquisition (SLA) studies have examined the acquisition of morphosyntax and grammar (Haastrup & Henriksen, 2001). The past few decades, however, have witnessed an expansion of work on L2 vocabulary. For instance, a number of studies have examined the effects of type, frequency, and distribution of practice on vocabulary acquisition (for reviews, see Nation, 2013; Schmitt, 2010). Nevertheless, upon consulting a number of books and book chapters on corrective feedback (henceforth, CF), we found that there is hardly ever any section discussing its relationship exclusively with vocabulary, whether it is oral CF (henceforth, OCF) or written CF (henceforth, WCF). This is perhaps partly derived from a belief that most vocabulary is learned incidentally from meaning-focused input (Doughty & Williams, 1998), and CF plays only a limited role in vocabulary development. However, possibly due to recent empirical evidence showing that form-focused activities facilitate L2 vocabulary learning more than meaning-focused activities (for a review, see Laufer, 2009), there is growing interest in the effects of CF on vocabulary acquisition (e.g., Dilāns, 2010).

CF can be given by interlocutors other than teachers, such as peers (i.e., other students). CF can also be computer-mediated, including online automated writing evaluation (e.g., Li, Link & Hegelheimer, 2015). WCF studies have also looked into the effects of conferences where teachers and students talk over drafts face to face while CF is being given. Owing to the limitations of space, however, these issues will not be addressed in the current chapter.

Those readers who are interested in these topics of CF are advised to refer to other chapters in this book as well as other book-length volumes (e.g., Hyland & Hyland, 2006; Nassaji & Kartchava, 2017).

Oral Corrective Feedback and Development of L2 Vocabulary

OCF can be broadly divided into two types: input-providing (henceforth, *reformulations*) and output-prompting / generating / pushing (henceforth, *prompts*). In the former, the teacher gives the correct answer to the student who made the error, whereas in the latter the teacher attempts to elicit the correct answer from the student, urging to self-correct. OCF can also be categorized according to the degree of explicitness. Explicit corrections, for instance, are usually considered more explicit than recasts. Table 18.1 gives a classification of OCF traditionally employed by existing studies (e.g., Sheen, 2004). An example of each type of OCF, in response to an error of lexical choice "My hobby is *gathering (collecting) stamps," is also provided. Note also that it is possible to provide more than one type of OCF at once, which is referred to as *multiple feedback* (e.g., Doughty & Varela, 1998; Loewen & Philp, 2006; Lyster & Ranta, 1997).

Classroom Practices of Oral Corrective Feedback on L2 Vocabulary

Past studies have shown that there are variations among L2 teachers in their use of OCF. Existing studies, for instance, found that recasts, which is the most typical kind of OCF (Lyster, Saito & Sato, 2013), account for 11–27.5 percent of the OCF moves for lexical errors (e.g., Loewen & Philp, 2006; Mackey, Gass & McDonough, 2000; Sheen, 2006). The variations may be in part due to a number of variables such as teacher beliefs (e.g., Kamiya, 2016) and contexts (e.g., Sheen, 2004) that are found to affect the use of OCF. Despite some variations, research also suggests that OCF on vocabulary is very common. Alcón and García Mayo (2008) report that 66 percent of OCF in an EFL classroom in Spain was on lexical or spelling errors, far outnumbering other types of errors. Lyster (1998a) has also indicated that lexical errors tend to induce OCF from teachers. He analyzed OCF given by four French immersion teachers in twenty-seven lessons in Canada. The errors were categorized into four: grammar, phonology, lexicon, and unsolicited use of L1. Lexical errors accounted for 18 percent of all errors, but 24 percent of all OCF moves were on them. Moreover, 80 percent of lexical errors were followed by OCF, which turned out to be the highest figure among all error types.

Effectiveness of Oral Corrective Feedback on L2 Vocabulary

Given that OCF on vocabulary is common, one might wonder to what extent OCF facilitates L2 vocabulary development. In his reformulated

Table 18.1 *Categorization of oral corrective feedback*

	Explicitness	Types	Corrective moves	Examples
Reformulation	Implicit	Recast	Reformulate the erroneous utterance while maintaining the original meaning.	My hobby is collecting stamps.
	Explicit	Explicit correction	Explicitly tell the student that the utterance was erroneous and provide the correct answer.	Not gathering. Collecting.
Prompt	Implicit	Clarification request	Let the student know that the utterance was erroneous or incomprehensible.	I'm sorry?
		Repetition	Repeat the erroneous part verbatim.	Gathering?
		Elicitation	Elicit the correct answer from the student by either pausing right before the erroneous part or asking a specific question.	My hobby is ...
	Explicit	Metalinguistic feedback / clue	Give the student a metalinguistic comment regarding the error.	When we get a number of things as a hobby, we say collect, not gather.

Note. In the table, OCF is given in order of explicitness following Lyster and Saito (2010). Explicit corrections, for instance, are usually considered more explicit than recasts. It should be noted, however, that explicitness can be manipulated by various features, such as the length or emphasis. For instance, if the teacher phonetically emphasizes the word *collecting* in the recast *My hobby is COLLECTING stamps*, the recast might be perceived as explicit as an explicit correction.

Interaction Hypothesis, Long (1996) argues that negative feedback given in the form of OCF should facilitate vocabulary development. Existing studies have yielded somewhat inconsistent results regarding the effects of OCF on grammatical and morphosyntactic features. The accumulation of these studies led researchers to conduct several meta-analyses in which OCF was the only or one of the independent variables (Li, 2010; Lyster & Saito, 2010; Mackey & Goo, 2007; Norris & Ortega, 2000; Russell & Spada, 2006; Spada & Tomita, 2010). Yet, although the effects of OCF are likely to differ depending upon what linguistic features are to be targeted (Gass, Behney & Plonsky, 2013), most of these meta-analyses did not examine whether OCF has differential effects on different target features. Mackey and Goo (2007) showed that the magnitude of effects is larger for the development of lexical knowledge than for grammatical knowledge. However, it should be noted that their analysis was on the effects of interaction in general, not OCF per se.

SLA researchers, nonetheless, have hypothesized that OCF on lexical (and phonological) errors should be more effective than on grammatical or morphosyntactic errors (e.g., Lyster et al., 2013), and a limited number of studies have supported this hypothesis. For instance, in Jeon (2007), forty-one learners of Korean in the United States participated in a variety of communicative tasks in which they received OCF from a Korean native speaker. The target features were relative clauses, honorifics, concrete nouns, and action verbs. The gain scores from the pre-test to the two post-tests indicated that OCF on nouns and verbs was more effective than that on honorifics, but it was equally effective for errors in relative clauses.

Gass and Torres (2005) compared the effects of the following four treatments: input only, interaction only, input followed by interaction, and interaction followed by input. The three treatments except the input only condition included OCF (elicitation, recast, and negotiation) as a part of interaction. English-speaking learners of Spanish participated in dyadic tasks where a native speaker of Spanish provided OCF on seven target words along with two grammatical features (gender agreement and the copula *estar*). The results of gain scores from the pre-test to the post-test showed that the three interaction groups receiving OCF outperformed the input only group ($p = 0.07$) only on vocabulary measures. The results suggest that vocabulary acquisition is more amenable to OCF than grammar acquisition. Gass and Torres argue that it is possibly because vocabulary is less complex and abstract compared to grammar.

There are several reasons to surmise promising effects of OCF on lexical errors. First, past studies suggest that OCF on lexical errors tends to be accurately perceived as CF, rather than responses to content or mere conversation moves (Carpenter et al., 2006; Mackey et al., 2007; Mackey et al., 2000; Roberts, 1995). For instance, in Mackey et al. (2000), learners of ESL and Italian as a Foreign Language participated in task-based dyadic interaction in which they received OCF on morphosyntactic, lexical, and phonological errors from (near-) native speakers. Upon the completion of the tasks, participants were asked to articulate their thoughts about each instance of OCF, while watching the video of interactions (i.e., stimulated recalls). The results showed that 83 percent and 66 percent of OCF moves on lexical errors were accurately construed as CF by ESL learners and Italian learners, respectively. These figures were higher than OCF on phonological errors (ESL: 60%; Italian: 21%) or morphosyntactic errors (ESL: 13%; Italian: 24%). Mackey and colleagues attribute the results to the potentially high *communicative value* (VanPatten, 1985) of vocabulary: In other words, vocabulary errors tend to interfere with comprehension more seriously than morphosyntax errors.

Second, with respect to recasts, those on lexical errors can be easily made salient by focusing on the single erroneous word, possibly along with phonetic emphasis on it. Leeman (2003) claims that enhanced saliency may increase learning because it helps learners to notice OCF, which is beneficial for learning, according to the Noticing Hypothesis (Schmidt, 1990, 1994; but see Truscott, 1998, for criticism). Schmidt (1994) argued that noticing is a prerequisite for input to be converted into intake. Although it is still controversial whether noticing is indispensable for learning (e.g., Williams, 2005), a series of studies corroborate the notion that it does facilitate it. Egi (2007b) demonstrated that recasts which learners interpreted as linguistic positive and/or negative evidence led to more improved test scores than those that they interpreted as responses to content. Alcón and García Mayo (2008) showed that the vocabulary items that EFL learners self-reported that they had learned from prompts were significantly correlated with the correct use of those words in translation tasks given both immediately ($r = 0.995$) and a week after the lesson ($r = 0.818$). Unlike recasts on lexical errors, recasts on grammatical errors are often given in the form of a whole sentence. This is likely to decrease the possibility that learners notice the OCF because recasts may be interpreted as mere conversation moves, rather than OCF (e.g., Ellis & Sheen, 2006; Nicholas, Lightbown & Spada, 2001), although the extent to which they notice OCF depends on its explicitness. The learners' failure to accurately interpret recasts as OCF is somewhat understandable because L2 teachers often use noncorrective repetition in response to students' well-formed utterances (Lyster, 1998b). The empirical evidence for the preponderance of shorter recasts comes from Loewen and Philp (2006). Logistic regression analyses showed that the length of recasts is one of the predictive variables for post-test scores; recasts with fewer than five morphemes were twice as effective as those with five or more. The advantage of shorter recasts over longer ones has also been reported by other studies (e.g., Egi, 2007a; Philp, 2003; Roberts, 1995; Sheen, 2006). For instance, Egi (2007a) showed that longer recasts are more likely to be interpreted as responses to content, whereas shorter recasts are more likely to be interpreted as positive and/or negative evidence.

Furthermore, the acquisition of lexicon is supposedly unconstrained by the developmental readiness of the learners, unlike some types of morphosyntax or grammar (e.g., Mackey & Philp, 1998), which suggests that the effects of OCF on lexical features are not affected by learners' proficiency. This perhaps explains failures by some learners to accurately interpret OCF on grammatical and morphosyntactic errors (see above). That is to say, the learners may have been developmentally *unready* to process them. Finally, unlike grammar, learners are not required to extrapolate rules from OCF void of metalinguistic comments, nor deal with exceptions. Thus, in a way, due to the less complex and abstract nature of vocabulary, it perhaps benefits more from OCF than grammar or morphosyntax (Gass & Torres, 2005).

Given the potential benefits of OCF on lexis, one might wonder what type of OCF is the most effective. Dilāns (2010) is probably the only study that has compared the effects of different types of OCF on vocabulary acquisition. In his study, twenty-three adult ESL learners received either recasts or prompts (elicitation and repetition) on ten target words, and their retention was measured by various tests measuring three dimensions of vocabulary knowledge: partial-precise, depth, and receptive-productive. The results indicated that both recasts and prompts were equally effective in the short term, but prompts were slightly more effective than recasts in the long run, especially for the acquisition of the depth dimension.

Pedagogical Implications

OCF is directly related to classroom practices and a topic of great concern among L2 teachers. However, because various factors may potentially influence the effects of OCF, researchers often hesitate to make concrete pedagogical recommendations; thus, their typical recommendation is often nothing more than to give various kinds of feedback (e.g., Loewen, 2012). Here we endeavor to proffer more specific suggestions, however tentative they are. One pedagogical implication is that teachers should make OCF salient because research suggests that OCF that is interpreted as CF facilitates learning. This can be done by keeping OCF short, and targeting the single erroneous word, possibly along with a phonetic emphasis on it.

Another implication is that teachers should use prompts, rather than reformulations, because research suggests that prompts facilitate vocabulary learning and retention more than reformulations (Dilāns, 2010). This recommendation is also supported by research showing that tasks which require learners to produce lexical items increase learning (de la Fuente, 2006; Laufer & Hulstijn, 2001; Loewen, 2012). One caveat, though, is that prompts are effective only when the learner knows the correct answer. When the teacher is not sure whether the learner knows the correct answer, *corrective recasts* (Doughty & Varela, 1998) may be used. Corrective recasts consist of two steps: prompts followed by recasts. First, the teacher uses prompts with a rising intonation, eliciting self-correction. (Although Doughty and Varela used only repetitions as an example of corrective recasts, we deem that any types of prompts can be used.) Second, only when the student fails to respond correctly does the teacher give recasts to provide the correct word. The teacher can then ask the student to repeat the word after them if time allows and it is appropriate to do so in the flow of discourse.

Written Corrective Feedback and Development of L2 Vocabulary

WCF is generally more explicit than OCF because WCF is visualized (Ellis, 2010; Sheen & Ellis, 2011), but it can also be implicit by, for instance, prompting to self-correct. WCF is often categorized as *direct* and *indirect*. In the former, the teacher directly corrects students' errors and provides the correct answer. In the latter, the teacher gives some kind of indication regarding the errors made and encourages the student to self-correct them in follow-up revisions or in new writing tasks. Just like OCF, multiple types of WCF can be used in combination (e.g., *highlight* and *coding*). Table 18.2 provides a list of major types of WCF without any intention to be exhaustive.

The studies on WCF can be roughly categorized into two strands. One is those conducted in the framework of L2 writing, in which researchers investigate how WCF contributes to the improvement of students' writing, namely, *feedback-for-accuracy* or *learning-to-write* language framework (Manchón, 2011). The other is those conducted in the framework of SLA, in which researchers investigate how WCF contributes to the development of learners' interlanguage, namely, *feedback-for-acquisition* or *writing-to-learn* language framework (Manchón, 2011). Whereas WCF is sometimes provided on lexical errors in studies conducted in the former framework, studies conducted in the latter typically focus on grammatical or

Table 18.2 *Categorization of written corrective feedback*

Directness	Explicitness	Types	Corrective moves
Direct	—	Direct correction	Directly correct the erroneous part and give the correct answer.
Indirect	Implicit	Model[a]	Provide the students with sample writing on the same prompt written by proficient writers, and have them compare with theirs and find errors on their own.
		Reformulation	Provide the students with the corrected writing of their own while retaining as much of the original meaning as possible, and have them compare with theirs and find errors on their own.
		Indication of errors	Simply indicate whether there is an error or not (in the whole text, each paragraph, or line, etc.).
		Number of errors	Tell the student how many errors the passage contains (in the whole text, each paragraph, or line, etc.).
		Highlight errors	Highlight the erroneous word(s) by textual enhancements, such as underlines, squares, circles, etc.
		Description / Coding of errors	Describe the type of error. For instance, the teacher writes "choice" (or simply "c") under an erroneous word, indicating that the word choice is wrong.
	Explicit	Metalinguistic comment	Write metalinguistic comments regarding errors.

Note. In the table, indirect WCF is given in order of explicitness, from the most implicit (models) to most explicit (metalinguistic comments), although the order is not meant to be definite.

[a] Models are also referred to as reformulations.

morphosyntactic features, and English articles *inter alia* (but see Van Beuningen, De Jong & Kuiken, 2012, for an exception).

In the L2 writing framework, the effectiveness of WCF is usually measured by whether WCF was incorporated in the subsequent revisions (e.g., Bitchener & Ferris, 2012). SLA researchers, however, argue that this cannot be considered as evidence of language acquisition; according to them, WCF can be proven to be effective only when it has been incorporated into a new text written under a new task (at the cost of ecological validity from the perspective of L2 writing researchers). While it may be possible to design tasks so that learners have to use certain grammatical or morphosyntactic features for which they received WCF previously, it is not very practical to do the same with lexical items. Thus, from SLA perspective, the effects of WCF on vocabulary acquisition are elusive due to methodological challenges. In a small number of studies where WCF was given to lexical errors, the results are often bundled with other types of errors and reported together (e.g., Chandler, 2003; Qi & Lapkin, 2001; Van Beuningen et al., 2012). This makes it virtually impossible to tease apart the effects of WCF on lexical errors from those on other kinds of errors, another factor that makes it even more difficult to evaluate the effectiveness of WCF on lexis.

Effectiveness of Written Corrective Feedback on L2 Vocabulary

In an influential article, Truscott (1996) proposed that WCF should be abandoned in L2 writing classes. Although his argument was mostly concerned with grammatical errors, its scope also extended to lexical errors because, as he claimed, lexicons are complex in the sense that they consist of "much more than a list of words: the meaning, form, and use of each word depend very much on its relationships to other words and to other portions of the language system, as well as to nonlinguistic cognitive systems" (p. 344). Nevertheless, some studies conducted under the learning-to-write framework have shown that WCF may lead to appropriate use of vocabulary in revisions as well as rewriting on the same prompt.

The first question to be posed is, like the case for OCF, whether learners notice WCF on vocabulary because noticing is crucial for the feedback to be incorporated in further writing (Schmidt, 1990). Studies have indicated that learners do notice WCF on vocabulary. In Storch and Wigglesworth (2010), forty-eight ESL students collaboratively wrote an English text based on a graph in pairs. WCF was given in the form of (a) reformulations or (b) highlights and error codes. After discussing the feedback in a pair, each pair revised their original text while talking to each other without visually referring to the feedback. Storch and Wigglesworth analyzed language-related episodes (LREs) observed in the discussion and revision sessions. LREs refer to a discussion between learners about language-related problems that they encountered (Swain & Lapkin, 1995). The results showed that around 50 percent of LREs in the discussion and revision sessions were on lexicon regardless of the type of WCF. The findings indicate that learners notice WCF on lexical errors.

Coyle and Roca de Larios (2014) also investigated the extent to which learners pay attention to WCF on lexis. In their study, twenty pairs of EFL children in Spain wrote a story based on a series of pictures. Half of the pairs received direct corrections, whereas the other half received two models. Each pair discussed the differences between their original text and the feedback, and LREs in the discussions were analyzed. The results showed that (a) regardless of the type of WCF and the English proficiency of the participants, the LREs were predominantly on lexis, and (b) models induced more LREs on lexis (83 percent) than direct corrections (56 percent). These findings also indicate that learners tend to notice WCF on lexical errors.

Given that learners often notice WCF on lexical errors, one might wonder to what extent these instances of noticing contribute to successful revisions and rewriting. In Adams (2003), intermediate Spanish learners were assigned to one of the three conditions: noticing, noticing and stimulated recall, and control. The participants formed dyads and each wrote a story collaboratively based on pictures, which served as the pre-test baseline. Those texts were then reformulated by (near-) native speakers of Spanish, which were given back to the participants (except for the control group). After that, the two groups (not the control group) participated in the noticing session, where each student dyad met with the researcher individually. They were asked to compare their original story and the reformulations, and find as many differences as they could. Following the noticing session, those in the noticing and stimulated recall group participated in a stimulated recall session. During the post-test, all of the participants reconstructed the story from the pictures individually, not in pairs. The results showed that in 32 percent of the instances where the participants noticed, the vocabulary use became more target-like, whereas in 21 percent of the cases, it became less target-like. These proportions were similar to those for grammatical errors. Moreover, the noticing and the noticing and stimulated recall groups significantly outperformed the control group, indicating that noticing facilitated a larger number of target-like corrections.

Similar results were also observed for models. In Hanaoka (2007), thirty-seven Japanese university students wrote a narrative based upon a picture prompt while taking notes regarding any problems that came to mind during writing. Then, two models were distributed, and participants took notes on any differences that they noticed between their original text and the models. After that, they revised the original text immediately and again after two months. The results showed that 63 percent of their tokens of noticing were on lexicon. When the answers were available in the models, they noticed 65 percent of them. Out of these, 92 percent were incorporated in the revision, and 37 percent in the delayed revision. Although higher-proficiency learners tended to perform better than lower-proficiency learners, the difference was not statistically significant.

Ferris and Roberts (2001) compared the effects of two types of WCF: underlines with or without error codes. In their study, sixty-seven ESL students in the United States were divided into three groups: control, underlines, and underlines with error codes. After writing an essay in English, participants were given their word-processed essays, and instructed to self-edit their essays. No WCF was given to the control group, whereas for the other two groups, errors were indicated with underlines with or without error codes. The results showed that 63 percent and 55 percent of errors in word choice were corrected by the underlines with error codes group and the underlines only group, respectively. The difference, however, was not statistically significant. A further analysis indicated that the rate of successful correction was moderated by the learners' proficiency. In other words, higher proficiency learners were more successful in correcting lexical errors ($r = 0.252$). A point worth noting is that even the participants who did not receive any WCF succeeded in correcting 31 percent of the lexical errors, which was the highest percentage among five error categories.

Finally, Suzuki (2012) examined to what extent learners were successful in incorporating direct correction into subsequent revisions. In his study, twenty-four native speakers of Japanese were asked to write essays in English. He found that 96 percent of lexical targets discussed in written LREs were successfully incorporated into the revisions. To summarize, existing studies indicate that WCF is effective for L2 vocabulary development to some extent, as long as it is noticed by learners.

However, it should be noted that all of the aforementioned studies measured the effects of WCF via revisions of the original texts or rewriting on the same topic, which is not necessarily indicative of language acquisition, according to SLA researchers. Ferris (2006) investigated whether the effects of WCF can be carried over to a new piece of writing. In her study, ninety-two ESL students in the United States wrote four essays outside of classes throughout the semester, for each of which they wrote three drafts. WCF was given on various linguistic features. Results showed that approximately 80 percent of lexical errors (e.g., lexical choice and spelling) were corrected in the revision following feedback, demonstrating its short-term effects. In order to investigate its long-term effects (i.e., acquisition), Ferris also compared the second drafts of Essays 1 and 4 of fifty-five students. The total number of lexical errors decreased from 13.58 to 11.78 on average, and a small effect size was observed ($p = 0.07$, $r = 0.25$). However, it should be noted that her study did not ensure that same lexical items were used in both essays. As a result, the decreased number of lexical errors in the second essay may be due to a number of reasons such as the nature of tasks (e.g., learners made more lexical errors in the first essay because the first essay required the use of more low-frequent, sophisticated vocabulary). To our knowledge, Ferris (2006) is the only study that has investigated the effects of WCF on L2 vocabulary in a new writing task. More studies along this line of research are warranted.

Effectiveness of Direct and Indirect Corrective Feedback on L2 Vocabulary

Given the potential benefits of WCF on vocabulary, one might wonder which type of WCF is more effective, direct or indirect. Sheen (2010) argues that explicitness is a crucial factor for feedback to be beneficial. This suggests that direct feedback, which is explicit in nature, is more effective than indirect feedback. Ferris (1999) also claims that lexical errors, such as word choice and idioms, are "untreatable" except, perhaps, for spelling errors (Ferris, 2006). This is because "there is no handbook or set of rules students can consult to avoid or fix those types of errors" (Ferris, 1999, p. 6). In other words, while learners may be able to self-correct spelling errors when highlighted, they might be unable to do so for word choice errors. Teachers, therefore, should perhaps give direct feedback or explicit types of indirect feedback to lexical errors, which L2 teachers have been instinctively doing (Ferris, 2006).

To examine the effects of direct and indirect feedback on vocabulary development, Santos, López-Serrano, and Manchón (2010) compared the effects of direct corrections and reformulations. In their study, four pairs of Spanish high school students collaboratively wrote a narrative in English based on a series of pictures. WCF was given in the form of reformulations and direct corrections alternately. Two days after each pair discussed the feedback, they individually revised their original text. The results showed that, when noticed, 75 percent of reformulations and 88 percent of direct corrections were incorporated in the revisions. However, it is not clear whether the difference was statistically significant. The analysis also found that the type of WCF (direct or indirect) had smaller effects on lexical errors, compared with other types of errors (forms and discourse).

Other studies, however, suggest that indirect feedback may be more effective for vocabulary development. In Coyle and Roca de Larios (2014), which is described earlier, a week after writing a story based on a series of pictures, participants rewrote the story based on the same pictures. The majority of the tokens of revisions were on lexis: 63 percent for direct corrections and 91 percent for models. The results suggest that models, a type of indirect feedback, may encourage learners to focus on lexis more than direct corrections. The authors ascribed the results to the differing characteristics of these two types of WCF: Whereas direct corrections help learners "to identify linguistic inadequacies in their output but did not provide them with alternatives to what was already correct in their original texts" (p. 478), models offer them "a set of L2 words beyond what they had written and content that they could draw on to express new meanings" (p. 478). Suzuki (2012) offers an alternative explanation. He speculates that whereas direct correction is likely to promote grammatical development, indirect feedback, such as models and reformulations, is more likely to facilitate vocabulary development. This is because learners tend to focus on lexical issues when they are left to their own devices to look for any changes made in their drafts. Suzuki (2012) also argues that lexical problems are easier to verbalize than grammatical problems. All in all, due to the shortage of empirical studies, we are still far from being able to conclude with conviction which type of WCF, direct or indirect, is more effective.

Pedagogical Implications

The above discussion indicates the potential benefits of WCF on L2 vocabulary. The evidence comes not only from immediate revisions. In Hanaoka (2007), the delayed revision incorporated as much as 37 percent of WCF. Albeit successful revisions do not guarantee acquisition, the finding that learners retained the feedback even two months after the feedback session can be considered an indirect sign that those words were stored in their long-term memory. The finding indicates the value of WCF on vocabulary.

Nevertheless, pedagogical recommendations should be made cautiously until more studies confirm the effectiveness of WCF on vocabulary acquisition. It seems reasonable to expect direct or explicit feedback to be more effective than indirect or implicit feedback for at least two reasons. First, the Noticing Hypothesis (Schmidt, 1990, 1994; Sheen, 2010) suggests that direct or explicit feedback, which is more likely to induce noticing than indirect or implicit feedback, is beneficial for learning. Second, the finding that form-focused activities facilitate L2 vocabulary learning more than meaning-focused activities (for a review, see Laufer, 2009) also suggests that direct or explicit feedback is more effective than indirect or implicit feedback. The results of past studies, however, are somewhat inconsistent (Coyle & Roca de Larios, 2014; Santos et al., 2010). Furthermore, although Ferris and Roberts (2001) and Hanaoka (2007) found that higher-proficiency learners incorporated more feedback than lower-proficiency learners, no consistent pattern emerged regarding the relationship between learners' proficiency and the number of LREs in Coyle and Roca de Larios (2014). In short, more studies are needed until we can draw pedagogical implications.

Suggestions for Further Research

Considering that research has shown that CF on lexis is common and facilitates noticing, further studies on both OCF and WCF will be useful. One area for future research is to examine whether different lexical items benefit differently from CF. In existing studies, all lexical items are treated uniformly as if they were equally susceptible to CF, and the results are reported altogether. It is, however, possible that the effects of CF are moderated by various lexical features, such as concreteness, cognate status, word length, or frequency, which are found to affect vocabulary learning (e.g., Chen & Truscott, 2010; de Groot & Keijzer, 2000; Schmitt, 2010). In future research, it may be useful to investigate whether these lexical features influence the effects of CF.

Another area for future research may examine how individual differences of learners moderate the effects of CF on vocabulary. Recent studies have found that a number of cognitive, conative, and affective variables may potentially influence the effects of both OCF and WCF (e.g., Goo, 2012; Sheen, 2007, 2008; Storch & Wigglesworth, 2010; Trofimovich, Ammar & Gatbonton, 2007). Studies on OCF, for instance, have shown that learner-related variables such as working memory capacity (e.g., Goo, 2012) or anxiety (e.g., Sheen, 2008) influence grammar acquisition. WCF studies have also found large standard deviations in the data (Adams, 2003; Ferris, 2006). The results indicate wide variations among learners in their ability to incorporate WCF, a finding consistent with those of grammar acquisition studies (Ferris & Hedgcock, 1998). Ferris and Roberts (2001) found that higher-proficiency learners are typically more successful in incorporating WCF. However, their study employed a series of correlation analyses; therefore, it is not clear whether there is a causal relationship between the proficiency levels and the successful incorporation of WCF. Further research examining what variables are responsible for variations among learners in their ability to incorporate OCF and WCF will be useful.

One limitation of existing studies is the paucity of research comparing the effects of different types of CF on vocabulary learning. A number of OCF studies have compared the effectiveness of recasts and prompts. However, because most studies have targeted only grammatical or morphosyntactic features (for an exception, see Dilāns, 2010), their effects on vocabulary acquisition are still unclear. Past studies on WCF also examined a limited number of types of WCF, typically comparing between direct corrections and reformulations, whose results are rather mixed. It may be valuable to compare the effects of different types of OCF and WCF on vocabulary learning in future research.

Another interesting area of research would be to examine the effects of timing of OCF on vocabulary learning. OCF can be provided immediately after the learner's erroneous utterance (immediate OCF) or after a delay (delayed

OCF). Although cognitive psychology literature on the distributed practice effect predicts the advantage of delayed OCF over immediate OCF, existing studies on grammar learning have provided little evidence for the benefits of delaying OCF (for a review, see Quinn & Nakata, 2017). However, it is possible that vocabulary acquisition benefits more from delayed OCF than grammar acquisition. This is because research has shown that the timing of instruction, not OCF, has larger effects on vocabulary learning (Nakata, 2015; Nakata & Webb, 2016) than grammar learning (e.g., Suzuki & DeKeyser, 2017). In future research, it may be useful to examine whether delaying OCF facilitates vocabulary learning.

From the perspective of vocabulary acquisition, one limitation of previous WCF studies is that the effectiveness of WCF has been typically measured by the degree of its incorporation in revisions. However, incorporating lexicon in revisions is relatively easy because learners simply need to replace a word with another. Although some studies have had learners rewrite a text for the same prompt as the pre-test, this does not necessarily mean that they have acquired the vocabulary in the sense that they can use it for another piece of writing. In other words, earlier studies may have investigated what Truscott (1996) refers to as *pseudo-learning*, "a superficial and possibly transient form of knowledge, with little value for actual use of the language" (p. 345). Our review of literature shows that no existing studies have examined whether WCF allows learners to correctly use vocabulary in a new piece of writing, rather than in revision or rewriting. It is true that Ferris (2006) found that the total number of lexical errors decreased across two writing assignments when learners received WCF. However, as described earlier, her study did not examine whether lexical items that received WCF were used correctly in subsequent writing tasks. Although ensuring that the same lexical items are used across multiple, independent writing tasks is methodologically challenging, in future research, it will be valuable to examine whether WCF facilitates the successful use of the same lexical items in a new writing task.

As a final note, although CF has been studied extensively in the field of SLA, our survey has found that the effects of CF on vocabulary learning are still under-researched. This is unfortunate considering the importance of vocabulary knowledge. As Wilkins (1972) once proclaimed, "Without grammar very little can be conveyed, without vocabulary nothing can be conveyed" (p. 111). We hope that our chapter encourages more researchers to examine the effects of CF on vocabulary acquisition.

References

Adams, R. (2003). L2 output, reformulation and noticing: Implications for IL development. *Language Teaching Research, 7*(3), 347–376. DOI:10.1191/ 1362168803lr127oa.

Alcón, E. & García Mayo, M. P. (2008). Incidental focus on form and learning outcomes with young foreign language classroom learners. In J. Philp, R. Oliver & A. Mackey (eds.), *Second language acquisition and the younger learner: Child's play?* (pp. 173–192). Amsterdam: John Benjamins.

Bitchener, J. & Ferris, D. (2012). *Written corrective feedback in second language acquisition and writing.* New York: Routledge.

Carpenter, H., Jeon, K. S., MacGregor, D. & Mackey, A. (2006). Learners' interpretations of recasts. *Studies in Second Language Acquisition, 28*(2), 209–236. DOI:10.1017/S0272263106060104.

Chandler, J. (2003). The efficacy of various kinds of error feedback for improvement in the accuracy and fluency of L2 student writing. *Journal of Second Language Writing, 12*(3), 267–296. DOI:10.1016/s1060-3743(03)00038-9.

Chen, C. & Truscott, J. (2010). The effects of repetition and L1 lexicalization on incidental vocabulary acquisition. *Applied Linguistics, 31*(5), 693–713. DOI:10.1093/applin/amq031.

Coyle, Y. & Roca de Larios, J. (2014). Exploring the role played by error correction and models on children's reported noticing and output production in a L2 writing task. *Studies in Second Language Acquisition, 36*(3), 451–485. DOI:10.1017/s0272263113000612.

de Groot, A. M. B. & Keijzer, R. (2000). What is hard to learn is easy to forget: The roles of word concreteness, cognate status, and word frequency in foreign-language vocabulary learning and forgetting. *Language Learning, 50*(1), 1–56. DOI:10.1111/0023-8333.00110.

de la Fuente, M. J. (2006). Classroom L2 vocabulary acquisition: Investigating the role of pedagogical tasks and form-focused instruction. *Language Teaching Research, 10*(3), 263–295. DOI:10.1191/1362168806lr196oa.

Dilāns, G. (2010). Corrective feedback and L2 vocabulary development: Prompts and recasts in the adult ESL classroom. *Canadian Modern Language Review, 66*(6), 787–816. DOI:10.3138/cmlr.66.6.787.

Doughty, C. & Varela, E. (1998). Communicative focus on form. In C. Doughty & J. Williams (eds.), *Focus on form in classroom second language acquisition* (pp. 114–138). New York: Cambridge University Press.

Doughty, C. & Williams, J. (1998). Pedagogical choices in focus on form. In C. Doughty & J. Williams (eds.), *Focus on form in classroom second language acquisition* (pp. 197–261). Cambridge: Cambridge University Press.

Egi, T. (2007a). Interpreting recasts as linguistic evidence: The roles of linguistic target, length, and degree of change. *Studies in Second Language Acquisition, 29*(4), 511–537. DOI:10.1017/S0272263107070416.

(2007b). Recasts, learners' interpretation, and L2 development. In A. Mackey (ed.), *Conversational interaction in second language acquisition* (pp. 249–267). Oxford: Oxford University Press.

Ellis, R. (2010). Epilogue: A framework for investigating oral and written corrective feedback. *Studies in Second Language Acquisition, 32*(2), 335–349. DOI:10.1017/s0272263109990544.

Ellis, R. & Sheen, Y. (2006). Reexamining the role of recasts in second language acquisition. *Studies in Second Language Acquisition*, 28(4), 575–600. DOI:10.1017/S027226310606027X.

Ferris, D. (1999). The case for grammar correction in L2 writing classes: A response to Truscott (1996). *Journal of Second Language Writing*, 8(1), 1–11. DOI:10.1016/S1060-3743(99)80110-6.

(2006). Does error feedback help student writers?: New evidence on the short- and long-term effects of written error correction. In K. Hyland & F. Hyland (eds.), *Feedback in second language writing: Contexts and issues* (pp. 81–104). Cambridge: Cambridge University Press.

Ferris, D. & Hedgcock, J. S. (1998). *Teaching ESL composition: Purpose, process, and practice.* Mahwah, NJ: Lawrence Erlbaum.

Ferris, D. & Roberts, B. (2001). Error feedback in L2 writing classes: How explicit does it need to be? *Journal of Second Language Writing*, 10(3), 161–184. DOI:10.1016/S1060-3743(01)00039-X.

Gass, S. M., Behney, J. & Plonsky, L. (2013). *Second language acquisition: An introductory course* (4th edn.). New York: Routledge.

Gass, S. M. & Torres, M. J. A. (2005). Attention when? An investigation of the ordering effects of input and interaction. *Studies in Second Language Acquisition*, 27(1), 1–31. DOI:10.1017/S0272263105050011.

Goo, J. (2012). Corrective feedback and working memory capacity in interaction-driven L2 learning. *Studies in Second Language Acquisition*, 34(3), 445–474. DOI:10.1017/S0272263112000149.

Haastrup, K. & Henriksen, B. (2001). The interrelationship between vocabulary acquisition theory and general SLA research. *EUROSLA Yearbook*, 1, 69–78.

Hanaoka, O. (2007). Output, noticing, and learning: An investigation into the role of spontaneous attention to form in a four- stage writing task. *Language Teaching Research*, 11(4), 459–479. DOI:10.1177/1362168807080963.

Hyland, K. & Hyland, F. (eds.). (2006). *Feedback in second language writing: Contexts and issues.* Cambridge: Cambridge University Press.

Jeon, K. S. (2007). Interaction-driven L2 learning: Characterizing linguistic development. In A. Mackey (ed.), *Conversational interaction in second language acquisition* (pp. 379–403). Oxford: Oxford University Press.

Kamiya, N. (2016). The relationship between stated beliefs and classroom practices of oral corrective feedback. *Innovation in Language Learning and Teaching*, 10(3), 206–219. DOI:10.1080/17501229.2014.939656.

Laufer, B. (2009). Second language vocabulary acquisition from language input and from form-focused activities. *Language Teaching*, 42(3), 341–354. DOI:10.1017/s0261444809005771.

Laufer, B. & Hulstijn, J. H. (2001). Incidental vocabulary acquisition in a second language: The construct of task-induced involvement. *Applied Linguistics*, 22(1), 1–26. DOI:10.1093/applin/22.1.1.

Leeman, J. (2003). Recasts and second language development: Beyond negative evidence. *Studies in Second Language Acquisition, 25*(1), 37–63. DOI:10.1017/S0272263103000020.

Li, J., Link, S. & Hegelheimer, V. (2015). Rethinking the role of automated writing evaluation (AWE) feedback in ESL writing instruction. *Journal of Second Language Writing, 27,* 1–18. DOI:10.1016/j.jslw.2014.10.004.

Li, S. (2010). The effectiveness of corrective feedback in SLA: A meta-analysis. *Language Learning, 60*(2), 309–365. DOI:10.1111/j.1467-9922.2010.00561.x.

Loewen, S. (2012). The role of feedback. In S. Gass & A. Mackey (eds.), *The Routledge handbook of second language acquisition* (pp. 24–40). New York: Routledge.

Loewen, S. & Philp, J. (2006). Recasts in the adult English L2 classroom: Characteristics, explicitness, and effectiveness. *Modern Language Journal, 90*(4), 536–556. DOI:10.1111/j.1540-4781.2006.00465.x.

Long, M. H. (1996). The role of the linguistic environment in second language acquisition. In W. C. Ritchie & T. K. Bhatia (eds.), *Handbook of second language acquisition* (pp. 413–468). San Diego, CA: Academic Press.

Lyster, R. (1998a). Negotiation of form, recasts, and explicit correction in relation to error types and learner repair in immersion classrooms. *Language Learning, 48*(2), 183–218. DOI:10.1111/j.1467-1770.2001.tb00019.x.

(1998b). Recasts, repetition, and ambiguity in L2 classroom discourse. *Studies in Second Language Acquisition, 20*(1), 51–81. DOI:10.1017/S027226319800103X.

Lyster, R. & Ranta, L. (1997). Corrective feedback and learner uptake: Negotiation of form in communicative classrooms. *Studies in Second Language Acquisition, 19*(1), 37–66. DOI:10.1017/S0272263197001034.

Lyster, R. & Saito, K. (2010). Oral feedback in classroom SLA: A meta-analysis. *Studies in Second Language Acquisition, 32*(2), 265–302. DOI:10.1017/s0272263109990520.

Lyster, R., Saito, K. & Sato, M. (2013). Oral corrective feedback in second language classrooms. *Language Teaching, 46*(1), 1–40. DOI:10.1017/s0261444812000365.

Mackey, A., Al-Khalil, M., Atanassova, G., Hama, M., Logan-Terry, A. & Nakatsukasa, K. (2007). Teachers' intentions and learners' perceptions about corrective feedback in the L2 classroom. *Innovation in Language Learning and Teaching, 1*(1), 129–152. DOI:10.2167/illt047.0.

Mackey, A., Gass, S. & McDonough, K. (2000). How do learners perceive interactional feedback? *Studies in Second Language Acquisition, 22*(4), 471–497. DOI:10.1017/S0272263100004022.

Mackey, A. & Goo, J. (2007). Interaction research in SLA: A meta-analysis and research synthesis. In A. Mackey (ed.), *Conversational interaction in second language acquisition* (pp. 408–452). Oxford: Oxford University Press.

Mackey, A. & Philp, J. (1998). Conversational interaction and second language development: Recasts, responses, and red herrings? *Modern Language Journal*, 82(3), 338–356. DOI:10.1111/j.1540-4781.1998.tb01211.x.

Manchón, R. M. (ed.). (2011). *Learning-to-write and writing-to-learn in an additional language*. Amsterdam: John Benjamins.

Meara, P. M. (1980). Vocabulary acquisition: A neglected aspect of language learning. *Language Teaching and Linguistics Abstracts*, 13(4), 221–246. DOI:10.1017/S0261444800008879.

Nakata, T. (2015). Effects of expanding and equal spacing on second language vocabulary learning. *Studies in Second Language Acquisition*, 37(4), 677–711. DOI:10.1017/s0272263114000825.

Nakata, T. & Webb, S. (2016). Does studying vocabulary in smaller sets increase learning? *Studies in Second Language Acquisition*, 38(3), 523–552. DOI:10.1017/s0272263115000236.

Nassaji, H. & Kartchava, E. (eds.). (2017). *Corrective feedback in second language teaching and learning: Research, theory, applications, implications*. New York: Routledge.

Nation, I. S. P. (2013). *Learning vocabulary in another language* (2nd ed.). Cambridge: Cambridge University Press.

Nicholas, H., Lightbown, P. M. & Spada, N. (2001). Recasts as feedback to language learners. *Language Learning*, 51(4), 719–758. DOI:10.1111/0023-8333.00172.

Norris, J. & Ortega, L. (2000). Effectiveness of L2 instruction: A research synthesis and quantitative meta-analysis. *Language Learning*, 50(3), 417–528. DOI:10.1111/0023-8333.00136.

Philp, J. (2003). Constraints on "noticing the gap": Nonnative speakers' noticing of recasts in NS–NNS interaction. *Studies in Second Language Acquisition*, 25(1), 99–126. DOI:10.1017/S0272263103000044.

Qi, D. S. & Lapkin, S. (2001). Exploring the role of noticing in a three-stage second language writing task. *Journal of Second Language Writing*, 10(4), 277–303. DOI:10.1016/S1060-3743(01)00046-7.

Quinn, P. & Nakata, T. (2017). The timing of oral corrective feedback. In H. Nassaji & E. Kartchava (eds.), *Corrective feedback in second language teaching and learning: Research, theory, applications, implications* (pp. 35–47). New York: Routledge.

Roberts, M. A. (1995). Awareness and the efficacy of error correction. In R. W. Schmidt (ed.), *Attention and awareness in foreign language learning* (pp. 163–182). Manoa, HI: Second Language Teaching Curriculum Center.

Russell, J. & Spada, N. (2006). The effectiveness of corrective feedback for the acquisition of L2 grammar. In J. Norris & L. Ortega (eds.),

Synthesizing research on language learning and teaching (pp. 133–164). Amsterdam: John Benjamins.

Santos, M., López-Serrano, S. & Manchón, R. M. (2010). The differential effects of two types of direct written corrective feedback on noticing and uptake: Reformulation vs. error correction. *International Journal of English Studies*, *10*(1), 131–154. DOI:10.6018/ijes.10.1.114011.

Schmidt, R. (1990). The role of consciousness in second language learning. *Applied Linguistics*, *11*(2), 129–158. DOI:10.1093/applin/11.2.129.

(1994). Deconstructing consciousness in search of useful definitions for applied linguistics. *AILA Review*, *11*, 11–26.

Schmitt, N. (2010). *Researching vocabulary: A vocabulary research manual*. Basingstoke: Palgrave Macmillan.

Sheen, Y. (2004). Corrective feedback and learner uptake in communicative classrooms across instructional settings. *Language Teaching Research*, *8*(3), 263–300. DOI:10.1191/1362168804lr146oa.

(2006). Exploring the relationship between characteristics of recasts and learner uptake. *Language Teaching Research*, *10*(4), 361–392. DOI:10.1191/1362168806lr203oa.

(2007). The effects of corrective feedback, language aptitude, and learner attitudes on the acquisition of English articles. In A. Mackey (ed.), *Conversational interaction in second language acquisition* (pp. 301–322). Oxford: Oxford University Press.

(2008). Recasts, language anxiety, modified output, and L2 learning. *Language Learning*, *58*(4), 835–874. DOI:10.1111/j.1467-9922.2008.00480.x.

(2010). Differential effects of oral and written corrective feedback in the ESL classroom. *Studies in Second Language Acquisition*, *32*(2), 203–234. DOI:10.1017/s0272263109990507.

Sheen, Y. & Ellis, R. (2011). Corrective feedback in language teaching. In E. Hinkel (ed.), *Handbook of research in second language teaching and learning* (Vol. II, pp. 593–610). New York: Routledge.

Spada, N. & Tomita, Y. (2010). Interactions between type of instruction and type of language feature: A meta-analysis. *Language Learning*, *60*(2), 263–308. DOI:10.1111/j.1467-9922.2010.00562.x.

Storch, N. & Wigglesworth, G. (2010). Learners' processing, uptake, and retention of corrective feedback on writing. *Studies in Second Language Acquisition*, *32*(2), 303–334. DOI:10.1017/s0272263109990532.

Suzuki, W. (2012). Written languaging, direct correction, and second language writing revision. *Language Learning*, *62*(4), 1110–1133. DOI:10.1111/j.1467-9922.2012.00720.x.

Suzuki, Y. & DeKeyser, R. (2017). Effects of distributed practice on the proceduralization of morphology. *Language Teaching Research*, *21*(2), 166–188. DOI:10.1177/1362168815617334.

Swain, M. & Lapkin, S. (1995). Problems in output and the cognitive processes they generate: A step towards second language learning. *Applied Linguistics*, *16*(3), 371–391. DOI:10.1093/applin/16.3.371.

Trofimovich, P., Ammar, A. & Gatbonton, E. (2007). How effective are recasts?: The role of attention, memory, and analytical ability. In A. Mackey (ed.), *Conversational interaction in second language acquisition* (pp. 171–195). Oxford: Oxford University Press.

Truscott, J. (1996). The case against grammar correction in L2 writing classes. *Language Learning*, 46(2), 327–369. DOI:10.1111/j.1467-1770.1996.tb01238.x.

⎯⎯⎯ (1998). Noticing in second language acquisition: A critical review. *Second Language Research*, 14(2), 103–135. DOI:10.1191/026765898674803209.

Van Beuningen, C. G., De Jong, N. H. & Kuiken, F. (2012). Evidence on the effectiveness of comprehensive error correction in second language writing. *Language Learning*, 62(1), 1–41. DOI:10.1111/j.1467-9922.2011.00674.x.

VanPatten, B. (1985). Communicative value and information processing in second language acquisition. In E. Judd, P. Nelson, & D. Messerschmitt (eds.), *On TESOL '84: A brave new world* (pp. 88–99). Washington, DC: TESOL.

Wilkins, D. A. (1972). *Linguistics in language teaching*. London: Arnold.

Williams, J. N. (2005). Learning without awareness. *Studies in Second Language Acquisition*, 27(2), 269–304. DOI:10.1017/S0272263105050138.

19

Effects of Corrective Feedback on Second Language Pronunciation Development

Kazuya Saito

In the field of second language acquisition (SLA), it has been well attested that corrective feedback (CF) on learners' linguistic errors is instrumental to the process and product of successful second language (L2) learning. The benefits of CF are theoretically attributed to its ability to promote learners' awareness, noticing, and understanding of linguistic form, especially when using their L2 for meaning conveyance (e.g., in task-based language learning, content-based classrooms) (Ellis, 2016; Long, 2007; Mackey, 2012). Furthermore, others have emphasized that CF provides ideal opportunities for learners to practice their L2 in communicatively authentic discourse, which in turn enhances their accurate, fluent, and automatic use in the long term (Lyster, Saito & Sato, 2013).

Over the past thirty years, the literature on CF has been largely concerned with the learning of L2 morphosyntax and has generated a number of insightful findings for researchers and teachers alike. For example, Li (2010) conducted a meta-analysis of thirty-four intervention studies focusing on CF and morphosyntax learning using pre-/post-test designs. Their results showed that CF positively influenced L2 learners' performance with medium effects when it was consistently directed to certain morphosyntactic errors. Similarly, focusing on fifteen classroom-based CF studies, Lyster and Saito's (2010) meta-analysis demonstrated that CF treatments led to medium-sized learning gains which were durable over an extensive period of time. Outside of morphosyntax, research has demonstrated the comparable effectiveness of CF for development in other domains of language as well, including L2 vocabulary (e.g., Dilāns, 2010) L2 pragmatics (Nguyen, Pham & Pham, 2012), and L2 pronunciation, which has received rapidly increasing interest in recent years (e.g., Saito & Lyster, 2012a, 2012b).

Given the increasing focus on the latter domain (CF and L2 pronunciation), it is timely and prudent to provide a piece of scholarly work which focuses on synthesizing and presenting the current state of affairs. Though a number of meta-analytic and narrative reviews have been published on the role of CF in SLA, this chapter is the very first attempt to provide a focused review for CF and L2 pronunciation in particular. The information provided by such a review could be useful for practitioners who are interested in how to use CF to assist L2 pronunciation learning in classroom settings; and for scholars with a wide range of backgrounds, including both those who are interested in instructed L2 speech learning in general (e.g., Derwing & Munro, 2015), and those who are interested in theory-driven pedagogical techniques (including CF) across different dimensions of language (grammar, vocabulary, phonology) (e.g., Solon, Long & Gurzynski-Weiss, 2017).

In what follows, I will provide a critical review on pronunciation-focused CF with three objectives in mind. First, I will explain what kinds of CF practices have been adopted in L2 pronunciation teaching and the instructed SLA literature, as well as how teachers and learners perceive them in various classroom settings. Next, I will synthesize the data from a range of recent quasi-experimental studies in order to elucidate the complex role of CF in L2 pronunciation development according to a range of affecting factors, including L2 learners' readiness (the presence/absence of explicit phonetic knowledge, conversational experience and perceptual awareness), types of CF (recasts vs. prompts), and instructional targets (segmentals vs. suprasegmentals). Finally, I will close the chapter by addressing, in particular, three topics worthy of future investigations: (a) the role of L2 learners' social and cognitive individual differences in the effectiveness of CF; (b) the need to integrate multiple analytic methods for assessing the effectiveness of CF; and (c) the differential impacts of CF for L2 speech perception vs. production learning.

How Has Pronunciation-Focused CF Been Used and Perceived in Classroom Settings?

In a broad sense, second language pronunciation proficiency can be considered as comprising four different dimensions of learners' sound production (for details of definition and outcome measures of L2 pronunciation proficiency, see Saito & Plonsky, 2019):

1. Segmental accuracy: Pronouncing new consonant and vowel sounds using L2 forms instead of using their L1 counterparts or interlanguage forms (a mixture of L1 and L2 forms).

2. Syllabic accuracy: Processing a range of syllable structures (e.g., Consonant-Consonant-Vowel [CCV]; CCVC; CCVCC) without deleting any consonant sounds or inserting any epenthetic vowels to consonant clusters.
3. Word stress accuracy: Assigning target-like word stress via enunciating stressed syllables with longer, louder or/and higher pitch.
4. Intonation accuracy: Demonstrating adequate intonational cues in the L2, using rising and falling tones at sentence boundaries.

Pronunciation-focused CF is generally provided by teachers, conversational partners, and/or computer software when L2 learners make pronunciation errors belonging to one or more of the above dimensions; thus, it is considered to be "production-based" by nature (see the section of Future Directions for a more detailed discussion on the role of CF during L2 perception training). During the 1950s, the dominant pedagogical practice (i.e., the audiolingual method) placed a strong emphasis on the mastery of pronunciation accuracy, particularly with reference to native-speaker models. According to this method, providing explicit CF was considered fundamental to L2 pronunciation learning and teaching, as any deviation from native norms needed to be amended immediately to prevent learners from fossilizing their errors. In the 1990s, however, researchers began to cast doubt on the importance (and possibility) of pursuing such native-like pronunciation forms in the first place. In fact, there emerged ample research evidence showing that few L2 learners can actually attain native-like pronunciation proficiency, and that accent is a normal characteristic of L2 speech (e.g., Flege, Munro & MacKay, 1995). Subsequently, a number of scholars have considered the attainment of adequately comprehensible (but still mildly accented) speech as a more "realistic" and "achievable" goal (e.g., Derwing & Munro, 2015; Isaacs, Trofimovich & Foote, 2017).

To date, researchers have exhaustively elucidated which pronunciation features should be taught and learned as a primary focus based on their relative impact on L2 speech comprehensibility. Such communicatively important features include word and sentence stress (Field, 2005; Hahn, 2004), prosody (Derwing, Munro & Wiebe, 1998; Kang, Rubin & Pickering, 2010), and segmentals with high functional load (Munro & Derwing, 2006; Suzukida & Saito, 2019). Though fewer in number, certain scholars have begun to explicate how we can teach these pronunciation features in the most efficient and effective way, especially by incorporating a range of focus-on-form techniques into the instruction, including via CF.

There are several ways to provide CF in L2 pronunciation pedagogy. For example, in explicit phonetic instruction, teachers can ask students to read aloud the target sounds and provide guidance on whether their pronunciation is sufficiently comprehensible and intelligible (i.e., isolated CF). To help ensure the accuracy of the feedback, some teachers can also rely on computer-assisted pronunciation teaching tools (e.g., De Bot, 1983;

Hincks, 2003; Hincks & Edlund, 2009). Corrective feedback can also be operationalized as teachers' post-hoc comments on the segmental, syllabic, and prosodic accuracy on students' audio recordings as a part of at-home assignments (e.g., Dlaska & Krekeler, 2013; Lord, 2005).

In the field of instructed SLA, researchers are generally interested in studying CF as a way to draw students' attention to phonological form during communication in a more spontaneous, naturalistic, and interactive fashion (i.e., integrated CF). Following Lyster and Ranta's (1997) oft-cited CF coding scheme, such CF can be delivered as recasts, which provide both negative (signaling the presence of errors) and positive evidence (presenting target-like pronunciation forms). Some examples for pronunciation-focused recast episodes are as follows:

Saito (2013)
STUDENT: I like **running** (mispronounced as [lʌn]) outside.
TEACHER: **Running** [ɹʌnɪŋ].
STUDENT: **Running** [ɹʌnɪŋ].

Sheen (2006)
STUDENT: Ho-, **Holland** (mispronounced as [hɒɹənd]).
TEACHER: **Holland** ([hɒlənd]), yeah.

In order to push L2 learners to modify their unclear pronunciation or mispronunciation, CF can also take the form of prompts, which provide negative evidence but without supplying model pronunciation forms. One example for such prompt techniques is clarification requests.

Gooch, Saito & Lyster (2016)
STUDENT: **Pray** (mispronounced as [pleɪ]).
TEACHER: Sorry? Can you say that again?
STUDENT: **Pray** ([pɹeɪ]).

Whereas recasts and prompts are thought to occur without interrupting the natural flow of communication, the provision of CF can also be more direct, taking the form of didactic, explicit correction, as in this example below in a French L2 classroom:

Lyster (1998)
STUDENT: Le renard gris, le loup, le coyote, le bison et la gr…**groue** (*the gray fox, the wolf, the coyote, the bison and the cr … crane*)
TEACHER: Et la **grue**. On dit "**grue**" (*And the crane. We say "crane"*)

To date, there have been a number of published studies descriptively probing the frequency of CF episodes during teacher and student interaction in various communicatively oriented classrooms all over the world. Brown's (2016) meta-analysis showed that teachers likely provide CF on students' grammar errors (42.7%) significantly more often than to their vocabulary (27.6%) and pronunciation (22.4%). Although pronunciation-focused CF does not frequently occur (especially compared to grammar-focused CF), students seem to be able to perceive the corrective intension of pronunciation-focused CF with greater ease and precision. In Lyster's (1998) oft-cited observational research on teacher–student interaction in French immersion classrooms in Quebec, for example, the audio-recorded data showed that young students corrected their pronunciation errors more following pronunciation-focused (62%) than grammar-focused CF (22%). In fact, this strong sensitivity to pronunciation-focused CF (i.e., repair ratio > 70%) has been found across learners with different ages, proficiency, and experience backgrounds in different classroom settings, such as adult L2 learners in English as a Second Language (ESL) classrooms in New Zealand (Ellis, Basturkmen & Loewen, 2001) and English as a Foreign Language (EFL) classrooms in Korea (Sheen, 2006).

Furthermore, some scholars have directly surveyed L2 learners' perceptions about receiving pronunciation-focused CF through stimulated recalls. For example, Mackey, Gass, and McDonough (2000) found that when asked to watch video recordings of their task-based interaction with native-speaker interlocutors, two groups of learners (learners of ESL and Italian as a Foreign Language) recognized pronunciation-focused CF more accurately than morphosyntax-focused CF (see also Carpenter et al., 2006; Kim & Han, 2007). Importantly, Mackey et al. (2000) argued that the learners' high-level awareness of their phonological errors might be due to the fact that inaccurate pronunciation has "more potential to seriously interfere with understanding" than morphosyntactic errors do (p. 493). Correspondingly, there is ample evidence that listeners tend to rely more on phonological information (40–50% of variance) than on lexicogrammatical information (30–40% of variance) during their assessment of accented L2 speech (Saito, Trofimovich & Isaacs, 2016, 2017).

Other research examining the perceptions of pronunciation-focused CF has yielded interesting nuances on the topic related to learning context. For instance, it has been found that students in foreign language classroom settings likely prefer to receive CF (and explicit instruction) on their linguistic errors overall (e.g., Schulz, 2001). Yet such a tendency seems to be weaker among students who are immersed in the target language speaking environment (Loewen et al., 2009). Additionally, in meaning-oriented classrooms, it has been shown that teachers generally have a more conservative attitude toward providing CF. According to previous observation studies, teachers in such contexts tend to correct only those errors which greatly hamper communication, arguably because they want to prioritize students' communication without too much interruption (Yoshida, 2008) and seek to avoid raising their anxiety levels by overly correcting them in front of their peers (Lasagabaster & Sierra 2005).

In addition to work on perceptions of CF, scholars have also explored learner and teacher *beliefs* about pronunciation-focused CF. For example, Baker and Burri (2016) interviewed five experienced ESL teachers in New

Zealand who all point to CF as a crucial component in L2 pronunciation teaching, especially when their students' errors hinder successful L2 communication. Huang and Jia (2016) administered a questionnaire to a total of seventy-five students and twenty-five teachers at a university in China surveying their beliefs on CF. The results pointed to the shared belief of the necessary role of CF in L2 pronunciation learning but revealed differences in their preferred CF strategies. Specifically, students preferred more indirect and less intrusive CF (e.g., recasts) while teachers preferred more pedagogically oriented CF (e.g., prompts or explicit correction).

Taken together, the observational and stimulated recall analyses presented in the aforementioned descriptive studies have generally indicated that L2 learners can notice the corrective and pedagogic message available in pronunciation-focused CF more unambiguously, promptly, and easily than grammar-focused CF (see Mackey et al., 2000). In addition, while some teachers may be cautious about whether or not to provide CF in meaning-oriented classrooms, it seems a majority of L2 learners are willing to receive CF and work on improving their errors for the ultimate goal of successful L2 communication. In addition, given that SLA is strongly linked to L2 learners' awareness of their interlanguage forms (Schmidt, 2001), the increased saliency of pronunciation-focused CF revealed across these studies seems to evidence its relative suitability for L2 development. In what follows, I will turn the review to answering whether, to what degree, and how, CF actually impacts on L2 pronunciation development.

How Beneficial Is Pronunciation-Focused Corrective Feedback?

To test the associations between CF and acquisition, many classroom and laboratory studies have been conducted using quasi-experimental, pre-test/post-test designs. These studies have generally shown that L2 learners can improve their pronunciation accuracy after receiving explicit pronunciation training (including CF) compared to learners not receiving any pronunciation-focused activities (e.g., Derwing et al., 1998; Hincks, 2003; Hincks & Edlund, 2009; Lord, 2005). The overall message of these studies is that explicit phonetic instruction (which includes CF) makes a difference in the development of L2 pronunciation (for meta-analytic reviews, see Lee, Jang & Plonsky, 2015; Saito & Plonsky, 2019).

More recently, a growing amount of attention has been directed toward examining precisely which components of explicit instruction are relatively crucial for L2 pronunciation development, using corrective feedback as an independent variable. As a part of stand-alone pronunciation training, Dlaska & Krekeler (2013) asked a total of 169 L2 learners of German to listen to and compare their own recorded utterances with native-speaker models. Those in the experimental group also received feedback from instructors on their pronunciation performance, while those in the control group did not. According to native listeners' judgments, the comprehensibility of the experimental group's speech (sentence reading) significantly improved compared to the control group.

Focusing on sixty-six Japanese learners of English with a varied length of residence experience in Canada (1 month to 13 years), Saito and Lyster (2012a) examined the effectiveness of pronunciation-CF on the acquisition of English [r] in a meaning-oriented classroom. All the participants engaged in a range of focused tasks where they were guided to use the target feature accurately (English [r]) while focusing on task completion (e.g., English debate activities). Throughout the training, those in the experimental group constantly received recasts from their instructor on unclear production or mispronunciations of English [r]. The results of pre-tests and post-tests showed that the participants significantly improved their English [r] production at both controlled (word and sentence reading) and spontaneous (timed picture description) speech levels. In a follow-up study, Saito (2015a) revisited the same dataset, finding strong practice effects; that is, the more CF the participants received, the more they self-corrected their interlanguage pronunciation forms following the CF moves, and the more gains they demonstrated during the project.

When it comes to L2 suprasegmental learning, Parlak and Ziegler (2017) examined how provision of pronunciation-focused CF could facilitate sixty-four Arabic L1 learners' acquisition of L2 English lexical stress. In their study, the participants engaged in an interactive role-play task via either face-to-face or oral synchronous computer-mediated communication. The experimental group received recasts on their lexical stress errors for certain target words, while the control group only performed the tasks. Results of acoustic analyses of the participants' pre-test/post-test performance (sentence reading, information-exchange task) showed that the experimental group appeared to pay more attention to the duration aspects of their speech (but not to pitch and intensity) to improve their L2 English lexical stress patterns.

Interestingly, whereas the existing literature generally supports the role of explicit phonetic instruction and CF in L2 pronunciation development, the degree of improvement seems to vary between participants to a great extent (e.g., Saito, 2015a). To this end, scholars have also begun to further push the research agenda ahead by expounding the mechanisms underlying the effectiveness of pronunciation-focused CF. Similar to L2 morphosyntax CF research (e.g., Lyster et al., 2013), a growing number of studies have been conducted to examine to what degree, when, why, and how the effectiveness of pronunciation-focused CF is subject to individual variability. In what follows, I will provide an overview on the potentials and limits of pronunciation-focused CF for improved L2 pronunciation proficiency according to commonly investigated learner internal and external factors.

Learner Readiness

One crucial factor moderating the effectiveness of pronunciation-focused CF concerns L2 learners' relevant experience with and knowledge of the target features – i.e., learner readiness. Using a design similar to Saito and Lyster (2012a), Saito conducted two experimental studies to test the impact of pronunciation-focused CF on L2 segmental and suprasegmental learning (Saito, 2015b for English [r]; Saito & Wu, 2014 for Mandarin tones). Unlike the original study, which was conducted with somewhat experienced L2 learners who had ample opportunities to use the target language in an L2 speaking environment (Japanese learners in Canada), the follow-up studies (Saito, 2015b; Saito & Wu, 2014) featured L2 learners in foreign language contexts, where such conversational experience was lacking. In contrast to Saito and Lyster (2012a), the results of Saito (2015b) and Saito and Wu (2014) showed (a) that engaging in meaning-focused activities led to significant improvements in pronunciation performance, but that (b) the benefits of adding pronunciation-CF remained unclear when learners were not developmentally ready (e.g., lacking in conversational experience or/and explicit phonetic knowledge).

Saito (2015b) attributed the lack of significant CF effects to the participants' insufficient explicit phonetic knowledge regarding how to repair target phonetic features on their own. Indeed, the post-hoc analysis of the video-recorded data showed that many of the participating students repeated the teachers' recasts throughout the treatment. However, they did so by simply substituting their L1 counterpart for the target sound – i.e., the Japanese tap [ɾ] instead of English [r]. Saito and Wu (2014) also argued that pronunciation-focused CF strongly implies modified output (e.g., students are strongly pushed to self-correct their interlanguage forms after pronunciation errors), which may be particularly overwhelming for inexperienced L2 learners with otherwise occupied, limited cognitive resources.

To further examine the relationship between readiness (operationalized as learner proficiency/language experience), CF, repair, and L2 pronunciation development, Saito and Akiyama (2017) tracked the longitudinal speech development of Japanese learners receiving CF from native-speaking interlocutors during computer-mediated dyads. Results indicated that while the inexperienced learners (who had studied L2 English only in EFL classrooms without any experience abroad) repeated their conversational partners' pronunciation-focused recasts, they nevertheless failed to demonstrate any significant improvement in terms of global L2 pronunciation proficiency. In contrast, not only did the experienced learners (i.e., more than one year of experience being abroad) successfully repeat their conversational partners' recasts, but they improved their pronunciation performance as well (Saito et al., 2019).

To date, several L2 morphosyntax studies have investigated how CF effectiveness can be influenced by learners' initial levels of proficiency, experience, and knowledge of target structures. Drawing on well-established developmental sequences of certain grammatical features, Mackey and Philp (1998) linked the effectiveness of CF to learners' initial proficiency levels. According to the results, CF (recasts) positively influenced learners who were developmentally ready to acquire the target feature (Stage 3), but not those who lacked developmental readiness (Stage 2) (for similar findings in the acquisition of English possessive determiners, see Ammar & Spada, 2006).

From a theoretical perspective, SLA is comprehension driven in that early-stage L2 learners establish and refine their linguistic representations through the noticing and understanding of input. These representations are then drawn on to produce target-like output in the later stages of SLA (Ellis, 1997 for a computational model of SLA; Flege, 2016 for the Speech Learning Model; VanPatten, 2002 for Input Processing). Consequently, many scholars have argued that providing CF on learners' production errors, which serves as one kind of output enhancement, *can* promote SLA, but only when L2 learners are developmentally ready (i.e., have sufficient proficiency, experience, and explicit knowledge of the target language). This is arguably because CF is believed to help consolidate what L2 learners have already learned rather than lead to the acquisition of entirely new knowledge (e.g., DeKeyser, 2007; Lyster et al., 2013; Nicholas, Lightbown & Spada, 2001).

Explicit Phonetic Knowledge

Reviewing the results of the above-mentioned studies (Saito, 2015b; Saito & Wu, 2014), we can draw the tentative conclusion that pronunciation-focused CF can positively impact acquisition when L2 learners are ready for it, i.e., have enough explicit phonetic knowledge for the CF to interact with. A valid question to ask is whether it is worth providing pronunciation-focused CF to lower proficiency learners. On a pedagogical front, it is crucial to further examine what teachers should do to help less experienced, less proficient, and less ready learners make the most of pronunciation-focused CF.

There is some evidence that providing explicit phonetic instruction before CF treatment may help these less experienced learners. For example, in Saito (2013), inexperienced Japanese learners (with little experience abroad) first received phonetic instruction on the articulatory properties of the target feature (English [r]) and were then guided to exaggerate the acoustic properties of the sound (with extra lip rounding, tongue retraction, and phonemic lengthening). Results indicated that learners in the group receiving CF (pronunciation-focused recasts on their mispronunciations) during post-instruction tasks significantly outperformed non-recast groups on all the outcome measures (perception, controlled/spontaneous production).

From a theoretical standpoint, it is important to ask what precisely constitutes explicit phonetic knowledge. L2 speech scholars have debated whether phonetic knowledge is principally realized on a perceptual basis (i.e., perceiving and distinguishing new sounds from L1 counterparts) (e.g., Flege, 2016) or on an articulatory basis (i.e., knowing how to use articulators to produce new sounds) (e.g., Best & Tyler, 2007), though both positions agree that the perception and production dimensions are interconnected (see Bundgaard-Nielsen et al., 2012). Pedagogically speaking, this has led to another kind of discussion on the relative importance of teaching the auditory vs. articulatory aspects of new sounds during explicit phonetic instruction (Celce-Murcia et al., 2010; Lee, Plonsky & Saito, 2020).

In the L1 speech literature on children with reading difficulties, it has been observed that adding articulatory training to phonological awareness development paradigms can be beneficial (e.g., Joly-Pottuz et al., 2008). It has been shown that intensive auditory training could lead L2 learners to enhance their performance at both perception and production levels (e.g., Bradlow et al., 1997); and that focusing on both listening exercises and articulatory explanation in explicit phonetic instruction is facilitative of L2 pronunciation learning (e.g., Saito, 2013).

Notably, some studies have revealed that an exclusive focus on articulatory phonetics may not necessarily lead to clear positive gains (Kissling, 2013). Further, recent empirical evidence has hinted that individual differences in L2 pronunciation learning may be unrelated to the presence/absence of their explicit articulatory knowledge (e.g., Saito, 2018, 2015a). Rather, it has been shown that successful L2 speech acquisition could be strongly tied to different amounts of learners' perceptual acuity (Kissling, 2014) and phonological awareness (Saito, 2018). The findings here are in line with major theoretical stances suggesting that learners' ability to perceive acoustic properties of new sounds is instrumental to L2 (Flege, 2016) as well as L1 (Kuhl, 2000) speech learning.

Types of CF

In the L2 morphosyntax CF literature, there has been extensive debate on which types of CF techniques are relatively beneficial for SLA (e.g., Goo & Mackey, 2013 vs. Lyster & Ranta, 2013). The discussion has been mainly concerned with how explicit or implicit CF should be (Ellis & Sheen, 2006), and to what degree it should be input-providing vs. output-prompting (Lyster et al., 2013). According to a series of meta-analytic (e.g., Li, 2010) and narrative (e.g., Lyster et al., 2013) reviews, explicit/output-prompting feedback (providing metalinguistic information and eliciting self-modified output while correcting) may be particularly effective in classroom settings, where a teacher typically interacts with a large number of students, and where L2 learners are reported to have difficulty noticing the corrective message in more implicit CF. In laboratory settings on the other hand, where L2 learners can receive individualized attention from their interlocutors, all CF techniques seem to be equally salient and effective.

To my knowledge, there is only one empirical study that has compared different types of pronunciation-focused CF in a meaning-oriented classroom. In the context of relatively advanced-level Korean learners of English, Gooch et al. (2016) partially replicated Saito and Lyster (2012a) by testing the effectiveness of two different types of CF – recasts vs. prompts (a combination of clarification requests [*pardon?*] and elicitation [*can you say that again?*]) – for speech development. The primary motivation of the study was to examine the role of positive evidence in speech development (recasts = positive and negative evidence; prompts = negative evidence only). In addition, the classroom interactions were video-recorded to provide additional data for more qualitative/online analysis.

While quantitative analysis revealed similar performance between the two CF groups, analysis of the video-recorded data revealed that the participants reacted differently to recasts and prompts. Whereas the recast group showed more attention to using more target-like English [r] by repeating the instructor's model pronunciation, the prompt group produced a high percentage of hybrid forms containing elements of both Korean [ɾ] and English [r], arguably because they were pushed to modify their errors while lacking a model of the target-like form. In short, the findings suggest that the effectiveness of pronunciation-focused CF can be attributed to both positive and negative evidence.

Types of Target Features

Many scholars have stressed that L2 pronunciation teaching syllabi should focus on those pronunciation features which most affect comprehensibility and intelligibility[1] (Isaacs et al., 2018) – a position concordant with the opinions of many teaching professionals as well (Baker & Burri, 2016). In Derwing et al.'s (1998) oft-cited study, adult ESL learners demonstrated

---

[1] A reviewer pointed out that the distinction between comprehensibility and intelligibility needs to be clarified in this chapter. Comprehensibility (i.e., ease of understanding) has been generally operationalized via rater judgments in existing L2 speech literature (see Derwing & Munro, 2015). Although intelligibility refers to listeners' actual understanding of L2 speech, this construct has been differently analyzed using a wide range of measures without a clear methodological consensus (for a review, see Isaacs, 2008). In essence, comprehensibility and intelligibility are two different phenomena. Having said that, in this chapter, I use these terms "together" (i.e., comprehensibility and intelligibility). In so doing, I intend to refer readers' attention to one global dimension of L2 pronunciation proficiency in a broad sense (i.e., how much L2 can make themselves successfully understood despite foreign accentedness) (for the distinction between global vs. specific L2 pronunciation proficiency and assessment, see Saito & Plonsky, 2019).

more gains from explicit instruction (including CF treatment) focused on L2 suprasegmentals (word and sentence stress, intonation) than from that on L2 segmentals. The authors attributed the relative effectiveness of suprasegmental-based instruction to the general observations among researchers that L2 suprasegmental accuracy is more directly linked to listeners' understanding of L2 speech (see also Kang et al., 2010 for cross-sectional evidence).

With respect to pronunciation-focused CF, Saito and Lyster (2012b) surveyed an instructor who was asked to provide CF selectively to Japanese learners' English [r] or English [æ] during four hours of meaning-oriented instruction. Although pre-test/post-test results found that students improved regardless of the target of instruction, the instructor pointed out that it was more difficult to correct English [æ] than English [r]. This was because the students' mispronunciation of the former sound was not as salient nor as detrimental to communication as that of the latter. Extending Baker and Burri (2016) and Derwing et al. (1998), the results of Saito and Lyster (2012b) suggest that pronunciation-focused CF could be a beneficial pedagogic activity, especially when it targets pronunciation errors which greatly affect L2 comprehensibility and intelligibility.

Similar observations have been reported for morphosyntax, with the noticeability of target features determining whether and how CF can be facilitative of SLA. CF studies in this domain have focused on the acquisition of relatively easy/simple (English past tense *-ed*) vs. difficult/complex (English comparative *-er*) features (Ellis, 2007), and the acquisition of exemplar- (regular past tense) vs. item-based (irregular past tense) features (Yang & Lyster, 2010). These studies have shown that the effectiveness of CF (regardless of its degree of explicitness) is particularly strong when target features are easy and salient (e.g., irregular past tense). For more difficult and complex features, it may be necessary to rely on more explicit CF which contains metalinguistic information.

How Should We Expand Pronunciation-Focused CF Research?

Compared to grammar, vocabulary, and pragmatics CF studies, there still exists much room for research on the complex relationship between CF and L2 speech learning. To close, I would like to suggest several topics worthy of future investigations, including (a) the relationship between CF-efficacy and cognitive and social individual differences; (b) the inclusion of multiple outcome measures to assess the efficacy of CF; and (c) perception-based CF.

Cognitive and Social Individual Differences and CF Effectiveness

While we have shown in this chapter that providing CF can positively affect L2 pronunciation learning, it should nevertheless be considered and investigated as a multifaceted phenomenon. Indeed, as discussed previously, the effectiveness of pronunciation-focused CF can vary substantially according to a range of independent variables (e.g., learner readiness, explicit phonetic knowledge, types of CF, target features). Among these variables, a growing amount of attention has been given to cognitive and social individual differences. Research in this area has shown that the process and product of L2 speech learning is influenced not only by experience-related factors (e.g., how L2 learners have practiced the target language) but by learner-internal factors as well (e.g., to what extent they are cognitively and socially adept at L2 speech learning).

For example, L2 learners with greater phonemic coding abilities (i.e., analyzing and remembering unfamiliar sounds) have been shown to produce better segmental accuracy in naturalistic (Granena & Long, 2013) and classroom (Saito, 2017) settings. Music aptitude (tonal and rhythmic imagery) also seems to play some role, especially for L2 suprasegmental learning (Li & DeKeyser, 2017; Saito, Sun & Tierney, 2019). Moreover, whereas the relationship between motivation and acquisition has remained controversial (Moskovsky et al., 2016), there is some evidence that certain kinds of motivation have an impact on L2 pronunciation learning, especially when the motivation is highly context-specific and strongly associated with L2 learning experience (e.g., Nagle, 2018 for the Ideal L2 Self; Saito, Dewaele & Hanzawa, 2017 for the idea of International Posture).

These studies suggest a tentative conclusion that the effectiveness of CF may indeed be mediated by certain cognitive and social individual differences. This conclusion has thus far been supported by grammar-focused CF studies focused on explicit aptitude and explicit CF (e.g., Yilmaz & Granena, 2016; cf. Li, 2013), and on anxiety and CF (Sheen, 2008). Following this line of thought, it would be intriguing for future studies to examine to what degree L2 learners with different aptitude, motivation and emotion profiles can differentially benefit from pronunciation-focused CF.

Multiple Outcome Measures

Many intervention studies have confirmed the effectiveness of instruction for L2 pronunciation development. However, Saito and Plonsky's (2019) research synthesis pointed out a range of methodological limitations in need of attention. Notably, in these primary studies, learner gains have been assessed predominantly via controlled speech tasks (e.g., word and sentence reading), using only lexical items exposed to learners during training. Rather than relying on such assessment methods, the impact of instruction (including CF treatment) should be probed by taking into account the complex, multidimensional nature of L2 speech learning.

To this end, it is worth looking at how L2 speech learning takes place in naturalistic settings. In essence, the initial stage of acquisition is lexically driven. For example, L2 learners' pronunciation of frequently occurring words (comprising 90–95 percent of the lexical items: Adolphs & Schmitt, 2003) may become easily comprehensible and intelligible, as these words are likely to be encountered and practiced repeatedly. In their longitudinal study with late L2 learners, Munro and Derwing (2008) found that a substantial amount of learning was observed especially when they were asked to pronounce common rather than infrequent words. The authors claimed that the word frequency factor could predict the extent to which L2 learners can develop "more accurate cognitive representations of the common items" (p. 495).

Once L2 learners increase their vocabulary size beyond the range of these most frequent words, they are forced to attend to fine-grained phonemic discrimination and identification (e.g., [i] vs. [ɪ], [p] vs. [b], [r] vs. [l]). As such, these learners become capable of accurately comprehending and producing speech by drawing on a large lexicon containing many confusing minimal pairs (e.g., *beat* vs. *bit*, *pit* vs. *bit*, *read* vs. *lead*). In terms of processing abilities, L2 learners of English have some initial difficulty accessing these newly developed phonetic representations, especially in meaning-focused communication. As L2 learners gain more experience through ample practice opportunities, they can increase their control over their phonetic knowledge so that they can use it more accurately, fluently, and automatically.

In light of the sequence of acquisition here, I argue that it is crucial to adopt multiple outcome measures to capture the intricate characteristics of L2 learners' developing phonetic knowledge. Given that L2 speech learning can be considered as a transition from vocabulary to sound learning, the impact of instruction and CF should be measured by examining the extent to which L2 learners can not only pronounce new sounds with trained lexical items but also generalize their newly acquired phonetic knowledge to novel and untrained lexical items not encountered during the training sessions. Additionally, learners' processing abilities should be analyzed by way of both controlled (e.g., word and sentence reading) and spontaneous (e.g., picture description and oral interview) measures. As has been the case in L2 grammar studies (e.g., Lyster & Saito, 2010), the pedagogical potential of CF should be most salient and obvious when it is assessed via tasks which can best mirror the way L2 is actually used naturalistically (i.e., free constructed responses).

Effectiveness of Perception-Focused CF

Whereas most of the discussion has thus far focused on CF and learners' pronunciation errors, feedback has been found to be similarly instrumental to acquisition when it targets L2 learners' perception errors (e.g., Lee & Lyster, 2016a; Logan, Lively & Pisoni, 1992; McCandliss et al., 2002; for a meta-analytic review, see Sakai & Moorman, 2018). During such perception-based treatment, L2 learners engage in a range of receptive activities where they are asked to identify and discriminate new target sounds without much pressure to produce them. In many training studies, providing CF (whether their answers are "correct" or "incorrect") has been a part of the treatment (e.g., Bradlow et al., 1997; Logan et al., 1992). Interestingly, McCandliss et al. (2002) demonstrated that the effectiveness of perception training significantly declined when the participants did not receive any feedback during the treatment.

To further examine the role of CF in L2 perception training, Lee and Lyster (2016a) implemented a range of activities to improve Korean learners' awareness of the English [i] and [ɪ] contrast. During the treatment, the participants consistently received CF from their instructor on whether they had made errors in perception. The results convincingly supported the benefits of perception-focused CF, as it enabled the learners to successfully restructure, confirm, and consolidate their developing phonetic representations in the target language. Lee and Lyster's (2016b, 2017) follow-up studies further examined the effectiveness of different types of CF on L2 perception development. According to the follow-up research, Korean learners demonstrated the largest and most robust gains when CF specified the target and nontarget forms involved in the error (e.g., *hit* but not *heat*). The authors argued that this combined CF treatment could be considered as the ideal type to strive for, as it allowed L2 learners to compare the phonetic properties of the target phonemic contrast (English [i] vs. English [ɪ]), without having to retrieve target and nontarget forms from their own memory. In contrast, only indicating the error (e.g., showing "wrong" on the computer screen) turned out to be the least effective strategy, an interesting finding given that this form of perception-focused CF has been frequently employed in previous L2 perception training studies (e.g., Logan et al., 1992).

As discussed earlier, many theoretical accounts have agreed that learners' performance in perception reflects the current state of their L2 phonetic representations/proficiency and that perception development can serve as an anchor for any aspect of L2 speech learning (e.g., Flege, 2016). Examining the CF-acquisition link enables researchers to control various elements of input (amount, quality, and timing of positive and negative evidence) as independent variables. To further the research agenda on successful L2 speech learning, therefore, it would be experimentally, theoretically, and pedagogically reasonable to include examinations of how L2 learners process various types of CF during perception-based training.

Conclusion

According to existing descriptive studies, both teachers and learners equally consider the provision of CF to be a crucial component of L2 pronunciation development, especially when the errors in question hinder successful communication. More recently, a growing number of scholars have investigated the acquisitional value of pronunciation-focused CF by conducting quasi-experimental studies with a pre-test/post-test design in both classroom and laboratory settings. Whereas the results have generally shown that pronunciation-focused CF facilitates the development of both segmental and suprasegmental accuracy, the effectiveness of such CF techniques appears to be subject to a great deal of individual variability. Specifically, the potentials of pronunciation-focused CF can be maximized (a) when L2 learners have enough phonetic knowledge, conversational experience, and perceptual awareness of target sounds; (b) when CF provides model pronunciation forms (e.g., recasts rather than prompts); and (c) when the target of instruction concerns communicatively important and salient features. A strong call is made for future studies to explore how pronunciation-focused CF can be implemented in the most efficient and effective manner. Such studies could examine, for example, how L2 learners with various motivation, emotion, and aptitude profiles can differentially benefit from CF when engaged in various types of training activities (perception vs. production-based training); and when their performance is assessed via multiple outcome measures (tapping into their transition from perception to production; from controlled to spontaneous processing abilities; and from vocabulary to sound learning).

References

Adolphs, S. & Schmitt, N. (2003). Lexical coverage of spoken discourse. *Applied Linguistics*, 24(4), 425–438.

Ammar, A. & Spada, N. (2006). One size fits all? Recasts, prompts, and L2 learning. *Studies in Second Language Acquisition*, 28(4), 543–574.

Baker, A. & Burri, M. (2016). Feedback on second language pronunciation: A case study of EAP teachers' beliefs and practices. *Australian Journal of Teacher Education*, 41, 1–19.

Best, C. & Tyler, M. (2007). Nonnative and second-language speech perception. In O. Bohn, & M. Munro (eds.), *Language experience in second language speech learning: In honour of James Emil Flege* (pp. 13–34). Amsterdam: John Benjamins.

Bradlow, A. R., Pisoni, D. B., Akahane-Yamada, R. & Tohkura, Y. I. (1997). Training Japanese listeners to identify English /r/ and /l/: Some effects of perceptual learning on speech production. *Journal of the Acoustical Society of America, 101*(4), 2299–2310.

Brown, D. (2016). The type and linguistic foci of oral corrective feedback in the L2 classroom: A meta-analysis. *Language Teaching Research, 20*(4), 436–458.

Bundgaard-Nielsen, R., Best, C., Kroos, C. & Tyler, M. (2012). Second language learners' vocabulary expansion is associated with improved second language vowel intelligibility. *Applied Psycholinguistics, 33*(3), 643–664.

Carpenter, H., Jeon, K. S., MacGregor, D. & Mackey, A. (2006). Learners' interpretations of recasts. *Studies in Second Language Acquisition, 28*(2), 209–236.

Celce-Murcia, M., Brinton, D., Goodwin, J. & Griner, B. (2010). *Teaching pronunciation: A course book and reference guide*. Cambridge: Cambridge University Press.

De Bot, K. (1983). Visual feedback of intonation: I. Effectiveness and induced practice behaviour. *Language and Speech, 26*(4), 331–350.

DeKeyser, R. (2007). Skill acquisition theory. In J. Williams. & B. VanPatten (eds.), *Theories in Second Language Acquisition: An introduction* (pp. 97–113). Mahwah, NJ: Lawrence Erlbaum.

Derwing, T. M. & Munro, M. J. (2015). *Pronunciation fundamentals: Evidence-based perspectives for L2 teaching and research*. Amsterdam: John Benjamins.

Derwing, T., Munro, M., & Wiebe, G. (1998). Evidence in favor of a broad framework for pronunciation instruction. *Language Learning, 48*(3), 393–410.

Dilāns, G. (2010). Corrective feedback and L2 vocabulary development: Prompts and recasts in the adult ESL classroom. *The Canadian Modern Language Review, 66*(6), 787–815.

Dlaska, A. & Krekeler, C. (2013). The short-term effects of individual corrective feedback on L2 pronunciation. *System, 41*(1), 25–37.

Ellis, R. (1997). *Second language acquisition*. Oxford: Oxford University Press.

(2007). The differential effects of corrective feedback on two grammatical structures. In A. Mackey (ed.), *Conversational interaction in second language acquisition: A collection of empirical studies* (pp. 407–452). Oxford: Oxford University Press.

(2016). Focus on form: A critical review. *Language Teaching Research, 20*(3), 405–428.

Ellis, R., Basturkmen, H. & Loewen, S. (2001). Learner uptake in communicative ESL lessons. *Language Learning, 51*(2), 281–318.

Ellis, R., & Sheen, Y. (2006). Re-examining the role of recasts in L2 acquisition. *Studies in Second Language Acquisition, 28*(4), 575–600.

Field, J. (2005). Intelligibility and the listener: The role of lexical stress. *TESOL Quarterly, 39*(3), 399–423.

Flege, J. (2016). *The role of phonetic category formation in second language speech acquisition.* Plenary address delivered at New Sounds, Aarhus University, Denmark, June 10–12, 2016.

Flege, J., Munro, M. & MacKay, I. R. A. (1995). Factors affecting degree of perceived foreign accent in a second language. *Journal of the Acoustical Society of America, 97*(5), 3125–3134.

Goo, J. & Mackey, A. (2013). The case against the case against recasts. *Studies in Second Language Acquisition, 35*(1), 127–165.

Gooch, R., Saito, K. & Lyster, R. (2016). Effects of recasts and prompts on L2 pronunciation development: Teaching English [r] to Korean adult EFL learners. *System, 60,* 117–127.

Granena, G. & Long, M. H. (2013). Age of onset, length of residence, language aptitude, and ultimate L2 attainment in three linguistic domains. *Second Language Research, 29*(3), 311–343.

Hahn, L. (2004). Primary stress and intelligibility: Research to motivate the teaching of suprasegmentals. *TESOL Quarterly, 38*(2), 201–223.

Hincks, R. (2003). Speech technologies for pronunciation feedback and evaluation. *ReCALL, 15*(1), 3–20.

Hincks, R. & Edlund, J. (2009). Promoting increased pitch variation in oral presentations with transient visual feedback. *Language Learning & Technology, 13*(3), 32–50.

Huang, X. & Jia, X. O. (2016). Corrective feedback on pronunciation: Students' and teachers' perceptions. *International Journal of English Linguistics, 6*(6), 245.

Isaacs, T., (2008). Towards defining a valid assessment criterion of pronunciation proficiency in non-native English-speaking graduate students. *The Canadian Modern Language Review, 64,* 555–580.

Isaacs, T., Trofimovich, P. & Foote, J. A. (2017). Developing a user-oriented second language comprehensibility scale for English-medium universities. *Language Testing, 35*(2), 193–216. DOI: 10.1177/0265532217703433.

(2018). Developing a user-oriented second language comprehensibility scale for English-medium universities. *Language Testing, 35,* 193–216.

Joly-Pottuz, B., Mercier, M., Leynaud, A. & Habib, M. (2008). Combined auditory and articulatory training improves phonological deficit in children with dyslexia. *Neuropsychological rehabilitation, 18*(4), 402–429.

Kang, O., Rubin, D. & Pickering, L. (2010). Suprasegmental measures of accentedness and judgments of English language learner proficiency in oral English, *Modern Language Journal, 94*(4), 554–566.

Kim, J. & Han, Z. (2007). Recasts in communicative EFL classes: Do teacher intent and learner interpretation overlap? In A. Mackey (ed.), *Conversational Interaction in Second Language Acquisition: A Series of Empirical Studies* (pp. 269–297). Oxford: Oxford University Press.

Kissling, E. M. (2013). Teaching pronunciation: Is explicit phonetics instruction beneficial for FL learners? *Modern Language Journal, 97*(3), 720–744.

(2014). What predicts the effectiveness of foreign-language pronunciation instruction? Investigating the role of perception and other individual differences. *Canadian Modern Language Review, 70*, 532–558.

Kuhl, P. K. (2000). A new view of language acquisition. *Proceedings of the National Academy of Science, 97*(22), 11850–11857.

Lasagabaster, D. & Sierra, J. M. (2005). Error correction: Students' versus teachers' perceptions. *Language Awareness, 14*(2), 112–127.

Lee, A. H. & Lyster, R. (2016a). The effects of corrective feedback on instructed L2 speech perception. *Studies in Second Language Acquisition, 38*(1), 35–64.

(2016b). Effects of different types of corrective feedback on receptive skills in a second language: A speech perception training study. *Language Learning, 66*, 809–833.

(2017). Can corrective feedback on second language speech perception errors affect production accuracy? *Applied Psycholinguistics, 38*, 371–393.

Lee, B., Plonsky, L. & Saito, K. (2020). The effects of perception- vs. production-based pronunciation instruction. *System.* DOI: https://doi.org/10.1016/j.system.2019.102185.

Lee, J., Jang, J. & Plonsky, L. (2015). The effectiveness of second language pronunciation instruction: A meta-analysis. *Applied Linguistics, 36*(3), 345–366.

Li, M. & DeKeyser, R. (2017). Perception practice, production practice, and musical ability in L2 Mandarin tone-word learning. *Studies in Second Language Learning, 39*(4), 593–620.

Li, S. (2010). The effectiveness of corrective feedback in SLA: A meta-analysis. *Language Learning, 60*(2), 309–365.

(2013). The interactions between the effects of implicit and explicit feedback and individual differences in language analytic ability and working memory. *Modern Language Journal, 97*, 634–654.

Loewen, S., Li, S., Fei, F., Thompson, A., Nakatsukasa, K., Ahn, S. & Chen, X. (2009). Second language learners' beliefs about grammar instruction and error correction. *Modern Language Journal, 93*(1), 91–104.

Logan, J., Lively, S. & Pisoni, D. (1992). Training Japanese listeners to identify English /ɹ/ and /l/: A first report. *Journal of the Acoustical Society of America, 89*(2), 874–886.

Long, M. H. (2007). *Problems in SLA.* Mahwah, NJ: Lawrence Erlbaum.

Lord, G. (2005). (How) can we teach foreign language pronunciation? On the effects of a Spanish phonetics course. *Hispania,* 557–567.

Lyster, R. (1998). Negotiation of form, recasts, and explicit correction in relation to error types and learner repair in immersion classrooms. *Language Learning, 48*(2), 183–218.

Lyster, R. & Ranta, L. (1997). Corrective feedback and learner uptake. *Studies in Second Language Acquisition*, 19(1), 37–66.

(2013). Counterpoint piece: The case for variety in corrective feedback research. *Studies in Second Language Acquisition*, 35(1), 167–184.

Lyster, R. & Saito, K. (2010). Corrective feedback in classroom SLA: A meta-analysis. *Studies in Second Language Acquisition*, 32(2), 265–302.

Lyster, R., Saito, K. & Sato, M. (2013). Oral corrective feedback in second language classrooms. *Language Teaching*, 46(1), 1–40.

Mackey, A. (2012). *Input, interaction, and corrective feedback in L2 learning*. Oxford: Oxford University Press.

Mackey, A., Gass, S. & McDonough, K. (2000). How do learners perceive interactional feedback? *Studies in Second Language Acquisition*, 22(4), 471–497.

Mackey, A. & Philp, J. (1998). Conversational interaction and second language development: Recasts, responses and red herrings? *Modern Language Journal*, 82(3), 338–356.

McCandliss, B. D., Fiez, J. A., Protopapas, A., Conway, M. & McClelland, J. L. (2002). Success and failure in teaching the [r]-[l] contrast to Japanese adults: Tests of a Hebbian model of plasticity and stabilization in spoken language perception. *Cognitive, Affective, & Behavioral Neuroscience*, 2(2), 89–108.

Moskovsky, C., Assulaimani, T., Racheva, S. & Harkins, J. (2016). The L2 motivational self system and L2 achievement: A study of Saudi EFL learners. *Modern Language Journal*, 100(3), 641–654.

Munro, M. & Derwing, T. (2006). The functional load principle in ESL pronunciation instruction: An exploratory study. *System*, 34(4), 520–531.

(2008). Segmental acquisition in adult ESL learners: A longitudinal study of vowel production. *Language Learning*, 58(3), 479–502.

Nagle, C. (2018). Motivation, comprehensibility, and accentedness in L2 Spanish: Investigating motivation as a time-varying predictor of pronunciation development. *Modern Language Journal*, 102(1), 199–217.

Nguyen, T., Pham, T. & Pham, M. (2012). The relative effects of explicit and implicit form focused instruction on the development of L2 pragmatic competence. *Journal of Pragmatics*, 44(4), 416–434.

Nicholas, H., Lightbown, P. & Spada, N. (2001). Recasts as feedback to language learners. *Language Learning*, 51(4), 719–758.

Parlak, Ö. & Ziegler, N. (2017). The impact of recasts on the development of primary stress in a synchronous computer-mediated environment. *Studies in Second Language Acquisition*, 39(2), 257–285.

Saito, K. (2013). The acquisitional value of recasts in instructed second language speech learning: Teaching the perception and production of English /ɹ/ to adult Japanese learners. *Language Learning*, 63(3), 499–529.

(2015a). Variables affecting the effects of recasts on L2 pronunciation development. *Language Teaching Research*, 19(3), 276–300.

(2015b). Communicative focus on L2 phonetic form: Teaching Japanese learners to perceive and produce English /ɹ/ without explicit instruction. *Applied Psycholinguistics*, 36(2), 377–409.

(2017). Effects of sound, vocabulary and grammar learning aptitude on adult second language speech attainment in foreign language classrooms. *Language Learning*, 67(3), 665–693.

(2018). Advanced segmental and suprasegmental acquisition. In P. Malovrh & A. Benati (Eds.), The handbook of advanced proficiency in second language acquisition (pp. 282–303). Hoboken, NJ: Wiley Blackwell.

(2019). Individual differences in second language speech learning in classroom settings: Roles of awareness in the longitudinal development of Japanese learners' English /ɹ/ pronunciation. *Second Language Research*, 35(2), 149–172.

Saito, K. & Akiyama, Y. (2017). Video-based interaction, negotiation for comprehensibility, and second language speech learning: A longitudinal study. *Language Learning*, 67(1), 43–74.

Saito, K., Dewaele, J.-M. & Hanzawa, K. (2017). A longitudinal investigation of the relationship between motivation and late second language speech learning in classroom settings. *Language and Speech*, 60(4), 614–632.

Saito, K. & Lyster, R. (2012a). Effects of form-focused instruction and corrective feedback on L2 pronunciation development of [r] by Japanese learners of English. *Language Learning*, 62(2), 595–633.

(2012b). Investigating pedagogical potential of recasts for L2 vowel acquisition. *TESOL Quarterly*, 46(2), 387–398.

Saito, K. & Plonsky, L. (2019). Effects of second language pronunciation teaching revisited: A proposed measurement framework and meta-analysis. *Language Learning*, 69(3), 652–708.

Saito, K., Sun, H. & Tierney, A. (2019). Explicit and implicit aptitude effects on second language speech learning: Scrutinizing segmental, prosodic and temporal sensitivity and performance via behavioral and neurophysiological measures. *Bilingualism: Language and Cognition*, 22(5), 1123–1140.

Saito, K., Suzuki, S., Oyama, T. & Akiyama, Y. (2019). How does longitudinal interaction differentially promote experienced vs. inexperienced learners' L2 speech learning? *Second Language Research*. https://doi.org/10.1177/0267658319884981.

Saito, K., Trofimovich, P. & Isaacs, T. (2016). Second language speech production: Investigating linguistic correlates of comprehensibility and accentedness for learners at different ability levels. *Applied Psycholinguistics*, 37(2), 217–240.

(2017). Using listener judgments to investigate linguistic influences on L2 comprehensibility and accentedness: A validation and generalization study. *Applied Linguistics, 38*(4), 439–462.

Saito, K. & Wu, X. (2014). Communicative focus on form and L2 suprasegmental learning: Teaching Cantonese learners to perceive Mandarin tones. *Studies in Second Language Acquisition, 36*(4), 647–680.

Sakai, M. & Moorman, C. (2018). Can perception training improve the production of second language phonemes? A meta-analytic review of 25 years of perception training research. *Applied Psycholinguistics, 39*(1), 187–224.

Schmidt, R. (2001). Attention. In P. Robinson (ed.), *Cognition and second language instruction* (pp. 1–32). Cambridge: Cambridge University Press.

Schulz, R. A. (2001). Cultural differences in student and teacher perceptions concerning the role of grammar instruction and corrective feedback: USA-Colombia. *Modern Language Journal, 85*(2), 244–258.

Sheen, Y. (2006). Exploring the relationship between characteristics of recasts and learner uptake. *Language Teaching Research, 10*(4), 361–392.

(2008). Recasts, language anxiety, modified output and L2 learning. *Language Learning, 58*(4), 835–874.

Solon, M., Long, A. Y. & Gurzynski-Weiss, L. (2017). Task complexity, language-related episodes, and production of L2 Spanish vowels. *Studies in Second Language Acquisition, 39*(2), 347–380.

Suzukida, Y. & Saito, K. (2019). Which segmental features matter for successful L2 comprehensibility? Revisiting and generalizing the pedagogical value of the Functional Load principle. *Language Teaching Research.* https://doi.org/10.1177/1362168819858246.

VanPatten, B. (2002). Processing instruction: An update. *Language Learning, 52*(4), 755–803.

Yang, Y. & Lyster, R. (2010). Effects of form-focused practice and feedback on Chinese EFL learners' acquisition of regular and irregular past-tense forms. *Studies in Second Language Acquisition, 32*(2), 235–263.

Yilmaz, Y. & Granena, G. (2016). The role of cognitive aptitudes for explicit language learning in the relative effects of explicit and implicit feedback. *Bilingualism: Language and Cognition, 19*(1), 147–161.

Yoshida, R. (2008). Teachers' choice and learners' preference of corrective feedback types. *Language Awareness, 17*(1), 78–93.

20

Corrective Feedback in Instructional Pragmatics

Kathleen Bardovi-Harlig and Yucel Yilmaz

Introduction

This chapter explores the potential for a role for corrective feedback (CF) in instructional pragmatics. Pragmatics can be defined informally as knowing how to say what to whom when, and the acquisition of L2 pragmatics as learning how to say what to whom when in the second language/culture (Bardovi-Harlig, 2013). More formally, pragmatics involves speakers' intentions and hearers' perceptions captured by Crystal's (1997) definition of pragmatics as "the study of language from the point of view of users, especially of the choices they make, the constraints they encounter in using language in social interaction and the effects their use of language has on other participants in the act of communication" (p. 301).

Pragmatic competence can be divided into two types of knowledge, sociopragmatics – the social rules of language use – and pragmalinguistics – control of the linguistic devices used to realize the sociopragmatic rules as well as to convey the intended illocutionary force of an utterance. The special nature of pragmatics and its relatively high variability and optionality make it a challenging context in which to consider the potential efficacy of CF.

This chapter begins with a brief introduction to CF. The next section considers the orientation of classic pragmatics literature toward feedback, exploring the ideological compatibility of L2 pragmatics research and the assumptions of CF research. The third section discusses studies that address CF in one or more research questions. The final section proposes ways to study and report the efficacy of CF in pragmatics instruction more reliably.

Corrective Feedback

Many L2 researchers (e.g., Gass, 1997; Long, 2007; Pica, 1988) believe that CF (i.e., input indicating that the learner's production is not target-like) has a beneficial role in L2 acquisition. Confirming evidence for this position has been found in studies investigating learners' immediate responses to feedback (e.g., repair [Sheen, 2004]), and their performance on individualized post-test items (e.g., Loewen & Philp, 2006). Confirming evidence has also been obtained in studies comparing the performance of feedback groups versus non-feedback groups (models [e.g., Leeman, 2003] or non-feedback control groups [e.g., Yilmaz, 2012]). In addition, reviews synthesizing the research on CF have demonstrated the benefits of CF for L2 development (Goo et al., 2015; Li, 2010; Long, 2007; Lyster, Saito & Sato, 2013; Nassaji, 2015; Yilmaz, 2016b).

Among the theoretical proposals that have motivated research on CF, the Interaction Hypothesis (Long, 1996) and the focus-on-form perspective (Long, 1991, Long & Robinson, 1998) are two of the most prominent. Both of these theoretical proposals have been influenced by the work of the researchers (Robinson, 1995; Schmidt, 2001; Tomlin & Villa, 1994) who have claimed that focal attention on language code features is necessary in order for those features to be acquired. The Interaction Hypothesis (Long, 1996) postulates that conversational interaction, especially when it involves CF, facilitates L2 acquisition by drawing learners' attention to L2 forms. Similarly, according to the focus-on-form perspective (Long, 1991; Long & Robinson, 1998), learners' attention should be drawn to formal elements of language in order for acquisition to take place. The focus-on-form perspective also specifies that this manipulation should be brief and performed when the need arises during a communicative or meaning-based activity (Long, 1991; Long & Robinson, 1998).

There are two widely accepted methods of classifying feedback types. One of these methods involves distinguishing between feedback types depending on whether they are explicit or implicit. Feedback types are considered explicit when they provide either one or both of the following: (a) metalinguistic information in the form of clues or rules (e.g., metalinguistic feedback); (b) information indicating that the learner's production is not target-like (e.g. explicit correction). Feedback types lacking both (a) and (b) are considered implicit (e.g., recasts). Another widely accepted method of classifying feedback types involves determining whether the feedback type pushes learners to repair their nontarget-like production. According to this distinction, feedback types that promote such a repair (e.g., elicitation, metalinguistic feedback, clarification request, and repetition) are referred to as prompts (Ranta & Lyster, 2007). Prompts are contrasted with reformulations (e.g., explicit correction, recasts), which restate learners' nontarget-like production into target-like sentences without pushing them to repair their initial production. Empirical studies that compared the relative effectiveness of explicit feedback and implicit feedback produced mixed results. Some studies showed an advantage for explicit feedback (Ellis et al. 2006; Goo, 2016; Sheen, 2007; Yilmaz, 2012, 2013), whereas several other studies reported no difference between implicit and explicit feedback (e.g., Goo, 2012; Loewen & Nabei, 2007). The findings of the studies comparing the relative effectiveness of prompts versus reformulations were also mixed. While some studies demonstrated an advantage for prompts over reformulations (e.g., Lyster, 2004), others reported no difference between the two feedback categories (e.g., Lyster & Izquierdo, 2009). It is important to bear in mind that several researchers (Goo & Mackey, 2013; Yilmaz, 2016b) have called for caution in interpreting the results of previous research because a considerable number of previous studies suffer from methodological problems.

A limitation of these observations is that they are based on a literature that exhibits a bias toward morphosyntactic targets. As a result, studies surveying the literature on CF include only a few that have investigated the effectiveness of CF in language domains such as pragmatics, which is the focus of this chapter. For example, a recent meta-analysis by Goo et al. (2015) included only two CF studies investigating pragmatic targets. Lyster, Saito, and Sato (2013), a narrative review focusing on classroom CF studies, included four such studies. Another meta-analytic study by Li (2010) limited its scope, excluding studies that investigated pragmatic targets. Given that pragmatic targets in the CF literature have been underinvestigated and are underrepresented, it is an empirical question whether the reported findings can be generalized to the pragmatic domain.

Feedback in Instructional Pragmatics

A Pragmatic Orientation
Instructional pragmatics and CF are not natural allies. In fact, a disinclination to correction may be built into the DNA of L2 pragmatics because correction implies a right way to do things, whereas in pragmatics, the key concept is choice. The underlying social rules – the sociopragmatics – may be seen as part of behavior. Sociopragmatics is realized through the linguistic system – or pragmalinguistics. Implementing CF in pragmatics potentially engages both behavior and language development. In this section, we consider what correcting pragmatic behavior might look like, the attitude of pragmatics researchers toward correcting behavior, the feasibility of sociopragmatic corrections, and the lack of pragmatic "rulebooks." We also consider contemporary pressure from instructed SLA research and pedagogical practice to expand correction to the pragmatic domain.

Let us begin to examine the potential for CF in pragmatics by considering the four-way analysis of speech-act performance used by Bardovi-

Harlig (1996): speech acts, semantic formulas, content, and form. The first three levels belong to sociopragmatics. As Kasper (2001) observes "pragmatics: sociopragmatics refers to the link between action-relevant context factors and communicative action (e.g., deciding whether to request an extension, complain about a neighbor's barking dog) and does not necessarily require any links to specific linguistic forms at all" (p. 51). Comparing a learner's production to the target language (a topic which is the subject of much debate in SLA, but a required step in CF), we may ask whether the learner produces the speech act preferred by the target language/culture for the particular real-world context. For example, when ending an appointment in an instructor's office, should a student thank the instructor for her time or apologize for taking her time? This is culturally determined. In the American Midwest, the preferred speech act is thanking (Bardovi-Harlig, 2009); in northern China, the preferred speech act is apologizing (Bardovi-Harlig & Su, 2018). Thus, American learners of Chinese need to learn a new speech act for the context as do Chinese ESL learners. Whereas speakers from both cultures express their indebtedness for the instructor's time and attention, learners must develop the feel for a speech act that is not preferred by their native pragmatics. CF at this level would amount to telling the American student in the Chinese setting "you should apologize" or telling the Chinese student in the American setting "you should say thank you."

The second level of analysis considers semantic formulas, the building blocks of speech acts. An apology, for example, has many semantic formulas, not all of which are realized in a single apology: [apology] [explanation] [responsibility] [promise of forbearance] [offer of repair]. While the head act in an apology, "I'm sorry" or "I apologize" is often present, an explicit statement taking responsibility for the offense, promising not to repeat the offense, or offering to repair the damage can be a matter of individual choice, but it may also be linked to the situation. Offering to replace a broken glass or clean a stained garment may be appropriate and within financial reach, but offering to replace a dog that one has run over seems callous. Whereas correcting the speech act was considered earlier, at this level learners would be admonished to include certain components, many of which are optional, highly personal, and vary according to context.

The next level is content. Bardovi-Harlig and Hartford (1993) demonstrated its importance in advising sessions. In an advising session, a graduate student may refuse an advisor's suggestion to take a particular course with an explanation. However, there are restrictions on the content. Legitimate explanation content includes time conflicts and a course being too easy. Illicit content includes claiming that a course is too hard or that a course is all new. Similarly, offering an alternative is a good move in a refusal, but legitimate alterative content includes a harder course or a course that provides a foundation, but not an easier course or no course at all. While we may prepare novices in a speech community about safe topics in advance of an event (such as coaching Ph.D. students before an on-campus interview in the United States *not* to talk about salary until the job offer is made), correction at this level might sound like "don't say that" or "don't talk about easy classes."

The last level is form. This is the level at which all the information at the other levels is encoded (Bardovi-Harlig, forthcoming; Kasper 2001). This is the domain of performatives, illocutionary force indicating devices (IFIDs), mitigation, aggravation, pragmatic routines and conventional expressions, address terms (and corresponding verbal morphology), discourse markers, intonation, and every other linguistic device that languages use to convey pragmatic variables. This level is sensitive to linguistic development (Bardovi-Harlig, 1999) and ultimately development of an L2 pragmatic system depends not only on the acquisition of target forms, but also the acquisition of alternatives in order for the use of the target forms to be meaningful (Bardovi-Harlig, 2017). CF at the pragmalinguistic level might look like "I was wondering if you could take a look at my paper" in response to the learner production "I want you to take a look at my paper" (Fukuya & Zhang, 2002). Corrections at the sociopragmatic level are akin to corrections of behavior, and corrections at the pragmalinguistic level are corrections of language. As Kasper notes, even at the level of form, "pragmatics is never only form" (2001, p. 51).

Takenoya (2003) articulates the difficulty with correction from the teacher's perspective. She notes that teachers are sometimes uncomfortable making corrections. She observes that teachers of Japanese may feel that they are forcing American learners to behave like Japanese, or that they themselves are acting like mothers who are teaching manners to young children, roles that fit neither participant. Thomas (1983) and Kasper (1997) voiced concerns similar to Takenoya's, emphasizing the social aspect of correction and adding the learners' perspective to that of the teachers':

> Correcting pragmatic failure stemming from sociopragmatic miscalculation is a far more delicate matter for the language teacher than correcting pragmalinguistic failure. Sociopragmatic decisions are *social* before they are linguistic, and while foreign learners are fairly amenable to corrections which they regard as linguistic, they are justifiably sensitive about having their social (or even political, religious, or moral) judgment called into question (p. 104, emphasis in original)

Closely related to issues of correcting behavior are considerations of learner subjectivity, or a learner's agency in accepting or resisting target-like norms (Eslami-Rasekh, 2005; Ishihara, 2007; Washburn, 2001). Eslami-Rasekh (2005) observed that "not all English language learners wish to behave pragmatically just like native speakers of the target language (Washburn 2001). An important issue to be considered by teachers is to acknowledge and respect learners' individuality and freedom of choice and their systems of values and beliefs" (p. 207).

Kasper (2001) raised two additional arguments: the difficulty of implementing sociopragmatic correction and the lack of firmly established norms. Building on the distinction of pragmalinguistics and sociopragmatics, Kasper notes the difficulty of applying principles developed for teaching grammar to teaching pragmatics.

> [T]he shift from pragmatic action to metapragmatic comment can be triggered by a contextually inappropriate pragmatic feature. As long as such problems are clearly pragmalinguistic, that is, the learner chooses an inappropriate *form* – a wrong discourse marker, routine formula, or modal verb to index illocutionary force or mitigation, for instance – *and* limited to short utterance segments, such problems may be fairly easy to identify and recast. But if the problem is sociopragmatic, things get murky."
>
> (p. 51)

She goes on to explain that sociopragmatically influenced errors may be difficult to locate. If a learner chooses a politeness style that is inappropriate for a speech event, markers of that style are distributed throughout the discourse; there is no single location of an error. The misidentification of the status (or power and distance) of an interlocutor can be pervasive.

Finally, correction assumes that there are rules. A compendium of knowledge is required, which teachers are unlikely to have at their fingertips (see also Wolfson, 1989, for the claim that native speakers do not have declarative knowledge of their own pragmatics); Bardovi-Harlig (2017) noted that there are no pragmatic reference books to which teachers can refer. Kasper (2001) raises an even more basic issue – the lack of firm sociopragmatic norms – as the "most serious reservation against instant identification and repair of sociopragmatic problems" (p. 52). As she points out, casual conversation has a wide range of allowable and unpredictable contributions which are negotiated in the flow of communication: "Such preferences and the options and constraints emerging from the interaction itself elude instant repair; they can most adequately be addressed in metapragmatic discussion" (p. 52).

Given the issues of correcting behavior, learner subjectivity, the feasibility of identifying error, and even the lack of firm norms to use in correction, it is no wonder that it has not played a significant role in the development of instructional pragmatics. Neither Ishihara and Cohen's (2014) comprehensive guide to the teaching of pragmatics nor Bardovi-Harlig's (2015) guide to designing instructional effects studies for pragmatics has a section on correction. Instead, the noticing approach to instruction is often implemented to allow learners to develop productive competence on their own terms (Bardovi-Harlig, 2018b). The disinclination to correct learner pragmatics is seen in the relatively few studies that have included feedback in pragmatics instruction. Taguchi's (2015) review of fifty-eight instructed pragmatics studies lists only twenty-nine that use feedback. Bardovi-Harlig (2015) reviewed eighty-one studies, only thirty-four of which reported some type of feedback. The studies identified a variety of responses to learner production such as peer feedback in telecollaboration, whole group discussions such as after-event debriefings, as well as teacher-provided feedback to both production and interpretation. In the studies that report on teacher-provided feedback, only four studies (Barekat & Mehri, 2013; Fukuya & Zhang, 2002, reported and expanded in Fukuya & Zhang Hill, 2006; Koike & Pearson, 2005; Takimoto, 2006) include CF in their research questions.

An Instructional Orientation
Contemporary to Kasper's (2001) seminal article, researchers of what would come to be known as instructed SLA viewed pragmatics as an unexplored testing ground for instruction, including CF. Early studies (e.g., Fukuya & Zhang, 2002; Yoshimi, 2001) investigated CF on pragmalinguistic errors and through both description and examples provide a starting point for the discussion in the next section.

Fukuya and Zhang (2002) developed a four-part grid for providing pragmalinguistic recasts. Recasts were given when utterances were pragmatically inappropriate by changing their head acts or when pragmatically appropriate but grammatically incorrect by changing the form of the head act, working with requests in English. They cite four possibilities: (1) correct form, correct usage in which no correction is given; (2) incorrect form, correct usage in which case utterances such as *I will be grateful if* was recast as *I would be grateful if* and *Would I mind* was recast as *Would you mind*; (3) correct form, incorrect usage in which *I want you to take a look at my paper next Monday* would be recast as *I was wondering if you could* ... and *Set up the table* was recast as *Do you want to set up the table*; and, (4) incorrect form and incorrect usage was recast by using one of four target expressions for each of high- and low-risk contexts.

A second example was provided by Yoshimi (2001) for interaction markers, a type of discourse marker used in Japanese narratives. Yoshimi provided delayed elaborated written CF using a transcript of learners' oral stories. The instructor and at least one teaching assistant – one of whom was a native speaker – and the researcher collaborated on the feedback. Yoshimi addresses the issue that teachers may not have declarative knowledge of the target pragmatics or that an immediate assessment may not always be available by delaying feedback and using a team of language specialists to provide feedback.

Both of these studies focused on CF for pragmalinguistics, providing examples of the feedback that was provided, but only Fukuya and Zhang's study made CF part of the research questions. In the next section we expand the search for studies of instructional pragmatics that isolate CF as a variable and we examine how feedback is conceptualized in those studies.

Corrective Feedback in Instructed Pragmatics as the Focus of Research

Literature Search and Selection Criteria

To identify studies in which feedback was one of the instructional features, we first checked the database used in Bardovi-Harlig (2015). We then searched the electronic databases of Academic Search (EBSCO), the Education Resources Information Center (ERIC), the Linguistic and Language Behaviors Abstracts (LLBA), PsycINFO, ProQuest Dissertations and Thesis, and Google Scholar with the key words *corrective/negative feedback, correction, pragmatics, pragmatic competence, speech acts*, and *politeness*. We used three inclusion criteria: studies (1) followed a pre-test/post-test design, (2) included research questions about the effectiveness of oral or written CF, (3) measured the development of specific L2 pragmatic targets.

Description of the Dataset and Design Features

Nine studies published between 2005 and 2017 met the inclusion criteria (Ajabshir, 2014; Barekat & Mehri, 2013; Fukuya & Zhang Hill, 2006; Guo, 2013; Koike & Pearson, 2005; Nguyen et al., 2015, 2017; Nipaspong & Chinokul, 2010; Takimoto, 2006). The majority of the studies (67 percent) were published after 2010, which indicated a recent increased interest in the role of CF in the acquisition of pragmatic competence. Eight of these studies were published in various academic journals, and one of them was an unpublished Ph.D. dissertation (Guo, 2013). Seven studies were quasi-experimental because they did not assign participants to treatment groups randomly, even though some of them used randomization at the class level (e.g., Nguyen et al. 2017). Only two studies were experimental. All the studies used some form of control group not receiving the feedback that feedback group(s) received. All the studies included a pre-test and a post-test, and six of them included at least one delayed post-test. Only six studies reported the timing of the tests they administered. Of these, four administered the pre-test several days before the first treatment session (ranging from two to seven), and two right before the first treatment session. In four studies, the first post-test was administered immediately after the last treatment session, and, in two, eight to ten days after the last treatment session. With the exception of Guo (2013) that included a three-week delayed second post-test, all the studies administered the second post-test four weeks after the treatment. Nguyen et al. (2017) included a third post-test administered eight months after the treatment. Written discourse-completion tasks were the most commonly used assessment task. They were used by eight studies. Two studies used multiple-choice tests, and one study used an oral role-play task.

All the published studies were carried out in a foreign language context. While the L1 of the participants varied greatly (Azeri, Chinese, Japanese, Persian, Thai, Vietnamese, and mixed), English was the target of eight studies, and Spanish was the only other target language. Out of eight studies that reported participants' proficiency level in the target language, six included intermediate-level learners, whereas the remaining two used participants from other proficiency levels (novice-high and intermediate-low in Koike & Pearson, 2005; and low-intermediate and high-intermediate in Nipaspong & Chinokul, 2010). Only Takimoto (2006) relied on the results of a standardized test to report on participants' proficiency, and the rest relied on participants' institutional status.

All nine studies were conducted in a classroom context. The length of the instruction learners received ranged from three sessions of 20 minutes to ten sessions of 90 minutes. It should be noted, however, that the reported length of instruction does not necessarily reflect how long the feedback treatment lasted. In a typical study, learners first received explicit information about a pragmatic target and then performed activities during which they received feedback. The reported length of the treatment indicated the total amount of time all instructional activities lasted in a study. The sample size in these studies ranged from 20 to 99 corrections with an average sample size of 50.11 (SD = 24.45).

Feedback Characteristics

The nine focal studies included seventeen different feedback conditions with six studies including more than one feedback condition. The most common feedback condition in this set of studies was metapragmatic feedback, which Nguyen et al. (2017) defined as "questions or comments related to the nature of the lapses in accuracy and/or appropriacy" (p. 17). Metapragmatic feedback was followed by recasts, which were used in four studies. Recasts were not always operationalized in the same way. For example, Fukuya and Zhang Hill (2006) used *focused recasts*, which involve the repetition of the inappropriate request form with a rising intonation followed by the question *"you said?"* and the provision of the appropriate request form. In other studies (e.g., Nguyen et al. 2017), recasts were defined as "a reformulation of an inaccurate/inappropriate expression" (Nguyen et al. 2017, p. 17). The reports rarely explicitly mentioned the timing of the feedback provided in the studies. Eight studies, however, reported sufficient information to infer when the feedback was provided in relation to the infelicitous production. In six studies, feedback was provided immediately following learners' infelicitous production, and in the remaining two studies, feedback was delayed until learners completed the task in which they produced the inappropriate output. The two studies that used delayed feedback were the only two studies that focused on written feedback, indicating a close relationship between modality and timing. The remaining studies included oral feedback.

In seven studies, feedback was provided during conversational interaction, whereas, in two of them, feedback was provided during noticing activities (Barekat & Mehri, 2013; Takimoto, 2006). This aligns with the emphasis on pragmatic awareness in instructional pragmatics but contrasts markedly with the CF attention to production. Unlike in the majority of the CF studies that were synthesized in the previous literature (e.g., Li, 2010; Yilmaz, 2016b), in six of the seven studies, feedback was not provided by an interlocutor, even though it was provided in the context of an interaction. Instead, feedback was provided by an instructor not involved in the interaction (e.g., Guo, 2013), and when learners performed a planned communicative activity in pairs, often in the form of a roleplay. Only Fukuya and Zhang Hill (2006) provided feedback by an instructor who was involved in the interaction.

A Pragmatic Perspective on Feedback Characteristics

All nine studies focused on speech acts, with six studies targeting requests, two refusals, and one suggestions. Five studies focused on pragmalinguistics and thus provided the type of feedback that Kasper (2001) suggested was the most feasible. Two studies additionally provided sociopragmatic information. In response to "Please give me more time to complete my work," Nguyen et al. (2015) give sociopragmatic information in the metapragmatic input condition, "The teacher has higher status than you. She also is not obliged to give you the extension" (p. 177). Nipaspong and Chinokul (2010) recast an utterance adding a semantic formula to metapragmatic information in Example (1).

(1) s: I'm sorry. I can't stay late today. I've a dentist's appointment.
    t: You may make it more polite by saying "I'd love to, but I've a dentist's appointment ..."

Not all studies provide examples of the feedback; however, all examples seem to be examples of *planned* feedback and no examples illustrate correction during an interaction. The paucity of examples suggests that CF has not been fully developed in instructional pragmatics. Some of the examples illustrate the difficulties with correction discussed in the previous section, adding correction of grammar for grammar's sake, providing unnecessary or questionable information, and inconsistent correction for the same infelicity across conditions. Grammatical correction in the service of pragmalinguistics, "a focus on grammatical forms in their role as pragmalinguistic resources ... that are used to express pragmatic intent, such as respect or politeness, in socially appropriate situations" (Félix-Brasdefer & Cohen, 2012, p. 561), is illustrated in examples (2) and (3) from Fukuya and Zhang (2006, p.24).

(2)   s: I was grateful if you VP.
       t: I'd be grateful if you VP. (recast)

(3)   s: Would I mind VP?
       t: Would you mind VP? (recast)

In contrast to pragmalinguistic corrections, some examples suggest purely grammatical corrections, as in the prompts and explicit correction provided by Nipaspong and Chinokul (2010) to refusals to an invitation in (4).

(4)   s: Oh.. I'm interesting, but I already have plans. I'm sorry.
       t: I'm interesting? I'm interest ...? (prompts)
       t: You should say "I'm interested." (explicit correction)

(5)   s: I'm sorry. I can't stay late today. I've a dentist's appointment.
       t: You may make it more polite by saying "I'd love to, but I've a dentist's appointment ..."

Some corrections appear to be as infelicitous as the learner production. In (1), repeated here as (5), a student refuses his or her boss's request to stay late to set up for a meeting (Nipaspong & Chinokul, 2010). The recast provided, "I'd love to," is not an appropriate response to a boss's work-related request but, rather, may be interpreted as overstated or sarcastic. An expression of willingness, such as, "Normally I would, but" or, "I would if I could, but" would be more appropriate to the work context.

Moreover, in the same study, the planned CF for the same utterance in (6) encodes different pragmatic information in the CF using metalinguistic clues plus elicitation and the CF using explicit correction. Thus, the students receive different information in the two conditions regarding the same infelicity.

(6)   s: I'm sorry. I can't help you today. I've a dentist appointment.
    a. t: Can you make "I can't help you today" softer? (metalinguistic clues + elicitation)
    b. t: You may make it more polite by saying "I'd love to, but I've a dentist's appointment ..." (explicit correction)

Finally, some suggested corrections may be unnecessary. In (7) Ajabshir (2014) provides a planned correction for a pragmatically infelicitous example from Bardovi-Harlig and Dörnyei (1998) in response to a teacher's request that the student check the bus schedules on the way home from school, "Could you check the bus times ...?"

(7) s: No, I can't tonight. Sorry.
    t: The form you used is not polite. You must use an apology formulae and/or an explanation.

However, there is an apology, "Sorry." In a pragmatics revision activity, ESL students corrected this response by moving "Sorry" to the beginning of the turn, "Sorry, I can't tonight," thus ameliorating the effect of the original response (Bardovi-Harlig & Griffin, 2005). Such a correction is precise, minimal, consistent with the learner's original contribution, and according to the empirical research, perceived as sufficient by learners.

Findings and the Validity of the Reported Findings

At first glance, the findings of these studies seem to show that CF is beneficial for the acquisition of specific pragmatic targets. As previously mentioned, all the studies used some form of control or comparison group that did not receive feedback. In five of these studies, the control group received an alternative form of instruction, in two, the control group did not receive any sort of additional treatment, and, in the remaining two, the control group completed the same production activity as the feedback group. Of the five control groups that received an alternative form of instruction, three followed their regular syllabus, one received TOEIC (Test of English for International Communication) practice, and one received delayed feedback. Six studies using this type of control group found that all feedback groups included in the study outperformed the control group, and eight found that at least one feedback group outperformed the control group. Guo (2013), which investigated the relative effectiveness of prompts in the form of metapragmatic feedback versus reformulations in the form of recasts in the acquisition of bi-clausal request forms, was the only study that did not find a positive effect for feedback.

However, the fact that the feedback groups performed better than the control group does not necessarily mean that the difference can be attributed to feedback. For such a claim to be made, the only difference between a control and a feedback group should be the presence or absence of the feedback. This was not always the case in these studies because feedback was accompanied by other instructional features in the feedback groups. Five studies that showed a significant difference between at least one feedback group and the control group included feedback groups that received metapragmatic information, and three included feedback groups that carried out other instructional activities, i.e., consciousness raising in Barekat and Mehri (2013), output production in Fukuya and Zhang (2006), and structured input activities in Takimoto (2006). It is not clear, therefore, whether the difference reported between the feedback groups and the control groups can be attributed to feedback. It could well be that the additional instructional feature, e.g., metapragmatic information, or combination of feedback and the additional instruction feature was responsible for the observed positive effect.

Fukuya and Zhang Hill's (2006) study was an exception in this regard because the researchers ensured that the feedback and the control group were different from each other only with respect to the provision of feedback which involved recasts on English requests. They accomplished this by asking the control group to perform the same role-play activity as the feedback group performed. Two other studies (Barekat & Mehri, 2013; Takimoto, 2006) were successful in isolating the effect of feedback by including a second no-feedback group other than the control group in their design and by exposing this group to the additional instructional feature that was given to the feedback group. This additional group helped them isolate the effect of feedback from the effect of the additional instructional feature. When the feedback groups in these studies were compared to these additional groups, it was shown that the feedback groups outperformed the no-feedback groups. Taken together, even though a large majority of the studies (eight of nine) reported positive effects for CF, only a small number of these studies had the appropriate research design to warrant the conclusion that CF had beneficial effects on the acquisition of specific pragmatic targets.

Six of the nine studies investigated the effectiveness of multiple feedback types, and thus, their results shed light on the question of whether the effectiveness of CF on pragmatic targets depends on CF type. Of these six studies, two reported no differences between the feedback types, whereas four reported an advantage for one of the feedback types. Ajabshir's (2014) study investigated the relative effectiveness of metapragmatic feedback versus recasts in the acquisition of English refusals. Ajabshir claimed that the metapragmatic group outperformed the recast group, but it is difficult to verify this interpretation because crucial information such as descriptive statistics is missing from the paper. Koike and Pearson (2005) investigated the relative effectiveness of four treatment groups combining one of two types of pre-instruction (explicit or implicit) and one of two types of feedback (i.e., implicit feedback in the form of clarification requests or explicit feedback in the form of metapragmatic corrections). The results were mixed. The group that received implicit pre-instruction with implicit feedback outperformed the other groups on the written DCT, whereas the group that received explicit instruction with explicit feedback outperformed the other groups on the multiple-choice test. Nipaspong and Chinokul (2010) focused on the relative effectiveness of prompts versus recasts and found an advantage for prompts over recasts in a multiple-choice test. Finally, Nguyen et al. (2015) investigated the relative effectiveness of metapragmatic feedback versus direct feedback, which they defined as "provision of the correct/suggested answer without explaining the correction" (p. 177). Their results were also mixed. The groups were not significantly different from each other on the discourse completion task, but the metapragmatic feedback group outperformed the direct feedback group on the delayed post-test of the multiple-choice test. These results need to be interpreted with caution because, in none of the studies that claimed to have found an advantage for one feedback type over another, was feedback the only instructional feature used.

Feedback groups in these studies also received metapragmatic instruction. The logic behind comparing two groups that are matched on explicit instruction (e.g., metapragmatic instruction) but different with regard to feedback type has been criticized in the previous CF literature on the grounds that it is not possible to attribute the observed effect to the feedback factor alone (Goo & Mackey, 2013; Yilmaz, 2016b). The effect obtained from the combination of explicit instruction and feedback might not be equal to the effect that could be obtained from feedback alone. The interpretation gets even more complicated in the quasi-experimental designs implemented in three of the four studies that reported a statistical difference between two feedback types. Since learners are not randomly assigned to treatment groups in quasi-experiments, it is likely that intact classes differ on variables that interact with the effectiveness of metapragmatic instruction. In other words, the use of unequal groups undermines the assumption that different groups would take advantage of metapragmatic instruction to the same degree. Another important threat to the internal validity of the studies relates to the extent to which the studies left room for exposure to learning targets outside of the experiment. Four of the nine studies reviewed did not administer their pre-tests immediately before the treatment, and two of the nine studies did not administer their post-tests immediately after the treatment. This makes it difficult to assume that the students did not gain explicit information about the learning target through sources such as the Internet, reference books or teachers, or receive positive evidence, including the learning target, inside or outside the classroom.

In addition to these potential threats to internal validity, some of the reporting practices in the synthesized studies not only decrease replicability of these studies but also prevent one from determining whether the studies suffer from additional validity issues. For example, no studies reported descriptive statistics showing the amount of feedback the groups received. It is usually considered a desirable design feature for studies comparing the relative effectiveness of different feedback types to balance the number of feedback instances. This type of control allows one to attribute any differences in learning gains to feedback type and not to the amount of feedback. The consistency with which feedback with different features was provided to feedback groups is another area where the reports are not clear. In all the studies, with the exception of two, feedback was provided to individual learners in a whole class or group setting. This creates three exposure conditions: learners who receive feedback on their own errors, learners who overhear the feedback provided to another learner, and learners who potentially are exposed to both (see Yilmaz, 2016a for a discussion of the role of exposure condition in feedback effectiveness). The studies reviewed did not report the extent to which each of these exposure conditions was represented in their feedback groups. Finally, in some studies, learners received feedback from a range of different feedback types that fall under the overarching category of prompts, but no information was reported as to the number of occurrences of each feedback type, what determined the selection of one feedback type over another, or whether only one or all of the feedback types were provided on a particular infelicitous production. In the absence of this crucial information, it is not possible to exactly replicate these studies or to fully evaluate the quality of the evidence they provide.

Planning Corrective Feedback for Instructional Pragmatics

The nine pioneering studies reviewed here show that the state of CF studies in instructed pragmatics is still in its infancy. Many of the issues raised in the second section of this chapter have surfaced in the scant examples provided by the reports. The majority of the corrections are pragmalinguistic; the rare examples show that at some points the corrections are purely grammatical and at others are infelicitous themselves. The minority are sociopragmatic.

On the basis of the present review, we can neither advocate for the implementation of CF in instructional pragmatics nor advocate against it. What we can do instead is to lay out some guidelines for principled investigations into CF in instructional pragmatics, drawing from research in both pragmatics and CF. The following five points outline essential design requirements. The decisions made for each should be described clearly in any report.

1. Include at least a pre-test and a post-test. Make sure that the pre-test is administered immediately before the treatment and the post-test immediately after the treatment.
2. Include assessment tasks that are matched with the task in which learners receive feedback for modality (Bardovi-Harlig, 2018a). Make sure to select tasks that can measure the extent to which learners display the knowledge in a real-life setting.
3. Make sure that feedback is the only instructional feature included in the treatment. If it is necessary to provide instruction including metapragmatic information and there is theoretical support for it, provide instruction to all groups before the pre-test. This allows researchers to classify learners with similar scores into subgroups and to make sure

that learners belonging to these subgroups are equally distributed across treatment groups.
4. Characteristics of the chosen feedback type should be predetermined by the researcher and included in the description of the feedback. The description should be precise enough to allow readers to reliably deduce how the feedback was provided after each infelicitous production. Feedback interactions (i.e., actual performed infelicity, feedback, and responses, if any) should also be reported.
5. If two feedback types are compared for a theoretically motivated difference, such as explicit vs. implicit, or prompts vs. reformulations, make sure that the only characteristic on which these feedback types differ is the characteristic specified by the theory. Other feedback characteristics, such as modality (e.g., written, oral), modified output opportunities (whether learners are provided with an opportunity to repair their initial infelicitous productions), timing of feedback (immediate or delayed), exposure condition (whether learners receive feedback on their own infelicitous productions or hear the feedback that is provided to other learners), should be controlled.

Whereas the five principles apply to CF investigations in any linguistic domain, within instructional pragmatics there are additional considerations as this review has highlighted. Sociopragmatic CF – and even pragmalinguistic CF – has to be carried out without seeming to challenge a learner's behavior. One way may be to delay provision of sociopragmatic information and/or to say it impersonally, allowing observations about what speakers of the target language do. "In this situation, speakers of English generally do X" or "speakers of Kiswahili generally open a conversation with ten greeting turns. Can you add one more turn sequence to your role play?"

Holden and Sykes (2013) invite us to explore the possibility of creating feedback uniquely suited for pragmatics instruction. The online game developed by Holden and Sykes, *Mentira*, has the potential for providing feedback without appearing to correct the learner's behavior. In *Mentira*, students are assigned to a family. Each family has specific values and speech characteristics (such as being direct). When students select speech that is inappropriate for the context (such as informal direct speech to a high status character who is part of the game), they could be reprimanded or corrected.

> Through these various contextualized interactions, learners see the impact of their pragmatic choices by learning to select behaviors relevant to each specific interaction or character. As a result, the same semantic formula has the effect of being extremely rude in one case and perfectly appropriate in another. A player is made aware of the success (or failure) of these choices through the NPCs' [nonplayer characters'] reactions and the assets that are awarded or taken away in the game (e.g., clues).
>
> (Holden & Sykes, 2013, p. 171)

Holden and Sykes also discuss the possibility of escalating the negative feedback provided when a learner does not meet the stated speech expectations, such as the family patriarch slamming a door or ending the conversation. The feedback in the game is immediate and individualized. Importantly, learners may restart the game and try a different pragmatic strategy (either sociopragmatic or pragmalinguistic) to effect a different outcome. Since other players in the game are the ones who provide the negative feedback, the risk to learner and instructor is removed.

This brings us to three avenues for future research. The first is testing the efficacy of delayed CF in instructed pragmatics. Delayed feedback could be a good choice in instructional pragmatics for the reasons discussed; however, it is important to determine whether it can be causally linked to the acquisition of pragmatic targets, as well as whether it is comparable to immediate feedback in effectiveness. The second avenue of investigation is to compare sociopragmatic feedback with pragmalinguistic feedback (acknowledging that means of sociopragmatic feedback must yet be developed). Given that sociopragmatics and pragmalinguistics constitute different types of knowledge, this represents a potentially informative comparison. The third avenue of investigation involves, first, designing online games, similar to the one developed by Holden and Sykes (2013), which can provide feedback uniquely suited for pragmatic instruction, and, second, evaluating the effectiveness of this feedback using valid assessment tasks that have the potential to measure learners' real-life pragmatic performance.

The development of pragmatic specific CF offers an exciting challenge to researchers, materials developers, and instructors working in instructional pragmatics. Careful documentation of such innovations will ultimately provide an empirical answer to the question of whether CF can facilitate L2 pragmatic development.

References

Ajabshir, Z. F. (2014). The effect of implicit and explicit types of feedback on learners' pragmatic development. *Procedia – Social and Behavioral Sciences*, 98, 463–471.

Bardovi-Harlig, K. (1996). Pragmatics and language teaching: Bringing pragmatics and pedagogy together. *Pragmatics and Language Learning*, 7, 21–39.

(1999). The interlanguage of interlanguage pragmatics: A research agenda for acquisitional pragmatics. *Language Learning*, 49(4), 677–713.

(2009). Conventional expressions as a pragmalinguistic resource: Recognition and production of conventional expressions in L2 pragmatics. *Language Learning*, 59(4), 755–795.

(2013). Developing L2 pragmatics. *Language Learning*, 63(Suppl. 1), 68–86.

(2015). Operationalizing conversation in studies of instructional effects in L2 pragmatics. *System*, *48*, 21–34.
(2017). Acquisition of pragmatics. In S. Loewen & M. Sato (eds.), *Handbook of instructed SLA* (pp. 224–245). New York; London: Routledge.
(2018a). Matching modality in L2 pragmatics research. *System*, *75*, 13–22.
(2018b). Pragmatic awareness in second language acquisition. In P. Garret & J. Maria Cots (eds.), *Routledge handbook of language awareness* (pp. 323–338). New York: Taylor & Francis.
(2019). Routines in L2 pragmatics research. In N. Taguchi (ed.), *Handbook of SLA and pragmatics* (pp. 47–62). New York: Routledge.
Bardovi-Harlig, K. & Dörnyei, Z. (1998). Do language learners recognize pragmatic violations? Pragmatic vs. grammatical awareness in instructed L2 learning. *TESOL Quarterly*, *32*(2), 233–259.
Bardovi-Harlig, K. & Griffin, R. (2005). L2 pragmatic awareness: Evidence from the ESL classroom. *System*, *33*(3), 401–415.
Bardovi-Harlig, K. & Hartford, B. S. (1993). Learning the rules of academic talk: A longitudinal study of pragmatic development. *Studies in Second Language Acquisition*, *15*(3), 279–304.
Bardovi-Harlig, K. & Su, Y. (2018). The acquisition of conventional expressions as a pragmalinguistic resource in Chinese as a foreign language. *Modern Language Journal*, *102*(4), 732–757.
Barekat, B. & Mehri, M. (2013). Investigating effects of metalinguistic feedback in L2 pragmatic instruction. *International Journal of Linguistics*, *5*(2), 197–208.
Crystal, D. (ed.). (1997). *The Cambridge encyclopedia of language* (2nd ed.). New York: Cambridge University Press.
Ellis, R., Loewen, S. & Erlam, R. (2006). Implicit and explicit corrective feedback and the acquisition of L2 grammar. *Studies in Second Language Acquisition*, *28*(2), 339–368.
Eslami-Rasekh, Z. (2005). Raising the pragmatic awareness of language learners. *ELT Journal*, *59*(3), 199–208.
Félix-Brasdefer, J. C. & Cohen, A. D. (2012). Teaching pragmatics in the foreign language classroom: Grammar as a communicative resource. *Hispania*, *95*(4), 650–669.
Fukuya, Y. & Zhang, Y. (2002). Effects of recasts on EFL learners' acquisition of pragmalinguistic conventions of request. *Second Language Studies*, *21*(1), 1–47.
Fukuya, Y. J. & Zhang Hill, Y. (2006). The effects of recasting on the production of pragmalinguistic conventions of request by Chinese learners of English. *Issues in Applied Linguistics*, *15*(1), 59–91.
Gass, S. (1997). *Input, Interaction and the second language learner*. Mahwah, NJ: Lawrence Erlbaum.
Goo, J. (2012). Corrective feedback and working memory capacity in interaction-driven L2 learning. *Studies in Second Language Acquisition*, *34*(3), 445–474.

(2016). Corrective feedback and working memory capacity: A replication. In G. Granena, D. O. Jackson & Y. Yilmaz (eds.), *Cognitive individual differences in second language processing and acquisition* (pp. 276–302). Amsterdam: John Benjamins.

Goo, J., Granena, G., Yilmaz, Y. & Novella, M. (2015). Implicit and explicit instruction in L2 learning: Norris & Ortega (2000) revisited and updated. In P. Rebuschat (ed.), *Implicit and explicit learning of languages* (Vol. IV, pp. 443–483). Amsterdam: John Benjamins.

Goo, J. & Mackey, A. (2013). The case against the case against recasts. *Studies in Second Language Acquisition, 35(1)*, 127–165.

Guo, L. (2013). Effects of recasts and metalinguistic feedback on developing ESL learners' pragmatic competence. Unpublished Ph.D. dissertation, University of Kansas, Lawrence.

Holden, C. L. & Sykes, J. M. (2013). Complex L2 pragmatic feedback via place-based mobile games. In N. Taguchi & J. M. Sykes (eds.), *Technology in interlanguage pragmatics research and teaching* (pp. 155–170). Philadelphia: John Benjamins.

Ishihara, N. (2007). Web-based curriculum for pragmatics instruction in Japanese as a foreign language: An explicit awareness-raising approach. *Language Awareness, 16(1)*, 21–40.

Ishihara, N. & Cohen, A. D. (2014). *Teaching and learning pragmatics: Where language and culture meet.* Abingdon: Routledge.

Kasper, G. (1997). The role of pragmatics in language teacher education. In K. Bardovi-Harlig & B. S. Hartford (eds.), *Beyond methods: Components of language teacher education* (pp. 113–136). New York: McGraw Hill.

(2001). Classroom research on interlanguage pragmatics. In K. Rose & G. Kasper (eds.), *Pragmatics in language teaching* (pp. 33–60). Cambridge: Cambridge University Press.

Koike, D. & Pearson, L. (2005). The effect of instruction and feedback in the development of pragmatic competence. *System, 33(3)*, 481–501.

Leeman, J. (2003). Recasts and second language development. *Studies in Second Language Acquisition, 25(1)*, 37–63.

Li, S. (2010). The effectiveness of corrective feedback in SLA: A meta-analysis. *Language Learning, 60(2)*, 309–365.

Loewen, S. & Nabei, T. (2007). Measuring the effects of oral corrective feedback on L2 knowledge. In A. Mackey (ed.), *Conversational interaction in second language acquisition* (pp. 361–377). New York: Oxford University Press.

Loewen, S. & Philp, J. (2006). Recasts in the adult L2 classroom: Characteristics, explicitness and effectiveness. *Modern Language Journal, 90(4)*, 536–556.

Long, M. (1991). Focus on form: A design feature in language teaching methodology. In K. De Bot, R. Ginsberg & C. Kramsch (eds.), *Foreign language research in cross-cultural perspectives* (pp. 39–52). Amsterdam: John Benjamins.

(1996). The role of the linguistic environment in second language acquisition. In W. Ritchie & T. K. Bhatia (eds.), *Handbook of second language acquisition* (pp. 413–468). New York: Academic Press.

Long, M. H. (2007). *Problems in SLA*. New York: Lawrence Erlbaum.

Long, M. H. & Robinson, P. (1998). *Focus on form in classroom second language acquisition*. New York: Cambridge University Press.

Lyster, R. (2004). Differential effects of prompts and recasts in form-focused instruction. *Studies in Second Language Acquisition*, 26(3), 399–432.

Lyster, R. & Izquierdo, J. (2009). Prompts versus recasts in dyadic interaction. *Language Learning*, 59(3), 453–498.

Lyster, R., Saito, K. & Sato, M. (2013). Oral corrective feedback in second language classrooms. *Language Teaching*, 46(1), 1–40.

Nassaji, H. (2015). *The interactional feedback dimension in instructed second language learning: Linking Theory, Research and Practice*. New York: Bloomsbury.

Nguyen, M. T. T., Do, H. T., Nguyen A. T. & Pham T. T. (2015). Teaching email requests in the academic context: A focus on the role of corrective feedback. *Language Awareness*, 24(2), 169–195.

(2017). The effectiveness of corrective feedback for the acquisition of L2 pragmatics: An eight-month investigation. *International Review of Applied Linguistics in Language Teaching (IRAL) early access*.

Nipaspong, P. & Chinokul, S. (2010). The role of prompts and explicit feedback in raising EFL learners' pragmatic awareness. *University of Sydney Papers in TESOL*, 5, 101–146.

Pica, T. (1988). Interlanguage adjustments as outcome of NS–NNS negotiated interaction. *Language Learning*, 38(1), 45–73.

Ranta, L. & Lyster, R. (2007). A cognitive approach to improving immersion students' oral language abilities: The awareness-practice-feedback sequence. In R. DeKeyser (ed.), *Practice in a second language: Perspectives from applied linguistics and cognitive psychology* (pp. 141–160). Cambridge: Cambridge University Press.

Robinson, P. (1995). Attention, memory, and the "noticing" hypothesis. *Language Learning*, 45(2), 283–331.

Schmidt, R. (2001). Attention. In P. Robinson (ed.), *Cognition and second language instruction* (pp. 3–32). Cambridge: Cambridge University Press.

Sheen, Y. (2004). Corrective feedback and learners' uptake in communicative classrooms across instructional settings. *Language Teaching Research*, 8(3), 263–300.

(2007). The effects of corrective feedback, language aptitude, and learner attitudes on the acquisition of English articles. In A. Mackey (ed.), *Conversational interaction in second language acquisition* (pp. 301–322). New York: Oxford University Press.

Taguchi, N. (2015). Instructed pragmatics at a glance: Where instructional studies were, are, and should be going. *Language Teaching*, 48(1), 1–50.

Takenoya, M. (2003). *Terms of address in Japanese: An interlanguage pragmatics approach*. Sapporo: Hokkaido University Press.

Takimoto, M. (2006). The effects of explicit feedback and form-meaning processing on the development of pragmatic proficiency in consciousness-raising tasks. *System, 34*(4), 601–614.

Thomas, J. (1983). Cross-cultural pragmatic failure. *Applied Linguistics, 4*(2), 91–111.

Tomlin, R., & Villa, V. (1994). Attention in cognitive science and second language acquisition. *Studies in Second Language Acquisition, 16*(2), 183–204.

Washburn, G. (2001). Using situation comedies for pragmatic language teaching and learning. *TESOL Journal, 10*(4), 21–26.

Wolfson, N. (1989). *Perspectives: Sociolinguistics and TESOL*. Rowley, MA: Newbury House.

Yilmaz, Y. (2012). The relative effects of explicit correction and recasts on two target structures via two communication modes. *Language Learning, 62*(4), 1134–1169.

(2013). The relative effectiveness of mixed, explicit and implicit feedback. *System, 41*(3), 691–705.

(2016a). The effectiveness of explicit correction under two different feedback exposure conditions. *Studies in Second Language Acquisition, 38*(1), 65–96.

(2016b). The linguistic environment, interaction and negative feedback. *Brill Research Perspectives in Multilingualism and Second Language Acquisition, 1*, 45–86.

Yoshimi, D. R. (2001). Explicit instruction and JFL learners' use of interactional discourse markers. In K. Rose & G. Kasper (eds.), *Pragmatics in language teaching* (pp. 223–244). Cambridge: Cambridge University Press.

21

Alphabetic Print Literacy Level and Noticing Oral Corrective Feedback in SLA

Elaine Tarone

Introduction

A stated goal of this handbook is to summarize cutting-edge research and recent developments in core areas of error correction and their implications for second language acquisition and instruction. The present chapter reviews a small body of research on error correction addressed to adult second language (and second-dialect) learners with emergent literacy. It is recognized that, although second languages (L2s) are regularly taught to adults who have low and emergent literacy skills, virtually all the research on error correction in second language acquisition (SLA) has focused on very literate second language learners. Low print literacy levels are a worldwide phenomenon; a UNESCO study (2017) found that 15 percent of all adults worldwide lacked basic reading and writing skills. Because almost all of them also are multilingual in several languages, it is likely they have acquired at least some of these languages through processes of SLA. There is simply little research on the processes of SLA this population engages in, so our understanding of the impact of error correction upon those processes is limited. Just in the period between 2012 and 2014, 41 percent of adult immigrants to the United States were functionally illiterate (Richwine, 2017); however, even now little SLA research in the United States has examined the impact of error correction on such immigrants' learning of English L2.

What reason is there to believe that alphabetic print literacy level might differentially affect the efficacy of oral error correction provided to second language learners? The answer to this question hinges on a central assumption: the use of oral corrective feedback (CF) assumes that L2 learners are able to "notice the gap" between their own linguistic output and that provided by CF (Schmidt & Frota, 1986, 310). Such an ability must rely in turn on learners' possession of phonemic and phonological awareness – the ability to notice and reflect on the linguistic forms that encode target language utterances. Yet growing evidence suggests that adults who lack minimal levels of alphabetic print literacy have low levels of phonemic and phonological awareness. Kurvers et al. (2006, p.84), for example, conclude, "For most illiterate adults, language is a referential system and a medium of communication, but not an object accessible to reflection, or a string of elements that can be parsed into structural units."[1] If this is true, then of what use is oral CF provided to illiterate and low-literate adult L2 learners?

In this chapter, I summarize a body of research in cognitive psychology on the phonemic and phonological awareness of adults with low levels of (or emergent) alphabetic print literacy, as well as a handful of SLA studies on the way adult L2 (and second dialect) learners with emergent literacy respond to error correction. The results of the small body of existing SLA research so far appear to suggest that oral CF with second language learners with low levels of alphabetic print literacy may not be particularly helpful in promoting second language acquisition. This conclusion would be reinforced by the fact that second language educators who work with adults with emerging literacy are evolving a knowledge base and set of effective pedagogical practices that, by and large, do not seem to make use of oral error correction (Martha Bigelow, personal communication, May 4, 2018).

I begin by reviewing the evidence we have about adult second language learners with low levels of alphabetic print literacy, their phonemic and phonological awareness, and the way they respond to oral error correction when using their developing L2s.

Alphabetic Print Literacy Improves Processing of Linguistic Forms in Oral Input

One line of research evidence comes from cognitive psychology. As Sheen (2010) states in her introduction to a thematic issue of *Studies in Second Language Acquisition*, support for oral CF in promoting interlanguage development in SLA derives from a number of cognitive and psycholinguistic theories, all of which claim that corrective feedback focused on erroneous forms produced by the learner "promotes learning because it induces noticing and noticing-the-gap" (p. 170). In other words, these theories posit that the efficacy of oral corrective feedback

---

[1] For background on the relationship of alphabetic print literacy and oral language processing, see Olson (1977) and Perfetti et al. (2001).

relies on the learner's ability to *notice* linguistic forms, specifically, the difference between his or her own oral production of an erroneous target form, and an interlocutor's oral production of the corresponding correct target form. However, as pointed out several times, starting more than fifteen years ago (Bigelow & Tarone, 2004; Bigelow et al., 2006; Tarone & Bigelow, 2007; Tarone, Bigelow & Hansen, 2009), claims for the efficacy of CF are based entirely on research on literate L2 learners – and, primarily, learners who can read alphabetic script (as opposed to Chinese characters, for example). The problem is that, as Bigelow, Tarone, and others point out, individuals who are not alphabetically literate have been shown in carefully designed experiments to process language almost entirely in terms of its meaning, and not its linguistic form. A respectable body of international research in cognitive psychology (e.g., Adrián, Alegria & Morais, 1995; Castro-Caldas et al., 1998; Dellatolas et al., 2003; Read et al., 1986; Reis & Castro-Caldas, 1997) documents controlled experiments in which literate and illiterate groups of adults performed the same sets of oral tasks. In these studies, statistical measurement of differences in the performance of these groups revealed that illiterate adult participants had significantly lower levels of phonological awareness, or ability to focus on linguistic forms, than matched groups of adults who were alphabetically literate. For example, Reis and Castro-Caldas (1997) studied fifteen pairs of adult sisters from the same village in Portugal, where one sister had gone to school and become alphabetically literate, while the other had to stay home to mind the siblings and did not learn to read. The pairs of sisters performed the same oral language processing tasks, some of which could be done using semantic processing and some of which required phonological processing. To illustrate, one semantic task required oral repetition of words the participants knew the meaning of, while one phonological processing task required oral repetition of pseudo-words which had no semantic content. The semantic task (recall of known words) was equally easy for readers and nonreaders, but the pseudo-word repetition task was significantly harder for adult nonreaders. In another pair of tasks, participants had to recall word lists that were related either semantically (e.g., names of animals) or phonologically (e.g., words that begin with /p/). Readers in the literate and nonliterate groups did equally well on the semantic processing recall tasks; however, the nonreaders performed significantly worse than the readers when asked to recall the phonological word lists. Reis and Castro-Caldas (1997, p. 445) conclude:

> Learning to match graphemes and phonemes is learning an operation in which units of auditory verbal information heard in temporal sequence are matched to units of visual verbal information, which is spatially arranged. ... visual-graphic meaning is given to units that are smaller

than words, and thus independent of their semantic representation ... Therefore learning to read and write introduces into the system qualitatively new strategies for dealing with oral language.

This line of research has even established a difference in measured brain function between literate and nonliterate adults in such tasks. Castro-Caldas et al. (1998) used PET scans to compare the brain activity of readers and nonreaders when performing real-word and pseudo-word repetition tasks. The brain scans showed that when both readers and nonreaders repeated meaningful words, similar areas of their brains activated; however, when the readers and nonreaders repeated pseudo-words, different areas of their brains were activated. Similarly, in an MRI study comparing literate and illiterate brain structure, Castro-Caldas et al. (1999) found significant differences in brain circuitry and physical structure in the parietal lobe. Castro-Caldas et al. (1998, p. 1053) conclude: "Our results indicate that learning to read and write [alphabetical script] during childhood influences the functional organization of the adult brain."

This line of research in cognitive psychology also suggests that alphabetic print literacy facilitates phonemic awareness. For example, certain tasks require phonemic awareness: deleting initial phonemes (e.g., "If we delete /g/ from the syllable /got/, we have ...?"), and reversing phonemes (e.g., in a study of Spanish-speaking adults, "How do you say /sal/ (salt) backwards?" Answer: "/las/"). Morais et al. (1979) and Adrián et al. (1995) compared the ability of adult readers and nonreaders to perform such phonemic awareness tasks. They found that readers consistently outperformed nonreaders. They conclude on the basis of these results that phonemic awareness develops in part as a consequence of the acquisition of alphabetic print literacy.

To determine whether character-based scripts and alphabetic scripts have the same impact on this kind of oral language processing, Read et al. (1986) replicated Morais et al. (1979) recruiting thirty Chinese adults working at Beijing Normal University with similar ages and levels of schooling. In their cohort, eighteen could only read Chinese characters (the non-alphabetic group), and twelve (the alphabetic group) could read both characters and an alphabetic script (Hanyu Pinyin). Both groups were asked to add or delete a single consonant (d, s, n) at the beginning of spoken Chinese syllables, all of which were permissible phonological sequences in Chinese; some targets were words and others non-words requiring processing entirely in terms of phonological form and not meaning. Read et al. found that the nonalphabetic Chinese group (even though they could read character-based script) resembled Morais et al.'s (1979) nonliterate participants: they could not add or delete individual consonants in spoken Chinese, and had most difficulty on with non-words. The alphabetic group could easily and accurately perform this task. The authors conclude,

"It is not literacy in general which leads to [oral] segmentation skill, but alphabetic literacy in particular" (p. 41).

These well-designed and carefully controlled experiments in cognitive psychology produced statistically significant findings that lead us to conclude that adults' alphabetic print literacy gives them the ability to cognitively represent oral language segments with visual symbols. It is this ability that can then function as a processing tool that significantly improves their ability to notice and manipulate linguistic forms perceived in oral input. Lack of alphabetic print literacy will hamper this ability.

Alphabetic Print Literacy Level Is Significantly Related to Uptake of Oral Corrective Feedback in SLA

The findings of cognitive psychologists regarding the relationship between alphabetic print literacy level and ability to process oral language in terms of its linguistic form led a handful of SLA researchers in the early 2000s to ask whether oral CF focused on form benefits adolescent and adult L2 learners with low levels of alphabetic print literacy. Did they notice the gap when their errors in L2 linguistic forms were corrected by oral CF? Was there evidence they were not likely to take up corrective feedback on L2 linguistic forms? Such questions seemed important given that L2 learners with emergent literacy were then, and still are, very numerous, given increased migration of multilingual and illiterate adult L2 learners worldwide and in the United States (Bigelow & Tarone, 2004). If corrective feedback is not, as generally assumed, universally facilitative of successful SLA, there are important implications for pedagogy with low-literate L2 learners.

Positing that the L2 learner's alphabetic print literacy level is significantly related to the ability to notice and incorporate oral CF on form, Bigelow et al. (2006) carried out a research study in Minnesota (referred to here as the "Somali study"). They partially replicated a previous study by Philp (2003) on uptake by university-level L2 learners when they were given CF focused on question formation. Bigelow et al.'s Somali study gathered data from a group of thirty-five recent Somali immigrants with interrupted formal schooling in a partial replication of Philps's recast study, adding an elicited imitation task (Hansen 2005) and a measure of the participants' alphabetic print literacy levels in L1 and L2. There were no completely illiterate L2 learners in the available participant group; since they were living in the United States, all had encountered, and had at least some rudimentary awareness of, print in the environment. The researchers decided to measure the participants' relative degree of alphabetic print literacy level in both L1 and L2 by applying an analytic rating rubric to their performance on a measure called the Native Language

Table 21.1 *Participant profiles (table modified from Bigelow et al., 2006)*

				Literacy level				Years of schooling		
Names	Age	Gender	SPEAK	L1	L2	Mean	Developmental stage	L1	L2	Years in USA
Low literacy group										
Abukar	15	M	50	4	6	5	5	0	4.5	4.5
Najma	27	F	40	5	6	5.5	5	7	1.5	3
Ubax	17	F	40	0	7	3.5	3	0	3	3
Fawzia	20	F	30	6	6	6	4	0	3	3
Moderate literacy group										
Khalid	16	M	50	8.5	8.5	8.5	5	0	7	7
Faadumo	18	F	40	9	9	9	4	0	3	3
Moxamed	17	M	40	9	9	9	5	0	7	7
Sufia	15	F	30	9	7	8	4	0	3	3

Literacy Screening Device (NLLSD).[2] To isolate the variable of alphabetic print literacy level, two subgroups of participants were formed: the four participants with the lowest literacy scores in L1 and L2 combined, and the four participants with the highest literacy scores in L1 and L2 combined. The recast performance of these two groups was then compared and the statistical significance of any differences in their performance was assessed. The two literacy groups in the Bigelow et al. study appear in Table 21.1.

In Table 21.1 the participants are listed with the first four constituting the low literacy group, and the second four a moderate literacy group; these groups were formed based on rubric-based ratings of their ability to read and write in Somali (L1) and in English (L2). The mean literacy scores of group 1 range from 3.5 to 6, and those of group 2 range from 8 to 9, on a 9-point scale. There was a 2-point difference between the lowest score (8) in the Moderate literacy group, and the highest score (6) in the Low literacy group. It is interesting that their years of reported schooling in L1 and L2 medium schools did not seem to relate at all to their measured literacy levels. Note that both groups had identical oral English proficiency levels, as measured by a test of spoken English (SPEAK). Their developmental stage, identified using Pienemann et al.'s (1988) framework, was established based on the way they formed questions.

For the Bigelow et al. study, as in Philp (2003), participants were engaged in an oral task in which they asked questions in English about events displayed in a series of pictures; they were told that sometimes the

---

[2] The NLLSD is described in detail in Bigelow et al. (2006, p. 672–673). The rubric developed by the researchers to rate literacy level based on performance on the NLLSD is available in Tarone et al. (2009), Appendix A. Further information on both the NLLSD and the rubric is available upon request.

researcher would say something while knocking on the table,[3] at which point the participant would need to repeat what the researcher had just said. Whenever the participant made an error in English question formation, the researcher would knock on the table and provide corrective feedback in the form of a recast. (Though a recast is considered to be a form of implicit corrective feedback, Philp used table-knocking to make the feedback more explicit; this technique should work well with participants of any literacy level.) As in Philp (2003), "noticing" was operationalized in the Somali study as accurate immediate recall of recasts of ill-formed English questions. The uptake of the two literacy level groups following recasts of their English L2 questions was classified as *correct*, *modified*, or *no recall*, and the statistical significance of the difference between them was established using exact permutation analysis, described in Bigelow et al. (2006). Table 21.2 displays the resulting quantitative findings.

These quantitative findings of the Somali study, reported in detail in Bigelow et al. (2006), Tarone et al. (2009), and elsewhere are clearly consistent with the outcomes of experiments by cognitive psychologists reported in the previous section. Alphabetic print literacy level correlates with improved cognitive processing of formal linguistic features in oral language required to notice and take up the recast. Whether the criterion was correct recall, or correct + modified recall, the moderate literacy group score always is higher than that of the low literacy group, whether the recast was long or short, asked for one change only, or two or more changes. But were these differences statistically significant? When the

Table 21.2 *Mean correct or modified recalls by literacy level (table modified from Bigelow et al., 2006, p. 680)*

	Correct or modified recall		
	Mean literacy level		
	Low	Moderate	
Recast type	1 to 6	8 or 9	p-value*
All	0.852	0.928	**0.043**
Long	0.827	0.907	0.086
Short	0.851	0.974	0.071
1 change	0.849	0.909	0.114
2+ changes	0.820	1.000	**0.014**

* All p-values are one-tailed

[3] The study by Philp (2003) introduced the idea of table-knocking while providing a recast in order to draw participants' attention to the recasts, to make error correction more explicit. Bigelow et al., Martin-Mejía, and Mueller all adopted this technique as part of their replications of the Philp study.

criterion was a combination of "correct or modified recall," Table 21.2 shows that the L2 group with moderate literacy had significantly (p=0.043) better recall of recasts on their overall question formation than the low literacy group, and an even bigger advantage (p=0.014) when the recast called for two or more changes. It can be argued that higher levels of alphabetic print literacy enabled L2 learners to notice the gap between linguistic forms in their own utterance and the oral recast, and take up that corrective feedback at significantly higher rates. This conclusion is consistent with the conclusions of cognitive psychologists cited above that alphabetic print literacy affords a cognitive tool that improves language processing in terms of linguistic forms, not just meaning. These experimental findings isolating the impact of the level of alphabetic print literacy raise serious questions about the efficacy of oral corrective feedback provided to adolescent and adult L2 learners before they have higher levels of alphabetic print literacy.

Qualitative data from the performance of Abukar, a participant with one of the lowest measured alphabetic print literacy levels (for detail, see Tarone & Bigelow, 2007), sheds additional light on the experimental findings reported above. Examination of Abukar's interaction with the researcher shows that he had little difficulty noticing a recast that focused on meaning. When the researcher said "jar," a new vocabulary word, Abukar immediately repeated the word to himself several times, and he used it correctly later in the same session. However, the researcher's recasts of linguistic forms such as copulas and grammatical morphemes that do not carry semantic meaning seemed to be very hard for Abukar to notice, even after several repetitions that included phonological stress on a persistently unnoticed copula:

Example 1 Abukar's difficulty with a grammatical recast

1	ABUKAR:	What he sit on, what he SIT on, or whatever?
2	MB:	What is he sitting on?
3	ABUKAR:	Mhm.
4	MB:	What is he sitting on? Again. Repeat.
5	ABUKAR:	What he sitting on?
6	MB:	What IS he sitting on?
7	ABUKAR:	Oh. What he sitting on?
8	MB:	What IS he sitting on?
9	ABUKAR:	What IS he sitting on?

(Tarone & Bigelow, 2007: 113–114)

Example 1 illustrates the difficulty a participant with low alphabetic print literacy can have in noticing the gap in linguistic forms between his own utterance "What he sit on?" where each word has at least some semantic content, and the researcher's five-word recast "What is he sitting on?" This recast in line 2 adds an unstressed copula and a present progressive verb ending – linguistic forms which carry grammatical information but don't really add new semantic content. It takes an exchange of four recasts over nine conversational turns, including efforts to make the recasts explicit, before Abukar, in line 9, finally produces approximate uptake. Indeed, in line 3 Abukar's initial response to the researcher's recast indicates that he is focusing on meaning, and mistakes line 2 as a confirmation of the meaning of his utterance in line 1. In line 4, the researcher repeats the recast along with an explicit command to repeat it. In line 5, Abukar does repeat, taking up the progressive ending but not the copula. The researcher then offers two repetitions of the same recast with emphatic stress added to draw his attention to the copula. In spite of this, in line 7 Abukar's attempt at uptake still lacks the copula. Only after a second recast with the copula stressed in line 8 does he notice and reproduce it, complete with *stressed* copula, in his uptake. He never does succeed in producing the *unstressed* form of the copula provided in the original recast in lines 2 and 4.

The cognitive psychology experiments reviewed in the second section of this chapter provide a plausible explanation for the difficulty that Abukar displays in Example 1: Lacking substantial alphabetic print literacy, he has not yet acquired the cognitive ability to represent phonemes with graphemes. The absence of this ability to mentally visualize the recast utterance decreases his capacity for explicit phonological processing of linguistic units which are not meaningful to him, like the unstressed copula and *-ing* ending. Like the illiterate adults in the experiments reviewed in the second section, however, Abukar has no difficulty processing feedback on the meaning of L2 words, repeating and later appropriately using the meaningful word "jar." He is processing oral language in terms of semantics, but not in terms of linguistic forms.

The Somali study (Bigelow et al., 2006; Tarone & Bigelow, 2007; Tarone et al., 2009), using an experimental design and evaluating findings using an inferential statistical measure, shows a significant relationship between alphabetic print literacy level and adult L2 learners' ability to notice and take up corrective feedback on linguistic form. However, this is just one study, based on only eight L2 learners, all of them Somali learners of English. It could be argued that, despite robust support from research on literacy in cognitive psychology outside the realm of SLA research, this is too small a database to rely on to make reliable generalizations about the cognitive processes underlying low-literate L2 learners' processing of CF on form. It is disappointing that, in the fifteen years since the publication of the Somali study, to my knowledge no other study has been published using an experimental design with inferential statistical measures to validate the claim that lack of alphabetic print literacy inhibits L2 learners' noticing of CF on errors of linguistic form. The claim is clearly important for L2 pedagogy, since it implies that oral CF on form may not be useful for the large numbers of adult L2 learners who are illiterate or have low alphabetic print literacy levels, and that its use in pedagogy should be minimized until these learners acquire alphabetic print literacy.

Even though, to my knowledge, no experimental replication studies have been published on the effectiveness of oral error correction with low-literate L2 learners, there are now some case studies that are generally supportive of the findings of the Somali study. These are reviewed in the next section.

Case Studies Relating Alphabetic Print Literacy Level to Uptake of Oral Corrective Feedback in SLA

Subsequent to the Somali study, some descriptive case studies have explored the claimed relationship between L2 learners' alphabetic print literacy and their processing of oral CF on form. This section reviews three such studies: Martin-Mejía (2011), Mueller (2013), and Steele (2014); it also reviews a descriptive study of oral language in a classroom for low-literate L2 learners that includes detail on their responses to oral recasts (Strube 2007, 2014) and a longitudinal study describing an adult L2 learner's simultaneous acquisition of literacy and oral syntax (Pettitt & Tarone 2015). Only one of these studies (Steele) employs statistical analysis of the output of learners at different literacy levels, and only three – Steele (with Oliver), Strube, and Pettitt & Tarone – have been published. All are of interest here because they provide descriptions and findings that test the Somali study claim that L2 learners' low levels of alphabetic print literacy interact with their ability to take up oral CF and develop specific features of oral morphology and syntax.

The first study, Martin-Mejía (2011), asked how accurately adult low-literacy English language learners recalled oral CF (recasts) on learner-generated questions. Eleven native speakers of Somali or Spanish, ranging in age from 24 to 67, were recruited through two local Adult Basic Education sites as recommended by their teachers and program coordinators. Martin-Mejía established the proficiency levels of her participants using the Test of Spoken English (TSE) rather than the OPI used in Bigelow et al. (2006). The literacy levels of the participants in both English and their native language were established by use of a slightly modified version of Bigelow et al.'s (2006) rubric rating of observed learner behavior during the administration of the NLLSD,[4] and, following the procedures used in Bigelow et al., two groups of participants were formed, as shown in Table 21.3, one labeled a Low literacy group and the other a Moderate literacy group.

---

[4] Detail on this test is provided in footnote 2.

Table 21.3 *Participant literacy levels (table modified from Martin-Mejía, 2011, p. 34)*

Participant	Native language literacy	English literacy	Literacy mean	Literacy group
FS	4	5	4.5	Low
MV	5	5	5	Low
MZ	5	5	5	Low
ER	5	6	5.5	Low
AC	7	6	6.5	Low
NN	7	6	6.5	Low
HH	9	6	7	Moderate
AD	7	8	7.5	Moderate
MR	7	8	7.5	Moderate
TP	8	7	7.5	Moderate
EA	9	8	8.5	Moderate

The two literacy level groups in Table 21.3 (Martin-Mejía) are not strictly comparable to the two literacy groups in Table 21.1 (Bigelow et al.). Where the mean literacy scores in Table 21.1 show a two point difference between the Low literacy group and the Moderate literacy group (6 vs. 8), Table 21.3 shows only a 0.5 difference between the two groups (6.5 vs. 7). In addition, half of the Moderate literacy group in Table 21.1 score 9s, while 80 percent of the Moderate group in Table 21.3 score 7 or 7.5, with the highest score being 8.5.

For the eleven participants in the Martin-Mejía study, as with the eight in Bigelow et al., there was no apparent relationship between years of reported schooling and measured literacy level using the NLLSD rating procedure.

Martin-Mejía's two Low and Moderate literacy groups performed a number of oral tasks, including question-asking tasks with recasts of ill-formed questions, and an elicited imitation task (similar to that in Hansen, 2005). A record was kept when participants asked questions as they performed spot-the-difference and story completion tasks. The percentage of questions that were correct was tabulated, and when the researcher recast any errors participants made in question formation, their responses to recasts were counted as correct, modified, or no recall, as in Bigelow et al. (2006). The results of these counts were displayed in tables, with no statistical analysis of significance of difference of scores.

Table 21.4, showing the two groups' accuracy in question formation and responses to recasts with table-knocking when performing the spot-the-difference task, displays differences between the scores of the Moderate and Low literate learners. For one thing, both groups had high rates of correct question formation at the outset of data collection, apparently needing less corrective feedback overall than the groups in the Bigelow et al. study. It is therefore possible that all the participants in the Martin-Mejía study were at a higher stage of question formation than were the

Table 21.4 *Recall of recasts of questions in spot-the-difference task (table modified from Martin-Mejía, 2011, p. 41)*

Low literacy	No recall of recast	Modified recall	Correct recall of recast	Total recasts of questions
Raw #	4	18	13	35
Percentages	11%	51%	37%	100%
Moderate literacy	No recall of recast	Modified recall	Correct recall of recast	Total recasts of questions
Raw #	3	4	21	28
Percentages	11%	14%	75%	100%

groups in Bigelow et al. (2006). The initial question formation of the Moderate literacy group was also more accurate than that of the Low literacy group overall, with 42 percent of their questions needing no recast at all, compared to 31 percent for the Low literacy group – a difference of 19 percent.

Table 21.4 shows that when Martin- Mejía's participants made errors that were recast on the spot-the-difference task, the Moderate literacy group appeared to have more correct recall (75 percent) of recasts than the Low literacy group (37 percent). These findings are consistent with those of Bigelow et al. (2006), supporting the view that literacy improves recall accuracy. The results on the story completion task (Martin-Mejía, 2011, p. 41) were in the same direction, but the differences between the two groups in their responses to recasts did not appear to be as great as those for the spot-the-difference task shown in Table 21.4.

Thus, the results of the Martin-Mejía (2011) study with regard to the relationship between literacy level and the ability to accurately recall recasts provided as corrective feedback are thus generally consistent with those of Bigelow et al. (2006), with results going more or less in the same direction: Lower literate learners appeared to notice and recall recasts with less accuracy than learners with even a slightly higher level of alphabetic print literacy. Of course the participants in the two studies were not directly comparable, since the Martin-Mejía participants appear to have been more proficient in English than the Bigelow et al. participants, and the mean literacy level ranges of the Low vs. Moderate literacy groups in the two studies also differed. But in general, the findings on the positive relationship between alphabetic print literacy level and ability to benefit from error correction are consistent with the findings of Bigelow et al. (2006). Martin-Mejía suggests that the uptake of her participants might have been influenced by the level of context in which the recast took place, which might provide a greater awareness of the meaning and function of the phrase being corrected.

The second descriptive case study, Mueller (2013), replicated and built upon Philp (2003), Bigelow et al. (2006), and Martin-Mejía (2011) in order to explore the three-way relationship among L2 learners' alphabetic print literacy level (low vs. moderate), their uptake of recasts of forms in the questions they asked, and oral tasks that provided varying levels of meaningful context (the latter suggested in Martin-Mejía). In an elicited imitation task (designated low-context), the researcher asked a question with no visual aids or conversational context, which the participant had to repeat, with a recast (along with table-knocking) provided if the participant's question was ungrammatical. In a jigsaw task (providing mid-level context) the participant was shown a picture of unrelated objects on a page and had to ask the researcher questions about the physical attributes of those objects; again, a recast with table-knocking was provided if the participant's question was ungrammatical. The third task (with the highest level of context) was the same story completion task used in Bigelow et al., where the participant asked questions about a series of pictures depicting familiar scenes, with a recast with table-knocking provided if the participant's question was ungrammatical.

Eleven adult learners of English L2 from one Adult Basic Education site took part in the Mueller study; their first languages were primarily Somali, other L1s being Arabic (two speakers), French, and Spanish. Table 21.5 displays their alphabetic print literacy scores (on the NLLSD) and their assignment to one of two literacy groups, five to a Low literacy group and six to a Moderate literacy group.

The range of mean literacy levels in each group in Mueller's study resembles that in Bigelow et al. somewhat more than was the case in Martin-Mejía; Mueller's Low literacy group mean scores ranged from 3.5 to 6.5 (compared to Bigelow et al.'s 3.5 to 6), and Mueller's Moderate literacy group scores ranged from 7.5 to 8.5, with almost all scoring 8.5 (compared to Bigelow et al.'s 8 to 9). The English proficiency of Mueller's participants was estimated based on their placement into speaking/

Table 21.5 *Participant literacy levels (table modified from Mueller, 2013, p. 41)*

Participant	Native language Literacy	English literacy	Literacy mean	Literacy group
IB	3	4	3.5	Low
SF	3	5	4	Low
MM	4	6	5	Low
RK	6	5	5.5	Low
RS	7	6	6.5	Low
AB	9	6	7.5	Moderate
UB	8	8	8	Moderate
ZA	8.5	8.5	8.5	Moderate
FN	9	8	8.5	Moderate
CA	9	8	8.5	Moderate
CR	9	8	8.5	Moderate

listening classes at one of three levels, beginner, high beginner, or low intermediate. No detail is provided on this placement process, so we cannot assume that the English proficiency levels of Mueller's participants were comparable to those in Bigelow et al.

Participants' questions and responses to recasts were recorded and transcribed, and analyzed in a way similar to that used in both Bigelow et al. and Martin-Mejía. Mueller asked if there were seeming but statistically unvalidated differences in the Low- and Mid-literacy L2 learners' responses to recasts of their questions in the tasks with three different levels of contextual support. After a consideration of uncontrolled variables affecting the impact of context in the study[5], Mueller (2013) concludes that "in this study the participants of the Moderate Literacy group outperformed the Low Literacy group in all three tasks" (p. 77) and that her findings were generally consistent with those of both the Bigelow et al. study and the Martin-Mejía study.

The third case study, Steele (2014; Oliver & Steele 2019), is a partial replication of the Bigelow et al. (2006) study extended to second-dialect (D2) learners; this study asks whether alphabetic print literacy levels affect Aboriginal English (AE) speakers' ability to notice and take up oral recasts of their oral output as they strove to acquire Standard Australian English (SAE) as their D2. The study asks, first, whether these D2 learners *noticed* dialectal differences between their AE utterances and SAE recasts, and whether such noticing was significantly related to the learners' literacy level; and second, whether these learners were able to *accurately reproduce* the SAE recasts provided, and whether the accuracy of their reproductions was significantly related to their literacy level.

The nineteen participants in the study were native speakers of Manyjilyjarra, an oral language, and spoke AE as a second language with limited confidence. Ranging in age from 8 to 16 years old, they were learning SAE as a second dialect in school. Their overall literacy scores were low, ranging from four to twenty-two out of a possible thirty, as based on a combination of their reading performance on the PM Benchmark Test (Nelson Australia, 2003), assessment of their writing using Australian Curriculum standards (Australian Curriculum Assessment & Reporting Authority, 2010), and their stage of oral English question formation, following Pienemann, Johnston & Brindley (1988). An oral spot-the-difference task was used to elicit questions, and the researcher provided CF in the form of recasts at a morphosyntactic level to match the participant's stage of question development. In response, the participant was asked (1) to indicate whether their question differed from the researcher's SAE recast, and (2) to reproduce the SAE recast. The following example is provided by Steele:

---

[5] For example, three of Mueller's participants seemed to recall recasts much better on Task 3; explanations for this could have been either that Task 3 provided more context OR that in Task 3, recasts were focused on the participants' self-generated utterances, whereas in Tasks 1 and 2, recasts focused on learners' attempts to reproduce utterances originally provided by the researcher.

PARTICIPANT TRIGGER:	Do your alien have two eyes?
RESEARCHER RECAST:	Does your alien have two eyes? Did I say the same thing or different?
PARTICIPANT RESPONSE:	Same thing.

The results of the Steele study are presented below[6]. First, all these low-literate D2 learners had great difficulty overall in accurately noticing differences between their AE questions and SAE recasts. Overall, more than 50 percent of the time, they were unable to correctly identify such differences. The data suggest that the rate of noticing was related to the number of changes presented in the recast; the accuracy of their noticing was greatest either if there were no changes at all (83% accurate noticing), or if four or more changes were made by the recast (70% accurate noticing). The accuracy of their noticing went down dramatically when one to three changes were made by the recast (37% accurate). These patterns of noticing were unrelated to the participants' literacy levels.

The study also found that the average uptake rate of these low-literate D2 learners, meaning the incorporation of any part of the recast, was only 59 percent; that is, even though recasts had been made at each learner's morphosyntactic level, the study participants had great difficulty incorporating those changes in their responses. The rate of uptake varied depending on the linguistic feature being changed; where the recast focused on word choice, the rate of uptake was highest at 60 percent, but uptake rate dropped dramatically when the focus was on articles (42%), pluralization (45%) or verb morphology (38%). The participants' success in reproducing recasts was positively and highly significantly correlated with their literacy levels ($r=0.83$, $p<0.0001$).

Steele (2014, p. 34) concludes, "These results have implications for both SLA theory and classroom practice. They suggest that there may be a need to reconsider how current theory pertains to low literate groups and second dialect learners, particularly with regard to the effectiveness of corrective feedback as a language/dialect teaching tool. While there are still examples of participant uptake during interactions, effectiveness is reduced." She issues an impassioned call for more research in this area, and stronger emphasis on teaching reading skills to L2 and D2 learners.

A fourth case study, Strube (2014[7]), focused on oral skills practice in adult education programs for illiterate and low-literate adult L2 learners in the Netherlands. Unlike the studies cited above, Strube made no attempt to measure the learners' literacy levels; her focus was on the oral

---

[6] To document noticing of CF, each participant's percentage of correct identification of difference between AE utterance and SAE recast was derived, and for each participant, this percentage was correlated with their literacy level using Pearson's correlation coefficient. To document uptake of corrective feedback, following Philp (2003), an uptake rate, or percentage, was calculated as the number of times participants used any part of the number of recasts provided, that enabled them to move toward target-like SAE production; this uptake rate was correlated with the participant's literacy level using Pearson's correlation coefficient.

[7] Strube (2007) is a related earlier publication.

interactions of very low-literacy L2 learners in intact classrooms. Part of the study focused on teachers' oral CF during oral skills lessons given to forty-one students across six different classes, and the students' responses, including their level of uptake of that feedback, using Lyster and Ranta's (1997) framework to track apparent interrelationships among types of CF, types of errors being treated (phonological, lexical, grammatical, use), and student uptake (with or without repair).

Strube found that the most prevalent form of CF was the recast, with a mean occurrence of 59 percent, but as with more literate learners, it was the least successful type of CF in producing repair. Indeed, Strube judged efforts to give metalinguistic feedback to often be relatively "opaque" to these learners (p. 205); because these students with limited formal schooling had little or no understanding of metalinguistic terms, sometimes teachers tried to paraphrase, though that often had no or limited success. Results for student repair in response to all forms of CF reveal a high percentage for no repair at all (mean 51 percent), though feedback for phonological or lexical error producing a somewhat higher rate of repair than feedback for grammatical error. Strube concluded, "while most corrective feedback was directed toward correcting grammatical errors (305 out of 483, or 63%), more than half of these resulted in no repair" (2014, p. 214). The disappointing responses of these very low-literate adult L2 learners to CF in several intact classes are consistent with more experimental studies reviewed earlier in this chapter.

In a final case study, Pettitt and Tarone (2015) recorded one Somali learner's development of alphabetic print literacy over a six-month period concurrently with his development of specific features of oral English. Over the six months, there was a modest increase in his suppliance of some semantically redundant morphemes and in syntactic complexity; at the same time his awareness of sound–symbol correspondence also developed. These findings are consistent with Tarone, Swierzbin, and Bigelow's (2006) suggestion that acquisition of "some more complex syntactic structures ... may benefit from, or even require, a base level of alphabetic print literacy" (p. 76). An important agenda for future SLA study is to explore this possibility and pinpoint the syntactic structures used orally by learners and ways these may develop as print literacy increases.

Conclusion and Implications

The research reviewed in the second section of this chapter, the significant findings of the Somali study described in the third section, and five case studies appearing since, reviewed in the fourth section, together make the case that an absence or limited amount of alphabetic print literacy substantially impairs L2 learners' ability to notice and take up form-focused corrective feedback. In several of these studies, feedback on form, even though it was termed a "recast," was supplemented with additional signals like table-knocking to make it explicit and noticeable. Yet this error correction was seldom noticed or taken up by learners with low literacy levels.

It is worth asking why research on the relationship between CF and alphabetic literacy level that has been documented in this chapter has failed to generate more interest on the part of SLA theorists, or more replication by university researchers interested in CF. Surely this gap cannot be because theorists and researchers feel low-literate learners are not important. One possible reason may be that it is much more difficult to do research in the immigrant communities in which L2 learning and low literacy levels coincide. As Ngo, Bigelow, and Lee (2014) point out, education research with immigrant populations presents extremely complicated issues of ethics and politics, issues that are usefully laid out in this guest-edited publication. Some advocates fear that education researchers may do more harm than good in such communities, and we must respect those fears.

The fact is, however, that populations of L2 learners currently being served by L2 teachers around the world have changed, and SLA research, theories, and methodologies should change with them. There is good reason to suspect that theoretical claims about the role of CF in the learning and teaching of L2 do not hold for large swathes of the L2 learning population, particularly for immigrants and refugees worldwide who lack alphabetic print literacy. For this population, the research reviewed in this chapter suggests that oral error correction may not be useful for such learners, and if this is the case, its use should be minimized until these learners in fact acquire alphabetic print literacy. Across the board, serious and ethically sensitive research is needed on the processes of SLA used by illiterate and low-literate adult L2 learners, both to evaluate the efficacy of oral error correction and to support alternative pedagogical practices with this population.

Until such research on the efficacy of error correction for low-literate adults is carried out, teachers of low-literate adult students may benefit from the research and exploratory practice of a group of educators and researchers in North America and Europe interested in Literacy Education and Second Language Learning for Adults (LESLLA, www.leslla.org). LESLLA maintains an active website documenting their work and communications at annual conferences, alternating annually between North America and Europe. In addition to conference proceedings posted on this website, notable publications on LESLLA learning and teaching include Vinogradov (2012, 2016) and Vinogradov and Bigelow (2010). Pedagogical approaches grounded in sociocultural and sociolinguistic theory may offer alternative ways to support L2 acquisition by learners with emergent literacy, such as that discussed by LaScotte and Tarone (2019); they show how learners who are invited to use the L2 to enact imagined "voices" of more proficient others in constructed dialogue in narration are able to improve grammatical accuracy. In other words, sociolinguistic, sociocultural, and other approaches to pedagogy can be actively explored to support SLA as alternatives to oral error correction for adults with emergent literacy.

References

Adrián, J. A., Alegria, J. & Morais, J. (1995). Metaphonological abilities of Spanish illiterate adults. *International Journal of Psychology*, 30(3), 329–353.

Australian Curriculum Assessment & Reporting Authority (ACARA). (2010). *F-10 Curriculum: English*. www.australiancurriculum.edu.au/f-10-curriculum/english/.

Bigelow, M., Delmas, R., Hansen, K. & Tarone, E. (2006). Literacy and the processing of oral recasts in SLA. *TESOL Quarterly*, 40(4), 665–689.

Bigelow, M. & Tarone, E. (2004). Doesn't *who* we study determine *what* we know? *TESOL Quarterly*, 38(4), 689–700.

Castro-Caldas, A., Petersson, K. M., Reis, A., Stone-Elander, S. & Ingvar, M. (1998). The illiterate brain: Learning to read and write during childhood influences the functional organization of the adult brain. *Brain: A Journal of Neurology*, 121(6), 1053–1063. www.ncbi.nlm.nih.gov/pubmed/9648541.

Castro-Caldas, A., Miranda, P. C., Canno, L., Reis, A., Leote, F., Ribero, C. & Ducla-Soares, E. (1999). Influence of learning to read and write on the morphology of the corpus callosum. *European Journal of Neurology*, 6(1), 23–28.

Dellatolas, G., Braga, L. W., Souza, L. D. N., Nunes Filho, G., Queiroz, E., & Deloche, G. (2003). Cognitive consequences of early phase of literacy. *Journal of the International Neuropsychological Society*, 9(5), 771–782.

Hansen, K. (2005). Impact of literacy level and task type on oral L2 recall accuracy. MA thesis, University of Minnesota, Twin Cities.

Kurvers, J., Vallen, T. & van Hout, R. (2006). Discovering language: Metalinguistic awareness of adult illiterates. In I. van de Craats, J. Kurvers & M. Young-Scholten (eds.), *Low-educated second language and literacy acquisition: Proceedings of the inaugural symposium* (pp. 69–88). Utrecht: LOT.

LaScotte, D. & Tarone, E. (2019). Heteroglossia and constructed dialogue in SLA. *Modern Language Journal*, 103, 95–112.

Lyster, R., & Ranta, L. (1997). Corrective feedback and learner uptake: Negotiation of form in communicative classrooms. *Studies in second language acquisition*, 19(1), 37–66.

Martin-Mejía, C. (2011). Low-literacy adult English language learners: Oral recall and recasts. MA thesis, School of Education, Hamline

University, St. Paul, Minnesota. https://digitalcommons.hamline.edu/hse_all/460/.

Morais, J., Cary, L., Alegría, J. & Bertelson, P. (1979). Does awareness of speech as a sequence of phones arise spontaneously? *Cognition*, 7(4), 323–331.

Mueller, R. (2013). How do context and low L1 literacy of non-native speakers of English affect their noticing of L2 learner recasts? MA thesis, School of Education, Hamline University, St. Paul, Minnesota. https://digitalcommons.hamline.edu/hse_all/531/.

Nelson Australia (2003). *The PM Benchmark Kit*. Toronto: Thomson Learning Australia.

Ngo, B., Bigelow, M. & Lee, S. (2014) What does it mean to do ethical and engaged research with immigrant communities? *Diaspora, Indigenous, and Minority Education: Studies of Migration, Integration, Equity, and Cultural Survival, Special Issue*, 8(1), 1–6.

Oliver, R. & Steele, C. (2019). Can print literacy impact upon learning to speak Standard Australian English? In A. Lenzing, H. Nicholas & J. Roos (eds.), *Widening contexts for processability theory: Theories and issues* (pp. 349–369). Amsterdam: John Benjamins.

Olson, D. R. (1977). From utterance to text: The bias of language in speech and writing. *Harvard Educational Review*, 47(3), 257–281.

Perfetti, C., Van Dyke, J. & Hat, L. (2001). The psycholinguistics of basic literacy. *Annual Review of Applied Linguistics*, 21(1), 127–149.

Pettitt, N. & Tarone, E. (2015). Following Roba: What happens when a low-educated adult immigrant learns to read. *Writing Systems Research*, 7(1), 20–38.

Philp, J. (2003). Constraints on "noticing the gap": Nonnative speakers' noticing of recasts in NS-NNS interaction. *Studies in Second Language Acquisition*, 25(1), 99–126.

Pienemann, M., Johnston, M. & Brindley, G. (1988). Constructing an acquisition-based procedure for second language assessment. *Studies in Second Language Acquisition*, 10(2), 217–243.

Read, C., Zhang, Y., Nie, H. & Ding, B. (1986). The ability to manipulate speech sounds depends on knowing alphabetic spelling. *Cognition*, 24 (1–2), 31–44.

Reis, A. & Castro-Caldas, A. (1997). Illiteracy: A cause for biased cognitive development. *Journal of the International Neuropsychological Society*, 3(5), 444–450.

Richwine, J. (2017). Immigrant literacy: Self-assessment vs. reality. *Center for Immigration Studies* (June 2017). https://cis.org/Immigrant-Literacy-Self-Assessment-vs-Reality.

Schmidt, R. & Frota, S. (1986). Developing basic conversational ability in a second language: A case study of an adult learner. In R. Day (ed.), *Talking to learn: Conversation in second language acquisition* (pp. 237–326). Rowley, MA: Newbury House.

Sheen, Y. (2010). Introduction: The role of oral and written corrective feedback in SLA. *Studies in Second Language Acquisition*, 32(2), 169–179.

Steele, C. (2014) Can print literacy impact upon learning to speak Standard Australian English? MA dissertation, Curtin University, Australia.

Strube, S. (2007). Recasts and learner uptake: The non-literate adult L2 classroom during oral skills practice. In Martha Young-Scholten (ed.), *Proceedings of the Third annual LESLLA Forum* (pp. 61–74). Newcastle upon Tyne: Newcastle University. Available at www.leslla.org.

(2014). Grappling with the oral skills: The learning and teaching of the low-literate adult second language learner. Ph.D. dissertation, Radboud University, Nijmegen, Netherlands.

Tarone, E. & Bigelow, M. (2007). Impact of literacy on oral language processing: Implications for second language acquisition research. In A. Mackey (ed.), *Conversational interaction in second language acquisition: A series of empirical studies* (pp. 101–121). Oxford: Oxford University Press.

Tarone, E., Bigelow, M. & Hansen, K. (2009). *Literacy and second language oracy*. Oxford: Oxford University Press.

Tarone, E., Swierzbin, B. & Bigelow, M. (2006). The impact of literacy level on features of interlanguage in oral narratives. *Rivista di Psicolinguistica Applicata*, 6(3), 65–77.

UNESCO eAtlas of Literacy (2017). https://tellmaps.com/uis/literacy/#!/tellmap/-601865091.

Vainikka, A. & Young-Scholten, M. (2012). The straight and narrow path. *Linguistic Approaches to Bilingualism*, 2(3), 319–323.

Vinogradov, P. E. (2012). "You just get a deeper understanding of things by talking:" Study circles for teachers of ESL emergent readers. *Journal of Research and Practice for Adult Literacy, Secondary, and Basic Education*, 1, 34–48.

(2016). Crossing contexts for teacher learning: Adult ESL teachers in kindergarten. In J. A. Crandall & M. A. Christison (eds.), *Teacher education and professional development in TESOL: Global perspectives* (pp. 161–175). New York: Routledge.

Vinogradov, P. E. & Bigelow, M. (2010). *Using oral language skills to build literacy of adult learners with emerging English literacy*. Washington, DC: Center for Applied Linguistics.

Part VI

Contexts of Corrective Feedback and Their Effects

22

Corrective Feedback in Second versus Foreign Language Contexts

Maria del Pilar García Mayo and Ruth Milla

Introduction

Corrective feedback (CF) is a fundamental construct in the field of second language acquisition (SLA). It refers to the correction that follows an incorrect utterance as in (1):

(1) LEARNER: Last night he was watching TV but then he fall asleep.
    TEACHER: He ...?
    LEARNER: He fell asleep.

Example (1) illustrates a typical CF episode (CFE) which is the usual context where CF occurs. These episodes arise within oral interaction and typically consist of three moves: error, CF, and uptake. In the example above, the learner produces a grammar error in the error move, which is followed by the teacher's prompt that tries to elicit a reformulation or a repair from the learner. Lyster and Ranta (1997, p. 49) defined the third move, uptake, as "a learner's utterance that immediately follows the teacher's feedback and that constitutes a reaction in some way to the teacher's intention to draw attention to some aspect of the learner's initial utterance." They claimed that uptake, whether it was a response that modified that learner's original output or simply acknowledgment of the receipt of feedback (*yes, ok*, etc.), shows that learners try to use the feedback provided. However, as Nassaji (2016, p. 539) points out, uptake has been operationalized in different ways. Thus, some studies view uptake as attempts that involve some degree of repair or modification of the original output by the learner (e.g., Mackey & Philp, 1998; Nassaji, 2011), which would make more sense "since the term uptake usually denotes that learners have somewhat benefited from the feedback, whereas responses of acknowledgement do not necessarily do so" (Nassaji, 2016, p. 539). The third move in a CFE may occur or not, as sometimes learners ignore the teachers' corrections or fail to notice them (for more information about key terms and definitions, see Chapter 29, this volume).

SLA research has reported that CF provision and subsequent learner uptake is affected by multiple factors such as learners' individual differences (IDs), types of CF, and instructional context. This chapter will focus on this last variable, that is, on how CF is addressed depending on whether the learning context is a second or a foreign language setting, as well as on how context affects learner uptake. Nassaji and Fotos (2011), among others, have pointed out that context is a crucial factor when examining CF, and Choi and Li (2012) have called for research that considers how content teachers address learners' errors. One should be careful, however, when trying to reach generalizations, because, as Nassaji (2016, p. 554) stated, context is a multifaceted construct and cannot simply be taken to refer to macro-level differences between settings such as English as a Second Language (ESL) or English as a Foreign Language (EFL). As Nassaji (2013) himself found, many variables influence the effectiveness of CF, such as lesson formats, activity and task types, and lesson topics.

Owing to space constraints, this chapter will focus on oral CF provided by the teacher (for oral peer CF the reader is referred to Sato (2017) and Chapter 13, this volume) and will present an overview of research in both second and foreign language contexts. The chapter will also summarize the few studies that compare CF provision and learner uptake in these contexts and will conclude with some pedagogical implications and lines for further research.

Corrective Feedback in Different Learning Contexts

The differences between second language (SL) and foreign language (FL) contexts have been acknowledged in different studies (Muñoz, 2007; Sheen, 2004). SL contexts include those where the target language is an official one and, as such, is used outside the instructional environment. Examples of this type of context are French immersion classrooms in Canada (Lyster & Mori, 2006). In SL settings, learners are exposed to more frequent and more varied types of input, in both oral and written format, which has an impact on the chances of learning a language in conditions similar to the ones in which children learn their first language (L1). Learners in these contexts have more opportunities to use the target language in a natural way outside class, and programs integrate language and content across the curriculum (Lyster, 2007). FL settings, in turn, include those in which the language taught is not the official one in the country, or is used as a school subject, or for mainly academic purposes. In general, the focus in FL contexts is on language as a formal system and as a subject. In these contexts, exposure to the target language is typically limited to 1–3 hours a week of timetabled lessons (doubled on average in content and language integrated learning (CLIL) programs), and there are very few opportunities to use the language outside class, although these have clearly improved thanks to the Internet and the possibility to interact with native speakers (Pinter, 2011).

The differences in the access to real input and the possibilities to use the language in natural interactions, together with variations in teachers' background and methodologies in these two contexts, may have an effect on pedagogical decisions about how to provide CF and pedagogical implications for how learners may react to CF (uptake). Thus, it would seem worthwhile to look at findings in each of the two settings in order to establish the potential influence of context in CF provision and effectiveness.

Studies in Second Language Contexts

This subsection will summarize the main findings of studies on oral CF carried out in SL contexts. Lyster and Ranta (1997) conducted a pioneering study in French immersion (FI) classrooms in Canada with English primary school learners (grades 4 and 5). The authors followed a classroom observation methodology, as is usual in these types of CF studies, and recorded the lessons without intervening in their natural development, hence maintaining the ecological validity of the data. Their findings showed that recasts (i.e., the correct reformulation of a learner's utterance) were the most frequently used type of CF (55 percent of the total number of turns contained feedback). However, they were the least likely to lead to learner uptake (only 31 percent of the recast moves resulted in uptake). The preference for recasts has been found in many other studies (e.g., Ellis, Basturkmen & Loewen, 2001; Panova & Lyster, 2002), although this type of CF has been shown to be useful only for some aspects of language. For example, Choi and Li (2012) reported beneficial effects of recasts only for the phonological errors produced by English primary school learners of different first languages in New Zealand. Their findings were in line with those of other studies (Lyster, 1998; Saito & Lyster, 2012). Recasts seem to be more effective when they are provided in an explicit way, as shown in Oliver and Grote (2010), a study in which the researchers recorded learners of different backgrounds studying English in a primary school in Australia.

More salient CF types, such as prompts (elicitation, metalinguistic cues, clarification requests, and repetitions), have been found to lead to higher rates of learner uptake and repair. Lyster (2004), for example, conducted a study in a French as a Second Language (FSL) learning environment where he found that prompts were more beneficial for learning than recasts or no feedback at all. Ellis, Loewen, and Erlam (2006) also found that metalinguistic cues seem to be particularly effective for adult learners in the New Zealand ESL setting. However, in a study with forty-two adult ESL learners and two native English teachers performing dyadic task-based interactions, Nassaji (2007) identified six different reformulation subtypes and five different elicitation subtypes. The analysis of the data for output accuracy following feedback showed that both reformulations and elicitations resulted in higher rates of accurate repair when they were combined with explicit intonational or verbal prompts compared to explicit prompts or no prompts. His findings pointed to the importance of salience and opportunities for pushed output, essential characteristics of effective feedback. In a more recent study with L1 French ESL learners, Kartchava and Ammar (2014) reported that CF types that seek learners' self-repair – prompts and a combination of prompts and recasts – were more noticeable than recasts alone. In general, researchers have argued for the superiority of prompts over recasts because of the explicitness of the former, which seems to highlight the teacher's corrective intention in a clearer way (but see Goo & Mackey, 2013, for a different position).

As for IDs, research has shown that age (Ellis, Basturkmen & Loewen, 2001), proficiency (Philp, 2003), and anxiety (Sheen, 2008) play a crucial role in the processing of CF, with adult learners obtaining more benefits than children, prompts being more beneficial for low-proficiency learners, and recasts being particularly effective for those learners with low levels of anxiety (for a detailed description, see Part VIII of this volume).

Research on CF in SL settings indicates that regardless of the learners' L1 or the second languages being learned, teachers prefer to use recasts over other CF types, probably because they feel that this CF strategy does not interrupt the conversation flow and is less face-threatening. However, recasts seem to be the CF type least likely to lead to learner uptake in SL contexts because they are less explicit than prompts and, therefore, the teacher's corrective intention is not so clear. In general, from the studies reviewed above, it would seem that the more explicit and output-prompting CF types, that is, those types that elicit the learner's production of self-repaired forms, appear to be more beneficial in SL settings, both for children and adult learners; this is because they draw the learners' attention to formal aspects of the language in lessons that are mainly focused on meaning. However, it is true that not all studies in SL contexts have shown superiority for elicitation; those that have were studies that combined elicitation with form-focused instruction. In a recent study, Nassaji (2019) analyzed pictured-cued oral production of relative clauses by fifty-four high- and low-proficiency ESL learners who were assigned to three groups, namely, recast, prompt, and control. His findings revealed an advantage for recasts over prompts and showed that the CF types varied in their effects on uptake.

Studies in Foreign Language Contexts

As mentioned above, FL learning environments are different from SL settings, but research on CF in the former context has examined similar intervening variables in CF provision and learner uptake.

Havranek and Cesnik (2001) analyzed the oral CF received by 207 German EFL learners (children and adults). Their findings showed that the success of such feedback as measured on a subsequent test was affected by its format, the type of error corrected, and certain learner characteristics. As in some of the SL studies reviewed above, the most successful format of correction, both for the learners receiving the feedback and for their peers, was feedback that successfully elicited self-correction in practice situations. Among the least successful formats, however, were recasts that did not promote additional comments or repetition by the corrected learner. The type of error addressed differed in the two groups: the learners whose output was corrected learned most from the correction of their grammatical errors and least from the correction of pronunciation errors, that is, the error type affected the results. Peers scored best on pronunciation items and gained least from correction of lexical errors. As for IDs, verbal intelligence, relative proficiency, and the learners' attitude toward correction proved to be most influential.

Other studies in FL settings have considered CF types, error types, task-related features, and IDs as well as their impact on CF provision and learner uptake (see Part VIII of this volume for detailed information). Regarding CF types, Samar and Shayestefar (2009) investigated the uptake and repair types of Persian EFL learners (aged 16–17) in communicative classrooms and found that metalinguistic and explicit CF types produced the largest amount of uptake, with the former yielding the highest rate of repair. Dabaghi and Basturkmen (2009) also studied the CF of Persian adult EFL learners, reporting that recasts were more effective for late features (i.e., those aspects of the language that have been claimed to be acquired at a later time in the SLA process – in their study: indefinite articles, regular past tense, relative clauses, active and passive voice and third-person -s) and explicit correction was most beneficial for such early developmental features as the definite article, irregular past tense, and plural -s. Yang and Lyster's (2010) results, however, differed in that in studying CF provision delivered to seventy-two Chinese undergraduate EFL learners, they found larger effects for prompts than for recasts in the learners' use of the regular past tense forms and similar effects for the two strategies in their use of the irregular past tense forms. Yilmaz (2012) reported that explicit correction was more effective than recasts when assessing the CF received by Turkish university EFL learners, whereas Goo (2012) reported no significant differences between recasts and metalinguistic feedback for the acquisition of the target feature (*that*-trace filter) by Korean university students.

From this brief overview of studies, it would seem that the use of prompts or metalinguistic feedback is favored in FL contexts, although there is a clear impact of other intervening variables, one of which is the type of linguistic feature addressed. In these contexts, where attention is mainly drawn to the form of the language, CF types that provide learners with the opportunity to self-repair appear to be more effective (see Alcón Soler & García Mayo, 2008, who found an increased effect in terms of learner uptake, particularly when learners initiated the CF episodes).

More recently, Rassaei (2014) carried out a study, from a sociocultural perspective (Vygotsky, 1978), with Iranian EFL learners (mean age = 23.2) and found that scaffolded feedback led to better results than the recasts in post-tests administered two days after the treatment. Example (2) illustrates a scaffolded feedback sequence of nine turns, where the teacher and learner negotiate and the teacher offers four levels of gradual assistance for self-repair, tailoring the CF moves to the learner's needs. In level 1, the teacher uses an elicitation move, followed by metalinguistic information in levels 2, 3, and 4:

(2) 1 LEARNER: What the boy do?
2 TEACHER: Would you repeat your sentence? (Level 1)
3 LEARNER: Um ... What the boy do?
4 TEACHER: No, think about the tense of your sentence. (Level 2)
5 LEARNER: Um ...
6 TEACHER: Present continuous ... what is ...? (Level 3)
7 LEARNER: What is the boy do?
8 TEACHER: No, for example, we say: What is that student doing? What are those men doing? (Level 4)
9 LEARNER: Doing, yes, what is the boy doing?

(Rassaei, 2014, p. 422)

Similarly, other studies have revealed the superiority of prompts over recasts for L2 grammar development (Jafarigohara & Gharbavib, 2014; Mifka-Profozic, 2014). Recasts have also been found to be less effective for morphosyntactic errors (Mackey, Gass & McDonough, 2000; Nabei & Swain, 2002), but learners seem to perceive the corrective intention of recasts more clearly when they are used to address lexical errors.

Researchers have also considered the impact of task-related features on the type of CF used in FL settings. In their study with a group of Spanish as a Foreign Language learners in an American university, Gurzynski-Weiss and Révész (2012) found that task-related features (meaning vs. form-focused, for example) played a crucial role on the type of CF used, amount of CF provided, and learners' use of that CF.

In a nutshell, certain similarities are apparent when comparing the findings of studies conducted in SL and FL settings. Thus, it seems that prompts and explicit feedback types are more beneficial in promoting accuracy than recasts are, although the linguistic target in focus clearly has a role to play. However, there are methodological differences among the studies reviewed above (e.g., use or absence of a control group, inferential statistics, delayed post-tests) as well as other intervening variables (learners' IDs) which make comparisons difficult. The next section is devoted to the few studies that have specifically considered learning context as a factor that might explain differences in CF provision and learner uptake.

A Comparison of Different Learning Contexts

A comparison of different learning contexts regarding CF provision is a topic that has clearly been underexplored in SLA. In their meta-analysis of oral CF in SLA, Lyster and Saito (2010) examined the potential influence of several factors on CF effectiveness, with one of those being instructional setting. They found no significant differences between SL and FL settings as to the effect of CF and attributed the results to the "too fluid" (Lyster & Saito, 2010, p. 292) distinction between SL and FL settings, referring to the fact that the differences between the two contexts were probably not clear enough, or maybe to the fact that CF does not activate different cognitive processes across instructional settings. In spite of their unexpected findings, Lyster and Saito refer to Mackey and Goo's (2007) meta-analysis in which a positive relationship was found between context and the effect of CF, with significant larger effects in FL settings ($d = 0.88$) than in SL settings ($d = 0.64$). Mackey and Goo (2007) analyzed CF as a type of interaction and considered its impact on grammar and vocabulary gains in a selection of twenty-eight classroom and laboratory-based studies. The different conclusions in Lyster and Saito's (2010) and Mackey and Goo's (2007) meta-analyses were probably due to the different nature of the studies selected in each, as Lyster and Saito considered fifteen classroom-based studies and excluded those conducted in laboratory settings. Lyster and Saito also adhere to Lyster and Mori's (2006) call for more qualitative types of research that contribute to "a better understanding of the relevant contextual variables that influence classroom learners' attentional biases toward one type of interactional feedback over another" (Lyster & Mori, 2006, p. 294, as cited in Lyster & Saito, 2010, p. 292).

In order to determine whether or not context has an important role to play in CF provision, more recent research has compared its findings with those reported in earlier studies. For example, in a study conducted in an ESL context with adults, Ellis et al. (2001) found higher uptake rates than Lyster and Ranta (1997) in FI classrooms. Sheen (2004) compared CF provision and learners' uptake in four different classroom settings: FI and ESL in Canada, ESL in New Zealand, and EFL in Korea. She focused on recasts due to the small proportion of the other CF types in her database. Her findings showed differences in CF provision and uptake: the use of recasts, although high in all the settings, was significantly higher in New Zealand and Korean classrooms compared to FI and ESL settings in Canada. Significant differences were also found between the number of recasts in Korean EFL and New Zealand ESL settings.

In addition to the differences in CF provision, the rate of uptake and repair in response to recasts was found to be higher in the Korean EFL and New Zealand ESL contexts than in Canadian ESL and immersion classrooms. Sheen (2004) attributes this difference to the learners' orientation to form rather than meaning in Korean EFL and New Zealand ESL, which consequently leads to greater noticing of this CF type. The fact that an ESL setting is oriented to form and not to meaning contrasts with other SL contexts, typically oriented to meaning. However, as the author explains, the New Zealand course was of an intensive nature that differed from the other SL settings in several aspects. These included a monolingual native English-speaking teacher and older (i.e., college students versus school children) speakers of varied L1s. These characteristics of the New Zealand ESL classrooms might explain the different lesson orientation and, therefore, the CF and uptake results in this particular setting, which were more similar to those in the Korean EFL classrooms. Sheen (2004) calls for more research on the impact of: (i) contextual factors on CF patterns and learner uptake, (ii) IDs (age, proficiency, and previous education) and perceptions of CF (since learners who had received formal instruction for longer periods showed higher rates of uptake and repair), and (iii) teachers' beliefs and learners' perceptions of CF provision and uptake (see Part VII of this volume). Sheen's research points to the very important issue of lesson orientation, which is of great relevance to other studies reviewed below.

Lyster and Mori (2006) also considered how instructional setting could be a relevant factor in CF provision. They observed and recorded intact lessons in two different learning settings at the elementary-school level. On the one hand, 18.3 audio-recorded hours of FI lessons delivered to English-speaking learners in Canada (i.e., FSL context) drawn from Lyster and Ranta's (1997) seminal study were studied. On the other hand, the data reported on in Mori (2002) were used; they contained video recordings of 14.8 hours of Japanese immersion (JI) lessons that targeted English speakers in the USA (i.e., Japanese as a Foreign Language [JFL] context). To obtain a realistic picture of CF in the two settings, no intervention was made by the researchers in the lessons either in respect of activities or content.

Lyster and Mori (2006) analyzed the lessons with Part A of the communicative orientation of language teaching (COLT) coding scheme used by Spada and Fröhlich (1995) and found that FSL lessons had a more experiential orientation and the focus of the lessons was generally on meaning and rarely on form. The JFL lessons had a more analytic orientation and their focus was predominantly on form. The authors then confirmed that the two settings were different regarding their pedagogical orientation and endeavored to examine and compare CFEs in each of them. The analysis revealed that the proportion of errors corrected by the teachers was similar in both settings (67% in FSL and 61% in JFL) and that CF types were used similarly across the two contexts, with recasts being the predominant type (54% in FSL and 65% in JFL of all CF moves), prompts occurring in a smaller proportion (38% in FSL and 26% in JFL), and explicit correction being relatively infrequent (7% in FSL and 9% in JFL).

However, uptake findings revealed differences. First, uptake and repair rates were higher in the JFL than the FSL setting. Second, there was more uptake after prompts in the FSL classrooms and after recasts in the JFL setting. Furthermore, there was more repair after prompts in the FSL setting and after recasts in the JFL context. Uptake and repair of explicit correction moves were similarly small in both settings, accounting for less than 10 percent.

Based on these findings the authors proposed the Counterbalance Hypothesis, which states that

> instructional activities and interactional feedback that act as a counterbalance to a classroom's predominant communicative orientation are likely to prove more effective than instructional activities and interactional feedback that are congruent with its predominant communicative orientation. (Lyster & Mori, 2006, p. 269)

Thus, the teachers in the meaning-focused lessons of the FSL context obtained more learner uptake with the use of form-focused teaching techniques, such as prompts. On the other hand, in the JFL classrooms, which were found to be more oriented to form, more meaning-focused or implicit types, such as recasts, resulted in larger rates of uptake and repair due to the learners' awareness of CF in this setting. The authors acknowledge the difficulty of classifying instructional context as purely analytic or experiential, but they explain that the COLT coding scheme can help to identify the orientation of a given classroom to form or to meaning. The analysis of the activities can help researchers to recognize not only the teachers' but also the learners' form/meaning orientation, which, in turn, seems to predict their ability to perceive and use the different CF types. However, since instruction is not focused exclusively on form or on meaning, the authors advocate for a balanced provision of CF, which uses different feedback strategies in order to enable learners to notice them. Lyster and Mori (2006) encourage future investigations on the relationship between learners' IDs and the Counterbalance Hypothesis. Moreover, they call for more "fine-grained" classroom research in settings that share the same target language and where FL classrooms are compared with immersion settings.

Lochtman (2007) is another example of a comparative study. The data were gathered in German as a Foreign Language (GFL) classrooms (Lochtman, 2002) and in FSL classrooms (Lyster & Ranta, 1997). The comparison revealed differences in CF provision in that the teachers in FL settings tended to prompt learners to self-correct errors, whereas the SL teachers reformulated erroneous utterances themselves by means of recasts. As for uptake, similar results were found, with higher rates in response to prompts in both settings, but in GFL recasts also yielded remarkable rates of repair. Thus, Lochtman's (2007) results echoed those of Lyster and Mori's (2006) in that the instructional context influences the three moves of CFEs, explained above.

Therefore, it seems that FL lessons tend to feature a focus on form, illustrated by teachers' preference for explicit CF types and prompts, and learners' uptake of all types of CF in general and recasts in particular. This usually implicit CF type (i.e. recasts) becomes more salient in FL classrooms and leads to higher rates of uptake. On the other hand, in SL contexts, teachers overlook most of the errors, but when they correct them, they prefer to reformulate them by means of recasts, which have been proven to be less effective than in FL classrooms.

In FL contexts, CLIL is a type of learning setting that has been clearly under-researched with regard to CF provision. Dalton-Puffer (2011, p.183) defines CLIL as "an educational approach where curricular content is taught through the medium of a FL, typically to learners participating in some form of mainstream education at the primary, secondary, or tertiary level." The notion of CLIL derives from immersion programs in Canada, but while these programs only considered language as the communicative vehicle to teach content, CLIL is a holistic approach whose aims are for learners to attain linguistic skills, communicative competence, and subject content knowledge. Language is not an end but a means to learn a variety of content. As Lasagabaster and Sierra (2010) point out, there are clear differences between immersion and CLIL. The language taught in immersion programs is the language spoken in the community, the teachers are native speakers of that language, the learners are exposed to it at an early age, the teaching materials are aimed at native speakers, and the goal is to be native-like. In CLIL programs, however, the language taught is a FL, the teachers are bilingual, the teaching materials are abridged, and the language objective is to reach an advanced proficiency level.

CLIL, therefore, "could be interpreted as a FL enrichment measure packaged into content teaching" (Dalton-Puffer, 2011, p. 184), but it is still an approach implemented in a FL context. Dalton-Puffer and Nikula (2014) emphasized that one of the areas where research is most needed in CLIL is on the type of feedback provided to learners. Unfortunately, there is very little CF research in this context. De Graaff et al. (2007) carried out one of the first studies examining pedagogical practices in CLIL in the Netherlands. They found that nonnative CLIL teachers were not very concerned about language rules and forms in their lessons as they considered this to be the responsibility of EFL teachers. The only CF that these subject teachers offered had to do with vocabulary errors. Lorenzo, Casal, and Moore (2010) presented findings from a large-scale project on CLIL in Andalusia (Southern Spain) and explained that language teachers are more likely to use CF than their subject content counterparts. However, to the best of our knowledge, only three studies to date have compared CLIL settings with more form-oriented FL contexts focusing on CF, namely: Llinares and Lyster (2014), Milla and García Mayo (2014), and Milla (2017); they are reviewed in what follows.

Llinares and Lyster (2014) compared CF and uptake in three different contexts: FSL in Canada, JFL in the USA, and CLIL classrooms in Spain. The researchers used data from Lyster and Mori's (2006) FSL and JFL classrooms and included a CLIL context. In this study, CLIL learners, primary school children, had Spanish as their L1 and were enrolled in a bilingual program, with English as the target language. Based on Lyster and Mori's (2006) comparison of the two different immersion classrooms, Llinares and Lyster (2014) performed a three-way analysis of CFEs by examining the frequency and distribution of CF types, the amount of repair and uptake these CF types yielded, and the factors that contributed to similarities and differences across the instructional settings.

Llinares and Lyster (2014) reported that CF types occurred in a similar proportion in the three settings, with recasts being the most frequently used type, followed by prompts; the least used type was explicit correction. As for uptake, the pattern was reversed with recasts producing uptake in the CLIL and JFL settings, whereas FSL learners responded more to prompts. Recasts were much more effective – in terms of repair – in CLIL classrooms, with the opposite happening in FSL classrooms. In JFL, similar high rates of repair were found for recasts, prompts, and explicit correction.

Finally, the researchers distinguish between conversational and didactic recasts (Sheen, 2006). Conversational recasts are more implicit, less direct; teachers use longer sentences to reformulate the error and, therefore, they tend to be a less salient type of CF. Didactic recasts, on the other hand, are more explicit and direct. Teachers use shorter reformulations of the erroneous utterance and isolate the repaired form to make it more apparent to the learners. In Llinares and Lyster (2014), the CLIL and JFL teachers used didactic recasts more than the FSL teachers, who preferred conversational recasts. This may be the reason for the differences in uptake and repair results found in the different contexts, since the explicitness of didactic recasts may bring their corrective focus to the forefront, increasing their effectiveness.

Llinares and Lyster (2014) examined classroom differences in order to clarify the impact of contextual characteristics on the quantity and quality of CFEs. They reported that interaction in CLIL and JFL shared more characteristics than interaction in JFL and FSL, termed as immersion contexts by Lyster and Mori (2006). The authors explain that this finding has to do with the fact that, as there are different types of CLIL programs (Lasagabaster & Sierra, 2010), immersion programs differ from one another as well (Tedick & Cammarata, 2012). Thus, in each of the contexts, teachers' beliefs and previous experience shape CF patterns and the type of instruction seems to influence learners' noticing of CF as well. The authors conclude that future research on teachers' beliefs and on the potential influences that these beliefs might have on their teaching practices, such as CF, should be carried out. Moreover, they consider it interesting to explore CFEs in secondary school classrooms, where CLIL teachers' background is different, since they are subject matter specialists and have no specific training as language teachers.

The lack of research on CF in CLIL classrooms was what prompted Milla and García Mayo (2014) to carry out another comparative study, where the corrective behavior of two teachers, CLIL and EFL, as well as the uptake and repair patterns of a group of thirty intermediate-level learners in different lessons were analyzed. The learners were 17–18 years old and belonged to an intact class in the second year of post-compulsory secondary education in a trilingual program (Spanish, Basque, and English), which included about 30 percent of the lessons in English. Following a classroom observation procedure, the authors audio-recorded a total of 377 minutes of three CLIL lessons (Business Studies in English) and four EFL lessons. As in Lyster and Mori (2006), the lessons were analyzed using the COLT scheme. The findings revealed that the CLIL lessons were clearly oriented to meaning, while EFL lessons were more form-oriented. This finding contrasts with Llinares and Lyster's (2014) CLIL classrooms, which were clearly form-oriented. The reason may lie in the fact that in Milla and García Mayo (2014) the CLIL teacher was a subject specialist with no specific training in language teaching, a regular occurrence in secondary education in Spain. Conversely, primary school CLIL teachers are generally English language teachers that also teach different subjects in English. Therefore, one would expect that CLIL secondary school teachers are less oriented to form and their lessons are more focused on meaning, as in immersion classrooms.

The type of feedback provided by the teacher was classified from the more explicit strategies (e.g., metalinguistic clues, explicit correction) or prompts (e.g., clarification requests or elicitations) to the more implicit (recasts) types. Milla and García Mayo (2014) also examined which type of feedback promoted immediate uptake, operationalized as any reaction on the part of the learner to the CF move, regardless of whether the error was repaired or not. The analysis of the CFEs in the two contexts revealed significant differences in the amount of errors corrected by the EFL (72 percent) and CLIL (53 percent) teachers. The authors also found that the CLIL teacher used recasts almost exclusively, as illustrated in example (3), while the EFL teacher used the whole spectrum of types, favoring explicit correction, elicitation, repetition, and metalinguistic feedback, as illustrated in (4):

(3) LEARNER: The value it has when the company start...
    TEACHER: Ok, when the company starts [recast]... and do you remember that in order to calculate we have a simple formula ok? It is...?
    (addressing another learner). Do you remember?

(4) LEARNER: ... instead of using the speech and rhyme to express meaning signers/*sɪŋɔrs/ use their hands in fact anything that can be expressed through spoken language can also be expressed through sign /*sɪŋ/ language.
    TEACHER: What was the problem with their speech? There was a very big problem, [explicit correction]... Now it was this (Teacher writes the word "sign" on the whiteboard [recast] that their text was about sign /saɪn/ language [recast]... and they invented a language: "singers were singing the language" [repetition] and you could see a person who wasn't singing at all, right? She was moving her hands! Be careful! Some pronunciation mistakes stop communication altogether! [metalinguistic cue]. How do you say this? [elicitation]
    LEARNERS: Sign /saɪn/!
    (Milla & García Mayo, 2014, p. 10)

These findings are in line with Lyster and Mori (2006), where the more form-oriented teachers (JFL) preferred prompts and the more meaning-oriented teachers (FSL) used recasts in a remarkably higher proportion with respect to other types. Milla and García Mayo (2014) showed that the differences in the use of CF in the two classrooms were not significant. The lack of significance could have been due to the small amount of data obtained from the recorded lessons. The authors were interested in unravelling the details of the CFEs occurring in the two contexts and carried out a qualitative analysis of CF moves to explore the differences found but not confirmed by the statistical analysis. The qualitative analysis revealed that the teachers not only provided different types of CF but also used the types in different ways.

The analysis of the uptake moves showed that CF was significantly more effective in the EFL (82 percent) than in CLIL (52 percent) lessons. Regarding the learners' immediate response to the CF types, it was found that there was a higher proportion of uptake after recasts and clarification requests in EFL and after elicitation and recasts in CLIL. Although these differences were not significant, the researchers reported that there was a tendency for learners to respond more positively to implicit types in form-oriented lessons and to explicit correction in the meaning-focused lessons of CLIL. These findings are in line with Lyster and Mori (2006) and, thus, could be explained by the Counterbalance Hypothesis.

With the aim of overcoming the limitations of previous studies and contribute to the need for more comparative research on CF in different learning settings, Milla (2017) conducted a classroom-based study with a group of learners (n=26) in their second year of secondary education (mean age = 17.11) enrolled in the same trilingual programs as those in Milla and García Mayo (2014). The learners attended the lessons of an EFL teacher (English language) and a CLIL teacher (Business Studies). Data from twelve CLIL and fifteen EFL lessons were recorded (22 hours and 43 minutes). To explore whether the participants' beliefs about CF influenced their classroom behavior, EFL and CLIL teachers along with their students completed a beliefs questionnaire.

The analyses of the 262 CFEs identified revealed differences between the two contexts. Significant differences were found between the teachers' corrective practices, not only with respect to the proportion of errors corrected (78% in EFL and only 20% in CLIL; p-value = 0) but also in relation to the types of CF used (p-value = 0). That is, the EFL teacher showed a great concern for accuracy by using more explicit types (elicitations and metalinguistic correction), while the CLIL teacher preferred to reformulate errors by means of recasts. Moreover, although recasts were the most frequently used CF type across the contexts (typical in classroom interaction), the types of recasts used differed in that more implicit or conversational recasts dominated the CLIL setting, whereas more explicit or didactic recasts were more frequent in the EFL context.

This study revealed an interesting finding: even though the group of learners was the same in the two classroom settings, their behavior changed depending on the type of lesson they were attending. In other words, they made more errors in CLIL than in EFL, and the types of errors were significantly different as well (p-value = 0). Moreover, the learners made an unsolicited use of their L1 very frequently in CLIL, while more pronunciation errors were found in EFL lessons. Furthermore, higher rates of uptake were found in the EFL lessons; this was especially the case after recasts (p-value = 0). This finding is probably due to the learners' increased attention to form in this context, plus the teacher's use of more explicit CF types and techniques that made the CF offered more salient. For instance, the EFL teacher used *multiple feedback* moves, which made CF types more salient and, therefore, potentially more effective. Consider (5), where the learner's pronunciation error is addressed with an explicit correction move followed by metalinguistic information, all in the same turn. This combination of CF types was codified as explicit correction, following Lyster and Ranta's (1997) conventions.

(5) Explicit correction + Metalinguistic cue = Explicit correction
 LEARNER: Suits [swiːts] and...
 TEACHER: Not sweets, sweet is something that you eat and is full of sugar. Suits [suːts] yes?

Finally, the analyses of the questionnaires revealed that the teachers' beliefs were similar in the two contexts, but inconsistencies were found in the comparison of beliefs and practices, especially for the CLIL teacher, who expressed positive attitudes about CF in the questionnaire but did not act on them in his corrective practices. This mismatch was attributed, as in previous studies (Mori, 2011; Yoshida, 2008), to curriculum constraints as well as to the fact that CLIL teachers might believe that while providing CF is beneficial, it may not necessarily be their duty. They leave this responsibility of taking care of form to their language teacher counterparts while they choose to focus primarily on meaning.

Regarding the learners' beliefs about CF, they were found to be significantly more positive than the teachers'. This finding is also consistent with previous research (Armheim & Nassaji, 2010; Lee, 2013) in that learners demand further correction from their teachers, while the latter are afraid of creating anxiety or interrupting the flow of communication by correcting too much.

Pedagogical Implications and Future Research

This chapter has summarized the main findings regarding the effect of the instructional context variable on CF provision and learner uptake in SL and FL settings. Although there are other intervening variables in CF provision, such as learners' ID, CF type, and task-related factors, instructional context seems to play an important role in the way teachers provide CF to oral errors as well as in learners' reaction to those errors (uptake). Lesson orientation appears to be a key factor and, thus, in those contexts where teachers, learners, and activities are focused on language forms, such as FL settings, CF seems to be more effective, especially when provided in the form of a recast. In classrooms which are more meaning or content-oriented, such as SL, immersion, or secondary school CLIL classrooms, the rates of uptake are lower, and more explicit CF types (such as metalinguistic information or elicitation) are needed.

Research on CF in second language teaching and learning is of utmost importance, since how to correct learner errors is a decision that every teacher needs to make (see Nassaji & Kartchava, 2017, for an update). Our review points to several pedagogical implications albeit caution should be exercised in implementing them in the classroom. First, teachers should be encouraged to strike a balance between meaning and form in their classes. They could guide learners' attention to formal aspects of language in CLIL classes by using different types of CF. In content-oriented classrooms, such as secondary school CLIL, teachers have been found to hold positive beliefs about CF that do not match their actual classroom behavior (see Li, 2017 for a recent overview of teacher and student beliefs on oral CF). CLIL and SL teachers do not address a high percentage of errors and resort mainly to recasts. Their provision of feedback is rather implicit and learners generally overlook these CF moves, which turn out to be not very effective. Higher rates of uptake have been found to occur after prompts and explicit CF in these meaning-focused classrooms (Lyster & Mori, 2006; Milla, 2017), so CLIL and SL teachers should provide these CF types to develop a more balanced language-content focus in their lessons. Another issue that teachers should take into account is that linguistic target also seems to play an important role regarding CF provision. As shown in several research studies, explicit feedback types seem to work better for morphosyntactic targets, whereas implicit CF types are perceived more when dealing with lexical and phonological items.

Second, both learner and teacher training on how to provide and receive CF in order to maximize its effectiveness should be emphasized. There are recent studies on learner training in how to provide CF (Fujii, Ziegler & Mackey, 2016; Sato & Ballinger, 2012; see also Chapter 28, this volume), which have shown that trained learners detected more errors than those who were not. Teachers should also be trained and be made aware of the different types of CF and their impact on learner development. CF should facilitate learners' noticing (Schmidt, 1990) of their errors especially in FL contexts in which access to input is restricted. The teachers' role is also crucial in constructing a collaborative learning environment in the classroom that may foster peer CF (see Sato, 2017; Chapter 13, this volume) in both SL and FL settings. In order to achieve this goal, teachers should be involved in research and informed about the findings, which will help them become aware about their own practices as well as gain knowledge about the effect of teaching techniques such as CF (see Sato & Loewen, 2019).

There is clearly a need for further research on the link between CF and the instructional context. For example, the issue of CF provision and uptake remains unexplored in child FL learning. Considering the worldwide trend to introduce English early (Enever, 2018; García Mayo, 2017), there are numerous avenues for research within that population. These may include a study of the type of CF provided by teachers for that age range (6–12), children's uptake of different CF types, peer CF, and the impact of such intervening variables as linguistic target, task-related features, and IDs. Research is also needed on oral CF provided in CLIL secondary schools to corroborate the findings reported by Milla (2017) and, moreover, on teachers' and learners' (adolescent and children) beliefs about CF. In sum, researchers should be able to reach more robust findings that can be transferred to practitioners in order for them to make research-informed pedagogical decisions.

References

Alcón Soler, E. & García Mayo, M. P. (2008). Incidental focus on form and learning outcomes with young foreign language classroom learners. In J. Philp, R. Oliver & A. Mackey (eds.), *Second language acquisition and the younger learner: Child's play?* (pp. 173–192). Amsterdam: John Benjamins.

Amrhein, H. R. & Nassaji, H. (2010). Written corrective feedback: What do learners and teachers prefer and why? *Canadian Journal of Applied Linguistics, 13*(2), 95–127.

Choi, S. & Li, S. (2012). Corrective feedback and learner uptake in a child ESOL classroom. *RELC Journal, 43*(3), 331–351.

Dabaghi, A. & Basturkmen, H. (2009). The effectiveness of implicit and explicit error correction on learners' performance. *System, 37*(1), 82–98.

Dalton-Puffer, C. (2011). Content and language integrated learning: From practice to principles. *Annual Review of Applied Linguistics, 31*, 182–204.

Dalton-Puffer, C. & Nikula, T. (2014). Content and language integrated learning (guest editorial). *The Language Learning Journal, 42*(2), 117–122.

De Graaff, R., Koopman, G. J., Anikina, Y. & Westhoff, G. (2007). An observation tool for effective L2 pedagogy in content and language integrated learning (CLIL). *International Journal of Bilingual Education and Bilingualism, 10*(5), 603–624.

Ellis, R., Basturkmen, H. & Loewen, S. (2001). Learner uptake in communicative ESL lessons. *Language Learning, 51*(2), 281–318.

Ellis, R., Loewen, S. & Erlam, R. (2006). Implicit and explicit corrective feedback and the acquisition of L2 grammar. *Studies in Second Language Acquisition, 28*(2), 339–368.

Enever, J. (2018). *Policy and politics in global primary English*. Oxford: Oxford University Press.

Fujii, A., Ziegler, N. & Mackey, A. (2016). Peer interaction and metacognitive instruction in the EFL classroom. In M. Sato & S. Ballinger (eds.), *Peer interaction and second language learning: Pedagogical potential and research agenda* (pp. 63–89). Amsterdam: John Benjamins.

García Mayo, M. P. (2017). *Learning foreign languages in primary school: Research insights*. Bristol: Multilingual Matters.

Goo, J. (2012). Corrective feedback and working memory capacity in interaction-driven SL learning. *Studies in Second Language Acquisition, 34*(3), 445–474.

Goo, J. & Mackey, A. (2013). The case against the case against recasts. *Studies in Second Language Acquisition, 35*(1), 127–165.

Gurzynski-Weiss, L. & Révész, A. (2012). Tasks, teacher feedback, and learner modified output in naturally occurring classroom interaction. *Language Learning, 62*(3), 851–879.

Havranek, G. & Cesnik, H. (2001). Factors affecting the success of corrective feedback. In S. Foster-Cohen & A. Nizegorodzew (Eds.), *EUROSLA Yearbook Volume 1* (pp.99–122). Amsterdam: John Benjamins.

Jafarigohara, M. & Gharbavib, A. (2014). Recast or prompt: Which one does the trick? *Procedia- Social and Behavioral Sciences, 98*, 695–703.

Kartchava, E. & Ammar, A. (2014). The noticeability and effectiveness of corrective feedback in relation to target type. *Language Teaching Research, 18*(4), 428–452.

Lasagabaster, D. & Sierra, J. M. (2010). Immersion and CLIL in English: More differences than similarities. *ELT Journal, 64*(4), 376–395.

Lee, E. (2013). Corrective feedback preferences and learner repair among advanced ESL learners. *System, 41*(2), 217–230.

Li, S. (2017). Student and teacher beliefs and attitudes about oral corrective feedback. In H. Nassaji & E. Kartchava (eds.), *Corrective feedback in second language teaching and learning* (pp. 143–157). New York; London: Routledge.

Llinares, A. & Lyster, R. (2014). The influence of context on patterns of corrective feedback and learner uptake: A comparison of CLIL and immersion classrooms. *The Language Learning Journal, 42*(2), 181–194.

Lochtman, K. (2002). Oral corrective feedback in the foreign language classroom: How it affects interaction in analytic foreign language teaching. *International Journal of Educational Research, 37*(3), 271–283.

(2007). Die mündliche Fehlerkorrektur in CLIL und im traditionellen Fremdsprachenunterricht: Ein Vergleich. In C. Dalton-Puffer & U. Smit (eds.), *Empirical perspectives on CLIL classroom discourse* (pp. 119–138). Frankfurt: Peter Lang.

Lorenzo, F., Casal, S. & Moore, P. (2010). The effects of content and language integrated learning in European education: Key findings from the Andalusian bilingual sections evaluation project. *Applied Linguistics, 31*(3), 418–442.

Lyster, R. (1998). Recasts, repetition and ambiguity in L2 classroom discourse. *Studies in Second Language Acquisition, 20*(1), 51–80.

(2004). Differential effects of prompts and recasts in form-focused instruction. *Studies in Second Language Acquisition, 26*(3), 399–432.

(2007). *Learning and teaching languages through content: A counterbalanced approach*. Amsterdam: John Benjamins.

Lyster, R. & Mori, H. (2006). Interactional feedback and instructional counterbalance. *Studies in Second Language Acquisition, 28*(2), 269–300.

Lyster, R. & Ranta, L. (1997). Corrective feedback and learner uptake: Negotiation of form in communicative classrooms. *Studies in Second Language Acquisition, 19*(1), 37–66.

Lyster, R. & Saito, K. (2010). Oral feedback in classroom SLA. A meta-analysis. *Studies in Second Language Acquisition, 32*(2), 265–302.

Mackey, A. & Goo, J. (2007). Interaction research in SLA: A meta-analysis and research synthesis. In A. Mackey (ed.), *Conversational interaction in second language acquisition* (pp. 407–472). Oxford: Oxford University Press.

Mackey, A., Gass, S. & McDonough, K. (2000). How do learners perceive interactional feedback? *Studies in Second Language Acquisition, 22*(4), 471–497.

Mackey, A. & Philp, J. (1998). Conversational interaction and second language development: Recasts, responses, and red herrings? *Modern Language Journal, 82*(3), 338–356.

Mifka-Profozic, N. (2014). Effectiveness of implicit negative feedback in a foreign language classroom. *EUROSLA Yearbook, 14*, 111–142.

Milla, R. (2017). Corrective feedback episodes in CLIL and EFL classrooms: Teachers' and learners' beliefs and classroom behaviour. Unpublished doctoral thesis. University of the Basque Country (UPV/EHU), Vitoria, Spain.

Milla, R. & García Mayo, M. P. (2014). Corrective feedback episodes in oral interaction: A comparison of a CLIL and an EFL classroom. *International Journal of English Studies, 14*(1), 1–20.

Mori, R. (2002). Teachers' beliefs and corrective feedback. *JALT Journal, 24*(1), 48–69.

(2011). Teacher cognition in corrective feedback in Japan. *System, 39*(4), 451–467.

Muñoz, C. (2007). CLIL: Some thoughts on its psycholinguistic principles. *Revista Española de Lingüística Aplicada (Models and practice in CLIL)* Vol. Extra 1, 17–26.

Nabei, T. & Swain, M. (2002). Learner awareness of recasts in classroom interaction: A case study of an adult EFL learner's second language learning. *Language Awareness. 11*(1), 43–63.

Nassaji, H. (2007). Elicitation and reformulation and their relationship with learner repair in dyadic interaction. *Language Learning, 57*(4), 511–548.

(2011). Correcting students' written grammatical errors: The effect of negotiated versus nonnegotiated feedback. *Studies in Second Language Learning and Teaching, 1*(3), 315–334.

(2013). Participation structure and incidental focus on form in adult ESL classrooms. *Language Learning, 63*(4), 835–869.

(2016). Anniversary article: Interactional feedback in second language teaching and learning: A synthesis and analysis of current research. *Language Teaching Research, 20*(4), 535–562.

(2019). The effects of recasts versus prompts on learning a complex target structure. In R. DeKeyser & G. P. Botana (eds.), *(Doing) SLA research* with implications for the classroom (reconciling methodological demands and pedagogical applicability) (pp. 107–126). Amsterdam: John Benjamins.

Nassaji, H. & Fotos, S. (2011). Teaching grammar in second language classrooms: Integrating form-focused instruction in communicative context. London: Routledge.

Nassaji, H. & Kartchava, E. (eds.). (2017). Corrective feedback in second language teaching and learning. Research, theory, applications, implications. New York; London: Routledge.

Oliver, R. & Grote, E. (2010). The provision and uptake of different types of recasts in child and adult ESL learners: What is the role of age and context? *Australian Review of Applied Linguistics*, 33(3), 26.1–26.22.

Panova, I. & Lyster, R. (2002). Patterns of corrective feedback and uptake in an adult ESL classroom. *TESOL Quarterly*, 36(4), 573–595.

Philp, J. (2003). Constraints on noticing the gap: Nonnative speakers' noticing of recasts in NS-NNS interaction. *Studies in Second Language Acquisition*, 25(1), 99–126.

Pinter, A. (2011). *Children learning second languages*. Houndsmills: Palgrave Macmillan.

Rassaei, S. (2014). Scaffolded feedback, recasts and L2 development: A sociocultural perspective. *Modern Language Journal*, 98(1), 417–431.

Saito, K. & Lyster, R. (2012). Effects of form-focused instruction and corrective feedback on L2 pronunciation development of / ɹ / by Japanese learners of English. *Language Learning*, 62(2), 595–633.

Samar, G. R. & Shayestefar, P. (2009). Corrective feedback in EFL classrooms: Learner negotiation strategies and uptake. *Journal of English Language Teaching and Learning*, 212, 107–134.

Sato, M. (2017). Oral peer corrective feedback. Multiple theoretical perspectives. In H. Nassaji & E. Kartchava (eds.), *Corrective feedback in second language teaching and learning. Research, theory, applications, implications* (pp. 19–34). New York; London: Routledge.

Sato, M. & Ballinger, S. (2012). Raising learner awareness in peer interaction. A cross-context, cross-method examination. *Language Awareness*, 21(1–2), 157–179.

Sato, M. & Loewen, S. (2019). Towards evidence-based second language pedagogy: Research proposals and pedagogical recommendations. In M. Sato & S. Loewen (eds.), *Evidence-based second language pedagogy: A collection of instructed second language acquisition studies* (pp. 1–24). New York: Routledge.

Schmidt, R. (1990). The role of consciousness in L2 learning. *Applied Linguistics*, 11(2), 129–158.

Sheen, Y. (2004). Corrective feedback and learner uptake in communicative classrooms across instructional settings. *Language Teaching Research*, 8(3), 263–300.

(2006). Exploring the relationship between characteristics of recasts and learner uptake. *Language Teaching Research*, 10(4), 361–392.

(2008). Recasts, language anxiety, modified output, and L2 learning. *Language Learning, 58*(4), 835–874.

Spada, N. & Fröhlich, M. (1995). *COLT. Communicative orientation of language teaching observation scheme: Coding conventions and applications.* Sydney: National Centre for English Language Teaching and Research.

Tedick, D. J. & Cammarata, L. (2012). Content and language integration in K-12 contexts: Learner outcomes, teacher practices and stakeholder perspectives. *Foreign Language Annals, 45*(1), 28–53.

Vygotsky, L. S. (1978). *Mind in society: The development of higher psychological processes.* Cambridge, MA: Harvard University Press.

Yang, Y. & Lyster, R. (2010). Effects of form-focused practice and feedback on Chinese EFL learners' acquisition of regular and irregular past tense forms. *Studies in Second Language Acquisition, 32*(2), 235–263.

Yilmaz, Y. (2012). The relative effects of explicit correction and recasts on two target structures via two communication modes. *Language Learning, 62*(4), 1134–1169.

Yoshida, R. (2008). Teachers' choice and learners' preference of corrective-feedback types. *Language Awareness, 17*(1), 78–93.

23

Corrective Feedback in Computer-Mediated versus Face-to-Face Environments

Luis Cerezo

Introduction

The potentially transformative power of computer-mediated communication (CMC) for additional language (L2) acquisition has inspired an active research agenda for the last three decades. Since early on, many interactionists hypothesized that CMC, particularly in its written and synchronous variety (written SCMC), could elicit more explicit, accurate, and complex output, enhance comprehension and attention to form, and promote more readily available and usable corrective feedback, due to features and affordances like the increased saliency of the written word, the lack of prosodic and paralinguistic markers, the ability to reinspect previous input, the additional processing time, or the purportedly reduced anxiety (e.g., Ortega, 1997).

Expectations, however, have not always found empirical validation. In her synthesis of last decade's work, Ortega (2009) compellingly showed that written SCMC may promote highly variable amounts of negotiation for meaning (NfM), corrective feedback, successful uptake, and L2 development, thus calling for "temperance and more research" (p. 244). Yet, as Ziegler and Mackey (2017) noted a decade later, the evidence remains "conflicting" for many variables (NfM, p. 83; noticing, p. 84; L2 development, p. 86). In addition, given the increased presence of technology in L2 classrooms, Ortega (2009) advocated for more "studies pursuing a direct comparison between the SCMC and FTF [face-to-face] modes" (p. 245). Dozens of comparative studies have since been published; most, however, await the scrutiny of a critical synthesis.

Through the critical synthesis of forty-one studies comparing written SCMC and FTF interaction, I will take stock on how the interactional environment may moderate the effectiveness of corrective feedback. Because such effectiveness is ultimately determined by feedback availability, usability, and use, I cast a wide net and include studies on learning processes and products. I will demonstrate that these studies, like their non-comparative counterparts, yield conflicting findings, which I will attribute to methodological issues (discrepancies in the architecture of experimental designs, construct operationalizations, and units of analysis) and substantive issues (a neglect of the notion of modality). To address these caveats and identify emerging trends, I will consider effect sizes, prioritize within-subjects designs, factor in moderating variables, and analyze the role of different tools and language learning objectives.

The Current Study

In this chapter I critically synthesize the results of forty-one empirical studies comparing the L2 developmental effects of written SCMC versus FTF interaction. To identify these primary sources, I mined the Linguistics and Language Behavior Abstracts database using the intentionally wide search query <"computer-mediated" AND "face to face">. This yielded 1,014 peer-reviewed publications as of March 18, 2018, which I canvassed one by one. Second, I inspected the reference sections of previous syntheses and meta-analyses. Third, I iteratively added relevant sources from the literature review sections of the selected studies. These last two steps were particularly useful to include oft-cited book chapters and dissertations.

To qualify for this review, studies had to empirically compare, through within- or between-subjects experimental designs, the effects of written SCMC versus FTF interaction on (a) L2 learning outcomes (e.g., grammar or vocabulary development, *as measured by pre-test/post-test comparisons*) or (b) L2 learning processes (e.g., *during-treatment* differences in terms of amount, complexity, and accuracy of output; participation rates; and meaning and form negotiation rates, including noticing of feedback, uptake, modified output, and self-corrections). Studies were excluded if (a) their treatment tasks were not comparable (e.g. if the written SCMC group received additional exposure to computerized drills, or if the FTF group only completed the assessment tests), or (b) they investigated socio-affective dependent measures (e.g., motivation, anxiety).

To glean emerging hypotheses from the admittedly limited body of research, I will consider Cohen's *d* effect sizes, whenever the reported data allowed for calculations. Based on Oswald and Plonsky's (2010) conservative benchmarks, 0.40, 0.70, and 1.00 will be respectively considered small, medium, and large effects. In addition, I will explain contradictory findings in light of methodological and substantive issues, as explained below.

Methodological Discrepancies Partly Explain Conflicting Findings

Comparative studies have vastly differed in their operationalizations of experimental variables, such as the size of the interacting groups and the type of interlocutors, tasks, instructions, settings, or linguistic targets. To illustrate this with one variable, the allotted time-on-task in Fitze (2006) was the same for both SCMC and FTF conditions, and respectively double and quadruple for SCMC in de la Fuente (2003) and Chang (2007).

Studies have also varied in their units of analysis. For example, learner participation rates have been compared via head-count percentages (Sullivan & Pratt, 1996), individual distances from the group mean words and turns (Freiermuth, 2001), or more complex statistical measures such as the Gini coefficient of inequality (Warschauer, 1996).

There are crucial architectural differences, too. Counterbalanced *within-subjects* designs have reported data from participants exposed to both environments; in *between-subjects* designs, participants have been split in two conditions; and in *indirect comparisons*, the performance of a single SCMC group has been compared against previous literature on FTF interaction. Various scholars (e.g., Rouhshad, Wigglesworth & Storch, 2016, p. 517; Zeng, 2017, p. 262) have criticized the last two types of studies because treatment and learner inconsistencies may yield strikingly discordant findings. For example, while in Zeng's (2017) within-subjects study SCMC yielded double the rate of language-related episodes (LREs); in indirect comparisons such as Zeng and Takatsuka (2009), this edge increased to sixty times more LREs; and in Loewen and Reissner's (2009) between-subjects study, it was actually the FTF condition that produced four to fourteen times more form-focused episodes (FFEs) per minute.

To minimize confounds, in this chapter I synthesize within- and between-subjects comparative studies exclusively, prioritizing the former and considering differences in construct operationalizations and analysis. Before that, though, I will draw attention to a substantive issue – the notion of *modality*.

The Overlooked Explanatory Power of Modality

As Lamy (2012) notes, modality has long been envisaged as a defining characteristic of computer-assisted language learning (CALL); however, it is often "ignored," "rarely defined," "used inconsistently," or "misunderstood" in the literature, thus hampering our understanding of the educational benefits that can be expected from technology (pp. 110, 121). A three-dimensional construct, modality comprises *tools*, *language learning objectives*, and *modes* (Lamy, 2012, p. 111).

Tools are the artifacts used to access, produce, and disseminate information. Consider the following examples: in Chatnet, the tool of choice in Fernández-García and Martínez Arbelaiz (2003), messages were restricted to three lines of text, the typing window fit only two lines, and there was no possibility to scroll up or down to edit text (pp. 118–119); in Böhlke's (2003b) version of OTChat, there was only one window to read and write messages, which "led to confusion for a few students because the text posted from other students would interrupt their own sentences" (p. 72); in Yilmaz's (2012) version of MSN Messenger, learners had full typing, scrolling, and editing capabilities before sending messages; and in Kaneko's (2009) DigiChat, words were transmitted in real time as they were being typed. Arguably, these affordances can differently impact the quantity and quality of learners' input and output per turn, learners' ability to notice forms in their own and partner's speech, and to self-edit, provide corrective feedback, and modify output; yet, they are often overlooked in the discussion sections.

Language learning objectives refer to the pedagogical goals envisaged for a particular tool, such as accessing authentic L2 input, producing output, receiving feedback, and so on. Take Rouhshad et al. (2016), where participants were told "please correct your peers throughout the task. For example, if they use 'goed' instead of 'went', you are encouraged to correct your peer." Now consider Zeng (2017), where participants did not receive special instructions. These studies matched in their goals (comparing rates of negotiation of form, NoF), architecture (within-subjects designs), construct operationalizations (dyadic interaction between nonnative speakers [NNSs], similar time-on-task), and units of analysis (amount of output was controlled for). Yet, they yielded different results. Rouhshad et al. (2016) found that FTF interaction triggered nonsignificantly more NoF, while in Zeng (2017) SCMC yielded significantly double the number of LREs. Arguably, the directions in Rouhshad et al. (2016), among other factors, may have contributed to this discrepancy by enhancing attention to form in FTF interaction, narrowing the gap with SCMC.

Finally, *modes* are the semiotic representations used to convey information, whether linguistic, visual, aural, gestural, or spatial (Guichon & Cohen, 2016, p. 510). When two or more modes are combined, we speak of *multimodality*. The most evident case is videoconferencing, where users are exposed to their interlocutor's image, oral speech, and sometimes, written output. From a psycholinguistic perspective, multimodality is a complex phenomenon in which quantitative and qualitative factors (the number and type of modes, their interaction, and the sensory channels invoked) impact our attention, understanding, and learning. Consequently, in order to understand how these factors contribute to L2 learning, separate comparisons between different iterations of FTF interaction and CMC (written, oral, video, synchronous, and asynchronous) are certainly warranted. For depth of focus, I will concentrate exclusively on written SCMC, arguably the most researched type.

Emerging Trends: L2 Learning Outcomes

Written SCMC May Amplify Feedback Effectiveness in Tutor–Learner Interaction

Researchers have only recently started to investigate whether corrective feedback may promote different learning outcomes in written SCMC and FTF contexts. In Yilmaz and Yuksel's (2011) seminal study, twenty-four Turkish learners completed two one-way information tasks individually with their tutor, receiving recasts on plural and locative morphemes. Time-on-task was about double in SCMC. Online recasts led to higher controlled oral development of the two morphemes, although the edge over FTF interaction only reached statistical significance for the plural, the more salient structure ($d = 0.85$). Doubling the sample size, Yilmaz (2012) additionally investigated the effects of explicit corrections. He found that recasts and explicit corrections combined were significantly more effective in SCMC, particularly with more formally-oriented tasks ($d = 0.97$). Explicit corrections generally promoted higher learning gains than recasts in both environments, and saliency made an independent rather than moderating contribution, because participants always learned the more salient structure better –Yilmaz (2012) attributed this discrepancy with Yilmaz and Yuksel (2011) to a caveat in their operationalization of salience (p. 1163). In a between-subjects study, Baralt (2013) did uncover a moderating variable, task complexity. Eighty-four Spanish learners completed a prompt-based story retell individually with her, either FTF or online in over twice the time, receiving recasts on the Spanish past subjunctive. Results from both FTF and online iterations of the treatment tasks showed that recasts promoted the highest development rates when delivered online, but only with less complex tasks ($d = 0.69$–0.99); conversely, FTF recasts led to the most learning with more complex tasks ($d = 0.33$–0.89).

Overall, these studies suggest that written SCMC may boost the developmental effects of corrective feedback, with medium to large effect sizes ($d = 0.69$–0.99), under specific circumstances: in untimed dyadic interaction with tutors; with formally oriented assessment tasks, and with controlled, less complex treatment tasks, because the additional negotiation involved with more complex tasks may dilute SCMC benefits like the immediate visual juxtaposition of recasts after errors (Baralt, 2013, p. 718). Crucially, though, because individualized tutor–learner interaction is not ecologically realistic in most curricula, the question that arises is whether the environment also moderates feedback effectiveness in peer interaction.

Written SCMC Has No Clear Developmental Edge in Peer Interaction

To my knowledge, no comparative studies have rigorously isolated the effects of peer correction on L2 development. The existing developmental studies can only inform about the role of feedback indirectly, given its natural occurrence in interaction; they all used between-subjects designs, so sampling errors cannot be discarded, and their results are mixed.

Some studies showed a developmental edge of written SCMC in a variety of treatments. In Beauvois (1998) eighty-three French learners participated in small-group and whole-class discussions for 50 minutes a week over a semester. In Payne and Whitney (2002) fifty-eight Spanish learners participated in twenty-one 50-minute sessions of communicative activities in small groups of four to six. In Abrams (2003) ninety-six German learners discussed readings in small groups of five for two 50-minute sessions. And in Blake (2009) twenty-four English learners completed twelve 60-minute sessions of free conversation, vocabulary review, and teacher-led discussion in groups of six to eight (FTF) or ten (SCMC). Their results provide support to skill transferability, with SCMC groups achieving significantly higher oral proficiency gains in holistic measures (Beauvois, 1998, $d = 0.46$; Payne & Whitney, 2002, $d = 0.29$), amount of words and C-units (Abrams, 2003, $d = 0.38$–0.39), and fluency (Blake, 2009, $d = 0.56$–0.83).

Other evidence, however, suggests no environmental impact. In the just-discussed study by Abrams (2003), oral proficiency gains in lexical and syntactic complexity were statistically similar across conditions. In Kost's (2004) study of ninety-four German learners, twelve 15–20 minute role-play sessions in groups of two to three yielded similar oral and written proficiency gains in quantity of speech, lexical complexity, and accuracy on subject-verb agreement and the present perfect. And in Hirotani's (2009) study of thirty-six Japanese learners, ten weekly 35-minute topic-based discussions in small groups of three to four propelled similar gains on eleven measures of quantity, complexity, accuracy, and cohesiveness of oral speech.

Finally, an edge for FTF interaction was found in de la Fuente (2003). Ten dyads of Spanish learners negotiated vocabulary items in two iterations of an information-gap task, with double the time allotment in SCMC (30 vs. 15 minutes). The FTF group performed best on all measures of vocabulary development, statistically better in the oral mode (d = 1.03–2.27) and nonsignificantly in the written mode.

In sum, there is disagreement as to the developmental effects of written SCMC versus FTF conditions in peer interaction. While some studies obtained an edge for written SCMC in oral proficiency development, with small to medium effect sizes (d = 0.29–0.83), others found no differences, and de la Fuente (2003) found an advantage for FTF interaction in vocabulary acquisition, with a large effect size (d = 1.03–2.27). More studies are surely warranted, prioritizing within-subjects designs and control for corrective feedback. Meanwhile, studies on how the environment affects learning processes may provide additional insight.

Emerging Trends: L2 Learning Processes

Amount of Output and Participation

Written SCMC Usually Promotes Lower Output Rates

Numerous within-subjects studies suggest that FTF interaction promotes higher output rates under a variety of circumstances. In Vandergriff (2006) six triads of German learners produced 2.3 times more C-units while carrying out consensus-building tasks FTF under 30 minutes. Six dyads of English learners in Lai and Zhao (2006) produced an average of thirty-three more words while completing a spot-the-difference task FTF in 22 fewer minutes. In Kaneko (2009) sixteen dyads of Japanese learners produced 2.75 times the number of morphemes when completing three communicative tasks FTF for 10 minutes each. The twenty-one English learners in Sauro (2012) produced 26 percent more tokens while performing two narrative tasks FTF (d = 0.55) alone with her in less than one-third of the time (2.5 minutes). In Rouhshad et al. (2016) twelve dyads of English learners produced almost double the number of words when completing a decision-making task FTF (d = 1.58) two and a half times faster (11 minutes). Sixteen dyads of English learners in Zeng (2017) produced more than double the number of words while completing jigsaw and dictogloss tasks FTF (d = 1.81) in almost one-third of the time (12 minutes per task). And the between-subjects studies by Nguyen and White (2011) and Sullivan and Pratt (1996) corroborate this edge.

There is, however, counterevidence. The twenty-seven English learners in Fitze (2006) produced similar word counts in both environments during two 20-minute discussions in large groups of thirteen to fourteen. Other studies even obtained an edge for SCMC. In Kern (1995), forty French learners produced 45 percent more words, two to three and a half times more turns, and two to four times more sentences online during 50-minute discussions in groups of fourteen to eighteen. The twenty-seven German learners in Böhlke (2003a) produced double the number of attributive adjectives (but identical predicate adjectives) during 12-to 15-minute online discussions in groups of four to five. Six out of the nine foursomes of English learners in Freiermuth and Jarrell (2006) produced more words when carrying out consensus-building tasks online, behind pseudonyms, for 45 minutes. And in Chang's (2007) between-subjects study of fifty English learners, the SCMC group produced significantly more words during individual discussions with their instructor (d = 0.39). Their time-on-task (12 minutes), though, quadrupled the amount allocated to the FTF group.

In sum, evidence largely indicates that learners produce more output when interacting FTF, with large effect sizes (d = 1.58–1.81). However, this gap may be narrowed when discussions are held one-on-one with the tutor, who may play an equalizing role (Sauro, 2012, d = 0.54) or in larger groups, where simultaneous online contributions can match (Fitze, 2006) or even surpass (Kern, 1995) FTF output rates. In addition, written SCMC may yield more output when strikingly different time allotments may disadvantage the FTF groups (Chang, 2007), when pseudonyms are used, likely lowering affective filters and enticing learners to be more vocal (Freiermuth & Jarrell, 2006), or when specific parts of speech are considered, particularly if they might be more frequent in the written mode (Böhlke, 2003a).

Written SCMC Usually Promotes More Equal Participation

Accumulating evidence shows that despite its generally lower output rates, written SCMC promotes more equal participation. In Kern's (1995) corpus of 50-minute large-group discussions, SCMC elicited participation from all students, while FTF interaction was dominated by a minority. Three out of four foursomes of English learners in Warschauer (1996) displayed significantly twice the equality of participation during 15-minute online discussions. The ten English learners in Pyun (2003) significantly approached the number of turns of the native speakers (NSs) they paired up with when exchanging opinions online for 15 minutes (d = 1.41). In Tan, Wigglesworth, and Storch's (2010) study of ten 2-hour weekly sessions, six dyads of Chinese learners collaborated and cooperated more often while completing seven writing tasks online, while in FTF interaction one partner was usually more dominant. And the between-subjects studies by Sullivan and Pratt (1996), Freiermuth (2001), and Nguyen and White (2011) confirmed this pattern.

Some studies, however, yielded mixed results. Böhlke (2003b) found that the within-group variance in participation was statistically four times smaller online, but only in groups of four rather than five students, and Fitze (2006) found statistically greater equality of participation in SCMC (d = 1.5) for one of his two classes only (n = 13–14). Finally, contra Tan et al. (2010) above, the twelve pairs of English learners in Rouhshad and Storch (2016) collaborated more while co-writing 150-word compositions FTF than online, where division of labor and dominance patterns prevailed. Possibly, this could result from their shorter treatment and task-tool interaction. Thirty minutes on average may have not been enough to build a collaborative relationship online, particularly given the logistical complexities of writing on Google Docs while communicating and editing in its small chat window (p. 285).

Overall, then, mounting evidence suggests that written SCMC may promote up to two Gini coefficients more equal participation than FTF interaction (Warschauer, 1996), although with less probability in larger groups, where some learners may be disincentivized by the multiplicity of voices and the speedy, disjointed communication, and in short-termed collaborative tasks that require writing in two tools (e.g., document and chat windows), where learners may opportunistically divide labor.

Complexity and Accuracy

Written SCMC Displays Shorter Utterances but Perhaps More Complex Grammar and Vocabulary

Incipient research suggests that FTF interaction may yield *longer utterances* per turn. The ten English learners in Pyun (2003) produced significantly (40 percent) longer T-units during dyadic FTF interaction with NSs ($d = 2.85$). One of the two dyads of English learners in Hamano-Bunce (2011) produced longer AS-units while completing two information-exchange tasks FTF. And in Nguyen and White's (2011) between-subjects study, triads of TESOL students produced FTF turns that were almost three times longer ($d = 2.82$), although due to more dominant participants stealing the floor. Conversely, the twenty-one English learners in Sauro (2012) produced similarly long AS-units while completing two narrative tasks with her in both environments, which could have resulted from her more inclusive operationalization of AS-units, as Sauro noted, as well as her equalizing role as a tutor. Overall, then, FTF interaction seems to elicit turns that are from 40 percent (Pyun, 2003) to three times (Nguyen & White, 2011) longer than SCMC, with very large effect sizes (up to $d = 2.85$). Among other reasons, this may be because in SCMC learners tend to keep their messages short to mark their social presence, make a point before the next incoming message, or elicit more responses, particularly when they possess limited typing skills (Nguyen & White, 2011, p. 29).

Longer FTF utterances, however, do not necessarily involve more syntactic *subordination*. While Pyun (2003) did find nonsignificantly 6 percent higher subordination in this modality ($d = 0.79$), Sauro (2012) found a comparable ratio of clauses to AS-units in both conditions, and Warschauer (1996) found significantly more subordination in SCMC, where only 18.5 percent of combined clauses were based on coordination, as opposed to 47.5 percent in FTF interaction.

Studies employing scales of *developmental stages* suggest a potential edge for SCMC. Salaberry's (2000) four Spanish learners displayed more advanced uses of past tense morphology when interviewing them online. However, since SCMC seemingly happened after FTF interaction, carry-over effects cannot be discarded. More compellingly, ten dyads of English learners in Kim (2017) produced significantly more advanced questions when completing three tasks online. Specifically, 50 percent of questions in SCMC ranked as stages IV and V (based on Pienemann & Johnston, 1987), as opposed to 21 percent in FTF interaction (d = 3.25–5.85). In contrast, the German learner foursomes in Böhlke (2003b) produced more advanced constructions FTF; Böhlke, however, neither reported inferential statistics nor controlled for the higher amount of speech in this modality.

Finally, at least two studies suggest that SCMC might elicit significantly more *lexical complexity*. Warschauer (1996) found a 4 percent higher type-token ratio and Fitze (2006) found an 18 percent higher standardized type-token ratio (d = 3.73). Sauro (2012), though, found statistically similar lexical complexity in both environments, a discrepancy which may result from differences in the types of interactors (peers in Warschauer's and Fitze's studies, tutor–learner in Sauro's) and units of analysis (Warschauer and Fitze both compared excerpts of equal length, while Sauro used Guiraud's index).

To sum up, incipient evidence tentatively suggests that in written SCMC learners may produce shorter utterances (Hamano-Bunce, 2011; Nguyen & White, 2011; Pyun, 2003), but possibly more complex grammar (Kim, 2017; Salaberry, 2000) and vocabulary (Fitze, 2006; Warschauer, 1996), with very large effect sizes (d = 2.85 for shorter utterances, 5.85 for more complex grammar, and 3.73 for more complex vocabulary). However, much more research is needed to validate these hypotheses and identify potential causes and moderators.

Written SCMC Might Display More Accurate Output

Very few studies have robustly compared output accuracy rates across environments. In Pyun (2003) ten English learners paired with NSs produced significantly (10 %) more error-free T-units online (d = 1.04), although there was no significant difference in the distribution of morphological, syntactic, and lexical errors. Similarly, the ten dyads of English learners in Kim (2017) produced significantly (around 3 %) more accurate uses of English articles online (d = 0.27–0.43). In contrast, Böhlke (2003a) found similar accuracy rates of attributive adjectives in her small groups of four to five German learners, and Hamano-Bunce (2011) reported similar percentages of accurate AS-units in his two dyads of English learners.

Finally, Chang's (2007) between-subjects study reported significantly (1.5 times) more accurate words per turn in the FTF group ($d = 0.99$).

Despite the mixed findings, a critical analysis of the evidence suggests a possible trend toward greater accuracy in written SCMC, at least in NNS dyadic interaction, with highly variable effect sizes ($d = 0.27–1.04$). The studies that reported comparable or inferior accuracy rates either entailed larger groups (Böhlke, 2003a), had small sample sizes (Hamano-Bunce, 2011), or implemented between-subjects designs with little detail about coding procedures (Chang, 2007). Hypothetically, SCMC's edge could result from its positive affordances (e.g., additional processing time) but also intrinsic challenges. As Kim (2017) noted, the overlapping turns, split interactions, and physical absence of the interlocutor that characterize SCMC may push learners to use more explicit statements and accurate deixis in order to avoid ambiguity (pp. 228, 231). This hypothesis, however, is in urgent need of more supporting evidence.

Negotiation for Meaning and of Form

Researchers are increasingly positing that L2 development may be facilitated not only through NfM – as contended by the original formulations of the Interaction Hypothesis – but via NoF that is not born out of incomprehension (Zeng, 2017, pp. 258–259). However, whether the environment moderates the quantity and quality of these negotiations, and the relative weight of each of these two factors for L2 development remain empirical questions.

Finding answers to these questions in the existing comparative literature is not straightforward, as many studies investigate NfM and NoF jointly or do not describe their coding protocols in detail. Recently, Rouhshad et al. (2016) coded their negotiation episodes as NfM when communication breakdowns were initiated by clarification requests, confirmation, or comprehension checks, and as NoF when there were no comprehension issues and episodes followed recasts, explicit corrections, and metalinguistic feedback. Admittedly, this classification is not without problems. For example, interrogative recasts may either indicate non-comprehension (as Rouhshad et al., 2016 coded them) or polite uptalk corrections. With this caveat in mind, I will use this classification to glean tentative patterns from the literature.

Written SCMC Usually Promotes Less NfM

Because L2 learners typically produce more speech during FTF interaction, there is also apt to be more NfM in this modality, unless amount of speech is controlled for. Indeed, studies reporting raw NfM counts showed either an edge for FTF interaction or, at worst, similar amounts in both environments, with no advantages for SCMC. The six dyads of English learners in Lai and Zhao (2006) displayed significantly higher rates of negotiation ($d = 1.68$) while completing spot-the-difference tasks FTF in one-third of the time. In Sim, Har, and Luan (2010), sixteen mixed proficiency dyads of English learners produced almost triple the amount of negotiation routines (188 vs. 66) when completing two decision-making tasks FTF in an unreported amount of time. And in Kim (2014) ten dyads of English learners supplied significantly thirteen times more instances of collaborative dialog (sixty-seven vs. five) while completing three communicative tasks FTF in about the same time. Some studies, though, yielded mixed findings. In Fernández-García and Martínez Arbelaiz (2003) the FTF modality yielded significantly triple the number of negotiation routines for NS–NNS dyads ($d = 1.27$) but comparable amounts for NNS–NNS dyads. Treatments involved exchanging personal information in L2 Spanish, with double the time allotment online. Similarly, in Yuksel and Inan (2014) and Loewen and Wolff (2016) the FTF condition produced significantly more confirmation checks (by an 11% edge, $d = 1.09$, and a 1,000% edge, $d = 2.47$, respectively) but similar amounts of comprehension checks and clarification requests. Yuksel and Inan's (2014) study involved thirty-two English learners completing jigsaw tasks, one-third faster in FTF, while in Loewen and Wolff's (2016) between-subjects study, eight dyads per condition performed three communicative tasks under the same time limit. Finally, some studies found no environmental effects. In Gurzynski-Weiss and Baralt (2014) twenty-four Spanish learners produced comparable amounts of NfM while completing an information-gap task individually with the researcher, online ($M = 2.92$), and FTF in half the time ($M = 3.12$).

When amount of speech is controlled for, some studies have still yielded an edge for FTF interaction. In Kaneko (2009) sixteen dyads of Japanese learners negotiated meanings twice more often (2% vs. 1% of all morphemes) in the FTF modality when completing three tasks in the same time. FTF negotiations were also qualitatively superior, with more extended negotiations (19% vs. 8%), fewer shortened negotiations (11% vs. 37%), and a wider array of strategies. Similarly, in Rouhshad et al. (2016) twelve dyads of English learners produced significantly twice as many instances of negotiation (0.35% vs. 0.17% of all words) while completing a decision-making task FTF 2.5 times faster. In contrast, Vandergriff (2006) found comparable percentages of "reception strategies" by C-units when six triads of German learners completed consensus-building tasks in both environments under 30 minutes, both overall (SCMC: 7%; FTF: 6%) and by subtypes. Furthermore, studies like Fitze (2006) found an edge for SCMC, where English learners produced almost three times more "interactive competence" (including confirmations and clarifications) in this mode (19% vs. 7%) in two 20-minute large-group discussions.

Overall, though, a critical evaluation seems to tilt the scale in favor of FTF interaction. Raw count reports show that FTF interaction may yield from 11percent (Yuksel & Inan, 2014) to thirteen times (Kim, 2014) more NfM than SCMC, with large effect sizes ($d = 1.09$–2.47), and the counter-evidence from normalized datasets seems tenuous – none of the relevant studies (Fitze, 2006; Vandergriff, 2006) isolated NfM proper (clarification requests, confirmation, and comprehension checks) from other discourse functions. Hypothetically, SCMC's lower NfM rates could result from the affordances of the written mode (e.g., additional processing time, ability to reinspect previous input), which may facilitate decoding (Fernández-García & Martínez Arbelaiz, 2003), and its reduced contextual cues, which may push learners to produce more complete utterances (Kim, 2014, p. 33). On the other hand, FTF's edge may surface for some moves only, like confirmation checks (Loewen & Wolff, 2016; Yuksel & Inan, 2014), or it may not surface at all; for example, when all interactants are NNSs (Fernández-García & Martínez-Arbelaiz, 2003) or have similar competence, or in highly controlled settings where tutors may negotiate meanings intensively and consistently across modalities (Gurzynski-Weiss & Baralt, 2014).

Written SCMC Might Promote Relatively Denser and More Explicit NoF

As above, SCMC has not been found to promote more NoF when amount of speech is left uncontrolled. Raw count reports indicate either an edge for FTF or no environmental impact. The two pairs of English learners in Hamano-Bunce (2011) produced four to nine times more LREs while performing two tasks FTF ($M = 34.5$ vs. 4.5). In Rouhshad and Storch (2016) twelve dyads of English learners English engaged in two and a half times more LREs while co-writing a report FTF ($M = 14.75$ vs. 5.91). And in Loewen and Wolff's (2016) between-subjects study, eight dyads of English learners produced significantly three times more LREs while completing three tasks FTF ($d = 1.67$). In contrast, in Gurzynski-Weiss and Baralt (2014) twenty-four Spanish learners produced comparable amounts of NoF while carrying out an information-gap task with their tutor, FTF ($M = 3.7$) and online ($M = 3.42$). Likewise, in the previous study by Loewen and Wolff (2016), both conditions exchanged statistically similar amounts of recasts (FTF: 1.16; SCMC: 0.88).

The studies investigating the density of NoF (by controlling for amount of output or time-on-task) have yielded mixed results. Some, like Loewen and Reissner's (2009) between-subjects study, found an edge for FTF. Learners interacting in this modality engaged in four to fourteen times more FFEs per minute (0.73) than SCMC groups (0.05–0.18). Other studies, conversely, found no environmental impact. The six dyads of English learners in Lai and Zhao (2006) produced similar amounts of recasts

(d = 0.16) with strikingly similar opportunities for response (ca. 70%). The twelve dyads of English learners in Rouhshad et al. (2016) produced non-significantly different amounts of NoF (FTF: 0.26%; SCMC: 0%). And the participants in Zeng (2017) exchanged statistically similar percentages of feedback (FTF: 23%; SCMC: 20%) and metatalk (15% of LREs). Finally, some evidence suggests an edge for SCMC. The sixteen dyads of Japanese learners in Kaneko (2009) produced significantly twice the amount of feedback in SCMC (0.05% vs. 0.025% of the morphemes). Likewise, in Zeng (2017) sixteen dyads of English learners produced significantly double the number of LREs while carrying out jigsaw and dictogloss tasks online (1.25% vs. 0.61%, d = 1.18).

Clearly, the evidence is very mixed. Yet, a critical inspection of the studies yielding an edge for FTF interaction reveals serious validity threats. For example, in Hamano-Bunce (2011) dyads were observed discussing language orally while engaged in chatroom tasks due to the proximity of computers (p. 429), which may have reduced the amount of online negotiation. In turn, Loewen and Reissner's (2009) design disadvantaged the SCMC group, which was "markedly" less familiarized with the treatment task (p. 111) and was also likely exposed to fewer form-focused instructor interventions (p. 110). Consequently, while any conclusions are necessarily tentative given the limited and contradictory nature of the literature, it seems that, between NfM and NoF, it is actually the latter where SCMC might have an advantage over FTF, if any. As Rouhshad et al. (2016) concluded in their within-subjects study, "in FTF mode there were more negotiations triggered by communication breakdown than ... by inaccuracies ... However, in SCMC mode, there was a rough balance between the two" (p. 527).

Beyond quantitative differences, accumulating evidence suggests that the environment may also play a role in the quality of NoF negotiations. While implicit feedback was the preferred choice among Kaneko's (2009) learners regardless of modality, SCMC did yield a more even distribution of implicit and explicit feedback types. Similarly, in Gurzynski-Weiss and Baralt (2014), the tutor was more explicit when correcting morphosyntactic errors online, where overt corrections, followed by recasts, were the most frequent feedback moves; the reverse happened in FTF interaction.

Written SCMC Is More Likely to Subvert the Negotiate-Over-Lexis-First Principle

Various comparative studies have found that in SCMC, as in FTF interaction (Mackey & Goo, 2007), learners prioritize lexical negotiations. Additionally, these studies have suggested no role for the environment in moderating the focus of learner negotiations, yielding mirror rankings for SCMC and FTF interaction. In Kaneko (2009), the ranking was lexis >

whole message, morphosyntax; in Zeng (2017), lexis > grammar > orthography, and in Gurzynski-Weiss and Baralt (2014), lexis > morphosyntax > semantics > phonology/spelling. In contrast, Rouhshad and Storch's (2016) ranking for both conditions was syntax/morphology > lexis > punctuation/phonology/spelling, which is not surprising given the linguistic orientation of their task (cowriting a report). Interestingly, though, learners negotiated over formal features (syntax and morphology) more frequently online (48%) than during FTF interaction (42%), and this trend has been confirmed by other studies that did yield different rankings across environments.

In Lai and Zhao (2006) SCMC negotiations focused mostly on morphosyntax (65%), while FTF negotiations prioritized vocabulary (39%). Yuksel and Inan (2014) reported slightly more grammatical than lexical negotiations in SCMC and the opposite for FTF (although the differences were almost negligible). In Rouhshad et al. (2016) SCMC negotiations focused mostly on form (58%) and were more equally distributed, while FTF negotiations focused more on meaning (63%). In Zeng (2017) SCMC triggered significantly more orthographical LREs. And in Loewen and Reissner's (2009) between-subjects study, the focus of FFEs in tutor-monitored SCMC groups was spelling/pronunciation (75%) > grammar (15%) > vocabulary (10%), while in FTF groups it was tied for vocabulary and grammar (36% each), followed by pronunciation and spelling (28%).

In sum, accumulating evidence suggests that while the negotiate-over-lexis principle typically holds true for both environments, learners might subvert this principle more often online than FTF. The pressing question now is whether learners notice these negotiations at different rates depending on the context.

Noticing, Uptake, Modified Output and Self-correction

Written SCMC May Boost Noticing of NfM in Stimulated Recalls of Peer Interaction

Various studies have employed stimulated recalls to investigate whether the environment moderates the frequency with which learners notice feedback. Some have answered this question affirmatively, showing an advantage for SCMC. In Lai and Zhao (2006) six dyads of English learners correctly identified NfM triggers (clarification requests, comprehension checks) more often online (45%) than FTF (24%). The difference did not reach statistical significance, but the effect size was large ($d = 0.83$). Similarly, the thirty-two dyads of English learners in Yuksel and Inan (2014) identified communication breakdowns significantly more often in SCMC, both of lexical (52% vs. 40%, $d = 0.87$) and grammatical (50% vs. 39%, $d = 0.81$) nature. Several caveats in their stimulated recall protocols, however, urge caution in interpreting these findings. Learners were explicitly asked to identify communication breakdowns (p. 342), which might have increased noticing rates, and the chat logs and video-screenings respectively used for the SCMC and FTF recall sessions might have created different opportunities for self-paced analysis.

On the other hand, in the just-discussed study by Lai and Zhao (2006) learners noticed recasts similarly across modalities (FTF: 18%; SCMC: 10%), although this analysis was based on data from only four participants. Likewise, in Gurzynski-Weiss and Baralt (2014) the environment did not moderate feedback noticing rates, both overall (SCMC: 71%; FTF: 68%) and by type of linguistic target. Notably, however, this study involved tutor–learner interaction, it lumped together nine different feedback types, and stimulated recalls focused only on a subset ($M = 10$) of feedback episodes.

Overall, the limited data suggest that SCMC might have a relative edge in promoting noticing of communication breakdowns during peer interaction. This may be due to the permanence of NfM triggers, as well as their more explicit nature (e.g., Lai & Zhao, 2006, pp. 112–113). However, stimulated recalls have not yet produced compelling evidence that SCMC might promote significantly more noticing of form-focused feedback (e.g., recasts) in peer interaction.

Written SCMC May Promote Less Successful Uptake and Maybe Less Modified Output

In addition to stimulated recalls, scholars have used constructs like successful uptake and modified output to assess learners' noticing of feedback. *Uptake* typically occurs when a learner incorporates the positive evidence in an input-providing feedback move (e.g., a learner repeats a recast), while *modified output* may follow output-promoting feedback (e.g., a learner modifies an utterance after a prompt). Increasingly, modified output is considered a more reliable indicator of noticing, with stronger links to learning because it originates from the learner (Nassaji, 2011). Moreover, incipient research suggests that partial modified output (that fixes only the part corrected in the feedback) may be a stronger predictor of noticing feedback than full modified output, as it involves more hypothesis reevaluation (Gurzynski-Weiss & Baralt, 2015).

Very few studies have compared successful uptake rates across environments, tentatively suggesting an edge for FTF interaction. In Kaneko (2009) sixteen dyads of Japanese learners produced significantly more successful uptake while completing three tasks FTF (77%) than online (18%). In Rouhshad et al. (2016) twelve dyads of English learners produced more successful uptake while completing a decision-making task FTF (59%) than in SCMC (31%). And in Baralt's (2010) between-subjects study of eighty-four Spanish learners, the FTF condition produced more uptake after recasts during an individual story retell with her, both for more complex (FTF: 70%; SCMC: 3%, d = 3.81) and less complex (FTF: 72%; SCMC: 5%, d = 4.31) versions of her task.

Relatively more studies have compared successfully modified output rates. In the just-discussed studies by Kaneko (2009) and Rouhshad et al. (2016), learners repaired ill-formed utterances more often in FTF interaction than online (in Kaneko, 2009, FTF: 84% vs. SCMC: 58%; in Rouhshad et al., 2016, FTF: 63% vs. SCMC: 27%). Similarly, in Gurzynski-Weiss and Baralt (2014) twenty-four Spanish learners modified their output significantly more in the FTF context, both for all linguistic targets combined (FTF: 68%; SCMC: 62%, d = 1.27) and in response to feedback on lexis, morphosyntax, and phonology/spelling. Conversely, in Sim et al. (2010) sixteen dyads of English learners modified their output more frequently while completing two decision-making tasks online, but only when they possessed high proficiency (SCMC: 65%; FTF: 46%) rather than low proficiency (FTF 32%; SCMC 25%). Sim et al. (2010), however, did not report inferential statistics, unlike Zeng (2017), where SCMC yielded significantly more correctly solved LREs (82% vs. 72%, d = 0.1) and fewer incorrectly solved LREs (5% vs. 13%, d = 0.75). His study involved sixteen dyads of English learners completing jigsaw and dictogloss tasks.

Overall, then, existing evidence indicates that SCMC may promote from 28% (Rouhshad et al., 2016) to 61% (Baralt, 2010) less uptake than FTF interaction, with very large effect sizes (up to d = 4.31), and possibly less successfully modified output, too, although results are mixed. Various scholars have questioned the validity of uptake in SCMC, at least as traditionally operationalized (Baralt & Leow, 2015; Smith, 2005), and Gurzynski-Weiss and Baralt (2015) recently suggested that full modified output in SCMC "may have more of a social function than a noticing one" (p. 1411). Consequently, future research must assess the reliability of uptake and modified output as indicators of attention to form, propose revised operationalizations, or switch the focus to alternative constructs, such as self-correction.

Written SCMC Seems to Promote More Self-correction

Studies have rarely compared self-correction rates in SCMC and FTF interaction, with some even avoiding them deliberately on the grounds that they are not part of peer interaction (e.g., Loewen & Wolff, 2016, p. 172; Rouhshad & Storch, 2016, p. 278); however, incipient evidence shows much promise for this construct as an indicator of noticing in SCMC. For example, Lai and Zhao (2006) found that six dyads of English learners self-corrected significantly two and a half times more frequently online (29% of words produced) than FTF (11%) while completing spot-the-difference tasks, and the effect size was large (d = 1.34). Similarly, in Zeng (2017), sixteen dyads of English learners produced significantly 2.4 times more self-corrections in SCMC (26% of LREs) than FTF interaction (11%) while completing jigsaw and dictogloss tasks ($d = 0.8$). Finally, while Loewen and Reissner (2009) did not measure self-correction in the FTF group of their between-subjects study, they found a high rate in their tutor-monitored SCMC groups (50% of FFEs) and no detected cases in their unmonitored SCMC groups, suggesting that, at least in small-group SCMC ($n = 3$–4), tutor monitoring may have a moderating role. In sum, then, existing evidence suggests that self-corrections can occur twice as frequently in SCMC than FTF interaction, with medium to large effect sizes ($d = 0.8$–1.34) and with instructor supervision increasing their occurrence. Clearly, though, much more research is needed to corroborate this edge and uncover moderating variables.

Conclusions and Recommendations for Future Research

Three decades of scientific inquiry have established that SCMC can impact L2 development processes, including corrective feedback, and their resulting products, in new and exciting ways. However, the high variability of the existing evidence calls for more theoretical and methodological rigor, and the proliferation of hybrid and online learning curricula makes it imperative to assess SCMC's contributions on the basis of sound comparisons with mirror FTF conditions.

In this chapter I have synthesized forty-one studies comparing the relative effects of written SCMC and FTF interaction on L2 development, filtering contradictory findings through the sieve of methodological validity and the notion of modality. Like every critical synthesis, this one involves a degree of subjectivity. Many of the hypotheses posited here await validation given the limited scope of the data, and they may contradict projections made in the non-comparative literature.

I have posited that written SCMC may amplify the developmental effectiveness of corrective feedback in untimed tutor–learner interactions with less complex treatment tasks and formally oriented assessment measures (e.g., Baralt, 2013; Yilmaz, 2012). However, despite several success stories (e.g., Blake, 2009; Payne & Whitney, 2002), there is disagreement as to whether written SCMC, at least as explored hitherto, may have a developmental edge over FTF conditions in peer interaction (e.g., de la Fuente, 2003; Hirotani, 2009). This merits special attention, since tutors are often unable to provide individualized instruction, and peer interaction is at the core of currently favored socio-constructivist pedagogical paradigms (Sato & Ballinger, 2016).

From a process-oriented perspective, though, mounting evidence carves out a place for written SCMC in peer interaction. Existing research shows that while completing a task through written SCMC typically yields less output, from 26 percent fewer tokens to 2.75 times fewer morphemes

(Kaneko, 2009; Sauro, 2012), it tends to promote more equal participation, by up to two Gini coefficients (Warschauer, 1996). Notably, several variables may moderate results. Learners may produce comparable or larger amounts of output online when shielded by face-saving pseudonyms (Freiermuth & Jarrell, 2006); for parts of speech that are more frequent in writing (Böhlke, 2003a); when given significantly more time to complete a task (Chang, 2007), or when interacting in larger groups. In this last case, simultaneous contributions can make up for the lower speeds of typing versus oral speech, yielding comparable (Fitze, 2006) or even larger amounts of output (Kern, 1995), but participation rates may also suffer (Böhlke, 2003b; Fitze, 2006), as some learners may feel disincentivized by the multiplicity of voices or the speedy and disjointed communication.

Incipient evidence suggests that learners typically produce shorter utterances in written SCMC, from 40% shorter T-units to three times shorter turns (Nguyen & White, 2011; Pyun, 2003). This may result from learners' desire to mark their social presence, make a point before the next incoming message, or elicit more responses, particularly when they possess limited typing skills. Yet, written SCMC has been shown to promote up to 29% more developmentally advanced structures (Kim, 2017), from 4% to 18% richer vocabulary (Fitze, 2006; Warschauer, 1996), and from 3% to 10% more accurate speech (Kim, 2017; Pyun, 2003), which might ensue from its unique affordances (e.g., additional processing time) but also intrinsic challenges (e.g., the physical absence of the interlocutor, overlapping turns, and split interaction routines).

In absolute terms, written SCMC does not seem to promote more negotiation of either meaning or form. Studies have yielded from 11% to thirteen times less NfM (Kim, 2014; Yuksel & Inan, 2014) and from comparable to nine times less NoF (Gurzynski-Weiss & Baralt, 2014; Hamano-Bunce, 2011). However, a more complex picture emerges when considering the density of negotiations. Written SCMC appears to promote up to two times less dense NfM (Kaneko, 2009; Rouhshad et al., 2016), probably because the extra processing time, ability to reinspect previous input, and increased accuracy and explicitness that characterize SCMC can make negotiation unnecessary. At the same time, these affordances have been found to promote up to two times more dense NoF (Kaneko, 2009; Zeng, 2017), boost the explicitness of negotiations (Gurzynski-Weiss & Baralt, 2014; Kaneko, 2009), and help subvert the negotiate-over-lexis-first principle in favor of more formal linguistic features like morphology, grammar, or orthography (e.g., Lai & Zhao, 2006; Rouhshad et al., 2016).

Because written SCMC may amplify the explicitness of negotiations and these remain on the screen, it could be posited that they could also be more noticeable. However, studies have had different success rates in establishing this link depending on the procedures and constructs used. Stimulated recalls have shown that learners are indeed better at noticing NfM online, correctly identifying from 11% to 21% more triggers like clarification requests and comprehension checks (Lai & Zhao, 2006; Yuksel & Inan, 2014); however, this has not been the case for recasts and other forms of NoF (Gurzynski-Weiss & Baralt, 2014; Lai & Zhao, 2006). Tallies of successful uptake and modified output have not helped either. Actually, studies have shown that FTF interaction can promote from 28% to 61% more incorporations of feedback (Baralt, 2010; Rouhshad et al., 2016) and from 6% to 36% more successful repairs (Gurzynski-Weiss & Baralt, 2014; Rouhshad et al., 2016), although with some counterevidence (Sim et al., 2010; Zeng, 2017). In contrast, incipient research indicates that learners can self-correct their own output over two times more frequently online (Lai & Zhao, 2006; Zeng, 2017), reclaiming a place for self-correction as a more reliable indicator of noticing in SCMC.

Looking forward, a first priority for future comparative research is to assess the validity of the emerging hypotheses presented here. Significant efforts should be devoted to developing the practically nonexistent body of replication studies, addressing methodological gaps to identify attributes and affordances that transcend a particular technology (Handley, 2018).

Another pressing issue is to uncover the moderating variables of learning processes and outcomes in each environment. Loewen and Sato's (2018) recent state-of-the-art article provides an exhaustive account for FTF interaction, including variables relative to the interlocutor (L1 status, L2 proficiency, individual differences), the task characteristics (conditions, complexity, participation structure), and the linguistic targets. This chapter has illustrated the interplay between the environment and some of these variables, but more comparative research is certainly warranted, especially for the understudied role of social and sociocognitive factors (Toth & Davin, 2016).

A third fruitful research direction is to explore the impact of more innovative iterations of written SCMC based on the aforementioned three-dimensional nature of modality. Beginning with *tools*, researchers should further investigate the disruptive power of real-time text (RTT). Because in RTT the receiving person can read messages character by character, as they are being typed, opportunities for vicarious learning are increased, particularly given the increased frequency of self-corrections in written SCMC. In addition, RTT might reduce the number of overlapping turns and split interaction routines that characterize written SCMC, as learners do not have to wait indefinitely for their peers to make a point. Unfortunately, despite the popularity of RTT among the deaf and hard-of-hearing, it has not yet gone mainstream, and many of the instant messaging applications that used to support it, like YTalk for Unix or AOL Instant Messenger, have been discontinued. Recently, however, some of the leading mobile operating systems (e.g., iOS 12.1, released October 30, 2018) have released RTT for Wi-Fi calling, thus opening a wealth of experimental opportunities.

Moving on to *language learning objectives*, researchers should strive to assess the contributions of written SCMC to L2 development more critically, avoiding unrealistic expectations and magnified conclusions on the basis of statistical significance and look instead at effect sizes and the interplay with contextual factors. For example, future written SCMC research should investigate how increased equality of participation and reduced amount of output counter each other to create feedback opportunities, or the developmental impact of the reportedly denser NoF in the context of overall low negotiation rates. Moreover, researchers should wonder whether we are expecting too much from technology and our learners in the first place. Recent metacognitive research shows that learning is maximized not only when pedagogical tasks are carefully crafted, but when learners are empowered as cognizant actors of their learning. For example, learners have been found to increase the provision and use of feedback after receiving instruction on how feedback works (Fujii, Ziegler & Mackey, 2016; Sato, 2013). Similar benefits should be expected from informing learners about the inner workings of SCMC. As Fischer (2012) put it, learner training should entail "not only guiding learners to make good pedagogical decisions ... but also instructing them how to use technological resources in support of those pedagogical decisions" (p. 28).

Finally, future research should continue to investigate the *mode* variable in the modality equation, comparing not only the effects of written SCMC against FTF interaction on L2 development processes and products but also those of oral and video SCMC (e.g., Parlak & Ziegler, 2016; Rassaei, 2017), including innovative iterations like three-dimensional virtual environments (Kartchava & Nassaji, 2019), augmented reality (Godwin-Jones, 2016) and video games (Reinhardt, 2019).

There has never been a time like this for rich, meaningful, situated, and contextualized multimodal communication. As the lines between researchers, teachers, and students become blurred in educational settings and scientific work becomes ever more robust and readily available, it is everyone's responsibility to inform ourselves and others about how the different components of linguistic interaction (input, output, and corrective feedback) and multimodality (tools, learning objectives, and modes) operate and interconnect if we are to unlock the full potential of these communication opportunities.

References

* denotes synthesized within-subjects comparative studies.
^ denotes synthesized between-subjects comparative studies.

^Abrams, Z. I. (2003). The effect of synchronous and asynchronous CMC on oral performance in German. *Modern Language Journal*, 87(2), 157–167.

^Baralt, M. (2010). Task complexity, the Cognition Hypothesis, and interaction in CMC and FTF environments. Unpublished doctoral dissertation, Georgetown University, Washington, DC.

^(2013). The impact of cognitive complexity on feedback efficacy during online versus face-to-face interactive tasks. *Studies in Second Language Acquisition*, 35(4), 689–725.

Baralt, M. & Leow, R. (2015). Uptake, task complexity, and L2 development in SLA: An online perspective. In R. Leow, L. Cerezo & M. Baralt (eds.), *A psycholinguistic approach to technology and language learning* (pp. 199–218). Boston: De Gruyter Mouton.

^Beauvois, M. H. (1998). Write to speak: The effects of electronic communication on the oral achievement of fourth semester French students. In J. A. Muyskens (ed.), *New ways of learning and teaching: Focus on technology and foreign language education* (pp. 93–115). Boston: Heinle & Heinle.

^Blake, C. (2009). Potential of text-based internet chats for improving oral fluency in a second language. *Modern Language Journal*, 93(2), 227–240.

*Böhlke, O. (2003a). Adjective production by learners of German in chatroom and face-to-face discussions. *Die Unterrichtspraxis/Teaching German*, 36(1), 67–73.

*(2003b). A comparison of student participation levels by group size and language stages during chatroom and face-to-face discussions in German. *CALICO Journal*, 21(1), 67–87.

^Chang, Y.-Y. (2007). The potential of synchronous text-based computer-mediated communication for second language acquisition. *Issues in Information Systems*, 8(2), 355–361.

^de la Fuente, M. J. (2003). Is SLA interactionist theory relevant to call? A study on the effects of computer-mediated interaction in L2 vocabulary acquisition. *Computer Assisted Language Learning*, 16(1), 47–81.

*Fernández-García, M. & Martínez Arbelaiz, A. (2003). Learners' interactions: A comparison of oral and computer-assisted written conversations. *ReCALL*, 15(1), 113–136.

Fischer, R. (2012). Diversity in learner usage patterns. In G. Stockwell (ed.), *Computer-assisted language learning: Diversity in research and practice* (pp. 14–32). Cambridge: Cambridge University Press.

*Fitze, M. (2006). Discourse and participation in ESL face-to-face and written electronic conferences. *Language Learning & Technology*, 10(1), 67–86.

^Freiermuth, M. R. (2001). Native speakers or non-native speakers: Who has the floor? Online and face-to-face interaction in culturally mixed small groups. *Computer Assisted Language Learning*, 14(2), 169–199.

*Freiermuth, M. R. & Jarrell, D. (2006). Willingness to communicate: Can online chat help? *International Journal of Applied Linguistics*, 16(2), 189–212.

Fujii, A., Ziegler, N. & Mackey, A. (2016). Peer interaction and metacognitive instruction in the EFL classroom. In M. Sato & S. Ballinger (eds.),

Peer interaction and second language learning: Pedagogical potential and research agenda (pp. 63–89). Amsterdam: John Benjamins.

Godwin-Jones, R. (2016). Augmented reality and language learning: From annotated vocabulary to place-based mobile games. *Language Learning & Technology*, 20(3), 9–19.

Guichon, N. & Cohen, C. (2016). Multimodality and CALL. In F. Farr & L. Murray (eds.), *The Routledge handbook of language learning and technology* (pp. 509–521). London: Routledge.

*Gurzynski-Weiss, L. & Baralt, M. (2014). Exploring learner perception and use of task-based interactional feedback in FTF and CMC modes. *Studies in Second Language Acquisition*, 36(1), 1–37.

*(2015). Does type of modified output correspond to learner noticing of feedback? A closer look in face-to-face and computer-mediated task-based interaction. *Applied Psycholinguistics*, 36(6), 1393–1420.

*Hamano-Bunce, D. (2011). Talk or chat? Chatroom and spoken interaction in a language classroom. *ELT Journal*, 65(4), 426–436.

Handley, Z. (2018). Replication research in computer-assisted language learning: Replication of Neri et al. (2008) and Satar & Özdener (2008). *Language Teaching*, 51(3), 417–429.

^Hirotani, M. (2009). Synchronous versus asynchronous CMC and transfer to Japanese oral performance. *CALICO Journal*, 26(2), 413–438.

*Kaneko, A. (2009). Comparing computer mediated communication (CMC) and face-to-face (FTF) communication for the development of Japanese as a foreign language. Unpublished doctoral dissertation, The University of Western Australia.

Kartchava, E. & Nassaji, H. (2019). Noticeability of corrective feedback in three dimensional virtual environments and face-to-face classroom contexts. In R. Leow (ed.), *Depth of processing in instructed second language acquisition* (pp. 407–420). New York: Routledge.

*Kern, R. G. (1995). Restructuring classroom interaction with network computers: Effects on quantity and characteristics of language production. *Modern Language Journal*, 79(4), 457–476.

*Kim, H. Y. (2014). Learning opportunities in synchronous computer-mediated communication and face-to-face interaction. *Computer Assisted Language Learning*, 27(1), 26–43.

*(2017). Effect of modality and task type on interlanguage variation. *ReCALL*, 29(2), 219–236.

^Kost, C. (2004). An investigation of the effects of synchronous computer-mediated communication (CMC) on interlanguage development in beginning learners of German: Accuracy, proficiency, and communication strategies. Unpublished doctoral dissertation, University of Arizona, Tucson.

*Lai, C. & Zhao, Y. (2006). Noticing and text-based chat. *Language Learning & Technology*, 10(3), 102–120.

Lamy, M.-N. (2012). Diversity in modalities. In G. Stockwell (ed.), *Computer-assisted language learning: Diversity in research and practice* (pp. 109–126). Cambridge: Cambridge University Press.

^Loewen, S. & Reissner, S. (2009). A comparison of incidental focus on form in the second language classroom and chatroom. *Computer Assisted Language Learning*, 22(2), 101–114.

Loewen, S. & Sato, M. (2018). Interaction and instructed second language acquisition. *Language Teaching*, 51(3), 285–329.

^Loewen, S. & Wolff, D. (2016). Peer interaction in F2F and CMC contexts. In M. Sato & S. Ballinger (eds.), *Peer interaction and second language learning: Pedagogical potential and research agenda* (pp. 163–184). Amsterdam: John Benjamins.

Mackey, A. & Goo, J. M. (2007). Interaction research in SLA: A meta-analysis and research synthesis. In A. Mackey (ed.), *Input, interaction and corrective feedback in L2 learning* (pp. 379–452). New York: Oxford University Press.

Nassaji, H. (2011). Immediate learner repair and its relationship with learning targeted forms in dyadic interaction. *System*, 39(1), 17–29.

^Nguyen, L. V. & White, C. (2011). The nature of "talk" in synchronous computer-mediated communication in a Vietnamese tertiary EFL context. *International Journal of Computer-Assisted Language Learning and Teaching*, 1(3), 14–36.

Ortega, L. (1997). Processes and outcomes in networked classroom interaction: Defining the research agenda for L2 computer-assisted classroom discussion. *Language Learning & Technology*, 1(1), 82–93.

(2009). Interaction and attention to form in L2 text-based computer-mediated communication. In A. Mackey & C. Polio (eds.), *Multiple perspectives on interaction* (pp. 226–253). New York: Routledge.

Oswald, F. L. & Plonsky, L. (2010). Meta-analysis in second language research: Choices and challenges. *Annual Review of Applied Linguistics*, 30, 85–110.

Parlak, Ö. & Ziegler, N. (2016). The impact of recasts on the development of primary stress in a synchronous computer-mediated environment. *Studies in Second Language Acquisition*, 39(2), 257–285. DOI:10.1017/s0272263116000310.

^Payne, J. S. & Whitney, P. J. (2002). Developing L2 oral proficiency through synchronous CMC: Output, working memory, and interlanguage development. *CALICO Journal*, 20(1), 7–32.

Pienemann, M. & Johnston, M. (1987). Factors influencing the development of language proficiency. In D. Nunan (Ed.), *Applying second language acquisition research* (pp. 45–147). Adelaide: National Curriculum Resource Centre, AMEP.

*Pyun, O. C. (2003). Effects of networked language learning: A comparison between synchronous online discussions and face-to-face discussions. (Unpublished master's thesis), Ohio State University, Columbus, OH.

Rassaei, E. (2017). Video chat vs. face-to-face recasts, learners' interpretations and L2 development: A case of Persian EFL learners. *Computer Assisted Language Learning*, 30(1–2), 133–148. DOI:10.1080/09588221.2016.1275702.

Reinhardt, J. (2019). *Gameful second and foreign language teaching and learning: Theory, research, and practice*. London: Palgrave Macmillan.

*Rouhshad, A. & Storch, N. (2016). Focus on mode: Patterns of interaction in face-to-face and computer-mediated contexts. In M. Sato & S. Ballinger (eds.), *Peer interaction and second language learning: Pedagogical potential and research agenda* (pp. 267–289). Amsterdam: John Benjamins.

*Rouhshad, A., Wigglesworth, G. & Storch, N. (2016). The nature of negotiations in face-to-face versus computer-mediated communication in pair interactions. *Language Teaching Research*, 20(4), 514–534.

*Salaberry, M. R. (2000). L2 morphosyntactic development in text-based computer-mediated communication. *Computer Assisted Language Learning*, 13(1), 5–27.

Sato, M. (2013). Beliefs about peer interaction and peer corrective feedback: Efficacy of classroom intervention. *Modern Language Journal*, 97(3), 611–633.

Sato, M. & Ballinger, S. (eds.). (2016). *Peer interaction and second language learning:Pedagogical potential and research agenda*. Amsterdam: John Benjamins.

*Sauro, S. (2012). L2 performance in text-chat and spoken discourse. *System*, 40(3), 335–348.

*Sim, T., Har, K. & Luan, N. (2010). Low proficiency learners in synchronous computer-assisted and face-to-face interactions. *The Turkish Online Journal of Educational Technology*, 9(3), 61–75.

Smith, B. (2005). The relationship between negotiated interaction, learner uptake, and lexical acquisition in task-based computer-mediated communication. *TESOL Quarterly*, 39(1), 33–58.

^Sullivan, N. & Pratt, E. (1996). A comparative study of two ESL writing environments: A computer-assisted classroom and a traditional oral classroom. *System*, 29(4), 491–501.

*Tan, L. L., Wigglesworth, G. & Storch, N. (2010). Pair interactions and mode of communication: Comparing face-to-face and computer mediated communication. *Australian Review of Applied Linguistics*, 33(3), 1–24.

Toth, P. D. & Davin, K. J. (2016). The sociocognitive imperative of L2 pedagogy. *Modern Language Journal*, 100(S1), 148–168.

*Vandergriff, I. (2006). Negotiating common ground in computer-mediated versus face-to-face discussions. *Language Learning & Technology*, 10(1), 110–138.

*Warschauer, M. (1996). Comparing face-to-face and electronic discussion in the second language classroom. *CALICO Journal*, 13(2–3), 7–26.

*Yilmaz, Y. (2012). The relative effects of explicit correction and recasts on two target structures via two communication modes. *Language Learning*, 62(4), 1134–1169.

*Yilmaz, Y. & Yuksel, D. (2011). Effects of communication mode and salience on recasts: A first exposure study. *Language Teaching Research*, 15(4), 457–477.

*Yuksel, D. & Inan, B. (2014). The effects of communication mode on negotiation of meaning and its noticing. *ReCALL*, 26(3), 333–354.

*Zeng, G. (2017). Collaborative dialogue in synchronous computer-mediated communication and face-to-face communication. *ReCALL*, 29(3), 257–275.

Zeng, G. & Takatsuka, S. (2009). Text-based peer-peer collaborative dialogue in a computer-mediated learning environment in the EFL context. *System*, 37(3), 434–446.

Ziegler, N. & Mackey, A. J. (2017). Interactional feedback in computer-mediated communication: A review and state of the art. In H. Nassaji & E. Kartchava (eds.), *Corrective feedback in second language teaching and learning: Research, theory, applications, implications* (pp. 80–94). London: Routledge.

24

Corrective Feedback in Mobile Technology-Mediated Contexts

Eva Kartchava and Hossein Nassaji

Introduction

Investigations into mobile-assisted language learning (MALL) have existed for over twenty-five years (Burston, 2014), having come into focus due to the centrality of technology, and mobile technology in particular, in our everyday reality. Because the use of mobile technology is expected to continue to grow, Ally (2013) has claimed that "we have entered the mobile era" (p. 7), whose impact will engender changes in the way we work, do business, interact, and learn. While the education sphere has, to a degree, benefited from some of these technological changes, MALL has largely stalled in taking advantage of the affordances of mobile technologies (e.g., portability and small size, freedom of access in both time and space, authenticity, situated learning, see Reinders & White, 2010; Stockwell & Hubbard, 2013), especially when it comes to pedagogical innovations (Burston, 2014). Although mobile technology has proven useful in the study of second/additional (L2) languages in general and in the development of specific skills, little is known to date about how mobile technology can best assist learners in the process of language learning. This is especially the case for corrective feedback, namely, information provided to L2 learners about the accuracy of their output.

Investigations into mobile-assisted feedback are necessary since corrective feedback is considered by many to play a crucial role in the development of one's linguistic knowledge and, as such, can be instrumental in helping learners notice, monitor, and improve their L2 output. Corrective feedback can alert a learner to the inaccuracy of the targeted L2 form and/or point to an existing gap in learners' knowledge of the form (Schmidt & Frota, 1986; Swain, 1993). This has been considered to be beneficial because learners receive feedback at the time when an error is made. Corrective feedback can help learners realize their errors, which, in turn, may promote a number of L2 processes such as hypothesis testing and form–meaning mapping, which have been considered to be crucial for language learning (e.g., Doughty & Varela, 1998). Repeated exposure to corrective feedback may push learners "to reflect on their output and consider ways of modifying it to enhance comprehensibility, appropriateness, and accuracy" (Swain, 1993, p. 160). Focusing on form in the moment of communication (when the meaning is clear) can enhance the effectiveness of corrective feedback and strengthen the established form–meaning connections (Long, 1996).

Mobile-assisted feedback can combine the affordances of mobile technology with corrective feedback and, therefore, may amplify the effects of the feedback. It can do so, for example, by the potential to be accessed on the go, adding to the amount of correction provided by a teacher in the classroom orally or in writing as well as ensuring that the feedback is provided consistently, with a particular intensity, immediately after an error is made, or following a predetermined delay.

The goal of this chapter is to discuss the role of corrective feedback in mobile technology-mediated contexts. It begins by briefly discussing the role of technology in language learning and teaching, focusing on mobile technology and explaining its affordances. It then examines the role that MALL can play in providing and monitoring corrective feedback in language learning. The chapter concludes with a discussion of the pedagogical implications as well as directions for future research on MALL-supported corrective feedback.

The Role of Technology

The ubiquitous nature of technology has permeated much of the contemporary world, including ways in which people communicate, consume information, engage with content, and exchange knowledge. Technology has also enabled individualization of these actions, allowing for the choice of what and how much information to produce/consume as well as the kinds of communicative practices and identities to adopt. In fact, individualization of learning has long been considered one of the major affordances of technology for the modern-day learners who not only "think and process information fundamentally differently" (Prensky, 2001, p. 1) from their predecessors but also have distinct expectations for using technology in ways that may facilitate and enhance learning (Prensky, 2005).

For L2 learners, technology has increased opportunities for language learning, practice, and use. More specifically, computer-mediated communication (CMC) has been considered to promote authentic L2 interactions with other learners and/or speakers of the language beyond the classroom (e.g., Golonka et al., 2014; Kern, 2006; Lin, 2015; Sykes, Oskoz & Thorne, 2008; Warschauer, 1996), increasing learner autonomy in directing communication (Chapelle, 2008), asking questions, debating, and reflecting on the target language use (e.g., Belz & Kinginger, 2003; Blake, 2000; Pellettieri, 2000; Reynolds & Anderson, 2015; Young & West, 2018), as well as augmenting "opportunities for linguistic practice, negotiation of meaning, and feedback" (Vandergriff, 2016, p. 6).

Many individual studies as well as several meta-analyses have confirmed the positive effects of technology-mediated instruction on enhancing L2 learning as a whole (e.g., Felix, 2005a, 2005b; Liu et al., 2002; Zhao, 2003; Ziegler, 2016) as well as various subskills, including the development of L2 writing (e.g., Kessler, 2009; Lee, 2010; Mak & Coniam, 2008) and reading and vocabulary skills (e.g., Abraham, 2008; Taylor, 2006). A recent meta-analysis comparing the effectiveness of technology-mediated instruction with traditional (technology-free) approaches (Grhurovic, Chapelle & Shelley, 2013) was, however, unable to unequivocally confirm the superiority of the former, with authors concluding that "second/foreign language instruction supported by computer technology was at least as effective as instruction without technology" (p. 191). Such results may be because of the interaction of the technology-based instruction with various context- and learner-related variables. As Vandergriff (2016) argued, they could also be due to the conflation of the various technologies employed in the selected studies, without differentiating their distinct impact on the reported results. In Grhurovic et al.'s (2013) meta-analysis CALL research spanned thirty-six years (1970–2006) and involved technologies that ranged from the static human-computer interactions of the 1970s to 1990s (i.e., Tutorial CALL, see Chapter 11, this volume) to the currently dynamic human–human interactions via a computer (i.e., Web 2.0 tools). Such a diversity in data collection makes it difficult to draw a unified conclusion about the effectiveness of technology overall (Vandergriff, 2016). Hence, considering the type of technology and the context in which it is used are essential in research that attempts to determine the impact of technology on L2 learning (Herring, 2007).

Such considerations are especially poignant for mobile technology in the context of language learning. This is because technology does not exist in a vacuum but interacts with its users. It not only responds to the users' goals for a particular tool but also shapes that interaction via various medium and situational factors, either inherent to a given tool or determined contextually. MALL is particularly susceptible to this medium-situational co-dependence since the type of device, its various applications (i.e., "apps"), and the setting in which they are used can individually and/or collectively determine the effectiveness of a language learning experience (Burston, 2014). For example, while mobile devices may facilitate additional exposure to L2 input beyond structured learning contexts (e.g., watching a movie, listening to a podcast, playing a language game), their mobile nature can also affect, and even change, the learning task. Watching a movie on a bus, for example, is different from watching it in the classroom, since additional distractions and increased noise levels can impact the attentional levels. Similarly, although various mobile apps can promote L2 learning by capturing audio (e.g., oral interaction, audio notes) and visual (e.g., video recording, photography) data in the real world, the setting in which mobile devices are used, can impact the type and amount of language produced. The use of audio, for instance, requires confidence to speak aloud and additional equipment (e.g., headset, microphone) to hear/record the output (Demouy & Kukulska-Hulme, 2010). However, not every L2 user may want or be able to engage in such practice publicly (e.g., Kim, 2014; Xu, Dong & Jiang, 2017).

Mobile-Assisted Language Learning

An area where technology has recently gained attention in L2 learning and teaching is mobile-assisted learning that uses mobile technology including various mobile devices such as mobile phones and tablets. Although many studies have examined the effects of technology in the past, theory and research on the use of mobile devices in language learning have just recently begun to gain attention. This has been because of the assumed positive effects of MALL in promoting and enhancing opportunities for language learning.

The advantages of MALL can be viewed in terms of the mobility of the learner and/or the device itself, in addition to other features such as accessibility, interactivity, and the potential for multimedia capabilities (Ally & Samaka, 2016). Palalas's (2011) definition of mobile-assisted learning combines the mobility of the learner with that of a device – "MALL can be defined as language learning enabled by the mobility of the learner and portability of handheld devices" (pp. 76–77). If we look at current research, we also see that almost all published research on MALL has in fact focused on these two features, that is "the use of hand-held devices in an out-of-class environment" (Burston, 2014, p. 345).

In other words, MALL can be part of a mobile pedagogy which can be taken to refer to not simply the use of mobile devices in the classroom but also to "learners and language learning being mobile, moving between places, linking classroom learning with work, home, play and other spaces and embracing varied cultural contexts, communication goals and people" (Kukulska-Hulme, Norris & Donohue, 2015). When the learner is the focus, mobility takes on a very broad meaning, with flexible access to technology becoming the main requirement. In this view, any technology that is available to the learner – be it a web-based program, computer, or printed book – is seen as a tool capable of supporting one's learning along with their preexisting learning preferences and habits. Here, learners are "opportunistically appropriating whatever technology is ready to hand as they move between settings, including mobile and fixed phones, their own and other people's computers, as well as books and notepads" (Sharples, Taylor & Vavoula, 2005, p. 5, cited in Burston, 2014). When the mobility of a device is prioritized, any technology that is portable and can be held in one's hand is seen as supportive of learning as it is "potentially available anytime, anywhere" (Kukulska-Hulme & Shield, 2008, p. 273).

It is, however, important to note that unlike CALL, MALL is said to "enable new ways of learning emphasizing continuity or spontaneity of access and interaction across different contexts of use" (Kukulska-Hulme & Shield, 2008, p. 273). The continuity of access across contexts is assured not only by various mobile devices that range from e-book readers and tablets to MP3/4 players and smartphones, but also by applications designed specifically for a particular purpose or in support of it. In language learning, for example, mobile applications developed specifically for the study of grammar can be used alone or in conjunction with automatic translation tools to support it. Similarly, text messages and email can be used to augment vocabulary learning and writing skills. Investigations into the effectiveness of such applications for language learning have found a number of advantages, including improvements in spelling, grammar, vocabulary learning, as well as listening and speaking (e.g., Abdous, Camarena & Facer, 2009; Ally et al., 2007; Demouy & Kukulska-Hulme, 2010; Kim, 2013; Shih, Lee & Cheng, 2015; Wu, 2015; Zhang, Song & Burston, 2011; also see Chapter 11, this volume).

Research on MALL

The effects of MALL in various areas of L2 learning and teaching, including reading, writing, listening, spelling, vocabulary, grammar, have, to date, been the primary focus of investigation. To this end, a number of studies and several meta-analyses have reported positive effects (e.g., Shi, Luo & He, 2017; Sung, Chang & Yang, 2015; Taj et al., 2016; Thornton & Houser, 2005) not only on the development of particular skills but also on the increase of confidence among language learners in their skill-specific and skill-external abilities. This, for example, was the case in Shih, Lee, and Cheng's (2015) examination of the effects of smartphones on English spelling among ESL college-level learners taking part in an eighteen-week optional course on English spelling. As part of the course, the learners were required to complete assignments on their smartphones after the class in addition to the classroom component. The online assignments were built on the material covered in class and required the use of a dictionary. These were also monitored by the instructor, who provided feedback on the quality of the submitted work. The learners demonstrated significant improvement in their spelling skills on the post-test and reported increased confidence in their spelling ability of the known and new vocabulary items.

The use of mobile devices in the study of vocabulary was also found to be fruitful for a group of Chinese learners of English, who, for twenty-six days, were tasked with learning 130 new words, which they received via text messages that contained five words each (Zhang, Song & Burston, 2011). The comparison group received the entire list of words in one of the in-class sessions and was free to sequence their vocabulary learning as they saw fit. The results indicated that although the vocabulary knowledge of the two groups at the onset of the study was not significantly different, the use of the mobile device, the authors argued, allowed the experimental group to benefit from the spaced and repeated exposure to vocabulary, resulting in developmental gains that were not observed for the comparison group. Although not supported statistically, higher retention rates were also observed for the experimental group five weeks later, on the delayed post-test. A similar effect for mobile technology was found in Wu's (2015) semester-long study that compared the effectiveness of learning 3,402 English words by Chinese EFL university students, who either used a traditional wordlist or the Word Learning CET-4 application installed on a smartphone. Although both groups were given the same wordlist at the beginning of the study, the experimental group also had the option to use the mobile software to practice the vocabulary. Two tests containing 100 words each, chosen at random from the target wordlist, were administered at the beginning and end of the term to determine changes in the participants' vocabulary learning. The results indicated that the experimental group not only outperformed the control group on the post-test but also was more effective at capitalizing on the affordances of mobile technology by engaging with vocabulary study "anytime, anywhere" without having to wait for text messages sent according to a schedule; furthermore, the participants were free in their selection of the words to study and were not limited to the preselected items sent to them via SMS messages.

MALL has been found to assist the development of L2 writing and grammar skills as well. Using Functional Systemic Linguistics and Genre Pedagogical Approaches as theoretical frameworks, Noriega (2016) conducted a case study that involved a 19-year-old university freshman student, who attended a narrative writing class and then used a mobile device after the class to learn about different text types. The analysis of the student's writing in terms of text types and linguistic features during an eight-week period revealed that when a genre approach was combined with MALL, it had a significant effect on the student's writing ability. To assess the flexibility and effectiveness of mobile technology in the learning of grammar, Ally et al.'s (2007) study asked learners to use their mobile phones to complete ten grammar units and accompanying exercises drawn from the digital content of a commercially available series (i.e., Penguin introductory English grammar and exercise books). The exercises were considered interactive, since they involved four different question types (multiple choice, true/false, matching, and changing the order of sentences), tested knowledge effectively, and were easy to complete on the go. The participants' grammatical knowledge was tested before, immediately after, and one week after the completion of the assigned lessons. The findings indicated positive effects for the mobile study of grammar, with increases in the learners' post- and delayed test scores. The participants appreciated having unrestricted access to the material outside the classroom but did not see it as an appropriate substitute for instructed learning and human interaction. They also identified a number of challenges. The cost of the Internet was seen as a drawback in using smartphones as well as the small screen size, which prevented the use of all the available question types, compelling the students toward the multiple-choice and true/false formats the most. To enhance the learning experience, the participants wished for more challenging module and exercise content, teacher supplied feedback, and the ability to use audio.

Investigations of the use of mobile technology for improvement of listening and speaking skills have pointed to opportunities for extending classroom-initiated practice and yielding perceived improvement. Demouy and Kukulska-Hulme (2010), for example, asked university-level French L2 learners in the UK to report on their experiences of using mobile devices for additional out-of-class listening and speaking practice. Two groups of participants with thirty-five students each were formed. Over six weeks, the students completed listening and speaking activities that accompanied the course and assessed their effectiveness. While the first group used iPods or MP3 players to access the material, the second group used smartphones instead. The second group could also review their audio responses, which were recorded over the phone. The findings showed that the first group used their mobile devices regularly (15 to 120 minutes a day) in a variety of settings (at work, in public spaces, at the supermarket) while "doing something else" (p. 222), whereas the smartphone group chose to complete the tasks mostly at home. This was precipitated by their feeling that the course tasks were difficult and required a high level of concentration. Hence, to this group, interactive speaking activities required a "quiet" spot and dedicated time, and could not be done in public places in front of others or while doing something else. Even though the second group participants could record their responses, they did not find the practice beneficial because they did not receive feedback on their correct answers unless they visited the course website that provided model answers. To many, this was a "useless" feature as there was no model to compare their performance with. In spite of this, the authors argue that the use of mobile devices helped the participants. Similarly, a positive impact for the use of podcasts on the development of language-related skills was reported by Abdous, Camarena, and Facer (2009). The researchers explored how American university-level learners of various languages

(English, Spanish, French, German, and Japanese) assessed their listening and speaking skills as a function of participation in courses that either integrated podcasts in the course or used podcasts as a supplement to the language course they were attending. The learners in the integrated podcasts classes, compared to their counterparts, rated their oral and production skills much improved by the end of the course. They also cited notable improvements in their vocabulary and grammar skills, suggesting that podcasting promoted learning of the different language skills.

Despite these positive findings, it is important to note that learners do not take full advantage of audio input and output capabilities inherent to mobile devices, given the practical (i.e., the need for a headset and/or external microphone) and environmental (i.e., settings where speaking out loud is considered appropriate and safe) constraints associated with using such devices (e.g., Demouy & Kukulska-Hulme, 2010). To address these shortcomings, several studies have recently begun to explore how peer engagement and interaction can take advantage of the affordances inherent to mobile learning (e.g., Comas-Quinn, Mardomingo & Valentine, 2009; Procter-Legg, Cacchione & Petersen, 2012). Comas-Quinn et al. (2009), for example, used a mobile blog to create a student-generated resource that promoted interaction and collaboration among British learners of Spanish pursuing a three-week study abroad program in Spain and those who stayed in the UK. The blog provided a means by which learners could engage with the foreign culture through creation, sharing, and reflection on their experiences with their peers, who were encouraged to respond to the content in the L2. Similarly, Vandergriff (2016) described Procter-Legg et al.'s (2012) study, in which learners used LingoBee, a language learning application, to communicate, comment on other users' entries, and to create, share, and consume content.

Yet, despite all the benefits, the affordances of mobile technology in the area of corrective feedback have yet to be fully explored (Burston, 2014). This is especially the case since feedback, if provided, tends to still be of the right/wrong variety, with virtually no interaction between the provider and recipient of the corrective information; and this is despite the evidence that learners view mobile-assisted feedback positively (e.g., Xu et al., 2017; Xu & Peng, 2017) and seek it when using mobile devices (Ally et al., 2007; Demouy & Kukulska-Hulme, 2010).

Corrective Feedback and MALL

As noted earlier, corrective feedback aims at improving learners' accuracy. Corrective techniques can range from implicit (e.g., recasts) to explicit (e.g., direct corrections) or input-providing (i.e., providing the correct form) to output-prompting (i.e., signaling the error without providing the correction) (Ellis, 2006). Research has shown positive effects for technology on delivering various corrective feedback types, in general (see Nassaji & Kartchava, 2017). However, although there is much less research on mobile-assisted feedback, there is evidence that it can enhance L2 learning. For example, studies have shown that the asynchronous nature of feedback provided in MALL can affect the types of strategies employed when error correction is supplied. Among the earliest attempts to provide learners of foreign languages with real-time feedback was that of Brown (2001), who had teachers answer the learners' questions over the telephone. The study, conducted in the Stanford Learning Lab, tested the effectiveness of several mobile prototypes which were developed in-house for providing opportunities for listening, speaking, and vocabulary practices. Housed in one integrated voice/data environment, the prototypes allowed learners to engage with the study of vocabulary, access online translation tools, test their developing knowledge, and interact with a human coach on the go, each time for a limited period ("30 seconds or 10 minutes at a time"). The results showed that while mobile access allowed for sustained exposure to foreign language and improved motivation, technology-based issues and short bursts of attention inherent to mobile learning caused frustration and led to fragmented learning. The live-voice coaching sessions, in particular, were challenged by poor sound reception, which made comprehension difficult at times, and by determining the amount of time one needed to spend with the coach to improve. The opportunity to interact with a foreign language expert was, however, seen as ideal for language practice.

The ESL learners in Li's (2009) study reported similar sentiments after participating in a semester-long investigation, during which they received text-based feedback on their out-of-class practice with vocabulary items introduced in class. After having been exposed to twenty-five new words in class on a weekly basis, the participants received text-based questions on their mobile phones to improve their understanding and test their knowledge of the target items. When sending in their responses, the students immediately received confirmation of the correct answers and, in the case of errors, they received feedback. Individual records of the students' results were emailed to them daily, and at the end of the week, a summative word test was administered in class. The results indicated that the use of mobile technology not only improved the participants' vocabulary learning but also stimulated their engagement with the word study, allowing for flexibility in terms of time and place. The engagement with the provided feedback, in particular, was claimed to have led to improvements in the participants' test scores.

Other studies (e.g., Hsu, Wang & Comac, 2008; Kim, 2014) have investigated the usefulness of integrating teacher-supplied feedback in response to audio blogs and digital stories created by language learners as a way to improve their oral proficiency. In Hsu, Wang and Comac's (2008) study, for example, ESL learners attending an advanced English conversation course used mobile phones to respond to comprehension questions about teacher-selected short listening texts as well as to record oral assignments, which they posted on their audio blogs, powered by the online audio recording/playing system *Evoca*. The teacher regularly accessed individual audio blogs to provide asynchronous spoken or written (via commenting function) feedback to suggest ways for the learners to improve their oral performance, including addressing what the authors termed as "serious errors" (p. 188) that were judged to impede the fluency and comprehension criteria needed for successful completion of the course. The results suggest that the learners not only found audio blogs to be useful but also felt satisfied with the teacher's individualized feedback that they overwhelmingly judged effective in advancing their language learning experience.

Similarly, in Kim's (2014) study, the instructor's feedback played an important role in affecting oral proficiency of college ESL learners of intermediate-advanced proficiency engaged in technology-supported independent study outside the classroom. Using online recording and speech-to-text programs (Vocaroo, VozMe, VoiceThread), the five learners recorded, practiced, and listened to nine stories they produced in response to predetermined weekly topics. Once or twice a week, the students voluntarily emailed their recording links to the instructor for (written) feedback on discourse, pronunciation, vocabulary, and sentence complexity issues that required attention. The teacher also provided guidance on ways to improve the participants' storytelling and suggested resources to address grammar and vocabulary concerns they had faced. Four times during the study, the participants' oral proficiency development was tested, showing significant improvement overall and in the areas of vocabulary, pronunciation, and sentence complexity. Kim (2014) claims that "a combination of [web-based] communication tools [coupled with instructor's guidance and feedback] gives ESL learners a positive learning which promotes self-confidence and autonomously develops their language skills" (p. 28).

Similarly, instruction realized via a mobile application and a teacher has produced significant results in L2 pronunciation development. Liakin, Cardoso, and Liakina (2017a) investigated the impact of using a mobile text-to-speech synthesizer (TTS), NaturalReader, to improve L2 French learners' pronunciation of the French liaison (i.e., pronouncing the latent word-final consonant of a word that precedes the following word that starts with a vowel). Three groups of participants, drawn from intact French as a second language classes, engaged in weekly sessions, during which they completed pronunciation activities and received feedback on the accuracy of their output either from the TTS or the teacher (non-TTS group); the third group interacted with the teacher but received no feedback (controls). Every Monday, the TTS group received a link to the weekly expressions (not all of which dealt with the targeted feature) and related tasks they were to practice using the mobile application. The non-TTS group worked with a teacher, who read the expressions out loud and had students repeat them, providing feedback as needed. The control group, in turn, engaged in oral discussion with the teacher on various topics "with the goal of practicing their conversation skills" (p. 333) but received no pronunciation-focused feedback. The participants' pronunciation skills measured by way of reading aloud pre-supplied sentences were tested before and immediately after the intervention, followed by a delayed test two weeks later. Although all groups improved their liaison production, only the TTS and non-TTS groups (i.e., instructed groups) significantly improved over time (i.e., from the pre-test to the post-test and from the pre-test to the delayed post-test). The authors suggest that, in addition to the in-class instruction, teachers consider incorporating the TTS tool to supplement and promote target input and practice.

Xu and Peng (2017) found that 70 percent of all the teacher feedback that Chinese L2 learners in China received on their recorded stories in WeChat, a popular smartphone social communication app, was explicit, with the remainder prompting students to self-correct. The authors claim that, unlike classroom feedback, mobile-assisted feedback precludes the use of recasts, which promote synchronous interaction and enable immediate clarification of an intended meaning, in favor of overt correction as a more efficient alternative for learning on the go. Additionally, despite the focus of investigation being on oral production, the teachers chose to focus mainly on errors of grammar (33%) and vocabulary (28.9%), addressing issues of phonology only 21.6% of the time (16.5% of feedback focused on content). Even so, the students overwhelmingly praised the effectiveness of the supplied feedback in enhancing their speaking ability and pronunciation, specifically. This result was explained by the participants' willingness to send in their stories for feedback, feeling less shy to record speech using the app compared to speaking in front of peers, and a desire to learn from the feedback. Even though similar findings were reported for EFL students in China (Xu et al., 2017), not all learners embraced mobile technology for speaking practice, citing discomfort having to speak into a smartphone instead of conversing directly with a real person (Demouy & Kukulska-Hulme, 2010; Xu & Peng, 2017). Yet, learner perceptions of a mobile tool being useful to language study is essential to its implementation and positive impact on the resulting learning (Ally, 2013).

The beginner French L2 learners in Liakin, Cardoso, and Liakina's (2014) study not only embraced using a free automatic speech recognition (ASR) application, Nuance Dragon Dictation, installed on their iPods and iPhones, but also found it helpful in improving pronunciation of the French vowel /y/, judged as problematic in production and perception alike. For a period of five 20-minute sessions, the students read aloud the words containing the target feature and received "immediate written visual feedback via an orthographic representation of their attempt"

(p. 9). For example, if a learner attempted to pronounce the word "pure," but "pour" or "pire" representations appeared on the screen, this signaled a need to re-attempt. A comparison (non-ASR) group completed the same activities one-on-one with a teacher and received immediate oral feedback on their pronunciation in the form of recasts and repetitions; the third (control) group participated in weekly 20-minute discussions with a teacher that did not focus on form. The participants' perception and production skills tested before and after the treatment showed no changes in the vowel perception among groups, but they showed a significant improvement in the production for the ASR group. Although the authors used the length of study and complexity of the target as the reasons why no differences in the perception results were found, it may be that a lack of perception practice and intensive focus on production played a role. That is, neither of the conditions allowed learners to practice noticing the target feature in the input, but instead required them to react (in some way) to the supplied feedback. While the need to react was imbedded in the ASR practice, it was optional (albeit welcomed) in the teacher interactions. Furthermore, the chosen feedback strategies can explain the superior production results for the ASR group, in that the explicit visual feedback highlighted the locus of the problem and required self-correction; recasts and repetitions used by the teacher, on the other hand, may have attracted learners' attention but did not necessarily direct it to the intended goal of correction or its focus.

    Interestingly, in their investigation of self-editing practices adopted by intermediate EAP learners, who used a web-based app, Grammar Clinic, when working on their course-bound assignments, Li and Hegelheimer (2013) found the participants better able to identify than to correct their errors. While this result may appear to be in stark contrast to the ASR findings in the Liakin et al.'s (2014) study discussed above, in that the participants were able to produce but not recognize more feedback in the mobile feedback condition, it may be argued that the task of editing one's writing promotes (and may even require) recognition of error in the input to enable the enactment of the necessary correction. Furthermore, the corrections came from the learners themselves in addition, not in lieu of, peer and teachers' feedback. Over the course of a term, the students were required to write several drafts of four major paper assignments and, between the first and second drafts, to complete three sets of Grammar Clinic tasks that focused on rule-based errors of sentence fragments, run-on sentences, and the use of verbs, articles, and prepositions. Second drafts were peer reviewed for content, revised, and submitted for evaluation. The findings showed positive effects for the use of the mobile app overall and for improvement on the five identified errors. The learners reported the editing software to be useful in increasing their L2 writing ability and confidence in identifying and correcting errors. Yet, Liakin, Cardoso, and Liakina (2017b) reported both positive and negative perceptions among

French as a second language learners using mobile TTSs and ASR tools to improve their L2 pronunciation. While they appreciated and took advantage of the affordances that the two applications offered, the learners found several shortcomings, such as the lack of accuracy in spelling out what they had said (with ASR) and the unnaturalness of the automatic voice they heard when using TTS. In addition, the implicit corrective feedback that the two tools provided (TTS via voice and ASR – through orthography) was judged as insufficient in allowing the learners to recognize and effectively address their pronunciation errors. Investigations such as these and those that integrate written feedback onto mobile platforms are rare, however, and hence require further research.

Conclusions, Pedagogical Implications, and Future Research Directions

This chapter reviewed theory and research in the field of MALL with a focus on how mobile technology can enhance opportunities for corrective feedback . The review suggests that mobile devices can promote opportunities for language learning both inside and outside language classrooms, including opportunities for corrective feedback. The available MALL research confirms its facilitative role in a number of areas including providing additional exposure to the target language, accommodating learners' study preferences and habits, and enhancing their performance in several L2 skills. MALL can also be used as a tool to facilitate learner engagement with both written and spoken feedback and, hence, can promote depth of learning in these areas.

An important implication drawn from research in this area is that teachers should familiarize themselves with such affordances and attempt to make use of them in their classrooms. What's more, teachers may need to think of strategies that can extend language learning outside the classroom. The use of mobile technology can play an essential role in facilitating this beyond the classroom learning, as the use of mobile devices makes such learning possible by removing physical barriers. Such devices often stress the role of the learners and their autonomy in language learning and, in doing so, may be considered to downplay the important role of the teacher. This, however, is not the case as language teachers can both use mobile technology in the classroom as a way of assisting learners and also combine it with other activities outside the classroom in a way that can promote learning. For example, when the students are giving an inside classroom presentation, the teacher can use his or her mobile device to jot down the areas students have problems with and provide feedback on these when an opportunity arises.

In their discussion of the use of mobile technology for language pedagogy, Kukulska-Hulme et al. (2015) highlighted a number of areas that can be promoted by the use of MALL. The four main categories they discuss are: outcomes, rehearsal, reflection, and inquiry or seeking information. Although these have been discussed with regard to the role of mobile pedagogy in general, all the areas could equally be enhanced when the mobile devices are used as a way of facilitating corrective feedback. Outcome, for example, concerns the question of how MALL can enhance language proficiency. But, as the authors pointed out, it can also address ways of how to promote other outcomes such as identifying gaps in knowledge, learning to notice, developing autonomy or learning to learn, connecting experts and non-experts, and also developing skills in using mobile devices. These outcome areas can be facilitated when learners participate in activities involving the use of mobile technology and receiving feedback, and therefore, teachers should consider them in their teaching. Inquiry, in turn, concerns the degree to which mobile technology can be used as a tool for seeking information about learning and teaching. Teachers can use mobile devices for capturing linguistic moments students have problems with and then use them as a way of providing feedback, by posing or answering questions when learners use commutative contexts.

Mobile devices can also be used as a tool for reflecting on the kinds of corrective strategies that do or do not work in a teaching context. As Kukulska-Hulme et al. (2015) pointed out, "The teacher's role includes modelling good practices (e.g., correct language forms) and, crucially, helping learners reflect on their learning – what has and has not been learnt or understood, how it may be applied, how to improve and progress, what new learning goals may be set and so on" (p. 9). Mobile devices can facilitate such reflection processes.

Teachers could use mobile devices to make sure that students have integrated the language form into their interlanguage system. This can be checked through rehearsal or practicing what students have learned. Mobile devices can provide "a supportive environment in which to prepare for target language communication outside the classroom" (Kukulska-Hulme et al., 2015, p. 9). However, they can also be used as a tool to help learners to practice, become aware of the problems they have, and receive feedback, even when the students are not inside the classroom.

As for research, although there is empirical evidence that mobile devices can facilitate language learning, little research has been conducted into how mobile technology can be incorporated effectively into teachers' routine classroom practices. This, claims Burston (2014), is due to the pedagogical, technical, and human challenges inherent to providing feedback that is not unidirectional (teacher to student) and is in line with the anytime/anywhere nature of mobile technologies. Another reason could be that much of this research has focused on the use of mobile technology as additional practice in formal language learning settings, with highly structured activities reminiscent of the

Tutorial CALL and not those that promote interaction and collaboration (Burston, 2014; Kukulska-Hulme & Shield, 2008). Even when interaction is the goal (e.g., Demouy & Kukulska-Hulme, 2010), the most-utilized mobile-based tasks resemble language drills, with predetermined correct responses, more than activities that promote engagement and interaction.

Therefore, research is needed in order to determine how MALL can be integrated into classroom practices as an instructional tool that can be built into the teacher's existing curriculum and lesson plans. Furthermore, although there is ample research on how MALL can be used in L2 teaching and learners have also been shown to view portable devices favorably and employ them regularly, the role of MALL in provision and effectiveness of corrective feedback is a relatively new area. Hence, little is known about how MALL assists L2 learning. There is also much more work needed to determine how MALL can be used as a way of providing and assessing the effectiveness of feedback in and outside classroom contexts as well as the effects of MALL on how teachers, other experts, and learners (peer or self) provide feedback and the challenges they face in the process. What is clear, however, is that MALL is here to stay and grow. This adds to the urgency of research in the area and the need for educators "to start using mobile technology to deliver education" that is learner-centered and available anytime, anywhere (Ally, 2013, p. 7).

References

Abdous, M., Camarena, M. M. & Facer, B. R. (2009). MALL technology: Use of academic podcasting in the foreign language classroom. *ReCALL, 21*(1), 76–95.

Abraham, L. B. (2008). Computer-mediated glosses in second language reading comprehension and vocabulary learning: A meta-analysis. *Computer Assisted Language Learning, 21*(3), 199–226.

Ally, M. (2013). Mobile learning: From research to practice to impact education. *Learning and Teaching in Higher Education: Gulf Perspectives, 10* (2), 1–10.

Ally, M., McGreal, R., Schafer, S., Tin, T. & Cheung, B. (2007). Use of mobile learning technology to train ESL adults. In *Proceedings of the Sixth International Conference on Mobile Learning* (pp. 7–12). Melbourne.

Ally, M. & Samaka, M. (2016). Guidelines for design and implementation of mobile learning. In B. H. Khan (ed.), *Revolutionizing modern education through meaningful e-learning implementation* (pp. 161–176). IGI Global. http://doi:10.4018/978-1-5225-0466-5.ch009.

Belz, J. A. & Kinginger, C. (2003). Discourse options and the development of pragmatic competence by classroom learners of German: The case of address forms. *Language Learning, 53*(4), 591–647.

Blake, R. J. (2000). Computer mediated communication: A window on L2 Spanish interlanguage. *Language Learning & Technology*, 4(1), 120–136.

Brown, E. (ed.). (2001). Mobile learning explorations at the Stanford Learning Lab. *Speaking of Computers* (issue 55, January 8). https://tomprof.stanford.edu/posting/289.

Burston, J. (2014). MALL: The pedagogical challenges. *Computer Assisted Language Learning*, 27(4), 344–357.

Chapelle, C. (2008). Computer assisted language learning. In B. Spolsky & F. M. Hult (eds.), *The handbook of educational linguistics* (pp. 585–595). Oxford: Blackwell.

Comas-Quinn, A., Mardomingo, R. & Valentine, C. (2009). Mobile blogs in language learning: making the most of informal and situated learning opportunities. *ReCALL*, 21(1), 96–112.

Demouy, V. & Kukulska-Hulme, A. (2010) On the spot: Using mobile devices for listening and speaking practice on a French language programme, *Open Learning: The Journal of Open, Distance and e-Learning*, 25(3), 217–232.

Doughty, C. & Varela, E. (1998). Communicative focus on form. In C. Doughty & J. Williams (eds.), *Focus on form in classroom second language acquisition* (pp. 114–138). New York: Cambridge University Press.

Ellis, R. (2006). Researching the effects of form-focused instruction on L2 acquisition. *AILA Review*, 19(1), 18–41.

Felix, U. (2005a). What do meta-analyses tell us about CALL effectiveness? *ReCALL*, 17(2), 269–288.

Felix, U. (2005b). Analyzing recent CALL effectiveness research – Towards a common agenda. *Computer Assisted Language Learning*, 18(1–2), 1–32.

Golonka, E. M., Bowles, A. R., Frank, V. M., Richardson, D. L. & Freynik, S. (2014). Technologies for foreign language learning: A review of technology types and their effectiveness. *Computer Assisted Language Learning*, 27(1), 70–105.

Grhurovic, M., Chapelle, C. & Shelley, M. (2013). A meta-analysis of effectiveness studies on computer technology-supported language learning. *ReCALL*, 25(2), 165–198.

Herring, S. C. (2007). A faceted classification scheme for computer-mediated Discourse. *Language@Internet*, 4, article 1. www.languageatinternet.org/articles/2007/761.

Hsu, H-Y., Wang, S-K. & Comac, L. (2008). Using audioblogs to assist English-language learning: an investigation into student perception. *Computer Assisted Language Learning*, 21(2), 181–198.

Kern, R. (2006). Perspectives on technology in learning and language teaching. *TESOL Quarterly*, 40(1), 183–210.

Kessler, G. (2009). Student-initiated attention to form in wiki-based collaborative writing. *Language Learning & Technology*, 13(1), 79–95.

Kim, H-S. (2013). Emerging mobile apps to improve English listening skills. *Multimedia-Assisted Language Learning*, 16(2), 11–30.

Kim, S. (2014). Developing autonomous learning for oral proficiency using digital storytelling. *Language Learning and Technology*, *18*(2), 20–35.

Kukulska-Hulme, A., Norris, L. and Donohue, J. (2015). *Mobile pedagogy for English language teaching: A guide for teachers*. London: British Council.

Kukulska-Hulme, A. & Shield, L. (2008). Overview of mobile assisted language learning: From content delivery to supported collaboration and interaction. *ReCALL*, *20*(3), 271–289.

Lee, L. (2010). Exploring wiki-mediated collaborative writing: A case study in an elementary Spanish course. *Calico Journal*, *27*(2), 260–276.

Li, A. & Hegelheimer, V. (2013). Mobile-assisted grammar exercises: Effects of self-editing in L2 writing. *Language Learning and Technology*, *17*(3), 135–156.

Li, C. (2009). SMS-based vocabulary learning for ESL students. Master's thesis, Auckland University of Technology, New Zealand. http://aut.researchgateway.ac.nz/bitstream/handle/10292/746/LiC.pdf?sequence=4&isAllowed=y.

Liakin, D., Cardoso, W. & Liakina, N. (2014). Learning L2 pronunciation with a mobile speech recognizer: French /y/. *CALICO*, *32*(1), 1–25.

  (2017a). The pedagogical use of mobile speech synthesis (TTS): focus on French liaison. *Computer Assisted Language Learning*, *30*(3–4), 325–342.

  (2017b). Mobilizing instruction in a second-language context: Learners' perceptions of two speech technologies. *Languages*, *2*(3), 11, 1–21. https://doi.org/10.3390/languages2030011.

Lin, H. (2015). Computer-mediated communication (CMC) in L2 oral proficiency development: A meta-analysis. *ReCALL*, *27*(3), 261–287.

Liu, M., Moore, Z., Graham, L. & Lee, S. (2002). A look at the research in computer-based technology use in second language learning: A review of literature from 1990–2000. *Journal of Research on Technology in Education*, *34*(3), 250–273.

Long, M. (1996). The role of the linguistic environment in second language acquisition. In W. C. Ritchie & T. K. Bhatia (eds.), *Handbook of language acquisition*. Vol. II: *Second Language Acquisition* (pp. 413–468). New York: Academic Press.

Mak, B. & Coniam, D. (2008). Using wikis to enhance and develop writing skills among secondary school students in Honk Kong. *System*, *36*(3), 437–455.

Nassaji, H. & Kartchava, E. (eds.). (2017). *Corrective feedback in second language teaching and learning: Research, theory, applications, implications*. New York: Routledge.

Noriega, H. S. R. (2016). Mobile learning to improve writing in ESL teaching. *TEFLIN Journal*, *27*(2), 182–202.

Palalas, A. (2011). Mobile-assisted learning: Designing for your students. In S. Thouësny & L. Bradley (eds.), *Second language teaching and learning with technology: Views of emergent researchers* (pp. 71–94). Dublin: Research-publishing.net.

Pellettieri, J. (2000). Negotiation in cyberspace: The role of chatting in the development of grammatical competence. In M. Warschauer & R. G. Kern (eds.), *Network-based language teaching: Concepts and practice* (pp. 59–86). New York: Cambridge University Press.

Prensky, M. (2001). Digital natives, digital immigrants part 1. *On the Horizon*, 9(5), 1–2.

—— (2005). Listen to the natives. *Educational Leadership*, 63(4), 8–13.

Procter-Legg, E., Cacchione, A. & Petersen, S. A. (2012). LingoBee and social media: Mobile language learners as social networkers. Paper presented at the International Association for Development of the Information Society (IADIS) International Conference on Cognition and Exploratory Learning in Digital Age (CELDA) (Madrid, Spain, Oct 19-21, 2012).

Reinders H. & White, C. (2010). The theory and practice of technology in materials development and task design. In N. Harwood (ed.), *Contemporary computer assisted language learning* (pp. 359–375). London: Continuum Books.

Reynolds, B. L. & Anderson, T. A. F. (2015). Extra-dimensional in-class communications: Action research exploring text chat support of face-to-face writing. *Computers and Composition*, 35, 52–64.

Schmidt, R. & Frota, S. (1986). Developing basic conversational ability in second language: A case study of an adult learner of Portuguese. In R. Day (ed.), *Talking to learn: Conversation in second language acquisition* (pp. 237–326). Rowley, MA: Newbury House.

Shi, Z., Luo, G. & He, L. (2017). Mobile-assisted language learning using WeChat instant messaging. *International Journal of Emerging Technologies in Learning*, 12(2), 16–26.

Shih, R.-C., Lee, C. & Cheng, T.-F. (2015). Effects of English spelling learning experience through a mobile LINE app for college students. *Procedia – Social and Behavioral Sciences*, 174, 2634–2638.

Stockwell, G. & Hubbard, P. (2013). *Some emerging principles for mobile-assisted language learning*. Monterey, CA: The International Research Foundation for English Language Education. www.tirfonline.org/english-in-the-workforce/mobile-assisted-language-learning.

Sung, Y., Chang, K. & Yang, J. (2015). How effective are mobile devices for language learning? A meta-analysis. *Educational Research Review*, 16 (Complete), 68–84.

Swain, M. (1993). The output hypothesis: Just speaking and writing aren't enough. *Canadian Modern Language Review*, 50(1), 158–164.

Sykes, J. M., Oskoz, A. & Thorne, S. L. (2008). Web 2.0, Synthetic immersive environments, and mobile resources for language education. *CALICO Journal*, 25(3), 528–546.

Taj, I. H., Sulan, N. B., Sipra, M. A. & Ahmad, W. (2016). Impact of mobile assisted language learning (MALL) on EFL: A meta-analysis. *Advances in Language and Literary Studies*, 7(2), 76–83.

Taylor, A. M. (2006). The effects of CALL versus traditional L1 glosses on L2 reading comprehension. *CALICO Journal*, *23*(2), 309–318.

Thornton, P. & Houser, C. (2005). Using mobile phones in English education in Japan. *Journal of Computer Assisted Learning*, *21*(3), 217–228.

Vandergriff, I. (2016). *Second-language discourse in the digital world: Linguistic and social practices in and beyond the networked classroom*. Amsterdam: John Benjamins.

Warschauer, M. (1996). Comparing face-to-face and electronic communication in the second language classroom. *CALICO Journal*, *13*(2), 7–26.

Wu, Q. (2015). Pulling mobile assisted language learning (MALL) into the mainstream: MALL in broad practice. *PLoS ONE*, *10*(5), e0128762.

Xu, Q., Dong, X. Q. & Jiang, J. (2017). EFL learners' perceptions of mobile-assisted feedback on oral production. *TESOL Quarterly*, *51*(2), 408–417.

Xu, Q. & Peng, H. (2017). Investigating mobile-assisted oral feedback in teaching Chinese as a second language. *Computer Assisted Language Learning*, *30*(3–4), 173–182.

Young, E. H. & West, R. E. (2018). Speaking practice outside the classroom: A literature review of asynchronous multimedia-based oral communication in language learning. *EuroCALL Review*, *26*(1), 59–78.

Zhang, H., Song, W. & Burston, J. (2011). Reexamining the effectiveness of vocabulary learning via mobile phones. *Turkish Online Journal of Educational Technology*, *10*(3), 203–214.

Zhao, Y. (2003). Recent developments in technology and language learning: A literature review and meta-analysis. *CALICO Journal*, *21*(1), 7–27.

Ziegler, N. (2016). Synchronous computer-mediated communication and interaction: A meta-analysis. *Studies in Second Language Acquisition*, *38*(3), 553–586.

25

Oral Corrective Feedback in Content-Based Contexts

Susan Ballinger

Background

Content-based contexts are defined broadly as approaches in which content is taught through a second language (L2) with the dual goals of developing both content and L2 knowledge (Cenoz, 2015; Dalton-Puffer et al., 2014; Lyster, 2017, 2018; Lyster & Ballinger, 2011). The focus and structure of content-based programs are diverse, but they have been conceptualized as falling along a continuum (Figure 25.1) that ranges from content-driven to language-driven (Lyster, 2017; Met, 1998). At the language-driven end of the continuum are programs, such as theme-based foreign language instruction, that prioritize language objectives and use content to facilitate language learning. Toward the middle of the continuum would be content and language integrated learning (CLIL) programs that pair foreign language classes with one or two subject classes taught through the target language. Finally, programs that hinge on achieving content objectives or that use language primarily as a vehicle for content learning would fall toward the content-driven end of the continuum. These might include English medium instruction (EMI) or immersion and CLIL programs that deliver 50 percent or more of the curriculum via the L2.

While certain content-based programs such as CLIL and immersion have received a greater amount of attention in the literature in recent decades, content-based approaches encompass an array of programs, including theme-based foreign or second language classes (Cammarata, 2016) and higher education programs such as EMI that use an L2 as the medium of instruction (Burger & Chrétien, 2001; Dafouz & Camacho-Miñano, 2016; Macaro et al., 2018). Other immersion programs target additional goals and types of learners. For instance, two-way immersion integrates L1 English speakers and L1 minority language speakers to promote learning and appreciation of both languages and cultures (Lindholm-Leary, 2001).

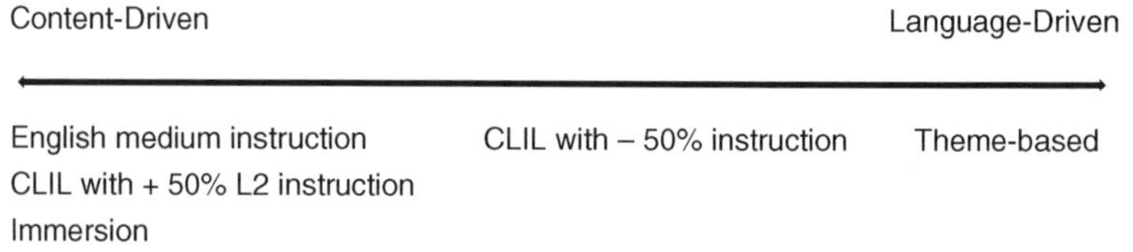

Content-Driven ←——————————————————————→ Language-Driven

English medium instruction   CLIL with – 50% instruction   Theme-based
CLIL with + 50% L2 instruction
Immersion

Figure 25.1 Continuum of content and language integration (Lyster, 2017; Met, 1998).

Indigenous and minority language immersion programs also seek to revitalize the role and status of the target language in the broader community (Hermes & Kawai'ae'a, 2014).

L2 learning outcomes from content-based classrooms such as immersion and CLIL have generally been found to be superior to those of non-content-based classrooms. These outcomes have been well-documented in immersion programs in the United States and Canada, where learners have been found to reach levels of L2 listening and reading comprehension that are comparable to native speakers. While immersion learners' L2 speaking and writing skills fall far short of those of native speakers, they are consistently found to be more advanced than those of non-immersion, foreign language students (Allen et al., 1990; Lindholm-Leary & Genesee, 2014). Studies in European CLIL programs have found similar positive outcomes (see Dalton-Puffer, 2011).

Canadian French immersion researchers have long noted that while these learners quickly become capable of communicating meaning in their L2, even at the time of graduation from the program, they continue to make basic grammar errors, lack sociolinguistic awareness, and demonstrate a limited range of vocabulary (Lindholm-Leary & Genesee, 2014). In fact, immersion students' speech production can be so nontarget-like that they have been described as "speaking immersion," rather than standard French (Lyster, 1987). Recent research has also uncovered a plateau effect in L2 oral proficiency development that tends to occur from grade five to grade eight, indicating the fossilization of certain errors in learners' speech (Fortune & Tedick, 2015). In sum, while content-based outcomes are superior to other language classroom contexts, there are still ample opportunities for teachers to provide content-based learners with oral corrective feedback (CF).

Diversity of Content-Based Programs

CLIL and immersion are widely available in North America and Europe, but they are also increasingly found in Asia (Dalton-Puffer, Nikula & Smit, 2010) and Australia (Oliver et al., 2019). While English is by far the most common target language in European and Asian contexts, French, Spanish, and Mandarin (among others) are also common foreign or heritage languages targeted in North America and Australia. EMI has long been found in South America, India, and Africa. However, due to the increasing power that English wields in business, arts, and scientific communities, this program has grown exponentially in recent years in Asia and Europe, particularly at the tertiary level (Dafouz & Smit, 2014; Macaro et al., 2018). Indigenous and minority language immersion programs can be found, for example, for Maori in New Zealand (May & Hill, 2005), for Quechua in South America (Hornberger, 2006), for Cherokee (Peter, 2014) and Ojibwe (Hermes, 2007) in North America, for Hawaiian in Hawaii (Wilson & Kamana, 2011), and for Basque (Lasagabaster, 2001) and Irish (Hickey, 2007) in Europe.

Clearly, the label "content-based" can refer to a wide range of structures, objectives, geographical locations, and languages. Adding to the ambiguity, a program labeled CLIL in one location may be labeled as immersion, content-based instruction (CBI), content-based language teaching (CBLT), or EMI in another location. In fact, the literature on content-based approaches has hosted debates over what label should be used, whether immersion, CLIL, and EMI should be categorized under one overarching term, and, if so, what that term should be. Macaro et al. (2018, p. 68), for example, note the need to "arrive at a model of the different learning situations in which content and language are at issue" and "to identify and then define relatively stable superordinate and subordinate terminology for these learning situations." Currently, some researchers (usually North American) prefer the term CBI or CBLT (Genesee & Lindholm-Leary, 2013; Lyster, 2017), while others (usually European) have argued that CLIL is a more accurate label for programs that "integrate" content and language (see, e.g., Morton & Llinares, 2017).

Convincing arguments have been made regarding the importance of both the similarities (Cenoz, Genesee & Gorter, 2014; Lyster, 2017, 2018; Lyster & Ballinger, 2011) and differences (Dalton-Puffer et al., 2014; Lasagabaster & Sierra, 2010; Morton & Llinares, 2017; Pérez-Cañado, 2012) of these programs. Nevertheless, the above researchers agree that there is a fair amount of overlap in the programs' structure and objectives. Namely, that using the communicative approach to promote effective and extensive communication among students in these programs is fundamental and that balancing content and language learning goals is at the heart of these programs.

These two foundations of content-based instruction – adherence to the communicative approach and the dual content-language focus – also happen to be at the heart of many cross-context issues related to the use of CF in content-based contexts. In the following section, the impact of these pedagogical principles on CF in these contexts will be examined in relation to generalizable pedagogical implications. Nevertheless, important differences, such as program structures and goals, languages of instruction, and students' age and cultural backgrounds, also exist among these contexts.

Therefore, a subsequent section will also examine literature demonstrating the impact that these differences may have on CF in these classrooms.

Relevant Research

Cross-Context Issues

Appropriateness of CF in Content-Based Contexts

Based on the nature of language production in content-based contexts as well as patterns of student L2 acquisition, targeted CF may be particularly appropriate and effective in these settings. First and most simply, CF is dependent upon student language production. Owing to the greater amount of time allocated to learning in the L2, the higher proficiency levels of the students, and the focus on communicative learning, there are, conceivably, numerous opportunities for CF to take place in these contexts. Second, content-based approaches emphasize the use of authentic communication (Swain & Johnson, 1997). In contrast with many foreign language contexts, where learners frequently engage in isolated practice of linguistic form (Huang, 2006; Nishimuro & Borg, 2013; Pahissa & Tragant, 2009; Yaghoubinejad, Zarrinabadi & Nejadansari, 2017), content-based learners must constantly use their L2 for authentic communicative functions, such as comprehending and analyzing new information or expressing opinions and ideas.

Several second language acquisition theories support the enhanced effectiveness of CF on learners' errors when they are engaged in authentic communication. For example, researchers grounded in interactionist and cognitivist approaches posit that CF during meaningful interaction is necessary for L2 acquisition (Long, 1996; Long & Robinson, 1998) and that it supports learners' ability to notice the gap in their L2 knowledge (Gass & Mackey, 2006). Sociocultural learning theory underlines the necessity of offering learners support (i.e., scaffolding) when they can proceed to the next level of learning only with assistance from an expert (i.e., their Zone of Proximal Development). It claims that this moment of support – which could include support in the form of CF – is precisely when learning takes place (Lantolf, 2000; Nassaji & Swain, 2000). Finally, Transfer Appropriate Processing (Lightbown, 2008) argues that learners will be better able to recall linguistic forms when they are applied in the same context in which they were learned. Therefore, if content-based students' errors are corrected during authentic communication, they will be better able to recall the error, and the corrected form, during future authentic communication. The above theories have been supported by research from a variety of L2 learning contexts demonstrating the general effectiveness of CF for L2 learning (Lyster, Saito & Sato, 2013).

While the strong theoretical grounding and positive research findings would seemingly make a strong case for targeted and ongoing use of CF in content-based contexts, CF's place in these contexts has been precarious from the start. As stated earlier, content-based pedagogy is founded on communicative language teaching (CLT), the strong version of which argues that L2 learning – similar to L1 acquisition – should take place through communication for meaning and that the L2 should not be taught explicitly but rather learned through exposure and use in the same way that a child acquires a first language (Howatt, 1984; Spada, 2007). The focus is on developing fluency, leaving "little room for error correction" (Ellis, 2017, p. 4). However, as immersion learners progressed through the original programs, findings emerged demonstrating the fossilization of certain errors in their oral production (Allen et al., 1990). Therefore, researchers began questioning the strong version of CLT, and they moved toward developing and promoting methods of incorporating an explicit language focus into the framework of content-based and communicative approaches. These included the development of the focus-on-form approach (see Doughty & Williams, 1998) as well as a heightened interest in the role of CF as a means of integrating a focus on language into content instruction (Lyster, 2017).

Use and Effectiveness of CF in Content-Based Contexts
While research on CF in L2 learning settings has examined the impact of a range of variables, such as the timing of CF and its effectiveness for learning various linguistic features, the bulk of CF literature has been taken up with an examination of the presence and effectiveness of implicit versus explicit CF. Feedback can be seen as falling along a continuum of implicit to explicit. Reformulations of a learner's incorrect utterance, which give no overt indicator to a learner that an error has occurred, are the most implicit form of feedback (Ellis, 2017). Other, more explicit, forms of feedback offer indications that the learner has committed an error, with the most explicit feedback type including a clear statement that the utterance was incorrect. Generally, across L2 learning settings, more explicit recasts have been associated with higher rates of uptake, which has been defined as a students' response to a teacher's CF and which can include both incorrect and correct attempts at repair (Lyster, Saito & Sato, 2013).

In their seminal study, which took place in a content-based setting, Lyster and Ranta (1997) examined CF use among four immersion teachers during classroom instruction. They quantified the teachers' CF use, identified six feedback types, and associated each CF type with learners' uptake and repair. The feedback types were explicit corrections, metalinguistic feedback, elicitations of students' self-repair, or repetition of the error, though these have been simplified as recasts, prompts, and explicit correction in subsequent studies. The teachers in their study provided CF for more than half of student errors (62 percent). They were also found to prefer recasting student errors over the other identified CF types.

Findings from subsequent studies of feedback provision in content-based settings have found a clear tendency for teachers to prefer reformulations (also see Chapter 22, this volume). For instance, in a study of two content-based ESL classes at a US university, Pica (2002) found that teachers generally engaged in very little incidental focus on form (including CF) during discussion activities. Lee (2007) found that, out of the total CF episodes, Korean teachers of English immersion for 8- to 9-year-olds used reformulations (53%), prompts (39%), and explicit corrections (8%). In Lyster and Mori (2006), out of the total CF episodes, teachers of Japanese immersion for 9- to 10-year-olds used recasts (65%), prompts (26%), and explicit corrections (9%). Llinares and Lyster (2014) found that, in two Spanish CLIL classes for 9- to 10-year-olds with English as the target language, teachers used recasts 57 percent of the time, prompts 29 percent, and explicit correction 14 percent of the time.

When CF use is language-focused, foreign language (FL) classrooms are compared with content-based classes, and a pattern emerges indicating that more CF and more prompts are used in language-focused or FL classes in comparison with content-based classes. Lochtman (2007) compared CF provision in FL classes from Lochtman (2002) with the CF in the immersion classes from Lyster and Ranta (1997), finding that FL teachers tend to prompt learners to self-correct while immersion teachers prefer to reformulate errors. Milla and García Mayo (2014) compared CF provision in EFL and English language CLIL classes among the same group of students at a Spanish secondary school, finding that the CLIL teacher used mainly reformulations, while the EFL teacher used more explicit forms of CF. The researchers also interviewed the teachers regarding their CF preferences, and indeed, the EFL teacher stated that she preferred to use more explicit, language-focused CF that pushed learners to correct their errors, while the CLIL teacher stated that he tried "to convey CF in an implicit way in order not to deviate learners' attention from content" (p. 6).

A number of studies have also examined the effectiveness of CF provision in content-based contexts, as represented by learner uptake and repair of errors or by the learning of grammatical forms targeted by CF. For the most part, these studies have found prompts to be more effective than recasts. Lyster and Ranta (1997) found that immersion students engaged in uptake after 55 percent of CF episodes and successfully repaired their errors in 27 percent of these episodes. Moreover, a clear pattern emerged indicating that learners engaged in uptake and repair more often after more explicit CF than after recasts. Milla and García (2014) found that while the EFL learners engaged in uptake in response to all but one CF type, explicit corrections, CLIL learners only engaged in uptake for elicitations and recasts. It is interesting to note that not only did the CLIL learners engage in uptake more often for the elicitations, they also responded to this particular CF type more than the EFL learners. Finally, Lee (2007) also found that English immersion learners in Korea engaged in uptake less frequently in response to recasts.

While the above studies were all observational in nature, Lyster (2004) conducted a quasi-experimental study of the differential effects of prompts and recasts on Grade four and five immersion students' learning of French grammatical gender in three classrooms. In one classroom, the teacher gave no feedback, in the second, only recasts were offered, and in the third, only prompts. Lyster found that the prompts were more effective than recasts in supporting learners' performance on post-tests and that both forms of feedback were more effective than no feedback. Ammar and Spada (2006) also conducted a quasi-experimental study in three Grade six intensive English[1] classrooms in Quebec, examining different types of CF provision on students' learning of possessive determiners. They found that students in both the prompt and the recast groups outperformed those in the control group on post-tests, but that the prompt group performed significantly better than the recast group.

There were two exceptions to the pattern of findings from the above studies. The Spanish CLIL students from Llinares and Lyster (2014) and the Japanese immersion learners in Lyster and Mori (2006) more frequently engaged in uptake and repair subsequent to a recast than a prompt. However, Llinares and Lyster (2014) offer an explanation for this divergence. In this study, which compares findings from French immersion (Lyster & Ranta, 1997), Japanese immersion (Lyster & Mori, 2006), and English CLIL in Spain, the authors make a distinction between conversational recasts and didactic recasts. They note that the former were used in the French immersion setting, while the latter were used in the Japanese immersion and English CLIL settings. Conversational recasts are reformulations that fit into the overall conversational pattern, making them theoretically more implicit and less noticeable to the learner. On the other hand, didactic recasts are argued to be more explicit because they isolate the error from its communicative function.

Some researchers have explained teachers' preference for recasts and students' lack of uptake after recasts by noting that teachers and students are more attuned to content material, rather than linguistic form, during interactions in content-based classrooms. Therefore, teachers are less likely to offer CF and students are less likely to notice or respond to it (Loewen, 2004). Others have noted that there is additional ambiguity surrounding teachers' preferred CF type – recasts – which may explain the lesser amount of uptake or repair found in most content-based classrooms (Lyster, 2017). Lyster (1998) found that French immersion teachers

---

[1] Intensive English is a half-year (five-month) program that does not teach content but focuses on themes in order to facilitate students' English acquisition. It would therefore fall at the language-driven end of the content-based continuum.

not only reformulated learners' incorrect utterances, but they also repeated almost one-third of learners' correct utterances. Under these circumstances, learners who are already more focused on meaning than language may hear a reformulated error as a repetition of what they have already said. This study also found that even when teachers did intend to recast learners' incorrect utterances, they often preceded the recast with a sign of approval (e.g., *Bravo!*, *Very good!*). This ambiguity surrounding the intention of teachers' CF extends to other CF types as well. For instance, in three Italian CLIL classes, Mariotti (2006) found that although CF was offered to learners, when teachers did use prompts in the form of clarification requests (2 percent of all feedback moves), their corrective intention was unclear to the learners. Koike and Pearson (2005) found that, following clarification requests, learners tended to give the same response, but with a louder voice.

In sum, research has found that while content-based teachers do engage in CF, the dual focus on content and language in these classrooms seems to impact CF's salience and effectiveness, particularly for content-based teachers' preferred CF type –the recast.

Cognitive Complexity of Oral CF in Content-Based Contexts

A second CF-related issue in content-based contexts that reaches across programs is the challenge that teachers face in trying to meet both content and language objectives. Lightbown and Spada (2013) have described this type of teaching as being a "two-for-one" approach (p. 171), which means that a single teacher must do the job of two. Lyster (2017) describes the practice of an effective content-based teacher as involving "counterbalanced instruction," or constant shifts between an instructional focus on meaning and form. He also divides the task of integrating content and language into "proactive" and "reactive" approaches. The proactive approach includes preplanning activities that target both content and language objectives. The reactive approach includes scaffolding and CF techniques in response to students' language production "to support student participation while insuring that oral interaction is a key source of [content and language] learning" (Lyster, 2018, p. 9).

In other words, during interactions with their students, content-based teachers must be able to give students support for and feedback on both content and language – a feat that requires a high level of attention on the part of the teachers. It is perhaps unsurprising that researchers have found that content-based teachers struggle to achieve this goal (Cammarata & Tedick, 2012; Fortune, Tedick & Walker, 2008). In a study that examined the experiences of immersion teachers involved in a professional development (PD) program, Cammarata and Tedick (2012) found that these teachers still had difficulty choosing which linguistic features to target in content lessons. In Fortune, Tedick, and Walker's (2008) study of US Spanish immersion teachers' content and language instruction practices, participating teachers stated that they were always engaged in language teaching. However, video observations showed that they did not do so in a planned or deliberate way, that their language teaching focused almost exclusively on vocabulary, and that most feedback in student–teacher interactions focused on the content, not the language, of students' production.

In other words, not only does the simultaneous attention to content and language seem to pose a substantial cognitive load for teachers, but the ability to determine the language focus of content lessons and, by extension, CF, also seems to require extensive training. In a study of a content-based teacher-training course, Tedick & Zilmer (2018) found that 87 percent of teachers ranked an assignment targeting teachers' scaffolding and CF provision as having a high impact on their learning, the second highest impact of any assignment in the class. In this assignment, teachers were required to video record themselves during an interactive lesson, to analyze their scaffolding and CF moves, to create an improvement plan, and to video record themselves once more to analyze their improvement. One Spanish immersion teacher stated, "I thought I was doing better with my feedback, and then I realized how much I was still recasting and not using prompting .... I felt like [this assignment] really changed my practice." While this study reveals the impact that PD can have on teachers' CF practice, this type of study is rare in content-based literature, and this type of training is unavailable to most content-based teachers.

Few CLIL or EMI-based studies have included an investigation of teachers' perspectives on CF provision. One exception is van Kampen et al. (2017) which sought to determine whether CLIL stakeholders in the Netherlands held similar views on what constitutes "ideal" CLIL pedagogy. They interviewed seven CLIL teachers and nine specialists (one policy expert, three teacher-educators, and five researchers), asking them open-ended questions about their perspectives on ideal CLIL goals and practices. Although the researchers did not specifically ask participants about their views on feedback, three teachers and five specialists mentioned that all CLIL teachers offer feedback in practice. However, only two participants, both specialists, mentioned that feedback should be provided on language form by all teachers, and one teacher stated that subject teachers should only give feedback on content.

Context-Specific Issues

Lack of Interaction-Focused Research
While some researchers based in EMI and CLIL contexts have called for an increase in studies focusing on interaction and CF in these contexts (García & Bastarrechea, 2017), at this point, the overall concern seems to be with more global issues related to classroom interaction and learning. More

specifically, the literature from this context notes the generalized need for training that focuses on teachers' language competence and knowledge of content-based methodologies. Pérez-Cañado (2016) describes CLIL teachers as being, "extremely motivated teachers with serious training deficits" (p. 268). In her pan-Europe needs analysis survey of 501 pre- and in-service teachers, she found that teachers ranked training in the theoretical underpinnings of CLIL as their greatest need and L2 training as their second greatest need. In EMI contexts, research has uncovered a similar concern for instructors' English competence, and many teachers do not distinguish between the pedagogical underpinnings of teaching a subject in English versus teaching it in the students' L1 (Macaro et al., 2018).

Similarly, in minority and indigenous language contexts, interactional research has not prioritized CF research. Rather, interaction research in minority language contexts, such as US two-way immersion or Irish immersion, has focused a great amount of attention on the manifestations of power relationships between majority and minority languages in these contexts and their impact on minority language learners (see Hickey, 2007; Potowski, 2007). Research in indigenous contexts has focused more on the historical, societal, and cultural considerations relevant to interaction, rather than on micro-level features of interaction such as CF (Palmer, Ballinger & Peter, 2014). This does not imply, of course, that teachers in the above contexts do not provide learners with CF or struggle with issues related to CF, but that researchers in these contexts have focused their attention elsewhere.

Context Variables Impacting CF

Another important context-specific issue to consider in relation to the prevalence and effectiveness of CF in content-based contexts is the impact of students' age, students' and teachers' cultural background(s), and the content- versus language-driven nature of the program. In foreign language classrooms, it has typically been found that older learners benefit from both implicit and explicit CF types, while younger learners require more explicit CF (Lyster, Saito & Sato, 2013). Considering the range of program types and student age ranges included in content-based contexts, it is important to consider the fact that most CF findings have been generated by studies in primary school immersion settings. Thus, they may not be generalizable to other programs such as EMI in higher education.

Similarly, it may also be important to consider where a content-based program may fall along the content- versus language-driven spectrum when gauging the potential effectiveness of CF types in a particular context. Lyster & Mori (2006) referred to this as the degree of "form orientation" in an instructional context. Their (2006) Counterbalance Hypothesis posits that the more form-oriented a classroom context is, the more oriented a learner will be toward CF on formal aspects of their production.

Thus, teachers in more language-driven programs may be more likely to provide learners with CF in general and explicit CF types specifically. Furthermore, their students may be more likely to notice and respond to all types of CF in those programs.

Finally, it may also be important to consider students' and teachers' cultural and sociolinguistic background when examining the role of CF. For one, there are different expectations for student–teacher interaction in various cultures. In cultures that expect a more teacher-centered classroom environment, learners may be more attuned to their teachers' evaluation of their response in the I-R-E sequence and more responsive to all CF types (Sato, 2011; Sheen, 2004; Yang, 2016). Additionally, cultures vary in the value they place on implicit versus explicit communication. In cultures that place more value on implicitness, recasts may be preferable to both teachers and students and more noticeable to students. This cultural contrast is nicely stated by a Japanese participant in Spack's (1997) longitudinal study of an international student's adjustment to academic expectations at a US university: "in Japan, you don't have to say everything you think or feel because certain things are 'understood' or even 'to be observed' … But then here in the States, no thoughts or feelings exist unless you express them." Thus, for learners accustomed to observing for and understanding the implicit during everyday interactions, recasts may be more salient.

Conclusions and Implications

There is a notable lack of CF research in content-based contexts. In the literature search done for this chapter, no studies were found that focused primarily on oral CF in EMI, two-way immersion, minority language, or indigenous language contexts. CLIL researchers have also noted the need for more CF research in that context (García & Basterrechea, 2017; Milla & García, 2014). Finally, while it may seem that more CF studies have taken place in immersion settings, it is important to point out that a number of the studies reporting CF-related findings from immersion settings are actually recycling data reported in Lyster and Ranta (1997) as a comparison point. Lochtman (2007), Llinares and Lyster (2014), and Lyster and Mori (2006) all draw on that same source of immersion data. In fact, Llinares and Lyster (2014) also recycle the data from the Japanese immersion setting in Lyster and Mori (2006). While these studies have served as a useful means of comparing CF across content-based contexts, they may give the impression that the interactional patterns found in a small number of immersion classrooms are more common than they actually are. The bottom line is that more studies of CF are needed to offer content-based educators a clearer picture of CF effectiveness and teachers' needs.

One specific area that merits further research is peer interaction and, specifically, peer CF in content-based contexts. Peer interaction has been shown to allow learners to engage in more turn-taking and more extensive L2 production than they do in whole-class discussions, to take more risks with language, to negotiate for meaning and form more frequently, to be exposed to more feedback, and to notice errors in their partner's speech (Philp, Adams & Iwashita, 2014; Sato & Ballinger, 2016). Because peer CF is reciprocal in nature, requiring a learner to both provide and receive CF, it has been theorized as achieving dual purposes that heighten the value gained from monitoring and noticing errors (Sato & Lyster, 2012). However, relatively little research on peer CF has taken place in any context, a phenomenon which has been attributed to teachers' reluctance to use peer interaction extensively in their classrooms.

While content-based contexts represent excellent opportunities for learners to engage in authentic peer interaction due to their emphasis on meaning and authentic communication, several studies have found that peer interaction is used far less frequently than whole-class interaction in this context. For instance, immersion teachers in Salomone's (1992) study estimated that up to 80 percent of the time in the kindergarten classroom and 65 percent of the time in the grade two classroom was dedicated to whole-class activities. Lyster and Mori (2006) found that only 14 percent of class time in both contexts was used for groupwork activities. In Austrian secondary CLIL classes, Dalton-Puffer (2007) found that teachers relied primarily on whole-class lectures and activities and only occasionally had students engage in groupwork activities. In a study of three, grade two Canadian French immersion classrooms Netten and Spain (1989) also found that the classrooms emphasized whole-class activities over groupwork. However, this study also found a higher level of L2 achievement in the immersion classroom that offered learners more opportunities for meaningful peer interaction.

Several studies based in Canadian French immersion have examined learners' focus on language – including peer CF – during collaborative interactions. These studies have been grounded in sociocultural theory (Lantolf, 2000), which posits that language is both a tool for communication and for thinking and that learning must first take place through external interaction with an expert and then internalized. Swain and Lapkin (1998, 2002) and Swain (2001) examined the integration of content and language that took place through peer dialogue as immersion learners worked on collaborative tasks and resolved both language and content problems. They found that pairs could engage in learning of linguistic form through language-related episodes (LREs) that occurred during these interactions. However, Swain and Lapkin (1998) also note that not all pairs of learners in their study benefited in the same way from their interactions, a finding which is common in peer interaction studies from other L2 learning contexts.

A small number of studies in and outside of content-based contexts have focused on training learners to engage in peer CF. For instance, in Ballinger (2013), Grade three and four Canadian French immersion learners were taught reciprocal learning strategies, which included giving and receiving peer CF, prior to engaging in paired collaborative activities. Similarly, Helgerson (2017) taught US Spanish immersion students strategies, including peer CF, to help them maintain Spanish during peer interaction. Both studies found that while learners quickly understood the purpose of the strategies, their ability to apply them appropriately varied greatly. The researchers attribute this to the short-term nature of the intervention as well as the fact that researchers, not teachers, led the strategy training.

Further findings from Ballinger (2013) underline the complex nature of peer CF. In her study, CF frequently resulted in conflict. Further, when CF episodes devolved into conflict, learners did not engage in uptake or repair. Those who did engage in uptake and repair following CF also used additional collaborative interactional moves such as seeking contributions from their partner and confirming their partners' understanding and approval of their own ideas. In other words, the surrounding collaborative interactional moves appeared to be just as important as the actual CF episode in ensuring the effectiveness of the CF. Considering the uniquely social nature of peer interaction (Sato, 2017), it seems crucial that future studies of peer CF closely examine the surrounding social behaviors, relationships, and "collaborative mindset" of learners in these situations.

A crucial area of future research in relation to oral CF in content-based contexts is that of teacher training. While some studies have examined content-based teachers' beliefs, perspectives, and current practices of integrating content and language, very few content-based studies have included teacher-training interventions. In fact, pre-service teacher-training programs are rare for immersion and CLIL, and even though PD support for in-service teachers has increased, the vast majority of content-based teachers do not have specialized training. Consistently, across contexts, researchers have called for training to support EMI teachers' language proficiency (Macaro et al., 2018), to improve immersion teachers' ability to better integrate content and language (Fortune, Tedick & Walker, 2008; Cammarata & Tedick, 2012), and to unify CLIL teachers' perspectives on CLIL pedagogy (van Kampen et al., 2017). Considering the cognitive complexity involved in using CF to integrate content and language during whole-class instruction, it is logical that teachers require highly effective and empirically tested training to be able to achieve this feat. Research still has a long way to go to fill this void.

In the more than twenty years since Lyster and Ranta (1997) made a compelling case for the use of explicit CF in content-based classrooms, teachers' CF practice has not changed. Teachers still tend to use it inconsistently and to worry that more explicit CF will impede learners' communication of meaning or discourage them from participating in discussions.

Ellis (2017, p. 4) points out the "notable differences in the perspectives of teachers and researchers" on this issue, and he draws on examples from teaching guides that emphasize the need to offset the "potentially damaging" (p. 5) nature of CF.

In light of this continued gap between theory and practice, one final argument this chapter will make is that classroom-based CF research should respond more seriously to teachers' concerns. CF episodes are face-threatening moments in which a novice presents their knowledge, or lack of it, for evaluation by an expert, often in front of a group of peers. It therefore makes sense that content-based CF research look at factors that may correlate with both extensive production *and* effective CF (based on uptake). For example, more effective CF within extensive production may occur with teachers who also successfully promote students' positive attitudes toward risk-taking and error-making. CF research that examines the full range of pedagogical methods employed by content-based teachers may reveal more than studies examining isolated CF episodes, and by taking teachers' concerns seriously, it may also have a greater long-term impact on content-based teacher training and classroom practice.

References

Allen, P., Swain, M., Harley, B. & Cummins, J. (1990). Aspects of classroom treatment: Toward a more comprehensive view of second language education. In B. Harley, P. Allen, J. Cummins & M. Swain (eds.), *The development of second language proficiency* (pp. 57–81). Cambridge: Cambridge University Press.

Ammar, A. & Spada, N. (2006). One size fits all? Recasts, prompts and L2 learning. *Studies in Second Language Acquisition, 28*(4), 543–574.

Ballinger, S. (2013). Towards a cross-linguistic pedagogy: Biliteracy and reciprocal learning strategies in French immersion. *Journal of Immersion and Content-Based Language Education, 1*(1), 131–148.

Ballinger, S., Lyster, R., Sterzuk, A. & Genesee, F. (2017). Context-appropriate cross-linguistic pedagogy: Considering the role of language status in immersion. *Journal of Immersion and Content-Based Language Education, 5*(1), 30–57.

Burger. S. & Chrétien, S. (2001). The development of oral production in content-based second language courses at the University of Ottawa. *Canadian Modern Language Review, 58*(1), 84–102.

Cammarata, L. (ed.). (2016). *Content-based foreign language teaching: Curriculum and pedagogy for developing advanced thinking and literacy skills*. New York: Routledge/Taylor & Francis.

Cammarata, L. & Tedick, D. (2012). Balancing content and language in instruction: The experience of immersion teachers. *Modern Language Journal, 96*(2), 251–269.

Cenoz, J. (2015). Content-based instruction and content and language integrated learning: the same or different?' *Language, Culture and Curriculum*, 28(1), 8–24.

Cenoz, J., Genesee, F. & Gorter, D. (2014). Critical analysis of CLIL: Taking stock and looking forward. *Applied Linguistics*, 35(3), 243–262.

Dafouz, E. & Camacho-Miñano, M. (2016). Exploring the impact of English-medium instruction on university student academic achievement: The case of accounting. *English for Specific Purposes*, 44, 57–67.

Dafouz, E. & Smit, U. (2014). Towards a dynamic conceptual framework for English-medium education in multilingual settings. *Applied Linguistics*, 37(3), 397–415.

Dalton-Puffer, C. (2007). *Discourse in content and language integrated learning (CLIL) classrooms*. Amsterdam: John Benjamins.

(2011). Content and language integrated learning: From practice to principles? *Applied Linguistics*, 31, 182–204.

Dalton-Puffer, C., Llinares, A., Lorenzo, F. & Nikula, T. (2014). "You can stand under my umbrella": Immersion, CLIL and bilingual education. A response to Cenoz, Genesee & Gorter (2013). *Applied Linguistics*, 35(2), 213–218.

Dalton-Puffer, C., Nikula, T. & Smit, U. (2010). Language use and language learning in CLIL: Current findings and contentious issues. In C. Dalton-Puffer, T. Nikula & U. Smit (eds.), *Language use and language learning in CLIL classrooms* (pp. 279–291). Amsterdam: John Benjamins.

Doughty, C. & Williams, J. (1998). *Focus on form in classroom second language acquisition*. New York: Cambridge University Press.

Ellis, R. (2017). Oral corrective feedback in L2 classrooms: What we know so far. In H. Nassaji & E. Kartchava (eds.), *Corrective feedback in second language teaching and learning* (pp. 3–18). New York: Routledge.

Fortune, T. & Tedick, D. (2015). Oral proficiency development of K–8 Spanish immersion students. *Modern Language Journal*, 99(4), 637–655.

Fortune, T., Tedick, D. & Walker, C. (2008). Integrated language and content teaching: Insights from the classroom. In T. Fortune & D. Tedick (eds.), *Pathways to multilingualism: Evolving perspectives on immersion education* (pp. 71–96). Clevedon: Multilingual Matters.

García Mayo, M. P. & Bastarrechea, M. (2017). CLIL and SLA: Insights from an interactionist perspective. In A. Llinares & T. Morton (Eds.), *Applied linguistics perspectives on CLIL* (pp. 33–50). Amsterdam: John Benjamins.

Gass, S. & Mackey, A. (2006). Input, interaction and output: An overview. *AILA Review*, 19(1), 3–17.

Genesee, F., & Linholm-Leary, K. (2013). Two case studies of content-based language education. Journal of Immersion and Content-Based Language Education, 1(1): 3–33.

Helgerson, E. (2017). The effects of supporting target language use in immersion. Unpublished master's thesis, McGill University, Montreal, QC.

Hermes, M. (2007). Moving toward the language: Reflections on teaching in an indigenous immersion school. *Journal of American Indian Education*, 46(3), 54–71.

Hermes, M. & Kawai'ae'a, K. (2014). Revitalizing indigenous languages through indigenous immersion education. *Journal of Immersion and Content-Based Language Education*, 2(2), 303–322.

Hickey, T. (2007). Children's language networks and teachers' input in minority language immersion: What goes in may not come out. *Language and Education*, 21(1), 46–65.

Hornberger, N. (2006). Voice and biliteracy in indigenous language revitalization: Contentious educational practices in Quechua, Guarani, and Maori contexts. *Journal of Language, Identity & Education*, 5(4), 277–292.

Howatt, A. (1984). Language teaching traditions: 1884 revisited. *ELT Journal*, 38(4), 279–282.

Huang, J. (2006). Understanding factors that influence Chinese English teachers' decision to implement communicative activities in teaching. *The Journal of ASIA TEFL*, 3(4), 165–191.

Koike, D. & Pearson, L. (2005). The effect of instruction and feedback in the development of pragmatic competence. *System*, 33(3), 481–501.

Lantolf, J. (2000). Introducing sociocultural theory. In J. Lantolf (ed.), *Sociocultural theory and second language learning* (pp. 1–26). Oxford: Oxford University Press.

Lasagabaster, D. (2001). Bilingualism, immersion programmes and language learning in the Basque Country. *Journal of Multilingual and Multicultural Development*, 22(5), 401–425.

Lasagabaster, D. & Sierra, J. M. (2010). Immersion and CLIL in English: More differences than similarities. *ELT Journal*, 64, 367–375.

Lee, J. (2007). Corrective feedback and learner uptake in English immersion classrooms at the primary level in Korea. *English Teaching*, 62(4), 311–334.

Lightbown, P. (2008). Transfer appropriate processing as a model for classroom second language acquisition. In Z. Han (ed.), *Understanding second language process* (pp. 27–44). Clevedon: Multilingual Matters.

Lightbown, P. & Spada, N. (2013). *How languages are learned*. Oxford: Oxford University Press.

Lindholm-Leary, K. (2001). *Dual language education*. Clevedon: Multilingual Matters.

Lindholm-Leary, K. & Genesee, F. (2014). Student outcomes in one-way, two-way, and indigenous immersion language immersion education. *Journal of Immersion and Content-Based Language Education*, 2(2), 165–180.

Llinares, A. & Lyster, R. (2014). The influence of context on patterns of corrective feedback and learner uptake: A comparison of CLIL and immersion classrooms. *Language Learning Journal*, 42(2), 181–194.

Lochtman, K. (2002). Oral corrective feedback in the foreign language classroom: How it affects interaction in analytic foreign language teaching. *International Journal of Educational Research*, 37, 271–283.

(2007). Die mündliche Fehlerkorrektur in CLIL und im traditionellen Fremdsprachenunterricht: Ein Vergleich. In C. Dalton-Puffer & U. Smit (eds.), *Empirical perspectives on CLIL classroom discourse* (pp. 119–138). Frankfurt: Peter Lang.

Loewen, S. (2004). Uptake in incidental focus on form in meaning-focused ESL lessons. *Language Learning*, 54(1), 153–188.

Long, M. (1996). The role of the linguistic environment in second language acquisition. In W. Ritchie & T. Bhatia (eds.), *Handbook of second language acquisition* (pp. 413–468). San Diego, CA: Academic Press.

Long, M. & Robinson, P. (1998). Focus on form: Theory, research, and practice. In C. Doughty & J. Williams (eds.), *Focus on form in classroom second language acquisition* (pp. 15–41). Cambridge: Cambridge University Press.

Lyster, R. (1987). Speaking immersion. *Canadian Modern Language Review*, 43(4), 701–717.

(1998). Recasts, repetition and ambiguity in L2 classroom discourse. *Studies in Second Language Acquisition* 20(1), 51–80.

(2004). Differential effects of prompts and recasts in form-focused instruction. *Studies in Second Language Acquisition*, 26(3), 399–432.

(2017). Content-based language teaching. In S. Loewen & M. Sato (eds.), *The Routledge handbook of instructed second language acquisition* (pp. 87–107). New York: Routledge.

(2018). *Content-based language teaching*. New York: Routledge.

Lyster, R. & Ballinger, S. (2011). Content-based language teaching: Convergent concerns across divergent contexts. *Language Teaching Research*, 15(3), 279–288.

Lyster, R. & Mori, H. (2006). Interactional feedback and instructional counterbalance. *Studies in Second Language Acquisition*, 28(2), 269–300.

Lyster, R. & Ranta, L. (1997). Corrective feedback and learner uptake: Negotiation of form in communicative classrooms. *Studies in Second Language Acquisition*, 19(1), 37–66.

Lyster, R., Saito, K. & Sato, M. (2013). Oral corrective feedback in second language classrooms. *Language Teaching*, 46(1), 1–40.

Macaro, E., Curle, S., Pun, J., An, J. & Dearden, J. (2018). A systematic review of English-medium instruction in higher education. *Language Teaching*, 51(1), 36–76.

Mariotti, C. (2006). Negotiated interactions and repair. *VIEWS Vienna English Working Papers*, 15, 33–41.

May, S. & Hill, R. (2005). Māori-medium education: Current issues and challenges. *International Journal of Bilingual Education and Bilingualism*, 8(5), 377–403.

Met, M. (1998). Curriculum decision-making in content-based second language teaching. In J. Cenoz & F. Genesee (eds.), *Beyond bilingualism:*

Multilingualism and multilingual education (pp. 35–63). Clevedon: Multilingual Matters.

Milla, R. & García Mayo, M. P. (2014). Corrective feedback episodes in oral interaction: A comparison of a CLIL and an EFL classroom. *International Journal of English Studies, 14*(1), 1–20.

Morton, T. & Llinares, A. (2017). Content and language integrated learning (CLIL): Type of programme or pedagogical model? In A. Llinares & T. Morton (eds.), *Applied linguistics perspectives on CLIL* (pp. 1–18). Amsterdam: John Benjamins.

Nassaji, H. & Swain, M. (2000). A Vygotskyan perspective on corrective feedback in L2: The effect of random versus negotiated help on the learning of English articles. *Language Awareness, 9*(1), 34–51.

Netten, J. & Spain, W. (1989). Student-teacher interaction patterns in the French immersion classroom: Implications for level of achievement in French language proficiency. *Canadian Modern Language Review, 45*(3), 485–501.

Nishimuro, M. & Borg, S. (2013). Teacher cognition and grammar teaching in a Japanese high school. *JALT Journal, 35*(1), 29–50.

Oliver, R., Sato, M., Ballinger, S. & Pan, L. (2019). Content and Language Integrated Learning classes for child Mandarin L2 learners: A longitudinal observational study. In M. Sato & S. Loewen (eds.), *Evidence-based second language pedagogy: A collection of instructed second language acquisition studies* (pp. 81–102). New York: Routledge.

Pahissa, I. & Tragant, E. (2009). Grammar and the non-native secondary school teacher in Catalonia. *Language Awareness, 18*(1), 47–60.

Palmer, D., Ballinger, S. & Peter, L. (2014). Classroom interaction in one-way, two-way, and indigenous immersion contexts. *Journal of Immersion and Content-Based Language Education, 2*(2), 225–240.

Pérez-Cañado, M. L. (2012). CLIL research in Europe: Past, present, and future. *International Journal of Bilingual Education and Bilingualism, 15*(3), 315–341.

(2016). Teacher training needs for bilingual education: in-service teacher perceptions. *International Journal of Bilingual Education and Bilingualism, 19*(3), 266–295.

Peter, L. (2014). Language ideologies and Cherokee revitalization: Impracticality, legitimacy, and hope. *Journal of Immersion and Content-Based Language Education, 2*(1), 96–118.

Philp, J., Adams, R. & Iwashita, N. (2014). *Peer interaction and second language learning*. New York: Routledge.

Pica, T. (2002). Subject matter content: How does it assist the interactional and linguistic needs of second language learners? *Modern Language Journal, 86*, 1–19.

Potowski, K. (2007). *Language and identity in a dual immersion school*. Clevedon: Multilingual Matters.

Salomone, A. (1992). Immersion teachers' pedagogical beliefs and practices: Results of a descriptive analysis. In E. Bernhardt (ed.), *Life in language immersion classrooms* (pp. 9–44). Clevedon: Multilingual Matters.

Sato, M. (2011). Constitution of form-orientation: Contributions of context and explicit knowledge to learning from recasts. *Canadian Journal of Applied Linguistics*, 14(1), 1–28.

(2017). Oral peer corrective feedback: Multiple theoretical perspectives. In H. Nassaji & E. Kartchava (eds.), *Corrective feedback in second language teaching and learning: Research, theory, applications, implications* (pp. 19–34). New York: Routledge.

Sato, M. & Ballinger, S. (2016). Understanding peer interaction: Research synthesis and directions. In M. Sato & S. Ballinger (eds.), *Peer interaction and second language learning: Pedagogical potential and research agenda* (pp. 1–30). Amsterdam: John Benjamins.

Sato, M. & Lyster, R. (2012). Peer interaction and corrective feedback for accuracy and fluency development: Monitoring, practice, and proceduralization. *Studies in Second Language Acquisition*, 34(4), 591–626.

Sheen, Y. (2004). Corrective feedback and learner uptake across instructional settings. *Language Teaching Research*, 8(3), 263–300.

Spack, R. (1997). The acquisition of academic literacy in a second language: A longitudinal case study. *Written Communication*, 14(1), 3–62.

Spada, N. (2007). Communicative language teaching: Current status and future projects. In J. Cummins & C. Davison (eds.), *International handbook of English language teaching* (pp. 271–288). New York: Springer.

Swain, M. (2001). Integrating language and content teaching through collaborative tasks. *Canadian Modern Language Review*, 58(1), 44–64.

Swain, M. & Johnson, R. (1997). Immersion education: A category within second language education. In M. Swain and R. Johnson (eds.), *Immersion education: International Perspectives* (pp. 1–16). New York: Cambridge University Press.

Swain, M. & Lapkin, S. (1998). Interaction and second language learning: Two adolescent French immersion students working together. *Modern Language Journal*, 82(3), 320–337.

(2002). Talking it through: Two French immersion learners' response to reformulation. *International Journal of Educational Research*, 37(3–4), 285–304.

Tedick, D. & Zilmer, C. (2018). Teacher perceptions of immersion professional development experiences emphasizing language-focused content instruction. *Journal of Immersion and Content-Based Language Education*, 6(2), 269–294.

Van Kampen, E., Meirink, J., Admiraal, W. & Berry, A. (2017). Do we all share the same values on content and language integrated learning (CLIL)? Specialist and practitioner perceptions of 'ideal' CLIL pedagogies in the Netherlands. *International Journal of Bilingual Education and Bilingualism.* DOI:10.1080/13670050.2017.1411332.

Wilson, W. & Kamana, K. (2011). Insights from indigenous language immersion in Hawai'i. In D. J. Tedick, D. Christian & T. Williams Fortune (eds.), *Immersion Education: Practices, Policies, Possibilities* (pp.36–57). Tonawanda, NY: Multilingual Matters.

Yaghoubinejad, H., Zarrinabadi, N. & Nejadansari, D. (2017). Culture-specificity of teacher demotivation: Iranian junior high school teachers caught in the newly-introduced CLT trap! *Teachers and Teaching, 23* (2), 127–140.

Yang, J. (2016). Learners' oral corrective feedback preferences in relation to their cultural background, proficiency level, and types of error. *System, 61,* 75–86.

Part VII

Learners' and Teachers' Feedback Perspectives, Perceptions, and Preferences

26

Teachers' and Students' Beliefs and Perspectives about Corrective Feedback

YouJin Kim and Tamanna Mostafa

Introduction

Over the last few decades, corrective feedback has received a lot of attention among second language researchers and practitioners from various theoretical perspectives in subfields of applied linguistics such as second language acquisition (SLA) and second language (L2) writing (see Bitchener & Storch, 2016). Several meta-analyses on corrective feedback (CF) have offered systematic and comprehensive syntheses of empirical research on the various aspects of CF (Brown, 2016; Kang & Han, 2015; Li, 2010; Lyster & Saito, 2010; Russell & Spada, 2006). There has also been scholarly interest in whether and how teachers' and learners' beliefs or attitudes toward CF impact the efficacy of CF (see Li, 2017). Beliefs are defined as ideas that people hold as true, that are implicit, have "a strong evaluative and affective component, provide a basis for action, and are resistant to change" (Borg, 2011, p. 370). Learners' beliefs have been identified as an important individual difference variable, and both teachers' and learners' beliefs have been investigated in relation to their implications for classroom pedagogical practices (Kamiya, 2016; Loewen et al., 2009). The purpose of the current chapter is to discuss teachers' and students' beliefs of oral and written CF. As Li (2017) mentions, there are fundamental differences between oral and written CF. Thus, the findings from the two fields are not comparable, and each topic needs to be examined on its own. Because of the scope of this chapter, our discussion on CF focuses on CF that is provided by teachers rather than peers. In particular, we focus on how teachers' and learners' beliefs about oral and written CF impact feedback provision practices, and uptake or response behavior, respectively.

Oral CF

Beliefs about oral CF have been investigated from both teachers' and students' perspectives (Bell, 2005; Brown, 2009; Li, 2017; Loewen et al., 2009; Mori, 2011; Oladejo, 1993; Ozmen & Aydın, 2015; Schulz, 1996, 2001; Vásquez & Harvey, 2010; Yang, 2016). In many cases, as with written CF studies, there have been discrepancies between teachers' stated beliefs about oral CF and their actual classroom practices (Basturkmen, Loewen & Ellis, 2004; Dilāns, 2016; Oskoz & Liskin-Gasparro, 2001). Additionally, learners' beliefs about oral CF have been shown to be influenced by different variables such as first language (L1) backgrounds, cultural differences, and individual difference factors such as proficiency and anxiety (Rassaei, 2015; Yang, 2016; Zhang & Rahimi, 2014).

Teachers' Beliefs about Oral CF

Most of the studies on teachers' beliefs about oral CF found discrepancies between teachers' beliefs and their actual classroom practices related to the use of different types of oral CF. Dilāns (2016) investigated teachers' beliefs about providing oral CF to learners of Latvian as an L2 and examined the relationships between those beliefs and the teachers' classroom practices of CF. The results showed that whereas in a survey, the teachers indicated that they used both elicitation and recasts equally as frequently, in their actual classroom practice, recasts alone accounted for 72 percent of the total instances of CF whereas elicitations accounted for only 13 percent. Similarly, in Dong (2012), although there were some congruences between oral CF beliefs and the practices of the two participating teachers of Chinese at a US university, there were also mismatches. For example, although the teachers expressed beliefs about instigating learners' self-repair, this belief was not reflected in the most frequent CF strategy used by them, which was recast. Oskoz and Liskin-Gasparro (2001) and Roothooft (2014) also found similar discrepancies between teacher's beliefs about CF and their actual CF practices in the classroom context. Oskoz and Liskin-Gasparro explored how the beliefs of one teacher about CF corresponded to her instructional practices in a Spanish as a Foreign Language context. The findings showed that contrary to her stated beliefs, the teacher provided CF to the majority of student errors in class. Likewise, Roothooft found that English as a Foreign Language (EFL) teachers' beliefs about the importance of fluency-based activities and methods of providing oral CF did not match their actual classroom practices. For example, whereas five of the ten teacher participants expressed beliefs against providing students with correct answers as feedback, the most frequent feedback type they used was recast.

In a similar vein, Basturkmen et al. (2004) investigated three intermediate-level English as a Second Language (ESL) teachers' beliefs about communicative language teaching and their provision of CF during focus-on-form episodes in which they had to make online decisions while interacting with students. Basturkmen et al. used three self-report data collection methods (interview, cued-response scenario, and stimulated recall) to indirectly investigate the teachers' beliefs. The study found that some of the teachers' beliefs matched their CF practices, for example, their lack of interest in student-initiated form-focused episodes. However, the results also showed that some of their beliefs differed from practice. For instance, contrary to their belief in providing CF to only the meaning-related errors, all the teachers chose to provide teacher-initiated feedback in the absence of any student error, and they also justified that feedback during the stimulated recall sessions. A clear distinction emerged between the beliefs that the teachers explicitly expressed and were aware of having ("technical knowledge") and the beliefs that were implicitly expressed in their behavior ("practical knowledge"; Basturkmen et al., 2004, p. 268). Basturkmen et al. argued that "enquiry into teachers' beliefs of unplanned elements of teaching needs to be based on both stated beliefs and observed behaviors" (p. 269). However, in research on teacher cognition, teacher beliefs about oral CF have usually been investigated separately from teachers' behaviors in the classroom.

Many studies have also investigated the effects of experience on teachers' cognition (see Li, 2017 for review). Basturkmen et al. (2004) argued that experience may help teachers to proceduralize their technical knowledge, which might lead to the disappearance of discrepancies between their beliefs and practice. However, Kamiya (2016) found mismatches between beliefs and practices for the most experienced teacher, whereas for the other three teachers, there was agreement between their beliefs and instructional practices. Hence, Kamiya refuted the idea expressed in Basturkmen et al. (2004) that the proceduralization of technical knowledge through experience can result in harmony between teachers' stated beliefs and classroom practices. In this regard, Kamiya proposed that the relationship between teachers' stated beliefs and their classroom practices might be "fluid rather than fixed" (p. 217). In their case study on two ESL teachers (one novice and one experienced), Junqueira and Kim (2013) found that compared to the novice, the experienced teacher used more diverse types of CF with learners, was more balanced in providing CF on different linguistic targets, and provided more CF overall, thus creating more learning opportunities. Interestingly, although they provided CF in class, which they perceived as part of communicating with learners, neither of the teachers believed in the efficacy of oral CF in oral communication class where fluency was the main focus of lessons. Additionally, their experience and previous educational training had no impact on this belief.

Rahimi and Zhang (2015) found significant differences between novice and experienced teachers' cognitions about the provision of CF in oral communication classes. Interviews with the experienced teachers revealed that their previous teaching experiences helped them be more conscious about the effects of different contextual, learner, and linguistic variables on the effectiveness of classroom CF compared to the novice teachers. In line with the findings of Junqueira and Kim (2013), Rahimi and Zhang (2015) also did not find any effect of formal teacher education instruction on either group of teachers' beliefs. These research findings support Kennedy's (1997) argument that changes in teachers' beliefs might not be caused by simply getting information or knowledge from a source. However, although previous educational and teaching experience might not have a strong impact on teachers' stated beliefs about oral CF, they may nevertheless positively impact teachers' practical efficiency in providing oral CF or enhance their awareness in this regard (Junqueira & Kim, 2013; Kamiya, 2016; Rahimi & Zhang, 2015).

In terms of the role of teacher training, Kamiya and Loewen (2014) investigated the effect of reading three academic articles about oral CF on the beliefs of an ESL teacher. The findings showed that being exposed to scholarly papers on oral CF did not cause any changes in the teacher's stated beliefs about CF. However, the act of reading the articles raised teacher's consciousness about using oral CF in the classroom, which might have some positive pedagogical implications (Kamiya & Loewen, 2014). Whereas the participant in Kamiya and Loewen's study was exposed to only academic articles, the participants in Vásquez and Harvey (2010) took part in a classroom-based research replication project, which affected their beliefs about oral CF. In Vásquez and Harvey, nine graduate students replicated Lyster and Ranta (1997)'s study on corrective feedback in Intensive English Program classes that they were teaching, and they wrote reflections on their experiences. The findings show that after participating in the replication project, the graduate students had expanded their awareness of the role of oral CF in classroom pedagogy. For example, whereas before the project they used to put more emphasis on students' feelings resulting from oral CF, after participating in the project, they developed a more sophisticated understanding of the efficacy of oral CF and of the relationship between oral CF, student uptake, and error type. Vásquez and Harvey also implied that such an expanded understanding might initiate possible changes in future teaching practices of the participants.

Similar to Vásquez and Harvey (2010), Busch (2010) found significant changes in pre-service teachers' beliefs after they participated in an introductory second language acquisition course; the changes in their beliefs were regarding several aspects of language learning such as the length of time required for learning a language, the role of error correction, and the importance of grammar. Not only were the participants in

Busch's investigation exposed to the academic course content, but each of them also had to tutor an ESL student throughout the course, both of which helped change their beliefs, as was revealed in their post-course reflections. Hence, in contrast to the participant in Kamiya and Loewen (2014)'s study who only read scholarly articles on oral CF, those in Vásquez and Harvey (2010) and Busch (2010) participated in experiential activities, such as replicating research and tutoring, which might explain why their beliefs had changed after such participation. It might be that professional coursework including both experiential and reflective components has stronger effects on teachers' belief systems than simple readings of academic articles (Busch, 2010). Li (2017) also agreed that "declarative knowledge obtained through reading the related literature must be processed and consolidated through reflective activities and proceduralized through hands-on practice activities" for the occurrence of any change in teachers' beliefs (p. 152).

One less explored area of research in this area is whether or how teachers' awareness of students' affective states influences teachers' oral CF beliefs. Li (2017)'s meta-analysis of studies on students' and teachers' beliefs about oral CF found that overall, students hold positive attitudes toward receiving oral CF, but teachers are not usually interested in providing much oral CF in the classroom. In Kamiya (2016), the four participating ESL teachers shared the belief about the necessity of creating a comfortable atmosphere for learners in the classroom, and hence, they consciously avoided any explicit oral CF for fear of embarrassing the students. Similarly, in Roothooft (2014), the participating teachers were sensitive to their learners' affective states while being corrected by their teachers in classroom oral CF. Likewise, in Junqueira and Kim (2013), both the novice and experienced teachers put more emphasis on communicating with learners in oral communication classes than on correcting them through feedback. Additionally, the teacher participants in Roothooft's study also believed in taking into consideration learners' personalities while giving oral CF because extrovert learners might respond to oral CF differently from introvert learners. In a similar vein, in the study by Mori (2011), the two teacher participants' provision of oral CF was influenced by variables such as time constraints, student personality, and the students' ability to communicate. Because the two teachers' prior experiences as language learners and EFL professionals also influenced their beliefs and practices of providing oral CF, Mori argued for the need to expand the scope of oral CF research to include related social, cultural, personal, and experiential factors. As previous research found mismatches between teacher and student beliefs about oral CF in instructional contexts (Brown, 2009; Lee, 2013; Li, 2017), a related question is whether taking into consideration learners' beliefs, personalities, or affective factors would help teachers provide classroom oral CF more effectively. Since research findings show that, in many cases, teachers tend to be sensitive to learners' affective or personality variables while giving oral CF, a yet-to-be-explored area of research seems to be whether tailoring oral CF to learners' affective states, beliefs about language learning, or personality traits can lead to better language learning.

Students' Beliefs about Oral CF

previous research found mismatches between teachers' beliefs and students' beliefs about oral CF (Agudo, 2014; Brown, 2009; Lee, 2013; Oladejo, 1993; Roothooft, 2014; Schulz, 1996, 2001). Lee (2013) reported that advanced-level adult ESL learners preferred to get explicit error corrections from their teachers even in the middle of conversational interactions, and hence, explicit correction was their most favored oral CF type. On the contrary, their teachers preferred to be selective while giving oral CF, as "they did not want to be forced to give error corrections when student errors occurred" (Lee, 2013, p. 224). Not surprisingly, recast was the CF type most favored by the teachers in Lee (2013). Similarly, in Oladejo (1993), both groups of ESL learners (secondary school students and university undergraduates) believed that "comprehensive, not selective" error correction was necessary for improving the accuracy and fluency of their oral communication skills (p. 78). Contrary to some widely held beliefs of teachers, the participants in Oladejo (1993) believed that grammatical accuracy should be prioritized over communication of meaning and that constant error corrections do not cause frustrations among students. In a similar vein, the ten EFL teacher participants in Roothooft (2014) expressed concerns about using too many oral CF, which can, in their opinions, not only interrupt the flow of communication in classrooms but also embarrass or frustrate students. However, those teacher-participants also recognized the value of providing oral CF as well as their learners' wish to be corrected while communicating in classrooms (Roothooft, 2014). Likewise, in Brown(2009)'s investigation of foreign language teachers' and learners' beliefs about language pedagogy, the teachers preferred meaning-focused activities with less emphasis on error correction, whereas their learners tended to prefer explicit CF and discrete grammar practices. Such disparities between teachers' and learners' beliefs is noteworthy because, as emphasized by Oladejo (1993), to ensure the effectiveness of oral CF, teachers' views and practices of oral CF need to be integrated with those of their learners. Schulz (1996) and Schulz (2001) also emphasized the need to diminish the often-existing distance between learners' beliefs and teachers' beliefs about oral CF in a language learning context for the sake of better learning.

Additionally, as research on oral CF has received growing interest over the last few decades, researchers have examined whether learners' perceptions of oral CF are influenced by various learner-internal, social, or contextual variables (Loewen et al., 2009; Rassaei 2015; Yang, 2016; Zhang &

Rahimi, 2014). These studies mainly used questionnaires, including Likert-scale items, to investigate learners' beliefs about oral CF as well as learner-internal variables, such as anxiety. Loewen et al. (2009) used questionnaire responses to investigate the beliefs of 754 foreign and second language students about grammar instruction and error correction. An exploratory factor analysis of the learners' responses to the Likert-scale questionnaire items revealed six underlying beliefs (factors) including negative attitude to error correction and negative attitude toward grammar instruction. Furthermore, learners studying various target languages differed significantly in their responses to those factors. For example, ESL learners were more interested in increasing their communication skills instead of grammar instruction and error correction compared to foreign language learners. Loewen et al. (2009) found that ESL learners, who were mostly Korean and Chinese L1 speakers, had a greater amount of previous grammar instruction compared to the foreign language learners who were mainly native English speakers. Loewen et al. (2009) argued that as the ESL learners had already had a large amount of grammar instruction in the past, they expressed their stronger interests in learning communication skills than the foreign language learners. Thus, the participants' previous educational experiences might have been a strong mediating factor on their beliefs about error correction and grammar instruction (Loewen et al., 2009).

Previous research also showed that learners' preferences for CF types were influenced by linguistic targets, learners' proficiency levels, and cultural backgrounds (Yang, 2016). In Yang (2016), learners perceived recasts as more useful CF for phonological errors than for grammatical or lexical errors. Furthermore, intermediate learners, in contrast to beginner learners, believed that clarification requests in response to pronunciation errors were effective, and explicit correction for pragmatic errors was viewed to be effective by learners from a Confucian cultural background. Yang also found that the learners' preferences for oral CF types were influenced by factors such as the linguistic features of their L1, their awareness of the corrective functions of CF, the affective states that particular CF types lead to, limited instructional time, and understanding of different cultural values.

Furthermore, learner anxiety as an individual difference variable has also been investigated as influencing learner beliefs about oral CF. Rassaei (2015) explored whether sixty upper-intermediate EFL learners' perceptions of recast and metalinguistic feedback were affected by their foreign language anxiety in the classroom. Based on the output of an anxiety questionnaire, the participants were placed in either a high- or low-anxiety group. The participants received oral CF during task-based interactions with interlocutors, and their perceptions of oral CF were investigated through stimulated recall interviews. The findings revealed that the low-anxiety participants were more successful in noticing the gap between their erroneous productions and the target-like forms, and they were also more successful in noticing both recasts and metalinguistic feedback as corrective feedback than the high-anxiety group.

On the contrary, Zhang and Rahimi (2014) did not find anxiety to be a mediating variable on learners' beliefs about oral CF. Zhang and Rahimi divided 160 Iranian EFL learner participants into high- and low-anxiety groups based on their responses on the five-point Likert-type foreign language classroom anxiety scale. The study did not find any significant difference between the high-anxiety and low-anxiety groups in their beliefs about CF. However, data on the CF beliefs in Zhang and Rahimi were only collected through a Likert-type scale. Inclusion of open-ended interview questions or stimulated recall methodology might have revealed richer insights about how learners of different anxiety groups perceive oral CF types in a classroom context. Rassaei (2015) and Zhang and Rahimi also had contradictory findings regarding the influence of anxiety on learner beliefs, which could be attributed to the methodological differences between the two studies. Future studies could use different methodological approaches, such as stimulated recall interviews and questionnaires, to measure learner anxiety and investigate to what extent it influences learners' beliefs and noticing of oral CF.

How Students' Beliefs about Oral CF Affect Learning Opportunities or Learning Outcomes

So far only a few studies have investigated how learners' beliefs can be related to learning opportunities. These studies have explored the noticing of CF, production of uptake/repair, and learning outcomes in instructional contexts (Akiyama, 2017; Kartchava & Ammar, 2013; Lee, 2013; Sheen, 2007). Lee (2013) investigated both teachers' and advanced ESL students' preferences or beliefs about oral CF. In Lee's study, teachers' and students' beliefs were investigated through questionnaires that included a Likert questionnaire, a rank of preferences for different CF types, and open-ended questions, follow-up interviews, and classroom observation. The findings revealed dissimilarities between the learners' preferred feedback type and the CF that the teachers provided in the classroom. For example, learners' most preferred feedback type was explicit correction, but in the class the most frequent CF type was a recast, which generated the highest percentage of learner repair (92.09 percent). Moreover, whereas 90.63 percent of clarification requests elicited learner repairs, these were the students' least preferred CF type, since they perceived clarification requests as "vague and unclear corrections" (p. 226). Hence, if learners' production of repair can be taken as an indication of their noticing of feedback, then the findings of Lee (2013) suggest that for learners to notice teachers' CF, their beliefs about CF do not necessarily need to be matched with the actual CF they receive in the classroom.

On the contrary, Akiyama (2017) had a different finding in her investigation on how learners' beliefs were related to CF practices in a fourteen-week-long instructional project using video chat between Japan and the USA. The participants were twelve learners of Japanese in the USA and twelve learners of English in Japan. Learners' beliefs were investigated through online survey questionnaires (from all participants) and interviews (from five selected participants). This mixed-method study found recast to be the preferred mode of CF by the participants, whose successful uptake rates were the highest when the CF they received matched their beliefs. However, learners' successful uptake may not be indicative of their learning even though successful uptake might signal that they have noticed feedback (Mackey & Philp, 1998; Nassaji, 2011). In this regard, both Sheen (2007) and Kartchava and Ammar (2013) examined the relationship between learners' attitude towards or beliefs about oral CF and their L2 learning.

Sheen (2007) investigated whether two learner individual variables – aptitude for language learning and attitude toward error correction – could mediate the participants' learning of English articles after they received two types of oral CF: recast and metalinguistic correction. Eighty participants in five intact classes were divided into three groups – recast, metalinguistic correction, and control – and completed both the aptitude tests and the attitude or belief questionnaire. The study found that for the participants in the metalinguistic CF group, who outperformed both the recast and the control groups, only the immediate post-test scores were significantly related to their attitudes to error correction. Yet for the recast group, who did not have significantly better scores than the control group, there was no significant relationship between their test scores and their attitudes towards error correction. However, in Sheen (2007), the participants completed the beliefs questionnaire after participating in the treatment sessions. Therefore, it is not clear whether their participation in the specific treatment sessions influenced their attitudes or beliefs toward oral CF. It is possible that those in the metalinguistic correction group noticed the feedback because they were provided with both the correction and metalinguistic information. Therefore, this experience might have affected their responses on the questionnaire and their test scores. On the contrary, those in the recast group might not have noticed recasts on a non-salient target form such as English articles. As a result, they couldn't improve their test scores over the control group, and there was no relationship between those scores and their attitudes to oral CF (Sheen, 2007).

Contrary to Sheen (2007), Kartchava and Ammar (2013) investigated not only noticing of oral CF and L2 learning but also the mediating effect of learner beliefs on these two variables. They measured learner beliefs using a questionnaire of forty statements. Using a Likert scale that ranged from one to five, the participants had to express the extent to which they agreed with each statement. Three ESL teachers and ninety-nine high-beginner ESL students participated in the experimental intervention in which they were divided into four groups: recast, prompt, mixed (prompt and recast), and control. The two target forms were past tense and questions. The treatment consisted of two 120-minute sessions during which the participants engaged in communicative tasks. To measure the noticeability of CF, Kartchava and Ammar used immediate recall during class activities and lesson reflection sheets as well as implemented two tasks for target forms before and immediately after the intervention. To examine common themes in the participants' beliefs, Kartchava and Ammar conducted an exploratory factor analysis on the participants' questionnaire responses. A Pearson analysis of correlation found a significant positive relation between learner beliefs about the importance of CF and effectiveness of recast and noticing. These findings suggest that if learners believe in the efficacy of a non-salient feedback technique such as recast, they are more likely to notice it. However, no such significant relation was found between beliefs and learning. Kartchava and Ammar attribute the lack of relationship between beliefs and learning to the inadequacy of the Likert scale responses in capturing a complex mental construct such as learner beliefs. They also argue that including a delayed post-test in the study design might have yielded a different result because it might take time for beliefs to exert any influence on learning outcomes. Neither Sheen nor Kartchava and Ammar found any significant relationship between learner beliefs and L2 learning (except for the metalinguistic correction group's gain on only the immediate post-test in Sheen, 2007). As Ellis (2008) argued, whether learners will act on their beliefs can be influenced by different factors such as context or lack of personal motivation. Such an indirect connection between beliefs and learning outcomes might explain the lack of relationship between these two variables in Sheen and Kartchava and Ammar.

Another important consideration is that learners' beliefs might not be static and might change over time (Ellis, 2008; Leontjev, 2016). Addressing this dynamic nature of learners' beliefs might prove to be crucial for ensuring the validity of studies that examine the relationship between beliefs and L2 learning. However, there is a scarcity of studies that take the dynamic nature of the belief construct into consideration. Leontjev (2016) is an exception in this regard. In the framework of sociocultural theory, Leontjev examined how L2 learners' beliefs about oral CF are transformed by their experiences of dynamic assessment and social interactions. Leontjev reported a case study of one participant and a study of a group of six participants in the EFL context of Russia. The case study found changes in the single participant's beliefs about oral CF within a period of six months. Similarly, the findings from the group study also suggest alterations in the participants' oral CF beliefs over the course of one research interview. These changes in beliefs were attributed to the learners' own experiences of receiving teachers' feedback and others' social interaction experiences during the group interviews and mediation. However, Leontjev (2016) did not relate such changes in beliefs to the students' learning opportunities or learning outcomes. Similarly, Akiyama (2017) captured the dynamic nature of beliefs by collecting online survey data multiple times (before, during, and after the project using video chat), reporting changes in the students' beliefs over these three periods. For example, over the period of fourteen weeks, there was a considerable increase in the number of participants who wanted to be corrected through recasts. Although Akiyama related learners' beliefs to their production of uptake during instructional interactions, the study did not examine the relationship between learners' beliefs and L2 learning.

Kartchava and Ammar (2013) examined such relationship, but they measured learners' beliefs using a Likert scale questionnaire, which, as the authors themselves admitted, might be too simplistic to measure learner beliefs that could be situational rather than static. Hence, future studies investigating the relation between learners' beliefs and L2 learning need to incorporate methodological innovations to tap into the dynamic construct of learner beliefs. In this regard, Ellis (2008) recommended the use of qualitative data collection methods such as interviews or diaries to measure learner beliefs over time.

Akiyama (2017) and Lee (2013) related learners' beliefs or preferences for CF types to their productions of repair (Lee, 2013) and uptake (Akiyama, 2017), which are argued to reflect learner noticing of CF. However, unlike the use of immediate recall and reflection sheets in Kartchava & Ammar (2013), neither Akiyama (2017) nor Lee (2013) used a specific method to measure learners' noticing of CF. As these studies offer mixed findings regarding the relationship between learners' beliefs about CF types and their actual noticing of that feedback (or production of uptake or repair), more research that uses specific methods for measuring learners' noticing of CF is needed. As an example, future studies might use introspective methods such as stimulated recall to investigate learner noticing of CF. Future studies might also use both quantitative and qualitative methods to examine learners' beliefs of CF and how learners' beliefs and noticing of CF are related.

Written CF

Since Truscott's (1996) article on written CF, researchers have proposed and responded to various claims about the role of written CF in students' writing development (see Bitchener & Storch, 2016 for review). However, compared to oral CF research, relatively little is known about teachers' and students' beliefs about written CF and the extent to which their beliefs translate into practice and revision behavior. While some studies have shown similar perceptions of receiving and providing written CF from both teachers and learners (Schulz, 2001), others (Amrhein & Nassaji, 2010) have found that although students wanted their teachers to correct their errors, teachers had mixed views on written CF provision.

Teachers' Beliefs about Written CF and Their Feedback Practices

One frequently asked question in the literature is regarding the relationship between teachers' beliefs and their written CF practices. Lee (2008) examined secondary school teachers' beliefs about written CF and their written CF practices in Hong Kong. Her study involved two sources: (1) teacher feedback on 174 texts provided by twenty-six secondary teachers and follow-up interviews with seven teachers, and (2) a questionnaire administered to 206 secondary teachers and follow-up interviews with nineteen of them. Lee presented ten mismatches between teachers' beliefs and feedback practices. For instance, teachers believed that good writing involves more than grammatical accuracy, but their written CF focused primarily on language form. Teachers also preferred selective written CF but provided comprehensive written CF on students' writing. Additionally, teachers continued to correct student writing although they believed that their effort did not pay off. Thus, Lee's large-scale study demonstrated several gaps between teachers' beliefs and their written CF practices.

Similarly, Ferris (2014) reported survey results on college teachers' (n=129) beliefs about feedback practice at eight post-secondary institutions and follow-up interview data. The interviews focused on the teachers' philosophies and beliefs about responding to students' errors. The results showed that the teachers believed in the value of individualized and conventional feedback. According to the findings, "teachers' approaches ranged from the noble (empower students as individual writers) to the compassionate (build students' confidence in themselves) to the pragmatic (manage the time demands) to the cynical (just give students models to follow because they don't care much and won't exert much effort)" (p. 21). Ferris also noted convergences and mismatches between teachers' reported feedback practices and their philosophies as well as what was actually observed in their written responses. Likewise, in a Saudi university context, Alshahrani and Storch (2014) collected three teachers' feedback on forty-five students' essays (fifteen students per teacher) and conducted interviews with the teachers. Their study reported similar findings in that teachers' feedback practice was not always in line with their beliefs about written CF. For instance, teachers believe that vocabulary should be the main focus of the feedback, whereas the majority of their feedback focused on mechanics, which they were unaware of.

A longitudinal case study approach to examining teachers' beliefs has been widely adopted in the literature. For instance, Min (2013) examined a Chinese writing teacher's beliefs about and practices of written CF by triangulating various data sources, including learning logs, reflection journal entries, and the teacher's feedback on the students' first and last papers on two different topics over a semester. The findings show that there was a structural change in the teacher's belief system. At the beginning of the semester, four guiding principles underlying her beliefs included clarifying writers' intentions, identifying problems, explaining problems, and making specific suggestions. However, by the end of the semester, her focus had shifted from fixing students' errors to understanding students' belief systems in more complex ways.

Junqueira and Payant (2015) also reported a one-semester-long contextualized case study which focused on one novice teacher's beliefs about written CF and her practices in a university ESL writing class. The case study results, which were based on a reflective journal, interviews, and the teacher's (Kim) feedback practices, showed a complex set of beliefs toward CF. The results showed that Kim did not always apply her beliefs about CF to her own practice, which is in line with the findings of previous studies (e.g., Lee, 2008). Similar to the in-service teachers in Lee's (2008) study, Kim also believed that CF provision takes a lot of time and is a tedious process. However, Kim adopted a coping strategy to deal with time constraint issues over the semester. For instance, the finding showed that 80.6 percent of her written CF moves focusing on local issues did not involve any explanations. Over the semester, Kim realized that feedback provision requires practice, and that it is crucial for her students' success in L2 writing. The findings of Junqueira and Payant highlight that beliefs are not static and as teachers gain experience, their beliefs toward CF changes and new beliefs evolve. Building on teacher cognition research (Borg, 2006), Junqueira and Payant did not perceive a mismatch between teacher beliefs about written CF and their practice as a negative phenomenon, but rather as an exciting opportunity for a deeper exploration of teacher cognition on CF. Junqueira and Payant also addressed important implications for reflectivity in longitudinal teacher education studies, particularly when topics that involve dynamic changes such as CF are explored.

Overall, previous research on the relationships between writing teachers' beliefs and practices have often pointed out mismatches (Lee, 2008; Min, 2013; Montgomery & Baker, 2007; Phipps & Borg, 2009). Additionally, as teachers gain experience with feedback practice, their beliefs and practice change over time. Accordingly, researchers have suggested that such mismatches should not be criticized, but instead be treated as opportunities for understanding teacher cognition and teaching.

Learners' Perceptions of Written CF and Their Revision Behavior

Within the research domain of perceptions of written CF, the examination of learners' perspectives is the least explored area. It is known that many L2 learners prefer teacher or expert feedback over peer written CF. Previous studies often used surveys to collect information on learner perceptions of written CF (Grami, 2005; Lee, 2004, 2008; Leki, 2006). These studies cover various instructional contexts including secondary school learners in Hong Kong (Lee, 2008), Saudi adult learners (Grami, 2005), and adult learners in the USA (Leki, 2006). In general, studies have shown that learners expect to receive written CF and have positive perceptions of it, particularly in the usefulness of written CF (Schulz, 2001). However, various factors, such as feedback type, learners' beliefs, or goals, have been shown to impact learner uptake or processing of written CF. For instance, in Storch and Wigglesworth (2010), one group of students received editing symbols and another group received reformulations as written CF types on essays that they wrote in pairs in response to a graphic prompt. The students' pair-talk during writing and in response to the CF they had received was analyzed for their processing and preferences or beliefs of the CF. Storch and Wigglesworth found that although editing instigated greater attention to CF and focus on form and uptake, reformulation helped the learners internalize the correct language forms. Furthermore, learners' affective factors, their goals, beliefs, and attitudes toward the CF influenced their retention of that CF.

In addition, there have been studies comparing teachers' and students' beliefs or perceptions regarding written CF. Amrhein and Nassaji (2010) conducted a survey study with thirty-three adult ESL students and thirty-one ESL teachers at two private English institutions in Canada. In order to compare students' and teachers' preferences for written CF and their reasons for such preferences, the researchers designed parallel questionnaires. The questionnaires focused on the participants' preferences for the amount and types of written CF as well as other conditions of feedback, such as the use of comments or the provision of clues, as a part of written CF. The results showed both similarities and differences between teachers and students in terms of their preferences in the provision of written CF. For instance, students preferred to receive written CF on as many errors as possible and particularly emphasized the importance of grammatical errors. However, although teachers also valued the importance of written CF, they discriminated between errors that they thought were more or less important to address. Furthermore, while students showed preferences for larger amounts of error correction on all error types, teachers were more selective and focused more on communication accuracy. Similar perceptions between the two groups include the pedagogical value of written CF and the importance of providing feedback to repeatedly occurring errors each time they are made.

One of the major lines of research in this area is to examine the relationship between learners' beliefs about written CF and learners' engagement with feedback. Han and Hyland (2015) reported multi-case studies with four non-English-major Chinese EFL learners and examined their engagement with written CF, using three dimensions (i.e., cognitive engagement, behavioral engagement, affective engagement). The data were collected over five weeks in a level three English class in a Chinese university context. The students wrote a letter to a friend, and their instructor provided various types of feedback (e.g., indirect written CF with revision clues, indirect written CF with clarification requests, and direct written CF). The researcher observed the class and interviewed both the instructor and the student participants at the beginning and the end of the research periods and collected class artifacts (e.g., syllabus, grading rubrics). The students also participated in a retrospective verbal report within 24 hours of their producing the final draft of their letter. With regards to learners' beliefs about written CF, the findings suggest that the students' L2 learning goals and beliefs about the effectiveness of written CF had a substantial impact on their use of meta-cognitive operations and how much they were willing to engage with written CF.

Han (2017) also examined how learners' beliefs mediate learners' engagement with written CF and to what extent learners' experience with written CF mediates their beliefs over time. The multiple-case study reported in Han revealed that, in general, learners' beliefs about written CF mediate their engagement with it both directly and indirectly. For instance, learners' emotional reactions to written CF, their use of external resources, and revision operations were impacted by their beliefs. Han also highlights the nonlinear relationship between learners' beliefs and learners' engagement with written CF and discusses L2 learners' often inconsistent and contradictory beliefs. In Han, the students' beliefs also changed as they became more experienced in processing and using written CF. Over time the students developed a more sophisticated view of written CF in terms of its benefits on improving drafts, enhancing written accuracy, and facilitating L2 development (Han, 2017). Han's study shed valuable insights into learners' beliefs about written CF in that the study reported longitudinal data (sixteen weeks) and captured how learners' beliefs can change.

Conclusion

Because of the emerging trend of dynamic complexity theory in applied linguistics and in SLA, learners' beliefs, in addition to other individual characteristics, are conceptualized as having both a static, trait-like dimension, and a situated, dynamic dimension (Han, 2017). From reviewing previous research on learners' and teachers' beliefs about oral and written CF, a clear pattern has emerged, in that researchers have begun to examine oral and written CF over time to capture the situational and dynamic patterns of learners' and teachers' beliefs. For example, in the literature on oral CF, there are studies that collect data on learners' beliefs multiple times to investigate any changes in those beliefs (Akiyama, 2017; Leontjev, 2016), but the way such dynamicity in learner beliefs is related to L2 learning has not yet been investigated. In terms of research methodology, studies which used either mixed or qualitative methods have contributed to disseminating detailed descriptions of changes in learners' and teachers' beliefs, and of how beliefs and feedback practices (for teachers) or engagement with feedback (for learners) are connected. There have also been arguments in the literature for using qualitative data collection methods for investigating a complex cognitive construct such as beliefs (Ellis, 2008).

The current literature, particularly within the domain of written CF, is still limited in that only a limited type of writing genre has been implemented in research, and a variety of writing prompts in different instructional contexts need to be explored. Furthermore, how teachers' and learners' beliefs about CF are converging and diverging from each other needs to be examined more systematically (e.g., Amrhein & Nassaji, 2010). Moreover, in the literature on oral CF, the relation between learners' beliefs, learners' noticing of CF, and L2 learning is still underexplored. Future research needs to use sophisticated data collection methods such as immediate or stimulated recall to investigate learners' noticing of oral CF during classroom interaction and open-ended interview questions for measuring learners/teachers' beliefs in this regard.

References

Agudo, J. D. D. M. (2014). Beliefs in learning to teach: EFL student teachers' beliefs about corrective feedback. *Utrecht Studies in Language and Communication*, (27), 209.

Akiyama, Y. (2017). Learner beliefs and corrective feedback in telecollaboration: A longitudinal investigation. *System, 64*, 58–73.

Alshahrani, A. & Storch, N. (2014). Investigating teachers' written corrective feedback practices in a Saudi EFL context. *Australian Review of Applied Linguistics, 37*(2), 101–122.

Amrhein, H. R. & Nassaji, H. (2010). Written corrective feedback: What do students and teachers think is right and why? *Canadian Journal of Applied Linguistics/Revue Canadienne de Linguistique Appliquee, 13*(2), 95–127.

Basturkmen, H., Loewen, S. & Ellis, R. (2004). Teachers' stated beliefs about incidental focus on form and their classroom practices. *Applied Linguistics, 25*(2), 243–272.

Bell, T. R. (2005). Behaviors and attitudes of effective foreign language teachers: Results of a questionnaire study. *Foreign Language Annals, 38* (2), 259–270.

Bitchener, J. & Storch, N. (2016). *Written corrective feedback for L2 development.* Bristol: Multilingual Matters.

Borg, S. (2006). The distinctive characteristics of foreign language teachers. *Language Teaching Research, 10*(1), 3–31.

— (2011). The impact of in-service teacher education on language teachers' beliefs. *System, 39*(3), 370–380.

Brown, A. V. (2009). Students' and teachers' perceptions of effective foreign language teaching: A comparison of ideals. *Modern Language Journal, 93*(1), 46–60.

Brown, D. (2016). The type and linguistic foci of oral corrective feedback in the L2 classroom: A meta-analysis. *Language Teaching Research, 20*(4), 436–458.

Busch, D. (2010). Pre-service teacher beliefs about language learning: The second language acquisition course as an agent for change. *Language Teaching Research, 14*(3), 318–337.

Cathcart, R. L. & Olsen, J. E. W. B. (1976). Teachers' and students' preferences for correction of classroom conversation errors. In J. F. Fanselow & R. Crymes (eds.), *On TESOL 76* (pp. 41–53). Washington, DC: TESOL.

Dilāns, G. (2016). Corrective feedback in L2 Latvian classrooms: Teacher perceptions versus the observed actualities of practice. *Language Teaching Research, 20*(4), 479–497.

Dong, Z. (2012). Beliefs and practices: A case study on oral corrective feedback in the teaching Chinese as a foreign language (TCFL) classroom. MA thesis, Arizona State University.

Ellis, R. (2008). Learner beliefs and language learning. *Asian EFL Journal, 10* (4), 7–25.

Ferris, D. R. (2014). Responding to student writing: Teachers' philosophies and practices. *Assessing Writing, 19*, 6–23.

Grami, M. (2005). The effect of teachers' written feedback on ESL students' perception: A study in a Saudi ESL university-level context. *Annual Review of Education, Communication and Language Sciences*, 1–12.

Han, Y. (2017). Mediating and being mediated: Learner beliefs and learner engagement with written corrective feedback. *System, 69*, 133–142.

Han, Y. & Hyland, F. (2015). Exploring learner engagement with written corrective feedback in a Chinese tertiary EFL classroom. *Journal of Second Language Writing, 30*, 31–44.

Junqueira, L. & Kim, Y. (2013). Exploring the relationship between training, beliefs, and teachers' corrective feedback practices: A case study of a novice and an experienced ESL teacher. *Canadian Modern Language Review, 69*(2), 181–206.

Junqueira, L. & Payant, C. (2015). "I just want to do it right, but it's so hard": A novice teacher's written feedback beliefs and practices. *Journal of Second Language Writing, 27,* 19–36.

Kamiya, N. (2016). The relationship between stated beliefs and classroom practices of oral corrective feedback. *Innovation in Language Learning and Teaching, 10*(3), 206–219.

Kamiya, N. & Loewen, S. (2014). The influence of academic articles on an ESL teacher's stated beliefs. *Innovation in Language Learning and Teaching, 8*(3), 205–218.

Kang, E. & Han, Z. (2015). The efficacy of written corrective feedback in improving L2 written accuracy: A meta-analysis. *Modern Language Journal, 99*(1), 1–18.

Kartchava, E. & Ammar, A. (2013). Learner beliefs as mediator of what is noticed and learned in language classrooms. *TESOL Quarterly, 48*(1), 86–109.

Kennedy, M. (1997). The connection between research and practice. *Educational Researcher, 26,* 4–12.

Larsen-Freeman, D. (2011). Complex dynamic systems: A new transdisciplinary theme for applied linguistics? *Language Teaching, 45,* 202–214.

Lee, E. J. E. (2013). Corrective feedback preferences and learner repair among advanced ESL students. *System, 41*(2), 217–230.

Lee, I. (2004). Error correction in L2 secondary writing classrooms: The case of Hong Kong. *Journal of Second Language Writing, 13,* 285–312.

 (2008). Ten mismatches between teachers' beliefs and written feedback practice. *ELT Journal,63*(1), 13–22.

Leki, I. (2006). "You cannot ignore": Graduate L2 students' experience of and response to written feedback practices within their disciplines. In K. Hyland & F. Hyland (eds.), *Feedback in ESL writing: Contexts and issues* (pp. 266–285). Cambridge: Cambridge University Press.

Leontjev, D. (2016). Exploring and reshaping learners' beliefs about the usefulness of corrective feedback: A sociocultural perspective. *International Journal of Applied Linguistics, 167*(1), 46–77.

Li, S. (2010). The effectiveness of corrective feedback in SLA: A meta-analysis. *Language Learning, 60*(2), 309–365.

 (2017). Teacher and learner beliefs about corrective feedback. In H. Nassaji & E. Kartchava (eds.), *Corrective feedback in second language teaching and learning: Research, theory, applications, implications* (pp. 143–157). New York: Routledge.

Loewen, S., Li, S., Fei, F., Thompson, A., Nakatsukasa, K., Ahn, S. & Chen, X. (2009). Second language learners' beliefs about grammar instruction and error correction. *Modern Language Journal, 93*(1), 91–104.

Lyster, R. & Ranta, L. (1997). Corrective feedback and learner uptake: Negotiation of form in communicative classrooms. *Studies in Second Language Acquisition*, 19(1), 37–66.

Lyster, R. & Saito, K. (2010). Oral feedback in classroom SLA: A meta-analysis. *Studies in Second Language Acquisition*, 32(2), 265–302.

Mackey, A. & Philp, J. (1998). Conversational interaction and second language development: Recast, responses, and red herrings? *Modern Language Journal*, 82, 338–356.

Min, H. T. (2013). A case study of an EFL writing teacher's belief and practice about written feedback. *System*, 41(3), 625–638.

Montgomery, J. L. & Baker, W. (2007). Teacher-written feedback: Student perceptions, teacher self-assessment, and actual teacher performance. *Journal of Second Language Writing*, 16(2), 82–99.

Mori, R. (2011). Teacher cognition in corrective feedback in Japan. *System*, 39(4), 451–467.

Nassaji, H. (2011). Immediate learner repair and its relationship with learning targeted forms in dyadic interaction. *System*, 39, 17–29.

Oladejo, J. A. (1993). Error correction in ESL: Learner's preferences. *TESL Canada Journal*, 10(2), 71–89.

Oskoz, A. & Liskin-Gasparro, J. (2001). Corrective feedback, learner uptake, and teacher beliefs: A pilot study. In A. Oskoz & J. Liskin-Gasparro (eds.), *The past, present, and future of second language research* (pp. 209–228). Somerville, MA: Cascadilla Press.

Ozmen, K. S. & Aydın, H. Ü. (2015). Examining student teachers' beliefs about oral corrective feedback: Insights from a teacher education program in Turkey. *Australian Journal of Teacher Education*, 40(12), 141–164.

Phipps, S. & Borg, S. (2009). Exploring tensions between teachers' grammar teaching beliefs and practices. *System*, 37(3), 380–390.

Rahimi, M. & Zhang, L. J. (2015). Exploring non-native English-speaking teachers' cognitions about corrective feedback in teaching English oral communication. *System*, 55, 111–122.

Rassaei, E. (2015). The effects of foreign language anxiety on EFL learners' perceptions of oral corrective feedback. *Innovation in Language Learning and Teaching*, 9(2), 87–101.

Roothooft, H. (2014). The relationship between adult EFL teachers' oral feedback practices and their beliefs. *System*, 46, 65–79.

Russell, J. & Spada, N. (2006). The effectiveness of corrective feedback for the acquisition of L2 grammar: A meta-analysis of the research. In J. Norris & L. Ortega (eds.). *Synthesizing research on language learning and teaching* (pp.133–164). Amsterdam: John Benjamins.

Schulz, R. A. (1996). Focus on form in the foreign language classroom: Students' and teachers' views on error correction and the role of grammar. *Foreign Language Annals*, 29(3), 343–364.

(2001). Cultural differences in student and teacher perceptions concerning the role of grammar instruction and corrective feedback: USA-Colombia. *Modern Language Journal*, 85(2), 244–258.

Sheen, Y. (2007). The effects of corrective feedback, language aptitude, and learner attitudes on the acquisition of English articles. In A. Mackey (ed.), *Conversational interaction in second language acquisition: A collection of empirical studies* (pp. 301–322). Oxford: Oxford University Press.

Storch, N. & Wigglesworth, G. (2010). Learners' processing, uptake, and retention of corrective feedback on writing: Case studies. *Studies in Second Language Acquisition*, 32(2), 303–334.

Truscott, J. (1996). The case against grammar correction in L2 writing classes. *Language learning*, 46(2), 327–369.

Vásquez, C. & Harvey, J. (2010). Raising teachers' awareness about corrective feedback through research replication. *Language Teaching Research*, 14(4), 421–443.

Yang, J. (2016). Learners' oral corrective feedback preferences in relation to their cultural background, proficiency level and types of error. *System*, 61, 75–86.

Zhang, L. J. & Rahimi, M. (2014). EFL learners' anxiety level and their beliefs about corrective feedback in oral communication classes. *System*, 42, 429–439.

27

Written Corrective Feedback and Learners' Objects, Beliefs, and Emotions

Neomy Storch

Introduction

Feedback provided on the writing of second language (L2) writers has received much research attention in recent years, and in particular feedback on language errors referred to as written corrective feedback (WCF). Much of this research has focused on what kind of corrective feedback is most effective. A large number of studies, for example, have compared the efficacy of direct versus indirect or targeted versus comprehensive written CF (see review in Bitchener & Storch, 2016), yielding mixed findings. The reasons for these mixed findings can be attributed to differences in research design (see synthesis in Liu & Brown, 2015) as well as how the efficacy or success of corrective feedback is defined and measured. Early studies tended to define and measure the success of written CF in terms of uptake; that is, the L2 learners' ability to incorporate the information received by the feedback and produce more accurate revised drafts. The current view among second language acquisition and L2 writing scholars (e.g., Bitchener & Ferris, 2012; Ellis, 2017; Polio, 2012) is that written CF is deemed effective if it leads to language development in the learners' writing and language use in the long term. Thus in current studies (see review in Bitchener & Ferris, 2012), researchers examine new texts rather than revised drafts and include a control group that receives no feedback. This research design enables them to determine whether learners' new texts show a higher degree of grammatical accuracy and linguistic complexity compared to their pre-treatment versions and compared to texts produced by those who did not receive written CF.

However, as Hyland (2010) correctly points out, the language learning potential of WCF is only realized if learners are willing and motivated to attend to the feedback. How learners respond to and engage with the feedback they receive is "a critical link that connects the provision of WCF with learning outcomes" (Han & Hyland, 2015, p. 31). If learners ignore or reject the feedback they receive, such feedback is unlikely to lead to long-term development. This view has led some researchers to explore the possibility that the effectiveness of different approaches to the provision of written CF may depend on individual affective variables.

Early studies on affective variables focused mainly on learners' preferences for the type of feedback they would like to receive (e.g., Hedgcock & Lefkowitz, 1994; Leki, 1991). In many of these studies, data consisted of one-off surveys, asking students about their preferences for feedback in general rather than the feedback that they actually received in their learning contexts. Furthermore, these studies did not investigate how the learners' preferences affected their response to the feedback provided. For example, there was no analysis of learners' revised texts to determine whether learners accepted and incorporated only preferred forms of feedback nor how they reacted to dispreferred forms of feedback.

A small number of subsequent studies (e.g. Hyland, 1998; Lee & Schallert, 2008) have examined learner response to feedback in greater depth, using a case study research design and utilizing rich qualitative data such as interviews and think-aloud protocols. Furthermore, these studies tend to be longitudinal, adopting a broader view of feedback: not a one-off, standalone occurrence but as part of an ongoing teaching activity taking place in a specific educational context. The feedback in these studies is provided by the regular classroom teacher. A salient feature of these studies is the view of learners as active agents whose engagement with the feedback provided is intentional, a view that resonates with sociocultural theoretical perspectives. Lantolf and Pavlenko (2001, p. 145), leading sociocultural theorists, urge researchers to view learners as people who "actively engage in constructing the terms and conditions of their learning."

Thus, in this chapter, I use sociocultural perspectives, and specifically activity theory (AT), to frame the discussion of individual affective factors that may explain the outcome of written CF. I believe that activity theory provides a systematic and comprehensive approach to investigate and ultimately understand learner response to written CF. Although the primary focus of discussion in this chapter is on individual learner factors, such factors can only provide a partial explanation of learner response to feedback. In order to fully understand how and why learners respond to feedback, it is also important to consider how individual factors interact with elements in the immediate instructional context as well as the broader social context in which the feedback activity takes place. It should be noted at the outset that although individual learner and context-related factors may explain learner response to feedback, regardless of whether the feedback is provided by teachers, peers or is computer generated, in this chapter I review and discuss primarily research on feedback that has been provided by classroom teachers.

I begin with a brief summary of activity theory, a theory that has evolved over time but has its roots in Vygotsky's sociocultural theory. I then draw on the small body of relevant research to discuss the factors that have been identified in these studies, including learners' overall learning goals and beliefs. This discussion suggests that learner background, previous language learning experiences, and desires may shape these goals and beliefs. The discussion also illustrates how individual and context-related factors interact to explain why feedback may or may not be effective for some learners or may even have unintentionally adverse effects on some learners. The chapter concludes with suggestions for pedagogy and for future research directions.

Activity Theory

Activity theory builds on the original writings of Vygotsky (1978) on sociocultural theory. Vygotsky's original concept of an activity, or a mediated act, was developed into a fully fledged theory by Leont'ev (1978, 1981) and subsequently revised and represented as increasingly more complex models by Engeström (1987, 2001). The main distinction between the models of activity put forward by the two scholars is their focus. Whereas Leont'ev was concerned mainly with individual actions and what drives these actions, Engeström was concerned predominantly with the context of collective activity (Kaptelinin, 2005). However, the underlying premise of all the models of AT is that human behavior in pursuit of achieving a certain outcome (*object*) is purposeful, mediated, and situated. Thus, in order to understand human behavior, we need to consider the following: (a) the human participants (referred to as *subjects*) and the goals that drive their actions, (b) the symbolic (e.g., language) or material (e.g., computers) artifacts (*tools*) that mediate actions, and (c) the context (referred to as *community*) in which the activity takes place, including the norms (*rules*) and the power hierarchies (*division of labour*) inherent in that context (for a fuller discussion of AT and the various models, see Bitchener & Storch, 2016).

The most frequently deployed graphic model of AT in second language (L2) research is Engeström's (2001) second generation (G_2) model (see Figure 27.1). The model has six key elements (see italicized terms mentioned above) with tools and signs at the apex of the activity triangle mediating the actions that individuals or groups take to achieve an overall goal or object. These actions take place within the constraints of context

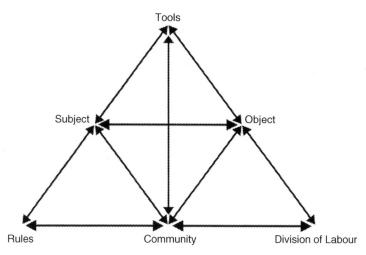

Figure 27.1 Second generation (G$_2$) model of AT (adapted from Engeström 2001)

variables leading to an outcome. Thus, analysis informed by this G$_2$ model of AT enables researchers to consider the interaction of individual and social forces simultaneously. The double-headed arrows between these key elements within the model denote that all these elements shape and are shaped by each other.

Before exemplifying how this model can be used to investigate teachers' feedback practices and learner response to feedback, it is important to note that this model, based as it is on Engeström's work, excludes explicit reference to actions and short-term goals. It focuses instead on the overall outcome and the context in which the activity takes place (community, rules, division of labour). Nevertheless, when applied to educational research, scholars often discuss individual short-term goals, and how they may be thwarted by institutional norms and power relations. For example, this model was used by Lee (2014) to reinterpret her earlier findings (2008a) on teacher feedback practices in secondary schools in Hong Kong. Lee showed how the expectations of parents and school administrators, key stakeholders within the community, influenced teachers' feedback practices rather than the teachers' own beliefs about effective feedback. Lee argued that using AT and identifying the elements within the feedback activity shed light on the tensions within the feedback activity in this context.

Operationalizing the provision and uptake of feedback as an activity means that the participants (teachers, learners) are the *subjects* whose actions (e.g., providing feedback, engaging with the feedback) are mediated by *tools*. These tools may be symbolic (e.g., language, symbols, gestures) or material tools (e.g., computer programs) which are used to deliver teachers' feedback and facilitate learner response to the feedback. The *community* is the classroom or educational program within which the feedback activity takes place. This community may have *rules* that determine appropriate behavior for teachers and students. For teachers, for example, these rules may determine the expected form of the feedback (e.g., direct or indirect, focused or comprehensive), what tools are used to deliver the feedback, and the frequency of feedback provision. For students, these rules relate to what is considered in this context to be appropriate learner response to the feedback (e.g., submission of revised drafts). The *division of labour* relates to the status of teachers vis-à-vis the students and other stakeholders in the educational institution (e.g., program coordinators) and beyond (e.g., local grading policies, government educational policies, parental expectations). However, rules and division of labour may also be shaped by society at large, by historical and cultural factors, such as beliefs concerning the importance of accuracy and the status of teachers (e.g., see Lee, 2008a).

If we focus only on learners as *subjects* in the feedback activity, the *object* toward which the entire activity is oriented and which gives meaning to the activity may be different for individual learners. For some, the overall goal or object may be improved linguistic accuracy, for others it may be improved L2 writing more generally or attaining a desired exam grade. To fulfill their long-term object, learners undertake certain actions mediated by the available *tools* (e.g., online dictionaries) in order to achieve shorter-term goals (e.g., comprehend feedback comments and symbols received). In specific contexts, expectations and power hierarchies (i.e., *rules* and *division of labour*) influence or constrain learners' actions. For example, the rules and power hierarchies in a particular context may determine whether it is considered appropriate to question or reject some of the feedback that teachers provide. It is the interaction of all these elements of the activity which ultimately determines the outcome and whether the desired object is achieved. Thus feedback affords students learning opportunities but will not guarantee actual learning.

As the above discussion suggests, activity theory offers a comprehensive framework that can capture the complexity of the feedback activity. Yet, most of the research on feedback has been largely informed by cognitive perspectives of SLA, the more traditional and entrenched perspectives in our field. Activity theory is less familiar, the terms used are at times ambiguous (e.g., see discussion of the term *object* in Kaptelinin, 2005), and the models of activity increasingly more complex. These factors can explain why to date only a small number of researchers have adopted activity theory when investigating learner response to feedback. These studies have focused on teachers' feedback practices (e.g., Lee, 2014) or learner response to peer feedback (e.g., Storch & Aldossary, 2019; Zhu & Mitchell, 2012). There is, however, a small body of research on learner response to teacher feedback which, although not making explicit reference to the theory, does make reference to sociocultural theories as informing the research (e.g., Han & Hyland, 2015). Moreover, and as mentioned in the introduction to this chapter, the fundamental premises in these studies align with key concepts in AT. Thus, in the section that follows I discuss key factors that can explain learner response to written CF by drawing on the findings of these studies and using the nomenclature of activity theory.

Learner Response to Written CF: Activity Theory Perspectives

A small number of studies have considered individual learner variables using a case study approach in longitudinal studies conducted in situ; that is, in authentic language or writing classes. Most of these studies were conducted with adult learners of English as a Second (ESL) or Foreign (EFL) Language. I discuss these studies, highlighting the three main affective variables that the studies identified to explain learner response to feedback. I then discuss the interaction of these affective variables with context-related variables, such as interpersonal relationships and expected norms of behavior that can explain more fully learner response to and engagement with written CF.

Individual Affective Variables: Objects, Beliefs, Emotions

Three affective individual variables or factors have been identified in longitudinal, qualitative studies that investigated how and why learners respond to the WCF provided by their teachers. These three key factors are: learners' overall goals and perceived language learning needs, captured by the term object in AT, beliefs about L2 writing and what constitutes effective feedback, and learners' emotions. It should be noted at the outset that these variables are inextricably linked. I begin with studies that have investigated learners' long-terms goals and their beliefs. Most of these studies have been conducted by Fiona Hyland (e.g., 1998, 2003) and her colleagues (e.g., Han & Hyland, 2015). I then discuss research by Mahfoodh (e.g., 2017; Mahfoodh & Pandian, 2011) that focused explicitly on emotions, an affective variable that has only recently received research attention.

One of the earliest studies to consider learners' overall goals (or objects) and beliefs in order to explain learner response and the outcome of a feedback activity is Fiona Hyland's longitudinal doctoral study, conducted with adult ESL learners in New Zealand over a semester. In the first published study based on the larger study (1998), Hyland examined not only the learners' immediate actions (response to feedback on successive drafts) but also the impact that the feedback had on the learners' perceived writing development and their confidence at the end of the semester. Hyland used the learners' language learning histories in an attempt to explain what may have shaped these learners' beliefs and expectations.

In the 1998 publication, Hyland focused on two female learners from her larger study who presented contrasting case studies. Maho, a Japanese student with low/intermediate English proficiency, showed the least uptake of the feedback provided by the teacher. Samorn, a more proficient Thai student, followed all the feedback points she received very closely. Although both students began the course with positive attitudes toward English writing and the role of feedback, at the end of the course they both felt that they had made no progress and had lost confidence in their L2 writing abilities. What explained their actions (response to the feedback) and outcome (perceived lack of progress) was their learning objects and beliefs concerning what constitutes valuable feedback.

Interview data with Maho revealed that she viewed writing as a means to communicate her ideas and her main object in attending the ESL course was to develop her L2 writing ability so that she could express her intended meaning clearly. Maho therefore preferred feedback on her ideas to feedback on accuracy. She also strongly believed that the act of writing helped her to develop her ideas. These beliefs shaped her immediate goals and actions. Her response to the feedback was to largely ignore the corrective feedback and instead rewrite large chunks of her texts. At the end of the writing course, she did not feel that she made any progress on her writing because the teacher did not provide positive comments on her ideas. The feedback she received clearly did not align with her object nor her underlying beliefs and expectations about the kind of feedback that would help her achieve her desired outcome.

In contrast, Samorn, had a very different object and set of beliefs. Samorn was very confident about her writing abilities, a confidence based on her past language learning experiences in Thailand. In Thailand she received positive feedback on her mastery of grammar from her teachers and peers. Her object in joining the ESL course in New Zealand was to gain greater grammatical accuracy and a wider range of vocabulary in order to further improve her written communication. She believed that corrective feedback could help her in achieving this object and thus expected the teacher to provide corrective feedback on all her language errors. Her actions in response to the comprehensive corrective feedback she received was to revise her writing by following very closely the feedback she received. However, Samorn was accustomed to receiving positive feedback on any language improvements made. The absence of such feedback in this class had unintentional adverse effects. Over time, Samorn lost confidence in her writing ability and her mastery of grammar, and she no longer enjoyed writing.

In subsequent publications (2003, 2011), Hyland reported on Keith, a third case study from her larger study, who unlike Maho and Samorn felt that he achieved progress in his writing over time. He was very positive about the feedback he received throughout the semester and attributed his perceived progress to the teacher feedback and the actions he took. Keith's ultimate object, like Samoran, was to improve the grammatical accuracy of his writing, particularly at the sentence level. He believed that a systematic response to comprehensive and indirect teacher corrective feedback would help him achieve his object. These beliefs were based on his previous language learning experience in Taiwan. He attributed his failure to improve his English writing in Taiwan to his actions; to the fact that he did not engage methodically with the feedback he received. He thus adopted a different approach to feedback in this class: he carefully read all the teacher feedback comments, sought assistance from peers and his teacher to clarify any problems, corrected all errors in response to the feedback received, and kept a log of his errors, which he consulted before writing his assignments. He also experimented with complex vocabulary and grammatical structures in his drafts in order to get feedback on his attempts. At the end of the writing course, Keith felt that his object had been achieved and that his writing showed gradual improvement. He was convinced that his sustained and proactive approach to the feedback received was the main reason why his accuracy improved. What these case studies clearly illustrate is how the learners' objects and beliefs interacted with the kind of feedback they received to explain their response to the feedback (actions). However, the cases of Keith and Samorn also show that even when the objects and actions seem to be similar, previous experiences and expectations may affect how learners evaluate the ultimate outcome of the feedback activity.

In a more recent study, Han and Hyland (2015) reported on four learners from a longitudinal study conducted in an EFL class in China. Here, too, the authors considered the learners' objects and beliefs about L2 learning and CF but linked these more closely to the actions the learners took in response to the feedback they received. Using Ellis's (2010) multiple dimensional model of engagement with corrective feedback, which they suggested aligns with sociocultural perspectives, the authors distinguished between two types of learner actions: cognitive and behavioral. Cognitive actions refer to how learners attended to the feedback; behavioral engagement considers the nature of revisions undertaken.

Of the four cases presented, only Ying was a highly motivated student who valued written CF because she believed that it would improve her accuracy in English. Achieving high accuracy in her writing was thus her object. To achieve this object, Ying engaged extensively with the feedback received and followed it very closely in her revisions. The authors noted that these actions were taken despite Ying's feeling disappointed about the amount of feedback she continued to receive.

The other three case study students engaged only minimally with the feedback, but their actions were driven by very different objects. Song viewed the EFL subject simply as a hurdle requirement. In the past she did very well in English with little effort and was thus very confident about the accuracy of her own writing. Given these past experiences, she was very skeptical about the benefits of feedback and also admitted to at times being overwhelmed by the amount of feedback she received. Thus her response to the feedback she received was often to simply ignore or reject it. Lin just wanted to pass the exams, and thus viewed the CF simply as a means to help him pass exams. He read the feedback comments only before the scheduled exams. Dai, like Maho in Hyland's (1998) earlier study, wanted to improve her content rather than accuracy, and thus her engagement with the WCF was also limited. Although she was often confused by the written CF, she did not seek the teacher's assistance.

What all these studies show is that adult learners are fully cognizant of their language learning objects and have firmly established beliefs, shaped by prior language learning experiences, about what kind of feedback is most effective in enabling them to achieve their objects. Their actions in response to the feedback are compatible with their own objects and their beliefs. Thus, although they may be seemingly participating in the same feedback activity, their objects and subsequent actions make it a very different activity for each of them and with different language learning outcomes.

Studies by Swain and Lapkin (2002) and subsequently by Storch and Wigglesworth (2010a, 2010b) also showed how learners' beliefs and previous language learning histories can explain learners' uptake or rejection of the feedback they receive. These studies used recorded pair dialogues of adult ESL learners' processing feedback they had received on their jointly composed texts. The studies found evidence of learners rejecting specific feedback points when the feedback was deemed to contradict what they had learned previously, when they could not understand the reasons for the corrections, or where the feedback offered, via reformulations, changed their intended meaning. Importantly, these studies suggest that even when feedback is noticed (an important stage in cognitive explanations of feedback processing, see Bitchener, Chapter 10, this volume) it does not mean that it will be accepted because learners exercising their agency may reject it.

Han and Hyland's (2015) study also showed that learners' response to feedback may be affected by emotional reactions to the nature and quantity of the feedback received. In their discussion they noted that their case study participants experienced emotions such as disappointment, confusion, and being overwhelmed. To date, the emotional response that feedback evokes has received little explicit research attention. As a number of scholars in the field of education (e.g., Barbalet, 2002; Värlander, 2008) and L2 research (e.g., Benesch, 2012; Imai, 2010; Swain, 2013) have pointed out, cognition and emotions continue to be treated separately and the role of emotions in learning is largely ignored or undervalued. Perhaps one of the reasons why emotions have been largely ignored is because they are difficult to measure (Imai, 2010) and hence to predict their potential impact on learning. I note that emotions have also been ignored in successive models of activity theory. Yet emotions pervade all social interaction and thus play a significant role in the very activity of learning.

Feedback being an inherently interactive activity can evoke a range of positive or negative emotions in both the feedback provider (teacher) and recipient (student). In the case of students, the nature of the feedback comments or even the absence of comments (e.g., praise) can evoke emotions toward the explicit or implicit message transmitted and toward the teacher providing the feedback. These emotions may shape the response or actions that follow. For example, students who like the feedback they receive and/or respect the teacher providing the feedback are perhaps more likely to accept the feedback and use it to revise their writing. On the other hand, feedback comments that evoke anger or frustration are perhaps more likely to be rejected or ignored. However, it is important to acknowledge that students' emotional response to feedback may also be affected by the asymmetrical power relationships between teachers and students and the expectations in some contexts that teacher expertise should be followed and that it cannot be questioned, even if not fully understood.

To date, despite some authors making reference to learners' emotional response to the feedback they receive (e.g., Han & Hyland, 2015; Lee, 2007), there has been very little research that has set out to explicitly examine learners' emotional reaction to feedback. The exception a study by Mahfoodh (2017) which built on the earlier study by Mahfoodh and Pandian (2011). The two studies were conducted with eight adult EFL learners in Yemen. Using think-aloud protocols and interview data, Mahfoodh and Pandian (2011) found that the feedback evoked a range of positive emotions such as happiness, satisfaction, agreement/acceptance as well as negative emotions such as frustration and displeasure. The authors reported that the main emotion the feedback evoked was acceptance (in over 85 percent of the data), followed by rejection (about 9 percent of the data). These emotions seemed to be related to the nature of the comments, with praise eliciting positive emotions; harsh criticism and feedback that was difficult to understand eliciting negative emotions. In the 2017 study, Mahfoodh attempted to link emotions to the learners' response to the feedback, finding, perhaps not surprisingly, that positive emotions led to successful revisions, whereas negative emotions led to rejection of the feedback provided or unsuccessful revision.

However, linking emotions only to revision behavior may be misleading, because it does not take into consideration two important elements of the feedback activity: *division of labour* (power hierarchies) and *rules* (expected norms of behavior). In studies conducted by Storch and Wigglesworth (2010a, 2010b), mentioned earlier, the authors found that the learners often incorporated feedback in their revised drafts even if they did not agree with the feedback received. Other studies (e.g., Hyland, 1998; Zhao, 2010) have also shown that learners incorporated teacher feedback even when they did not understand it, simply because it was provided by the teacher, the perceived expert. What these findings suggest is that feedback which is noticed but not understood or not accepted may lead to revisions, because of context-related expectations and power relations. In their studies, Storch and Wigglesworth also found that their participants often reverted to the use of the same erroneous structures when producing new texts despite receiving feedback and it in the revised drafts. The researchers suggest that feedback which is not accepted, or which is not understood, may lead to revision but not necessarily to learning.

I now turn to studies which investigated not only affective individual variables but also how these variables interact with context-related variables. Learner response to feedback can only be partially attributed to their goals and beliefs. Feedback is a situated, social activity. It takes place in interactions between people in a particular educational and cultural context. As a number of scholars (e.g., Goldstein, 2006; Hyland, 2010; Hyland & Hyland, 2006) have argued, studies investigating feedback need to consider important context variables, including the ethos in the classroom, the type of institution, the interpersonal relationship between students and teachers, as well as the broader sociocultural context.

Context-Related Variables

As in the case of affective variables, there have been very few studies that have considered the impact of local and broader context-related factors on learner response to feedback. Such studies are more difficult to implement because they require collecting qualitative data from multiple sources, often beyond the immediate instructional context. However, and as I note in the concluding remarks and elsewhere (Storch, 2018), it is these kinds of studies that should constitute the future research agenda on written CF.

One of the earliest studies to consider the instructional context in which the feedback is delivered is Lee's (2008b) longitudinal study, conducted with Hong Kong secondary EFL students over an academic year. Although Lee's studies (e.g., 2008a) focus predominantly on investigating teachers' feedback practices, in this study she considered the factors that impacted on both teachers and students. Using classroom observations and questionnaires, her study found that the students' attitudes to written CF was affected by how their teachers dealt with feedback in the classes. Students whose teacher was observed to be encouraging and who provided his or her learners with opportunities to engage with the feedback in the classes displayed a more positive attitude to written CF. In contrast, those whose teacher adopted a more traditional, teacher-centered approach were less interested in feedback and felt quite frustrated by it. However, the study did not consider the learners' goals nor their revision behavior.

The study by Lee and Schallert (2008), conducted in Korea with adult EFL learners, is a fascinating investigation which examined the complexities of the feedback activity by considering individual affective variables and key contextual variables in the one study. Using two contrasting case studies, the researchers demonstrate how learners' language learning goals and attitudes toward feedback and toward their language teacher impacted on their response to the feedback they received as well as on the teacher's feedback practices and the outcome of the feedback activity.

The two case studies reported on, Sangho and Jongmin, were two male students enrolled in an EFL class taught by the same female teacher. Sangho considered himself a poor learner of English who did not take studying English seriously throughout his school years. However, he was much more motivated to study English as an adult. His object in attending the EFL class was to improve his English in order to enable him to eventually study abroad. He viewed the teacher as the ultimate L2 expert, trusting and valuing all the feedback she provided on his writing. He thus read and responded to her feedback closely by editing and rewriting his texts carefully. This behavior, according to the authors, is fairly typical of Korean students, who tend to respect and comply with teachers' feedback. Furthermore, unlike his peers, Sangho came to individual conferences prepared with a list of questions. This diligence impressed his teacher. She thought that Sangho was a very good student and that he showed progress over time. She thus rewarded him with a very high final grade, the highest grade in the class.

The contrasting case is of Jongmin who had lived and studied in English-speaking countries for ten years. He was very fluent in English (and Korean) and very confident about his English abilities, as evident by his active classroom participation. In fact, he felt more confident in speaking and writing English than Korean. Jongmin's primary reason for undertaking this English course was purely pragmatic. The course was offered in an intensive mode during the summer semester. Unlike Sangho, Jongmin did not perceive the teacher as an L2 expert because she did not train in an English-speaking country. According to the teacher participant in this study, such low regard of teachers trained in Korea is widely held in Korea and is used to discriminate particularly against female academics. Because Jongmin did not always trust the teacher's feedback on his writing nor agree with the suggestions given, he often ignored it. The teacher, on the other hand, felt that Jongmin overestimated his L2 writing abilities and underestimated her expertise. She thus continued to provide him with feedback on his writing, partly out of obligations in her role as a teacher but also to demonstrate to him her expertise in English writing. She also gave him low grades on his writing to penalize him for ignoring her feedback. This volume of feedback and poor grades led over time to an even greater deterioration in the student–teacher relationship.

The study thus highlights the interpersonal dimension of the context, a dimension that has not been considered in previous studies. The relationship learners and teachers form influences not only the learner response to the feedback provided but also, arguably, the teacher's feedback and perhaps even grades. This reciprocal activity (which may hence be better captured by two intersecting activity systems, as suggested in Bitchener & Storch, 2016) is shaped not only by classroom and feedback interactions but also by widely held beliefs in the broader context, such as beliefs about the importance of compliance and about the status of teachers.

The studies discussed in this section provide us with a glimpse of the complexity of the feedback activity and the impact that affective and context-related variables can have on learner response to written CF. In the concluding section I make some tentative suggestions about pedagogical practices and future studies that may enhance teachers' and students' understanding of the potential efficacy of written CF for language learning and, in turn, encourage greater learner engagement with the feedback they receive.

Conclusion: Pedagogical and Research Suggestions

The research discussed in this chapter has shown that learner response to and engagement with feedback is complex and also unpredictable. Yet encouraging learners to engage with feedback is important. The language learning potential of feedback is realized only if learners engage with it (Ellis, 2010; Hyland, 2010). One pedagogical recommendation made by a number of researchers (e.g., Han & Hyland, 2015) is to have open dialogues between teachers and students about feedback expectations. Such dialogues may provide teachers and students with opportunities to gain a shared understanding of their respective goals, beliefs, and expectations. Establishing a shared understanding at the beginning of the course may help teachers provide more effective feedback. It may also assist in creating a classroom environment that will encourage learners to engage more deeply with the feedback provided, seeking clarification and assistance, if needed.

The small number of studies discussed in this chapter reflects the current state of research on learner response to the feedback they receive. As Han and Hyland (2015) argue, learner response and engagement with written CF is under-conceptualized and under-explored. Furthermore, although there is a growing recognition from leading L2 scholars that certain individual and context-related variables can moderate and influence cognitive processes (e.g., Bitchener, 2017, Chapter 10, this volume; Kormos, 2012), much of the research on written CF does not consider fully the context in which feedback is provided and tends to treat learners as devoid of agency and emotions.

There is clearly a need for further investigation of variables such as learners' emotional responses to the feedback they receive, on the impact that teacher/student relationships have on feedback receivers and providers, and on how power and status, dimensions inherent in all social interactions, impact on learners' goals, beliefs, and their actions. Such research also needs to consider one other element that has not been discussed in this chapter, namely the tools used in the feedback activity. Future studies, for example, could investigate how language is used in feedback comments or whether feedback delivered online and using the more impersonal bank of comments available to teachers impacts on learners' emotional responses to the feedback (for more concrete examples of suggested studies and their research design, see Storch, 2018). Such research needs to be longitudinal and conducted in a range of language learning contexts, beyond adult learners of English. A diversity of contexts could provide researchers and practitioners with greater understanding of the role that learner and context-related variables play in a written CF activity.

I believe that activity theory provides researchers with a conceptual framework to investigate the affective and context-related variables as well as the interaction between them in a systematic and comprehensive manner. The diagrammatic model of activity brings these variables to the foreground and shows how they are linked. The use of the model, as demonstrated by Lee (2014), could also identify the potential paradoxes and tensions in the feedback activity in a specific language learning context, and how these could be addressed.

References

Baker, N. L. (2014). "Get it off my stack": Teachers' tools for grading papers. *Assessing Writing, 19*, 36–50.

Barbalet, J. (2002). *Emotions and sociology*. Oxford: Blackwell.

Benesch, S. (2012). *Considering emotions in critical English language teaching: Theories and praxis*. New York; London: Routledge.

Bitchener, J. (2017). Why some L2 learners fail to benefit from written corrective feedback. In H. Nassaji & E. Karchava (eds.), *Corrective feedback in second language teaching and learning* (pp. 129–140). New York: Routledge.

Bitchener, J. & Ferris, D. (2012). *Written corrective feedback in second language acquisition and writing*. New York: Routledge.

Bitchener, J. & Storch, N. (2016). *Written corrective feedback for L2 development*. Bristol: Multilingual Matters.

Ellis, R. (2010). Cognitive, social, and psychological dimensions of corrective feedback. In R. Batstone (ed.), *Sociocognitive Perspectives on Language Use and Language Learning* (pp. 151–165). Oxford: Oxford University Press.

(2017). Oral corrective feedback in L2 classrooms: What we know so far. In H. Nassaji & E. Kartchava (eds.), *Corrective feedback in second language teaching and learning* (pp. 3–18). New York: Routledge.

Engeström, Y. (1987). *Learning by expanding: An activity-theoretical approach to developmental research*. Helsinki: Orienta-Konsultit Oy.

(2001). Expansive learning at work: Toward an activity theoretical reconceptualization. *Journal of Education and Work, 14*, 133–156.

Goldstein, L. (2006). Feedback and revision in second language writing: Contextual, teacher, and student variables. In K. Hyland & F. Hyland (eds.), *Feedback in second language writing: Contexts and issues* (pp. 185–205). Cambridge: Cambridge University Press.

Han, Y. & Hyland, F. (2015). Exploring learner engagement with written corrective feedback in a Chinese tertiary EFL classroom. *Journal of Second Language Writing, 30*, 31–44.

Hedgcock, J. & Lefkowitz, N. (1994). Feedback on feedback: Assessing learner receptivity in second language writing. *Journal of Second Language Writing, 3*, 141–163.

Hyland, F. (1998). The impact of teacher written feedback on individual writers. *Journal of Second Language Writing, 7*(3), 255–286.

(2003). Focusing on form: Student engagement with teacher feedback. *System, 31*(2), 217–230.

(2010). Future directions in feedback on second language writing: Overview and research agenda. *International Journal of English Studies, 10*(2), 171–182.

(2011). The language learning potential of form-focused feedback on writing: Students' and teachers' perceptions. In R. Manchón (ed.), *Learning-to-write and writing-to-learn in an additional language* (pp. 159–180). Amsterdam; Philadelphia: John Benjamins.

Hyland, K. & Hyland, F. (2006). Contexts and issues in feedback on L2 writing: An introduction. In K. Hyland & F. Hyland (eds.), *Feedback in ESL writing: Contexts and issues* (pp. 1–20). Cambridge: Cambridge University Press.

Imai, Y. (2010). Emotions in SLA: New insights from collaborative learning for an EFL classroom. *Modern Language Journal, 94*(2), 278–292.

Kaptelinin, V. (2005). The object of activity: Making sense of the sense-maker. *Mind, Culture and Activity, 12*(1), 4–18.

Kormos, J. (2012). The role of individual differences in L2 writing. *Journal of Second Language Writing, 21*(4), 390–403.

Lantolf, J. P. & Pavlenko, A. (2001). (S)econd (L)anguage (A)ctivity theory: Understanding second language learners as people. In M. Breen (ed.),

Learner contributions to language learning (pp.141–158). London: Longman.
Lee, G. & Schallert, D. (2008). Meeting in the margins: Effects of the teacher–student relationship on revision processes of EFL college students taking a composition course. *Journal of Second Language Writing*, 17(3), 165–182.
Lee, I. (2007). Preparing pre-service English teachers for reflective practice. *ELT Journal*, 61(4), 321–329.
  (2008a). Understanding teachers' written feedback practices in Hong Kong secondary classrooms. *Journal of Second Language Writing*, 17(2), 69–85.
  (2008b). Student reactions to teacher feedback in two Hong Kong secondary classrooms. *Journal of Second Language Writing*, 17(3), 144–164.
  (2014). Revisiting teacher feedback in EFL writing from sociocultural perspectives. *TESOL Quarterly*, 48(1), 201–2013.
Leki, I. (1991). The preferences of ESL students for error correction in college-level writing classes. *Foreign Language Annals*, 24(3), 203–218.
Leont'ev, A. N. (1978). *Activity, consciousness, and personality*. Englewood Cliffs, NJ: Prentice Hall.
  (1981). The problem of activity in psychology. In J. V. Wertsch (ed.), *The concept of activity in Soviet Psychology* (pp. 37–71). Armonk, NY: Sharpe.
Liu, Q. & Brown, D. (2015). Methodological synthesis of research on the effectiveness of corrective feedback in L2 writing. *Journal of Second Language Writing*, 30, 66–81.
Mahfoodh. O. H. A. (2017). "I feel disappointed": EFL university students' emotional responses towards teacher written feedback. *Assessing Writing*, 31, 53–72.
Mahfoodh, O. H. A. & Pandian, A. (2011). A qualitative case study of EFL students' affective reactions to and perceptions of their teachers' written feedback. *English Language Teaching*, 4(3), 14–27.
Polio, C. (2012). The relevance of second language acquisition theory to the written error correction controversy. *Journal of Second Language Writing*, 21(4), 375–389.
Storch, N. (2018). Written corrective feedback from sociocultural theoretical perspectives: A research agenda. *Language Teaching*, 51(2), 262–277.
Storch, N. & Aldossary, M. (2019). Peer feedback: An activity theory perspective on givers' and receivers' stances. In M. Sato & S. Loewen (eds.), *Evidence-based second language pedagogy: A collection of instructed second language acquisition studies* (pp. 123–144). New York: Routledge.
Storch, N. & Wigglesworth, G. (2010a). Learners' processing, uptake and retention of corrective feedback on writing: Case studies. *Studies in Second Language Acquisition*, 32(3), 303–334.

(2010b). Students' engagement with feedback on writing: the role of learner agency/beliefs. In Batstone R (ed.), *Sociocognitive perspectives on language use and language learning* (pp. 166–185). Oxford: Oxford University Press.

Swain, M. (2013). The inseparability of cognition and emotion in second language learning. *Language Teaching*, 46(2), 195–207.

Swain, M. & Lapkin, S. (2002). Talking it through: Two French immersion learners' response to reformulation. *International Journal of Educational Research*, 37(3–4), 285–304.

Värlander, S. (2008). The role of students' emotions in formal feedback situations. *Teaching in Higher Education*, 13(2), 145–156.

Vygotsky, L. S. (1978). *Mind and society: The development of higher psychological processes*. Cambridge, MA: Harvard University Press.

Zhao, H. (2010). Investigating learners' use and understanding of peer and teacher feedback on writing: A comparative study in a Chinese English writing classroom. *Assessing Writing*, 15(1), 3–17.

Zhu, W. & Mitchell, D. (2012). Participation in peer response as activity: An examination of peer response stances from an activity theory perspective. *TESOL Quarterly*, 46(2), 362–386.

28

The Role of Training in Feedback Provision and Effectiveness

Eva Kartchava

Introduction

While the utility of corrective feedback (CF) – information provided to second language (L2) learners about the accuracy of their output – in L2 development has chiefly been ascertained (e.g., Li, 2010; Lyster & Saito, 2010; Mackey & Goo, 2007; Nassaji, 2015, 2016; Nassaji & Kartchava, 2017a; Russell & Spada, 2006), the understanding of the intricacies of and the processes inherent to the phenomenon remains largely incomplete. This is evidenced by the recurring view of CF as "a complex phenomenon" (Nassaji & Kartchava, 2017b, p. 179), whose effectiveness is dependent, among other things, on a number of factors that are driven by the differences among learners, teachers, pedagogical tasks, and contexts in which CF is provided. The need to better comprehend this complexity has, in turn, yielded a standing call for additional research "into how corrective feedback is used and contributes to L2 acquisition in various areas and contexts" (Nassaji & Kartchava, 2017b, p. 182). This call is supported further by the burgeoning need for "systems thinking" in the larger field of L2 acquisition that would allow for "a credible, useful, and usable understanding of second language learning [made possible by] identifying systems and uncovering their mechanism and inner workings" (Han & Nassaji, 2019, pp. 394–395). A more nuanced understanding of the inner workings of the CF system may, then, shed light on the processes involved. One way to begin to understand the complexity of CF is by examining the various theoretical lenses through which error correction has been viewed; this is because the perception of the kinds of underlying processes involved as well as their role and effects differ from one theory to another. The interactionist perspectives on CF, for example, prioritize meaning-based communication and relegate feedback to instances of form-based breakdowns, where the intended meaning is unclear or inappropriate but necessary for a successful exchange (see Chapter 2, this volume). The cognitive perspective, in turn, is multifaceted (see Chapter 3) but tends to attribute a more prominent role to CF, since attention to error is believed to play a role in L2 development in general and information processing in particular. Still, the sociocultural perspectives (see Chapter 4) view CF as facilitative in the process of language learning; this assistance is personalized, gradual, systematic, and provided during interaction, with the goal of encouraging more learner autonomy (self-regulation) and less reliance on outside help (other-regulation).

Regardless of the role attributed to CF within each perspective, the act of correction itself implies that some level of input processing on the part of the receiver of feedback needs to occur. However, attentional resources needed for the successful processing and use of the corrective information (i.e., turning input into intake, Schmidt, 1990, 2001) may differ from one individual to another and/or be shaped by such factors as instructional context, error type, feedback strategy, and its explicitness (Nassaji & Kartchava, 2017a, 2017b). Research has repeatedly shown, for example, that explicit CF strategies (whose corrective intent is overt; see Ellis, 2017, for a typology of CF strategies) not only are preferred by learners (e.g., Li, 2017) but also bring about opportunities for increased feedback noticing (Egi, 2007). Although implicit feedback may also be noticed, especially in the form of uptake, i.e., learner responses to feedback (Lyster & Ranta, 1997) or uptake-induced self-repair (Nassaji, 2011), explicit CF types may yield more L2 learning (e.g., Ammar & Spada, 2006; Ellis, Loewen & Erlam, 2006; Lyster, 2004, but see Li, 2010). This is because, when the corrective intent of a CF move is made clear to learners, not only are they more likely to notice the correction but they may also act on this noticing and improve their knowledge/use of the targeted feature. Nevertheless, much of the descriptive research on the distribution of CF strategies across instructional contexts continues to show that among feedback types recasts – a largely implicit strategy – are still the most widely used CF technique (e.g., Dilans, 2016; Ellis, Basturkmen & Loewen, 2001; Lyster & Mori, 2006; Lyster & Ranta, 1997; Sheen, 2004; but see Lyster, Saito & Sato, 2013).

The concern with this practice is twofold. First, implicit CF types tend to be more difficult for L2 learners to process and, consequently, to act on. This is especially true for recasts that target non-salient forms such as grammar errors, which tend to receive more CF compared to lexical and phonological errors, whose saliency is more pronounced (e.g., Brown, 2016; Mackey, Gass & McDonough, 2000). The increased saliency has been shown to result in more uptake and learning gains for vocabulary and phonological targets, but not for non-salient grammatical features (e.g., Mackey & Goo, 2007). Moreover, although saliency of recasts may be increased as learners become more proficient (Ammar, 2008; Ammar & Spada, 2006; Mackey & Philp, 1998), teachers who solely rely on implicit CF strategies may put their learners at a disadvantage by curtailing the opportunities to benefit from other types of feedback or provide feedback in ways whose effectiveness can be enhanced in L2 classrooms (Kartchava et al., 2020). While "no one instructional method or feedback strategy can address all problems learners have" (Nassaji, 2016, p. 553), understanding how to provide CF within one's teaching context may allow teachers to be more effective, yet consistent, in their CF choices. Kartchava et al. (2020) argue that in order to gain this understanding, teachers may need to engage in targeted training on CF, that is, feedback that builds on teacher attitudes toward feedback and, at the same time, addresses concepts specific to feedback provision. Such training may also be useful to learners, who receive instruction on both how to recognize and provide CF, with the goal of improving their L2 developmental results.

This chapter addresses the topic of training in feedback provision and effectiveness. The chapter begins by discussing the role and importance of training and practice in language learning in general and then discusses how feedback training can assist feedback provision and processing. To this end, empirical studies on both teacher and student training of feedback and their implications will be discussed. It is important to note that this discussion is limited to oral CF since much of the research on feedback training concerns oral feedback although there are discussions of the role of feedback training on written feedback (see, for example, Tigchelaar & Polio, 2017, for a discussion on written peer CF training).

Training as a Concept

There is no singular definition for the term "training" in L2 acquisition, and research in this area has adopted various terms such as instruction, teaching, intervention, practice, or, simply, training. While the implied connotations of each term may differ somewhat, the main shared focus is, arguably, on the development of expertise and expert performance through guided instruction. Here, viewed from the psychological perspective, expertise refers to "the characteristics, skills, and knowledge that distinguish experts from novices and less experienced people" (Ericsson, 2006a, p. 3), and expert performance is defined as "[consistent ability] to exhibit superior performance for representative tasks in a domain" (p. 3). This expert-led guidance, then, can be thought of as "training of expert performance" (p. 16) where experts assist novices in mastering the necessary skills to become effective and/or autonomous providers of the actions required in a particular field or trade. The skill mastery, in turn, requires "deliberate practice" (p. 16) – i.e., activities specifically designed for the improvement of performance – that is extensive and yielding of the real-world performance (e.g., Ericsson, 1996, 2004).

In L2 learning, the deliberateness of practice is often mistakenly equated with the rote drill-induced audiolingual period that favored mechanical repetition of externally predetermined language forms that carried no meaning-based significance to the learner. This lack of engagement, DeKeyser (1998) posited, can prevent learners from participating in the form–meaning mapping necessary for L2 processing and learning. Yet, according to the skill acquisition theory, meaningful repetition is an important element of practice and is helpful as it promotes proceduralization of declarative knowledge, increasing skill competence – "the ability to routinely, reliably and fluently perform goal-directed activities as a result of practice with those activities" (Carlson, 1997, p. 45, cited in DeKeyser, 2007). Proceduralization is facilitated when practice focuses on the elements already known to the learner and also when it draws learners' attention to new forms in the input with the goal of unearthing new insights and/or restructuring the interlanguage (Larsen-Freeman, 2003; Robinson, 2007).

Proceduralization is also facilitated with feedback on practice. In the general sense, feedback refers to information on one's performance after the said performance has been demonstrated. In this sense, feedback is a "consequence of performance" (Hattie & Timperly, 2007). In L2 acquisition, feedback is provided in response to learner output and can focus on its content, accuracy, and/or appropriateness. While feedback can be positive (as in agreement or encouragement to continue with the demonstrated performance) or negative (as in provision of corrective information or alternative strategy to modify original performance), L2 acquisition research has primarily focused on the latter type (i.e., negative/corrective feedback) and its role in the language learning process.

Research has shown that CF contributes to L2 development. Particularly important to this process is practice which, according to the skill acquisition perspective, promotes automatization of L2 knowledge. CF supplied with practice within a meaningful context may yield more attention to declarative knowledge, leading to fewer errors and increased competence in L2 use (e.g., Lyster & Saito, 2010; Ranta & Lyster, 2007). Such practice can also help the proceduralization of non-target-like structures to be minimized (Leeman, 2007). Finally, providing learners with feedback and deliberate practice is likely to increase their engagement by helping them to pay attention to and seek the information needed in the learning process.

Deliberate practice is equally important to the development of expert performance in L2 teaching and teacher preparation. The training that novices receive as part of their formal education is often rudimentary and requires additional experience in the field. Yet even this experience, according to Ericsson (2006b), is not enough to achieve mastery because experience on its own allows only for "a stable, average level of performance [which if maintained at the initial level, remains] pedestrian for the rest of their [i.e., trainees'] careers" (p. 683). Extensive experience combined with deliberate practice, however, bring about continuous yet incremental improvement that leads to advanced levels of expert performance (Ericsson, 1996, 2004).

In addition, to ensure improvement, trainees need to be exposed to and engage in challenging tasks that focus on specific areas of the desired performance. Such engagement should be further refined through feedback and targeted repetition. This is important as deliberate practice requires attention to and understanding of the supplied information along with concentration needed for problem-solving. These, together can "refine cognitive mechanisms to support continued learning and improvement" (Ericsson, 2006b, p. 694). To Ericsson, deliberate practice helps experts to resist automaticity (i.e., arrested development) in performance and ensures ongoing development. Furthermore, deliberate practice engenders predictive skills that allow experts to anticipate context-dependent behaviors of the novices and guide them toward improvement and eventual success. According to this view, expertise and expert performance are processes that require targeted training, reflection on performance, and establishing advanced goals for further improvement (Tsui, 2005). Understanding these processes and their mediating structures is "crucial [since this knowledge] would enable mentor teachers and teacher educators to identify emerging characteristics of expertise among young members of the profession and to ensure that they are well supported and appropriately challenged at the various phases of their development" (Tsui, 2005, p. 185).

Teachers' views about CF and their corrective practices are among the processes that require such understanding, since feedback provision belongs to "incidental aspects of teaching ... in responding to [which] teachers might largely draw on automatic and generally unexamined behaviours" (Basturkmen, 2012, p. 291). Yet research on teacher cognition has provided evidence that teacher practices exist in a bi-directional and ever-changing relationship with their beliefs (Arnett & Turnbull, 2008; Borg, 2003); these beliefs originate in experiences the teachers may have undergone as language learners, teacher trainees, or practicing language teachers (Borg, 2003, 2006). Teachers' CF responses, in particular, may also depend on contextually derived constraints, including curricular and administrative limitations placed on teachers by their teaching contexts, and opportunities (freedoms allotted for teachers to exercise when, for example, designing courses and planning individual lessons) (Clark & Peterson, 1986), as well as advice given on the topic in teacher guides (Ellis, 2017). It then stands to reason that targeted training (i.e., deliberate practice) in CF has a role to play in helping teachers develop expertise and engage in expert performance when providing feedback to learners. Another reason for feedback training is the theory–practice gap that currently exists between research findings and teaching practice (Nassaji, 2012). Such training can help bridge this gap by communicating to teachers what research has shown about how and when CF could be provided to be effective.

Teacher Training and CF

Before considering empirical evidence on teacher CF training, the link between teachers' beliefs about CF and practices needs to be examined. Understanding what pre-service/new teachers think about CF prior to training is well-regarded and even promoted in teacher cognition research to help teacher educators (i.e., experts) to tailor instruction and facilitate "in time" learning (Peacock, 2001). For experienced teachers, identifying their views on the topic can be enlightening for their own benefit and that of their students, since the teachers may unknowingly hold "incorrect beliefs about CF" (Li, 2017, p. 155), which may negatively affect their practice in general and student engagement in particular. Research has repeatedly shown that because beliefs – i.e., attitudes, views or opinions on an aspect/aspects of L2 teaching or learning – define and affect learner performance (e.g., Breen, 2001; Horwitz, 1985, 1999; Mori, 1999; Tanaka, 2004), withholding corrective information from the learners who believe in its importance and wish to receive it may yield negative attitudes toward the teacher and the learning process as a whole (Horwitz, 1990; Nunan, 1989). Yet, numerous investigations into teacher and learner beliefs about CF have revealed a disconnect, with teachers choosing not to provide CF as often as learners, regardless of the instructional context, expect to be corrected (Amrhein & Nassaji, 2010; Cathcart & Olsen, 1976; Jean & Simard, 2011; Karim & Nassaji, 2015; Li, 2017; Schulz, 1996, 2001; Kim & Mostafa, Chapter 26, this volume). For pre-service teachers, even if their belief in the importance of CF is strong, the disconnect may primarily rest in their lack of knowledge and experience in providing feedback (Kartchava et al., 2020; Rankin & Becker, 2006). This is exactly what Mackey, Polio, and McDonough (2004) found in their investigation of CF use by experienced and inexperienced teachers, when the latter group did not provide as much feedback as the former group despite both groups having engaged in similar levels of negotiation with learners. The inexperienced teachers cited difficulty in implementing CF into their practice even after the awareness-raising workshop that the researchers engaged this group in.

The level of experience is often attributed as the main reason why teachers differ in the amount of CF they provide. This is true of studies that have shown experienced teachers provide more CF in meaning-based classrooms than their less-experienced counterparts (e.g., Mackey et al., 2004) as well as investigations that reported more favorable CF attitudes among experienced teachers compared to the novices (e.g., Rahimi & Zhang, 2015). Experience is also important in the choice of CF techniques teachers use. This is because experienced teachers are more likely to vary the types of CF they use (Junqueira & Kim, 2013; Rahimi & Zhang, 2015, but see Dilāns, 2016), whereas new and less experienced teachers, if they choose to provide CF at all, may prefer to employ a single strategy, most likely recasts or indirect feedback that they view as face-saving yet effective (Bell, 2005; Kartchava et al., 2020; Rahimi & Zhang, 2015). Novices may shy away from using more direct CF types, such as explicit correction (Rahimi & Zhang, 2015), in order to avoid feelings of anxiety (Lasagabaster & Sierra, 2005) and embarrassment (Kamiya, 2014) among their students as well as to prevent unnecessary interruptions in communication (Brown, 2009; Roothooft, 2014; Sepehrinia & Mehdizadeh, 2018). Yet even experienced teachers worry that CF may break the communicative flow and negatively affect their students' motivation (Jean & Simard, 2011); some may also choose to avoid CF altogether in meaning-based interactions in which the focus, they feel, should exclusively be on fluency work (Junqueira & Kim, 2013; Kamiya, 2014). CF-related issues such as when to provide feedback, to what types of error, and by whom cannot, to date, be explained in terms of teacher experience. This is because, according to Li's (2017) synthesis of the empirical research on teacher and learner beliefs about CF, the instruments used to study the issues (primarily, written surveys) either have not addressed all the possible facets of the issue under consideration (e.g., timing of CF) or have used categorical phrasing (e.g., "only," "all," "every," p. 151) to probe attitudes; what's more, an insufficient number of investigations on the topics make it difficult to reach conclusions about teachers' thoughts on these issues and their likely practices.

There is evidence, however, that targeted training on CF can make a difference in how teachers, experienced or not, view feedback and the kinds of corrective practices they may choose to adopt in their lessons. Two oft-cited studies that investigated changes in the attitudes that student-teachers held about CF before and after training are those by Vásquez and Harvey (2010) and Busch (2010). Working with nine graduate students enrolled in a required SLA course, Vásquez and Harvey (2010) designed a research project that required the students to engage in partial replication of a published study on CF (i.e., Lyster & Ranta, 1997). Specifically, working in groups, the students were asked to analyze a teaching video of a member's authentic ESL lesson for instances of CF and to reflect on the project and the findings. The students also completed pre- and post-course questionnaires, and kept a reflective journal; at the end of the course, some volunteered to participate in a focus group interview. The reflective journals revealed that at the beginning of the course, the participants had either very limited or no knowledge of CF and that those with some (mostly, EFL) teaching experience were concerned with the affective dimensions of CF, worrying about the negative influences of feedback on the learners' self-esteem and motivation. According to the questionnaire responses, however, at the end of the course, there was a marked shift in the participants' views of CF. These reflected a more expanded yet informed understanding of

CF issues and pointed to a departure from the teacher-participants' initial concerns about the affect toward the need to raise awareness in their learners' engagement with and correction of their errors. The authors claim that the teachers became, in particular, cognisant of "the relationship between feedback and uptake, the interaction between error type and feedback, [and] understanding the differences between various feedback moves that supply learners with correct responses versus those feedback moves that do not" (Vásquez & Harvey, 2010, p. 437) and expressed intention to amend their future CF-related practices in accordance with their newly acquired and newly experienced understanding of the topic.

Busch (2010) also studied the impact of an SLA course on teacher trainees' beliefs about L2 learning and teaching. In addition to completing the BALLI questionnaire (Horwitz, 1988) at the onset and end of the course, the 381 pre-service teachers were also asked to compare their responses, explaining any differences in a written report. During the course, they engaged in experiential and reflective activities that included tutoring a child or adult ESL learner and analyzing their L2 output. The comparative reports revealed a general shift in the teachers' beliefs about language learning and pointed to a different understanding of the role of error correction in the process. At the beginning of the course, the participants saw CF as "the most important part of language teaching", felt that speaking a language "perfectly" was the goal, and, to avoid fossilization, deemed it necessary to hold off speaking L2 until that time when they could speak it free of errors. After the course, the teachers began to view errors as "a natural part of language acquisition" and developed opinions about when CF should happen, what it should address, and how it should be done (Busch, 2010, p. 330). Busch argued that the observed changes were generated for the topics, such as error correction, that were "most relevant to the teachers in their future teaching" (p. 335). Similarly, Kartchava et al. (2020) found that the SLA course made a difference in how the 99 pre-service teachers in Canada felt about the timing of CF in that those who had taken the course (n=20) expressed a more pronounced effect in supplying corrective information immediately after an error had been made compared to those who had not taken the course (n=79). Although it is unclear what the students were asked to do in the course that brought on this particular change, the authors argue that a combination of the theoretical content and in-class discussions on the topic of CF may "have 'trained' the pre-service teachers to see the timing of CF differently" (Kartchava et al., 2020, p. 235); such discussions and a chance to engage in research replication were said to be the reasons why the student-teachers in the Vásquez and Harvey's study experienced change in CF attitudes; the same explanation may apply to the student-teachers who tutored real L2 learners in Busch's study.

Together, these studies point to a change in CF beliefs as a function of an explicit focus on the topic, but they do not show, nor can accurately predict, whether these attitudinal changes can amend the trainees' in-class practices. Although Kartchava et al. showed a link between the participants' stated preferences for recasts and their actual use of the technique when providing feedback, this finding may be due to the fact that the written survey the participants were presented with targeted their thoughts about hypothetical, not real-life situations. As such, the teachers' in-class corrective behaviour may not be representative of their beliefs about CF and similarly, their beliefs may not be reflective of their actual classroom practices. This was the case in a study of CF preferences and use among experienced teachers of Latvian as an L2 (Dilāns, 2016). The participants (n=66) first reported the frequencies with which they used specific CF types (recasts, explicit correction, repetition, and elicitation) and then, some of the teachers (n=13) were observed to compare the reports with the actual CF use in the classroom. The findings show a disconnect in that while the teachers appeared not to differentiate the frequencies with which they imagined themselves use the four CF strategies, opting to most frequently choose "sometimes" as the marker of frequency, the observations revealed that recasts were used the most (72% of the time), followed by explicit correction (13%), elicitation (13%), and repetition (2%).

Kamiya and Loewen (2014) took a different approach to investigate the link between teachers' stated beliefs about CF, training, and corrective practices. They asked an experienced ESL teacher to read three articles, of which he read two, with different perspectives on the issues of oral CF effectiveness and noticeability as well as to participate in two semi-structured interviews, with one conducted before the reading and another afterwards, to probe the teacher's initial and post-reading views on CF. Although the readings did not impact the teacher's initial CF views, reading about CF research brought to the forefront the need for the teacher to reflect on his corrective practices and provided empirical evidence that informed his existing views and allowed for a better way to articulate them (Borg, 2011; Busch, 2010; Kamiya, 2016; Vásquez & Harvey, 2010). The researchers suggest that incorporating academic articles into training of new and experienced teachers alike may engage them in the necessary self-reflection and raise awareness of their practices. This recommendation finds support in Kamiya's (2016) follow-up study with four ESL teachers, whose stated beliefs about CF and classroom feedback practices did not change as a result of reading academic research, but the teachers "became more conscious of CF than before" (p. 344). Similarly, Rankin and Becker's (2006) study showed a pre-service teacher of German, after reading three academic articles about CF as part of a course requirement, align his stated beliefs about CF with classroom practices, albeit he struggled to consistently act on his beliefs in the classroom. Li (2017), however, goes further to suggest that such exposure to information, albeit with some advantages, may not be enough on its own and that some kind of practical application of the information consumed may be required for a transformation in views and practices to occur. This, of course, was the case in the studies by Vásquez and Harvey and Busch detailed above. Li's suggestion finds additional support not only in Ericsson's (1996, 2004) views on the importance of deliberate practice in bringing about expertise and expert performance, but also echoes Tsui's (2005) assertions for the need of targeted and extensive training coupled with recurring reflection on performance and setting of higher goals for continued development.

Student Training and CF

The effectiveness of training learners to recognize the goals behind feedback provision depends, in part, on the attitudes they hold about CF and the extent to which they engage with the corrective information in the input. There is ample evidence that learners from various instructional settings (e.g., Kartchava, 2016) are generally in favour of having their errors corrected in some way (e.g., Li, 2017; Kim & Mostafa, Chapter 26, this volume), suggesting that learners who hold positive views about CF are more likely to notice (e.g., Kartchava & Ammar, 2014b) and benefit from correction (Sheen, 2007). Learners also differentiate between various CF strategies (Kartchava, 2016) and hold preferences for the ones they view as effective (Brown, 2009; Kartchava & Ammar, 2014b; Lee, 2013; Yoshida, 2008). Learners with positive attitudes towards recasts, for example, have been shown to notice this corrective technique in the CF provided by their teacher in response to the errors with the English past tense and questions in the past (Karchava & Ammar, 2014b).

In terms of the kinds of errors that CF should target, learners vary in their opinions, with some gravitating toward a comprehensive treatment of error (Jean & Simard, 2011; Oladejo, 1993) and others preferring a selective approach (Brown, 2009; Jean & Simard, 2011; Kartchava, 2016; Lee, 2013). While language students hold opinions about when CF is best provided, with the majority wanting to be corrected by the teacher immediately after an error has been made, they also see benefits in being corrected by both peers and the teacher (Li, 2017). Knowing what students think about CF and how they process it is important to the teacher wishing to maximize the benefits of the practice, especially if the teacher's views differ from the learners'. Similarly, for the learner, understanding the corrective intent of CF is equally important not only to take advantage of the information it contains, but also to improve their L2 overall. One way to enable improvement is through training and deliberate practice in CF. The effects of such training, to date, have primarily been addressed in research on peer feedback with a very limited focus on whole-class training.

Recognizing the link between learner beliefs and learning outcomes, Sato (2013) investigated the effects of training on learners' attitudes toward and engagement in peer interaction and peer feedback provision. Japanese EFL learners (n=167) completed a beliefs questionnaire before and after the training that raised the learners' awareness about the benefits of peer interaction and instructed some of them on how to provide feedback to each other; a subset of thirty-six also participated in follow-up interviews. Analysis of the twenty-six-item questionnaire completed before the training revealed that the students were generally in favour of peer interaction, seeing it as an essential step in improving their speaking skills, since it allows for repeated practice and provides additional opportunities for L2 output. Yet, they posited, the effectiveness of the practice depends in large part on the set up of the classroom and social relationships between interlocutors (see Sato, 2017, for discussion on the social dynamics of peer CF). The learners also welcomed CF from a peer, appearing to trust the quality of their correction, but worried about breaking the communicative flow with CF and possible negative affects that could arise from the act of correction. While all the participants engaged in peer interaction instruction that included a discussion of the benefits of peer interaction for L2 development and weekly fluency-focused collaborative tasks, only two groups received peer feedback training. One of the groups was taught to recognize and provide recasts in response to grammatical errors, and the other – prompts. The training followed the Modeling, Practice, and Use-in-Context sequence. The students first witnessed a role-play between the two participating teachers, during which they supplied each other with CF, but were then instructed to practice using their assigned CF technique during a role-play and to continue using it in the weekly fluency-focused activities. The beliefs expressed prior to the training appeared intensified afterwards since all the learners reported increased confidence in their peers as learning resources, and those with CF training became more willing to and confident about providing CF, the quantity of which increased over time.

To investigate the impact of peer feedback training on the amount of the supplied CF and its effectiveness, working with the same population described above for Sato (2013), Sato and Lyster (2012) trained two of four groups of learners to provide each other with CF – either by using recasts (n=46) or prompts (n=41) – during fluency-focused tasks. The remaining groups either participated in the tasks without CF focus (i.e., peer interaction group, n=42) or served as the controls (n=38). The CF training included modeling of a role-play, in which one of the teachers made errors that the other corrected using the feedback technique assigned to the observing group. In the practice stage, working in groups of three, the learners engaged in a similar role-play with peers, where each was assigned the role of speaker, observer, or feedback provider. Each student received a different scenario for the role-play along with a list of errors to include in the story they would create in the role of the speaker. As the speaker relayed the story, the feedback provider identified the errors and gave feedback whereas the observer kept a tally of the errors that were and were not addressed. In the final stage, the students participated in an information-exchange activity, in which they had to change partners, relay the information received from the previous partner to the new one in the same amount of time, and to provide CF. L2 development was assessed with two tasks. Administered at the beginning and end of the term, Task 1 elicited the participants' spontaneous production by having them individually narrate a story prompted by a set of pictures. To examine learners' interactional patterns, Task 2, administered at the end of the term, had students working in pairs on a decision-making activity. The results show that while the learners who received CF training improved both in accuracy and in fluency, those who participated in interaction only outperformed the controls overall. In terms of the CF types, the recast group corrected more than the prompt group. The authors suggest that because the learners were both receivers and providers of feedback, the benefits of CF were twofold. By receiving feedback within meaningful peer interaction, learners were prompted "to reassess non-target structures retrieved from long-term memory by reprocessing them in working memory with the help of declarative knowledge ... [and] giving CF to one another triggered an ideal proceduralization loop in which learners started to rely on procedural knowledge during spontaneous production" (p. 611). The study confirms positive effects for CF training and highlights the proactive role learners can play in promoting their own and peer L2 development.

Using a similar approach in training learners to provide each other with CF, Fujii, Mackey, and Ziegler (2016) employed a four-part "metacognitive instruction session" to alert a group of low-intermediate EFL learners in Japan about the importance of CF and to show them ways to provide feedback in interaction with peers. The training began with a presentation of the benefits of meaning-based instruction (vs. form-based teaching prevalent in this instructional context) and the developmental effects of interaction. Video examples of successful teacher–learner interactions during a decision-making task were shown next, and the learners were presented with "useful phrases" (i.e., interactional feedback in the form of clarification requests, confirmation requests, and recasts) that could be used to negotiate the intended meaning in interaction. In the final phase, learners engaged in two picture-difference tasks – one done with the teacher and another with a classmate. Showing learners how to initiate negotiation and provide CF, the teacher-led task modelled how it was to be performed with a peer. In addition to the training, the experimental group was asked to complete a questionnaire detailing their impressions about the instructional session. Both the experimental (n=23) and control (n=16) groups also completed pre- and post-tests in the form of two information-gap tasks. The results showed that the CF training positively impacted the experimental group in terms of the rate of feedback provision in learner–learner interactions and led to greater recognition of the benefits of CF to L2 development.

Since peer feedback does not "necessarily contain pedagogical intent to assist language development of another learner" (Sato & Ballinger, 2012, p. 159), but teacher CF does, it is necessary to investigate the effects of training learners to recognize the corrective nature of teacher-provided CF. Few studies have attempted whole-class explicit CF training (Bouffard & Sarkar, 2008; Kartchava, 2019). Bouffard and Sarkar (2008), for example, devised training to help Grade three French immersion students in Quebec, Canada (n=43) focus on the accuracy of their L2 output. Using twenty-three video-recorded communicative class activities (e.g., presentations, storytelling) during which the teacher supplied CF (mostly prompts in the form of elicitation, metalinguistic clues, and repetition), the researchers identified 287 episodes of the error-feedback-repair sequence (one error per episode) and presented them to the students (n=38) to discuss in groups. As they watched each video, the teacher prompted children to notice, identify, and repair errors; these discussions were audio-recorded and analyzed. The data revealed three levels of focus on form: (1) noticing was attributed to instances when the children located or repaired the error; (2) language awareness was manifested when the students identified the locus of the error and used metalanguage to explain it; (3) analysis referred to the instances when learners engaged in grammatical analysis of error. The discussions also pointed to improvement in the way students discussed and analyzed errors, becoming better able to articulate their understanding of the reasons for the supplied CF. This echoes the teachers' improved ability to use technical terminology to discuss CF reported by Vasquez and Harvey (2010), suggesting that such awareness-raising activities can be as effective with language learners since "articulation and reflection are reciprocal processes. One needs the words to talk about what one does and in using those words one can see it more clearly" (Freeman, 2002, p. 11).

Adopting a different approach, Kartchava (2019) investigated whether a classroom-based feedback training would help L2 learners recognize the corrective intent behind recasts supplied by a teacher during meaning-based tasks. While three groups of French L1 learners of English in Canada (n=62) participated in a whole-class communicative task, recasts were provided to only two groups (recasts only and recasts + training) in response to their errors with the past tense, with one of the groups (recasts + training) receiving CF training prior to the task; the third group served as a control. The training consisted of students watching two video clips of an ESL teacher correcting a learner and reflecting on what they saw. Then, they were told that the teacher provided the learner with CF and the recasts used in the videos were highlighted, with alternative iterations of recasts offered. For additional practice with recasts (Part 2), the students were asked to identify errors in three additional sentences (one error per sentence) and to suggest ways to correct them. Then the students were told that they would participate in a whole-class communicative task, during which the teacher would address their errors using recasts (Part 3). To measure L2 development on the target feature, all the students engaged in a written picture description task before and after the treatment. Noticing, in turn, was measured with uptake operationalized as learners' immediate reaction to feedback. The results show that the "trained" learners produced fewer errors overall, had a higher CF-uptake ratio, and repaired more than the "recasts only" learners; still, no differences in the learning outcomes for any of the groups were found.

What these studies collectively show is that learners are willing to engage in CF training and are likely to benefit from it in both learner-to-learner interactions and in whole-class discussions with the teacher. The more extensive training sessions, however, appear to be more effective as was the case in Sato and Sato and Lyster, with learners spending at least 10 hours practicing providing and receiving feedback; the same was true in Bouffard and Sarkar's study that engaged learners in over 167 minutes of awareness-raising discussions. Yet, even 10 minutes spent on training along with a 60-minute practice session in Kartchava (2019) appears to have yielded some recognition of the corrective intent of recasts among the trained participants. This training, however, did not yield any L2 gains. This result may be due to the fact that the learners were not given opportunity to verbalize grammatical analyses they engaged in, unlike the learners in Bouffard and Sarkar, precluding feedback on performance required for proceduralization of knowledge to occur. After all, training on its own may not be enough to improve performance in a large-group setting, but training coupled with practice and reflection on that practice may lead to marked development.

Conclusion and Future Research Directions

The chapter has argued that targeted training in CF can be helpful to both L2 teachers and learners not only to improve their feedback practices but to also help them to become expert consumers and users of the information CF contains. Deliberate practice and reflection on this practice yield expert performance that allows teachers to understand and improve their feedback provision skills as well as to recognize the expertise and knowledge that learners themselves bring to the task of correcting and language learning. For learners, engagement with information about CF coupled with deliberate practice and reflection may promote informed attitudes about feedback and enable knowledgeable engagement with it, which, in turn, may lead to L2 gains (e.g., Sato, 2013; Sato & Lyster, 2012). Still, to yield results that are not only sustained but also continue to be incrementally improved, deliberate practice, as conceived by Ericsson (1996, 2004), needs to be regular, consistent, and long term. The extant research on CF training has, to date, investigated short-term effects of such training and, in some cases, produced a limited number of inquiries investigating its particular aspect (e.g., learner whole-class CF training). While the student–teacher investigations generally lasted longer (about a term) than the ones done with L2 learners (but see Sato, 2013; Sato & Lyster, 2012), it is unclear whether the effects of this training will continue into the teachers' future practice and, if they do, to what extent they are to remain unchanged or grow; alternatively, in the absence of new knowledge, reflection, and practice, how likely are the effects of training to degrade or return to the pre-training levels altogether?

After all, initial teacher preparation and time spent in a job does not equal expertise, since "level of training and experience frequently has only a weak link to objective measures of performance" (Ericsson, 2006b, p. 686). Even if teachers read research to inform their practice, the impact is likely to be limited, especially with experienced teachers (Kamiya & Loewen, 2014). Nassaji (2012) has shown that experienced ESL and EFL teachers do not consume research often, citing lack of time, difficulty understanding the language used in research articles, and general lack of interest as the reasons; many felt that published research had little relevance to their in-class behavior and that teaching experience was the best way to improve their practice. If teachers try something new in their teaching and fail, they will likely abandon the initiative; still, if they succeed, the likelihood of them maintaining the practice without some kind of feedback on that practice is limited. Similarly, long-term effects on the learners' CF training is questionable, especially if the learners are not exposed to CF regularly, not given opportunities to practice providing feedback to others, and are not encouraged to engage in grammatical analysis. Even though the recent meta-analysis on instructed SLA (Kang, Sok & Han, 2019) has not found a clear advantage for longer or intensive instruction, the bigger question when it comes to the effects of CF training is their longevity. Hence, future investigations should consider and, possibly, address this issue.

While research on CF training among peers is burgeoning in oral and written CF (Tigchelaar & Polio, 2017), studies that focus on training learners to recognize teacher's feedback in the classroom are few. Yet this type of training is especially important in light of the high likelihood that learners will encounter CF in the classroom and that it will be supplied by a teacher. Since there is extensive evidence that learners can struggle to recognize the corrective intent of CF or its strategies, helping learners to focus their attentional resources on the processing of form in the input may be achieved through CF training. Doing so may alert learners to the presence of corrective information and prompt them to take advantage of it to improve their L2 knowledge. This training may also alert learners to the need to let the teacher know – by way of a signal, response, or grammatical analysis – that the supplied correction has been noticed and/or understood. After all, if teachers do not receive feedback on their CF practice from the learners, they may cease to offer it or continue with the same technique(s) they are used to providing without reflecting on its utility and effectiveness. This, needless to say, may affect their own development and that of their learners. Hence, additional investigations on CF training in the classroom are needed. Inquiries into CF training with the help of the computer or an electronic device are also merited since there is evidence that decontextualized computer-administered feedback can help learners notice the corrective intent of recasts (Sagarra & Abbuhl, 2013). Finally, as research on CF training grows, scholars may choose to ask innovative questions, adopt original research methods, and answer Han and Nassaji's (2019) call to "step out from the long shadow of our familiar territory, unafraid of wading into unchartered waters" (p. 395).

References

Ammar, A. (2008). Prompts and recasts: Differential effects on second language morphosyntax. *Language Teaching Research*, 12, 183–210.

Ammar, A. & Spada, N. (2006). One size fits all?: Recasts, prompts, and L2 learning. *Studies in Second Language Acquisition*, 28(4), 543–574.

Amrhein, H. R. & Nassaji, H. (2010). Written corrective feedback: What do students and teachers prefer and why? *Canadian Journal of Applied Linguistics*, 13(2), 95–127.

Arnett, K. & Turnbull, M. (2008). Teacher beliefs in second and foreign language teaching: A state-of-the-art review. In H. J. Sisken (ed.), *From thought to action: Exploring beliefs and outcomes in the foreign language program* (pp. 9–29). Boston, MA: Thomson Heinle.

Basturkmen, H. (2012). Review of research into the correspondence between language teachers' stated beliefs and practices. *System*, 40(2), 282–295.

Bell, T. (2005). Behaviours and attitudes of effective foreign language teachers: Results of a questionnaire study. *Foreign Language Annals*, 38(2), 259–270.

Borg, S. (2003). Teacher cognition in language teaching: A review of research on what language teachers think, know, believe, and do. *Language Teaching*, 36(2), 81–109.

(2006). *Teacher cognition and language education: Research and practice.* London: Continuum.

(2011). The impact of in-service teacher education on language teachers' beliefs. *System*, 39(3), 370–380.

Bouffard, L. A. & Sarkar, M. (2008). Training 8-year-old French immersion students in metalinguistic analysis: An innovation in form-focused pedagogy. *Language Awareness, 17*(1), 3–24.

Breen, M. P. (2001). *Learner contributions to language learning: New directions in research.* Harlow: Pearson Education Limited.

Brown, A. V. (2009). Students' and teachers' perceptions of effective foreign language teaching: A comparison of ideals. *Modern Language Journal, 93*(1), 46–60.

Brown, D. (2016). The type and linguistic foci of oral corrective feedback in the L2 classroom: A meta-analysis. *Language Teaching Research, 20*(4), 436–458.

Busch, D. (2010). Pre-service teacher beliefs and language learning: The second language acquisition as an agent for change. *Language Teaching Research, 14*(3), 318–337.

Cathcart, R. & Olsen, J. (1976). Teachers' and students' preferences for correction of classroom conversation errors. In J. Fanselow & R. Crymes (eds.), *On TESOL' 76* (pp. 41–53). Washington, DC: TESOL.

Clark, G. & Peterson, P. L. (1986). Teachers thought processes. In C. M. Wittrock (ed.), *Handbook on Research on Teaching* (pp. 255–296). New York: Macmillan.

DeKeyser, R. M. (1998). Beyond focus on form: Cognitive perspectives on learning and practicing second language grammar. In C. Doughty & J. Williams (eds.), *Focus on form in classroom second language acquisition* (pp. 42–63). New York: Cambridge University Press.

(2007). Introduction: Situating the concept of practice. In R. M. DeKeyser (ed.), *Practice in second language: Perspectives from applied linguistics and cognitive psychology* (pp. 1–18). Cambridge: Cambridge University Press.

Dilāns, G. (2016). Corrective feedback in L2 Latvian classrooms: Teacher perceptions versus the observed actualities of practice. *Language Teaching Research, 20*(4), 479–497.

Egi, T. (2007). Recasts, learners' interpretations, and L2 development. In A. Mackey (ed.), *Conversational interaction in second language acquisition: A collection of empirical studies* (pp. 249–267). Oxford: Oxford University Press.

Ellis, R. (2017). Oral corrective feedback in L2 classrooms: What we know so far. In H. Nassaji & E. Kartchava (eds.), *Corrective feedback in second language teaching and learning: research, theory, applications, implications* (pp. 3–18). New York: Routledge.

Ellis, R., Basturkmen, H. & Loewen, S. (2001). Learner uptake in communicative ESL lessons. *Language Learning, 51*(2), 281–318.

Ellis, R., Loewen, S. & Erlam, R. (2006). Implicit and explicit corrective feedback and the acquisition of L2 grammar. *Studies in Second Language Acquisition, 28*(2), 339–368.

Ericsson, K. A. (1996). The acquisition of expert performance: An introduction to some of the issues. In K. A. Ericsson (ed.), *The road to excellence:*

The acquisition of expert performance in the arts and sciences, sports, and games (pp. 1–50). Mahwah, NJ: Lawrence Erlbaum.

(2004). Deliberate practice and the acquisition and maintenance of expert performance in medicine and related domains. *Academic Medicine*, 79(10), S70–S81.

(2006a). An introduction to the Cambridge handbook of expertise and expert performance: Its development, organization, and content. In K. A. Ericsson, N. Charness & P. J. Feltovich (eds.), *Cambridge handbook of expertise and expert performance* (pp. 3–19). Cambridge: Cambridge University Press.

(2006b). The influence of experience and deliberate practice on the development of superior expert performance. In K. A. Ericsson, N. Charness & P. J. Feltovich (eds.), *Cambridge handbook of expertise and expert performance* (pp. 683–703). Cambridge: Cambridge University Press.

Freeman, D. (2002). The hidden side of the work: Teacher knowledge and learning to teach. *Language Teaching*, 35(1), 1–13.

Fujii, A., Ziegler, N. & Mackey, A. (2016). Peer interaction and metacognitive instruction in the EFL classroom. In M. Sato & S. Ballinger (eds.), *Peer interaction and second language learning: Pedagogical potential and research agenda* (pp. 63–89). Amsterdam: John Benjamins.

Han, Z. & Nassaji, H. (2019). Introduction: A snapshot of thirty-five years of instructed second language acquisition. *Language Teaching Research*, 23(4), 393–402. DOI: 10.1177/1362168818776992.

Hattie, J. & Timperley, H. (2007). The power of feedback. *Review of Educational Research*, 77(1), 81–112.

Horwitz, E. K. (1985). Using student beliefs about language learning and teaching in the foreign language methods course. *Foreign Language Annals*, 18(4), 333–340.

(1988). The beliefs about language learning of beginning university foreign language students. *Modern Language Journal*, 72(3), 283–294.

(1990). Attending to the affective domain in the foreign language classroom. In S. Magnan (ed.), *Shifting the instructional focus to the learner* (pp. 15–33). Middlebury, VT: Northeast Conference on the Teaching of Foreign Languages.

(1999). Cultural and situational influences on foreign language learners' beliefs about language learning: a review of BALLI studies. *System*, 27(4), 557–576.

Jean, G. & Simard. D. (2011). Grammar learning in English and French L2: Students' and teachers' beliefs and perceptions. *Foreign Language Annals*, 44(4), 465–492.

Johnson, K. E. & Golombek, P. R. (2002). Inquiry into practice: Teachers' personal and professional growth. In K. E. Johnson & P. R. Golombek (eds.), *Teachers' narrative inquiry as professional development* (pp. 1–14). Cambridge: Cambridge University Press.

Junqueira, L. & Kim, Y. (2013). Exploring the relationship between training, beliefs, and teachers' corrective feedback practices: A case study of a novice and an experienced ESL teacher. *Canadian Modern Language Review, 69*(2), 181–206.

Kamiya, N. (2014). The relationship between stated beliefs and classroom practices of oral corrective feedback. *Innovation in Language Learning and Teaching, 10*(3), 206–219.

(2016). What effect does reading academic articles on oral corrective feedback have on ESL teachers? *TESOL Journal, 7*, 328–349.

Kamiya, N. & Loewen, S. (2014). The influence of academic articles on an ESL teacher's stated beliefs. *Innovation in Language Learning and Teaching, 8*(3), 205–218.

Kang, E. Y., Sok, S. & Han, Z. (2019). Thirty-five years of ISLA on form-focused instruction: A meta-analysis. *Language Teaching Research, 23*(4), 428–453. DOI:10.1177/1362168818776671.

Karim, K. & Nassaji, H. (2015). ESL students' perceptions towards written corrective feedback: What type of feedback do they prefer and why? *The European Journal of Applied Linguistics and TEFL, 4*(1), 5–26.

Kartchava, E. (2016). Learner beliefs about corrective feedback in the language classroom: Perspectives from two international contexts. *TESL Canada Journal, 33*(2), 19–45.

(2019). Training learners to notice corrective feedback. In *Noticing oral corrective feedback in the second language classroom: Background and evidence* (pp. 81–115). Lanham, MD: Lexington Books.

Kartchava, E., & Ammar, A. (2014a). The noticeability and effectiveness of corrective feedback in relation to target type. *Language Teaching Research, 18*(4), 428–452.

(2014b). Learners' beliefs as mediators of what is noticed and learned in the language classroom. *TESOL Quarterly, 48*(1), 86–109.

Kartchava, E., Gatbonton, E., Ammar, A. & Trofimovich, P. (2020). Corrective feedback: Novice ESL teachers' beliefs and practices. *Language Teaching Research, 24*(2), 220–249. DOI: 10.1177/1362168818787546.

Larson-Freeman, D. (2003). *Teaching language: From grammar to grammaring.* Boston: Heinle.

Lasagabaster, D. & Sierra, J. M. (2005). Error correction: Students' versus teachers' perceptions. *Language Awareness, 14*(2–3), 112–127.

Lee, E. J. E. (2013). Corrective feedback preferences and learner repair among advanced ESL students. *System, 41*(2), 217–230.

Leeman, J. (2007). Feedback in L2 learning: Responding to errors during practice. In R. M. DeKeyser (ed.), *Practice in second language: Perspectives from applied linguistics and cognitive psychology* (pp. 111–137). Cambridge: Cambridge University Press.

Li, S. (2010). The effectiveness of corrective feedback in SLA: A meta-analysis. *Language Learning, 60*(2), 309–365.

(2017). Student and teacher beliefs and attitudes about oral corrective feedback. In H. Nassaji & E. Kartchava (eds.), *Corrective feedback in second language teaching and learning: Research, theory, applications, implications* (pp. 143–157). New York: Routledge.

Lyster, R. (2004). Differential effects of prompts and recasts in form-focused instruction. *Studies in Second Language Acquisition, 26*(3), 399–432.

Lyster, R. & Mori, H. (2006). Interactional feedback and instructional counterbalance. *Studies in Second Language Acquisition, 28*(2), 269–300.

Lyster, R. & Ranta, L. (1997). Corrective feedback and learner uptake: Negotiation of form in communicative classrooms. *Studies in Second Language Acquisition, 19*(1), 37–66.

Lyster, R. & Saito, K. (2010). Oral feedback in classroom SLA. *Studies in Second Language Acquisition, 32*(2), 265–302.

Lyster R., Saito, K. & Sato, M. (2013) Oral corrective feedback in second language classrooms. *Language Teaching, 46*(1), 1–40.

Mackey, A. (2006). Feedback, noticing and instructed second language learning. *Applied Linguistics, 27*(3), 405–430.

Mackey, A., Gass, S. M. & McDonough, K. (2000). How do learners perceive implicit negative feedback? *Studies in Second Language Acquisition, 22*(4), 471–497.

Mackey, A. & Goo, J. (2007). Interaction research in SLA: A meta-analysis and research synthesis. In A. Mackey (ed.), *Conversational interaction in second language acquisition: A collection of empirical studies* (pp. 407–452). Oxford: Oxford University Press.

Mackey, A. & Philp, J. (1998). Conversational interaction and second language development: Recasts, responses, and red herrings? *Modern Language Journal, 82*(3), 338–356.

Mackey, A., Polio, C. & McDonough, K. (2004). The relationship between experience, education and teachers' use of incidental focus-on-form techniques. *Language Teaching Research, 8*(3), 301–327.

Mori, Y. (1999). Epistemological beliefs and language learning beliefs: What do language learners believe about their learning? *Language Learning, 49*(3), 377–415.

Nassaji, H. (2011). Immediate learner repair and its relationship with learning targeted forms. *System, 39*, 17–29.

(2012). The relationship between SLA research and language pedagogy: Teachers' perspectives. *Language Teaching Research, 16*(3), 337–365.

(2015). *Interactional feedback dimension in instructed second language learning*. London: Bloomsbury Publishing.

(2016). Anniversary article: Interactional feedback in second language teaching and learning: A synthesis and analysis of current research. *Language Teaching Research, 20*(4), 535–562.

Nassaji, H., & Kartchava, E. (eds.). (2017a). *Corrective feedback in second language teaching and learning: Research, theory, applications, implications*. New York: Routledge.

(2017b). Conclusion, reflections, and final remarks. In H. Nassaji & E. Kartchava (eds.), *Corrective feedback in second language teaching and learning: Research, theory, applications, implications* (pp. 174–182). New York: Routledge.

Nunan, D. (1989). Hidden agendas: The role of the learner in programme implementation. In R. Johnson (ed.), *The second language curriculum* (pp. 176–186). Cambridge: Cambridge University Press.

Oladejo, J. (1993). Error correction in ESL: Learners' preferences. *TESL Canada Journal*, *10*(2), 71–89.

Peacock, M. (2001). Pre-service ESL teachers' beliefs about second language learning: A longitudinal study. *System*, *29*(2), 177–195.

Rahimi, M. & Zhang, L. (2015). Exploring non-native English-speaking teachers' cognitions about corrective feedback in teaching English oral communication. *System*, *55*, 111–122.

Rankin, J. & Becker, F. (2006). Does reading the research make a difference? A case study of teacher growth in FL German. *Modern Language Journal*, *90*(3), 353–372.

Ranta, L. & Lyster, R. (2007). A cognitive approach to improving immersion students' oral language abilities: The Awareness-Practice-Feedback sequence. In R. M. DeKeyser (ed.), *Practice in a second language: Perspectives from applied linguistics and cognitive psychology* (pp. 141–160). Cambridge: Cambridge University Press.

Robinson, P. (2007). Aptitudes, abilities, contexts, and practice. In R. M. DeKeyser (ed.), *Practice in second language: Perspectives from applied linguistics and cognitive psychology* (pp. 256–286). Cambridge: Cambridge University Press.

Roothooft, H. (2014). The relationship between adult EFL teachers' oral feedback practices and their beliefs. *System*, *46*(1), 65–79.

Russell, J. & Spada, N. (2006). The effectiveness of corrective feedback for second language acquisition: A meta-analysis of the research. In J. Norris & L. Ortega (eds.), *Synthesizing research on language learning and teaching* (pp. 131–164). Amsterdam: Benjamins.

Sagarra, N. & Abbuhl, R. (2013). Optimizing the noticing of recasts via computer-delivered feedback: Evidence that oral input enhancement and working memory help second language learning. *Modern Language Journal*, *97*(1), 196–216.

Sato, M. (2013). Beliefs about peer interaction and peer corrective feedback: Efficacy of classroom interaction. *Modern Language Journal*, *97*(3), 611–633.

(2017). Oral peer corrective feedback: Multiple theoretical perspectives. In H. Nassaji & E. Kartchava (eds.), *Corrective feedback in second language teaching and learning: Research, theory, applications, implications* (pp. 19–34). New York: Routledge.

Sato, M. & Ballinger, S. (2012). Raising language awareness in peer interaction: A cross-context, cross-method examination. *Language Awareness, 21*(1–2), 157–179.

Saito, K. & Lyster, R. (2012). Effects of form-focused instruction and corrective feedback on L2 pronunciation development of /ɹ/ by Japanese learners of English. *Language Learning, 62*(2), 595–633.

Schmidt, R. (1990). The role of consciousness in second language learning. *Applied Linguistics, 11*(2), 129–158.

(2001). Attention. In P. Robinson (ed.), *Cognition and second language instruction* (pp. 3–32). Cambridge: Cambridge University Press.

Schulz, R. A. (1996). Focus on form in the foreign language classroom: students' and teachers' views on error correction and the role of grammar. *Foreign Language Annals, 29*(3), 343–364.

(2001). Cultural differences in student and teacher perceptions concerning the role of grammar instruction and corrective feedback: USA – Columbia. *Modern Language Journal, 85*(2), 244–258.

Sepehrinia, S. & Mehdizadeh, M. (2018). Oral corrective feedback: Teachers' concerns and researchers' orientation. *Language Learning Journal, 46*(4), 483–500.

Sheen, Y. (2004). Corrective feedback and learner uptake in communicative classrooms across instructional settings. *Language Teaching Research, 8*(3), 263–300.

(2007). The effects of corrective feedback, language aptitude, and learner attitudes on the acquisition of English articles. In A. Mackey (ed.), *Conversational interaction in second language acquisition: A collection of empirical studies* (pp. 301–322). Oxford: Oxford University Press.

Tanaka, K. (2004). *Changes in Japanese students' beliefs about language learning and English language proficiency in a study-abroad context.* Unpublished doctoral dissertation, University of Auckland, New Zealand.

Tigchelaar, M. & Polio, C. (2017). Language-focused peer corrective feedback in second language writing. In H. Nassaji & E. Kartchava (eds.), *Corrective feedback in second language teaching and learning: Research, theory, applications, implications* (pp. 97–113). New York: Routledge.

Tsui, A. B. M. (2005). Expertise in teaching: Perspectives and issues. In K. Johnson (ed.), *Expertise in second language learning and teaching* (pp. 167–189). New York: Palgrave Macmillan.

Vásquez, C. & Harvey, J. (2010). Raising teachers' awareness about corrective feedback through research replication. *Language Teaching Research, 14*(4), 421–443.

Yoshida, R. (2008). Teachers' choice and learners' preference for corrective-feedback types. *Language Awareness, 17*(1), 78–93.

29

Perceptions and Noticing of Corrective Feedback

Reiko Yoshida

Noticing and Corrective Feedback

In this chapter, noticing of corrective feedback in different contexts – between teachers and learners, between peers, and in computer-mediated situations – is discussed, together with factors that affect noticing. Owing to limited space, the focus is on corrective feedback (CF) in oral communication; however, cases of CF in text communication are included, particularly in relation to computer-mediated chat.

According to Schmidt (2010), noticing means "the conscious registration of attended specific instances of language" (p. 725). Schmidt emphasizes that people only learn target language items to which they pay attention, and that second language acquisition, at least for adult learners, involves some level of conscious attention to form. Noticing forms part of "perception," which is defined as "a process which involves the recognition and interpretation of stimuli" (Rookers & Wilson, 2000, p. 1). Perception is thus broader in definition than noticing, including not only the recognition or registration but also the interpretation of a specific instance of language. It is worth noting that there is some debate about the importance of learners' noticing in second language (SL) or foreign language (FL) learning. For example, Tomlin and Villa (1994) suggest that learning without awareness is possible. However, Rosa and O'Neil (1999) point out that the majority of researchers agree that noticing is a crucial component of SL learning (Rosa & O'Neil, 1999; Schmidt, 1990, 1995). In his Noticing Hypothesis, Schmidt (1990) states that noticing is important for changing input into intake, which is crucial for language learning – unless learners recognize a specific instance of language, they cannot interpret and understand that instance for their learning. Therefore, noticing may be regarded as a first step for language learning. While the Noticing Hypothesis has received the criticism that noticing in itself does not develop learners' competence in SL/FL (e.g., Truscott, 1998), noticing is generally considered as important for learning in SL/FL classrooms.

It has been claimed that noticing may occur after CF, which is direct or indirect feedback in response to an error made by a learner and is usually carried out by a teacher. Based on their own earlier categorization (Lyster & Ranta, 1997) and also on Lyster's (2004) distinction between recasts (reformulations of errors) and prompts (a variety of different signals to indicate errors, with the exception of correct forms), Ranta and Lyster (2007) categorize CF into two types: (1) reformulations and (2) prompts. Reformulations include the following two types of feedback:

a. explicit correction (explicit provision of a correct form)
b. recasts (partial or complete reformulation of a learner's error).

Prompts consist of the following four types of feedback:

a. clarification requests (asking for clarification of a learner's utterance)
b. metalinguistic clues (comments, information, or questions related to the ill-formedness of a learner's utterance)
c. elicitation (asking a learner to reformulate their utterance)
d. repetition (repeating a learner's erroneous utterance).

What a learner needs to notice depends on the type of CF provided by the teacher. When CF includes a reformulation of a learner's error, the learner needs to notice the difference between the correct form and their error, a phenomenon known as "noticing the gap" (Schmidt, 1990). When a teacher provides prompts, a learner needs to perceive the teacher's utterance as CF and notice clues for a reformulation of their own problematic utterance if the CF includes such clues.

When a learner notices CF, they may or may not respond to it, and may or may not reformulate their incorrect utterance after being given it. When a learner does respond to CF, this is called uptake, and according to Lyster and Ranta (1997), it can include an acknowledgment such as *yes* or *ok*, or a full or partial reformulation of their error. This definition of uptake has frequently been used in studies of CF (e.g., Mackey & Philp, 1998; Panova & Lyster, 2002). More recently, Nassaji (2009, 2016) defined uptake as a response that involves some modification of the learners' output. Recasts would seem to be the type of CF that occurs most frequently in SL classrooms (Doughty, 1994; Lyster & Ranta, 1997), and recasts consist of 57 percent while prompts comprise 30 percent of all CF in SL/FL classes in Brown's (2016) meta-analysis. However, a review of FL studies (Lyster, Saito & Sato, 2013) notes that prompts occurred more frequently than recasts in some English, Spanish, and German classrooms.

The Noticing of Corrective Feedback

As stated earlier, CF is usually thought of as being provided by teachers, and this was the focus when researchers began investigating learners' noticing of CF. For this reason, the first two subsections here discuss studies which examine this type of feedback, first considering laboratory-based studies and then studies carried out in classroom settings. While much CF is provided by teachers, researchers began to realize that CF also occurred between learners, and so the third subsection here looks at those studies which have examined the noticing of CF in peer interactions. More recently, with developments in technology and its use in language learning contexts, researchers have started exploring the noticing of CF in computer-mediated language learning, as discussed in the final subsection here.

Laboratory Studies of Feedback Noticing

On the basis of the earlier findings of Doughty and of Lyster and Ranta, mentioned above, researchers carrying out laboratory studies (that is, studies conducted outside of the classroom) have particularly focused on learners' noticing of recasts. They have measured this by considering uptake (Mackey & Philp, 1998) and a learner's ability to recall CF online and retrospectively (Egi, 2007, 2010; Mackey, Gass, & McDonough, 2000; Mackey et al., 2002; Philp, 2003; Trofimovich, Ammar & Gatbonton, 2007), and also measured the noticing of recasts using tests before and after an experiment (Leeman, 2003).

Learners tend to notice recasts relatively often in these studies – for example, Philp (2003) found that learners of English as a Second Language (ESL) noticed 60 to 70 percent of recasts, which in her study were provided around errors related to English question forms in communication tasks with native speakers. In these types of studies, learners receive feedback from native speakers or teachers in pair interactions in laboratory situations (Egi, 2010; Mackey et al., 2000; Mackey & Philp, 1998; Nassaji, 2009), and feedback is provided on particular target forms (McDonough, 2007; Philp, 2003). Nicholas, Lightbown, and Spada (2001) have pointed out these characteristics of laboratory studies and stated that the participants are "in some sense 'ready' to receive the recast" (p. 749), which probably contributes to learners' higher attention to CF in these studies.

However, uptake may not always mean that a learner has noticed a recast as being error correction. In particular, if a learner gives a simple acknowledgment after a recast, this does not necessarily mean that they have noticed the existence of CF, although the acknowledgment would be treated in many studies as uptake, as noted earlier. Even the repetition of a recast by a learner does not show that the learner has noticed the differences between their error and the correct form, that is, that they have noticed the gap. To test this, Egi (2010) examined whether uptake did indicate noticing by learners of Japanese as a Foreign Language (JFL) by using stimulated recall reports after recast episodes. In recast episodes where learner uptake occurred, learners' reports showed that they perceived recasts as CF significantly more frequently compared to episodes where uptake did not occur. In episodes where learners repaired their errors, their reports indicated that they had recognized corrective recasts and noticed the gap significantly more frequently than episodes where repairs did not occur. This suggests that uptake does provide evidence of learners' noticing of CF, at least to some extent.

The noticeability of recasts has been shown to be influenced by (1) the characteristics of the CF, in particular the length and salience of recasts (Leeman, 2003; Philp, 2003); (2) the type of learner error, whether it was lexical, semantic, phonological, or morphosyntactic (Mackey et al., 2000); and (3) individual differences between learners, such as working memory capacity, phonological memory, attention control, analytical ability, and their proficiency level in the target language (Mackey & Philp, 1998; Mackey et al., 2002; Trofimovich et al., 2007). Shorter and more visually and auditorily prominent recasts are more noticeable for learners compared to recasts without those characteristics (Leeman, 2003; Philp, 2003). Learners notice recasts after lexical, semantic, and phonological errors more frequently than recasts after morphosyntactic errors (Mackey et al., 2000). Recasts are more noticeable for learners with a higher proficiency in the target language than for those with lower proficiency (Mackey & Philp, 1998). Learners with a larger working memory capacity report more frequent noticing of recasts (Mackey et al., 2002), and similarly learners with a larger phonological memory, a more extensive working memory span, more efficient attention control, and a stronger analytical ability tend to notice the feature targeted by the recasts more often than learners who do not have those characteristics (Trofimovich et al., 2007). Individual differences in terms of affective factors are also relevant here – Sheen (2011) investigated how anxiety influences ESL learners' noticing of CF and found that oral recasts were beneficial for learning only for learners with low levels of anxiety.

Braidi (2002) has pointed out that recasts can be focused on single or multiple errors and can occur in a number of different interaction patterns. She examined ESL learners' noticing of recasts in one-signal negotiated interactions, extended negotiated interactions, and nonnegotiated interactions, by investigating their responses to the CF. Recasts occurred in all these interaction patterns, and learners noticed recasts for multiple errors slightly more often than recasts for single errors; however, the difference was not statistically significant.

Egi (2007) researched how JFL learners' noticing of the positive and negative evidence in recasts was associated with their learning of lexis and morphosyntactics, by using stimulated recalls and post-tests. Noticing of negative evidence was defined as cases where learners reported that they had made errors and/or received recasts, but they did not notice the target-like models in the recasts. Noticing of positive evidence was seen in situations where the learners reported that they had found target-like models in recasts without showing attention to their errors. Learners' noticing of positive evidence alone or noticing of both positive and negative evidence was related to both lexical and morphosyntactic learning. Learners' noticing of positive evidence far more obviously contributed to their lexical learning than their morphosyntactic learning.

While most laboratory studies have examined recasts, researchers have also compared English language learners' noticing of CF between recasts and prompts, by investigating uptake (McDonough, 2007), by using stimulated recall of CF with video-watching (Ammar, 2008), and by looking at immediate recall of CF (Nassaji, 2009). In this research, learners notice clarification requests – a type of prompt – more frequently than recasts; however, both clarification requests and recasts facilitate the development of a targeted linguistic form (McDonough, 2007). The intent of prompts to provide a correction was noticed more often by learners than the intent of recasts (Ammar, 2008). On the other hand, learners show a higher rate of correction of their errors after recasts than they do after elicitation in immediate recall protocols; more explicit recasts and elicitations result in more frequent correction (Nassaji, 2009). Nassaji states that the explicitness of CF is a key factor for learners' noticing of CF and reformulations of their errors. Lin and Hedgcock (1996) investigated Spanish language learners' noticing of native speakers' metalinguistic input – another type of prompt – by looking at whether the learners incorporate the CF in their responses. They found that higher-proficiency learners notice and incorporate CF more frequently than lower-proficiency learners. This result supports the findings of Mackey and Philp (1998) in relation to the noticing of recasts.

Learners seem to notice recasts and prompts to different degrees when these are provided by native speakers or teachers in the context of laboratory studies. The noticeability of CF appears to be influenced by the salience and length of the CF, the error type that triggered the CF, and by learners' individual differences, such as working memory, analytical ability, their level of anxiety, and their proficiency level in the target language.

Classroom Studies of Feedback Noticeability

Studies carried out in the classroom which have investigated learners' noticing following CF from teachers have primarily looked at uptake (e.g., Fu & Nassaji, 2016; Loewen & Philp, 2006; Lyster & Mori, 2006; Lyster & Ranta, 1997; Ohta, 2001); some studies have also carried out stimulated recall interviews on CF episodes while watching or listening to a recording of the class (Mackey et al., 2007; Moroishi, 2002; Nabei & Swain, 2002; Yoshida, 2008, 2009, 2010). While most of the studies discussed in this section are observational, a few experimental studies which were carried out in classrooms (Lyster, 2004; Mackey, 2006; Sheen, 2008) are also included; in the observational studies, researchers examined naturally occurring CF in classrooms, while the experimental studies involved control groups, experimental activities, or teacher training prior to the classroom-based investigation.

Uptake rates after recasts in classroom contexts were 55 percent in Lyster and Ranta (1997), 40 percent in Panova and Lyster (2002), and 38 percent in Ohta (2001), all of which are lower than the 60 to 70 percent in Philp's (2003) experimental study. While uptake was defined in Lyster and Ranta (1997) and Panova and Lyster (2002) to include learner acknowledgments such as *yes*, uptake in Ohta (2001) was restricted to learners' full or partial reformulations of errors, which perhaps explains the slightly lower rate (38 percent) in that study. Learners seem to react to recasts less frequently in classroom than in laboratory studies, probably because there are more distractions for learners in classroom contexts, such as the existence of classmates, compared to the contexts of face-to-face pair interactions with native speakers in laboratory studies such as those in Philp (2003).

Lyster (1998) points out that the ambiguous nature of recasts, which are very similar to non-corrective repetitions, contributes to learners' infrequent noticing of recasts. Lyster (2004) also notes that recasts are less noticeable than other CF, such as elicitation or metalinguistic clues, especially for child learners in the communicatively oriented SL classrooms of an immersion program. After Ellis and Sheen (2006) pointed out that recasts can be given in different forms, such as implicit/explicit or intensive/extensive recasts, some researchers have investigated the relationship between noticing and different types of recasts. Loewen and Philp (2006) reexamined the data of an earlier study by Loewen (2004) about uptake following CF in English classes, and found that recasts with stress, declarative intonation, one change, and multiple feedback moves are more noticeable for learners. This result supports the findings of laboratory studies of Philp (2003) and Leeman (2003) that learners are likely to notice short and salient recasts more often than the longer and less salient ones.

In social contexts, such as language classrooms, learners sometimes notice recasts that have been provided to other learners – those incidental contrasts between learners' erroneous utterances and teachers' recasts directed to other learners are called incidental recasts in Ohta (2001). The noticeability of direct versus incidental recasts has been compared in some studies (Nabei & Swain, 2002; Ohta, 2001; Yoshida, 2009). Learners notice direct recasts (recasts that are directed to them, not to other learners) more often than incidental recasts, according to Nabei and Swain (2002). However this finding contrasts with those of other studies, which show that learners notice both direct and incidental recasts almost equally (Ohta, 2001; Yoshida, 2009). Because Nabei and Swain's (2002) research was carried out in a meaning-focused English class, they suggest that the learner's focus on meaning rather than form in the teacher's recasts led to the learner not noticing grammatical recasts unless they were directly provided to the learner. On the other hand, Ohta (2001) and Yoshida (2009) investigated Japanese language classes which were more focused on linguistic structure, and this may have contributed to the learners paying greater attention to their teachers' incidental recasts. Thus, the characteristics of different language classes seem to affect learners' noticing of recasts.

According to Lyster and Mori (2006), it is not only learners' noticing of CF that varies between different language classrooms, but also the relative occurrence of recasts and prompts. In a French language classroom, prompts were used more frequently than recasts, and learners noticed them more; while in a Japanese language classroom, recasts occurred more frequently and learners noticed them more often than prompts. Lyster and Mori suggest that the tendency of learners in the Japanese class to frequently repeat their teachers' models may have contributed to the learners' more frequent noticing of the teachers' recasts, which are more implicit as CF than prompts. Learners do notice targeted linguistic forms more often when prompts or recasts are provided than when no CF is provided (Mackey, 2006), and according to Mackey, the rate of noticing of CF also depends on the linguistic forms which are being targeted: CF related to question forms in English is more noticeable than CF around plurals and past tense, for example.

Learners' noticing of CF would appear to also be related to the type of error which triggers the CF. Moroishi (2002) found that more than 50 percent of teacher recasts were noticed and accurately perceived by Japanese language learners, and that morphosyntactic feedback was noticed and perceived more accurately than phonological and lexical feedback. This result contrasts with the findings of a laboratory study by Mackey et al. (2000) that English and Italian language learners notice and more accurately perceive CF on lexical, semantic, and phonological errors than on morphosyntactic errors. In a later study by Mackey et al. (2007), learners of Arabic generally noticed and understood morphosyntactic and lexical CF provided by teachers, but generally did not understand phonological CF. The form-focused nature of these Japanese and Arabic classrooms may have contributed to the more frequent noticing of morphosyntactic CF, compared to the English and Italian classrooms.

As noted in the previous subsection, laboratory studies have found that individual cognitive differences between learners, such as their working memory capacity or analytical ability, affect their noticing of CF (Mackey et al., 2002; Trofimovich et al., 2007), and that at least one affective factor, anxiety, also influence learners' noticing of CF (Sheen, 2011). Sheen (2008) examined how learners' noticing of recasts is influenced by their language anxiety in classrooms by using a language anxiety questionnaire and looking at the learner responses to recasts. She found that "low anxiety" groups of learners notice recasts more often than "high anxiety" groups.

Researchers have also focused on teachers' intentions in providing CF and learners' interpretations of the CF. For example, Roberts (1995) investigated how teachers' CF is noticed or understood by Japanese language learners, who were asked to categorize CF in a video of one of their classes; on average, approximately 35 percent of the CF was noticed and approximately 21 percent was correctly identified. Kim and Han (2007) explored the extent to which teachers' intentions in providing recasts and learners' interpretations of them overlap in an English as a Foreign Language (EFL) class, and whether learners recognize gaps between their errors and the linguistic information in the recasts. More than 50 percent of the corrective recasts were recognized in their study, and the gaps were noticed in more than 40 percent of the recasts, but more than 30 percent of the recasts were not recognized by the learners. These results suggest that relatively many recasts are not recognized or not understood even though they are recognized.

While the studies discussed so far have focused on oral interactional feedback, Han's (2001) longitudinal case study examined written feedback by considering the perceptions of a Thai student learning Norwegian. The learner's errors on a particular form were persistent in her written output, despite the teacher's repeated corrections, which provided the correct form. In an interview, Han found that the learner perceived both her output and the teacher's correction as acceptable. Han (2001) thus observes that even when learners notice feedback, they do not necessarily recognize the true difference between the corrected forms and their own output – here the learner noticed the particular forms in the feedback as well as the gaps between the teacher forms and her own output, but she did not perceive this as CF. Yoshida (2009) supports Han's (2001) conclusions. A Japanese language learner, who repeated a recast that had been provided by her teacher, reported in her stimulated recall interview that she had understood the teacher's recast as an alternative to her (erroneous) utterance and perceived both of them as correct. Cases such as these cannot be discovered using classroom recordings of the speech of teachers and learners – it is important to carry out stimulated recall interviews to learn about aspects of learners' noticing of CF that do not surface in the data of interactions between teachers and learners.

In Yoshida's (2009, 2010) studies, learners sometimes did not notice their teachers' CF or did not understand why their answers were incorrect compared to the correct forms in the CF, even when they responded to the feedback. However, the teachers tended to assume that those learners whom they perceived as "strong" had noticed and/or understood their CF, even when the learners did not in fact notice and/or understand it. The teachers also reported that they provided "strong" learners with prompts, because they perceived that they would be able to reformulate their errors without being given the correct forms (Yoshida, 2008). Thus teachers' perceptions of particular learners seem to influence their provision of CF to those learners. This may then affect the learners' noticing and/or understanding of the CF – those "strong" learners sometimes did not notice and/or understand the less overt CF provided to them by the teacher (Yoshida, 2009). This suggests that it is necessary to implement stimulated recall interviews with teachers as well as learners in order to understand teachers' perceptions of CF and of particular learners, since this in turn potentially influences learners' noticing of CF.

Overall, then, it would seem that learners quite often do not appear to notice their teachers' CF, especially recasts, in SL/FL classrooms. The characteristics of different language classrooms, such as whether they are form-focused or meaning-focused, seem to affect the occurrence of different types of CF and also affect learners' noticing of this CF. The type of error made by a learner in different language classrooms, the explicitness of CF, and the degree of learner anxiety similarly all seem to influence learners' noticing of CF. There are also discrepancies between teachers' intentions in giving CF and learners' interpretations of that CF. Perhaps most interestingly, stimulated recall interviews reveal that learners' repetition of a recast does not always show that they noticed their teacher's recast as CF.

The Noticing of Corrective Feedback in Peer Interactions

The studies discussed so far have focused on CF in interactions between teachers and learners, but CF also occurs between peers. This subsection discusses a number of studies on learners' noticing of CF which was provided by other learners. These studies include both classroom experimental studies, in which pairs of learners are given particular tasks in class (Sato, 2016; Sato & Ballinger, 2012; Sato & Lyster, 2012; Storch, 2001, 2002), and laboratory studies, in which pairs of learners and pairs of learners and native speakers are given tasks in order to compare the different types of pairs (Mackey, Oliver & Leeman, 2003; Oliver, 2002; Sato & Lyster, 2007; Shehadeh, 2001). In addition to studies designed specifically to look at peer CF, some studies of CF in the classroom have considered peer CF as well as teacher CF. In Ohta's (2001) study mentioned earlier, for example, recasts were provided by learners in peer work in classrooms, in addition to the teacher CF, and more than 70 percent of those learner recasts were noticed. In Yoshida (2009), the rates of learners' noticing of CF provided by other learners in peer-work situations (50% in the first semester and 56% in the second semester) was very similar to or even higher than their rates of noticing teacher CF in teacher-fronted situations (55% in the first semester and 35% in the second semester). Moreover, in classroom pair-work, learners overheard and noticed CF provided to other learners in pairs sitting close to them, and reformulated their own errors (Ohta, 2001; Yoshida, 2009).

Interactions with native speakers have traditionally been considered as more effective for learners than interactions with other learners – this follows from the Interaction Hypothesis (Long, 1996), which considers that learners need to be given comprehensible input, CF, and opportunities to produce output through negotiation for meaning (see Chapter 2, this volume). In order to find out more about learners' noticing of CF in learner–learner interactions, laboratory studies have compared interactions in dyads of native speaker and nonnative speaker with those of two nonnative speakers (e.g. Mackey et al., 2003; Oliver, 2002). It was found that more self-initiated repairs (Shehadeh, 2001) and more modified output after CF (Sato & Lyster, 2007) were produced in English language learner–learner dyads. Those results show that learners notice both their own errors and CF more frequently in interactions with other learners than with native speakers. Similarly, more opportunities for responses after CF have been found in child learner–learner dyads (Oliver, 2002), and this may potentially contribute to more frequent noticing and reformulation of errors. However, in the study of Mackey et al. (2003), although *child* learner-learner dyads noticed CF and reformulated errors more frequently than learner–native-speaker dyads, there was no significant difference between *adult* learner–native and learner–learner dyads when it came to learners' noticing of CF and modification of their output.

To find out why learners notice CF more frequently in peer interactions, researchers have explored learners' perceptions of interactions with different types of interlocutors. Sato and Lyster (2007) examined the perceptions that EFL learners had of their interactions with other learners and with native speakers. The learners perceived the interactions with other learners as more comfortable and nonthreatening than the interactions with native speakers, and felt that they had more time to think about what to say. The learners also commented that when they made errors, native speakers sometimes used elicitations as CF but then went on to provide the correct form in the continuing interaction in any case. So learners felt that they did not need to modify their utterances following elicitations, since the native speakers would provide the appropriate form anyway, and thus the learners perhaps did not attend to linguistic form and CF in these situations. The environment of the interaction and the characteristics of the interaction itself seems to influence learners' noticing of CF by their peers and by native speakers.

Sato (2016) examined the relationship between the noticing of CF and learners' interactional mindset by investigating the interactional behaviors of learners and their SL development after the interactions. The interactional mindset was defined as "a disposition toward the task and/or during the interlocutor prior to and/or during the interaction" (Sato, 2016, p. 255). He found that dyads with a collaborative interaction mindset were likely to notice and accept their partners' CF and develop their FL skills, compared to dyads with a more non-collaborative interaction mindset. Sato thus concluded that learners' interaction mindset can determine whether CF will be noticed or unnoticed. Storch (2001, 2002) similarly found that collaborative pairs of English language learners, who share goals and focus more on the learning processes than on performance, achieve more language learning than dominant/dominant and dominant/ passive pairs. Storch's collaborative pairs presumably have a collaborative interaction mindset, in Sato's terms, and this influences their noticing of peer CF.

Some researchers have investigated peer CF after they have trained learners to provide CF, hypothesizing that this will make peer CF more noticeable and more effective for learning. In a series of studies (Sato & Ballinger, 2012; Sato & Lyster, 2012), FL learners of English and French were taught how to provide CF and collaborate in peer interactions, and the learners' ability to notice CF was researched, looking at uptake and using pre- and post-tests. Sato and Ballinger (2012) found that collaborative pairs, in which both learners provided similar amounts of CF, showed higher language awareness and more noticing of CF produced by their interlocutors. On the other hand, the least collaborative pair, in which the learners' contributions to a task were unbalanced, often did not notice each other's CF. Sato and Ballinger contend that the most important factors for noticing of peer CF are trust and respect between the peers, and that a collaborative mindset is crucial to develop this trust and respect. According to Sato and Lyster (2012), not only in receiving but also in providing CF in peer interactions, learners' noticing of CF and their repair of errors increases. CF does not impede fluency but, rather, contributes to faster processing through noticing, which results in the development of fluency (Sato & Lyster, 2012). Sato and Lyster conclude that providing and receiving CF alike improve learners' noticing of both peer CF and errors. The learners' increased conscious awareness of linguistic forms, developed through providing CF to their interlocutors, may promote their own noticing of CF that is given to them.

Thus, studies suggest that the more comfortable and nonthreatening nature of peer interaction results in more frequent noticing of CF. However, dominance by one of the peers seems to affect the noticing of CF – collaboration appears to be key in the noticing of CF in peer interactions. Socio-affective factors, such as trust and respect, are important for facilitating collaboration, which in turn contributes to the noticing of CF in peer communication. When learners are both providers and receivers of CF, they seem to be more likely to notice both the errors of their peers and also CF which they receive, compared to when they are only receivers of CF.

The Noticing of Corrective Feedback in Synchronous Computer-Mediated Communication

While the focus so far has primarily been on oral interactions, CF has also been studied where it occurs in synchronous computer-mediated communications (SCMCs) using text, audio, or video, and this subsection discusses studies in this more recent area of research. Those studies include learners' noticing of computer-mediated CF provided by teachers (Blake, 2005; Loewen & Erlam, 2006; Shintani, 2015), a researcher (Gurzynski-Weiss & Baralt, 2014a), other learners (Baralt, Gurzynski-Weiss & Kim, 2016; Lai & Zhao, 2006; Pellettieri, 2000; Smith, 2004, 2009; Smith & Gorsuch, 2004; Yuksel & Inan, 2014), and native speakers (who are neither teachers nor researchers) as well as other learners (O'Rourke, 2005; Sotillo, 2005, 2009), and the noticing of CF generated by particular language learning computer programs (Heift, 2004; Heift & Rimrott, 2008).

Learners' noticing of a gap after a teacher's CF has been seen to occur in text SCMCs in a distance language course (Blake, 2005), and after other learners' CF in text SCMCs (Shintani, 2015). In stimulated recall interviews after task-based interactions, learners' recall of CF that occurred in text SCMCs has been found to be as accurate as their recall of CF that occurred in face-to-face interactions (Gurzynski-Weiss & Baralt, 2014a). This suggests that learners notice CF in text SCMCs just as they do in face-to-face interactions.

Researchers have found some positive features in relation to the noticing of CF in text SCMCs. In some stimulated recall protocols, learners recall grammatical and/or lexical CF that is given in text SCMCs more frequently than CF that is produced in face-to-face interactions (Lai & Zhao, 2006; Yuksel & Inan, 2014). Learners notice not only CF but also self-errors more often in text SCMCs (Lai & Zhao, 2006; Shintani, 2015; Smith, 2009) compared with face-to-face interactions. Text-based SCMCs encourage learners to pay a higher degree of attention to linguistic forms and function in meaningful communications (e.g., O'Rourke, 2005; Smith & Gorsuch, 2004). The written mode of communication, the explicitness and re-readability of messages, and the longer processing time due to the slower communication seem to contribute to learners' frequent noticing of CF and self-errors (Pellettieri, 2000; Shintani, 2015; Smith, 2004).

On the other hand, researchers have also found negative aspects related to the noticing of CF in SCMCs. CF, including recasts, can occur three or four turns after the errors in text SCMCs between a teacher and a learner and between learners (Lai & Zhao, 2006; Loewen & Erlam, 2006), and this delayed CF tends to go unnoticed by learners (Sotillo, 2005). Modified output and opportunities for modified output have been found more often in face-to-face communication between learners compared to SCMCs (Gurzynski-Weiss & Baralt, 2014a). This suggests that there is more noticing and more opportunities for noticing in face-to-face communication than in SCMCs. According to Gurzynski-Weiss and Baralt (2014b), full modified output in their study was connected most often with noticing in face-to-face interactions, while partial modified output was connected most frequently with noticing in text SCMCs, although both types of modified output were rare in the SCMCs. Full modified output in the SCMCs was associated more with social moves (actions to make communication smoother) rather than with noticing, showing a response to interlocutors – they were carried out using the copy-and-paste function, and interlocutors' feedback had not been processed or well understood. In a further study, Baralt et al. (2016) examined the relationship between learners' attention to form and their affective and social engagement by using chat logs and a questionnaire after SCMCs and face-to-face communication; they found that learners' cognitive engagement was influenced by their affective and social engagement. Affective engagement in social interactions led the learners to develop their awareness of form in face-to-face interactions, while in text SCMCs, which involve more independent work and less affective and social engagement, there was less cognitive engagement, potentially influencing the noticeability of CF. The researchers concluded that it is important to enhance learners' social and affective engagement in SCMCs to increase the noticing of linguistic forms and CF in text SCMCs.

Researchers have also investigated the noticing of CF in SCMCs between different types of interlocutor and between different modes (text, audio, and video). Sotillo (2005, 2009) compared SCMC communications between learners and native speakers with those between learners and advanced learners. In SCMC using text, audio, and video, more error-related communication episodes and more opportunities for error corrections were found in communications between the learners, which resulted in more frequent noticing of CF (Sotillo, 2005). Native speakers provided significantly less CF than learners, and much of the CF from the native speakers was indirect, which negatively influenced the learners' noticing of the CF. Sotillo (2009) found that the rate of occurrence of CF episodes was similar between video and text SCMCs, and that learners noticed the CF provided by both native speakers and advanced learners, and also noticed their own errors with no CF. Noticing occurred in only 45 percent of cases of CF in the video SCMCs, compared with 75 percent of cases of CF in text SCMCs. The visual salience of text messages and the longer processing time may have contributed to the higher rate of noticing of CF in the text SCMCs.

CF can also be provided by a computer in SL/FL learning programs. Heift (2004) found that in this case metalinguistic feedback with errors highlighted was the most noticeable CF for learners, and this was supported by Heift and Rimrott (2008), who studied CF in an online parser-based program for German.

In summary, studies show that CF in SCMCs enables noticing. Some studies have found that learners notice CF more often in text SCMCs, and that they recall CF in the SCMCs more frequently than CF in face-to-face communication. Learners have also been reported to notice their own errors more frequently in SCMCs than in face-to-face interactions, and learners often accurately perceive CF in SCMCs. The slowness of text communication and the saliency and re-readability of text CF appear to allow learners to attend to CF and errors more often. However, disadvantages of SCMCs have also been reported when it comes to noticing CF. Some studies have shown that modified output is found less often in SCMCs than in face-to-face interactions, which suggests there is less frequent noticing of CF in SCMCs. Delayed CF, which often occurs in SCMCs, is not likely to be noticed by learners. The use of the copy-and-paste function to respond to CF does not contribute to learners' processing of the CF. The very nature of SCMCs, which involve more independent work, seems to affect learners' cognitive engagement, because they have less social and affective engagement, and this may negatively affect the noticing of CF. Within SCMCs, different modes and different interlocutors seem to influence the noticing of CF. Thus, SCMCs have both positive and negative aspects when it comes to the noticing of CF, and the combination of those aspects seems to contribute to the different results found in different studies.

Teaching Implications and Suggestions for Future Studies

In laboratory studies, learners' noticing of CF has been examined using a number of different measures – uptake, online or retrospective recalls of CF, and pre-/post-tests. These studies have found that the noticeability of CF is affected by the type of error, the length and salience of the CF, the proficiency level of the learner, and their working memory capacity, attention control, and analytical ability. In classroom studies, learners' noticing of CF has been investigated using uptake, and some studies have also implemented stimulated recall interviews of CF episodes with audio or video recordings. The different focus of different language classrooms seems to affect the occurrence of different types of CF and also learners' noticing of the CF. The explicitness of the CF and learners' anxiety in language classrooms additionally influence their noticing of CF in the classroom. A further finding of studies is that there are discrepancies between teachers' intentions in giving CF and learners' interpretations of that CF.

Researchers have also examined the noticeability of CF in peer interactions and SCMCs, in association with learners' perception of the interactions and their interlocutors. Through these studies, it has been revealed that social aspects, such as the relationship between learners in peer interactions, are closely related to cognitive aspects, such as the noticing of CF.

Some teaching implications can be drawn from the results found in previous CF studies. Recasts should be salient in terms of their length and the number of errors they are correcting, and they should be visually and auditorily prominent. Teachers also need to consider learners' individual differences, such as their proficiency level, when providing CF. Recasts are more noticeable for learners with higher proficiency than those with lower proficiency (Mackey & Philp, 1998), and thus more explicit CF should be provided to learners with lower proficiency. However, teachers should be careful to avoid the common belief that "strong" learners always understand CF and be aware that just because learners repeat recasts does not necessarily show that they have noticed the errors and/or the CF – teachers may need to confirm whether learners have noticed the CF and give explanations when necessary. It is also crucial for teachers to understand that learners' anxiety impedes their noticing of CF (Sheen, 2008, 2011), so developing a relaxed and friendly classroom atmosphere will help to enhance learners' noticing of CF. Dyads with a collaborative interaction mindset tended to notice their partners' CF more often than dyads with a non-collaborative interaction mindset (Sato, 2016). When particular learners are dominant in pair- or group work, changing partners or group members to provide more cooperative interactions may be helpful to enhance the noticing of CF, and the development of a classroom atmosphere in which learners can cooperate with each other may similarly be helpful in promoting the noticing of CF. Computer-based text chats have certain strengths in terms of contributing to learners' noticing of CF, such as the slow pace of the communication and the re-readability of the text messages. The less obtrusive nature of text chat compared to face-to-face interaction may also be helpful for anxious learners. Using text chat as part of a lesson or an assessment task may be useful in promoting learners' attention to form and their noticing of CF.

While there have been a range of previous studies of CF and noticing, and the results have implications for teaching, there seem to be certain aspects that have largely been overlooked. When it comes to noticing, it is not always clear exactly what learners notice in CF episodes. Learners may notice: (1) the existence of feedback; (2) the existence of an error; (3) the correct form; or (4) the difference between the error and the correct form (the gap). Being able to notice the correct form or the gap may depend on the type of CF provided. According to the noticing hypothesis, noticing the correct form or the gap is necessary for learning. However, understanding – such as realizing why one's own output is incorrect compared to the correct form provided in CF (cf. Yoshida, 2009, 2010) – also needs to be examined, because understanding the nature of an error in comparison to the correct form is more facilitative for learning. In future studies, it will be necessary to examine more precisely what the learner notices and how this noticing is effective for learning; and how and when noticing leads to understanding should be also investigated to explore the process of deeper learning. Implementation of stimulated recall interviews is essential to understand those cases where learners do not notice the corrective intention of CF even though they notice the gaps. In recent SCMC studies, an eye-tracking system has been found to be an effective tool to probe learners' noticing (Smith & Renaud, 2013). This method may be very useful in combination with interviews to investigate what learners actually notice and what they perceive when the noticing occurs.

Affective factors clearly influence learners' cognitive engagement, as Baralt et al. (2016) have found. Sheen (2008, 2011) found that anxiety influenced noticing of CF. However, more studies about learners' affect and CF are essential so that teachers comprehend how learners' affect influences their noticing and understanding of CF. Studies have also found that anxiety affects language learning (Gardner, Tremblay & Masgoret, 1997; Hewitt & Stephenson, 2011; Horwitz, Horwitz & Cope, 1986; MacIntyre & Legatto, 2010), and positive psychology suggests that positive emotions enhance learners' attention as well as their resilience and motivation (Frederickson, 2001; Frederickson & Branigan, 2005; Frederickson & Joiner, 2002). Future studies could explore how positive emotions influence the noticing and understanding of CF.

The majority of studies of noticing and CF have examined this among learners of the English language or learners of European languages such as Spanish or French. More studies looking at the learning of Asian languages and other less commonly taught languages are necessary. This is particularly important, since previous studies have found that teachers and learners of Asian and less commonly taught languages tend to perceive CF more positively than learners of English or European languages (Brown, 2009; Schulz, 1996, 2001), and consequently the beliefs of the teachers and learners of those languages may influence the teachers' use of CF and the learners' interpretations of CF. Because adult learners – primarily university students – have been the participants in the majority of studies, more studies about child learners need to be carried out in the future to find out whether the types of CF that are noticed vary between child and adult learners. In group situations, such as classrooms or group work in SCMCs, incidental CF and noticing of this CF can occur, as Ohta (2001) and Yoshida (2009) found in Japanese language classrooms. How and when incidental CF is noticed in different learning contexts should also be investigated in future studies in order to understand not only explicit noticing but also how more implicit noticing occurs in classroom interactions.

References

Ammar, A. (2008). Prompts and recasts: Differential effects on second language morphosyntax. *Language Teaching Research*, *12*(2), 183–210.

Baralt, M., Gurzynski-Weiss, L. & Kim, Y. (2016). Engagement with the language: How examining learners' affective and social engagement explains successful learner-generated attention to form. In M. Sato & S. Bellinger (eds.), *Peer interaction and second language learning: Pedagogical potentials and research agenda* (pp. 209–239). Amsterdam: John Benjamins.

Blake, R. J. (2005). Bimodal CMC: The glue of language learning at a distance. *CALICO Journal*, 22(3), 497–511.

Braidi, S. M. (2002). Reexamining the role of recasts in native-speaker/nonnative-speaker interactions. *Language Learning*, 52(1), 1–42.

Brown, A. V. (2009). Students' and teachers' perceptions of effective foreign language teaching: A comparison of ideals. *Modern Language Journal*, 93(1), 46–60.

Brown, D. (2016). The type and linguistic foci of oral corrective feedback in the L2 classroom: A meta-analysis. *Language Teaching Research*, 20(4), 436–458.

Doughty, C. (1994). Fine-tuning of feedback by competent speakers to language learners. In J. Alatis (ed.), *Georgetown University Round Table (GURT) 1993* (pp. 96–108). Washington, DC: Georgetown University Press.

Egi, T. (2007). Recasts, learners' interpretations, and L2 development. In A. Mackey (ed.), *Conversational interaction in second language acquisition* (pp. 249–267). Oxford: Oxford University Press.

(2010). Uptake, modified output, and learner perceptions of recasts: Learner responses as language awareness. *Modern Language Journal*, 94(1), 1–21.

Ellis, R. & Sheen, Y. (2006). Reexamining the role of recasts in second language acquisition. *Studies in Second Language Acquisition*, 28(4), 575–600.

Frederickson, B. L. (2001). The role of positive emotions in positive psychology: The broaden-and-build positive emotions. *American Psychologist*, 56(3), 218–226.

Frederickson, B. L. & Branigan, C. (2005). Positive emotions broaden the scope of attention and thought-action repertoires. *Cognition and Emotion*, 19(3), 313–332.

Frederickson, B. L. & Joiner, T. (2002). Positive emotions trigger upward spirals toward emotional well-being. *Psychological Science*, 13(2), 172–175.

Fu, T. & Nassaji, H. (2016). Corrective feedback, learner uptake, and feedback perception in a Chinese as a foreign language classroom. *Studies in Second Language Acquisition*, 6(1), 159–181.

Gardner, R. C., Tremblay, P. F. & Masgoret, A.-M. (1997). Towards a full model of second language learning: An empirical investigation. *Modern Language Journal*, 81(3), 344–362.

Gurzynski-Weiss, L. & Baralt, M. (2014a). Exploring learner perception and use of task-based interactional feedback in FTF and CMC modes. *Studies in Second Language Acquisition, 36*(1), 1–37.

(2014b). Does type of modified output correspond to learner noticing of feedback? A closer look in face-to-face and computer-mediated task-based interaction. *Applied Psycholinguistics, 36,* 1393–1420.

Han, Z. (2001). Fine-tuning corrective feedback. *Foreign Language Annals, 34*(6), 582–599.

Heift, T. (2004). Corrective feedback and learner uptake in CALL. *ReCALL, 16*(2), 416–431.

Heift, T. & Rimrott, A. (2008). Learner responses to corrective feedback for spelling errors in CALL. *System, 36*(2), 196–213.

Hewitt, E. & Stephenson, J. (2011). Foreign language anxiety and oral exam performance: A replication of Phillips's MLJ study. *Modern Language Journal,* 1–20.

Horwitz, E. K., Horwitz, M. B. & Cope, J. (1986). Foreign language classroom anxiety. *Modern Language Journal, 70*(2), 125–132.

Kim, J. H. & Han, Z. (2007). Recasts in communicative EFL classes: Do teacher intent and learner interpretation overlap? In A. Mackey (ed.), *Conversational interaction in second language acquisition* (pp. 269–297). Oxford: Oxford University Press.

Lai, C. & Zhao, Y. (2006). Noticing and text-based chat. *Language Learning and Technology, 10*(3), 102–120.

Leeman, J. (2003). Recasts and second language development, beyond negative evidence. *Studies in Second Language Acquisition, 25*(1), 37–63.

Lin, Y. H. & Hedgcock, J. (1996). Negative feedback incorporation among high-proficiency and low-proficiency Chinese-speaking learners of Spanish. *Language Learning, 46*(4), 567–611.

Loewen, S. (2004). Uptake in incidental focus on form in meaning-focused ESL lessons. *Language Learning, 54*(1), 153–188.

Loewen, S. & Erlam, R. (2006). Corrective feedback in the chatroom: An experimental study. *Computer Assisted Language Learning, 19*(1), 1–14.

Loewen, S. & Philp, J. (2006). Recasts in the adult English L2 classroom: characteristics, explicitness, and effectiveness. *Modern Language Journal, 90*(4), 536–556.

Long, M. H. (1996). The role of the linguistic environment in second language acquisition. In W. C. Ritchie & T. K. Bhatia (eds.), *Handbook of second language acquisition* (pp. 413–468). San Diego: Academic Press.

Lyster, R. (1998). Recasts, repetition, and ambiguity in L2 classroom discourse. *Studies in Second Language Acquisition, 20*(1), 51–81.

(2004). Differential effects of prompts and recasts in form-focused instruction. *Studies of Second Language Acquisition, 26,* 399–432.

Lyster, R. & Mori, H. (2006). Interactional feedback and instructional counterbalance. *Studies in Second Language Acquisition, 28*(2), 269–300.

Lyster, R. & Ranta, L. (1997). Corrective feedback and learner uptake, negotiation of form in communicative classrooms. *Studies in Second Language Acquisition*, 19(1), 36–66.

Lyster, R., Saito, K. & Sato, M. (2013). Oral corrective feedback iin second language classrooms. *Language Teaching*, 46(1), 1–40.

MacIntyre, P. D. & Legatto, J. J. (2010). A dynamic system approach to willingness to communicate: Developing an idiodynamic method to capture rapidly changing affect. *Applied Linguistics*, 32(2), 149–171.

Mackey, A. (2006). Feedback, noticing and instructed second language learning. *Applied Linguistics*, 27(3), 405–430.

Mackey, A., Al-Khalil, M., Atanassova, G., Hama, M., Logan-Terry, A. & Nakatsukasa, K. (2007). Teachers' intentions and learners' perceptions about corrective feedback in the L2 classroom. *Innovation in Language Learning and Teaching*, 1(1), 129–152.

Mackey, A., Gass, S. & McDonough, K. (2000). How do learners perceive interactional feedback? *Studies in Second Language Acquisition*, 22(4), 471–497.

Mackey, A., Oliver, R. & Leeman, J. (2003). Interactional input and the incorporation of feedback: An exploration of NS-NNS and NNS-NNS adult and child dyads. *Language Learning*, 53(1), 35–66.

Mackey, A. & Philp, J. (1998). Conversational interaction and second language development: Recasts, responses, and red herrings? *Modern Language Journal*, 82(3), 338–356.

Mackey, A., Philp, J., Egi, T., Fujii, A. & Tatsumi, T. (2002). Individual differences in working memory, noticing of interactional feedback and L2 development. In P. Robinson (ed.), *Individual differences and instructed language learning*. (pp. 181–209). Amsterdam: John Benjamins.

McDonough, K. (2007). Conversational interaction in second language acquisition. In A. Mackey (ed.), *Conversational interaction in second language acquisition* (pp. 323–338). Oxford: Oxford University Press.

Moroishi, M. (2002). Recasts, noticing and error types: Japanese learners' perception of corrective feedback. *Daini Gengo to shite no Nihongo no Shuutoku Kenkyuu (Acquisition of Japanese as a Second Language)*, 5, 24–41.

Nabei, T. & Swain, M. (2002). Learner awareness of recasts in classroom interaction: A case study of an adult EFL student's second language learning. *Language Awareness*, 11(1), 43–62.

Nassaji, H. (2009). Effects of recasts and elicitations in dyadic interaction and the role of feedback explicitness. *Language Learning*, 59(2), 411–452.

(2016). Interactional feedback in second language teachig and learning: A synthesis and analysis of current research. *Language Teaching Research*, 20(4), 535–562.

Nicholas, H., Lightbown, P. M. & Spada, N. (2001). Recasts as feedback to language learners. *Language Learning*, 51(4), 719–758.

O'Rourke, B. (2005). Form-focused interaction in online tandem learning. *CALICO Journal*, 22(3), 433–466.

Ohta, A. S. (2001). *Second language acquisition process in the classroom: Learning Japanese*. Mahwah, NJ: Lawrence Erlbaum.

Oliver, R. (2002). The patterns of negotiation for meaning in child interactions.*Modern Language Journal*, 86(1), 97–111.

Panova, I. & Lyster, R. (2002). Patterns of corrective feedback and uptake in an adult ESL classroom. *TESOL Quarterly*, 36(4), 573–595.

Pellettieri, J. (2000). Negotiation in cyberspace: The role of chatting in the development of grammatical competence. In M. Warshauer & R. Kern (eds.), *Network-based language teaching: Concepts and practice* (pp. 59–86). Cambridge: Cambridge University Press.

Philp, J. (2003). Constraints on noticing the gap, nonnative speakers' noticing of recasts in NS–NNS interaction. *Studies in Second Language Acquisition*, 25(1), 99–126.

Ranta, L. & Lyster, R. (2007). A cognitive approach to improving immersion students' oral language abilities: The awareness-practice-feedback sequence. In R. M. Dekeyser (ed.), *Practice in a second language: Perspectives from applied linguistics and cognitive psychology* (pp. 141–160). Cambridge: Cambridge University Press.

Roberts, M. A. (1995). Awareness and the efficacy of error correction. In R. Schmidt (ed.), *Attention and awareness in foreign language learning* (pp. 163–182). Manoa: Second Language Teaching & Curriculum Center, University of Hawaii.

Rookers, P. & Wilson, J. (2000). *Perception: Theory, development and organisation*. London: Routledge.

Rosa, E. & O'Neil, M. D. (1999). Explicitness, intake, and the issue of awareness: Another piece to the puzzle. *Studies in Second Language Acquisition*, 21(4), 511–556.

Sato, M. (2016). Interaction mindsets, interactional behaviors, and L2 development: An affective-social-cognitive model. *Language Learning*, 67(2), 249–283.

Sato, M. & Ballinger, S. (2012). Raising language awareness in peer interaction: A cross-context, cross-methodology examination. *Language Awareness*, 21(1–2), 157–179.

Sato, M. & Lyster, R. (2007). Modified output of Japanese EFL learners: Variable effects of interlocutor versus feedback types. In A. Mackey (ed.), *Conversational interaction in second language acquisition* (pp. 123–142). Oxford: Oxford University Press.

(2012). Peer interaction and corrective feedback for accuracy and fluency development. *Studies in Second Language Acquisition*, 34, 591–626.

Schmidt, R. (1990). The role of consciousness in second language learning. *Applied Linguistics*, 11(2), 129–158.

(1995). Consciousness and foreign language learning: A tutorial on the role of attention and awareness in learning. In R. Schmidt (ed.),

Attention and awareness in foreign language learning (pp. 1–64). Manoa: Second Language Teaching & Curriculum Center, University of Hawaii.

(2010). *Attention, awareness, and individual differences in language learning.* In W. M. Chan, S. Chi, K. N. Cin, J. Istanto, M. Nagami, J. W. Sew, T. Suthiwan & I. Walker (eds.), *Proceedings of CLaSIC 2010, Singapore, December 204* (pp. 721–737). Singapore: National University of Singapore, Centre for Language Studies.

Schulz, R. A. (1996). Focus on form in the foreign language classroom: Students' and teachers' views on error correction and the role of grammar. *Foreign Language Annals, 29*(3), 343–364.

(2001). Cultural differences in student and teacher perceptions concerning the role of grammar instruction and corrective feedback: USA-Colombia. *Modern Language Journal, 85*(2), 244–258.

Sheen, Y. (2008). Recasts, language anxiety, modified output, and L2 learning. *Language Learning, 58*(4), 835–874.

(2011). *Corrective feedback, individual differences and second language learning.* Dordecht: Springer.

Shehadeh, A. (2001). Self- and other-initiated modified output during task-based interaction. *TESOL Quarterly, 35*(3), 433–457.

Shintani, N. (2015). The effects of computer-mediated synchronous and asynchronous direct corrective feedback on writing: A case study. *Computer Assisted Language Learning, 29*(3), 517–538.

Smith, B. (2004). Computer-mediated negotiated interaction and lexical acquisition. *Studies in Second Language Acquisition, 26*(3), 365–398.

(2009). The relationship between scrolling, negotiation, and self-initiated self-repair in an SCMC environment. *CALICO Journal, 26*(2), 231–245.

Smith, B. & Gorsuch, G. J. (2004). Synchronous computer mediated communication captured by usability lab technologies: New interpretations. *System, 32,* 553–575.

Smith, B. & Renaud, C. (2013). Using eye tracking as a measure of foreign language learners' noticing of recasts during computer-mediated writing conferences. In K. McDonough & A. Mackey (eds.), *Second language interaction in diverse educational contexts* (pp. 147–166). Amsterdam: John Benjamins.

Sotillo, S. (2005). Corrective feedback via instant messenger learning activities in NS–NNS dyads. *CALICO Journal, 22*(3), 467–496.

(2009). Learner noticing, negative feedback, and uptake in synchronous computer-mediated environments. In L. B. Abraham & L. Williams (eds.), *Electronic discourse in language learning and language teaching* (pp. 87–110). Amsterdam: John Benjamins.

Storch, N. (2001). How collaborative is pair work? ESL tertiary students composing in pairs. *Language Teaching Research, 5*(1), 29–53.

(2002). Patterns of interaction in ESL pair work. *Language Learning, 52*(1), 119–158.

Tomlin, R. & Villa, V. (1994). Attention in cognitive science and SLA. *Studies in Second Language Acquisition, 16*(4), 183–204.

Trofimovich, P., Ammar, A. & Gatbonton, E. (2007). How effective are recasts? The role of attention, memory, and analytical ability. In A. Mackey (ed.), *Conversational Interaction in Second Language Acquisition* (pp. 171–195). Oxford: Oxford University Press.

Truscott, J. (1998). Noticing in second language acquisition: A critical review. *Second Language Research, 14*(2), 103–135.

Yoshida, R. (2008). Teachers' choice and learners' preference of corrective-feedback types. *Language Awareness, 17*(1), 78–93.

(2009). *Learners in Japanese language classrooms: Overt and covert participation.* London: Continuum.

(2010). How do teachers and learners perceive corrective feedback in the Japanese language classroom? *Modern Language Journal, 94*(2), 293–314.

Yuksel, D. & Inan, B. (2014). The effects of communication mode on negotiation of meaning and its noticing. *ReCALL, 26*(3), 333–354.

Part VIII

Individual Differences, Tasks, and Other Language- and Learner-Related Factors

30

Age and Corrective Feedback

Alyssa Vuono and Shaofeng Li

Despite the enormity of the body of research on corrective feedback, one factor that has been almost entirely ignored is age. The bulk of the research concerns adult learners, over the age of 18, while studies investigating child learners, or language learners between the ages of 7 and 12 years, are few and far between. While comparisons have been made to illuminate feedback provided to learners of different ages (Mackey, Oliver & Leeman, 2003), no experimental studies have investigated age as an independent variable impacting the efficacy of feedback for child and adult learners. The limited research on child learners (Ammar & Spada, 2006; Li, Ellis & Zhu, 2016; Lyster, 2004) does not refer to age as a main explanatory factor for the reported results. This chapter seeks to provide an extensive and in-depth discussion of the age factor from various perspectives. Given that the research on adult learners has been extensively discussed and synthesized in other chapters, we focus on the studies of child learners. We start by presenting the different theoretical positions regarding the relevance of age to the effects of feedback on second language (L2) development. We proceed to review the research on the role of feedback in first language (L1) learning before synthesizing the literature on feedback in L2 learning. Finally, we conclude the chapter by discussing the implications for researchers and teachers.

Theoretical Accounts on the Relationship between Age and Corrective Feedback

There are several theories related to the relevance of feedback to language acquisition, but they do not make overt claims about the impact of age in relation to feedback provision nor efficacy. For instance, Krashen (1982) argues that only positive evidence is necessary to acquisition and that negative evidence, in the form of corrective feedback or otherwise, is not only irrelevant but would actually hinder language development in child and adult learners alike. The Interaction Hypothesis emphasizes the importance of embedding feedback in negotiated interaction in facilitating learners' communicative competence. However, the theory and the related research do not distinguish adults and children (Long, 1991). In other words, researchers championing the Interaction Hypothesis attach importance to interactional feedback regardless of whether the learners are adults or children. A similar stance is embraced by those who base their research on skill acquisition theory (e.g., Lyster, 2004). These researchers argue that the primary function of feedback, especially prompts, is to push the learner to retrieve, practice, and proceduralize previously learned linguistic knowledge. The research based on this theory has been conducted with both adult (e.g., Yang & Lyster, 2010) and young L2 learners (e.g., Lyster, 2004), assuming that feedback is effective regardless of learners' age.

Whereas the theories hitherto described maintained the notions that acquisition is the same for all learners with no consideration for differences on the basis of age, the Fundamental Difference Hypothesis (Bley-Vroman, 1990) identifies age differences as the logical problem in language learning. This hypothesis identifies various ways in which adults and children vary when acquiring a second or other language, highlighting the overall failure of adult learners to the extent that Bley-Vroman (1990) claims that adults who do gain native-like success are as much of an anomaly as native-speaking children who are unable to do so. He suggests that adults rely on problem-solving abilities because they no longer have access to Universal Grammar, or domain-specific mechanisms, which are available to children when acquiring a first or other language. For this reason, according to the Fundamental Difference Hypothesis, children are better able to rely on implicit or intuitive means of acquiring language, whereas for adults the process is more explicit and strenuous. Based on this theory, corrective feedback, which affords negative evidence and facilitates explicit learning, is essential for adult language learning but unnecessary for child language acquisition. As Moulton and Robinson (1981) pointed out, "while it is debatable exactly how much deliberate shaping the average child receives, no one would claim that deliberate feedback and control over the child's linguistic experience is necessary" (p. 245).

Because adults are perceived as more capable of learning and applying metalinguistic components of language and children less so, teaching of different age groups reflects the notion that younger children do not benefit from explicit or grammatical instruction (Lichtman, 2016). In line with these ideas, teachers are normally trained to teach language to children using implicit techniques and to teach adult learners applying a more explicit approach. However, there is evidence that children benefit from explicit instruction as much as adults (Lichtman, 2016). Lichtman (2016) proposes that the explicit and implicit debate has evolved into a chicken and egg problem. She developed the Instructional Hypothesis, claiming that implicit pedagogical practices impact the learning habits of children, while adults, who are typically taught using explicit or metalinguistic pedagogy, may exhibit habits that correlate with their preparedness to learn explicitly. To investigate the Instructional Hypothesis, Lichtman (2016) taught an artificial mini-language to child and adult learners either explicitly or implicitly. When tested, seven days later, all participants were able to learn various components of the mini-language and to generate creative sentences in the language as well as to identify grammatical and ungrammatical sentences in the target language. If explicit instruction is beneficial to both children and adults, as demonstrated by Lichtman's (2016) findings, it follows that negative feedback may also be useful for all age groups, depending upon the feedback with which they are most frequently provided.

Feedback from Caregivers in L1 Acquisition

Similar to the assertions made by the Fundamental Difference Hypothesis, Aljaafreh and Lantolf (1994) claim that "error correction is apparently neither a necessary nor a sufficient condition for L1 learning in children" (p. 465). They argue that because learning is implicit in the first language, and negative evidence in the form of error corrections can be regarded as explicit, children stand to gain nothing from corrective feedback in their native tongues. Nonetheless, parents, caregivers, and siblings provide negative evidence to toddlers as they acquire their first language.

In an investigation of recordings available in the CHILDES Archive of parent–child interactions in both French and English, Chouinard and Clark (2003) discovered that parents provided corrections for 48–67 percent of their children's erroneous utterances. They also found that when as little as six months had lapsed, parents were more likely to ignore their child's errors and less inclined to provide feedback than they had six months prior. Chouinard and Clark (2003) speculate that the cause for this decrease in corrections occurred not because of the decrease in the frequency of errors but rather because of the comprehensibility of the errors. As the toddlers grew from 2 to 4 years old, their parents were better able to decipher what was being said, and so there was a decreased need to negotiate meaning. Their findings indicate that toddlers progressed to using more adult-like forms over the span of time investigated. That is, the toddlers exhibited fewer errors and their errors were more likely to be ignored by their parents as they got older. Furthermore, a greater proportion of errors were left ignored or uncorrected by caregivers as the children matured.

Another possible explanation for the decrease in error correction through provision of meaning-focused feedback is that parents become more directive as their children age (Illmann, 1995). Through use of more directive, question-based feedback as toddlers develop, greater opportunity is provided for the child to modify their output as well as recognize their own errors, thus encouraging self-correction. As Illmann (1995) describes, feedback provided in the L1 shifts from input-providing to output-prompting as children get older. Furthermore, Farrar (1990) found recasts to be effective at particular developmental stages in the child's morphological acquisition but not "prior to the time the children are cognitively ready to extract a morpheme or once they have successfully extracted it" (p. 621). Therefore, the developmental preparedness of the learner, or *linguistic readiness*, should be considered in determining when it is appropriate to begin the transition from recast-type to output-prompting feedback methods, although parents and caregivers seem to intuitively make this shift.

Parents are not the only people who provide input and feedback to emergent L1 users. In an investigation of interactions with children averaging 27 months old, Strapp (1996) found that older siblings, who averaged 4 years of age, provided less corrective feedback than their parents. Interestingly, relatively the same amount of feedback was provided if they were in dyads with one parent, triads with both parents, or tetrads with their parents and sibling. That is to say that regarding the quantity of feedback, the size of the group was insignificant, but the members of the group were highly relevant.

To sum up, the recurring trend in studies presented here shows an overall shift in feedback provided to toddlers as they age. At early stages of L1 development, parents and caregivers provide extensive feedback with a focus on meaning, most typically in the form of recasts. As the child's language abilities develop, instances of feedback maintain a focus on meaning, but the correct forms and verbiage are elicited through use of questioning and other forms of negotiation-based feedback. Also, as children get older and are less likely to exhibit errors in their language production, their errors are more likely to be ignored, and feedback is provided less frequently. That is, as children gain proficiency, they are less likely to commit errors, but even if they do, those errors are more likely to be ignored by a caregiver. It follows that the same may be true for L2 learners in that, as they gain proficiency and become more able to fluently convey their intended meaning, form-focused corrections may occur less frequently than at early stages of acquisition. However, in the language classroom where linguistic forms are more often the focus of instruction, corrective feedback is likely more frequent than in other contexts, regardless of learner proficiency. Unfortunately, prior research on oral feedback provided in the L1 has maintained a focus on parents and caregivers, with no studies on oral corrective feedback provided in the L1 classroom; yet one might expect corrective feedback to occur in the English language arts classroom.

Feedback in Second Language Research

Before considering feedback provision and feedback efficacy in various contexts, we must first provide a taxonomy of feedback. In order to make the studies comparable, we employed Ellis's (2016) categorizations of feedback types as being either input-providing or output-prompting. Input-providing feedback includes any feedback in which the learner is provided with the correct form of their erroneous statement. Conversely, output-prompting feedback aims to elicit the correct form from the learner. Table 30.1 provides examples of possible input-providing and output-prompting feedback made in response to the erroneous statement, "Yesterday, I play in the park."

Table 30.1 *Types of corrective feedback with examples of correction to a student's erroneous utterance *"Yesterday, I play in the park"*

Input-providing	Output-prompting

• Recasts
   o "You played."
• Explicit correction
   o "Not play, played."
• Explicit correction + metalinguistic explanation
   o "No, yesterday is in the past, you played."
	• Repetition
	   o "Yesterday you play?"
	• Clarification requests
	   o "Sorry?"
	• Metalinguistic comments
	   o "Try again in the past tense."
	• Elicitation
	   o "You ... ?"
	• Paralinguistic signal
	   o "Yesterday you play." (with stress)

Source. Adapted from Ellis, 2016, p. 418

Feedback Provided in the Classroom Context by Age

A number of studies have examined the incidence and distribution of corrective feedback in child language classes. The observational studies in Table 30.2 represent some major trends that emerged from the research. The studies were selected through a thorough search of LLBA and ERIC databases as well as top journals in the field of second language acquisition. The articles were selected to illustrate trends rather than to reach conclusions. The quantity of feedback provided to learners, which could be the result of several different factors, is reported as both total observed corrective feedback moves as well as the ratio of moves per hour. The data show that the quantity of feedback provided in each of these contexts varies greatly, with some students receiving as little as two corrections per hour (Simard & Jean, 2011) and others nearly forty corrections per hour (Lochtman, 2002; Lyster & Ranta, 1997). Similarly, there is great variability in the duration of observations, ranging from 100 utterances to as many as sixty-four lessons.

Table 30.2 Feedback provided by age in the classroom

Context	Age	Observed hours	Total CF moves	Moves per hour	Input-providing (%)	Output-prompting (%)
1. English & Spanish immersion (Vicente-Rasoamalala, 2009)	5–10 and 13–14 years	70	1186	17	12	88
2. ESOL program (Choi & Li, 2012)	6–12 years 2nd–6th grade	8	147	18	85	15
3. Intensive ESL (Oliver, 2000)*	8–12 years	first 100 utterances			36	12
4. English immersion (Lee, 2007)	8–9 years	10	133	13	53	47
5. Japanese immersion (Mori, 2002)	9–10 years	15	259	17	65	35
6. French immersion (Lyster & Ranta, 1997)	9–10 years	18	686	38	55	45
7. EFL (Havranek, 2002)	10–university age	48–64 lessons	1,700	26–35	47	53
8. FSL (Simard & Jean, 2011)	11–16 years	12	73	6	25	75
9. ESL (Simard & Jean, 2011)	11–16 years	8	235	28	41	59
10. FSL (Simard & Jean, 2011)	11–16 years	31	73	2	32	68
11. ESL (Simard & Jean, 2011)	11–16 years	29	235	8	48	52
12. EFL (Yang, 2009)	12–13 and 16–17 years	6	36	6	31	69
13. German FL (Lochtman, 2002)	15–16 years	10	394	39	30	70

Source. Adapted from Lyster, Saito & Sato, 2013, p. 6

Note: The representative studies in Table 30.2 were selected based on a thorough search in top journals in the field of second language acquisition. It should not be considered an exhaustive list, nor should conclusions be reached on the basis of this list. The studies referenced in Table 30.2 were used for identifying trends within existing published data.

* Percentages reported by Oliver (2000) exclude ignored learner errors.

With regard to the distribution of different feedback types, the majority of oral corrective feedback is provided through input-providing techniques to children under 12 years old (studies 1–8), most frequently in the form of recasts. It appears that in the immersion setting, regardless of location, children are more likely to receive recasts than output-prompting forms of feedback, with the exception of Vicente-Rasoamalala's (2009) study. The lack of differentiation between child (5–10 years old) and adolescent (13–14 years old) classrooms may have impacted the heightened frequency of metalinguistic feedback in Vicente-Rasoamalala's results. It is also possible that the foreign language learning environment may have impacted the heightened frequency of output-prompting feedback in Senegal immersion programs (Vicente-Rasoamalala, 2009), although that was not the case among other immersion programs such as Japanese immersion in the United States (Mori, 2002) or English immersion in Korea (Lee, 2007), with participant ages ranging from 9 to 10 and 8 to 9 years respectively. However, in non-immersion EFL classes in Germany, output-prompting was the preferred form of feedback provided to child and adolescent learners, even though feedback provided was recorded for 10-year-old to college-aged students without differentiation (Havranek, 2002). We are uncertain why corrections provided in this context deviated from the findings of other observational studies within this age group. One of the reasons may be that the classes observed took place in the foreign language environment, which typically has a strong focus on form with limited opportunity for communicational practice outside of the classroom and may lend itself to more output-prompting feedback in the form of metalinguistic cues. In the same vein, because the nature of foreign language classes is more form-focused, teachers may be more willing to devote more class time to prompting feedback, spending more time eliciting the correct response from the learner rather than providing the student with the correct linguistic form and proceeding with the lesson. Alternatively, in the immersion context, in which content area subjects are taught in the target language without explicit language instruction, prompts may be viewed as more interruptive of lessons. Teachers in immersion classrooms may provide recasts more frequently to save class time and maintain the focus of the lesson on course content rather than on linguistic components. Similarly, second language classes, where the target language is the lingua franca of the geographical region, are more conducive to implicit, meaning-focused, feedback such as recasts. Teachers may also prefer using input-providing feedback as a way of scaffolding learning for children, particularly when language use may not be the focus of the lesson.

Although their observations revealed the occurrence of more input-providing than output-prompting feedback in a children's (6–12 years) ESOL classroom, Choi and Li (2012) found explicit correction to be more prevalent in the classroom than what Lyster and Ranta (1997) reported in the grade 5 immersion context. They elaborated that the discrepancy may be due, in part, to the differences between immersion and ESOL settings. Because the ESOL setting has a greater focus on linguistic outcomes, there is likely to be more focus on language and, therefore, explicit correction of errors. However, in the immersion context, the focus is on content and, therefore, implicit corrections with a focus on meaning are more likely to occur.

In every study with adolescent participants, or learners aged 12–17 (studies 8–13 in Table 30.2), output-prompting feedback was preferred by middle and high school teachers. This heightened frequency of prompting feedback was observed in studies focused exclusively on adolescent classrooms as well as the studies which considered children and adolescents simultaneously. It is possible that because immersion is less common for this age group, input-providing feedback seemed less favored. Another possibility is that teachers of adolescents view their students as more capable of correcting their own erroneous utterances, potentially because of heightened metalinguistic awareness and greater attentional resources available to them at this age. It is also conceivable that teenagers need more push and discipline, which output-prompting feedback may promote, as they tend to be more easily distracted than adults.

While the studies represented in Table 30.2 focused on observations of children and adolescents, we now turn our attention to studies of adult language learners to compare the findings to the observations made in child and adolescent classrooms. Interestingly, while it should be expected that adult learners' attentional resources and metalinguistic awareness are more advanced than those of adolescents' and that teachers would continue to provide output-prompting feedback to adult learners, recasts remain the most frequent form of feedback provided to adults over the age of 17 (Ellis, Basturkmen & Loewen, 2001; Kamiya, 2016; Oliver, 2000; Panova & Lyster, 2002; Sheen, 2004). There is a possibility that teachers refrain from using output-prompting feedback with adults because adults are more self-conscious and are likely to perceive explicit output-prompting feedback as face-threatening (Kamiya, 2016).

The number of corrective feedback instances per hour did not seem to vary much between the studies. Overall, there appear to be fewer instances and less variability across contexts of corrective feedback provided to adults compared to children and adolescents, with the exception of Panova and Lyster's (2002) observation of adult ESL students in Quebec. Panova and Lyster (2002) also had the largest range of ages reported (17–55 years) among studies in which age was specified rather than grouped into the "adults" category. There is a chance, as was demonstrated with children learning their L1, that as people age, more errors are ignored and fewer corrections are provided.

It is worth noting that the patterns regarding age and feedback are speculative and that age has rarely been discussed as a moderating factor for the incidence of feedback in the classroom. Among the studies included in Table 30.2, Choi and Li's (2012) study was the only one that discussed the role of age in the findings, saying that "the higher percentage of explicit correction in this context than in adult ESL/EFL classes may be due to the teacher's belief that the young children were not attentive enough to notice the corrective force of more implicit types of feedback and might therefore need more explicit cues as attention grabbers" (p. 346). They suggest that feedback be made more explicit and more salient to promote the child's recognition of the corrective nature of the feedback provided to them. The ESOL teacher in Choi and Li's (2012) study appears to oppose the notions mentioned previously regarding the impact of age on instruction, in line with the Instruction Hypothesis (Lichtman, 2016) which states that children can learn explicitly and should be taught that way. However, the quantity of feedback provided may be impacted by the opportunities for learners to generate erroneous utterances, as Oliver (1996) showed.

Oliver (1996) reported that teachers were more likely to provide feedback to adults than to children by a ratio of 60 percent to 52 percent. She later elaborated that age influenced the opportunity learners were given to commit errors, and, therefore, impacted the provision of feedback (Oliver, 2000). According to Oliver, teachers seemingly have greater expectations for their adult students than they do for children and hence encourage more risk-taking behaviors from adult students, enabling them to commit more errors than children would be able to. These findings are contrary to those of L1 acquisition which claim that as children age, they receive less feedback (Chouinard & Clark, 2003; Illmann, 1995) because, in fact, children are provided fewer opportunities to make errors in the classroom. The discrepancies in feedback provided in the L1 and L2 may be further explained by who is providing the feedback. While acquiring the L1, children learn from their parents and the feedback provided to them is largely meaning-focused. In learning an L2, teachers, as opposed to parents, are more likely to aid the students by focusing on a greater variety of language components than on meaning alone to further advance the learners' knowledge.

To summarize, in the classroom studies reported in Table 30.2, there appears to be a trend in that children receive more input-providing feedback, teenagers more output-prompting feedback, and adults more input-providing feedback again. Furthermore, it seems clear that there is much variability within age groups and across settings. It must be pointed out that the majority of the observational studies described did not highlight age as a factor nor interpret their findings in the context of child language learning, giving the impression that the findings are true for all language classes and language learners.

Feedback Provided in Laboratory Contexts by Age

Observational outcomes in the laboratory setting with children using their L2 somewhat resemble those of the L1 parent–toddler interactions discussed previously. Recall that L1 learners were more likely to negotiate meaning in age-paired peer interactions than in interactions with adults, a phenomenon Philp, Adams, and Iwashita (2014) attributed to perceptions of equity in expertise of child interlocutors. That is, when children interact with one another, they do not see their peer as an expert as they do with an adult; they share expertise. To investigate the impact of perceived expertise in L2 interaction, Oliver (1995) observed the role of negotiation between native (NS) and non-native speaking (NNS) children (8–13 years old) in the laboratory setting. She found that (1) 39 percent of erroneous utterances made by NNSs, while completing a one-way or two-way language task, were ignored by their NS peers; (2) 39 percent of errors were negotiated to decipher the NNS's intended meaning; and (3) the remaining 22 percent of errors were met with recasts or other input-providing forms of feedback. The children worked together collaboratively and reciprocally to complete the task provided, relying on negotiation of meaning. That is, NS interlocutors took the role of an equal rather than a language expert, working with their age-paired NNS peer to clarify areas of confusion rather than to explicitly correct language errors. While there were no linguistic differences identified in the interactions on the basis of the learners' ages, cognitive and maturational differences were observed. For instance, older children were more likely to stay on task and to repeat the same utterances with minor changes in order to complete the tasks, indicating reduced cognitive involvement in the tasks.

Oliver (2000) compared child (aged 8–12) and adult (mean age 25.19) interactions, demonstrating a greater likelihood for NNS children to negotiate meaning with NS peers, whereas adult NS were more inclined to provide corrections in the form of recasts. However, the age-related comparison should be interpreted with caution as Oliver (2000) identified the difficulty of coordinating tasks which were age appropriate and engaging for both children and adults. It stands to reason that differences in negotiation and feedback provided may have been impacted by participants' engagement with the task. It is also possible that NS adults did not want to embarrass the NNS counterparts when they made an error and thus provided the correct form through the use of recasts rather than by drawing more attention to the learners' errors through negotiation of meaning. Conversely, Mackey et al. (2003) did not report a difference in cognitive engagement in their comparative investigation of the nature of NS and NNS dyadic tasks between adults, fourth-year college students, and children, aged 8–12 years. No statistically significant difference was found in regard to the quantity or nature of feedback provided to learners based on dyadic formation or age. In fact, the only significant difference reported in relation to age was that children produced more modified output than did adults, even though there was no significant difference in opportunity to produce modified output across age groups. In adult dyads, modified output was found to be similar for learners paired with NS and NNSs (Pica et al. 1996).

The Effectiveness of Feedback

In order to determine the efficacy of various feedback types, there are three common methods employed: uptake, tailor-made tests, and pre- and post-tests. In classroom observational studies, uptake and tailor-made tests have been implemented. Uptake, as defined by Lyster and Ranta (1997), includes "student responses to corrective feedback" (p. 40). Student responses may be indicative of learning or, at the very least, noticing of the corrective nature of feedback provided to them. Responses made by students can include repetition of the correction or affirmations such as "yes" as well as other acknowledgements of the correction made. There has been some debate over the efficacy of uptake as a measure of learning (e.g., Mackey & Philp, 1998). Therefore, some researchers prefer to use tailor-made post-tests, or individualized tests targeting linguistic items that received feedback during learner–interlocutor (or teacher) interaction (Loewen, 2005; Nassaji, 2010). In the laboratory setting, where there is more control, pre- and post-tests are used to measure learning outcomes resulting from different feedback types provided.

Effectiveness of Feedback Indexed by Uptake and Gains on Tailor-Made Tests

In observational studies of corrective feedback, it is common practice for uptake to be regarded as evidence of learning a corrected form (e.g., Lyster & Ranta, 1997). While uptake may indicate that the learner has noticed the gap between their erroneous utterance and the target form or even recognized the corrective nature of negative feedback they have received, it has been argued that uptake may simply be a mimicking behavior following recasts (Gass, 2003). Gass's argument has received support from Nassaji (2011), who found that repairs (successful uptake) following recasts are qualitatively different from those following elicitations (prompts). Specifically, while the two types of repairs showed similar effects on learning gains measured through tailor-made tests immediately after an interactive task, recast-generated repairs, especially those involving mere repetitions rather than incorporation of recasts in expanded utterances, were not as effective as repairs following elicitations on the delayed post-tests. In the same vein, Loewen and Philp (2006) reported that uptake was predictive of learning (measured through tailor-made tests) only when it followed prompts (such as elicitation and clarification) but not recasts.

Table 30.3 shows the uptake levels after feedback reported by classroom studies conducted with different age groups. As can be seen, with the exception of one observational study (Lyster & Mori, 2006), output-prompting feedback consistently resulted in greater uptake across age

Table 30.3 *Feedback forms with the most reported uptake in classroom observational studies*

Context	Age	Hours observed	Uptake level
ESOL program (Choi & Li, 2012)	6–12 years	8 hours	output-prompting > input-providing
Japanese immersion (Lyster & Mori, 2006)	9–11 years	33 hours	input-providing > output-prompting
French immersion (Lyster & Mori, 2006)	8–10 years	33 hours	output-prompting > input-providing
French immersion (Lyster & Ranta, 1997)	9–12 years	18.3 hours	output-prompting > input-providing
EFL (Havranek, 2002)	10–university	48–64 lessons (lesson length not reported)	output-prompting > input-providing
ESL (Panova & Lyster, 2002)	17–55 years	10 hours	output-prompting > input-providing

Note: The representative studies in Table 30.3 were selected based on a thorough search in top journals in the field of second language acquisition. It should not be considered an exhaustive list, nor should conclusions be reached on the basis of this list. The studies referenced in Table 30.3 were used for identifying trends within existing published data.

groups. The Japanese immersion context in Lyster and Mori's (2006) observational study of grade 4 and 5 learners was the only investigation we found that identified input-providing feedback resulting in greater uptake than output-prompting feedback. They attribute this difference to the nature of the class, indicating that the Japanese immersion context utilized much more repetition of the teachers' utterances, and so the children were likely primed to repeat statements made by the teacher than in other contexts. Again, what is typical in the classroom impacts learners' habits and the way that learners react to instruction as well as feedback (Lichtman, 2016).

Although production-focused feedback types have a greater positive effect on acquisition than other forms, there is great variance in the provision of feedback by type to learners. Mackey and Philp (1998) considered learner preparedness as a factor impacting uptake through input-providing feedback, saying that "provided the level is appropriate, recasts may be used eventually by some learners, regardless of their immediate response to the recast" (p. 352). They claim that proficiency and preparedness have a greater impact on acquisition than does uptake. Mackey and Philp (1998) go on to state that input-providing feedback places learners at a disadvantage because of the limited opportunity for modified output. Alternatively, Sheen (2004) reported that the uptake rates after recasts in adult ESL classes in New Zealand and Korea were considerably higher than in Canadian immersion programs. While the researcher attributed this finding to the nature of the instructional context (i.e., intensive language programs vs. immersion), one could argue that age may also play a role. Because immersion programs are most commonly available for children and early-adolescents, age rather than context may be the factor impacting uptake and opportunities for modified output rather than the immersion context alone. There has only been one study conducted with child participants which employed tailor-made tests (Havranek, 2002). Havranek (2002) found that recasts were the most frequently employed form of feedback in the German EFL classes he observed, with learners ranging from 10 years old to university aged. He created tailor-made tests based on the feedback provided to learners in the observed lessons. Not only did his findings reveal greater benefits for output-prompting feedback, he also discovered that when learners were exposed to a peer receiving output-prompting feedback, they were more likely to retain the structure for future use. That is, learners receiving corrections performed with 50 percent accuracy for the structures that received a correction, while their classmates performed with 60 percent accuracy after witnessing their peers' errors being corrected. However, because the nature of tailor-made tests makes employment of pre-tests impossible, there is a chance that the test results demonstrated preexisting knowledge of the structures as well as gains resulting from feedback.

Effectiveness of Feedback Measured by Pre-tests and Post-tests

Whereas observational studies use uptake as an index of feedback effectiveness, experimental studies gauge learning gains through pre-tests and post-tests. Typically, in an experimental study, learners perform one or more focused tasks designed to elicit the production of a certain linguistic target. Learners are divided into groups, and each group receives the type of feedback assigned to them consistently on their nontarget-like use of the specific structure of focus. Statistical analysis is conducted to determine whether one feedback type is significantly more effective than another or than a control group which does not receive feedback treatment. Table 30.4 provides an overview of the findings of several experimental studies conducted with young learners, organized by age. The studies represented make it clear that young learners gain more from feedback than no feedback, whether it is input-providing or output-prompting, further supporting the notion that feedback is useful for all ages. These studies also show that output-prompting feedback seems to be more effective than input-providing feedback. This may suggest that output-prompting feedback (mostly metalinguistic clues) may work particularly well for young learners because compared with adults, young learners may need more external prodding in order for them to attend to errors and reflect on their L2 production. However, these studies only examined children, not adults, so we cannot make strong claims about the

Table 30.4 *Findings of experimental effectiveness studies*

Context	Treatment	Age	Findings
French immersion (Lyster, 2004)	8–10 hours of FFI	10–11 years	Output-prompting > input-providing > control
French immersion (Lyster, 2004)	8–10 hours of FFI	10–11 years	Output-prompting > input-providing > control
Intensive ESL (Ammar & Spada, 2006)	1 instruction session and 11 practice sessions	11–12 years	Output-prompting > input-providing > control
Intensive ESL (Ammar, 2003)	PPP for 4 weeks	11–12 years	Output-prompting > input-providing > control
Spanish EFL (Alcón-Soler, 2009)	teacher-led conversation	14–15 years	Output-prompting > input-providing
German FL (Van de Guchte et al., 2015)	3 task-based lessons	mean age 14.3 years	Output-prompting > input-providing > control

Note: The representative studies in Table 30.4 were selected based on a thorough search in top journals in the field of second language acquisition. It should not be considered an exhaustive list, nor should conclusions be reached on the basis of this list. The studies referenced in Table 30.4 were used for identifying trends within existing published data.

influence of age on feedback effectiveness. In this regard, Lyster and Saito's meta-analysis is more revealing.

Lyster and Saito's (2010) meta-analysis investigated age as a moderating variable for the effectiveness of corrective feedback in classroom settings. Lyster and Saito aggregated the results of fifteen classroom studies and found an overall advantage for output-prompting feedback over input-providing feedback. The researchers divided the studies into three groups based upon reported age means, namely children (10–12 years), young adults (17–20 years), and adults (23 and over). However, the reported age groups were not considered separately, possibly because of the limited literature available in relation to children and feedback, and a regression analysis was used to measure differences across ages on a continuum. Along this continuum, Lyster and Saito (2010) found larger gains for child learners than adults, again with more support for prompts than recasts. However, because the analysis on age effects did not distinguish different feedback types, it is unclear whether different feedback types worked differently for learners of different ages. Also, the variable of age was created by the researchers based on learners' demographic data reported in the primary studies, and age was not examined as an independent variable in the studies. Therefore, the findings need to be confirmed in further research. Notwithstanding, Lyster and Saito provided some convincing explanations for the age-related findings of their meta-analysis.

They argue that children are likely more responsive to feedback than adults because corrective feedback facilitates implicit learning in oral production tasks, which were used as treatment tasks in the primary studies. In congruence with the claims made by Bley-Vroman (1990) in relation to the implicitness of learning, children are better at implicit learning than adults. However, Lyster and Saito's (2010) findings indicate that the younger a learner is, the more likely they are to benefit from corrective feedback, which is in direct contrast to the Fundamental Difference Hypothesis. The distinction between children and adults may be due in part to the duration of the studies, as research investigating the impact of corrective feedback on children lasted considerably longer than that with adults. When length of study was considered a factor in the same meta-analysis, Lyster & Saito (2010) found that longer treatments led to greater outcomes than treatments of short or medium duration. However, the researchers argued that because of the long history of the impact that both age and cognitive development have on acquisition, it may be justifiable to say that age has a greater impact than length of study although further exploration of this phenomenon in relation to corrective feedback is encouraged. Length and intensity of treatment for children and adults would make for an interesting comparison in future studies.

The only experimental study that has been conducted to make a direct comparison between child and adult learners was through a partial replication of Mackey's (1999) investigation of feedback efficacy for adult learners. Mackey and Oliver (2002) explored the impact of interactional feedback provided by an adult, in the form of recasts and negotiation of meaning (Long, 1991), on children's language acquisition. All twenty-two children (8–12 years old) participated in interactions with adults, but only half received feedback. Interestingly, and contrary to the Fundamental Difference Hypothesis, the feedback group demonstrated significant and sustained development compared to the group which participated in interactions without feedback. While feedback and control groups received similar quantities of input as well as opportunities for output in their interactions, feedback had a positive and lasting impact, as demonstrated in the results of one immediate and two delayed post-tests. Mackey and Oliver (2002) identified that adult learners were much more actively involved in the interactions than were children and that adult learning was more pronounced. Unfortunately, learner involvement was not measured in Mackey and Oliver's (2002) work with children, as it was in the previous study with adults (Mackey, 1999), although the authors report that the children were actively engaged in the task throughout the treatment. Mackey and Oliver (2002) report that "feedback seemed to lead to more immediate interlanguage destabilization and restructuring [among children], and the effects of interactional feedback on L2 development were observed earlier than has been reported in adults" (pp. 474–475). That is, while adults were more actively involved in tasks, children were more likely to make immediate gains on the basis of interactions and feedback provided to them albeit feedback types were not considered separately.

The effects of feedback have been found to be constrained by various factors. For instance, Ammar and Spada (2006) investigated whether the comparative effects of output-prompting and input-providing feedback for grade 6 EFL learners varied as a function of learners' proficiency level. They found output-prompting feedback to be significantly more effective than input-providing feedback for low-proficiency learners, but for high-proficiency learners in the same study, there was no statistically significant difference between the two forms of feedback nor the control groups. That is, high- proficiency learners had relatively the same gains from both feedback types and no feedback at all. Similarly, task modality and target structure may also impact gains made in response to various feedback types. With a focus on the French grammatical gender, Lyster's (2004) study, which involved grade 5 students in an immersion program, revealed that the effects of feedback were different depending on the task used to measure treatment effects. While there was no significant difference found on the basis of feedback type in oral production tasks, the students who received prompting feedback had significantly greater accuracy on subsequent written production tasks than did the learners who received recasts. Lyster (2004) also highlighted the importance of structure salience in relation to corrective feedback provided, indicating that less salient structures may require more form-focused instruction (FFI) and feedback than more salient structures. The French gender is a non-salient structure and may require feedback that is more explicit and that requires deeper cognitive processing, hence the advantage of output-prompting feedback (primarily metalinguistic clues) over input-providing feedback (recasts).

To sum up, experimental research for learners of all ages indicates that output-prompting feedback leads to greater linguistic gains than input-providing feedback when the two are analyzed separately. The only experimental study which directly explored the impact of age on acquisition found that children reap greater short-term gains from interactions with feedback provided to them, although learning was more pronounced in adult interactions (Mackey & Oliver, 2002). The findings of Lyster and Saito's meta-analysis indicate that children make greater gains than adults from feedback, with both age groups gaining more from output-prompting than input-providing feedback. It is worth noting, however, that provision of feedback, regardless of type, always led to greater linguistic gains than control groups who did not receive feedback of any form.

Conclusions and Implications

Implications for Researchers

This chapter has outlined various approaches to feedback research with a focus on children and adults in various contexts. While there has been considerably more focus on the frequency and efficacy of corrective feedback in adult language learning, a large gap remains in feedback research comparing child and adult learners. The majority of studies related to children are based on observations rather than experimental design. Furthermore, with the exclusion of Mackey and Oliver's (2002) comparative study and Lyster and Saito's (2010) meta-analysis, the comparison of differences among adult and child learners has not been examined as an independent variable. Therefore, we propose that more experimental studies be employed to investigate (1) the phenomenon of corrective feedback in studies with children, (2) the effects of different feedback types on different age groups, and finally, (3) teacher and child learners' beliefs related to feedback.

The few experimental studies that have been conducted including child learners (e.g., Lyster, 2004) utilized samples of learners' ages ten and older participating in up to 10 hours of interaction, identifying output-prompting feedback to be more effective than input-providing feedback. However, theories related to children's language acquisition claim that implicit learning is more effective for children than explicit instruction (Bley-Vroman, 1990; Krashen, 1982). We suggest that future studies elucidate this phenomenon to identify if and how the mechanisms used in first language acquisition impact the way feedback is received in the second language. Longitudinal design is recommended as implicit knowledge typically takes considerably longer to acquire than explicit knowledge (Lichtman, 2016), and the relatively short duration of the feedback studies that have been conducted with children (no more than 10 hours) may have led to the overall trend of output-prompting feedback leading to greater learning than input-providing feedback.

Research investigating age as an independent variable and making a direct comparison between adults and children is particularly needed. Such studies must involve both child and adult learners, who receive the same treatment, with age being the only difference between the treatment groups. Great care should also be taken to control for participant proficiency at the time of the study as well to ensure that the adult and child learners are equally prepared to learn the target structure under investigation (Illmann, 1995; Pienemann, 1989). A large sample size is also recommended to limit the impact that other individual differences and extraneous variables may have on learning outcomes resulting from feedback provided.

Finally, while data related to teacher perspectives and beliefs in relation to the feedback they provide to adolescent and adult learners are available (see Chapter 26, this volume), no research has been done on the beliefs of children's teachers on the feedback they provide, nor on children's preferences for varied forms of feedback. Although surveying teachers of children could be as simple as distributing questionnaires, interviews preceding and following observations may be advised because of the dissonance found between teacher beliefs and the feedback they provide their adult students (Kamiya, 2016). While surveying children to identify preferences in learning has been effective (e.g., Shak & Gardner, 2008), we advise researchers to identify child learner preferences regarding feedback to ensure they receive different types of feedback along with the opportunity to identify their preferences. For instance, learners may engage in similar tasks with different teachers or adults who provide exclusively one form of corrective feedback, for example, prompts or recasts. After participating in interactions with each teacher and receiving the two forms of feedback, the children can be asked which teacher they preferred interacting with, and what they did and did not enjoy about the interaction, as a means of identifying the preferred type of feedback.

Implications for Teachers

While the previous section highlighted several gaps in the research, the existing literature can still illuminate and inform practices for teachers of children. As Nassaji (2016) summarized, "if research has found that something is effective for language teaching, it does not necessarily mean that L2 teachers can apply it in their teaching" (p. 553). The truth is, there is no single answer for what teachers should do in their classrooms. However, that is not to say that teaching practice should be approached in an uninformed manner. In this section, we will make several suggestions for teachers to enhance their feedback practices in the classroom including (1) providing opportunity for errors to occur, (2) considering learner developmental preparedness and proficiency, (3) prioritizing errors while providing intensive and focused feedback, and (4) using a variety of feedback types.

Oliver (2000) showed that adults were more likely to receive feedback than children because teachers are more likely to promote risk-tasking behaviors in adults through open communicative tasks as compared to children, who participate in more controlled activities with fewer opportunities to make errors. As Gass, Mackey, and Pica (1998) identified, interaction with the target structure is certainly not the cause of acquisition but helps to enhance saliency of familiar, although yet unmastered, forms providing greater potential for learning. Recall, recasts, and negotiation for meaning in interactive tasks had positive and lasting effects on children's acquisition (Mackey & Oliver, 2002). Therefore, we suggest that teachers employ more communicative, small group tasks to encourage children to take risks, receive feedback, and increase saliency of target structures in the classroom environment.

Lyster and associates (e.g., Lyster, 2004; Lyster & Ranta, 1997) found that prompts were more effective than recasts in terms of uptake and learning gains in French immersion classes. The learners of the studies happened to be young learners (grades 4–6). While the generalizability of their findings to other contexts is questionable, it would seem that prompts may work particularly well for children whose attention span is short and whose attention needs to be directed toward the error in question. We would like to further argue that from a pedagogical perspective, and in the spirit of maximizing instructional effects, the best way to provide feedback is to utilize a hybrid feedback package consisting of a prompt to encourage self-repair, followed by a recast in the absence of self-repair (Li et al., 2016).

Li (2018) recommends that learner errors be prioritized with focus and intensity provided for the most pressing concerns (or forms the lesson is focused on) while either ignoring or providing unfocused feedback for errors of other forms. Providing the appropriate quantity of feedback can help prevent learner overload, particularly with beginners whose errors could not possibly be corrected exhaustively. Errors interfering with intended meaning should be addressed before errors related to form alone.

Even though the preceding discussion has shown that input-providing feedback may not be as effective to language acquisition as the output-prompting alternative, recasts are still found to be more effective to language acquisition than no feedback at all. As Goo & Mackey (2013) wrote, "making a case against recasts is neither convincing nor useful for advancing the field" (p. 127). In order to make recasts more effective, they suggest that recasts be kept short. When a recast is short, a learner can focus on the error and the correction, rather than the entire utterance in which the error occurred (Ellis & Sheen, 2006). We recommend that teachers use a range of feedback types – in a principled way. Although some would argue that children are less capable of learning explicitly (e.g., Bley-Vroman, 1990), there is evidence that children benefit from explicit instruction (Lichtman, 2016). Therefore, it does not seem reasonable to withhold from providing explicit feedback to children.

While the Fundamental Difference Hypothesis (Bley-Vroman, 1990) claims that feedback is not necessary for young learners, the literature indicates a clear and positive impact of feedback being useful for L2 acquisition in children as well as adults, if not more so for child learners. Less noticeable or less salient forms, typically the target for more advanced learners, are more likely acquired through explicit instruction than more salient forms (Long, 2007). As discussed previously, it is important for the teacher to keep the learners' proficiency levels and readiness in mind when providing various forms of feedback as beginning learners benefit more from output-prompting feedback, whereas varied feedback forms are equally effective for advanced learners (Ammar & Spada, 2006).

References

Alcón-Soler, E. (2009). Focus on form, learner uptake and subsequent lexical gains in learners' oral production. *International Review of Applied Linguistics in Language Teaching*, 47(3–4), 347–365.

Aljaafreh, A. & Lantolf, J. P. (1994). Negative feedback as regulation and second language learning in the zone of proximal development. *Modern Language Journal, 78*(4), 465–483.

Ammar, A. (2003). Corrective feedback and L2 learning: Elicitation and recasts. Doctoral thesis, McGill University, Montreal.

Ammar, A. & Spada, N. (2006). One size fits all? Recasts, prompts, and L2 learning. *Studies in Second Language Acquisition, 28*(4), 543–574.

Bley-Vroman, R. (1990). The logical problem of foreign language learning. *Linguistic Analysis, 20*(1–2), 3–63.

Choi, S. & Li, S. (2012). Corrective feedback and learner uptake in a child ESOL classroom. *RELC Journal, 43*(3), 331–351.

Chouinard, M. M. & Clark, E. V. (2003). Adult reformulations of child errors as negative evidence. *Journal of Child Language, 30*(3), 637–669.

Ellis, R. (2016). Anniversary article focus on form: A critical review. *Language Teaching Research, 20*(3), 405–428.

Ellis, R., Basturkmen, H. & Loewen, S. (2001). Learner uptake in communicative ESL lessons. *Language Learning, 51*(2), 281–318.

Ellis, R. & Sheen, Y. (2006). Reexamining the role of recasts in second language acquisition. *Studies in Second Language Acquisition, 28*(4), 575–600.

Farrar, M. (1990). Discourse and the acquisition of grammatical morphemes. *Journal of Child Language, 17*(3), 607–624.

Gass, S. M. (2003). Input and interaction. In C. J. Doughty & M. H. Long (eds.), *The handbook of second language acquisition* (pp. 224–255). Malden, MA: Blackwell Publishing.

Gass, S. M., Mackey, A. & Pica, T. (1998). The role of input and interaction in second language acquisition: Introduction to the special issue. *Modern Language Journal, 82*(3), 299–307.

Goo, J. & Mackey, A. (2013). The case against the case against recasts. *Studies in Second Language Acquisition, 35*(1), 127–165.

Havranek, G. (2002). When is corrective feedback likely to succeed? *International Journal of Educational Research, 37*(3–4), 255–270.

Illmann, C. (1995). Contextual influences on parental declarative speech style. Doctoral dissertation, University of Windsor, Canada.

Kamiya, N. (2016). The relationship between stated beliefs and classroom practices of oral corrective feedback. *Innovation in Language Learning and Teaching, 10*(3), 206–219.

Krashen, S. (1982). *Principles and practice in second language acquisition*. Oxford: Pergamon.

Lee, J. (2007). Corrective feedback and learner uptake in English immersion classrooms at the primary level in Korea. *English Teaching, 62*(4), 311–334.

Li, S. (2010). The effectiveness of corrective feedback in SLA: A meta-analysis. *Language Learning, 60*(2), 309–365.

(2018). Corrective feedback in L2 speech production. *The TESOL Encyclopedia of English Language Teaching*, 1–9.

Li, S., Ellis, R. & Zhu, Y. (2016). Task-based versus task-supported language instruction: An experimental study. *Annual Review of Applied Linguistics*, 36, 205–229.

Lichtman, K. (2016). Age and learning environment: Are children implicit second language learners. *Journal of Child Language*, 43(3), 1–24.

Lochtman, K. (2002). Oral corrective feedback in the foreign language classroom: How it affects interaction in analytic foreign language teaching. *International Journal of Educational Research*, 37(3–4), 271–283.

Loewen, S. (2005). Incidental focus on form and second language learning. *Studies in Second Language Acquisition*, 27(3), 361–386.

Loewen, S. & Philp, J. (2006). Recasts in the adult English L2 classroom: Characteristics, explicitness, and effectiveness. *Modern Language Journal*, 90(4), 536–556.

Long, M. H. (1991). Focus on form: A design feature in language teaching methodology. In K. De Bot, R. Ginsberg & C. Kramsch (eds.), *Foreign language research in cross-cultural perspective* (pp. 39–52). Amsterdam: John Benjamins.

(2007). *Problems in SLA*. Mahwah, NJ: Lawrence Erlbaum.

Lyster, R. (2004). Differential effects of prompts and recasts in form-focused instruction. *Studies in Second Language Acquisition*, 26(3), 399–432.

Lyster, R. & Mori, H. (2006). Interactional feedback and instructional counterbalance. *Studies in Second Language Acquisition*, 28(2), 269–300.

Lyster, R. & Ranta, L. (1997). Corrective feedback and learner uptake: Negotiation of form in communicative classrooms. *Studies in Second Language Acquisition*, 19(1), 37–66.

Lyster, R. & Saito, K. (2010). Oral feedback in classroom SLA: A meta-analysis. *Studies in Second Language Acquisition*, 32(2), 265–302.

Lyster, R., Saito, K. & Sato, M. (2013). Oral corrective feedback in second language classrooms. *Language Teaching*, 46(1), 1–40.

Mackey, A. (1999). Input, interaction, and second language development: an empirical study of question formation in ESL. *Studies in Second Language Acquisition*, 21(4), 557–587.

Mackey, A. & Oliver, R. (2002). Interactional feedback and children's L2 development. *System*, 30(4), 459–477.

Mackey, A., Oliver, R. & Leeman, J. (2003). Interactional input and the incorporation of feedback: An exploration of NS–NNS and NNS–NNS adult and child dyads. *Language Learning*, 53(1), 35–66.

Mackey, A. & Philp, J. (1998). Conversational interaction and second language development: Recasts, responses, and red herrings? *Modern Language Journal*, 82(3), 338–356.

Mori, H. (2002). Error treatment sequences in Japanese immersion classroom interactions at different grade levels. Doctoral dissertation, University of California.

Moulton, J. & Robinson, G. (1981). *The organization of language*. Cambridge: Cambridge University Press.

Nassaji, H. (2010). The occurrence and effectiveness of spontaneous focus on form in adult ESL classrooms. *Canadian Modern Language Review*, 66(6), 907–933.

(2011). Immediate learner repair and its relationship with learning targeted forms. *System: An International Journal of Educational Technology and Applied Linguistics*, 39(1), 17–29.

(2016). Anniversary article interactional feedback in second language teaching and learning: A synthesis and analysis of current research. *Language Teaching Research*, 20(4), 535–562.

Oliver, R. (1995). Negative feedback in child NS–NNS conversation. *Studies in Second Language Acquisition*, 17(4), 459–481.

(1996, January). *Input and feedback to adult and child ESL learners*. Paper presented at Pacific Second Language Research Forum, Victoria University, Wellington, New Zealand.

(2000). Age differences in negotiation and feedback in classroom and pairwork. *Language Learning*, 50(1), 119–151.

Panova, I. & Lyster, R. (2002). Patterns of corrective feedback and uptake in an adult ESL classroom. *TESOL Quarterly*, 36(4), 573–595.

Philp, J. (2003). Constraints on "noticing the gap": Nonnative speakers' noticing of recasts in NS–NNS interaction. *Studies in Second Language Acquisition*, 25(1), 99–126.

Philp, J., Adams, R. & Iwashita, N. (2014). Age related characteristics and peer interaction. In L. Babb-Rosenfeld (ed.), *Peer interaction and second language learning* (pp. 103–119). New York: Routledge.

Pica, T., Lincoln-Porter, F., Paninos, D. & Linnell, J. (1996). Language learners' interaction: How does it address the input, output, and feedback needs of L2 learners? *TESOL Quarterly*, 30(1), 59–84.

Pienemann, M. (1989). Is language teachable? Psycholinguistic experiments and hypotheses. *Applied Linguistics*, 10(1), 52–79.

Shak, J. & Gardner, S. (2008). Young learner perspectives on four focus-on-form tasks. *Language Teaching Research*, 12(3), 387–408.

Sheen, Y. (2004). Corrective feedback and learner uptake in communicative classrooms across instructional settings. *Language Teaching Research*, 8(3), 263–300.

Simard, D. & Jean, G. (2011). An exploration of L2 teachers' use of pedagogical interventions devised to draw L2 learners' attention to form. *Language Learning*, 61(3), 759–785.

Strapp, C. M. (1996). Language development in the family setting: Comparing sources of linguistic input. Doctoral Dissertation, University of Nevada.

Van de Guchte, M., Braaksma, M., Rijlaarsdam, G. & Bimmel, P. (2015). Learning new grammatical structures in task-based language learning: The effects of recasts and prompts. *Modern Language Journal, 99*(2), 246–262.

Vicente-Rasoamalala, L. (2009). Teachers' reactions to foreign language learner output. Doctoral dissertation, Universitat de Barcelona, Spain.

Yang, Y. (2009). Feedback and uptake in Chinese EFL classrooms: In search of instructional variables. *The Journal of ASIA TEFL, 6*(1), 1–22.

Yang, Y. & Lyster, R. (2010). Effects of form-focused practice and feedback on Chinese EFL learners' acquisition of regular and irregular past tense forms. *Studies in Second Language Acquisition, 32*(2), 235–263.

31

Gender Effects

Rebecca Adams and Lauren Ross-Feldman

Introduction

This chapter considers the role of gender in the provision and use of feedback in second language. Second language theorists have long posited a role for gender in second language learning in general (Pavlenko & Piller, 2001) and for the provision of feedback specifically (e.g., Long, 1996). While the role of gender in feedback provision has not been frequently researched, a growing body of evidence suggests that this factor may play a substantial role in determining how feedback is provided across a range of settings. In this chapter, we will first examine the rationale for considering gender in research on feedback and then present key findings on the role of gender in the provision of feedback in teacher/native speaker feedback and in peer interaction.

However, before we begin, we wish to acknowledge the disparity between the extant research on gender and feedback in second language acquisition and research on gender and language use in sociolinguistics. As we will see, researchers examining second language feedback have tended to view gender as a fixed variable, whereas sociolinguists increasingly view gender as more mutable, a socially constructed reflection of identity that is negotiated and performed differently in different contexts of communication. This view of gender and language is not currently reflected in research on second language feedback, which has tended to rely on the argument (expressed by Green & Oxford, 1995) that "there might be some consistent differences in the ways that females as a group learn a language, compared with males as a group, although variability also exists within groups" (p. 266). Our focus in this chapter will be on current research, which has sought to find consistent differences between the ways males and females provide and respond to feedback, but we will consider how this gap can be bridged later in this chapter.

Why Might Gender Impact Second Language Feedback Provision?
There is considerable evidence that gender plays a role in first language (L1) use in both casual (e.g., Aries, 1976; Cameron, 2003; Goodwin, 1990; Holmes, 1998; Tannen, 1990) and educational (e.g., Eckert, 1998) settings. Gender has been shown to influence L1 communication in a number of ways, including interactional style (Goodwin, 1990), conflict-resolution strategies (Sheldon, 1990), and giving and receiving compliments (Holmes, 1998). This role is, however, not biologically fixed, but mediated by cultural background (e.g., Aries, 1996; Cook-Gumperz & Szymanski, 2001). Gender has also been shown to play a role in educational attainment, both in L1 (Sadker & Sadker, 1994) and in second language (L2) (Mady & Seiling, 2017) settings. These differences extend to the provision of feedback given to male and female students in L1 settings, in both oral (Fassinger, 1995; Foote, 2002) and written modes (Haswell & Haswell, 1996; Read, Francis, & Robson, 2005; Susanti, 2013).

In L2 settings, gender has influenced the communication strategies learners develop and select for use (Green & Oxford, 1995), their willingness to communicate in the target language (MacIntyre et al., 2002), and the assessment of their language skills (O'Loughlin, 2002). Similarly, gender has been shown to play a role in L2 communication. Gass and Varonis (1986), for example, found that males dominated talk in L2 interactions, producing more talk and nominating more topics than the female learners they worked with. These findings, however, may vary based on the learner's cultural background and the language they are interacting in (Itakura, 2001). Because gender influences how learners engage in interactions and in the work of L2 classrooms, it also impacts how feedback is given and received.

Gender Differences in Second Language Feedback
Relatively few studies have examined how gender influences the provision of and response to second language feedback, and the results of these studies are not consistent. At this point, any conclusions about the role of gender in L2 feedback are tenuous. In this section, we review studies of gender and feedback, beginning with studies of feedback provided to learners by teachers and/or native speakers and followed by studies of feedback provided by peers in learner–learner interactions. We have necessarily cast a wide net in selecting literature for this chapter, including studies of canonical feedback moves like recasts and explicit correction, but also including studies that examine negotiation of meaning and form (which provide learners with implicit feedback that their original output may not have been successfully communicative) as well as language-related episodes (where learners engage in discussion of language form, frequently in response to an error).

How Does Gender Impact the Nature of Feedback Provided by Teachers/Native Speakers?

Several studies have considered how male and female teachers provide feedback differentially to male and female students. Early findings in these studies suggested that male students received more help than female students in these interactions. For example, Pica et al. (1989) conducted a study of feedback and responses to feedback produced by ten L1 Japanese students (five male and five female) interacting with female native speakers of English on meaning-focused tasks. While not initially designed as a study of gender, their findings suggested that the interactions had been more beneficial for male learners. They noted that the NS interlocutors engaged in negotiation of meaning more often with the males: they provided more clarification requests and confirmation requests with males than with females. These moves can provide learners with implicit feedback about the nativelikeness of their utterances and give learners chances to modify their output toward the target. Because their study was not designed to examine gender differences, Pica et al. were appropriately cautious in making claims about their findings, suggesting that further research on interactional feedback should consider both gender and ethnicity of participants.

In a follow-up study, Pica et al. (1991) examined the interactions of twenty dyads composed of male and female English NS and male and female Japanese ESL learners. Each native speaker interacted with five male and five female participants, resulting in five male NS/male nonnative-speaker (NNS) dyads, five female NS/female NNS dyads, five male NS/female NNS dyads, and five female NS/male NNS dyads. Pica et al. examined interactions on four information-gap and opinion-gap tasks. While there were no significant differences according to dyad type, when Pica et al. looked at individual learner language production, they found that "[n]egotiation and [the number of] negotiation utterances appeared to be affected by gender, but it was the gender of the NS rather than the NNS member of the dyads that seemed particularly crucial" (p. 356), meaning that it was the differences between the dyads with a female NS and those with a male NS that were significant, rather than the differences between dyads with a female NNS and a male NNS. In their findings, being a male student did not lead to receiving more feedback; rather, learners of both genders received more feedback from the female NS than the male NS.

Similar findings on the importance of the gender of the NS in the provision of feedback were found by other studies, including those by Alcón and Codina (1996) and Zuengler and Wang (1993). Both studies showed that the gender of the teacher was a better predictor of the provision of feedback and the feedback strategies used than the gender of the learner. Alcón and Codina paired a male teacher and a female teacher with both male and female students who then engaged in an information-gap task and a discussion task. While they did not find any differences in terms of negotiation of meaning during the information-gap task, they did find that both male and female students engaged in more negotiation of meaning with the female teacher, receiving more feedback on the comprehensibility of their communication. They hypothesize that learners felt more at ease with the female NS, and because of this engaged more readily in negotiation of meaning, giving them greater access to feedback on their language use. Alcón and Codina cautioned, however, that the differences found were slight and suggested that the learners overall may have been intimidated by communicating one-on-one with a native speaker. They note that patterns of feedback in interaction may be different in a more familiar and lower-anxiety context, such as interacting in class with a peer.

While the research cited above suggests that female teachers may provide more feedback, it is not clear that this always translates into more learning from feedback. Rassaei and Tavakoli (2012) found that learning rates from the interaction varied depending on whether the learners interacted with an interlocutor of the same or the opposite gender. The learners in the study met over a period of six weeks with either a mixed- or matched-gender interlocutor. They engaged in meaning-focused tasks, but the interlocutors were trained to give corrective feedback in the form of recasts followed by metalinguistic feedback, as in Example 1 below.

Example 1
1   STUDENT: Man is running.
2   TEACHER: The man is running. You should use definite article because it is known to us and you have already mentioned it.
(Rassaei & Tavakoli, 2012, p. 161)

The interlocutors were instructed to provide feedback on four broadly defined, high-frequency target structures. Following the final session, individual post-tests were prepared for learners based on the feedback they had received in the interaction sessions. For each of the four structures, learners in the matched-gender group retained significantly more learning from feedback than the learners in the mixed-gender group. The researchers note that in the Iranian cultural context, males and females are segregated in education settings from a young age, and speculate that the learners in their study may have been more able understand and learn from feedback from an interlocutor who was socialized into similar communication patterns. The researchers do not present data on the amount of feedback provided in each group, which may have also influenced awareness and learning. They also did not separate the results according to gender among the matched groups – any differences between female–female (FF) and male–male (MM) groups are not considered in this analysis.

A more recent study by Nakatsukasa (2017) suggests that females in particular may benefit from feedback provided by a matched-gender interlocutor. In this study, the female researcher provided recasts on prepositions of location to male and female ESL students from a variety of L1 backgrounds. Two different types of feedback were provided – some learners received oral recasts only and the rest received gesturally enhanced recasts. For gesturally enhanced recasts, the researcher accompanied the recast with a hand gesture symbolizing the meaning of the locative, for example, "on" was accompanied by a gesture of putting an object on something. Learners participated in oral pre- and post-tests consisting of oral grammar-focused activities and communicative activities designed to elicit prepositions.

Females increased their test scores more than the males in both conditions, but this effect only rose to the level of significance for the group that received gesture-enhanced recasts. Nakatsukasa notes that this distinction may be related to differences in memory capacity between males and females, suggesting that the relatively more implicit oral recasts may have triggered procedural processing, where males are more likely to have a cognitive advantage (e.g., Reiterer et al., 2011). On the other hand, adding gestures to the recasts presented the information to the learners in two modes (oral and visual), which may have made it more likely for the new information to be retained in long-term memory, an area of cognition where females may outperform males (e.g., Harsthone & Ullman, 2006).

To date, the handful of studies that have considered NS/teacher feedback to learners have shown mixed results in terms of the role the gender of the learner or the interlocutor may play in the provision of feedback and learning outcomes. Considering the small number of studies that have addressed this question and the range of other variables of interest, this is not surprising. Research on the role of gender in L2 instruction and use has consistently found that teacher gender, learner gender, culture, task, and context all intersect in complex ways. Sunderland (1995) points out that in oral interview testing, the gender of the tester has been shown to influence success, but not uniformly across settings. Some studies have found that females score higher on oral proficiency tests if the tester is a female (Buckingham, 1997); others have alternately found that students of both genders fare better with male test providers (Porter, 1991) or with female test providers (O'Sullivan, 2000). This range of contradictory findings likely relates to differences in cultural backgrounds and settings. Because gender identities are culturally conditioned and performed rather than biologically fixed (Meyerhoff, 2014), ideal gender pairings from one language learning context and cultural setting should not be expected to translate exactly, if at all, to another. The intersection of gender, context, culture, and language performance in oral test settings has been shown to be too complex for consistent biases to arise in different settings (O'Loughlin, 2002). Given the similarity between oral testing settings and second language communicative interaction between teachers or native speakers and learners, it is not surprising that inconsistent findings have surfaced among the few studies that have examined the role of gender in the provision and use of feedback.

How Does Gender Impact the Nature of Feedback Provided by Language Learning Peers?

We turn now to feedback provided by peers to one another in learner–learner interactions. While we chose to discuss peer feedback studies separately from teacher feedback studies because of the well-attested social and discursive differences between teacher–learner and peer interaction (cf. Philp, Adams & Iwashita, 2014, for a fuller account), the findings of peer feedback studies echo the conclusion reached above: the gender of both interlocutors as well as the context, culture, and task all influence the way that feedback is provided.

Early findings on gender and feedback suggested that males provide more feedback to their interlocutors than do females in peer interactions. One of the earliest studies to consider the role of gender in interaction was conducted by Gass and Varonis (1985). While they did not design their study to investigate gender differences in interaction, they did observe some differences between males and females. Males more often indicated that they did not understand their interlocutor's utterances (by initiating negotiation sequences) than did females. On one-way tasks, they also signaled a need to negotiate more overtly than females. These findings suggested that peer interactions tended to promote feedback targeted to the needs of male rather than female participants. Gass and Varonis point out, however, that their findings could also be interpreted in two other ways: first, that females interacting with males do not feel confident enough to indicate a lack of understanding and initiate feedback sequences or, second, that the females had higher proficiency and did not need feedback as much. The small number of participants did not allow for further investigation.

Gass and Varonis (1986) followed their earlier study with one designed specifically to investigate the effect of mixed and matched-gender dyads on negotiation and feedback (as well as amount of talk and other interactional features). Twenty adult speakers of Japanese studying ESL at a US university were divided into ten dyads: three MM (male male), three FF (female female), and four male–female (MF). They completed two tasks: a conversation and a picture drawing task. The findings indicated that FF dyads engaged in the least amount of negotiation, followed by MM dyads, and finally by MF dyads, who engaged in the greatest amount of negotiation. Both males and females initiated more negotiation in the mixed than the matched groupings, leading the researchers to speculate that it might be the gender pairing, rather than the gender of the individual, that affects negotiation. However, the small number of participants and the fact that individuals participated in only one type of gender pairing (mixed or matched) means that it is possible that the amount of negotiation and feedback was influenced by individual interaction styles, rather than gender pairings.

Further studies have also shown male students providing more feedback moves than females. Kasanga (1996) examined the interactions of fifty-four Zairean EFL students performing a map task and a free talk task in mixed-gender pairs. Across both tasks, she found that males provided their female interlocutors with more interactional feedback and produced more modified output during feedback exchanges. This included negotiation moves like clarification requests and confirmation checks (including implicit recasts) that provide interlocutors with implicit feedback on the comprehensibility of their language production as well as producing elaborations of their own and their partners' output while negotiating understanding of meaning. Interestingly, males provided more feedback and more responses to feedback whether they had higher, lower, or equivalent language proficiency to their female interlocutor. Unusually for gender and interaction studies, these patterns held across task types, pointing to a strong effect of gender on interactional feedback among her participants. She also collected perception data from her participants, who reported a consistent belief that male students provided more repairs than female students. Matched-gender dyads were not included in this study, but the pattern of findings within mixed-gender dyads pointed to a clear role for gender in negotiation of meaning and the provision of interactional feedback in peer dyadic interactions.

Gender played a similar role in the provision of feedback in Oliver's (2002) study of children's L2 interaction. Her study of 192 child ESL learners aged 8–13 considered age groups (older dyads and younger dyads), proficiency (higher, lower, and mixed proficiency dyads), and gender (MM and FF dyads). The study looked at NS–NS, NS–NNS, and NNS–NNS dyads, the latter of which we focus on here. These forty-eight learner–learner dyads performed two tasks, a one-way task and a two-way task. Oliver examined the frequency of negotiation and implicit feedback moves including clarification requests, confirmation checks, and self- and other-repetition (which Ranta & Lyster, 2007, categorize as a feedback prompt). Oliver found that differences in both age and proficiency level were associated with differences in the frequency of feedback moves. For gender, no statistically significant differences were found in the provision of feedback between MM and FF dyads overall, but Oliver noted a trend suggesting that older MM and FF dyads (i.e., those aged 11 to 13 years) differed more from one another than did the younger MM and FF dyads (i.e., those aged 8 to 10 years). While it did not reach the level of statistical significance, the data pointed to older boys providing implicit negative feedback more frequently than younger boys, while older girls used these same feedback moves less frequently than younger girls. Oliver suggested that these results may indicate gendered differences in peer interactions emerging as children grow older, with older children increasingly following patterns noted in studies of the interaction of adult learners, where males provide more implicit feedback through engagement in negotiation of meaning than females.

It should be noted that other studies, notably Ross-Feldman (2005), did not find that male and female learners differed substantially in terms of the provision of feedback in mixed-gender pairs. The sixty-four L1 Spanish learners in her study each interacted in both mixed- and matched-gender dyads, doing tasks quite similar to those in Kasanga's study. On only one task (a picture placement task), did Ross-Feldman find that males produced more negotiation signals through comprehension checks than females in mixed-gender dyads, but she found no differences in the amounts of implicit feedback through clarification requests or confirmation checks provided by males and females on either of the other tasks. There were, however, individual female students who used more confirmation checks and fewer comprehension checks when they worked with males in mixed-gender dyads than when they interacted in matched-gender dyads. Ross-Feldman notes that the emerging trend, then, is one of males increasing their use of comprehension checks and females increasing their use of confirmation checks when they work together, suggesting that this may reflect cultural expectations. If males are socialized to avoid showing weakness, giving feedback to a partner on their comprehension may be more face-threatening in interaction between two males than it is in interaction between a male and a female.

Other studies of gender and feedback have not found that males provide more feedback. Ross-Feldman (2007), for example, used a counterbalanced design that allowed her sixty-four L1 Spanish learners to complete three information gap tasks in both a mixed- and matched-gender dyad. The tasks all involved an information gap. In two of the tasks, there were no differences among participants in terms of engagement in focus on form, but in the picture narrative task, learners in the MM dyads engaged in significantly less focus on form than learners in either the FF or the MF conditions. Because the learners engaged in both mixed- and matched-gender interactions, Ross–Feldman could compare their performance in both contexts. She found that females, regardless of whether they were working with a male or another female, were more likely to initiate a focus on linguistic form. However, while males initiated fewer instances of focus on form, when they did so the topic was more likely to be discussed and resolved; instances of female-initiated focus on form were more likely to be dropped or ignored, as in the following example from a picture narrative task about a luggage mishap.

Example 2
1   FEMALE LEARNER: Interchange their bags. What is the word?
                      I don't know.

2	MALE LEARNER:	After that they ...
3	FEMALE LEARNER:	Their bags.
4	MALE LEARNER:	They went to the cafeteria and drink cup of coffee.

(Ross-Feldman, 2007, p. 72)

The female learner in this instance is attempting to get feedback on her use of vocabulary. She is using the word "bag" to describe suitcases, but would like to use a more specific term, which she does not know. She asks her male interlocutor for help, but he ignores her request and tries to continue the task, beginning a description of the next part of the narrative. She interrupts him, emphasizing the word "bag" to try to focus his attention on her query. He again ignores her attempt to gain feedback and continues with the story. Ross-Feldman found that males were more likely to remain focused on continuing the discussion of content, as in this example, while females were substantially more likely than males to pick up on a request to discuss language use and to provide feedback to their interlocutors. Thus for any learner, interacting with a female rather than a male made it more likely for them to receive feedback on their language use.

Ross-Feldman notes that this pattern is reflective of L1 gendered interactions, in which researchers have noted that the presence of a female could "change the all-male style of interacting" (Aries, 1976, p. 14), with females often being more effective communication partners than males (e.g., Holmes, 1998). Fishman (1978), for example, found in L1 English interactions that topics initiated by females were frequently abandoned, while topics initiated by males were generally picked up by their interlocutor and continued, concluding that "women do the work necessary for interaction to occur smoothly, but men control what will be produced as reality by the interaction" (p. 405). West and García (1988) echo this point, claiming that men changed topics more frequently than women, during a wider variety of conversational moves, and frequently changed topics to avoid conversational activities they were disinclined to engage in. Ross-Feldman points out that engagement in focus on form is very much like a new topic initiation in nonlanguage-focused communication – one interlocutor signals a need for feedback on language use, much like initiating a new conversational topic, and this signal can be picked up or ignored. This suggests that female L2 learners may be more likely to engage in aspects of conversation that attend to their interlocutor's needs. Because engagement in focus-on-form episodes has been strongly linked to subsequent learning (e.g., Adams, 2007), male learners picking up fewer of their interlocutor's attempts to initiate a focus on form could result in interactional activities that are more beneficial for male learners than their female interlocutors in MF dyads.

Alcón and Codina (1996) also found that female participants did more of the work of the interaction, even if there were not differences in the amount of feedback provided. Their study looked at interactions between L1 Spanish EFL learners at the university level. This study also found more negotiation of meaning in mixed-gender dyads than in matched-gender dyads, and that both males and females used more feedback moves in mixed- than in matched-gender dyads, though the types of feedback moves used by males and females differed. Female participants were more likely to use implicit feedback moves that asked for clarification of their partner's utterances and verified their understanding of their partner's speech, while males were more likely to use negotiation moves to check their partner's understanding of their own speech. Alcón and Codina note that female learners tend to "work hard in keeping the conversation going until mutual understanding or agreement is achieved, while male learners tend to abandon conversation" (p. 28).

Sadeghi and Sagedi (2013) also found more feedback in FF and MF dyads than in MM dyads in their study of twenty-four Iranian EFL students (L1 Azeri Turkish) working together on one- and two-way tasks that required information and opinion exchange. They examined the interactional transcripts for all instances of nontarget-like production and coded whether or not feedback was provided, using a broad definition of implicit negative feedback including confirmation checks, clarification requests, recasts, and requests for help, as in the following example of feedback on erroneous lexical usage.

Example 3
1 MALE 2: There is three candies on the cake and two of them are burning?
2 MALE 1: What?
3 MALE 2: Candies, we put them on cakes and light them.
4 MALE 1: Oh, three candles are on the cake.
5 MALE 2: Yes, candles.
(Sadeghi & Sagedi, 2013, p. 122)

They found that around 60 percent of nontarget-like utterances received feedback in MF dyads and 57 percent in FF dyads, compared to 50 percent in MM. It should be noted though that substantially more feedback was produced in the FF dyads, because there were not as many errors in the MF dyads, perhaps suggesting care in language production when working in a mixed-gender grouping, possibly due to the participants' lack of experience interacting in mixed-gender groupings. Regardless, in light of earlier findings that male students provide more feedback than females, it is striking that in this data set, MM dyads produced the lowest rate of feedback to errors and substantially fewer feedback moves overall than in dyads with a female interlocutor, reinforcing Ross-Feldman's (2007) argument that females do much of the work of attending to language form in an interaction. These findings suggest that males do not universally provide more feedback than females. The researchers propose that the gender dynamics of pairing (mixed- versus matched-gender) may play a larger role than an individual's gender in terms of provision of feedback.

Shehadeh's (1994) study compared matched-gender NS–learner and learner–learner pairs with mixed-gender learner groups. The twenty-seven mixed-L1 ESL learners completed a picture dictation task and an opinion exchange task in pairs (either with another learner or with a native speaker) and then worked in mixed-gender groups on a decision-making task. Regardless of whether the learners worked with a native speaker or another learner, Shehadeh found that the females in matched-gender pairs provided more repair than the males. However, when the learners interacted in mixed-gender groups, the males requested clarification, initiated repair, and produced comprehensible output more than the females, suggesting that males may not inherently provide a greater volume of feedback than females, but rather that they provide feedback differently depending on whether they are paired with a male or female peer.

Su and Huang (2013) similarly found more focus-on-form sequences in mixed-gender dyads than in matched-gender dyads. In their data, both males and females in MF dyads initiated more feedback sequences than their counterparts in matched-gender dyads. Su and Huang considered whether solidarity with the interlocutor might have influenced these findings. The L1 Chinese participants in their study were more accustomed to studying and interacting with matched-gender peers in their educational setting. The researchers noted that the interactions were longer and more conversational in the matched-gender dyads, while the talk in mixed-gender dyads was more factual and task-focused, with less personal talk. The learners in MF dyads seemed less engaged with their interlocutors, which may have allowed them to focus more on language. A lack of solidarity may have made them more careful in the focus-on-form resolutions they offered. This analysis again points to the centrality of the gender pairing in terms of feedback-providing behavior.

Azkarai's (2015) findings reinforce the point that mixed-gender dyads may be more beneficial for males but also suggest advantages of mixed-gender interactions for female students. She explored what happened when forty-four L1 Spanish university EFL learners solicited feedback or attempted to discuss linguistic form with their interlocutor while working together on dictogloss and text editing tasks. She examined each instance of learners attempting to discuss language or asking for feedback on language forms to determine if the attempt led to a target-like resolution, a nontarget-like resolution, or no resolution at all, either because the topic was discussed and discarded without coming to a conclusion or because the attempt was ignored outright, as in Example 4.

Example 4
1	SERGIO:	... eats ...
2	IRIA:	... times year? Ay...
3	SERGIO:	On average San Francisco eat...
4	IRIA:	San Franciscans. People from San Francisco.
5	SERGIO:	Ah, yes.

(Azkarai, 2015, p. 21)

The learners in this excerpt are attempting to edit a text. As they work together, Iria questions a phrase ("times year") in the passage, which she reads with questioning intonation. Sergio's attention is drawn to a different phrase, and he ignores Iria's turn. A chance to correct a textual error and to discuss language form is missed.

Azkarai found that attention to form in mixed-gender dyads favored female students, with more female attempts to discuss form ending in resolutions than male attempts. On the other hand, there were advantages for males too – when they interacted with females, their attempts to focus on form were taken up at a higher rate than in interactions with males, when more attempts were ignored. These findings reinforce Ross-Feldman's argument about female learners being more helpful interlocutors in terms of discussing meaning. While the males in this study did not overall provide more feedback than the females, they did provide feedback in different ways, as illustrated in Example 5.

Example 5
1	CANDELA:	[...] Louise Woodward was the eighteen year nanny convicted in nineteen no sé qué [whatever] by a court in the United States of America for murder. No. Convicted for murder? No sé [I don't know]. For murder the infant? Of murder...
2	CARLOS:	For the murder.
3	CANDELA:	For the murder?
4	CARLOS:	Sí. Y quitando [Yes. And leaving off] "of."

(Azkarai, 2015, p. 25)

The learners in this example are engaged in the text editing task. The female learner, Candela, questions how the text should be edited and suggests how to phrase it. Her male interlocutor, Carlos, gives her feedback on the phrasing, which she confirms, before making a suggestion. Azkarai notes this style of feedback, which is provided through direct, authoritative responses, was given more often by males than females. Overall, males tended to frame their contributions as feedback or answers, while females framed theirs as suggestions. This observation implies that the differences in male and female feedback may not be limited to the amount of feedback given, but also according to the conversational style used.

Complicating this picture is the fact that other studies have found more feedback occurring in matched- rather than mixed-gender dyads. Ross-Feldman (2005) examined the interactions of adult L1 Spanish learners. She found that there were more recasts in matched- than mixed-gender dyads, noting that the results may be related to the face-threatening nature of providing recast feedback. Ross-Feldman explains that "[r]ecasts may be a fairly face threatening interactional move; when one learner recasts another, he is not only telling the other learner that she is wrong, he is saying that he knows what is correct. Both males and females in this study were more willing to take this risk with an interlocutor of the same gender than with an interlocutor of a different gender" (p. 192). Azkarai (2015) and Gass and Varonis (1986) also found that females initiate more negotiation when working with other females than with males. They suggest that matched-gender dyads may be particularly beneficial for female learners, because they have more conversational control than when they interact with male learners. Ross-Feldman (2005) suggests that her similar findings reflect that it is working with a female interlocutor that may make the difference for feedback provision and use. So for males, mixed-gender dyads may be more beneficial, and for females, matched dyads may be more beneficial.

Similar to the research carried out on NS–learner feedback, there are reasons to accept findings on peer interactional feedback and gender with caution. Again, there has been noticeably little research in this area, and only a few studies have had substantial participant pools. Studies have not consistently revealed gender effects on feedback. Bitchener (2003), for example, found no differences between MM and FF dyads in terms of implicit feedback through negotiation of meaning among thirty-six L1 Japanese and Korean ESL learners, despite gender differences in L1 communication in these cultures. Participants in his study indicated in post-treatment interviews that they avoided providing feedback to each other, feeling that it would be face threatening and unnecessary. He points out that even for L1 communication, gender differences are diminished in certain communicative settings, for example in friendly, same-gender talk in a tightly controlled experimental setting (cf. Freed & Greenwood, 1996). Examining peer interactions in controlled quasi-experimental settings may not provide a full reflection of how males and females provide feedback to peers in actual language classrooms.

When studies have shown differences according to learner gender or gender pairing, these effects seem to be at least partly an artifact of the tasks that were used. Ross-Feldman (2005) found that task was an intervening variable for gender effects; on one task, a one-way picture description task, males used more comprehension checks than females in MF dyads, and on that same task, there were significantly more recasts in matched-gender dyads than in mixed. Azkarai and García Mayo (2012) similarly found an interaction of gender and task in their study; not only did the amount of focus on form generated depend on the task, a finding consistent with previous research, but gender roles were more clearly delineated on some tasks than others. They note that, in their study, gender seemed to play an important role in the use of feedback in the information-gap task, but not in the discussion task. They hypothesize that the difference might be tied to the locus of control in the different tasks. In the free discussion activity, learners could determine what they would contribute, but in the information-gap task, learners have an individual responsibility to share their information, which might increase provision of feedback, revealing gendered differences.

Future Directions for Gender and Feedback Research

There has been relatively little research on gender and L2 feedback, leaving uncertainty and substantial gaps in our understanding of how gender shapes learning opportunities through feedback. In particular, we highlight four issues that should be addressed by future research.

The first is the intersection of gender and culture. We have several times in this chapter noted that contradictory findings may be related to differences among different cultural groups. Gendered behavioral norms are not biologically fixed. There is, as Cameron (2003) explained, "no universal essence of masculinity or femininity" (p. 188) and gender norms differ substantially across cultural and social groups (Meyerhoff, 2014). While L1 cultural norms do not translate directly into L2 learning and use (Itakura, 2001), a learner's culturally informed expectations about gender likely mediate the ways that learners engage in L2 learning and use. Research on gender and feedback among a wider sample of cultural groups is needed to clarify this relationship.

Similarly, even within a single society or community, gender norms can vary widely (Cameron, 2003). Just as cultural differences may inform gendered behavior, so too, may differences in educational attainment and research settings. Azkarai (2015) and Ross-Feldman (2007) reported different effects of learner gender on focus on form in peer interactions, despite striking similarities in research design. Azkarai attributes these distinctions to different cultural backgrounds (as language socialization experiences of the Central American participants in Ross-Feldman's study might have differed substantially from those of the Spanish participants in her own study) as well as to possible distinctions in L2 cultural understandings of learners in EFL and ESL settings. A further distinction may have been experience with formal education; Ross-Feldman's participants were enrolled in an adult education program, with few having education in their home countries beyond secondary education, while Azkarai's participants were college students in their home countries. It is possible that their additional education may have influenced the patterns of their interaction and the effect of gender on those interactions, as it has been shown to do in L1 interactions (Meyerhoff, 2014). Again, more research conducted among learners with different backgrounds might help unravel the relationships among cultural background, educational setting, and gender effects in interaction and feedback.

On a related note, much of the research on gender and feedback has taken place in English learning settings, generally in either ESL or EFL contexts. While learners do bring cultural expectations about gendered behavior to interactions, they may also be influenced by their growing understanding of the target culture. In a study of pronunciation among L1 English learners of Japanese, Ohara (2001) found that female learners were aware of the use of pitch in Japanese to express femininity. The learners spoke with higher pitch when they were seeking to express alignment with Japanese culture, but used lower pitch to express their identity as foreigners. It is possible as well that language learners (particularly those in L2 settings) are aware of target culture gendered expression and may seek to exhibit this as they interact and respond to feedback. Research conducted in a broader range of language learning settings is needed to understand how exposure to new cultural norms mediates the ways that different students provide and respond to feedback.

The second area in need of further research is the role of gender in L2 language writing and feedback. While there is substantial evidence that both the gender of the teacher and that of the student mediate the amount and types of feedback provided in L1 writing in educational settings (e.g., Haswell & Haswell, 1996; Read et al., 2005; Susanti, 2013), there is a dearth of corresponding research for L2 writing. Part of our language socialization is awareness of cultural attributions of femininity and masculinity to writing. It is likely that these tacit understandings carry over to L2 teaching, prompting differences in the ways that feedback is provided to male and female language learners by both their teachers and peers. Empirical inquiry is required to understand these relationships.

A third gap is research investigating how differences in the provision of feedback to males and females may impact language learning. The studies of feedback and gender reviewed here have been primarily descriptive, looking at how feedback is provided. However, as Ross-Feldman (2005) noted, descriptive differences do not necessarily lead to divergent developmental outcomes. Alcón and Codina (1996), for example, found that despite differences in interactional feedback between males and females in their study, there was no difference in vocabulary learning during the study. Research on gender and language strategy use, as another example, has found differences according to learner gender that have not mapped onto learning success (Ehrman & Oxford, 1989). Likewise, developmental research is required to illuminate the relationship among gender, feedback, and language learning.

Fourth, we observe that the treatment of gender in L2 feedback studies is misaligned with current understandings of the role of gender in language use. As we noted earlier in this chapter, feedback studies that have considered gender have simply divided learners into groups based on their biological sex, rather than considering how gendered behaviors might be constructed and performed by different learners. As Meyerhoff (2014) points out, our understanding of gender and language has evolved from early models that simply categorized participants as male and female, taking an anthropological and critical perspective that gender is socially constructed and language differences are due less to inherent, biological sex-related qualities than to societal constructions of gender roles. This perspective, rather than studying gender as a binary deterministic variable, considers the "ideologies of gender" (Pavlenko & Piller, 2001, p. 23) and how gender is constructed, negotiated, and performed in a given context. In short, L2 feedback research continues to treat gender as something participants "have," while sociolinguistic research has increasingly examined gender as something learners "do" in their first and second language use. For this reason, as Pavlenko and Piller (2001) have pointed out, "the role of gender in second language acquisition (SLA) continues to be under-theorized and under-researched" (p. 1). This certainly applies to studies of L2 feedback and gender.

Related to this, research on gender and feedback has generally considered gender as a binary (male vs. female) variable, while sociolinguistic research has increasingly considered the complex ways transgender, fluid, and queer identified individuals use language to shape and reflect gendered identities (e.g., Hall, Zimman, & Davis, 2009). Future studies should consider gendered language use and responses to feedback beyond binary divisions of gender, adopting qualitative and critical discourse analysis perspectives to understand how gendered language socializations impact L2 interactional language use.

Finally, it is worth remembering that some aspects of how males and females provide, respond to, and learn from feedback may be related to biological sex rather than to socially constructed gender. Tannen (1994) points out that some gendered differences are linked to biological sex, while others might be linked to gendered associations expressed in specific cultures. As Nakatsukasa (2017) points out, research from cognitive psychology has generally found differences in memory capacity and cognitive processing speeds between men and women. While her small-scale study did not provide evidence of an impact on learning from feedback, it is possible that larger-scale studies could find cognitive advantages for interaction and feedback for men or women. For example, if women are better at storing new information in long-term memory, that might suggest an advantage for learning vocabulary from feedback. More research is needed to understand how such factors might play a role in language learning from interaction and feedback.

Clearly, there are many open avenues of empirical research for future explorations of the role of gender in L2 feedback. The discussion in this chapter will hopefully provide a base from which further exploration of these issues can emerge. Research carried out in diverse teaching settings, linked to an understanding of gender and language identity as expressed in both the first and second language, and using a wider range of analytic approaches is needed to clarify how gender impacts the way language students receive and use feedback for learning.

References

Adams, R. (2007). Do second language learners benefit from interacting with each other? In A. Mackey (ed.), *Conversational interaction in second language acquisition* (pp. 29–51). Oxford: Oxford University Press.

Alcón, E. & Codina, V. (1996). The impact of gender on negotiation and vocabulary learning in a situation of interaction. *International Journal of Psycholinguistics*, 12(1), 21–35.

Aries, E. J. (1976). Interaction patterns and themes of male, female, and mixed groups. *Small Group Behavior*, 7(1), 7–18.

(1996). *Men and women in interaction: Reconsidering the differences.* New York: Oxford University Press.

Azkarai, A. (2015). Males and females in EFL task-based interactions: Does gender have an impact on LREs? *Vigo International Journal of Applied Linguistics*, 12, 9–35.

Azkarai, A. & García Mayo, M. P. (2012). Does gender influence task performance in EFL? Interactive tasks and language related episodes. In E. Alcón Soler & M. P. Safont-Jordá (eds.), *Language learners' discourse across L2 instructional settings* (pp. 249–278). Amsterdam: Rodopi.

Bitchener, J. (2003). The effects of individual learner factors and task type on negotiation: A study of advanced Japanese and Korean ESL learners. *Australian Review of Applied Linguistics*, 26(2), 63–83.

Buckingham, A. (1997). Oral language testing: Do the age, status and gender of the interlocutor make a difference? Unpublished MA dissertation, University of Reading, UK.

Cameron, D. (2003). Gender and language ideologies. In J. Holmes & M. Meyerhoff (eds.), *Handbook of language and gender* (pp. 447–467). Oxford: Blackwell.

Cook-Gumperz, J. & Szymanski, M. (2001). Classroom "families": Cooperating or competing – Girls' and boys' interactional styles in a bilingual classroom. *Research on Language and Social Interaction*, 34(1), 107–130.

Eckert, P. (1998). Gender and sociolinguistic variation. In J. Coates (ed.), *Language and gender: A reader* (pp. 64–75). Oxford: Blackwell.

Ehrman, M. & Oxford, R. (1989). Effects of sex differences, career choice, and psychological type on adult language learning strategies. *Modern Language Journal*, 73(1), 1–13.

Fassinger, P. A. (1995). Understanding classroom interaction: Students' and professors' contributions to students' silence. *The Journal of Higher Education*, 66(1), 82–96.

Fishman, P. M. (1978). Interaction: The work women do. *Social Problems*, 25(4), 397–406.

Foote, C. (2002). Gender differences in attribution feedback in the elementary classroom. *Research in the Schools*, 9(1), 1–8.

Freed, A. F. & Greenwood, A. (1996). Women, men, and type of talk: What makes the difference? *Language in Society*, 25(1), 1–26.

Gass, S. M. & Varonis, E. (1985). Task variation and nonnative/nonnative negotiation of meaning. In S. M. Gass & C. Madden (eds.), *Input in second language acquisition* (pp. 149–161). Rowley, MA: Newbury House.

(1986). Sex differences in NNS/NNS interactions. In R. R. Day (ed.), *Talking to learn: Conversation in second language acquisition* (pp. 327–351). Rowley, MA: Newbury House.

Goodwin, M. H. (1990). Tactical uses of stories: Participation frameworks within girls' and boys' disputes. *Discourse Processes*, 13(1), 33–71.

Green, J. & Oxford, R. (1995). A closer look at learning strategies, L2 proficiency, and gender. *TESOL Quarterly*, 29(2), 261–297.

Hall, K., Zimman, L. & Davis, J. (2009). Gender, sexuality, and the "third sex." In C. Llamas & D. Watt (eds.), *Language and Identities* (pp. 166–78). Edinburgh: Edinburgh University Press.

Hartshorne, J. K. & Ullman, M. T. (2006). Why girls say "holded" more than boys. *Developmental Science*, 9(1), 21–32.

Haswell, R. H. & Haswell, J. T. (1996). Gender bias and critique of student writing. *Assessing Writing*, 3(1), 31–83.

Holmes, J. (1998). Complimenting: A positive politeness strategy. In J. Coates (ed.), *Language and gender: A reader* (pp. 100–120). Oxford: Blackwell.

Itakura, H. (2001). *Conversational dominance and gender: A study of Japanese speakers in first and second language contexts*. Philadelphia: John Benjamins.

Kasanga, L. A. (1996). Effect of gender on the rate of interaction: Some implications for second language acquisition and classroom practice. *I.T.L. Review of Applied Linguistics*, 111–112, 155–192.

Long, M. H. (1996). The role of the linguistic environment in second language acquisition. In W. C. Ritchie & T. K. Bhatia (eds.), *Handbook of research on language acquisition. Vol. II: Second language acquisition* (pp. 413–468). New York: Academic Press.

MacIntyre, P. D., Baker, S. C., Clement, R. & Donovan, L. A. (2002). Sex and age effects on willingness to communicate, anxiety, perceived competence, and L2 motivation among junior high school French immersion students. *Language Learning*, 52(3), 537–564.

Mady, C. & Seiling, A. (2017). The coupling of second language learning and achievement according to gender. *Theory and Practice in Language Studies*, 7(12), 1149–1159.

Meyerhoff, M. (2014). Variation and gender. In S. Ehrlich, M. Meyerhoff & J. Holmes (eds.), *The handbook of language, gender, and sexuality* (pp. 85–102). Hoboken, NJ: John Wiley & Sons.

Nakatsukasa, K. (2017). Gender and recasts. In L. Gurzynski–Weiss (ed.), *Expanding individual difference research in the interaction approach: Investigating learners, instructors, and other interlocutors* (pp. 100–119). Philadelphia: John Benjamins.

O'Loughlin, K. (2002). The impact of gender in oral proficiency testing. *Language Testing*, 19(2), 169–192.

O'Sullivan, B. (2000). Exploring gender and oral proficiency interview performance. *System*, 28(1), 1–14.

Ohara, Y. (2001). Finding one's voice in Japanese: A study of the pitch levels of L2 users. In A. Pavlenko, A. Blackledge, I. Piller & M. Teutsch-Dwyer (eds.), *Multilingualism, second language learning, and gender* (pp. 231–254). New York: Mouton de Gruyter.

Oliver, R. (2002). The patterns of negotiation for meaning in child interactions. *Modern Language Journal*, 86(1), 97–111.

Pavlenko, A. & Piller, I. (2001). New directions in the study of multilingualism, second language learning, and gender. In A. Pavlenko, A. Blackledge, I. Piller & M. Teutsch–Dwyer (eds.), *Multilingualism, second language learning, and gender* (pp. 17–52). New York: Mouton de Gruyter.

Philp, J., Adams, R. & Iwashita, N. (2014). *Peer interaction and second language learning*. New York: Routledge.

Pica, T., Holliday, L., Lewis, N. E., Berducci, D. & Newman, J. (1991). Language learning through interaction: What role does gender play? *Studies in Second Language Acquisition*, 13(3), 343–376.

Pica, T., Holliday, L., Lewis, N. E. & Morgenthaler, L. (1989). Comprehensible output as an outcome of linguistic demands on the learner. *Studies in Second Language Acquisition*, 11(1), 63–90.

Porter, D. (1991). Affective factors in the assessment of oral interaction: Gender and status. In S. Arnivan (ed.), *Current developments in language testing* (pp. 92–102). Singapore: SEAMEO Regional Language Centre.

Ranta, L. & Lyster, R. (2007). A cognitive approach to improving immersion students' oral language abilities: The Awareness–Practice–Feedback sequence. In R. DeKeyser (ed.), *Practice in a second language: Perspectives from applied linguistics and cognitive psychology* (pp. 141–160). Cambridge: Cambridge University Press.

Rassaei, E. & Tavakoli, M. (2012). Corrective feedback in the L2 classroom: Matched-gender and mixed-gender dyads in focus. *Iranian EFL Journal, 52*(1), 157–166.

Read, B., Francis, B. & Robson, J. (2005). Gender, "bias," assessment and feedback: Analyzing the written assessment of undergraduate history essays. *Assessment and Evaluation in Higher Education, 30*(3), 241–260.

Reiterer, S. M., Hu, X., Erb, M., Rota, G., Nardo, D., Grodd, W., Winkler, S. & Ackermann, H. (2011). Individual differences in audio–vocal speech imitation aptitude in late bilinguals: Functional neuro-imaging and brain morphology. *Frontiers in Psychology, 2*, 271. http://doi.org/10.3389/fpsyg.2011.00271.

Ross-Feldman, L. (2005). Task-based interactions between second language learners: Exploring the role of gender. Unpublished doctoral dissertation, Georgetown University, Washington, DC.

  (2007). Interaction in the L2 classroom: Does gender influence learning opportunities? In A. Mackey (ed.), *Conversational interaction in second language acquisition: A collection of empirical studies* (pp. 52–77). Oxford: Oxford University Press.

Sadeghi, K. & Sagedi, S. P. (2013). Modified output in task-based EFL classes across gender. *The Journal of Teaching Language Skills, 32*(2), 113–135.

Sadker, M. & Sadker, D. (1994). *Failing at fairness: How our schools cheat girls.* New York: Charles Scribner's Sons.

Shehadeh, A. (1994). Gender differences and second language acquisition. *Research Journal of Aleppo University (Arts and Humanities Series), 26*(2), 73–98.

Sheldon, A. (1990). Pickle fights: Gendered talk in preschool disputes. *Discourse Processes, 13*(1), 5–31.

Su, I.-R. & Huang, C.-N. (2013). The influence of gender on task-based conversational interactions in a foreign language. *English Teaching and Learning, 37*(4), 1–54.

Sunderland, J. (1995). Gender and language testing. *Language Testing Update, 17,* 24–35.

Susanti, R. (2013). Students' perceptions towards the effective feedback practices in the large EFL writing class based on participants, gender, and English proficiency level. Unpublished MA thesis, Indiana University of Pennsylvania, Indiana, PA.

Tannen, D. (1990). Gender differences in topical coherence: Creating involvement in best friends' talk. *Discourse Processes, 13*(1), 73–90.

  (1994). *Gender and discourse.* New York: Oxford University Press.

West, C. & García, A. (1988). Conversational shift work: A study of topical transition between women and men. *Social Problems, 35*(5), 551–575.

Zuengler, J. & Wang, H. (1993). Gender and communication strategy use. Paper presented at the Xth International Congress of Applied Linguistics, Amsterdam.

32

Feedback, Aptitude, and Multilingualism

Beatriz Lado and Cristina Sanz

Introduction

In the last twenty years, the field of second language acquisition (SLA) has witnessed a growing interest in the role of individual differences (IDs) as it continues to investigate "the nature of the specific IDs and the degree to which they affect specific aspects of second language (L2) acquisition" (Sanz, 2005, p. 14). Cognitive variables such as aptitude, including linguistic analytic ability, rote memory, working memory (WM), or phonological short-term memory, and language experience (i.e., multilingualism[1]) are among the IDs where scholarship has grown the most. This includes investigations of how cognitive variables and prior language experience moderate the effectiveness of different components of language pedagogy, including corrective feedback. The present chapter is an attempt to bridge the gap between research and pedagogy by informing researchers, teachers, and practitioners about the role that two IDs, aptitude and multilingualism, play across different learning conditions, and specifically those in which feedback is involved.

Cognitive Aptitudes

In the field of SLA, the term *aptitude* has often been used to refer to cognitive abilities implicated in language learning (e.g., Robinson, 2005a). The construct has undergone considerable modifications over the course of time, starting with Carroll's view of aptitude as "an individual's initial state of readiness and capacity for learning a foreign language, and probable facility in doing so given the presence of motivation and

---

[1] In this chapter, the term *multilingualism* refers to knowledge of more than one language by an individual, including different degrees of early and late bilingualism and multilingualism. Our definition is in line with approaches that consider that "bilingualism begins with learning of more than a single language variety" (De Houwer & Ortega, 2019).

opportunity" (Carroll, 1981, p. 86). Aptitude has frequently been equated to the set of abilities measured by the Modern Language Aptitude Test (MLAT), developed by Carroll and Sapon in 1959, when Behaviorist approaches to learning in psychology and audiolingualism in the language teaching profession were popular. The MLAT contained five sections: (1) number learning, (2) phonetic script, (3) spelling cues, (4) words in sentences, and (5) paired associates, which attempted to measure rote learning ability and memory, phonetic coding ability, inductive language learning, and grammatical sensitivity. A similar test developed at that time was Pimsleur's Language Aptitude Battery (PLAB; Pimsleur, 1966) designed for younger learners. Despite the MLAT's shortcomings (Skehan, 1998) and profound changes in approaches to language development and to teaching methodology, this test is still widely used and is considered one of the most successful predictors of language learning, both in instructional contexts (Ehrman & Oxford, 1995; Erlam, 2005; Harley & Hart, 1997; Winke, 2013) and laboratory studies (De Graaff, 1997; Robinson, 1997). Significant correlation coefficients between MLAT scores and different measures of foreign language progress, including grades, have been found (see Sparks, Javorsky & Ganschow, 2005, for a summary). Current research prefers to report results on specific subtests of the MLAT, a procedure considered to be more informative and that reflects a change in the concept of *aptitude*, now seen as multicomponential. Two of the best predictors of language success are the *Paired Associates* subtest (e.g., Hummel, 2009; Robinson, 1997), which measures rote memory, and the *Words in Sentences* subtest (e.g., Erlam, 2005; Li, 2013), which measures linguistic analytic ability. Both Skehan and Robinson acknowledge the multicomponential and dynamic nature of aptitude. In Skehan's (1998, 2002) view, the cognitive processes involved in the developmental stages of SLA (e.g., noticing, linguistic pattern identification, pattern restructuring) result from the interaction of multiple aptitude components. Similarly, Robinson's (2005a) "Aptitude complexes" framework relates different cognitive abilities to specific language tasks.

One of the subcomponents of aptitude that has received more attention is memory. At the time when the MLAT was developed, Atkinson and Shiffrin (1968) considered short-term memory a storage mechanism through which information was transferred to long-term memory by means of rehearsal. Baddeley and Hitch (1974) later argued that the traditional storage-based short-term memory (STM) should be replaced with WM, concerned not only with storage but also with active processing. Miyake and Shah (1999) defined WM as "those mechanisms or processes that are involved in the control, regulation, and active maintenance of task-relevant information in the service of complex cognition, including novel as well as familiar skilled tasks" (p. 450). One of the most cited models of WM is the Multiple-Component model developed by Baddeley and Hitch (1974) and later modified by Baddeley (2000, 2017), which views

WM as a hierarchical system consisting of (a) a phonological loop, involved in retaining verbal information in a temporary store, (b) a visuo-spatial sketch pad, which maintains visual or spatial information, (c) an episodic buffer, a temporary storage system that integrates the information processed in the other subsystems and long-term memory, and (d) a central executive, to control and regulate attention. Baddeley suggests that the combination of the processing and storage components of WM can help predict individual differences in such cognitive skills as reading, comprehension, and reasoning. In addition, this model considers the central executive as an attentional system (Baddeley & Logie, 1999) crucial for successful language learning.

Research on WM in SLA looks at the role of the phonological loop on L2 acquisition with the implementation of phonological short-term memory (PSTM) tests, or at the role of both storage and processing capacity with sentence span tests (Daneman & Carpenter, 1980) as WM measures. Both lines of investigation have found that there is a relationship between WM and second language learning (see Li, 2017 and Williams, 2012, for reviews).

In line with their multicomponent approach to aptitude, Skehan (2002) and Robinson (2005a) suggested expanding the traditional view of aptitude by integrating WM measures into "a much broader battery of aptitude subtests than operationalized in MLAT and other traditional tests" (Robinson 2005a, p. 51). Other scholars have also called for a reevaluation of the construct (Gardner, 1990; McLaughlin, 1995; Parry & Stansfield, 1990; Sawyer & Ranta, 2001; Wen, Biedron & Skehan, 2017), which has led to the inclusion of aptitude in information-processing[2] perspectives of language acquisition. For this reason, many scholars are now adopting a perspective in which WM plays a significant role (Wen et al., 2017) and are talking about *cognitive aptitudes* (Suzuki & DeKeyser, 2017) in order to account for the multicomponent view of the construct. With these theoretical perspectives in mind, new tests that incorporate WM have offered new alternatives to operationalize cognitive aptitudes: The CANAL-F test (Cognitive Ability for Novelty in Acquisition of Language-Foreign) developed by Grigorenko, Sternberg, and Ehrman (2000), and the LLAMA aptitude test (Meara, 2005). As Skehan (2012) describes it, the CANAL-F was developed with an understanding of attentional functions in cognitive psychology. The different sections measure inductive language learning, paired associates, attentional processing, and WM. The LLAMA test includes measurements of WM, phonemic coding ability, inductive language learning, and paired associates. The recent High-Level Language Aptitude Battery (Hi-LAB) (Doughty et al., 2010; Linck et al. 2013)

---

[2] Information-processing approaches look at second language learning from the perspective of human information processing, which derives from contemporary cognitive psychology and its concern for the processes of learning, perception, memory, problem-solving, and decision-making (McLaughlin, Rossman & McLeod, 1983).

was developed with an advanced L2 population in mind and includes twelve measures of seven cognitive abilities; PSTM, implicit learning, and rote memory were revealed as significant predictors of advanced L2 learning. Recently, Granena (2019) has shown that the LLAMA and the Hi-LAB include tests that tap the same constructs. Despite the posited link between aptitude and WM, Li (2017) argues for more research on the "theoretical and empirical links between traditional aptitude and WM" (p. 401).

Cognitive Aptitudes and Pedagogical Conditions

An important issue that has obvious implications for second language learning and teaching is whether the role of cognitive aptitudes varies depending on the type of instruction. This emerging line of research is known as aptitude-treatment interaction (ATI) research (see Vatz et al., 2013).

Although Krashen (1981) claimed that aptitude influences language learning only when the approach to teaching promotes explicit learning (see Robinson, 2002, 2005a, for a discussion on this issue), other researchers such as Skehan (1998, 2002) argue that aptitude plays a larger role in more informal (e.g., nonclassroom immersion) contexts as learners are under more pressure when processing input.[3]

Robinson (1997, 2002, 2005b) contributed to this discussion with evidence from two studies. In Robinson (1997), 104 ESL students were distributed into four different treatments to learn an "easy rule" (subject-verb inversion is allowed in sentences where adverbials of movement/location are fronted) and a "hard rule" (how to form pseudo-clefts of location). The four conditions varied depending on whether participants were instructed to comprehend the stimuli (incidental), to memorize it (implicit), to look for rules (rule-search), or were exposed to the rules in advance (instructed). Aptitude was measured using the "words in sentences" (linguistic analytic ability) and "paired associates" (rote memory) subtests of the English MLAT. Results on a grammaticality judgment test revealed that linguistic analytic ability significantly correlated with learning in the implicit, rule-search, and instructed conditions, but not in the incidental condition. Moreover, results revealed correlations between the most explicit condition (i.e., instructed) and rote memory, and between the rule-search condition (i.e., the second most explicit) and rote memory (for the hard rule). These findings seem to indicate that aptitude influences language learning in both explicit and implicit conditions. However, when the conditions are more explicit and include formal rule learning, it appears that more aptitude constructs are involved than when conditions are more implicit.

---

[3] We chose to start with studies that include different pedagogical variables as they contribute to the issue of whether learning is more successful under more or less explicit conditions. Some of the studies are also included because they show that language development is possible in the absence of feedback (e.g., Tagarelli et al., 2016).

The lack of relationship between these aptitude measures and language learning in the incidental condition was later partially supported by Robinson (2002, 2005b). This study showed that in conditions involving processing for meaning rather than focus on form, traditional measures of aptitude were not good predictors of immediate language learning. Specifically, the analyses showed that aptitude (as measured by the Language Aptitude Battery for the Japanese, similar to the MLAT) was related to performance in the more explicit learning condition. On the contrary, WM was found to be related only to incidental learning on immediate and one-week delayed listening grammaticality judgment post-tests and on one-week and six-months delayed guided production post-tests.

More recently, Tagarelli, Borges Mota, and Rebuschat (2015) have also explored the way in which WM (as measured by an operation word span task and a letter-number ordering task) interacts with instructional conditions (incidental, intentional, and control) in the learning of a semi-artificial language. A positive correlation between performance and WM was found only for the intentional (rule discovery) group on grammatical items. Similarly, Tagarelli et al. (2016) looked at the interaction between WM (as measured by a reading span task) and learning conditions (incidental and instructed with provision of rule) but found no significant correlations between WM and learning when considering all items in the test. However, when the items were separated, the results revealed a positive correlation between WM and performance on complex items in the incidental group, which researchers attributed to the saliency of the items in the less structured condition.

Laboratory studies such as those by Robinson (1997, 2002, 2005b) and Tagarelli and colleagues (2015, 2016) show a messy picture: results vary with the learning condition, the cognitive measure, and the complexity of the form. An important issue to be considered is the nature of the abilities measured by the aptitude tests implemented (Granena, 2016). It seems that tests such as the MLAT may be measuring abilities associated with explicit and attention-driven cognitive processes (e.g., explicit inductive learning, rote memory, and linguistic analytical ability) as supported by the literature (e.g., Li, 2015). An investigation by Granena (2013) also revealed that three of the four LLAMA subtests (B, E, and F[4]) tap into explicit cognitive processes involved in explicit inductive learning, explicit associative learning, and rote learning ability, a combination that she named Explicit Language Aptitude (ELA).

Traditional measurements may not capture the relationship between cognitive aptitudes and learning under more implicit conditions; some

---

[4] The four subtests of the LLAMA are: LLAMA B, a test of vocabulary learning, LLAMA D, a test of sound recognition that requires previously heard sound sequences to be identified in new sequences, LLAMA E, a test of sound–symbol associations, and LLAMA F, a test of grammatical inferencing (Granena, 2013).

researchers (Granena, 2013, 2016; Linck et al., 2013) have suggested other measurements, such as Serial Reaction Time (SRT), hypothesized to rely on implicit processing. The development of tests such as the Hi-LAB (Doughty et al., 2010; Linck et al., 2013), mentioned above, shows promise as it incorporates measurements intended to tap into both explicit and implicit learning cognitive aptitudes.

Cognitive Aptitudes and Feedback

Do learners with high cognitive aptitudes benefit more from corrective feedback than those with low cognitive aptitudes? What cognitive aptitudes benefit learning when receiving implicit forms of feedback such as recasts, and which ones are related to learning under explicit corrective feedback conditions (e.g., right/wrong correction with or without grammar rules)? What type of feedback is effective regardless of learners' cognitive aptitudes? In what follows, we review studies that have attempted to answer these questions.[5]

Ever-growing evidence from both laboratory and classroom studies suggest that there is a relationship between some cognitive aptitudes and different types of corrective feedback (DeGraaf, 1997; Erlam, 2005; Goo, 2012; Lado, 2017; Li, 2013; Mackey et al., 2002; Sagarra & Abbuhl, 2013a, 2013b; Sanz et al., 2016; Sheen, 2007; Yilmaz, 2013; Yilmaz & Granena, 2016). Importantly, whereas laboratory studies tend to include feedback during accuracy-based computerized practice (e.g., DeGraaf, 1997; Lado, 2017; Sanz et al., 2016), many classroom-based studies provide feedback during communicative tasks (e.g., Goo, 2012; Sheen, 2007). The different approaches have obvious implications for the development of knowledge (more or less implicit) and for the role of cognitive aptitudes.

A frequently cited study by De Graaff (1997) investigated the learning of a language adapted from Esperanto (eXperanto) in a laboratory setting. Fifty-four participants were asked to learn simple and complex morphological and syntactic forms in 150 hours of computer-based lessons, during which they had to read dialogue translations, complete vocabulary activities, and practice interpreting and producing the target forms. There were two groups, which varied in degrees of explicitness: (1) an explicit group, with explicit rules presented before practice and during the provision of feedback on the correctness of their answers in the activities, and (2) an implicit group, with the same corrective feedback (right/wrong) but without rule presentation before or during the activities. Aptitude was measured by an adaptation of the MLAT in Dutch containing the "words in sentences" and "paired associates." The results from the aptitude tests were collapsed so that correlations could be run. It was found that aptitude

---

[5] Here, we begin with some studies where feedback appears in combination with other pedagogical practices (provision of rule, etc.). We choose to include some of these studies to provide a broader view of the role of feedback on second language instruction.

correlated with overall performance on language tests (grammaticality judgment and production), but there was no interaction between aptitude and treatment. In other words, aptitude was positively related to language performance regardless of how the language was taught, including how corrective feedback was provided (i.e., with or without metalinguistic information).

A recent laboratory study by Sanz et al. (2016), conducted within the Latin Project[6] paradigm, investigated the relationship between WM capacity and language learning in two conditions that varied in the presence or absence of a grammar lesson given before input-based practice with explicit feedback. Participants were L2 Spanish intermediate learners who were exposed to Latin (L3) for the first time. WM predicted a positive change in the ability to interpret written and aural input only in the absence of the pre-practice grammar lesson, suggesting that WM capacity may play more of a role when metalinguistic information is limited to reactive feedback. Also within the Latin Project, Lado (2017) investigated linguistic analytic ability and rote memory (as measured by the MLAT), WM, and PSTM on L3 learning under two computerized conditions (without a pre-practice grammar lesson) that differed in the provision of metalinguistic information as part of the feedback. The results supported those in Sanz et al. (2016), as they also revealed that WM played a role during learning when feedback included metalinguistic information. Linguistic analytic ability also gave learners an advantage under the metalinguistic condition when processing sentences for meaning, but only WM (and rote memory to a lesser extent) had a role in the development of grammatical sensitivity to the form. In contrast, except rote memory in immediate aural interpretation, none of the aptitude measures predicted learning under the right/wrong corrective feedback condition. Given these results, Lado suggested that the less explicit approach may have been more democratic, i.e., it was equally suitable for learners with both high and low cognitive aptitudes. It may be the case that, when learners are not given grammatical explanations, they have to use alternative strategies that do not involve conscious metalinguistic reflection. Those learners with high linguistic analytic ability and WM capacity may still make use of these abilities while trying to come up with the rules by themselves, but those with low linguistic analytic ability and WM capacity may rely more on chunking.

Mackey et al. (2002) and Trofimovich, Ammar, and Gatbonton (2007) looked at the role of cognitive aptitudes in the noticing of feedback. Mackey et al. (2002) included an adaptation of the Daneman and Carpenter's WM test (1980) and a PSTM test. Their findings showed that participants with higher WM capacity noticed implicit feedback (i.e., recasts) more than those with lower WM capacity. In contrast, in

---

[6] The Latin Project (Lado, 2017; Lado et al., 2014, 2017; Lenet et al., 2011; Sanz et al., 2009; Sanz et al., 2016) adopts an interactive perspective to the study of individual differences and learning contexts.

Trofimovich et al. (2007), WM did not seem to be associated with the noticing of recasts, perhaps due to the measures implemented or different saliency in the feedback provided. Trofimovich et al. (2007) measured phonological memory and WM with a non-word recognition task and a letter-number string test respectively. Additionally, the authors included language analytic ability (as measured by the words in sentences MLAT test) and attention control. Learners completed several picture description tasks and received oral computerized recast. Three target forms were included: English possessives (grammatical), intransitive verbs (lexical), and possessives and transitive forms combined (mixed). Language analytic ability was associated with language development on the grammatical forms, but not on the lexical forms. Moreover, whereas phonological memory seemed to determine the effectiveness of recasts on the delayed test, WM did not predict or explain any of the accuracy results.

A number of additional studies have also explored the role of aptitude on the effect of different types of corrective feedback (e.g., recasts, metalinguistic feedback[7]) under an interactionist approach (Goo, 2012; Li, 2013; Sagarra & Abbuhl, 2013a, 2013b; Sheen, 2007; Yilmaz, 2013; Yilmaz & Granena, 2016). Sheen (2007) investigated aptitude by means of the Otto test (Otto, 2002) (a multiple-choice translation test where learners need to analyze grammatical markers supplied in a glossary) and corrective feedback (oral recast, and correction with metalinguistic feedback) during a two-way classroom information-gap activity to learn the indefinite and definite English articles. The findings revealed that aptitude played a role on the effects of metalinguistic correction but not on the effects of recasts.

Goo (2012) investigated whether WM mediated acquisition of the English *that*-trace filter under three different conditions in a classroom study: oral recast, oral metalinguistic feedback (correction with explanation of the rule), and control. Participants were fifty-four Korean EFL learners completing two one-way information-gap activities as well as pre- and post- grammaticality judgment and written production tests. WM was measured using a reading span task and an operation span task. The results revealed that WM mediated learning only in the oral recast group. Caution is needed when interpreting these results due to the low sample size of the recast group (n=14) and the lack of a delayed test.

WM was also one of the cognitive aptitudes included in Li (2013). He investigated whether the effect of recasts or metalinguistic feedback on the acquisition of an opaque linguistic structure (Chinese perfective -*le*) was mediated by linguistic analytic ability and WM as measured by the words in a sentences subtest of the MLAT and a listening span test, respectively. WM was negatively correlated with performance on the delayed grammaticality judgment test in the metalinguistic feedback group.

---

[7] Metalinguistic feedback is frequently operationalized in interaction studies as provision of the correct form followed by explicit rule explanation (e.g., Li, 2013; Sheen, 2007).

Linguistic analytic ability, however, was positively correlated with the same test scores, confirming that linguistic analytic ability plays an important role under conditions where learners receive feedback with metalinguistic explanations. The role of aptitude-mediating grammar learning under explicit conditions is further supported by Li's (2015) meta-analysis, Skehan's (2015) critical overview, and additional ATI studies (Yilmaz, 2013; Yilmaz & Granena, 2016). Yilmaz (2013) investigated the relationship between WM (as measured by an operation span task), linguistic analytic ability (as measured by LLAMA F), and L2 learning (Turkish plural and locative morphemes) under explicit correction or recast conditions. The results revealed that explicit correction worked better than recasts when learners had high cognitive abilities (both WM and linguistic analytic ability). Yilmaz and Granena (2016) also looked at the interaction between cognitive aptitudes (as measured by the three subtests of the LLAMA hypothesized to tap into explicit language learning, i.e., ELA) and L2 learning under explicit correction, recast, or no feedback conditions. ELA only predicted learning immediately after the treatment and under explicit correction conditions (direct rejection of the learner's answer plus correction of the error), not under recast conditions.

Another study on interactive feedback by Sagarra and Abbuhl (2013a) investigated the role of WM on the development of gender and number agreement in L1 English/L2 Spanish learners distributed in six experimental treatments that provided different types of feedback: written or oral utterance rejection, written or oral unenhanced recasts, and written (with bold and capitalized font) or oral (with stress) enhanced recasts. Participants were required to complete a computerized fill-in-the-blank activity with the correct form of the adjective. WM was found to be related to written and oral accuracy as well as to production in a face-to-face interactional post-test for the enhanced and unenhanced oral recasts. In a follow-up study (2013b), feedback was provided to four groups as follows: written enhanced recasts, written unenhanced recasts, written unenhanced recasts with a pre-task grammar explanation, and no feedback. Unlike in their first study, WM did not play a significant role in L2 learning perhaps due to the fact that all feedback in this second study was written, suggested to be easier to process than aural feedback and therefore less sensitive to WM effects. These studies on interaction seem to indicate again that cognitive aptitudes, such as linguistic analytic ability, benefit learning when metalinguistic information is provided during feedback (Li, 2013; Yilmaz, 2013; Yilmaz & Granena, 2016). WM (as measured by a sentence span test), on the contrary, is more beneficial under implicit forms of feedback such as recasts although the benefits may be more evident when recasts are provided orally (Goo, 2012; Sagarra & Abbuhl, 2013a). Disparate findings (Trofimovich et al. 2007; Yilmaz, 2013), however, surely warrant further research on the role of WM when implicit forms of feedback are provided.

In sum, results from laboratory and classroom research conducted with adult learners of different languages suggest that the effects of feedback on language development are constrained by a number of cognitive aptitudes (e.g., De Graaff, 1997; Goo, 2012; Lado, 2017; Li, 2013; Sanz et al., 2016; Sheen, 2007; Yilmaz, 2013; Yilmaz & Granena, 2016). Specifically, learners with high WM seem to benefit more from corrective feedback than those with low cognitive capacity. Furthermore, under conditions that provide explicit correction with metalinguistic explanations, the positive relationship between linguistic analytic ability and rote memory and language learning seems to be consistent as measured by tests such as the MLAT (Lado, 2017; Li, 2013) or the LLAMA (Yilmaz, 2013; Yilmaz & Granena, 2016). WM also appears to be related to language learning when rules are provided reactively during computerized feedback but not before practice (Lado, 2017; Sanz et al., 2016), or when providing oral recasts, an implicit form of feedback, during interaction (Goo, 2012; Mackey et al., 2002; Sagarra & Abbuhl, 2013a) albeit counterevidence for this last claim also exists (Trofimovich et al., 2007; Yilmaz, 2013).

Pedagogical Implications

We first look at laboratory studies (e.g., Lado, 2017; Sanz et al., 2016), which are key to understanding the role of computerized feedback in current online, hybrid, and regular face-to-face classrooms with an online component (also see Chapter 11, this volume). In computer-assisted language learning (CALL), computers provide feedback that is usually "immediate, provided only when needed, individualized, and focused on the key form" (Sanz, 2004, p. 12). Often, teachers assign exercises after going over the grammar (either at home or in class) without really reflecting on whether this approach could be beneficial for all learners. Does this technique help level the field for all learners (Erlam, 2005)? Computerized practice similar to that presented in the laboratory studies reviewed above suggests that learning also occurs without provision of rules prior to practice (Lado, 2017; Sanz et al., 2016) as long as there are enough opportunities for practice and the input is rich. Additionally, there is evidence that computerized practice with non-metalinguistic corrective feedback (i.e., right/wrong) may be beneficial for all learners regardless of cognitive aptitudes (Lado, 2017; Sagarra & Abbhul, 2013a). Learning under such conditions may require more time, but asking students to practice before being exposed to grammar may lead to more implicit learning and consequently result in greater retention of gains as opposed to more metalinguistic conditions, where students perform well in the short term but where gains are rapidly lost (Lado et al., 2014; Li, 2010).

Classroom-oriented studies reveal that learners with high linguistic analytic ability benefit from correction with metalinguistic feedback (Li, 2013; Sheen, 2007; Yilmaz, 2013; Yilmaz & Granena, 2016), but it is less clear whether WM also plays a role when providing this type of explicit feedback (Goo, 2012; Li, 2013) or when receiving recasts (Trofimovich et al., 2007; Yilmaz & Granena, 2016). Overall, these results seem to indicate that when teachers focus on providing feedback with grammatical rules, they may be favoring those students with higher levels of grammatical sensitivity. For that reason, teachers should provide different forms of feedback in the classroom in order to take into account differences in cognitive abilities among learners.

Prior Language Experience (Multilingualism)

Even though multilingualism is the norm rather than the exception, prior language experience has been traditionally overlooked in *second* language research, as the name itself suggests, partly due to the monolingual bias (Cook, 1992, 2007) that predominates in Western societies, especially in the United Kingdom and the USA, where most of the pedagogical research has been conducted. Traditionally, research in SLA has compared the L2 learner's linguistic behavior against a native monolingual standard, making multilingualism invisible (Ortega, 2014). Until late, the field has seldom taken into account that the multilingual's competence is very different from that of a monolingual's (Grosjean, 2008), and, consequently, that acquiring a second language is very different from acquiring an additional language beyond the second (Cenoz, 2013). Fortunately, research on third language acquisition (Cenoz, 2013), or what is also called multilingual acquisition (Lado & Sanz, 2016), continues to grow as evidenced by the number of volumes and articles on the factors involved, including but not limited to crosslinguistic influence (e.g., Sanz, Park, Lado, 2014). In this section, we focus on research that explores if and how prior language experience affects additional language learning, and if those effects, as suggested by research in cognitive psychology (Bialystok, 2001, and elsewhere), vary with external conditions, such as instructional variables, including feedback.

Multilingualism and Additional Language Learning

Outcome-oriented research conducted in the 1990s and early 2000s explored the role of early bilingual education on L3 learning in adults (e.g., González-Ardeo, 2000) and children or adolescents living in bilingual communities (e.g., Brohy, 2001; Cenoz & Valencia, 1994; Keshavarz & Astaneh, 2004; Lasagabaster, 2000; Muñoz, 2000; Sagasta, 2003; Sanz, 2000, 2007; Swain et al., 1990). Additionally, research with immigrant populations also investigated bilingualism and its role in learning an additional language (e.g., Clyne, Hunt & Isaakidis, 2004; Thomas, 1988). These studies revealed that bilingualism predicts overall L3 proficiency (Brohy 2001; Cenoz & Valencia 1994; Lasagabaster, 2000; Muñoz, 2000; Sagasta, 2003; Sanz, 2000, 2007), vocabulary learning (e.g., Keshavarz & Astaneh, 2004), or grammar development (e.g., Sanz, 2007). Counterevidence also exists (Gibson, Hufeisen & Libben 2001; Okita & Jun Hai, 2001; van Gelderen et al., 2003; Wagner, Spratt & Ezzaki, 1989), likely due to different socioeconomic factors associated with migrant populations and minoritized languages, which are often accompanied by lack of biliteracy (Okita & Jun-Hai 2001), such as the case of Berber in Wagner et al.'s study. This factor, biliteracy, is frequently linked to positive effects of bilingualism, which suggests that developing literacy skills may be required for bilingualism to positively affect additional language learning in instructional contexts (Sanz 2007; Thomas, 1988). Higher levels of metalinguistic awareness and a wider range of learning strategies and of linguistic repertoires (see Bowden, Sanz & Stafford, 2005, and Cenoz, 2013, for reviews) have also been proposed. In the next section we look at the way these factors interact with explicitness in pedagogical conditions, including more or less explicit feedback, to influence language development.

Multilingualism and Instruction

Laboratory studies allow for the manipulation of external tasks and provide a controlled environment to study the interaction between cognitive demands set by the external tasks, such as presence or absence of information about how the language works as feedback, and multilingualism. This research reveals that multilingualism leads to an advantage at learning additional languages that varies with the instructional conditions, including explicit feedback (e.g., Lado et al., 2017; Nation & McLaughlin, 1986).

McLaughlin and colleagues[8] (Nation & McLaughlin, 1986; Nayak et al., 1990) conducted a series of studies with monolinguals, bilinguals, and multilinguals learning an artificial language under implicit (exposure without instructions) and explicit (with instructions to find rules) conditions. In Nation and McLaughlin (1986), multilinguals outperformed their peers only in the implicit condition. Nayak et al. (1990) expanded on this study and exposed multilinguals and monolinguals to a "memory" and a "rule discovery" condition. Here, multilinguals did not outperform monolinguals, but group differences in processes (through verbalizations) were observed: multilingual learners were more capable of adjusting their strategies to the demands of the tasks and had more flexibility in using a wider variety of strategies.

A number of studies under The Latin Project continued this line of research but investigated the role of amount of prior experience on learning a natural language, Latin, as the L3. These studies do not just compare monolinguals with bilinguals, but also look at differences inherent to multilingualism, including age of acquisition and level of experience with the language. For example, Stafford, Sanz, and Bowden (2010) compared early and late Spanish L1–English L2 bilinguals during the first

---

[8] Just as we did with aptitude earlier, we first present research on the relationship between multilingualism and learning under different conditions, to focus later on feedback.

stages of learning Latin through exposure to a highly explicit instructional condition – a treatment consisting of a grammar lesson and practice with metalinguistic feedback (i.e., correction plus provision of the rule). The findings revealed that three weeks later, late bilinguals retained more of what they had learned as compared to early bilinguals. As later explained (Lado et al., 2017), the results were surprising, as the authors had initially assumed that an earlier age of arrival and exposure to the L2 would be associated with a higher level of bilingual expertise and, therefore, better L3 learning. The explanation put forward was that late bilinguals benefited from their greater familiarity with traditional foreign-language classroom-based instruction, which, like the lesson in the study, often provides grammatical rules before and during practice. These results reveal the importance of contextual factors (above and beyond knowledge) when learning a language (for more on the role of context, see Chapter 22, this volume).

Within the same paradigm, Lado et al. (2017) compared four different levels of late-learned L1-English/L2-Spanish bilinguals: beginner, intermediate, advanced, and very advanced.[9] In Experiment 1, learners were exposed to practice and feedback that included explicit correction (right/wrong) and metalinguistic information (grammar rules) on the target form. In Experiment 2, the feedback provided indicated only if learners' responses were correct or incorrect. The results revealed that, when the feedback included metalinguistic information, intermediate learners outperformed beginners when tested right after the lesson, but only the most advanced group of bilinguals showed retention of gains three weeks later. In contrast, when the feedback did not include grammar rules, only the very advanced learners had an advantage over beginners at immediate and delayed post-test. The authors concluded that adults' formal L2 experience can make learning an additional language more successful, but when learners are not exposed to feedback that includes grammar explanations, only advanced bilingualism may provide learners with an advantage at processing and internalizing input.

The most recent research within The Latin Project paradigm looks at how aging can moderate the interaction between prior experience and learning context (Cox, 2017; Cox & Sanz, 2015; Lenet et al., 2011). Lenet et al.'s results showed a clear interaction between age and type of feedback in that aging learners outperformed their college-aged counterparts (all monolingual) when the feedback did not provide information on how the language worked; it seems that for aging learners, explicit feedback, instead of serving as a scaffold, overloads the learners' system. Park (2000) suggested the main deficits that occur with cognitive aging are decreases in WM capacity, processing speed, and inhibitory control.

---

[9] The groups included college Spanish learners: Beginner (first and second semester); Intermediate (third and fourth semester); Advanced (fifth and sixth semester); and Very Advanced (senior Spanish majors and graduate students).

However, inhibitory control may explain bilinguals' advantage in certain cognitive tasks and L3 learning, as it helps suppress irrelevant input (Sanz, 2000). So Cox (2017) and Cox & Sanz (2015) set out to investigate the role of bilingualism in L3 development among young and older bilinguals who were exposed to grammar prior to practice. When combined, their results show that for aging late-learned bilinguals, aged 65–92, learning a new language can be as successful as for young bilinguals, and that practice plays a key role as the driver of success. Importantly, their results also show that older bilinguals, compared to their monolingual counterparts, can take advantage of grammar explanations when they are provided as an advanced organizer, possibly due to the bilinguals' higher metalinguistic awareness, and that older learners are handicapped by feedback that includes grammar rules that overwhelm their cognitive capacity.

In sum, laboratory studies under an information-processing approach reveal that more explicit instruction with grammar explanations provided before practice or as feedback neutralize the effect that bilingualism has on additional language learning (Lado et al., 2017; Stafford et al., 2010) although these results seem to be less apparent for learners who are not at their cognitive prime (Cox, 2017). However, as the positive effects associated with grammar and metalinguistic feedback are not consistently maintained weeks after the lesson (Cox & Sanz, 2015; Lado et al., 2017), future research that explores whether these benefits are maintained over time with continued exposure is warranted.

Results also suggest that, for young adults, very advanced late-learned bilingualism is associated with cognitive advantages that emerge in more demanding conditions, i.e., conditions in which learners need to inhibit attention to unhelpful cues and/or figure out the rules on their own when processing aural input – arguably more demanding than written input due to the memory constraints placed by its volatility (Lado et al., 2017). This behavior is consistent with the posited link between prior language experience and executive control (Bialystok, 2001), as bilinguals have been claimed to outperform monolinguals on tasks that require interference suppression, i.e., "inhibitory control" (Bialystok & Senman, 2004; Bialystok & Shapero, 2005). However, counterevidence also exists (Bialystok, 2009; Hilchey & Klein, 2011; Paap & Greenberg, 2013), so there is certainly room for further research.

Finally, a very limited number of studies have also looked at the role that prior language experience plays in how learners benefit from written corrective feedback. For example, Bitchener and Knoch (2008) investigated two groups of L2 English learners in New Zealand: international students with previous formal exposure to English, and immigrants with more limited formal exposure to English. Three different forms of written corrective feedback were provided to help students improve accuracy on the English articles: direct error correction alone, direct error correction with written metalinguistic explanations, and direct error correction with written and oral metalinguistic explanations. The results revealed that more formal exposure did not benefit learners' accuracy or their writing as a result of the feedback. Results are inconclusive, however, as some immigrant students had also received formal exposure to English, like their international student counterparts. Given the growing presence of migrants and refugees in highly literate countries around the world and the enormous differences in educational background among individuals, studying how different populations of multilinguals can better benefit from written feedback, both when learning to write and when writing to learn their new language, is a worthwhile research endeavor.

Pedagogical Implications
Although research on the role of prior language experience and type of instruction is limited, the findings to date seem to indicate that multilingualism provides young adults with an advantage during lessons with less scaffolding (i.e., in the absence of feedback with grammar rules). Also, while learners over 65 benefit greatly from practice, their learning experience appears to be negatively affected by the presence of explicit feedback with grammar, which they perceive as an excess of information. However, when grammatical information is presented prior to practice, it seems to give older bilinguals an edge compared to their monolingual counterparts. It is important to note, however, that regardless of cognitive capacity or prior language experience, practice alone can lead to language development that results in long-lasting retention, even in the absence of grammatical explanations.

What are the implications of these findings for the language classroom? Although grammar may be beneficial for all learners during the initial stages of learning a language, when learners have a high level of L2 experience, teachers should favor an inductive approach and avoid overusing grammar explanations when providing feedback. When learners are older bilinguals who are used to traditional approaches to language teaching, assigning a mini grammar lesson for homework is advisable. In every case, it is beneficial to provide learners with lots of opportunities to interact with the language in ways that push them to make form–meaning connections during practice with simple correct/incorrect feedback. Populations that may benefit from this approach include classes in bi/multilingual educational contexts, such as Spanish/Basque bilinguals taking L3 English in bilingual educational programs in the Basque Country, or learners in countries with high levels of functional multilingualism like the Netherlands, or in contexts where the majority of learners are international or bilingual or have similarly high levels of L2 experience, such as students in "Portuguese for Spanish speakers" courses. As the number of L3 classes for experienced L2 learners grows, teachers need to be informed of the idiosyncrasies of this population so that students make the most of their time in the classroom. Given that prior language experience provides learners with higher levels of metalinguistic awareness and a wider and more frequent use of successful strategies, implicit approaches in which students are provided with numerous instances of contextualized and meaningful input – as in task-based or content-based approaches with more implicit forms of feedback – should be given priority. As bi/multi-linguals "look for more sources of input and make an early effort to use the new language" (Bowden et al., 2005, p.122), they will immerse themselves in cognitively engaging learning while they form and test their own hypotheses, which should lead to successful language learning. This type of approach also benefits learners in superdiverse urban contexts, such as New York City, where institutions may have a large number of first or second-generation immigrants with knowledge of one or two additional languages. Many of these immigrant students may have had formal exposure to their first and/or second language in their home country and are no strangers to learning a new language in a formal context; therefore, instructors should ask students to reflect on their prior linguistic knowledge as they engage in activities that help them incorporate the new language into their linguistic repertoire. Finally, as more and more aging adults in developed nations remain healthy and active, the number of nontraditional students who return to the classroom later in life keeps growing. Teachers should be aware that for late-learned older bilinguals, providing a carefully designed combination of explicit instruction *prior* to practice that avoids taxing their cognitive capacities the way explicit feedback does may eliminate some of the effects associated with aging. We recommend that practitioners include a background questionnaire at the beginning of the semester to collect information on students' prior language experience and learning strategies in order to better account for this and other individual differences, including age (see Chapter 30, this volume) and cognitive abilities.

References

Atkinson, R. C. & Shiffrin, R. M. (1968). Human memory: A proposed system and its control processes. In K. W. Spence & J. T. Spence (eds.), *The psychology of learning and motivation: Advances in research and theory* (Vol. II, pp. 89–195). New York: Academic Press.

Baddeley, A. (2000). The episodic buffer: A new component of working memory? *Trends in Cognitive Sciences*, 4(11), 417–423.

(2017). Modularity, working memory and language acquisition. *Second Language Research*, 33(3), 299–311.

Baddeley, A. & Hitch, G. (1974). Working memory. In G. H. Bower (ed.), *The psychology of learning and motivation: Advances in research and theory* (Vol. VIII. pp. 47–90). San Diego, CA: Academic Press.

Baddeley, A. & Logie, R. H. (1999). Working memory: The multiple-component model. In A. Miyake & P. Shah (eds.), *Models of working memory: Mechanisms of active maintenance and executive control* (pp. 28–61). New York: Cambridge University Press.

Bialystok, E. (2001). *Bilingualism in development: Language, literacy, and cognition*. New York: Cambridge University Press.

(2009). Bilingualism: The good, the bad, and the indifferent. *Bilingualism: Language and Cognition*, 12(1), 3–11. DOI:10.1017/S1366728908003477.

Bialystok, E. & Senman, L. (2004). Executive processes in appearance–reality tasks: The role of inhibition of attention and symbolic representation. *Child Development*, 75, 562–579.

Bialystok, E. & Shapero, D. (2005). Ambiguous benefits: The effect of bilingualism on reversing ambiguous figures. *Developmental Science*, 8, 595–604.

Bitchener, J. & Knoch, U. (2008). The value of written corrective feedback for migrant and international students. *Language Teaching Research*, 12(3), 409–431.

Bowden, H., Sanz, C. & Stafford, C. A. (2005). Individual differences: Age, sex, working memory, and prior knowledge. In C. Sanz (ed.), *Mind and context in adult second language acquisition: Methods, theory, and practice* (pp. 105–140). Washington, DC: Georgetown University Press.

Brohy, C. (2001). Generic and/or specific advantages of bilingualism in a dynamic plurilingual situation: The case of French as official L3 in the school of Samedan (Switzerland). *International Journal of Bilingual Education and Bilingualism*, 4, 38–49.

Carroll, J. B. (1981). Twenty-five years of research on foreign language aptitude. In K. C. Diller (ed.), *Individual differences and universals in language learning aptitude* (pp. 83–118). Rowley, MA: Newbury House.

Carroll, J. B. & Sapon, S. M. (1959). *Modern Language Aptitude Test*. New York: The Psychological Corporation/Harcourt Brace Jovanovich.

Cenoz, J. (2013). The influence of bilingualism on third language acquisition: Focus on multilingualism. *Language Teaching*, 46, 71–86.

Cenoz, J. & Valencia, J. F. (1994). Additive trilingualism: Evidence from the Basque Country. *Applied Psycholinguistics*, 15, 195–207.

Clyne, M., Rossi Hunt, C. & Isaakidis, T. (2004). Learning a community language as a third language. *International Journal of Multilingualism*, 1(1), 33–52.

Cook, V. J. (1992), Evidence for multicompetence. *Language Learning*, 42, 557–591.

(2007). The goals of ELT: Reproducing native-speakers or promoting multi-competence among second language users? In J. Cummins & C. Davison (eds.), *International handbook on English language teaching*, Springer International Handbooks of Education Vol. 15 (pp. 237–248). Boston: Springer.

Cox, J. (2017). Explicit instruction, bilingualism and the older adult learner. *Studies in Second Language Acquisition*, 39(1), 29–58.

Cox, J. & Sanz, C. (2015). Deconstructing PI for the ages: Explicit instruction vs. practice in young and older adult bilinguals. *IRAL: International Review of Applied Linguistics*, 53(2), 225–248.

Daneman, M. & Carpenter, P. A. (1980). Individual differences in working memory and reading. *Journal of Individual Learning and Verbal Behavior*, 19, 450–466.

De Graaff, R. (1997). The eXperanto experiment: Effects of explicit instruction on second language acquisition. *Studies in Second Language Acquisition*, 19(2), 249–276.

De Houwer, A., & Ortega, L. (2019). *The Cambridge handbook of bilingualism*. Cambridge: Cambridge University Press.

Doughty, C., Campbell, S., Mislevy, M., Bunting, M., Bowles, A. & Koeth, J. (2010). Predicting near-native ability: The factor structure and reliability of Hi-LAB. In M. Prior, Y. Watanabe & S. Lee (eds.), *Selected proceedings of the 2008 Second Language Research Forum* (pp. 10–31). Somerville, MA: Cascadilla Proceedings Project.

Ehrman, M. & Oxford, R. (1995). Cognition plus: Correlates of language learning success. *Modern Language Journal*, 79(1), 67–89.

Erlam, R. (2005). Language aptitude and its relationship to instructional effectiveness in second language acquisition. *Language Teaching Research*, 9(2), 147–171.

Gardner, R. (1990). Attitudes, motivation, and personality as predictors of success in foreign language learning. In T. S. Parry & C. W. Stansfield (eds.), *Language aptitude reconsidered* (pp. 179–221). Englewood Cliffs, NJ: Prentice Hall Regents.

Gibson, M., Hufeisen, B. & Libben, G. (2001). Learners of German as an L3 and their production of German prepositional verbs. In J. Cenoz, B. Hufeisen & U. Jessner (eds.), *Cross-linguistic influence in third language acquisition* (pp. 138–148). Clevedon: Multilingual Matters.

Goo, J. (2012). Corrective feedback and working memory capacity in interaction-driven L2 learning. *Studies in Second Language Acquisition*, 34(3), 445–474.

González-Ardeo, J. M. (2000). Engineering students and ESP in the Basque Country: SLA versus TLA. In J. Cenoz, B. Hufeisen & U. Jessner (eds.), *Looking beyond second language acquisition: Studies in tri- and multilingualism* (pp. 75–95). Tübingen: Stauffenburg.

Granena, G. (2013). Cognitive aptitudes for second language learning and the LLAMA Language Aptitude Test. In G. Granena & M. H. Long (eds.), *Sensitive periods, language aptitude, and ultimate L2 attainment* (pp. 105–129). Amsterdam: John Benjamins.

(2016). Explicit and implicit cognitive aptitudes and information-processing styles: An individual differences study. *Applied Psycholinguistics*, 37(3), 577–600.

(2019). Cognitive aptitudes and L2 speaking proficiency: Links between LLAMA and HI-LAB. *Studies in Second Language Acquisition*, 41(2), 313–336. DOI:10.1017/S0272263118000256.

Grigorenko, E. L., Sternberg, R. J. & Ehrman, M. E. (2000). A theory-based approach to the measurement of foreign language learning ability: The canal-F theory and test. *Modern Language Journal*, 84(3), 390–405.

Grosjean, F. (2008). *Studying bilinguals*. Oxford: Oxford University Press.

Harley, B. & Hart, D. (1997). Language aptitude and second language proficiency in classroom learners of different starting ages. *Studies in Second Language Acquisition*, 19, 379–400.

Hilchey, M. D. & Klein, R. M. (2011). Are there bilingual advantages on nonlinguistic interference tasks? Implications for the plasticity of executive control processes. *Psychon Bulletin & Review*, 18(4), 625–658.

Hummel, K. (2009). Aptitude, phonological memory, and second language proficiency in nonnovice adult learners. *Applied Psycholinguistics*, 30(2), 225–249.

Keshavarz, H. M. & Astaneh, H. (2004). The impact of biliguality on the learning of English vocabulary as a foreign language (L3). *Bilingual Education and Bilingualism*, 7(4), 295–302.

Krashen, S. D. (1981). Aptitude and attitude in relation to second language acquisition and learning. In K. C. Diller (ed.), *Individual differences & universals in language learning* (pp. 155–175). Rowley, MA: Newbury House.

Lado, B. (2017). Aptitude and pedagogical conditions in the early development of a nonprimary language. *Applied Psycholinguistics*, 38(3), 679–701.

Lado, B., Bowden, H., Stafford, C. & Sanz, C. (2014). A fine-grained analysis of the effects of negative evidence with and without metalinguistic information in language development. *Language Teaching Research*, 18 (3), 320–344.

Lado, B., Bowden, H. W., Stafford, C. & Sanz, C. (2017). Two birds, one stone, or how learning a foreign language makes you a better language learner. *Hispania*, 100(3), 361–378.

Lado B. & Sanz, C. (2016). Methods in multilingualism research. In K. King, Y. J. Lai & S. May (eds.), *Research methods in language and education: Encyclopedia of language and education* (3rd ed.). Cham: Springer.

Lasagabaster, D. (2000). Three languages and three linguistic models in the Basque educational system. In J. Cenoz & U. Jessner (eds.), *English in Europe: The acquisition of a third language* (pp. 179–197). Clevedon: Multilingual Matters.

Lenet, A. E., Sanz, C., Lado, B., Howard, J. H. J. & Howard, D. V. (2011). Aging, pedagogical conditions, and differential success in SLA: An empirical study. In C. Sanz & R. P. Leow (eds.), *Implicit and explicit language learning: Conditions, processes, and knowledge in SLA and bilingualism* (pp. 73–84). Washington, DC: Georgetown University Press.

Li, S. (2010). The effectiveness of corrective feedback in SLA: A meta-analysis. *Language Learning*, 60(2), 309–365.

(2013). The differential roles of two aptitude components in mediating the effects of two types of feedback on the acquisition of an opaque linguistic structure. In C. Sanz & B. Lado (eds.), *Individual differences, L2 development & language program administration: From theory to application* (pp. 32–52). Boston: Cengage Learning.

(2015). The associations between language aptitude and second language grammar acquisition: A meta-analytic review of five decades of research. *Applied Linguistics*, 36(3), 385–408.

(2017). Cognitive differences and ISLA. In S. Loewen & M. Sato (eds.), *The Routledge handbook of instructed second language acquisition* (pp. 396–417). New York: Routledge.

Linck, J., Hughes, M., Campbell, S., Silbert, N., Tare, M., Jackson, S., Smith, B., Bunting, M. & Doughty, C. (2013). Hi-LAB: A new measure of aptitude for high-level language proficiency. *Language Learning*, 63(3), 530–566.

Mackey, A., Philp, J., Fujii, A., Egi, T. & Tatsumi, T. (2002). Individual differences in working memory, noticing of interactional feedback, and L2 development. In P. Robinson and P. Skehan (eds.), *Individual differences in L2 learning* (pp. 181–208). Amsterdam: John Benjamins.

McLaughlin, B. (1995). Aptitude from an information-processing perspective. *Language Testing*, 12(3), 370–387.

McLaughlin, B. & Nayak, N. (1989). Processing a new language: Does knowing other languages make a difference? In H. W. Dechert & M. Raupach (eds.), *Interlingual processes* (pp. 5–16). Tübingen: Gunter Narr.

McLaughlin, B., Rossman, T. & McLeod, B. (1983). Second language learning: An information-processing perspective. *Language Learning*, 33(2), 135–158.

Meara, P. (2005). *LLAMA language aptitude tests: The manual*. Swansea: Lognostics.

Miyake, A. & Shah, P. (1999). *Models of working memory: Mechanisms of active maintenance and executive control*. Cambridge: Cambridge University Press.

Muñoz, C. (2000). Bilingualism and trilingualism in school students in Catalonia. In J. Cenoz & U. Jessner (eds.), *English in Europe: The acquisition of a third language* (pp. 157–178). Clevedon: Multilingual Matters.

Nation, R. & McLaughlin, B. (1986). Novices and experts: An information processing approach to the "good language learner" problem. *Applied Psycholinguistics*, 7(1), 41–55.

Nayak, N., Hansen, N., Krueger, N. & McLaughlin, B. (1990). Language-learning strategies in monolingual and multilingual adults. *Language Learning*, 40(2), 221–244.

Okita, Y. & Jun Hai, G. (2001). Learning of Japanese Kanji character by bilingual and monolingual Chinese speakers. In J. Cenoz, B. Hufeisen

& U. Jessner (eds.), *Looking beyond second language acquisition: Studies in tri- and multilingualism* (pp. 63–73). Tübingen: Stauffenburg.

Ortega, L. (2014). Ways forward for a bi-multilingual turn in SLA. In S. May (ed.), *The multilingual turn: Implications for SLA, TESOL, and bilingual education* (pp. 32–53). New York: Routledge.

Ottó, I. (2002). *Magyar Egységes Nyelvérzékmérö-Teszt* [Hungarian Language Aptitude Test]. Kaposvar: Mottó-Logic Bt.

Paap, K. R. & Greenberg, Z. (2013). There is no coherent evidence for a bilingual advantage in executive processing. *Cognitive Psychology, 66* (2), 232–258.

Park, D. C. (2000). The basic mechanisms accounting for age-related decline in cognitive function. In D. C. Park & N. Schwarz (eds.), *Cognitive aging: A primer* (pp. 3–21). Philadelphia: Psychology Press.

Parry, T. S. & Stansfield, C. W. (1990). *Language aptitude reconsidered.* Englewood Cliffs, NJ: Prentice Hall Regents.

Pimsleur, P. (1966). *The Pimsleur language aptitude battery.* New York: Harcourt Brace Jovanovich.

Robinson, P. (1997). Individual differences and the fundamental similarity of implicit and explicit adult second language learning. *Language Learning, 47*(1), 45–99.

(2002). Effects of individual differences in intelligence, aptitude and working memory on incidental SLA: A replication and extension of Reber, Walkenfield and Hernstadt (1991). In P. Robinson (ed.), *Individual differences and instructed language learning* (pp. 211–266). Philadelphia: John Benjamins.

(2005a). Aptitude and second language acquisition. *Annual Review of Applied Linguistics, 25,* 45–73.

(2005b). Cognitive abilities, chunk-strength, and frequency effects in implicit artificial grammar and incidental L2 learning: Replications of Reber, Walkenfeld, and Hernstadt (1991) and Knowlton and Squire (1996) and their relevance for SLA. *Studies in Second Language Acquisition, 27*(2), 235–268.

Sagarra, N. & Abbuhl, R. (2013a). Optimizing the noticing of recasts vis computer-delivered feedback: Evidence that oral input enhancement and working memory help second language learning. *Modern Language Journal, 97*(1), 196–216.

(2013b). Computer-delivered feedback and L2 development: The role of explicitness and working memory. In C. Sanz & B. Lado (eds.), *Individual differences, L2 development & language program administration: From theory to application* (pp. 53–70). Boston, MA: Cengage Learning.

Sagasta, M. (2003). Acquiring writing skills in a third language: Positive effects of bilingualism. *International Journal of Bilingualism, 7*(1), 27–42.

Sanz, C. (2000). Bilingual education enhances third language acquisition: Evidence from Catalonia. *Applied Psycholinguistics, 21*(1), 23–44.

(2004). Computer delivered implicit vs. explicit feedback in processing instruction. In B. VanPatten (ed.), *Processing instruction: Theory, research, and commentary* (pp. 241–255). Mahwah, NJ: Lawrence Erlbaum.

(2005). Adult SLA: The interaction between internal and external factors. In C. Sanz (ed.), *Mind and context in adult second language acquisition: Methods, theory, and practice* (pp. 3–20). Washington, DC: Georgetown University Press.

(2007). The role of bilingual literacy in the acquisition of a third language. In C. Pérez Vidal, A. Bel & M. Juan Garau (eds.), *A portrait of the young in the new multilingual Spain* (pp. 220–240), Clevedon: Multilingual Matters.

Sanz, C., Lin., H., Lado, B., Bowden, H. B. & Stafford, C. A. (2009). Concurrent verbalizations, pedagogical conditions, and reactivity: two CALL studies. *Language Learning*, 59(1), 33–71.

(2016). One size fits all? Learning conditions and working memory capacity in ab initio language development. *Applied Linguistics*, 37(5), 669–692.

Sanz, C., Park, H. I. & Lado, B. (2014). A functional approach to cross-linguistic influence in ab initio L3 acquisition. *Bilingualism: Language & Cognition*, 18(2), 236–251.

Sawyer, M. & Ranta, L. (2001). Aptitude, individual differences, and instructional design. In P. Robinson (ed.), *Cognition and second language instruction* (pp. 319–353). Cambridge: Cambridge University Press.

Sheen, Y. (2007). The effects of corrective feedback, language aptitude, and learner attitudes on the acquisition of English articles. In A. Mackey (ed.), *Conversational interaction in second language acquisition* (pp. 301–322). New York: Oxford University Press.

Skehan, P. (1998). *A cognitive approach to language learning*. Oxford: Oxford University Press.

(2002). Theorising and updating aptitude. In P. Robinson (ed.), *Individual differences in instructed language learning* (pp. 69–93). Philadelphia: John Benjamins.

(2012). Language aptitude. In S. Gass & A. Mackey (eds.), *Handbook of second language acquisition* (pp. 381–395). New York: Routledge.

(2015). Foreign language aptitude and its relationship with grammar: A critical overview. *Applied Linguistics*, 36(3), 367–384.

Sparks, R. L., Javorsky, J. & Ganschow, L. (2005). Should the modern language aptitude test be used to determine course substitutions for and waivers of the foreign language requirement? *Foreign Language Annals*, 38(2), 201–210. DOI:10.1111/j.1944-9720.2005.tb02485.x.

Stafford, C., Sanz, C. & Bowden, W. H. (2010). An experimental study of early L3 development: age, bilingualism and classroom exposure. *International Journal of Multilingualism*, 7(2), 162–183.

Suzuki, Y. & DeKeyser, R. (2017). The interface of explicit and implicit knowledge in a second language: Insights from individual differences in cognitive aptitudes. *Language Learning*, 67(4), 747–790.

Swain, M., Lapkin, S., Rowen, N. & Hart, D. (1990). The role of mother tongue literacy in third language learning. *Language, Culture and Curriculum*, 3(1), 65–81.

Tagarelli, K. M., Borges Mota, M. & Rebuschat, P. (2015). Working memory, learning context, and the acquisition of L2 Syntax. In W. Zhisheng, M. Borges Mota & A. McNeill (eds.), *Working memory in second language acquisition and processing: Theory, research and commentary* (pp. 224–247). Bristol: Multilingual Matters.

Tagarelli, K. M., Ruiz, S., Moreno, J. L. & Rebuschat, P. (2016). Variability in second language learning: The roles of individual differences, learning conditions, and linguistic complexity. *Studies in Second Language Acquisition (Special Issue): Cognitive Perspectives on Difficulty and Complexity in SLA*, 38(2), 293–316.

Thomas, J. (1988). The role played by metalinguistic awareness in second and third language learning. *Journal of Multilingual and Multicultural Development*, 9(3), 235–246.

Trofimovich, P., Ammar, A. & Gatbonton, E. (2007). How effective are recasts? The role of attention, memory, and analytical ability. In A. Mackey (ed.), *Conversational interaction in second language acquisition* (pp. 171–195). New York: Oxford University Press.

van Gelderen, A., Schoonen, R., de Glopper, K., Hulstijn, J., Snellings, P., Simis, A. & Stevenson, M. (2003). Roles of linguistic knowledge, metacognitive knowledge, and processing speed in L3, L2, and L1 reading comprehension: A structural equation modeling approach. *International Journal of Bilingualism*, 7(1), 7–25.

Vatz, K., Tare, M., Jackson, S. & Doughty, C. (2013). Aptitude-treatment interaction studies in second language acquistition: Findings and methodology. In G. Granena, & M. H. Long (eds.), *Sensitive periods, language aptitude, and ultimate L2 attainment* (pp. 273–292). Amsterdam: John Benjamins.

Wagner, D., Spratt, J. & Ezzaki, A. (1989). Does learning to read in a second language always put the child at a disadvantage? Some counterevidence from Morocco. *Applied Psycholinguistics*, 10(1), 31–48.

Wen, Z., Biedroń, A. & Skehan, P. (2017). Foreign language aptitude theory: Yesterday, today and tomorrow. *Language Teaching*, 50(1), 1–31. DOI:10.1017/S0261444816000276.

Williams, J. N. (2012). Working memory and SLA. In S. M. Gass & A. Mackey (eds.), *The Routledge handbook of second language acquisition* (pp. 427–441). New York: Routledge.

Winke, P. (2013), An investigation into second language aptitude for advanced Chinese language learning. *Modern Language Journal*, 97(1), 109–130.

Yilmaz, Y. (2013). Relative effects of explicit and implicit feedback: The role of working memory capacity and language analytic ability. *Applied Linguistics, 34*(3), 344–368.

Yilmaz, Y. & Granena, G. (2016). The role of cognitive aptitudes for explicit language learning in the relative effects of explicit and implicit feedback. *Bilingualism: Language and Cognition, 19*(1), 147–161.

33
Corrective Feedback and Affect

Jaemyung Goo and Takaaki Takeuchi

Introduction

Second language (L2) research to date has provided convincing evidence that corrective feedback (CF) plays a nontrivial role in L2 development (Li, 2010; Lyster & Saito, 2010; Lyster, Saito & Sato, 2013; Mackey & Goo, 2007; Nassaji, 2016; Russell & Spada, 2006). As empirical evidence for CF being beneficial to L2 learning has accumulated to a great extent, more recent research has shifted its direction to how/when CF can possibly benefit L2 learners in an optimal way. To this end, researchers have investigated various potential factors that likely mediate the effectiveness of CF in the L2 learning process and overall results (see Lyster et al., 2013; Nassaji, 2016; Nassaji & Kartchava, 2017 for recent reviews). Affect, *inter alia*, is one such domain that scholars have begun to show interest in examining (e.g., Di Loreto & McDonough, 2013; Kartchava & Ammar, 2014; Lee, 2013, 2016; Rassaei, 2015a, 2015b; Sheen, 2007, 2008; Zhang & Rahimi, 2014).

Affect, defined as emotions or feelings, has been one of the most neglected areas in L2 research (Dörnyei, 2009; Dörnyei & Ryan, 2015), with the possible exception of language anxiety. Emphasizing the importance of affect in the L2 learning process, Dörnyei and Ryan (2015) view L2 learning as an emotionally demanding experience. Swain (2013) also argues that L2 learning involves both cognitive and emotional processes, and that the two processes are interdependent or rather inseparable. In fact, as mentioned in Ortega (2009), the distinction between cognition and affect is often blurred because they influence each other. In other words, they are not mutually exclusive, and this potential interdependence provides every reason for conducting empirical research to explore the role of affect in L2 learners' cognitive processing and overall L2 development. Nevertheless, affect has been considered as a peripheral issue and treated as such. This overall lack of scholarly attention to affect appears to be even more evident in the case of CF research.

The significance of investigating how affect interacts with CF lies in the possibility that it may influence the amount of learner attention to CF provided, and, as a consequence, the level of noticing considered critical for L2 learning (Schmidt, 1990, 2001). Of course, learner noticing of CF does not always guarantee L2 learning (e.g., Mackey, 2006, 2012), but there appears no denying that noticing facilitates learners' overall L2 processing and learning through CF in various ways (e.g., Egi, 2010; Gurzynski-Weiss & Baralt, 2015; Loewen & Philp, 2006; Philp, 2003). It should also be noted that interaction between CF and affect is bidirectional. That is, CF may change the shapes and colors of affect in a positive or negative way depending on L2 learners' own experiences with CF, which may influence their future course of learning.

The current chapter discusses this relatively under-explored area, describing empirical research conducted so far in relation to whether, and if so, how affective variables influence or are influenced by CF-driven L2 learning or teaching. Given a scarcity of relevant research and a space limit, the chapter focuses mainly on language anxiety, learner beliefs/attitudes, emotions, and other related issues (e.g., motivation, self-efficacy). The brief overview of research illustrated in this chapter suggests that affect mediates L2 learning processes involving CF, and that learners' affective states are often influenced by teacher feedback. Findings also indicate that L2 learners's experience changes in affective domains, which in turn leads to varying degrees of intra-individual variability in their perceptions of CF (e.g., Akiyama, 2017; Zhang & Rahimi, 2014). As expected from a complex dynamic systems perspective, research evidence shows that L2 learners' affective characteristics can be viewed as multifaceted malleable factors possibly interacting with each other (see Dörnyei & Ryan, 2015). Nevertheless, currently insufficient empirical research concerning the relationship between affect and CF-driven L2 learning and teaching renders it quite unlikely to reach any reasonable level of consensus or generalization.

Our discussion begins with language anxiety in terms of whether it relates to learner noticing, modified output production, L2 development, and overall CF-based learning processes. In the section that follows, we discuss a potential link between teacher feedback and learner beliefs/attitudes with respect to noticing of CF, uptake, L2 learning, and learner engagement with teacher feedback. Then, we review research on whether L2 learners' emotional responses to CF and other related factors (e.g., motivation, self-efficacy) affect learner engagement with CF. The chapter ends with a brief summary of research discussed and concluding remarks that include pedagogical implications.

Language Anxiety

We begin our discussion with (foreign) language anxiety, one of the most widely-researched affective factors (Horwitz, 2001, 2010; Horwitz, Horwitz

& Cope, 1986). Language anxiety is defined as "the feeling of tension and apprehension specifically associated with second language contexts, including speaking, listening, and learning" (MacIntyre & Gardner, 1994b, p. 284) and considered "fundamental to our understanding of how learners approach language learning, their expectations for success or failure, and ultimately why they continue or discontinue study" (Horwitz, 2001, p. 121). Horwitz et al. (1986) conceptualized foreign language anxiety as a situation-specific multifaceted anxiety distinct from other academic or nonacademic (general trait) anxiety and responsible for L2 learners' negative emotional reactions to language learning. They developed the Foreign Language Classroom Anxiety Scale (FLCAS) designed to measure three aspects of L2 learners' language anxiety: communication apprehension, test anxiety, and fear of negative evaluation, which has been employed intact or adapted in a number of studies. Unsurprisingly, especially given the intuitive assumption that anxiety likely impedes language learning, foreign language anxiety has received much scholarly attention and has been investigated in terms of its impact on L2 achievement, sources of language anxiety, its relation to other learner variables, anxieties related to specific areas in L2 learning (e.g., listening, reading, and writing), multilingualism, and other relevant issues (see Dörnyei & Ryan, 2015; Horwitz, 2001, 2010).

Despite evidence that language anxiety interferes with L2 learning (see Horwitz, 2010 for a summary of related studies), Sparks and his colleagues (Sparks & Ganschow, 1991, 1995; Sparks, Ganschow & Javorsky, 2000; Sparks et al., 2009), in their Linguistic Coding Differences Hypothesis (LCDH), argue that language anxiety is not a cause, but rather an affective consequence of poor L2 performance caused by L1 linguistic processing/learning deficits (mainly in the phonological/orthographic domains). MacIntyre (1995a, 1995b) and Horwitz (2000) contested Sparks and his colleagues' position, pointing out that anxiety impedes almost all kinds of learning, that language learning involves more than sound–symbol correspondences, and that contextual and nonlinguistic aspects are also associated with language learning anxiety. Later, MacIntyre and Gregersen (2012) stated, emphasizing its complex, multifaceted nature, that anxiety can be "both a cause and effect, part of a non-linear, ongoing learning and performance process" (p. 106). Regardless of the causality debate, language anxiety has been explored in relation to various aspects of, and approaches to, L2 learning (Dörnyei & Ryan, 2015). Interaction research is not an exception, albeit not sufficient enough to arrive at any definitive conclusion (e.g., Baralt & Gurzynski-Weiss, 2011; Rassaei, 2015a, 2015b; Révész, 2011; Sheen 2008).

The relevance of language anxiety to the effectiveness of CF lies in the possibility that high anxiety interferes with L2 cognitive processing while performing a given task at various stages (e.g., MacIntyre & Gardner, 1994a, 1994b). Learner noticing of CF, especially CF delivered in an implicit form (e.g., recasts), requires much focused attention. Language anxiety may come into play in this cognitive process of noticing. To elaborate, for high-anxiety learners, the noticing of CF may be a more challenging task, compared to low-anxiety learners, because cognitive attempts to combat language anxiety while engaging in interaction are so taxing as to deplete their attentional resources, leaving little or no cognitive space for noticing. This potential disparity in the amount of noticing of CF between high- and low-anxiety learners may have a nontrivial bearing on modified output production and overall L2 development. Likewise, language anxiety has been researched in terms of L2 learners' perceptions or noticing of CF, modified output, and L2 development (e.g., Jang, 2011; Rassaei, 2015a, 2015b; Sheen, 2008).

Rassaei (2015a) examined the relationship between language anxiety and English as a Foreign Language (EFL) learners' perceptions of two different CF moves (recasts vs. metalinguistic feedback) provided during task-based interactions. A fourteen-item anxiety questionnaire adapted from Horwitz et al.'s (1986) FLCAS was employed to divide learners into high- and low-anxiety groups: one standard deviation above (for those with high anxiety) and below (for those with low anxiety) the mean. Data from stimulated recall interviews were categorized into three types: noticing the gap (being able to identify the error or locate the mismatch), feedback recognition (being able to recognize the corrective nature of CF, but unable to locate the source of the error), and other (not being able to recognize CF). It was observed that much more noticing or recognizing transpired among low-anxiety than high-anxiety learners, regardless of the type of CF. The finding confirms the assumption that language anxiety affects the level of learner noticing of CF.

As stated above, attention has also been paid to the production of modified output and L2 development. For instance, Sheen (2008) investigated the impact of language anxiety on the production of modified output following recasts and the effectiveness of recasts in the development of English articles. Language anxiety was measured via an eight-item anxiety questionnaire. Her study found that the low-anxiety recast group performed significantly better than the high-anxiety recast group in both speeded dictation and writing post-tests (post-tests 1 and 2). The low-anxiety recast group also outperformed the low-anxiety control group on both measures (the speeded dictation post-tests 1 and 2 and the writing post-test 1). Also observed was that the low-anxiety recast group produced much more modified output than did the high-anxiety recast group. The findings showed a clear advantage for low-anxiety learners in terms of modified output production and L2 learning.

Jang (2011) expanded on Sheen's (2008) study by adding one more variable, that is, the type of CF, recasts and prompts (elicitations and metalinguistic clues). In other words, he examined possible interactions between the level of language anxiety (high vs. low) and the two CF moves different in nature (input-providing vs. output-prompting) in the development of English question formation. Stage 5 questions (e.g., *What should I do?*) according to Pienemann, Johnston, and Brindley's (1988) developmental sequence were selected as the target structure. Language anxiety was measured via an adapted version of Sheen's eight-item questionnaire. Contrary to Sheen's finding, Jang did not find any significant role for language anxiety in the amount of modified output following recasts; only the CF type made a noticeable difference in favor of prompts. However, language anxiety appeared to mediate the efficacy of recasts on the production of learner repair (successful uptake) and explicit knowledge development (measured via a substitution test), favoring low-anxiety learners in both cases. For those who received prompts, language anxiety seemed to exert no influence on learner performance in any respect.

Similarly, Rassaei (2015b) examined whether language anxiety mediates the effectiveness of recasts and metalinguistic feedback for the development of English articles among Iranian EFL learners. Results showed that with regard to low-anxiety learners, metalinguistic feedback was found significantly more effective than recasts on all three dependent variable measures (writing, error correction, and oral production tasks). However, as for high-anxiety learners, those who received recasts performed significantly better than their counterparts who received metalinguistic feedback on the writing and oral production tasks, with no significant difference in their performance on the error correction task. Furthermore, although recasts were found effective for low-anxiety learners on the two free production measures (writing and oral production), metalinguistic feedback did not appear to be beneficial for high-anxiety learners on the measures. The findings suggest a rather clear interaction between the level of language anxiety and the type of CF. That is, while such implicit, nonobtrusive CF as recasts are more felicitous for high-anxiety learners due to their affective sensitivity, explicit, obtrusive CF such as metalinguistic feedback appears to be relatively more suitable for low-anxiety learners.

As mentioned earlier, language anxiety has also been examined in relation to other learner-internal individual variables. Zhang and Rahimi (2014), for example, investigated learner beliefs. They explored whether language anxiety mediates learner beliefs about oral CF, especially in terms of the necessity, frequency, and timing of CF, the types of errors that should be corrected, CF types, and choice of correctors. No significant difference was found between the two anxiety levels with respect to their beliefs about CF. However, albeit nonsignificant, the low-anxiety learners appeared to feel the necessity of CF more than did the high-anxiety learners. Both anxiety groups preferred explicit types of feedback (e.g., explicit correction and metalinguistic feedback) to implicit feedback (e.g., clarification requests and recasts), and, similar to Schulz (2001), the learners, regardless of their level of anxiety, preferred teachers, not peers, as CF providers.

More recently, Lee (2016) collected and analyzed data from a questionnaire, interviews, and classroom observations to investigate the relationship between different CF moves and affective variables (anxiety, attitude, motivation, and self-confidence). Some questionnaire items were adapted from Sheen's (2011) study and others were developed by the researcher. With regard to language anxiety, she found that most CF moves provided by English as a Second Language (ESL) teachers contributed to substantially lowering their learners' self-rated language anxiety in all three aspects (anxiety about speaking English, fear of speaking in front of classmates, and embarrassment about communicating in English). Nonetheless, certain clarification requests (e.g., *What?*) made L2 learners feel anxious, frustrated, and sometimes even annoyed, increasing their level of anxiety or emotional discomfort.

Lee's (2016) findings suggesting the positive role of CF in reducing learner anxiety were further confirmed in a written CF (WCF) context. Di Loreto and McDonough (2013) showed that continued instructor feedback contributed to reducing ESL learners' writing test anxiety. Their results also revealed a significant negative correlation between learners' perceptions of teacher feedback and writing test anxiety. In other words, less anxiety was related to more positive perceptions about instructor feedback. That is, the careful and continued provision of WCF can decrease writing anxiety and pave the way for learners to perceive teacher CF in a much more favorable manner.

Overall, CF researchers have shown that language anxiety relates to learner noticing of CF moves, production of modified output, and L2 development. Relevant findings suggest that more noticing of CF may occur among low-anxiety learners than high-anxiety learners (Rassaei, 2015a; Sheen, 2008). Also, low-anxiety learners seem to be better able to produce modified output or learner repair (Jang, 2011; Sheen, 2008). The type of CF appears to mediate the relationship between language anxiety and L2 development. Sheen (2008) and Jang (2011) provided evidence of positive impact of low anxiety on the effectiveness of recasts in L2 development. Rassaei (2015b) found an interaction effect between the level of language anxiety and the type of CF in the development of English articles, with recasts befitting high-anxiety learners and metalinguistic feedback lending itself to low-anxiety learners. Moreover, low-anxiety learners appear to believe in the necessity of CF more than high-anxiety learners (Zhang & Rahimi, 2014). Continued exposure to CF may contribute to reducing the overall level of language anxiety (Di Loreto & McDonough, 2013; Lee, 2016). Nevertheless, certain clarification requests (e.g., *What?*) still tend to provoke and increase language anxiety due mainly to their output-prompting nature (Lee, 2016). This potential link between CF and language anxiety merits much more future research because learner anxiety may have an effect on the amount of attention paid to CF and the overall effectiveness of CF. Important to note is that the relationship between language anxiety and CF is bidirectional with the two variables likely to influence each other in one way or another. From a pedagogical perspective, this bidirectionality makes classroom applications of previous CF research findings a rather complicated task. Empirical evidence that has shown pedagogical advantages for prompts over recasts in classroom contexts (see Lyster & Saito, 2010 for a meta-analysis) should be interpreted with care for a number of reasons, one of which is language anxiety.

Learner Beliefs and Attitudes

L2 learners' beliefs (and attitudes reflected in their beliefs) have traditionally been considered as a "highly individual, relatively stable, and relatively enduring" (Grotjahn, 1991, p. 189) learner characteristic and examined in relation to L2 learning outcomes by means of a specifically designed questionnaire, for example, Horwitz's (1988) Beliefs About Language Learning Inventory (BALLI) (see Dörnyei & Ryan, 2015 for a brief history of research on learner beliefs). Currently, learner beliefs are viewed as a complex, malleable, dynamic factor interacting with other affective variables (e.g., emotions), possibly influenced by interaction with other interlocutors and polished by reflections on the existing beliefs (Barcelos & Kalaja, 2011). Learner beliefs from both perspectives (viewing beliefs as a trait-like individual difference factor and as a dynamic learner characteristic) have been discussed in L2 CF research.

It makes intuitive sense that L2 learners' mental and psychological readiness to receive CF, which is reflected in their beliefs about (and attitudes toward) CF, may determine the extent to which they attend to it, influencing the quality and quantity of learner noticing and possibly L2 learning. Accordingly, learner beliefs and attitudes toward CF, as potential variables likely to mediate the effectiveness of CF, have also been considered worthy of investigation (e.g., Akiyama, 2017; Kartchava & Ammar, 2014; Loewen et al., 2009; Schulz, 1996, 2001; Sheen, 2007; Yoshida, 2008). Relevant research has indicated that teachers' and learners' beliefs about grammar teaching and CF often do not overlap, and, in fact, L2 learners' attitudes toward the role of error correction appear noticeably different from teachers' attitudes (Schulz, 1996, 2001). Summarized below are several studies that have investigated a link between learner beliefs/attitudes and CF-based learning. These studies have examined learner beliefs and/or attitudes in terms of learners' CF preferences, noticing of CF, uptake, L2 development, learner engagement with CF, learners' orientation to CF, and motivation (Akiyama, 2017; Han, 2017; Kartchava & Ammar, 2014; Loewen et al, 2009; Schulz, 1996, 2001; Sheen, 2007; Waller & Papi, 2017).

Schulz (1996, 2001) observed that an overwhelming number of the learners surveyed accepted teacher feedback as a vital component of the learning process with approximately 90% or more showing positive attitudes towards teacher CF. However, teacher perceptions of CF exhibited somewhat different patterns, with approximately 25% of the teachers predicting learners' negative emotional reactions to CF. Also, approximately 95% of the learners agreed with the necessity of error correction, whereas only 48% of the teachers did. This teacher–learner discrepancy appeared to be even wider in the case of oral CF. Most learners would like their teachers to offer CF on their erroneous oral output (97% and 90% in Colombia and the USA, respectively), whereas only 39% and 30% of the teachers in the Colombian and the US samples, respectively, agreed that they should provide CF on learners' oral errors.

Loewen et al. (2009) showed that different target language (TL) groups may differ in their perceptions of grammar instruction and error correction in terms of negative attitudes toward error correction, importance of grammatical accuracy, and priority of communication. They also suggested that past learning experiences along with learning contexts may contribute to shaping learner beliefs. For instance, ESL learners with much focus on grammar in their previous learning experiences seemed to disfavor error correction as well as grammar instruction. They would rather prioritize communication over linguistic knowledge through grammar instruction in order to improve their communicative skills. This teacher–learner discrepancy likely occurs in their CF preferences with teachers more likely to provide recasts irrespective of their pedagogical beliefs, and learners showing differing preferences depending on L2 learning contexts (e.g., Akiyama, 2017; Lee, 2013, 2016; Yang, 2016; Yoshida, 2008; Zhang & Rahimi, 2014). Yoshida's (2008) Japanese as a Foreign Language learners in Australia preferred to have some time to think about their erroneous utterances and possible corrections rather than receiving correct answers through recasts or explicit correction.

Empirical evidence of learner beliefs being a dynamic variable was obtained in Akiyama's (2017) study. Akiyama conducted a longitudinal video-chat telecollaboration study where twelve learners of Japanese in the United States and twelve learners of English in Japan engaged in task-based interactions. Twelve English-Japanese tutor–tutee dyads were formed; each pair consisted of one Japanese-speaking learner of English in Japan and one English-speaking learner of Japanese in the United States. The learners spent half of each hour-long video-chat session speaking in Japanese and the other half in English. That is, a tutor of one language for the first half of the session became a tutee for the other language for the remaining half. Her learners' preference for recasts significantly increased over time. In fact, the majority of learners eventually viewed recasts as the most effective method of providing and receiving CF. Akiyama also found that CF types preferred by the learners tended to result in more successful uptake. Furthermore, as evidenced in other similar studies (e.g., Yoshida, 2008), the Japanese tutors' beliefs about which CF to offer did not overlap with their actual practices. Akiyama's findings clearly indicate that L2 learners' feedback experience can change their beliefs about CF.

With respect to a potential link between learner attitudes and L2 learning through CF, Sheen (2007) explored whether language attitudes about error correction (measured via a nine-item six-point Likert scale questionnaire) related to the effectiveness of recasts and/or metalinguistic corrections (metalinguistic explanation + recasts). Language attitudes were found to be significantly correlated with the efficacy of metalinguistic corrections, whereas no significant correlation was found between attitudes and the efficacy of recasts on L2 learning. She attributed this nonsignificant attitudes–recasts link to the possibility that the corrective nature of recasts went undetected on many occasions.

Similarly, Kartchava and Ammar (2014) investigated whether learner beliefs about CF affect the noticing of oral CF provided in the classroom and the development of two target features (past tense and questions in the past) under three CF conditions (i.e., recasts, prompts, and a combination of the two). While learner noticing was measured via immediate recall and lesson reflection sheets, learner beliefs were collected by means of a questionnaire. Results showed that learner noticing was positively correlated with learners' beliefs about the effectiveness of recasts as well as the importance of CF in general. Learner beliefs regarding the effectiveness of prompts and potential negative consequences of CF were found unrelated to learner noticing. Also, no significant correlations were observed between learner beliefs and noticing of either of the two targets across the feedback conditions. Furthermore, learner beliefs were not significantly correlated with the learning of the target features. Even then, their findings suggest that learner beliefs about the positive role of CF in general and recasts in particular are likely to facilitate learner noticing of CF, which, in turn, may bring about L2 development.

Learner beliefs have also been researched in relation to learner engagement with WCF (e.g., Han, 2017). Based on Fredricks, Blumenfeld, and Paris's (2004) tripartite construct of student engagement (cognitive, behavioral, and emotional engagement), Ellis (2010) stated that learner engagement with CF can be reflected and illustrated in three dimensions: (1) the cognitive dimension referring to L2 learners' cognitive attention to the CF they receive, (2) the behavioral dimension referring to L2 learners' responses to CF (uptake or revisions), and (3) the attitudinal dimension referring to attitudes toward, or affective responses to, CF. Several studies employing Ellis's explanation of learner engagement have begun to appear in CF research (Han, 2017; Han & Hyland, 2015; Zhang & Hyland, 2018). Introduced in the next paragraph as a relevant example is Han's

(2017) investigation into the relationship between learner beliefs and learner engagement with WCF.

Han (2017) collected data from six Chinese EFL university students via interviews, retrospective verbal reports, and reflective accounts. Results showed that overall, learner beliefs (person-related, task-related, and strategy-related) mediated the learners' cognitive, behavioral, and affective engagement with WCF both directly (e.g., guiding learners' selection of learning strategies and revision approaches, shaping emotional reactions to WCF, etc.) and indirectly (e.g., shaping learner expectations and motivation). The study further revealed that the learners' continuous engagement with WCF influenced their beliefs about it in terms of its positive role in improving written drafts, enhancing written accuracy, and promoting L2 learning. In fact, their engagement with WCF contributed to developing "a more sophisticated and balanced view of WCF" (p. 140). As was the case with language anxiety (Di Loreto & McDonough, 2013; Lee, 2016), the findings suggest some level of bidirectional relationship between learner beliefs and learner engagement with WCF, mutually affecting and shaping each other, as expected in a complex dynamic perspective on learner beliefs (see Barcelos & Kalaja, 2011; Dörnyei & Ryan, 2015 for relevant discussion; see also Kim & Mostafa, Chapter 26, this volume).

L2 learners' beliefs about their overall writing abilities have also been found to have an impact on motivation which "affects learners' attention paid to feedback and their further development in creating text revisions" (Kormos, 2012, p. 399) and their attitudes toward WCF. Waller and Papi (2017) explored this interesting aspect of learner beliefs. Based on Dweck's (2000) implicit theory of intelligence, whether to view intelligence either as dynamic and malleable (incremental theory) or as fixed and unchangeable (entity theory), Waller and Papi examined learner perceptions of writing intelligence/abilities with respect to learners' attitudes toward WCF and motivation. The study reported that L2 learners' incremental theory of writing intelligence significantly predicted their feedback-seeking orientation and L2 writing motivation. L2 learners' entity theory of writing intelligence (perceiving their writing intelligence as fixed and unchangeable) was found to be a significant predictor of their feedback-avoiding orientation. Unsurprisingly, L2 learners' writing motivation was strongly correlated with feedback-seeking orientation. The findings suggest that learners' positive attitudes and mindset regarding their writing abilities likely provide motivational support, helping them to orient their attentional resources to WCF, not to avoid it.

In sum, learner beliefs and/or attitudes have been investigated in regard to learner noticing of CF, uptake, L2 learning, learner engagement with CF, L2 learners' orientation to CF, and motivation. Relevant research findings provide quite a complex picture of how learner beliefs and attitudes relate to L2 learning processes. Learners' beliefs about CF have been found to vary according to L2 learning contexts, target languages, and past learning experiences (Leowen et al., 2009; Schulz, 1996, 2001). Kartchava and Ammar (2014) found learner beliefs about the effectiveness of CF were significantly correlated with noticing. Moreover, they observed that different CF moves appear to have differentially influenced the level of learner noticing. Learner beliefs about the effectiveness of recasts, but not of prompts, were found to be significantly correlated with overall CF noticing. Regarding learner uptake, Akiyama's (2017) study suggests that CF moves congruent with learner beliefs likely lead to more successful uptake. In terms of L2 learning, Sheen (2007) provided evidence of the type of CF (recasts vs. metalinguistic corrections) being a mediating variable that can influence a potential link between learner attitudes and the effectiveness of CF. Kartchava and Ammar, despite a significant role of learner beliefs on the efficacy of recasts in noticing, found no significant recast–prompt differences in L2 gains. In addition, positive learner beliefs about WCF and L2 writing ability resulted in more active cognitive and affective engagements with WCF, heightening learners' motivation and feedback-seeking orientation (Han, 2017; Waller & Papi, 2017). Nonetheless, research evidence is scarce, and this state of affairs renders it hardly likely to reach any level of consensus on the relationship among learner beliefs, CF-led learning processes, and the effectiveness of CF.

Emotions and Other Issues

When L2 learners receive teacher CF, various emotional responses such as frustration and embarrassment may transpire. We cannot neglect learners' emotional responses to CF because they are likely to influence the level of their engagement with CF, motivation, and other attitudinal aspects. Moreover, learners' emotional responses to CF may affect the amount of noticing of CF and L2 development as a consequence. Thus, examining these emotional experiences is essential to gain a better understanding of how affect relates to the effectiveness of CF in the process of L2 learning.

Emotional discomfort was investigated with respect to L2 learners' CF preferences (e.g., Lee, 2013, 2016; Yang, 2016). For instance, Lee (2013) found that her advanced ESL learners chose clarification requests as the least preferred CF type because, in addition to their vagueness of what error was being targeted, clarification requests engendered emotional discomfort such as nervousness and embarrassment in front of peers. This psychological discomfort led some frustrated learners to disengage from further conversational interactions. Her participants suggested for teachers to utilize more follow-up questions after clarification requests to make the intended nature of the teachers' clarification requests more explicit. Lee's results were confirmed in Yang's (2016) study. Yang's interview data indicate that clarification requests sometimes function as an anxiety-provoking corrective attempt, lower L2 learners' self-confidence, and make them question their ability to appropriately respond to the CF immediately after it is provided. These findings are in line with Lee's (2016) results regarding L2 learners' overall disapproval of clarification requests.

Most often, L2 learners' emotions have been examined in written feedback research, in terms of whether emotions affect learner engagement with CF, motivation, and L2 writing performance, and if so, how (e.g., Busse, 2013; Han & Hyland, 2015; Mahfoodh, 2017; Tang & Liu, 2018; Zhang & Hyland, 2018). Han and Hyland (2015) utilized Ellis's (2010) learner engagement framework mentioned in the previous section. Their observations of four Chinese EFL learners indicated that all three perspectives (cognitive, behavioral, affective engagement) appeared to be intertwined, reflecting a complex nature of learner engagement with WCF. Regarding the attitudinal/affective engagement, they found evidence that, as Truscott (1996) claims, WCF causes negative emotions, hinders, and/or slows down L2 writing development. However, these negative feelings and other emotional responses to WCF were also dependent on learners' expectations and self-efficacy beliefs. Furthermore, their results suggest that learner engagement with WCF is mediated by motivation, learning goals, beliefs about the effectiveness of WCF and their own writing abilities.

Han and Hyland's finding that learner engagement with WCF interacts with other seemingly nontrivial variables (e.g., motivation, beliefs, proficiency, etc.) was confirmed in Zhang and Hyland's (2018) recent study. They investigated the relationship between the type of CF source and learner engagement. Two Chinese learners of English (highly engaged more-proficient vs. moderately engaged less-proficient) received teacher CF and machine-generated CF (automated writing evaluation: AWE). For the highly engaged more-proficient learner, her affective engagement precipitated cognitive and behavioral engagement with both teacher WCF and AWE feedback. With an increasing level of motivation, she actively engaged in revising drafts. Her initial frustration by the AWE feedback in fact motivated intense behavioral engagement with the feedback. The less-proficient learner showed a very low level of engagement with both types of feedback. The AWE feedback had a more negative impact on the less-proficient learner's engagement, compared to the teacher WCF. Emotional discomfort or negative emotions caused by the AWE incapacitated his cognitive and behavioral engagement with the AWE-generated feedback. In addition to proficiency, the authors suggested learner beliefs about learning to be another potentially crucial factor that is likely to mediate the level of L2 learners' cognitive and affective engagement.

As indicated above, motivation, in addition to emotional responses to CF and learner beliefs, appears to influence learner engagement with CF. That is, learner motivation is assumed to be another variable that may relate to the cognitive and affective functions of CF in L2 learning and learning processes (e.g., Busse, 2013; Fernandez-Toro & Hurd, 2014; Waller & Papi, 2017). Concerning the role of CF in developing motivation, Fernandez-Toro and Hurd (2014) noted that effective feedback is that which contributes to motivating L2 learners to make the necessary efforts to close the gap between ideal and possible selves by narrowing the discrepancy between actual and ideal performances through cognitive and affective engagement. Teacher feedback that reinforces L2 self-efficacy beliefs is one potential candidate that can increase L2 motivation (Busse, 2013) and, thus, enhance the level of learner engagement with CF (Han, 2017; Han & Hyland, 2015).

For instance, Busse (2013) observed this WCF-motivation link (in relation to self-efficacy) among first-year German learners with high motivation but low self-efficacy beliefs. The learners viewed WCF as a crucial factor for L2 writing motivation. The absence of teacher CF made them feel insecure and become unwilling to exert efforts to engage in writing tasks and develop their L2 writing skills. It should also be noted that they often felt frustrated and demotivated when WCF was insufficient and/or too general to be useful and when it was provided with little positive encouragement from the teacher (see Lipnevich & Smith, 2009 on a positive effect of praise on learner emotions). The study suggested that learner motivation and self-efficacy beliefs may, to a great degree, depend on the way, and the extent to which, WCF is provided (see also Lee, 2013, 2016; Yang, 2016 in this regard).

With respect to L2 learners' writing development, Mahfoodh (2017) observed that EFL learners in Yemen for the most part accepted WCF, which likely led to successful revisions. When rejected, teacher feedback did not seem to result in revisions. Also, the learner responses of surprise, disappointment, and frustration also contributed to successful revisions, which may be due, according to the author, to "EFL students' strong beliefs in the authority of their teachers" (p. 66). In addition, learners' emotional responses were found to differ depending upon the type of teacher feedback (Busse, 2013; Tang & Liu, 2018). These diverse emotional responses to WCF may determine the extent of successful revisions. Interesting to note is that Mahfoodh's learners displayed more favorable attitudes toward teacher CF, compared to those in other studies (e.g., Busse, 2013). That is, as evidenced in Schulz (2001) and Loewen et al. (2009), learning contexts and target languages may play a role in shaping L2 learners' affective responses to teacher feedback.

Similarly, Tang and Liu (2018) investigated the role of short affective comments (e.g., *A lovely intro! I like your story*, etc.) in the efficacy of indirect coded CF (ICCF; e.g., VT for verb tense) on learners' writing performance, uptake, and motivation. They compared two CF groups, ICCF-alone versus ICCF with short affective comments. Significant improvements were evidenced in the learners' overall writing performance and uptake, irrespective of the CF mode. It was observed, however, that teachers' short affective comments served as an effective tool for shaping a positive mindset, furthering learners' motivation to take more active steps and make the necessary efforts to improve writing skills.

This section focuses mainly on L2 learners' emotional aspects and how they relate to learner engagement with CF. Learner motivation is also discussed in terms of whether it affects L2 learners' cognitive and affective engagement with CF. Relevant findings indicate that learner motivation and emotional reactions to teacher feedback are likely to influence the level of learner engagement with CF. For instance, clarification requests could cause emotional discomfort that may lower motivation and hinder learner engagement with teacher feedback. Affective comments and positive self-efficacy beliefs, on the other hand, have been found to contribute to developing learner motivation, which in turn increases learners' cognitive and affective engagement with teacher feedback.

Conclusion

This chapter discusses language anxiety, learner beliefs/attitudes, emotional responses to CF, and other relevant issues such as motivation in terms of learner engagement with CF, noticing of CF, modified output or uptake, and L2 development. With respect to language anxiety, research findings indicate that low-anxiety learners tend to be better able to notice teacher feedback and produce more modified output or repair compared to high-anxiety learners. Also, low-anxiety learners appear to benefit more from recasts than high-anxiety learners. When compared to metalinguistic feedback, however, recasts may work better for high-anxiety learners, and metalinguistic feedback for low-anxiety learners. Certain clarification requests provoke anxiety due to their output-prompting nature. One more thing to note is that learner anxiety can be reduced by continuous teacher feedback.

CF research on beliefs and attitudes shows that learning contexts, target L2, and past learning experiences may influence learner beliefs about CF. Beliefs affect the amount of uptake and relate to learner noticing and L2 learning, with the type of CF often playing a mediating role. Positive learner beliefs about L2 writing ability appear to contribute to increasing the level of L2 learners' cognitive and affective engagement with WCF, motivation, and feedback-seeking orientation. Concerning emotions and motivation, research evidence suggests that emotional responses to CF and learner motivation affect learner engagement with CF. Also, clarification requests likely cause emotional discomfort, which may lower motivation and hinder learner engagement, whereas affective comments and positive self-efficacy beliefs may increase the level of motivation and facilitate learner engagement.

Despite the overall significant role of both oral and written CF in L2 development, relevant research to date has indicated that the effectiveness of CF, regardless of its mode, is mediated by affective variables and related factors (e.g., language anxiety, learner beliefs/attitudes, emotions, and motivation). However, the exact nature of the observed moderating effects is still unclear due mainly to rather complex interactions among various affective issues across dimensions (see Dörnyei & Ryan, 2015 for discussion on this complexity) and a dearth of related empirical research. In fact, the current state of affairs does not offer more than a potential link between CF and affective variables, and, of course, is inconclusive in terms of the extent to which these seemingly important affective variables influence the way CF contributes to L2 learning process and overall development.

One important issue to bear in mind is that, as Dörnyei and Ryan (2015) rightly acknowledge, recent research views learner characteristics and individual differences from a complex dynamic systems perspective. That is, "IDs are better seen as ongoing, evolving constructs rather than stable learner traits" (Dörnyei & Ryan, 2015, p. 8). Dörnyei and Ryan further note that "the most significant contribution of a complex dynamic systems approach is in its role as an overriding guiding principle that positions *change* [italics in original] rather than stability as the norm, moving us away from static conceptualizations of learners toward embracing notions of change and growth within a synergic relationship of agent and its context" (p. 11), which inevitably makes it quite challenging to configure an affect–learning relationship. More specifically, this newly emerging complex dynamic systems paradigm, somewhat expectedly, although in no way invalidating the well-established findings on the positive role of CF in L2 learning, adds much complexity to our current understanding of how CF contributes to refining L2 knowledge and skills. Notwithstanding this added complexity, the approach seems likely to offer valuable opportunities to gain more sophisticated insights into the role of CF. Until we firmly uncover the systematicity of multifaceted affective and other relevant variables, the burden of proof is still on CF researchers. Much more research is needed to reach a reasonable conclusion concerning how affect interacts with the effectiveness of CF.

From a pedagogical perspective, it is of particular importance that L2 teachers bear in mind that, as evidenced in some of the studies described earlier, learner characteristics in affective domains are subject to change in various shapes and colors, whether rapidly or relatively slowly, depending on time and context. What makes language teaching more complicated is that these changes are not isolated phenomena but are rather interconnected in most cases despite the possibility that some trait-like learner characteristic may still remain relatively intact at a particular moment even after undergoing some level of expected change. Careful observations are likely to allow teachers to become aware of potential changes in their learners' affective states. These changes should be reflected in their teaching methods and techniques. For instance, depending on where learners stand in terms of language anxiety, teachers may try utilizing explicit, obtrusive CF moves (e.g., metalinguistic feedback) for low-anxiety learners and implicit, non-obtrusive CF moves (e.g., recasts) for high-anxiety learners. Still, care must be taken when teachers provide clarification requests, among other implicit CF moves, to emotionally sensitive learners. It should also be noted that L2 teachers' continuous practice of offering CF in a judicious manner can alleviate language anxiety or any emotional discomfort caused by CF itself or the way it is provided. Given learner beliefs may influence the level of motivation and engagement with CF, L2 teachers should help learners develop positive beliefs about the effectiveness of CF in L2 learning. Learners' positive beliefs about CF can motivate them to pay more attention to teacher CF and enhance their affective and cognitive engagement with CF; these two outcomes contribute to boosting chances of learner noticing of CF, and thus, L2 development as a consequence. Teachers should make an array of pedagogical attempts to induce positive changes in their learners' affective domains that pave the way for further development. Of course, their attention to relevant research findings on affective variables and how they influence CF-based learning is one integral step.

References

Akiyama, Y. (2017). Learner beliefs and corrective feedback in telecollaboration: A longitudinal investigation. *System, 64*, 58–73.

Baralt, M. & Gurzynski-Weiss, L. (2011). Comparing learners' state anxiety during task-based interaction in computer-mediate and face-to-face communication. *Language Teaching Research, 15*(2), 201–229.

Barcelos, A. M. F. & Kalaja, P. (2011). Introduction to beliefs about SLA revisited. *System, 39*(3), 281–289.

Busse, V. (2013). How do students of German perceive feedback practices at university? A motivational exploration. *Journal of Second Language Writing, 22*(4), 406–424.

Di Loreto, S. & McDonough, K. (2013). The relationship between instructor feedback and ESL student anxiety. *TESL Canada Journal, 31*(1), 20–41.

Dörnyei, Z. (2009). *The psychology of second language acquisition.* Oxford: Oxford University Press.

Dörnyei, Z. & Ryan, S. (2015). *The psychology of the language learner revisited.* New York: Routledge.

Dweck, C. S. (2000). Self-theories: Their role in motivation, personality, and development. Philadelphia, PA: Psychology Press.

Egi, T. (2010). Uptake, modified output, and learner perceptions of recasts: Learner responses as language awareness. *Modern Language Journal*, 94 (1), 1–21.

Ellis, R. (2010). Epilogue: A framework for investigating oral and written corrective feedback. *Studies in Second Language Acquisition*, 32(2), 335–349.

Fernandez-Toro, M. & Hurd, S. (2014). A model of factors affecting independent learners' engagement with feedback on language learning tasks. *Distance Education*, 35(1), 106–125.

Fredricks, J., Blumenfeld, P. C. & Paris, A. (2004). School engagement: Potential of the concept, state of the evidence. *Review of Educational Research*, 74(1), 59–109.

Grotjahn, R. (1991). The research programme: Subjective theories. *Studies in Second Language Acquisition*, 13(2), 187–214.

Gurzynski-Weiss, L. & Baralt, M. (2015). Does type of modified output correspond to learner noticing of feedback? A closer look in face-to-face and computer-mediated task-based interaction. *Applied Psycholinguistics*, 36(6), 1393–1420.

Han, Y. (2017). Mediating and being mediated: Learner beliefs and learner engagement with written corrective feedback. *System*, 69, 133–142.

Han, Y. & Hyland, F. (2015). Exploring learner engagement with written corrective feedback in a Chinese tertiary EFL classroom. *Journal of Second Language Writing*, 30, 31–44.

Horwitz, E. K. (1988). The beliefs about language learning of beginning university foreign language students. *Modern Language Journal*, 72(3), 283–294.

(1995). Student affective reactions and the teaching and learning of foreign languages. *International Journal of Educational Research*, 23(7), 573–579.

(2000). It ain't over till it's over: On foreign language anxiety, first language deficits, and the confounding of variables. *Modern Language Journal*, 84(2), 256–259.

(2001). Language anxiety and achievement. *Annual Review of Applied Linguistics*, 21, 112–126.

(2010). Foreign and second language anxiety. *Language Teaching*, 43(2), 154–167.

Horwitz, E. K., Horwitz, M. B. & Cope, J. (1986). Foreign language classroom anxiety. *Modern Language Journal*, 70(2), 125–132.

Jang, S.-S. (2011). Corrective feedback and language anxiety in L2 processing and achievement. *English Teaching*, 66(2), 73–99.

Kartchava, E. & Ammar, A. (2014). Learners' beliefs as mediators of what is noticed and learned in the language classroom. *TESOL Quarterly*, 48(1), 86–109.

Kormos, J. (2012). The role of individual differences in L2 writing. *Journal of Second Language Writing*, 21(4), 390–403.

Lee, E. J. (2013) Corrective feedback preferences and learner repair among advanced ESL students. *System*, 41(2), 217–230.

(2016). Reducing international graduate students' language anxiety through oral pronunciation corrections. *System*, 56, 78–95.

Li, S. (2010). The effectiveness of corrective feedback in SLA: A meta-analysis. *Language Learning*, 60(2), 309–365.

Lipnevich, A. A. & Smith, J. K. (2009). I really need feedback to learn: Students' perspectives on the effectiveness of the differential feedback messages. *Educational Assessment, Evaluation and Accountability*, 21(4), 347–367.

Loewen, S., Li, S., Fei, F., Thompson, A., Nakatsukasa, K., Ahn, S. & Chen, X. (2009). Second language learners' beliefs about grammar instruction and error correction. *Modern Language Journal*, 93(1), 91–104.

Loewen, S. & Philp, J. (2006). Recasts in the adult English L2 classroom: Characteristics, explicitness, and effectiveness. *Modern Language Journal*, 90(4), 536–556.

Lyster, R. & Saito, K. (2010). Oral feedback in classroom SLA: A meta-analysis. *Studies in Second Language Acquisition*, 32(2), 265–302.

Lyster, R., Saito, K. & Sato, M. (2013). Oral corrective feedback in second language classrooms. *Language Teaching*, 46(1), 1–40.

MacIntyre, P. D. (1995a). How does anxiety affect second language learning? A reply to Sparks and Ganschow. *Modern Language Journal*, 79(1), 90–99.

(1995b). On seeing the forest and the trees: A rejoinder to Sparks and Ganschow. *Modern Language Journal*, 79(2), 245–248.

MacIntyre, P. D. & Gardener, R. C. (1994a). The effects of induced anxiety on three stages of cognitive processing in computerized vocabulary learning. *Studies in Second Language Acquisition*, 16(1), 1–17.

(1994b). The subtle effects of language anxiety on cognitive processing in the second language. *Language Learning*, 44(2), 283–305.

MacIntyre, P. D. & Gregersen, T. (2012). Affect: The role of language anxiety and other emotions in language learning. In S. Mercer, S. Ryan & M. Williams (eds.), *Psychology for language learning: Insights from research, theory & practice* (pp. 103–118). Basingstoke: Palgrave.

Mackey, A. (2006). Feedback, noticing and instructed second language learning. *Applied Linguistics*, 27(3), 405–430.

(2012). *Input, interaction and corrective feedback in L2 classrooms*. Oxford: Oxford University Press.

Mackey, A. & Goo, J. (2007). Interaction research in SLA: A meta-analysis and research synthesis. In A. Mackey (ed.), *Conversational interaction in second language acquisition: A collection of empirical studies* (pp. 407–452). Oxford: Oxford University Press.

Mahfoodh, O. H. A. (2017). "I feel disappointed": EFL university students' emotional responses towards teacher written feedback. *Assessing Writing, 31*, 53–72.

Nassaji, H. (2016). Interactional feedback in second language teaching and learning: A synthesis and analysis of current research. *Language Teaching Research, 20*(4), 535–562.

Nassaji, H. & Kartchava, E. (2017). *Corrective feedback in second language teaching and learning: Research, theory, applications, implications.* New York: Routledge.

Ortega, L. (2009). *Understanding second language acquisition.* London: Hodder Education.

Philp, J. (2003). Constraints on noticing the gap: Nonnative speakers' noticing of recasts in NS–NNS interaction. *Studies in Second Language Acquisition, 25*(1), 99–126.

Pienemann, M., Johnston, M. & Brindley, G. (1988). Constructing an acquisition-based procedure for second language assessment. *Studies in Second Language Acquisition, 10*(2), 217–243.

Rassaei, E. (2015a). The effects of foreign language anxiety on EFL learners' perceptions of oral corrective feedback. *Innovation in Language Learning and Teaching, 9*(2), 87–101.

(2015b). Oral corrective feedback, foreign language anxiety and L2 development. *System, 49*, 98–109.

Révész, A. (2011). Task complexity, focus on L2 constructions, and individual differences: A classroom-based study. *Modern Language Journal, 95* (Supp.), 162–181.

Russell, J. & Spada, N. (2006). The effectiveness of corrective feedback for the acquisition of L2 grammar: A meta-analysis of the research. In J. M. Norris & L. Ortega (eds.), *Synthesizing research on language learning and teaching.* Amsterdam: John Benjamins.

Schmidt, R. (1990). The role of consciousness in second language learning. *Applied Linguistics, 11*(2), 129–158.

(1995). Consciousness and foreign language learning: A tutorial on the role of attention and awareness in learning. In R. Schmidt (ed.), *Attention and awareness in foreign language learning* (pp. 1–63). Honolulu: University of Hawai'i Press.

(2001). Attention. In P. Robinson (ed.), *Cognition and second language instruction* (pp. 3–32). Cambridge: Cambridge University Press.

Schulz, R. A. (1996). Focus on form in the foreign language classroom: Students' and teachers' views on error correction and the role of grammar. *Foreign Language Annals, 29*(3), 343–364.

(2001). Cultural differences in student and teacher perceptions concerning the role of grammar instruction and corrective feedback: USA–Colombia. *Modern Language Journal, 85*(2), 244–258.

Sheen, Y. (2007). The effects of corrective feedback, language aptitude, and learner attitudes on the acquisition of English articles. In A. Mackey (ed.), *Conversational interaction in second language acquisition* (pp. 301–322). Oxford: Oxford University Press.

(2008). Recasts, language anxiety, modified output, and L2 learning. *Language Learning, 58*(4), 835–874.

(2011). *Corrective feedback, individual differences and second language learning.* New York: Springer.

Sparks, R. L. & Ganschow, L. (1991). Foreign language learning difficulties: Affective or native language aptitude differences? *Modern Language Journal, 75*(1), 3–16.

(1995). A strong inference approach to causal factors in foreign language leanring: A response to MacIntyre. *Modern Language Journal, 79*(2), 235–244.

Sparks, R. L., Ganschow, L. & Javorsky, J. (2000). Déjà vu all over again: A response to Saito, Horwitz, and Garza. *Modern Language Journal, 84*(2), 251–255.

Sparks, R. L., Patton, J., Ganschow, L. & Humbach, N. (2009). Long-term relationships among early first language skills, second language aptitude, second language affect, and later second language proficiency. *Applied Psycholinguistics, 30*(4), 725–755.

Swain, M. (2013). The inseparability of cognition and emotion in second language learning. *Language Teaching, 46*(2), 195–207.

Tang, C. & Liu, Y.-T. (2018). Effects of indirect coded corrective feedback with and without short affective teacher comments on L2 writing performance, learner uptake and motivation. *Assessing Writing, 35*, 26–40.

Truscott, J. (1996). The case against grammar correction in L2 writing classes. *Language Learning, 46*(2), 327–369.

Waller, L. & Papi, M. (2017). Motivation and feedback: How implicit theories of intelligence predict L2 writers' motivation and feedback orientation. *Journal of Second Language Writing, 35*, 54–65.

Yang, J. (2016). Learners' oral corrective feedback preferences in relation to their cultural background, proficiency level and types of error. *System, 61*, 75–86.

Yoshida, R. (2008). Teachers' choice and learners' preference of corrective feedback types. *Language Awareness, 17*(1), 78–93.

Zhang, Z. & Hyland, K. (2018). Student engagement with teacher and automated feedback on L2 writing. *Assessing Writing, 36*, 90–102.

Zhang, L. J. & Rahimi, M. (2014). EFL learners' anxiety level and their beliefs about corrective feedback in oral communication classes. *System, 42*, 429–439.

34

Corrective Feedback, Developmental Readiness, and Language Proficiency

Miroslaw Pawlak

Introduction

Few second language acquisition (SLA) researchers currently question the beneficial role of corrective feedback (CF). This type of pedagogic intervention can be regarded as an integral component of form-focused instruction (FFI), comprising "any attempt on the part of the teacher to encourage learners to attend to, understand or gain greater control over targeted language features, whether they are grammatical, lexical, phonological or pragmalinguistic in nature" (Pawlak, 2014, p. 2). The positive contribution of CF is recognized by dominant theoretical positions in SLA (e.g., skill learning theory, Interaction Hypothesis, Output Hypothesis, sociocultural theory, connectionism). There is also copious empirical evidence that such pedagogical intervention is effective for a variety of features in different target languages (TL), it drives the development of both explicit and implicit knowledge (Ellis, 2009a; Nassaji, 2017a), and it can work not only immediately but also in the long run. There are also pedagogical reasons why CF is needed in most contexts, such as scant out-of-class exposure, the nature of classroom interaction, the need to inform learners of their progress, or simply the desire to cater to their beliefs or preferences (e.g., Ellis, 2016, 2017; Loewen, 2015; Nassaji, 2015; Nassaji & Kartchava, 2017; Pawlak, 2014; Sheen & Ellis, 2011).

This said, it should be emphasized that, just as is the case with FFI in general, the value of CF hinges on a number of factors, and its effects can also be conceived of in disparate ways. As illustrated in the framework for the study of CF proposed by Ellis (2010) and modified by Pawlak (2014, 2017a), the first thing to consider is the type of CF, the medium in which it is provided, its scope as well as timing (e.g., oral vs. written, explicit vs. implicit, input-providing vs. output-prompting, focused vs. unfocused, immediate vs. direct). While the bulk of research has focused on the effects of such instructional choices, much less attention has been given to the mediating influence of individual difference (ID) variables, linguistic factors, and contextual issues, all of which affect learner engagement (i.e., behavioral, cognitive, affective) with CF and thus to a large extent determine the learning of the targeted features. Such learning, in turn, can be operationalized in many ways, ranging from overall, more or less objective, proficiency measures to carefully designed indices of explicit and implicit second language (L2) knowledge.

The chapter aims to consider the role of developmental readiness and proficiency. These two variables have been shown to moderate the effectiveness of various CF options but at the same time can be adopted as key points of reference when evaluating learning outcomes that accrue from feedback. An attempt will first be made to illuminate the two constructs and their relationship to L2 knowledge. This will be followed by an overview of the main findings of research that has addressed the role of the two factors in moderating the effects of CF. Finally, the pedagogical relevance of developmental readiness and proficiency will be considered and suggestions will be made on how research-based insights can inform classroom practice.

Developmental Readiness, Proficiency, and Second Language Knowledge

Before synthesizing relevant research into the role of developmental readiness and proficiency as well as considering its pedagogical implications, it is warranted to shed light on how these constructs can be understood and how they are related to L2 knowledge. At the outset, however, it makes sense to highlight some key characteristics that the two variables have in common. For one thing, developmental readiness and proficiency are not easily categorized and doubts can arise whether they can be seen as ID characteristics. Developmental readiness, for example, can be regarded as an attribute of the learner, who may or may not have reached the requisite stage of interlanguage development. At the same time, it can be seen as a property of a given linguistic feature which is acquired before other features because, for example, it is easier to process (Pawlak, 2014). When it comes to proficiency, it is typically excluded from discussions of ID factors. This happens on the grounds that while it represents an independent variable that surely mediates the provision of instruction (e.g., intensity, target, type), it must also be considered a dependent variable since its measures provide information about the effects of pedagogic intervention (Pawlak, 2017b). Second, both factors can be understood and operationalized in disparate ways, which can clearly affect research outcomes and have far-reaching consequences for the comparability of the studies conducted. Third, the relevance of developmental readiness and proficiency will inevitably vary depending on the type or aspect of L2 knowledge being tapped into. Fourth, the mediating role of both variables hinges on the conditions in which CF is provided, such as the medium (i.e., oral or written), the context (i.e., task type), the targeted structure (e.g., its difficulty, however it is defined), or the corrective strategy (e.g., more or less explicit or direct, including a requirement for self-correction or not). Fifth, developmental readiness and proficiency can be seen as two sides of the same coin, with the former logically constituting one way in which the latter can be established.

Loewen and Reinders (2011) define developmental readiness as "the learner's potential to acquire a particular linguistic item" (p. 51). They add that "a learner is considered developmentally ready to acquire a given structure when he or she is at the required stage of the developmental sequence of that structure" (p. 51). Over several decades SLA research has generated some evidence for the existence of relatively fixed stages in the acquisition of linguistic features in different L2s, such as English, German, Spanish, or Italian. Learners need to gradually progress through such stages and this process may not be amenable to pedagogic intervention, including different variants of CF (cf. Ellis, 2008; Gass & Selinker, 2008; Larsen-Freeman & Long, 1991; Ortega, 2009). Examples of such developmental stages include a consistent order of acquisition of grammatical morphemes (e.g., Larsen-Freeman, 1976), the tense-aspect system (e.g., Klein, 1995), and some syntactic structures, such as interrogatives, negatives, relative pronouns, or word order (e.g., Dulay, Burt & Krashen, 1982). In the case of question formation in English, which has often been adopted as a point of reference in CF studies, the following five main stages can be identified: (1) reliance on canonical (i.e., subject–verb–object) word order and questioning intonation, (2) fronting of question words or the auxiliary *do* with no inversion, (3) the appearance of pseudo-inversion, whereby an auxiliary or modal is used sentence-initially in *yes/no* questions and the copula and the subject change positions in *wh*-questions, (4) the emergence of inversion proper with the accurate word order being used, and (5) the omission of inversion in indirect questions, at least in more formal contexts (Loewen & Reinders, 2011; Mackey, 1999). In effect, when learners are only beginning to change word order to signal interrogatives, CF directed at inversion on different auxiliaries may be ineffective, particularly in the short run. This is because learners are believed to go through relevant stages at their own pace and with different degrees of success, which may simply not match externally supplied CF.

Even though developmental readiness can be understood in several ways, such as the mastery of requisite functional categories (Zobl & Liceras, 1994) or prototypicality (Anderson & Shirai, 1996), Meisel (2013) points out that "a more promising solution seems to be to rely on processing mechanisms as well as on grammatical properties of sentences" (p. 171). This is in fact the explanation that has been typically adopted in research into CF which has primarily drawn on the assumptions of processability theory and teachability hypothesis (e.g., Pienemann, 1989, 1998). As Pienemann and Lenzing (2015) elucidate, "at any stage of development the learner can produce and comprehend only those second language (L2) linguistic forms which the current state of the language processor can handle" (p. 159). In other words, the mastery of TL features depends on the learner's ability to perform syntactic operations necessary to transfer grammatical information both within and between phrases in a sentence. Pienemann (1998) distinguishes six stages in his original processability hierarchy: (1) no procedure, (2) category procedure, (3) noun phrase procedure, (4) verb phrase procedure, (5) sentence procedure, and (6) subordinate clause procedure. Thus, for example, when a learner has not yet reached stage 5, he or she may not be able to add the third person -*s* because this often requires transferring information between different phrases in a sentence. Obviously, such constraints are unlikely to apply in equal measure to all types of L2 knowledge (i.e., implicit or explicit) and they may be of more relevance for production than comprehension (Pawlak, 2006, 2014), issues that will be elaborated on later. There are also other reservations concerning the operation of developmental sequences. In particular, our knowledge is limited in terms of the number of structures and languages that have been investigated. Moreover, these languages comprise not only developmentally constrained features but also variational ones that do not require the capacity to perform complex syntactic operations (Mellow, 1987). There is also empirical evidence that appropriately tailored FFI can speed up the acquisition of TL items that manifest crosslinguistic markedness relations, such as relative clauses (e.g., Doughty, 1991). Additionally, some theoretical positions, such as skill acquisition theory (DeKeyser, 1998), posit that mastery of TL structures can be achieved through carefully graduated practice, even if these structures are developmentally constrained. Thus, as Ortega (2009) comments, "although there is much merit in the principle of learner readiness, it should not be followed slavishly" (p. 138).

While developmental readiness has been predominantly investigated in its own right, it can also be seen as a dimension of proficiency, understood as attainment in L2, irrespective of whether this factor acts as a mediating (i.e., independent) or outcome (i.e., dependent) variable. It is possible to adopt a very narrow perspective on proficiency, as when it is established with respect to the command of a specific structure (e.g., the use of the passive in different tasks). Proficiency can also be conceived of more broadly, as when an attempt is made to gain a snapshot of learners' entire communicative competence or its components (e.g., grammar, pronunciation, pragmatics). In the latter case, a wide array of indices can be employed. These can range from scores on standardized examinations, through classroom test results, course or examination grades, performance on tasks, which in itself can be operationalized differently (e.g., in terms of accuracy, complexity, and fluency; Michel, 2017), to diverse forms of self-assessment. While such measures evidently vary in sensitivity, sophistication, or demands placed on the researcher, a question inevitably arises about their validity or the extent to which they yield reliable information about attainment (cf. Pawlak, 2017b). In particular, especially in experimental and quasi-experimental studies, care should be taken to go beyond test scores or holistic evaluations. While such measures may be easy to come by, they cannot shine a light on all dimensions of L2 knowledge, especially communicative TL use. Equally importantly, the measures applied to differentiate between higher and lower proficiency levels need to have sufficient discriminatory power. For instance, when examining the role of proficiency as a moderating variable in interactions among advanced learners, it is easy to fall into the trap of failing to adequately distinguish between different levels when judgments are based solely on written examination scores. When this happens, the design of the study will be to some extent compromised and researchers will be hard-pressed to tease out the mediating effects of attainment.

The discussion of developmental readiness and language proficiency would surely be incomplete without relating the two concepts to L2 knowledge and the ways in which CF contributes to the development of this knowledge. Of pivotal importance is the distinction between explicit and implicit knowledge as well as the relationship between them, as these issues lie at the core of most SLA theories (cf. Ellis, 2009a; Nassaji, 2017a; Pawlak, 2019). Although there are many nuances when it comes to the two types of representation (e.g., DeKeyser, 1998, 2003, 2010, 2017), the discussion here is confined to their most salient properties. Explicit knowledge is conscious, declarative, it is not subject to developmental or age-related constraints, it can be verbalized, but it is often imprecise and can only be assessed in controlled processing when adequate time is available. In contrast, implicit knowledge is intuitive, procedural, variable but systematic, it is constrained by developmental stages and age limitations, it cannot be verbalized, but it is easily accessed in automatic processing, indispensable in spontaneous, real-time performance (Ellis, 2004, 2005, 2009a). An important caveat is that it may be difficult to talk about genuine implicit knowledge in the case of L2 learners who have passed the critical period, mainly because they are likely to keep falling back on consciously known rules. Thus, it makes more sense to talk about *highly automatized explicit knowledge*, which is functionally indistinguishable from implicit knowledge (DeKeyser, 2003, 2010; DeKeyser & Juffs, 2005) even if these two constructs may ultimately be distinct (Suzuki & DeKeyser, 2017). Nonetheless, following current trends in the literature, the terms *explicit* and *implicit* are used in this chapter. The meaning of the latter, however, is extended to include situations in which explicit knowledge of a TL feature is automatized to a degree that allows effortless spontaneous performance.

When it comes to the role of CF in fostering the development of L2 knowledge, much depends on the medium, conditions, and ways in which errors are responded to (Pawlak, 2014). It is reasonable to assume that written correction, which is by default explicit to a greater or lesser extent (see Suzuki, Nassaji & Sato, 2019), mainly drives the development of explicit knowledge. However, such knowledge can subsequently trigger the development of a parallel implicit representation or become automatized, which testifies to the beneficial, even if delayed, effects of explicit FFI, including written CF (cf. Ellis, 2002; Lightbown, 1985; Nassaji, 2017a; Spada & Tomita, 2010). As regards the contribution of oral CF, the decisive issue is whether it is provided during accuracy-based activities or fluency-oriented tasks. The former entail text-manipulation (Ellis, 1997) and include a wide array of controlled exercises (e.g., paraphrasing, translation), allowing learners to consciously apply and practice TL rules. The latter may take the form of text-creation activities (Ellis, 1997), according learners opportunities to employ the targeted forms to convey their own messages (e.g., role-plays, simulations). Fluency can also be fostered through focused and unfocused communication tasks. The former are designed in such a way that the use of a TL feature is encouraged or even required for task completion, whereas in the latter a variety of forms are likely to be experimented with (Ellis, 2003). CF provided in accuracy-based activities, which is typically immediate and explicit, affects in the main the growth of explicit knowledge. However, yet again, it may have a delayed effect or foster automatization. In the case of fluency-oriented tasks, the role of CF in the development of TL knowledge is much more complex. On the one hand, when the task induces excessive attention to form, as might happen with memorized role-plays or when the teacher suspends interaction to address an egregious error, the intervention may feed into explicit knowledge, with ensuing scenarios reflecting those described above. On the other hand, when CF, whether it involves a recast or a prompt, occurs interactionally within the window of cognitive opportunity (Doughty, 2001), it may directly trigger the development of implicit knowledge or foster automatization of existing explicit knowledge (DeKeyser, 1998, 2007; Pawlak, 2014).

In view of such considerations, it stands to reason that developmental readiness will be relevant only to feedback which is provided interactionally in tasks involving meaning and message conveyance. This is the case when such readiness is viewed as an independent variable mediating the efficacy of CF (e.g., a clarification request may fail to work when the learner has not reached the required stage of interlanguage development). This reasoning also applies when developmental readiness is regarded as a dependent variable used to determine the impact of CF on learning outcomes (i.e., it is pertinent only for measures necessitating reliance on implicit knowledge). It should be noted though that the role of developmental readiness may itself be moderated by the difficulty of the targeted feature in terms of implicit knowledge, which is related to salience, frequency, transformational properties, communicative value, or regularity (Ellis, 2006; DeKeyser, 2005). It appears obvious that developmental readiness does not pertain to situations in which learners have ample time to resort to consciously known rules, particularly in text-manipulation activities. This is mainly because explicit knowledge is not subject to processing constraints and its development hinges more on cognitive maturity, intelligence, aptitude, or adept use of strategies. It is also not clear to what extent developmental stages mitigate comprehension of targeted features, since, in contrast to production, this process relies more on semantic cues rather than syntactic transformations (cf. Swain, 1985). By contrast, broadly conceived proficiency, whether treated as an independent or dependent variable, is pertinent to the development of both explicit and implicit knowledge, in relation to their productive and receptive dimensions. For example, when attainment is operationalized as scores on a final examination, it may moderate the impact of CF supplied in controlled exercises, since, for example, lower-level learners may be unable to self-correct even when they have ample time to apply rules. At the same time, it may also mediate the efficacy of CF supplied in communicative tasks because less proficient learners may fail to interpret a recast as negative evidence directing their full attention to content. The effect of proficiency will also be mediated by the difficulty of TL features, in terms of not only implicit knowledge, but also explicit knowledge. As regards the latter, such factors come into play as conceptual clarity, crosslinguistic similarity, and/or need to employ metalanguage. Somewhat similarly, when pre-test/post-test gains in proficiency are established following the provision of CF, this can be done with respect to both explicit and implicit knowledge, sometimes taking into account their productive and receptive dimensions. The final point is that developmental readiness and proficiency are bound to interact with ID (e.g., working memory, motivation, willingness to communicate) and contextual (e.g., program type, prior instruction) factors. This is a critical issue that has been largely overlooked in the relevant studies which will be overviewed in the following section.

Overview of Research Findings

The present section provides a succinct overview of research that has investigated the role of developmental readiness and proficiency as variables mediating the effects of CF. However, some caveats need to be mentioned at the outset. First, although, as has been shown above, both factors can serve as independent and dependent variables, the focus will mainly be on their mediating role, as space limitations preclude detailed discussion of outcome measures employed in different studies. Second, for the same reason, only the most representative studies will be considered and emphasis will be placed on the variables in question even though other issues, such as CF options or other mediating factors, may have been investigated as well. Third, no attempt will be made to draw a distinction between studies of oral and written CF or those conducted in classrooms, under laboratory conditions or in online environments. Fourth, although the two concepts sometimes overlap, studies related to developmental readiness and proficiency will be discussed in separate subsections. General observations will be included in yet another subsection which takes stock of the research conducted thus far.

Developmental Readiness and CF

Two early studies that reported the constraining impact of developmental readiness are those carried out by Long and Ortega (1997) and Long, Inagaki, and Ortega (1998), which compared the effectiveness of recasts and prompts. The first examined the acquisition of adverb placement and object topicalization in Spanish by thirty young adults and showed that recasts are more beneficial. However, this held only for adverb placement because both forms of CF proved to be ineffective in the case of object topicalization, presumably because the participants were not developmentally ready to acquire the more complex feature. Similar findings were reported by Long et al. (1998), who conducted two studies involving young adults. The first focused on adjective and locative constructions in Japanese and the second concentrated on direct object and adverb placement in Spanish. Although in this case, too, recasts were found to be superior to models for adverb placement, CF did not produce statistically significant gains for direct object placement and the two Japanese structures. The findings were also accounted for in terms of participants not having reached the requisite developmental stage to be able to benefit from CF. The mediating role of developmental readiness was also hypothesized by Ishida (2004), who examined the effect of intensive recasts on the acquisition of Japanese aspectual forms. Although durable accuracy gains were reported in relation to the frequency of CF, recasts did not work for the progressive meaning of the targeted form, a finding that was explained in terms of the failure to reach the requisite developmental stage. What should be emphasized, though, is that none of these studies attempted to establish the developmental stages that the participants represented with respect to instructional targets. Thus, explanations were offered *a posteriori* and the ineffectiveness of CF might just as well have been a function of the overall proficiency of the participants or the complexity of the structures under investigation.

Considerably more insightful are the results of studies in which developmental readiness is carefully operationalized. Such operationlization typically involves adopting as a point of reference the developmental stages posited by processability theory (Pienemann, 1998). One example is the research project undertaken by Mackey and Philp (1998), who explored the effect of intensive recasts and negotiated interaction on the acquisition of interrogatives in L2 English. Using the five-stage sequence of the development for English question formation proposed by Pienemann and Johnston (1986), they divided thirty-five beginner and low-intermediate participants into four groups with respect to presence or absence of CF and the developmental stage. Their performance on immediate and delayed post-tests indicated that intensive recasting was more beneficial for more advanced, developmentally ready learners because they exhibited the greatest improvement in stage increase. The sequence for question development was also used, this time as an outcome measure, by McDonough and Mackey (2006), who investigated the effects of recasts provided in four communicative tasks conducted over nine weeks. They found that CF was an important predictor of progress along the developmental sequence, but this was not the case for immediate repetition of the reformulated utterances or their parts (i.e., immediate uptake).

There are also studies which have looked into the way in which developmental readiness interacts with specific types of CF as well as other moderating variables, in particular ID factors. Ammar (2008), for example, investigated the effects of recasts and prompts in the acquisition of English third-person possessive determiners by French learners. The analysis of participants' performance on a picture description task at the individual level demonstrated that prompts were more effective than recasts in allowing advancement through the stages of pre-emergence, emergence, and post-emergence (White, 1998). In particular, it was the less advanced learners that benefited the most from this type of CF. Varnosfadrani and Basturkmen (2009) explored the effects of explicit and implicit correction on grammar errors committed by Iranian learners as they were retelling a text. In line with the results of much of FFI research (see Nassaji, 2017a), explicit CF proved to be more effective overall. However, the analysis of individualized tests indicated that while the explicit corrective strategy benefited developmentally early features, implicit feedback was superior for developmentally late forms. Li, Zhu, and Ellis (2016) compared the effects of immediate and delayed feedback in the form of a prompt followed by a recast on errors in the use of English past passive construction which was, by and large, new to Chinese participants. While immediate CF was more effective, the gains could be seen only on a measure of explicit knowledge (i.e., a grammaticality judgment test) but not implicit knowledge (i.e., an elicited imitation test). This finding was accounted for in terms of learners not being developmentally ready to acquire the targeted feature. Developmental readiness has also been taken into consideration in studies of working memory (WM). For example, Mackey et al. (2002) reported that although greater WM capacity is likely to promote the noticing of recasts and aid better use of the negative evidence embedded in them, these positive effects are mediated by developmental constraints. Mackey et al. (2010), in turn, found a positive relationship between WM and output production in communicative tasks when prompts were geared to the participants' developmental level with respect to the problematic features.

Proficiency and CF

There is also some research that has investigated the relationship between more broadly defined proficiency and the effectiveness of different types of feedback. In general, it could be argued, as Nassaji (2015) does with respect to interactional CF, that "learners who have higher levels of language proficiency may be better able to process and benefit from feedback than those who do not [because] ... in order to be able to attend to linguistic forms during meaning-focused interaction, learners need to have reached a level of language proficiency wherein they can focus on the language form" (p. 158). This assumption finds support in the study undertaken by Lin and Hedgcock (1996) who divided eight Chinese learners of Spanish into low and high proficiency on the basis of one-on-one interviews during which CF was provided. It was found that although less advanced learners received four times as much feedback, they were able to improve their output only in 7.1 percent of instances, compared to 69.5 percent for higher-proficiency participants. Williams (2005), in turn, demonstrated that more proficient adult learners working in dyads were more likely to attend to TL features than less proficient students whose attentional resources were insufficient to allow simultaneous focus on form and meaning. Indirect support for the assumption that higher-level learners benefit more from CF also comes from studies exploring written error correction. Ferris and Robert (2001), for instance, suggested that self-editing was likely to be more successful for learners who scored higher on a pre-test focusing on grammar. Some reformulation studies (e.g., Watanabe & Swain, 2007) indicate as well that proficiency may be an important factor moderating the focus, nature, and outcomes of collaborative discussions of original and reformulated texts.

The picture that emerges from the findings of other studies, however, is more complex, suggesting that proficiency interacts with CF type, instructional target, or learning conditions and that its effects may depend on how attainment is established. Ammar and Spada (2006) investigated the effects of prompts and recasts on the acquisition of possessive determiners in English as a function of proficiency determined on the basis of participants' performance on a pre-test. They found that while both types of CF were beneficial for higher-proficiency students, prompts were more advantageous for lower-proficiency learners, which was connected with the transparency of their corrective function. They concluded that "there is not one CF technique that is ideal or ... one size does not fit all. The effectiveness of any CF technique needs to be evaluated in relation to learners' proficiency level" (2006, p. 566). Similar results were reported by Trofimovich, Ammar, and Gatbonton (2007), who focused on the role of attention, memory, and analytical ability as mediating factors in the noticing and production of recasts in a picture description task. They also uncovered that the provided feedback was more beneficial for higher-proficiency participants. More recently, Li (2014) examined the effectiveness of recasts and metalinguistic correction on the acquisition of Chinese classifiers and perfective -*le* by American university students who were divided into higher and lower proficiency based on standardized test performance. In the case of classifiers, recasts turned out to be effective irrespective of the proficiency level, but only higher-level learners benefited from them with respect to perfective -*le*. Metalinguistic correction was more effective for lower-level students, but both CF types worked well for higher-level participants. The intricacies of the moderating role of proficiency also emerge from the study by Li, Ellis, and Shu (2016), who divided 120 Chinese learners of English into low level and high level based on exam scores. Participants at both levels completed two dictogloss tasks focusing on the English passive voice in four conditions: immediate CF, delayed CF, task only, and control. While low-proficiency learners benefited from immediate CF but not from any other condition, high-proficiency participants improved when they were provided with either feedback type or simply performed communicative tasks. The researchers ascribed such results to proficiency-related differences in cognitive demands rather than distinct learning conditions. In the case of written correction, Allen and Mills (2014) investigated the quantity, type, and incorporation of peer feedback offered in dyads as a function of proficiency. More proficient reviewers were found to offer more suggestions while low-proficiency writers tended to incorporate fewer meaning-related comments into their revisions than their high-level counterparts.

Of particular interest is the study by Iwashita (2001), since it failed to produce evidence for the impact of proficiency on the provision of CF or the occurrence of output modifications in three pairs matched for proficiency (i.e., low-low, high-high, low-high) that were performing communicative tasks. The finding was explained in terms of the interaction between proficiency and ID factors as well as the fact that the differences between participants may have been too small, a potential pitfall that was signaled in the previous section. There is also evidence that proficiency may not mediate the effects of written CF, whether delivered manually or by means of the computer. Martoccio (2018), for example, showed that both learners with high prior knowledge and those with low prior knowledge of Spanish personal *a* benefited from computer-generated explicit instruction and feedback, as measured on a grammaticality judgment test and a picture description task. López, Van Steendam, and Buyse (2019), in turn, compared the contribution of direct feedback, metalinguistic feedback with rule reminders, and self-correction on the accuracy of grammar use in immediate revisions and improvement in such accuracy in four pieces of writing. They found that while the intervention was equally effective for low- and high-level university L2 learners, proficiency was related to attitudes toward CF and preferences concerning its provision.

Evaluation of Available Empirical Evidence

When examining the studies which have focused on the link between developmental readiness and proficiency and the outcomes of CF, one is immediately struck by the obvious paucity of the empirical evidence and the difficulty in detecting general patterns. In fact, one can hardly avoid the impression that although it is easy to refer to these two variables in situations when the effects of different types of feedback prove to be difficult to interpret, such explanations are more speculative than firmly grounded in the collected data. With respect to developmental readiness, it is used rather randomly as an independent or dependent variable. Moreover, it has also been investigated in relation to just a few structures (e.g., questions) in a handful of languages (i.e., primarily English), taking into account a very limited repertoire of corrective strategies (i.e., mainly recasts). When it comes to proficiency, it is operationalized in a variety of ways. However, the measures used not only often fail to distinguish between explicit and implicit knowledge but are also usually too crude (e.g., scores on standardized tests or tasks tapping into a single TL subsystem, skill, or aspect of communicative competence) to enable reliable discrimination among participants. Overall, the interface between CF and these two variables has been investigated in relation to very few linguistic features. Additionally, almost no attention has been given to possible interactions of developmental readiness and proficiency with other variables potentially mediating the effects of CF, that is ID factors and contextual considerations. It could be hypothesized, for instance, that developmental readiness might be of limited relevance in the case of output-providing feedback if the learner lacks motivation or his or her willingness to communicate is low. Similarly, differences in globally measured proficiency might prove to be less important in shaping the effects of CF than recent instruction aimed at the targeted feature. It is also disconcerting that some researchers tend to, as if by default, equate developmental readiness with proficiency. Such a position is evident in the following quote from Loewen (2012): "Learners' proficiency levels are also a consideration, with studies suggesting that learners need to be developmentally ready to benefit from feedback" (p. 29). This is certainly an oversimplification because, although developmental readiness can be seen as a facet of proficiency, the mediating effects of the two variables are evidently a function of the conditions under which CF occurs and its potential for contributing to the development of explicit and implicit knowledge. A key question arises, though, whether carefully operationalized overall proficiency is not a better candidate for investigation as a factor mediating the effects of feedback than the somewhat elusive, intangible, and perhaps pedagogically untenable concept of developmental readiness.

Pedagogical Implications

As can be seen from the critical evaluation of the research, the empirical evidence is tenuous and it hardly provides a sound basis for making concrete and feasible pedagogical proposals. This, however, has not precluded researchers investigating FFI in general and CF in particular from offering such recommendations, mainly with respect to developmental readiness, some of which are more realistic than others. Nassaji and Fotos (2011), for example, make the following comment: "Learners learn best when they are developmentally ready. Thus, the teacher should attempt to adjust the feedback to the learners' developmental level" (p. 82). They hasten to add, however, that this approach "may not easily work in practice as it is difficult to determine whether a particular learner is developmentally ready to process a particular feedback type" (p. 82). They also suggest that one possible solution is to rely on negotiated feedback that caters to learners' abilities and needs. Sheen and Ellis (2011) offer somewhat less feasible advice to teachers: "If learner self-correction is the goal of CF, then this might be best achieved by means of CF that is fine-tuned to individual learners' level of L2 development and their capacity to benefit from CF. One way in which this might be achieved is by teachers systematically probing for the most implicit form of CF that will enable the learner to self-correct" (p. 607). Based on existing research, Nassaji (2015) writes that "teachers should take into account learners' developmental readiness and provide feedback in such a way that matches learners' developmental level" (p. 213) but admits the daunting challenges involved in implementing such guidelines. Following Ellis (2009b), Nassaji (2015) suggests taking advantage of a variety of corrective strategies on different occasions and opting for negotiated scaffolded feedback of the kind described by Aljaafreh and Lantolf (1994).

A crucial question at this juncture concerns the true value that such recommendations may represent for practitioners. As someone who worked as a secondary school teacher for over a decade and has also been teaching English for many years to English majors at the university level, I would argue that these proposals are of limited relevance to everyday classroom practice for a few reasons. First, there are still many unknowns about developmental sequences and few of these, apart from question formation, have been investigated by CF research, which renders any pedagogical proposals speculative at best. Second, the available empirical evidence is far from conclusive, which is the corollary of the fact that the concept of developmental readiness has been operationalized, measured, and used in different ways in different studies, as has been the construct of TL development as such (Mackey, 2012). Third, as aptly pointed out by Lyster, Lightbown, and Spada (1999), the belief that the only beneficial type of CF is the one that is tailored to the learner's developmental stage is untenable. They argue that there is copious evidence to the contrary and that feedback can be successfully integrated into communicative activities even when developmental stages are ignored. Fourth, and by far most importantly, even if the research findings were more compelling and conclusive, it would be unrealistic to expect teachers to be able to establish the developmental readiness of, say, twenty or thirty learners with respect to different TL features in mixed-level classes. What is more, it is sheer wishful thinking to believe that practitioners can in fact use such information to adjust their corrective strategies to respond to errors committed in ongoing interaction when the decisions about whether, what, when, and how to correct must often be made instantaneously in real time. A more feasible solution is to provide focused CF (Sheen, 2007) on features that have recently been the focus of instruction. At the same time, it is warranted to ignore most other inaccuracies or deal with only the most egregious errors which arise in unfocused communication tasks (i.e., such that do not call for the use of specific TL features). Also promising is Nassaji's (2015) advice to employ varied CF strategies or negotiate feedback in order to best adjust it to learners' needs. An important caveat here is that the usefulness of the latter option may be considerably limited by acute time constraints in most classrooms. Learners' developmental readiness would probably be easier to capitalize on in accuracy-based activities when time pressure is less of an issue. However, as elucidated above, this concept is not applicable to CF supplied under such circumstances, as accuracy-based activities are designed to cater to the development of explicit knowledge. All of this indicates that, somewhat similarly to aptitude or working memory, developmental readiness may be of interest to theorists and researchers, but it is difficult to see how this construct can successfully inform decisions about CF in everyday teaching practice.

It is easier to think of the ways in which proficiency could be taken into account when correcting errors. For one thing, it is warranted to assume that CF supplied to beginners, whether this happens in controlled exercises or communicative tasks, should not be directed at features that exceed students' capacity to process both as explicit and as implicit knowledge. For example, when learners are struggling to produce the present simple and fail to accurately use the present perfect by saying *I know her for a long time** instead of *I have known her for a long time*, CF, whatever form it assumes, is only likely to create confusion and introduce chaos into the L2 system being constructed. It also stands to reason that proficiency could be a factor informing decisions concerning CF in communicative activities performed in the classroom. In focused communication tasks, which are intended to ensure the use of a given structure, more implicit types of feedback, such as recasts, elicitations, or clarification requests, should in most cases be sufficient irrespective of proficiency, as long as CF is mainly confined to the targeted form. In unfocused communication tasks, where a number of errors in different domains are bound to be committed, lower-level learners should in most cases be corrected when these errors get in the way of expressing their intended messages. In light of the research findings, more explicit, output-inducing types of CF might work better in such tasks as well. When it comes to written correction, it would make sense to provide less advanced learners with more direct feedback types, accompanied by extensive comments, explanations, or examples, although not necessarily metalinguistic information. At the same time, indirect CF should be reserved for higher-level learners who are more likely to successfully self-correct (e.g., Bitchener & Storch, 2016). In fact, even when a correction code is devised, it would seem that lower-level learners would only really benefit from it if they were given ample opportunities to discuss and negotiate the comments (Nassaji, 2017b). This could surely happen in dedicated tutorial sessions, but while this option is feasible in writing courses, such tutorials are an unrealistic proposition in classes with a general focus on all TL skills and subsystems. Obviously, whatever research findings suggest, every classroom is unique and it ultimately falls upon teachers to decide how to factor in proficiency level when making decisions about CF. What should also not be forgotten is the role of ID factors that may trump the mitigating effects of learners' level. Therefore, as Nassaji (2015) suggests, in many instances variety may be the most obvious, most viable, and perhaps also most effective option when providing CF.

Conclusion

From both a theoretical and an empirical perspective, developmental readiness and proficiency indeed constitute potentially important mediating variables with respect to the provision of CF. They should also be taken into account when determining the effects of different types of feedback on learning outcomes. However, there are two crucial problems concerning the utility of these variables for informing classroom practice. First, the available empirical evidence is scant, confined to a small set of structures, languages, CF types, and task conditions, seldom tapping into interactions with other moderating variables. Second, while teachers can at least to some extent harness what they know about learners' proficiency when implementing CF, it is difficult to see how they could base their decisions on the evidently scarce knowledge of how CF is constrained by developmental sequences. Even if we knew considerably more in this area, it would be a major, perhaps even impossible, challenge to provide practitioners with feasible guidelines on how to establish their learners' developmental readiness and fine-tune feedback provided in spontaneous interactions accordingly. Such realities do not mean in the least that research on developmental readiness or proficiency should be abandoned. In fact, well-designed studies, drawing on what we know about relationships between various corrective options, L2 knowledge, task conditions, and ID factors are urgently needed. This is because even if insights from such studies may not find direct application in the classroom, they can aid the development of more general pedagogical recommendations on how different CF types can contribute to the development of explicit and implicit knowledge in a variety of instructional conditions.

References

Aljaafreh, A. & Lantolf, J. P. (1994). Negative feedback as regulation and second language learning in the zone of proximal development. *Modern Language Journal*, 78(4), 465–483.

Allen, D. & Mills, A. (2014). The impact of proficiency in dyadic peer feedback. *Language Teaching Research*, 20(4), 498–513.

Ammar, A. (2008). Prompts and recasts: Differential effects on second language morphosyntax. *Language Teaching Research*, 12(2), 183–210.

Ammar, A. & Spada, N. (2006). One size fits all? Recasts, prompts, and L2 learning. *Studies in Second Language Acquisition*, 28(4), 543–574.

Andersen, R. W. & Shirai, Y. (1996). The primacy of aspect in first and second language acquisition: The pidgin–creole connection. In W. C. Ritchie & T. K. Bhatia (eds.), *Handbook of research on second language acquisition* (pp. 527–570). New York: Academic Press.

Bitchener, J. & Storch, N. (2016). *Written corrective feedback for L2 development*. Bristol: Multilingual Matters.

DeKeyser, R. (1998). Beyond focus on form: Cognitive perspectives on learning and practicing second language grammar. In C. Doughty & J. Williams (eds.), *Focus on form in classroom second language acquisition* (pp. 42–63). Cambridge: Cambridge University Press.

(2003). Implicit and explicit learning. In C. J. Doughty & M. H. Long (eds.), *The handbook of second language acquisition* (pp. 313–348). Oxford: Blackwell.

(2005). What makes learning second-language grammar difficult? A review of issues. *Language Learning*, 55(Suppl. 1), 1–25.

(2007). The future of practice. In R. DeKeyser (ed.), *Practice in a second language: Perspectives from applied linguistics and cognitive psychology* (pp. 287–304). Cambridge: Cambridge University Press.

(2010). Cognitive-psychological processes in second language learning. In M. H. Long & C. J. Doughty (eds.), *The handbook of language teaching* (pp. 117–138). Oxford: Wiley-Blackwell.

(2017). Knowledge and skill in SLA. In S. Loewen & M. Sato (eds.), *The Routledge handbook of instructed second language acquisition* (pp. 15–32). New York and London: Routledge.

DeKeyser, R. & Juffs, A. (2005). Cognitive considerations in L2 learning. In E. Hinkel (ed.), *Handbook of research in second language teaching and learning* (pp. 437–454). Mahwah, NJ: Lawrence Erlbaum.

Doughty, C. J. (1991). Second language instruction does make a difference: Evidence from an empirical study of ESL relativization. *Studies in Second Language Acquisition*, 13(4), 431–469.

(2001). Cognitive underpinnings of focus on form. In P. Robinson (ed.), *Cognition and second language instruction* (pp. 206–257). Cambridge: Cambridge University Press.

Dulay, H., Burt, M. K. & Krashen, S. D. (1982). *Language two*. Rowley, MA: Newbury House.

Ellis, R. (1997). *SLA research and language teaching*. Oxford: Oxford University Press.

(2002). Does form-focused instruction affect the acquisition of implicit knowledge? A review of the research. *Studies in Second Language Acquisition*, 24(2), 223–236.

(2003). *Task-based language learning and teaching*. Oxford: Oxford University Press.

(2004). The definition and measurement of explicit knowledge. *Language Learning*, 54(2), 227–275.

(2005). Measuring implicit and explicit knowledge of a second language: A psychometric study. *Studies in Second Language Acquisition*, 27(2), 141–172.

(2006). Modeling learning difficulty and second language proficiency: The differential contributions of implicit and explicit knowledge. *Applied Linguistics*, 27(3), 431–463.

(2008). *The study of second language acquisition* (2nd ed.). Oxford: Oxford University Press.

(2009a). Implicit and explicit learning, knowledge and instruction. In R. Ellis, S. Loewen, C. Elder, R. M. Erlam, J. Philp & H. Reinders (eds.), *Implicit and explicit knowledge in second language learning, testing and teaching* (pp. 3–25). Bristol; Buffalo; Toronto: Multilingual Matters.

(2009b). Corrective feedback and teacher development. *L2 Journal*, 1(1), 3–18.

(2010). Epilogue: A framework for investigating oral and written corrective feedback. *Studies in Second Language Acquisition, 32*(2), 335–349.

(2016). Focus on form: A critical review. *Language Teaching Research, 20*(3), 405–428.

(2017). Oral corrective feedback in L2 classrooms: What we know so far. In H. Nassaji & E. Kartchava (eds.), *Corrective feedback in second language teaching and learning: Research, theory, applications, implications* (pp. 3–18). London and New York: Routledge.

Ferris, D. R. & Roberts, B. (2001). Error feedback in L2 writing classes: How explicit does it need to be? *Journal of Second Language Writing, 10*(3), 161–184.

Gass, S. M. & Selinker, L. (2008). *Second language acquisition: An introductory course* (3rd ed.). London; New York: Routledge.

Ishida, M. (2004). Effects of recasts on the acquisition of the aspectual form "-te i-(ru)" by learners of Japanese as a foreign language. *Language Learning, 5*(2), 311–394.

Iwashita, N. (2001). The effect of learner proficiency on interactional moves and modified output in nonnative–nonnative interaction in Japanese as a foreign language. System, *29*(2), 267–287.

Klein, W. (1995). The acquisition of English. In R. Dietrich, W. Klein & C. Noyau (eds.), *The acquisition of temporality in a second language* (pp. 31–68). Amsterdam; Philadelphia: John Benjamins.

Larsen-Freeman, D. (1976). An explanation for the morpheme acquisition order of second language learners. *Language Learning, 26*(1), 125–134.

Larsen-Freeman, D. & Long, M. H. (1991). *An introduction to second language acquisition research*. London: Longman.

Li, S. (2014). The interface between feedback type, L2 proficiency, and the nature of the linguistic target. *Language Teaching Research, 18*(3), 373–396.

Li, S. Ellis, R. & Shu, D. (2016). The differential effects of immediate and delayed feedback on learners of different proficiency levels. *Foreign Languages and Foreign Language Research, 286,* 1–15.

Li, S. Zhu, Y. & Ellis, R. (2016). The effects of the timing of corrective feedback on the acquisition of a new linguistic structure. *Modern Language Journal, 100*(1), 276–295.

Lightbown, P. M. (1985). Can language acquisition be altered by instruction? In K. Hyltenstam & M. Pienemann (eds.), *Modeling and assessing second language acquisition* (pp. 101–112). Clevedon: Multilingual Matters.

Lin, J. H. & Hedgcock, J. (1996). Negative feedback incorporation among high-proficiency and low-proficiency Chinese-speaking learners of Spanish. *Language Learning, 46*(4), 567–611.

Loewen, S. (2012). The role of feedback. In S. M. Gass & A. Mackey (eds.), *The Routledge handbook of second language acquisition* (pp. 24–40). New York; London: Routledge.

(2015). *Instructed second language acquisition*. New York; London: Routledge.

Loewen, S. & Reinders, H. (2011). *Key concepts in second language acquisition*. New York: Palgrave Macmillan.

Long, M. H., Inagaki, S. & Ortega, L. (1998). The role of implicit negative feedback in SLA: Models and recasts in Japanese and Spanish. *Modern Language Journal*, 82(3), 357–371.

Long, M. H. & Ortega, L. (1997). The effects of models and recasts on the acquisition of object topicalization and adverb placement by adult learners of Spanish. *Spanish Applied Linguistics*, 1(1), 65–86.

López, M. B., Van Steendam, E. & Buyse, K. (2019). Comprehensive corrective feedback on low and high proficiency writers: Examining attitudes and preferences. *International Journal of Applied Linguistics*, 168(1), 91–128.

Lyster, R., Lightbown, M. P. & Spada, N. (1999). A response to Truscott's "What's wrong with oral grammar correction?" *Canadian Modern Language Review*, 55(4), 457–467.

Mackey, A. (1999). Input, interaction, and second language development: An empirical study of question formation in ESL. *Studies in Second Language Acquisition*, 21(4), 557–587.

(2012). *Input, interaction, and corrective feedback*. Oxford: Oxford University Press.

Mackey, A., Adams, R., Stafford, C. & Winke, P. (2010). Exploring the relationship between modified output and working memory capacity. *Language Learning*, 60(3), 501–533.

Mackey, A. & Philp, J. (1998). Conversational interaction and second language development: Recasts, responses, and red herrings? *Modern Language Journal*, 82(3), 338–356.

Mackey, A., Philp, J., Egi, T., Fujii, A. & Tatsumi, T. (2002). Individual differences in working memory, noticing of interactional feedback, and L2 development. In P. Robinson (ed.), *Cognition and second language instruction* (pp. 181–209). Cambridge: Cambridge University Press.

Martoccio A. (2018). How does prior explicit knowledge affect the efficacy of explicit instruction and feedback? The case of the personal a in L2 Spanish. *Language Teaching Research*, 22(4), 379–397. DOI:10.1177/1362168816689802.

McDonough, K. & Mackey, A. (2006). Responses to recasts: Repetition, primed production, and language development. *Language Learning*, 56(4), 693–720.

Meisel, J. M. (2013). Development in second language acquisition. In P. Robinson (ed.). *The Routledge encyclopedia of second language acquisition* (pp. 165–173). London and New York: Routledge.

Mellow, J. D. (1987). On the primacy of theory in applied studies: A critique of Pienemann and Johnson. *Second Language Research*, 12(3), 304–318.

Michel, M. (2017). Complexity, accuracy, and fluency in L2 production. In S. Loewen & M. Sato (eds.), *The Routledge handbook of instructed second language acquisition* (pp. 50–68). London; New York: Routledge.

Nassaji, H. (2015). *The interactional feedback dimension in instructed second language learning: Linking theory, research and practice.* London: Bloomsbury.

(2017a). Grammar acquisition. In S. Loewen & M. Sato (eds.), *The Routledge handbook of instructed second language acquisition* (pp. 205–223). London; New York: Routledge.

(2017b). Negotiated oral feedback in response to written errors. In H. Nassaji & E. Kartchava (eds.), *Corrective feedback in second language teaching and learning: Research, theory, applications, implications* (pp. 114–128). London; New York: Routledge.

Nassaji, H. & Fotos, S. (2011). *Teaching grammar in second language classrooms: Integrating form-focused instruction in communicative context.* New York; London: Routledge.

Nassaji, H., & Kartchava, E. (2017). Conclusions, reflections, and final remarks. In H. Nassaji & E. Kartchava (eds.), *Corrective feedback in second language teaching and learning: Research, theory, applications, implications* (pp. 174–182). London; New York: Routledge.

Ortega, L. (2009). *Understanding second language acquisition.* London: Hodder Education.

Pawlak, M. (2006). *The place of form-focused instruction in the foreign language classroom.* Poznań–Kalisz: Adam Mickiewicz University Press.

(2014). *Error correction in the foreign language classroom: Reconsidering the issues.* Heidelberg; New York: Springer.

(2017a). Individual difference variables as mediating influences on success or failure in form-focused instruction. In E. Piechurska-Kuciel, E. Szymańska-Czaplak & M. Szyszka (eds.), *At the crossroads: Challenges of foreign language learning* (pp. 75–92). Heidelberg: Springer Nature.

(2017b). Overview of learner individual differences and their mediating effects on the process and outcome of interaction. In L. Gurzynski-Weiss (ed.), *Expanding individual difference research in the interaction approach: Investigating learners, instructors, and other interlocutors* (pp. 19–40). Amsterdam; Philadelphia: John Benjamins.

(2019). Tapping the distinction between explicit and implicit knowledge: Methodological issues. In B. Lewandowska-Tomaszczyk (Ed.), *Contacts and contrasts in educational contexts and translation.* Heidelberg: Springer Nature.

Pienemann, M. (1989). Is language teachable? Psycholinguistic experiments and hypotheses *Applied Linguistics, 10*(1), 52–79.

(1998). *Language processing and second language development: Processability theory.* Amsterdam; Philadelphia: John Benjamins.

Pienemann, M. & Johnston, M. (1986). An acquisition-based procedure for second language assessment. *Annual Review of Applied Linguistics*, 9 (1), 92–122.

Pienemann, M. & Lenzing, A. (2015). Processability theory. In B. VanPatten & J. Williams (eds.), *Theories in second language acquisition* (2nd ed., pp. 159–179). London: Routledge.

Sheen, Y. (2007). The effect of focused written corrective feedback and language aptitude on ESL learners' acquisition of articles. *TESOL Quarterly*, 41(2), 255–283.

Sheen, Y. & Ellis, R. (2011). Corrective feedback in language teaching. In E, Hinkel (ed.), *Handbook of research in second language teaching and learning* (pp. 593–610). London and New York: Routledge.

Spada, N. & Tomita, Y. (2010). Interactions between type of instruction and type of language feature: A meta-analysis. *Language Learning*, 60(2), 263–308.

Suzuki, W., Nassaji, H. & Sato, K. (2019). The effects of feedback explicitness and type of target structure on accuracy in revision and new pieces of writing. *System*, 81, 135–145.

Suzuki, Y. & DeKeyser, R. M. (2017). The interface of explicit and implicit knowledge in a second language: Insights from individual differences in cognitive aptitudes. *Language Learning*, 67(4), 747–790.

Swain, M. (1985). Communicative competence: Some roles of comprehensible input and comprehensible output in its development. In S. Gass & C. Madden (eds.), *Input in second language acquisition* (pp. 235–253), Rowley, MA: Newbury House.

Trofimovich, P., Ammar, A. & Gatbonton, E. (2007). How effective are recasts? The role of attention, memory, and analytical ability. In A. Mackey (ed.), *Conversational interaction in second language acquisition* (pp. 171–195). Oxford: Oxford University Press.

Varnosfadrani, A. D. & Basturkmen, H. 2009. The effectiveness of implicit and explicit error correction on learners' performance. *System*, 37(1), 82–98.

Watanabe, Y. & Swain, A. (2007). Effects of proficiency differences and patterns of pair interaction on second language learning: Collaborative dialogue between adult ESL learners. *Language Teaching Research*, 11(2), 121–142.

White, J. (1998). Getting the learners' attention: A typographical input enhancement study. In C. J. Doughty & J. Williams (eds.), *Focus on form in classroom second language acquisition* (pp. 85–113). Cambridge: Cambridge University Press.

Williams, J. (2005). The effectiveness of spontaneous attention to form. *System*, 29(3), 325–340.

Zobl, H. & Liceras, J. (1994). Functional categories and acquisition orders. *Language Learning*, 44(1), 159–180.

35

Corrective Feedback and Grammatical Complexity: A Research Synthesis

Gisela Granena and Yucel Yilmaz

Background

The Notion of Grammatical Complexity

In the field of second language acquisition (SLA), the notion of complexity has long attracted the attention of researchers. Some researchers focus on the complexity of second language (L2) learners' performance, or the structural complexity of a text (e.g., Pallotti, 2015), from the point of view of lexical, morphological, syntactic, and phonological complexity. Others investigate the complexity of language features as a factor that contributes to the ease or difficulty of their acquisition (e.g., DeKeyser, 2005). As in DeKeyser (2005), the present chapter focuses on the complexity of grammatical structures (i.e., grammatical complexity), a notion of complexity that is essential for instructed SLA research, due to its potential impact on the effectiveness of different types of L2 instruction. Rather than phonology or the lexicon, we restrict this chapter to morphosyntax and to the complexity of morphosyntactic structures considering form and form–meaning relationships.

There is no doubt that L2 instruction is likely to have a differential impact depending on the type of target structure. There is also agreement in the field that complexity is inherent to a target structure, while difficulty is relative and experienced by the learners as a result of factors such as first language (L1) background, proficiency level, and other learner and contextual factors (DeKeyser, 2003; Hulstijn & De Graaff, 1994). Scholars further concur that these two constructs, complexity and difficulty, are not completely independent. As DeKeyser (2005) points out, grammatical complexity is one of the factors contributing to grammatical difficulty. Similarly, Bulté and Housen (2012) explain that complexity, which they refer to as "absolute complexity," is one of the objective factors determining difficulty, or "relative complexity."

The field has not reached consensus, however, on the definition of grammatical complexity in L2 acquisition. Part of the reason is that different approaches (pedagogical, cognitive, or linguistic) can be taken to define complexity. Pedagogical approaches define complexity by relying on teacher and/or textbook judgments (e.g., Robinson, 1996). These are approaches that are seen as having high face validity and that are empirically supported, since teachers build their judgments based on what their learners can do (Robinson, 1996). However, while they can be used to operationalize complexity in a particular research study, they do not address the issue of what complexity is from a theoretical perspective or, in other words, what actually causes some features to be easy or difficult.

From a cognitive perspective, several proposals have been made. For example, Hulstijn and De Graaff (1994) defined complexity in cognitive terms as the number (and/or type) of grammatical criteria[1] taken into account in order to arrive at a correct form. The more criteria, the less likely spontaneous noticing and processing will be. To illustrate the differences in the cognitive complexity of grammatical rules, Hulstijn and De Graaff provided two examples from hypothetical languages. In these languages, a rule with different endings for three different tenses/aspects is considered more complex than a rule with different endings for two different tenses/aspects. Similarly, a rule that includes two plural suffixes, one for nouns ending on a vowel, or a consonant, with a front vowel in the penultimate syllable, and one for nouns ending on a consonant with a back vowel in the penultimate syllable, is considered more complex than a rule that includes the same two suffixes, but one for nouns ending on a vowel and one for nouns ending on a consonant. Other proposals within the cognitive approach have defined complexity in terms of processing constraints that can make language features difficult to process if the learner is not developmentally ready for them (Clahsen, 1984; Pienemann, 1989; Pienemann & Johnston, 1987).

Linguistically, DeKeyser (2005) distinguished between complexity of meaning, complexity of form, and complexity of form–meaning mapping. Problems of meaning can arise from factors such as novelty and abstractness, especially if the learner's L1 lacks the grammatical structure in question. For example, the meaning of articles in English can be a source of difficulty for native speakers of languages such as Chinese, Japanese, or Korean, due to their abstractness. Problems of form have to do with the choice and placement of morphemes and allomorphs. No semantics is involved. These problems are particularly common in highly inflected languages. For example, grammatical gender agreement in Spanish is a well-known learning problem for native speakers of English because in

---

[1] By "criteria" Hulstijn and De Graaff meant realizations/transformations of a grammatical concept. For example, the concept of noun plurality has different suffixes (i.e., realizations/transformations).

addition to being a formal feature, English lacks this particular language feature. Finally, problems of form–meaning mapping arise as a result of the link between a form and its meaning not being transparent. DeKeyser (2005) lists three factors that trigger such lack of transparency: (1) redundancy, (2) optionality, and (3) opacity. The link between form and meaning may not be transparent because the meaning of the form in question is conveyed by another element in the sentence making it redundant (for example, an adverb of time such as *yesterday* in the case of a past *-ed* form). The form–meaning link can also be hard to establish when a form is optional, such as null subjects in Spanish. Finally, form–meaning mapping can be problematic when multiple forms have the same meaning or the same form has multiple meanings. For example, the morpheme *-s* in English functions both as plural and third-person singular suffix. Other examples of opaque form–meaning mapping relationships, according to DeKeyser (2005), are irregular morphemes (e.g., irregular past forms) and certain discourse-motivated word order patterns, such as verb-subject (VS) order in Spanish. Other proposals from a linguistic perspective have suggested perceptual salience, understood as the ease in which grammatical features can be noticed in the input, as a source of difficulty (e.g., Doughty & Williams, 1998). Goldschneider and DeKeyser (2005), for example, were able to account for a considerable percentage of the variance in the order of morpheme acquisition in English by means of salience, defined as a combination of phonological salience, semantic complexity, morphological regularity, and frequency.

This brief review of the literature on the notion of grammatical complexity has summarized several useful proposals. It is clear that defining complexity is not easy, due to the number of factors involved, and to the fact that, as DeKeyser (2005) points out, these factors interact with one another in such a way that the extent to which one factor (e.g., frequency) contributes depends on the extent to which another factor (e.g., transparency) does, making complexity very difficult to pin down. Defining and operationalizing grammatical complexity is especially relevant for SLA studies that investigate the effectiveness of different instructional interventions by focusing on particular target structures. In this type of research, complexity becomes an independent variable that can have an impact on the learning outcomes of a particular treatment. A type of instructional intervention that has attracted the attention of the SLA field and that has generated an increasingly growing body of research since the mid-1990s is corrective feedback, defined as those comments on the appropriateness or accuracy of L2 learners' production or comprehension (Li & Vuono, 2019). In this chapter, we will review corrective feedback studies that investigated specific target structures in order to determine the extent to which the grammatical complexity of the target structures investigated had an impact on the effectiveness of the feedback intervention.

Instructed SLA and Grammatical Complexity

The difficulty in defining complexity may be one of the reasons behind the lack of empirical studies comparing the effectiveness of instructional interventions on target forms with varying complexity. The most widely cited studies were conducted in the 1990s (DeKeyser, 1995; Hulstijn & De Graaff, 1994; Robinson, 1996; and Williams & Evans, 1998) and all of them focused on teaching methods or on L2 learning conditions. Hulstijn and De Graaff (1994) argued that the effects of L2 instruction should be greater with complex language features because these features are more difficult to notice spontaneously and, therefore, instruction should facilitate their learning. Specifically, Hulstijn and De Graaff proposed that explicit instruction should be more effective than implicit instruction with complex rather than with simple grammatical rules. De Graaff (1997) tested Hulstijn and De Graaff's claim in his eXperanto experiment. Using an artificial language, De Graaff investigated whether explicit grammar instruction would be more effective in the acquisition of complex rather than of simple structures. His operationalization of complexity followed Hulstijn and De Graaff's (1994) definition of complexity as the number of different grammatical criteria that have to be taken into account in order to process a language structure. The results of the experiment, however, yielded only partial support for the hypothesis. No significant interactions were found between complexity and type of instruction (operationalized as presence or absence of explicit grammar instruction), but there was a significant difference between the two types of instruction with regards to the syntactic structures. Specifically, the explicit group performed significantly better than the group with no instruction on the complex syntactic structure. In the case of the morphological structures, however, the explicit group performed significantly better on the simple morphological structure, failing to support the complexity hypothesis.

Unlike Hulstijn and De Graaff (1994), other researchers (e.g., Krashen, 1982, 1994; Reber, 1989) argue that explicit instruction can only be helpful in the case of simple rules and that complex grammar can only be learned implicitly. Robinson (1996) tested this claim by looking at whether implicit learning was more effective than explicit learning in the acquisition of complex grammar in English as an L2. The experiment included four learning conditions: (1) implicit, which consisted in memorizing sentences, (2) incidental, which consisted in reading and understanding the meaning of the stimuli, (3) rule-search, which consisted in searching for rules, and (4) instructed, which provided formal rule explanation. Following the pedagogical approach, Robinson's operationalization of complexity relied on experienced L2 teachers' judgments to identify an easy and a hard rule. In relation to the hard rule, the study showed that participants' performance under the instructed condition was significantly more accurate than under the rule-search condition, and, contrary to expectations, also more accurate than under the implicit or incidental conditions, even though these differences were not significant. In relation to the easy rule, the instructed condition was significantly better than the rule-search and the implicit conditions, and marginally significantly better than the incidental condition. Robinson concluded that his study provided support for Krashen's and Reber's claim regarding the possibility to learn simple rules via explicit L2 instruction, but failed to provide support for the claim that complex rules can only be learned implicitly.

Williams and Evans (1998) investigated, among other issues, whether some forms are more amenable to focus on form than others. They chose a simple form (i.e., participial adjectives of emotive verbs) and a complex form (i.e., the passive). Their instructional treatments included a group that received input flood with no explicit rules or feedback and a group that received explicit instruction with feedback in addition to input flood. Their results showed that not all forms are equal in terms of the effectiveness of focus on form. The explicit treatment was only effective with the simple form. In this case, the explicit instruction group showed significantly greater increases than the input flood group and the control group. There were no differences between explicit instruction and input flood, however, with regard to the complex form. Williams and Evans concluded that "forms that are easily misinterpreted or misanalysed by learners, but also easily explained, are excellent candidates for instruction containing more explicit focus on form, including the use of negative evidence" (p. 152). Williams and Evans's conclusion provides support to Krashen's and Reber's claims regarding the usefulness of explicit instruction with simple grammatical structures and fails to support Hulstijn and De Graaff's (1994).

Finally, DeKeyser (1995) conducted an experiment with a miniature linguistic system in order to test whether explicit-deductive learning would be better than implicit-inductive learning for simple rules and whether implicit-inductive learning would be better than explicit-deductive learning for prototypicality patterns, where no clear-cut rules apply. The study showed that explicit-deductive learning was statistically significantly better for simple rules than implicit-inductive learning. The study also showed that complex patterns where no clear-cut rules apply were better learned under the implicit-inductive condition, at least at the descriptive level (i.e., no statistical testing was performed).

The findings of these four studies are consistent with the claim that explicit instruction is more helpful with simple structures. In the case of complex structures, results are more mixed, but, in general, the studies show that explicit instruction is as effective as implicit instruction. In addition to the studies reviewed above, Spada and Tomita (2010) carried out a meta-analysis on the interactions between type of instruction and type of language feature. The study investigated the effects of explicit and implicit types of instruction on simple and complex grammatical features in English. The target structures in a pool of forty-one studies were coded following Hulstijn and De Graaff's (1994) definition of complexity. Simple structures included tense, articles, plurals, prepositions, SV inversion, possessive determiners, and participial adjectives, while complex structures included dative alternation, question formation, relativization, passives, and pseudo-cleft sentences. The study found that the effects of explicit instruction were statistically significant for both simple and complex features and, therefore, that there was no interaction between type of instruction and language feature, while the effects of implicit instruction were only significant for complex features. The largest effect size was reported for explicit instruction and complex forms on free production measures, while the effect sizes for implicit instruction were small, both for simple and complex structures.

The result that explicit instruction is more beneficial than implicit instruction for both simple and complex forms is in part consistent with studies that provided partial support for explicit instruction (i.e., De Graaff, 1997; DeKeyser, 1995; Robinson, 1996; Williams & Evans, 1998). The clear superiority reported for explicit instruction with complex forms, however, is surprising. As the authors acknowledge, this result may have been due to the small number of sample studies contributing to a particular effect size. As the authors also acknowledge, a different definition of complexity could have yielded different findings. Particularly, they mention that their criteria (i.e., number of linguistic transformations; Hulstijn & De Graaff, 1994) did not incorporate the dimension of semantic complexity. The same concern was raised by De Graaff (1997), a study that used the same operationalization of complexity. De Graaff (1997) explained the lack of differential effects of explicit instruction on simple versus complex morphological features by arguing that semantic salience had not been controlled for. He explained that, depending on the structure, successful form processing also depends on meaning and, therefore, that the form–meaning connections a particular structure establishes (i.e., whether transparent or opaque) should be considered as part of the complexity of that structure. According to De Graff (1997), "future research should keep the salience variable constant or specifically study the interaction between semantic salience and complexity" (p. 270).

Given the lack of systematic reviews and meta-analyses on grammatical complexity in the area of corrective feedback, and in line with the overall theme of this volume, the goal of the current chapter was to review corrective feedback studies that targeted specific grammatical structures in order to determine the extent to which the effectiveness of a feedback intervention varies depending on the grammatical complexity of the target structure investigated. Following Hulstijn and De Graaff's (1994) suggestion, we defined complexity by combining formal and semantic criteria. Specifically, we added the semantic redundancy and opacity of the form–meaning connection that a structure establishes to the formal grammatical criteria considered by Hulstijn and De Graaff in order to see if the superiority reported for explicit methodological interventions with complex forms also characterizes corrective feedback interventions.

Present Study

Following De Graff's call, and given the lack of studies focusing on the effects of corrective feedback on the acquisition of simple and complex grammatical features, the present chapter reviewed corrective feedback studies that investigated the effectiveness of this particular instructional intervention on specific target structures in English as an L2. While corrective feedback studies tend to focus on specific target structures, they do not operationalize them along the complexity dimension. This chapter further focused on English as an L2 due to the number of corrective feedback studies available and the need to have a study pool as large as possible for the sake of statistical power. According to Li's (2010) meta-analysis on the effectiveness of corrective feedback, English is the most frequently investigated L2, followed by French.

The research synthesis reported in this chapter was guided by the following general question:

> Does the effectiveness of corrective feedback differ depending on the level of grammatical complexity of the target structure in English as an L2?

For the purpose of this study, we defined corrective feedback as those reactions language learners receive from their interlocutors indicating that the learners' language production is not target-like. After reviewing the literature on how simple and complex features had been defined, we decided to adapt Hulstijn and De Graaff's (1994) definition of complexity, which relies on formal grammatical criteria, by incorporating the dimension of semantic complexity. In order to do so, we followed DeKeyser's (2005) proposal and focused on complexity due to problems of form–meaning mapping. This is one of the three problems DeKeyser identifies, the other two being problems of meaning and of form. Our rationale to focus on form–meaning mapping problems was that we could apply both formal and semantic criteria to operationalize them since they involve both. In addition, as DeKeyser argues, form–meaning mapping plays an important role in determining the difficulty of acquisition and it is a common source of learning problems. Even if form and meaning are not particularly problematic, acquiring the form–meaning mapping can still be a problem.

Thus, following Hulstijn and De Graaff (1994) and DeKeyser (2005), we operationalized complexity along two dimensions, formal and semantic. This yielded a 2x2 categorization matrix. For the sake of coding, we relied on discrete categories. Note, however, that the notion of complexity is better understood in terms of a continuum, rather than in terms of discrete categories. This is particularly true when formal and semantic criteria are combined to define complexity, like in the present chapter, since semantic salience is a trigger of complexity that we add to formal complexity. In our matrix, formal grammatical criteria were used to categorize structures along one of the axes and semantic criteria along the other. The criteria used were the following: one transformational rule (simple form) or two or more transformations (complex form; same as Spada & Tomita, 2010, based on Hulstijn & De Graaff, 1994), and, based on DeKeyser (2005), either redundant or opaque (simple form–meaning mapping) or both redundant and opaque (complex form–meaning mapping). The four possible resulting categories were, therefore: [simple form, simple form–meaning mapping], [complex form, simple form–meaning mapping], [simple form, complex form–meaning mapping], and [complex form, complex form–meaning mapping].

Method

Identifying Primary Studies
We initially checked studies referenced in published state-of-the-art articles and meta-analyses (such as Goo et al., 2015; Li, 2010; Spada & Tomita, 2010; Yilmaz, 2016) to locate the studies that focused on the effects of corrective feedback on English target structures. We also searched databases such as Academic Search (EBSCO), the Education Resources Information Center (ERIC), Web of Science, and Google Scholar with different combinations of the following keywords: *corrective feedback, negative feedback, explicit correction, recasts, prompts, reformulations, complexity/difficulty, second language, language acquisition/learning, and English*. Our search revealed ninety-five studies.

Inclusion/Exclusion Criteria
We assessed whether each study met the following inclusion and exclusion criteria to determine whether they qualified for our research synthesis.

Inclusion Criteria
1. The study investigated the effects of a corrective feedback type that is delivered orally during an interactive task;[2]
2. The study measured learners' improvement using a variation of a pre-test/post-test control group design;
3. The study focused on the development of at least one English morphosyntactic linguistic target;
4. The study was published in a refereed journal or edited collection;

---

[2] Written non-interactional feedback is usually delayed, whereas oral interactional feedback is immediate with respect to the occurrence of learners' errors. Since we did not know how this difference may interact with the role of grammatical complexity in the effectiveness of corrective feedback, we kept the studies included in our synthesis as homogenous as possible by excluding written feedback studies.

5. The study reported descriptive statistics that are necessary for the calculation of effect sizes separately for every target structure investigated in the study.

Exclusion Criteria
1. The effects of feedback were investigated under conditions in which either task complexity or an individual difference factor is experimentally manipulated. We excluded these studies because it is not possible to determine to what extent the effect of feedback in these studies is comparable to the effect of feedback in studies where these factors are not controlled.
2. The complexity of the grammatical structure investigated in the study is due to problems of form. Dative alternations investigated in Carroll and Swain (1993) and *that*-trace filter investigated in Goo (2012, 2016) are examples of such structures.[3] The source of the complexity is not related to the link between form and meaning in these structures.

Dataset

Eleven studies published between 2006 and 2018 qualified for our research synthesis (Ammar & Spada, 2006; Ellis, 2007; Ellis, Loewen & Erlam, 2006; Guo & Yang, 2018; Kartchava & Ammar, 2014; Li, Zhu, & Ellis, 2016; Loewen & Nabei, 2007; Nassaji, 2017; Sheen, 2007; Yang & Lyster, 2010; Yilmaz, 2013). Three of these studies were published in *Studies in Second Language Acquisition*, two in the *Modern Language Journal*, one in *Language Teaching Research*, one in *System*, one in the *Journal of Psycholinguistic Research*, and three in an edited volume (Mackey, 2006). All but two studies (Nassaji, 2017; Yilmaz, 2013) were carried out in a classroom. Nassaji (2017) and Yilmaz (2013) were carried out in a lab context, and together with a classroom study (Li et al., 2016), they were the only three studies that used random assignment of subjects to treatment groups. All eleven studies used a comparison group that did not receive any feedback but performed the communicative task during which treatment groups received feedback. The comparison groups of two studies (Ammar & Spada, 2006; Guo & Yang, 2018), in which the feedback groups received explicit instruction on the target forms, also received explicit instruction. Two studies (Li et al., 2016; Loewen & Nabei, 2007) included true control groups which took the same tests the experimental groups took but did not receive any treatment.

---

[3] 'In dative alternations and that-trace, no semantics is involved and no meaning gets lost because of the mistake, in principle, even though indirectly it could sometimes make understanding harder' (R. DeKeyser, personal communication, 21 March 2019).

Except for two studies that only included an immediate post-test (Kartchava & Ammar, 2014; Loewen & Nabei, 2007), all studies included a delayed post-test, the timing of which ranged from twelve days (Ellis et al., 2006) to two months (Yilmaz, 2013) after the treatment.

Five studies were carried out in an English as a Foreign Language (EFL) context, whereas the remaining six were carried out in an English as a Second Language (ESL) context. Two studies targeted adolescent learners (Ammar & Spada, 2006; Li et al., 2016), whereas the remaining nine studies targeted adult learners. Learners' proficiency levels ranged from high beginner to high intermediate based on eight studies that reported the relevant information. Six studies controlled for their participants' L1 (Chinese, French, Japanese, and Turkish), whereas the remaining five studies had mixed L1 learners.

Treatment Characteristics

Feedback in nine studies was provided in a whole-class or group setting where not only the person who commits the error, but also the other learners listening to the exchange between the teacher/researcher and the learner could benefit indirectly from the feedback. In the other two studies (Nassaji, 2017; Yilmaz, 2013), feedback was provided to individual learners, and no second-hand (indirect) feedback opportunity was given.

Various feedback conditions were used in our focal studies. Although all eleven studies included at least one recast condition, the way the studies operationalized recasts varied considerably (see below for the narrative review of individual studies). Both metalinguistic feedback and prompts were included in four studies (see Table 35.1). Mixed feedback including either a combination of prompts and recasts (Kartchava & Ammar, 2014) or a combination of explicit correction and recasts (Yilmaz, 2013) were included in two, and clarification requests were included in only one study (Loewen & Nabei, 2007).

Review of Focal Studies

The following is a narrative review of the results of the studies that focused on the performance of the feedback groups as compared to other groups that performed the treatment tasks without receiving any feedback (e.g., comparison groups). One study (Li et al., 2016) included both a comparison group and a group that only took the pre-test and post-test without performing the treatment tasks. We excluded this control group from this review because it cannot be used to isolate the feedback effect from other instructional features the experimental groups experienced (e.g., producing output during interactive treatment tasks). Feedback conditions that were not similar to the majority of the feedback conditions that were included in this synthesis in terms of intensity (the reduced-explicit condition in Yilmaz, 2013) or timing (the delayed condition in Li et al., 2016) were also excluded.

Three studies focused on English articles (Nassaji, 2017; Sheen, 2007; Yilmaz, 2013), more specifically, on the first mention function of the indefinite article and on the anaphoric reference function of the definite article. Yilmaz (2013) and Sheen (2007) compared the effectiveness of recasts (partial recasts in Yilmaz and full or partial recasts in Sheen) vs. explicit feedback types (explicit correction in Yilmaz, and metalinguistic correction in Sheen). Yilmaz's study also included a mixed feedback condition which involved the provision of both explicit corrections and recasts. Nassaji (2017) compared an intensive recast condition in which learners received full or partial recasts only on their article errors to an extensive recast condition in which learners received recasts not only on their article errors but also on any other error they made during communicative tasks. The results of Sheen and Nassaji with respect to recasts differed from Yilmaz because Sheen and Nassaji found no difference between the no-feedback conditions and feedback conditions, whereas Yilmaz found a difference in favor of recasts on the immediate posttest. In all three studies, the feedback condition compared to intensive recasts (i.e., explicit correction, metalinguistic correction, and extensive recasts) always performed significantly better than the comparison groups (except on the written story-retelling task in Nassaji, 2017), and they were statistically better than intensive recasts whenever there was a statistical difference between them.

Two studies focused on the past *-ed* form (Ellis et al., 2006; Yang & Lyster, 2010). Ellis et al. (2006) compared the relative effectiveness of feedback involving a metalinguistic explanation about how to correct the mistake after the repetition of the error (e.g., "kiss–you need past tense") and recasts including reformulations of the erroneous segments of learners' utterances. They reported that the metalinguistic group performed statistically better than the recast group on the delayed oral production task and on the untimed grammaticality judgment tests, and better than the no-feedback group only in the delayed oral production test. Other comparisons were not statistically significant. Yang and Lyster (2010) compared the relative effects of prompts, which took the form of metalinguistic clues, repetitions (or clarification requests), or elicitations versus recasts, which could be partial or full. Although Yang and Lyster focused on both regular and irregular past tense forms, we did not include in the review their results on irregular past tense forms, which are not rule-based, as the authors also acknowledged.[4] The study

---

[4] We excluded Yang and Lyster's (2010) results on irregular past tense forms to ensure homogeneity across the linguistic targets of the included studies in terms of the cognitive processes they require. Researchers (e.g., Ellis, 2005) have stated that there are no clear rules for irregular past tense forms, and therefore, the acquisition of these forms is exemplar or item based, involving the use of declarative memory (Pinker & Ullman, 2002). However, the rest of the

did not reveal any significant differences between the feedback and no-feedback groups or between the two feedback groups.

Ellis (2007), using the same participants as in Ellis et al. (2006), compared learners' performance on the past *-ed* to the comparative form *-er*. He evaluated the learning difficulty of the two targets based on eight criteria and concluded that the comparative rule was more difficult.[5] He argued, for example, that the knowledge of the syllabic structure of adjectives is necessary in comparatives to determine whether the morphemic or periphrastic construction should be used, whereas the *-ed* is easier because it only involves the addition of *-ed* to the base form of the verb to refer to completed actions in the past. Ellis reported that the recast group performed similarly on both structures, whereas the metalinguistic group made larger gains for the comparative on the immediate post-test, and larger gains for past *-ed* on the delayed post-test. Ellis did not report on the statistical difference between the performance of each feedback group and the performance of the no-feedback group.

Loewen and Nabei (2007) investigated the relative effectiveness of full recasts, metalinguistic feedback (i.e., learners were asked to think about the form of their utterances), and clarification requests (e.g., "Pardon?") on the acquisition of English question formation. The results of one of the outcome measures (i.e., untimed grammatical judgement task ([GJT]) did not show any differences between the groups, but the results of the other outcome measure (i.e., timed GJT) showed that the feedback groups outperformed the no-feedback group, but there were no differences between the feedback groups.

Kartchava and Ammar (2014) focused on two target structures: past tense and questions in the past. They investigated the relative performance of three feedback groups: a group that received various forms of recasts (full, partial, interrogative, or integrated reformulations), a group that received various forms of prompts (full or partial repetitions, elicitations, or metalinguistic information), and a group that received a mixture of both prompts and reformulations. The study showed that feedback types were not more effective than the no-feedback control group in promoting development from pre-test to post-test. There were no differences among the different feedback types either. It should be noted, however, that the context in which some of the feedback instances were provided was unusual due to a methodological feature used in the study. The researchers were interested in learners' noticing of feedback, in addition to their pre-test/post-test development, and, in order to

---

targets included in our synthesis are governed by rules, which makes the acquisition of them rule based (Ellis, 2005), requiring computation and the use of procedural memory (Pinker & Ullman, 2002).

[5] Since Ellis aimed at determining the difficulty level of the two target structures and difficulty is a broader concept than complexity (Bulté & Housen, 2012), he used more criteria to operationalize difficulty. Nevertheless, two of the criteria Ellis used, "explicit knowledge" and "formal semantic redundancy," are similar to our criteria, "formal complexity" and "form–meaning complexity," respectively.

measure noticing, they asked learners to write down their thoughts whenever one of the researchers lifted a red card during the task. This procedure might have increased the noticeability of feedback instances in general by increasing learners' alertness.

Li et al. (2016) focused on the English past passive in a study whose main purpose was to investigate the effects of feedback timing. There were two feedback-timing conditions in the study. The immediate group received corrective recasts which included the provision of the repetition of the learner's error ("the driver was arrest?"), followed by a reformulation ("the driver was arrested") after each error. There was also a delayed group in the study that received explicit feedback at the end of the treatment task. The results for the delayed group, however, are not relevant for our review because it is not comparable to the feedback provided in the rest of the studies. The results for the immediate group revealed that the difference between the no-feedback (referred to as "task-only" in the study), and the immediate group was not significant across outcome measures and test times. The difference, however, was nearly significant in one of the outcome measures (i.e., grammaticality judgment) at the immediate post-test.

Guo and Yang (2018) compared the effects of prompts and recasts on the development of the third-person -s, following a pre-test-immediate post-test-delayed post-test design. The recast group received partial or full reformulations of learners' erroneous utterances, whereas the prompt group received repetitions of learners' errors. Both groups received form-focused instruction on the target structure in addition to the feedback they received. The no-feedback comparison group also received form-focused instruction. The results of one of the outcome measures (a written test asking learners to write a composition in 15 minutes) were not clear at the post-test. The prompt group was better than the recast group, but neither the recast nor the prompt group was statistically better than the no-feedback group. The results were clearer on the delayed post-test. The prompt group outperformed the no-feedback group and the recast group. There were no differences between the groups on the other outcome measure (i.e., text completion) at either time point (immediate or delayed).

Ammar and Spada (2006) focused on possessive determiners and compared a group that received various prompt moves (e.g., metalinguistic clues) versus a group that received various types of recasts (e.g., full, partial). Although the study included two outcome measures, a passage correction and oral production tasks, we excluded the results for the passage correction task because the descriptive statistics for the no-feedback comparison group were not reported in the study. The results for the oral production task revealed that the prompt group performed significantly better than the recast group at the delayed post-test, and both feedback groups performed significantly better than the no-feedback group at both times.

Coding

Two coders (i.e., the two authors) classified all the studies in the dataset in terms of target structure complexity into one of four categories: [simple form, simple form–meaning mapping], [complex form, simple form–meaning mapping], [simple form, complex form–meaning mapping], and [complex form, complex form–meaning mapping]. Except for Kartchava and Ammar (2014) and Ellis (2007), which focused on two target forms, all studies focused on only one target form. The agreement rate was 90 percent, and differences between the two coders were resolved through discussion. This discrepancy involved the classification of comparatives as [simple form, complex form–meaning mapping] or [complex form, complex form–meaning mapping]. Based on Ellis's (2007) criteria and his conclusion that comparatives are a more complex structure than the *-ed* past tense, comparatives were finally classified as [complex form, complex form–meaning mapping].

We categorized the passive, question formation, and comparatives as [complex form, complex form–meaning mapping]. Four studies in our dataset investigated at least one of these structures (Ellis, 2007; Kartchava & Ammar, 2014; Li et al., 2016; Loewen & Nabei, 2007). These structures have in common the fact that two or more grammatical criteria need to be applied to arrive at the correct target form (i.e., multiple features determine their specific form), which makes them complex in form. In addition, these are structures that are both redundant and opaque from the point of view of form–meaning mapping, because their meaning can be derived from other elements in the sentence and because they involve a form that has multiple meanings (e.g., *-ed*, auxiliary *do*) or a meaning that is conveyed by multiple forms (e.g., *more* and *-er*).

We categorized the past *-ed* form, third-person *-s*, and articles as [simple form, complex form–meaning mapping]. Eight studies in our dataset investigated at least one of these structures (Ellis, 2007; Ellis et al., 2006; Guo & Yang, 2018; Kartchava & Ammar, 2014; Nassaji, 2017; Sheen, 2007; Yang & Lyster, 2010; Yilmaz, 2013). These structures are both redundant and opaque from the point of view of form–meaning mapping, but their specific form is determined by a single feature, which makes them simple from the point of view of form. Finally, we categorized possessive as [simple form, simple form–meaning mapping]. This target structure was only investigated by one study (Ammar & Spada, 2006). None of the studies that qualified for this research synthesis focused on a target structure that could be considered as having [complex form, simple form–meaning mapping]. A summary of the main features of the studies is provided in Table 35.1.

Table 35.1 *Study features*

Study	Participants	Target feature	Outcome measures	Design	Feedback types
Ammar & Spada (2006)	64 mixed-L1 adults	possessive determiners = simple form, simple form–meaning	oral production	pre-post-del, quasi-experimental	prompts, recasts
Ellis (2007)	34 mixed-L1 adults	comparatives = complex form, complex form–meaning	elicited imitation, untimed GJT	pre-post-del, quasi-experimental	metalinguistic, recasts
Ellis et al. (2006)	35 mixed-L1 adults	past -*ed* = simple form, complex form–meaning	elicited imitation, untimed GJT	pre-post-del, quasi-experimental	metalinguistic, recasts
Guo & Yang (2018)	175 Chinese-L1 adults	third person -*s* = simple form, complex form–meaning	written production, text-completion	pre-post-del, quasi-experimental	prompts, recasts
Kartchava & Ammar (2014)	99 French-L1 adults	past -*ed* = simple form, complex form–meaning; questions = complex form, complex form–meaning	oral production	pre-post, quasi-experimental	prompts, recasts, mixed
Li et al. (2016)	120 Chinese-L1 adolescents	passives = complex form, complex form–meaning	elicited imitation, untimed GJT	pre-post-del, experimental	recasts
Loewen & Nabei (2007)	66 Japanese-L1 adults	questions = complex form, complex form–meaning	untimed and timed GJT	pre-post, quasi-experimental	clarification requests, metalinguistic feedback, recasts
Nassaji (2017)	48 mixed-L1 adults	articles = simple form, complex form–meaning	oral production, written storytelling, untimed GJT	pre-post-del, experimental	prompts, recasts
Sheen (2007)	99 mixed-L1 adults	articles = simple form, complex form–meaning	speeded dictation, written production, error correction	pre-post-del, quasi-experimental	metalinguistic, recasts
Yang & Lyster (2010)	72 Chinese-L1 adults	past -*ed* = simple form, complex form–meaning	oral production, written production	pre-post-del, quasi-experimental	prompts, recasts
Yilmaz (2013)	80 Turkish-L1 adults	articles = simple form, complex form–meaning	guided oral production, story retelling, spot-the-difference	pre-post-del, experimental	recasts, explicit correction, mixed

Results

Following our categorization matrix, possessive determiners were classified as [simple form, simple form–meaning mapping]. The results of the only study that focused on possessive determiners (Ammar & Spada, 2006) showed that both feedback types (recasts and prompts) were effective since they were both significantly better than the control group at both times.

Regarding [simple form, complex form–meaning mapping], this was the category that was most frequently targeted by our focal studies (Ellis et al., 2006; Guo & Yang, 2018; Kartchava & Ammar, 2014; Nassaji, 2017; Sheen, 2007; Yilmaz, 2013). The grammatical structures that we coded under this category were third-person -s, past -ed, and articles. In five of the seven studies in this group, at least one feedback group significantly outperformed the no-feedback group in one outcome measure or time point.

Finally, we considered question formation, passive construction, and comparatives as [complex form, complex form–meaning mapping]. Of the four studies that targeted one of these structures (Ellis, 2007; Kartchava & Ammar, 2014; Li et al., 2016; Loewen & Nabei, 2007), only three reported information about the statistical difference between the feedback groups and no-feedback groups (Ellis, 2007; Li et al., 2016; and Loewen & Nabei, 2007), and, of these three, only one study showed that feedback groups were statistically significantly better than the no-feedback comparison groups. Therefore, it seems that fewer studies found an effect for feedback with grammatical structures that were both complex in form and form–meaning mapping than with structures that were simple in form, but complex in form–meaning mapping, or with structures that were simple both ways. However, no studies were identified with structures that could be coded as [complex form, simple form–meaning mapping]. Therefore, it is not possible to discuss how this category would compare to the [complex form, complex form–meaning mapping] category. In addition, an approach based on counting studies that could not find significant effects for a factor has limitations, since the lack of statistical significance can be due to low statistical power (Borenstein et al., 2011). To provide a more fine-grained analysis of the existing research, we also summarized the effect sizes for each complexity category.

We used Comprehensive Meta-analysis Version 3.3 (Borenstein et al., 2014) to compute effect sizes for each study and synthesize the effects. We used Hedges' g (Hedges, 1981) as the effect size index because it has been argued that Cohen's d tends to overestimate the absolute value of the effect size parameter in small samples and that Hedges' g corrects for this bias (Hedges, 1981). An effect size was calculated for each outcome measure (e.g., oral production, grammaticality judgment), comparison type (e.g., recast vs. control, prompts vs. control), and time point (e.g., immediate post-test, delayed post-test) based on changes in (gain) scores between pre-test and immediate post-test and between pre-test and delayed post-test. The effect size for each study indicated the magnitude of the difference between the gain scores of the feedback groups and the gain scores of the no-feedback comparison groups. Rather than using separate effect sizes for each outcome measure and comparison type to calculate summary effects, we averaged the effect sizes for different outcome measures and comparison types within a study in order to arrive at one effect size per study. This was done to avoid the treatment of separate outcomes and comparison types coming from the same study as providing independent information, which leads to "improper estimate of the precision of the summary effect" (Borenstein et al., 2011, p. 226). We also used random-effects models because the methodological heterogeneity across our focal studies prevented us from assuming that the true effect size of each study was the same, an assumption that needs to be satisfied in order to be able to carry out fixed-effects models. Finally, we performed separate analyses for different time points (immediate and delayed). Even though Kartchava and Ammar (2014) investigated the effects of two different target structures, we only included their results for question formation in an attempt to have a single effect size per study, as Borenstein et al. (2011) suggest. Our decision to include question formation instead of past -*ed* was motivated by the observation that the [complex form, complex form–meaning mapping] category, under which question formation was classified, was represented by fewer studies than the [simple form, complex form–meaning mapping] category, under which past -*ed* was classified. With this choice, we hoped to increase the reliability of the overall effect size estimate for the [complex form, complex form–meaning mapping] category. Finally, although Ellis (2007) investigated two target structures, we only included the results reported for comparatives, because the results for past -*ed* were reported in Ellis et al. (2006). Table 35.2 provides a summary of the results of our analysis including information about the effectiveness of feedback on target structures with different complexity levels, the number of studies representing each category, mean effect size, standard error, and 95 percent confidence interval for each effect size by the two time points combined and each time point separately. Following Cohen (1988), effects between 0.20 and 0.49 were considered small, effects between 0.50 and 0.79 were considered medium, and effects larger than 0.80 were considered large.

As can be seen, the combined effect of feedback on [complex form, complex form–meaning mapping] target structures was small ($g = 0.25$). The immediate and delayed effects on these targets ($g = 0.27$ and $g = 0.23$, respectively) were also small. The effects on these targets were the smallest among the three target structure categories identified in the dataset. The effect of feedback on [simple form, complex form–meaning mapping] target structures was medium, regardless of whether both time points

Table 35.2 *Feedback effects by time and target complexity*

Effect type	Groups	k	Mean ES (g)	SE	95% CI Lower limit	95% CI Upper limit
Immediate effects	complex form complex form–meaning	4	0.27	0.17	−0.05	0.60
	simple form complex form–meaning	6	0.69	0.38	−0.05	1.43
	simple form simple form–meaning	1	0.55	0.35	−0.14	1.23
Delayed effects	complex form complex form–meaning	2	0.23	0.22	−0.21	0.67
	simple form complex form–meaning	6	0.50	0.25	0.02	0.99
	simple form simple form–meaning	1	0.74	0.35	0.05	1.43
Combined effects	complex form complex form–meaning	4	0.25	0.16	−0.08	0.57
	simple form complex form–meaning	6	0.60	0.32	−0.03	1.22
	simple form simple form–meaning	1	0.64	0.35	−0.04	1.33

were considered together ($g = 0.60$) or separately (immediate, $g = 0.69$; delayed, $g = 0.50$). Finally, the effect of feedback on [simple form, simple form–meaning mapping] target structures was also consistently medium, regardless of whether time points were considered together ($g = 0.64$) or separately (immediate, $g = 0.55$; delayed, $g = 0.74$). The combined and delayed effects of this category were the largest among the three complexity categories. Finally, except for the confidence intervals of the delayed effects on the [simple form, complex form–meaning] category and [simple form, simple form–meaning] category, confidence intervals of all other effects included zero, indicating statistically nonsignificant effects.

Discussion

This research synthesis sought to determine whether the effectiveness of corrective feedback as an instructional intervention in the acquisition of L2 English varied depending on the grammatical complexity of the target structure investigated. Following De Graaff's (1997) suggestion, not only was our definition of complexity based on formal criteria but it incorporated a semantic component from the perspective of the redundancy and transparency of the form–meaning mapping (DeKeyser, 2005). This allowed us to code a structure such as English articles as simple in terms of form, but as complex in terms of form–meaning mapping, thus avoiding the problematic categorization of this structure as a simple language feature by Spada and Tomita (2010).

In terms of the magnitude of the effect, the effectiveness of corrective feedback depending on target structure complexity for the two time points (immediate/delayed) combined was as follows: ([simple form, simple form–meaning mapping] = [simple form, complex form–meaning mapping]) > [complex form, complex form–meaning mapping]. The smallest effect corresponded to those structures categorized as complex both in terms of form and in terms of form–meaning mapping. These were structures such as the passive, question formation, and comparatives. The finding that corrective feedback as an instructional intervention is less beneficial for the most complex features compared to simpler ones fails to provide support to Hulstijn and De Graaff's (1994) argument that the effects of L2 instruction should be greater with complex language features because these features are more difficult to be noticed spontaneously than simple ones. It also differs from the results reported in Spada and Tomita's (2010) meta-analysis, where the difference between simple and complex, when averaged across implicit and explicit treatments, was practically nonexistent: 0.54 for simple features and 0.57 for complex features. A possible explanation for these results is that instruction that includes only corrective feedback is not sufficient in the case of complex grammatical structures, or, at least, it is not as effective as instruction types that include other instructional features (e.g., explicit information) in addition to corrective feedback. Alternatively, it could also be that feedback interventions involving complex grammar need a longer time to be effective compared to other types of instruction. Finally, a possible interaction between modality and target structure complexity might explain why our study showed smaller effect sizes for complex targets than what was reported in Spada and Tomita (2010): the studies included in our synthesis used only the oral modality, whereas the studies included in Spada and Tomita's meta-analysis used any modality type (i.e., written, oral, or both). A comparison of the effectiveness of implicit versus explicit feedback interventions in the case of simple rules and more complex grammar could throw more light on this issue, but, unfortunately, this was beyond the scope of this research synthesis.

Our results also showed that the distinction between simple and complex form–meaning mapping did not seem to have an effect on the benefits of corrective feedback when the form was simple. In both cases, [simple form, simple form–meaning mapping] and [simple form, complex form–meaning mapping], the effect size was similar when both testing times (immediate and delayed) were considered together (0.64 and 0.60, respectively). Only when the effect sizes of delayed post-tests were considered separately did simple form–meaning mapping correspond to a larger effect size than complex form–meaning mapping, yielding the following ranking of categories in decreasing order of effect size: [simple form, simple form–meaning mapping] > [simple form, complex form–meaning mapping] > [complex form, complex form–meaning mapping]. The most complex structures consistently showed small effects for both immediate and delayed post-tests.

The overall findings of this research synthesis indicate that, in general, corrective feedback is more effective for simpler grammatical features. Contrary to Spada and Tomita's (2010) findings, this provides support to the hypothesis that the type of language feature interacts with the effectiveness of instruction and that it is a relevant dimension to consider in the design of instructional interventions based on corrective feedback.

Conclusion and Implications

One of the goals of this research synthesis was to bring the field's attention to the role of target structure features in the effectiveness of feedback and to propose a categorization method that takes into account both formal and semantic complexity features and that can be used in future studies. Indeed, there is a need to investigate the relationship between complexity of target structure and corrective feedback effectiveness, since this is a question that has not been investigated in primary studies so far. The conclusions that can be drawn from the present synthesis, however, are only tentative. First, only a small number of studies qualified for inclusion in this study. Second, the majority of the confidence intervals for the effect sizes included zero, which means that the effects were not statistically significant. Finally, the qualifying studies diverged from one another methodologically. For example, six different feedback types were used in our eleven focal studies, and the same feedback type was often operationalized differently in different studies. Given the fact that previous research has revealed feedback type as a major source of variability in feedback effectiveness, there is good reason to investigate the interaction between feedback type and target complexity in future research.

This research synthesis has implications for L2 instructors and L2 researchers alike. It can help instructors have more realistic expectations about the effectiveness of the feedback they provide to their students. Comments on the correctness of simpler features, as long as they are simpler both formally and semantically, can be expected to be more effective than comments on the correctness of features that are simpler formally, but not semantically, such as articles in English. Similarly, this research synthesis can help SLA researchers deepen their understanding of the varying effects of instruction on different target structures. Our definition of complexity further provides a foundation on which later studies can elaborate or expand. However, the findings of this research synthesis are only tentative, given the small number of studies included, and should be viewed as a call for more theoretical and empirical research into the role of grammatical complexity in L2 instruction.

References

* Studies included in the current research synthesis are marked with an asterisk.

*Ammar, A. & Spada, N. (2006). One size fits all? Recasts, prompts, and L2 learning. *Studies in Second Language Acquisition*, 28(4), 543–574.

Borenstein, M., Hedges, L. V., Higgins, J. P. T. & Rothstein, H. R. (2011). *Introduction to meta-analysis*. Chichester: Wiley & Sons.

  (2014). *Comprehensive meta-analysis (Version 3.3) [computer software]*. Englewood, NJ: Biostat.

Bulté, B. & Housen, A. (2012). Defining and operationalising L2 complexity. In A. Housen, F. Kuiken & I. Vedder (eds.), *Dimensions of L2 performance and proficiency: Investigating complexity, accuracy and fluency in SLA* (pp. 21–46). Amsterdam; Philadelphia: John Benjamins.

Carroll, S., & Swain, M. (1993). Explicit and implicit negative feedback: An empirical study of the learning of linguistic generalizations. *Studies in second language acquisition*, 15(3), 357–386.

Clahsen, H. (1984). The acquisition of German word order: A test case for cognitive approaches to second language acquisition. In R. Andersen (ed.), *Second languages* (pp. 219–242). Rowley, MA: Newbury House.

Cohen, J. (1988). *Statistical power analysis for the behavioral sciences*. Hillside, NJ: Lawrence Erlbaum.

De Graaff, R. (1997). The eXperanto experiment: Effects of explicit instruction on second language acquisition. *Studies in Second Language Acquisition*, 19(2), 249–297.

DeKeyser, R. M. (1995). Learning second language grammar rules: An experiment with a miniature linguistic system. *Studies in Second Language Acquisition*, 17(3), 379–410.

  (2003). Implicit and explicit learning. In C. Doughty & M. Long (eds.), *The handbook of second language acquisition* (pp. 313–348). Oxford: Blackwell.

  (2005). What makes learning second-language grammar difficult? A review of issues. *Language Learning*, 55(Suppl. 1), 1–25.

Doughty, C. & Williams, J. (1998). Pedagogical choices in focus on form. In C. Doughty & J. Williams (eds.), *Focus on form in classroom second language acquisition* (pp. 197–261). Cambridge: Cambridge University Press.

Ellis, R. (2005). Measuring implicit and explicit knowledge of second language: A psychometric study. *Studies in Second Language Acquisition*, 27(2), 141–172.

  *(2007). The differential effects of corrective feedback on two grammatical structures. In A. Mackey (ed.), *Conversational interaction*

in second language acquisition (pp. 339–360). Oxford: Oxford University Press.
*Ellis, R., Loewen, S. & Erlam, R. (2006). Implicit and explicit corrective feedback and the acquisition of L2 grammar. *Studies in Second Language Acquisition*, 28(2), 339–368.
Goldschneider, J. M. & DeKeyser, R. M. (2005). Explaining the "natural order of L2 morpheme acquisition" in English: A meta-analysis of multiple determinants. *Language Learning*, 55(Suppl. 1), 27–77.
Goo, J. (2012). Corrective feedback and working memory capacity in interaction-driven L2 learning. *Studies in Second Language Acquisition*, 34(3), 445–474.
   (2016). Corrective feedback and working memory capacity. In G. Granena, D. O. Jackson, & Y. Yilmaz (Eds.), Cognitive individual differences in second language processing and acquisition, 3, (pp. 279–302). John Benjamins.
Goo, J., Granena, G., Yilmaz, Y. & Novella, M. (2015). Implicit and explicit instruction in L2 learning. In P. Rebuschat (ed.), *Implicit and explicit learning of languages* (pp. 443–482). Amsterdam: John Benjamins.
*Guo, X. & Yang, Y. (2018). Effects of corrective feedback on EFL learners' acquisition of third-person singular form and the mediating role of cognitive style. *Journal of Psycholinguistic Research*, 47(4), 841–858.
Hedges, L. V. (1981). Distribution theory for Glass's estimator of effect size and related estimators. *Journal of Educational Statistics*, 6(2), 107–128.
Hulstijn, J. H. & De Graaff, R. (1994). Under what conditions does explicit knowledge of a second language facilitate the acquisition of implicit knowledge? A research proposal. *AILA Review*, 11, 97–112.
*Kartchava, E. & Ammar, A. (2014). The noticeability and effectiveness of corrective feedback in relation to target type. *Language Teaching Research*, 18(4), 428–452.
Krashen, S. (1982). *Principles and practice in second language acquisition*. Oxford: Pergamon.
   (1994). The input hypothesis and its rivals. In N. Ellis (ed.), *Implicit and explicit learning of languages* (pp. 45–77). London: Academic Press.
Li, S. (2010). The effectiveness of corrective feedback in SLA: A meta-analysis. *Language Learning: A Journal of Research in Language Studies*, 60(2), 309–365.
Li, S. & Vuono, A. (2019). Twenty-five years of research on oral and written corrective feedback in *System. System*, 84, 93–109.
*Li, S., Zhu, Y. & Ellis, R. (2016). The effects of the timing of corrective feedback on the acquisition of a new linguistic structure. *Modern Language Journal*, 100(1), 276–295.
*Loewen, S. & Nabei, T. (2007). Measuring the effects of oral corrective feedback on L2 knowledge. In A. Mackey (ed.), *Conversational interaction*

in second language acquisition (pp. 361–377). Oxford: Oxford University Press.
Mackey, A. (ed.). (2006). *Conversational interaction in second language acquisition*. Oxford: Oxford University Press.
*Nassaji, H. (2017). The effectiveness of extensive versus intensive recasts for learning L2 grammar. *Modern Language Journal*, 101(2), 353–368.
Pallotti, G. (2015). A simple view of linguistic complexity. *Second Language Research*, 31(1), 117–134.
Pienemann, M. (1989). Is language teachable? Psycholinguistic experiments and hypothesis. *Applied Linguistics*, 10(1), 52–79.
Pienemann, M. & Johnston, M. (1987). Factors influencing the development of language proficiency. In D. Nunan (ed.), *Applying second language acquisition research* (pp. 45–141). Adelaide: National Curriculum Resource Centre.
Pinker, S. & Ullman, M. (2002). The past and future of the past tense. *Trends in Cognitive Science*, 6(11), 456–463.
Reber, A. S. (1989). Implicit learning and tacit knowledge. *Journal of Experimental Psychology: General*, 118(3), 219–235.
Robinson, P. (1996). Learning simple and complex second language rules under implicit, incidental, rule-search and instructed conditions. *Studies in Second Language Acquisition*, 18(1), 27–67.
*Sheen, Y. (2007). The effects of corrective feedback, language aptitude, and learner attitudes on the acquisition of English articles. In A. Mackey (ed.), *Conversational interaction in second language acquisition* (pp. 301–322). Oxford: Oxford University Press.
Spada, N. & Tomita, Y. (2010). Interactions between type of instruction and type of language feature: A meta-analysis. *Language Learning*, 60(2), 263–308.
Williams, J. & Evans, J. (1998). What kind of focus and on which forms? In C. Doughty & J. Williams (eds.), *Focus on form in classroom second language acquisition* (pp. 139–155). Cambridge: Cambridge University Press.
*Yang, Y. & Lyster, R. (2010). Effects of form-focused practice and feedback on Chinese EFL learners' acquisition of regular and irregular past tense forms. *Studies in Second Language Acquisition*, 32(2), 235–263.
*Yilmaz, Y. (2013). The relative effectiveness of mixed, explicit and implicit feedback in the acquisition of English articles. *System*, 41(3), 691–705.
  (2016). The linguistic environment, interaction and negative feedback. *Brill Research Perspectives in Multilingualism and Second Language Acquisition*, 1, 48–86.

36

The Role of Task in the Efficacy of Corrective Feedback

Pauline Foster and Martyn McGettigan

Introduction

This chapter addresses the question of how classroom tasks can be a conduit for corrective feedback (CF) to second language learners. To explore this, we acknowledge both the theoretical issues in second language acquisition (SLA) research about the place of negative evidence and also the practical issues in identifying where, when, and by whom learner errors are best treated. We start with a definition of the word *task* itself, to set it apart from other pedagogic activities commonly used in language classrooms. We then move to why a task-rich and meaning-focused classroom is argued to provide better opportunities for SLA than a form-focused one. We consider the theoretical underpinnings of Long's Interaction Hypothesis (1983, 1996) and how this meshes with an important feature of classroom tasks: that they provide the learner with a platform for interacting with other learners or with a teacher, and through interaction to be guided implicitly and incidentally to noticing shortcomings in their L2 knowledge. A role for CF in such an environment is not obvious, especially in interactions between learners, and in reviewing research studies into the place of tasks in CF research, and the place of CF in task research, we note the two perspectives seem seldom to intersect. The final sections of this chapter address task design and implementation factors that seek to create space for CF without compromising the essentially meaning-focused nature of task interaction. These include the affordances of computer-mediated interaction and task implementation sequences in which CF is delayed till the post-task stage, or fed-forward at the pre-task stage.

How Should We Define Task?

On first consideration, the word does not conjure a linguistic context. It conjures rather the broader context of human life and the mundane "bits of work" required of us all. Indeed, Long (1985) presents a list of examples of everyday tasks, some of which would involve little if any language:

> painting a fence, dressing a child, filling out a form, buying a pair of shoes, making an airline reservation, borrowing a library book, taking a driving test, typing a letter, weighing a patient, sorting letters, taking a hotel reservation, writing a check, finding a street destination, and helping someone across a road.
>
> (p. 89)

Long's objective here is to show that tasks-in-the-world are carried out for their own sake, with a goal in mind that is obviously not the display of particular linguistic structures. In this view, the language used to complete a task is part of the means to its end, and not the end in itself. How successfully a task has been carried out is assessed not by the language it generates, but simply by whether or not its purpose has been achieved: the fence has been painted, the shoes bought, the book borrowed, the patient weighed, and the room reserved. This conception of task stands in contrast to language classroom activities, such as drills and sentence transformations, which are designed precisely to give learners context-free practice in using particular linguistic structures, and which are assessed on whether the structures are displayed accurately or not. For an activity, the focus on language structure relegates language meaning to the position of a car used for a driving test; it does not matter what destination the car is headed to, only how skillfully it is driven.

To distinguish a classroom *task* from a classroom *activity*, and to bring it from the wider world into the classroom, Skehan (1998) and Ellis (2003) set out criteria that capture a task's essentially communicative nature. For both authors, the key defining element in a task is an overarching concern for meaning relatable to the world. This does not mean that tasks must be simulations of authentic daily life. Ellis (2003) gives the example of tasks like finding differences between two pictures, which might happen only occasionally in real life, but which nevertheless involve "processes of language use," such as asking and answering questions, and these "reflect those that occur in real-world communication" (p. 10). In the same vein, Long (1985) distinguishes between real-world tasks (which learners will ultimately need to accomplish outside the classroom) and pedagogic tasks (which are used inside the classroom to build the task-specific knowledge and skill for real-life deployment).

Ellis (2009) adds another criterion for the definition of language task, that its design should create a need for the task-takers to convey information, express an opinion, or to infer meaning. This need to communicate clearly brings the learner to make the best use of his or her language resources to complete the task successfully. Ellis and Shintani (2014) note that a learner should not be relying on having "useful" language pre-taught before the task begins, but classroom tasks can be designed with predetermined linguistic forms in mind that are "task-essential," and where pre-task teaching would be a pedagogically useful form of pre-task planning (Loschky & Bley-Vroman, 1993).

While tasks are predominantly conceived as oral, Ellis (2003) reminds us they could be solitary undertakings such as reading or writing. As long as the reading and writing are meaning-focused and being done for a clearly defined communicative purpose, they come within the definition of task. Nor should it be assumed that individual tasks are stand-alone elements of a lesson. They can be designed in sequences (Willis, 1996) such that a solitary reading or writing task can productively feed into or arise from an interactive task undertaken by a group of learners.

The Locus of Focus in Language Classrooms: Theoretical Background

In this section we explore the reasoning behind task-based language learning and teaching (TBLT) and why meaning-focused tasks are thought to offer more effective, more frequent, and more varied opportunities for second language development than form-focused activities. This entails three acronyms: Focus on Forms (FonFs), Focus-on-Meaning (FonM) and Focus-on-Form (FonF). They were coined by Long (1988) at a time when communicative approaches to language teaching were spurning the first, and advocating the second or the third. FonFs characterizes the traditional method of encouraging the development of explicit knowledge of linguistic elements through explicit teaching. An exclusive FonM characterizes Krashen's (1981, 1985) position that only by understanding meaning (i.e., comprehensible input) are learners able to develop the implicit knowledge of language structures necessary for fluent performance. FonF reflects Long's position whereby learners' attention is incidentally brought to bear on linguistic elements during interactions that are otherwise meaning-based. Thus, a FonFs approach to teaching invites immediate and systematic CF, a FonM approach abjures it entirely, while a FonF approach provides negative evidence when communication is compromised.

Krashen's (1981, 1985) input model of SLA has no role for output, let alone CF to output. This position was challenged by Gregg (1984) who noted that even after years of successfully comprehending input (as in L2 immersion settings), adult learners can still fall a long way short of L2 proficiency, and this cannot be explained away through the operations of a sensitive and capricious Affective Filter. Indeed, VanPatten (1990) showed that adult language learners, especially beginners, have difficulty in attending to language form and meaning simultaneously, and choose to pay attention to form only so far as is necessary for them to understand the meaning it encodes. This suggests that an overriding FonM in classroom tasks would actually provide the ideal circumstances for learners *not* to develop their L2 knowledge. Schmidt's (1990, 2001) Noticing Hypothesis argues the essential starting point for the acquisition of any grammatical feature is that, at some level of awareness, the learner pays attention to it. Long's Interaction Hypothesis (1985, 1996) takes the position that understanding meaning is a necessary but insufficient condition for SLA; learners must create messages as well as understand them. During FonM task interactions, Long argues (1996, p. 425), there will be points where communication breaks down. This will provoke the learners to switch to FonF at precisely the moments it is most needed, allowing the speaker or listener to become aware of the inadequacy in their L2 knowledge that has led them to not understand or not to be understood. The speaker and listener then work together on the problem utterance to confirm or clarify the meaning, provide the missing information, and create opportunities for acquisition. Instances of such "negotiations for meaning" (e.g., Doughty & Pica 1986; Duff, 1986; Gass & Varonis, 1985) are especially prized in FonM interaction because they provide individual learners with timely, incidental, and tailor-made negative evidence, which a deliberate, teacher-prompted FonFs does not.

Troubleshooting Interactions, Conversational Interactions, and Task Design

The early research into FonF through negotiations for meaning (NfM) explored the independent variables relating to task design, comparing the different impact on learner–learner interaction of the direction of information flow between participants (one-way or two-way), the need to exchange this information (optional vs. required), the interactional set-up (dyad vs. group) and the task goals (convergent vs. divergent). The dependent variables were typically three interactional moves supposed to indicate a problem had occurred in understanding: confirmation checks (e.g., *Do you understand?*); comprehension checks (e.g., *Is this what you mean?*); and clarification requests (e.g., *I don't understand/What do you mean?*). Results indicated that in a learner–learner dyadic set-up, with an exchange of information in which both speakers had to give and receive task-specific information in the pursuit of a convergent goal, more communication breakdowns occurred, giving rise to more NfM and thus more opportunities for acquisition (See Pica, 1994, for a full review). Typical examples of two-way required information exchange tasks include "jig-saw" pictures, narratives, map navigations, and "spot-the-differences," all useful for learners interacting with each other, rather than with a teacher, giving each participant the chance to process input and produce output.

The pedagogic implications in these early studies suggested classroom task design could be deliberately recruited to shepherd pairs of learners into communication breakdowns, creating opportunities for NfM, and maximizing the opportunities that individuals would get to "notice" where their L2 knowledge was lacking. Setting aside the risk of a boring classroom diet of two-way required information exchange pairwork, the success of a strategy that puts learners into task situations where they would negotiate for meaning was very much dependent on provoking communication failures large enough to require a FonF. This is more difficult than might be imagined, as a host of grammatical errors can pass without compromising a speaker's meaning, or setting the listener off in a pursuit for clarity. Subsequent studies in learner–learner interaction (Eckerth, 2009; Foster, 1998; Foster & Ohta, 2005; Rouhshad et al., 2015) showed little evidence of or appetite for NfM in tasks, explained by participants' natural disinclination to lose face or threaten face by highlighting their own or their task partner's failings. This was compounded by the fact that interactional moves having the surface structure of an opening for NfM can actually represent a listener's polite interest in the content of a partner's language, and not a problem with its form (Foster & Ohta, 2005). In the case of learner–teacher task interactions, genuine NfM is unlikely to be initiated on the teacher's side because language teachers are professionally practiced at understanding ill-formed L2 utterances. A teacher reaction to an ill-formed utterance would be deliberate CF, and not an incidental negotiation to resolve a communication impasse.

As interest in the value of interaction to SLA expanded, "communication trouble" as the narrow genesis of NfM gave way to something much less confined. Indeed, Mackey (1999, p. 584, footnote) explicitly equates the terms *negotiated interaction*, *conversational interaction*, and *negotiation* because "(t)hey have often been used throughout the literature to refer to the same concept." *Conversational* is a very broad term indeed, suggestive of a low-stakes interaction where learners communicate with each other to whatever degree of clarity they might choose. Accordingly, other interactional features moved inside the research purview, loosely labelled as language-related episodes (LREs) in which learners choose to talk about the language forms they are using, explicitly reflecting on accuracy and sharing whatever linguistic resources they possess to communicate with each other (e.g., Swain & Lapkin, 1998). LREs might more properly be called negotiations for form (NfF), providing FonF at moments when meaning is not an issue but how to express it best in the L2 is recognized as tricky. The expansion of the inherent value of interaction to SLA from troubleshooting to reflective collaboration moved it outside the original conception of the Interaction Hypothesis, with implications for classroom task design. There is no longer any sense in designing tasks that set the stage for NfM over communication failures when LREs and NfF will crop up during communication success.

Corrective Feedback in Interactive Tasks

For Ellis (2003), the impetus for feedback is different for a teacher than it is for a learner. In teacher–learner interactions the function is pedagogic; in learner–learner interactions the function is communicative. This means teacher–learner interactions are a natural habitat for CF, while learner–learner interactions are not. Learner–learner interactions are more suited to mutual engagement in information exchange, and to expressions of opinion, interest, and sympathy. Unsurprisingly therefore, in a study by Adams, Alwi, and Newton (2015), where learners were instructed to take on a pedagogic function by giving implicit or explicit corrections to their task partners, their implicit recasts did not have any impact on learning, and their explicit corrections had a negative impact on it; the learners either disliked CF from a peer, or they did not expect it, so did not notice it (but see Chapter 13, this volume).

Teacher-generated CF can be delivered in a variety of ways, but for the purposes of this discussion on task-based interaction, the most relevant are immediate *teacher prompts* and *teacher recasts*. Teacher prompts draw a learner's attention to the presence of an error in what he or she has just said and implicitly invite the learner to attempt a correction. The prompt may be followed by the teacher's metalinguistic explanation of the error, explicitly inviting the learner to attempt a correction. Whatever their type, prompts bring the task to a halt until the learner has responded satisfactorily, and as such are noticeable, and noticeably didactic (Ammar, 2008; Kartchava & Ammar, 2014). Recasts, on the other hand, happen when a teacher, in spite of understanding the meaning of an ill-formed utterance, recasts it with a well-formed equivalent, incidentally and implicitly providing feedback to the learner with didactic intent. For learners on the receiving end, recasts are not unmistakeably didactic. Lyster and Ranta (1997) showed their inherent ambiguity. In their study, while teacher recasts were the most abundant form of feedback in the classes they investigated, the learners did not reliably perceive them as corrective and accordingly were not likely to notice the feedback they implied. Panova and Lyster (2002) reported similar findings; recasts were seen as confirming the speaker's message as much as (or even more than) disconfirming its form. Mackey, Gass, and McDonough (2000) reported a small study on teacher–learner task interactions and showed that recasts involving morphology were the least likely to be noticed by the learners when compared to recasts involving phonology or lexis. In contrast, Ellis, Basturkman, and Loewen (2001) reported higher levels of learner attention to teacher recasts, possibly because the learners in their study had been exposed to form-focused instruction before the meaning-focused tasks and were therefore more alert to when the teacher's language implied correction. There was no role for task design variables here to encourage learners to pick up on the corrective intent of recasts; the important ingredient was not the task itself, but the context of the pre-task stage: explicit FonFs teaching.

In sum, CF through recasts preserves the task interaction, but its implicit nature means its corrective force can pass unnoticed; CF through prompts is a task-stopping move in which a teacher deliberately and obviously draws a learner's attention to error. The more explicit and more noticeable form of CF in interactive tasks is thus the least congruent to the defining element of tasks noted above: the maintenance of a primary focus on meaning.

The Place of Task in Corrective Feedback Research

Corrective feedback is such a widely researched area in SLA that robust meta-analyses have been possible. Li, Zhu, and Ellis (2016) report on four of these (Li, 2010; Lyster & Saito, 2010; Mackey & Goo, 2007; Russell & Spada, 2006), revealing the wide range of independent variables in use. These include setting (laboratory vs. classroom); target feature (grammar, vocabulary, or pronunciation); type of CF (implicit vs. explicit, output-providing vs. output-prompting); length of treatment (short, medium, or long); durability of effect (immediate vs. delayed); outcome measures (comprehension vs. production, free vs. constrained); and learner characteristics (age, L1, L2 proficiency). Significantly for the theme of this chapter, Li et al.'s list includes nothing about task variables. In the meta-analyses, the role of task is that of generating samples of learner language, most commonly through picture-based narratives, designed to elicit some predetermined L2 structure (e.g., the English definite article or the past tense suffix). Development in the chosen structure is then assessed by comparing pre-test and post-test scores. In Nassaji's recent survey of factors influencing the effectiveness of CF (2016), task also takes a back seat. Among a host of independent variables, including target structure, gender, working memory, language anxiety, analytic ability, developmental readiness, and error type, there is only one mention of task (in Gass, Mackey & Ross-Feldman, 2005), and this is in relation to NfM. Task design emerges as a contingent and inert factor in CF research.

By way of recent examples, Kartchava and Ammar's (2014) study of CF does not involve task as a variable. The authors looked at the noticeability of two kinds of implicit CF (prompts and recasts) on two kinds of error in English (questions in the past and past tense forms). Their findings indicate that participants noticed CF on past tense errors more than on question forms, and that prompts were more effective than recasts in getting the learners to understand the corrective intention of the teacher. No significant difference in accuracy was detected in the pre-test to post-test comparison. Similarly, Li et al. (2016) comparing timing of CF (immediate vs. delayed) on the acquisition of the English past passive construction, employed a dictogloss-*cum*-narrative task to generate the oral data. Using an elicited imitation test (EIT) and a grammaticality judgment test (GJT), the authors found no gains on the EIT for either kind of CF, though both delayed and immediate types were related to gains on the GJT. No task variables were involved in this study. Adams, Nuevo, and Egi (2011) investigated implicit and explicit CF on noun–adjective agreement in French as a Foreign Language, using learner–learner task interactions. They did not involve the task as a variable and found no significant advantage for either type of CF.

A different tack was taken by Kartchava and Gatbonton (2014) in a study that set out to explore how task design would enhance the noticeablity of teacher-generated CF. They used ACCESS, a TBLT methodology originally developed by Gatbonton and Segalowitz (2005), in which tasks are specifically designed to fit three criteria: to be genuinely communicative, inherently repetitive, and inherently formulaic. They propose that these design factors taken together promote automatization of L2 structures through repetition of task-specific formulae. Kartchava and Gatbonton's results suggest that the ACCESS task enabled learners to pay greater attention to the teacher's CF. There was, however, no comparison of the ACCESS task performance with other task types, and the control group showed a similar gain in post-task accuracy.

The Place of Corrective Feedback in Task-Based Teaching Research

While the early research into NfM, mentioned above, explored tasks that promoted L2 development through maximizing communication breakdowns, studies in task-based learning and teaching (TBLT) look more broadly at how different types of classroom tasks can be designed or implemented to best support it. Typically, the studies employ task types (narratives, descriptives, and discussions) which are designed to be more or less cognitively taxing for learners, depending on, *inter alia*, how many elements they involve, their modality, and their demands on working memory (Robinson, 2001; Skehan, 1998, 2009). Task implementation conditions include pre-task planning, task repetition, during-task time pressure, and post-task requirements. In this research, learner task performances are assessed through a host of complexity, accuracy, lexis, and fluency measures, known collectively as CALF. A key aim is to show how a learner's performance in each CALF dimension is manipulated by the conditions of the task he or she is given to do; i.e., whether a task results in measurably significant differences in how fluent, how accurate, how varied, and how complex the performance is. The broader point is that greater attention to language form, which may never break the surface as an observable LRE, can be facilitated by different degrees of cognitive complexity in the task content, different lengths of pre-task planning time, and different numbers of task repetitions. Significantly for this chapter, a large majority of task-based performance investigations look at learner monologues or learner–learner interactions in oral or written tasks, and unsurprisingly, the studies do not address how a task design might encourage greater opportunities for CF from a teacher. Rather, they look at how a learner may be supported by the task conditions to perform at the high end of their L2 proficiency, maintaining an overall attention to L2 meaning but enabled at the same time to pay attention to different aspects of L2 form.

A recent example of task-based research that did not involve CF is Rafie, Rahmany, and Sadeqi (2015) who investigated task implementation conditions by looking at the effects on oral monologues of different sorts of planning: task rehearsal, 10-minute pre-task planning, no planning without task time limit, and no planning with task time limit. Comparing accuracy in participant monologues across these four conditions, they showed that the most supportive condition was rehearsal, in which participants repeated the task after a two-week interval. No corrective feedback was involved here as the data was monologic. Similarly, Kim's (2017) investigation manipulated task modality (face-to-face communication vs. synchronous computer-mediated communication) and showed more accurate use of the definite article and more developmentally advanced question forms in the latter mode, but no role for CF. Gilabert, Baron, and Llanes (2009) manipulated the inherent cognitive complexity of task structure. Their participants worked in dyads on two versions of three tasks, one deemed cognitively simple and the other deemed cognitively complex. The resulting transcripts were coded for frequency of NfM and assorted LREs, described by the authors as "interactional" feedback. This was found to be more frequent in cognitively complex versions of the task, which the authors claim could be linked to greater opportunities for acquisition. There is only one reference to CF in the paper, and this is in relation to the previous work on task design and NfM.

Task-related and CF-related studies might appear to be pursuing separate agendas. Certainly the early research into how tasks could manipulate a learner's attention regarded confirmation checks, comprehension checks, and clarification requests as incidental FonF leading to noticing, rather than anything explicitly didactic or "corrective." However, the term *interactional feedback* suggests a conflation of a learner's incidental *noticing* (a gap in his or her L2 knowledge) and a teacher's deliberate *correction* (of a learner's performance error). Indeed, Nassaji (2016, p. 536) is explicit in deeming interactional feedback per se to be corrective in nature. This conflation is parallel to the broadening of NfM (during communication failure) to include interaction (during communication success), and ultimately to the simple asking and answering of content questions (Mackey, 1999). This means that learners engaged in L2 interaction, of a problem-solving type or not, with a teacher or a fellow learner, can be exposed conversationally to additive L2 information, and didactically to corrective L2 information.

Task Manipulations to Support Noticing/Negative Evidence in Interactional Feedback

As discussed above, task-based pedagogies seek ideally to preserve for learners a real-time, meaning-based flow of oral interaction, allowing windows of opportunity to open briefly for a learner to shift to FonF. Recasts are common ways of teachers providing such windows during teacher–learner interactions, but as we have seen, the corrective intention is often lost on learners who may feel they are in the midst of successful conversation rather than a pedagogic exercise. The option of learners collaborating on a piece of writing, as in a dictogloss task (Swain & Lapkin 1998, 2001), creates extended time for a FonF as they co-write a text. This stretches Long's Interaction Hypothesis some way from its original conceptualization in spoken L2 interaction, especially because the learners' deliberations are likely to be in their shared L1. Nevertheless, the FonF is abundant and easy to track, if perilously close to FonFs. In recent years a third modality has become possible: synchronous computer-mediated communication (SCMC). As an alternative to face-to-face interaction, it affords learners a way of engaging in live interactions via instant messaging (see Chapter 11 and Chapter 23, this volume). The pressure of real-time spoken communication is relieved as learners type out their contributions and wait for their task partner to type back; in effect, the FonF window stays open longer. As we noted above, Kim (2017) used text-based SCMC to afford space for learners to reflect on the messages they were sending to their interlocutor, with the option of deleting and retyping before they hit "send." This exploratory study (only twenty participants) compared SCMC performance with face-to-face (F2F) performance on three tasks: spot-the-difference, story sequencing, and decision-making. The results showed the F2F condition as characterized by paralinguistic cues and simple syntax, while the SCMC condition was characterized by more accurate use of the definite article and more developmentally advanced interrogatives. Kim concludes that the SCMC condition relieved the participants of the pressure of real-time language processing, made space for revision, and thus allowed greater attention to form that underpinned their greater accuracy and complexity in the target structures. There was no corrective feedback involved here, just an assumption that the learners were able to monitor themselves and thus perform at a higher level of L2 proficiency than real-time task performance would allow.

Rouhshad, Wigglesworth, and Storch (2015) also compared task modality in learner–learner interaction. Their participants did two similar two-way information exchange tasks in either F2F interactions or SCMC interactions and were encouraged to correct their interlocutor when they noticed an error; i.e., they were told to give CF. The resulting data were coded for incidences of NfM and NfF (in the guise of recasts) and for explicit and metalinguistic CF. The results showed that mode of interaction was an important variable. NfM in SCMC was less frequent than in the F2F condition, in both conditions NfM was scarce, and NfF scarcer still. The authors, citing Rouhshad (2014), ascribe this to the participants' lack of confidence in their own knowledge, their fear of appearing rude, and being satisfied with a partial understanding of their interlocutor's meaning. The less frequent use of NfM or NfM in the SCMC mode is nevertheless interesting and was perhaps due to the extra time allowed for each participant to reflect and resolve communication issues by simply scrolling back and re-reading. Sheen (2010) compared oral recasts with written direct corrections on a narrative task focusing on the use of English articles. She found implicit oral recasts were least effective unless accompanied by metalinguistic explanation, while all forms of written corrective feedback were effective. She concludes that the degree of explicitness in CF was the key rather than the modality, but it is also possible that the longer time taken by learners to process metalanguage and read the written language facilitated their uptake of the corrections.

Pedagogical Applications

We can sum up the previous sections by distilling their main observations. SLA is argued to be more effectively driven by interactive, meaningful engagement with the L2 than explicit teaching about the L2. Classroom tasks need to be genuinely communicative, preserving a learner's overall FonM with switches to FonF at fleeting "windows of opportunity" contiguous to signs of insufficient L2 knowledge. No language form can be acquired without it being "noticed" at some level of awareness. Learners have insufficient attentional capacity to be aware of language form and content at the same time. They are adept at interacting successfully with each other without noticing insufficiencies in their L2 knowledge, and also adept at interacting successfully with a teacher without reliably interpreting teacher feedback as corrective. Learners may not necessarily welcome or trust CF from a peer. New technologies allow learners to interact meaningfully off-line through SMCM, creating extra attentional capacity that can be devoted to L2 form, whether that be manifested in complexity or accuracy, of syntax or lexis.

That said, there must always be a degree of tentativeness in putting forward pedagogical recommendations. A lot of SLA research is exploratory, small-scale, cross-sectional, and carried out in a laboratory setting, using participants who tend to be educated and from the developed world, and very little research is backed up by replications. With these caveats in mind, however, we offer the suggestions below on how a classroom task can be manipulated to support the feedback it engenders from fellow learners and teachers.

"Structure-Trapping" in Task Design

A task designer can set out to make use of a particular grammatical structure or lexical items that are natural and essential to the transaction of the task. For two English examples, a task about plans for the near future will probably involve the present continuous, while a task about speculating what the pocket contents of a lost jacket says about the owner will probably involve modal verbs (Samuda, 2001). In other words, the FonF is pre-set to a given target (Skehan, 1998). The usual criteria for a task are unchanged; it must relate to real life, involve communication, and be essentially meaning-focused. It is not easy to design tasks that will reliably constrain a learner's language choices (Loschky & Bley-Vroman, 1993) as humans can employ communication strategies to get round gaps in their language knowledge. But it is more likely that learners can be corralled into processing a particular linguistic form if given a priming reading task where it is essential to comprehension. If the interaction is teacher–learner, the pre-task priming means that the teacher's recasts of errors with the targeted structure will be more readily understood as corrective. If the interaction is learner–learner, the teacher could deliver post-task CF to the class as a whole, but only if the task has gone according to plan, and learners have, in fact, been using the forms the task designer was intending to trap. It remains debatable whether structure-trapping is in the wider spirit of TBLT, and Long (2015) has explicitly rejected it on the grounds that it is neither desirable nor practical for a teacher to determine if a whole class of learners will benefit from the chosen focus.

Delayed Corrective Feedback in Tasks

We noted above that a task does not have to be seen as an isolated performance but can sit between a pre-task and post-task phase. Accordingly, CF by the teacher can be delayed till the main task has been completed by groups of learners, and a follow-up post-task has started which involves the whole class. The teacher's role during a task becomes easier: to monitor the group interactions from the sidelines, to "collect" whatever errors appear most ripe for negative evidence, and then to deliver post-task CF that everyone is invited to listen to. This avoids any inappropriate and distracting interruption of the learners' FonM, and does not spoil what may have been shaping up to be an enjoyable interaction where all the learners felt engaged and successful. It is debatable whether such delayed FonF misses the boat as far as the Interaction Hypothesis is concerned because it does not coincide with the incidental and momentary noticing of any gap in knowledge. There remains the question of how a teacher should organize delayed CF for the class as a whole. Ellis and Shintani (2014, p. 277) suggest that the teacher could decide on a certain type of error (e.g., a grammatical form or a group of forms) and give CF only on that (cf. Doughty & Varela, 1998), but this does not address the problem of uncorrected errors appearing to be implicitly endorsed, or of the CF being less relevant to some learners than to others.

Task Repetition and Corrective Feedback

Setting aside the possible risk of boredom, there is no reason why a task should not be performed more than once. After the first iteration, there can be a period of encouraging the learners to reflect on their performance, and the performance of their peers, before doing the task again (and possibly a third time), taking into account the errors they had noticed, or their peers had noticed or the teacher had noticed. There is some evidence for the effectiveness of this strategy. Hawkes (2012) showed that when learners were given a form-focused session after the first iteration of a task and then repeated the task, there was greater accuracy and self-correction among students in the second iteration. The form-focused session did not consist of explicit CF, but rather of consciousness-raising related to useful forms in the task materials (see also Bygate, 2001; Lynch & Maclean, 2000). Foster and Hunter (2016) suggest repetition be used as a pedagogic tool whereby learners notice and reduce their own errors.

Rather than having students repeat the task under the same conditions, they could be asked to do it again in different conditions, e.g., in front of the rest of the class. Foster and Skehan (1999) found a small effect for this on accuracy, and in a subsequent study (2013) they operationalized post-task activity differently, and more effectively. Participants were told they would be recorded during the task, and then be given a copy of the recording to transcribe later. This was done to test the effect which *anticipation* of a post-task transcription would have on the initial performance. Foster and Skehan found it supported both accuracy and complexity in the during-task phase. While not part of their study, the actual recording made by the participants of their own performance provided a resource whereby they could give tailor-made CF to themselves, offline, without the risk of loss of face inherent in correction proffered by someone else, teacher or fellow learner. With readily available recording devices in every mobile phone, this is a practice which teachers can easily encourage in their classrooms.

Task Cycles

For Willis and Willis (2007) the "strongest" form of TBLT comprises task cycles, in which a pre-task prepares for the task itself, and a review stage looks back upon it. In the pre-task, the learners get to know what the task expects of them and may even watch a model task being done by the teacher. In the task itself, groups of learners perform the task and the teacher circulates as observer or troubleshooter if necessary. In the review stage, the learners' performance is subject to comments from peers or the teacher, including explicit CF. In this way CF is supplied reactively, but still within the cycle, and ties up with the pre-task focus on what the task itself is likely to involve. The learners are explicitly guided to remain alert to three kinds of information: the meanings expressed in the task, the language forms used to express those meanings, and the CF offered when the meaning or the form is inadequate.

Stretching Out Time: Computers as Task Mediators

A feature of recent years is the emergence and astonishing popularity of instant messaging via text, email, WhatsApp, Twitter, Facebook, and other platforms. It has not taken long for these methods of communication to be exploited by language pedagogy; if learners are already accustomed to messaging where not long ago they would have resorted to letters, postcards, phone calls or conversation, then it will seem natural for them to do interactive tasks via smartphone or computer. The advantage of this form of interaction is, as we have seen, that it hybridizes speech and writing and allows greater time for reflection on the language used to create the message. This, in turn, allows for FonF as a learner types a message, or re-reads what the task partner has already written while waiting for the next message to arrive. Ultimately the stream of text chat becomes a transcript of the interaction, and as such allows a teacher to give post-task CF on it, tailor-made for the writer. It is possible for groups of learners to collaborate on creating and reading the messages, talking about what the "designated typist" should write, offering CF on spelling, grammar, and vocabulary choices, as well as discussing what might be problematic in the messages they are getting back (see Chapter 11 and Chapter 23, this volume). The affordances of computer-mediated interaction are only just beginning to be explored, but their main benefit is already clear: they allow space for FonF and CF to flourish without compromising the interactive and meaning-oriented nature of TBLT.

Concluding Observations and Directions for Future Research

This chapter has attempted to resolve two notions which, on first consideration, might seem antithetical: corrective feedback on L2 forms in the environment of meaning-focused L2 tasks. Indeed, much of the research we have covered appears to be interested in one rather than the other. However, by seeing TBLT in terms of task sequences and not the individual stand-alone types used in much of the research, some tentative pedagogical suggestions for teachers and TBLT syllabus designers have emerged that are practical, meaning oriented, and allow CF a place before, during, or after a task performance. These are, in no particular order of importance: an explicit grammatical focus in a teacher-fronted stage before the learners embark on a task interaction with each other; tasks designed with a particular L2 structure in mind with targeted CF on this structure in a post-task stage; tasks designed with no particular L2 structure in mind can have a post-task stage added where the teacher gives CF on errors observed to be common to much of the class; a pre-task planning stage can be included where learners prepare for the task by reflecting on its content and language useful to its completion; tasks can be repeated and interspersed with learners reflecting on their own performance, or teachers giving targeted CF; and lastly, in a world where even the poorest people have access to mobile devices, the pedagogic possibilities of instant messaging can be explored and exploited.

The future research paths of CF and of TBLT may productively continue on their separate ways, but there is some scope for intersection. For example, we noted above the exploratory study of Kartchava and Gatbonton (2014) into enhancing the noticeablity of teacher-generated CF through using ACCESS tasks (Gatbonton & Segalowitz, 2005). Kartchava and Gatbonton's task asked learners to create and repeatedly defend an alibi to a crime, thus fitting the required ACCESS criteria of being inherently communicative, repetitive, and formulaic. Their result suggested that, in regard to the English simple past and past tense question forms, the alibi task did support greater attention to teacher CF. The challenge now would be to look at the development of a range of ACCESS-type tasks, on other L2 structures, especially in a longitudinal design. But there is perhaps more research scope in taking the tentative pedagogical implications laid out in the paragraph above, and looking at how they stand up under the conditions of actual classroom practice, with learners of different L2 proficiencies, from a variety of educational backgrounds, with different expectations of the role of the teacher and design of the pedagogic material.

References

Adams, R., Alwi, N. A. N. M. & Newton, J. (2015). Task complexity effects on the complexity and accuracy of writing via text chat. *Journal of Second Language Writing, 29,* 64–81.

Adams, R., Nuevo, A. M. & Egi, T. (2011). Explicit and implicit feedback, modified output, and SLA: Does explicit and implicit feedback promote learning and learner-learner interactions? *Modern Language Journal, 95*(Suppl.), 42–63.

Ammar, A., (2008). Prompts and recasts: Differential effects on second language morphosyntax. *Language Teaching Research, 12*(2), 185–210.

Bygate, M. (2001). Effects of task repetition on the structure and control of oral language: In M. Bygate, P. Skehan, & M. Swain (eds.), *Researching pedagogic tasks: Second language learning, teaching and testing* (pp. 23–48). London: Longman.

Doughty, C. & Pica, T. (1986). Information-gap tasks: Do they facilitate second language acquisition? *TESOL Quarterly, 20*(2), 305–326.

Doughty, C. and Varela, E. (1998). Communicative focus on form. In C. Doughty & J. Williams (eds.), *Focus on form in classroom second language acquisition* (pp. 114–138). Cambridge: Cambridge University Press.

Duff, P. (1986). Another look at interlanguage talk: taking task to task. In R. Day (ed.), *Talking to learn: Conversation in second language acquisition.* (pp. 147–181) Rowley, MA: Newbury House.

Eckerth, J. (2009). Negotiated interaction in the L2 classroom. *Language Teaching, 42*(2), 109–130.

Ellis, R. (2003). *Task-based language learning and teaching.* Oxford: Oxford University Press.

(2009). Task-based language teaching: Sorting out the misunderstandings. *International Journal of Applied Linguistics, 19*(3), 221–246.

Ellis, R., Basturkman, H. & Loewen, S. (2001). Learner uptake in communicative ESL lessons. *Language Learning, 51*(2), 281–318.

Ellis, R. & Shintani, N. (2014). *Exploring language pedagogy through second language acquisition.* London: Routledge.

Foster, P. (1998). A classroom perspective on the negotiation of meaning. *Applied Linguistics, 19*(1), 1–23.

Foster, P. & Hunter, A. (2016). When it's not what you do but the way that you do it: How research into second language acquisition can help teachers make the most of their classroom materials. In B. Tomlinson (ed.), *SLA and materials development for language teaching* (pp. 280-293). New York: Routledge.

Foster, P. & Ohta, A. (2005). Negotiation for meaning and peer assistance in classroom language tasks. *Applied Linguistics, 26*(3), 402–430.

Foster, P. & Skehan, P. (1999). The influence of source of planning and focus of planning on task-based performance. *Language Teaching Research*, 3(3), 215–247.

(2013) The effects of post-task activities on the accuracy of language during task performance. *Canadian Modern Language Review*, 69(3), 249–273.

Gass, S., Mackey, A. & Ross-Feldman, L. (2005). Task-based interactions in classroom and laboratory settings. *Language Learning*, 55, 575–611.

Gass, S. & Varonis, E. (1985). Task variation and non-native/non native negotiation of meaning. In S. M. Gass and C. G. Madden (eds.), *Input and second language acquisition* (pp. 149–162). Rowley, MA: Newbury House.

Gatbonton, E. & Segalowitz, N. (2005). Rethinking communicative language teaching: A focus on access to fluency. *Canadian Modern Language Review*, 61, 325–353.

Gilabert, R., Baron, J. & Llanes, A. (2009). Manipulating cognitive complexity across task types and its impact on learners' interaction during oral performance. *International Review of Applied Linguistics in Language Teaching*, 47(3–4), 367–395.

Gregg, K. (1984). Krashen's Monitor and Occam's razor. *Applied Linguistics*, 5(3), 79–100.

Hawkes, M. (2012). Using task repetition to direct learner attention and focus on form. *ELT Journal*, 66(3), 327–336.

Kartchava, E. & Ammar, A. (2014). The noticeability and effectiveness of corrective feedback in relation to target type. *Language Teaching Research*, 18(4), 428–452.

Kartchava, E. & Gatbonton, E. (2014). ACCESS-TBLT and adult ESL learners' noticing of corrective feedback. *CONTACT: Refereed Proceedings of TESL Ontario Research Symposium*, 40, 32–50.

Kim, H. Y. (2017). Effect of modality and task type on interlanguage variation. *ReCALL: The Journal of EUROCALL*, 29(2), 219–236.

Krashen, S. (1981). *Second language acquisition and second language learning*. Oxford: Pergamon Press.

(1985). *The input hypothesis: Issues and implications*. Oxford: Pergamon Press.

Li, S. (2010). The effectiveness of corrective feedback in SLA: A meta-analysis. *Language Learning*, 60(2), 309–365.

Li, S., Zhu, Y. & Ellis, R. (2016). The effects of the timing of corrective feedback on the acquisition of a new linguistic structure. *Modern Language Journal*, 100(1), 276–295.

Long, M. (1983). Native speaker/non-native speaker conversation in the second language classroom. In M. Clark & J. Handscombe (eds.), *On TESOL '82: Pacific perspectives on language learning* (pp. 207–225). Washington, DC: TESOL.

(1985). A role for instruction in second language acquisition: Task-based language teaching. In K. Hylstenstam & M. Pienemann (eds.), *Modelling* and assessing second language acquisition (pp. 77–99). Clevedon: Multilingual Matters.

(1988). Instructed interlanguage development. In L. Beebe (ed.), *Issues in second language acquisition: Multiple perspectives*. (pp. 115–141). Rowley, MA: Newbury House.

(1996). The role of the linguistic environment in second language acquisition. In W. Ritchie & T. Bhatia (eds.), *Handbook of second language acquisition* (pp. 413–446). San Diego: Academic Press.

(2015). *Second language acquisition and task-based language teaching*. Chichester: John Wiley.

Loschky, L. & Bley-Vroman, R. (1993). Grammar and task-based methodology. In G. Crookes & S. Gass (eds.), *Tasks and language learning: Integrating theory and practice*. Philadelphia: Multilingual Matters.

Lynch, T. & Maclean, J. (2000). Exploring the benefits of task repetition and recycling for classroom language learning. *Language Teaching Research*, 4(3), 221–250.

Lyster, R. & Ranta, L. (1997). Corrective feedback and learner uptake: negotiation of form in communicative classrooms. *Studies in Second Language Acquisition*, 19(1), 37–66.

Lyster, R. & Saito, K. (2010). Oral feedback in classroom SLA: A meta-analysis. *Studies in Second Language Acquisition*, 32(2), 265–302.

Mackey, A. (1999). Input, interaction, and second language development: An empirical study of question formation in ESL. *Studies in Second Language Acquistion*, 21(4), 557–587.

Mackey, A., Gass, S. & McDonough, K. (2000). How do learners perceive interactional feedback? *Studies in Second Language Acquisition*, 22(4), 471–498.

Mackey, A. & Goo, J. (2007). Interaction research in SLA: A meta-analysis and research synthesis. In A. Mackey (ed.), *Conversational interaction in second language acquisition: a series of empirical studies* (pp. 407–453). Oxford: Oxford University Press.

Nassaji, H. (2016). Interactional feedback in second language teaching and learning: A synthesis and analysis of current research. *Language Teaching Research*, 20(4), 535–562.

Panova, I. & Lyster, R. (2002). Patterns of corrective feedback and uptake in an adult ESL Classroom. *TESOL Quarterly*, 36(4), 573–595.

Pica, T. (1994). Research on negotiation: What does it reveal about second-language learning conditions, processes, outcomes? *Language Learning*, 44(3), 493–527.

Rafie, Z. F., Rahmany, R. & Sadeqi, B. (2015). The differential effects of three types of task planning on the accuracy of L2 oral production. *Journal of Language Teaching and Research*, 6(6), 1297–1304.

Robinson, P. (2001). Task complexity, cognitive resources, and syllabus design: A triadic framework for investigating task influences on SLA.

In P. Robinson (ed.), *Cognition and second language instruction* (pp 287–318). New York: Cambridge University Press.

Rouhshad, A. (2014). The nature of negotiations in computer-mediated and face-to-face modes with/without writing modality. Unpublished doctoral dissertation, University of Melbourne, Australia.

Rouhshad, A., Wigglesworth, G. & Storch, N. (2015). The nature of negotiations in face-to-face versus computer-mediated communication in pair interactions. *Language Teaching Research*, 20(4), 514–534.

Russell, J. and Spada, N. (2006). The effectiveness of corrective feedback for the acquisition of L2 grammar: A meta-analysis of the research. In J. Norris & L. Ortega (eds.), *Synthesizing research on language learning and teaching* (pp. 133–164). Amsterdam: John Benjamins.

Samuda, V. (2001). Guiding relationships between form and meaning during task performance: The role of the teacher. In M. Bygate, P. Skehan & M. Swain (eds.), *Researching pedagogic tasks: Second language learning, teaching, and testing* (pp. 119–140). Harlow: Pearson Education.

Schmidt, R. (1990). The role of consciousness in second language learning. *Applied Linguistics*, 11(2), 129–158.

  (2001). Attention. In P. Robinson (ed.), *Cognition and second language instruction* (pp. 3–32). Cambridge: Cambridge University Press.

Sheen, Y. (2010). Differential effects of oral and written corrective feedback in the ESL classroom. *Studies in Second Language Acquisition*, 32(2), 203–234.

Skehan, P. (1998). *A cognitive approach to language learning*. Oxford: Oxford University Press.

  (2009). Modelling second language performance: Integrating complexity, accuracy, fluency, and lexis. *Applied Linguistics*, 30(4), 510–532.

Swain, M. & Lapkin, S. (1998). Interaction and second language learning: Two adolescent French immersion students working together. *Modern Language Journal*, 82(3), 320–337.

  (2001). Focus on form through collaborative dialogue: Exploring task effects. In M. Bygate, P. Skehan, & M. Swain (eds.), *Researching pedagogic tasks: Second language learning, teaching and testing* (pp. 99–118). Harlow: Pearson Education.

VanPatten, B. (1990). Attending to form and content in the input. *Applied Linguistics*, 12(3), 287–301.

Willis, D. & Willis, J. (2007). *Doing task-based teaching*. Oxford: Oxford University Press.

Willis, J. (1996). *A Framework for Task-Based Learning*. London: Longman.

Index

accuracy, 25, 171, 208, 210–213, 275, 289, 291, 311–313, 373–374, 380, 408–409, 503–504
  accuracy-based activities, 738, 746
  grammatical, 171, 370, 371, 372, 581
  increased, 7, 96, 285, 288, 353, 479, 512, 527, 588, 609, 740
Acquisition-Learning Hypothesis, 68
action research, 134, 160
Activity Theory, 14, 583–590, 594
affect, 381, 565, 566, 567, 574, 575, 582–583, 586, 592, 593, 635, 723–726
aptitude, 6, 51, 313, 351, 419, 422, 569, 739, 746
aptitude-treatment interaction research, 692, 697
assessment, 113, 156, 411, 419, 435, 463, 498, 511, 634
  dynamic assessment, 101, 356, 570
attention, 45–46, 49, 72, 73, 78, 132, 743
  alertness, 74
  detection, 74, 76
  increased, 280, 282
  level of, 78, 782
  orientation, 74
  selective, 86, 111
attention to form. *See* focus on form
automatization, 48, 76, 77, 78, 284, 601, 738
awareness, 70, 72, 79, 132, 282, 285, 288, 671
  level of awareness, 69, 70, 72–73, 75, 78, 79, 81, 343, 358, 780

behaviorism, 9, 23–30, 36, 37, 49, 66, 690
brain function, 453,

child language acquisition, 2, 646
child learners, 55, 658, 661, 663, 674
clarification requests, 281, 410, 505, 506, 508, 621, 670, 674, 675, 718, 723
  anxiety, 718, 726,
classroom interaction, 100, 149, 160, 201, 547, 733
classroom management, 152, 262
classroom-based research, 130, 131, 132, 133–135, 141–142, 143–144, 309, 350–351, 407, 552, 610
  effect size, 310

  interventionist quasi-experimental, 134
  noninterventionist quasi-experimental, 134
  observational, 134
cognitive load, 90, 547
cognitive perspective, 51, 54, 85, 86, 103, 282–284, 304, 599
cognitive processes, 56, 67, 69, 75–76, 81, 210, 213–218, 275, 479
  impact of emotions, 593, 716
  reactivation and reconsolidation, 333, 335
cognitive psychology, 451–454, 457, 458
cognitive-interactionist perspective, 2, 86, 101, 187, 281, 282–283, 341
collaboration, 88, 89, 92, 527, 534, 630
communication breakdown, 85, 278, 286, 504, 507, 508, 780, 784
communicative goals, 54, 283, 523
competence, 32–38, 89, 103, 601
comprehensibility, 417, 418, 521, 647, 670, 671, 674
Comprehensible Input Hypothesis. *See* Input Hypothesis
comprehension, 49, 73, 261–263, 390, 529, 736, 739
comprehension checks, 132, 504, 505, 506, 508, 513, 675, 680, 780
comprehensive corrective feedback, 4, 213, 301, 312, 566, 572, 581, 587, 588
computer delivered feedback. *See* technology-mediated feedback
computer-assisted language learning, 226, 524
  intelligent computer-assisted language learning, 231–232
  learner-computer interactions, 226, 227, 232
  learner-learner interactions, 226
  pronunciation tools, 237, 409
  Tutorial CALL, 227, 231–232, 522, 534
computer-mediated communication, 5, 6, 11, 13, 52, 324, 521
  asynchronous, 117, 324
  effectiveness, 522
  environments, 117
  instruction, 131
  synchronous, 117, 123, 324, 336, 413, 494, 504, 514

Index

text-chat, 117, 790
computer-mediated feedback. *See* technology-mediated feedback
confirmation checks, 506, 670, 674, 780
confirmation requests. *See* confirmation checks
Connectionism, 733
consciousness-raising, 48, 69, 112, 440, 789
Content and Language Integrated Learning, 151, 475, 488, 539
content-based classrooms, 69, 407, 540, 545, 551
contextual features, 10, 148, 150, 156, 160
Contrastive Analysis Hypothesis, 25
curriculum, 133, 148, 150, 153, 156, 474, 487, 534, 539

declarative knowledge, 2, 48, 76–78, 275, 283, 342, 434, 435, 565, 601, 609
delayed feedback, 12, 120, 200, 377, 438, 440, 445, 741, 743, 766, 771, 788–789
depth of processing, 69, 70–71, 76, 78–81
developmental level, 88, 89, 102, 344, 380, 455, 742, 745
developmental readiness, 6, 15, 354, 380, 391, 415, 742, 744, 783
direct feedback, 3, 7, 65, 113, 176, 191, 208, 209, 323, 324, 397, 441, 734, 744, 747
dual coding theory, 257, 259, 260, 263

effectiveness of corrective feedback, 15, 94–99, 178, 195–198, 209, 265, 534, 657–660, 764, 772, 773
  affecting factors, 51, 56, 178, 201, 598, 738
  contextual factors, 198, 199, 275, 284, 286, 289, 313, 480, 514, 576, 754
  evidence, 142, 170
  feedback quality, 283
  introspective measurements, 117–122
  sociocultural perspective, 102, 103
  using tasks, 112–115
efficacy of corrective feedback. *See* effectiveness of corrective feedback
elicitations, 3, 48, 116, 139, 193, 343, 368, 390, 392, 484, 621, 716
emotions. *See* affect
enactment theory, 257,
engagement, 605, 608, 632, 635, 721–722, 723, 724–725, 726,
  facilitated, 285, 532
  lack of, 601
English as a foreign language, 53, 101, 147, 151, 156, 198, 256, 262, 525, 681, 763
English as a second language, 147, 151, 152, 156, 254, 259, 524, 681, 763
English for Academic Purposes, 235
explicit correction. *See* explicit feedback
explicit feedback, 56, 57, 101, 192–193, 252, 348, 544, 761, 772
explicit instruction, 24, 76, 132, 154, 176, 264, 290, 759, 762
explicit knowledge, 5, 7, 50, 77, 138, 264, 733, 736, 738, 739, 747
explicit learning, 67, 68, 71, 79, 81, 82, 115, 646, 692, 693, 757
extensive corrective feedback, 4, 7, 65, 199, 300, 310, 379, 648

face-to-face communication, 6, 13, 52, 117, 379, 413, 625, 631–633, 634, 697, 785, 786

feedback moves, 54, 94, 193, 198, 473–474, 486, 605, 625, 649, 674, 677,
feedback orientation, 277–279
feedback quality, 279–281
feedback strategies, 153, 157, 341, 344, 345, 348, 350, 358, 375, 379, 481, 670
  use of, 149, 682, 739
first language acquisition, 1, 32, 33, 68, 661
first language interference, 24, 25, 26, 66
fluency, 25, 50, 57, 133, 373, 374, 381, 563, 604, 608, 738, 784
  increased, 288, 609
focal attention, 72, 75, 430
focus on form, 1, 7, 50, 154, 196, 254–255, 288, 777, 779, 786, 788
Focus on Forms, 49, 779, 783
focus on meaning, 1, 50, 57, 255, 626, 648, 777, 779, 780, 783
focused corrective feedback, 4, 65, 156, 207, 208, 220, 323, 324, 662, 734, 746
foreign language contexts, 6, 13, 53, 153, 154, 158, 265, 474, 477–479, 542, 544
form-focused feedback, 302, 309, 465, 509
form-focused instruction, 35, 36, 261, 370, 476, 660, 733, 738, 741, 745, 766, 783
form-meaning connections. *See* form-meaning mapping
form-meaning mapping, 12, 45, 263, 521, 759, 760
  complex, 761, 770, 773
  simple, 761, 773
fossilization, 29, 34, 49, 409, 540, 543, 605
frequency of feedback, 585, 740

generativist perspective, 44, 45
gestures, 122, 276, 672,
  beats, 253, 259
  deictic, 253, 255, 259, 263
  emblems, 253
  iconic, 258, 259
  learner beliefs, 262
  meaningless, 257
  metaphoric, 253,
grammar, 124, 166, 168, 174, 179, 263–264, 266, 495, 524, 529
  grammatical complexity, 15, 771, 774
  instruction, 34, 37, 142, 171, 176, 304, 374, 566–567, 720, 757
  terminology, 243
grammaticality judgment test, 115, 328, 329, 352, 357, 692, 696, 741, 744, 764
guided practice, 283, 290

habit formation, 24, 25, 66
heritage learners, 157
history of corrective feedback, 66
hypothesis testing, 29, 45, 48, 70, 78, 80, 305, 333, 521

immediate feedback, 12, 120, 188, 199, 200, 242, 377, 445, 734, 741, 743, 766
immediate recall, 5, 118, 456, 570, 624, 721
immersion programs, 151, 349, 539–541, 543, 549, 651
  Canadian French immersion, 69, 149, 154, 475, 610
implicit feedback, 56, 57, 252, 348, 484, 674, 677, 741, 772

implicit instruction, 358, 757, 758, 759,
implicit knowledge, 5, 7, 77, 264, 733, 736, 739, 747
implicit learning, 67, 68, 75, 79, 81, 82, 115, 175, 342, 659, 661, 698, 757
incidental learning, 693, 757
indirect feedback, 3, 7, 65, 191, 207, 208, 397-398, 588, 604, 621
individual differences, 102, 118, 149, 190, 214, 215-220, 221, 264-265, 734, 747
   age, 200, 264, 265, 291, 411, 459, 476, 541, 548, 671, 674, 737
   analytic ability, 6, 219, 690, 692, 695-697
   cognitive differences, 419
   cultural background, 56, 541, 548, 567, 669, 672, 681,
   gender, 6, 56, 264, 265
   identity, 54
   social factors, 56, 198-199, 419
inductive learning, 693, 758
innatism, 9, 30-36, 37
input, 32, 48, 187, 226, 257
   input processing, 72, 74, 78, 599
   modified input, 44, 48, 54
   visual, 259
Input Hypothesis, 45, 48, 69, 210
input-providing feedback, 3, 48, 57, 140, 252, 276, 282, 283, 285, 289, 291, 527
instructional contexts, 132, 178, 349, 481, 487, 591, 700
intake, 72, 73, 75, 78, 215, 343, 391, 599
intensive corrective feedback, 4, 7, 65, 199, 278, 300-302, 303, 310, 316, 356, 383, 662
interaction, 85-87, 88, 91, 92-93, 100-101, 119, 142, 149-150, 284, 547-549, 623, 698
   oral interaction, 94, 118, 355, 465, 473, 546, 627, 786
   peer interaction, 132, 277, 283, 285, 499-500, 508-509, 550-551, 608-609, 628-630, 673, 680
Interaction Hypothesis, 44, 67, 73-76, 86, 282, 430, 646, 733, 777, 780, 786
interactional feedback, 2, 6, 73, 374, 479, 481, 646, 670, 674, 680
interactionist perspective, 2, 9, 85, 494, 542, 598
interlanguage, 66, 190, 281, 283, 372, 451, 533, 601, 659, 734
interlocutor, 137-138, 139, 143, 192, 286-287, 387, 438, 496, 629-630, 632, 633, 671-672, 760
   gender, 673, 674, 676, 678, 679
   native speaker, 283, 357, 414, 654, 670
   physical absence, 504, 512
   relationship, 275, 284, 608
internalization, 88, 91, 92, 331
international students, 156-157, 159
intervention studies, 140, 153, 256, 259, 263, 407, 419

L1 interference. *See* first language interference
laboratory-based research, 52, 139-141, 148, 175, 196, 261, 309, 479, 622
   advantages, 346
   effect size, 310
Language Acquisition Device, 2
language features, 280, 291, 733, 739, 754, 755, 757, 772
learned linguistic behavior, 33, 36

learned linguistic knowledge, 33-35, 36, 37, 646
learner anxiety, 137, 476, 487, 567-568, 604, 623, 626, 635, 713, 714-719, 726
learner autonomy, 51, 199, 230, 521, 599
learner beliefs, 197, 200, 284, 290, 530, 574-575, 719-723
learner goals, 155, 156, 574
learner needs, 103, 157, 200, 621
learning context, 154, 190, 474-487, 542, 594
learning environments, 116, 137, 232, 475, 477, 488, 651
learning outcomes, 51, 53, 153, 157, 195, 369, 739
listening, 155, 372, 416, 524, 526, 527, 528, 529, 540, 624, 693, 715,
literacy, 6, 13, 55
   illiterate learners, 464, 466
   low literate learners, 13, 451, 455, 459, 466
   low print literacy levels, 450
   phonemic awareness, 451, 453
   phonological awareness, 451, 452
Literacy Education and Second Language Learning for Adults, 466

meaning-focused input, 387
meaning-focused instruction, 57, 783
meaning-focused interaction, 85, 742
mechanistic approach. *See* behaviorist perspective
mediation, 90-91, 102, 275, 330, 336, 357, 571
   mediating tools, 70
mental representation, 2, 283, 333, 335
meta-analysis, 165-166, 167, 168, 169, 170, 171-175, 177
metacognitive instruction, 140, 286, 609
metalinguistic awareness, 69, 652, 700, 702, 704
metalinguistic feedback, 52, 150, 208, 277, 465, 621, 671, 744
metalinguistic information, 122, 139, 276, 747, 766
methodological synthesis, 165, 167
mobile-assisted language learning, 14
   affordances, 521, 523
   applications, 522-523
   asynchronous, 528
   automatic speech recognition, 530-532
   contexts of use, 524
   synchronous, 530
   text-to-speech synthesizer, 529
modality, 257, 438, 443, 495, 496-498, 511, 513, 660, 772, 784, 785, 786
Model of the L2 learning process in ISLA, 67, 78
   input processing stage, 68, 69, 73, 78, 81
   intake processing stage, 78, 79
   knowledge processing stage, 78, 79
modelling, 49, 51, 290, 533
moderator analysis, 166, 174, 178
Monitor Model, 67, 69
motivation, 76, 199, 200, 307, 419, 604, 726

Native Language Literacy Screening Device, 455, 459
nativist theory, 2, 66
negative data, 32-37
negative evidence, 1, 44-45, 85, 111, 188, 190, 410, 645, 777, 779, 780, 786-787
negative feedback, 75, 389, 436, 445, 647, 655, 674, 677, 761

negotiated feedback, 96, 98, 99, 309, 745
negotiation for meaning, *See* negotiation of meaning
negotiation of form, 85, 497, 506–507
negotiation of meaning, 2, 49, 51, 73, 75, 85, 654, 669–670, 674, 677, 680, 780
nonverbal feedback, 3, 11, 178, 251
  gesture. *See* gestures
  headshaking, 255
  nodding, 255
noticing, 45–48, 75, 119, 132, 452, 456, 508–510, 599, 607, 715, 718, 765
  ability, 458, 465, 695
  difficulty, 417, 457, 757, 782
  facilitated, 1, 85, 218, 399, 484, 599
  noticing the gap, 70, 333, 568, 621, 789
  rate, 464, 480, 714, 723
  spontaneous, 755, 757
Noticing Hypothesis, 35, 46, 67, 71–73, 190, 391, 398, 508–509, 780

opportunities for corrective feedback, 112, 115, 116, 233, 532
oral feedback, 3, 140, 166, 171, 174, 175, 176, 276–284, 309–311, 315, 531, 600
output, 2, 49, 70, 71, 73, 74, 85, 111, 210, 520, 747
  modified output, 3, 47, 80, 118, 444, 509–510, 629, 631, 633, 716, 726
  partial modified output, 47
Output Hypothesis, 48, 67, 69–71, 75, 81, 283, 342, 733
output-prompting feedback, 3, 48, 57, 140, 252, 276, 282, 286, 291, 369, 660

participation, 24, 175, 495, 496, 501–502, 527, 546, 565, 569, 592
peer feedback, 4, 12, 30, 54, 193, 201, 285–290, 680
  effectiveness, 289, 290
  factors affecting, 286–287
  frequency, 286
  perceptions of, 287–288
peer review. *See* peer feedback
performance, 32–34, 765, 779, 789
  complexity, 754
  enhanced, 282, 407, 416, 532, 601–602, 611
  spontaneous, 738
positive evidence, 1, 44–45, 85, 111, 188, 191, 192, 276, 417, 442, 509, 623, 645
pragmatics, 13, 53, 407, 435, 436–440, 443–445
  pragmalinguistics, 429, 433, 434, 435, 445, 733
  sociopragmatics, 429, 431, 434, 445
primary linguistic data, 32–35, 37
priming, 47, 75, 116, 656, 788
prior knowledge, 54, 71, 73, 75, 79, 81, 380–381, 744
procedural knowledge, 2, 48, 77, 283–284, 331, 343, 609, 737
proceduralization, 48, 76, 77, 275, 333, 601, 611
processability theory, 736, 741
production, 48, 71, 75, 87, 112, 117, 133, 190, 194, 433, 435, 736
  erroneous, 192, 226, 443, 444, 760
  oral, 79, 452
proficiency, 6, 15, 52, 138, 289, 599, 674, 744, 754, 763, 779

enhanced, 533
oral, 499, 529
prompts, 193–195, 342, 368, 370, 373, 475–476, 543–545, 608, 621
  effectiveness, 52, 196, 441, 477, 544, 662, 740, 741
pronunciation, 11, 166, 174, 179, 237–243, 259–261, 407, 682
  accuracy, 237, 241
  intonation, 57, 259, 266, 351, 392, 418, 433, 735
  pitch, 237, 238, 240, 242, 260, 266, 682
  prosody, 252, 253, 260, 261, 409
  stress, 239, 243, 253, 259, 266, 346, 409, 458
  tone, 260, 261, 409
prototypicality. *See* developmental readiness
psycholinguistics, 27, 69, 257

reaction time, 77, 115, 118, 122, 373,
reading, 258, 416, 450, 463, 499, 530, 540, 565, 691, 696, 779
  self-paced, 167
  sentence reading, 413, 420
recall, 117, 257, 258, 259, 452, 461, 542, 622, 633
recasts, 192, 345–355, 373, 608, 655–657
  effectiveness, 52, 195, 357, 369–370, 459–461, 475–476, 483, 498–499, 648, 740, 743
  extensive, 377–378
  frequency of use, 151, 152, 252, 621, 651, 652, 680
  learner perceptions, 606, 716, 723
  noticeability, 343, 459–464, 544–545, 622, 623–627, 634, 695
reflection, 281, 527, 533, 564, 565, 570, 602, 607, 611, 721, 790
reformulation, 3, 44, 74, 201, 546, 621, 741, 742, 761, 766
regulation, 91–94, 330, 690
  other-regulation, 90, 91, 92, 93, 94, 102, 599
  self-regulation, 51, 92, 94, 99, 101, 102, 104, 191, 196, 235, 344, 356, 599
reinforcement, 23, 25, 31
  negative reinforcement, 24
  positive reinforcement, 24
repair, 351, 414, 465, 477, 484, 551
  individual differences, 674, 678, 726
  rate, 480, 481, 545
  self-repair, 3, 30, 193, 510–511, 629, 739, 745
repetition, 195, 280, 621, 741, 766

saliency, 70, 118, 253, 276, 376–379, 633, 693, 756
  increased, 196, 390, 412, 662
  low-saliency, 142, 226
scaffolded feedback, 101, 103, 356–357, 478, 745
scaffolding, 50, 89–90, 99, 103, 122, 187, 196, 275, 284, 546, 651, 701, 703
second language contexts, 6, 53, 153, 669, 682, 715
segmentation, 74, 280, 454
selective corrective feedback, 28, 301, 302, 303, 310, 313, 418, 566, 572
self-correction. *See* self-repair
self-efficacy, 15, 217, 714, 724, 725, 726, 727
short-term memory. *See* working memory
Skill Acquisition Theory, 2, 48, 67, 76–78, 281, 283–284, 331–332
Skill Learning Theory, 733

sociocognitive perspective, 55, 281, 284
sociocultural learning theory. *See* sociocultural theory
sociocultural perspective, 9, 94, 187, 196, 304, 305, 316, 478, 588
sociocultural theory, 50, 70, 86–94, 284, 330–331, 344, 356, 357, 466, 542, 550, 733
sociolinguistic theory, 466
speaking, 282, 526, 527, 528, 608
spelling, 231, 232, 388, 396, 524–525, 532
stimulated recall, 119–120, 124, 219, 262, 266, 395, 411, 412, 508, 509, 622, 631

task-based language teaching, 6, 10, 16, 133, 138, 167, 704, 779
 confederate scripting technique, 115
 instruction, 115–117
 task completion, 277
 task conditions, 748
 task cycle, 790
 task design, 16, 788
 task manipulation, 786
 task performance, 784, 791
 task repetition, 789
 task-based interaction, 91, 114, 390, 411, 476, 567, 631, 716, 720, 783
TBLT. *See* task-based language teaching
teacher attitudes. *See* teacher beliefs
teacher beliefs, 57, 152, 158, 262, 388, 411, 562–566, 573, 661
technology-mediated feedback, 6, 11, 139, 171, 226, 232, 237, 244
 automated corrective feedback, 233, 234, 236
 automated writing evaluation, 237, 724
 automatic speech recognition, 240–243
 grammar checker, 228
 spell checker, 227–231
Test of English for International Communication, 440
think alouds, 117, 118, 219, 582, 590
Thorndike Law of Effect, 24
training, 14, 600–602
 learner training, 235, 488, 514, 611
 teacher training, 552, 564, 600, 607
translation tools, 524, 528
transparency, 45, 167, 177, 756, 771
types of feedback, 3–4, 65, 132, 138, 140, 195–198, 199, 209, 252, 280, 733, 747, 773
types of tasks, 143

consensus, 112, 113–114
dictogloss, 117, 132, 329, 500, 511, 678, 743, 784
discussion, 681
grammaticality judgment, 115, 155, 765
imitation, 115, 454, 462
information gap, 499, 671, 681
jigsaw, 112, 114–115, 462, 505
narrative, 500, 502, 675, 784
oral production, 101, 659, 660, 764, 766
picture depiction, 112–113, 741
repetition, 151, 452, 453
role-play, 288, 499, 608
spot-the-difference, 460, 461, 463, 500, 505, 510
story completion, 460, 462
writing, 324, 336, 501

UG. *See* Universal Grammar
unfocused corrective feedback, 4, 7, 12, 65, 207, 210, 213–214, 220, 310, 323, 734
Universal Grammar, 2, 31, 45, 646
uptake, 121–122, 473–474, 482, 483, 484, 509–510, 574, 581, 589, 605, 655–657
 immediate, 741
 rate, 55, 252, 309, 464, 479, 480, 481, 486, 543

virtual classroom, 137, 143, 160,
visual feedback, 237–240
vocabulary, 174, 499, 502–503, 525, 572
 instruction, 254
 low-frequency, 133
 range, 540, 587
 size, 420

willingness to communicate, 70, 669, 744
working memory, 46, 72, 78, 118, 333, 343, 609, 624, 742, 746, 783
 capacity, 57, 265, 314, 399, 623, 633
writing, 11, 29, 70, 155–156, 207–208, 232–234, 393–397, 585, 779, 790
 automated, 387
 collaborative, 121, 193
 drafts, 118, 243, 323
written feedback, 3, 113, 171–173, 175, 232, 234, 311–313, 323, 532, 627, 703, 724

Zone of Proximal Development, 87–89, 90, 95, 102, 196

Printed in the United States
by Baker & Taylor Publisher Services